Employment Law in Ireland

Employment Law in Ireland

Dr Neville Cox
LLB, PhD, BL, FTCD, Barrister-at-Law

Val Corbett
BCL, LLM (NUI)

Desmond Ryan
LLB (Dub), BCL, MA (Oxon), Barrister-at-Law

CLARUS
PRESS

Published by
Clarus Press Ltd,
Griffith Campus,
South Circular Road,
Dublin 8.

Typeset by
Marsha Swan

Printed by
MPG Books Ltd
Victoria Square, Bodmin, Cornwall.

ISBN
978-1-905536-26-9

Disclaimer
Whilst every effort has been made to ensure that the contents of
this book are accurate, neither the publisher or authors can accept
responsibility for any errors or omissions or loss occasioned to any
person acting or refraining from acting as result of any material in
this publication.

For Ronnie & Jean Russell (NC)

For Niamh and Jessica (VC)

For my parents, Maureen and Kevin Ryan (DR)

Foreword

'It is sufficient to say that public policy and the dictates of constitutional justice require that statutes, regulations or agreements setting up machinery for taking decisions which may affect rights or impose liabilities should be construed as providing for fair procedures.'

I usually have difficulty locating that sentence in the seminal majority decision of the Supreme Court in *Glover v BLN Ltd.* [1973] IR 388, and so it was on this occasion. The sentence is to be found in the judgment of Walsh J at page 425. The factual background to the action was that Mr. Glover's contract of employment with the defendant companies had provided that his employment might be terminated, without giving rise to compensation, for serious misconduct or serious neglect, subject to the unanimous opinion of the board of directors of one of the companies, the holding company, that the serious misconduct injuriously affected the reputation, business or property of the holding company or of the subsidiary companies. As Walsh J stated in his judgment, the Constitution had been relied upon on behalf of Mr. Glover, in particular, Article 40, s.3, in support of the argument that there should be implied into Mr. Glover's contract a term that the inquiry to be conducted by the board of directors and the determination should be fairly conducted. The sentence I have quoted was preceded by the observation of Walsh J that he considered that it was not necessary to discuss the full effect of Article 40 in the realm of private law or indeed public law. However, the importance of the decision, and the sentence in which it is encapsulated, is that for almost forty years it has been settled law in this jurisdiction that procedural fairness is an essential element in disciplinary action by an employer against an employee. Understandably, the authors devote a chapter to the topic.

The authors have undertaken a formidable task in attempting to cover a subject as broad as *Employment Law in Ireland*. The scope of the subject is well explained in the Introduction in Chapter 1, in which they outline the sources of our employment law – the Constitution (as exemplified by the *Glover* decision), the European Convention on Human Rights, European Union law, statute law, whether 'home-grown' or the transposition of European Union law, the common law and the decisions of the Courts and the various statutory tribunals and agencies in which jurisdiction in relation to various areas is reposed by the Oireachtas. Indeed, as is pointed out in Chapter 1, a key distinguishing feature of employment litigation in this jurisdiction is the multiplicity of different fora which have jurisdiction in particular areas and in which claims may be brought, ranging from the Labour Court to the Employment Appeals Tribunal to the Health and Safety Authority. A body of jurisprudence has developed in the courts in consequence of the Court's involvement in the decisions of those specialist bodies, both arising from enforcement of their decisions and appeals on a point of law.

Foreword

In implementing their task, the authors have produced a very comprehensive, yet incisive, publication. It is one which I predict not only legal practitioners, but also employers, employer bodies and trade unions will come to regard as invaluable. The range of topics covered addresses the usual workplace issues from employment terms to termination and redundancy. Significantly, it also covers a number of topics one might be pleasantly surprised to find, including industrial relations law, data protection in the context of privacy and transfer of undertakings. Throughout, the authors helpfully and generously refer the reader to other texts and to articles in journals and suchlike, which deal with particular topics covered.

The overall picture which emerges from this publication is how Irish employment law has evolved in the last four to five decades and continues to evolve. In general, in its evolution, it has striven to maintain a fair and just balance between the employer and the employee. It is, however, a truism that old habits die hard. As late as 1973, in the head note to the *Glover* case in the Irish Reports, the action was characterised as a matter relating to 'master and servant'. That terminology has, in the main, been replaced by reference to employer and employee or worker. The attitude which the expression 'master and servant' reflected and which was epitomised in the judgment of Asquith J in *Collier v Sunday Referee Publishing Company* [1940] 2 KB 647 is also, I hope, a thing of the past. There, in the context of whether a master is obliged to provide his servant with work, Asquith J remarked: 'Provided I pay my cook her wages regularly she cannot complain if I chose to take any or all of my meals out.'

This publication is a very welcome exposition of the range and complexity of employment law in Ireland.

The Hon. Ms Justice Laffoy
The High Court
7 December 2009

Preface

The discipline of employment law is a rapidly expanding one in this jurisdiction. More and more practitioners now describe themselves as specialised employment lawyers, practising in the multiplicity of distinct employment law fora such as the Employment Appeals Tribunal, the Labour Relations Commission, the Equality Tribunal and the Labour Court. Furthermore, from these various bodies as well as from the civil courts has come an enormous wealth of decisions and statements of principle which operate in tandem with an ever-increasing number of Irish statutes and EC laws (both regulatory and in the form of decisions of the European Court of Justice and the Court of First Instance) on discrete areas of employment law. Finally, the quantity and quality of scholarship on such topics is also ever increasing with a number of important legal texts in the area and two dedicated employment law journals. To repeat what was said at the outset, Employment law is a discipline which has expanded significantly over the last two decades in Ireland and continues to do so.

To this end, the authors have attempted to provide a comprehensive text in which all the relevant aspects of the legal framework (including case law and the decisions of the specialist tribunals) in this area are identified and analysed. Because of the vastness of the topic, and because so much 'general law' (from criminal law to commercial law) will inevitably exert an impact on the operation of a workplace, an editorial decision was taken to focus only on those areas of law which, in the authors' view, could properly be regarded as *employment law*. Thus we do not deal in detail with issues such as taxation law, pensions law and bankruptcy and insolvency law, regarding them instead as discrete areas of law which touch on the workplace and which are discussed in other specialised texts. Similarly, whereas we include a chapter on industrial relations law, this deals exclusively with issues pertaining to the jurisdiction of the Labour Relations Commission and Labour Court in so far as trade disputes are concerned: we do not consider, for example, questions of the right to join trade unions and the law relating to industrial actions. We appreciate, however, that other lawyers in this field may disagree with us on the question of what should properly appear in a book of this nature and we respect such views.

Finally, it is our pleasant task to acknowledge with gratitude the very many people who have helped us in our work.

We are most grateful to our colleagues in Trinity College Dublin, Independent Colleges Dublin and at the Irish Bar for their support. In particular we would like to thank Professor William Binchy, Professor Hilary Delany, Marguerite Bolger SC, Cliona Kimber BL, Professor Gerry Whyte, Dr Oran Doyle BL, Dr Caoimhín MacMaoláin, Alex Schuster BL, Ray Ryan BL, Paul Coughlan BL, Joseph Bolger, Lindsay Hoopes, Grainne Ahern, Catherine Finnegan, Kelley McCabe and Michelle Quinn. We would in particular like to thank Nadia Bhatti LLB for her truly excellent work as a Research Assistant during the busy final months of the project.

We are most grateful to our publishers Clarus Press and in particular to David McCartney for his (extreme) patience with us during the writing and publication process and for his many very helpful editorial comments and good natured professionalism. It has been nothing but a pleasure to work with him. And we are most honoured, delighted and grateful that the Hon Ms Justice Laffoy has generously taken time out of her busy schedule to write the foreword to the book.

Finally the authors would like personally to acknowledge and thank a number people who have provided support and assistance at various stages.

Neville Cox would like to thank Mike Allen, Cliona Kimber BL, Ben Neill, Alan Cox, Jennie Hudson, Des Cox, Jean Cousins and especially his mother Wendy, his wife Sharon and his children Jessica, Jamie and Martha.

Val Corbett would like to thank those whose quiet support made the completion of this project so much easier. In particular, Val would like to thank his mother, Mary, as well as Liam, Maura B and Larry and Joan Doolan. Val would like to especially thank his wife, Niamh, and his daughter, Jessica whose constant encouragement throughout this process was so important.

Desmond Ryan would like to thank a number of leading employment lawyers who have deepened and influenced his understanding of the subject. He is particularly grateful to Marguerite Bolger SC for her constant encouragement and guidance. Professor Mark Freedland, Professor Sandra Fredman, and Cathryn Costello, Fellow of Worcester College Oxford, were and are inspiring teachers of Employment Law at Oxford University. Desmond wishes to thank his parents, Maureen and Kevin, as well as Ray and Louise and a number of friends for their support in general and for their patience during this project in particular.

In this book we attempt to state the law as it stands on 30 November 2009. While it is designed to give the reader a detailed insight into the current state of employment law in this jurisdiction no liability can be accepted for any errors or omissions contained in or missing from this text. For the avoidance of doubt, the book cannot and should not be regarded as a substitute for legal advice. The authors would, however, welcome any comments in respect of the book, especially comments noting any errors that we have made.

Neville Cox
Val Corbett
Desmond Ryan
Dublin, 4 December 2009

Contents

Contents

PART V: THE BREAKDOWN OF THE EMPLOYMENT RELATIONSHIP

Table of Cases

M

Table of Constitutional Provisions

Table of Statutes (Ireland)

Equal Pay Act 1970

Organisation of Working Time Act

Table of Statutory Instruments (Ireland)

RULES

BILLS

Table of Statutes and Regulations (Other Jurisdictions)

Table of EU Directives and Regulations

Table of Treaties and Conventions

PART I

Introduction to Employment Law

CHAPTER I

Introduction

This book is intended to provide a comprehensive account and analysis of the ever-burgeoning rules and principles of Irish employment law. In so doing it is necessary not merely to focus on the various statutes and other laws that provide employers and employees with rights and responsibilities, but also to focus both on the nature of employment law and of the processes by which it operates in Ireland. As such, in this introductory chapter we shall consider some basic and underlying features of Irish employment law, focusing *inter alia* on the specialist bodies that, in large measure, are charged with overseeing and enforcing the law.   [1–01]

For convenience, the structure of the book will loosely follow the chronology of a characteristic employment relationship and will assess the legal issues that can and do arise throughout this relationship.

In Part II we consider the nature of the employment relationship, focusing on the manner by which the status of a given worker can be assessed (including the often pivotal question of when a worker can be seen as an employee rather than an independent services provider), as well as the structure and content of a typical contract of employment. In addition we consider the position of what are often termed atypical workers and, briefly, the specific rules in relation to employment permits that apply in the case of migrant workers.   [1–02]

Part III is devoted to the hugely significant issue of employment equality and, following an introduction to the issue, considers the formative issue of equal pay, the various listed grounds on which an employer may not discriminate and, finally, the relatively novel prohibition of harassment and victimisation under equality law.   [1–03]

Part IV focuses on the operation of the employment relationship, and the various rules governing the same. Thus we consider the rules in respect of working time, wages, entitlement to protective leave, and the obligations on employers to inform and consult with employees in respect of the major developments affecting the undertaking in which they are employed. We also consider issues that may be said to relate to the general well being of employees while they are employed (above and   [1–04] beyond statutory and contractual entitlements): namely health and safety obligations, stress and bullying in the workplace, and privacy and data protection.

[1–05] Part V deals with the various legal issues that may arise in the event of difficulties in and specifically the breakdown of the employment relationship. Here we consider the various rules governing the manner in which an employer can institute and operate a disciplinary process in respect of an employee. We then move to look at notice requirements for an employee whose employment is being terminated, as well as the different contexts in which legal issues may arise on foot of such termination, namely unfair dismissal, redundancy and other miscellaneous forms of termination. Lastly we consider the increasingly complex legal rules and principles that apply where there is a transfer of undertakings situation, and also the role of what has become colloquially known as the 'employment injunction'.

[1–06] Finally, we include (as Chapter 2) an analysis of what may loosely be termed industrial relations law. This does not fit neatly into any of the above sections inasmuch as it is conceptually different to employment law *per se*. Nonetheless its importance cannot be overstated and accordingly an attempt is made in Chapter 2 to identify and analyse this framework that is so critical for the resolution of many employment law disputes.

1. Sources of Employment Law

[1–07] As will be seen throughout this book, employment law is a genuinely multi-sourced discipline. There are clear constitutional dimensions that come into play – most obviously the right to earn a livelihood,[1] the right to freedom of association,[2] the right to fair procedures,[3] the right to privacy,[4] the right to equality,[5] the right to join a trade union[6] and the right to go on strike.[7] In addition (albeit to a lesser extent),

---

1. *Murtagh Properties v Cleary* [1972] IR 330; *Murphy v Stewart* [1973] IR 97; *Attorney General v Paperlink* [1983] IEHC 1, [1984] ILRM 373; *In re Article 26 and the Employment Equality Bill, 1996* [1997] 2 IR 321; *Greally v Minister for Education (No. 2)* [1999] 1 IR 1, [1999] 2 ILRM 296. There are different judicial dicta on the question of whether the constitutional right to a livelihood, which is protected against 'unjust attack', derives from Article 40.3.1, 40.3.2 or 43 of the Constitution.
2. Article 40.6.1 (iii).
3. Article 40.3. *In re Haughey* [1971] IR 217; *Mooney v An Post* [1998] 4 IR 288; *Glover v BLN Ltd.* [1973] IR 388; and *Gallagher v Revenue Commissioners* [1995] 1 IR 55, [1995] 1 ILRM 241.
4. Article 40.3.1. See *Cogley v RTÉ*; *Aherne v RTÉ* [2005] 4 IR 79, [2005] 2 ILRM 529; *Herrity v Associated Newspapers* [2008] IEHC 249, [2009] 1 IR 316.
5. Article 40.1. See *In re Article 26 and the Employment Equality Bill, 1996* [1997] 2 IR 321. Generally, see Doyle, *Constitutional Equality Law* (Thomson Round Hall, 2004).
6. Article 40.6.1 (iii).
7. *Brendan Dunne Limited v Fitzpatrick* [1958] IR 29; *Educational Company v Fitzpatrick (No.2)* [1961] IR 345.

certain articles of the European Convention on Human Rights[8] will be of relevance – particularly in the areas of privacy (under Article 8 of the Convention), freedom of association (under Article 11 of the Convention) and freedom from discrimination (under Article 14 of the Convention).[9] Most importantly, as will be obvious throughout the course of the book, the role of the law of the European Union in shaping vast swathes of Irish employment law – generally with the purpose of improving the lot of workers generally, and of historically disadvantaged workers in particular – can scarcely be overstated.[10]

Beyond this, employment law is an area in which there has been a vast amount of legislative activity in the last 30 years, and indeed before this time. These statutes – many of which were enacted for the purpose of transposing EC law developments into Irish law – are considered in the course of the book as we focus on specific areas of employment law, as also are the many decisions of the Irish High Court and Supreme Court that are formative of Irish employment law. [1–08]

What makes Irish employment law unique as far as its sourcing is concerned, however, is the fact that, whereas these 'traditional sources' are enormously influential, the law has, in addition, been developed in innumerable and very significant ways by the determinations, decisions and other opinions of specialist and quasi-judicial bodies, to whom authority is given in specific statutes to enforce the terms of those statutes.[11] Indeed it is true to say that, perhaps more than in respect of any other body of law, Irish employment law provides a multiplicity of different fora in which claims can be brought. Accordingly, it is of primary importance for a person seeking to enforce the terms of any particular statute to be aware of the appropriate forum or fora in which to institute his or her claim. In the course of this book, and as we analyse the various employment law statutes, the question of how and where that statute is to be enforced will be considered. In this introductory chapter, we now turn to consider the nature of the specialist tribunals under discussion. [1–09]

2. Employment Law Fora

As has been mentioned, whereas naturally the courts can be and indeed are involved in some of the most crucial developments pertaining to employment law in the state (for example, in respect of claims for personal injuries arising [1–10]

---

8. See also the European Convention on Human Rights Act 2003.
9. See O'Dempsey, *Employment Law and the Human Rights Act 1998* (Jordans, 2001).
10. Generally, see Barnard, *EC Employment Law* (3rd ed., Oxford University Press, 2006); and Fay, 'An Overview of the European Union's Influence on Employees' Rights and Industrial Relations within Ireland', 22 *ILT* (2004), 282.
11. It seems clear that these bodies, when exercising judicial functions, fall into the category of quasi-judicial bodies envisaged by Article 37.1 of the Constitution. This is significant, not least because it seems likely that their proceedings would be protected in the context of a defamation action by the defence of absolute privilege. See Cox *Defamation Law* (Firstlaw, Dublin 2007), at Chapter 7.

out of workplace stress, or in respect of the so called 'employment injunction'), and whereas legal issues in respect of some aspects of the employment contract will only be enforceable through the courts (for example common law actions for wrongful dismissals or simple breach of contract claims) nonetheless it is the case that all of the specific employment law statutes considered in this book provide for the enforcement of their terms, at least in the first instance,[12] in various specific employment law fora. In addition, as is considered in Chapter 2, much of the business of promoting good industrial relations in the State is left in the hands of specific bodies created for this purpose; indeed, as far as these bodies are concerned, there is something of a cross-over in this regard between Industrial Relations law and employment law proper, in that they will often also have functions under a number of the general employment law statutes.

[1–11]   It can thus be said that a key distinguishing feature of Irish employment litigation is the multiplicity of different fora in which claims may be brought. Very often, one set of facts giving rise to an employment dispute will trigger multiple causes of action. For example, allegations of inappropriate behaviour in the workplace may give rise to a claim for, *inter alia*, discrimination before the Equality Tribunal, with parallel personal injuries proceedings in the Circuit or High Court. Similarly, a stress claim may result in a constructive dismissal case being brought before the Employment Appeals Tribunal in addition to a personal injuries action in the Circuit or High Court. In either or both of these examples, the potential for additional fora may be engaged due to the status of the claimant, as where, for example, he or she is a fixed-term employee. Because of the complex overlap between the different fora, it is essential to be aware of the key practical features of each forum.

[1–12]   The specialist bodies in question (which are now considered briefly in turn and which are dealt with individually in detail in various chapters in this book) are:

- The Labour Court
- The Labour Relations Commission
- The Rights Commissioner Service
- The Employment Appeals Tribunal
- The Equality Tribunal
- The Health and Safety Authority
- The Labour Inspectorate of the Department of Enterprise, Trade and Employment
- The National Employment Rights Agency

---

12. Most such statutes further provide that where the terms of a determination by a specific employment law body (such as the Employment Appeals Tribunal) are not carried out, then application may be made to the Circuit Court for an order in the terms of the determination. Moreover, again such statutes in general provide that appeals on a point of law from determinations of such bodies may be made to the High Court.

2.1. The Labour Court

The Labour Court was established under s.10(1) of the Industrial Relations Act [1–13]
of 1946 and has a myriad of different functions. Many of these functions (which
are considered in different chapters of this book) arise under specific employment
law statutes (including, for example, the Organisation of Working Time Act, the
Employment Equality Act and the Fixed Term Workers Act). Indeed as far as such
specific pieces of legislation are concerned, the Labour Court has become something
of an 'employment law court' where employment law matters of different kinds can
be resolved. The primary function of the Labour Court, however, is as a piece of
industrial relations machinery – the purpose for which it was originally created.

Originally, the Labour Court was a relatively small body consisting of a chairman [1–14]
and four 'ordinary members'[13] of which half would be representative of the interests of workers and half of employers, which gives the determinations of the
Labour Court the seal of being representative of all relevant players within the
industrial relations paradigm.[14] Thus the chairman would originally be appointed
by the Minister for Industry and Commerce (now the Minister for Enterprise,
Trade and Employment) and would hold office on such terms as would be fixed
by the Minister.[15] Moreover, the Minister would nominate an organisation representative of trade unions of workers and a trade union representative of employers
to nominate persons who would be appointed as 'ordinary members'.[16] Under the
original statutory scheme, the plan was for the court to have two divisions[17] of
three members, comprising two ordinary members (one representative of workers
and one representative of employers) and either the chairman of the court or a

---

13. An ordinary member is appointed for five years (s.10(7) Industrial Relations Act 1946) or, if
   appointed by regulations under s.10(5), the appointment is for five years or until the relevant
   ministerial regulations are revoked or annulled. Equally the appointee can be removed from
   office for stated reasons and with the consent of the organisation that nominated him if it is
   still in operation: s.10(8) *ibid.*

14. s.10(2) Industrial Relations Act 1946. An ordinary member is not permitted to hold any
   office or be a committee member of a trade union, or hold any office or employment that
   would prevent him from being available at all times for the work of the court (s.10(11) *ibid.*)
   and [s]he must be ordinarily resident in the State (s.10(12) *ibid.*).

15. s.10(3) *ibid.* On the other hand, the role of the chairman is expressly deemed to be a full-
   time job (s.10(10) *ibid.*).

16. s.10(4) *ibid.* Alternatively, if at the time of a vacancy there was more than one relevant
   workers' union from which a nominee might be chosen, and if the procedure under s.10(4)
   was felt by the Minister to be inappropriate, the Minister could invite the various trade
   unions to nominate persons for appointment and, by regulation, could choose an appointee
   from the list of such nominees: s.10(5) *ibid.*

17. s.11(1) *ibid.* It was provided that this notion of a two-division court would apply at the
   direction of the chairman whenever he was of the opinion that this would be expedient for
   the speedy dispatch of the court. Section 11 has been replaced by s.3 of the Industrial Relations Act 1969 to allow for the possibility of further divisions of the court being set up. In
   all instances the Chairman assigns the relevant business to the divisions and each division is
   deemed to have the powers of the court generally.

deputy chairman appointed by the Minister under s.12 of the 1946 Act. As a result of the amount of work done by the court, however, provision was made under the 1969 Industrial Relations Act to increase the number of ordinary members to 6 (again half of whom would represent workers, and half of whom would represent employers)[18] and the number of deputy chairman to two[19] in order that there be three divisions. Finally, since the Industrial Relations Act of 1976, the Minister is allowed to appoint as many more ordinary members[20] and deputy chairmen[21] (and thus as many new divisions of the Court) as [s]he regards as expedient.

[1–15]   The Labour Court is given a statutory power to make provision for its own procedures.[22] Thus for the purposes of both the Industrial Relations Act 1946[23] and any investigation under the Industrial Relations (Amendment) Act of 2001[24] the Court may summon witnesses, examine such witnesses on oath, and compel production by a witness of any document in his or her power or control.[25] Necessarily the level of fair procedures that will be required of the Labour Court in such cases will depend on the seriousness of what is at stake.[26] Moreover, according to statute, a witness in such a matter is entitled to the same immunities and privileges as if [s]he was a witness before the High Court.[27] It is an offence for a prospective witness who has been summoned to fail to attend a Labour Court hearing, or to refuse to take an oath, produce any document as [s]he is required by the Court, or to refuse to answer any question on which the Court may legally require an answer.[28]

---

18. s.2 Industrial Relations Act 1969.
19. s.4 *ibid.*
20. s.8 Industrial Relations Act 1976.
21. ss.8 and 9 *ibid.*
22. s.20(5) Industrial Relations Act 1946. So, for example, the Court may at its discretion hold any sitting or part thereof in private (s.20(7) *ibid.*) and may provide for cases in which persons can appear through solicitors or counsel: s.20(6) *ibid.*
23. s.21 Industrial Relations Act 1946.
24. s.4 Industrial Relations (Amendment) Act 2001.
25. As we shall see, in *Ryanair v Labour Court* [2007] IESC 6, [2007] 4 IR 199 the Supreme Court held that proceedings before the Labour Court had been otherwise than in accordance with fair procedures because the Court had determined questions of fact against Ryanair despite having heard no oral testimony from the relevant union that would support such a finding, even where testimony leading to a conflicting conclusion *had* been heard by the Court. This has essentially come to mean that it will be necessary for the Labour Court to have sufficient testimony before it to justify any finding of fact that it intends to make.
26. *Ryanair v Labour Court* [2007] IESC 6, [2007] 4 IR 199. Generally on this principle see *Flanagan v UCD* [1988] IR 724.
27. s.21(2) Industrial Relations Act 1946.
28. Under s.56 of the Industrial Relations Act 1990 a document with the seal of the Court stating that the person named was summoned to appear as a witness before the Court pursuant to s.21 of the Industrial Relations Act 1946, when a sitting of the Court was held on that day and [s]he defaulted in attending on that day shall, in a prosecution of that person for such default, be received in evidence of the matters so stated without further proof.

The precise impact of a decision of the Labour Court[29] is perhaps somewhat nebu-   **[1–16]**
lous in that there is no formal machinery available for enforcing such decision, nor
is it binding on any of the parties to the process.[30] This general rule is, however,
subject to two exceptions such that a Labour Court decision *is* binding:

(a) where the Labour Court, pursuant to its jurisdiction under various
employment law statutes, is hearing an appeal from a decision of a
tribunal of original jurisdiction; and
(b) where as a matter of contract (including a provision in a Registered
Employment Agreement) the parties agree to be bound by such decision.

Finally, no appeal lies from a decision of the Labour Court on any matter within
its jurisdiction to any court of law.[31]

The Court is empowered to appoint further officers to assist in its general work of   **[1–17]**
furthering industrial relations. So, for example, it may appoint industrial officers[32]
to perform any duties assigned to them by the Court or the Chairman of the
Court. In particular the role of industrial officers is to assist in the resolution of
trade disputes *inter alia* through facilitating negotiations and discussions between
employees and employers. Furthermore, the Minister can appoint technical asses-
sors,[33] registrars and other officers and servants of the Court.[34]

2.2. Rights Commissioners

A particularly important development both in terms of Industrial Relations   **[1–18]**
law and the enforcement of employment law generally is the creation of the
office of the Rights Commissioner[35] under s.13 of the Industrial Relations Act

---

29. It is only the decision of the Court and not any dissenting or assenting judgments that are published: s.20(4) Industrial Relations Act 1946.
30. It should be noted that the Court is not permitted to publish information that has arisen in the course of proceedings and that would not otherwise be in the public domain relating to any business carried on by any person or as to any trade union without the consent of that person or that trade union: s.22 *ibid.*
31. s.17 *ibid.* In addition, s.4 of the Documentary Evidence Act of 1925 applies to every order of the Court.
32. s.16 Industrial Relations Act 1946. Under s.16 these officers were called conciliation officers but have been renamed industrial officers under s.6 of the Industrial Relations Act 1969.
33. s.14 Industrial Relations Act 1946.
34. s.13 *ibid.*
35. Rights Commissioners are appointed by the Minister from time to time (s.13(1) Industrial Relations Act 1969) on such conditions as are determined by the Minister (s.13(4) *ibid.*). A Rights Commissioner is appointed for three years but may be re-appointed for a further term or terms (s.34 Industrial Relations Act 1990). Thus the Minister can appoint more than one Rights Commissioner at any given time or indeed at a time when one or more Rights Commissioner stands appointed (s.13(7) Industrial Relations Act 1969). On the other hand, the Minister is restricted to appointing as a Rights Commissioner someone on a panel of persons nominated by the Labour Relations Commission (s.34 Industrial Relations Act 1990).

1969.[36] The role of the Rights Commissioner is a varied one, with most employment law statutes now requiring prospective litigants thereunder to have recourse to the Rights Commissioner as a primary port of call. These instances are discussed in detail throughout this book. Significantly, however, the Rights Commissioner service also has an important Industrial Relations function.

[1–19] The nature of the Rights Commissioner service – and the significant degree to which the Rights Commissioner service has evolved over time to encompass an increasingly quasi-judicial role – is well captured in the following extract from the most recent report of the Rights Commissioner service:

> At its commencement, the service was expected to perform a problem-solving role by helping to resolve small-scale disputes in a non-legalistic manner. The rationale for creating the service was to ensure that relatively minor employment disputes were resolved without impacting on the wider collective bargaining industrial relations, causing unnecessary conflict between employers, trade unions & employees. In the period since its establishment, however, the role, function and indeed importance of the Rights Commissioner Service within the public dispute resolution architecture has changed significantly. Although Rights Commissioners have retained their function of providing a non-adversarial problem solving approach to dispute resolution within the industrial disputes arena, they have also gradually acquired a more encompassing quasi-judicial role in respect of the adjudication on employment rights.[37]

[1–20] The Rights Commissioner operates as a service of the Labour Relations Commission,[38] and is expressly required to be independent in the performance of his or her functions.[39] Under s.13 of the Industrial Relations Act of 1969, a party to any trade dispute (either existing or apprehended) other than one relating to rates of pay, hours of work or the annual holidays of workers, may refer the matter to a Rights Commissioner[40] who will investigate the matter. The Rights Commissioner investigation may involve a hearing[41] and the Rights Commissioner himself or herself is empowered to make provision for the regulation of any such proceedings.[42] The Rights Commissioner, having investigated the matter, will make recommendations

---

36. Under s.35 of the Industrial Relations Act 1990, Rights Commissioners now operate as a service of the Labour Relations Commission.
37. Rights Commissioner Service, Digest of Decisions 2008, at p.6.
38. s.35(1) Industrial Relations Act 1990.
39. s.35(2) *ibid.*
40. s.13 (2) Industrial Relations Act 1969.
41. It is provided that such investigations shall take place in private: s.13(8) *ibid.*
42. s.13 (6) *ibid.* Again, provision is made that whereas generally no solicitor or barrister is permitted to represent a party in an investigation by a Rights Commissioner, the Rights Commissioner may provide for cases in which this is permissible: s.13(6) *ibid.*

to the person who has sought his or her advice,[43] and notify the Labour Court of such recommendations.[44]

Any party to the dispute can appeal the Rights Commissioner's recommendation   [1–21] to the Labour Court.[45] It is provided under s.13(9) of the Industrial Relations Act 1969 that the parties to the dispute shall be bound by the decision of the Labour Court on any such appeal. This is, however, something of a misnomer given, as we have seen, that outside of a situation where the parties agree contractually to be bound by such decision, the Labour Court cannot issue binding rules. Thus it is suggested that the best interpretation of s.13(9) of the 1969 Act is that an appeal to the Labour Court represents the final point of appeal for parties to any such trade dispute.[46] Finally, and outside of such an appeal scenario, the Labour Court is not permitted to investigate a trade dispute in relation to which a Rights Commissioner has made a recommendation.[47]

2.3. The Labour Relations Commission

The third major organ dealing with Industrial Relations matters in Ireland is the   [1–22] Labour Relations Commission, established under s.24 of the Industrial Relations Act 1990. The Labour Relations Commission (LRC) is a body corporate comprising a Chairman and six ordinary members.[48] The chairman is appointed by the Minister following consultation with organisations that the Minister regards as being representative of workers and employers, and is appointed for

---

43. Such recommendation cannot include any confidential or private information about a person or organisation without the consent of that person or organisation: s.14 Industrial Relations Act 1969.

44. s.13(3) *ibid.* A Rights Commissioner is not permitted to investigate a dispute if the Labour Court has already made a recommendation in respect of it, or if a party to the dispute informs him or her in writing that he objects to the matter being dealt with by the Rights Commissioner.

45. s.13(9) *ibid.* As a generalisation it would appear that the Labour Court will not disturb a Rights Commissioner's determination where it is 'reasonable and appropriate' (*Peamount Hospital v A Worker* CD/08/451 AD 0869, 16 October 2008) or 'fair and reasonable' (*Concern v Manufacturing Science Finance* CD 94564 AD 9497, 22 December 1994), *Anchor Training Ltd. v A Worker* CD/08/489 AD 0876, 3 November 2008) or where there is no legitimate basis for so doing (*HSE South v A Worker* CD/07/232 AD 0877, 17 November 2008) or where the Rights Commissioner has not erred in his determination (*HSE Ambulance Service v A Worker* CD/08/426 AD 0874, 30 October 2008). On the other hand, the Labour Court has deemed it appropriate to overturn a Rights Commissioner decision where changed circumstances since that determination have rendered it now inappropriate (*Peter O'Brien Catering Company Ltd. v SIPTU* CD90600 AD 9060, 21 December 1990).

46. See Moffat, ed., *Employment Law* (2nd ed., Law Society of Ireland, 2006), at p.351.

47. s.13(10) Industrial Relations Act 1969.

48. s.24(3) Industrial Relations Act 1990. The LRC is permitted to act notwithstanding the existence of not more than two vacancies in its membership: s.27(1) *ibid.*

such period and on such terms and conditions as the Minister determines.[49] Of the ordinary members, two are nominated by such organisation or organisations as the Minister regards as being representative of workers, two are nominated by such organisation or organisations as the Minister regards as being representative of employers, and two are nominated by the Minister.[50] In addition, there is a chief executive, appointed by the Minister in consultation with the LRC (on terms of conditions of service to be determined by the Minister).[51]

[1–23] With the consent of the Minister for Finance, the Minister for Enterprise, Trade and Employment may appoint staff to the LRC to aid it in the performance of its functions.[52] The LRC can also appoint members of its staff to act as industrial relations officers, with the role of assisting in the prevention and settlement of trade disputes as well as doing any further duties assigned to them by the LRC through its chairman or chief executive officer.[53] Finally, the LRC may also appoint members of staff, including Industrial Relations officers to give advice on Industrial Relations matters to management or workers or their representatives.[54]

[1–24] The functions of the LRC[55] are set out in s.25 of the Industrial Relations Act 1990 – subject to its general responsibility for promoting the improvement of industrial relations[56] and assisting in the resolution of trade disputes before they come to the Labour Court.[57]

---

49. Both the chair and the ordinary members can be removed by the Minister for stated reasons.
50. The rules in respect of the nomination of the members of the LRC are contained in the 4th Schedule to the Industrial Relations Act 1990.
51. s.28 Industrial Relations Act 1990. It is possible, with the consent of the Minister, for the Chief Executive and the Chairman to be the same person.
52. s.32 *ibid.*
53. s.33 *ibid.*
54. s.33(3) *ibid.*
55. See www.lrc.ie for the Labour Relations Commission's *Statement of Strategy 2008–2010.*
56. The LRC may, from time to time, make rules regarding its own procedure and business (including rules relating to quorums) and must furnish the Minister with a copy of the same: s.27(3) *ibid.*
57. Under s.26 of the Industrial Relations Act 1990, the Labour Court cannot investigate a trade dispute unless the LRC has certified in a report that there is nothing more that it can do to advance the resolution of the dispute, or alternatively (under s.26(3) of the 1990 Act), unless the Chairman of the LRC (or someone authorised by him) notifies the Court that it waives its entitlement to exercise its conciliatory functions in the matter, or unless the parties to the dispute request the Court to hear the matter, or where there are exceptional circumstances justifying the Court from hearing the matter without the normal certification from the LRC (s.26(5) of the 1990 Act) – for example, where the urgency or sensitivity of the matter requires this. See, for example, *Irish Aviation Authority v IMPACT* CD/08/84, recommendation no. LCR 19158, 25 February 2008; *An Post v Communication Workers Union* CD/05/1172, recommendation no. LCR 18405, 22 November 2005.

These specific functions are as follows: [1–25]

- to provide a conciliation service[58];
- to provide an industrial relations advisory service;
- to prepare codes of practice relevant to industrial relations after consultation with unions and employer organizations.[59] Thus under s.42 of the Industrial Relations Act 1990, the LRC is required to prepare[60] draft codes of practice for submission to the Minister either at its own behest or following a request by the Minister. If the Minister wishes to do so, [s]he may then (by order) designate the code as a Code of Practice for the purposes of the Act,[61] in which case that code is admissible in evidence (that is, it must, where relevant, be taken into account) in any proceedings before the Labour Court, LRC, Employment Appeals Tribunal, a Rights Commissioner, or an Equality Officer.[62] Throughout this book we consider the importance of such codes of practice.
- to offer guidance on codes of practice and help to resolve disputes concerning their implementation. In addition, the Labour Court may, on the application of one or more parties to a dispute, give its opinion as to the interpretation of a Code of Practice (provided that notice of the application is given to any other parties to the dispute[63]) and may investigate any alleged breaches of the Code of Practice[64] with a view to issuing a recommendation setting out its opinion on the matter and outlining the steps which, in its view, a party in breach of the Code of Practice should take or cease from taking in order to become compliant with the code.[65]
- to appoint Equality Officers of the Commission and provide staff and facilities for the Equality Officer Service;

---

58. Under s.36 of the Industrial Relations Act 1990, the LRC is not permitted to exercise its conciliation functions in respect of a dispute on which a Rights Commissioner has made a recommendation.

59. The LRC has currently published 11 codes of practice, available at http://www.lrc.ie/ViewDoc.asp?fn=/documents/publications/codes/index.htm&CatID=23&m=u.

60. Before preparing the Code of Practice, the LRC is required to seek and consider the views of organisations representing both employers and workers and such other groups as it considers appropriate: s.42(2) Industrial Relations Act 1990.

61. In addition, the Minister may subsequently revoke a Code of Practice: s.42(6) *ibid.*

62. s.42(3) *ibid.* On the other hand, a failure on the part of any person to observe any provision of a Code of Practice does not of itself render him or her liable to any proceedings.

63. s.43(1) *ibid.* See, for example, *Wright Window Systems v SIPTU* CD/06/131, opinion no. INT 062, 2 October 2006; *Iarnród Eireann v ATGWU* CD/01/282, opinion no. INT 013, 25 July 2001.

64. This is on condition that the complaint has been referred to the Court by a party directly involved and also that the complaint has first been considered by the LRC (s.43(2) Industrial Relations Act 1990). See, for example, *Eircom Ltd. v A Worker* CD/07/114, recommendation no. LCR 18919, 18 June 2007; *Dunnes Stores Tralee v Mandate* CD/05/344, recommendation no. LCR 18364, 1 November 2005.

65. s.43(3) Industrial Relations Act 1990.

- to select and nominate persons for appointment as Rights Commissioners and provide staff and facilities for the Rights Commissioner service;
- to conduct or commission research into matters relevant to industrial relations;
- to review and monitor developments in the area of industrial relations;
- to assist joint labour committees and joint industrial councils in the exercise of their functions;
- on its own behalf or following a request, to provide such advice as it thinks is appropriate on matters concerned with Industrial Relations to employers or employers associations or workers or trade unions[66];
- to publish an annual report of its activities and to make such observations as it thinks proper relating to trends and developments in industrial relations in Ireland, including trends and developments relating to pay[67]; and
- to supply the Minster with such information as [s]he may from time to time require regarding its activities.[68]

[1–26] Finally, it is provided that the LRC may, at the request of one or more parties to a trade dispute or on its own initiative, offer the parties its appropriate services with a view to bringing about a settlement.[69] In addition, and unless there is some specifically agreed provision whereby a trade dispute will be heard *ab initio* by the Labour Court, the default position is that all trade disputes are first referred to the LRC or to the appropriate branch of the LRC.[70]

2.4. The Employment Appeals Tribunal

[1–27] The EAT was established by s.39 of the Redundancy Payments Act 1967 and is the forum for claims for unfair dismissal. It should be noted, however, that the EAT is also the forum for determining complaints both at first instance and on appeal in a number of employment law areas dealt with in this book.

A very significant point to be made at this stage is that the EAT enjoys far-reaching powers of redress where it finds a dismissal to have been unfair: it can, for example, make an order for re-instatement or re-engagement. The most frequent award made, however, is one for compensation (which can be up to two years' remuneration, which term is widely defined to include benefits such as bonuses, etc.). It is essential to note that the EAT may only award compensation for losses suffered by

---

66. s.25(5) *ibid.*
67. s.27(3) *ibid.* The Minister must cause copies of this report to be laid before each House of the Oireachtas.
68. s.27(4) *ibid.*
69. s.25(2) *ibid.*
70. s.25(3) *ibid.*

the employee in terms of loss of income – it has no jurisdiction to make an order for damages or compensation to reflect wrongful treatment.

2.5. The Equality Tribunal

Established under the Employment Equality Act 1998, the tribunal is responsible [1–28] for overseeing the Employment Equality Acts 1998–2008 outlawing discrimination in the workplace on nine grounds. The tribunal's functions are quasi-judicial. It hears or mediates claims of unlawful discrimination under the equality legislation. Claims taken before it may be the subject of mediation through equality mediation officers. A tribunal mediator will facilitate parties to reach a mediated agreement that is legally binding. Where parties object to mediation, a case will be heard by a tribunal Equality Officer, who will hear evidence from both parties before issuing a legally binding decision. Failing mediation, the matter is determined by Equality Officers, whose decision can be appealed to the Labour Court.

Where the tribunal upholds a claim of discrimination, it awards redress and, [1–29] significantly, it can direct an employer to take specific action. It should be emphasised that many recent determinations of the equality tribunal display a willingness on the part of the equality tribunal to invoke its jurisdiction pursuant to s.82 of the 1998 Act to make awards solely addressed at reflecting the effects of the discrimination, notwithstanding what might be termed the lack of either causation or loss in the particular circumstances.[71]

2.6. The Health and Safety Authority

The Health and Safety Authority was established under the Safety, Health and [1–30] Welfare at Work Act 1989. Although this piece of legislation was repealed by the Safety, Health and Welfare at Work Act 2005 – analysed in detail in Chapter 15 of this book – s.32 of the latter Act expressly provides that the authority shall continue in existence. The chief responsibility of the authority is for the promotion and enforcement of workplace health and safety in Ireland. Its far-reaching powers also have implications for other areas. In the context of workplace bullying, harassment and stress, for instance, the HSA has introduced a Code of Practice, discussed in detail in Chapter 16.

2.7. Labour Inspectorate

Various employment law statutes considered in this book envisage the possi- [1–31] bility of their terms being enforced *inter alia* through the work of inspectors[72] or

---

71. For detailed discussion, see Chapters 7–10.
72. Specifically the Industrial Relations Acts 1946 to 1990, National Minimum Wage Act 2000, the Organisation of Working Time Act 1997 and the Protection of Young Persons (Employment) Act 1996.

'authorized officers'[73] appointed thereunder.[74] The precise powers of such inspectors for the purposes of any particular statute, are contained within that statute but in general such inspectors are authorised to come onto the employer's property at reasonable times; to interview employees and take statements; to require the production of, examine and take copies of records; to initiate prosecution of certain offences under various Acts; and to institute civil proceedings on behalf of a worker in specific circumstances.[75] Moreover, it is an offence under these statutes to obstruct or hinder the work of such inspectors or to decline to answer questions put by the inspector and to fail to answer such questions truthfully.

Controversy has surrounded the question of what may be done by an inspector with material that has come to light in the course of the inspection process. In particular, it has proved controversial as to whether such findings may be published generally,[76] or whether they can only be conveyed to specific persons.

[1–32] This was the issue at stake in *Gama Endustri Tesisleri Imalat Montag A.S v Minister for Enterprise Trade and Employment & Anor.*[77] In February 2005, Mr Joe Higgins TD made a statement in the Dáil alleging that the applicant company had been guilty of various infractions of employment laws and on a wide scale. Specifically it was alleged that it had breached its obligations towards its employees under the Organisation of Working Time Act 1997, and the Minimum Wage Act 2000. In response the Minister for Enterprise, Trade and Employment directed the Labour Inspectorate (and specifically its head, Edward Nolan) to investigate the matter. Following an investigation (which, the Supreme Court accepted, was conducted in accordance with fair procedures) a report was produced, which, so it would appear, was intended for general publication. Having obtained interlocutory relief from Kelly J in April 2005 restraining general publication of the report – though not its publication to various named entities being enforcement agencies in the state,[78] the company sought a full judicial review of the inspection process and

---

73. Redundancy Payments Acts 1967 to 1991, Protection of Employment Act 1977, Employment Agency Act 1971, European Communities (Safeguarding of Employees Rights on Transfer of Undertakings) Regulations 1980, Protection of Employees (Employers Insolvency) Acts 1984 to 1991 and Payment of Wages Act 1991.

74. As is noted later in this chapter, the Employment Compliance Bill 2008, if and when enacted, will transfer responsibility to the National Employment Rights Association (NERA), created under s.6 of the bill.

75. For analysis of this, see the comments of Kearns J in the Supreme Court in *Gama Endustri Tesisleri Imalat Montag A.S. v Minister for Enterprise Trade and Employment & Anor* [2009] IESC 37.

76. It should be noted that there is express reference to the preparation of a report by an inspector within s.34(4) of the National Minimum Wage Act 2000, but in no other statute.

77. [2009] IESC 37, [2005] IEHC 210.

78. The specific agencies in question to which Kelly J concluded that the Minister for Enterprise, Trade and Employment was 'perfectly entitled' to send the report were the Competition Authority, the Department of Finance, the Department of Transport, the Director

into the legitimacy of the report, claiming an injunction restraining publication of the report, a declaration that the investigation and the preparation of the report were unlawful and an order quashing the report.

In the High Court, Finlay Geoghegan J concluded that the powers afforded to the   [1–33] inspectors under the relevant sections of the Organisation of Working Time Act and the Minimum Wage Act[79] were expressly *for the purposes of the Acts*. In other words, these were not powers to be exercised generally, but rather were specific to the statutes. Hence the extent of such powers were entirely circumscribed by the terms of the legislation. In particular, such powers did not include an incidental or consequential power on the part of the inspector to prepare a report outlining the results of his or her investigation into a particular workplace, nor was it legitimate for the Minister to circulate or publish such a report. On the other hand, the judge, referring to the well known precedent in *Desmond v Glackin (No. 2)*[80] did make the important statement:

> An Inspector must…have an implicit or consequential power under the relevant Employment Acts to pass to the Minister and persons concerned with the civil enforcement procedures information, documents or evidence gathered pursuant to the Inspector's express statutory powers for the purposes of those persons enforcing the obligations imposed by the Acts on employers either by way of civil procedures or by prosecuting alleged offences. I have reached such conclusion by reason of the very limited role for an Inspector provided in the civil enforcement procedures and the limited offences which an Inspector may prosecute. It would render almost useless the express powers conferred on an Inspector to gather and obtain information for the purposes of enforcing the obligations imposed by the Acts unless he had a power to pass on the information gathered.[81]

The Supreme Court on appeal accepted all of these conclusions of Finlay   [1–34] Geoghegan J. On the other hand, it did not accept her conclusion that, inasmuch as there had been *ab initio* an intention that the fruits of the investigation be put into a report that was to be published generally, therefore the report itself was invalid in its entirety and should be quashed. Rather Kearns J held that there was no need to 'conflate the concept of publication with the purposes of the investigation itself'[82]; in other words, the investigation could still be regarded as valid even

---

of Corporation Enforcement, the Garda Fraud Squad, the Garda National Immigration Bureau, the Incorporated Law Society, the Irish Auditing and Accounting Supervisory Authority, the Irish Financial Services Regulatory Authority, the Joint Body of Local Authorities, the National Roads Authority and the Revenue Commissioners.

79. In both the High Court and the Supreme Court it was concluded that the inspector in the particular case was appointed pursuant to the relevant legislation and not on the basis of some floating executive power.

80. [1993] 3 IR 67.

81. [2009] IESC 37 at p.11 of the judgment.

82. [2009] IESC 37 at p.15 of the judgment.

though there had been an invalid intention *vis-à-vis* what should be done with the report when compiled. Alternatively, if this was not a correct statement of the law, Kearns J was nonetheless content that 'the issue of publication is one which in this case can readily be severed from the commissioning of the investigation and the preparation of the ensuring report'.[83]

[1–35]   The net conclusions therefore of the judgments of the Supreme Court and High Court in *Gama* can be stated as follows:

1.   An inspector acting in fulfillment of his or her statutory obligations under any of the relevant pieces of legislation is confined to the exercise of the specific powers and functions contained in or referred to in the legislation.

2.   Such power includes an incidental power to prepare a report for the Minister and for that report to be circulated to relevant statutory agencies.

3.   Such power does *not*, however, include a power to have such a report circulated or published in any more general fashion.

4.   Equally, the validity of both the investigation and of the preparation of the report is not compromised by the fact that the Minister appoints the inspector intending that his or her report will be published in a manner that is not valid under the terms of the legislation.

2.8. The National Employment Rights Agency

[1–36]   Under the terms of the Employment Law Compliance Bill 2008 (discussed below) it would appear that many of the functions currently exercised by the Labour Inspectorate of the Department of Enterprise Trade and Employment are to be transferred to 'authorised officers', appointed under s.35 of the 2008 bill by the Director of the National Employment Rights Authority (NERA) a body which is itself set up and given statutory authority under s.6 of the 2008 bill. At the time of writing, and despite the fact that the statutory basis for its existence has not yet come into being, NERA *is*, nonetheless, already in existence, providing an information service for employers and employees, operating a licensing system under the Protection of Young Persons (Employment) Act 1996, prosecuting offences under the relevant legislation, and taking on the role of inspectors under the relevant pieces of legislation.[84]

[1–37]   NERA (as it currently exists) was set up in 2007 (with an interim director appointed by the Minister for Enterprise, Trade and Employment) and pursuant to the 2006 Partnership Agreement 'Towards 2016'. Equally, and whereas there is mention in that agreement of the perceived need for legislation to be enacted with the aim of

---

83.   [2009] IESC 37 at p.16 of the judgment.

84.   Generally, see Callanan, 'The Power of NERA: An Overview of the New Employment Rights Authority', 2 *Employment Law Review* (2008), 10.

increasing compliance with employment statutes and of a proposal that a new office of Director for Employment Rights Compliance be established, the statutory basis for NERA's existence and operation is exclusively contained within the 2008 Bill. In other words, it is difficult to see the source of the *vires* of the work of NERA *prior to* the coming into being of the bill – and given the tenor of the decision of the Supreme and High Courts in the *Gama* case in which the courts stressed that it was necessary that the work of entities in enforcing employment law statutes be entirely statutorily based, such work may be open to a challenge by way of judicial review. On the other hand, as far as the work of NERA employees as inspectors under the various employment law statutes are concerned, it is simply provided that the Minister may (in writing) appoint inspectors for the purposes of the Act. Hence, provided that this individual written appointment has occurred, there does not appear to be anything problematic in the fact that such appointees are also connected with NERA.

2.9. Relationship between Civil Courts and Specialist Tribunals

The rarity of the circumstances in which the High Court will overturn a decision of [1–38] a specialist tribunal such as the Labour Court has been emphasised by the superior courts in many cases, of which the best-known example is *Henry Denny & Sons (Ireland) Ltd. v Minister for Social Welfare.*[85] In that case Hamilton CJ warned that:

> The courts should be slow to interfere with the decisions of expert administrative tribunals. Where conclusions are based upon an identifiable error of law or an unsustainable finding of fact by a tribunal such conclusions must be corrected. Otherwise it should be recognised that tribunals which have been given statutory tasks to perform and exercise their functions, as is now usually the case, with a high degree of expertise and provide coherent and balanced judgments on the evidence and arguments heard by them it should not be necessary for the courts to review their decisions by way of appeal or judicial review.[86]

This passage invites consideration of another fundamental question: when will a [1–39] determination of the Labour Court properly be characterised as amounting to a matter of law, and when one of fact? On this point, it is instructive to have regard to the more recent Supreme Court decision in *National University of Ireland Cork v Ahern*[87] where the Supreme Court considered what was meant by a 'question of law' in the context of an appeal from the Labour Court (in that case, under s.8(3) of the Anti-Discrimination Pay Act 1974). McCracken J, with whom the other members of the Supreme Court agreed, stated:

> The respondents submit that the matters determined by the Labour Court were largely questions of fact and that matters of fact as found by the Labour Court

---

85. [1997] IESC 9, [1998] 1 IR 34.
86. [1998] 1 IR 34, 37.
87. [2005] IESC 40, [2005] 2 IR 577, [2005] 2 ILRM 437.

must be accepted by the High Court in any appeal from its findings. As a statement of principle, this is certainly correct. However, this is not to say that the High Court or this court cannot examine the basis upon which the Labour Court found certain facts. The relevance, or indeed admissibility, of the matters relied on by the Labour Court in determining the facts is a question of law. In particular, the question of whether certain matters ought or ought not to have been considered by the Labour Court and ought or ought not to have been taken into account by it in determining the facts, is clearly a question of law, and can be considered on an appeal.[88]

3. Future Legislative Developments: The Employment Law Compliance Bill 2008

[1–40] Finally, it is appropriate that brief mention be given to an important future legislative development, which appears to be imminent but which does not predate publication of this book, namely enactment of the Employment Law Compliance Bill 2008. This bill, if and when enacted, is likely to have a radical influence on Irish employment law. Born out of the *Towards 2016* Partnership agreement, its key provisions include the following:

- the establishment of a new statutory office of the Director of the National Employment Rights Authority;
- the strengthening of inspection and enforcement powers in order to ensure compliance with employment legislation in line with 'state-of-the-art' provisions in Revenue, Social Welfare and Consumer Protection legislation; and
- the stipulating of the specifications of statutory employment records to be maintained by employers and the provision of high penalties for breaches of these and other aspects of employment legislation.

[1–41] The implications of these and other far-reaching provisions of the Employment Law Compliance Bill 2008 are at the time of writing the subject of a considerable amount of debate and discussion, not least because the bill envisages a considerable redoubling of the sanctions potentially to be imposed upon employers for lack of compliance with employment law statutes. If enacted, such a regime will harbinger the closer alignment of employment law with other areas of protective regulation: in this regard, it is significant that the Explanatory Memorandum to the 2008 bill expressly refers to the existing models of Revenue, Social Welfare and Consumer Protection legislation as providing inspiration for the compliance model espoused in the 2008 bill. Such a development would clearly bring Irish employment law yet further still away from the *laissez faire* contractual paradigm of the master and servant relationship; its other ramifications remain to be seen.

---

88. [2005] 2 IR 577, 580.

CHAPTER 2

Industrial Relations Law

Introduction

The focus of this chapter is upon aspects of Irish industrial relations law. This body [2–01] of law operates alongside both statutory employment law and basic principles of contract law to govern the relationship between employer and employee. In doing so it takes account of one of the basic realities of the Irish workplace, namely the role of collective lobbying groups – be they workers' trade unions or employers' groups – in determining the manner by which individual employer/employee relationships are to be regulated. Put simply, the development in the 20th century of more sophisticated use by trade unions of collective bargaining procedures and the endorsement of such procedures under industrial relations statutes[1] has meant that, in many cases, an individual worker will enjoy more than that to which [s]he is entitled under statute in terms of pay and conditions, leave entitlements and hours of work, including holidays.

1. The Operation of the Industrial Relations Machinery

For the purposes of this chapter, we will consider three principal areas in which [2–02] the industrial relations machinery (considered in Chapter 1) operates:

(a) in dealing with trade disputes – and as we shall see, since 2001 the ability of the Labour Court to investigate a trade dispute has been significantly increased in circumstances where an employer has no collective bargaining machinery in place;

(b) in the use of Registered Employment Agreements (REAs);

(c) in the work of Joint Labour Committees (JLCs) and Joint Industrial Councils (JICs).

---

1. It is noted throughout this book that in many areas the law permits exceptions to be made to the general statutory procedures that apply in order to allow the results of such collective negotiations to be given effect, such that they will be read into an employee's contract of employment.

[2–03]   In this respect it should be stressed that this is not a book about Irish trade union law, although excellent books on this subject exist.[2] Hence we will not be focusing on the constitutional position of trade unions, the question of whether there should be mandatory recognition of trade unions by employers,[3] and the law, both constitutional and statutory in respect of strikes and other forms of industrial action. Our essential focus in this chapter is rather on the manner by which industrial relations legislation supplements general employment law.[4]

1.1. The Resolution of Trade Disputes

[2–04]   One of the primary functions of the industrial relations machinery in Ireland is in the resolution of trade disputes, and in this respect, the concept of a 'trade dispute' is given a wide definition at Irish law.[5] Under s.3 of the Industrial Relations Act 1946, a trade dispute is defined as 'any dispute or difference between employers and workers[6] or between workers and workers connected with the employment

---

2.   See, for example, Forde, *Industrial Relations Law* (Round Hall Press, 1991); Kerr & Whyte, *Irish Trade Union Law* (Abingdon; Professional Books, 1985).

3.   See, for example, Howlin & Fitzpatrick, 'The Feasibility of Mandatory Trade Union Recognition in Ireland', 29 *DULJ* (2007), 179. For a comparative perspective', see Rosnic, 'Irish and European Law and the *Irish Ferries* Trade Dispute: An American Lawyer's View of What's Wrong with Irish Industrial Relations Legislation', 6 *Employment Law Review* (2005), 131.

4.   Furthermore, historically it is perhaps more accurate to regard what has been termed 'collective labour law' in this area as supplementing the traditionally voluntary processes of industrial relations negotiations (see Gibbs, 'Beyond Voluntarism in Collective Labour Law', 2(1) *IELJ* (2005), 3). Equally, as we shall see later in this chapter, the general thrust of industrial relations law in Ireland since 2001 has been towards reform of the voluntarist nature of this traditional system.

5.   In *Bell Security v TEEU*, CD/07/654 10 April 2008, the Labour Court rejected the suggestion from an employer that a trade dispute could not occur where the internal dispute-resolution procedures within a company had not been exhausted, and hence, in order to prove that a trade dispute existed one would also have to prove that such internal procedures no longer worked.

6.   Under s.23 of the Industrial Relations Act 1990, a 'worker' is defined as 'any person aged 15 years or more who has entered into or works under a contract with an employer whether the contract be for manual labour, clerical work or otherwise, whether it be express or implied, oral or in writing, and whether it be a contract of service or of apprenticeship or a contract personally to execute any work or labour'. In *BATU & Scott v Labour Court and Others* [2005] IEHC 109, Murphy J held that this definition was sufficiently broad to include persons providing services personally and whether under a contract of service or a contract for services and was also broad enough to include sub-contractors. This approach has been consistently followed by the Labour Court in subsequent cases. See *Headland Homes Ltd. v BATU*, CD/06/973, REA 0823, 11 March 2008; *Headland Homes v BATU*, CD/06/838, REA 0821, 2 April 2008; *Murphy & O'Sullivan t/a Skellig Construction v BATU*, CD/06/961, REA 0767, 23 November 2007; *EP Lynam Properties Ltd. v BATU*, CD/06/588, REA 075; 19 January 2007. In addition, it would appear that a person who *used* to work for his or her employer but has since been dismissed or made redundant is still a worker for the purposes of s.23 of the 1990 Act: *Galway Clinic v SIPTU*, CD/06/1143, recommendation no. 18815,

or non-employment[7] or the terms of the employment or with the conditions of employment of any person'.[8]

The breadth of this definition was temporarily enhanced when the Labour Court, [2–05] in interpreting the term in its decision in *Ryanair v IMPACT*,[9] took the view that there is a distinction to be drawn between the terms 'dispute' and 'difference' within the statutory provision, and that a *difference* could be something falling short of a *dispute*.[10] In other words, the statutory provisions relating to trade disputes could apply to a situation where there was a disagreement *inter partes* but where the parties had not yet become so entrenched in their positions that the matter had turned into a dispute proper.[11] The Supreme Court, however, rejected this distinction in the appeal taken by Ryanair against this determination by the Labour Court[12] (which will be considered in detail later). Thus it held that:

> It is common in statutes to include overlapping nouns or adjectives. For instance, if Ryanair and a particular group of its employees with which it was dealing were in disagreement over the dismissal of some employee, that would incontrovertibly be a *'dispute'*. On the other hand if the disagreement related to interpretation of say a collective agreement, it might at least be argued that that was not a *'dispute'*. The inclusion of the word *'difference'* is intended only to indicate the wider meaning of *'trade dispute'*. In the definition itself both words come within the expression *'trade dispute'*. The Labour Court in considering whether there was a *'trade dispute'* should have investigated whether there was internal machinery for resolving the perceived problem and whether that machinery had been exhausted.[13]

---

18 January 2007; *Goulding Chemicals v Bolger* [1977] IR 211; *Bradbury Ltd. v Duffy* [1984] JISLL 86.

7. It has been held that a dispute concerning dismissal is still a trade dispute for the purposes of s.3 of the 1946 Act in that it is connected with 'the employment or non-employment' of workers. *Galway Clinic v SIPTU*, CD/06/1143, recommendation no. 18815, 18 January 2007; *Goulding Chemicals v Bolger* [1977] IR 211.

8. A slightly more restricted definition of a trade dispute is given in Part II of the Industrial Relations Act 1990 and for the purposes of Part II, which deals with industrial action.

9. *Ryanair v Irish Municipal and Civil Trade Union/Irish Airlines Pilot Association*, CD/04/1199, DECP 051, 25 January 2005. The point has also been made that the concept of a trade dispute under the Industrial Relations Act 1946 is so broad that it could be used to cover situations that would otherwise arise, for example, before the Employment Appeals Tribunal. See Moffat, ed., *Employment Law* (2nd ed., Oxford University Press, 2006), at para.10.2.1.

10. For a similar conclusion, see *O'Connor Meats Ltd. v SIPTU*, CD/06/379, recommendation no. 18583, 22 May 2006.

11. This distinction was accepted by the High Court in *Ryanair v Labour Court* [2005] IEHC 330, [2006] ELR 1 and in other Labour Court decisions occurring prior to the Supreme Court decision in the *Ryanair* case. See, for example, *O'Connor Meats v SIPTU*, CD/06/379, recommendation no. 18583, 22 May 2006.

12. *Ryanair v Labour Court & IMPACT* [2007] IESC 6, [2007] 4 IR 199, [2007] ELR 57. See Turner, 'Case and Comment', 4(1) *IELJ* (2007), 24.

13. *Ryanair v Labour Court & IMPACT* [2007] 4 IR at 216 (emphasis added).

[2–06]   Finally, and whereas the concept of a Labour Court investigation of a trade dispute is commonly associated with a relatively large-scale conflict between unions and employers, it can also cover a situation where there is a localised dispute between a single employer and an employee.[14]

[2–07]   Under the legislation, there are in essence two methods by which an investigation of a trade dispute can be heard, one of which applies generally (under s.20 of the Industrial Relations Act 1969) and one of which applies in circumstances where the employer has refused to deal collectively with a union (under the Industrial Relations (Amendment) Act 2001 as amended by the Industrial Relations (Supplemental Provisions) Act 2004). As we shall see, this latter procedure is particularly significant in that it appears to strike at the hitherto voluntarist nature of Irish industrial relations law.

1.1.1. Section 20 of the Industrial Relations Act 1969

[2–08]   As we have seen, one of the principal functions of the Industrial Relations Acts 1946–2004 is to authorise the use of the State's industrial relations machinery to deal with trade disputes.[15] So, for example, under s.20 of the Industrial Relations Act 1969, provision is made for workers concerned in a trade dispute or their trade union[s] to request the Labour Court to investigate the dispute as a whole or for the parties to a trade dispute to request the Labour Court to investigate a specified issue or issues within the dispute.[16] In such circumstances, and provided that the relevant parties undertake beforehand to accept the recommendation of the Labour Court in respect of the same, then the Court shall investigate the dispute[17] and make a recommendation.[18] Such recommendation will set forth the Court's opinion on the merits of the dispute and the terms on which it feels that it should be settled. The recommendation must be communicated to all parties to the dispute and to such other persons as the Court thinks fit.[19]

---

14. See, for example, *Little Rascal Creche v SIPTU*, CD/06/636, recommendation no. 18648, 24 July 2006.

15. So, for example, under s.70 of the Industrial Relations Act 1946 it is provided that where a trade dispute has occurred or is apprehended, the Court, with the consent of all the parties concerned, may refer the dispute to the arbitration of one or more persons or may itself arbitrate upon the dispute. See *Waterford Crystal v ATGWU*, CD 94660 ARB 951, 4 May 1995.

16. s.20(2) Industrial Relations Act 1969.

17. Such investigations are heard in private but, if a party to the dispute requests it, the Court must conduct it in public, and if it is conducted in public then the Court may at its discretion conduct in private any aspects of the dispute it thinks should be treated as confidential: s.8 *ibid.*

18. The Labour Court is prohibited from issuing a recommendation in respect of a claim that is based on the restoration of a pay differential between an employee and another employee who has secured or is to secure an increase in pay as a result of the passing of the National Minimum Wage Act: s.43(1) National Minimum Wage Act 2000.

19. s.68 Industrial Relations Act 1946.

Under the 1990 Industrial Relations Act, however, primary responsibility for [2–09] dealing with trade disputes – certainly as a tribunal of first resort – passes to the Labour Relations Commission. Thus under s.25(2) of the 1990 Act it is provided that the LRC, at the request of one or more parties to a trade dispute or on its own initiative, may offer the party its appropriate services with a view to bringing about a settlement. Moreover, it is further provided that save where there is specific provision for a matter to be referred *ab initio* to the Labour Court, a trade dispute is to be referred first to the Labour Relations Commission or its appropriate services.[20] Thus the current position is that the Labour Court may not investigate a trade dispute unless it has received a report from the LRC stating that it is satisfied that no further efforts on its part will advance the resolution of the dispute and moreover that the parties have requested the Court to investigate the dispute,[21] or alternatively, unless the chairman of the commission (or some member or officer authorised by the chairman) notifies the Court that in the circumstances it waives its function of conciliation in the dispute and, again, that the parties to the dispute have requested the Court to investigate it.[22] Finally, the Labour Court may also investigate a dispute if, having consulted with the LRC, it is of the opinion that this is warranted by the exceptional circumstances of the case.[23]

Under s.13(2) of the Industrial Relations Act 1969, it is possible for a party to a [2–10] trade dispute *other than one dealing with rates of pay, hours or times of work of or annual holidays of a body of workers* to refer that dispute to a Rights Commissioner for investigation and in such circumstances the Rights Commissioner is required to investigate the matter, make a recommendation to the parties setting out his or her opinion on the merits of the dispute, and notify the Court as well as the Minister and the LRC[24] of the recommendation. On the other hand, the Rights Commissioner may not investigate such a dispute if the Court has made a recommendation in relation to it, or if one of the parties to the dispute, within three weeks of the date on which notice of the reference of the dispute to the commissioner has been posted to him, notifies the Rights Commissioner of his objection to the dispute being investigated by him.[25] A recommendation of a Rights Commissioner in relation to a trade dispute may be appealed to the Labour Court[26] but notice of such appeal must be given by the prospective appellant to

---

20. s.25(3) Industrial Relations Act 1990.
21. s.26(1) Industrial Relations Act 1990. Under s.26(2) *ibid.* it is provided that such report will include information on the issues in dispute, the attempts made to resolve the dispute, and any other information the LRC considers to be of assistance to the Labour Court.
22. s.26(3) *ibid.*
23. s.36(5) *ibid.*
24. s.36(3) *ibid.* The LRC is precluded from exercising its function of conciliation on a dispute on which a Rights Commissioner has made a recommendation: s.36(4) *ibid.*
25. s.13 (3)(b)(ii) Industrial Relations Act 1969 and s.36(1) Industrial Relations Act 1990.
26. s.13(9)(a) Industrial Relations Act 1969. The statute provides that the parties to the dispute shall be bound by the decision of the Court on appeal, though it is difficult to see how this could be possible in the absence of any enforcement powers within the Labour Court.

the Court within six weeks of the making of the recommendation by the Rights Commissioner.[27]

[2–11]   Finally, where the Minister is of the opinion that a trade dispute, whether actual or apprehended, affects the public interest, then [s]he may refer the matter to the Court or commission, which shall endeavour to resolve the dispute.[28] Alternatively, if the Minister is of the opinion that the dispute is one of *special importance* [s]he may request the LRC or the Labour Court (or another person or body) to conduct an enquiry into the dispute and to furnish a report to him or her on the findings.[29] It is, perhaps, uncertain, at least in theory, as to how to distinguish between a dispute that is of special importance and a dispute that affects the public importance, but this is a matter that is at the discretion of the Minister and depends on his or her view.

[2–12]   In this respect it is worth noting the conclusion of the Supreme Court in *Ryanair v IMPACT*[30] that, whereas it may be legitimate for the Labour Court to define its own procedures, equally it was a breach of fair procedures for it to reach conclusions of fact that were not supported by any oral testimony.[31] This conclusion is an interesting one with ramifications well beyond the facts of this case. Traditionally, after all, as Doherty notes[32] the approach of the courts in Ireland towards the Labour Court had been one of comparative deference – similar, in a sense, to the approach the courts take, for example, to bodies charged under statute with the application of planning law. Thus the view appeared to be that the Labour Court was a body of experts in this area of law whose decisions, recommendations and procedures the civil courts should consequently be slow to disturb.[33] Yet the effect of the Supreme Court's considerably less deferential decision in *Ryanair* must surely be radically to alter the manner in which the Labour Court does business.[34]

---

27. s.36(2) *ibid.*

28. s.38(1) *ibid.*

29. s.38(2) *ibid.*

30. [2007] IESC 6, [2007] 4 IR 199, [2007] ELR 57. It should be noted that this case was not a referral of a trade dispute under the 1990 Act.

31. See, for example, *Castle Furniture Ltd. v SIPTU*, CD/07/248, recommendation no. 19002, 1 October 2007, for the view that by application of the principles laid down by the Supreme Court in *Ryanair*, the Labour Court would be bound to find *against* an employer on questions of fact where the employer had not turned up to the Labour Court hearing and consequently had not presented evidence on its own behalf.

32. See Doherty, 'Union Sundown? The Future of Collective Representation Rights in Irish Law', 4(4) *IELJ* (2007), 96.

33. See, for example, the approach of Clarke J in *Ashford Castle Ltd. v SIPTU* [2006] IEHC 201, [2007] 4 IR 70, and that of Hanna J in the High Court in *Ryanair v Labour Court and IMPACT* [2005] IEHC 330, [2006] ELR 1. Generally, see Ryan, 'Leaving it to the Experts – In the Matter of the Industrial Relations (Amendment) Act 2001: *Ashford Castle Limited v SIPTU*', 3(4) *IELJ* (2006), 118; and Smith, 'Ryanair and IMPACT: The Dispute so Far', 5 *Employment Law Review* (2007), 2.

34. Doherty predicts that the Supreme Court decision 'will likely have the effect of encour-

This is not to say that such a step is inappropriate – indeed if existing procedures were fundamentally unfair or flawed then plainly it *is* appropriate that they not be allowed to stand simply because they have been created by an 'expert body'. Nonetheless what occurred in this aspect of the Supreme Court's decision in the case may turn out to be as significant as any other.[35]

1.1.2. *The Industrial Relations (Amendment) Act 2001*

A newer and more controversial procedure for dealing with trade disputes is [2–13] prescribed under s.2(1) of the Industrial Relations Act 2001 as amended by the Industrial Relations (Miscellaneous Provisions) Act 2004.[36] This procedure arguably represents a more forceful approach towards the resolution of industrial disputes generally, and in particular in circumstances where a worker or workers can be regarded as being disadvantaged by the fact that it is not the normal practice of his or her employer to negotiate collectively with unions or similar groups. Moreover, as has been recognised by a number of commentators, the new procedure could have been the basis for a gradual dismantling of the traditionally voluntarist approach to trade dispute resolution that had previously existed within Irish industrial relations law, and may indeed have amounted to an incentive for employers to recognise and deal with trade unions.[37]

---

aging a greater formality in respect of Labour Court hearings and perhaps encourage a further justification of the process' and suggests that it might well lead to 'the extension of higher evidential standards into other cases heard in the Labour Court...[which]...could make Labour Court hearings more legalistic and more akin to ordinary civil Court actions', and that ultimately this will likely lead to 'more lawyers, more delays and more costs'. See Doherty, 'Union Sundown? The Future of Collective Representation Rights in Irish Law', 4(4) *IELJ* (2007), 96. See also Sheehan, 'Labour Court's Guidelines for 2001–2004 Cases in wake of "*Ryanair*" judgement', 14 *Industrial Relations News* (2007), 1, for a list of changes that the Labour Court has adopted as far as its own procedures are concerned.

35. The Labour Court has interpreted the decision of the Supreme Court in *Ryanair* as meaning not that all of the workers who are complainants in a case must give evidence before the Court, but rather that 'credible and cogent evidence (if required) be given by the complainants in the case as to the status of their complaint': *Headland Homes v BATU*, CD/06/838, REA 0821, 2 April 2008. Thus in that case the Labour Court found that where one worker appeared in Court and testified that he had worked for the company, this was sufficient to establish that the identified employees were the workers referred to by the union in the case.

36. For analysis of the 2004 Act see Kerr, 'Legislative Developments', 1(3) *IELJ* (2004), 98. The general thrust of both the 2001–2004 Acts as well as the relevant codes of practice in this area emerges out of the discussions and recommendations that went towards the 'Partnership 2000' and 'Sustaining Progress' industrial relations negotiations. See Doherty, 'Union Sundown? The Future of Collective Representation Rights in Irish Law', 4(4) *IELJ* (2007), 96 and Ryan, 'Leaving it to the Experts – In the Matter of the Industrial Relations (Amendment) Act 2001: *Ashford Castle Limited v SIPTU*', 3(4) *IELJ* (2006), 118.

37. See, for example, Purdy, 'The Industrial Relations (Amendment) Act 2001 and the Industrial Relations (Miscellaneous Provisions) Act 2004', 1(5) *IELJ* (2004), 142, for the view that the 2001 Industrial Relations Act represented 'the first move against this country's voluntarist system'. See also Gibbs, 'Beyond Voluntarism in Collective Labour Law', 2(1) *IELJ* (2005), 3.

[2–14] This prospect, however, now seems considerably more remote in light of the seminal decision of the Supreme Court in *Ryanair v Labour Court*,[38] which is considered shortly. Nonetheless, the new legislative procedure, whereas it is not aimed at requiring a mandatory system of collective bargaining,[39] is nonetheless likely (and intended[40]) to have a significant impact in a situation where employees in a workplace in which there is no system of collective bargaining do not receive concessions from employers (in relation *inter alia* to pay, terms and conditions of employment, and availability of grievance procedures) that tend to exist within workplaces in which a system of collective bargaining has been in place.[41] As such, the 2001–2004 Acts, as well as various codes of practice that have come into force through ministerial regulations, represent the culmination of various efforts by trade unions to generate a legal culture where this can occur.[42]

For the view that the 2001 Act originally had a 'minimal impact on the industrial relations landscape in Ireland', see Connolly, 'Industrial Relations (Miscellaneous Provisions) Act 2004 – Implications for Industrial Relations Law and Practice of the Supreme Court Decision in *Ryanair v Labour Court and IMPACT*', 4(2) *IELJ* (2007), 37. Generally, see Purdy, 'The Industrial Relations (Amendment) Act 2001 and the Industrial Relations (Miscellaneous Provisions) Act 2004 – Have They Helped?', 1(5) *IELJ* (2004), 142.

38. [2007] IESC 6, [2007] 4 IR 199, [2007] ELR 57.

39. See Connolly, 'Industrial Relations (Miscellaneous Provisions) Act 2004 – Implications for Industrial Relations Law and Practice of the Supreme Court Decision in *Ryanair v Labour Court and IMPACT*', 4(2) *IELJ* (2007), 37 for the view that in cases like *Junk v Kuhnel* [2005] EUECJ C18803, [2005] 1 CMLR 42, [2005] IRLR 310, the ECJ has blurred the lines between the notions of employee consultation (which, as we shall see in Chapter 14, is required by Irish law) and mandatory negotiations with employees (which is not). See also Doherty, 'Union Sundown? The Future of Collective Representation Rights in Irish Law', 4(4) *IELJ* (2007), 96.

40. In *Ryanair v Labour Court and IMPACT* [2007] IESC 6, [2007] 4 IR 199, [2007] ELR 57, the Supreme Court expressly took a purposive interpretation of the statute and concluded that the intention behind it was that an employer have some appropriate system in place whereby it would negotiate collectively with employees. See Smith, 'Ryanair and IMPACT: The Dispute so Far', 5 *Employment Law Review* (2007), 2 at p.5.

41. See *SIPTU v GE Healthcare*, CD/04/678, recommendation no. 18013 19 November 2004; *Johnson Matthey v SIPTU*, CD/05/ 819, recommendation no. 18387, 11 November 2005. Generally, see Connolly, 'Industrial Relations (Miscellaneous Provisions) Act 2004 – Implications for Industrial Relations Law and Practice of the Supreme Court Decision in *Ryanair v Labour Court and IMPACT*', 4(2) *IELJ* (2007), 37; Smith, 'Ryanair and IMPACT: The Dispute so Far', 5 *Employment Law Review* (2007), 2; Purdy, 'The Industrial Relations (Amendment) Act 2001 and the Industrial Relations (Miscellaneous Provisions) Act 2004 – A Critique, an Employer's Perspective', 1 *Employment Law Review* (2005), 23.

42. It is worth noting that whereas there is no requirement of mandatory trade union recognition under Irish law, and whereas the 2001–2004 Acts represent the most significant change in this regard in Irish legal history, nonetheless it was always possible under the 1946 and 1990 Industrial Relations Acts that the failure of an employer to recognise trade unions could represent a trade dispute, which could be referred to the Labour Court or Labour Relations Commission and that it could be recommended by such bodies that the employer recognise the trade union and indeed negotiate with it. See Kerr, 'Legislative Developments', 1(3) *IELJ* (2004), 98.

Prior to the 2001 Industrial Relations (Amendment) Act, the only approach for a   **[2–15]**
union that was unable to secure employer acceptance of any Labour Court recommendations in respect of trade disputes that had been referred to it or, indeed, that
was simply unable to get an employer to negotiate collectively on any level, was
to take industrial action against that employer.[43] Since the 2001 Act, however, the
Labour Court can issue binding recommendations in respect of terms and conditions of employment with which an employer who does not negotiate collectively
with employees must comply. Moreover, prior to the decision of the Supreme
Court in the *Ryanair* case (discussed below) it was possible that the 2001–2004
Acts could have led to a situation where in reality an employer would have to
choose between meeting face-to-face with unions on the one hand, or being
required to comply with a binding Labour Court recommendation in respect of
terms and conditions on the other.[44] This decision, however, as we shall see, has
meant that, whereas the legislation still provides a strong incentive to an employer
to negotiate collectively with workers, this may be on his or her terms, nor will it
commit him or her to the traditional form of collective bargaining, which involves
recognition of and negotiation with trade unions.[45]

1.1.2.1. Prerequisites to an Investigation under the 2001–2004 Acts
Under s.2(1) of the Industrial Relations (Amendment) Act of 2001 (as amended[46])   **[2–16]**
the investigatory powers of the Labour Court under the Act generally can only be
activated provided that certain criteria are fulfilled. Thus, apart from being clear
that a 'trade dispute' exists,[47] the Court must be satisfied that[48]:

---

43. See Doherty, 'Union Sundown? The Future of Collective Representation Rights in Irish
    Law', 4(4) *IELJ* (2007), 96.
44. See Gibbs, 'Beyond Voluntarism in Collective Labour Law', 2(1) *IELJ* (2005), 3, for the view
    that the transition from complete voluntarism to a more directive system was made more
    incremental and less sudden by virtue of the absence of 'speedy enforcement procedures' for
    Labour Court recommendations. It may be suggested that in fact it was the limitations of
    the original 2001 Code of Practice that was of most significance in this regard. Generally,
    see Connolly, 'Industrial Relations (Miscellaneous Provisions) Act 2004 – Implications for
    Industrial Relations Law and Practice of the Supreme Court Decision in *Ryanair v Labour
    Court and IMPACT*', 4(2) *IELJ* (2007), 37, for the view that the impact of the legislation has
    resulted in a situation that sees the Labour Court 'increasingly directing employers who do
    not recognise trade unions for collective bargaining purposes to deal with trade unions for a
    wide range of purposes'.
45. See Doherty, 'Union Sundown? The Future of Collective Representation Rights in Irish
    Law', 4(4) *IELJ* (2007), 96, for the view that such legislation may play a considerably
    reduced role in the resolution of further disputes following *Ryanair*, not least because of
    Geoghegan J's statement in the case that the ability of employers to refuse to deal with trade
    unions was protected by law, and that no law could be passed undermining that ability.
46. The original s.2 of the 2001 Act was replaced under the terms of s.2 of the Industrial Rela-
    tions (Miscellaneous Provisions) Act 2004.
47. The question of the definition of a 'trade dispute' has been considered earlier at para.1.1.
48. As defined in s.6 of the Trade Union Act of 1941, as amended by the Trade Union Act of
    1942. In *Ryanair v Labour Court and IMPACT*, the Supreme Court held that if there was

1. It is not the practice of the employer to engage in collective bargaining negotiations in respect of the grade, group or category of workers who are party to the trade dispute and the internal dispute resolution procedures (if any) normally used by the parties concerned have failed to resolve the dispute,

2. Either

    (i) the employer has failed to observe—

    (I) a provision of the Code of Practice on Voluntary Dispute Resolution under s.42 of the Industrial Relations Act 1990 specifying the period of time for the doing of any thing (or such a provision of any code of practice amending or replacing that code), or

    (II) any agreement by the parties extending that period of time or,

    (ii) the dispute having been referred to the Commission for resolution in accordance with the provisions of such code, no further efforts on the part of the Commission will, in the opinion of the Commission, advance the resolution of the dispute and the Court has received a report from the Commission to that effect,[49]

3. The trade union or the excepted body or the employees as the case may be have not acted in a manner which, in the opinion of the Court has frustrated the employer in observing a provision of such code of practice and

4. The trade union or the excepted body or the employees as the case may be have not had recourse to industrial action after the dispute in question was referred to the Commission in accordance with the provisions of such code of practice.

[2–17] Where these criteria have been met (and the Court has the discretion to hold a preliminary hearing for the purposes of determining whether or not this has happened or simply to allow this question to form part of its investigation),[50] the Labour Court can investigate a trade dispute irrespective of whether or not the employer agrees and, as we shall see, can issue a binding determination following its investigation, which can be enforced by the Circuit Court.

---

an Employee Representative Committee in place whereby employees could negotiate on a collective basis with management, then this would constitute an excepted body for the purposes of the legislation.

49. This conclusion may, for example, be reached where an employer has attended an advisory service hearing pursuant to the 2004 Voluntary Code of Practice (considered below) but, as a result of an entrenched opposition to the idea of granting the union any degree of recognition, that employer has refused to participate meaningfully in proceedings. Purdy, 'The Industrial Relations (Amendment) Act 2001 and the Industrial Relations (Miscellaneous Provisions) Act 2004 – Have They Helped?', 1(5) *IELJ* (2004), 142.

50. s.3 Industrial Relations (Amendment) Act 2001, as amended by s.3 of the Industrial Relations (Miscellaneous Provisions) Act 2004. It would appear that the Labour Court will only hold such a preliminary hearing on the application of one of the parties to the case. Where it decides *not* to hold a preliminary hearing, the Court's normal practice is to hear submissions on the jurisdictional issue, reserve judgement thereon, and then proceed to hear the parties on the substantive issue, although it would seem that either party to the matter could object to such procedure: *O'Connor Meats Ltd. v SIPTU*, CD/06/379, recommendation no. 18583, 22 May 2006.

Many applications to the Labour Court under the 2001 Act will entail a prelimi- [2–18]
nary enquiry into the question of whether the above prerequisites exist (and
consequently, whether the Court has jurisdiction over the matter). In this respect,
three key questions derive from the various criteria contained in s.2:

(a) Is it the normal practice of the employer to engage in collective
bargaining and have the internal dispute-resolution procedures normally
used by the parties have failed?

(b) Has the employer failed to observe a provision of a relevant Code of
Practice on voluntary dispute resolution? and

(c) Have the employees/trade union acted in a way that has reduced the
legitimacy of their standing, either through acting in a manner that
frustrates the employer's ability to observe a relevant term in a Code of
Practice or by commencing industrial action when the matter is already
before the LRC?

These three questions are now considered in turn.

A. Is it the normal practice[51] of the employer to engage in collective bargaining
and have the internal dispute-resolution procedures normally availed of by the
parties concerned failed to resolve the dispute?

There are two separate aspects to this prerequisite under s.2 of the 2001 Act and [2–19]
we will consider them separately, but prior to doing so, it is worth noting the
significance of the use of the conjunctive '*and*' (rather than 'or') in the section.
Essentially, it would seem that a union must prove *both* that it is not normal
practice of the employer to engage in collective bargaining and *also* (and even if it
proves this first point) that any internal dispute-resolution procedures normally
availed of by the parties have failed to resolve the dispute. In other words, the best
advice for an employer who wishes to avoid collective bargaining and also to avoid
the application of the procedures under the Industrial Relations Acts 2001–2004
would be simply to create some internal dispute-resolution procedures and ensure
that they are capable of resolving the relevant dispute.

---

51. By 'practice' in this sense, the Labour Court has inferred a requirement that the employer
'normally or routinely' engage in collective bargaining (*Ryanair v IMPACT*, CD/04/1199,
DECP 051, 25 January 2005). In the Supreme Court decision in *Ryanair* the Court required
a machinery to be in place that would have obliged the management to sit around the table
with representatives of workers and discuss matters of pay and conditions. This definition
has been adopted subsequently by the Labour Court (*Bell Security v TEEU*, CD/07/654,
recommendation no. 19188, 10 April 2008). Generally, see Purdy, 'The Industrial Relations
(Amendment) Act 2001 and the Industrial Relations (Miscellaneous Provisions) Act 2004
– Have They Helped?', 1(5) *IELJ* (2004), 142, for the view that the legislation clearly implies
that such a process must already be in place at the time of the dispute.

Is it the normal practice of the employer to engage in collective bargaining in respect of the grade, group or category of workers who are party to the trade dispute?

[2–20] Again, within this aspect of s.2 of the Act of 2001 two sub-questions emerge:
(1) What is meant by a normal practice of collective bargaining?
(2) What is meant by 'the grade, group or category of workers who are party to the trade dispute'?

[2–21] *Defining Collective Bargaining:* This issue is a major one as far as interpretation of the 2001–2004 Industrial Relation Acts is concerned, in that there are two possible approaches that the courts (and in particular the Labour Court) could theoretically adopt. The first is to define collective bargaining by reference to the traditional and highly formalised process of negotiations that occur between a union and an employer who recognises such union.[52] Were such an approach to be adopted, the Labour Court would have to conclude that any informal mechanisms whereby an employer negotiates with workers at a general or collective level (rather than individually) would not constitute collective bargaining under the Act if they did not resemble the traditional employer/unions negotiations structure.

[2–22] The alternative approach is to look to the purpose of the 2001 Act (as is manifest in the report of the High Level Group, which was, itself, the basis for the 2001 Act), which sought to achieve an increased degree of negotiations between workers and management but to do so without creating a legal environment in which an employer was compelled to recognise or negotiate with unions. Were such an approach to be adopted, the reference to 'collective bargaining' in s.2 of the 2001 Act would have to be interpreted in a broad sense and be deemed to include even any informal practices whereby employers and workers are engaged in negotiations pertaining to terms and conditions of employment.

---

52. It is arguable that this is the approach taken by the Labour Court prior to the Supreme Court decision in *Ryanair*. See, for example, *Little Rascal Creche v SIPTU*, CD/06/636, recommendation no. 18648, 24 July 2006; and especially *Ashford Castle Ltd. v SIPTU*, CD/03/658, DECP 032, 19 November 2003, in which the Labour Court specifically said that for the purposes of the 2001 Act, collective bargaining 'is synonymous with the approach to the determination of pay and conditions of employment typically found in unionised employments but not the various internal systems of communication and employee consultation typically found in the non-unionised sector'. See Purdy, 'The Industrial Relations (Amendment) Act 2001 and the Industrial Relations (Miscellaneous Provisions) Act 2004 – A Critique, an Employer's Perspective', 1 *Employment Law Review* (2005), 23 at 25 for a criticism of this narrow approach to interpretation of the term (as adopted by the Labour Court in *Ryanair v IMPACT*, CD/04/1199, DECP 051, 25 January 2005) on the basis that it goes against the legislative intention underpinning the 2001–2004 Acts by essentially requiring workers to engage in negotiations with unions.

The question of which of these approaches is appropriate was one of the core [2–23] matters under discussion by the Supreme Court in *Ryanair v The Labour Court*.[53] This case began life as an application under s.2 of the 2001–2004 Acts by IMPACT and the Irish Airline Pilots Association in respect of the Ryanair company.[54] The unions in question argued that there was a trade dispute between its workers and Ryanair, and that, inasmuch as the criteria under s.2 of the 2001 Act were fulfilled (that is, that Ryanair did not as a matter of normal practice engage in collective bargaining, that the relevant internal dispute procedures had failed to resolve the dispute, and that Ryanair had not complied with the relevant provisions of the 2000 Code of Practice), the Labour Court had jurisdiction to investigate the matter under the 2001 Act as amended. Ryanair for its part argued that the Labour Court did *not* have jurisdiction to deal with the matter *inter alia* because Ryanair *did* engage in collective bargaining with employees, albeit in an informal manner and through what were termed 'town hall meetings', and via Employee Representative Committees (ERCs).[55]

The Labour Court had held that this did not constitute a normal practice of collec- [2–24] tive bargaining for the purposes of the act.[56] This was for a number of reasons. First, in its view, the ERC approach was essentially merely a basis for the provision of information by management; secondly, it argued that had these procedures amounted to collective bargaining for the purposes of the Act then matters such as the manner by which the ERCs had been established, as well as matters relating to pension benefits and training arrangements, would have been discussed; thirdly it argued that the ERC process could not amount to collective bargaining because (so it was alleged) by the time the action came before the Labour Court, the pilots had actually withdrawn from such ERCs.

The Supreme Court took the view that the unilateral withdrawal by the pilots [2–25] from the ERC process could not, of itself, ground the claim that there was no collective bargaining process in place for employees.[57] More generally it accepted

---

53. *IMPACT v Ryanair* [2005] ELR 99, Labour Court; *Ryanair v Labour Court and IMPACT* [2005] IEHC 330 [2007] 1 ILRM 45, [2006] ELR 1, High Court; *Ryanair v Labour Court* [2007] IESC 6, [2007] 4 IR 199, [2007] ELR 57, Supreme Court.
54. For an analysis of the facts of the relevant dispute, see Doherty, 'Union Sundown? The Future of Collective Representation Rights in Irish Law', 4(4) *IELJ* (2007), 96.
55. As we have seen, Ryanair further claimed that it had been denied fair procedures in the Labour Court and that the Labour Court decision was irrational in that it had reached a finding of fact without any oral testimony to support it.
56. The Labour Court had held that the word *practice* in the Act suggests that the employer must normally engage in collective bargaining with the relevant workers.
57. The Court took the view that the Labour Court's conclusion that the fact of such unilateral withdrawal meant that internal procedures had failed was based on a mistaken understanding of the Supreme Court's decision in *Iarnród Éireann v Holbrooke* [2001] IESC 7, [2001] 1 IR 237, where the Supreme Court had essentially concluded that an 'excepted body' did not exist because the employer refused to negotiate with the employees. See Murray

that the concept of collective bargaining was something of a term of art and it cited the definition of collective bargaining used by the Labour Court in *Ashford Castle Ltd. v SIPTU*[58]:

> Collective bargaining comprehends more than mere negotiation or consultation on individual employment related issues including the processing of individual grievances in relation to pay or conditions of employment. In the industrial relations context in which the term is commonly used it connotes a process by which employers or their representatives negotiate with representatives of a group or body of workers for the purpose of concluding a collective agreement fixing the pay and other conditions of employment applicable to the group or collective of workers on whose behalf the negotiations are conducted.

> Normally the process is characterised by the involvement of a trade union representing workers but it may also be conducted by a staff association which is an excepted body within the meaning of the *Trade Union Act 1941*, as amended. However, an essential characteristic of collective bargaining, properly so called, is that it is conducted between parties of equal standing who are independent in the sense that one is not controlled by the other.[59]

[2–26] Equally, the Supreme Court felt that this definition was an overly rigid one, which derived from, and was applicable only to, a workplace in which there was employer recognition of unions. It would, however, have no application in a workplace situation where (as was the case with Ryanair) negotiations with workers took place on a more informal basis. Yet pivotally, according to the Supreme Court, such informal negotiations could still be held to amount to collective negotiations.[60] In other words, according to the Supreme Court, what was needed was an ordinary as distinct from a 'special trade union meaning' of the term 'collective bargaining', nor did such a practice (for the purposes of s.2 of the 2001–2004 Acts) necessarily require the type of activity that would be associated with trade union negotiations with employers. All that was needed, as far as the Supreme Court was concerned, was that there be some permanent machinery in place that obliged management

---

Smith, 'Ryanair and IMPACT: The Dispute so Far', 5 *Employment Law Review* (2007), 2.

58. [2004] ELR 214.
59. [2004] ELR 214 at 217.
60. Again the Supreme Court took the view that employers' representatives had testified that this *was* a collective bargaining situation and, in the absence of conflicting oral testimony from employees who were party to such disputes, it would be inappropriate to arrive at a different conclusion on this issue of fact. See Connolly, 'Industrial Relations (Miscellaneous Provisions) Act 2004 – Implications for Industrial Relations Law and Practice of the Supreme Court Decision in *Ryanair v Labour Court and IMPACT*', 4(2) *IELJ* (2007), 37, for the view that this approach of the Supreme Court may open the door for employers to resist the jurisdiction of the Labour Court over an alleged trade dispute by pointing to informal consultation and negotiation mechanisms that were in place, and claiming that they amount to mechanisms for collective bargaining.

to discuss matters pertaining *inter alia* to pay and conditions with representatives of employees.[61] For present purposes, the Supreme Court concluded that the ERC approach adopted by Ryanair (certainly in the absence of contradictory evidence from the employees in the case) could constitute collective bargaining and, *inter alia* for this reason, the Labour Court did not have jurisdiction under s.2 of the 2001–2004 Acts to hear the matter.[62] Since the decision in *Ryanair* the Labour Court has adopted the approach of the Supreme Court in that case, holding that 'The only requirement (in order for a collective bargaining situation to arise) appears to be that the object of the discussions must be to reach agreement if possible'.[63]

What is the grade, group or category of workers who are party to the trade dispute? Again [2–27] this can be a troubling issue for employers. Of particular concern is the question of whether the reference to the 'parties to the trade dispute' in s.2 of the 2001–2004 Acts relates to the parties before the Court or the parties to the trade dispute itself. If the former was the case, after all, the position would become virtually impossible for the employer who does not want to negotiate with unions, in that the party before the Court will almost inevitably be a union, yet the very reason why

---

61. Doherty, 'Union Sundown? The Future of Collective Representation Rights in Irish Law', 4(4) *IELJ* (2007), 96, argues that this 'loose' definition of the term may mean that Ireland is out of line with international obligations in this regard, including International Labour Organisation conventions, Article 140 of the EC Treaty, Article 28 of the Charter of Fundamental Rights, and Article 11 of the European Convention on Human Rights. See also Murray Smith, 'Ryanair and IMPACT: The Dispute so Far', 5 *Employment Law Review* (2007), 2. In *Bell Security v TEEU*, CD/07/654, recommendation no. 19188, 10 April 2008, the union involved contended that the Labour Court should adopt the ILO definition of collective bargaining as laid down in its 1998 Declaration on Fundamental Principles and Rights at Work, but this appears not to have been accepted by the Labour Court in light of the Supreme Court decision in *Ryanair*.

62. Doherty makes the point that the Supreme Court did not, however, give any guidelines as to the minimum thresholds an ERC-type process would have to cross if it was to be found to be a collective bargaining practice. As he points out, 'It is clear from the Supreme Court judgement that employers would be free to determine the form, structure and organisation of any internal collective bargaining units, as long as these have a degree of permanency and are not *ad hoc*' (Doherty, 'Union Sundown? The Future of Collective Representation Rights in Irish Law', 4(4) *IELJ* (2007), 96). The same author suggests that some assistance in assessing such minimum thresholds (assuming they exist) may be found in the approach to employee consultation taken in legislation (and the grounding EC Directive) requiring consultation and provision of information to employees, which we discuss in Chapter 14 of this book.

63. *Bell Security v TEEU*, CD/07/654, recommendation no. 19188, 10 April 2008. See also *Specialist Training Services t/a Fernley Airport Services v Independent Workers Union*, CD/07/2, recommendation no. 18845, 26 February 2007; *Federal Security Services Ltd. v Independent Workers Union*, CD/06/552, recommendation no. 18621, 4 July 2006, for the view that a collective bargaining situation would exist where an employer had an agreement to negotiate with a union, even if it was not the union of choice of every employee within the workplace.

the matter will have come to the Labour Court at all is because the employer does *not* negotiate with unions and hence naturally will not have collectively bargained with such a party.[64] It is thus appropriate that in *Ryanair v Labour Court and IMPACT*[65] the Supreme Court made it clear that the reference to 'parties' in s.2 of the 2001–2004 Acts was to the parties to the dispute and not the parties before the Court, and moreover, that this applied equally to the question of whether the channels normally used by the parties as internal dispute resolution procedures had failed.[66] It is worth noting further that the Labour Court had already rejected the argument that the reference to the 'parties concerned' could be taken as applying to the employer and his or her employees generally, but would need to mean the employer and the specific employees who were parties to the particular trade dispute.[67]

[2–28] In discussing the question of the 'parties to the dispute' it is important to highlight a further point of difficulty for employers as far as the application of the legislation is concerned, namely that the procedure under the 2001–2004 Acts does not require that the trade union bringing the application disclose the names or other identifying details of the workers whom it represents,[68] nor need it actually represent any of the workers engaged in any trade dispute with the employers. In particular, the legislation does not specify a threshold number of workers to be represented by that union as a prerequisite to bringing a claim.[69] In other words, a union could make a claim on behalf of even a tiny minority of workers in a workplace, where the vast majority of workers had no dispute with the employer.

---

64. See Purdy, 'The Industrial Relations (Amendment) Act 2001 and the Industrial Relations (Miscellaneous Provisions) Act 2004 – Have They Helped?', 1(5) *IELJ* (2004), 142.
65. [2007] IESC 6, [2007] 4 IR 199, [2007] ELR 57.
66. In addition, it is worth noting that in *Ryanair v Labour Court and IMPACT* the Supreme Court appears to have been influenced by its view that IMPACT may have been exploiting the terms of the legislation in an attempt effectively to force Ryanair to recognise and negotiate with it. See Murray Smith, 'Ryanair and IMPACT: The Dispute so Far', 5 *Employment Law Review* (2007), 2 at p.7. On the other hand, a similar finding did not appear to influence the Labour Court in holding in favour of the relevant union in *Irish Guide Dogs for the Blind v SIPTU*, CD/06/547, recommendation no. 18692, 18 September 2006.
67. *Ashford Castle Ltd. v SIPTU*, CD/03/658, DECP 032, 19 November 2003.
68. See, for example, *Genesis Group v AMICUS*, CD/05/672, DIR 0511, 22 September 2005. Thus in *Analog Devices v SIPTU*, CD/05/5, recommendation no. 18137, 16 March 2005, the Labour Court simply accepted the assurances of the union that it was representative of the employees of the company who were in dispute with their employer, despite the fact that the union did not actually produce any evidence to this effect. It is difficult to see how such an approach could survive the Supreme Court decision in *Ryanair*.
69. *Swords Packaging and Logistics Ltd. v SIPTU*, CD/07/420, DIR 081, 16 January 2008. See Connolly, 'Industrial Relations (Miscellaneous Provisions) Act 2004 – Implications for Industrial Relations Law and Practice of the Supreme Court Decision in *Ryanair v Labour Court and IMPACT*', 4(2) *IELJ* (2007), 37, for the view that this means an employer could engage with the process under the Industrial Relations (Amendment) Act of 2001 without even being aware of the numbers of workers who would be affected by the result.

The vulnerability of the employer in this regard was compounded by the fact that formerly the approach of the Labour Court was to permit the union in question to make its arguments exclusively using written submissions and without actually identifying the workers whom it was representing. It is of huge significance, therefore, that in *Ryanair v Labour Court and IMPACT*[70] the Supreme Court held that complete non-disclosure of the identity of such workers was not permissible where there were factual questions in dispute and, equally importantly, that in the absence of conflicting oral testimony from such workers, the Labour Court was not entitled to depart from the version of facts given in oral testimony by any representatives of the employers in question, and that, by doing so in the present case, the Labour Court had conducted itself unfairly.[71]

Have the internal dispute-resolution procedures normally[72] availed of by the parties concerned failed to resolve the dispute?
Naturally, this will be a question of fact in any case, however, various principles [2–29] emerge from decisions of the Labour Court and latterly of the Supreme Court that may assist in answering the question.[73]

(a) The reference to the 'parties concerned', like the reference earlier in s.2 to the 'grade, group or category of workers who are party to the trade dispute' can be taken as meaning not the parties who could theoretically avail of the procedures (that is, any employees and the employer within the relevant workplace), nor the parties who are before the Court, but simply the parties who are involved in the particular trade dispute currently being investigated by the Court whether or not they themselves are before the Court.[74]

(b) Such procedures must be generally available to deal with group or grade disputes (pertaining *inter alia* to terms and conditions of employment of a category of workers) rather than being specific and existing to resolve individual grievances.[75]

---

70. [2007]IESC 6, [2007] 4 IR 199, [2007] ELR 57.
71. The Labour Court had, in fact, decided the case largely on the basis of supposed omissions in Ryanair's documentation and on the basis of the view of the trade union that was a party to the case. See Murray Smith, 'Ryanair and IMPACT: The Dispute so Far', 5 *Employment Law Review* (2007), 2; Doherty, 'Union Sundown? The Future of Collective Representation Rights in Irish Law', 4(4) *IELJ* (2007), 96.
72. The word 'normally' in this context has been taken to connote a procedure that 'is routinely and consistently resorted to and has become established over time as the normal model of dispute resolution': *Ashford Castle Ltd. v SIPTU*, CD/03/658, decision no. DECP 032, 19 November 2003.
73. See Purdy, 'The Industrial Relations (Amendment) Act 2001 and the Industrial Relations (Miscellaneous Provisions) Act 2004-Have They Helped?', 1(5) *IELJ* (2004), 142.
74. *Ashford Castle Ltd. v SIPTU*, CD/03/658, decision no. DECP 032, 19 November 2003.
75. *Radio Kerry v MANDATE*, CD/04/363, recommendation no. 17919, 27 July 2004; *Ryanair v IMPACT* Labour Court, CD/04/1199, decision no. DECP 051, 25 January 2005; *Irish Guide*

(c) Such procedures must be 'normally used' – which indicates both that very new procedures and procedures which were used only occasionally could not fulfil the statutory description.[76]

(d) Where there *are* such procedures in place, the fact that relevant workers who are parties to the dispute decline (for whatever reason) to use them or unilaterally withdraw from such procedures does not mean that they will thereby be able to claim that such procedures have failed to resolve the dispute.[77]

(e) The Labour Court will seek to give effect to the purpose behind the relevant section of the legislation, which was to give employers some fair chance to be put on notice of any issues of contention in its workplace and to resolve the issues internally before the jurisdiction of the Labour Court was invoked.[78]

(f) It was not appropriate to say that such internal procedures could not be regarded as having been exhausted until an employer put forward his final position on an issue because if this were the case 'the whole purpose of the Act could be frustrated by an employer who, instead of flatly rejecting the workers' demands embarked on a process of putting forward proposals and counter proposals *ad nauseam* until the other side was simply worn down'.[79]

[2–30] Again in *Ryanair v Labour Court and IMPACT*[80] the Supreme Court considered the question of whether the internal procedures relied on by the employers had failed to resolve the dispute and again it came to the view that this finding could not be reached in the absence of sworn supporting testimony from employees.

B. Non-Fulfilment of Relevant Provisions of Codes of Practice on Voluntary Dispute Resolution

[2–31] As we have seen, s.42 of the Industrial Relations Act 1990 provides for the preparation of draft codes of practice by the LRC for submission to the Minister, and for the Minister to make an order declaring that a draft Code of Practice shall be an official Code of Practice for the purposes of the Act, which can be used as evidence in Court. Under s.2 of the 2001–2004 Acts, it is a prerequisite to application of the investigatory powers of the Labour Court under this legislation that the employer has failed to live up to its obligation under any Code of Practice on voluntary dispute resolution that is in place.

Dogs for the Blind v SIPTU, CD/06/547, recommendation no. 18692, 18 September 2006.
76. *Ashford Castle Ltd. v SIPTU*, CD/03/658, decision no. DECP 032 17675, 19 November 2003; *Radio Kerry v MANDATE*, CD/04/363, recommendation no. 17919, 27 July 2004.
77. *Banta Global Turnkey v SIPTU*, CD/03/890, recommendation no. DECP 041, 31 May 2004.
78. *Bell Security v TEEU*, CD/07/654, recommendation no. 19188, 10 April 2008.
79. *ibid.*
80. [2007] IESC 6, [2007] 4 IR 199, [2007] ELR 57.

In 2000, the LRC published a Code of Practice on voluntary dispute resolution, [2–32] which was declared to be a Code of Practice for the purposes of the Act under the Industrial Relations Act 1990.[81] This Code of Practice was created in response to the recommendations set out in the 'Report of the High Level Group on Trade Union Recognition'[82] and its main stated objective was to provide a recognised framework that had the full support of all parties for the processing of disputes arising in situations where negotiating arrangements were not in place and where collective bargaining fails to take place.

In such circumstances, the code provided that the following process should be put [2–33] in place. In the first instance the matter would be referred to the LRC, which would appoint an officer from its advisory service to assess the issues in dispute, and that officer would work with the parties to attempt to resolve the issues in dispute. If it was found that the issues in dispute were not capable of early resolution by the LRC intervention then an agreed cooling-off period would be put in place, during which time, the LRC advisory service would continue to work with the parties in an attempt to resolve any outstanding issues. Moreover, the code specifically provided that the Commission could engage expert assistance, including the involvement of ICTU and IBEC, should that prove helpful to resolve such differences. If after the cooling-off period the issues remained unresolved, the LRC was required to make a written report to the Labour Court on the situation, who would consider the position of the employer and the union and issue recommendations on outstanding matters.[83]

The relative ineffectiveness of the code,[84] coupled with the perceived need to [2–34] change the statutory position as it then existed in the 2001 Act, was highlighted in Article 8.9 of the Sustaining Progress Social Partnership Agreement 2003–2005. As a direct result, the 2004 Act was introduced (and, as we have seen, it made significant changes to its 2001 predecessor) and also a new draft Code of Practice was recognised as a Code of Practice for the purposes of the 1990 Act under the terms of the Industrial Relations Act 1990 Enhanced Code of Practice on Voluntary Dispute Resolution (Declaration) Order 2004.[85]

---

81. Code of Practice on Voluntary Dispute Resolution (Declaration) Order 2000, SI no. 145 of 2000.

82. This group was established under para.9.22 of Partnership 2000 for Inclusion, Employment and Competitiveness.

83. If after the end of the cooling-off period all issues *had* been resolved, then the LRC would disengage from the process, but could make proposals to the parties for the peaceful resolution of any further grievances or disputes.

84. Purdy, 'The Industrial Relations (Amendment) Act 2001 and the Industrial Relations (Miscellaneous Provisions) Act 2004 – Have They Helped?', 1(5) *IELJ* (2004), 142, describes the procedure under the 2000 Order as 'cumbersome' and notes that it comprises 11 steps and could take up to 18 months to complete. See also Ryan, 'Leaving it to the Experts – In the Matter of the Industrial Relations (Amendment) Act 2001: *Ashford Castle Limited v SIPTU*', 3(4) *IELJ* (2006), 118.

85. SI no. 76 of 2004.

[2–35] Under this new code (which is the relevant code for the purposes of s.2 of the 2001–2004 Acts) it is provided that there should be prescribed time limits in which the trade dispute in question should be resolved (26 weeks, with provision for a maximum of 34 weeks), and also that the Court could become engaged in the dispute as a result of such time limits not being adhered to (which, as we have seen, is the position under s.2 of the 2001 Act as amended by the 2004 Act). Thus under the code it is now provided that the dispute should last for a period of six weeks from the date of receipt by the other party of a written invitation from the LRC to participate in the process. This six-week period should consist of two weeks to arrange meetings and commence discussions on the issues in dispute and four weeks for substantive engagement on the issues.[86] On the other hand, in the event that the parties are making substantial progress towards resolving the matter, it is provided that this time period can be extended by agreement.

[2–36] It is further provided under the code that the matter should in the first instance be referred to the LRC and that the LRC will appoint an advisory officer to facilitate the procedure.[87] Such advisory officer will issue a written invitation to the other party to the dispute to participate in the procedure, and should the other party fail to reply indicating a willingness to proceed within two weeks, this will then be deemed to be a breach of the relevant time frame.[88] Should the other party respond positively, then the advisory officer will work with the parties in an

---

86. Purdy suggests that these time limits were included at the behest of unions who felt that without them, employers might be tempted to delay the process. Equally he argues (correctly, it is submitted) that in practice, such time limits within which an employer must consider his or her position, take legal advice and devise a relevant strategy, which may possibly (in the case, for example, of a multinational company) require consultation with a company based outside of Ireland, are 'totally unrealistic'. This view is shared by IBEC. See Purdy, 'The Industrial Relations (Amendment) Act 2001 and the Industrial Relations (Miscellaneous Provisions) Act 2004 – Have They Helped?', 1(5) *IELJ* (2004), 142; Doherty, 'Union Sundown? The Future of Collective Representation Rights in Irish Law', 4(4) *IELJ* (2007), 96.
87. See Purdy, 'The Industrial Relations (Amendment) Act 2001 and the Industrial Relations (Miscellaneous Provisions) Act 2004 – A Critique, an Employer's Perspective', 1 *Employment Law Review* (2005), 23, for the view that the statistics so far indicate that this preliminary stage of the procedure is highly unlikely to be effective, and hence it might make more sense for these matters simply to be referred directly to the Labour Court.
88. As has been noted, the main reason why an employer would tend not to attend at an initial LRC hearing is to avoid generating any inference that [s]he be seen to be recognising the union even on a *de facto* basis and irrespective of the fact that the Act prohibits the Labour Court from issuing any recommendation on collective bargaining. See Purdy, 'The Industrial Relations (Amendment) Act 2001 and the Industrial Relations (Miscellaneous Provisions) Act 2004', 1(5) *IELJ* (2004), 142. The same author suggests that the Labour Court is likely to take a dim view of an employer's refusal to participate at this early stage in the process, either by not attending (*Marble & Granite Supplies Ltd. v SIPTU*, CD/03/525, recommendation no. 17699, 9 December 2003), or by attending but not participating in any meaningful manner (*Irish Express Cargo v SIPTU*, CD/02/698, recommendation no. 17469, 15 April 2003).

attempt to resolve the dispute over a four-week period. During this period (which can be extended by agreement if substantial progress is being made, in which case there will be an agreed cooling-off period put in place) the LRC can engage expert assistance, including that of ICTU and IBEC, should that prove helpful. If at the end of the relevant time period the matter has been resolved, then the advisory officer will disengage and the procedure will be deemed to be completed (and, before disengaging, the advisory officer can make proposals for the peaceful resolution of any further grievance disputes). If not, then the advisory officer will make an immediate written report to the Labour Court on the situation.

Prior to the 2004 Industrial Relations Act it had been provided in s.2 (1)(b) of the [2–37] 2001 Act that (in the event of the other prerequisites we have considered being in place) the matter could also be dealt with by the Labour Court where the employer had failed to observe any provision of the relevant Code of Practice *in good faith.*[89] It may be strongly argued that whereas the removal of this particular clause from the amended version of s.2(1) of the 2004 Act means that the requirement of good-faith compliance is no longer applicable in determining whether or not an investigation under s.2 may validly occur, equally given that such investigation *may* still occur where the LRC has dealt with the matter pursuant to the Code of Practice and reports that it can do nothing further to resolve the dispute, the failure of the employer to act in good faith – that is, by engaging in 'a constructive effort to address and resolve the issues referred to by the other side and to do so with expedition'[90] may still (if reported by the LRC) have a bearing on the matter in practice.[91]

C. Frustration by employees/union of the employer's ability to observe a term of the Code of Practice

Finally, it is provided that the Labour Court cannot take cognisance of the matter [2–38] if, in its view, the trade union, excepted body or employees have frustrated the employer in observing a provision of the Code of Practice,[92] or where the trade

---

89. For analysis, see *Ashford Castle Ltd. v SIPTU*, CD/03/658, DECP 032, 19 November 2003.
90. *Irish Express Cargo v SIPTU*, CD/02/698, recommendation no. 17469, 15 April 2003.
91. See Purdy, 'The Industrial Relations (Amendment) Act 2001 and the Industrial Relations (Miscellaneous Provisions) Act 2004 – Have They Helped?', 1(5) *IELJ* (2004), 142.
92. s.2(1)(c) Industrial Relations (Amendment) Act 2001 as amended. In *The Kildare Hotel and Golf Club v AMICUS*, CD/06/720, recommendation no. 18672, 14 August 2006, the Labour Court, in assessing what an employer would need to demonstrate in order to show that it had been frustrated in its efforts to fulfil the obligations of the Code of Practice, stated that 'an employer would have to show that the conduct of the union was such as to prevent an employer from complying with a relevant provision of the Code. This could arise, for example, where a Union fails to make itself available for meetings within the specified time frame or where it refuses to specify its claims with sufficient particularity so as to allow the employer to meaningfully respond'. On the other hand, the Labour Court felt that this type of frustration would not occur where the union had been publicly critical of the approach of the employer while the process was ongoing.

union/excepted body/employees have had recourse to industrial action after the dispute in question was referred to the LRC in accordance with the provisions of such Code of Practice.[93]

1.1.2.2 The Effect of Section 2 of the 2001–2004 Acts

[2–39] The net affect of this section from the employer's perspective is an interesting one and provides him or her with a stark choice. Either [s]he continues to refuse to negotiate collectively with unions, both generally and in the manner envisaged by the Code of Practice (with its requirement of participation before the advisory officer), in which case [s]he leaves him or herself open to the Labour Court making an order against him or her pertaining to terms and conditions of employment (which, as we shall see, may be enforced by the Circuit Court), or else [s]he bites the bullet and engages, even in a limited way, in some form of face-to-face discussion with unions. Whichever approach is taken it seems clear that the ability of employers simply to decide on issues pertaining to terms and conditions of employment by themselves and without outside interference (beyond minimum statutory standards) is now seriously compromised.

1.1.2.3. Investigations, Recommendations and Determinations under the 2001–2004 Acts

[2–40] Where it is determined that the terms of s.2 of the 2001 Act have been met in a particular case, the Labour Court may investigate the dispute.[94] Having done so, it may issue a recommendation[95] giving its opinion on the matter and stating, where appropriate, its view as to the action that should be taken, having regard to terms and conditions of employment and to dispute-resolution and disciplinary procedures.[96] Equally (and in line with the view that Irish law continues not to

---

93. s.2(1)(d) Industrial Relations (Amendment) Act 2001 as amended. See, for example, *Ashford Castle Ltd. v SIPTU*, CD/03/658, recommendation no. DECP 032, 19 November 2003; and also *Ashford Castle Ltd. v SIPTU*, CD/06/1142, recommendation no. 18820, 22 January 2007, for an analysis of what constitutes industrial action in this context.

94. It is notable that the Labour Court has been prepared to investigate a matter under the 2001–2004 Acts even in circumstances where the employer does not agree to participate in proceedings. *The Oval Creche v SIPTU*, CD/06/511, recommendation no. 18601, 14 June 2006.

95. Such recommendation will seek to balance the reasonable aspirations of the employees as represented by their union on the one hand and the financial and commercial circumstances of the employer on the other. *Carlingford Nursing Home v SIPTU*, CD/04/729, DIR 054, 21 April 2005.

96. s.5 Industrial Relations (Amendment) Act 2001. It has been suggested that, having regard to the legislative history of the 2001 Act and the fact that the procedure contained therein represents a radical departure from the traditionally voluntarist nature of the Irish industrial relations system, the power to issue recommendations under the Act should be used sparingly. Thus in *Bank of Ireland v IBOA*, CD/03/154, recommendation no. 17745, 28 January 2004, the Labour Court held: 'It seems to the Court that, having regard to the voluntary nature of our industrial relations system, such an intervention is only appropriate where it is necessary in order to provide protection to workers whose terms and conditions of employment, when viewed in their totality, are significantly out of line with appropriate standards.' See also *Analog Devices v SIPTU*, CD/05/5, recommendation no. 18137, 16 March

require mandatory recognition of trade unions) such recommendations may not provide for arrangements for collective bargaining.[97]

Where a dispute that was the subject of such a recommendation has still not been resolved,[98] the Court may, at the request of a trade union or excepted body and following a review of all relevant matters, make a determination.[99] Such determination[100] may have regard to the terms and conditions of employment in the relevant workplace as well as to issues pertaining to dispute-resolution and disciplinary processes that apply.[101] This determination must be in the same form as the recommendation that had been made in the case, save where a variation has been agreed by the parties and the Court, or where a part of the initial recommendation is now deemed to have been based on unsound or incomplete information.[102] The

[2–41]

2005; *GE Healthcare v SIPTU*, CD/04/678, recommendation no. 18013, 19 November 2004. See Purdy, 'The Industrial Relations (Amendment) Act 2001 and the Industrial Relations (Miscellaneous Provisions) Act 2004 – Have They Helped?', 1(5) *IELJ* (2004), 142, for criticism of the view (taken, for example, in *Analog Devices v SIPTU*, CD/05/5, recommendation no. 18137, 16 March 2005) that the burden of proving that one's employees are treated equivalently to those in 'unionised' workplaces should rest with the employer, who must produce documentation to support such claim. Purdy contends that the unfairness of this approach is exacerbated by the fact that the Labour Court does not require anything like such a burden of proof to rest on the union (*Goode Concrete Case*, CD/04/633, recommendation no. 18037, 9 December 2004), nor indeed does it feel constrained in its own determinations by any lack of evidence before supporting such recommendations. It may, however, be argued that since the Supreme Court decision in *Ryanair v Labour Court and IMPACT* [2007] IESC 6, [2007] 4 IR 199, [2007] ELR 57 more is required of the union to prove its case under the 2001–2004 Acts.

97. s.5(2) of the Industrial Relations (Amendment) Act 2001. In *Genesis Group v AMICUS*, CD/05/672, DIR 0511, 22 September 2005, the Labour Court held that, whereas it was precluded from making a recommendation on arrangements for collective bargaining, equally it was *not* precluded from making recommendations for the representation of individuals in matters of difference with their employer not involving collective bargaining. It may be suggested that this line of authority is somewhat doubtful following the decision of the Supreme Court in *Ryanair*.

98. The Labour Court has held that 'in a normal industrial relations sense an issue in dispute can only be regarded as resolved when both parties are satisfied that it is resolved… [that is] when the recommendation is accepted by both parties and is either implemented or a timeframe is agreed for its implementation'. See *Dunnes Stores v MANDATE*, CD/06/400, DIR 064, 19 April 2006.

99. s.6 Industrial Relations (Amendment) Act 2001. Again this may not provide for collective bargaining. Moreover, under s.11 of the 2001 Act, an appeal on a point of law may be brought to the High Court by any party to the dispute.

100. Such determination must be in writing and include a statement of the reasons underpinning it: s.7 *ibid.*

101. s.6(2) *ibid.*

102. s.6(3) *ibid.* The normal judgment of the Labour Court in such matters tends to be to endorse the earlier decision, often in circumstances where it concludes that, whereas there may have been deficiencies in the information that had been available to it at the earlier

Court may, as it thinks proper and by order, give effect to any such determination from such date as is specified in the order[103] (and the order must be served on the parties to the dispute).[104]

[2–42] Somewhat confusingly, it is further provided (under s.8 of the 2001 Act) that the Labour Court must cease its investigation *under s. 6* (that is, where a s.5 recommendation has been made but where the dispute has still not been resolved and hence the issue is under further investigation by the Labour Court prior to it issuing a determination) if, following a request by an employer or at its own behest, the Court comes to the conclusion that industrial action in relation to the matter under investigation has taken place. It would appear from the mandatory language of s.6(1) that – subject to the terms of s.8(2) of the 2001 Act – it *must* cease such investigation even where the industrial action in question has already ceased, provided only that it has, at some time, taken place.

[2–43] The precise time at which such industrial action must have taken place in order for s.8 to have application, is, however, curious. After all, under s.2 of the Act, the Labour Court is precluded from taking cognizance of the matter if industrial action has taken place after the matter was referred to the LRC pursuant to the relevant codes of practice. Hence the industrial action at issue under s.8 must have taken place *after* the date on which the Labour Court decided that an investigation under s.2 was warranted. The logical conclusion is that the reference to industrial action in s.8 of the 2001 Act was intended to denote industrial action that occurred after the Court issued a recommendation under s.5 and before it converted that recommendation into a determination under s.6. Moreover, where there is no preliminary hearing to enquire into the question of whether the Labour Court has jurisdiction over the matter under s.2 this will inevitably be the case. But, what is less clear is whether s.8 will have application in circumstances where such a preliminary hearing *does* take place but where industrial action occurs between the date of the preliminary hearing and the date of the hearing for the purposes of investigation under s.5. There is, after all, nothing in s.5 to say that the Labour Court in making a recommendation in relation to a dispute is required or indeed permitted to have regard to any industrial action that occurred since it took jurisdiction over the matter. On the other hand, under s.8 of the Act, the Court *must* have regard to such industrial action (that is industrial action that occurred after it took jurisdiction and before or during the period when it was engaged in the s.5

---

stage, equally such decision was not based on such unsound or incomplete information. See, for example, *Fournier Laboratories v SIPTU*, CD/06/905, DIR 072, 18 January 2007. In other words, provided that the substance of the argument justifying or opposing the recommendation is presented to the Court, it does not matter that the argument is made in a more documented and particularised form subsequently. *Bayfield Supplies Ltd. v MANDATE*, CD/06/1182, DIR 071, 9 January 2007; *Carlingford Nursing Home v SIPTU*, CD/04/729, DIR 054, 21 April 2005.

103. s.7(2) Industrial Relations (Amendment) Act 2001.
104. s.7(3) *ibid.*

process) in deciding whether or not to make a determination in the matter, and if it finds that such industrial action has occurred then it must withdraw the s.5 recommendation. As has been said, s.8 was clearly aimed at providing an incentive to workers not to engage in industrial action in the period between the making of a recommendation and the making of a determination, but it would perhaps have made sense, therefore, for s.5 to have contained a sub-clause equivalent to that in s.8 prohibiting the Court from making even a recommendation if industrial action had taken place since it took jurisdiction over the matter.

Furthermore, it is provided that the general rule in s.8 shall not apply where the [2–44] procedures under ss.2, 5 and 6 have been exhausted.[105] Given, however, that s.8 only applies in the context of an ongoing Labour Court investigation under s.6 (and hence the procedure under s.6 could not possibly have been exhausted) this is probably unnecessary. It may, however, be taken to mean that a Circuit Court is not permitted to have regard to such industrial action where it is endorsing the determination of the Labour Court under s.10 of the 2001 Act. Finally, s.8 further provides that even where there has been industrial action, the general rule (that the Labour Court must refuse to investigate the matter and withdraw its s.5 determination) can be set aside and the Court proceed with its investigation where, in all the circumstances, it is satisfied by a trade union or excepted body that it is reasonable for it to do so.[106]

What is key as far as the whole thrust of the Act is concerned is that where an [2–45] employer does not fulfil the terms of such determination in the time period specified therein,[107] a trade union or excepted body may apply to the Circuit Court for an order directing the employer to carry out the terms of the determination.[108] In those circumstances, the Circuit Court must make such order without hearing the employer or any other evidence (other than in relation to the question of his or her failure to carry out the terms of the Labour Court determination).[109] Hence the 'new' process of investigating trade disputes under the 2001–2004 Acts is a genuinely radical one in that it creates a process that may lead to a *binding* Court order requiring an employer who does not negotiate collectively with employees to take certain measures nonetheless, to improve the position of such employees. To that extent, it may be argued that, at least on one level, it would be preferable for the employer to negotiate collectively with such employees and thereby to retain some measure of control over how issues such as pay and terms and conditions

---

105. s.8(3) *ibid.*
106. s.8(2) *ibid.*
107. If no such time period is specified then, under s.10(1) *ibid.* as inserted by s.4 of the Industrial Relations (Miscellaneous Provisions) Act of 2004, the obligations must be fulfilled as soon as may be after the determination is communicated to the parties.
108. Such applications should be brought pursuant to Order 57 Rule 11 of the Circuit Court Rules 2001 as inserted by the Circuit Court Rules (Industrial Relations Acts) 2007, SI no. 12 of 2007.
109. s.10 Industrial Relations (Amendment) Act 2001.

in his or her workplace are to be determined, which [s]he will lose should the matter simply fall to be resolved by the Labour Court and Circuit Court.

2. Registered Employment Agreements

[2-46] The concept of a Registered Employment Agreement (REA) – essentially a negotiated agreement between workers and employers within a particular sector of the economy, which is registered with and can be enforced by the Labour Court – first received legislative expression in Ireland under Part III of the Industrial Relations Act of 1946.

Within this section an employment agreement is defined as

> an agreement relating to the remuneration or the conditions of employment of workers of any class, type or group made between a trade union of workers and an employer or trade union of employers or made, at a meeting of a registered joint industrial council, between members of the council representative of workers and members of the council representative of employers.[110]

[2-47] Thus an REA is deemed to govern the employment relationship of all employees and employers working in the relevant industry to which the agreement relates.[111] Most significantly, given that the agreement essentially relates to an entire classification of workers, it will apply irrespective of whether a particular employee within that classification (or his or her employer) is in fact a party to the agreement or wishes to be bound by its terms[112] (although naturally an individual contract of employment of a particular worker may provide for a level of pay and/or terms and conditions in excess of that provided for in the REA). Hence if the employment contract of a particular worker to whom the agreement applies provides that [s]he should be paid a rate of pay or enjoy terms and conditions at a level that is less favourable than those provided for in the REA, the terms of the REA will effectively be read into his or her contract, such that his or her contractual rate of pay or minimum terms and conditions will, in fact, be those contained in the REA.

---

110. s.25 Industrial Relations Act 1946.
111. So, for example, under s.42(b) of the National Minimum Wage Act 2000 its terms are deemed to be in addition to and not in derogation of REAs, save where the minimum rate of pay in an REA is less than the national statutory minimum rate of pay, in which case the latter will apply. In addition, the Labour Court may not register or vary an REA that is, in its view, based, or partly based, on the restoration of a pay differential between an employee and another employee who has secured or is to secure an increase in pay as a result of the passing of the National Minimum Wage Act: s.43(3) National Minimum Wage Act 2000.
112. s.30(1) Industrial Relations Act 1946.

2.1. Registration of an Agreement

Under s.26 of the Industrial Relations Act of 1946, the Labour Court is required to [2–48]
maintain a register to be known as the Register of Employment Agreements[113] and
any party to an employment agreement may apply to the Court to register this
agreement in that register.[114] On receipt of such application (and provided that
various administrative and logistical requirements are complied with)[115] the Court
must determine whether or not the agreement can validly be registered, and must,
in fact, register it if it is satisfied[116]:

(a) that, in the case of an agreement to which there are two parties only,
both parties consent to its registration and, in the case of an agreement
to which there are more than two parties, there is substantial agreement
amongst the parties representing the interests of workers and employers,
respectively, that it should be registered,

(b) that the agreement is expressed to apply to all workers[117] of a particular
class, type or group and their employers[118] where the Court is satisfied
that it is a normal and desirable practice or that it is expedient to have a
separate agreement for that class, type or group,

(c) that the parties to the agreement are substantially representative of such
workers and employers,

---

113. s.26 *ibid.* Currently there are 46 REAs on the register.

114. s.27(1) *ibid.*

115. Thus under s.27(4) of the Industrial Relations Act 1946 it is provided that the Court may
require specified parties to the agreement to publish particulars of the agreement in such
manner as, in the opinion of the Court, is best calculated to bring the application to the
notice of all parties concerned, nor shall the Court register an REA until 14 days after publication of such particulars (s.27(5)(a) *ibid.*), during which time the Court must consider any
objections that it receives to registration of the agreement (other than those that it considers
frivolous), including hearing all parties whom the Court regards as being interested and
desiring to be heard. If, on the basis of such representations and objections, the Court
concludes that the agreement does not conform to the requirements in s.27(3) it must refuse
to register the agreement s.27(5)(b) *ibid.*

116. s.27(3) *ibid.*

117. A 'worker' in this context is defined under s.3 of the 1990 Act.

118. The Labour Court, while maintaining that the normal principles of contractual interpretation
should apply to an REA, has consistently rejected arguments that an REA will not cover, for
instance, sole traders within the relevant industry (*O'Boyle v TEEU*, CD/06/726, REA 0757,
11 October 2007). Moreover it has also held that a company that uses sub-contractors is to be
regarded (for the purposes of an REA) as the employer of workers used by that sub-contractor
(EP *Lynam Properties v BATU*, CD/06/588, REA 075, 19 January 2007). In essence its conclusion
on this point is that it is necessary to give a broad definition to the notion of a firm or company
employing workers within the relevant industry if the purpose of the REA (that is, to ensure
that the standards contained therein are generally applicable throughout the relevant industry)
is to be achieved, nor should employers be able to avoid their obligations under the legislation
by relying on semantics: *CK Decoratorss v INP&DTG*, CD/06/72, REA 072, 10 January 2007;
Horan Homes (Castlemaine) Ltd. v BATU, CD/06/534, REA 06121, 21 November 2006.

(d) that the agreement is not intended to restrict unduly employment generally or the employment of workers of a particular class, type or group or to ensure or protect the retention in use of inefficient or unduly costly machinery or methods of working,

(e) that the agreement provides that if a trade dispute occurs between workers to whom the agreement relates and their employers a strike or lock-out shall not take place until the dispute has been submitted for settlement by negotiation in the manner specified in the agreement,[119] and

(f) that the agreement is in a form suitable for registration.

[2–49] In *National Union of Security Employers v Labour Court*[120] Flood J stressed that the Labour Court could not simply rubber stamp a request to register the agreement but was bound to follow fair procedures in determining whether such agreement *should* be registered. Moreover, in assessing whether it was satisfied of the matters referred to above, the Labour Court should have regard to

- the fact that the overall purpose of any REA is to create harmony within the industry as a whole,
- the fact that an REA is intended to bind all employers and employees in the industry, the fact that sanctions will flow from breach of the agreement, and
- the fact that parties to the agreement are substantially representative of workers and employers in the industry.

2.2. Breach of a Registered Employment Agreement

[2–50] The effect of registration[121] (notice and particulars of which must be published in such manner as the Court thinks fit[122]) is essentially to give the Labour Court jurisdiction over the employment relationship between employers and employees to whom the agreement is expressed to apply. Thus, in the event of a perceived breach of the REA by an employer, a trade union that is representative of workers

---

119. See *Headland Homes Ltd. v BATU*, CD/06/973, REA 0823, 11 March 2008. The High Court is particularly willing to grant interlocutory injunctive relief to restrain industrial action in breach of a disputes procedure contained in an REA (*Action and Jordan v Duff*, unreported, High Court, Carroll J, 12 July 1982). On the other hand, the Labour Court clearly requires that both employers and unions participate appropriately in this process. *LM Developments v BATU*, CD/06/1113, REA 0815, 26 February 2008.

120. [1994] 10 JISLL 97.

121. It should be noted that the REA can be varied if this possibility is provided for within its terms. An application to vary the agreement may be made to the Labour Court by any party thereto: s.28 Industrial Relations Act 1946.

122. s.31(1) *ibid.*

affected by an REA[123] (and not necessarily the trade union that actually represents a worker affected by the breach) or alternatively, a different employer or trade union representative of employers[124] can make a complaint to the Court that such breach has allegedly occurred.[125] Where this happens the Court is required to consider the complaint (including hearing from all parties that appear to be interested and desiring to be heard) and if, following such consideration, the Court is satisfied that the complaint is well founded, it *may* by order[126] direct the employer in question to do such things as are necessary to ensure compliance with the agreement – including paying any sum due to a worker by way of remuneration due under the terms of the agreement. Failure to comply with such an order is an offence.[127]

An employer (or a trade union that is representative of employers) affected by   [2–51]
an REA may make a complaint that a trade union representative of employees is promoting or assisting out of its funds a strike that, to the knowledge of the general committee of the workers' union, is in contravention of the REA and is being undertaken with the aim of forcing the employer to provide pay or conditions to workers other than those fixed by the terms of the REA.[128] Where this happens, the Court must again consider such complaint (including hearing interested witnesses) and if it is satisfied that such complaint is well founded, it again *may* (by order) either direct the union to stop assisting out of its funds in the

---

123. s.32(1) *ibid*.

124. s.10(1) Industrial Relations Act 1969. This would happen, for example, where the Construction Industry Federation (as distinct from a trade union) feels that an employer within the construction industry is not fulfilling its obligations under the REA governing the construction industry. See *PA Dunne Construction Ltd. v Construction Federation Operatives Pension Scheme*, CD/03/980, REA 0430, 15 July 2004; *GMP Plant Hire Ltd. c. CIF*, CD/96/39, REA 976, 3 April 1997. In fact the Construction Industry Federation or some related body has been a party to every case heard by the Labour Court under s.10 of the 1969 Act.

125. The Labour Court has stressed that it takes seriously its duty under s.32 to ensure that all parties adhere to both the spirit and the letter of the legally binding obligations that they incur under the REA, such that 'the Court will use the full powers available to it under the Section so as to ensure that these obligations are fulfilled'. *O'Malley Construction Co Ltd. v BATU*, CD/06/1110, REA 0773, 24 December 2007.

126. It is notable that there is not a requirement that the Court *must* take such a step.

127. s.32(4) Industrial Relations Act 1946.

128. s.32(2) *ibid*. On the other hand, where a strike is *not* in contravention of the REA, the Labour Court has no jurisdiction to hear the matter. Thus in *P. Elliot v BATU*, CD/06/1075, REA 0615, 9 October 2006, the relevant REA provided that no such strike could occur until the Labour Court had investigated the dispute, but on the facts, the Labour Court *had* investigated the dispute, the dispute still existed and it was only at *that* point that the workers went on strike. The Labour Court then declined jurisdiction under s.32(2), concluding that what the workers had done was not in violation of the terms of the REA, in that they had not taken industrial action before the initial Labour Court investigation.

maintenance of the strike or cancel[129] the registration of the agreement.[130] It is an offence not to follow the direction contained in such order.

[2–52] For the purposes of monitoring potential breaches of the REA, relevant employers are bound to keep such records as are necessary to show that the REA is being complied with and to retain such records for three years.[131] Moreover, the Minister may appoint an inspector under s.51 of the Industrial Relations Act 1946 to investigate whether or not there has been a breach of the Act.[132] In addition to the normal powers of inspectors considered in Chapter 1, where an inspector is of the view that a sum is due from an employer to a worker to whom the REA applies or that the employer has failed to comply with a condition of the REA [s]he may institute civil proceedings on behalf of that worker[133] to recover the relevant sum of money or have the condition enforced.[134]

2.3. Variation and Cancellation of a Registered Employment Agreement

[2–53] Where an REA provides for its variation, then under s.46 of the Industrial Relations Act 1946, any party to the agreement may apply to the Labour Court to vary it *in its application to any worker or workers to whom it applies*.[135] The Court is required to consider this application and to hear all persons that appear to the Court to be interested and desiring to be heard.[136] Having considered such application, the Court then has a discretion to decide whether or not to accede to the application and also may vary the agreement (should it decide to do so) as it thinks proper.[137] In *Serco Services Ltd. v Labour Court*[138] Carroll J stressed that,

---

129. An REA can be cancelled more generally pursuant to s.29 of the 1946 Act, either on the consent of all parties, or where the Court finds that there has been a substantial change in the circumstances of the trade or business to which it relates, or generally within 12 months of registration in circumstances where the REA does not provide for its own duration or termination, or at the end of any period specified in the Act as the period of duration of the agreement.

130. Payments made in assistance of a strike are expressly deemed not to include payments made to members of a trade union whose pay or conditions of employment are not the subject of a strike, yet who are unable or decline to work while the strike continues: s.32(3) Industrial Relations Act 1946.

131. s.51(1) Industrial Relations Act 1990. It is an offence both to fail to keep such records (s.51(2) *ibid.*) and to keep or produce false records (s.51(3) *ibid.*).

132. For an analysis of the limitations of the powers enjoyed by such inspectors, see the decision of the Supreme Court and High Court in *Gama Endustri Tesisleri Imalat Montaj A.S. v Minister for Enterprise, Trade and Employment* [2009] IESC 37, [2005] IEHC 210 considered in Chapter 1.

133. This is without prejudice to the worker's ability to institute proceedings on behalf of him or herself: s.54(2) Industrial Relations Act 1990.

134. s.54(1) *ibid.* In such circumstances an order may be made for the payment of costs by the inspector, but not by the worker.

135. s.28(1) Industrial Relations Act 1946.

136. s.28(2)(a) *ibid.*

137. s.28(2)(b) *ibid.* Where it decides to vary the agreement, then the agreement shall be deemed to be varied not earlier than the date specified by the Court in the order: s.28(2)(c) *ibid.*

138. [2001] IEHC 125.

because s.28 of the 1946 Act specifically states that the agreement could only be varied in its application 'to any worker or workers to whom it applies'[139], therefore, by definition, a variation could not have the effect of extending the agreement to workers or employers to whom it formerly did not apply.[140]

In *Construction Industry Federation v CIC and ICTU*[141] the Labour Court (in the   **[2–54]** context of a dispute referred to it under s.26(1) of the Industrial Relations Act 1990) rejected an application by the Construction Industry Federation that, on the basis of the difficult economic times facing Ireland in the Spring of 2009, coupled with the falls in interest rates and other deflations leading to a consequent reduction in the cost of living, the REA for the Construction Industry should be revisited. The CIF, having rejected the proposals contained in the draft 'towards 2016– Review and Transitional Agreement: 2008–2009', argued that the REA for the construction industry was 'an anachronistic and inflexible restriction on the construction industry', and that its terms should be amended to provide for a 10 per cent reduction in the rates of pay to be paid to workers under the terms of this agreement.

The Labour Court rejected the claims of the CIF. It accepted that at the time of   **[2–55]** the hearing the construction industry was facing enormous difficulties, but noted that in the 'good times' where there was considerable competition in the labour market for the construction sector, 'the REA rates tended to operate as a floor rather than a ceiling'. In other words, because of the formerly inflated rates of pay in the industry, it would be possible for construction workers to be paid less whilst the terms of the REA would still be met. Thus rates of pay, according to the Labour Court, would fall logically to a level at or near the REA rates. Moreover (in the Court's view) a further reduction in the *minimum* rates under the REA would not serve to create or maintain employment in the construction industry.

In addition, if all parties to the agreement apply in this regard, and if the Court is   **[2–56]** satisfied that all parties have voluntarily consented to the application, the Court may cancel the REA.[142] Alternatively, the Court may cancel the registration of the agreement (presumably not necessarily on the application of the relevant parties) where it is satisfied that there has been a substantial change in the circumstances of the business to which the REA relates since the registration of the REA, such that its continued existence is no longer desirable.

---

139. [2001] IEHC 125 at para.41.
140. This approach was accepted by Murphy J in *BATU and Scott v Labour Court and Others* [2005] IEHC 109, although in this case the judge concluded that the variation in the agreement was one of classification and did not involve extending the agreement to a worker or workers to whom it did not originally apply.
141. CD/08/885, recommendation no. 19489 (31 March 2009).
142. s.29(1) Industrial Relations Act 1946.

2.4. Interpretation of a Registered Employment Agreement

[2–57] Finally, and more generally, the court may at any time on the application of *any person* (not necessarily a party to the agreement) give its decision on any question as to the interpretation of the REA or its application to a particular person.[143] Moreover, a court of law in determining any question arising in proceedings before it as to the interpretation of an REA or its application to a particular person must have regard to any decision of the Labour Court on the said agreement that is referred to it in the course of proceedings,[144] and indeed if a question of this nature arises in the course of proceedings before a court of law, the relevant court may, if it thinks proper, refer the question to the Labour Court whose decision on the matter shall be final.[145]

[2–58] It is arguable, however, given that all such matters *may* be dealt with by the Labour Court in the first instance (including the question of the applicability of the REA to a specific worker, and the question of whether there has been a breach of the agreement) and given indeed that it is clearly the legislative intention that the Labour Court should be the first port of call in this regard,[146] that it is inappropriate that a case should be brought *ab initio* before a civil court where what is being sought is solely the interpretation or enforcement of an REA. Rather it would seem that the jurisdiction under s.33(3) should only arise where questions of enforcement or interpretation are peripheral to some more substantive aspect of the matter – for example, where the manner in which the Labour Court had registered an REA is being judicially reviewed, or where a prosecution is being taken in the civil courts against an employer for failing to comply with a Labour Court order directing him or her to make good a breach of an REA,[147] or where a civil action is being taken by an inspector on behalf of a worker.[148] Indeed, by analogy, it is notable that in *An Employer v An Employee*[149] the EAT determined that neither it nor the Rights Commissioner had any jurisdiction under the Payment of Wages Act 1991 to enforce the terms of a REA on an employer.

---

143. s.33(1) Industrial Relations Act 1946. For recent examples of Labour Court decisions of this nature see *Kilkenny Tarmac Limited v SIPTU* CD/08/271, decision no. REA 0916, 18 May 2009, *De Bros Marble Work Limited v A Worker* CD/09/197, decision no. INT 093, 14 May 2009, *Corlin Developments Limited v Two Workers* CD/09/85, decision no. INT 092, 11 May 2009. A similar power is given under s.7 of the Industrial Relations Act 1969 more generally in the context of any agreement between an employer/trade union of employers, and a worker/trade union of workers, where what is at issue is the interpretation of the agreement or its application to any person. *Aer Lingus v IMPACT*, CD/04/217, INT 041, 26 April 2004.

144. s.33(2) Industrial Relations Act 1946.

145. s.33(3) *ibid.*

146. Indeed the Labour Court has accepted that it has the 'primary arbitral role' in respect of REAs. See *CK Decorators v INP&DTG*, CD/06/72, REA 072, 10 January 2007; *Horan Homes (Castlemaine) Ltd. v BATU*, CD/06/534, REA 06121, 21 November 2006.

147. *Joe Madden Construction Ltd. v CIF*, CD 94382, INT 943, 28 September 1994.

148. *Shree Ltd. v Carew*, CD 94275, INT 941, 3 August 1994.

149. PW92/2007 (Decision of 25 June 2008).

Thus in *Serco Services Ltd. v Labour Court*[150] – a case in which the applicant sought [2–59]
to judicially review the Labour Court's variation of an existing REA – Carroll
J considered whether or not to exercise her discretion under s.33(3) to refer the
matter to the Labour Court, but concluded that this would be inappropriate in
light of the fact that the Labour Court had not sought to be involved in the
hearing of the case before the High Court.

Moreover, more recently in *McCarthy Building and Civil Engineering Contractors* [2–60]
v BATU[151] the Labour Court held that it was inappropriate for the interpretation
procedure under s.33 of the 1946 Act to be used as a mechanism for resolving
a matter relating to the implementation or application of a clause in an REA.
Rather in such circumstances the matter should be referred to the NJIC for the
industry.[152]

3. Joint Labour Committees and Employment Regulation Orders

Part IV of the 1946 Act envisages the possibility of the establishment by the Labour [2–61]
Court of Joint Labour Committees (JLCs), which are responsible for the creation
of proposals that will be used as the basis for Employment Regulation Orders
(EROs), which in turn will lay down minimum standards for both remuneration[153] and/or terms and conditions for workers to whom the ERO applies.[154]

3.1. Establishment Orders

Under s.36 of the 1946 Act, the Minister or a trade union or any organisation [2–62]
of persons that claims to be representative of a group of workers or employers[155]
may apply to the Labour Court for an order establishing a JLC in respect of that
group of workers described in the order.[156] The Court is precluded from making
an establishment order unless it is satisfied

---

150. [2001] IEHC 125.

151. CD/08/805, decision no. INT 094, 22 May 2009.

152. For further discussion on the question of when it is appropriate for the Labour Court to take
jurisdiction over an issue relating to an REA see *CMH Construction & Civil Engineering Ltd.
v OPATSI* CD/08/16, decision no. REA 0934, 30 July 2009.

153. In addition, under s.58 of the Industrial Relations Act 1946, the Court may of its own initiative or on the application of any interested party fix what it regards as the appropriate weekly
wage for (as is specified) a male adult worker performing unskilled work in a particular area.
This is not binding in any sense.

154. Under s.53 *ibid.* all trade boards existing before the commencement of the act were expressly
deemed to become JLCs following commencement of the Act.

155. s.36 *ibid.*

156. s.35 *ibid.* It should be noted that specific provision is made for the creation of a JLC in
respect of agricultural workers within the Industrial Relations Act of 1976.

(a) that the claim by the applicant group that it is representative of the relevant workers or employers is well founded, and also

(b) either that there is substantial agreement between such workers and employers as to the establishment of a JLC *or* that the existing machinery for effective regulation of remuneration and conditions of employment of such workers is inadequate or is likely to cease to be adequate *or* that, having regard to the existing rates of remuneration of conditions of employment of such workers, it is expedient that a JLC should be established.[157]

[2–63] Significantly therefore, from an industrial relations perspective, the fact that, for example, it would be expedient or indeed desirable that a JLC be created will not of itself justify the making of an establishment order, unless the court is satisfied that the applicants for such order are representative of the relevant workers *or* their employers. On the other hand, the legislation does seem to leave open the possibility that the court might consider an application where, for example, it concludes that it would be expedient that a JLC should be established and where the application for such an order comes from a group representing employees, but where there is no agreement from employers in this regard.

[2–64] When an application is made to the Labour Court for an establishment order, the court is bound to consider the application and, following consultation with such parties as it thinks necessary, it must prepare a draft establishment order.[158] The court must then publish a notice stating that it proposes to hold an inquiry into the application on a date not less than 30 days from the publication of such notice but not more than 60 days from the receipt of the original application by the court[159] and indicating the place where copies of the draft may be obtained. Written objections to the draft may be submitted to the Court before the date of the holding of such enquiry and must state both the grounds of objection and such omissions, additions or modifications to the order as are being sought[160]; in holding the enquiry in question, the court is required to consider any objections to the draft that have been submitted.

[2–65] Having held such enquiry, the Court may, if it thinks fit, make the order either in terms made in the application or in some modified version.[161] Such order must be published in the prescribed manner and shall come into operation on the date

157. s.37 Industrial Relations Act 1946.
158. s.38(a) *ibid.*
159. s.38(b)(ii) *ibid.* as amended by s.45(1) Industrial Relations Act 1990.
160. s.38(c) Industrial Relations Act 1946.
161. s.39 *ibid.* When the establishment order is in force creating a JLC, the Court, on the application of the Minister, any trade union (therefore not necessarily one representative of the workers to whom the order relates), or any organisation or group of persons that claims to be and is, in the opinion of the Court, representative of such workers or employers to whom the order relates, may abolish or amend the JLC in question.

specified in the order. The Court is, moreover, required to make an establishment order or make known its decision *not* to do so, within 42 days of the completion of the enquiry.[162]

3.2. The Work of Joint Labour Committees

The constitution and proceedings of JLCs[163] are set out in the 5th schedule to the   **[2–66]** Industrial Relations Act of 1990.[164] Thus a committee is required to have one independent chairman appointed by the Minister[165] and an equal number of persons appointed by the Court to be representative of employers and workers[166] in relation to whom the committee is to operate.[167] Whereas the minutiae of such procedures is set out in this schedule, it is clear from the decision of the Supreme Court in *Burke v Minister for Labour and Others*[168] that inasmuch as the JLC has had powers delegated to it by the legislature, it is required in exercising these powers to act in accordance with justice and fairness, and with due regard to natural and constitutional justice, and in accordance with the framework and terms and objects of the legislation.[169] The most important function of the JLC is to submit proposals to the Court for fixing the minimum rate of pay[170] (either generally or for any particular work) or regulating the conditions of employment for all or any of the workers in relation to whom the committee operates.[171]

---

162. s.45(2) Industrial Relations Act 1990.

163. There are at present 19 JLCs in operation.

164. Moreover, under s.47 of the Industrial Relations Act 1990, the Court either on its own initiative or at the request of a JLC may arrange for the provision of a report on the industry or trade covered by the JLC and the position of its workforce, having regard to the purpose for which the committee was established.

165. The Minister will also appoint an independent person to act as independent member and chairman in the absence of the chairman.

166. If the representative member in question ceases to be representative of the group whom [s]he is representing, then his or her membership of the JLC is determined. Moreover, the Court may in its discretion determine the membership of any representative member of a JLC at any time.

167. para.2 of the Fifth Schedule. Before appointing such representative members, the Court must consult as far as is reasonably practicable with any organisation of employers or workers concerned.

168. [1979] 1 IR 354.

169. In this case Henchy J referred to the very significant nature of the powers of the JLC, not least in the fact that where an ERO is made by the Labour Court this is not subject to any parliamentary or ministerial control and, 'no matter how erroneous, ill-judged or unfair [the ERO] may be', the JLC is debarred from even hearing proposals for change for six months, even if the parent statute under which the ERO was made is repealed (*per* Henchy J at 359). Similar comments were made in the case by O'Higgins CJ.

170. This may include a minimum weekly wage.

171. s.42 Industrial Relations Act 1946. Such proposals must be conveyed by employers to employees in the prescribed manner, and failure to do so is an offence (s.49(2) *ibid.*). A JLC may not submit proposals for revoking or amending an existing ERO unless the order has been in force for at least six months (s.42(3) *ibid.*).

[2–67] Where such proposal is formulated, the JLC in question must publish a notice stating the place where copies of the proposals may be obtained, and also that representations in respect of the same may be made to the JLC within 21 days after the date of such publication.[172] It is only having considered any such representations that the JLC may submit proposals for an ERO to the Court, accompanied by a report on the circumstances surrounding their adoption.[173]

3.3. Employment Regulation Orders

[2–68] On receipt of such proposals, the Court may, as it thinks proper, give effect thereto by way of an ERO,[174] which will operate from the date specified.[175] Alternatively, if it is not satisfied with such proposals, it may submit amended proposals to the JLC that it *would* be willing to accept, and the JLC may, if it wishes, resubmit the amended proposals to the Court with or without modifications and the Court may give effect as it thinks proper to such re-submitted proposals.[176] In any event, when an ERO is made, the Court is required to give notice of the making thereof in the prescribed manner.[177]

[2–69] The significance of the making of an ERO is that an employer[178] (to whom it relates) is required to provide workers (to whom it relates) with no less than the standards of pay[179] and conditions provided for in the ERO[180] (and it should be noted that where the Act refers to 'statutory minimums' for remuneration and conditions, this is to be taken as meaning the minimum level of pay and conditions contained in an ERO and applying to an individual worker[181]), such that,

---

172. s.48(1) Industrial Relations Act 1990.
173. ss.48(2) and (3) *ibid.*
174. An ERO cannot prejudice any statutory rights of a worker (s.43(3) Industrial Relations Act 1946) and may contain different provisions for different descriptions of workers (s.43(5) *ibid.*). Moreover, it may amend or revoke a previous ERO (s.43(4) *ibid.*).
175. s.48(4) Industrial Relations Act 1990.
176. s.48(5) *ibid.*
177. There are currently 18 EROs in operation.
178. Under s.50(1) of the Industrial Relations Act 1946, an immediate employer of a worker, as well as someone who is the employer of that direct employer and on whose premises the worker is employed, will jointly be deemed to be the employers of the worker.
179. Payment in this context generally relates to the amount of money to be obtained in cash from an employer clear of all deductions other than those authorised by law, but an ERO may authorise certain benefits to be provided to an employee in lieu of cash, and where this happens such benefits are also to be factored into the calculation of what constitutes pay (s.47 *ibid.*). Moreover, where a worker to whom an ERO relates is an apprentice or learner, it is an offence for the employer to receive any payment by way of premium for him or her (s.48 *ibid.*).
180. It is possible to apply to the relevant JLC for a permit authorising the employer to pay less than the minimum level of remuneration under the ERO to an employee who is affected by infirmity or physical incapacity, which renders him incapable of earning that minimum remuneration: s.46 *ibid.*
181. s.34 *ibid.* Moreover, the reference to 'statutory conditions of employment' is to be taken as

where the worker's contract provides for less than this, the terms of the ERO are effectively read into that contract and replace the provisions relating to pay and/or conditions contained therein.[182] A failure on the part of an employer[183] to comply with the terms of the ERO is an offence.[184] Moreover, if convicted of such offence, the employer may be ordered not merely to alter the pay and conditions of the employee in question,[185] but also to compensate him or her for the period of his or her employment where his or her pay or conditions fell below the minimum threshold laid down in the ERO.[186] The prosecution must serve notice of intention to seek such 'payment in arrears' when serving the summons, warrant or complaint.[187] It has been suggested that because the sums that may be ordered to be paid in arrears may be sufficiently substantial to render the offence under s.45 of the 1946 Act a 'non-minor' one, consequently the section in question is unconstitutional in that it permits the District Court the power to try non-minor criminal offences, but this question has not been resolved.[188]

---

meaning the conditions of employment other than those relating to payment. *Minister for Labour v Costello* [1988] 1 IR 235.

182. s.44 *ibid.* So, for example, under s.42(b) of the National Minimum Wage Act 2000, its terms are deemed to be in addition to and not in derogation of EROs, although logically if the minimum rate of pay referred to in an ERO is less than the statutory minimum, it is the latter that should prevail. In addition, the Labour Court may not by an ERO give effect to a proposal from a JLC that is, in its view, based, or partly based, on the restoration of a pay differential between an employee and another employee who has secured or is to secure an increase in pay as a result of the passing of the National Minimum Wage Act: s.43(2) National Minimum Wage Act 2000.

183. Provision is made in the legislation for a prosecution to be taken (by an inspector) against some other person (or alternatively for that other person to be joined by the employer as a form of co-defendant) in circumstances where it was that other person's fault that the breach of the ERO occurred: s.50 Industrial Relations Act 1946.

184. In this respect, the burden of proof rests with the employer to show that [s]he has paid the relevant level of pay and provided the requisite conditions under the terms of the ERO. ss.45(5) and (6) *ibid.*

185. ss.45(2) and 45(3) *ibid.*

186. s.45(4) *ibid.* The power given under the Act to require the employer to pay such compensation to the employee is without prejudice to the latter's right to recover such sums in civil proceedings, though it would appear logical that the employer not be required to pay a double compensation to the employee. Finally, an inspector duly appointed under the terms of the Act may institute such civil proceedings on behalf of an employee, although again this is without prejudice to the employee's entitlement to issue such proceedings on his own behalf. The merit from the employee's perspective in permitting an inspector to take such proceedings is that where this happens, any order for costs made will be against the inspector rather than the employee: s.52(5) *ibid.* and s.49 Industrial Relations Act 1990.

187. In *Minister for Labour v Costello* [1988] 1 IR 235, O'Hanlon J concluded that the terms of s.45(2) of the 1946 Act could not authorise payment of compensation save in respect of specific nominated instances of failure to comply with the statutory minimum rate of pay (that is, the rate provided for under the relevant ERO) that had occurred within the limitation period for issuing a summons.

188. The question arose on a case-stated basis in *Minister for Labour v Costello* [1988] 1 IR 235, but

[2–70] In order to monitor compliance with the ERO, employers of workers to whom an ERO relates are required to keep such records as are necessary to show that their obligations under the ERO and under Part IV of the Act generally are being complied with and failure to do so is also an offence.[189] As with the enforcement of the terms of an REA, the Minister may appoint inspectors for the purposes of Part IV of the Act[190] and such inspectors have powers *inter alia* to enter at all reasonable times onto premises where they have reasonable grounds for believing that an employee to whom an ERO applies is employed, to require the production of relevant work sheets or other significant records and to examine any employer or worker to whom, in their reasonable belief, an ERO applies.[191]

[2–71] As with REAs, provision is made whereby the Labour Court can deal with any questions of interpretation as to whether a JLC or an ERO applies to a particular worker,[192] and a Court of law, in determining any related question that arises in proceedings, is required to have regard to any such determinations.[193] Moreover, should such a question arise in the course of proceedings before a Court of law, that Court may, if it thinks proper, refer the matter to the Labour Court.[194]

[2–72] Finally, the decision both to make an establishment order and to make an ERO can be challenged in the High Court by way of judicial review proceedings[195]. In this respect, the point has been made that, because of the impact an ERO has on a body of employers and employees, and because a challenge thereto would naturally run the risk of meaning that structural changes that had been taken on foot of the ERO would have to be revisited if the judicial review application was successful, an application for judicial review of a ERO should be resisted if there is significant (and presumably inexcusable) delay in issuing proceedings.[196]

O'Hanlon J concluded that it was not open to the defendant to plead the unconstitutionality of a statute before the District Court having regard to the terms of Article 34.3.2 of the Constitution, and also that it was not permissible to raise the issue of the constitutionality of a statute by way of case stated from the District Court.

189. s.49 Industrial Relations Act 1946.
190. s.51 *ibid.*
191. s.52(1) *ibid.* The inspector can require such a person to sign a declaration of the truth of the answers to such questions: s.52(1)(c) *ibid.*
192. s.57(1) *ibid.* See, for example, *Butlers Chocolate Ltd. v NERA* CD/09/254, decision no. DEC-091, 4 September 2009, ISS *Contract Cleaners Ltd. v SIPTU*, CD/00/190, DEC-001, 28 July 2000; *Lowe Alpine Ltd. v SIPTU*, CD 97/70, DEC-971, 10 July 1997. See also *Professional Contract Services Ltd. v SIPTU*, CD/96/427, decision no. 971, 9 January 1997, where, instead of pronouncing definitively on the question of whether or not the workers in question were covered by the relevant JLC, the Labour Court instead recommended that the JLC readdress the matter in light of changes in the contract cleaning industry since the JLC came into effect.
193. s.57(2) Industrial Relations Act 1946.
194. s.57(3) *ibid.*
195. For analysis of instances in which such proceedings have been taken, including cases which, at the time of writing are pending, see Compton and Dillon, 'Practice and Procedure', 6(3) *IELJ* (2009), 83.
196. *Noonan Services and Others v Labour Court* [2004] IEHC 42.

4. The Industrial Relations (Amendment) Bill 2009

Finally it is worth noting that in August 2009 a new Industrial Relations (Amend-   [2–73]
ment) Bill was published, with the aim of strengthening the process for making
of EROs and REAs and of ensuring the continued operation of such orders. The
new Bill *inter alia* provides for the following:

- s. 27 of the 1946 Industrial Relations Act is amended by the insertion of
  a new s.27(5a) which requires the Labour Court, following registration
  of a REA to forward a copy thereof to the Minister who must by order
  confirm the terms of the agreement. Similar provision is made for the use
  of Ministerial order to confirm any variation to or cancellation of a REA
  through amendments to ss.28 and 29 of the 1946 Act
- On this basis, s.25 of the 1946 Act is amended, such that there is a redefi-
  nition of the term 'Registered Employment Agreement' differentiating
  between those agreements registered prior to the commencement of the
  Bill when enacted (which are registered by the Labour Court) and those
  registered after the commencement thereof which must be confirmed by
  Ministerial order.
- In similar vein, s.43 of the 1946 Act is amended and a new s.43(2a) added,
  which provides that from the point of commencement of the 2009 Bill,
  an Employment Regulation Order will be made by the Minister rather
  than the Labour Court.[197]
- Again on this basis, s.34 of the 1946 Act is amended to provide a definition of an ERO which differentiates between those EROs made before
  commencement of the 2009 Bill (which come into force by an order
  made by the Labour Court), and those made *after* commencement of the
  2009 Bill which come into force through Ministerial order.
- Section 42 of the 1946 Act is amended by the insertion of a new s.42(2a)
  which lists certain matters to which a JLC must have regard when formulating proposals to submit to the court namely (a) the legitimate interests
  of workers and employers (b) the prevailing economic circumstances (c)
  the prevailing employment circumstances of workers and commercial
  circumstances of employers and (d) the terms of any national agreement
  relating to pay and conditions for the time being in force
- Under a proposed new s.42(4) of the 1946 Act it will be possible for a
  JLC to submit proposals for revoking or amending an ERO which has
  been force for less than six months where the JLC is satisfied that the
  ERO contains an error or that exceptional circumstances exist which
  warrant the revocation or amendment.
- Minor changes are made to the definition of 'worker' under s.23 of the
  Industrial Relations Act 1990 essentially to permit VEC officers other

---

197. Moreover, whenever the Labour Court adopts the proposals of a JLC, a copy of such proposals
will be submitted to the Minister.

than teachers to come within the definition, thereby providing them with access to the Industrial Relations machinery of the state.

- The Bill amends s.48 of the 1990 Act and provides for tightened procedures to be followed by the JLC and the Court in terms of submitting and dealing with proposals for an ERO as well as accompanying submissions.

- Finally it is proposed that the 5th schedule to the 1990 Act will be amended to provide that the term of office of a Chairman of a JLC will not exceed five years (or three years for an existing chairperson following the enactment of the 2009 Bill) and that such Chairperson shall cease to hold office on reaching the age of 65.

5. Joint Industrial Councils

[2–74]   Under s.61 of the 1946 Industrial Relations Act, the Labour Court can register an association as a Joint Industrial Council (JIC),[198] whose name is to be listed in the register of JICs which the Labour Court is obliged to maintain.[199] In order for an association to be registered as such, the Labour Court must be satisfied[200] that it fulfils the definition of a JIC,[201] namely that it be substantially representative of workers of a particular group, class or type and their employers, that its object be the promotion of harmonious relations between such workers and employers, and that its rules provide that if a trade dispute arises between such workers and employers, no strike or lock out will occur until the dispute has been referred to the association and considered by it.[202] The Court can cancel the registration of a JIC, either on the application of the relevant association or where it is of the opinion that the association has either ceased to exist or has ceased to fulfil the definition of a JIC.[203]

[2–75]   There are currently three Joint Industrial Councils in operation, and the Labour Court facilitates their work both by making available an officer of the Court to act as secretary at their meetings and by providing an Industrial Relations Officer of the LRC to act as chairperson of their meetings.

---

198. Where this happens the Labour Court must register the name of the association, its secretary and its principal office: s.61(3) Industrial Relations Act 1946.

199. s.60 *ibid.*

200. Thus an application for registration from an association must be accompanied by copies of its rules and any such other information with respect to the association as the Court may require (s.61(2) *ibid.*). Moreover, once it has been registered, the rules of a JIC must be open for public inspection at the offices of the Labour Court at such times as may be fixed by the Court: s.63 *ibid.*

201. s.61(1) *ibid.* A registered JIC is a board in relation to which s.3 of the Trade Union Act 1942 is applicable.

202. s.59 *ibid.*

203. s.62 *ibid.* See, for example, *Daru Blocklaying v BATU* [2002] IEHC 125 for an indication of the difficulties that can arise where a JIC effectively breaks down.

PART II

The Nature of the Employment Relationship

CHAPTER 3

Employment Status

Introduction

In employment law terms, a worker may be deemed to be either an employee [3–01] engaged under a *contract of service* or an independent contractor engaged under a *contract for services*. The distinction between the two forms of relationship is critical as the classification will significantly affect the rights, duties and obligations of both parties to the relationship.

For employment law purposes, a worker deemed to be an independent contractor [3–02] will be excluded from many of the protective statutory measures that have been introduced into Irish law in recent years and which are discussed throughout this book. Furthermore, employees are given additional protections under the common law, which are not extended to independent contractors. Thus, under the tort of negligence, an employer owes a special duty of care towards his employees that does not necessarily apply to independent contractors.[1] The distinction between employee and independent contractor can also be of significance to the rights of third parties. As we shall see, under the doctrine of vicarious liability an employer can, as a general proposition, only be held liable for the negligent acts of employees committed in the course of their employment.[2] Finally, the classification of the relationship will have financial as well as legal repercussions. So, for example, an employer is liable to pay PRSI on behalf of all employees but not independent contractors. Additionally, income tax in the form of PAYE is deducted from the worker's salary at source in cases where the relationship is characterised as one of employer and employee.

In the vast majority of circumstances, the classification of the relationship does [3–03] not give rise to much controversy. The typical employee is employed to do work for his or her employer and is not in business on his or her own; [s]he is referred to as an employee in the contract of employment; [s]he has income tax deducted at source and is paid holiday pay; and [s]he is exclusively engaged by and is subject to the direction or control of his or her employer. The typical independent contractor, on the other hand, is engaged in business on his or her own account,

---

1. *Dalton v Frendo*, unreported, Supreme Court, 15 December 1977.
2. *Phelan v Coillte Teo* [1993] 1 IR 18, [1993] ELR 56.

is not referred to as an employee under the contractual agreement, deals with his or her own tax affairs, is not paid when not working, is free to engage others to complete the work on his or her behalf, and is not subject to the direction or control of the employer who engaged him or her.

[3–04]   However, not all working relationships are so clearly defined. In the modern economy, where increased competitiveness and greater worker specialisation has led to the creation of more flexible working relationships, it is increasingly likely that business relationships outside of the employer/employee model will include some elements of all of these characteristics. As a consequence, the demarcation between employer and employee or employer and independent contractor can become blurred.

1. Determining Whether the Worker is an Employee

[3–05]   Given the changing nature of the employment relationship and the far-reaching consequences of defining a relationship as a contract of service or as a contract for services, one might be forgiven for assuming that the courts, tribunals or legislature would have developed a definitive test for determining the issue with some degree of certainty. Unfortunately, that has not yet occurred and consequently it is difficult to identify a unifying theme through the case law.

[3–06]   Much would appear to depend on the background policy considerations at play in any given case. For example, when determining the status of a worker for the purposes of imposing vicarious liability in tort, the dominant guiding criterion has traditionally been the element of control exercised by the employer over the work. This would appear to be on the basis *inter alia* that policy dictates that if the employer 'controlled' what the employee did then [s]he is responsible for the injuries caused by that employee during the course of his or her employment as if [s]he directly caused them him or herself.[3] In *Lane v Shire Roofing Company (Oxford) Ltd.*,[4] the Court of Appeal of England and Wales held that, for the purposes of a negligence claim, a worker who fell from a ladder while carrying out work for the defendant company was an employee. This was so notwithstanding the fact that the claimant had his own business as a builder, dealt with his own tax affairs and did not work under the control or supervision of the defendant company. Henry LJ concluded that 'when it comes to the question of safety at work, there is a real public interest in recognising the employer/employee relationship when it exists'.[5] On the other hand, if the question is posed by the Revenue Commissioners for tax purposes or the Department of Social Welfare for insurance purposes, the financial arrangements agreed between the parties may be of greater significance in determining the issue.

---

3.   *ibid.*
4.   [1995] IRLR 493.
5.   [1995] IRLR 493, 495.

The question as to whether the worker is an employee or an independent contractor is therefore one fraught with difficulty and much will depend on who is asking the question. However, the aim should be at all times 'to identify correctly those who should fall within the embrace of Employment Law and to exclude those who have sufficient economic independence to make it unnecessary to protect them'.[6] [3–07]

The leading Irish decision in this area was delivered by Keane J in *Henry Denny & Sons (Ireland) Ltd. v Minister for Social Welfare*,[7] where he stated that 'each case must be considered in the light of its particular facts and of the general principles which the courts have developed'.[8] In the High Court decision of *Minister for Agriculture and Food v Barry*,[9] Edwards J stated that the approach as outlined by Keane J was not intended to create a single overarching test: [3–08]

> Contrary to a misapprehension held in some quarters, I do not believe that it is a correct interpretation of the passage in question to regard it as the formulation by Keane J. of '*a single composite test*' either for determining the nature of the work relationship between two parties, or even for determining whether a particular employment is to be regarded as governed by a contract for service or a contract of service which is a somewhat narrower issue. To the extent that this passage from his judgment has given rise to a degree of confusion, I believe that this confusion derives primarily from misguided attempts to divine in the judgment the formulation of a definitive, '*one size fits all*', test in circumstances where the learned judge was not attempting to formulate any such test. In relation to the rush to discern a test, and to label it, it seems to this court that this is a classic example of the type of situation where a particular approach that has been advocated is subsequently labelled conveniently, but mis-characteristically, as the '*such and such test*', a step that is taken with the intention that it should be helpful, but which proves to be ultimately unhelpful, because the so called test turns out to be insufficiently discriminating. Put simply, such loose labelling can often create more problems than it solves. In the context of trying to correctly characterise the nature of a work relationship between two parties I think it can sometimes be unhelpful to speak of a '*control test*', or of an '*integration test*', or of an '*enterprise test*', or of a '*mixed test*', or of a '*fundamental test*' or of an '*essential test*', or of a '*single composite test*' because, in truth, none of the approaches so labelled constitutes a '*test*', in the generally understood sense of that term, namely, that it constitutes a measure or yardstick of universal application that can be relied upon to deliver a definitive result.[10]

---

6. Upex, Benny and Hardy, *Labour Law* (2nd ed., Oxford University Press, 2006), at 46.
7. [1997] IESC 9, [1998] 1 IR 34.
8. [1998] 1 IR 34, 49.
9. [2008] IEHC 216, [2009] 1 IR 215, [2008] ELR 245.
10. [2009] 1 IR 215, *per* Edwards J at 239.

1.1. Was the Worker in Business on His or Her Own Account?

[3–09] Whether the worker was business on his or her own account is the overarching question that must be answered in determining the employment status of the worker. Initially, when reaching a determination on this issue, the 'control test' was dominant. This test provided that if the employer controlled what the employer did, how [s]he was to do it and when [s]he was to do it, [s]he was an employee.[11] This test was developed during the 19th century when the words 'master' and 'servant' were commonly used to describe the nature of the employment relationship. At that time most work was not as highly skilled or technical, thereby making it capable of being the subject of such control. With the increasing complexity and professionalism of work this test soon became outdated and, while still relevant, is no longer the determinative factor, at least in employment law cases.[12] For a time, the 'integration test' was fashionable. This test provided that if the work was considered integral to the employer's business then the worker would be labelled as an employee.[13] However, difficulties in determining whether the work was integral or not meant that this test did not hold sway for long.

[3–10] It would seem that the approach that has now found favour in both Ireland[14] and the United Kingdom[15] is a general, multifaceted one. This approach views the relationship between the parties holistically and may be summarised by the question: was the worker in business on his or her own account? Variations of this have been called the 'mixed test', the 'multiple-factor test' or the 'economic-reality test'.

[3–11] One of the earliest applications of this approach arose in the United States Supreme Court case of *United States v Silk*.[16] In that case, the court was asked to consider whether two classes of workers engaged by the respondent should be considered employees or independent contractors. The respondent sold coal at retail. In the first instance, workers unloaded coal from railway cars and provided their own tools, worked only when they wished to work, and were paid an agreed price to unload the cars. In the second instance, truck drivers were engaged by the respondent to deliver the coal. They owned their own trucks, paid the expenses of their operation, employed their own helpers and received compensation on a piecework or percentage basis. In finding that the unloaders were employees, the Supreme Court observed that 'they provided only picks and shovels. They had no opportunity to gain or lose except from the work of their hands and these simple tools. That the unloaders did not work regularly is not significant. They did work in the course of the employer's trade or business.'[17] The Supreme Court distinguished the truckers' case from that of the unloaders on the basis that:

---

11. *Performing Right Society Ltd. v Mitchell and Booker (Palais de Danse) Ltd.* [1924] 1 KB 762.

12. *Henry Denny & Sons (Ireland) Ltd. v Minister for Social Welfare* [1997] IESC 9, [1998] 1 IR 34.

13. *Stevenson, Jordan & Harrison Ltd. v Macdonald and Evans* (1952) 1 TLR 101.

14. *supra*, n. 10

15. *Market Investigations Ltd. v Minister of Social Security* [1969] 2 QB 173, [1969] 2 WLR 1, [1968] 3 All ER 732.

16. 331 US 704 (1947).

17. *ibid.*, 717-718.

where [the arrangements leave the driver owners so much responsibility [for] the investment and management as here, they must be held to be independent contractors. These driver owners are small businessmen. They own their own trucks. They hire their own helpers. In one instance, they haul for a single business, in the other, for any customer. The distinction, though important, is not controlling. It is the total situation, including the risk undertaken, the control exercised, the opportunity for profit from sound management, that marks these driver owners as independent contractors.[18]

Effectively, the US Supreme Court weighed all the relevant factors and concluded that the truck drivers were not employees but rather 'small businessmen' working for themselves.

Silk was cited with approval by the Queen's Bench Division of the High Court [3–12] of England and Wales in *Ready Mixed Concrete Ltd. (South East) v Minister of Pensions.*[19] In that case, the Minister claimed that the plaintiff company was liable to pay national insurance contributions relating to a driver who was engaged by the plaintiff company to transport concrete. The contract between the driver and the company stated that he was an independent contractor. Under the contract, he purchased the truck, which he used to transport the company's concrete on hire purchase from the company. He was obliged to wear the company's uniform and the truck was to be painted in the company's colours and logo. The driver was responsible for all repair costs. Should he so choose, the driver could engage substitute drivers to carry out the work. Having reviewed the entirety of the relationship, MacKenna J stated that the essential characteristics of the employment relationship were as follows:

1. The employee agrees that in consideration of a wage or other remuneration he or she will provide his or her own work and skill in the performance of some service for the employer.
2. The employee agrees, expressly or impliedly, that in the performance of that service he or she will be subject to the other's control in a sufficient degree to make that other the employer.
3. That the other conditions of the contract are consistent with it being a contract of service.[20]

Applying the test to the case at hand, the court concluded that the driver was a [3–13] 'small businessman' running a business of his own. MacKenna J noted that the drivers' obligations were 'more consistent, I think, with a contract of carriage than with one of service. The ownership of the assets, the chance of profit and the risk of loss in the business of carriage are his and not the company's'.[21] Crucially, the

---

18. *ibid.*, 719.
19. [1968] 2 QB 497, [1968] 2 WLR 775, [1968] 1 All ER 433.
20. [1968] 2 QB 497, 515.
21. [1968] 2 QB 497, 526.

court noted that the driver had greater freedom to make his own choices as to how the business was run. In particular, MacKenna J noted that the driver:

> is free to decide whether he will maintain the vehicle by his own labour or that of another, and, if he decides to use another's, he is free to choose whom he will employ and on what terms. He is free to use another's services to drive the vehicle when he is away because of sickness or holidays, or indeed at any other time when he has not been directed to drive himself. He is free again in his choice of a competent driver to take his place at these times, and whoever he appoints will be his servant and not the company's. He is free to choose where he will buy his fuel or any other of his requirements, subject to the company's control in the case of major repairs. This is enough. It is true that the company are given special powers to ensure that he runs his business efficiently, keeps proper accounts and pays his bills. I find nothing in these or any other provisions of the contract inconsistent with the company's contention that he is running a business of his own. A man does not cease to run a business on his own account because he agrees to run it efficiently or to accept another's superintendence.[22]

[3–14] The approach adopted by the courts in *Silk* and *Ready Mixed Concrete* was further clarified by Cooke J in *Market Investigations Ltd. v Minister of Social Security*[23] when he stated that:

> The fundamental test to be applied is this: 'Is the person who has engaged himself to perform these services performing them as a person in business on his own account?' If the answer to that question is 'yes', then the contract is a contract of services. If the answer is 'no', then the contract is a contract for service. No exhaustive list has been compiled and perhaps no exhaustive list can be compiled of the considerations which are relevant in determining that question, nor can strict rules be laid down as to the relative weight which the various considerations should carry in particular cases. The most that can be said is that control will no doubt always have to be considered, although it can no longer be regarded as the sole determining factor; and factors which may be of importance are such matters as whether the man performing the services provides his own equipment, whether he hires his own helpers, what degree of financial risk he takes, what degree of responsibility for investment and management he has, and whether and how far he has an opportunity of profiting from sound management in the performance of his task.[24]

[3–15] The Irish Supreme Court approved Cooke J's formula in the pivotal case of *Henry Denny & Sons (Ireland) Ltd. v Minister for Social Welfare*.[25] In that case, the appellants had engaged in-store product demonstrators on yearly contracts. The contrac-

---

22. [1968] 2 QB 497, 526.
23. [1969] 2 QB 173.
24. [1969] 2 QB 173 at 184–185.
25. [1997] IESC 9, [1998] 1 IR 34.

tual arrangement between the parties provided that a demonstrator would be contacted by the appellants when a store requested a product demonstration. The demonstrator would submit an invoice to the appellants, which would be signed by the store manager. The demonstrators were paid by the day and were given a mileage allowance. However, the demonstrators were not entitled to become members of the appellants' pension scheme or trade union. The demonstrator in question was engaged under renewable contracts. The written contract described her as an independent contractor and made her responsible for her own tax affairs. While the demonstrators were not directly supervised by the appellants, she was provided with written instructions as to how she was to carry out her work. She was supplied with the materials to carry out the demonstrations and required the consent of the appellants prior to sub-contracting any of the demonstrations she was requested to carry out to another. In finding that the demonstrator was an employee, Keane J (as he then was) stated:

> while each case must be determined in the light of its particular facts and circum-stances, in general a person will be regarded as providing his or her services under a contract of service and not as an independent contractor where he or she is performing those services for another person and not for himself or herself. The degree of control exercised over how the work is to be performed, although a factor to be taken into account, is not decisive. The inference that the person is engaged in business on his or her own account can be more readily drawn where he or she provides the neces-sary equipment or some other form of investment, where he or she employs others to assist in the business and where the profit which he or she derives from the business is dependent on the efficiency with which it is conducted by him or her.[26]

The fact that there was no continuous supervision of the demonstrator by the [3-16] appellants, that she was provided with the clothing and equipment necessary for the demonstration and made no contribution, financial or otherwise, to the busi-ness were all indicators that she was an employee. She had the limited authority to request another person do the work if necessary, but that person had to be approved by the appellants. While the written agreement had been carefully drafted in an attempt to ensure that the demonstrator would be regarded as an independent contractor, Keane J held that the Appeals Officer was perfectly entitled to arrive at the conclusion that the demonstrator was, in fact, an employee.

The decision in *Henry Denny* was followed by the Supreme Court in *Castleis-* [3-17] *land Cattle Breeding Society Ltd. v Minister for Social and Family Affairs.*[27] In that case, the Society appealed to the High Court the decision of the Chief Appeals Officer regarding a decision that categorised a Mr Walsh – who worked as an artificial inseminator – as an employee for social welfare purposes. In upholding the appeal, O'Donovan J was of the opinion that the Appeals Officer had ignored

---

26. [1998] 1 IR 34, 50.
27. [2004] IESC 40, [2004] 4 IR 150.

key elements relating to the reality of the relationship between the Society and Mr Walsh. It was noted that the inseminator was obliged to provide his own transport and communication system suitable for him to carry out his duties at his own expense. The inseminator was required to arrange his own insurance cover and to indemnify the Society against all claims arising out of the use by him of such transport. The inseminator was obliged to carry out his work at his own risk at all times, to arrange for appropriate insurance cover, and to indemnify the Society from all claims arising from the inseminator's negligence. The inseminator was free to provide other services and engage in other businesses without permission if such engagements did not interfere with his work for the Society or was not in competition with the latter's business. Finally, the agreement could be terminated by the Society without notice.

[3–18]   Having reviewed the agreement in its entirety, O'Donovan J concluded that:

> those provisions of the said agreement and the fact (if it be so) that the nature of the agreement was such that the inseminator, by his own devices, could influence the amount of profit which he derived from the arrangement, were very relevant to the determination of the nature of the relationship between the parties to the said agreement and, if it be the case, as submitted by the appellant, that, in making her determination of the 7th February, 2001 the Appeals Officer, in fact, ignored those matters to which I have referred and if it be the case that this is manifest from her report, then I am of the view that that was a mistake on her part; a mistake in relation to the law because, in my view, a finding which ignores basic facts is an error of law. It follows, of course, that, if the determination of the Appeals Officer is erroneous by reason of some mistake having been made in relation to the law or the facts, then, in turn, the decision of the Chief Appeals Officer of the 5th July, 2001 is vitiated.[28]

[3–19]   The High Court decision in *Castleisland* was upheld on appeal by the Supreme Court where Geoghegan J affirmed the findings of O'Donovan J.[29] In particular, Geoghegan J found that two factors were fundamental. First, Mr Walsh knew quite well why his contract as an employee with the Society was terminated and new contractual arrangements with independent contractors were entered into. As a consequence of these new arrangements, Mr Walsh (and the other workers who were in a similar position) became self-employed for tax purposes, had to carry their own insurance and lost pension entitlements. Secondly, Geoghegan J referred to the point that the Society's retaining a degree of control over who could carry out the work was an indication that Mr Walsh was in reality still an employee. This argument was based on the fact that because the business of artificial inseminators of cattle is regulated by statute and statutory instrument imposed by the Department of Agriculture, any contract entered into by the

---

28. [2003] IEHC 133.
29. [2004] IESC 40, [2004] 4 IR 150.

Society had to contain such terms as were necessary to ensure strict compliance with the Department of Agriculture's regulations. Consequently, the Society had included a term in the contract that required its approval of the appointment of any substitute inseminators, or a term that limited his ability to assign the contract. However, Geoghegan J refused to accept this argument as evidence of control exercised by the Society and held that it was simply a requirement imposed by statute regarding the performance of the inseminator's function and not evidence that the inseminator was an employee.[30]

The question as to what the correct test is to be applied in determining the legal status of a worker remains a vexed and complex one. From the decisions in *Henry Denny* and *Castleisland Cattle Breeding Society Ltd.*, it would seem that the overarching question to be answered is whether the worker was in business on his or her own or was working for another. Thus factors such as whether the worker is using his or her own equipment to carry out his or her responsibilities or whether [s]he could profit from his or her own efficiency under the agreement can prove crucial in this regard. However, there are a number of subsidiary issues that, depending on the facts of a particular case, can prove equally critical in determining whether the worker is in business of his or her own account. Some of the factors that will be taken into consideration in answering this question are dealt with below: [3–20]

1. mutuality of obligation;
2. control;
3. parties' own description of the relationship; and
4. personal service.

1.1.1. Mutuality of Obligation

Before examining other aspects of the relationship in detail, the adjudicating body will first assess whether or not there exists what is called a 'mutuality of obligation' between the parties. In essence, mutuality of obligation is a requirement that there exist mutual obligations on the employer to provide work for the employee and on the employee to perform work for the employer. If such mutuality is not present there cannot be a contract of service. Edwards J, in *Minister for Agriculture and Food v Barry*,[31] explained the concept thus: [3–21]

> the mutuality of obligation test provides an important filter. Where one party to a work relationship contends that that relationship amounts to a contract of service, it is appropriate that the court or tribunal seized of that issue should in the first instance examine the relationship in question to determine if mutuality of obligation is a feature of it. If there is no mutuality of obligation it is not necessary to go further. Whatever the relationship is, it cannot amount to a contract of service. However, if mutuality of obligation is found to exist the mere fact of its existence

---

30. *ibid.*, at p.162.
31. [2008] IEHC 216, [2009] 1 IR 215,[2008] ELR 245.

is not, of itself, determinative of the nature of the relationship and it is necessary to examine the relationship further.[32]

[3–22] In *Barry*, the respondents were veterinarian surgeons who worked for the appellant as temporary veterinarian inspectors at the Galtee Meats plant in Mitchelstown in Cork. Following the closure of the plant, the respondents claimed redundancy payments from the appellant on the basis that they were employees. The appellant maintained that the respondents were not employees and refused to make the payments. The Employment Appeals Tribunal held that the respondents were employees and this decision was appealed on a point of law to the High Court. The court concluded that there was no evidence before the Tribunal from which it could be concluded that there had been an 'implied agreement' reached between the parties whereby the respondents agreed to carry out inspection of meat and the certification of same on behalf of the appellant. This conclusion was bolstered by the fact that the appellant did not have any control over the level of work provided to the respondents as this was entirely subject to the control of the processing plants. Consequently, the appellant was unable to give a commitment at any stage as to the level of work available to them and the respondents were aware of this. Furthermore, the court found that the arrangements entered into between the parties provided that the respondents 'were entitled to decline to work at the very least 16 per cent of the shifts offered to them without that refusal having any consequences for their contracts.'[33] On this basis it was held that no mutuality of obligation existed and the appeal was allowed.

1.1.2. Control

[3–23] While the actual control exerted by the employer over the employee's work may no longer be the critical feature of the employment relationship that it once was, it still remains a factor relevant to the determination of the ultimate issue. As Keane J has noted, 'The degree of control exercised over how the work is to be performed, although a factor to be taken into account, is not decisive.'[34] In recent years, the control test has been modified to reflect the changing nature and increased specialisation of the workplace. Now, rather than focusing on the actual control exercised by the employer on the mechanics of the work, emphasis is placed on the potential control that is exercisable by the employer over different aspects of the work.

[3–24] Holland and Burnett have called this as the 'who, what, where, when and how' test.[35] This approach examines the control exercised, or the control that could potentially be exercised over different aspects of the employee's work. A number of relevant questions flow from this approach.

---

32. [2009] 1 IR 215, 230-231 *per* Edwards J.
33. *ibid.*, at p.231.
34. *Henry Denny & Sons (Ireland) Ltd. v Minister for Social Welfare* [1998] 1 IR 34 at 50.
35. Holland and Burnett, *Employment Law* (Oxford University Press, 2006), at p.18.

- Did the employer retain control over *who* did the work? Personal service is one of the hallmarks of the employment relationship. In *Ready Mixed Concrete Ltd. (South East) v Minister of Pensions*,[36] it was held that the fact that the drivers of the lorries were entitled – with the consent of the company – to employ substitute drivers to do their work was evidence that the drivers were independent contractors.
- Did the employer control *what* the employee did (that is to say, the work that was done)?
- Did the employer control *when* the employee did the work (that is, the hours that were worked)?
- Did the employer control w*here* the work was done?
- Finally, did the employer control *how* the work was to be done? In other words, did the employer retain residual, if not actual, control over the employee's manner of doing the work?

The control test proved determinative, albeit in a case involving the doctrine of [3–25] vicarious liability, in the Supreme Court decision in *O'Keeffe v Hickey*.[37] In that case, the appellant was a pupil at a national school. The first defendant was a school teacher and principal at the school who had sexually abused the appellant. The school was a Catholic School in the diocese of Cork and Ross. The manager of the school was a Canon Strich, but it appeared that due to an infirmity he was unable to carry out his duties and the *de facto* manager of the school was Fr O'Ceallaigh. A number of complaints were made regarding the first defendant by other parents. Following a number of meetings arranged by Fr O'Ceallaigh, the first defendant resigned. He later took up a position as a teacher in another school. As manager, Fr O'Ceallaigh wrote to the Department of Education and informed it that the first defendant had resigned (although the letter did not state why) and that he planned to appoint another teacher in his place. In her action against the first defendant, the appellant claimed that the Department of Education was the teacher's employer and was therefore vicariously liable for his actions in the circumstances.

The majority of the Supreme Court held that the Department of Education was [3–26] not responsible on the basis that the teacher was not an employee of department and that, regardless, his actions were outside the course of his employment. In his judgment, Fennelly J focused on the tripartite relationship between the teacher, the school (through its manager) and the State. Fennelly J, for example, concluded that while the department had the ultimate power to withdraw recognition of the teacher's qualifications (thereby prohibiting him from teaching in any school) the actual contract of employment – and the employer/employee relationship was with the manager of the school because:

> Responsibility for day-to-day management and, in particular, the hiring and firing of teachers remains with the manager. In this latter respect, it is important to

---

36. [1968] 2 QB 497, [1968] 2 WLR 775, [1968] 1 All ER 433.
37. [2008] IESC 72, [2009] 1 ILRM 490.

distinguish between, on the one hand, recognition and, on the other, employment of a teacher. A teacher may not be employed if his qualifications are not recognised by the Minister and, if the Minister withdraws recognition, he may be unemployable. Nonetheless, it is the manager and not the Minister who decides on which teacher to employ. The contract of employment is between the manager and the teacher. The manager may dismiss the teacher without the sanction of the Minister.[38]

[3–27] The extent of control the employer can exercise over the worker's ability to do other work, to engage a substitute to do the work for him or her, and how the work will be done are significant factors in determining the nature of the relationship between the parties. The fact that the worker is not exclusively engaged by the employer or the fact that the worker is free to do work other than for the employer would raise an inference that the worker is not an employee but an independent contractor. In *Electricity Supply Board v Minister for Social Community & Family Affairs & Others*,[39] the appellant appealed a decision of the Appeals Officer of the first named respondent to classify six contract meter readers as being engaged under a contract of service rather than a contract for services for the purposes of social welfare contributions. Specifically, the appellant claimed that the Appeals Officer erred in law in failing to have regard for the written terms of the contract between the parties. The ESB engaged such meter readers on a contractor basis to read electricity meters. The readers were paid a fee at an agreed rate in respect of the number of customer visits completed by the reader. A higher fee was paid for such readings in rural areas as against urban areas. According to the written terms of the contract, the reader was responsible for making appropriate income tax and social welfare contributions. When making her decision, the Appeals Officer found that the two issues were fundamental in relation to the employment of the meter readers. First, any substitute nominated by the reader to do the work must have had ESB approval and was required to carry an ESB ID card. To obtain such a card the reader was required to apply to the ESB for approval of a nominated substitute; this procedure allowed the ESB to veto a nominated substitute (this had apparently already occurred on one occasion). Secondly, the meter readers were provided with a handheld computer terminal, which replaced meter books completed in writing. This terminal was the property of the ESB and allowed data obtained to be downloaded on a daily basis, thereby providing the ESB with instant information as

---

38. [2009] 1 ILRM 490, *per* Fennelly J at 533. Notwithstanding the reasoning of the Court it could be argued that, while the school manager may have been more directly involved with the day-to-day running of the school, it was the Department that retained the greater control over the teacher. Not only did it pay the teacher's salary and pension, and monitor that the appropriate curriculum was being taught to the children, but it also held the ultimate power over the teacher – it could withdraw recognition of his or her qualifications, thereby preventing any such teacher from teaching anywhere within the State. Had the Department been more informed it could have acted to prevent the teacher's transfer to another school, where he continued to teach for a further 20 years after the incidents that gave rise to the case.

39. [2006] IEHC 59.

regards the day's meter readings. The meter readers were obliged to enter the data at the time the reading was taken and the meter readers were not allowed to take manual readings and enter them at a later date. Furthermore, the meter readers were prohibited from taking meter readings after dark. Thus, the equipment belonged to the ESB, the time period during which the information must be collected by the ESB was dictated by the ESB, and the method of transmission of that information was also dictated by the ESB. Gilligan J refused to overturn the finding by the Appeals Officer that, notwithstanding the expressed terms of the contract, the meter readers were in fact employees and not independent contractors:

> I take the view that the Appeals Officer adopted a reasoned approach in deciding the issue before her. She was entitled to look beyond the contract and in particular the stipulation as contained therein that part-time meter readers were engaged in a contract which is not 'an employment contract'. The Appeals Officer comes to the conclusion that it was not necessary for her to consider in depth as to whether or not meter readers were free to engage in other work while under contract to the ESB and she accepts that it may well be that at different hours of the day, other work could be carried out by the meter readers, however the level of control exercised indirectly by the ESB would in her opinion preclude carrying out other business on meter reading visits.

1.1.3. Parties' Own Description of the Relationship

The parties to an employment agreement do not enjoy the same freedom that [3–28] parties entering other kinds of contract typically enjoy, not least because it is so likely that an employer will be in a vastly superior bargaining position to a prospective employee and could use such superiority to negotiate unfair terms with the employee, who might feel compelled to accept them in order to secure the work. Given these dangers, the courts and other adjudicating bodies have been wary of placing too much faith in the parties' own description of their relationship focusing on the objective reality of the relationship, rather than on the labels attached to the relationship by the parties.[40]

In *Ferguson v John Dawson & Partners (Contractors) Ltd.*,[41] the claimant was engaged [3–29] on the basis of an oral agreement that he was a 'labour-only sub-contractor'. No deductions for tax or national insurance were made from his pay by the defendant and he was obliged to follow the defendant's instructions as to what to do and when to do it. When equipment was required for the work it was supplied by the defendant company. The claimant was subsequently injured on the defendant's site. In order to ascertain whether he was entitled to a claim for industrial injuries' benefit it was necessary for him to establish that he was an employee (such benefits were

---

40. *Davis v New England College of Arundel* [1977] ICR 6. See also *ESB v Minister for Social Welfare* [2006] IEHC 59, dealt with above at para.3-27 where the court held that it was free to consider factors beyond the expressed terms of the contract.
41. [1976] 1 WLR 1213, [1976] 3 All ER 817, [1976] IRLR 346.

not made available in the circumstances to independent contractors). Notwith-standing the parties' own description of the arrangement, the majority of the court held that the claimant <u>was an employee.</u> While the label attached to the arrangement could be a factor to be taken into consideration, it was the majority's view that it should be ignored where the remainder of the evidence indicated that the relationship was in reality something different. In a dissenting judgment Lawton LJ, concerned that the approach of the majority would allow the worker to avail of the best of both worlds, noted that:

> I can see no reason why in law a man cannot sell his labour without becoming another man's servant even though he is willing to accept control as to how, when and where he shall work. If he makes his intention not to be a servant sufficiently clear, the implications which would normally arise from implied terms do not override the prime object of the bargain. In my judgement this is such a case.[42]

[3–30] The Irish courts have adopted a similar approach towards the issue. In *In re Sunday Tribune Ltd.*,[43] an arrangement by journalists (agreed with the Revenue Commissioners) where, for tax purposes, they were considered to be independent contractors, was held not to be a determinative factor when assessing the relationship. Carroll J emphasised the need to look further than the parties' own description of the arrangement, stating, 'The Court must look at the realities of the situation in order to determine whether the relationship of employer and employee in fact exists, regardless of how the parties describe themselves.'[44] In *Henry Denny & Sons (Ireland) Ltd. v Minister for Social Welfare*[45] the Supreme Court confirmed that while the terms of the contract may be relevant, if the reality of the relationship is different to that expressed in the contract, an adjudicating body is entitled to draw its own conclusions from the reality.

[3–31] However, where it is clear that both parties genuinely wished to clarify their working relationship and drafted a formal contract to this end, greater regard will be had to the terms of such a contract when determining the status of the worker. In *Massey v Crown Life Insurance Co Ltd.*,[46] Mr Massey worked as a branch manager for one of the insurance company's offices. His pay was partly based on commission. After receiving financial advice, Mr Massey thought it would be more economically advantageous for him to alter his status from that of employee to independent contractor. His employer agreed and arrangements were made to formalise the position. When he was later dismissed he sought to refer a claim under the unfair dismissals legislation. Lord Denning MR of the Court of Appeal held that the facts of the case disclosed sufficient evidence of a genuine intention to change Mr Massey's status:

---

42. [1976] 1 WLR 1213, 1226-1227.
43. [1984] IR 508.
44. [1984] 1 IR 508, 508.
45. [1997] IESC 9, [1998] 1 IR 34.
46. [1978] IRLR 31.

It seems to me on the authorities that, when it is a situation which is in doubt or which is ambiguous, so that it can be brought under one relationship or the other, it is open to the parties by agreement to stipulate what the legal situation between them shall be... So the way in which the parties draw up their agreement and express it can be a very important factor in defining what the true relation was between them. If they declare that one party is self-employed, that may be decisive.[47]

The decision in *Massey* must be viewed with caution and should not be interpreted   **[3–32]** as elevating the status of what was contractually agreed between the parties to the point where it can be considered the key factor in determining the status of the worker. The decision in *Massey* was possibly motivated by the fact that it would be unfair to allow Mr Massey to request that his contractual status be altered in order to alleviate his tax liability and then later when it suited him to seek the protection offered to employees under the unfair dismissals legislation. *Massey* can probably best be interpreted as authority for the proposition that in circumstances where both parties genuinely wish to alter the status of the worker (and in *Massey* it must be borne in mind that it was Mr Massey who suggested changing his status and not his employer) then the law should give effect to the intentions of the parties, but only if all the other evidence is inconclusive.

The potential scope of the finding in *Massey* was diminished by another decision   **[3–33]** of the Court of Appeal in *Young & Woods Ltd. v West*.[48] In that case, Mr West was a sheet-metal worker who chose to operate as an independent contractor for tax purposes. He was paid an hourly wage, used the respondent's equipment and was working under the same supervision as the other employees he worked along-side. When he was dismissed he claimed that he had been an employee all along and was therefore entitled to refer his claim under the unfair dismissals legisla-tion. While not dismissing the validity of his argument entirely, Stephenson LJ certainly was not convinced by its evidential strength:

> I am satisfied that the parties can resile from the position which they have deliber-ately and openly chosen to take up and that to reach any other conclusion would be, in effect, to permit the parties to contract out of the [Employment Rights] Act [1996] and to deprive, in particular, a person who works as an employee within the definition of the Act under a contract of service of the benefits which the statute confers upon him. If I consider the policy of the Act I can see the dangers, pointed out by Lord Justice Ackner in the course of the argument, of employers anxious to escape from their statutory liabilities under this legislation or the Factories Acts offering this choice to persons whom they intend to employ, as Mr West was employed, as employees within the definition of the Act and pressing them to take that employment – it may be even insisting upon their taking that employment

---

47. *ibid.*, at 34.
48. [1980] IRLR 201.

– on the terms that it shall not be called that employment at all, but shall be called a contract for services with a self-employed person.[49]

[3–34]   In reaching this conclusion Stephenson LJ emphasised the fact that it could not be said that Mr West was 'in business on his own account' and accepted that the decision in the case could be deemed contradictory by some:

> Unjust as it may seem in this case that Mr. West should be able to get away from the bed which he has made, or to eat his cake and still keep it, or to wear two hats according to which one happens to suit him at the time – whatever metaphor is used – nevertheless it is in my judgment the duty of an Industrial Tribunal, once a person goes to it and says, 'Though I was self-employed, nevertheless I am an employee entitled to enforce my statutory rights,' to see whether the label of self-employed is a true description or a false description by looking beneath it to the reality of the facts, and it must be its duty to decide on all the evidence whether the true legal relationship accords with the label or is contradicted by it.[50]

To ensure that Mr West did not benefit from 'the best of both worlds' Stephenson LJ did recommend that if he was deemed to be an employee as he had now claimed, the Inland Revenue should reclaim the tax deductions that had been granted to him as a self-employed person.

[3–35]   In *Lynch (Inspector of Taxes) v Neville Brothers Ltd.*,[51] the Irish High Court confirmed that while no one single test was decisive in determining the issue, the label attached to the relationship by the contract could be significant. In that case, the respondent company had engaged merchandisers to unload products from delivery vehicles at retail outlets they supplied. The written agreement between the parties referred to the merchandisers as independent contractors. The company did not direct the merchandisers as to how to do the work. The merchandisers could delegate the work to others without seeking the prior approval of the company and were free to provide merchandise services for other companies. The merchandisers were paid a fixed rate and did not supply their own equipment, nor did they invest in the business in any other way. The matter came before the High Court, which upheld the decision of the lower court and decided that the merchandisers were indeed independent contractors. Carroll J concluded:

> It is correct that the relationship between the respondent and the merchandiser cannot be defined merely by labeling it as a contract for services in the contract between them but the reality of the situation is that there is nothing in the contract or in the factual matrix of this case to cast doubt on the designation of the relationship in the contract.[52]

---

49. [1980] IRLR 201, 207.
50. [1980] IRLR 201, 207.
51. [2004] IEHC 375, [2005] 1 ILRM 536.
52. [2005] 1 ILRM 536, 540.

When attempting to determine the status of a worker, the description the parties [3–36] put on the relationship must always be regarded with a degree of circumspection. Two competing arguments are at play in such circumstances. On the one hand, the parties to the agreement can claim that they enjoy the freedom to contract on such terms as they please and short of illegality or fraud the law has no business in interfering with the agreed arrangements between the parties. On the other hand, it may be suggested that in the context of employment relationships, such an argument does not hold up well. Given the potential power imbalance between an employer and a worker the possibility exists that the worker will be coerced or unduly influenced into agreeing to terms that may not necessarily be favourable or fair. Simply following the declared intentions of the parties in such circumstances may allow such abuse to flourish.

Following *Henry Denny*, the Irish courts will consider the declared intent of the [3–37] parties and it would appear in cases where there is ambiguity as to the precise status of the arrangement (as occurred in *Massey*) the declared intention of the parties can be determinative. However, the importance of the parties' description is not to be overestimated and it is only in circumstances where the reality of the relationship corresponds with description or where the other evidence is contradictory that the label will be considered to be a determinative factor.

1.1.4. Personal Service

A contract of employment is one of exclusive service. The presence of an unre- [3–38] stricted right to delegate within the contract is not consistent with an employer/ employee relationship. In *Ready Mixed Concrete Ltd. (South East) v Minister of Pensions*,[53] MacKenna J stated that if the worker agrees, 'in consideration of a wage or other remuneration, he will provide his own work and skill in the performance of some service for his master'[54] then such agreement will be an indicator that the relationship is one of employment.

The right to delegate proved determinative in *Kane v McCann*.[55] In that case, the [3–39] claimant and respondent had entered into a partnership agreement regarding the operation of a pilot boat. It was the claimant's contention that he was an employee of the respondent and that he had been unfairly dismissed without notice. The respondent claimed that the agreement between them was one of partnership, which had been dissolved *inter alia* because the claimant had on certain days failed to appear to drive the boat or accompany the respondent on the boat. The claimant argued that the contract allowed him to send someone else to do the work for him and he often did so. The tribunal held that the all the evidence indicated that the contractual relationship between the claimant and respondent was not one of employer and employee. In particular, it held that the fact that the

---

53. [1968] 2 QB 497, [1968] 2 WLR 775, [1968] 1 All ER 433.
54. [1968] 2 QB 497, 515.
55. [1995] ELR 175.

claimant could send another to do the work for him, and repeatedly did so, was a determinative factor in this regard.[56]

[3–40]   The significance of the question of whether the worker is required to provide his services exclusively or not has links to the control test discussed earlier. If the worker has the authority to decide who does the work, then this is evidence that control as to who does the work lies with the worker and will be consistent with a finding that the worker is an independent contractor. In *Henry Denny & Sons (Ireland) Ltd. v Minister for Social Welfare*,[57] the Supreme Court upheld a finding that the fact that the demonstrator could not 'engage other people to stand in for her except in exceptional circumstances and then only with the approval of the company',[58] was a factor that indicated she was an employee. While the worker did have a right to delegate, this was restricted and subject to the authority of the employer. Thus a restrictive right to delegate where the employee is unable to do the work will not necessarily be fatal to a finding that the relationship is one of employee or employer.[59]

[3–41]   The existence of a right to delegate must be real and not illusory. A Tribunal must guard against unscrupulous employers who could insert 'substitution' or 'delegation' clauses into contracts with workers simply to avoid such agreements being classified as contracts of employment. Where substitution is in actual fact impossible and the clause is in effect a sham designed to avoid a determination that the agreement is one of employment, then it will be ignored when investigating the legal relationship between the parties.[60]

2. Agency Workers

[3–42]   During the heyday of the 'Celtic Tiger' and Ireland's booming economy the use of employment agencies became commonplace.[61] The purpose of such agencies is to supply businesses (the end-users) with suitably qualified workers on either a permanent or temporary basis. In the case of workers appointed on a temporary basis, the employment agency mechanism creates a triangular relationship between the worker, the employment agency and the end-user. From the point of view of employment status, these relationships raise legal questions as to who (if anyone) is the employer of the worker in such circumstances?

---

56. See also *Ryan v Shamrock Marine (Shannon) Ltd.* [1992] ELR 19.
57. [1997] IESC 9, [1998] 1 IR 34.
58. [1998] 1 IR 34, 44.
59. *Staffordshire Sentinel Newspapers Ltd. v Potter* [2004] UKEAT 0022 04 DM, [2004] IRLR 752.
60. *Ministry of Defence Dental Services v Kettle* [2007] UKEAT 0308 06 3101, [2007] All ER 301.
61. For broader discussion of the current and changing domestic and European legal landscape concerning agency workers see Regan, 'Agency Workers – Status and Rights', 5 *IELJ* (2008), 86.

The traditional view, as exemplified by the decision in *Construction Industry* [3–43]
Training v Labour Force Ltd.,[62] has been that workers operating under such conditions were neither employees of the employment agency nor of the end-user but
were instead engaged under a contract *sui generis*. In that case, the respondents
were an employment agency that supplied workers to various building contractors
who required labour. The workmen were paid by the agency on the basis of the
hours they had worked for these contractors and, while the end-users controlled
the workers and provided the work, the workers were paid by the agency and had
an express contractual relationship with the agency but not the end-users. The
Construction Industry Training Board applied a levy to the agency based on the
number of construction industry employees that they had apparently 'engaged'.
The agency contended that they had no such employees and argued that the
contracts with the workers were not ones of employment. The court held that
no contract of employment existed between the agency and the workers or the
workers and the construction firms. Cooke J concluded that:

> I think there is much to be said for the view that, where A contracts with B to
> render services exclusively to C, the contract is not a contract for services, but a
> contract *sui generis*, a different type of contract from either of the familiar two.[63]

The Irish High Court adopted a similar approach in *The Minister for Labour v* [3–44]
PMPA Insurance Company.[64] In that case, PMPA had employed a typist on
a temporary basis. The typist had been engaged by PMPA via an employment
agency. Under the terms of the contract, payment would be made to the agency
by PMPA and it was PMPA who controlled and supervised the typist's work.
Following the decision in *Labour Force*, Barron J held that two separate contracts
existed. One was a contract between PMPA and the agency and the other was
between the typist and the agency. There was, however, no contract, express or
implied, between the typist and PMPA. In conclusion, Barron J stated:

> So far as [PMPA] was concerned its rights and duties in relation to the employee
> were enforceable solely under its agreement with the [agency] and against the
> [agency]. So far as the employee was concerned her rights and duties equally were
> enforceable solely under the terms of her agreement with the [agency] and against
> the [agency]. In such a contractual situation I see no room for any implied contrac-
> tual relationship between [PMPA] and the employee.[65]

---

62. [1970] 3 All ER 220.
63. *ibid.*, at 225.
64. [1986] JISLL 215.
65. *ibid.*, at 217.

2.1. Mutuality of Obligation

[3-45] The approach adopted towards agency workers in the above cases left such workers in an isolated position. Consequently, in recent years, English cases regarding agency workers have sought to resolve the issue on the basis of whether a 'mutuality of obligation' existed between the parties. Mutuality of obligation has been described as 'an irreducible minimum'[66] of a contract of service.

[3-46] However, the 'mutuality of obligation' approach can also produce harsh results for a worker seeking to establish an employment relationship with another party, as typified by the decision in *Carmichael and Leese v National Power Plc.*[67] In that case, the applicants worked as power-station tour guides. They were engaged on 'a casual as required basis'. They were paid after the deduction of income tax and national insurance payments from their wages. They wore the company uniform, received company training and used a company vehicle when necessary. Upon their initial engagement they were working an average of three hours per week, but those hours had increased over time to an average of 25 hours per week. Difficulties arose when the applicants sought written particulars of their employment from National Power Plc, the successor to Blyth Power Stations, formerly operated by the Central Electricity Generating Board (CEGB). The House of Lords upheld the industrial tribunal's finding (which had been upheld by the Employment Appeals Tribunal but overturned by the Court of Appeal) that the applicants were not employees. In particular, on examining the documentation signed by the parties – although not to be taken as the exclusive memorial of such relationships generally – Lord Irvine LC concluded:

> that the documents did no more than provide a framework for a series of ad hoc contracts of service or for services which the parties might subsequently make; and that when they were not working as guides they were not in any contractual relationship with the CEGB. The parties incurred no obligations to provide or accept work, but at best assumed moral obligations of loyalty in a context where both recognised that the best interests of each lay in being accommodating to the other... (T)he words imposed no obligation on Mrs Leese and Mrs Carmichael, but intimated that casual employment on the pay terms stated could ensue as and when the CEGB's requirements for the services of the guides arose...

> If this appeal turned exclusively – and in my judgement it does not – on the true meaning and effect of the documentation of March 1989, then I would hold as a matter of construction that no obligation of the CEGB to provide casual work, nor on Mrs Leese and Mrs Carmichael to undertake it, was imposed. There would therefore be an absence of that irreducible minimum of obligation necessary to create a contract of service...[68]

---

66. *Nethermere (St Neots) Ltd. v Taverna and Gardiner* [1984] IRLR 240.
67. [1999] 1 WLR 2042, [1999] 4 All ER 897, [1999] ICR 1226, [1999] IRLR 43.
68. [1999] ICR 1226, 1229-1330.

To alleviate the perceived harshness of the mutuality of obligation test as it would   [3–47]
be applicable to agency workers, the English Court of Appeal has sought imaginative ways to give effect to the practical realities of the working relationship.
In *Dacas v Brook Street Bureau (UK) Ltd.*,[69] a contract of employment between
the worker and the end-user was implied in the absence of an express agreement
between the parties notwithstanding the fact that there was no direct express
contractual link between the worker and the end-user. Such a contract was also
implied on the basis of the threefold test outlined by MacKenna J in *Ready Mixed
Concrete (South East) Ltd. v Minister of Pensions and National Insurance*[70] already
discussed above.

In *Dacas*, Mrs Dacas was registered with an employment agency (Brook Street   [3–48]
Bureau). The agreement expressly stated that it did not give rise to a contract of
employment between Mrs Dacas and the agency. Mrs Dacas was assigned by the
agency to work as a cleaner in a hostel for Wandsworth Borough Council. Her
work was done at the council's premises and under its supervision and control.
In a separate contract with the council, the agency set her rates of pay and paid
her wages from payments made to it by the council. Mrs Dacas was dismissed
following an incident where it was alleged that she swore at a visitor to the hostel.
The tribunal held that she was neither employed by the agency nor the council.
While Mrs Dacas only appealed the judgment against the agency, the court did
consider what the position would have been as against the council. It was of
the opinion that the Employment Tribunal may have been so distracted by the
different contractual arrangements between the parties that it did not consider
the possibility that the facts of the case may have led to a finding that an implied
contract of employment existed between Mrs Dacas and the council. Mummery
LJ noted that:

> The formal written contracts between Mrs Dacas and Brook Street and between
> Brook Street and the Council relating to the work to be done by her for the Council
> may not tell the whole of the story about the legal relationships affecting the work
> situation. They do not, as a matter of law, necessarily preclude the implication of a
> contract of service between Mrs Dacas and the Council. There may be evidence of
> a pattern of regular mutual contact of a transactional character between Mrs Dacas
> and the Council, from which a contract of service may be implied by the tribunal.
> I see no insuperable objection in law to a combination of transactions in the trian-
> gular arrangements, embracing an express contract for services between Mrs Dacas
> and Brook Street, an express contract between Brook Street and the Council and
> an implied contract of service between Mrs Dacas and the Council, with Brook
> Street acting in certain agreed respects as an agent for Mrs Dacas and as an agent
> for the Council under the terms of the express written agreements.

---

69. [2004] EWCA Civ 217, [2004] ICR 1437, [2004] IRLR 358.
70. [1968] 2 QB 497, 515.

I approach the question posed by this kind of case on the basis that the outcome, which would accord with practical reality and common sense, would be that, if it is legally and factually permissible to do so, the applicant has a contract, which is not a contract of service, with the employment agency, and that the applicant works under an implied contract, which is a contract of service, with the end-user and is therefore an employee of the end-user with a right not to be unfairly dismissed. The objective fact and degree of control over the work done by Mrs Dacas at West Drive over the years is crucial. The Council in fact exercised the relevant control over her work and over her. As for mutuality of obligation, (a) the Council was under an obligation to pay for the work that she did for it and she received payment in respect of such work from Brook Street, and (b) Mrs Dacas, while at West Drive, was under an obligation to do what she was told and to attend punctually at stated times.[71]

Thus, based on the element of control exercised over Mrs Dacas and the existence of mutuality of obligation the court concluded that Mrs Dacas was an employee of the council in the absence of evidence inconsistent with that finding contained within the contract between the parties.

[3–49]   The Court of Appeal in *James v Greenwich London Borough Council*[72] did limit the circumstances in which a contract of employment could be implied between the end-user and the worker. Such a contract could only be implied in situations where it was necessary to do so in order to explain the relationship between the parties. In that case, Ms James worked for the council for a number of years as a social care support worker. Ms James worked under the control of the council, who provided her with her work instructions and materials. During the course of her work she wore a staff badge with the council's logo. Some time after beginning work with the council, Ms James changed agencies. The new agency assumed responsibility for her work with the council. She signed a new agreement with this agency because it provided her with a better hourly wage. The agency was responsible for the payment of her remuneration. The agency entered into an agreement with the council, under which payment would be made by the council to the agency to cover the worker's pay and other expenses in relation to the contract. Ms James was paid by the agency and could not avail of the council's sick or holiday pay provisions that were applicable to its employees.

[3–50]   Between August and September 2004 Ms James was absent from work through sickness and did not inform the council but instead provided medical certificates to the agency. The agency sent another worker to take her place with the council. When she returned to work she was informed that her services were no longer required. Ms James sought to bring an action for unfair dismissal against the council. To do so, it was first necessary to determine whether she was an employee

---

71. *ibid.*, at paras.52–53.
72. [2008] EWCA Civ 35, [2008] ICR 545.

of the council and the court found that no contract (implied or otherwise) existed between Ms James and the council. Rather Mummery LJ agreed with the Employment Tribunal's approach, observing that it was:

> entitled to conclude that Ms James was not an employee of the Council because there was no express or implied contractual relationship between her and the Council. Her only express contractual relationship was with the employment agency, as she recognised when she changed agencies rather then employers in order to obtain a higher wage. The Council's only express contractual relationship was also with the agency. There were no grounds for treating the express contracts as other than genuine contracts.

> The ET was not perverse in holding that it was unnecessary to imply a third contract between Ms James and the Council. What Ms James did and what the Council did were fully explained in this case by the express contracts into which she and the Council had entered with the employment agency. The Council provided work to Ms James for several years, but the ET found that it was not under any implied obligation to do so. The mere passage of time did not generate a legal obligation on the part of the Council to provide her with work any more than it generated a legal obligation on her to do the work. The provision of work by the Council, its payments to the employment agency and the performance of work by Ms James were all explained in this case by their respective express contracts with the employment agency, so that it was not necessary to imply the existence of another contract in order to give business reality to the relationship between the parties.

> In brief, the circumstances in which the Council received and paid for work done by Ms James for the Council and the facts about the working relationship between them did not lead irresistibly to the result that they were only explicable by the necessary existence of a contract of service between them.[73]

Mummery LJ also pointed out that the mutuality of obligation test was only of critical importance in deciding whether the agreement between two parties is a contract of employment or something else and not of significant assistance in cases such as this where the question is whether or not a contract existed between the parties at all: [3–51]

> I add that I agree with the EAT that in this case the question of the presence of the irreducible minimum of mutual obligations, which was addressed by the ET and by Mr Jonathan Cohen on behalf of the Council in his skeleton argument, was not the essential point. The mutuality point is important in deciding whether a contract, which has been concluded between the parties, is a contract of employment or some other kind of contract. In this case, on the findings of fact by the ET about the arrangements, how they operated in practice, about the work done by

---

73. *ibid.*, at paras.41–44.

Ms James and the conduct of the Council, there was no contract at all between Ms James and the Council: there was no express contract and there were insufficient grounds for requiring the implication of a contract.[74]

[3–52]   In *Diageo Global Supply v Mary Rooney*,[75] the Irish Labour Court resisted applying the implied contract approach and instead preferred to apply the approach of MacKenna J in *Ready Mixed Concrete (South East) Ltd. v Minister of Pensions and National Insurance*[76] to the question of the employment status of agency workers. Thus factors such as the mutuality of obligation, the control exercised over the worker and the terms contained in the contract were seen to be the determining features of the relationship.

[3–53]   In that case, Ms Rooney worked on a part-time basis for the respondent company. She applied to the company for the position and negotiated her terms and conditions with the company. Ms Rooney worked under the control and supervision of the respondent company but her wages were paid through a recruitment agency, Irish Recruitment Agency (IRC). Ms Rooney claimed that she had been treated less favourably than a comparable full-time employee of the company. The respondent company claimed that Ms Rooney was not their employee. By applying the *Ready Mixed* three-pronged test, the Labour Court held that Ms Rooney was an employee of the respondent company.

[3–54]   First, it held that she did work under a contract for the respondent company:

> Whilst the agreement was not reduced to writing it defined the rights and duties of the parties *inter se*, and there was valuable consideration. There was also mutuality of obligations in the sense that the respondent undertook to provide work and the claimant undertook to perform that work. Whilst it was agreed that the consideration, in the form of wages, would be paid through IRC, this does not mean that consideration did not pass from the respondent. The Court is satisfied that IRC were acting on behalf of the respondent in paying the claimant's wages from funds provided by the respondent.[77]

Secondly, it held that this contract was one of service largely because of the control exercised over Ms Rooney's work by the respondent company. In particular, the court found that the respondent company directed Ms Mooney as to her work at all material times. The respondent determined her hours of work and she was contractually bound to attend for work when contacted.

Thirdly, whilst acknowledging that payment of her remuneration through the IRC was not consistent with the finding of a contract of employment, the court

74. *ibid.*, at para.45.
75. [2004] ELR 133.
76. [1968] 2 QB 497, [1968] 2 WLR 775, [1968] 1 All ER 433.
77. [2004] ELR 133, 139.

was satisfied that the IRC was at all times operating on behalf of the respondent. All other aspects of the contractual relationship between the respondent and Ms Mooney were consistent with a finding that she was an employee. Under that contract the respondent was required to make work available to Ms Mooney, which she would personally perform. She worked exclusively for the respondent for 11 years and was accepted as part of their staff, as evidenced by the fact that she always attended the Christmas party.

3. Vicarious Liability

The status of the worker may also have implications, in terms of civil liability, for the party who engaged that worker. Where an employee commits a tortious wrong during the course of his or her employment, not only may that employee be directly liable for that wrong, but the employer may also be made vicariously liable to the injured third party for the resulting damage caused by the employee.[78] [3–55]

3.1. Justifications for Vicarious Liability

As a strict form of tortious liability, the doctrine is only applied in limited circum- [3–56] stances. Thus it is most commonly applied where the wrongdoer is an employee of the defendant employer (and hence the analysis in the previous section in respect of when a contract of employment will be deemed to exist is of obvious relevance), and the employer will only be made vicariously liable for the actions of the employee where that employee was acting in the *scope* or *course* of his or her employment.

Because it is an exceptional form of liability, which essentially places blame on an [3–57] employer who is not at fault (in the traditional legal sense), much debate exists as to the underlying rationale for the application of the doctrine.[79] Fleming has observed that the doctrine represents:

---

78. Generally, see McMahon and Binchy, *Law of Torts* (3rd ed., Butterworths, 2000), at pp.1091–1118; Healy, *Principles of Irish Torts* (Clarus Press, 2006), at pp.43–52; Ryan, ch.9 in Regan, ed., *Employment Law* (Tottel Publishing, 2009).
79. For example, in *Majrowski v Guy's and St Thomas's NHS Trust* [2006] UKHL 34, [2007] 1 AC 224, [2006] 3 WLR 125, [2006] 4 All ER 395, [2006] IRLR 695, Lord Nicholls said (at [9]): 'Stated shortly, these factors are that all forms of economic activity carry a risk of harm to others, and fairness requires that those responsible for such activities should be liable to persons suffering loss from wrongs committed in the conduct of the enterprise. This is 'fair', because it means injured persons can look for recompense to a source better placed finan- cially than individual wrongdoing employees. It means also that the financial loss arising from the wrongs can be spread more widely, by liability insurance and higher prices. In addi- tion, and importantly, imposing strict liability on employers encourages them to maintain standards of "good practice" by their employees.' On enterprise theory see further Brodie, 'Justifying Vicarious Liability', 27 *OJLS* (2007), 493.

a compromise between two conflicting policies: on the one hand, the social interest in furnishing an innocent tort victim with recourse against a financially responsible defendant; on the other, a hesitation to foist any undue burden on business enterprise.[80]

[3–58] Its application has also been justified on the basis that as the employer was in control of the employee's actions – in that the employer was in a position of authority or responsibility over the employee – then the employer should be made vicariously liable for that employee's actions (including those that were wrongful).[81] Another justification is that because the employee would not have been in a position to commit the wrong but for the fact of his or her employer's activities, then it is only fair that the employer should be made liable, as 'the master set the whole thing in motion'.[82] Yet another justification is that the doctrine acts as a loss-distribution mechanism. The loss is shifted, in economic terms, from the wrongdoer to another party who is usually in a better position to absorb the loss (the employer).[83]

[3–59] Given the different justifications for its existence, it is perhaps not surprising that the courts have failed to apply the doctrine, as we shall see, in any consistent, logical or predictable manner. In the words of Professor Glanville Williams:

> Vicarious liability is the creation of many judges who have had different ideas of its justification or social policy, or no idea at all. Some judges may have extended the rule more widely or confined it more narrowly than its true rationale would allow; yet the rationale, if we can discover it, will remain valid so far as it extends.[84]

In order to establish vicarious liability, the plaintiff must prove that the wrongdoer committed a tort, that [s]he was an employee of the third party[85] and that the tort was committed during the scope or course of the wrongdoer's employment. We have already considered the question of whether and when a contract of employment can be deemed to exist, hence we now turn to the question of when an employee can be said to be acting in the course of his or her employment.

---

80. Fleming, *The Law of Torts* (9th ed., LBC Services, 1998), at 409–410.
81. *Moynihan v Moynihan* [1975] IR 192.
82. *Hutchinson v The York, Newcastle and Berwick Railway Co* (1850) 5 exch.343 at 350.
83. *ibid.*
84. Williams, 'Vicarious Liability: Tort of the Master or of the Servant?', 72 *LQR* (1956), 201 at 231.
85. Identifying whether or not the wrongdoer was an employee of the third party will depend on the principles discussed earlier in this chapter. In cases involving vicarious liability the Irish courts have emphasised the control exercised by the employer over the worker. See *Phelan v Coillte Teo* [1993] IR 18; *O'Keeffe v Hickey & Others* [2008] IESC 72, [2009] 1 ILRM 490.

3.2. The Scope or Course of Employment

The scope or course of employment tests have been used interchangeably by the [3–60]
courts when assessing whether or not the employee's actions impose liability on
the shoulders of the employer. An employer will only be liable for the wrongs
committed by his or her employee where it can be said that those wrongs were
committed during the *scope* or *course* of his or her employment. The authorities
would appear to conflict with each other in this area and it can be difficult to
predict the outcome in any given case as to whether the employee was acting
within the scope or course of employment. As a general rule, it would seem that
the courts will expand the tests for vicarious liability 'if by doing so they are
serving better an "important purpose"'.[86]

3.2.1. The Scope of Employment/Implied Authority Test

Whether or not an employee's actions are within the scope of his or her employ- [3–61]
ment is a question of fact.[87] Under this test, liability is imposed on the employer
on the basis that the employee is authorised to do the acts in question.[88] Thus
an employee would be considered to have been acting within the scope of his
or her employment where it could be established that [s]he was working within
the implied delegated authority of the employer. The extent of the employee's
implied authority can vary depending on the circumstances of the case and the
competing interests at play. In *Poland v Parr & Sons*,[89] an employer was found
vicariously liable for the actions of his employee where that employee struck a
child because he reasonably believed that the child was stealing his employer's
property. The court held that the employee had the authority to act in defence
of his employer's property in emergency circumstances. His actions, while not
advisable, could be considered to be within his delegated authority and therefore
his employer was liable.

It is not sufficient for the plaintiff to establish that the acts were done within the [3–62]
employee's implied delegated authority, those acts must also be done *for* the employer,
that is, with the intention to benefit the employer or further the employer's objectives. In other words, an act of assault or battery committed by the employee may
be within the scope of employment where it is done in an emergency situation to
protect the employer's property as outlined above,[90] but similar actions would be
considered to have been committed outside the scope of employment where they are
committed out of personal vengeance or spite.[91] In *Farry v GN Rly Co*,[92] a dispute
arose as to whether or not the plaintiff had the appropriate ticket for a train journey.

---

86. Deakin, Johnston and Markesinis, *Markesinis & Deakin's Tort Law* (6th ed., Oxford University Press, 2008), at 679.
87. *Kirby v National Coal Board* (1958) SC 514 at 532 *per* Lord President Clyde.
88. *Tuberville v Stamp* (1697) 1 Ld. Raym. 264.
89. [1927] 1 KB 236.
90. *Poland v Parr & Sons* [1927] 1 KB 236.
91. *Warren v Henlys Ltd.* [1948] 2 All ER 935.
92. [1898] 2 IR 352.

A station employee detained the plaintiff, forcing him to give up his ticket. In assessing whether the defendant should be made liable for the false imprisonment, Palles CB outlined the limitations on the scope of employment test as follows:

> In actions of this class, two separate things are to be considered: first, the act done; secondly, the purpose for which it is done... If the act is outside the scope of the servant's employment, the master is not responsible, and in such a case it is unnecessary to consider the purpose... But, when the act... is one within the ordinary scope of the servant's employment then arises the question whether the act complained of was done for the employer; as, if the act, although of a class within the scope of the employment, was done by the servant, for his own purposes, such, for instance, as wreaking his own vengeance or spite upon a particular person, the act, although capable of being done within the scope of employment, is not in fact done within such scope, it is not done *for* the employer.[93]

Interpreted narrowly, the scope of employment test can be very limiting and, despite some imaginative applications,[94] deliberate wrongdoing by an employee is unlikely to render an employer vicariously liable under the scope of employment test as it will be unusual to find circumstances where the employer has authorised the commission of the deliberate wrongful act.[95]

3.2.2. *The Course of Employment Test*

[3–63] The course of employment test was explained thus by Lord Goff, 'an employee is acting in the course of his employment when he is doing what he is employed to do... or anything which is reasonably incidental to his employment'.[96] The course of employment test therefore takes into consideration the practical realities of the modern workplace and just because the employee is not doing *exactly* what [s]he was employed to do at the time of the incident does not necessarily take him or her outside the course of employment for the purposes of vicarious liability. Thus in *Kay v ITW*,[97] a fork-lift driver was held to be acting in the course of his employment when he reversed a lorry out of the way of the entrance to a warehouse, which he was trying to gain access to as part of his work. The employee was trying to do his job, even if he was not authorised to drive the lorry, when the accident occurred.

[3–64] In this respect, the time and place the accident occurred will be relevant in determining whether or not the employee's actions are considered to have been committed during the course of employment. In *Boyle v Ferguson*,[98] a car salesman was found to be acting in the course of his employment when he crashed a car owned by his employer on a Saturday evening whilst in the company of two

---

93. [1898] 2 IR 352, 355.
94. *Lloyd v Grace, Smith & Co* [1912] AC 716.
95. *Daniels v Whetstone Entertainments Ltd. and Allender* [1962] 2 Lloyd's LR 1.
96. *Smith v Stages* [1989] 1 All ER 833 at 836.
97. [1968] 1 QB 140, [1967] 3 WLR 695, [1967] 3 All ER 22.
98. [1911] 2 IR 489.

women. The court held that, notwithstanding the time and place of the accident, the salesman was acting in the course of his employment as his employer was paying for the petrol and the court accepted that the salesman was simply trying to encourage the women to purchase a car.

A number of cases have arisen from incidents where employees have been involved [3–65] in road traffic accidents coming to or from work. In *Compton v McClure*,[99] the employer was found vicariously liable when the employee (who was late for work) drove too fast while on the employer's premises in an effort to 'clock-in' on time and injured the claimant due to his careless driving. The court held that the employer was vicariously liable for the employee's wrongdoing on the basis that 'the conditions giving rise to vicarious liability are fulfilled when the employee comes onto his employer's premises in order to start the work that he is employed to do'. In *Smith v Stages*,[100] the House of Lords set out a number of principles in order to determine cases of this kind. In that case, two men were employed to install insulation in power stations. Most of their work was based in the Midlands in England. However, on this occasion they were asked by their employer to work at a power station in Wales. They were paid travelling expenses in addition to their normal wages. Following completion of the work, the employees were driving back when the car – driven by the first named defendant – left the road and crashed through a brick wall. The employee brought an action in negligence against the first named defendant – the uninsured driver of the car – and the second named defendant, who was the first named defendant's employer, on the basis of vicarious liability. The House of Lords held that the driver of the car was acting within the course of his employment at the time of the accident. In so doing, Lord Lowry laid down the following general guidelines to assist in the determination of the issue[101]:

1. In general an employee travelling from his ordinary residence to his or her place of work is not travelling in the course of his or her employment.
2. If the employee is travelling on his or her employer's time between workplaces then [s]he will be considered to be acting within the course of employment.
3. Receipt of wages by an employee will be an indication that the employee is travelling on the employer's time.
4. An employee travelling on the employer's time will be considered to be travelling in the course of his or her employment, i.e. travelling from his or her ordinary place of residence to a workplace other than his or her regular workplace.
5. A deviation or detour (unless it is merely incidental to the journey) will temporarily take the employee outside the course of his or her employment.
6. Return journeys are treated in the same manner as outward journeys.

---

99. [1975] ICR 378.
100. [1989] AC 928, [1989] 2 WLR 529, [1989] 1 All ER 833, [1989] ICR 272.
101. [1989] AC 928, 955-956.

3.2.3. Unauthorised Modes of Doing Authorised Acts

[3–66]   In his famous and oft-quoted statement, Salmond sought to expand the doctrine of vicarious liability beyond the limitations of the implied-authority test. He explained it thus:

> A master is not responsible for a wrongful act done by his servant unless it is done in the course of his employment. It is deemed to be so done if it is either (1) a wrongful act authorised by the master, or (2) a wrongful and unauthorised mode of doing some act authorised by the master.[102]

Under Salmond's formulation an employee who commits an unlawful act is acting in the course of employment where [s]he is doing a wrongful act authorised by the employer or is doing an act authorised by the employer in an unauthorised way. Thus not only can an employer be held liable for the acts of his or her employee but also for the manner in which [s]he does those acts. In *Century Insurance Co Ltd. v Northern Ireland Road Transport Board*,[103] an employer was held vicariously liable for the negligence of his employee who was doing his job (admittedly, very badly) when he caused the harm. The employee was a petrol lorry driver who, while transferring petrol from a tanker to the tank, lit a cigarette and threw away the lighted match he had used to light the cigarette. As a consequence, there was an explosion and the resulting fire caused extensive damage. While the act of lighting the cigarette and throwing away the match was not done for the benefit of the employer, what had occurred was part and parcel of his work. The lighting of the cigarette and the throwing away of the lighted match was an improper way of doing his work, which involved the safe transfer and delivery of the petrol. Similarly, in *Limpus v London General Omnibus Co*,[104] a bus driver, in contravention of his employer's instructions, raced a bus he was driving and caused a collision. The employer was held vicariously liable for the driver's actions. While racing the bus was contrary to his employer's instructions, he was still doing his job (driving a bus) at the time of the collision.[105] His actions were simply an unauthorised mode of doing something authorised by his employer.

---

102. Salmond and Heuston, *Salmond & Heuston on the Law of Torts* (Round Hall Sweet and Maxwell, 1996), at p.443.
103. [1942] AC 509, [1943] 1 All ER 491.
104. (1862) 1 H&C 526; 158 ER 993.
105. It would appear that, following *Limpus*, if an employee's actions are in direct contravention of his or her employer's instructions that fact alone will not automatically take the employee outside the course of his or her employment if the prohibition affects the *manner* in which the employee does the job. On the other hand, if the prohibition is intended to delineate the limits of the employee's authority, then the actions of the employee in contravention of such prohibition may be sufficient to take that employee outside of the course of his or her employment as [s]he exceeded his or her authority: *Conway v George Wimpey & Co Ltd.* [1951] 2 KB 266, [1951] 1 All ER 56; *Rose v Plenty* [1976] 1 WLR 141, [1976] 1 All ER 97.

3.2.4. Intentional Wrongs and the Sufficiency of Connection Test

The unauthorised-mode approach was an improvement on the implied-authority [3–67] test as it took into consideration the practical realities of the workplace rather than relying on an artificial construct of implied authority. However, it is ill-suited to determining whether or not an employer should be made vicariously liable for the intentional wrongs committed by an employee.[106] Applying Salmond's words literally, it is difficult to imagine circumstances in which an intentional wrong could ever be considered a mode of doing work giving rise to vicarious liability (indeed, if an intentional wrong was expressly authorised by an employer, then it would most likely give rise to primary direct liability on the part of the employer). The inadequacy of the unauthorised-mode approach in this regard was highlighted by the decision of the Court of Appeal of England and Wales in *Trotman v North Yorkshire County Council*.[107] In that case, a teacher committed sexual assault on a mentally disabled child while on a school trip abroad. It was held that the acts of sexual assault carried out by the school teacher in these circumstances could not be considered to be an improper mode of carrying out an authorised act for his employer (the Council). Butler-Sloss LJ held that such conduct was so far removed from the employee's duties as a teacher that it was in fact 'a negation of the duty of the Council to look after children for whom it was responsible'.[108] A similar conclusion was reached by the Irish High Court in *Health Board v B.C.*,[109] where it was held that an employer was not vicariously liable for a sexual assault carried out by one employee against another. This was on the basis that the court could not envisage a circumstance where such an assault could be regarded as being so connected with the employment to be considered within its scope.

Recent decisions on vicarious liability in Canada and the UK have evidenced [3–68] a move away from the unauthorised-mode approach, and instead have focused on what has became known as the sufficiency of connection test, whose foundations can be seen in the second part of Salmond's test. This lesser known part of Salmond's test provides that:

> But a master, as opposed to the employer of an independent contractor, is liable even for acts which he has not authorised, provided they are so connected with acts which he has authorised, that they may rightly be regarded as modes – although improper – modes of doing them.[110]

Under this approach, if the plaintiff can establish that there was a 'close connec- [3–69] tion' between the employment and the employee's conduct then that could be

---

106. For detailed analysis of this area, see Ryan, 'Making Connections: New Approaches to Vicarious Liability in Comparative Perspective', 15(1) *DULJ* (2008), 41.

107. [1998] EWCA Civ 1208, [1999] LGR 584.

108. *ibid.*, at 591.

109. [1994] ELR 27.

110. Salmond and Heuston, *Salmond &Heuston on the Law of Torts* (Round Hall Sweet and Maxwell, 1996), at p.443.

sufficient to attract the application of vicarious liability in certain circumstances. This approach to the issue of employer's liability for intentional wrongs committed by his or her employees was developed further in the Canadian Supreme Court decision of *Bazley v Curry*.[111] In that case, the appellant was a non-profit organisation that operated two residential-care facilities for the treatment of emotionally troubled children. The appellant acted as a 'parent' for these troubled children and its employees were to do everything a parent would do, from general supervision to intimate duties like bathing and putting the children to bed each night. The appellant hired a particular employee to work in one of its homes. The appellant did not know that this employee was a paedophile and had been advised that he was a suitable employee for such work. Following a complaint about the employee and after verifying that he had abused a child in one of its homes, the appellant dismissed him. That employee was convicted of 19 counts of sexual abuse, two of which related to the respondent. The respondent brought an action against the appellant for compensation for the injury he suffered while in its care on the basis that the appellant was vicariously liable for the actions of its employee in the circumstances. The matter came before the Supreme Court of Canada, which conducted an extensive analysis of the policy factors underpinning the doctrine of vicarious liability.

[3–70] Delivering the judgment of the court, McLachlin J referred to Salmond's famous quotation. It was obvious in this case that the employer had not authorised the sexual abuse. Therefore, the question was whether the wrong was so connected to an authorised act that it could be regarded as a mode of doing that act. McLachlin J approached the question in two steps. First, it was necessary to determine whether precedent unambiguously determined the issue one way or the other. If no such precedent existed, then one must decide whether or not vicarious liability should be imposed based on the policy rationales underpinning vicarious liability. Having reviewed the case law in this area, the court noted that no similar case had arisen before a higher court (apart from the decision in *Trotman*). McLachlin J then reviewed the case law involving employers who were held vicariously liable for the unauthorised wrongs of employees in an effort to find underlying recurring policy considerations. The cases were divided into three categories: (1) where the employee was acting in furtherance of the employer's aims[112] (2) where the employment creates a situation of friction,[113] and (3) the dishonest employee cases.[114] The common thread among these cases according to the court was that in each case the employer's enterprise had created the risk that produced the employee's wrongful act. Therefore, vicarious liability could be justified on the basis that 'where the employee's conduct is closely tied to a risk that the employer's enterprise has placed in the community, the employer may justly be held vicariously liable for the employee's wrong'.[115]

111. [1999] 2 SCR 534; (1999) 174 DLR (4th) 45.

112. *Kay v ITW Ltd.* [1968] 1 QB 140, [1967] 3 WLR 695, [1967] 3 All ER 22.

113. *Daniels v Whetstone Entertainments Ltd.* [1962] 2 Lloyd's Rep 1.

114. *Lloyd v Grace, Smith & Co* [1912] AC 716.

115. [1999] 2 SCR 534; (1999) 174 DLR (4th) 45, para.22.

Having found no precedent that resolved the issue, McLachlin J moved to the [3–71] second stage of her inquiry, which involved a consideration of the policy reasons for vicarious liability.[116] Having reviewed the underlying rationales for the imposition of vicarious liability, she agreed with Fleming,[117] who had identified the following factors as being the twin policies that lay at the heart of vicarious liability: '(1) the provision of a just and practical remedy for the harm; and (2) deterrence of future harm'.[118] The policy aim of providing a just and practical remedy was justified on the basis that the person who introduces a risk to society should be held responsible for those who may be injured by it. Vicarious liability would also ensure that the person injured by this activity would have a greater opportunity of recovering compensation from a financially viable defendant rather than a 'man of straw'. Furthermore, McLachlin J was of the view that vicarious liability was fair in the sense 'that the employer is often in the best position to spread the losses through mechanisms like insurance and higher prices, thus minimizing the dislocative effect of the tort within society'.[119] On the second policy aim of deterring future harm, the court noted that holding the employer vicariously liable for the employee's wrongs would encourage the employer to take steps to minimise the risk of future harm through more effective administration and supervision. McLachlin J then linked these underlying policies to the connection between the work and the wrong:

> A wrong that is only coincidentally linked to the activity of the employer and duties of the employee cannot justify the imposition of vicarious liability on the employer. To impose vicarious liability on the employer for such a wrong does not respond to common sense notions of fairness. Nor does it serve to deter future harms. Because the wrong is essentially independent of the employment situation, there is little the employer could have done to prevent it. Where vicarious liability is not closely and materially related to a risk introduced or enhanced by the employer, it serves no deterrent purpose, and relegates the employer to the status of an involuntary insurer. I conclude that a meaningful articulation of when vicarious liability should follow in new situations ought to be animated by the twin policy goals of fair compensation and deterrence that underlie the doctrine, rather than by artificial or semantic distinctions.[120]

---

116. McLachlin J did consider, and criticise, the Court of Appeal decision in *Trotman*, stating that: 'the opinion's reasoning depends on the level of generality with which the sexual act is described. Instead of describing the act in terms of the employee's duties of supervising and caring for vulnerable students during a study trip abroad, the Court of Appeal cast it in terms unrelated to those duties. Important legal decisions should not turn on such semantics.' (at para.24).

117. Fleming, *The Law of Torts* (9th ed., LBC Services, 1988), at 410.

118. [1999] 2 SCR 534; (1999) 174 DLR (4th) 45., para.29.

119. *ibid.*, at para.31.

120. *ibid.*, at para.36.

[3–72]   Having considered precedent and policy, McLachlin J summarised the legal principle as turning on the question of whether or not there is a connection or nexus
between the employment and the wrong that justifies the imposition of vicarious
liability on the employer. While acknowledging that the connection between the
tort and the employment was broad, McLachlin J did state that the employer's enterprise must have 'materially enhanced' the risk of the wrongful act occurring.[121]

[3–73]   After this exhaustive examination of vicarious liability, McLachlin J stated that the
courts should be guided by the following principles when determining whether an
employer should be liable for an employee's unauthorised, intentional wrongs:

> (1) They should openly confront the question of whether liability should
>   lie against the employer, rather than obscuring the decision beneath
>   semantic discussions of 'scope of employment' and 'mode of conduct'.
>
> (2) The fundamental question is whether the wrongful act is *sufficiently
>   related* to conduct authorized by the employer to justify the imposition
>   of vicarious liability. Vicarious liability is generally appropriate where
>   there is a significant connection between the *creation or enhancement
>   of a risk* and the wrong that accrues therefrom, even if unrelated to
>   the employer's desires. Where this is so, vicarious liability will serve
>   the policy considerations of provision of an adequate and just remedy
>   and deterrence. Incidental connections to the employment enterprise,
>   like time and place (without more), will not suffice. Once engaged in
>   a particular business, it is fair that an employer be made to pay the
>   generally foreseeable costs of that business. In contrast, to impose liability
>   for costs unrelated to the risk would effectively make the employer an
>   involuntary insurer.
>
> (3) In determining the sufficiency of the connection between *the employer's
>   creation or enhancement of the risk* and the wrong complained of,
>   subsidiary factors may be considered. These may vary with the nature
>   of the case. When related to intentional torts, the relevant factors may
>   include, but are not limited to, the following:
>   (a) the opportunity that the enterprise afforded the employee to abuse
>   his or her power;
>   (b) the extent to which the wrongful act may have furthered the
>   employer's aims (and hence be more likely to have been committed
>   by the employee);
>   (c) the extent to which the wrongful act was related to friction,
>   confrontation or intimacy inherent in the employer's enterprise;
>   (d) the extent of power conferred on the employee in relation to the victim;
>   (e) the vulnerability of potential victims to wrongful exercise of the
>   employee's power.[122]

---

121. *ibid.*, at para.39.
122. *ibid.*, at para.41 (emphasis in original).

Applying these guidelines to the facts of the case, the court concluded that the [3–74] employer should be held vicariously liable for the sexual abuse by its employee. In particular, the employee was permitted or required to be alone with the child for extended periods of time, was expected to supervise the child in intimate activities, and was in a position of power over the child. All of these factors materially enhanced the risk of the abuse occurring and, in light of the underlying policy themes, the circumstances justified the imposition of vicarious liability on the employer.

On the same day as it delivered its judgment in *Bazley*, the Supreme Court of [3–75] Canada delivered a decision in *Jacobi v Griffiths*, another case where an action was taken claiming that an employer could be vicariously liable for acts of sexual abuse committed by an employee.[123] In that case, the respondent – a Boys' and Girls' Club – which was a non-profit organisation, employed the respondent as a program director. In this role the employee was required to supervise volunteer staff and organise recreational activities and the occasional outing for the children. The acts of abuse committed by the employee were committed at his home outside working hours. The majority of the Supreme Court[124] held that the respondent was not vicariously liable for the sexual assaults. The majority held that it was not enough to show that the employer provided the employee with the opportunity of committing the wrong; there also had to be a strong connection between the employment and the wrong. The court held that that strong connection was absent in the case as – unlike in *Bazley* – the relationship between the employee and the appellants in *Jacobi* was not the same in terms of the power it granted the employee over the appellants, nor did the job create the same level of intimacy as existed in *Bazley*. Such a connection is even more critical, the court held, when dealing with non-profit organisations as they may not be in the same position as commercial employers to 'internalise their costs'. To find such organisations liable too readily could have negative policy effects, as Binnie J noted, '[Children's recreation is not a field that offers monetary profits as an incentive to volunteers to soldier on despite the risk of personal financial liability.'[125]

The Canadian Supreme Court reached, by a majority,[126] a similar conclusion in *EB* [3–76] *v Order of Oblates of Mary Immaculate in the Province of British Columbia*,[127] where it once again emphasised the fact that simply because the employment gave the employee the opportunity to commit the wrong was not alone sufficient to impose vicarious liability on the employer. In that case, the wrongdoer was a lay employee of a school run by the Oblates. He was employed as a baker, boat driver and odd-job man, and lived in a building on the school grounds. The employee sexually

---

123. [1999] 2 SCR 570; (1999) 174 DLR (4th) 71.
124. A dissenting judgment of L'Heureux-Dubé, Bastarache and McLachlin JJ was delivered by McLachlin J.
125. *ibid.*, at para.75.
126. With a strong dissenting judgment by Abella J.
127. [2005] 3 SCR 45; (2005) DLR (4th) 385. For analysis, see Feldthusen, 'Civil Liability for Sexual Assault in Aboriginal Residential Schools: The Baker Did It', 22 *Can J L & Soc* (2007), 61.

assaulted one of the schoolchildren over a period of years. The Supreme Court held that the school should not be made vicariously liable for the actions of the employee as there did not exist a sufficiency of connection between the employee's actions and the work. In particular, it was held that the employee was not permitted or required to be with the children, apart from supervised boat trips – his conduct was not in furtherance of his employer's aims; his work was limited to baking, maintenance and driving the boat; intimacy with the children was prohibited; the employee's living quarters were 'off limits' to the students and his employment did not confer any power on him over the children. Binnie J concluded:

> The trial judge suggested that the 'operational characteristics' of the school swept virtually all employees into the same 'enterprise risk' for which the respondent employer should be held vicariously liable, but this pushes vicarious liability too far. While vicarious liability does not require a claimant to establish that the wrongful employee was placed in a 'parent-like' position of authority, it does require consideration of the job-created power and the nature of an employee's duties as a fundamental component of determining if a particular enterprise increased the risk of *the employee's* wrongdoing in relation to the claimant... The appellant's global inclusion of all employees, including odd-job men, in the 'enterprise risk' paints with too broad a brush. It goes against the policy goal of ensuring that compensation is both effective and *fair*.[128]

[3–77]   The House of Lords was confronted with the same issue in *Lister v Hesley Hall*.[129] In that case, the claimants were residents in a boarding school, which was owned by the defendant. The defendants employed a warden whose responsibilities included supervising the boys, disciplining them and ensuring that they went to bed each evening and got up each morning. The warden sexually abused some of the schoolboys, who sued the defendant on the basis that it was vicariously liable for the wrongful acts. The House of Lords held that the defendant was liable and reiterated the principle that providing the employee with an opportunity to commit the wrong does not of itself make the employer vicariously liable – there must be a sufficient connection between the employment and the wrong. Lord Hobhouse further held that in order to establish whether a sufficient connection exists one had to first identify the duty owed by the employee to the employer that was breached and then identify the connection between that breach and the contractual duties of the employee to the employer. In *Lister*, the defendant had a duty to protect and care for the children attending the school. The warden was engaged to assist the defendant in that duty. Instead, he acted in breach of his contractual duties by sexually abusing some of the schoolchildren entrusted to his care. Hence his actions could be seen as occurring in the course of employment and hence the employer was vicariously liable in respect of the same.

---

128. *ibid.*, at paras.29–30.
129. [2001] UKHL 22, [2002] 1 AC 215, [2001] 1 WLR 1311, [2001] 2 All ER 769, [2001] ICR 665, [2001] IRLR 472.

While the claimants in *Lister* succeeded in their action, the status of *Bazley* as [3–78] authority remained unclear. Lord Hobhouse certainly did not think it appropriate to follow the decision, observing that:

> The judgments contain a useful and impressive discussion of the social and economic reasons for having a principle of vicarious liability as part of the law of tort which extends to embrace acts of child abuse. But an exposition of the policy reasons for a rule (or even a description) is not the same as defining the criteria for its application. Legal rules have to have a greater degree of clarity and definition than is provided by simply explaining the reasons for the existence of the rule and the social need for it, instructive though that may be. In English law that clarity is provided by the application of the criterion to which I have referred derived from the English authorities.[130]

In England, therefore, the theoretical position is that a person is acting in the [3–79] course of employment (and vicarious liability therefore arises) where the conduct of the employee was so closely connected with the nature and circumstances of the employment, and/or the risk of the breach was one so reasonably incidental to it, that it would be fair and just and reasonable to hold the employer vicariously liable for it.[131] This is, however, a question of fact to be answered on a case-by-case basis.[132] On this basis, for example, authorities in charge of children's homes have been held liable for sexual assaults perpetrated by employees thereof,[133] as has a nightclub where a bouncer (trained to act aggressively) who had been hit by someone he ejected from the defendants' club returned to his flat, found a knife and stabbed the claimant.[134] Similarly the employers of a policeman were held vicariously liable where he assaulted someone while off duty, having told the victim that he was a police officer.[135] Perhaps even more controversially, on this basis the Privy Council found a security company vicariously liable for the action of one of its employees in shooting dead (from two paces) a man who was trying to gain entry to a football stadium.[136] By contrast, vicarious liability has not been found, for example, where a policeman who offered to escort an inebriated female to a police station actually took her to his house and raped her as she slept,[137] or

---

130. *ibid.*, at para.60.
131. *Majrowski v Guy's and St Thomas's NHS Trust* [2005] QB 848, [2005] ICR 977.
132. *Dubai Aluminium Co Ltd. v Salaam* [2003] 2 AC 366, [2002] 3 WLR 884, [2003] IRLR 608.
133. *Lister v Hesley Hall Ltd.* [2001] UKHL 22, [2002] 1 AC 215, [2001] 1 WLR 1311, [2001] 2 All ER 769, [2001] ICR 665, [2001] IRLR 472; *Bernard v Attorney General of Jamaica* [2005] IRLR 398; *Bazley v Curry* [1999] 174 DLR (4th). A less expansive approach to this question is perhaps manifest in the decision in *Godden v Kent and Medway Strategic Health Authority* [2004] EWHC 1629, Queen's Bench, 8 July 2004.
134. *Mattis v Pollock* [2003] EWCA Civ 887, [2003] 1 WLR 2158, [2004] All ER 851, [2003] ICR 1335, [2003] IRLR 603.
135. *Weir v Chief Constable of Merseyside Police* [2003] ICR 708.
136. *Brown v Robinson* [2004] UKPC 56, 14 December 2004.
137. *N v Chief Constable of Merseyside Police* [2006] EWHC 3041.

where a policeman while off duty simply and randomly shot someone with his service revolver.[138]

[3–80] The Irish High Court was faced with the issue of vicarious liability and sexual assault in *Delahunty v South Eastern Health Board*.[139] In that case, the plaintiff as a young boy visited a friend in an industrial school where he was sexually assaulted by a house parent at that institution. He brought a claim that the school and the Minister for Education and Science should be made vicariously liable for the acts of employee. O'Higgins J, having reviewed the decisions in *Bazley*, *Jacobi* and *Lister* concluded that even if those authorities were to apply to the case at hand there was an absence of a strong connection between the perpetrator's employment and the wrong. The victim was a visitor to the school in respect of whom the perpetrator had no particular duties, quite unlike *Bazley* and *Lister* where the perpetrator, as part of his employment duties, had a close relationship with the victims. The High Court also held that the Minister for Education and Science also could not be held vicariously liable as the connection between the Minister and the plaintiff was 'quite remote'.

[3–81] *Delahunty* did little to clarify the law on the potential liability of an employer for the sexual assaults committed by its employees. However, shortly after *Delahunty* the Supreme Court was provided with the opportunity of ruling on the strong-connection test and the *Bazley* and *Lister* lines of authority in *O'Keeffe v Hickey & Others*,[140] 'a test case governing a significant number of pending cases'[141]. In that case, (the facts of which have been considered earlier in this chapter) the majority of the Supreme Court held that the Department of Education should not be held vicariously liable for the sexual abuse by the teacher as the teacher was not an employee of the department. Even though his finding that the teacher was not an employee essentially brought the main issue to an end, Hardiman J did consider the arguments put to him in favour of a broader basis for vicarious liability when considering whether or not the teacher's actions were in the course of his employment.

[3–82] Hardiman J was not impressed by the Canadian Supreme Court decisions in *Bazley* and *Jacobi*. He noted that a finding of vicarious liability can have serious consequences not only for the defendant but society in general. He also criticised the basis of liability as outlined in the Canadian decisions and dismissed the 'deep pockets' rationale on the basis that it did not automatically justify the imposition of such liability on a defendant who should not otherwise be found liable.[142]

---

138. *AG of British Virgin Islands v Hartwell* [2004] 1 WLR 1273.
139. [2003] 4 IR 361.
140. [2008] IESC 72, [2009] 1 ILRM 490, analysed by Feeney, 'The Supreme Court and Vicarious Liability – Implications for Employers', 6 *IELJ* (2009), 43.
141. *O'Keeffe v Hickey* [2009] IESC 39 (Ruling of the Supreme Court on the Question of Costs), unreported, Supreme Court, 6 May 2009, *per* Murray CJ at [6].
142. While Hardiman J rejected in no uncertain terms the development of a broader basis of

Hardiman J also expressed concern regarding the knock-on effects on society of imposing vicarious liability in such circumstances. He commented on the 'chilling effect' such a finding could have on the work of schools and other similar organisations and the negative effect that the imposition of a broad basis for vicarious liability would have on insurance costs. Hardiman J also dismissed the enterprise risk basis of liability on the facts of the case on the basis that, in his opinion, the State could not be considered an enterprise in the sense that other commercial entities could. Furthermore, he could not see how the State could be considered to be creating a risk by simply by facilitating the operation of the school.

Having dismissed the policy justifications outlined in *Bazley* as not being applicable to the case before him, Hardiman J held that the teacher's actions were not within the course of his employment, being in fact a negation of what he was employed to do.[143] He stated that the traditional Salmond test (unauthorised mode of doing an authorised act) was that which was to be applied in future Irish cases. In his opinion, the approach adopted in *Bazley*, which justified the imposition of vicarious liability on the employer in such circumstances only if it was fair and just, was 'utterly lacking in rigour, and perhaps even in meaning',[144] stating, 'It is utterly useless as a predictive tool… a modern version of the "Chancellor's foot", an old legal metaphor for an uncontrolled highly subjective discretion.'[145] Hardiman J also rejected the analysis in *Bazley* and *Lister*, which held that the close-connection test emanated from Salmond's famous statement of the law, concluding that: [3–83]

> I do not believe that the passage quoted above from the first edition of *Salmond* is at all capable of being the 'germ' of the close connection test. It is true Salmond in his first edition referred to acts which the employer had not authorised but which were 'so connected with acts which he has authorised…'. But the result of this close connection, in Professor Salmond's exposition, is that the acts in question are so connected *with acts (a) which the employer has authorised, and (b) that they may rightly be regarded as modes – although improper modes – of doing them.*
>
> Properly understood, there is no rational connection between this formulation and the Canadian one of 'close connection', or a ground of vicarious liability, except that the word 'connection' is used in both. But Professor Salmond's 'explanation'

---

liability in this area, it is arguable that his justification for doing so is somewhat problematic. He dismissed the 'deep pockets' theory as a rationale for the imposition of vicarious liability by making the point that simply because the employer is in a better position financially to absorb the loss is not sufficient reason to fix him or her with liability for the wrongs of his or her employees, but failed to consider in any great detail the other policy justifications for the imposition of liability, for example as an incentive for the employer to ensure that there is proper scrutiny of the actions of his or her employees.
143. para.23.
144. para.26.
145. *ibid.*

as Lord Steyn regards it, requires that the close connection be with acts which the employer has authorised and be such that what is actually done can be regarded as a mode, though an improper and unauthorised one, of doing what the employer has authorised. At the very least, the Canadian Supreme Court wholly dispensed with the second part of this test, requiring that what was in fact done must be a mode of doing what was authorised. The importance of the subject matter compels me to repeat, at the risk of tedium, that I cannot see anywhere in Professor Salmond's treatment of this subject the smallest 'germ' of what the Canadian Supreme Court did almost a century after Professor Salmond had first propounded his test.[146]

[3–84] On the other hand, Fennelly J in his judgment appeared to favour the close-connection test, stating that:

> The close-connection test is both well established by authority and practical in its content. It is essentially focussed on the facts of the situation. It does not, in principle, exclude vicarious liability for criminal acts or for acts which are intrinsically of a type which would not be authorised by the employer. The law regards it as fair and just to impose liability on the employer rather than to let the loss fall on the injured party. To do otherwise would be to impose the loss on the entirely innocent party who has engaged the employer to perform the service. The employer is, of course, also innocent, but he has, at least, engaged the dishonest servant and has disappointed the expectations of the person to whom he has undertaken to provide the service. There is no reason, in principle, to exclude sexual abuse from this type of liability. That is very far, as I would emphasise, from saying that liability should be automatically imposed... All will depend on a careful and balanced analysis of the facts of the particular case. In *Bazley*, the employees of the care home were required to provide intimate physical care for the residents. The sexual abuse was held to be closely connected.[147]

[3–85] Thus Fennelly J was of the view that the close-connection test was a justifiable method of determining whether or not vicarious liability should be imposed on an employer for intentional wrongdoing committed by his or her employee. While not expressing a concluding view one way or the other on the facts of the case, Fennelly J noted that the application of the close-connection test would not automatically mean that the employer would be made vicariously liable in every case; consideration would have to be taken in this case of the fact the music lessons were not part of the school curriculum and that the sexual abuse had occurred outside normal school hours. Furthermore, he noted that the sexual abuse in *Bazley* and *Lister* occurred in the more intimate surroundings of residential schools and the case could be distinguished on this basis.[148]

---

146. [2009] 1 ILRM 490, 521 (emphasis in original).
147. para.63.
148. para.64.

Geoghegan J, in his strong dissenting judgment, would have allowed the appeal [3–86] and would have imposed vicarious liability on the basis that in the circumstances of the relationship between Church and State at issue in *O'Keeffe*, to exempt the State from liability would not be just. On the question of the status in Irish law of *Lister* and *Bazley*, Geoghegan J described the Canadian innovation as perhaps 'the leading modern case' and went on to conclude that he would have allowed Ms. O'Keeffe's appeal on the basis of an application of 'the general modern principles underlying vicarious liability'.[149]

It is submitted that the decision of the majority of the Supreme Court in this [3–87] case is not without difficulties. Quite apart from the nuances of the different tests to be applied in vicarious liability claims such as these, the factual matrix of the case is undoubtedly one that triggers a strong impulse for the granting of recovery. Ultimately, it could be argued that by employing the principal, who was entrusted with the care and responsibility of the children attending his school, the employer in this case did enhance the risk of such abuse occurring. That is different from saying that such abuse was foreseeable. That teacher's responsibilities were to educate and care for the child whilst in his care. The teacher enjoyed a position of great power over the appellant who, as an eight-year-old schoolgirl, was extremely vulnerable. The offences occurred on school property, although not during school time – although it could be argued that playbreak constitutes part of school time. Furthermore, while the music lessons were not strictly part of the school curriculum, they were delivered on school property where the teacher would have retained his authority over the child, even though it did not necessarily involve school work. In other words, it may surely be argued that it is at least possible that there was a 'sufficient connection' between the abuse by the teacher and that teacher's work. This is not to say that an employer will always be vicariously liable for sexual assaults or other deliberate wrongs committed by their employees. Different facts will of course produce different results. Central to the decision in *Jacobi*, for example, was the fact that the perpetrator of the wrongdoing did not have a relationship of an intimate nature with the victim nor did he have the same authority over the victim that existed in *Bazley*. In *Delahunty* the fact that the victim was a visitor to the institution meant that the relationship of intimacy or power did not exist to such an extent as would bring the abuser's actions within the course of his employment.

The Supreme Court decision in *O'Keeffe* was revisited shortly afterwards by the same [3–88] court in *Reilly v Devereux & Others*.[150] In that case the plaintiff was employed as a member of the Defence Forces. He complained that he had been sexually assaulted on a number of occasions during the course of his employment by the first named defendant, who was a sergeant major in the Army and the plaintiff's superior officer. Kearns J emphasised how the plaintiff in the appeal in *Reilly* relied 'almost

---

149. *ibid.*, at 560.
150. [2009] IESC 22.

exclusively on the principles laid down in the *Bazley* case'. In so doing, three parallels were sought to be drawn between the factual backgrounds in *Bazley* and *Reilly*. First, the environment of the Defence Forces was such that the normal rules of adult interaction did not apply, since the disparity in rank between the plaintiff, who was a gunner, and the perpetrator, a sergeant major, led to a situation where the latter 'exercised great power over the plaintiff and could command unquestioning obedience from him'. Secondly, it was argued that 'an element of intimacy and camaraderie was encouraged in the Army in circumstances where employees worked in close quarters together'. Finally, it was suggested that within a culture where complaining was both discouraged and 'largely fruitless', a person in the plaintiff's position was particularly vulnerable to the wrongful exercise of power by a superior officer.

[3–89] Rejecting the attempt to draw these parallels between the facts of *Bazley* and *Reilly*, Kearns J did not accept that the nature of the employment relationship in *Reilly* supported the imposition of vicarious liability. The relationship between the plaintiff and defendant 'could hardly be more different' from that between a school teacher and a child at a residential school; nor was there intimacy or a quasi-parental role implicit in the relationship, as had been the case in *Bazley*.

[3–90] What is significant about the approach of Kearns J in *Reilly* in distinguishing *Bazley* is the strong suggestion in the judgment that, were the parallels with the latter case more strongly resounded on the facts of *Reilly*, then *Bazley* would govern the court's vicarious liability inquiry. With respect, this analysis is entirely question-begging since, as we have seen, the Supreme Court in *O'Keeffe* three months earlier not only did not resolve the status of *Bazley*, but indicated a sharp division of approach even amongst the members of the majority as to this fundamental question.

[3–91] A further source of confusion arising from *Reilly* is a degree of inconsistency arguably apparent within the judgment of Kearns J. It is, for example, confusing that Kearns J, in declining to impose vicarious liability in *Reilly*, invoked the following passage from the judgment of Hardiman J in *O'Keeffe*:

> In my view, both justice and the basic requirements of an ordered society require that the imposition of strict liability on a no fault basis be done (if at all) only on the clearest and most readily understandable basis. I do not regard the Canadian cases cited as providing such a basis: quite the opposite, as the two conflicting decisions cited demonstrate, in my view. I do not believe that the expanded basis of vicarious liability represents the law in this jurisdiction, or can be made to do so except by legislation. The consequences of doing this, social as well economic, would be immense...

Given Kearns J's emphasis on how *Bazley* could be distinguished in *Reilly*, it is difficult to see why support would then be drawn from that passage of Hardiman J's judgment in *O'Keeffe*, which explicitly rejects the very notion that *Bazley* could represent the law in this jurisdiction.

This confusion is deepened in the following passage of Kearns J's analysis of the   [3–92]
position of Hardiman J in *O'Keeffe*:

> Hardiman J. went on to note the 'chilling effect' of any extension of the doctrine of
> vicarious liability whereby the State would become liable for criminal activities of
> those in their employment in circumstances where there was no fault attaching to
> the State. To do so would be not only to make the taxpayer liable for the criminal
> acts of employees of State bodies, but it would also affect that body's actions in
> ways which would require to be considered as a matter of policy before such an
> extension of the law could be allowed.

On the basis of the above passage, it appears that Kearns J is signalling a strong   [3–93]
note of caution about the acceptance of the *Bazley* and *Lister* approaches in Irish
law. Once again, however, this is rendered less than clear by the passage immediately following this statement, in which Kearns J observes:

> While the able submissions advanced on behalf of the plaintiff make reference
> to the *Bazley* principles, they do so in a necessarily limited way and counsel was
> obliged to frankly concede that not all of the criteria elaborated by the Canadian
> Supreme Court were met in the instant case. I believe this case falls short by a
> considerable margin of establishing the prerequisites for a finding that the defend-
> ants should be held vicariously responsible for the criminal activities of the first
> named defendant in this case.

With respect, the references in this passage to the *Bazley* 'criteria' being 'met' and   [3–94]
to the 'prerequisites' for vicarious liability could be interpreted as suggesting that
the *Bazley* approach applies in Ireland. This view is, however, extremely difficult
to reconcile either with the passages from Kearns J's judgment, quoted above, in
which reliance is placed on the Hardiman approach in *O'Keeffe*, or indeed with
the complicated picture emerging from the various judgments in the latter case
already analysed above in this Chapter.

On the question of vicarious liability, Kearns J appeared to consider the *Bazley*   [3–95]
approach rejected by Hardiman J in *O'Keeffe*, but on the facts of the case denied
the plaintiff's claim:

> I cannot accept that the nature of the employment relationship between the plain-
> tiff and the defendants in this case was such as would support a finding of vicarious
> liability. While undoubtedly the first named defendant exercised a supervisory and
> disciplinary role where the plaintiff was concerned, he was not in the same posi-
> tion as a school teacher or boarding house warden in relation to a child. Nor was
> the nature of the employment one which would have encouraged close personal
> contact where some inherent risks might be said to exist as, for example, might
> arise if the first named defendant had been a swimming instructor in close physical
> contact with young recruits. There was no intimacy implicit in the relationship

between the plaintiff and the first named defendant nor was there any quasi-parental role or responsibility for personal nurturing which was found to exist in the cases where vicarious liability was established. To hold otherwise would be to extend to the Defence Forces a virtual new species of liability where the defendants would be liable for virtually every act or omission of an employee.

CHAPTER 4

The Contract of Employment

Introduction

While recent legislative activity in this area may have diminished its importance [4–01] somewhat, the contract of employment remains the foundation of the legal relationship between the employer and employee. Courts and tribunals continue to be guided by the contract between the parties when interpreting and applying protective legislation[1] and, in many cases, the various statutory rules of employment law are expressly deemed to be read into an employee's contract of employment.

It has been suggested by some commentators that contracts of employment do not [4–02] sit comfortably within traditional common law contract principles.[2] In particular, it has been noted that the inequality of bargaining power that traditionally existed (and in many cases continues to exist) between employer and employee undermines the 'bargain theory' aspect of traditional contract law doctrine. Equally, it may in the alternative be noted that this theory is arguably of limited importance to contract law as a whole. Thus Honeyball has correctly pointed out that the contract law maxim that 'consideration need not be adequate but must be sufficient' appears to endorse the existence of contracts founded on inequality of bargaining power.[3]

1. Formation of the Employment Contract

As a general rule there are no special requirements necessary for the formation [4–03] of a valid contract of employment other than those which generally apply to

---

1. For example, it may be crucial in constructive dismissal cases to determine whether or not the employer acted in breach of the contract with the employee and indeed as is noted throughout this book, in many cases the relevant statutes provide for their terms to be read into the employee's contract of employment.
2. Selwyn, *Selwyn's Law of Employment* (15th ed., Oxford University Press, 2008), at 76; Honeyball, *Honeyball & Bowers' Textbook on Labour Law* (9th ed., Oxford University Press, 2006), at 38–39; Freedland, *The Personal Employment Contract* (Oxford University Press, 2003).
3. Honeyball, *Honeyball & Bowers' Textbook on Labour Law* (9th ed., Oxford University Press, 2006), at 39.

any kind of contract.[4] In other words, provided that a valid exchange of offer and acceptance has occurred, the parties have provided consideration,[5] and an intention to create legal relations exists,[6] then in the vast majority of cases a valid contract of employment may come into existence so long as it does not have an illegal purpose.

1.1. Conditional Offers of Employment

[4–04] An offer of employment, once made by the employer and accepted by the employee, cannot be withdrawn. Any attempt by the employer to revoke such an offer can give rise to a cause of action for breach of contract even where that employee has not yet commenced work.[7] Therefore, an employer would be unwise to make an unconditional offer to any employee before being fully satisfied as to that employee's suitability for the work. The following are matters upon which an employer may typically wish to make an offer of employment conditional:

1.1.1. References

[4–05] An employer will often make an offer of employment conditional upon the production of a satisfactory reference from a former employer of the employee. In *Wishart v National Association of Citizens Advice Bureaux*,[8] the claimant was offered a position 'subject to receipt of satisfactory written references'. When the reference was produced it indicated that the claimant had taken a considerable amount of sick leave in a previous employment. On the basis of this reference, the employer decided to withdraw the offer. The claimant sought an injunction restraining the appointment of another person to the position, arguing that the reference would have been satisfactory to the reasonable employer. However, the Court of Appeal held that in such circumstances as long as no bad faith existed, a subjective test was more appropriate and thus the focus was on whether or not the reference was satisfactory as far as the particular employer was concerned. Gibson LJ stated *obiter*:

> I will assume, without deciding, that there was in this case a conditional contract. If there was I think it is at least highly probable that upon the true construction of the contract no objective test is applicable to the satisfactoriness of the references and that no obligation in law rested upon the defendants in considering the references other than in good faith to consider them and to decide whether they were

---

4. In exceptional circumstances there may be a requirement for the contract to be in writing, e.g. in relation to merchant seamen under the Merchant Shipping Act 1894 or apprentice solicitors under the Solicitors Act 1894.
5. *Melhuish v Redbridge Citizens Advice Bureau* [2005] EWCA Civ 73, [2005] IRLR 419.
6. *R v Lord Chancellor's Department, ex p Nangle* [1992] 1 All ER 897, [1991] ICR 743, [1991] IRLR 343.
7. *Sarker v South Tees Acute Hospitals NHS Trust* [1997] ICR 673, [1997] IRLR 328.
8. [1990] ICR 794, [1990] IRLR 393.

satisfactory to the defendants. No allegation of bad faith is made… It seems to me difficult to see on the material now before this Court on what basis the plaintiff can hope to show that the defendants were not entitled, assuming them to be bound by a contractual obligation, to treat the condition as not satisfied.[9]

In this respect, an employer is, in general, not obliged to provide a reference to an employee.[10] However, such a requirement could be implied into the contract of employment where it is the custom and practice in the industry or a regulatory requirement to do so.[11] Furthermore, an employer must ensure that when deciding whether to provide a reference or not [s]he must treat all employees equally (having regard to the listed grounds of discrimination in the equality legislation[12]) lest [s]he leave him or herself open to a claim of illegal discrimination under the Employment Equality Acts 1998–2008. Moreover, it is worth making the point that it is not impossible that the requirement that a prospective employee furnish references could in and of itself be indirectly discriminatory on, for example, the race ground within the Employment Equality legislative framework given the difficulty which a migrant worker might face in obtaining such references.[13]   [4–06]

Where an employer chooses to provide a reference for an employee [s]he is under a duty to take reasonable care in the preparation of that reference.[14] In *Spring v Guardian Assurance Plc,*[15] the plaintiff was dismissed following a takeover of his company by Guardian Royal Exchange. He applied for a similar position with another insurance company. The reference provided by his former employer stated *inter alia* that he was dishonest and tried to sell an unsuitable policy to a customer simply to increase his own commission. Not surprisingly, the reference effectively finished his career in the industry. Judge Lever QC, at first instance, accepted the plaintiff's counsel's description of the reference as being 'the kiss of death' to his career in insurance.[16] The House of Lords held that an employer owed his employee a duty of care in preparing a reference. It was reasonable to   [4–07]

9. [1990] ICR 794, 805.
10. *Lawton v BOC Transhield Ltd.* [1987] 2 All ER 608, [1987] IRLR 404.
11. *Spring v Guardian Assurance Plc* [1995] 2 AC 296, [1994] 3 WLR 354, [1994] ICR 596, [1994] IRLR 460, where employers in the life insurance industry were obliged under the Life Assurance and Unit Trust Regulatory Organisation rules to produce references for employees.
12. These listed grounds are considered in Chapter 9.
13. On this point, see the determination of the Equality Tribunal in *Czerski v Ice Group* [2007] ELR 221. Although an appeal to the Labour Court was allowed on this point (ADE/06/14, determination no. EDA0812, 16 May 2008), this was on the basis of findings of fact made in the Labour Court concerning assurances given to the prospective applicant that she could furnish a character reference in place of a second employment reference.
14. *Hedley Byrne & Co Ltd. v Heller & Partners Ltd.* [1964] AC 465.
15. [1995] 2 AC 296, [1994] 3 WLR 354, [1994] ICR 596, [1994] IRLR 460.
16. Quoted in the judgment of Lord Woolf in *Spring v Guardian Assurance Plc* [1995] 2 AC 296 at 342.

impose a duty of care on the employer in such circumstances given the proximity of relationship that existed between the parties, which meant that it was foreseeable in such circumstances that the negative reference would cause economic loss to the plaintiff.

[4–08] While *Spring v Guardian Assurance Plc* focused on the duty of the employer to take reasonable care in providing an accurate reference, it would appear there is a further duty on the employer to ensure that a reference does not create a misleading impression. In *Bartholomew v London Borough of Hackney* [17] the claimant was the subject of disciplinary proceedings when he decided to leave his employment with the council by availing of a voluntary severance package. The council provided the claimant with a reference that stated he was the subject of disciplinary proceedings at the time of his departure but did not mention the fact that he had denied the allegations or the fact that he had brought his own claim of racial discrimination against his former employer. The Court of Appeal held that an employer was under a duty not only to prepare a truthful reference, it must also be 'fair and balanced' and must not create a misleading impression. On the facts of this case, it was held that the statements made by the council were true and did not, on the whole, create a misleading impression. However, while the Court did hold that the reference had to be fair and balanced the duty in relation to the preparation of the reference did not extend to the employer providing a full and comprehensive reference. The Court stated:

> The reference must not give an unfair or misleading impression overall, even if its discrete components are factually correct. However the duty of care owed by an ex-employer to an ex-employee in accordance with *Spring v Guardian Assurance plc* does not mean that a reference must in every case be full and comprehensive. In the present case though the form of the reference might have been improved upon in some respects it was not, as a whole, unfair, inaccurate and false. Had the defendants omitted all reference to the suspension they might have considered themselves as failing in their duty not to be unfair or misleading to the recipient of the reference.[18]

[4–09] In a negligence action of this kind, the employee need only prove that the employer acted unreasonably in the preparation of the reference[19] and in this regard, the duty of an employer in relation to the preparation of a reference was clarified in *Kidd v AXA Equity & Law Life Assurance*,[20] where the High Court of England and Wales held that the essential duty of the referee was not to give misleading information *inter alia* by providing unfairly selective information, or by including

---

17. [1999] IRLR 246.
18. [1999] IRLR 246, at 246.
19. Generally, see Kobayashi and Middlemiss, 'The Legal and Human Resources Issues for Employers Providing References – Part 1', 24 *ILT* (2006), 156.
20. [2000] IRLR 301.

information which would generate a false or misleading inference in the mind of the reasonable reader.

Finally, it should be noted that, in writing a reference for an employee, an employer   [4–10] may be leaving him or herself open to a claim for defamation, should that reference contain defamatory statements of the employee. Equally, it is beyond doubt that the occasion of writing a reference is one of qualified privilege, and thus a referee will have a defence against such an action save where [s]he has acted maliciously – that is in abusing the occasion of privilege – most usually in circumstances where [s]he has written something about the employee that [s]he knows to be false.[21]

1.1.2. Medical Assessments

As in the case of references, an employer may make an offer to a prospective   [4–11] employee conditional on the completion of a satisfactory medical report. In such circumstances, the employer is entitled to withdraw the conditional offer if not satisfied with the results of the report.

In the United Kingdom it has been held that a medical practitioner engaged by   [4–12] an employer to carry out a medical report of a prospective employee does not owe a duty of care in negligence to that employee. In *Kapfunde v Abbey National Plc*[22] the claimant was employed on a temporary basis by the respondent. She applied for a permanent position. As part of her application she was obliged to complete a standard medical questionnaire. In so doing, she disclosed a medical condition, which had already caused her to be absent from work. The respondent forwarded the completed questionnaire to a medical practitioner for assessment. It was the medical practitioner's view that the condition was likely to cause her to suffer from a higher level of absenteeism in future. Based on this medical advice, the claimant's application was rejected. The claimant brought an action in negligence against the medical practitioner. It was held that the medical practitioner did not owe the claimant a duty of care in the circumstances. While it may have been foreseeable that any negligent advice by the medical practitioner could cause economic loss to the claimant (due to the loss of the opportunity of employment) there was no proximate relationship between the parties that could justify the imposition of such a duty. The medical practitioner was engaged by the respondent and the claimant did not rely on the advice given by the medical practitioner. The case was distinguished from *Spring v Guardian Assurance Plc*[23] as the duty of care in that case was established on the basis of the relationship that had previously existed between the employer and his former employee. No such relationship existed between the medical practitioner and the claimant.

---

21. *Kirkwood Hackett v Tierney* [1952] IR 185.
22. [1999] ICR 1, [1998] IRLR 583.
23. [1995] 2 AC 296, [1994] 3 WLR 354, [1994] ICR 596, [1994] IRLR 460.

While an offer of employment may be made conditional upon receipt of a satisfactory medical report, an employer must be wary of not discriminating unlawfully against a prospective employee on the basis of disability.[24]

2. Access to Written Particulars of Terms of Employment

[4–13] It is not necessary that the contract of employment be reduced to writing to be considered enforceable. However, certain statutory provisions do provide that upon the request of the employee particular information regarding the terms of the contract of employment must be provided to that employee in writing. Thus formerly, s.9(1) of the Minimum Notice and Terms of Employment Act 1973 required that an employer furnish an employee with a written statement of certain terms and conditions of that employee's employment and s.14 of the Unfair Dismissals Act 1977 required the employer to inform the employee in writing of the procedure the employer would observe before and for the purpose of dismissing the employee.

The principal rules governing the obligations of employers to give employees appropriate details of their terms of employment are now, however, contained in the Terms of Employment (Information) Act of 1994.[25] The Act lays down certain minimum requirements as to the information that must be given to employees by an employer and the time period within which such information must be given.

2.1. To Whom Does the Act Apply?
[4–14] In general, the provisions of the 1994 Act apply to all workers employed under a contract of employment. There are, however, exceptions to this rule. Thus they do not apply either to employment in which the employee is normally expected to work for less than eight hours a week[26] or employment in which the employee has

---

24. *Gannon v Milford Care Centre*, DEC-2004-048, 19 August 2004. In that case the respondent failed to provide the claimant, who was suffering from a long-term disability, with a reference. This action was not considered unlawful only by virtue of the fact that the incident had predated the Employment Equality Act 1998.

25. This Act was aimed at implementing Council Directive no. 91/553/EEC on an Employer's Obligation to Inform Employees of the Conditions Applicable to the Contract of Employment Relationship. In case C-350/99 *Lange v Georg Schuenemann GmbH* [2001] ECR I-1061, [2001] IRLR 244, the ECJ suggested that the purpose of this Directive was to ensure that the essential elements of the contract of employment are communicated to the employee. See also case C-253/96 *Kampelmann v Landschaftsverbrand Westfalen-Lippe* [1997] EUECJ C-253/96, [1997] ECR I-6907.

26. s.2(1)(a) Terms of Employment (Information) Act 1994.

been in continuous service[27] for less than a month.[28] In addition, following consultations with representatives of both employers and employees within a particular class of employment, the Minister may, by order, declare that the Act (or provisions thereof) should not apply to that class of employment – but such a step should only be taken provided that it is justified by objective considerations.[29]

2.2. Entitlements under the Act

From the standpoint of the employee the most important section of the Act is s.3, [4–15] which sets out the major obligations of the employer to provide the employee with the terms of his or her employment. Under s.3(1) it is provided that, within two months after the commencement of an employee's employment,[30] [s]he must be given a written statement[31] containing the following particulars[32]:

(a) the full names of the employer and the employee;

(b) the address of the employer in the State or, where appropriate, the address of the principal place of the relevant business of the employer in the State or the registered office (within the meaning of the Companies Act 1963);

(c) the place of work or, where there is no fixed or main place of work, a statement specifying that the employee is required or permitted to work at various places;

---

27. Under s.2(3) *ibid.* it is provided that, in assessing continuous service in this respect, regard should be had to the first schedule to the Minimum Notice and Terms of Employment Act 1973, save that the reference in that schedule to 21 hours should be taken as a reference to eight hours, and the reference in the schedule to an employee shall be construed as references to an employee within the meaning of the 1994 Act.

28. s.2(1)(b) Terms of Employment (Information) Act 1994. In this respect the rules for assessing continuous service are those to be found in the first schedule to the Minimum Notice and Terms of Employment Act 1973 (s.2(2)(3) of the 1994 Act). The reference in the schedule to 21 hours is taken for the purposes of s.2 of the 1994 Act to be a reference to eight hours.

29. s.2(2) Terms of Employment (Information) Act 1994. The Minister can revoke or amend an order made under this section: s.2(4) *ibid.*

30. This statement has to be given even where the employee's employment ends before the end of that two-month period: s.3(2) *ibid.*

31. The statement must be signed and dated by the employer (s.3(4) *ibid.*) and must be retained by the employer during the period of the employee's employment and for one year thereafter (s.3(5) *ibid.*). The EAT has further held that where terms and conditions are not given to an employee (in the form of a contract of employment), then his or her right to natural justice may have been compromised: *An Employer v An Employee* TE60/2007.

32. The mandatory requirement to give such information as a matter of course arises where the contract of employment begins *after* commencement of the 1994 Act (s.3(7)). If the contract was entered into *before* commencement of the Act then the employee can still *request* a statement under s.3 or s.4, and this must be given to him or her within two months of the request being made (s.6). See *Murphy v Tesco*, TE 7/1999 for the view that there must be evidence that such request was made if a claim for a breach of s.6 is to be upheld.

(d) the title of the job or nature of the work for which the employee is employed;

(e) the date of commencement of the employee's contract of employment;

(f) in the case of a temporary contract of employment, the expected duration thereof or, if the contract of employment is for a fixed term, the date on which the contract expires;

(g) the rate or method of calculation of the employee's remuneration;

(h) the length of the intervals between the times at which remuneration is paid, whether a week, a month or any other interval;

(i) any terms or conditions relating to hours of work (including overtime);

(j) any terms or conditions relating to paid leave (other than paid sick leave);

(k) any terms or conditions relating to –
   (i) incapacity for work due to sickness or injury and paid sick leave; and
   (ii) pensions and pension schemes;

(l) the period of notice the employee is required to give and entitled to receive (whether by or under statute or under the terms of the employee's contract of employment) to determine the employee's contract of employment or, where this cannot be indicated when the information is given, the method for determining such periods of notice[33]; and

(m) a reference to any collective agreements that directly affect the terms and conditions of the employee's employment including, where the employer is not a party to such agreements, particulars of the bodies or institutions by whom they were made.

[4–16] The Minister may, by order, require that additional particulars be given to employees (and subsequently can amend or revoke such order[34]). So, for example, an employer must also now provide an employee with particulars of the times and duration of rest periods and breaks and of any terms and conditions relating to such rest periods and breaks available to the employee under the Organisation of Working Time Act of 1997.[35] Similarly, an employer who employs a child or young person is required, not later than one month after that child or young person starts work, to give him or her a copy of the abstract of the Protection of Young Persons (Employment) Act of 1996.[36]

[4–17] Specific rules apply where an employee is employed *outside* the State for not less than one month. Where that is the case [s]he is entitled to particulars of the following[37]:

---

33. The particulars referred to in para.(g)(l) can be given by reference to statutes, laws or collective agreements that govern those particulars, provided that they can be read by the employee during the course of his or her employment and are otherwise reasonably accessible to him or her.

34. s.3(6) Terms of Employment (Information) Act 1994.

35. Terms of Employment (Additional Information) Order 1998, SI no. 49 of 1998.

36. See para.2 of the Terms of Employment (Information) Act 1994, s.3(6) Order of 1997, SI no. 4 of 1997.

37. s.4(1) Terms of Employment (Information) Act 1994. Again such particulars can be given by

(a) the period of employment outside the State;

(b) the currency in which the employee is to be remunerated in respect of that period;

(c) any benefits in cash or kind for the employee attendant on the employment outside the State; and

(d) the terms and conditions, where appropriate, governing the employee's repatriation.

Finally, when a statement under ss.3, 4 or 6 has been given to an employee but changes are made or occur in respect of any particular within that statement, the employee must be notified of such change not later than one month after the change or, if the employee is working outside the State and the change relates to this fact, not later than one month after his or her departure.[38]

2.3. Enforcement

An employee may bring a complaint to the Rights Commissioner for a breach by [4–18] his or her employer of any or all of ss.3, 4, 5 or 6.[39] Under the legislation, a Rights Commissioner shall not entertain a complaint if it is presented to the Commissioner after a period of six months beginning on the date of termination of the employment concerned.[40] In essence, this means that there is no limitation period in cases of this nature where the employee is still employed by the employer. In addition, it is notable that there is no power (as there is in other legislation[41]) whereby the Rights Commissioner can extend the time limit for bringing such a complaint.

Such complaint must be in writing[42] and must be copied to the other party con- [4–19] cerned.[43] Following a (non-public) hearing[44] of the matter in which the parties are given an opportunity to be heard and to present evidence,[45] the Rights

---

reference to statutes or collective agreement, although unlike s.3 there is no requirement that such statutes, particulars or collective agreements be reasonably accessible to such employees.

38. s.5(1)(b) *ibid.* See *An Employer v An Employee* TE 47-49/2008. Surprisingly, an employer does not need to inform an employee of any changes that are made to a statute, law or collective agreement to which [s]he has referred in a statement under s.3 or s.4: s.5(2) *ibid.*

39. s.7(1) *ibid.* The notion of the employer in this context also refers to someone who has become entitled to ownership of the business of the original employer after the contravention to which the complaint relates: s.7(2) *ibid.*

40. s.7(3) *ibid.*

41. For example, the Organisation of Working Time Act 1997.

42. s.7(4)(a) Terms of Employment (Information) Act 1994.

43. s.7(4)(b) *ibid.*

44. s.7(5) *ibid.* The Minister may, by regulations, make provision for the procedures governing such hearings: s.7(7) *ibid.*

45. s.7(1) *ibid.*

Commissioner must issue a recommendation (and communicate it to the parties and to the Employment Appeals Tribunal)[46] doing one of the following[47]:

(a) declaring that the complaint was or was not well founded;
(b) (i) confirming all or any of the particulars contained or referred to in any statement furnished by the employer under ss.3, 4, 5 or 6; or

   (ii) altering or adding to any such statement for the purpose of correcting any inaccuracy or omission and the statement as so altered or added to shall be deemed to have been given to the employee by the employer; or

(c) requiring the employer to give or cause to be given to the employee concerned a written statement containing such particulars as may be specified by the Commissioner.[48]

In addition the Rights Commissioner may order the employer to pay such compensation to the employee as is just and equitable having regard to all the circumstances.[49] Such compensation cannot, however, exceed four weeks' remuneration calculated in accordance with the employee's terms of employment.[50]

[4-20] The decision of the Rights Commissioner can be appealed to the EAT.[51] Such an appeal, which is initiated by a notice in writing to the EAT, must be made within six weeks of the date on which the Rights Commissioner's determination was communicated to the party taking the appeal.[52] It is provided in s.8(3)(g) that the Minister may make provision for the extension by the EAT for the time limit for initiating such appeals, but this is a curious provision given that there is no provision within the Act itself whereby the tribunal can have a discretion to extend such time limits, and it is unclear how such a significant power could be vested in the EAT exclusively by ministerial regulation. Indeed it may be argued that allowing

---

46. s.7(6) *ibid.*
47. s.7(2) *ibid.*
48. s.7(2) *ibid.* The references to an employer in this section are also taken to refer (where appropriate) to someone entitled to ownership of the business where such ownership has changed after a contravention to which the complaint relates.
49. Significantly, for tax purposes it has been held that such awards by the Rights Commissioner or the EAT represent compensation, not remuneration: *Archbold v CMC (Ireland) Ltd.*, TE 05/2003.
50. s.7(2)(d) Terms of Employment (Information) Act 1994. This is calculated in accordance with regulations under s.17 of the Unfair Dismissals Act 1977. Under s.7(7) of the 1994 Act, the Minister may (by regulation) vary the maximum amount of compensation that can be given under the section.
51. s.8(1) Terms of Employment (Information) Act 1994. Such appeals should be brought pursuant to the rules and procedures laid down in the Terms of Employment (Information) (Appeals and Complaints) Regulations 1994, SI no. 244 of 1994.
52. s.8 (2) Terms of Employment (Information) Act 1994.

the clear legislative position (that no such possibility for time limits to be extended) to be amended by ministerial regulation is of doubtful constitutionality.[53]

As things stand, however, and in the absence of any such regulations, the Rights Commissioner has no jurisdiction to deal with cases brought outside the six-month time limit and no apparent jurisdiction to extend the time limit, and there is no provision for the EAT to cure such lack of jurisdiction. Hence if a complaint is brought outside the six-month time period, there does not appear to be any further avenue open to the complainant. The notice of appeal (which the Tribunal must send as soon as possible to the other party) must state the intention of the party to appeal and contain any such particulars as are required by ministerial regulation. Moreover the Minister may make regulations providing for various procedural rules relating to the hearing and for anything consequential thereon or incidental or ancillary thereto.[54] It is further worth noting that claims both to the Rights Commissioner and to the EAT may, of course, be struck out for want of prosecution.[55] Finally, a party to the proceedings before the EAT can appeal its determination to the High Court on a point of law.[56] In addition and at the request of the Tribunal, the Minister can refer a question of law arising in the proceedings to the High Court for final determination.[57] [4–21]

On the other hand, when the terms of a recommendation of a Rights Commissioner have not been carried out by the employer and the time limit for bringing an appeal has expired, the employee concerned can bring a complaint to the EAT (by notice in writing), and the Tribunal, without hearing any evidence including that of the employer, shall make a determination in the same terms as the recommendation.[58] If the employer fails to carry out what is required of him or her by [4–22]

---

53. Thus in *Mulcreevy v Minister for the Environment, Heritage and Local Government* [2004] IESC 5, [2004] 1 IR 72 (at 87), Keane CJ for the Supreme Court commented: 'It is well established that the exclusive role assigned to the Oireachtas in the making of laws by this Article does not preclude the Oireachtas from empowering Ministers or other bodies to make regulations for the purpose of carrying into effect the principles and policies of the parent legislation. [See *Cityview Press Ltd. v An Chomhairle Oiliúna* [1980] IR 381.] But it is also clear that such delegated legislation cannot make, repeal or amend any law and that, to the extent that the parent Act purports to confer such a power, it will be invalid having regard to the provisions of the Constitution.'

54. s.8(3) Terms of Employment (Information) Act 1994. See the Terms of Employment (Information) (Appeals and Complaints) Regulations 1994, SI no. 244 of 1994.

55. See *An Employer v An Employee* TE 57/2007. On the other side of the coin, on the regular occasions where the employer does not attend the hearing despite being on notice of it, all findings of fact will inevitably favour the employee. See for example, *An Employer v An Employee* TE 24/2007.

56. s.8(4)(b) Terms of Employment (Information) Act 1994. Such determination shall be final and conclusive.

57. s.8(4)(a) *ibid.*

58. s.8(6) *ibid.* See, for some of the very many examples of this occurring, *Suchenka v Mitchell*, TE 2/2008 ; *An Employer v An Employee* TE 46/2008; *An Employer v An Employee* TE 66/2008.

a determination of the tribunal within six weeks of the date on which that determination is communicated to the parties, the District Court, on the application of the employee, the employee's trade union or, where appropriate, the Minister, shall make an order directing the employer to carry out the terms of the determination.[59] Moreover, where the order includes a requirement to pay compensation, the District Court may direct the employer to pay interest to the employee on such compensation, in respect of the whole or any part of the period beginning six weeks after the date on which the determination of the tribunal is communicated to the parties and ending on the date of the order.[60]

2.4. Status of the Written Statement of Terms

[4–23] It is unclear whether or not the written statement of terms required by the legislation may itself be considered to have contractual status. In the United Kingdom it would seem that the position is that such a statement is not the contract of employment. However, the written statement of terms is strong evidence of content of that contract. In *System Floors (UK) Ltd. v Daniel*,[61] Browne-Wilkinson J. said the following of the status of such written particulars:

> It provides very strong *prima facie* evidence of what were the terms of the contract between the parties, but does not constitute a written contract between the parties. Nor are the statements of the terms finally conclusive: at most, they place a heavy burden on the employer to show that the actual terms of contract are different from those which he has set out in the statutory instrument.[62]

Thus where the employer is disputing the proposition that the written statement of terms reflect the terms of the employee's contract, the courts tend to regard the probative weight of such statement as being extremely high. However, as Browne-Wilkinson J noted, where it is the employee challenging the accuracy of the written statement, that statement is regarded as being of 'persuasive' evidence only.

[4–24] Consequently, the parties should be careful to ensure that the written statement of particulars accurately reflects what was agreed before signing such a document. By signing, it could be interpreted that they have actually signed a new contract of employment on the terms outlined in the signed document. However, it would seem that for this to occur the parties must sign the written statement of particulars as the new contract of employment and not simply as a receipt of the written particulars.[63]

---

59. s.9(1) Terms of Employment (Information) Act 1994. Such enforcement applications are brought pursuant to the District Court (Terms of Employment Information) Rules 2003, SI no. 409 of 2003, amending ord. 99B of the District Court Rules 1997, SI no. 93 of 1997.
60. s.8(2) Terms of Employment (Information) Act 1994.
61. [1982] ICR 54, [1981] IRLR 475.
62. [1982] ICR 54, 58.
63. *Gascol Conversions Ltd. v Mercer* [1974] ICR 420, [1974] IRLR 155.

3. Express Terms of the Contract

The express terms agreed by the parties and which form the basis of the contract [4–25] of employment may be made orally or in writing. Obviously, however, from an evidential point of view, an express term in writing is preferable to one expressed orally.

3.1. Incorporation of Express Terms

An express term may be written directly into the contract of employment, but [4–26] may also be incorporated from an outside source, for example through a staff handbook or a collective agreement. Some of the most prominent ways in which such terms may be incorporated are considered below.

3.1.1. Works' Rules

Works' rules are generally rules of practice or behaviour the employer may have [4–27] set out for the workplace. These policies may be incorporated into the contract of employment, either expressly or implicitly, if they are sufficiently precise. These rules are usually contained in employer booklets or as notices. In addition to forming part of the contract of employment, they may also be used to interpret terms of the contract. Where it is argued that the rules have been implicitly incorporated into the contract, it must be established that the employer had provided the employee with reasonable notice of the rules. In the words of Browne-Wilkinson J in *Duke v Reliance Systems Ltd.*[64]:

> A policy adopted by management unilaterally cannot become a term of the employees' contracts… unless it is at least shown that the policy has been drawn to the attention of the employees or has been followed without exception for a substantial period.[65]

To incorporate another document as part of the contract of employment it is best practice to specifically reference the document and attach it to the contract. In *Jowitt v Pioneer Technology (UK) Ltd.*[66] the contract guaranteed the employee coverage under a disability scheme. This scheme had been underwritten by the employer under an insurance policy. The employer tried to incorporate the policy into the contract of employment by summarising its contents instead of simply referencing the policy and attaching it to the contract. In so doing, the employer omitted some key points and as a result exposed himself to much greater liability not covered by the insurance policy.

---

64. [1982] IRLR 347.
65. *ibid.*, at 347.
66. [2003] ICR 1120, [2003] IRLR 356.

3.1.2. *Custom and Practice*

[4–28] An express term may also be incorporated into the contract of employment on the basis of 'custom and practice'. The custom or practice in question must be sufficiently long established, generally well known and reasonable.[67] For example, in *Sagar v H Ridehalgh & Son Ltd.*[68] an employer successfully sought to make deductions from the wages of a cotton weaver because of poor workmanship on the basis that such a term had been the practice in the employer's factory for over 30 years and was customary in the trade.

3.1.3. *Collective Agreements*

[4–29] A collective agreement is one that is entered into between employers' associations or employers and trade unions.[69] If sufficiently precise, such agreements may be expressly incorporated into the individual employee's contract of employment.[70] Such agreements may also be implicitly incorporated into the contract of employment, but it may be difficult to establish such incorporation. In *Joel v Cammell Laird*,[71] it was held that before a collective agreement could be incorporated by way of implication there must be (a) specific knowledge of the agreement; (b) employee conduct that shows [s]he accepts the incorporation of the agreement; and (c) some indication of incorporation of the agreement into the contract.

3.2. Standard Express Terms

[4–30] The express terms of a contract of employment are, of course, specific to that contract. Equally there are certain express terms which may be regarded as being so common as to be 'standard terms'. Some examples of such standard express terms in an employment contract include the following:

(1) Date of Commencement and the Parties to the Contract

[4–31] The date of commencement of the employment relationship should be clearly expressed in the contract of employment not least because this date is crucial for determining the service requirements necessary for redundancy and unfair dismissals legislation, for example. Furthermore, the contract of employment should clearly express the identity of the parties to the agreement. While in many cases this may not be problematic, certain employment relationships may be more complicated – for example, where the employer is part of a group of companies.

(2) Job Specification

[4–32] The contract of employment should contain an express term that details the employee's function, obligations and responsibilities. Such a term may include a

---

67. *Devonald v Rosser & Sons* [1906] 2 KB 728.
68. [1931] 1 Ch. 310.
69. For more detailed discussion, see Chapter 2.
70. *National Coal Board v Galley* [1977] IRLR 351.
71. [1969] ITR 206.

certain amount of flexibility as regards the employee's duties and it may provide that the duties will, within reason, develop and change over time.

(3) Hours of Work

The contract of employment should specify the hours of work of the employee. It should also specify the breaks to which the employee is entitled[72]. In particular, the Terms of Employment (Additional Information) Regulations[73] provide that employers, from 1 March 1998, must provide employees with a written statement of particulars regarding the times and duration of such breaks and rest periods.[74]   [4–33]

(4) Place of Work

The contract of employment should state the normal place of work of the employee, i.e. the address of the employer's normal place of business or elsewhere, or whether the employee is expected to travel as part of their work.[75]   [4–34]

(5) Probation

An employee may be subject to a probationary period upon the commencement of the contract of employment. The inclusion of a probationary period as a term in the contract[76] gives the employer greater scope to dismiss the employee during that period without fear of sanction. Section 3(1) of the Unfair Dismissals Acts 1977–2003 provides that the legislation shall not apply to an employee dismissed during a probationary period at the commencement of employment if the contract of employment is in writing and the duration of the probationary period is one year or less and is specified in the contract.[77] Depending on the construction of the term, an employee may be dismissed at any time during that probationary period. In *Dalgleish v Kew House Farm*[78] the employee was employed under a contract that provided for a probationary period of three months, at which stage his performance was to be reviewed. He was dismissed for unsatisfactory performance after three weeks. It was held that the employers were not obliged to retain the employee for the full length of his probationary period.   [4–35]

(6) Remuneration

The contract of employment should contain an express term precisely setting out the remuneration to be paid to the employee. This term should include the rate of pay per week or per hour. The timing of the payment (weekly/monthly) should   [4–36]

---

72. Generally, see Chapter 11.
73. SI no. 49 of 1998.
74. For more detailed discussion, see Chapter 11.
75. *Rank Xerox Ltd. v Churchill* [1988] IRLR 280.
76. That is, in advance of the employment commencing. For the difficulties that can arise when such a clause is sought to be later introduced, see *Doyle v Grangeford Precast Concrete Ltd.* [1998] ELR 260.
77. Such a clause must be inserted at the time the contract was agreed. See *Doyle v Grangeford Precast Concrete Ltd.* [1998] ELR 260.
78. [1982] IRLR 251.

be stated and the manner of payment should also be outlined.[79] Any deductions from the employee's wages or salary should be clearly outlined in the contract. While the parties may agree the amount of remuneration, it will be subject to the national minimum wage.[80] In agreeing remuneration, the employer must ensure that it is not discriminating against other employees under the provisions of the Employment Equality Acts 1998–2008.

(7) Sick Pay

[4–37] The employer is not statutorily obliged to pay his or her employees' sick pay. However, such a term could be implied through custom and practice, and the employer would be advised to include an express term in the contract stating whether sick pay was provided or not.[81] An employer may be liable for a failure to make a sick-pay scheme available to a part-time employee where one is available to a full-time employee.[82] An employer is required to provide an employee with the details of any term or condition relating to incapacity for work due to sickness or injury and sick pay.[83]

(8) Holidays

[4–38] The contract of employment should clearly outline the employee's statutory paid annual leave and public holidays.[84]

(9) Retirement Age

[4–39] Particularly in cases where the employee avails of a pension scheme as part of his employment, the contract of employment should also contain an express term specifying the employee's retirement age. Employers should have regard to the principles of age discrimination enshrined under the Employment Equality Acts 1998–2008 when setting retirement ages in the contract of employment.[85]

(10) Pension

[4–40] Express reference should be made to pension entitlements where these are a feature of the employment relationship. In this regard, equality concerns are particularly relevant since different treatment in relation to pension may amount to unlawful discrimination under the Employment Equality Acts 1998–2008.[86]

---

79. Subject to the Payment of Wages Act 1991. For more detailed discussion see Chapter 12.
80. The National Minimum Wage Act 2000. For more detailed discussion see Chapter 12.
81. *Charlton v Aga Khan's Studs* [1999] ELR 136; *Mullarkey v Irish National Stud Company Ltd.* [2004] ELR 172.
82. *Diageo v Rooney* [2004] ELR 133.
83. s.3(1)(k), Terms of Employment (Information) Act 1994.
84. The Organisation of Working Time Act 1997. For more detailed discussion, see Chapter 11.
85. See Chapter 9.
86. See Chapter 9.

(11) Notice

The employee is entitled to a statutory minimum notice period under the Minimum [4–41]
Notice (Terms of Employment) Act 1973–2001. However, an employer may agree a
longer period with the employee by way of an express term in the contract.[87]

(12) Disciplinary and Grievance Procedures

The contract of employment should contain express terms outlining the disci- [4–42]
plinary and grievance procedures that may apply to the employee. Section 14(1)
of the Unfair Dismissals Act 1977 provides that an employer must, within 28
days of entering into the contract of employment, give to the employee notice
in writing setting out the procedure that the employer will observe before and
for the purpose of dismissing the employee.[88] The Industrial Relations Act 1990
(Code of Practice on Grievance and Disciplinary Procedures) (Declaration) Order
2000[89] sets out general guidelines on how grievance and disciplinary procedures
should be applied and promotes best practice in this context. The code provides
that grievance and disciplinary procedures should be in writing and presented in
a form and language that can be easily understood. Copies should be given to all
employees at the commencement of the employment relationship and included in
employee training programmes. One of the most significant legal considerations
surrounding grievance and disciplinary procedures is the question of fair procedures, discussed in detail in Chapter 18.

(13) E-mail and Internet Use

It is clearly very important that employers ensure that a comprehensive policy [4–43]
concerning the use of e-mail and Internet facilities is in place and brought to the
attention of employees.[90] Among the many significant legal issues surrounding the
use of such facilities is the potential for the employer itself to be held vicariously
liable for wrongs committed by employees via these media in the course of employment such as, for example, defamation, breach of copyright or sexual harassment.

3.3. Restrictive Covenants

One relatively common albeit occasionally controversial type of express clause [4–44]
in a contract is what is known as a restrictive covenant – a clause which essentially imposes limitations on the employee's freedom of action either during, or
following the operation of the contract of employment. Put simply, whereas much
of the contract of employment will seek to regulate the relationship between the
parties for the duration of the contract of employment, the parties may expressly
provide for further regulation for a period of time after the contract comes to an
end.[91] An employer may expressly agree with an employee that for a period of time

---

87. For more detailed discussion, see Chapter 20.
88. For more detailed discussion, see Chapter 18.
89. SI 146/2000.
90. For more detailed discussion see Chapter 17.
91. Generally, see McDermott, *Contract Law* (LexisNexis Butterworths, 2001), ch.16.

after the conclusion of the contract, that employee's ability to carry on a trade or set up a business, alone or with others, will be restricted in some manner. Otherwise known as restraint of trade clauses, such terms essentially seek to protect the employer's business from unfair competition by former employees who, through their past association with the employer, have gained particular knowledge of the employer's business.[92]

3.3.1. Burden of Proof

[4–45] In assessing the validity of restraint of trade clauses the courts are involved in a balancing exercise between the employer's right to protect his or her business and the employee's right to move freely to a competitor or to set up in competition. The courts will treat such clauses as *prima facie* void unless they can be justified[93] and the onus will rest with the party alleging that the clause is justified, and therefore enforceable, to prove that it is so.[94]

3.3.2. Reasonableness

[4–46] A restraint of trade clause will be enforceable where it can be justified. In *Nordenfelt v Maxim Nordenfelt*,[95] Lord MacNaghten stated that 'it is a sufficient justification, and indeed it is the only justification, if the restriction is reasonable'.[96] Costello J expanded on this concept of reasonableness in the Irish case of *John Orr Ltd. and Vestcom BV v John Orr*,[97] where he stated:

> All restraints of trade in the absence of special justifying circumstances are contrary to public policy and are therefore void. A restraint may be justified if it is reasonable in the interests of the contracting parties and in the interests of the public. The onus of showing that a restraint is reasonable between the parties rests on the person alleging that it is so. Greater freedom of contract is allowable in a covenant entered into between the seller and buyer of a business than in the case of one entered into between an employer and employee... A covenant by an employee not to compete may... be valid and enforceable if it is reasonably necessary to protect some proprietary interest of the covenantee such as may exist in a trade connection or trade secrets.[98]

[4–47] Much debate has centered on whether this test of reasonableness is a single overarching one or whether it is made of two separate tests to be considered by the courts, namely a test of reasonableness *inter partes* or a separate test of reasonableness based on the public interest. In *Esso Petroleum Company Ltd. v Harper's*

---

92. For analysis, see Kimber, 'Restrictive Covenants in Employment Law', 3(3) *IELJ* (2006), 85.
93. *Nordenfelt v Maxim Nordenfelt* [1894] AC 535.
94. *John Orr Ltd. and Vestcom BV v John Orr* [1987] ILRM 702; *Mulligan v Corr* [1925] 1 IR 169.
95. [1894] AC 535.
96. *ibid.*, at 565.
97. [1987] ILRM 702.
98. *John Orr Ltd. and Vestcom BV v John Orr* [1987] ILRM 702 at 704.

Garage (Stourport) Ltd.[99] Lord Hodson appeared to adopt a single approach to the question of reasonableness, which was rooted in public policy, when he stated:

> Public policy, like other unruly horses, is apt to change its stance; and public policy is the ultimate basis of the Courts' reluctance to enforce restraints. Although the decided cases are almost invariably based on unreasonableness between the parties, it is ultimately on the ground of public policy that the Court will decline to enforce a restraint as being unreasonable between the parties. And a doctrine based on the general commercial good must always bear in mind the changing face of commerce. There is not, as some cases seem to suggest, a separation between what is reasonable on grounds of public policy and what is reasonable between the parties. There is one broad question: is it in the interests of the community that this restraint should, as between the parties, be held to be reasonable and enforceable?[100]

On the other hand, in *Murgitroyd and Co Ltd. v Purdy*[101] Clarke J preferred to apply a two-fold test, which enquired whether (a) the term was reasonable between the parties and (b) it was consistent with the interests of the public.[102]

In many cases it can be difficult to separate the interests of the parties from the **[4–48]** interests of the public. In the words of Lord Macnaghten in *Nordenfelt*: 'All interference with individual liberty of action in trading, and all restraints of trade of themselves, if there is nothing more, are contrary to public policy, and therefore void'.[103] However, there are other cases where the public interest may be more obvious and will require the Court's intervention regardless of the reasonableness of the agreement between the parties themselves. Whatever approach is preferred, the case law indicates that reasonableness in the context of most restrictive covenants contained within a contract of employment will be examined by assessing (i) whether a legitimate proprietary interest exists which can be deemed to be deserving of protection; and (ii) whether the restraint goes too far in providing adequate protection to that interest. Public policy may be used in exceptional cases to strike down a restraint that, although satisfactory in terms of the interest to be protected and the scope of protection afforded, is nevertheless considered to be contrary to public policy.[104]

---

99. [1968] AC 269, [1967] 2 WLR 871.
100. [1967] 2 WLR 871, 902. See also, for example, Blair JA of the Ontario Court of Appeal in *Tank Lining Corporation v Dunlop Industrial Ltd.* (1982) 140 DLR (3d) 659 at 671, where he said: 'The considerations relevant to the interests of the parties and of the public are separate and distinct and this has become more apparent in recent years. The dual test in the doctrine recognizes that the assertion of a private right can create a public wrong.' For further discussion of the public interest aspect, see McDermott, *Contract Law* (LexisNexis Butterworths, 2001), at paras.16.40–16.41.
101. [2005] IEHC 159, [2005] 3 IR 12.
102. *Tank Lining Corporation v Dunlop Industrial Ltd.* (1982) 140 DLR (3d) 659 at 671.
103. [1894] AC 535, at 565.
104. *Kores Manufacturing Co v Kolok Manufacturing Co* [1958] 2 WLR 858, [1958] 2 All ER 65.

3.3.3. Legitimate Proprietary Interest

[4–49] In order to be enforceable, a restraint of trade clause must be reasonable as between the parties. Any attempt to restrain an employee in this manner can only be justified where the employer is seeking to do so in order to protect a 'legitimate proprietary interest'. In other words, to be considered reasonable as between the parties the clause must seek to protect – within reason – the employer's property. These proprietary interests were described as follows by Stephenson LJ in *Spafax Ltd. v Harrison*[105]:

> An employer is entitled to take and enforce promises from an employee which the employer can prove are reasonably necessary to protect him, the employer, his trade connection, trade interests and goodwill, not from competition by the employee if he leaves his employment, or from his then using the skill and knowledge with which his employment had equipped him to compete, but from his then using his personal knowledge of his employer's customers or his personal influence over them, or his knowledge of his employer's trade secrets, or advantages acquired from his employment, to his employer's disadvantage.[106]

[4–50] Thus the employer is entitled to protect his or her property, the goodwill [s]he has built up in the business, and any specialised information to which the employee gained access while in the employment of the employer. Therefore, unless the restrictive covenant isolates and identifies the specific interest to be protected it is unlikely to be upheld.[107] The following types of interests have been deemed to be proprietary interests that may legitimately be protected by way of a restrictive covenant:

(a) trade secrets and confidential information;
(b) trade connections; and
(c) existing employees.

(a) Trade Secrets and Confidential Information

[4–51] The main difficulty with the enforcement of restrictive covenants purporting to protect trade secrets and confidential information is one of definition of the terms 'trade secret' and 'confidential'.

A trade secret is information not generally available that will be likely to cause economic harm to the employer if it is released to competitors. Whether or not information amounts to a trade secret is a question of fact in each case. In *Forster & Sons v Suggett*[108] the defendant was employed as a works engineer by the plaintiff company involved in the glass-making industry. During the course of his work

105. [1980] IRLR 442.
106. *ibid.*, 443.
107. *Office Angels Ltd. v Rainer-Thomas & O'Connor* [1991] IRLR 214.
108. (1918) 35 TLR 87.

the defendant learned of the secret processes used by the plaintiff company in the manufacture of glass. The Court upheld a restrictive covenant imposed on the defendant, which prevented him from divulging these secret processes, and a covenant that prohibited the defendant from working for a competitor anywhere in the United Kingdom for five years after leaving the plaintiff's employment.

The line between knowledge that can be considered a trade secret and that which [4–52] the employee has developed due to his or her own intelligence, experience or skill is not always an easy one to draw. However, the distinction is important. Knowledge of the former kind is the property of the employer and [s]he has a legitimate interest in protecting it, while knowledge of the latter kind is that of the employee and restrictive covenants limiting its use will not be enforceable. In *Herbert Morris Ltd. v Saxelby*[109] Lord Shaw distinguished between 'objective knowledge', which was the property of the employer, and 'subjective knowledge', which was the property of the employee. In that case, an engineer had covenanted not to work for a competitor of his employer for a period of seven years after he left his employment. The covenant was found to be unenforceable as it attempted to impose a restraint on the engineer's technical skill, which he had developed as a result of his own intelligence, industry and experience. This knowledge was the employee's subjective knowledge and could not be the subject of such restraint.

In *SBJ Stephenson Ltd. v Mandy*[110] the employee worked in the insurance industry. [4–53] During the course of his employment he gained knowledge of details of his employer's customers: for example, identity, renewal dates, price and so forth. When he left his employment his former employer sought to enforce a covenant against him restricting him from using the information. The Court held that this information was objective knowledge, which was the property of the employer and in the circumstances the covenant was reasonable and therefore enforceable. In *Printers and Finishers Ltd. v Holloway*,[111] the claimant sought to restrain a former manager from disclosing certain information that came into the manager's possession while employed by the claimant. Some of the information concerned was contained in documents that the manager had taken with him. The restrictive covenant was applied to this information. However, the Court could not as easily distinguish the knowledge of the claimant's general business, which the manager had learned and committed to memory as a result of working for the claimant. Restricting the use of this information was not considered to be reasonable. It would seem, therefore, that if the knowledge is the product of the employer's labour and is not generally known to the public, it shall be considered the employer's property. However, if the knowledge has been acquired by the employee himself through his own skill, intelligence and observation, then it is more likely to be considered the employee's property.

---

109. [1916] 1 AC 688 at 714.
110. [2000] IRLR 233.
111. [1964] 3 All ER 731.

[4–54] An employer's confidential information may be protected by an implied term of loyalty and fidelity in the contract.[112] Such protection can be enhanced by the inclusion of an express restrictive covenant. In *Faccenda Chicken v Fowler*,[113] Neill LJ of the Court of Appeal of England and Wales held that whether or not information could be considered confidential depended, in particular, on the following factors:

(a) The nature of the employment. Thus employment in a capacity where 'confidential' material is habitually handled may impose a high obligation of confidentiality because the employee can be expected to realise its sensitive nature to a greater extent than if [s]he were employed in a capacity where such material reached him or her only occasionally or incidentally.

(b) The nature of the information itself. The information will only be protected if it can be classified as a trade secret or as material that, while not properly to be described as a trade secret, is in all the circumstances of such a highly confidential nature as to require the same protection as a trade secret *eo nomine*.

(c) Whether the employer impressed on the employee the confidentiality of the information. While the employer cannot prevent use or disclosure merely by telling the employee that the information is confidential, his attitude may provide assistance in determining the question as to how confidential the information actually is.

(d) Whether the information can easily be isolated from other information that the employee is free to use or disclose. So the fact that the alleged confidential information is part of a package where the remainder is not confidential would be likely to throw light on whether or not the information is, in reality, a trade secret.

In an Irish context, Clarke J summarised the legal position as established in *Faccenda Chicken*, which he described as the 'leading authority', as follows:

It is clear from that authority that no term will be implied into a contract of employment which precludes the employee, after his employment has ceased, from the disclosure of confidential information short of a trade secret. Therefore in summary, the law is clear. In the absence of an express term in a contract of employment the only enduring obligation on the part of an employee after his employment has ceased is one which precludes the employee from disclosing a trade secret.[114]

---

112. See below at 4.2.6.
113. [1987] Ch. 117, [1986] 3 WLR 288, [1986] 1 All ER 617, [1986] IRLR 69.
114. *The Pulse Group Limited v O'Reilly* [2006] IEHC 50 at paras.3.3–3.4.

In *Poeton Industries Ltd. & Another v Michael Ikem Horton & Another*[115] Morritt   [4–55]
LJ emphasised that in order for information to be considered confidential it is
important not only to consider the nature of the employment and the nature of
the information but also 'whether the employer impressed on the employee the
confidentiality of the information and whether such information may be easily
isolated from other information which the employee is free to use or disclose.'[116]
Moreover, it would appear that even if the information is deemed to be confidential, the courts will not restrict its disclosure if it is considered to be in the
public interest. Thus in *National Irish Bank Ltd. v RTÉ*[117] the Supreme Court held
that the disclosure of confidential information could be justified where it exposed
wrongdoing.[118]

(b) Trade Connections

An employer is entitled to protect the goodwill in his or her business that [s]he   [4–56]
has built up through his or her trading with customers and clients. These trade
connections may be protected through 'non-solicitation' or 'non-competition'
clauses, which seek to prevent former employees from unfairly using their personal
knowledge of the employer's trade connections or using such connections to set
up a competing business.

A general prohibition in this regard will not be upheld. In order for the restric-   [4–57]
tive covenant to be enforceable, it must be shown that the employer had suffered
harm as a result of the employee's actions. If the employee had no direct relationship with customers/clients it will be difficult to see how [s]he could have exercised influence over them to his or her former employer's disadvantage. In *Strange
v Mann*,[119] for example, the employee worked as a manager of a bookmakers'
shop. A covenant in his contract of employment prevented him from operating a
competing business within a 12-mile radius of his employer upon the termination
of his employment, and not to solicit the customers of his former employer. It
was held that there was no legitimate interest to protect. Most of the employee's
contact with customers was over the telephone and as such he did not build up a
close relationship of such a nature with them that it could be said he could exercise
influence over them.

It is therefore necessary that the employee has had direct contact with the customers   [4–58]
or clients in question. Otherwise it is difficult for an employer to argue that the
employee could have exercised such influence over the customers or clients that
they would have followed him or her when [s]he left the employer's employment.
In *Marley Tile Co Ltd. v Johnson*[120] the employer attempted to enforce a covenant

---

115. [2000] EWCA Civ 180.
116. [2000] EWCA Civ 180 at para.18.
117. [1998] IESC 2, [1998] 2 IR 465, [1998] 2 ILRM 196.
118. See also *Initial Services Ltd. v Putterill* [1968] 1 QB 396.
119. [1965] 1 WLR 629, [1965] 1 All ER 1069.
120. [1982] IRLR 75.

that restricted the solicitation by a former employee of any customers of the employer who were customers for the 12-month period prior to the termination of the employee's employment. As the covenant covered thousands of customers it was not possible that the employee could have dealt with any more than a small percentage of them, and hence the clause was deemed to be excessive. There was no evidence that the former employee could have developed a relationship with all of these customers of such a kind whereby he could exercise influence over them.

[4–59] The nature of the employment will be of relevance in assessing whether a restraint on using trade connections will be considered reasonable. The greater the influence exercised by the employee over the customer or client, the greater the likelihood that any proposed restraint will be upheld as reasonable. In *Attwood v Lamont*[121] the employee worked in the tailoring department of a store. He had agreed not to carry on a business as a 'tailor, dressmaker, general draper, milliner, hatter, haberdasher or outfitter', in competition with his employer. The clause was unreasonable as there was no evidence that his position was such that if [s]he were to leave his or her employment, his or her employer's customers would follow him. Thus the question of the influence that the employee could exert over the customers is critical – that is, would they follow the employee if [s]he left?[122]

[4–60] Where the relationship between the employee and the customers or clients is a recurring one, it is more likely that a non-solicitation clause will be upheld as reasonable. In *Bowler v Lovegrove*,[123] the employee worked for an estate agent and did most of his work with customers over the phone. It was held that the fact that the employee did not deal directly with customers, and because the nature of the business was non-recurring, any restraint on the employee was unreasonable as the employer had no trade connection to protect.

[4–61] Any proposed restraint on post-contractual engagement with customers or clients of the employer who were not customers or clients during the employee's employment will be considered unreasonable. An employer has no legitimate interest in preventing his or her former employee from dealing with customers or clients who were not part of the employer's business while the employee worked there. In *Murgitroyd and Co Ltd. v Purdy*,[124] the plaintiffs were in the business of providing intellectual property services and had several offices throughout Europe. The defendant was a patent agent who was hired to work in the plaintiff's Dublin office. When the defendant terminated his employment, the plaintiff sought to enforce a covenant against him that provided that he could not engage in any business in competition with the plaintiff in the Republic of Ireland for a period of 12 months. The High Court refused to enforce the covenant on the basis that

121. [1920] 3 KB 571.
122. *Hinton & Higgs (UK) Ltd. v Murphy and Valentine* [1989] IRLR 519.
123. [1921] 1 Ch. 642.
124. [2005] IEHC 159, [2005] 3 IR 12.

it did not protect the plaintiff's legitimate interest, namely in trade connections. Clarke J stated:

> A prohibition on dealing with (in addition to soliciting of) customers of the plaintiff would, in my view, have been reasonable and sufficient to meet any legitimate requirements of the plaintiff. The wider prohibition which restricts dealing with those who might be, but are not, such customers is excessive.
>
> There may be types of business where it is not practical to distinguish between customers and non-customers. This is not one of them. On the evidence, the number of customers is small and identifiable. A prohibition on dealing with those identified customers would be sufficient to prevent the defendant taking advantage of the plaintiff's trade connections. The wider restriction which prohibits competing for business in which the plaintiff might have an interest but where the client was not an existing customer, could not be directed to that end but to the wider aim of restricting competition as such.[125]

Similarly, in *Gledhow Autoparts v Delaney*,[126] the defendant was employed as a   [4–62] commercial traveller by the claimants. Upon termination of his contract he was subjected to a restrictive covenant that prevented him from operating in the area where he had previously operated for the claimants. The covenant prevented the employee from dealing not only with the existing customers of the claimants but also those within the area who were not the customers of the claimants. As such it was anti-competitive and unenforceable.

A non-solicitation clause cannot prevent an employee from dealing with former   [4–63] customers and clients of his former employer if they approach him or her to do so. In *European Paint Importers v O'Callaghan*[127] the plaintiffs sought to enforce a covenant against its former employees that prohibited them, for one year after the termination of their employment, from 'directly or indirectly seek[ing] to procure orders from, or do[ing] business with, any person, firm or company who has at any time during the one year immediately preceding such cessation of employment done business with the Company'.[128] In an *obiter* passage, Peart J questioned the validity of the clause, as, not only did it prohibit solicitation of customers, it also appeared to prohibit the plaintiffs from dealing with those customers who approached them unsolicited:

> For a period of twelve months the defendants must not only not seek out orders, but having done so, and when approached by such a customer, who perhaps for some reason does not wish to do business any longer with the plaintiff, must refuse

---

125. [2005] 3 IR 12, 21.
126. [1965] 1 WLR 1366, [1965] 3 All ER 288.
127. [2005] IEHC 280.
128. At p.1 of the judgment.

that custom forcing the customer to go to another competitor in the same marker, other that the plaintiff… would amount to an unwarranted restriction, and serve only to unreasonably and unjustifiably place an obstacle in the way of a fledging company which is legitimately entitled to try and get off the ground. It seems to me that the most which ought to be required of the defendants is not to take any positive steps to seek business from existing customers of the plaintiff for a period of up to twelve months.[129]

This passage suggests that it would be unreasonable to prevent former customers of the former employer from going to the new undertaking, where the customer's business had not been solicited by the former employee.

[4–64] It should, however, be added that on the facts in the *European Paint Importers* case, an interlocutory injunction was granted restraining the defendants from seeking to procure orders from, or doing any business with any person, firm or company who had at any time in the previous year been a customer of the plaintiff, regardless of whether the business in question was sought out by the said defendants or not.

(c) Existing Employees

[4–65] Traditionally, employees were not considered to be assets of the employer or business that could be considered a protectable interest of the employer. In *Hanover Insurance Brokers Ltd. v Schapiro*[130] the employer sought to enforce a restrictive covenant that provided that the departing employees were not to 'solicit or entice any employees of the company to the intent or effect that such employee terminates the employment'.[131] The Court noted that an employee has the right to work for any employer who will hire him or her. It held that the clause in question was unreasonable as it was too wide because it applied to all employees 'irrespective of expertise or juniority' and would also apply to employees who only joined the firm after the defendants had left.

[4–66] Increasingly, however, it has been recognised that certain employees, depending on the nature of the business, can be considered key to the organisation as a whole.[132] In such circumstances, where it can be established that a 'non-poaching' covenant applies to a specific class of employee of particular importance to the employer's business, and is generally limited to those employees who were former colleagues of the departing employee, then the courts are willing to uphold such clauses as reasonable.[133] In *Dawnay Day & Co Ltd. v De Braconier D'Alphen*[134] the Court of Appeal of England and Wales – distinguishing *Hanover* – upheld a

---

129. At p.3 of the judgment.
130. [1994] IRLR 82.
131. [1994] IRLR 82, at 82.
132. See *Ingham v ABC Contract Services Ltd.*, CA, 12 November 1993; *Alliance Paper Group Plc v Prestwich* [1996] IRLR 25.
133. *TSC Europe (UK) Ltd. v Massey* [1999] IRLR 22.
134. [1997] IRLR 442.

restrictive covenant that sought to prevent the poaching of key members of the employer's staff. In so doing, it identified 'the employer's interest in maintaining a stable trained workforce'[135] as deserving of protection if the covenant used to do so was reasonable in its scope.

While such clauses will generally only apply to the enticing of employees who were former colleagues of the departing employee, the High Court of England and Wales in *SBJ Stephenson v Mandy*[136] has upheld a 'non-poaching' covenant applied to all employees on the basis that such protection was necessary for the employer because the employees were 'prime assets' of the company. The Court concluded that the plaintiff was deserving of such protection in the circumstances because it had: [4–67]

> invested a great deal in the training of its staff… Insurance broking was a business
> which developed and flourished through the efforts of staff and the relationships
> they built up with clients, but it was not just the stability of broking staff which
> was important to SBJ. Its support staff had been trained and became experienced
> in its procedures and computer systems.[137]

In *Finnegan v J & E Davy*,[138] a decision discussed in detail later in this chapter, Smyth J of the High Court held that the withholding of the payment of a bonus that had been earned by the plaintiff could be considered a restraint of trade. In that case, the plaintiff received a bonus paid at the end of the year. Some years later, the plaintiff was told that the bonus was not going to be paid in the same way as previous bonus payments. The plaintiff was simply informed that he was no longer to be paid his bonus at the end of year to which it referred (as had been the case in the past) and some of it was to be deferred over a two-year period, which meant that the plaintiff would be obliged to work two further years before he would be entitled to payment of the bonus he had already earned. The plaintiff was also informed that if he left for a competitor before this time, the bonus would not be paid. The Court rejected the defendant's argument that this provision was not in restraint of trade and that it was simply an economic incentive for the plaintiff to remain with the defendant. The Court held that this new provision as regards the payment of the bonus had not been agreed upon and was in effect a restraint of trade. Furthermore, the Court could not find a 'genuine proprietary interest of the defendant that required the imposition of the provision imposed upon the plaintiff'[139] that would have justified such restraint.   [4–68]

---

135. [1997] IRLR 442, 443.
136. [2000] IRLR 233.
137. [2000] IRLR 233, 238.
138. [2007] IEHC 18, [2007] ELR 234.
139. [2007] ELR 234, 244.

3.3.4. *The Scope of the Restraint*

[4–69] In order to be enforced, the restrictive covenant must not only protect a legitimate proprietary interest, but also the extent of any such protection must be reasonable – that is, it must go no further than is reasonably necessary to protect that legitimate proprietary interest.[140] Assessment of the reasonableness of the extent of the restraint may be undertaken on the basis of the duration of the restraint and its geographical extent, in both cases having regard to the interest sought to be protected. Thus, a restraint of trade that had worldwide effect was deemed to be enforceable in *Nordenfelt v Maxim Nordenfelt*,[141] while a restraint that was limited to an area within 1,000 metres of the employer's business in *Office Angels Ltd. v Rainer-Thomas & O'Connor*[142] was deemed to be excessive. Consequently, reliance on precedent in this area can be dangerous.

The Duration of the Restraint

[4–70] The restraint must be no longer in terms of duration than is reasonably necessary to allow the employer the opportunity to make efforts to protect the business from the effects of the employee's departure. As Holland and Burnett put it:

> The restraint can last no longer than the projected useful life of that information. An obvious difference lies in the considerations applied to ex-employees of organizations famed for their 'secret recipes' and those, say, in the fashion industry, where the secrecy of next season's designs has a limited lifespan. It may be reasonable in the former case to impose a lifetime ban; in the latter case, probably no more than a few months.[143]

[4–71] In *Nordenfelt v Maxim Nordenfelt*,[144] a restraint preventing a former owner of a munitions company from competing with the new owner for a period of 25 years after the sale of the business was upheld on the basis that it was reasonable considering the nature of the business, its international market and the consideration paid to the dealer following the sale of the business. However, because '[g]reater freedom of contract is allowable in a covenant entered into between the seller and buyer of a business than in the case of one entered into between an employer and employee',[145] it is unlikely that clauses of similar duration will be upheld in cases involving straightforward contracts of employment.[146] In cases such as *Nordenfelt*, the vendor is paying for the goodwill of a business and should be entitled to protect that goodwill. In cases involving employees, the courts must also consider

---

140. *Herbert Morris Ltd. v Saxelby* [1916] 1 AC 688.
141. [1894] AC 535.
142. [1991] IRLR 214.
143. Holland and Burnett, *Employment Law* (Oxford University Press, 2006), at 214.
144. [1894] AC 535.
145. *per* Costello J in *John Orr Ltd. and Vestcom BV v John Orr* [1987] ILRM 702 at 704.
146. This will, of course, depend on the interest to be protected, i.e. trade secrets or confidential information in the possession of departing employees may be subject to lengthier restraint: *Fitch v Dewes* [1921] 2 AC 158.

the right of the employee to seek alternative (including similar) employment. Thus clauses of 12 months' duration, such as that in *Murgitroyd and Co Ltd. v Purdy*,[147] are more likely to be enforceable and tend to be more the norm.

When assessing the reasonableness of the duration of the restraint, regard must also   **[4–72]** be had to it geographical extent. In terms of duration, a longer restraint may be justified if the geographic area is quite limited. For example, in *Fitch v Dewes*,[148] a clause provided that a solicitor's managing clerk could not practice for life within seven miles of Tamworth Town Hall. While quite long in terms of duration, the clause was nevertheless upheld in light of the narrowness of its geographic extent. In the Irish Supreme Court decision of *Mulligan v Corr*,[149] Fitzgibbon J observed:

> The restriction imposed must not be greater than is reasonably required for the protection of the covenantee. If it exceeds in area or duration the limits which the Court considers reasonable it is void. The question of reasonableness is one of law for the Court to decide. A restriction though unlimited as to space may be reasonable if confined to a period of reasonable duration.[150]

The Geographic Limitations of the Restraint

The geographic extent of the restraint must also not be any wider than is reason-   **[4–73]** able necessary to protect the employer's legitimate interests and must be justified by virtue of the interest to be protected, such as the location of the employer's market, customers and so on. Again, each case must be examined in light of its particular facts. In *Nordenfelt*,[151] a restraint that had worldwide effect was enforce-able given the international nature of the market to be protected. By contrast, in *Commercial Plastics Ltd. v Vincent*,[152] a restraint with no geographical limitation was deemed unenforceable. Because it did not have any geographical limitation it was interpreted as having worldwide effect and, as the employer only operated in the United Kingdom, the restraint went beyond what was reasonably necessary to adequately protect the business and was void.

In *Mulligan v Corr*,[153] a solicitor sought to enforce a restraint of trade clause against   **[4–74]** a former apprentice. The clause provided that the former apprentice could not practice within 30 miles of Ballina or Charlestown, Co. Mayo, or within 20 miles of Ballaghadereen, Co. Roscommon. The solicitor at that time had offices in both Ballina and Charlestown. The Supreme Court refused to enforce the restraint as it went beyond what could be considered reasonably necessary to provide adequate

---

147. [2005] IEHC 159, [2005] 3 IR 12.
148. [1921] 2 AC 158.
149. [1925] 1 IR 169.
150. *ibid.*, at 175.
151. *Nordenfelt v Maxim Nordenfelt* [1894] AC 535.
152. [1965] 1 QB 623, [1964] 3 WLR 820, [1964] 3 All ER 546.
153. [1925] 1 IR 169.

protection to the solicitor's business. The clause as drafted would have excluded the former apprentice from practicing in Sligo town (the capital of a neighbouring county). Furthermore, the solicitor could not seek to restrain the employee from operating in a geographic location in which he did not have a business (Balla-ghadereen). In response to the solicitor's argument that his prospects of setting up an office in that area would be hampered without the restraint, Fitzgibbon J stated that 'a restriction imposed to protect a business which was not in fact being worked and might never be set up at all was quite unreasonable'.[154]

[4–75] The specialised nature of the work may justify the imposition of a wider geographic restraint. In *Murgitroyd and Co Ltd. v Purdy*,[155] Clarke J held that a restraint on a patent agent that extended throughout Ireland was justifiable given the nature of the business:

> Having heard the evidence presented on behalf of the plaintiff as to the nature of the business in Ireland I am satisfied that there are only 10 (or perhaps 11 if one includes the defendant) patent attorneys operating in Ireland and that they all operate from Dublin. No difficulty would appear to be encountered in servicing the demands of the Irish business from Dublin. In those circumstances it does not seem to me that a geographical restriction based upon the jurisdiction of the Irish state is unreasonable having regard to the way in which the business operates in Ireland.[156]

[4–76] A restraint of trade can be deemed unreasonable if it is considered to be excessive in light of the interest to be protected. For example, in *Office Angels Ltd. v Rainer-Thomas & O'Connor*,[157] a restraint of 1,000 metres was considered excessive when applied to the city of London. The restraint ruled out the possibility of the employee seeking similar employment anywhere in the city of London. Such a clause was deemed not to be necessary to protect the employer's clients, as most of the work was conducted with them over the telephone and as such the location of the office was not important to them. In *Hollis & Co v Stocks*,[158] the English Court of Appeal of England and Wales upheld a restraint of trade clause that prevented a solicitor from representing clients within a 10-mile radius of certain locations. The clause was quite specific in terms of its geographic scope. The solicitor was prohibited from representing clients at Sutton-in-Ashfield (where his former employer's office was located); Mansfield Police Station or Mansfield Magistrates' Court. The clause was carefully drafted to protect the employer's business and was not simply an anti-competitive measure as evidenced by the fact that the clause did not seek to prevent the solicitor from practising in a number of other large towns in the East Midlands region. In upholding the validity of the geographical extent of the

---

154. *ibid.,* at 177.
155. [2005] IEHC 159, [2005] 3 IR 12.
156. *ibid.,* at 21.
157. [1991] IRLR 214.
158. [2000] IRLR 712.

clause, the Court of Appeal stated that the trial judge was in the best position to make such a determination because, 'he knew the area well... being the county Court judge in the particular area'.[159]

3.3.5. Restraint of Trade Clauses and Competition Law

Restraint of trade covenants may also be governed by the Competition Act 2002. [4–77] Section 4(1) of the Act provides that:

> all agreements between undertakings, decisions by associations of undertakings and concerted practices which have as their object or effect, the prevention, restriction or distortion of competition on trade of any goods or services in the State or any part of the State are prohibited and void...

In the context of employment contracts, it would appear that the definition of 'undertakings' in s.3(1) of the Act does not apply to employees as individuals but only as economic entities.[160] However, where an employee left his employment to establish his own business, then that individual may be considered to be an undertaking for the purposes of the legislation.[161]

In *Apex Fire Protection v Murtagh*[162] the Competition Authority was notified [4–78] (pursuant to s.7(1) of the Competition Act 1991), for the purpose of obtaining a certificate under s.4(4) or, in the event of a refusal, a licence under s.4(2) of a restraint of trade clause, which the company sought to enforce against a former employee. Mr. Murtagh had been a former employee of the company who had resigned his position and set up another company in competition with his former employers. The clause in question sought to prevent Mr. Murtagh from soliciting any customers of his former employer or from divulging any information gained as a result of his employment with the company for a period of two years after his departure and within the area he had formerly operated. The Competition Authority ultimately refused to grant a licence to the agreement between the parties on the basis that the clause in question was unreasonable.

- First, the Authority held that as Mr. Murtagh owned and controlled his own business, which provided goods and services for gain, he was an 'undertaking' within the meaning of s.3(1) of the Act.

- Secondly, the Authority found that the non-solicit aspect of the clause was reasonable in that it sought to protect a legitimate interest of the employer. In particular, the Authority noted that:

---

159. [2000] IRLR 712, 713.
160. This view would be in line with that adopted by the European Commission with regards to European Union Competition law. See *Suker-Unie v Commission* [1975] ECR 1663.
161. *Notice on Employee Agreements and the Competition Act 1991*, Iris Oifigiúil, 18 September 1992.
162. [1993] ELR 201.

Mr. Murtagh remains free to transact unsolicited business with Apex customers within the designated area, all business with Apex customers elsewhere, and all business with non-Apex customers everywhere. He may engage in normal forms of advertising to attract customers. After the expiry of the restriction, he will be completely free to carry on business everywhere without any restriction.[163]

However, the Authority held that the extent of the clause was excessive in that it applied to *all* customers of Apex, including those who had ceased to be customers of Apex before Mr. Murtagh had established his business.

- Thirdly, the Authority did not see how a two-year restraint was justifiable in the circumstances:

> In coming to this view, the Authority has taken into account the fact that the period of time during which items of fire protection equipment normally require servicing is one year. A one-year period of protection, in the view of the Authority, would provide the company with ample opportunity to confirm its business connection and goodwill with its existing customers prior to facing competition for those customers from Mr. Murtagh subsequently.[164]

In summary, the Authority concluded that:

> Apex Fire Protection Ltd. and Mr. Noel Murtagh are undertakings within the meaning of the *Competition Act* and the contract of employment between them, dated 29 October 1991 (CA/1130/92), is an agreement between undertakings. The agreement, as amended in the letter of 28 May 1993, offends against *section 4(1)* of the Act insofar as it contains a restriction on soliciting certain customers which exceeds what is required for the legitimate commercial interests of Apex in that it still applies for a period of 18 months after termination of employment. The agreement may not benefit from the provisions of *section 4(2)* of the Act because it contains terms which are not indispensable to the attainment of any benefits achieved by the agreement. The Authority therefore refuses to grant a licence to the agreement between Apex Fire Protection Ltd. and Mr. Noel Murtagh.[165]

3.3.6. Remedies

[4–79] An employer may seek to enforce a valid restraint of trade clause by way of an application for an injunction.[166] Furthermore, damages may be awarded where a valid clause has been breached by the employee, although assessing the employer's loss may be difficult to quantify.[167] In *European Paint Importers v O'Callaghan*,[168]

---

163. [1993] ELR 201, 211.
164. [1993] ELR 201, 212-213.
165. [1993] ELR 201, 214-215.
166. *Ardex Optical Corporation v McMurray* [1958] Ir Jur Rep 65.
167. *Lennon v Doran*, unreported, High Court, 20 February 2001.
168. [2005] IEHC 280.

at the time at which the plaintiff sought an injunction to enforce a restrictive covenant (which sought to prevent the defendants from actively soliciting clients of the plaintiff and those clients of the plaintiff that approached the defendants of their own accord) the covenant had already been breached. The plaintiff claimed that he had suffered damage to his business as a result. Peart J granted an injunction ordering that the defendants could not solicit any further clients of the plaintiff, nor do any further business with clients already solicited. It was Peart J's view, however, that an award of damages was inappropriate as it was impossible to determine which of the clients' orders had come as a result of active solicitation (in breach of the clause) and those that had arisen independently (no breach).

3.3.7. The Doctrine of Severance

Where a restraint of trade clause, or part thereof, is deemed unenforceable, the [4–80] Court may in limited circumstances edit the clause by deleting the offending elements, thereby allowing the remainder to stand.[169] In this regard, a distinction must be drawn between two different types of severance: 'blue pencil' severance and 'notional severance'. This distinction was helpfully restated in the Supreme Court of Canada judgment in *Shafron KRG Insurance Brokers (Western) Inc.*[170] Rothstein J explained the two types of severance in the following passage:

> Where severance is permitted, there appears to be two types: 'blue-pencil' severance and 'notional' severance. Both types of severance have been applied in limited circumstances to remove illegal features of a contract so as to render the contract in conformity with the law. Blue-pencil severance was described in *Attwood v Lamont*, [1920] 3 K.B. 571 (C.A.), by Lord Sterndale as 'effected when the part severed can be removed by running a blue pencil through it' (p. 578). In *Transport North American Express Inc. v New Solutions Financial Corp.*, 2004 SCC 7, [2004] 1 S.C.R. 249, Bastarache J., in dissent, described this form of severance at para. 57:

> Under the blue-pencil test, severance is only possible if the judge can strike out, by drawing a line through, the portion of the contract they want to remove, leaving the portions that are not tainted by illegality, without affecting the meaning of the part remaining.

> Notional severance involves reading down an illegal provision in a contract that would be unenforceable in order to make it legal and enforceable (see *Transport*, at para. 2). In *Transport*, the contract provided that interest was to be charged at a rate exceeding 60 percent contrary to s. 347 of the *Criminal Code*. There was no evidence of an intention to contravene this provision, and this was not a case of loan sharking. Arbour J. applied the doctrine of notional severance to effectively read down the interest rate to the legal statutory maximum of 60 percent.[171]

---

169. The doctrine of severance has been given statutory effect under s.7 of the Competition Act 1991.
170. 2009 SCC 6, Supreme Court of Canada, 23 January 2009.
171. *ibid.*, at [29]–[30].

[4–81] Rothstein J, delivering the judgment of the Court in *Shafron*, emphasised that blue-pencil severance should be resorted to only sparingly, and only in cases where 'the part being removed is clearly severable, trivial and not part of the main purport of the restrictive covenant'. This did not affect the 'general rule' that an ambiguous or unreasonable restrictive covenant will be void and unenforceable.[172] Rothstein J continued his analysis by rejecting the contention that notional severance has any place in the construction of restrictive covenants in employment contracts. He did so for two reasons: first, that there is no 'bright-line test' for reasonableness, giving rise to the concern – expressed by Rothstein J as a conclusion – that '[a]pplying notional severance in these circumstances simply amounts to the Court rewriting the covenant in a manner that it subjectively considers reasonable in each individual case'.[173]

[4–82] The Supreme Court of Canada also based its rejection of notional severance on another justification: the imbalance of power between employees and employers at the heart of the employment relationship. Rothstein J explained:

> The restrictive covenant is sought by the employer. The obligation is on the employee. Having regard to the generally accepted imbalance of power between employers and employees, to introduce the doctrine of notional severance to read down an unreasonable restrictive covenant to what is reasonable provides no inducement to an employer to ensure the reasonableness of the covenant and inappropriately increases the risk that the employee will be forced to abide by an unreasonable covenant.[174]

Under the 'blue pencil' test, on the other hand, the courts use an imaginary blue pencil to draw a line through the offending aspects of the clause in order to remove words or sentences that may render the clause unreasonable.[175] For example, in *Mulligan v Corr*,[176] the Supreme Court held that a restraint of trade clause that prohibited the employee from working within 30 miles of Ballina, Charlestown and Ballaghadereen was excessive in its geographic scope, particularly as the employer's office was located in Ballina. Consequently, the Court severed the references to Charlestown and Ballaghadereen and granted an

---

172. *ibid.*, at [36].
173. *ibid.*, at [39].
174. *ibid.*, at [41].
175. For example, in *Sadler v Imperial Life Assurance Co of Canada Ltd.* [1988] IRLR 388, the following conditions were imposed on the operation of the severance doctrine: (a) the unenforceable provisions could be removed without the need to add or modify the wording of what remains; (b) the remaining terms continue to be supported by adequate consideration; (c) the removal of the words or sentences did not change the character of the clause or contract, i.e. make it substantially different to what was already agreed; and (d) the severance must be consistent with public policy underlying the avoidance of the offending clause.
176. [1925] 1 IR 169.

injunction preventing the employee from practising as a solicitor within 30 miles of Ballina.[177]

It is not the function of the Court to rewrite a contract already agreed between the parties. Consequently, the doctrine is reluctantly applied by the courts. Otherwise, parties might be encouraged to draft such restraints widely, safe in the knowledge that the clause would either be upheld by the courts or, if not, would be edited using the expertise of the courts in such a way as to make it enforceable. Thus in *Cussen v O'Connor*,[178] Andrews J observed: [4–83]

> We cannot vary the contract between the parties, so as to make an unreasonable and void contract a reasonable and valid one; but in dealing with a valid contract we may, as a Court of Equity, have regard to the effect upon the defendant, of the injunction we are asked to grant, and modify its severity, if injustice be not thereby done to the plaintiff.[179]

Severance will only be applied where the removal of the offending words or sentences do not create any grammatical difficulty or render the clause incomprehensible.[180] Severance will not be applied where to do so would leave the contract without adequate consideration, i.e. the restraint in question was the whole or part of the consideration of the contract.[181] Commentators have noted that severance is more likely to be applied in circumstances where the contract is drafted in such a way as to facilitate severability, that is, where the clause is drafted in such a way that it comprises several distinct sub-clauses.[182] Such an approach would allow the deletion of the offending clauses while retaining those deemed to be valid.[183]

3.3.8. Repudiatory Breach

An employer cannot enforce a restraint of trade clause in a contract of employment where he has repudiated that contract.[184] The breach must be a fundamental one (for example, where the employee has been wrongly dismissed by the [4–84]

---

177. In *Skerry v Moles* (1907) 42 ILTR 46, a teacher was subjected to a restraint of trade that prohibited him from teaching within a radius of seven miles of Belfast, Dublin and Cork. The employer feared that on his departure some students would have followed him. However, the teacher was employed in Belfast only. The Court held that a restraint that extended to Dublin and Cork in these circumstances was excessive. The reference to Dublin and Cork was severed from the contract and the reference to Belfast was upheld.

178. (1893) 32 LR (IR) 330.

179. *ibid.*, at 339.

180. *Business Seating (Renovations) Ltd. v Broad* [1989] ICR 729.

181. *Marshall v NM Financial Management Ltd.* [1997] IRLR 449.

182. See McDermott, *Contract Law* (LexisNexis Butterworths, 2001), at p.880; and the 'shopping list' approach discussed in Holland and Burnett, *Employment Law* (Oxford University Press, 2006), at pp.208–209.

183. *Attwood v Lamont* [1920] 3 KB 571.

184. *General Billposting Co Ltd. v Atkinson* [1909] AC 118.

employer,[185] where there has been the dissolution of a partnership in breach of contract,[186] or where there is a deliberate refusal to pay agreed remuneration under the contract[187]). Where a repudiatory breach exists, a restraint cannot be enforced by the insertion of a clause providing that the restraint is valid regardless of how the termination of the contract of employment comes about.[188]

4. Implied Terms

[4–85]   The parties to the contract of employment will not always adequately provide for all relevant matters incidental to the employment relationship through the incorporation of express terms. When such an eventuality does arise, a term dealing with it may be implied into the contract.

The implication of terms into employment contracts is subject to ordinary principles of contractual theory.[189] The source of such implied terms may arise from custom and practice, collective agreements, or statute.[190] However, the courts may also be asked to imply such terms into a contract of employment from the facts or from law.

4.1. Terms Implied from the Facts

[4–86]   When implying a term from the facts of the situation, the courts aim to give effect to the presumed intentions of the parties at the time they entered into the contract of employment. In *DP Refinery (Westernport) Pty Ltd. v Shire Hastings*[191] the Privy Council summed up the circumstances under which a term will be implied into a contract:

> (i)   the term must be reasonable;
> (ii) it must be necessary to give business efficacy to the contract;
> (iii) it must be so obvious that it goes without saying;
> (iv) it must be capable of clear expression;
> (v)   it must not contradict any other express term of the contract.

---

185. *ibid.*
186. *Briggs v Oates* [1990] 1 All ER 407, [1990] ICR 473, [1990] IRLR 472.
187. *Cantor Fitzgerald International v Callaghan* [1999] ICR 639, [1999] IRLR 234.
188. *Briggs v Oates* [1990] 1 All ER 407, [1990] ICR 473, [1990] IRLR 472; *Living Design (Home Improvements) Ltd. v Davidson* [1994] IRLR 69.
189. Generally, see McDermott, *Contract Law* (LexisNexis Butterworths, 2001), ch.7.
190. For example, s.20 of the Employment Equality Act 1998 implies a term into all contracts of employment providing for equal pay between men and women. It also provides that this implied term will override any express term to the contrary contained in the contract of employment. See Chapter 8.
191. [1978] 52 AJLR 43.

A term will not be implied into a contract of employment simply because it might seem reasonable with the benefit of hindsight to do so,[192] nor can the courts improve the contract by redrafting it at a later stage. As O'Higgins CJ noted in *Tradax (Ireland) Ltd. v Irish Grain Board Ltd.*,[193] 'The Courts have no role in acting as contract makers, or as counselors, to advise or direct which agreement ought to have been made by two people, whether businessmen or not, who chose to enter into contractual relations with each other.'[194]

Furthermore, the courts will not imply a term that contradicts another express **[4–87]** term of the contract.[195] The courts are seeking to give effect to the presumed intentions of the parties and to imply a term in such circumstances would be acting contrary to those expressed intentions. In *McGrath v Trintech Technologies*,[196] the plaintiff's contract of employment expressly provided that employees could avail of a permanent health insurance (PHI) scheme subject to certain exclusions and limitations. Payment under the scheme was expressed to continue until the termination of the plaintiff's employment. When the plaintiff's employment was terminated on the grounds of redundancy he challenged the decision on the basis *inter alia* that it was in breach of an implied term, which provided that the employer could not terminate the employee's employment when he was on certified sick leave and availing of the permanent health insurance scheme. Laffoy J disagreed:

> I am not persuaded by the authorities cited that there should be implied into the plaintiff's contract of employment a term on the lines pleaded. What is suggested is that it was an implied term of the contractual relationship that the defendant would not terminate the plaintiff's contract of employment by notice if two conditions existed: that he was on certified sick leave; and that he was reliant on the prospect of permanent health insurance cover. To imply such a term would be inconsistent with the express terms of the contract of employment, in that it was expressly provided that the plaintiff's employment could be terminated on one month's notice and that, even where payment had commenced under the PHI scheme, it would cease on the termination of the employment.[197]

The courts have adopted two tests to assist them in determining what the true **[4–88]** intentions of the parties were at the time of entering into the contract, the 'business efficacy' test and the 'officious bystander' test.[198] Under the 'business efficacy' test, the Court is trying to give such business efficacy to the contract that

---

192. *Liverpool City Council v Irwin* [1977] AC 239, [1976] 2 WLR 562, [1976] 2 All ER 39.
193. [1984] IR 1.
194. [1984] IR 1, 14.
195. *Carroll v National Lottery* [1996] IEHC 50, [1996] 1 IR 443; *Aga Khan v Firestone* [1991] IEHC 3, [1992] ILRM 31.
196. [2004] IEHC 342, [2005] 4 IR 382.
197. *ibid.*, at 400.
198. Generally, see McDermott, *Contract Law* (LexisNexis Butterworths, 2001), at [7.45]–[7.86].

the parties must have intended because without such a term it would not make commercial sense.[199] The 'officious bystander' test provides that the courts should imply a term into the contract when, based on all the surrounding circumstances, it was a term that was so obvious that the parties would have inserted it had they given any thought to the matter. The test was described as follows by MacKinnon J in *Southern Foundries Ltd. v Shirlaw*[200]:

> *Prima facie* that which in any contract is left to be implied and need not be expressed is something so obvious that it goes without saying; so that, if, while the parties were making their bargain, an officious bystander were to suggest some express provision for it in the agreement, they would testily suppress him with a comment of 'Oh, of course!'[201]

4.2. Terms Implied by Law

[4–89] Terms may be implied by law regardless of the intention of the parties, and in the absence of an express term on the point, if the contract is of a type that has shared characteristics with other contracts of that type, for example, sale of goods contracts, hire purchase agreements, contracts between landlord and tenant, and contracts for the sale of land.[202] As the courts have dealt regularly with such contracts they have over time developed special rules in relation to them. Contracts of employment are another example of these types of contracts. In *Mears v Safecar Security Ltd.*,[203] Stephenson LJ observed that:

> There are contracts which establish a relationship... which demand by their nature and subject matter certain obligations, and those obligations the general law will impose and imply, not as satisfying the business efficacy or officious bystander tests applicable to commercial contracts where there is no such relationship, but as legal incidents of those other kinds of contractual relationship. In considering what obligations to imply into contracts of these kinds which are not complete, the actions of the parties may properly be considered. But the obligation must be a necessary term; that is, required by their relationship. It is not enough that it would be a reasonable term.[204]

Thus these terms or 'incidents of the employment relationship' are deemed to be obligations or duties that are considered necessary or required by the relationship and will therefore be implied into the employment contract if there is no express provision for such matters within the contract. We now consider the nature of some of the more common implied terms in an employment contract.

---

199. *The Moorcock* (1889) 14 PD 64. Generally, see McDermott, *Contract Law* (LexisNexis Butterworths, 2001), at 7.45–7.68.
200.[1939] 2 KB 206.
201. *ibid.*, at 227.
202.*Carna Foods Ltd. v Eagle Star Insurance* [1997] 2 IR 193, [1997] 2 ILRM 499.
203. [1983] 1 QB 54.
204.*ibid.*, at 78.

4.2.1. Provision of Work

At the heart of the employment relationship is a promise by the employer to [4–90]
remunerate the employee, in return for which the employee agrees to perform
specified duties or work. While it is accepted that the employer is obliged to pay
the employee the agreed remuneration in accordance with the contract, there does
not appear to be an additional obligation on the employer to provide work to the
employee in return for that remuneration. The position was summed up rather
quaintly by Asquith J in *Collier v Sunday Referee*,[205] when he stated, 'Provided I
pay my cook her wages regularly, she cannot complain if I choose to take any or
all of my meals out.'[206]

However, the law has recognised that there are exceptions to the general principle [4–91]
that the employer is not obliged to provide the employee with work. Where the
employee is paid on commission or on a piecemeal basis based on work done, then
the employer may be obliged to furnish the employee with work in order that the
employee can earn his remuneration.[207] In *Devonald v Rosser*,[208] the employee worked
in a factory and was paid by the piece, i.e. based on the work that he actually did. He
was provided with six weeks' notice of the termination of his contract. The Court
held that the employer had an implied duty to provide the employee with a reasonable amount of work during the notice period. The courts have also recognised an
exception to the general rule where the employee argues that his reputation will be
damaged where he is deprived of work for a prolonged period. This would particularly apply to actors, singers and other performers who rely on their reputations and
publicity to earn a living. In such cases the right to work may be as important as
the right to be paid. In *Marbé v George Edwardes (Daly's Theatre) Ltd.*,[209] an actress
had agreed to take a part in a play and had also agreed that her name would feature
prominently in advertisements associated with the play. Before the commencement
of the play, her employers refused to allow her play the part. The Court of Appeal
held that her employers were obliged to allow her appear in the play as agreed. The
argument that the failure to provide the work as agreed could cause damage to the
employee's reputation may also be extended to an implied obligation to provide a
certain quality of work. In *Hebert Clayton & Jack Waller Ltd. v Oliver*,[210] an actor
had been engaged to act in the leading part in a play. He was then given a lesser part,
but retained his original salary. It was held that the employer was under an implied
obligation to provide the actor with work of a certain quality, given the importance
of the work and its quality to the actor's reputation.

Traditionally, the courts have not implied an obligation on an employer to provide [4–92]
work to an employee simply on the basis that not to do so would diminish the

---

205. [1940] 2 KB 647, [1940] 4 All ER 234.
206. *ibid.*, at 650.
207. For more detailed discussion see Chapter 11.
208. [1906] 2 KB 728.
209. [1928] 1 KB 269.
210. [1930] AC 209.

employee's skills.[211] However, this principle may be questionable following the Court of Appeal decision in *William Hill Organisation Ltd. v Tucker*,[212] where the Court held that an employer may not always be able to insist that an employee stay away from work for the duration of his or her notice period even where such an employee is continued to be paid his or her remuneration. In that case, the employee, a 'spread-betting' dealer, had a contract of employment containing a six months' notice provision. When the employee left the employment following only one months' notice, his employers sought an injunction restraining him from taking up employment elsewhere for the full duration of the six-month period. The employers argued that as long as they paid his salary during the relevant period, they were not obliged to provide him with any work and were entitled to prevent him working elsewhere for the duration of his notice. The Court rejected the employers' application for an injunction. It found that the employers had an obligation to provide the employee with work, and failure to do so would render them in breach of contract. The Court found against the employers based *inter alia* on the construction of the employee's contract and the fact that the employee's skills were such that required constant practice and experience. In essence, the employers had effectively sought to have a gardening-leave clause implied into the contract of employment, which would have entitled them to send the plaintiff home and pay him his remuneration with no corresponding obligation to provide him with work. The Court refused to imply such a term, which would allow the notice provisions of the plaintiff's contract be utilised as a garden-leave clause. Morritt LJ observed that to do so, 'an employer will need to stipulate for an express power to send his employee on garden leave in all cases in which the contract imposes on him an obligation to permit the employee to do the work'.[213]

[4–93] Further evidence that the traditional view may be changing can be seen from the Irish High Court decision of *Cronin v Eircom Ltd.*[214] The plaintiff was employed by the defendant since 1999. In April 2000 she was seconded to a UK subsidiary on the proviso that once the secondment ended she would continue to work with Éircom Ltd. in accordance with her existing terms and conditions of employment. Whilst on secondment she was promoted to the position of accounts manager. Her salary increased and she was promised that a commission scheme would be introduced. In April 2001, due to a restructuring, the plaintiff was informed that her position as accounts manager could no longer be sustained and she was repatriated. Her salary in sterling for the accounts manager position was paid from April 2001 to April 2003. From that time she was told that her current pay treatment would be revised to her substantive grade and payment would be in euro. At this time the plaintiff was advised that all possible assistance would be given to her in order that she might find an alternative suitable position within the

211. *Turner v Sawdon & Co* [1901] 2 KB 653.
212. [1998] EWCA Civ 615, [1999] ICR 291, [1998] IRLR 313.
213. [1998] EWCA Civ 615, at para.24. See also, and more generally, Chapter 20.
214. [2006] IEHC 380, [2007] 3 IR 104, [2007] ELR 84.

company. However, while she attended some interviews, nothing came of these. In May 2002 the plaintiff, while still an employee, instigated legal proceedings against her employer. In February 2005 the plaintiff was offered a position as a product support executive. The plaintiff did not think that the job offered was a good match for her skill set; it positioned her back to the grade and pay scale that she enjoyed prior to her secondment, despite the fact that she had actually been promoted *during* that secondment. The plaintiff sought injunctive relief and damages to enforce the contract of employment. In a departure from the traditional view that an employer was not obliged to provide work, or indeed a certain standard of work, Laffoy J was prepared to hold that failing to place her in an appropriate position in the years after her secondment ended amounted to a breach of her contract of employment. Laffoy J noted that:

> As the plaintiff is still an employee of the defendant it seems to me that the issue which arises is whether the defendant as her employer was under a contractual obligation, beyond the payment of her salary, to provide her with work so that she would have an opportunity to gain experience, pursue promotion in her job and advance her career. In my view, the defendant was under such an obligation, if not expressly (which I believe is the correct interpretation, because under the letter of appointment dated March 25, 1999 the plaintiff was engaged not only to receive pay but to work in a particular capacity) then under an implied term in the plaintiff's contract of employment, whether as a facet of the obligation to maintain mutual trust and confidence or otherwise. Further, I consider that the defendant was in breach of that obligation.[215]

The recent decisions in *William Hill* and *Cronin* indicate that the courts may [4–94] be willing in certain circumstances to impose an obligation on an employer to provide certain work for an employee. Whether such a term will be implied into the contract will depend on the position of the employee within the organisation and the construction of the express terms of their contract of employment. The position is now such that an employer would be advised to include an express term in the contract of employment denying that he or she is under a duty to provide work to the employee.

4.2.2. Provision of Sick Pay

As has been mentioned, there is no general obligation on an employer to provide [4–95] his or her employee with sick pay. The position is summarised by Halsbury's Laws of England as follows:

> Whether any such private sick pay is payable, its amount, its duration, and its relationship with statutory sick pay or any other benefit depends entirely on the terms of the individual employee's contract, since there is no rule of law that it either is or is not payable. The relevant term may be expressed in the contract and

---

215. [2007] 3 IR 104, 125-126.

this is common. If not so expressed a term may be implied. It is rather a case of considering all the evidence in the particular case, including the normal method of remuneration, custom and practice, and any pronouncement by the employer.[216]

[4–96] Thus, while no general presumption exists in favour of the payment of sick pay, it may be implied into the contract of employment by custom or practice or based on the intention or conduct of the parties. In *Mears v Safecar Security Ltd.*,[217] the employee was ill for a period of months. There was no express reference to the payment of sick pay by his employer in the contract of employment. The employer had not paid sick pay to employees in the past, nor did the employee ask for sick pay while ill. Based on the surrounding circumstances it was held that there was no evidence that sick pay was intended to be a term of the employee's contract of employment, and the employee was not entitled to such payment.

4.2.3. Duty to Indemnify Expenses

[4–97] The contract of employment normally will include a clause that provides that the employer is obliged to indemnify the employee for all reasonable expenses incurred by the employee in the course of his employment. If no such express term exists, one may be implied by the courts. The duty to indemnify will only extend to 'reasonable' expenses. Whether an employee is entitled to be indemnified for expenses incurred during the commission of a wrongful act will depend on whether or not the wrongful act was committed on behalf of the employer or with his authority.[218] Selwyn has explained the distinction as follows:

> For example, if an employer requires an employee to take out the firm's van, which has a defective tyre, and the employee is consequently fined, then it is reasonable to expect the employer to reimburse the amount, even though he may be prosecuted in addition. But if the work can be done in a lawful and unlawful manner, and the employee chose the latter option, the employer would not be required to reimburse such expenditure. For example, if the employee, in order to deliver some goods, parks illegally, then unless he was told to perform his work in this manner, he must bear any subsequent fine himself.[219]

4.2.4. Health and Safety

[4–98] Aside from statutory obligations,[220] the employer has an implied common law duty of care to take reasonable care to provide the employee with a safe and healthy work environment.[221] This common law duty specifically requires the employer to provide the employee with a safe place of work,[222] a safe system or method

---

216. *Halsbury's Laws of England* (4th ed., vol. 16, Butterworths, 1998), para.14.
217. [1983] QB 54, [1982] 3 WLR 366, [1982] 2 All ER 865, [1982] ICR 626, [1982] IRLR 183.
218. *Gregory v Ford* [1951] 1 All ER 121; *Re Famatina Development Corporation Ltd.* [1914] 2 ch.271.
219. Selwyn, *Selwyn's Law of Employment* (15th ed., Oxford University Press, 2008), at 272.
220. See Chapter 15.
221. *Wilsons & Clyde Coal Co Ltd. v English* [1937] 3 All ER 628.
222. *Kielthy v Ascon Ltd.* [1970] IR 122.

of doing the work,[223] safe equipment,[224] and also includes an obligation on the employer to engage competent staff.[225] These duties are subject to greater analysis elsewhere in the text.[226]

4.2.5. Mutual Trust and Confidence

The employment relationship has moved on from the early days of master and [4–99] servant, where the power rested primarily with the employer. It has now developed to such a point where the employee is entitled to be treated with the same respect traditionally accorded to the employer.[227]

The concept of 'mutual trust and confidence' is an amorphous one, and Honeyball has described it as an implied duty of cooperation imposed on both parties.[228] The term has been commonly used in cases involving constructive dismissal.[229] Essentially, a term of 'mutual trust and confidence' is one that, if breached, renders further performance of the contract impossible.[230]

The type of behaviour or activity that can lead to a finding that the term has been [4–100] breached is wide and varied. In *Woods v WM Car Services (Peterborough) Ltd.*,[231] Browne-Wilkinson J described the nature of the implied term as follows:

> It is clearly established that there is implied in a contract of employment a term that the employers will not, without reasonable and proper cause, conduct themselves in a manner calculated or likely to destroy or seriously damage the relationship of confidence and trust between employer and employee… To constitute a breach of this implied term it is not necessary to show that the employer intended any repudiation of the contract: the tribunal's function is to look at the employer's conduct as a whole and determine whether it is such that its effect, judged reasonably and sensibly, is such that the employee cannot be expected to put up with it.[232]

---

223. *Guckian v Scully*, unreported, Supreme Court, 9 March 1972.
224. *Burke v John Paul & Co Ltd.* [1967] IR 277.
225. *Hough v Irish Base Metals Ltd.*, unreported, Supreme Court, 8 December 1967.
226. See Chapter 15.
227. *Donovan v Invicta Airways* [1970] 1 Lloyds Rep 486.
228. Honeyball, *Honeyball and Bowers' Textbook on Labour Law* (9th ed., Oxford University Press, Oxford), at 59. Generally, see Brodie, 'The Heart of the Matter: Mutual Trust and Confidence', 25 *ILJ* (1996), 121; Brodie, 'Mutual Trust and Confidence: Catalysts, Constraints and Commonality', 37 *ILJ* (2008), 329; Bolger and Ryan, 'The Mutual Duty of Fidelity in the Contract of Employment: Significant Recent Developments', 4(4) *IELJ* (2007), 112; Maguire, 'Implied Terms and Conditions and the Contract of Employment', 1(5) *IELJ* (2004), 146; Redmond, 'The Implied Obligation of Mutual Trust and Confidence – A Common Law Action for "Unfair" Dismissal?', 6(2) *IELJ* (2009), 36.
229. See Chapter 21.
230. For more detailed discussion see Chapter 19.
231. [1981] ICR 666. The appeal to the Court of Appeal ([1982] ICR 693) is not relevant for this point.
232. [1981] ICR 666, 670–671.

[4–101]   In *Malik v BCCI*,[233] it was held that the employee was entitled to 'stigma damages' due to the damage caused to his professional reputation by his employer's fraudulent conduct. The employer's behavior was deemed to be in breach of the implied term of 'mutual trust and confidence' and the employee was entitled to damages where he struggled to find alternative work because of the damage to his reputation.[234] In *French v Barclays Bank Plc*,[235] an employee was required to move to a different location and was offered a loan by the company to assist in the move. However, when the employee had difficulty in finding a buyer for his house, the offer was withdrawn. As a consequence, the employee's need to sell his house became more urgent and he sold it at a lower price. It was held that the employer's actions in granting the loan and then withdrawing it after the employee had acted in reliance on the arrangement was in breach of the mutual duty of trust and confidence.

[4–102]   The Irish High Court has confirmed that the specific manner by which an employee is treated by an employer can give rise to a breach of contract based on the mutual duty of trust and confidence.[236] In *Berber v Dunnes Stores Ltd.*,[237] the plaintiff had been employed for 21 years by the defendant. He suffered from Crohn's Disease since his teens and his employer was aware of the condition. The plaintiff had worked his way up in the defendant's company to the position of buyer.

[4–103]   In 2000 he noticed a perceptible change in management's attitude towards him. In that year he did not travel abroad on as many business trips and he noticed an increased interest in his health from his employers. At this stage he was asked by the managing director to report his condition to the defendant's HR department. In October 2000, the plaintiff was informed that he was being transferred from his role as buyer to that of department manager. The plaintiff saw this as a demotion and demanded a meeting with the managing director. The managing director informed him that he was to take a change of career within the company. It was proposed that he be 'fast tracked' through training in order to become a store manager in the company's flagship store in the Blanchardstown shopping centre. He was to begin work in the ladies wear department. However, he was later informed by a Mr. McNiffe, the store operations' manager for the Blanchardstown branch, that he was to report to work in the homes ware department. The plaintiff was upset at this change to the agreement that he believed he had with the managing director. He refused to go to work in Blanchardstown until he spoke with the managing director. Following a number of meetings with Mr. McNiffe, the plaintiff was suspended with pay. In response, the plaintiff's solicitors explained in writing to the defendant that the plaintiff was not acting unreasonably and

---

233. [1998] AC 20, [1997] ICR 606, [1997] IRLR 462.
234. This decision was expressly approved by the Irish High Court in *Cronin v Eircom Ltd.* [2006] IEHC 380, [2007] 3 IR 104, [2007] ELR 84.
235. [1998] IRLR 646.
236. See also *Cronin v Eircom Ltd.* [2006] IEHC 380, [2007] 3 IR 104, [2007] ELR 84.
237. [2006] IEHC 327, [2007] ELR 1.

simply wanted to speak to the managing director regarding the move. The plaintiff's solicitors also informed the defendant that the stress from the incident caused him to become ill. The plaintiff eventually reported for work in Blanchardstown, but worked very little time there because of ill health. Eventually, after a row with the store manager, the plaintiff wrote to Mr. McNiffe, claiming that his behaviour and that of the company generally amounted to a repudiation of his contract of employment and that he was treating it as at an end. He referred to the medical advice he had been given that he should cease to work in that environment immediately. Laffoy J upheld the plaintiff's claim for breach of contract stating that:

> The manner in which the defendant dealt with the plaintiff in the knowledge of the precarious nature of his physical and psychological health viewed objectively amounted to aggressive conduct. It was likely to seriously damage the employer/ employee relationship and it did so. Accordingly, the defendant breached its obligation to maintain the plaintiff's trust and confidence.[238]

Although the Supreme Court allowed the employer's appeal in *Berber*,[239] this does not affect the statements of law made by Laffoy J in this regard, which remain intact.

[4–104] Other examples of behaviour that has amounted to a breach of the term of mutual trust and confidence include situations where an employer criticised managers in front of junior staff,[240] required an employee to submit to a psychiatric examination before allowing him to return to work after suspension when no good reason existed for such an examination,[241] used foul and abusive language regularly towards staff,[242] or punished a staff member arbitrarily by refusing to treat him in the same manner as other employees by not giving him a pay rise that others received.[243]

4.2.6. Duty of Fidelity
[4–105] An employee is obliged to act faithfully towards his employer. Much like the duty of trust and confidence, this is a difficult concept to pin down. Smith and Thomas have described the term as: 'An act which is inconsistent with the terms of the contract, express or implied, and which is injurious to the employer and his interest will amount to a breach of the duty of faithful service.'[244] The implied

238. [2007] ELR 1, 17.
239. [2009] IESC 10, [2009] ELR 61. For analysis, see Cox and Ryan, 'Bullying, Harassment and Stress at Work: The Implications of the Supreme Court Decisions in *Quigley* and *Berber*', 1 *Employment Law Review* (2009), 17.
240. *Associated Tyre Specialists (Eastern) Ltd. v Waterhouse* [1977] ICR 218, [1976] IRLR 386.
241. *Bliss v South East Thames Regional Health Authority* [1987] ICR 700.
242. *Horkulak v Cantor Fitzgerald Internationale* [2003] IRLR 756.
243. *Gardner v Beresford* [1978] IRLR 63.
244. Smith and Thomas, *Smith & Wood's Employment Law* (9th ed., Oxford University Press, 2008), at p.165.

duty of fidelity encapsulates a number of obligations, the most common of which relate to secret profits, misconduct, competition and confidential information.

(a) Secret Profits

[4–106] The implied duty of fidelity places an obligation on the employee not to make a secret profit as a result of his or her position as an employee, and to account for such profits to the employer where they are made. To do otherwise would amount to a fundamental breach of the contract of employment. In *Boston Deep Sea Fishing and Ice Co v Ansell*,[245] the defendant was the managing director of the plaintiff company. He entered into contracts on behalf of the company for the supply of ships. He received a commission from the shipbuilding company for this contract, of which his employer was not aware. The plaintiff also had a shareholding in a company that supplied ice to his employer. He received a bonus as a shareholder for these sales. The defendant's subsequent dismissal was deemed to be lawful as he had been in breach of his implied duty to act faithfully towards his employer. While the defendant employee in this case was also a director and therefore also owed a fiduciary duty to the company, it would seem that the principle would also apply to 'ordinary' employees.[246]

(b) Misconduct

[4–107] The employment relationship is not a fiduciary one and there is no obligation on an employee to declare to an employer his misdeeds that might have an effect on the employer or the employment relationship.[247] While it would appear that there is no obligation on an employee to declare the misconduct of his fellow employees, there has been some doubt cast on that principle by the decision in *Sybron Corporation v Rochem Ltd*.[248] In that case, the employee was a manager of the company's European operations. It was discovered by the company that the manager, with other employees of the company, had been defrauding the company. The Court of Appeal held that the manager, particularly given his senior position within the company, had a duty to reveal the wrongdoing of his fellow employees. It could be argued that the obligation to inform on fellow employees, however, is an obligation that will only be imposed on those employees who hold senior management positions.

(c) Competition

[4–108] During the course of his or her employment it is not unlawful for an employee to enter into competition with his or her employer. Where the employer does not expressly provide for a term in the contract that restricts the employee from competing, the employer may rely on an implied obligation on the employee

---

245. (1888) 39 Ch. D 339.
246. *Sinclair v Neighbour* [1967] 2 QB 279.
247. *Bell v Lever Bros* [1932] AC 161, [1931] All ER 1.
248. [1983] 2 All ER 707, [1983] IRLR 253.

not to do so. In *Nova Plastics Ltd. v Froggatt*,[249] the employee was employed as a handyman. During his time off he worked for a rival employer. The employee was not in breach of his contract as the work he was doing was so routine it could not, without evidence, be considered to have caused damage to his employer.

Thus, if such an implied term is to be successfully relied upon it must be estab- [4–109] lished that the employee's activities have caused harm to his employer. In *Hivac v Park Royal Scientific Instruments Ltd.*,[250] two skilled employees who worked on the manufacture of hearing aids also did similar work for a competitor of the employer. Given the highly skilled nature and importance of the work, it was held that it was capable of harming their employer's business and amounted to a breach of their duty of fidelity. Lord Greene MR rationalised the decision as follows:

> It would be most unfortunate if anything we said should place an undue restraint on the right of the workman, particularly a manual workman, to make use of his leisure for his profit. On the other hand, it would be deplorable if it were laid down that a workman could, consistently with his duty to his employer, know- ingly, deliberately and secretly set himself to do in his spare time something which would inflict great harm on his master's business.[251]

Simply forming an intention to set up in competition does not amount to breach [4–110] of the duty of fidelity.[252] However, acting on those intentions by misusing the employer's trade connections or confidential information will amount to a breach of the duty of fidelity. In *Wessex Dairies Ltd. v Smith*,[253] an employee was lawfully dismissed when, on his last day at work as a milkman, he asked the customers to give him their business. Similarly, in *Robb v Green*[254] the copying of the employer's customer list with the intention of soliciting those customers after he set his own business in competition was held to be a breach of the duty of fidelity.

(d) Confidential Information

We have earlier considered the efficacy of express terms in contracts restraining [4–111] the employee's ability to compete with his or her employer at the expiration of his or her contract of employment. Beyond such express clauses, the implied duty of fidelity also prohibits the misuse and unauthorised disclosure of confiden- tial information. However, an employer seeking protection of such information would be well advised to include an express provision dealing with same in the contract of employment.

249. [1982] IRLR 146.
250. [1946] 1 All ER 350.
251. *ibid.*, at 356.
252. *Laughton & Hawley v Bapp Industrial Supplies* [1986] ICR 634, [1986] IRLR 245.
253. *Wessex Dairies Ltd. v Smith* [1935] 2 KB 80.
254. [1895] 2 QB 315.

[4–112] The extent of the implied duty is difficult to measure. In particular, the courts have grappled with the issue as to what kind of information can be deemed to be confidential and subject to protection. In *Faccenda Chicken Ltd. v Fowler*,[255] the respondent was a manager employed by the appellant, who was in the business of selling chickens. The respondent left his employment and set up a competing business to that of the appellant. A number of the appellant's staff also left to join the respondent's business. The majority of the respondent's customers had been customers of the appellant. The appellant alleged that the respondent had breached his contract of employment by using confidential information relating to his customers to the disadvantage of his former employer. In dismissing the claim, the Court of Appeal classified confidential information as being of two types: that which is of such a highly confidential nature (trade secrets) that the employee could be prevented from disclosing it even after the employment relationship has been terminated, and that which, if disclosed during the course of the employment relationship would be in breach of the implied duty of fidelity, but after an employee's employment has ended, he or she could not be restrained by an implied term from disclosing or using that information. An express covenant in the contract of employment would be necessary if one were to prevent the employee from disclosing this 'less confidential' information. In order to determine whether information fell within the first, better protected category, the Court highlighted the following factors as being relevant:

(a) the nature of the employment;
(b) the nature of the information itself;
(c) whether the employer impressed on the employee the confidentiality of the information; and
(d) whether the information can easily be isolated from other information the employee is free to use or disclose.

[4–113] The appellant argued *inter alia* that the respondent used information on pricing that constituted a 'trade secret' and was therefore deserving of the greatest protection by the implied term. The Court rejected the claim on the following basis:

(1) The sales information contained some material that Faccenda conceded was not confidential if looked at in isolation.
(2) The information about the prices was not clearly severable from the rest of the sales information.
(3) Neither the sales information in general, nor the information about the prices in particular, though of some value to a competitor, could reasonably be regarded as plainly secret or sensitive.
(4) The sales information, including the information about prices, was necessarily acquired by the respondents in order that they could do their work. Moreover, as the judge observed in the course of his judgment,

---

255. [1987] Ch. 117, [1986] 3 WLR 288, [1986] 1 All ER 617, [1986] ICR 297, [1986] IRLR 69.

each salesman could quickly commit the whole of the sales information relating to his own area to memory.

(5) The sales information was generally known among the van drivers who were employees, as were the secretaries, at quite a junior level. This was not a case where the relevant information was restricted to senior management or to confidential staff.

(6) There was no evidence that Faccenda had ever given any express instructions that the sales information or the information about prices was to be treated as confidential.

Thus the courts will more readily impose a duty not to disclose confidential information on an employee during their employment with the employer, for example copying a list of the employer's customers before leaving the employment,[256] or soliciting customers of the employer while still employed by him.[257]

4.2.7. *Duty to Obey Lawful and Reasonable Orders*

It is one of the employee's fundamental duties that [s]he obeys his or her employer's lawful and reasonable orders. This obligation is considered so fundamental to the contract of employment that the employee's failure to do so can amount to a repudiatory breach, which entitles the employer to terminate the contract of employment.[258] Lord Evershed MR in *Laws v London Chronicle Ltd.*[259] described the importance of the obligation thus:

> wilful disobedience of a lawful and reasonable order shows a disregard... of a condition essential to the contract of service, namely the condition that the servant must obey the proper orders of the master, and that unless he does so the relationship is, so to speak, struck at fundamentally.[260]

To amount to an act of repudiation, the refusal to obey the orders must be such that it shows that the employee is repudiating the contract, is willful, and connotes 'a deliberate flouting of the essential contractual conditions'.[261] It can be difficult to define what level of disobedience amounts to a misconduct of such a nature that justifies the termination of the contract of employment. Generally, if the disobedience is a once-off and not extremely serious in nature, it cannot justify dismissal.[262] However, where the willful disobedience is the 'last straw' in a series of incidents of poor conduct, dismissal may be justified.[263]

[4–114]

[4–115]

---

256. *Robb v Green* [1895] 2 QB 315.
257. *Wessex Dairies Ltd. v Smith* [1935] 2 KB 80.
258. *Pepper v Webb* [1969] 1 WLR 514, [1969] 2 All ER 216.
259. [1959] 1 WLR 698, [1959] 2 All ER 285.
260. [1959] 1 WLR 698, 700.
261. [1959] 1 WLR 698, 701.
262. *Laws v London Chronicle Ltd.* [1959] 1 WLR 698, [1959] 2 All ER 285.
263. *Pepper v Webb* [1969] 1 WLR 514, [1969] 2 All ER 216.

[4–116] The duty does not extend to requiring the employee to complete an illegal act. In *Morrish v Henlys (Folkstone) Ltd.*,[264] an employee's dismissal because he would not falsify accounts was held to be unfair. Furthermore, if the orders are deemed unreasonable, the employee may be justified in refusing to obey them. In *Ottoman Bank v Chakarian*,[265] an employee refused to obey his employer's order to remain in Constantinople because he had been previously sentenced to death there. However, the refusal to obey must be reasonable and a general or vague fear will not justify a refusal. Thus, in *Walmsley v UDEC Refrigeration Ltd.*,[266] an employee's refusal to move to work in Co. Wexford on the basis that it was an area known for IRA activity was deemed unreasonable. The claim was too vague and unspecific to justify his refusal to obey the order.

4.2.8. Duty to Adhere to Natural Justice and Fair Procedures

[4–117] The contract of employment shall contain an implied term that the employer is obliged to follow natural justice and fair procedures in his or her dealings with the employee. In *Re Haughey*,[267] the Supreme Court held that the right to fair procedures was among the personal rights guaranteed under Art. 40.3 of the Constitution. Moreover, the Supreme Court decision in *Glover v BLN Ltd.*[268] provided that such a term places procedural and substantive limitations on the employer's right to dismiss. The disciplinary process and the attendant right to fair procedures are discussed in greater detail in Chapter 18.

4.3. Terms Implied by Statute

[4–118] The plethora of protective employment legislation that has been enacted over the past 35 years would count for very little if employers could simply contract out of its provisions. Thus statute can imply terms into contracts of employment irrespective of the intentions of the parties. The manner in which various employment statutes imply entitlements into contracts of employment is considered throughout this chapter.

4.4. Terms Implied by Custom and Practice

[4–119] If a contract is entered into by the parties involved in a particular industry, terms may be implied into that contract of employment in order to give effect to the custom and practice of that industry. Thus in *O'Conaill v Gaelic Echo*,[269] a term was implied into a journalist's contract of employment that he would receive holiday pay on the basis of evidence that holiday pay for journalist was customary in Dublin. In order for a term to be implied in this manner, the custom must be relatively obvious in that anyone enquiring about it would be informed of its existence.

---

264. [1973] 2 All ER 137, [1973] ICR 482, [1973] IRLR 61.
265. [1930] AC 277.
266. [1972] IRLR 80.
267. [1971] IR 217.
268. [1973] IR 388.
269. (1958) 92 ILTR 156.

5. Illegality

An illegal contract is one that is created or is to be performed in a manner that is [4–120] contrary either to legislation or to the common law. Such agreements may be struck down as being contrary to public policy and declared void.[270] In the employment context, the consequences of declaring a contract illegal can be severe. As the basis of the relationship between the parties is the contract of employment and much of the protective legislation is only applicable to employees, a determination of illegality could deprive that employee of his or her statutory rights. In *Tomlinson v Dick Evans 'U' Drive*,[271] it was held that, 'the rights, though creatures of statute, in our judgement depend on, or arise from the contract'.[272]

Notwithstanding this complication, the common law has adopted a very strict [4–121] approach to such situations and has continued to hold that, regardless of fault, a contract of employment tainted by illegality must fall. In *Lewis v Squash Ireland*,[273] the manner in which the claimant's contract of employment operated represented a fraud on the Revenue Commissioners. The claimant received £16,000 per annum. However, only £14,000 of this was recorded as salary with the Revenue. In an attempt to reduce its tax liability, the remaining £2,000 was falsely described as 'expenses' in the company's accounts. After the claimant had been dismissed, the Employment Appeals Tribunal declined jurisdiction to hear the claim for unfair dismissal on the basis that:

> It is public policy that Courts and this Tribunal, should not lend themselves to the enforcement of contracts either illegal on their face or in which the intended performance of obligations thereunder was illegal to the knowledge of the party seeking to enforce the contract.[274]

The legislature has sought to ameliorate some of the potential unfairness of the [4–122] common law position in this regard. Thus, s.7 of the Unfair Dismissals (Amendment) Act 1993 now provides that an employee shall be entitled to redress for unfair dismissal under the legislation notwithstanding that the contract of employment in question is in contravention of Income Tax Acts or the Social Welfare Acts. However, where such a contravention has occurred, the relevant tribunal must notify the Revenue Commissioner of the Minister for Social Welfare as appropriate of the situation.[275] Similar legislative provisions have been introduced elsewhere.[276]

---

270. Generally, see McDermott, *Contract Law* (LexisNexis Butterworths, 2001), ch.15.
271. [1978] IRLR 77, [1978] ICR 638.
272. *ibid.*, at 642.
273. [1983] ILRM 363.
274. [1983] ILRM 363, 369.
275. s.8(12) of the Unfair Dismissals (Amendment) Act 1993.
276. For example, s.40(1) National Minimum Wage Act 2000.

6. Variation of Terms

[4–123] Any alteration to the terms of the contract of employment as originally agreed amounts to a variation. In order to vary the terms of the contract both parties must agree to the alteration.[277] Any variation of the original contract must be supported by fresh consideration, although where the contract is executory, the agreement of both parties not to bring an action for breach of contract will be sufficient consideration.[278] The consent to the variation must be informed.[279]

[4–24] There must, moreover, be evidence that the employee consented to the variation. The fact that the employee continued to work for the employer after the unilateral variation is not evidence that the employee consented to the alteration. In *Hill v Peter Gorman Ltd.*,[280] the employee continued to work after his employer had unilaterally reduced the employee's salary by 10 per cent. The Court held that the fact that the employee did not leave could not necessarily lead to the conclusion that the alteration had been accepted. Similarly, in *McCarroll v Hickling Pentecost & Co*,[281] the employee worked as a foreman in a factory. He was demoted to his former position of a machine operator. Whist very unhappy with these developments, the employee worked in his new position for another ten days before resigning. It was held that his decision to remain in employment for the short period between his demotion and his resignation did not indicate that he had acquiesced in the alteration of the terms and conditions of his employment. However, where the employee continues to work for the employer for a substantial period of time after the variation to the contract, [s]he may be taken to have agreed to that change.[282]

[4–123] On the other hand, if the variation does not immediately affect the employee, then the fact that [s]he continues to work cannot be used as evidence that [s]he has consented to the change, even if [s]he continues to do so for a substantial period of time. In *Jones v Associated Tunnelling Co Ltd.*,[283] the employee's contract of employment was altered and a mobility clause was included. Four years later the employer sought to enforce the clause and argued that as the employee had continued to work for a substantial period of time after the alteration the employee had consented to the change. The Court rejected this argument as the employee's consent could not be implied solely on the basis that he had not objected to a

---

277. *Clarke v Kilternan Motor Co* [1996] IEHC 39.
278. *Scott v Midland Great W Rly* (1853) 6 Ir Jur 73.
279. *Cowey v Liberian Operators Ltd.* [1966] 2 Lloyds Rep 42.
280. (1957) 9 DLR (2d) 124.
281. [1971] NI 250.
282. See *Henry v London General Transport Services Ltd.* [2001] EWCA Civ 574, [2002] ICR 910, [2002] IRLR 472, CA, where the Court of Appeal of England and Wales held that employees who operated a new rota system for two years were held to have consented to the variation in their terms and conditions of employment.
283. [1981] IRLR 477.

clause at the time it was introduced when it had not had immediate effect on him at that point.

An employer may include an express term in the contract of employment that allows him the flexibility unilaterally to alter that contract. Such a clause will be interpreted reasonably[284] and will be construed strictly against the employer.[285]

Difficulties can arise where the employer seeks unilaterally to alter the terms of the contract. A very significant development in this regard is the judgment of the High Court in *Finnegan v J & E Davy*,[286] a decision that is at the time of writing understood to be under appeal to the Supreme Court.[287] This widely discussed ruling has important implications for restraint of trade issues.[288] It also marks the first significant Irish contribution to a growing line of case law, principally from the English courts, concerning the exercise of discretion by employers in awarding, and arriving at the amount of, bonus payments.[289]   [4–126]

The plaintiff was a stockbroker who sued his former employer for €260,000 in deferred bonus payments earned in 1998 and 1999. The plaintiff worked for Davy between 1990 and 2000. His bonuses were tied to the firm's profitability and his own performance, with the amounts being decided at a yearly meeting with his superiors, where his performance was assessed. He did not receive a bonus in 1992, but in every other year between 1990 and 1997, he earned bonuses of between £3,000 and £30,000. The entire sum was paid shortly after the annual review.   [4–127]

In 1997, the firm began deferring part of the payments. The timeline of events here is significant. At the beginning of 1998, it was agreed that the plaintiff's bonus for 1997 would be £100,000. He was paid £60,000 immediately, but £40,000 was deferred for a year. Its payment was conditional on his remaining with the firm. The plaintiff objected to this, particularly the condition that he stay with the company, but was told that Davy's biggest shareholder, Bank of Ireland, stipulated that bonuses be paid in this way. It was, however, agreed that he would receive the interest earned on the money. A year later, his bonus for 1998 was set at £200,000, payable in three installments, the first immediately, the second a year later and the third a year after that. His 1999 bonus was fixed at £210,000, payable in three equal installments over two years. All deferred payments depended on his remaining with the company. The plaintiff left Davy to join a rival firm in September 2000. As a result, he did not receive one installment of his 1998 bonus and two-thirds   [4–128]

---

284. *BBC v Beckett* [1983] IRLR 43.
285. *Lister v Fram Gerrard Ltd.* [1973] ITR 610.
286. [2007] IEHC 18, [2007] ELR 234.
287. Appeal lodged 15 March 2007.
288. See, for example, Ennis, 'An Examination of the Law on Restraint of Trade and Discretionary Bonus Schemes in the Light of *Finnegan v J & E Davy*', 4(1) *IELJ* (2007), 9.
289. For detailed treatment of this line of case law, see Ryan and Ryan, 'Bonus Points: Employers' Discretion in the Determination of Bonus Payments', 14(8) *CLP* (2007), 166.

of his 1999 payment, a total equivalent to just over €260,000. He argued that the attempt to change the terms of the bonus payment scheme was:

1. a unilateral attempt by the defendant to alter the terms of the employment contract, which was not accepted by the plaintiff and which was ineffective;
2. in breach of the employment contract as being an irrational exercise of the employer's discretion; and
3. an unenforceable term as being in restraint of trade.

[4–129] On behalf of the defendant employer, it was argued that such a deferred payment scheme was a legitimate means of 'incentivising' employees and an attempt to generate loyalty. For present purposes, then, the question of whether the duty of fidelity of the employee could be invoked by the employer to justify its approach to the bonus scheme in this case, is relevant. Smyth J. emphatically rejected the argument that the deferral acted to 'incentivise' employees and instead found as a fact that the real reason for the deferral was 'to create a financial and practical restriction on employees who wished to continue to act as stockbrokers going to another firm of stockbrokers'.[290]

[4–130] The plaintiff argued that in circumstances where bonus payments were calculated by reference to profitability of the firm in a calendar year and the individual performance of the plaintiff during that year, it was arbitrary and irrational to seek to make the payment of that bonus conditional upon the plaintiff remaining in the employment of the defendant for the following two years. The effect of this stipulation would be to change the criteria for the awarding of the bonus from one of profitability and performance to one of loyalty in the future. Smyth J accepted this argument and deemed the provision, which amounted to a restraint of trade, to constitute an improper exercise of discretion. Another significant finding of fact in this regard was that those employees who left the firm when outstanding elements of bonuses were unpaid, but who did not go into competition, were paid the outstanding monies. This finding of fact supported the conclusion that if the deferral provision was part of a contract it was part of a contract in restraint of trade.

[4–131] In terms of the broader implications of this ruling, it is significant that the unilateral attempt at alteration by the employer was regarded by the Court as particularly objectionable. As Smyth J observed, such a unilateral decision could 'hardly constitute the proper exercise of a discretion as to the level of bonus to which the plaintiff was entitled and his entitlement to receive it when ascertained and declared'.[291] This passage illustrates the danger of taking decisions without properly consulting and informing employees, an approach that attracts criticism for

---

290. [2007] ELR 234, 240.
291. [2007] ELR 234, 241.

its failure to involve an employee in decision-making connected to the contractual agreement between the parties. This theme is strongly in evidence in the judgment of Smyth J in *Finnegan*, most notably in the acceptance of the counsel's description of the employer's conduct in the case as 'somewhat Dickensian for not only had Mr. Finnegan, like Oliver Twist in effect to say *'Please, Sir, may I have some more?'*; he also had to make a case as to why he should get more, but unlike Bob Cratchit Mr. Finnegan could not and would not be patronised'.[292]

6.1. Variation in Work Practices

Having signed a contract of employment, it is not reasonable for the employee to [4–132] expect that the manner in which [s]he does his work will never change without his or her consent. Employers must be allowed, within reason, to update work processes and change the way the work is done in order that they may reduce costs or become more efficient. Thus, while an employer is not entitled unilaterally to alter the core terms of the contract of employment, [s]he can make changes to work practices that have developed over time or through custom, but do not have contractual status. In *Cresswell v Board of Inland Revenue,*[293] the Court was required to deal with the differentiation between the two. In that case, the employees worked for the UK Inland Revenue administrating the PAYE tax scheme. The scheme was administered manually but was updated and computerised. The employees refused to operate the new system on the basis that it was outside the express terms of their contracts of employment. In response, the employer suspended the employees' pay until such time as they agreed to operate the new system. The Court held that the employer's request did not so alter the job functions of the relevant employees as outlined in their contracts of employment that they fell outside that original description. The Court concluded that:

> After computerisation of the PAYE scheme each of jobs in question was the same as it was before though in part done in a different way. Computerisation merely introduced up-to-date methods for dealing with bulk problems. Though there may have been some loss of job satisfaction on the part of the employees concerned that was regrettable but by itself provided no cause of action.[294]

The difference between contractual terms (which cannot be unilaterally altered) [4–133] and work practices (which can be unilaterally altered) was examined by the Irish courts in *Kenny v An Post*.[295] In that case, the employees, who were postal sorters, reached an agreement with their supervisor in 1969 where it was agreed that they could take a 15-minute paid rest break. In 1983, An Post decided to remove this break. The question arose as to whether the agreement in 1969 could be elevated

---

292. [2007] ELR 234, 238.
293. [1984] 2 All ER 713, [1984] ICR 508, [1984] IRLR 190.
294. [1984] IRLR 190, 191.
295. [1988] IR 285.

to contractual status; if so An Post's attempts at its removal would be deemed a unilateral variation and would amount to a breach of contract. In examining this issue, the Court noted that the 1969 arrangement had never been the subject of a formal written agreement between the employer and the employees or their representatives. Furthermore, notice of the arrangement never went higher than the supervisor, and the Department of Posts and Telegraphs (as it then was) never sanctioned it. Ultimately, O'Hanlon J determined that the 1969 arrangement was a work practice that did not have contractual effect. He observed:

> [I]t is not clear to me that when the Act refers to 'conditions of service' it includes within its ambit conditions of service which were not legally enforceable as terms of the contract of employment, but were merely customs and usages practiced in a particular section. On the view I have taken of the arrangement… the work practice in question was one which the employer was entitled to terminate unilaterally at any time… without being involved in any breach of the contractual rights of the workers.[296]

[4–134]   More recently, in *Rafferty v Bus Éireann*,[297] the Irish courts were asked once again to consider the distinction between work practices and contractual terms. In that case, the plaintiff and his colleagues were bus drivers for the defendant company. Their employer sought to make certain changes to their rostering arrangements, abolish certain duties, and replace them with others. The employer justified these changes on the basis that they were necessary as a cost-saving exercise as the company was in serious financial difficulties. Whilst acknowledging that these proposals required the plaintiffs to undertake duties they had not been previously required to do, their jobs ultimately remained the same – they were drivers. They did not involve changes to key issues such as rates of pay, length of holidays, sick leave or pension rights. The High Court concluded that these changes were ones that involved work practices rather than changes in conditions of service, which the employer was entitled to unilaterally alter.

296.[1988] 1 IR 285, 289.
297.[1996] IEHC 33, [1997] 2 IR 424.

CHAPTER 5

Employment Permits

Introduction

Unsurprisingly, there is a good deal of law in place dealing specifically with the position of foreign nationals[1] working in Ireland.[2] Thus, most obviously, EC law is, in large part, devoted to ensuring that there is a genuine ability of workers within the territory of the EU to travel within the EU providing services and establishing undertakings. Similarly, it is conceivable that the actions of international workers employed by foreign-based multinational companies will raise issues of private international law. These issues are, however, well traversed in EC law and conflicts of laws textbooks and it is not proposed to deal with them in this book. Rather our consideration in this chapter is a specific one, which is of fundamental importance to foreign workers seeking to work in Ireland, namely the rules governing the grant of employment permits, without which a large percentage of such foreign nationals are not permitted to work in this jurisdiction.[3] [5–01]

1. Legislation, Ministerial Regulations and Departmental Schemes

The rules relating to employment permits are, in theory, derived from the parent statutes – the Employment Permits Acts 2003 and 2006 – and regulations made thereunder.[4] Equally, as we shall see, in practice many of the rules, both as to what [5–02]

---

1. A foreign national for the purposes of the Employment Permits Acts 2003 and 2006 is someone who is a non-national (and prior to enactment of s.39 of the 2006 Act, Irish employment permits legislation referred to non-nationals, rather than foreign nationals) for the purposes of the Immigration Act 1999. A non-national for the purposes of this Act is someone who is an alien for the purposes of the Aliens Act 1935 (that is, someone who is not a citizen of Ireland) and to whom an order under s.10 of the 1935 Act does not apply. For present purposes, therefore, it may be taken that the legislation is referring to persons who are not citizens of Ireland

2. See, for example, the consideration in Chapter 14 of the rules relating to the obligations on business that are transnational in nature to provide information to their employees.

3. Generally, see Cashman, 'Migrant Workers and the Law', 2(2) *IELJ* (2005), 40; and Gallagher, 'The Employment Permits Bill 2005: A New Era or More of the Same?', 2 *ELR* (2006), 34.

4. The 2006 Employment Permits Act (which forms the basis for the vast bulk of the law in this

must be done in order to apply for an employment permit, and indeed as to when an employment permit will be granted, are based on policy decisions taken by the Department of Enterprise, Trade and Employment. It may be suggested that the impact of such policy decisions and the various administrative schemes that have been created by the department in fulfilment of such decisions has been so enormous that, in large measure, they have come to represent the law in this area. In this light, and as will be discussed throughout this chapter, it is perhaps a matter of some controversy as to whether it is either appropriate or legitimate that such schemes should be developed without having a basis in ministerial regulations.

1.1. Ministerial Regulations

[5–03] In order properly to assess whether the day-to-day operation of the Department of Enterprise, Trade and Employment in this area is appropriate or even legitimate, it is necessary to consider the approach within the Employment Permits Acts 2003 and 2006 to the question of ministerial regulations.

[5–04] Generally under s.30 of the Employment Permits Act 2006, the Minister is entitled to make regulations in relation to any matter referred to in the Act as prescribed or to be prescribed. There are, moreover, two more specific contexts in which such regulations may be made.

[5–05] First, under s.14 of the Employments Permit Act 2006, the Minister is permitted to make regulations in respect of a number of matters connected with the grant of employment permits. [S]he must, in making such regulations, have regard to a number of factors,[5] namely:

- the qualifications or skills (of employees) that, in the opinion of the Minister, are required for economic and social development and competitiveness in the period to which the regulations concerned will relate[6];
- the economic sector or sectors that, in the opinion of the Minister, will be involved in the achievement of such economic and social development and competitiveness[7];
- the qualifications or skills that, in the opinion of the Minister, are required for the proper functioning of such economic sector or sectors in the relevant period[8]; and
- if, in the opinion of the Minister, there is likely to be, during the relevant period, a shortage or surplus in respect of such qualifications or skills, an

---

area) came into force on 1 January 2007. See Employment Permits Act 2006 (Commencement) Order 2006, SI no. 682 of 2006.

5. The factors in question are listed in s.15(1) Employment Permits Acts 2003 and 2006.

6. s.15(1)(a) *ibid.*

7. s.15(1)(b) *ibid.*

8. s.15(1)(c) *ibid.*

estimate as best the Minister may make (and which estimate the Minister is, by virtue of this section, required to make) of what the extent of that shortage or surplus will be.[9]

Having had regard to these factors, the Minister in dealing with original applications for permits (and where, having regard to the factors mentioned above [s]he considers it appropriate, in dealing with applications for renewal of permits[10]) may make regulations covering the following[11]: [5–06]

- the maximum number of employment permits that may be granted during the appropriate period either generally or in respect of a specified economic sector[12];
- categories of employment (by reference to the economic sector or sectors into which they fall) that may be or may not be the subject of the grant of an employment permit during the appropriate period[13];
- the minimum amount of remuneration (being an amount greater than the national minimum wage) that shall be payable in respect of an employment as a condition for the grant of an employment permit in respect of it[14];
- the qualifications or skills that a foreign national, in respect of whom, or by whom, an application for an employment permit is made during the appropriate period, is required to possess in order for a grant of the permit to be made[15];
- whether (pursuant to s.8(5) of the 2006 Act) it is appropriate to grant an employment permit for longer than the normal two-year period.[16]

As we shall see, a number of these matters appear to be currently dealt with as a matter of departmental schemes without having been prescribed in ministerial regulations. It may be suggested that, in light of the fact that the Act specifically provides that they *should* be dealt with by regulations, this approach is of doubtful legitimacy. [5–07]

Secondly, under s.29 of the Employment Permits Act 2006, the Minister is entitled to make regulations providing for the procedure to be followed when making [5–08]

---

9. s.15(1)(d) *ibid.*
10. s.14(2) *ibid.* The Minister may also make regulations specifying (for the purposes of s.20(3)) that a permit be renewed for longer than three years.
11. For so long as such regulations remain in force, the relevant powers of the Minister under the Act must be exercised subject to and in accordance with such regulations (s.14(3) *ibid.*), to the extent that they override even the application of s.2(11) of the Act in terms of determining whether or not an employment permit should be granted: s.14(4) *ibid.*
12. ss.14(1)(a) and (b) *ibid.*
13. s.14(1)(c) *ibid.*
14. s.14(1)(d) *ibid.*
15. s.14(1)(e) *ibid.*
16. s.14(1)(f) *ibid.*

an application either for an original employment permit or for the renewal of an existing permit.[17] Such procedural matters include *inter alia* the form in which such an application is to be made, the period in which documents or information should be submitted in respect of an application, and the evidence that may be required by the Minister to verify any information or documents submitted to the Minister.[18] Finally, the Minister may make regulations governing the procedure by which submissions are to be made (and accompanying information furnished) where an employee is seeking a review of a decision to refuse an employment permit or to revoke an existing permit.[19]

2. The Obligation to Have an Employment Permit

[5–09] The essence of the law in respect of employment permits is that a foreign national is not permitted either to enter the service of an employer in the State or be in employment in the State,[20] nor is an employer permitted to employ a foreign national[21] except in accordance with an employment permit granted by the Minister for Enterprise, Trade and Employment.[22] Moreover, this applies whether the employment concerned results from the foreign national being directly employed within the State, or being employed by a person outside the State to perform duties in the State as a result of an agreement between the contractor and another person, or as a result of any other arrangement.[23] It is an offence for a foreign national to work without an employment permit, or for someone to employ such foreign national to work without a permit.[24]

2.1. To Whom Do these Obligations Apply?

[5–10] Quite obviously, these general obligations under the legislation could not validly apply to *all* non-Irish workers seeking to work in Ireland, not least because this would represent a clear violation of EC law. To this extent, provision is made in

---

17. s.29(1) *ibid.*
18. s.29(2) *ibid.*
19. s.29(3) *ibid.*
20. s.2(1) *ibid.*
21. s.2(2) *ibid.*
22. In addition, where one person (A) enters into an agreement with another (B), whereby B agrees to cause or arrange for services to be rendered on behalf of A and in circumstances where either as a result of custom within the relevant trade or by reason of the circumstances in which the agreement is entered into it must have been in the contemplation of the parties that this will involve services being rendered by persons employed by a third party, it becomes the responsibility of A to take all reasonable steps to ensure that all such persons if they are foreign nationals are employed in accordance with an employment permit: s.2(2A) and s.2(2B) *ibid.*
23. s.2(1A) *ibid.*
24. s.2(3) *ibid.* It is also an offence to fail to take the steps prescribed in s.2(2B) above.

the legislation for various categories of non-Irish worker to whom the legislation does not apply:

- a person in respect of whom a declaration under s.17 of the Refugee Act 1996 is in force[25];
- a person entitled to enter the State pursuant to either s.18[26] or s.24[27] of the Refugee Act 1996[28];
- a person who is entitled to enter the State and be employed there pursuant to the treaties governing the European Communities[29];
- a person who is permitted to remain in the State by the Minister for Justice, Equality and Law Reform and who is employed in the State without an employment permit pursuant to a condition of that permission[30]
- a person who is a national of the Czech Republic, Republic of Estonia, Republic of Latvia, Republic of Lithuania, Republic of Hungary, Republic of Poland, Republic of Slovenia, and Slovak Republic,[31] being States which became Member States of the European Union after the passing of the Employment Permits Act 2003 and to which Articles 1–6 of Council Regulation (EEC) no. 1612/68 of 15 October 1968 on freedom of movement of workers within the Community do not apply in accordance with the Treaty of Accession.[32] In respect of this last category of exempted workers, it is further provided that during the transitional period of membership for those States (as defined in the relevant Treaty of Accession with that State) and if, in the opinion of the Minister, the Labour Market is experiencing a disturbance,[33] then [s]he may make an

---

25. s.2(10)(a) *ibid.* A declaration under s.17 of the Refugee Act 1996 is essentially a declaration that a person is a refugee as defined by the Act. The entitlement under s.2(10)(a) of the Employment Permits Acts 2003 and 2006 mirrors the general entitlement in s.3(2)(a)(i) of the Refugee Act 1996 of a refugee to seek and enter employment, to carry on any business, trade or profession, and to have access to education and training in the State in a like manner and to a like extent in all respects of an Irish citizen.

26. Under s.18 of the Refugee Act 1996 and on the application by a refugee, the Minister may permit a family member of the refugee to enter the State.

27. Section 24 of the Refugee Act 1996 refers to 'programme refugees', that is, a person to whom leave to enter and remain in the State for temporary protection or resettlement as part of a group of persons has been given by the government, and whose name is entered in a register established and maintained by the Minister for Foreign Affairs, whether or not such person is a refugee within the meaning of the definition of 'refugee' in the 1996 Act.

28. s.2(10)(b) Employment Permits Acts 2003 and 2006.

29. s.2(10)(c) *ibid.*

30. s.2(10)(d) *ibid.*

31. Although there is no specific provision in the legislation in this regard, the Department of Enterprise Trade and Employment has confirmed (in a telephone conversation with the authors) that workers from Cyprus and Malta do not require employment permits.

32. ss.3(1) and (2) *ibid.*

33. The concepts of 'disturbance' and 'labour market' are to be construed in accordance with the relevant Treaty of Accession.

order[34] providing that the general requirements in relation to employment periods will apply for a specified period or periods.[35] Equally such
an order cannot apply to a worker from such States who has been in
remunerated employment in the State for a period of not less than six
weeks immediately before the commencement of the order.[36]

2.1.1. The Case of Romania and Bulgaria

[5–11] In accordance with the general Irish approach to the relevant accession agreements, it is provided that the requirement to obtain an employment permit *does*
apply to a foreign national who is a national either of Romania or the Republic
of Bulgaria[37] and even after the date of accession of these States to the European Union.[38] It is further provided in respect of Romania and Bulgaria that the
Minister *may* make an order providing that the general requirements to obtain
employment permits under s.2 do not apply to nationals of these States for the
duration of such an order,[39] but may only do so if, in his or her opinion, this is
desirable in the interests of the proper functioning of the economy and if employment is likely to become available on a continuous basis for such nationals in the
24-month period following the making of the order.[40] Given that the five-year
transitional period in respect of Romania and Bulgaria is coming to an end, and
also that, at the time of writing, it would appear that Ireland is facing into a period
of serious unemployment that is likely to continue for the duration of the transitional period, it seems inconceivable that such an order will ever now be made.[41] It

---

34. Such order may be amended or revoked: s.3(5) Employment Permits Acts 2003 and 2006.
35. s.3(3) *ibid.* Where such an order is made, the Minister, in determining which applications
for employment permits should be granted, is obliged to give preference to applications
from nationals of a State in respect of which an order of this kind is in force.
36. s.3(4) *ibid.*
37. Under s.2A(1) *ibid.* it is provided that s.2 does not apply to nationals of Bulgaria or Romania,
who fall within the second or third sub-paragraph of para.2 of Annex VI of the Treaty of
Accession with Bulgaria or Romania, or to a person of any nationality falling within para.8
of Annex VI. In fact, Annex VI only refers to the position in respect of Bulgaria. Thus,
paras.2(2) and (3) relate to workers who have been working in a Member State for 12 months
either at or following the date of accession of Bulgaria, and para.8 makes provision in respect
of spouses and dependents of workers. It is Annex VII of the Treaty of Accession that makes
equivalent provision for workers from Romania, but this is not mentioned in s.2A of the
2003 and 2006 Acts.
38. s.2(10) Employment Permits Acts 2003 and 2006. The general application of s.2 to citizens
of Romania and Bulgaria continues for a period of five years from the accession date for
these states or, where an order made under s.3A (considered below) is revoked by a subsequent order, made either at the end of, or within two months before the end of, that five-
year period, then for a period of seven years from the date of accession: s.2A(2) *ibid.*
39. s.3A(1) *ibid.*
40. s.3A(2) *ibid.*
41. Under s.2A(3) *ibid.* an order of this kind may be revoked by a subsequent order, which may
only be made where the Minister is of the view that the labour market is experiencing or is
likely to experience a disturbance. Should such a second order be made, it does not apply to a

is notable that at the end of 2008, the government announced that from 1 January 2009 it would continue to restrict access to the Irish labour market for nationals of Bulgaria and Romania, but that the system would be comprehensively reviewed before the end of 2011.[42]

Finally, however, in determining which applications for employment permits [5–12] should be granted, the Minister *is* required to give priority *inter alia* to applications from nationals of Bulgaria and Romania to whom the general obligations under the legislation currently apply.[43]

3. Applications for an Employment Permit

Under the 2003 and 2006 Acts, an application for an employment permit[44] may [5–13] be made either by a person proposing to employ a foreign national or by the foreign national him or herself,[45] with the one caveat that the foreign national him or herself may only make such an application if an offer of employment in the State has been made in writing to him or her within 60 days before the date of the making of the application.[46] In either instance, however, the application for the employment permit must be expressed to be an application for the grant of such a permit *to the foreign national concerned*, and, if granted, it is granted to the foreign national concerned (rather than to his or her employer).[47] Moreover, in both cases, the employer of the foreign national (whether or not the employer is the applicant for the permit) is prohibited from making any deductions from the remuneration of the foreign national employee or charging him or her any fee or expense arising out of the application for the permit (or the application to renew an existing permit), the recruitment of the permit holder or indeed any amount previously paid to the permit holder in respect of any travelling expenses incurred in connection with taking up employment in the State.[48]

Bulgarian or Romanian national who has been employed in the State for a period of not less than six weeks immediately before the commencement of this second order.

42. For a statement of the current position in respect of Bulgarian and Romanian workers, see http://www.entemp.ie/publications/labour/2008/emppermitinformation-bulgarians-nov2008.pdf and http://www.entemp.ie/publications/labour/2008/emppermitinformation-romanians-nov2008.pdf.

43. s.2(11) Employment Permits Acts 2003 and 2006.

44. An application for such a permit must be in writing and accompanied by the appropriate fee as contained in the Employment Permits Act 2006 (Prescribed Fees and Miscellaneous Procedures) Regulations 2006, SI no. 683 of 2006: s.5(2) *ibid.*

45. s.4(1) Employment Permits Acts 2003 and 2006. In the case of the arrangement under s.2(1)(A) referred to above, application may either be made by the contractor referred to in the section or any person who is party to the relevant arrangement: s.4(2) *ibid.*

46. s.4(3) *ibid.* and para.7 Employment Permits Act 2006 (Prescribed Fees and Miscellaneous Procedures) Regulations 2006, SI no. 683 of 2006.

47. s.5(1) Employment Permits Acts 2003 and 2006.

48. ss.23(1) and (2) *ibid.*

[5–14] Where the application is made by a proposed employer of the foreign national and is successful, the employer is required to retain a record of the employment for the duration of the period of employment as also is the employer of a foreign national who has successfully applied for a work permit on his or her own behalf.[49] Such records as may be prescribed must be retained[50] (and must be available for inspection by an authorised officer[51]) for a period of five years or, where the foreign national is employed for longer than five years by the employer, for the period of his or her employment.[52] On the other hand, the employer is prohibited from retaining any personal document belonging to the permit holder, including a passport, driving licence, document relating to an account held by a financial institution, travel document or document relating to the skills, experience and qualifications of the permit holder.[53]

3.1. Contents of an Application for an Employment Permit
[5–15] The contents of an application (which must be accompanied by the relevant fee[54]) for an employment permit vary depending on whether the application is to be made by a putative employer of a foreign national or directly by the foreign national him or herself.

3.1.1. An Application Made on Behalf of a Foreign Worker
[5–16] In the former case, the application must do the following:

- provide a full and accurate description of the employment in respect of which the application is made (the 'employment concerned') and the terms and conditions, including the hours of work in each week, of the employment and the duration of the employment[55];

---

49. ss.27(1) and (2) *ibid*. Where the foreign national has applied for an employment permit on his or her own behalf it is necessary to keep a record of the employment [s]he performs, the duration of the employment and the particulars of the permit.
50. Specifically, it is necessary to retain records concerning the remuneration paid to the foreign national, records concerning the trade or business to which the relevant employment relates, and, if more than one foreign national is employed by the relevant employer, records of the number of foreign nationals employed who are (a) nationals of a Member State of the EEA and (b) nationals of a state other than an EU or EEA Member State: s.27(4) *ibid*.
51. s.27(3) *ibid*.
52. s.27(5) *ibid*.
53. ss.23(3) and (5) *ibid*.
54. The current fees in respect both of original and renewal applications are specified in Regulations 3 and 4 of the Employment Permits Act 2006 (Prescribed Fees and Miscellaneous Procedures) Regulations 2006, SI no. 683 of 2006. It is understood that new regulations setting out a revised fee structure will be published either in late 2009 or early 2010. For information as to the relevant fees at the time of writing, see http://www.entemp.ie/publications/labour/2009/guidelines-fees-april2009.pdf.
55. s.6(a) Employment Permits Acts 2003 and 2006.

- provide information in respect of the qualifications, skills or experience that are required for the employment concerned[56];
- provide information and, where appropriate, any relevant documents in respect of the qualifications, skills or experience of the foreign national concerned[57];
- specify the place at or in which the employment concerned is to be carried out[58];
- specify the remuneration and any deductions, where agreed, for board and accommodation or either of them in respect of the employment concerned[59];
- in respect of the foreign national concerned, specify whether or not [s]he has sought permission to land in the State on a previous occasion or has been in the State on a previous occasion without permission to land, and, where [s]he is in the State at the time of the application, provide information and documents relating to the permission granted to him or her to land in the State[60];
- provide the applicant's registered number with the Revenue Commissioners and (if the applicant is a company registered under the Companies Acts) the number assigned to it by the registrar of companies on its registration[61];
- provide the personal public service number, if any, of the proposed grantee of the employment permit[62];
- contain two photographs of the proposed grantee, each of the same size as the size of the photograph required by the Minister for Foreign Affairs to be contained in a passport issued by that Minister of the Government[63];
- provide information as to the number of nationals (if any) of Member States of the EEA and the Swiss Confederation employed, at the time of the application, by the applicant[64];
- provide such other information as may be prescribed, or which the Minister may request and which, in the Minister's opinion, might materially assist in the making of a decision on the application[65];
- be signed and dated both by the applicant and also by the proposed grantee (that is to say, the foreign national in question).[66]

56. s.6(b) *ibid.*
57. s.6(c) *ibid.*
58. s.6(d) *ibid.*
59. s.6(e) *ibid.*
60. s.6(f) *ibid.*
61. para.6(1)(a) Employment Permits Act 2006 (Prescribed Fees and Miscellaneous Procedures) Regulations 2006, SI no. 683 of 2006.
62. para.6(1)(b) *ibid.*
63. para.6(1)(c) *ibid.*
64. para.6(1)(d) *ibid.*
65. s.6(g) Employment Permits Acts 2003 and 2006.
66. para.6(3)(a) Employment Permits Act 2006 (Prescribed Fees and Miscellaneous Procedures) Regulations 2006, SI no. 683 of 2006.

[5–17] In addition, if an application is to be successful, the applicant must satisfy the Minister both that [s]he had taken all steps reasonably open to him or her to offer the employment in respect of which the application is made, either to a citizen or to a foreign national referred to in s.2(10) of the 2003 and 2006 Acts, or to whom s.3 thereof applies,[67] and also that at the time of the application, more than 50 per cent of his or her employees are nationals of either a Member State of the EEA or the Swiss Confederation or a combination of both.[68] The Minister will accept as proof that reasonable steps were taken to offer the job to a citizen or a foreign national to whom s.2 or s.3 applies, evidence that the relevant job was advertised on the FÁS/EURES employment network for at least eight weeks and in a newspaper in the State for at least six days before the date of the application.[69]

3.1.2. An Application Made Directly by a Foreign Worker

[5–18] On the other hand, where the application is to be made by the foreign national him or herself, it must do the following:

- provide such information and documents concerning the foreign national's qualifications, skills and experience as the Minister may request[70];
- specify whether or not [s]he has sought permission to land in the State on a previous occasion or has been in the State on a previous occasion without permission to land[71];
- provide – where the applicant is in the State at the time of the application – information and documents relating to the permission granted to him or her to land in the State[72];
- provide such information and documents concerning the offer of employment made to him or her as the Minister may request and provide information in respect of the qualifications, skills or experience that are required for the employment referred to[73];
- provide a full and accurate description of the employment that will result

---

67. s.10(2)(a) Employment Permits Acts 2003 and 2006. This requirement is expressly deemed to be supplementary to Council Regulation EEC no. 1612/68 of 15 October 1968 on freedom of movement of workers within the Community.

68. s.10(2)(b) Employment Permits Acts 2003 and 2006. Under s.3B *ibid.* the Minister may make an order providing that the requirements under s.10 do not apply for a specified time to nationals from Bulgaria or Romania. Such an order should not be made unless, having regard to conditions of the labour market in the State at the time, the Minister is of the opinion that it is desirable in the interests of the proper functioning of the economy that such an order is made: s.3(B)(2) *ibid.*

69. reg.8 Employment Permits Act 2006 (Prescribed Fees and Miscellaneous Procedures) Regulations 2006, SI no. 683 of 2006.

70. s.7(a) Employment Permits Acts 2003 and 2006.

71. s.7(b) *ibid.*

72. s.7(c) *ibid.*

73. ss.7(d) and (e) *ibid.*

if that offer of employment is accepted (the 'employment concerned')
and the terms and conditions, including the hours of work in each week
of the employment, and the duration of the employment[74];

- specify the place at or in which the employment concerned is to be
  carried out[75];
- specify the proposed remuneration and any deductions, where agreed,
  for board and accommodation or either of them in respect of the
  employment concerned[76];
- provide the personal public service number, if any, of the proposed
  grantee of the employment permit[77];
- contain two photographs of the proposed grantee, each of the same
  size as the size of the photograph required by the Minister for Foreign
  Affairs to be contained in a passport issued by that Minister of the
  Government[78];
- provide such other information as may be prescribed, or which the
  Minister may request and which, in the Minister's opinion, might
  materially assist in the making of a decision on the application[79]; and
- be signed and dated by the foreign national applicant.[80]

4. Consideration of the Application for an Employment Permit

It seems clear under the legislation that the decision whether or not to grant an   [5–19]
employment permit is entirely one for the discretion of the Minister.[81] Equally,
however, this is not an unfettered discretion[82] and, as we shall shortly see, the
terms of the 2003 and 2006 Acts provide for various matters that may and must
be borne in mind by the Minister in determining whether or not an employment
permit should be granted in a particular case. In addition, however, as has been
mentioned, a relatively detailed administrative scheme has developed within the
Department of Enterprise, Trade and Employment for determining whether or
not to grant such permits, such that, if an application is to be successful, the applicant must bring his or her case within one of such schemes. Both the statutory

---

74. s.7(f) *ibid.*
75. s.7(g) *ibid.*
76. s.7(h) *ibid.*
77. para.6(1)(b) Employment Permits Act 2006 (Prescribed Fees and Miscellaneous Procedures)
    Regulations 2006, SI no. 683 of 2006.
78. para.6(1)(c) *ibid.*
79. s.7(i) Employment Permits Acts 2003 and 2006.
80. para.6(3)(b) Employment Permits Act 2006 (Prescribed Fees and Miscellaneous Procedures)
    Regulations 2006, SI no. 683 of 2006.
81. Thus s.8(1) Employment Permits Acts 2003 and 2006 simply provides that 'the Minister
    may, on application made to him or her, grant an employment permit'.
82. s.8(1) *ibid.* provides that the discretion of the Minister is subject to ss.2(11), 10, 12 and 14 of
    the 2006 Act.

factors that must be considered and the nature of such administrative schemes are now discussed. The point has already been made that it is arguable that the scheme in question is so detailed and has such an impact in practice that it is both inappropriate and invalid that it should operate without being grounded in ministerial regulation, not least in that ss.11(3), (4) and 12(3) seem to envisage that guidance on the question of whether and when an employment permit should be granted should be provided by way of ministerial regulation.

4.1. Factors that Must Be Considered under Statute

[5–20] As we have seen earlier, apart from any other factors to be considered by the Minister in determining whether or not to grant an employment permit, [s]he is required to give preference to applications in respect of nationals from Bulgaria or Romania, and nationals of a State in relation to which an order under s.3 is in force.[83] Beyond this, in considering an application for an employment permit, the Minister is required to have regard to five separate factors:

- the extent to which a decision to grant the permit would be consistent with current government economic policy;
- whether the skills or qualifications which, according to the applicant or, where the application is made by the foreign national, according to the person who has made the job offer to the foreign national, are required for the relevant employment are in fact necessary for or relevant to that employment[84];
- the various information required under ss.6 and 7 to accompany the application[85];
- any regulations made pursuant to s.14 of the Act[86];
- the application of paras (a) to (j) of s.12(1).

Section 12(1) in turn sets out various factors on the basis of which the Minister *may* refuse to grant a permit. These factors can be divided into three categories, as follows:

4.1.1. Flaws in the Application Itself

[5–21] The application may be refused where the applicant has failed to provide necessary information required pursuant to the 2006 Act,[87] or has failed to pay the relevant

---

83. s.2(11) Employment Permits Acts 2003 and 2006.
84. s.11(1)(b) *ibid.* Where such skills or qualifications are not, in fact, relevant for the job, then the Minister *may* refuse to grant the relevant permit: s.12(1)(k) *ibid.*
85. s.11(1)(c) *ibid.* Under s.11(2) the Minister is entitled to take such steps as [s]he considers necessary to establish the accuracy or authenticity of the information provided in respect of the application.
86. ss.11(3) and (4) *ibid.* Where the grant of a permit would contravene the regulations in question then the Minister *shall* refuse to grant the permit: s.12(3) *ibid.*
87. s.12(1)(a) *ibid.*

fee,[88] or where there has been a material misrepresentation in the application[89] or a forged or fraudulent document submitted with the application.[90]

4.1.2. Illegality

Thus the application may be refused where the applicant has been convicted of an offence under the 2003 and 2006 Acts as well as any acts mentioned in the First Schedule to the 2006 Act in the period of five years before the date of the application,[91] where the foreign national concerned lands or has landed or is or has been in the State without permission,[92] or where the remuneration proposed to be paid to the foreign national in respect of the proposed weekly hours of work is less than the standard working week[93] remuneration.[94]   [5–22]

4.1.3. Policy

Perhaps most significantly, the Minister may refuse to grant the permit in question if in his or her opinion to do so would be manifestly inconsistent with economic policy for the time being of the government,[95] or if it is in the public interest[96] to do so,[97] or where there is already in force an employment permit granted to the applicant and less than 12 months has elapsed since [s]he first commenced employment in the State.[98]   [5–23]

Hence it would seem that under the terms of the Employment Permits Acts 2003 and 2006, provided that: [5–24]

- the application is complete and the relevant statutory requirements are fulfilled, and the terms of any regulations are not violated;
- the applicant or relevant foreign national have not acted illegally; and
- the applicant is correct in stating that the particular skills and qualifications possessed by the relevant employee are necessary for the job in question,

---

88. s.12(1)(b) *ibid.*
89. s.12(1)(g) *ibid.*
90. s.12(1)(h) *ibid.*
91. s.12(1)(c) *ibid.*
92. s.12(1)(i) *ibid.*
93. The concept of 'standard working week remuneration' means the weekly remuneration that the foreign national would receive if [s]he were to work a 39-hour week either at the national minimum hourly rate of pay or any higher rate of pay provided for in a relevant Employment Regulation Order or Registered Employment Agreement: s.12(6) *ibid.*
94. s.12(1)(j) *ibid.*
95. s.12(1)(d) *ibid.*
96. Public interest for the purposes of the Act includes public order, national security, public health and safety, and the need to protect the labour market: s.1 *ibid.*
97. s.12(1)(f) *ibid.*
98. s.12(1)(e) *ibid.*

then the only remaining relevant considerations for the Minister are policy-centered ones – and essentially whether it would be in accordance with governmental policy and the public interest for the relevant employment permit to be granted. In other words, the decision whether or not to grant the permit becomes one for ministerial discretion having regard to policy considerations.

4.2. Administrative Schemes and Policies

[5–25] In one sense it may be argued that inasmuch as the question of whether or not to grant an employment permit is one for the discretion of the Minister, the current approach[99] of the Department of Enterprise, Trade and Employment to the issue of employment permits, in creating a range of administrative schemes into which a prospective applicant must bring his or her case, is thus simply the application of ministerial discretion.[100] It should be stressed again, however, that these are merely schemes and whereas they will dictate in virtually all instances whether or not an employment permit is to be granted, equally they may be open to challenge in that, not being based on ministerial regulations their creation and operation may be *ultra vires* the power of the Minister under the Act, not least because in certain cases they make provision for matters which, under the Employment Permits Acts 2003 and 2006, are specifically stated to be matters appropriate for treatment by way of regulations.

[5–26] The Department of Enterprise, Trade and Employment currently divides employment permits into five types: green card permits, work permits, inter-company transfer permits, spouse and dependents' permits, and graduate schemes.

4.2.1. Green Card Scheme

[5–27] The first of these, the green card scheme (which replaces the former work visa/work authorisation scheme), allows permits to be issued for an initial period of two years and in respect of occupations[101] where high-level strategic skills shortages exist.[102] Significantly, there is no need to fulfill a labour market needs test (as there is with other work permits) in order to make an application for a green card. Green card applications can be made for all occupations where the salary on offer is €60,000 or more (other than those which are contrary to the public interest),

---

99. The material in this section relates to the departmental policy in place at the time of writing. There is no guarantee that it will remain departmental policy. Hence it is necessary for anyone seeking to be aware of the up-to-date departmental position to have regard to the department's website: www.entemp.ie.
100. The administrative schemes operated by the department are best accessed online at www.entemp.ie/labour/workpermits.
101. For a list of recent changes in the occupations eligible for green card permits, see http://www.entemp.ie/labour/workpermits/revisedgreencard.htm.
102. The most recent department guidelines for green card permits (at time of writing, May 2009) are published at http://www.entemp.ie/publications/labour/2009/guidelines-green-cards-may09.pdf.

and for certain specified strategically important occupations where the salary on offer is between €30,000 and €59,000.[103] Thus a green card cannot be awarded for a job where the salary on offer is less than €30,000.

It is worth remembering, however, that this scheme and the green card to which [5–28]
reference is made is simply an employment permit as defined under the 2003 and 2006 Acts. In this respect, whereas aspects of the scheme are quite clearly merely the fulfillment of the statutory obligations (for example, the rule that the relevant foreign national must possess the skills, qualifications and experience required for the employment, the requirement that such worker not be paid below the minimum wage and the rule that the permit is always granted to the employee), equally others seem to go well beyond the terms of the Act. Thus s.4(3) of the 2006 Act simply requires that where a foreign national is applying for an employment permit, [s]he must have a job offer from an employer. Under the green card scheme, however, there are significant specifications as to the nature of this job offer including, most importantly, the requirement that it be an offer for at least two years' employment. Finally, it is notable that, as we have seen, under s.14 of the Act the question of the minimum salary someone must earn in order to obtain a work permit (other than the requirement that [s]he not be paid less than the minimum wage) is one which the Act envisages would be dealt with by ministerial regulation.[104] Again it is thus a matter of some concern that the current approach of the department is to create such a *de facto* rule without grounding it in regulations.

4.2.2. Work Permits Scheme

Where so-called green card permits are not available, prospective employers or [5–29]
foreign employees may still apply for work permits.[105] Applications are considered for occupations (other than those contrary to the public interest) where the salary on offer is in excess of €30,000 and in exceptional cases where it is below €30,000 and no applications are considered in respect of a defined list of job categories. Under the most recent changes to the departmental scheme,[106] operative from June 2009, it is further required that a vacancy in respect of which an application for a work permit is being made must be advertised with the FÁS/EURES employment network for at least eight weeks and in local and national newspapers for six days, and that evidence of this fact be submitted with the application.[107]

---

103. The list of occupations in respect of which green card permits may be made and where the salary is between €30,000 and €59,000 is provided in Appendix A of the department guidelines at http://www.entemp.ie/publications/labour/2009/guidelines-greencards-may09.pdf.

104. s.14(1)(d) Employment Permits Acts 2003 and 2006.

105. Guidelines in respect of such non green card work permits, including the list of ineligible job categories, is provided at http://www.entemp.ie/publications/labour/2009/guidelines-workpermits-may2009.pdf.

106. See http://www.entemp.ie//labour/workpermits/revisedworkpermitarrangements%20-%20june%202009.htm.

107. This is in order to ensure that in the first instance a national of the EEA or Norway, Iceland, Liechtenstein and Switzerland and, in the second instance, of Bulgaria or Romania, cannot be found to fill the vacancy.

4.2.3. *Intra-Company Transfer Permits*

[5–30] The department has also designed a scheme whereby senior management or key personnel of a multinational company who are foreign nationals (as well as those undergoing a training programme) may apply to transfer to work in Ireland. The scheme is strictly limited to such categories of person, who must earn a minimum annual salary of €40,000 and have been working for a minimum period of 12 months with the overseas company prior to transfer. No labour market needs test is required in respect of such transfers. It would seem from the department guidelines that it is only the host organisation in Ireland (as distinct from the foreign national him or herself) which can apply for the employment permit in such circumstances. Indeed in some respects it is difficult to ascertain from department guidelines whether what is at issue here is an employment permit at all (and whether, for example, all the statutory requirements in relation to employment permits apply to this kind of permit). Obviously if this is *not* the case, then – whether such a scheme is valid or not – it is not related to what is provided for under the 2003 and 2006 Acts.[108]

4.2.4. *Work Permits for Spouses and Dependents of Employment Permit Holders*

[5–31] The department has also developed a scheme whereby the spouses[109] and dependents of certain categories of employment permit holder may also apply for an employment permit to work in the State.[110] Again it should perhaps be noted that, aside from the case where such foreign national spouses/dependents apply on their own behalf and in the usual manner for an employment permit, there is nothing in the legislation that envisages the possibility of spousal/dependent permits of this kind.[111] The essence of the scheme was formerly that the spouse and dependents of an employment permit holder would be able to apply for an employment permit in respect of most occupations without their prospective employer having to undertake a labour market test in respect of such matter and where the application is exempt from a fee,[112] but since 1 June 2009 these concessions have been

---

108. The most recent department guidelines (which intimate that the scheme is envisaged by the 2003 and 2006 Acts – which it clearly is not) are contained at http://www.entemp.ie/publications/labour/2009/guidelines-ict-april2009.pdf.

109. For the position of persons in *de facto* non-marital relationships with an employment permit holder, see http://www.entemp.ie//labour/workpermits/defacto.htm.

110. In addition, in a policy change since July 2009, spouses and dependents of hosting agreement holders will have greater ease of access to employment in the State. See http://www.entemp.ie//labour/workpermits/researchers.htm.

111. Thus, for example, the scheme requires the applicant spouse or dependent to submit additional information and material with his or her application to which reference is not made in the legislation, including a passport clearly indicating the most recent immigration stamp, a marriage certificate (in the case of an applicant spouse) and correspondence from the employer of the employment permit holder confirming that [s]he is in employment with that employer and indicating how long they have been in employment, their job title and salary.

112. regs.5(1) and (2) of the Employment Permits Act 2006 (Prescribed Fees and Miscellaneous

removed. In order for such an application to be made (either by the employee or prospective employer), the employment permit holder (whose spouse/dependents are seeking to make the application) must either have a valid so-called Green Card permit, a valid employment permit or hosting agreement in respect of a researcher position, a valid work permit of 12 months' or more duration (where his or her first work permit application must have been received by the department before 1 June 2009[113]), a valid working visa or work authorisation issued before 31 December 2006, or a valid intra-company transfer permit of 12 months' duration or more. Most importantly, the application must have been received by the department before 1 June 2009 and the employment permit holder must still be working within the terms of the employment permit. Furthermore, the applicant spouse/dependents must be legally resident in the State with the employment permit holder at the time of making the application.[114]

4.2.5. Graduate Scheme

The purpose of this scheme is to allow legally resident non-EEA third-level graduates to remain in Ireland for the purpose of seeking employment and applying for a Green Card or Work Permit.[115] Thus a non-EEA student who has, on or after 1 January 2007, acquired a primary degree, an honours degree, a higher diploma – equivalent of an honours degree, a masters degree, a post-graduate diploma or a doctorate degree from an Irish third-level educational institution will be permitted to apply for the scheme.[116] [5–32]

Persons who qualify under this scheme will be granted one non-renewable six-month extension to their current student permission to stay in Ireland and will be permitted to work for up to 40 hours per week without an employment permit but may not engage in self-employment or operate a business in the State.[117] [5–33]

Again this scheme bears no obvious relation to the procedure for obtaining employment permits under the 2003 and 2006 Acts. It should be remembered that s.2 of the 2003 Act makes it clear that as a blanket rule and save in the limited circumstances considered above, a foreign national may not enter into or be in [5–34]

Procedures) Regulations 2006, SI no. 683/2006, provide for the possibility of the Minister determining that a particular class of applications should attract a reduced fee or a zero fee.

113. If the work permit was applied for *after* 1 June 2009 then the spouse or dependents of the employment permit holder must apply for a permit in his or her own right and with none of the concessions contained in this scheme.

114. Guidelines in respect of the work-permit scheme for spouses and dependents can be found at http://www.entemp.ie/publications/labour/2009/guidelines-spousals-july2009.pdf.

115. Generally, see http://www.entemp.ie/labour/workpermits/graduatescheme.htm.

116. The student at the time of application must hold a current Certificate of Registration issued by the Garda National Immigration Bureau.

117. In addition, the department is willing to consider work-permit applications for a starting salary lower than €30,000 if it can be shown that this is the industry norm for certain graduate occupations. See http://www.entemp.ie/labour/workpermits/policygraduates.htm.

employment in the State without an employment permit. It is difficult to see how this clear statutory provision can be circumvented by a departmental scheme that is not even underpinned by regulations.

4.2.6. Departmental Policies

[5–35] As well as the schemes referred to above, it should be noted that the department currently has specific policies in place in respect of nurses and doctors[118] and sports professionals, which specify the manner by which employment permits are to be sought for such persons.[119]

5. The Decision on the Application

[5–36] On the basis of all of the above, the Minister may decide either to grant or to refuse the employment permit. Should [s]he grant the permit[120] then its effect is to permit the relevant foreign worker to work in the State in the employment specified in the application,[121] or, where the application was made by the foreign national him or herself, in the economic sector[122] specified in the application.[123] The permit should also specify the extent of its duration, which must not exceed two years or such longer period as may be specified by regulations made pursuant to s.14,[124] and should give a description either of the employment (including a statement of the remunerations and any deductions agreed for board and accommodation to which the employee is entitled) or the economic sector in respect of which it has been granted.[125] It must also include a statement that the foreign worker is to be paid no less than the minimum wage[126] and must include or be accompanied by a summary of the principal employment rights of the employee.[127] Finally it must include a statement that a new application for the grant of an employment permit may be made in respect of the foreign national concerned.[128]

---

118. http://www.entemp.ie/labour/workpermits/doctorsandnurses.htm.
119. http://www.entemp.ie/labour/workpermits/sportsprofessionals.htm.
120. Where the permit is granted, the original is issued to the relevant foreign worker and a copy thereof is issued to his or her employer: s.9(1) Employment Permits Acts 2003 and 2006.
121. s.8(2) *ibid.*
122. Economic sector in this respect means a sector of the economy concerned with a specific economic activity requiring specific qualifications, skills or knowledge: s.1 *ibid.*
123. s.8(3) *ibid.*
124. ss.8(4) and (5) *ibid.*
125. ss.9(2)(a) and (b) *ibid.*
126. s.9(2)(c) *ibid.*
127. s.9(3) *ibid.* The requirements of s.9 are expressly in addition to any other provisions of the Act or of regulations made pursuant to s.29(2) specifying matters to be included in an employment permit: s.9(4) *ibid.*
128. s.9(2)(d) *ibid.*

Where a decision to grant (or to renew) a permit is taken, the Minister is obliged   [5–37] to record this on a register of employment permits (which [s]he is bound to establish and maintain).[129] This register should indicate the name and address of the relevant foreign national and of the applicant (should the applicant not be the foreign national) or of the foreign national's employer.[130] It should also indicate the employment or economic sector to which it relates,[131] the duration of the permit and its commencement and expiry dates,[132] and whether it has been renewed,[133] revoked[134] or surrendered.[135]

Alternatively the Minister may decide to refuse to grant such permit, in which   [5–38] case [s]he must inform the applicant in writing of his or her decision and the reasons for it[136] and must return to him or her such portion of the application fee as is prescribed in regulations.[137] The applicant may submit such refusal to the Minister for review[138] within 21 days of the date on which [s]he was notified of the decision.[139] Where this happens the review must be undertaken by an officer of the Minister other than (and more senior than) the one who made the original decision.[140] Having afforded the person who submitted the matter for review the opportunity to make representations in respect of the matter, the relevant officer may confirm the decision or else may cancel it and grant the relevant foreign national the employment permit.[141]

---

129. s.28 *ibid.*
130. ss.28(a) and (c) *ibid.*
131. s.28(b) *ibid.*
132. s.28(d) *ibid.*
133. s.28(e) *ibid.*
134. s.28(f) *ibid.*
135. s.28(g) *ibid.*
136. s.12(4) *ibid.*
137. s.12(5) *ibid.* Under reg.5(7) of the Employment Permits Act 2006 (Prescribed Fees and Miscellaneous Procedures) Regulations 2006, SI no. 683/2006, an applicant is currently entitled to a refund of 100 per cent of his or her application fee. In addition, under reg.5(6) the relevant fee *may* be refunded to the applicant where his or her application for a permit is withdrawn before the issue of the relevant permit.
138. s.13(1) Employment Permits Acts 2003 and 2006. Submission of decisions for review should be in writing and should specify the grounds as to why the decision should be cancelled. See reg.9 Employment Permits Act 2006 (Prescribed Fees and Miscellaneous Procedures) Regulations 2006, SI no. 683 of 2006.
139. s.13(2) Employment Permits Acts 2003 and 2006.
140. s.13(3) *ibid.*
141. s.13(4) *ibid.*

6. Termination of an Employment Permit

[5–39] There are various circumstances in which an employment permit can be terminated. In the first place it may be revoked by the Minister either if there has been
some irregularity in the manner in which it was obtained,[142] if there has been an
abuse of the permit either by the employer or the foreign national[143] or if, in his
or her view, it is in the public interest for it to be revoked.[144] Where the Minister
decides to revoke the permit [s]he is required to notify both the relevant employer
and the foreign national concerned in writing of the decision, of the reasons for
the decision and of the fact that either or both of them may submit the decision[145] for review within 28 days.[146] As with a review of a decision to refuse a
permit, a review of a decision to revoke a permit must be undertaken by an officer
appointed by the Minister other than and in a position superior to the officer who
made the decision under review.[147] Having given the person who submitted the
decision for review the opportunity to make written representations in relation to
the matter, such officer may confirm[148] or cancel the decision.[149]

[5–40] Secondly, an employment permit will cease to be in force in relation to a foreign
national in respect of whom an order under s.3 (deportation orders) or s.4 (exclusion orders) of the Immigration Act 1999 is made.[150] Should such an order be

---

142. This arises where the permit was obtained by fraud or misrepresentation, where materially
false or misleading information was provided with the application, or where the permit was
granted by reason of an administrative error. ss.16(1)(c), (d) and (e) *ibid.*
143. ss.16(1)(a) and (b) *ibid.* Such abuse arises either where the holder of the permit has been
convicted of an offence under the Act, or where (under s.19) either the employer or the foreign
national has purported to transfer the permit to another person, to use it to allow another
foreign national to enter into employment in the State, or to use the permit to facilitate the
foreign national in entering into employment other than that specified on the permit.
144. s.16(1)(f) *ibid.*
145. Submission of decisions for review should be in writing and should specify the grounds as to
why the decision should be cancelled. See reg.9 Employment Permits Act 2006 (Prescribed
Fees and Miscellaneous Procedures) Regulations 2006, SI no. 683 of 2006.
146. s.16(2) Employment Permits Acts 2003 and 2006. Where in the Minister's opinion the
circumstances are such that it is appropriate in the public interest that the expiration of the
permit should take place immediately, then this will happen (s.16(5) *ibid.*). If this happens
and the decision to revoke the permit is cancelled on review, then the period for which the
permit was revoked is not counted in assessing the overall duration of the permit (s.17(5)
ibid.). Otherwise, the permit will expire 28 days after the date of notification (s.16(3) *ibid.*).
Where a decision to revoke is submitted for review under ss.17(1) and (2) *ibid.*, this has the
effect of suspending the decision until either the review is determined or the submission of
the decision for review is withdrawn (s.16(4) *ibid.*).
147. s.17(3) *ibid.*
148. Where the decision is confirmed, the person who submitted the decision for review must be
notified in writing of the reasons for the confirmation: s.17(4)(a) *ibid.*
149. s.17(4) *ibid.*
150. s.21(1) *ibid.*

revoked or cease to be in force, the relevant employment permit is thereby revived[151] and the period of its duration shall not include the period for which it was not in force.[152]

Finally, in cases other than those where the application for the employment permit was made by the foreign national him or herself (that is, where it was made by his or her employer) and where the employment of the relevant foreign national is terminated or ceases for whatever reason, then within four weeks from the date of such cessation or termination, the holder must surrender to the Minister the original of the permit and the employer must surrender the copy of the permit.[153] Failure to do so is an offence[154] although it is a defence for either the foreign national or the employer to show that they took all reasonable steps to surrender the relevant document within the four-week period.[155] It would appear that there is no equivalent obligation on a foreign national who has applied for his or her own permit and who has been made redundant to surrender that permit. In this respect, and since 28 August 2009, a foreign national who has previously been in possession of an employment permit but who was made redundant may stay in the country for up to six months in order to look for work.[156] The Department of Enterprise, Trade and Employment has, furthermore, indicated that it will look favourably on applications for employment permits from persons who were valid employment holders and who have been made redundant in the last three months.[157] [5–41]

7. Renewal of Employment Permits

Inasmuch as employment permits are of limited duration, the Minister may, from time to time and on application either of the employer or of the foreign national who originally applied for the permit, renew such permit.[158] Again this is a matter for the discretion of the Minister, and again in exercising this discretion [s]he is bound to give consideration to the matters that, under ss.11 and 13 of the 2003 and 2006 Acts, must be borne in mind when considering an application for an [5–42]

---

151. s.21(2) *ibid.*
152. s.21(3) *ibid.*
153. s.24(1) *ibid.*
154. s.24(2) *ibid.*
155. s.24(3) *ibid.*
156. See http://www.inis.gov.ie/en/INIS/Pages/PR09000180. The position prior to this date had been that such workers only had three months in which to stay in the country in order to find work.
157. See http://www.entemp.ie/labour/workpermits/redundant.htm for the current approach of the department. It should be noted that since June 2009 the position for persons applying for work permits for such workers has become more difficult, in that, for example, it is now necessary for them to show that the job it is proposed to give to the foreign national has been advertised in FÁS/EURES for eight weeks before the date of the application.
158. s.20(1) Employment Permits Acts 2003 and 2006.

original employment permit.[159] The application for renewal must be made within such period either before or after the expiration of the employment period as is prescribed.[160] Typically, the period for which such permit is renewed cannot exceed three years (or such longer period as may be provided for in regulations – and at the time of writing no such longer period has been prescribed),[161] however, if at the date of the making of the renewal application the permit has been in force (including the periods for which it has been previously renewed) for five or more years, then it may be renewed for an unlimited period and irrespective of whether the worker is made redundant during this time.[162]

[5–43] The application for renewal must be accompanied by the prescribed fee[163] and must contain such information (similar to that referred to in ss.6 and 7 in the context of an original application for a permit) as is specified by the Minister[164] in a written direction.[165] Currently, the renewal application is required to

- provide, in cases where the applicant is not the foreign national worker, the applicant's registered number with the Revenue Commissioners and, if the applicant is a company registered under the Companies Acts, the number assigned to it by the registrar of companies on its registration[166];
- provide the personal public service number, if any, of the proposed grantee of the employment permit[167];

---

159. s.20(9) *ibid.* The Minister, in considering a renewal application, is not to give consideration to the issues referred to in s.11(1)(b) – that is, whether the particular skills, qualifications or experience allegedly required for the employment are in fact so required: s.20(9)(a) *ibid.*

160. s.20(2) *ibid.* No such period has thus far been prescribed in regulations.

161. s.20(3) *ibid.*

162. s.20(4) *ibid.* For the relevant departmental policy on unlimited permits, see http://www.entemp.ie/labour/workpermits/elements/unlimited.htm.

163. Under reg.5(6) of the Employment Permits Act 2006 (Prescribed Fees and Miscellaneous Procedures) Regulations 2006, SI no. 683 of 2006, it would appear that whereas a fee submitted with a renewal application may be refunded should the application be withdrawn, on the other hand (unlike a situation where a fee is submitted with an original application), no such refund is possible where the application is unsuccessful.

164. For renewal applications received after 1 June 2009, the applicant will need to satisfy a labour market test, namely to show that the job it is proposed that the foreign national will continue to work in was advertised on the FÁS/EURES employment network for at least eight weeks and in a newspaper in the State for at least six days before the date of the application. No such requirement applies in the case of so-called green card permit holders.

165. s.20(6)(a) Employment Permits Acts 2003 and 2006. Such direction may be published by the Minister in any manner that [s]he regards as appropriate, and hence does not need to be in the form of regulations (s.20(7) *ibid.*). In addition the Minister may request a statement or evidence confirming that the applicant has complied with the terms of the original employment permit that it is now sought to be renewed (s.20(6)(b) *ibid.*).

166. para.6(1)(a) Employment Permits Act 2006 (Prescribed Fees and Miscellaneous Procedures) Regulations 2006, SI no. 683 of 2006.

167. para.6(1)(b) *ibid.*

- contain two photographs of the proposed grantee, each of the same size as the size of the photograph required by the Minister for Foreign Affairs to be contained in a passport issued by that Minister of the Government[168];
- provide, in cases where the applicant is not the foreign national worker, information as to the number of nationals (if any) of Member States of the EEA and the Swiss Confederation employed, at the time of the application, by the applicant[169];
- include a copy of the relevant foreign national's P60 forms for each of the years in which [s]he was employed pursuant to the relevant employment permit[170];
- be signed and dated by the foreign national and by the applicant where the applicant is not the foreign national.[171]

From 1 June 2009, the Department of Enterprise, Trade and Employment has [5-44] announced that, where a so-called green card permit is at issue, and subject to the holder having complied with his or her previous immigration and employment permit conditions and being of good character, [s]he will not have to apply for a renewal permit but will simply receive a Stamp 4 permission of one year's duration in his or her passport, which will enable him or her to work without an employment permit for the duration of this period.[172] It would appear that this is a temporary change in arrangements pending enactment of the Immigration, Residence and Protection Bill of 2008, which will allow such persons to apply for long-term residence. Given that the statutory requirement in s.2(3) of the 2003 Act is quite explicit on the requirement that foreign workers must have an employment permit, it is, once again, difficult to see how this can be circumvented by a departmental scheme.

8. Enforcement of the Legislation

Enforcement of the Employment Permits Acts 2003 and 2006 occurs, in the main, [5-45] through use of criminal prosecutions. There is also, however, as we shall see, provision for complaints to be made to the Rights Commissioner under the Acts. Provision is made in the 2006 Act for the appointment of authorised officers to oversee the operation of the Act.[173] Such authorised officers fulfill the same role in all material ways as the inspectors appointed under other employment legislation and to whom reference is made throughout this book. Thus they may come onto the employer's property, question employees and the employer, demand production

---

168. para.6(1)(c) *ibid.*
169. para.6(1)(d) *ibid.*
170. para.6(2) *ibid.*
171. para.6(3) *ibid.*
172. http://www.entemp.ie/labour/workpermits/greencardrenewal.htm.
173. s.22 Employment Permits Acts 2003 and 2006.

of records and inspect, copy, remove or retain such records. Accordingly the limitations on the powers of such inspectors discussed in Chapter 1 and deriving from the decisions of both the High Court and the Supreme Court in *Gama Endustri Tesisleri Imalat Montag A.S. v Minister for Enterprise, Trade and Employment & Anor*[174] will naturally apply to such authorised officers as well.

8.1. Offences under the Act

[5–46] Various offences are created under the Act, namely:

- as a foreign national, entering into the service of an employer or being employed in the State otherwise than in accordance with an employment permit; and as an employer, employing a foreign national otherwise than in accordance with an employment permit.[175] In both these cases the convicted offender on summary conviction is liable to a fine not exceeding €3,000 and/or 12 months' imprisonment.[176] Moreover, where it is the employer who is the offender [s]he may also be prosecuted on indictment and may be liable for a fine of no more than €250,000 and/or 10 years' imprisonment.[177] Such an employer will, however, have a defence if [s]he can show that [s]he took all reasonable steps as were open to him or her to ensure compliance with the legislation.[178]
- forging a document or using a forged document purporting to be an employment permit, altering or permitting the alteration of an employment permit or using or permitting the use of an employment permit in each case with intention to deceive[179];
- as an employer, transferring the employment permit to another person, using the employment permit to employ a foreign national other than the person in respect of whom it was granted, or using the employment permit in respect of employment other than that for which it was granted[180];
- as a foreign national holder of a permit, transferring it to another foreign national, allowing another foreign national to use it to enter into or be in employment in the State, or using the permit to enter into a contract of employment or to be in employment in an economic sector other than that in respect of which the permit was granted[181];

---

174. [2009] IESC 37, [2005] IEHC 210, [2009] 2 ILRM 179.
175. s.2(3) Employment Permits Acts 2003 and 2006.
176. s.2(3)(a) *ibid.*
177. s.2(3)(b) *ibid.*
178. s.2(4) *ibid.* The legislation makes provision for gardaí to obtain a warrant to search any place where it is suspected that there is an offence under s.2(3) of the 2003 and 2006 Acts being committed. See ss.2(5)–2(9) of the 2003 Act and s.34 of the 2006 Act.
179. s.18 Employment Permits Acts 2003 and 2006.
180. s.19(1) *ibid.*
181. s.19(2) *ibid.*

- as an employer, making deductions from the remuneration of a foreign national employee or seeking otherwise to impose a fee or expense arising out of the application process, whether or not the application was made by the employer or the foreign national[182];
- as an employer, retaining a personal document of an employment permit holder in violation of s.23(3) of the 2006 Act[183];
- furnishing false information to the Minister in any application either for an original permit or for renewal of an existing permit[184];

A person guilty of the previous six offences is liable on summary conviction[185] to a   [5–47]
fine not exceeding €5,000 and/or 12 months in prison and on indictment to a fine not exceeding €50,000 and/or five years in prison.[186]

- obstructing or impeding the work of an Authorised Officer under s.22 of the 2006 Act, failing to comply with a lawful requirement made by such officer or, in purported compliance therewith, providing information that is false or misleading in any material respect[187];
- failure to keep records as required s.27 of the Act[188]; or
- failure to surrender an employment permit or a copy thereof to the Minister within four weeks from the date of termination or cessation of the relevant employment to which the employment permit relates.[189]

A person guilty of these last three offences is liable on summary conviction[190] to a fine not exceeding €5,000 and/or 12 months in prison.[191]

In all cases, where the offence is committed by a body corporate and is proved to   [5–48]
have been committed with the consent or connivance of or to have been attributable to the neglect on the part of any director, manager, secretary or other officer of the body corporate, that person as well as the body corporate may be prosecuted for such offence.[192] Finally, and unsurprisingly given the international nature of

---

182. s.23(4) *ibid.*
183. s.23(4) *ibid.*
184. s.25 *ibid.*
185. Notwithstanding s.10(4) of the Petty Sessions (Ireland) Act 1851, summary proceedings may be brought (by the Minister) within 24 months from the date of the alleged offence. ss.32(3) and (4) Employment Permits Acts 2003 and 2006.
186. s.32(1) Employment Permits Acts 2003 and 2006.
187. s.22(10) *ibid.*
188. s.27(6) *ibid.*
189. s.24(2) *ibid.*
190. Notwithstanding s.10(4) of the Petty Sessions (Ireland) Act 1851, summary proceedings may be brought by the Minister within 24 months from the date of the alleged offence. ss.32(3) and (4) Employment Permits Acts 2003 and 2006.
191. s.32(2) Employment Permits Acts 2003 and 2006.
192. S 33(1) of the 2006 Act and ss.2(13) and 2(14) of the 2003 Act.

the legislation, provision is made for evidence to be given by live television link by someone who is outside the State.[193]

8.2. Prohibition on Penalisation of an Employee and Complaints to the Rights Commissioner

[5–49] In keeping with the various other employment law statutes considered in this book, an employer is prohibited from penalising or threatening to penalise an employee for making a complaint to a member of the gardaí or the Minister that a provision of the 2003 and 2006 Acts is not being complied with, or giving evidence in proceedings under the Acts, or giving notice of his or her intention to do either of these things.[194] Penalisation in this context means any act or omission that affects to his or her detriment an employee with respect to any term or condition of his or her employment.[195]

[5–50] Where any alleged penalisation has occurred, the employee is entitled to make a complaint (within six months of the date of the alleged contravention[196]) to the Rights Commissioner following the procedures in the Second Schedule to the 2006 Act.[197] Having heard the matter,[198] the Rights Commissioner may in his or her decision declare that the complaint was or was not well founded, may require the employer to take a specified cause of action and may require the employer to pay such compensation[199] as is just and equitable in the circumstances.[200]

193. s.35(1) Employment Permits Acts 2003 and 2006.

194. s.26(3) *ibid.*

195. s.26(1) *ibid.* Without prejudice to this general definition, penalisation includes suspension, lay-off, dismissal, demotion or loss of opportunity, transfer of duties, change of location of place of work, reduction in wages, changes in working hours, imposition of any discipline, reprimand or other penalty (including a financial penalty) coercion or intimidation: s.26(2) *ibid.*

196. para.1(4) of the Second Schedule to the Employment Permits Acts 2003 and 2006. This six-month period may be extended by up to a further six-month period by the Rights Commissioner where [s]he concludes that the failure to bring the complaint within time was due to reasonable cause: para.1(5) *ibid.*

197. s.26(4) Employment Permits Acts 2003 and 2006. Equally, where the penalisation is in the form of a dismissal, the employee may not obtain relief under both the 2006 Act and the Unfair Dismissals Acts 1977– 2005.

198. As usual, complaints before the Rights Commissioner are heard other than in public: para.1(8) of the Second Schedule to the Employment Permits Acts 2003 and 2006.

199. Any such compensation represents a priority debt to be paid under s.285 of the Companies Act 1963 in the event of the winding up of a company (para.5(1) of the Second Schedule to the Employment Permits Acts 2003 and 2006) and under s.81 of the Bankruptcy Act 1988 in the event of bankruptcy (para.5(2) *ibid.*).

200. para.1(3) of the Second Schedule to the Employment Permits Acts 2003 and 2006. It is notable that, unlike the other statutes to which reference is made in this book, there is no rule that such compensation is capped at the level of two years' salary for the employee.

As with other statutes considered in this book, the decision of the Rights Commis-   [5–51]
sioner can be appealed to the Labour Court within six weeks from the date on
which it was communicated to the prospective appellant, or such greater period as
the Labour Court may determine in the circumstances,[201] and the Labour Court,
following a hearing of the matter, may affirm, vary or set aside the decision of the
Rights Commissioner.[202] The decision of the Labour Court may be appealed by
either party to the High Court on a point of law,[203] and the Minister may, at the
request of the Labour Court, also refer a question of law arising in proceedings
before it to the High Court for determination.[204]

Where a decision of a Rights Commissioner has not been carried out and the time   [5–52]
for bringing an appeal has passed, then on application by the employee concerned,
the Labour Court shall, without hearing the matter, make a determination in the
terms of the decision of the Rights Commissioner.[205] Moreover, where the determination of the Labour Court has not been carried out within six weeks of being
communicated to the parties (and no appeal has been brought against such decision), then on the application either of the employee, any trade union of which
[s]he is a member (with his or her consent) or the Minister, the Circuit Court,
without hearing the matter, shall make an order directing the employer to carry
out the determination in accordance with its terms.[206]

---

201. paras.2(1) and (2) of the Second Schedule to the Employment Permits Acts 2003 and 2006.
202. para.2(1) *ibid.*
203. para.2(6) *ibid.*
204. para.2(5) *ibid.*
205. para.3(2) *ibid.*
206. para.4(1) *ibid.* Such order may include an order to pay interest on any outstanding
  compensation owed by the employer to the employee: para.4(3) *ibid.*

CHAPTER 6

Atypical Workers:
Part-Time and Fixed-Term Workers

Introduction

The purpose of this chapter is to provide a detailed analysis of two distinct but [6–01]
heavily related categories of atypical worker in Irish law: part-time workers and
fixed-term workers. Although the subject of separate pieces of legislation – the
Protection of Employees (Part-Time Work) Act 2001 ('the 2001 Act') and the
Protection of Employees (Fixed-Term Work) Act 2003 ('the 2003 Act'[1]) – both
areas have a number of features in common. In relation to this connection
between these two pieces of protective legislation, it has been held that the 2003
Act should be construed *in pari materia* with the 2001 Act.[2] For this reason,
throughout this chapter the overlap between the two areas will be emphasised
wherever appropriate.

1. Part-Time Workers

1.1. Background to the Protection of Employees (Part-Time Work) Act 2001
The law relating to part-time workers in Ireland was radically changed by the [6–02]
introduction of the 2001 Act,[3] which seeks to provide for the removal of discrimination against part-time workers. The purpose of the 2001 Act was to effect the
transposition into Irish law of Council Directive 97/81/EC concerning the Framework Agreement on part-time work concluded by the general cross-industry
organisations at European level. This Framework Agreement between the Union
of Industrial and Employers' Confederations of Europe (UNICE), the European
Trade Union Confederation (ETUC) and the European Centre of Enterprises

---

1. For detailed annotated commentary on the provisions of both the 2001 and the 2003 Acts,
   see Kerr, *Consolidated Irish Employment Legislation* (Thomson Round Hall, Release 22, June
   2009), Division H. See also Ryan, chapters 9 and 10, in Regan, ed., *Employment Law* (Tottel
   Publishing, 2009).
2. *ESB v McDonnell*, PTW/07/8, determination no. PTD 081, 6 March 2008.
3. The Act came into operation on 20 December 2001: see SI no. 636 of 2001. The 2001 Act
   repeals in its entirety the Worker Protection (Regular Part-Time Employees) Act 1991.

with Public Participation (CEEP) was concluded on 6 June 1997 and the agreement was adopted as Directive 97/81/EC on 15 December 1997.

[6–03] At the outset, it is critical to gain an understanding of the Framework Agreement in relation to part-time workers, given the requirement that transposing legislation must be interpreted and applied in light of the purpose and wording of the Directive so as to achieve the objectives pursued by the Directive.[4] The first and second paragraphs of the preamble to the Framework Agreement state:

> This Framework Agreement is a contribution to the overall European strategy on employment. Part-time work has had an important impact on employment in recent years. For this reason, the parties to this agreement have given priority attention to this form of work. It is the intention of the parties to consider the need for similar agreements relating to other forms of flexible work.

> Recognising the diversity of situations in Member States and acknowledging that part-time work is a feature of employment in certain sectors and activities, this Agreement sets out the general principles and minimum requirements relating to part-time work. It illustrates the willingness of the social partners to establish a general framework for the elimination of discrimination against part-time workers and to assist the development of opportunities for part-time working on a basis acceptable to employers and workers.

The objective of the Framework Agreement on part-time work is two-fold, as follows:

- First, it seeks to prevent discrimination against part-time workers and to improve the quality of part-time work. Clause 4 of the Agreement lays down the principle of non-discrimination, namely that, in respect of employment and conditions, part-time workers should not be treated in a less favourable manner than comparable full-time workers solely because they work part-time, save where the difference in treatment can be justified on objective grounds.
- Secondly, it aims to facilitate the development of part-time work on a voluntary basis and to contribute to the flexible organisation of working time in a manner that takes into account the needs of both employers and workers.[5] Clause 5(2) states that an employee's refusal to transfer from full-time to part-time status or *vice versa* should not constitute a valid reason for termination of employment (without prejudice to termination for other reasons such as may arise from the operational requirements of the establishment concerned). In light of these objectives

---

4. C-14/83, *Von Colson and Kamann v Land Nordrhein-Westfalen* [1984] EUECJ R-14/83, [1984] ECR 1891.
5. Framework Agreement on Part-Time Work (OJ no. L14, 20 January 1998, at p.9), clause 1.

and provisions of the Framework Agreement, an overview of the 2001 Act can now be offered.

1.2. Overview of the 2001 Act

The introduction of the 2001 Act was long overdue in Irish employment law. [6–04] Long before it was introduced, part-time workers had not only come to represent a considerable proportion of the workforce; they were also denied access to crucial protective legislation (such as the Unfair Dismissals Act 1977, with its stipulated threshold of 18 hours a week) and, indeed, to the social welfare system.[6] While piecemeal legislative measures were introduced to improve the lot of the part-time worker on both fronts in the early 1990s,[7] a unified legislative framework protecting part-time workers remained lacking.

In general terms, the 2001 Act pursues the objective in the Framework Agreement of ensuring that part-time employees will not be treated less favourably than comparable full-time employees unless there are objective grounds for the less favourable treatment; where a benefit is determined by the number of hours an employee works, it shall be on a *pro rata* or proportionate basis to part-time employees.

At this juncture, some fundamental points in relation to the influence of the 2001 [6–05] Act on litigation involving part-time workers should be made:

1. There is no provision in the 2001 Act, or elsewhere in Irish employment law, for a statutory entitlement to part-time work. Rather, the Act is concerned with preventing unfavourable treatment of part-time workers where such treatment cannot be objectively justified on a ground that is unrelated to the employee's part-time status.
2. Another obvious[8] point to clarify at the outset is that a part-time worker's grievance must relate to his or her status as a part-time worker in that it must be capable of being characterised in such a way as to bring the grievance within the scope of the scheme of redress laid down in this legislation.
3. The 2001 Act also makes provision for the Labour Relations Commission to carry out studies for the purposes of identifying obstacles that may exist in particular industries or sectors to access to part-time work, and

---

6. For detailed discussion of these points see Kerr, *Consolidated Irish Employment Legislation* (Thomson Round Hall, Release 22, June 2009), Division H.
7. *ibid.*
8. Though still one that was recently required to be stated by the Labour Court in *Top Security Ltd. v Jun Yu Wang*, determination no. PTD 061, 27 February 2006. The point can also become difficult where a person claims that a portion of their employment duties require to be characterised as representing a discrete part-time employment, a claim that was unsuccessfully made by the employee in *Eileen Peters v Wesley College*, PTW/05/2, determination no. PTD 054, 4 October 2005.

for the commission, in consultation with the social partners, to prepare a Code of Practice that would be of practical benefit to employers and employees in addressing such obstacles.[9]

4. Section 3 of the 2001 Act provides definitions of many key terms, a number of which are common to the protective legislation generally in this jurisdiction. Thus, the definition of 'collective agreement', for example, is identical to that in s.2(1) of the Organisation of Working Time Act 1997; so too does the definition of 'contract of employment'[10] raise the perennial question of whether a person is employed under a contract of service or a contract for services.[11]

1.3. Part-Time Work and the Rights of Part-Time Employees

1.3.1. Who is a Part-Time Worker?

[6–06] The 2001 Act straightforwardly defines a 'part-time employee' as 'an employee whose normal hours of work are less than the normal hours of work of an employee who is a comparable employee in relation to him or her'.[12] In the same section of the 2001 Act, the concept of 'normal hours of work' is defined as meaning the average number of hours worked by the employee each day during a reference period; the reference period, in turn, is defined as a period that complies with the following conditions:

(a) the period is of not less than seven days nor more than 12 months;
(b) the period is the same period by reference to which the normal hours of work of the other employee referred to in the definition of 'part-time employee' in this section is determined; and
(c) the number of hours worked by the employee concerned in the period constitutes the normal number of hours worked by the employee in a period of that duration.

In terms of the definition of part-time employee, the 2001 Act can be regarded as relatively generous to persons seeking to come within its ambit. Thus, there is recent Labour Court authority to the effect that seasonal workers are included

---

9. For analysis of the LRC Code, see below in this chapter.
10. Defined as meaning: '(a) a contract of service or apprenticeship, and (b) any other contract whereby an individual agrees with another person, who is carrying on the business of an employment agency within the meaning of the Employment Agency Act 1971, and is acting in the course of that business, to do or perform personally any work or service for a third person (whether or not the third person is a party to the contract), whether the contract is express or implied and, if express, whether it is oral or in writing'.
11. For fuller discussion of the overlap in nomenclature between the definitions in s.3 of the 2001 Act and other pieces of employment legislation, see Kerr, *Consolidated Irish Employment Legislation* (Thomson Round Hall, Release 22, June 2009), Division H.
12. s.7(1) of the 2001 Act.

within the meaning of part-time employees, that is, the contract of employment does not have to extend over the entire reference period in order for the employee to be considered a part-time employee under the 2001 Act.[13]

The 2001 Act does, too, envisage a broader definition being given to the phrase [6–07] 'contract of employment' than, for example, that used in the context of the Protection of Employees (Fixed-Term Work) Act 2003, to be considered later in this chapter. The 2001 Act provides, for example, that apprentices are included within its ambit, which is not the case under the 2003 Act.[14] It should also be noted that the Labour Court has been prepared to regard agency workers as being part-time employees of the organisation to whom the employee is referred by the agency where that organisation exercises sufficient control over the agency worker.[15]

1.3.2. Meaning of Comparable Employee

Of fundamental importance in the context of part-time employment is the [6–08] notion of the comparator. Pursuant to s.7(3) of the 2001 Act, an employee will be a comparator for the purposes of a claim by a part-time employee if one of the following circumstances is met:

(a) the employee and the relevant part-time employee are employed by the same employer or associated employers and one of a number of conditions (set out below) is satisfied in respect of those employees;

(b) in case (a) does not apply (including a case where the relevant part-time employee is the sole employee of the employer), the employee is specified in a collective agreement applying to the relevant part-time employee, to be a type of employee who is to be regarded for the purposes of the 2001 Act as a comparable employee in relation to the relevant part-time employee;

(c) in case neither (a) nor (b) applies, the employee is employed in the same industry or sector of employment as the relevant part-time employee is employed in and one of the conditions referred to below is satisfied in respect of those employees.

Section 7(3) continues by setting out the conditions to be satisfied for establishing [6–09] a comparator. It should be noted that only one of the following conditions must be fulfilled in order to establish the comparator. The conditions are:

- both of the employees concerned perform the same work under the same or similar conditions or each is interchangeable with the other in relation to the work;

---

13. *ESB v McDonnell*, PTW/07/8, determination no. PTD 081, 6 March 2008.
14. In the context of apprenticeships, the decision of the Labour Court in *ESB Networks v Kingham* [2006] ELR 181 reversed a decision of the Rights Commissioner that an apprenticeship scheme could come within the scope of protection of the 2003 Act.
15. *Diageo Global Supply v Rooney* [2004] ELR 133.

- the work performed by one of the employees concerned is of the same or a similar nature to that performed by the other and any differences between the work performed or the conditions under which it is performed by each, either are of small importance in relation to the work as a whole or occur with such irregularity as not to be significant;
- the work performed by the relevant part-time employee is equal or greater in value to the work performed by the other employee concerned, having regard to such matters as skill, physical or mental requirements, responsibility and working conditions.

It should be noted that the Act states that, for the avoidance of any doubt, a comparable full-time employee refers to such an employee either of the opposite sex to the part-time employee concerned or of the same sex as him or her.[16] It is, moreover, noteworthy that s.7(3) of the 2001 Act is drafted in terms similar to the definition of 'like work' in s.7 of the Employment Equality Act 1998. In at least one important way, however, the 2001 Act is more generous to claimants in this respect: unlike the position under the 1998 Act, in the absence of a comparable full-time employee in the employment where the part-time employee is employed, the comparator may be drawn from the same industry or sector of employment.

1.3.3. Approach of Labour Court in Blackrock College v Browne[17] and Catholic University School v Dooley[18]

[6–10] The determinations of the Labour Court in 2009 in *Blackrock College v Browne*[19] and *Catholic University School v Dooley*[20] involved a Labour Court appeal under the 2001 Act in which the Labour Court afforded detailed consideration to the question of identifying a legitimate comparator for the purposes of a claim of discrimination on grounds of part-time status. Given the striking similarity of the two cases, the *Browne* case will be analysed in detail, but reference will be made to *Dooley* as appropriate.

The claimant in *Browne*, a part-time teacher employed by the respondent college, taught 14 hours per week in comparison to full-time teachers, who teach 22 hours. As a private school, the respondent paid some teachers out of its own funds and other teachers were remunerated by the Department of Education and Science. Those paid by the department were on a scale agreed with the relevant trade union. Those paid directly by the college, including the claimant, were paid at a lower rate and their conditions of employment were generally less favourable. Thus, the

---

16. s.9(5) of the 2001 Act.
17. *Blackrock College v Browne* PTW/08/9, determination no. PTD 091, 2 February 2009.
18. *Catholic University School v Dooley*, PTW/08/8, determination no. PTD 092, 22 April 2009.
19. PTW/08/9, determination no. PTD 091, 2 February 2009.
20. *Catholic University School v Dooley*, PTW/08/04, determination no. PTD 092, 22 April 2009. See also *Catholic University School v Keogh*, PTW/08/04, determination no. PTD 093, 22 April 2009.

claimant was not entitled to sick pay and did not have access to the respondent's occupational health scheme. Some full-time teachers were paid directly by the school and other full-time teachers were paid by the department.

The claimant brought a claim before a Rights Commissioner alleging less favour- [6–11] able treatment in terms of her pay and conditions of employment compared to full-time colleagues paid by the department. She succeeded before the Rights Commissioner. On appeal to the Labour Court, the respondent sought a ruling on the preliminary issue of whether the claimant in fact had a cause of action under the Act; accordingly, this was the sole question addressed by the Labour Court (the issue of objective justification being deferred until (if at all) necessary).

The Labour Court began by finding that the claimant and the comparator were [6–12] employed by the same employer, even though the funds to pay the comparator came from the department and the claimant's wages came from the college. However, in turn the respondent argued that as it also employed full-time teachers it paid out of its own resources, that was the appropriate comparison for the part-time claimant to make rather than the nominated comparator paid for by the department who had a different status. As a result, given that full-time teachers paid directly by the college were employed on the same terms and conditions *pro rata* as the part-time claimant, there was no less favourable treatment involved. In rejecting this argument, the Court examined its decision in the case of *McArdle v State Laboratory*.[21] It will be recalled that in *McArdle* an unestablished civil servant working on a fixed-term contract successfully compared her treatment with an established permanent civil servant with whom she was engaged in like work. In that case the Labour Court, following the decision of the High Court (O'Sullivan J) in *Wilton v Steel Company of Ireland*,[22] concluded that it was for the claimant to choose his or her comparator provided the statutory criteria were met. The only test was whether or not the claimant and the comparator were engaged in like work.

The Labour Court in *Browne* then addressed the question of like work. The respondent argued that there were a number of differences in the conditions applicable to privately paid teachers and those paid directly by the department. Amongst these were requirements relating to registration, qualifications, negotiation arrangements, probation, access to posts of responsibility, career breaks and job sharing.

The Court observed that, while these differences might be relevant to the contractual terms under which both categories were employed, they were not relevant to assessing whether or not like work is being performed. As the claimant and

---

21. FTC/05/11, determination no. FTD 063. 4 April 2006 (the appeal to the High Court on a point of law, reported at [2007] 2 ILRM 438, is not relevant for this point but is discussed in detail below in this chapter in the context of fixed-term workers).
22. [1998] IEHC 87, [1999] ELR 1.

comparator were both secondary school teachers (although teaching different subjects) their work was 'undoubtedly of the same or a similar nature within the meaning of s.7(2)(b) or 7(2)(c) of the [2001] Act'.

[6–13] Another point of significance about *Browne* and *Dooley* was that a number of complex arguments were advanced on behalf of the respondent in each case concerning the extent to which the Irish legislation correctly transposed the Framework Agreement on Part-Time Work. It was contended in *Browne*, for example, that a part-time teacher paid by the college would be entitled to claim equal pay and conditions with a full-time teacher paid by the department, but a full-time teacher paid by the college could not claim such equal treatment. This would inevitably result in a reduction in opportunities for part-time teaching work, which would run counter to the purpose of the legislation and the EU Framework Agreement, one of the aims of which is to facilitate the development of part-time work and to contribute to the flexible organisation of working time in a manner that takes into account the needs of both employers and workers.[23] It is respectfully submitted that the Labour Court's determination in *Browne* does not comprehensively address this argument. Instead, the Court focused on the second (but related) submission put forward on behalf of the respondent, namely that clause 4 of the Framework Agreement – which provides that in respect of employment conditions, part-time workers shall not be treated in a less favourable manner than comparable full-time workers solely because they work part-time, unless the different treatment is justified on objective grounds – should influence the interpretation of the transposing domestic legislation, that is, the 2001 Act. In essence, it was argued (in both *Browne* and *Dooley*) that if the less favourable treatment was not related to the claimant's part-time status but to the status of the comparator as alleged in this case, discrimination had not taken place. The Court did not accept this interpretation of clause 4, on the basis that to do so would mean that any consideration unrelated to an employee's part-time status that influenced the decision to treat him or her less favourably would provide a full defence. Even if this interpretation were correct, the Court held that clause 6 of the Framework Agreement specifically permitted Member States to provide better protection for part-time workers in its domestic legislation. Ultimately, the Labour Court in *Browne* concluded that the claimant's complaint was legitimately made and that she was entitled to succeed in her claim unless the impugned treatment could be shown to be justified on objective grounds.[24] Similarly, in *Dooley*, the Labour Court in upholding the claim (under both the 2001 and 2003 Acts) rejected the argument of objective justification advanced by the school since it related solely to cost which, as will be discussed below in this chapter, is in and of itself not capable of amounting to objective justification.

---

23. Framework Agreement on Part-Time Work (OJ no. L14, 20 January 1998, at p.9), clause 1.
24. It is understood at the time of writing that the evidence as to the respondent's objective grounds is to be presented at a resumed hearing.

1.3.4. Assessment of 'Like Work'

In relation to the assessment of like work as between part-time workers and their [6–14] chosen comparators, the approaches of both the Rights Commissioner Service and the Labour Court display extremely detailed assessments of the value of ostensibly similar work, with one of the most helpful determinations of the Labour Court on this point being its determination in *Bus Éireann v Group of Workers*,[25] where part-time bus drivers were held not to come within the scope of the s.7 'like work' requirement when compared with full-time drivers. The Court's assessment included an exhaustive analysis of the skills, physical and mental requirements and responsibilities of each employee and relied on the differences it identified in these categories to reject the part-time workers' claim. Another consideration that may be relevant to be taken into account is the existence of any formal title distinguishing the complainant from the desired comparator in terms of employment function[26]; though the comparator's length of service is, it seems, irrelevant.[27] It should be emphasised, however, that the inquiry of whether or not the comparator is engaged in 'like work' with the claimant is a question to be resolved on a case-by-case basis, with courts and tribunals being reluctant to articulate any binding criteria that must govern the inquiry.

1.4. Conditions of Employment for Part-Time Employees

The relevant law on conditions of employment for part-time employees is set out [6–15] in s.9 of the 2001 Act. Its key provisions are as follows:

- A part-time employee shall not, in respect of his or her conditions of employment, be treated in a less favourable manner than a comparable full-time employee, unless that less favourable treatment can be justified on objective grounds.[28]
- In so far – but only in so far – as it relates to any pension scheme or arrangement, the prohibition of less favourable treatment does not apply to a part-time employee whose normal hours of work constitute less than 20 per cent of the normal hours of work of a comparable full-time employee.[29]

This section thus gives effect in Irish law to clause 4(1) of the Framework Agreement. As noted, a key feature of the section is the provision in s.9(2) that a part-time employee may, in respect of a particular condition of employment – which includes,

---

25. PTW/06/7, determination no. PTD 071, 18 May 2007.
26. *O'Leary v Cahill May Roberts*, PTW/04/3, determination no. PTD 044, 4 May 2004 (claim upheld on basis of a work inspection that revealed no comparator had any formal title that would distinguish the selected comparator from her fellow workers).
27. *Dunnes Stores Letterkenny v A Group of Workers*, PTW/03/12, determination no. PTD 046, 12 May 2004.
28. Subject to ss.9(4) and 11(2) of the 2001 Act.
29. s.9(4) of the 2001 Act.

inter alia, access to employee-ownership schemes,[30] entitlements to sick pay[31] and service pay[32] – be treated less favourably than a comparable full-time employee if that treatment can be justified on 'objective grounds'. The objective grounds must be based on considerations other than the status of the employee as a part-time worker and the less favourable treatment must be for the purpose of achieving a legitimate objective of the employer and must be necessary for that purpose. This is explicitly set out in s.12 of the 2001 Act, which provides as follows:

> A ground shall not be regarded as an objective ground for the purposes of any provision of this Part unless it is based on considerations other than the status of the employee concerned as a part-time employee and the less favourable treatment which it involves for that employee is for the purpose of achieving a legitimate objective of the employer and such treatment is appropriate and necessary for that purpose.

[6–16] The concept of objective justification – which 'requires the Court to balance the detriment suffered by the worker against the benefit accruing to the employee'[33] – thus coheres with the classic European Court of Justice formulation in *Bilka-Kaufhaus*.[34] As discussed in Chapter 8, in that case the ECJ set out a three-stage test by which an indirectly discriminatory measure may be justified. The Court held that the measure must:

- meet a 'real need' of the employer;
- be 'appropriate' to meet the objective which it pursues; and
- be 'necessary' in order to achieve that objective.

1.4.1. Requirement to Consider Alternative Options Less Detrimental to Employee

[6–17] In considering a claim under the 2001 Act, the Labour Court in *Diageo Global Supply v Rooney*[35] held that in order to satisfy the requirement of objective justification, an employer is obliged to give consideration to alternative options whose effects would be less serious for the employee affected:

> In the normal course, an employer would be expected to have considered alternative means of achieving the objective being pursued which might have a less detrimental effect on the part-time worker concerned. It is only if it can be

---

30. *ESB v McDonnell*, PTW/07/8, determination no. PTD 081, 6 March 2008.
31. *Dunnes Stores Letterkenny v SIPTU*, PTW/05/11, determination no. PTD 052, 26 January 2005; *Dunnes Stores Cavan v A Group of Workers*, PTW/03/11determination no. PTD 045, 12 May 2004.
32. *Dunnes Stores Cavan v A Group of Workers*, PTW/03/11, determination no. PTD 045, 12 May 2004.
33. *Catholic University School v Dooley*, FTC/08/8, determination no. PTD 092, 22 April 2009.
34. C-170/84, *Bilka-Kaufhaus v Weber von Hartz* [1986] EUECJ R-170/84, [1986] ECR 1607.
35. [2004] ELR 133.

demonstrated that there are no viable, less discriminatory means of achieving the objective being pursued can the defence of objective justification succeed.[36]

1.4.2. Requirement that Objective Grounds not be based on Part-Time Status

As to the requirement that the objective grounds must not be based on the status of [6–18] the employee as a part-time worker, it is instructive to consider the interesting case of *Mullaney Brothers v Two Workers*,[37] concerning the granting by the employer of so-called 'Christmas shopping leave' to full-time, but not part-time, employees in a drapery and travel business. The half-day paid shopping leave had applied to the claimant workers since they commenced employment until November 2004, when it was withdrawn from part-time staff on the grounds that it had been given as a concessionary measure and applied only to full-time workers who were working six days per week in the two weeks prior to Christmas. (It was found as a fact, however, that the concession was also restored to full-time staff in the travel business, who did not work a six-day week.) The Labour Court, upholding the Right Commissioner's determination on this point,[38] held that the employer had contravened the 2001 Act, since the only basis upon which the benefit was withdrawn from the claimants was that they were part-time employees. This clearly could not, the Court noted, constitute objective grounds within the meaning of s.12 of the Act.

By contrast, the Labour Court in *Louth VEC v Martin*[39] accepted that the require- [6–19] ment for teachers to be fully qualified before proceeding upon the incremental scale corresponded to a real need on the part of the employer to ensure that all persons teaching in its schools had the appropriate academic qualifications. It further accepted the employer's contention that it was appropriate and necessary to have such a financial sanction in order to encourage employees to obtain the necessary qualifications, and that there was no alternative means by which this objective could be achieved.

1.4.3. Objective Grounds Must Justify Less Favourable Treatment of Part-Time
Workers as Distinct from More Favourable Treatment of Full-Timers

In *Abbott Ireland Ltd. v SIPTU*[40] the union claimed that part-time workers [6–20] were entitled to rest breaks on a *pro rata* basis with full-time employees and that part-time employees working between 4pm and midnight were entitled to shift premium payments on a *pro rata* basis with comparable full-time employees. Both claims were successful, with the Labour Court emphasising in its determination that in relation to objective justification there is a distinction between less favourable treatment of part-time workers and more favourable treatment of full-time workers being capable of justification:

---

36. [2004] ELR 133, 143.
37. PTW/05/6, determination no. PTD 066, 22 September 2006.
38. But not on the question of *pro rata* allocation of the benefit: see below in this chapter.
39. PTW/04/2, determination no. PTD 051, 13 January 2005.
40. PTW/03/3, determination no. PTD 043, 28 January 2004.

The purpose of this Act is to prevent part-time employees being less favourably treated than comparable full-time employees. In this case, the full-time employees receive a thirty minute break during their four hour shift. The fact that the break given to full-time employees is in line with their entitlements under the Organisation of Working Time Act cannot be used as objective justification for the less favourable treatment of part-time employees. Indeed the Act is quite clear in what must be justified is not the more favourable treatment of full-time employees, but the less favourable treatment of part-time employees…

If the part-time employee works the same hours as a full-time employee and the full-time employee receives an unsocial shift premium for those hours then the part-time employee is also entitled to that premium unless there are objective grounds for its non-payment.

1.4.4. *Temporal Considerations Relevant to Pleas of Objective Justification*

[6–21] In the context of an employer attempting to advance an objective justification, it is important to stress that treatment that was objectively justifiable in the past may subsequently become unjustifiable, with the Labour Court having indicated that it will scrutinise justifications valid at one period of time to assess whether they remained valid at the time of the impugned treatment.[41]

1.5. The *Pro Rata* Principle under the 2001 Act

[6–22] In securing the provision of equal treatment in conditions of employment for part-time workers, the 2001 Act operates on the principle of proportionate provision or *pro rata temporis*. This is explained in s.10 of the Act, which provides:

(1) The extent to which any condition of employment… is provided to a part-time employee for the purposes of complying with section 9(1) shall be related to the proportion which the normal hours of work of that employee bears to the normal hours of work of the comparable full-time employee concerned.

(2) The condition of employment mentioned in subsection (1) is a condition of employment the amount of the benefit of which (in case the condition is of a monetary nature) or the scope of the benefit of which (in any other case) is dependent on the number of hours worked by the employee.

To date, the jurisprudence in relation to proportionate provision has been characterised by a rigorous assessment of whether *pro rata* approaches are strictly necessary: if the benefits in question do not have a sufficiently strong connection with the actual number of hours worked by the employee, then the employer's *pro rata* approach may be impugned. Thus, in *Department of Education and Science*

---

41. *O'Leary v Cahill May Roberts*, PTW/04/3, determination no. PTD 044, 4 May 2004.

v Gallagher,[42] the Labour Court said that s.10(2) must be construed in harmony with clause 4(2) of the Framework Agreement, which provides that the principle of non-discrimination could be satisfied by applying conditions of employment *pro rata* where appropriate. This, the Court said, recognised that the *pro rata* principle was not of universal application. Accordingly, the Court explained that the type of benefits contemplated by s.10(2) were 'connected to those which by their nature are appropriately dependent on the number of hours worked by the employee'.

Evidence of this strict necessity approach is further in evidence in a number of [6–23] later decisions of the Labour Court. A good example is the Court's decision in *Mullaney Brothers v Two Workers*,[43] a case discussed above in this chapter involving the granting of a half-day's leave to full-time but not part-time workers for the purposes of Christmas shopping, where the Court held the scope of the benefit at issue was not dependent on the hours worked by employees to whom it applied since it applied equally to full-time staff who worked a five-day week or a six-day week. Consequently it would be inappropriate that the benefit be pro-rated having regard to the provision of s.10(2) of the Act.

Another instructive authority in this context is the Labour Court's decision in *Department of Justice, Equality and Law Reform v Ennis*.[44] There the claimant was employed as a part-time traffic warden. In 2002 the claimant was redeployed from Dublin City to Dun Laoghaire. She claimed that she and 14 other part-time workers received a lower rate of travel allowance than full-time colleagues, in contravention of the 2001 Act. The allowance was not contingent on the number of hours worked but was dependent on the distance travelled to work. She claimed that her treatment was based on her part-time status and that there was no objective ground for less favourable treatment. The employer claimed that the travel allowance was an intrinsic part of the basic pay of the complainant and it was therefore consistent with the provisions of the Act to pay the allowance on a *pro rata* basis. The Rights Commissioner found that the travel allowance was not dependent on the number of hours worked but on the distance to the employee's place of work. The Commissioner found that the claim was well founded and ordered the respondent to treat the claimant no less favourably than a full-time warden. This finding was upheld by the Labour Court. The Court found that the allowance could not be regarded as part of the claimant's pay, but was compensation for the time and expense involved in travelling to work. It held that no objective grounds were put forward to justify paying the claimant on a *pro rata* basis.

So too did an employer's attempt at making *pro rata* payments attract the criticism of the Labour Court in *Department of Education and Science v Gallagher*,[45] an important authority demonstrating that an employer's bona fide view that the

42. PTW/03/13, determination no. PTD 047, 21 May 2004.
43. PTW/05/6, determination no. PTD 066, 22 September 2006.
44. PTW/03/10, determination no. PTD 041, 14 January 2004.
45. PTW/03/13. determination no. PTD 047, 21 May 2004.

part-time employee was fairly entitled to a *pro rata* payment is irrelevant for the purposes of determining whether the payment meets the strict necessity test being applied to s.10 of the 2001 Act. In that case the employee worked as a home economics teacher in a secondary school under a job-sharing contract, working half of the class contact hours done by her full-time counterparts. In April 2003 the Department of Education authorised a retrospective payment of €1,000 for supervision and substitution duties between September 2001 and March 2002. The claimant received €499, although she had done the same amount of supervision and substitution as her full-time colleagues. She claimed that the only reason she was paid half the amount paid to her comparator was her status as a part-time teacher. The department claimed that because the level of substitution and supervision undertaken by teachers differed in individual schools and between schools, it had decided that the only practical way of rewarding teachers for having undertaken these duties was by way of an *ex gratia* payment. It was not intended to reflect the quantum of hours worked by individual teachers. The payment was agreed with the teacher unions; the agreement was not designed to discriminate against part-time teachers and did not discriminate as the payment was not based on hours worked. The Labour Court, upholding the decision of the Rights Commissioner, found that while the payment was based on the bona fide understanding of the parties that teachers would have undertaken substitution and supervision duties in proportion to their contract hours, this did not happen in the instant case. The claimant was rostered for the same amount of duty as the comparator and in those circumstances the Court was satisfied that the claimant was treated less favourably because she was a part-time employee, which could not constitute an objectively justifiable reason.

1.6. Part-Time Employees Working on a Casual Basis

[6–24] The 2001 Act also makes provision for part-time employees working on a casual basis. Section 11(2) provides that a part-time employee may, if such less favourable treatment can be justified on objective grounds, be treated, in respect of a particular condition of employment, in a less favourable manner than a comparable full-time employee. By virtue of s.12(2), however, what may not be considered as an objective ground in relation to a part-time employee may be considered an objective ground in relation to a casual part-time employee.

1.6.1. Who is a Casual Part-Time Employee?

[6–25] Section 11(4) goes on to provide that a part-time employee shall, at a particular time, be regarded as working on a casual basis if:

- at that time [s]he has been in the continuous service of the employer for a period of less than 13 weeks, and that period of service and any previous period of service by him or her with the employer are not of such a nature as could reasonably be regarded as regular or seasonal employment;

or
- by virtue of his or her fulfilling, at that time, conditions specified in an approved collective agreement[46] that has effect in relation to him or her, [s]he is regarded for the purposes of that agreement as working on such a basis.

The Act states that the service of an employee shall be deemed to be continuous unless that service is terminated either by the dismissal of him or her by the employer, or by the employee voluntarily leaving his or her employment.[47]

1.7. Obstacles to the Performance of Part-Time Work

An important feature of the 2001 Act – inspired by the Framework Agreement [6–26] – is the commitment it embodies to the need to keep performance of part-time work under review. In considering this commitment, it is helpful to focus on two distinct questions: first, what are examples of obstacles to part-time work, and, secondly, what steps have to date been taken in Ireland in relation to this commitment to monitor such potential obstacles?

An interesting example of an obstacle to part-time work contained in domestic law was the measure at issue in the preliminary reference before the European Court of Justice in the joint cases *Michaeler and Subito GmbH*.[48] The relevant national legislation in Italy imposed an obligation on employers to send a copy of a part-time employment contract to the provincial office of the Labour and Social Security Inspectorate, within 30 days of signature of the part-time contract. Failure to comply with this obligation resulted in the imposition of administrative fines. The ECJ held that such a measure comprised an obstacle to the objective of promoting part-time work. The Court noted that there had been no indication given to it that a similar procedure was in place in relation to full-time employment contracts.[49] The Italian government contended that the obligation to give notice was justified 'by the need to combat undeclared work and to keep the authorities informed of employers' practices', a contention that the Court rejected as being 'unconvincing'. This was on the basis of its inherently disproportionate reach: there were other, less restrictive measures that would have enabled the Italian government to achieve its stated objectives of combating fraud and undeclared work. When looked at in its totality, both the administrative burden on employers and the potential threat of a fine combined to set up a system that the Court felt would discourage employers from making use of part-time work. The

---

46. That is, a collective agreement approved by the Labour Court under the Schedule to the 2001 Act.

47. ss.11(7)–11(9) set out a framework for review whereby the Minister shall from time to time cause to be reviewed, in such manner as [s]he determines, the operation of this section in relation to part-time employees.

48. C55/07 and C56/07, [2008] EUECJ C-55/07, 24 April 2008.

49. *ibid.*, at [24].

Court further noted[50] that, owing to the cost and the penalties, the obligation to notify the authorities of part-time contracts risked particularly affecting small and medium-sized undertakings which, because they would not have the same resources as larger undertakings, may 'consequently be inclined to avoid that form of organisation of work, namely part-time work, which it is the aim of Directive 97/81 to promote'.[51]

1.7.1. LRC Code of Practice on Access to Part-Time Working

[6–27]   As explained above, the 2001 Act enshrines a commitment to monitor obstacles to the performance of part-time work. To this end, s.13 provides a mechanism whereby the Labour Relations Commission may (and, at the request of the Minister, shall) study every industry and sector of employment for the purposes of identifying obstacles that may exist in that industry or sector to persons being able to perform part-time work, and make recommendations as to how any such obstacles so identified could be eliminated. The section provides, *inter alia*, for the possibility of the LRC's preparing and publishing codes of practice with respect to the steps that could be taken by employers for the purposes of clause 5.3 of the Framework Agreement. Acting under this section, the LRC has prepared a Code of Practice on access to part-time working, which has been implemented by the Industrial Relations Act 1990 (Code of Practice on Access to Part-Time Working) (Declaration) Order 2006.[52]

The stated objectives of the Code of Practice are:

- to encourage best practice and conformity with the provisions of both the Employment Equality Acts 1998–2004 and the 2001 Act;
- to promote the development of policies and procedures to assist employers, employees and their representatives, as appropriate, to improve access to part-time work for those employees who wish to work on a part-time basis;
- to promote discussion and encourage employers, employees and their representatives, as appropriate, to consider part-time work and to address any barriers that may exist;
- to stimulate employers – where consistent with business requirements – to provide wider access to part-time work options;
- to provide a framework and practical guidance on procedures for accessing part-time work; and
- to inform those who are interested in part-time work.

---

50. *ibid.*, at [29].

51. *ibid.*, at [29]. A separate feature of the case of interest was the *Bilka* argument to the effect that because the majority of part-time workers are women, such an administrative rule constituted indirect discrimination. In light of its finding above, however, the Court did not consider it necessary to rule on this interpretation of the principle of equal treatment of men and women.

52. SI no. 8 of 2006.

This Code of Practice should be consulted when advising employers about considering part-time work within their organisations.

As to the status of codes of practice introduced pursuant to s.13 of the 2001 Act,   [6–28]
such as the 2006 LRC Code, s.42(4) of the Industrial Relations Act 1990 provides
that such codes shall be admissible in evidence in any proceedings before a court,
the Labour Court, the Labour Relations Commission, the Employment Appeals
Tribunal or the Equality Tribunal, and any provision of the code that appears to
the body concerned to be relevant to any question arising in the proceedings shall
be taken into account in determining that question. The LRC Code of Practice
was declared to be a Code of Practice for the purpose of the Industrial Relations
Act 1990 by the Industrial Relations Act 1990 (Code of Practice on Access to Part-
Time Working) (Declaration) Order 2006.[53] A failure on the part of any person
to observe any provision of a Code of Practice does not of itself render him or her
liable to any proceedings.

1.8. Prohibition of Penalisation of Part-Time Workers
The 2001 Act contains a strong prohibition on penalisation of employees. The   [6–29]
wording of the relevant section, s.15, is as follows:

(1) An employer shall not penalise an employee—
  (a) for invoking any right of the employee to be treated, in respect of the
    employee's conditions of employment…, or
  (b) for having in good faith opposed by lawful means an act which is unlawful
    under this Act, or
  (c) for refusing to accede to a request by the employer to transfer from
    performing—
    (i) full-time work to performing part-time work, or
    (ii) part-time work to performing full-time work,
                                or
  (d) for giving evidence in any proceedings under this Act or giving notice of his
    or her intention to do so or to do any other thing referred to in paragraph
    (a), (b) or (c).

1.8.1. *What Amounts to Penalisation under the 2001 Act*
Section 15(2) provides that an employee is penalised if [s]he is dismissed,[54] suffers   [6–30]
any unfavourable change in his or her conditions of employment or any unfair
treatment (including selection for redundancy), or is the subject of any other
action prejudicial to his or her employment. The penalisation prohibition in

---

53. SI no. 8 of 2006.
54. s.15(3) specifically provides that if penalisation of an employee constitutes dismissal within
    the meaning of the unfair dismissals legislation, relief may not be granted to the employee
    in respect of that penalisation under both legislative schemes.

the 2001 Act contains an important exception: where the prejudicial action is in respect of an employee's refusal to transfer status (from part-time to full-time or *vice versa*), this shall not amount to penalisation as long as *both* of the following conditions are complied with:

- having regard to all the circumstances, there were substantial grounds both to justify the employer's making the request concerned and the employer's taking that action consequent on the employee's refusal, and
- the taking of that action is in accordance with the employee's contract of employment and the provisions of the protective legislation generally.

A part-time worker's claim for penalisation under s.15 was upheld in *Beacon Automotive v A Worker.*[55] There the Labour Court found as a fact that the employer had decided to dismiss the employee when she refused to switch from part-time to full-time work. Upon returning to work from a week's holiday, the employee found someone else in her place; she was allowed to remain at work all day without any explanation being offered; and was dismissed that evening. Unsurprisingly, the Labour Court identified all three occurrences as manifest breaches of s.15(2)(a) of the 2001 Act.

2. Fixed-Term Workers

[6–31]   The adoption of the Protection of Employees (Fixed-Term Work) Act 2003[56] ('the 2003 Act') in order to implement Directive 99/70/EC has introduced an entirely new legal regime in Ireland in relation to fixed-term workers.[57] Although only so recently introduced, the 2003 Act has provoked a considerable amount of litigation both before the Rights Commissioner and Labour Court, and there is indeed by now significant case law from the High Court concerning the interpretation

of the 2003 Act. Moreover, owing to the failure of the Irish government to implement Directive 99/70/EC by 10 July 2001 as required,[58] complex questions of the direct effect of Community law in light of a State failure to transpose timeously the Directive have arisen. Most recently, the consequences of this failure have been illustrated by the preliminary ruling from the European Court of Justice in April 2008 in *Impact v Minister for Agriculture and Food & Others.*[59] There is thus

---

55. PTW/07/2, determination no. PTD 072, 17 July 2007.

56. For detailed annotated commentary on the provisions of the 2003 Act, see Kerr, *Consolidated Irish Employment Legislation* (Thomson Round Hall, Release 22, June 2009), Division H. See also Ryan, Chapter 10, in Regan, ed., *Employment Law* (Tottel Publishing, 2009).

57. Prior to the introduction of the 2003 Act, there existed some minimal, piecemeal protection for fixed-term workers via the avenues of both gender equality and unfair dismissal legislation. For discussion, see Higgins, 'Protection of Fixed-Term Workers', 1(1) *IELJ* (2004), 12.

58. The 2003 Act came into force on 14 July 2003.

59. C-268/06 [2008] EUECJ C-268/06, [2008] ELR 181.

much legal complexity to be grappled with in attempting to analyse the current state of employment law concerning fixed-term workers. As one commentator has observed, '[t]he huge changes in the law, the ambiguity of certain aspects of the legislation pertaining to fixed-term workers, as well as the uncertainty surrounding the issue of direct effects of the Directive, has made the treatment of fixed-term workers by employers a complex one, both for employers and their legal advisers.'[60] In this section, a comprehensive analysis is conducted both of the key legislative provisions introduced by the 2003 Act and of the now considerable body of case law of both the European Court of Justice and the Irish courts and tribunals concerning fixed-term workers.

2.1. Background to the 2003 Act

The background to Council Directive 1999/70 of 28 June 1999 is the Framework   [6–32]
Agreement on fixed-term work concluded by ETUC, UNICE and CEEP.[61] At the outset, it is critical to gain an understanding of the Framework Agreement in relation to fixed-term workers, given the requirement that transposing legislation must be interpreted and applied in light of the purpose and wording of the Directive so as to achieve the objectives pursued by the Directive.[62]

An important initial point to make about the Framework Agreement is that it   [6–33]
proceeds on the premise[63] that employment contracts of indefinite duration are the general form of employment relationship, while recognising that fixed-term employment contracts are a feature of employment in certain sectors or in respect of certain occupations and activities. In essence, the Framework Agreement and the Directive (and consequently the transposing Irish legislation) embody two specific purposes, set out in clause 1 of the Framework Agreement. These are:

- To improve the quality of fixed-term work by ensuring the application of the principle of non-discrimination;
- To establish a framework to prevent abuse arising from the use of successive fixed-term employment contracts or relationships.

Clause 4 of the Framework Agreement, 'Principle of non-discrimination', attempts   [6–34]
to flesh out the first aim of non-discrimination. It provides:

- In respect of employment conditions, fixed-term workers shall not be treated in a less favourable manner than comparable permanent workers

---

60. Kimber, 'Fixed-Term Workers – Where Are We Now?', 4(4) *IELJ* (2007), 103.
61. [1999] OJ L175/43.
62. *Von Colson and Kamann v Land Nordrhein-Westfalen* [1984] EUECJ R-14/85, [1984] ECR 1891, recently referred to by the Labour Court in the context of the 2003 Act in *Our Lady's Children Hospital Crumlin v Khan*, FTC/07/19, determination no. FTD 0813, 28 July 2008.
63. Framework Agreement, 'General Considerations', paras.6 and 8.

solely because they have a fixed-term contract or relation unless different treatment is justified on objective grounds.
- Where appropriate, the principle of *pro rata temporis* shall apply.
- The arrangements for the application of this clause shall be defined by the Member States after consultation with the social partners and/or the social partners, having regard to Community law and national law, collective agreements and practice.
- Period-of-service qualifications relating to particular conditions of employment shall be the same for fixed-term workers as for permanent workers except where different length-of-service qualifications are justified on objective grounds.

[6–35] The second of the twin aims – that of the prevention of abuse – is dealt with in clause 5(1) of the Framework Agreement, which obliges Member States to introduce (in a manner takes account of the needs of specific sectors and/or categories of workers) one or more of the following measures:

(a) a requirement of objective reasons justifying the renewal of such contracts or relationships;
(b) a specification of the maximum total duration of successive fixed-term employment contracts or relationships;
(c) a limit on the number of renewals of such contracts or relationships.

[6–36] Although more will be said in the context of clause 5 presently,[64] suffice to note that the language here is conditional and open-ended. The clause requires Member States to introduce measures to guard against the abuse of fixed-term contracts, but leaves open to Member States a number of options as to how that objective is to be achieved, which include defining those circumstances regarded as constituting abuse. Ireland has chosen to implement clause 5 by prohibiting the placing of employees on fixed-term contracts for more than four years, unless the use of such a contract is capable of being objectively justified. If an employee's contract exceeds the four-year threshold, and there is no objective justification for this, the 2003 Act deems the employee to have what is termed a 'contract of indefinite duration'. Analysis now turns to the 2003 Act and to a consideration of how the Framework Objective is reflected in that Act.

[6–37] The twin objectives of the Framework Agreement find direct expression in the 2003 Act. Thus, s.6 of the 2003 Act confers an entitlement on a fixed-term employee not, in respect of his or her conditions of employment, to be treated in a less favourable manner than a comparable permanent employee, unless the less favourable treatment can be justified on objective grounds.

---

64. See below, in particular discussion of the 2008 European Court of Justice preliminary ruling in C-268/06, *IMPACT v Minister for Agriculture and Food & Others* [2008] EUECJ C-268/06, [2008] ELR 181.

Secondly, the prevention of the abuse of successive fixed-term contracts is provided [6–38] for in s.9 of the 2003 Act, which states that an employer may not renew a fixed-term contract so as to bring the aggregate period for such a contract to more than four years, except where there are objective grounds justifying such renewal. Section 9(3) of the 2003 Act provides that, where a provision in a fixed-term contract purports to contravene the prohibition on renewing the contract over the four-year limit, that provision 'shall have no effect and the contract concerned shall be deemed to be a contract of indefinite duration' unless there is an objective ground justifying such renewal.

It can therefore be seen that this twin approach of the 2003 Act confers two separate and distinct entitlements upon fixed-term workers: the entitlement to equal treatment *vis-à-vis* permanent workers, and an entitlement to the recognition of a change in status for fixed-term workers once the fixed-term worker can satisfy certain conditions. Each of these separate and distinct conditions will be analysed later in this chapter.[65]

2.2. Who is a Fixed-Term Employee?

Pursuant to s.2 of the 2003 Act, a fixed-term employee is defined as a person [6–39] having a contract of employment entered into directly with an employer where the end of that contract is determined by an objective condition, such as arrival at a specific date, completion of a specific task or the occurrence of a specific event.

A number of employees are specifically excluded from the scope of the Act. Thus, [6–40] s.2 of the Act provides that it does not apply to agency workers placed by a temporary work agency at the disposition of a user enterprise. Section 2 also excludes from the definition of fixed-term employees: employees in initial vocational training relationships or apprenticeship schemes, or employees with a contract of employment that has been concluded within the framework of a specific public or publicly supported training, integration or vocational retraining programme. Other employees excluded from the scope of the Act are set out in s.17. Pursuant to s.17, the Act does not apply to a contract where the employee is (a) a member of the Defence Forces, (b) a trainee garda, or (c) a trainee nurse.

Notwithstanding the relative clarity of these exclusions, litigation under the 2003 [6–41] Act has sought to test their parameters. Thus, in the context of apprenticeships, the decision of the Labour Court in *ESB Networks v Kingham*[66] reversed a decision of the Rights Commissioner that an apprenticeship scheme could come within the scope of protection of the 2003 Act. An interesting example of a case in which an employee's status as fixed-term worker was in dispute is the Labour Court

---

65. See below, sections entitled '2.4. Fixed-Term Work and the Rights of Fixed-Term Workers under the 2003 Act' and '2.7. Successive Fixed-Term Contracts'.
66. [2006] ELR 181. See also the determination of the Labour Court in *ESB Networks v Group of Workers*, FTC/06/6, determination no. FTD 074, 7 March 2007.

determination in *Irish Prison Service v Donal Morris.*[67] There the complainant, a Catholic priest, was appointed prison chaplain in Castlerea prison. At the time of his appointment in September 1998 there were no agreed terms or conditions of appointment. Agreement was reached on this matter in 2004 and the claimant signed a contract in June 2005, the terms of which were retrospective to July 2002. This contract provided for the termination of his employment by the Minister upon revocation of his nomination by the bishop. In August 2005 the bishop informed the Minister that he was revoking the claimant's nomination. His employment as chaplain ended the following month. The claimant claimed that he was a fixed-term worker for the purposes of the 2003 Act and that his employment had terminated as a result of the occurrence of a specific event, as provided for in the Act. He submitted that he was employed continuously for seven years and for the last four years and nine months on a temporary contract. He thus claimed that he was entitled to a contract of indefinite duration. Rejecting the claimant's argument, both the Rights Commissioner and the Labour Court held that the procedure to terminate the employment relationship and the potential to utilise this procedure did not constitute a 'specific event' determining the contract for the purpose of the Act and therefore the claimant was not a fixed-term worker within the meaning of the Act. The rationale for this approach was that if the revocation of the bishop's nomination and the claimant's recall by the bishop and his consequent reassignment were to be taken as 'the occurrence of a specific event' within the meaning of the Act, then so could the occurrence, for example, of a redundancy situation that is a normal occurrence within employment relationships. Accordingly the Labour Court found that the claimant was not a fixed-term worker within the meaning of the Act and the court had no jurisdiction to hear the matter.

[6–42] A more recent determination of the Labour Court has focused attention on the question of whether the 2003 Act definition of fixed-term worker will apply in the relatively unusual situation of workers being engaged on a month-to-month basis.[68] Here the Labour Court answered this question in the affirmative, giving its reason for so doing in the following passage:

> If it were to be held that the protection of the Act does not extend to the use of contractual arrangements under which the continuation of an employment relationship could be opened to reconsideration on a month-to-month basis (as an alternative to providing a fixed termination date) the purpose of the Framework Agreement would be subverted and the attainment of its object would be seriously compromised.[69]

---

67. FTC/06/10, determination no. FTD 073, 2 March 2007.
68. *Dublin Port Authority – Shannon Airport v Keehan and Flannery* [2008] ELR 281.
69. *ibid.*

In *Doyle v National College of Ireland*[70] the High Court confirmed that the ability of the parties to bring a fixed-term contract to an end at an earlier date by the giving of notice did not alter the status of that contract as a fixed-term contract.

2.3. Direct Effect: The ECJ's 2008 Ruling in *IMPACT*

Ireland's delay in transposing the Directive resulted in many litigants claiming [6–43] that the Directive gave rise to directly enforceable rights in the period between 10 July 2001 and 14 July 2003, relying on the EC law doctrine of direct effect.[71] As is well known, this doctrine enables litigants in domestic courts in the Member States to invoke a piece of European law directly, as long as the law meets certain conditions of precision and unconditionality. In the fixed-term work context, this question of direct effect has been particularly pressing given the frequency with which fixed-term contracts are utilised by large public-sector employers. Owing to this frequency of use, a great number of State and public-sector employees have sought to rely on the protection of the Directive in an attempt to realise the vindication of the rights contained in the Directive in the period between July 2001 to July 2003, before the 2003 Act was in force. This issue was the subject of a high-profile preliminary reference ruling by the European Court of Justice in *Impact v Minister for Agriculture and Food & Others*.[72]

The complainants in the Irish proceedings the subject of the preliminary reference [6–44] were all unestablished civil servants working in various civil service departments under fixed-term contracts, which had commenced at various times prior to the date of Ireland's transposition of the Directive on 14 July 2003. A number of complainants had more than three years' continuous service and were claiming, in addition to equality of employment conditions *vis-à-vis* permanent employees, contracts of indefinite duration. (Indeed, in the period immediately before the 2003 Act came into force, a certain number of the complainants had their contracts renewed for a fixed term of up to eight years.) Some of the complainants had less than three continuous years' service as fixed-term employees and those complainants were thus claiming employment conditions equal to those of comparable permanent employees.

The complainants brought proceedings before the Rights Commissioner seeking [6–45] redress for alleged abuse of fixed-term contracts by the government departments. Their complaints were based on clauses 4 and 5 of the Framework Agreement as regards the period between 10 July 2001, the deadline for transposing Directive 1999/70, and 14 July 2003, the date on which the provisions transposing the Directive into Irish law entered into force. As regards the period after 14 July 2003, the complaints were based on s.6 of the 2003 Act.

---

70. [2006] ELR 267.
71. For detailed treatment of this doctrine in the context of the 2003 Act, see Kimber, 'Fixed-Term Workers – Where Are We Now?', 4(4) *IELJ* (2007), 103.
72. C-268/06 [2008] EUECJ C-268/06, [2008] ELR 181.

[6–46] The Government departments challenged the jurisdiction of the Rights Commissioner to entertain the complaints to the extent that they were grounded on the Directive. They contended that the Rights Commissioner's jurisdiction was confined to adjudicating on complaints alleging a contravention of the relevant domestic law. Furthermore, the government departments contended that clauses 4 and 5 were neither unconditional nor sufficiently precise and thus could not be relied upon by individuals before their national court. The Rights Commissioner found that she did enjoy jurisdiction to entertain the totality of the complaints and that clause 4 was directly effective but that clause 5 was not. This was appealed to the Labour Court (with the Union also cross-appealing on the Rights Commissioner's determination in respect of clause 5); the Labour Court then referred five questions by way of the Art 234 EC preliminary reference procedure to the Court of Justice. For ease of analysis, it will be convenient to deal immediately below with each question followed by the Court of Justice's answer to that question, in turn.

The first question referred to the Court of Justice in *IMPACT* was as follows:

> 1. Do the Rights Commissioner and Labour Court have jurisdiction to apply a directly effective provision of the Directive where they have not been given express jurisdiction to do so under domestic law and where individuals can pursue alternate claims?

[6–47] Answering this question in the affirmative, the Court of Justice held that Community law, and in particular the principle of effectiveness, requires that a specialised court, which is called upon under the (albeit optional) jurisdiction conferred on it by the 2003 Act to hear and determine a claim based on an infringement of that legislation, must also have jurisdiction to hear and determine an applicant's claims arising directly from the Directive itself in respect of the period between the deadline for transposing the Directive and the date on which the transposing legislation entered into force, if it is established that the obligation on that applicant to bring, at the same time, a separate claim based directly on the Directive before an ordinary court would involve procedural disadvantages liable to render excessively difficult the exercise of the rights conferred on him by Community law. The ECJ held that it was for the Labour Court to undertake the necessary checks in that regard.[73]

[6–48] The second question referred to the Court of Justice in *IMPACT* was as follows:

> 2. If the answer to question 1 is in the affirmative, are clauses 4 and 5 of the Framework Agreement unconditional and sufficiently precise to be relied upon by individuals before their national courts?

---

73. C-268/06 [2008] ELR 181,, [55].

The Court of Justice, as had the Rights Commissioner, found that clause 4 was sufficiently unconditional and precise, but that clause 5 was not.

In relation to clause 4, the Court of Justice noted that the prohibition of discrimi- [6–49] nation was worded 'in a general manner and in unequivocal terms': its subject-matter was thus sufficiently precise to be relied upon by an individual and to be applied by the national court. Significantly, the ECJ rejected Ireland's submission that the fact that there was no definition of 'employment conditions' in clause 4 rendered that provision incapable of being applied by a national court to the facts of a dispute. In rejecting that argument, the ECJ invoked its previous case law to the effect that the provisions of a Directive can be said to be sufficiently precise notwithstanding the absence of a Community definition of the social law terms included in those provisions[74]; that the fact that directives do not require the adoption of any further measure of the Community institutions militates in favour of a finding of direct effect[75]; and that the application of a qualification (here the objective grounds qualification to the prohibition on less favourable treatment) is subject to judicial control.[76] Taken together, these principles led the Court towards a finding of direct effect in relation to clause 4.

By contrast, clause 5 was again found not to enjoy direct effect, principally on the basis that it was not possible to determine sufficiently the minimum protection that should, on any view, be implemented pursuant to clause 5(1) of the Framework Agreement.

The third question referred to the Court of Justice in *IMPACT* was as follows:

> **3.** Does clause 5 prohibit an employer from renewing a fixed-term contract for up to eight years after the Directive came into force but before it was enacted in domestic law?

The ECJ answered this third question in the affirmative – a conclusion that may [6–50] initially seem surprising in light of its finding concerning clause 5(1). When analysed closely, however, the Court's response here is readily understandable. Emphasising the second of the twin objectives of the Directive – the prevention of abuse of fixed-term contracts – and drawing on both Art. 10 EC, and the third paragraph of Art. 249 EC, the ECJ held that Directive 1999/70 must be interpreted as meaning that an authority of a Member State acting in its capacity as a public employer may not adopt measures contrary to the objective pursued by that Directive and the Framework Agreement as regards the prevention of the abusive use of fixed-term contracts. This was the case in *IMPACT* because of the

---

74. C-6/90 and C-9/90, *Francovich v Italy* [1991] EUECJ C-6/90, [1991] ECR I-5357.
75. C-41/74, *Van Duyn v Home Office* [1974] EUECJ R-41/74, [1974] ECR 1337.
76. C-212/04, *Adeneler v Ellinikos Organismos Galaktos* [2006] EUECJ C-212/04, [2006] ECR I-6057.

renewal of the employees' contracts for an unusually long term in the period – as noted, eight years in some cases – between the deadline for transposing Directive 1999/70 and the date on which the transposing legislation entered into force.

[6–51] The fourth question referred to the Court of Justice in *Impact* was as follows:

> 4. If the answer to question 1 or 2 is in the negative, are the Rights Commissioner and Labour Court required to interpret domestic law in accordance with the wording and purpose of a Directive and if so are they required to interpret the provisions of the 2003 Act as having retrospective effect to the date on which the Directive should have been transposed?

The Court replied that the answer to this question must be that, insofar as Irish law contains a rule that precludes the retrospective application of legislation unless there is a clear and unambiguous indication to the contrary, a national court hearing a claim based on an infringement of a provision of national legislation transposing Directive 1999/70 is required, under Community law, to give that provision retrospective effect to the date by which that Directive should have been transposed only if that national legislation includes an indication of that nature capable of giving that provision retrospective effect. This, the ECJ held, was a matter for the Labour Court to determine.[77]

The fifth and final question referred to the Court of Justice in *IMPACT* was as follows:

> 5. If the answer to question 1 or 4 is in the affirmative, are remuneration and pensions included in the meaning of 'employment conditions' referred to in clause 4 of the framework agreement?'

[6–52] The ECJ held that clause 4 of the Framework Agreement must be interpreted as meaning that employment conditions within the meaning of that clause encompass conditions relating to pay and to pensions that depend on the employment relationship, excluding conditions relating to pensions arising under a statutory social-security scheme. As the Framework Agreement was associated with the improvement of living and working conditions and the existence of proper social protection for fixed-term workers, in the light of those objectives, clause 4 of the Framework Agreement must be interpreted as articulating a principle of Community social law that cannot be interpreted restrictively. The Court held that to interpret clause 4 of the Framework Agreement as categorically excluding from the term 'employment conditions' for the purposes of that clause, financial conditions such as those relating to remuneration and pensions would be effectively to reduce – contrary to the very objective of to that clause – the scope of the protection against discrimination for the workers concerned by introducing a

---

77. [2008] ELR 181, at [104].

distinction based on the nature of the employment conditions, which the wording of that clause did not in any way suggest.

The Court placed further emphasis on the fact that, as the Advocate General [6–53] had noted in her opinion,[78] such an interpretation would render the reference in clause 4(2) of the Framework Agreement to the principle of *pro rata temporis* meaningless, that principle being intended by definition only to apply to divisible performance, such as that deriving from financial employment conditions linked, for example, to remuneration and pensions.

2.3.1. Broader Implications of IMPACT Ruling

The ruling of the Court of Justice in *IMPACT* will clearly have significant implica- [6–54] tions for many other cases currently at various stages of progression in the domestic fora in Ireland. Perhaps the most discussed example of another such case is that of *Scoil Íosagáin v Martin Henderson*.[79] The complainant was a teacher employed on a fixed-term contract between August 2002 and August 2003. In May 2003, the employer placed an advertisement in a national newspaper seeking applications for permanent teaching posts. The claimant was not informed of the vacancy and did not see the advertisement. He claimed that the failure of the employer to inform him of the vacancy contravened the 2003 Act when it came into force in July 2003 and/or in the alternative contravened clause 6.1 of the Directive. He argued that through the application of the doctrine of direct effect he was entitled to rely on the Directive in proceedings against the employer prior to the coming into force of the domestic legislation. Before the Rights Commissioner, the employer submitted that the Rights Commissioner had no jurisdiction to hear the complaint as the Act was not in force at the time of the alleged contravention. The employer further argued that the claimant could not rely on the doctrine of direct effect, as one of the conditions necessary before a provision of a Directive can have direct effect is that the action must be taken against the State and that the claimant's contract was not with the State but with the board of management of the school in which he was employed. The Rights Commissioner declined juris-diction to hear the complaint as the matters complained of occurred prior to the enactment of the 2003 Act in July of that year. On appeal to the Labour Court, the Labour Court did not directly address the matter of the jurisdiction or direct effect. The Court determined that the provision of primary education was a public service performed under the control of the State, and that the employer was an emanation of the State. It concluded, therefore, that the Directive was directly effective in an action taken against the board of management, and that the school was in breach of the requirement of the Directive and of the 2003 Act. It is inter-esting to note that the High Court appeal in *Henderson* was withdrawn following the *IMPACT* ruling.[80]

---

78. Opinion of Advocate General Kokott delivered on 9 January 2008, [161].
79. [2005] ELR 211.
80. For another example of *IMPACT* influencing domestic proceedings, see the approach of the

2.4. Fixed-Term Work and the Rights of Fixed-Term Workers under the 2003 Act

[6–55] Our focus now moves from the question of the direct effect of the 2003 Act to a detailed consideration of the scope of the legislation and the considerable body of litigation that has resulted from it in the domestic context.[81] Part II of the 2003 Act sets out the rights of fixed-term workers. It is convenient to identify each of the rights owed to fixed-term workers under the 2003 Act at this point. The rights are:

- the right not to be treated, in respect of his or her conditions of employment, in a less favourable manner than a comparable permanent employee;
- the right to receive written statements at engagement and renewal;
- the right, in certain circumstances, to be deemed to be employed on a contract of indefinite duration;
- the right to be informed by the employer of vacancies that become available to ensure that the fixed-term employee shall have the same opportunity to secure a permanent position as other employees;
- the right to have the employer facilitate, as far as practicable, access by a fixed-term employee to appropriate training opportunities to enhance his or her skills, career development and occupational mobility;
- the right to be taken into account for the purposes of calculating the threshold above which employees' representative bodies may be constituted in an undertaking in accordance with s.4 of the Transnational Information and Consultation of Employees Act 1996; and
- the right not to be penalised for, *inter alia*, invoking the protections of the 2003 Act.

2.4.1. Less Favourable Treatment Regarding Conditions of Employment for Fixed-Term Workers

[6–56] The term 'employment conditions' is defined in s.2 of the Act as including conditions in respect of remuneration, which in turn is defined as including pensions. However, in relation to pensions, s.6(5) provides that the requirement of equal treatment does not apply where the normal hours of work of the fixed-term employee constitute less than 20 per cent of the normal hours of work of a comparable permanent employee. Moreover, pursuant to ss.6(6) and 6(7) of the Act, the *pro rata* principle applies in relation to any benefit the amount or scope of which is dependent on the number of hours worked by the employee. Thus, the entitlement of the fixed-term employee to a given benefit is limited to the proportion of hours worked by that employee as compared to those worked by the comparable

---

Labour Court in *NUI Galway v Morley*, FTC/05/8, determination no. FTD 093, 2 March 2009.

81. For a detailed overview of earlier case law, see Meenan, 'Protection of Employees (Fixed-Term Work) Act 2003', 3(2) *IELJ* (2006), 39; Kimber, 'Fixed-term Workers – Where Are We Now?', 4(4) *IELJ* (2007), 103.

permanent employee. One of the most significant judicial authorities interpreting 'conditions of employment' in the context of the 2003 Act is the judgment of Laffoy J in *Minister for Finance v McArdle*,[82] to be analysed later in this chapter. There Laffoy J held that this term does not include conditions as to duration or tenure of employment.[83]

2.4.2. Meaning of 'Comparable Permanent Employee'

In order to establish the existence of a difference in treatment in the employment conditions applicable to fixed-term and permanent employees, it is necessary to identify a comparable permanent employee. Section 5 of the 2003 Act sets out three situations in which fixed-term and permanent employees can be considered comparable. First, where the permanent employee and the fixed-term employee are employed by the same employer or by an associated employer; secondly, if the first situation is not applicable, where the comparable permanent employee is specified in a collective agreement; thirdly, if neither of the above situations applies, where the comparable permanent employee is employed in the same industry or section of employment as the fixed-term employee. In relation to the first and third of these situations, one of the following conditions must be met under s.5(2) in order for the permanent employee to be a valid comparator: [6–57]

(a) both of the employees concerned perform the same work under the same or similar conditions or each is interchangeable with the other in relation to the work;

(b) the work performed by one of the employees concerned is of the same or a similar nature to that performed by the other and any differences between the work performed or the conditions under which it is performed by each either are of small importance in relation to the work as a whole or occur with such irregularity as not to be significant;

(c) the work performed by the relevant fixed-term employee is equal or greater in value to the work performed by the other employee concerned, having regard to such matters as skill, physical or mental requirements, responsibility and working conditions.

2.5. Claims of Less Favourable Treatment of Fixed-Term Workers and the Concept of Objective Justification

2.5.1. Less Favourable Treatment not simply Different Treatment

An important, if elementary, point to be noted here is that simply establishing a difference in treatment will not necessarily amount to establishing that that treatment is less favourable. That the need to show less favourable treatment may involve complex issues of proof is well illustrated in the Labour Court's determi- [6–58]

---

82. [2007] IEHC 98, [2007] 2 ILRM 438.
83. The case is discussed below in this chapter.

nation in *Eircom v McDermott*,[84] where the Labour Court considered that it was not possible to determine whether a fixed-term worker's being afforded access to one type of pension scheme was less favourable than another.

2.5.2. Non-Renewal of Fixed-Term Contract not in itself Capable of Amounting to Less Favourable Treatment

[6–59] The Labour Court has held on a number of occasions that the non-renewal of a fixed-term contract is not in itself capable of constituting less favourable treatment for the purposes of this section. So, in *Prasad v Health Service Executive*,[85] the Court held that, except in the circumstances envisaged by s.9 of the 2003 Act, a fixed-term employee does not have an automatic right to have his or her fixed-term contract renewed on its expiry. In so deciding the Court adopted the reasoning of the English Court of Appeal in *Department for Work and Pensions v Webley*,[86] in particular the following passage in the judgment of Wall LJ:

> Once it is accepted, as it must be, that fixed-term contracts are not only lawful, but are recognised in the Preamble to Directive 99/70 as responding, 'in certain circumstances, to the needs of both employers and workers', it seems to me inexorably to follow that the termination of such a contract by the simple effluxion of time cannot, of itself, constitute less favourable treatment by comparison with a permanent employee. It is of the essence of a fixed-term contract that it comes to an end at the expiry of the fixed-term. Thus unless it can be said that entering into a fixed-term contract is *of itself* less favourable treatment, the expiry of a fixed-term contract resulting in the dismissal of the fixed-term employee cannot, in my judgment, be said to fall within regulation 3(1).[87]

[6–60] The Labour Court had taken a similar view in the earlier case of *Aer Lingus v A Group of Workers*.[88] More recently, in *Dublin Port Company v McKraith and Kieran*[89] the Labour Court held that as far as the 2003 Act was concerned, the employer 'would have been perfectly entitled' to terminate the employment of the claimants if they had not been appointed to permanent vacancies. The rationale for this approach by the Labour Court is explained by its statement in another determination: 'If the conclusion of a fixed-term contract was to be regarded as less favourable treatment within the meaning of clause 4 of the Directive and s.6 of the Act, all fixed-term contracts would be *prima facie* unlawful. This could not have been intended.'[90] The Court in *Prasad* concluded that neither the Directive

---

84. FTC/04/11, determination no. FTD 051, 16 February 2005.
85. FTC/05/4, determination no. FTD 062, 7 April 2006.
86. [2004] EWCA Civ 1745, [2005] ICR 577, [2005] IRLR 288.
87. [2005] ICR 577, 585, *per* Wall LJ (with whom Jacob and Ward LJJ agreed) (emphasis in original). The reference to reg.3(1) is to the Fixed-Term (Prevention of Less Favourable Treatment) Regulations 2002.
88. [2005] ELR 261.
89. [2008] ELR 14.
90. *Our Lady's Children Hospital Crumlin v Khan* [2008] ELR 314.

nor the 2003 Act required 'that a fixed-term contract of employment must be renewed unless the employer can show that the requirement for the work being performed by the fixed-term employee [has] ceased'.

2.5.3. *Can Renewal of a Fixed-Term Contract Amount to Less Favourable Treatment?*

As analysed above, the position adopted by the courts in relation to the non-renewal of a fixed-term contract is that it cannot in and of itself amount to less favourable treatment. But what of the corollary situation: can the *renewal* of a fixed-term contract amount to less favourable treatment within the meaning of that term in the 2003 Act? As a matter of statutory construction, the answer to this question appears plainly to be in the affirmative: s.7(1) of the 2003 Act states (albeit parenthetically) that less favourable treatment 'may include the renewal of a fixed-term employee's contract for a further fixed term'. It would appear to follow that the 2003 Act does envisage that the fact of renewal of a fixed-term contract can in and of itself amount to less favourable treatment. In the case of *Our Lady's Children Hospital Crumlin v Khan*,[91] however, the Labour Court rejected this construction, preferring instead to explain the wording used in brackets in s.7 as relating to s.9(4) of the 2003 Act[92] rather than to s.6. Section 9(4) expressly requires objective justification for the renewal for a further fixed-term of a contract that would otherwise become one of indefinite duration by operation of s.9(1) or 9(2) of the Act. The Court observed:

[6–61]

> A reading of the Act as a whole suggests that the reference in s.7... is intended to convey that the standard of objective justification required for the purpose of derogating from the requirements of s.9 are [*sic*] the same as those required to derogate from s.6. However, these words do not imply that a person who cannot avail of s.9 of the Act to obtain a contract of indefinite duration, because he or she does not meet the requirements of that section, could achieve the same result by relying upon s.6.

With respect, it is submitted that this interpretation places a somewhat strained construction on the clear wording of s.6, which appears plainly to countenance the further renewal of a fixed-term contact as being capable of comprising less favourable treatment.

2.5.4. *The Meaning of Objective Justification*

The issue of what constitutes objective justification of less favourable treatment is one that requires detailed analysis. Section 7(1) of the 2003 Act, which lays down the requirement of objective justification of less favourable treatment, provides as follows:

[6–62]

---

91. [2008] ELR 314. See also *NUI Galway v Morley*, FTC/05/8, determination no. FTD 093, 2 March 2009.
92. See below in this chapter.

A ground shall not be regarded as an objective ground for the purposes of any provision of this Part unless it is based on considerations other than the status of the employee concerned as a fixed-term employee and the less favourable treatment which it involves for that employee (which treatment may include the renewal of a fixed-term employee's contract for a further fixed term) is for the purpose of achieving a legitimate objective of the employer and such treatment is appropriate and necessary for that purpose.

[6–63] In *Health Service Executive v Prasad*,[93] the Labour Court observed that the second limb of s.7(1) – that the grounds relied upon must be justified as being for the purpose of achieving a legitimate objective of the employer and that such treatment must be appropriate and necessary for that purpose – amounted to a restatement of the 'three tier test for objective justification in indirect discrimination cases' formulated by the European Court of Justice in its celebrated ruling in *Bilka-Kaufhaus*.[94] The *Bilka* test – mentioned earlier in this chapter in the context of part-time workers – is effectively now set out in s.22(1)(a) of the Employment Equality Act 1998.[95] Although there is a difference in wording between s.7 of the 2003 Act and the *Bilka* formulation, the Labour Court recently confirmed that s.7 comprises 'essentially the same test' as that laid down in *Bilka*.[96] In reaching this conclusion the Labour Court placed emphasis on the recent ruling of the Court of Justice in *Adeneler and Others v Ellinikos Organismos Galakto*.[97] In its ruling in *Adeneler* the Court of Justice referred to the need to show that the ground relied upon 'respond to a genuine need, is appropriate for achieving the objective pursued and is necessary for that purpose'.[98] The Court stressed that that the concept of 'objective reasons' within the meaning of clause 5 of the Framework Agreement could only be understood as referring to 'precise and concrete circumstances characterising a given activity' that might result from the specific nature of the inherent characteristics of the tasks or from pursuit of a legitimate social policy objective of a Member State. This builds on previously well-established principles in relation to objective justification, which include that the employer bears the burden of proof of establishing the objective reasons and that monetary considerations cannot in and of themselves be sufficient to discharge that burden.

[6–64] Examples of pleas of objective justification in defence of less favourable treatment that have been accepted as amounting to objective justification include public pay policies[99]; those in which the defence has been rejected have included arguments

---

93. FTC/05/4, determination no. FTD 062, 7 April 2006.
94. C-170/84, *Bilka-Kaufhaus v Weber von Hartz* [1986] EUECJ R-170/84, [1986] ECR 1607.
95. For detailed analysis of the various elements of the test, see the determination of the Labour Court in *Inoue v NBK Designs Ltd.* [2003] ELR 98.
96. *HSE v Ghulam* [2008] ELR 325.
97. C-212/04 [2006] EUECJ C-212/04, [2006] ECR I-6057.
98. C-212/04 [2006] ECR I-6057, at [74].
99. *28 Workers v Courts Service* [2007] ELR 212.

as to industrial relations issues,[100] and differences in collective bargaining processes.[101] It is important to emphasise, however, that the inquiry into the existence of objective justification is one that will be conducted against the backdrop of the full context of the working environment.[102]

Section 7(2) of the 2003 Act provides that less favourable treatment may be justi- [6–65] fied if the terms of the fixed-term employee's contract of employment are, when considered in their totality, at least as favourable as the terms of the comparable permanent employee's contract of employment. This was well captured by Laffoy J in the course of her judgment in *Minister for Finance v McArdle*[103] when she observed of s.7(2) that:

> In essence, sub-s. (2) provides that what would otherwise be a discriminatory contractual term shall be regarded as justified on objective grounds if the overall 'package' of terms of the fixed-term employee is at least as favourable as the overall 'package' of the comparable permanent employee.[104]

It is thus important to stress the distinction between this provision in the fixed-term workers' legislative scheme and the position obtaining under the Employment Equality Acts 1998–2004, since under the latter regime this broad, totality approach is not permissible: there, each individual element of the contract of employment must be compared *vis-à-vis* the claimant and a comparator.

2.6. Fixed-Term Workers' Rights to Receive Written Statements at Recruitment on Renewal

Section 8 of the 2003 Act confers an entitlement upon fixed-term employees to be [6–66] informed in writing as soon as practicable by the employer of the objective condition determining the contract, whether that condition is the arrival at a specific date, completion of a specific task, or the occurrence of a specific event. Furthermore, s.8(2) provides that where an employer proposes to renew a fixed-term contract, the fixed-term employee shall be informed in writing by the employer of the objective grounds justifying the renewal of the fixed-term contract and the failure to offer a contract of indefinite duration, at the latest by the date of the renewal. The Labour Court has observed that the requirement to give the information in writing is imposed so as to avoid 'the type of uncertainty or misunderstanding that can occur with verbal communications'.[105]

---

100. *McGarr v Department of Finance*, DEC-E2003/036, 3 September 2003.
101. C-127/92, *Enderby v Frenchay Health Authority* [1993] EUECJ C-127/92, [1993] ECR I-5535.
102. *28 Workers v Courts Service* [2007] ELR 212.
103. [2007] IEHC 98, [2007] 2 ILRM 438.
104. [2007] 2 ILRM 438, 443-444.
105. *Board of Management of North Dublin Muslim School v Naughton*, FTC/08/1, determination no. FTD 0811, 21 May 2008.

[6–67] The written statements referred to in s.8 are expressly deemed to be admissible as evidence in any proceedings under the 2003 Act.[106] Very significantly, if either the Rights Commissioner or the Labour Court in such proceedings takes the view that an employer omitted to provide a written statement or has provided one that is evasive or equivocal, then the Rights Commissioner or the Labour Court may 'draw any inference he or she or it consider just and equitable in the circumstances'.[107] These provisions thus demonstrate that the requirements under s.8 are capable of being used so as to effect robust protection of fixed-term workers. Employers will make light of their statements obligations under s.8 at their peril. This conclusion is, indeed, supported by case law. Thus, the Labour Court has characterised s.8 (2) as 'a mandatory provision admitting of no exceptions'.[108] As a result, a failure to provide the written notice before the renewal of the contract, even where this is due to inadvertence rather than wilful non-compliance, 'can neither be overlooked nor excused'.[109] Thus the employer's contention in *Clare County Council v Power*[110] that its breach of s.8 was 'a technical breach and was not motivated by any bad faith' did not avail the employer in that case.[111] More recently, the Labour Court has used more trenchant language still in relation to the s.8(4) obligation, stating that:

> There is no doubt that the failure to provide such a statement is a breach of the provisions of the Act. The failure to provide a written statement of these grounds is to be deplored and in normal circumstances would put the Respondent in a position of considerable difficulty.[112]

[6–68] In *Khan v HSE, North Eastern Area*[113] the Labour Court took the view that the requirement to provide a written statement of objective grounds is designed, in part, to ensure that a ground subsequently relied upon for renewing a fixed-term contract beyond the period normally permitted by s.9 is the real or operative reason justifying a derogation from the provisions of that section. The Labour Court went on to observe:

> Moreover, a purposive interpretation of section 9 indicates that a Respondent must establish that the reason relied upon as constituting objective grounds was the

---

106. s.8(3) of the 2003 Act.
107. s.8(4) of the 2003 Act. For an example of the Labour Court drawing such an inference, see *Irish Rail v Stead*, FTC/04/5, determination no. FTD 052, 1 March 2005.
108. *Galway City Council v Mackey*, FTC/06/5, determination no. FTD 065, 23 June 2006.
109. A phrase that the Labour Court repeated in *HSE v Ghulam* [2008] ELR 325.
110. FTC/07/14, determination no. FTD 0812, 3 June 2008.
111. Although it should be noted that the Labour Court did expressly find that the breach here was culpable. It is submitted, however, that the emphasis placed upon this culpability was merely to illustrate the seriousness of the breach and its impact on the employee rather than to suggest that inadvertent breaches are to be regarded with leniency under the 2003 Act.
112. *HSE v Ghulam* [2008] ELR 325.
113. [2006] ELR 313.

operative reason for the failure to offer a contract of indefinite duration at the time the fixed-term contract was renewed. This suggests that the Respondent must at least have considered offering the Claimant a contract of indefinite duration before renewing his or her fixed-term contract and decided against doing so for the reason relied upon.

Section 8(2) is also of considerable significance on this point. It seems to the Court that the purpose of Section 8 is not just to ensure that a fixed-term employee is informed of the reason why his or her contract is being renewed. On a reading of the Section as a whole it is clear that it is intended to ensure that the employer definitively commits itself, at the point at which the contract is being renewed, to the grounds upon which it will rely if subsequently pleading a defence under Section 9(4). Thus where an employer fails to provide a fixed-term employee with a statement in writing, in accordance with Section 8(2), it is apt to infer, in accordance with Section 8(4) of the Act, that the grounds subsequently relied upon were not the operative grounds for the impugned decision and it would be for the employer to prove the contrary.

More recently, the Labour Court in *Clare County Council v Power*[114] helpfully   [6–69]
provided a description of the type of conduct that will trigger censure under s.8:

> The Court has taken the view that the Respondents decided to, as it were, leave the gate open. They could not make up their minds whether to employ the Complainant on a full time and decided to have the best of both worlds by renewing her contract for another year. This is exactly the type of conduct which this Act was enacted to prevent and, in the view of this Court, represents more than a technical breach of Section 8.

2.6.1. Information Must Be Made Available in Writing 'As Soon as Practicable'

Section 8(1) of the 2003 Act requires that an employer inform a fixed-term   [6–70]
employee in writing 'as soon as practicable' of the objective condition determining the contract. The meaning of this phrase 'as soon as practicable' was recently considered by the Labour Court in *Board of Management North Dublin Muslim School v Naughton*[115], where the Court referred in detail to the decision of the Supreme Court in *McC. and McD. v Eastern Health Board*.[116] There the Supreme Court approved an earlier decision of Costello J (as he then was) on the meaning of the expression in *Hobbs v Hurley*.[117] In *McC. and McD. v Eastern Health Board*[118] it was held that in construing the phrase, regard must be paid to the context in which the words were used and all the surrounding circumstances and, in particular, the nature and purpose of the statutory obligation on the respondent. It was

---

114. FTC/07/14, determination no. FTD 0812, 4 June 2008.
115. FTC/08/1, determination no. FTD 0811, 21 May 2008.
116. [1997] 1 ILRM 349.
117. Unreported, High Court, 10 June 1980.
118. [1997] 1 ILRM 349.

held that the phrase was not synonymous with 'as soon as possible'. Relying on this authority, the Labour Court concluded as follows:

> It seems to the Court that the nature of the obligation imposed by the Section is to inform a fixed-term employee of the duration of his or her employment or, where this is indeterminable, of the circumstances in which it will expire. At least one purpose of the obligation is to ensure that the fixed-term employee knows the duration [of] the employment so as to be in a position to arrange his or her affairs accordingly. This suggests that the information should be given in close proximity to the commencement of the employment. The authorities also suggest that regard should also be had to any practical difficulties which might impede the [employer] in providing the information. Since the existence of any such difficulties are necessarily within the particular knowledge of the [employer] it is for it to explain any delay in providing the information.

2.7. Successive Fixed-Term Contracts

[6–71] As noted at the outset of this section, in addition to ensuring equal treatment for fixed-term workers, the Framework Agreement and thus the 2003 Act also seek to guard against the potential abuse of successive fixed-term contracts. Section 9(1) provides that where a fixed-term employee completes or has completed his or her third year of continuous employment, then his or her fixed-term contract may be renewed by that employer on only one occasion and any such renewal shall be for a fixed term of no longer than one year.[119] Section 9(2) provides that where a fixed-term employee is employed on two or more continuous fixed-term contracts and the date of the first such contract is subsequent to the date on which the 2003 Act was passed, the aggregate duration of such contracts shall not exceed four years.

[6–72] Once again, this section comprises a vigorous pursuit of the aims of the Framework Agreement: here, to guard against the abusive deployment of successive fixed-term contracts by employers. The strength of the provision is seen in s.9(3), which provides that where any term of a fixed-term contract purports to contravene s.9(1) or 9(2) that term shall have no effect and the contract concerned shall be deemed to be a contract of indefinite duration. However, the strength of the section is perhaps diluted somewhat by the fact that the provisions of ss.9(1) and 9(2) do not apply where there are objective grounds justifying the renewal.

---

119. It is thus important to note that a fixed-term employee could be employed on a number of successive contracts that cumulatively amount to less than four years and could thereby become entitled to a contract of indefinite duration, a point noted, with reference to Rights Commissioner authority, by Ennis and O'Sullivan, 'Fixed Term Workers, Contract Renewals and Less Favourable Treatment: Recent Developments', 6 *Employment Law Review – Ireland* (2007), 2, at p.9.

2.7.1. *The Meaning of Contract of Indefinite Duration*

A number of questions arise from the provisions in the 2003 Act concerned with [6–73] avoiding contracts of indefinite duration. First, the term itself requires consideration. The term 'contract of indefinite duration' is not defined in the 2003 Act but it has been judicially defined outside the context of the 2003 Act as meaning no more than a contract terminable upon the giving of reasonable notice. The most prominent recent example of this judicial definition is the judgment of the Supreme Court in *Sheehy v Ryan*,[120] where the Supreme Court affirmed the approach taken by Carroll J to the effect that a 'contract of indefinite duration' was essentially a contract terminable upon the giving of reasonable notice.[121]

From the standpoint of the 2003 legislation and the meaning to be accorded to the term 'contract of indefinite duration', a number of authorities now assist in understanding the term.

In *Health Service Executive (North Eastern Area) v Khan*,[122] the Labour Court [6–74] ruled that the contract of indefinite duration to which a fixed-term employee might become entitled by operation of s.9(3) 'is identical in its terms, including any express or implied terms as to training and qualifications, as the fixed term contract from which it was derived'. The effect of s.9(3), then, is to transform a contract of definite duration into one of indefinite duration: no more and no less. This interpretation was confirmed in the important case of *Minister for Finance v McArdle*,[123] where Laffoy J held that the Labour Court had erred in law in accepting that the employee's conditions as to duration or tenure of her employment must not be less favourable that that of her chosen comparator.[124]

2.7.2. *The High Court Decision in McArdle*

The leading authority to date on the meaning of the term 'contract of indefinite [6–75] duration' in the 2003 Act is the decision of the High Court in *Minister for Finance v McArdle*.[125] The kernel of the High Court ruling is perhaps best encapsulated in Laffoy J's observation in respect of s.9(3) that it 'only impacts on one aspect of a contract of employment when it comes into play: its duration'.[126]

The background to this case was that Ms McArdle commenced employment in [6–76] the State Laboratory in her capacity as a laboratory technician in March 2000, on a fixed-term contract for one year. Her contract was renewed on an annual basis thereafter until 21 March 2004. From that point onwards her contract was not managed appropriately, such that it was not until 31 May 2005, that she was

---

120. [2008] IESC 14, [2008] 4 IR 258.
121. [2004] ELR 87.
122. [2006] ELR 313.
123. [2007] 2 ILRM 438.
124. See also *HSE v Arefi*, FTC/07/6, determination no. FTD 081, 21 February 2008.
125. [2007] ELR 165.
126. [2007] 2 ILRM 438, 453.

furnished with a renewed contract, which purported to be in respect of the period from 22 March 2004 until 21 March 2005. The Minister for Finance accepted that the contract furnished did not comply with the 2003 Act and that as a result Ms McArdle became entitled to a contract of indefinite duration with effect from 22 March 2004. However, the issue still to be decided was what precisely was meant by a 'contract of indefinite duration'.

[6-77] The Rights Commissioner defined the contract of indefinite duration as being one that should be 'no less favourable than an established civil servant', that is, that the claimant should enjoy the same tenure on the same basis and subject to the same procedure as an established civil servant. The Labour Court adopted the finding of the Rights Commissioner on this point; the employer appealed to the High Court.

[6-78] In the High Court, Laffoy J found that the Labour Court had erred in law in concluding that the defendant acquired security of tenure similar to the security of tenure enjoyed by the comparator, namely an established civil servant. Laffoy J found that the effect of s.9(3) of the 2003 Act was that where an employee is given a renewed fixed-term contract in contravention of s.9(1) or (2), then s.9(3) operates to render void *ab initio* the term of the contract that purports to provide for its expiry by passing of time or the occurrence of event. Accordingly, by operation of law the offending term is severed from the contract, 'transmuting' its character from one of definite duration or fixed term to one of indefinite duration. Crucially, the remaining terms of the contract are unaffected – including terms as to pensionability and termination. Laffoy J held that the terms and conditions of a contract of indefinite duration that come into operation under s.9(3) must therefore be the same as those pertaining to the fixed-term contract from which it is derived in all respects other than its definite duration.

2.7.3. Objective Justification for Offering further Fixed-Term Contracts or not Offering a Contract of Indefinite Duration

[6-79] As already noted, s.9(3) of the 2003 Act provides, in essence, that once the four-year threshold has expired then the fixed-term contract is transmuted into a contract of indefinite duration by operation of law, unless there is objective justification for not altering the status of the contract in this way. Section 9 of the 2003 Act also prevents the renewal of a fixed-term contract such as to bring the aggregate period of such periods to more than four years, except where there are objective grounds for renewal. However, as with objective justification for less favourable treatment, there is no further detail in the legislation as to what amounts to an objective justification contravening the four-year threshold in the 2003 Act. There now exists, however, a considerable body of case law providing guidance on the question of when successive contracts will be objectively justified. From this case law it is possible to identify a number of key principles. First, significant restructuring that the employer is obliged to undertake for the purposes of economic viability will likely pass muster as an objective justification for repeated

recourse to fixed-term contracts. This is well illustrated by the case of *Aer Lingus v Group of Workers*,[127] where the Labour Court found that there were objective grounds for the non-renewal by Aer Lingus of fixed-term contracts of employees. The complainants were cabin-crew members whose contracts had expired and were renewed; nevertheless, the employer had advertised vacancies internally for temporary cabin crew positions. The complainants had only been employed on contracts of nine months' duration; candidates for the new temporary cabin crew positions were required to have at least 12 months' service with the employer. At the time the company was undertaking a major re-organisation of its operation and an increasing number of staff posts were being made redundant.

The claimants contended that the employer was in breach of the 2003 Act by not [6–80] renewing the contracts when there was a continuing requirement for the work they performed. They claimed that the existence of such work *required* that their contracts be renewed. Both the Rights Commissioner and the Labour Court rejected the claim, holding that there was no obligation on the company under the 2003 Act to renew a contract even where there was an ongoing requirement for work of that kind. They further accepted that the claimants were treated the same as permanent workers in that permanent workers were also subject to the 12 months' service requirement. In light of the fact that the airline was engaged in the process of seeking to redeploy long-serving staff in circumstances of redundancy and engaging in reorganisation, the Court concluded that the imposition of a service qualification was objectively justified.

In *University College Hospital Galway v Awan*[128] the complainant was employed [6–81] as a consultant anaesthetist between January 1999 and June 2004 on a succession of fixed-term contracts. He claimed that he became entitled to a contract of indefinite duration with effect from January 2004. He further complained that the employer failed to provide him with a written statement of the objective reasons relied upon in renewing his fixed-term contracts, and submitted that he was treated less favourably than a comparable permanent employee when the employer advertised the post he held and required him to apply for that post in open competition. The claimant did not participate in the competition: he believed that he was already legally entitled to hold the post permanently.

The employer contended that the appointment of consultant doctors in the public [6–82] health sector is governed by the Local Authority (Officers and Employees) Act 1926 and the Health Act 1970 and accordingly the Health Board was precluded from making appointments to permanent positions other than by way of public competition. It submitted that the constraints imposed under those Acts constituted objective reasons for the continued renewal of his employment for a fixed term. Strongly rejecting this argument, the Labour Court held that the post the

---

127. [2005] ELR 261.
128. [2008] ELR 64.

claimant held since 1999 on a succession of fixed-term contracts became one of indefinite duration by law on 1 January 2004. The Court held that national legislative measures could not be relied upon as objective reasons for derogating from the obligations imposed by the EU Directive on fixed-term work.

2.7.4. The Meaning of 'Continuous Employment' in the Context of Successive Fixed-Term Contracts

[6–83] A key issue in relation to fixed-term workers' litigation is the question of how the courts are likely to characterise successive fixed-term contracts. In particular, what is the position when the fixed-term contracts have been renewed, but only following a break in service? What length of a break will destroy the element of continuity such that the contract will be deemed not to be successive? This question was considered in *Department of Foreign Affairs v A Group of Workers*[129] where the claim was brought by a group of temporary clerical workers employment by the Department of Foreign Affairs on a number of fixed-term contracts between 2001 and 2006. The breaks between the various fixed-term contracts amounted to a number of weeks or months in each case. Their claim turned on the interpretation of 'continuous employment' within s.9 of the 2003 Act, for the employer argued that each employee's continuity of employment was broken by virtue of the expiry of each fixed-term contract. Thus, the employer argued, none of the claimants had completed his or her third year of continuous employment, the condition required to open the door to the operation of s.9(1) of the 2003 Act.

[6–84] In a determination that marks a generous approach to the question of continuity of service from the perspective of employees, the Labour Court held that an employee is continuously employed for the purposes of the 2003 Act even where there are breaks of weeks or months between successive contracts and that such breaks are to be considered as periods of 'lay-off' provided that the employee has a reasonable belief that [s]he will be re-employed and this does in fact occur. In considering whether there was a break in contracts and if so what break would lead litigants to fall outside s.9, the Labour Court noted that:

> there appears, at first sight, to be a conflict between s 9 of the Act and clause 5 of the Framework Agreement. This arises from the fact that clause 5 of the Framework Agreement applies to fixed-term contracts which are successive thus giving it a considerably wider scope than if its application was confined to employment relationships which were continuous. It seems to the Court that there is a significant qualitative difference between the concept of a continuous employment relationship and one which is successive. The former connotes an employment relationship without interruption whereas the latter indicates a series of relationships which follow each other but can be separated in time.

---

129. [2007] ELR 332.

It will be noted that clause 5.2(a) of the Framework Agreement permits Member States to define, *inter alia*, the conditions under which fixed-term contracts will be regarded as successive. This provision, however, could hardly authorise a Member States to define the concept of successive employment as meaning something which is qualitatively different and narrower in scope than that term would normally bear.[130]

In so holding, the Labour Court placed heavy reliance on the determination of **[6–85]** the European Court of Justice, discussed above, in *Adeneler and Others v Ellinikos Organismos Galaktos*,[131] where the Court ruled that clause 5 of the Framework Agreement was to be interpreted as 'precluding a national rule under which only fixed term employment contracts that are not separated from one another by a period of time longer than 20 working days are to be regarded as "successive"'.

It is instructive to quote a passage from the judgment of the European Court in *Adeneler* in its entirety:

It is clear that a national provision under which only fixed-term contracts that are separated by a period of time shorter than or equal to 20 working days are regarded as successive must be considered to be such as to compromise the object, the aim and the practical effect of the Framework Agreement.

As observed by the referring court and the Commission, and by the Advocate General in points 67 to 69 of her Opinion, so inflexible and restrictive a definition of when a number of subsequent employment contracts are successive would allow insecure employment of a worker for years since, in practice, the worker would as often as not have no choice but to accept breaks in the order of 20 working days in the course of a series of contracts with his employer.

Furthermore, a national rule of the type at issue in the main proceedings could well have the effect not only of in fact excluding a large number of fixed-term employ-ment relationships from the benefit of the protection of workers sought by Directive 1999/70 and the Framework Agreement, largely negating the objective pursued by them, but also of permitting the misuse of such relationships by employers.[132]

Having referred to the above passage in *Adeneler*, the Labour Court in *Depart-* **[6–86]** *ment of Foreign Affairs* thus upheld the finding of the Rights Commissioner that the claimants were employed on continuous contracts for the purpose of s.9 of the 2003 Act. The decision thus constitutes the conferral of an extremely broad latitude to fixed-term employees seeking to characterise as continuous several contracts that may have been interspersed by not insubstantial break periods.[133]

---

130. [2007] ELR 322, 339.
131. C-212/04 [2006] EUECJ C-212/04, [2006] ECR I-6057.
132. C-212/04 [2006] ECR I-6057, [84]–[86].
133. For a similarly generous approach to the question of continuous employment see the more

[6–87]   Furthermore, it is important to note that the Labour Court rejected the employer's argument that 'seasonal' or 'fluctuating' need could be capable of constituting objective justification in the circumstances for the continued use of fixed-term contracts, thus once again illustrating how high the bar will be set in relation to employers' attempts at establishing objective justification.

2.8. Rights of Fixed-Term Workers to Information on Employment and Training Opportunities

[6–88]   Section 10 of the 2003 Act enshrines fixed-term employees' rights to information on employment and training opportunities. Section 10(1) obliges an employer to inform a fixed-term employee in relation to vacancies that become available, so as to ensure that the fixed-term employee has the same opportunity to secure a permanent position as other employees. This information may be provided by means of a general announcement at a suitable place in the undertaking or establishment.[134] The High Court has held that the section carries 'a concomitant obligation to allow the employees to apply for such vacancies'.[135] Section 10(3) states that an employer shall, as far as practicable, facilitate access by a fixed-term employee to appropriate training opportunities to enhance his or her skills, career development and occupational mobility.

[6–89]   The scope of the employer's obligation to inform of vacancies was considered by the Labour Court in *Aer Lingus v A Group of Workers*.[136] There the Labour Court concluded that, whilst fixed-term employees had the right to receive information concerning vacancies for which they were qualified to apply, this provision did not restrict the right of an employer to determine the content of those qualifications.

[6–90]   The obligation imposed on employers by s.10 of the Act is to inform fixed-term employees of permanent vacancies so as to provide them with an opportunity to secure a permanent post. The nature of the obligation was considered by the Labour Court in *Henderson v Scoil Íosagáin*.[137] Here it was held that the mere placing of an advertisement in a newspaper was insufficient: the Court found that notification must be delivered to the fixed-term employee in person or a notice must be placed in a prominent position in the workplace.

[6–91]   The Labour Court further considered this provision in *Board of Management North Dublin Muslim School v Naughton*,[138] where a notice concerning vacancies for permanent posts that were to be filled in September was posted in the

---

recent determination of the Labour Court in *Health Service Executive v Oshodi*, FTC/08/20, determination no. FTD 0913, 24 September 2009.
134. s.10(2) of the 2003 Act.
135. *Minister for Finance v McArdle* [2007] IEHC 98, [2007] 2 ILRM 438.
136. [2005] ELR 261.
137. [2005] ELR 271.
138. FTC/08/1, determination no. FTD 0811, 21 May 2008.

complainant teacher's school in July. This was during the school holidays when the claimant was not at work. It was conceded ('rightly', according to the Labour Court), on behalf of the employer that this could not have discharged the obligation under this section. In *Naughton*, however, there was evidence that the employer also instructed its solicitors to write to the claimant informing him of the vacancies and enclosing a copy of the advertisement that had been placed in the public press. The Labour Court stated that it was satisfied that 'in causing the notification to be sent to the Claimant by post the Respondent did all that it could to fulfil its obligation under the Section'.

The High Court has held that subsection (1) is not limited to vacancies for posts at the same level as a post occupied by a fixed-term employee: it also includes promotions.[139]

2.9. Prohibition on Penalisation of Fixed-Term Workers

We have already encountered earlier in this chapter the concept of penalisation [6–92] in relation to part-time workers. Just as the Protection of Employees (Part-Time Work) Act 2001 contains a strong prohibition on penalisation of employees,[140] so too does the 2003 Act prohibit the penalisation of fixed-term employees by their employer. As the Labour Court has recently confirmed in the context of this aspect of the 2003 Act, 'penalisation must always be regarded as a serious matter'.[141] The wording of the relevant section, s.13, is as follows:

(1) An employer shall not penalise an employee—
  (a) for invoking any right of the employee to be treated, in respect of the employee's conditions of employment, in the manner provided for by this Part,
  (b) for having in good faith opposed by lawful means an act which is unlawful under this Act,
  (c) for giving evidence in any proceeding under this Act or for giving notice of his or her intention to do so or to do any other thing referred to in paragraph (a) or (b), or
  (d) by dismissing the employee from his or her employment if the dismissal is wholly or partly for or connected with the purpose of the avoidance of a fixed-term contract being deemed to be a contract of indefinite duration under section 9(3).
(2) For the purposes of this section, an employee is penalised if he or she—
  (a) is dismissed or suffers any unfavourable change in his or her conditions of employment or any unfair treatment (including selection for redundancy), or
  (b) is the subject of any other action prejudicial to his or her employment.

---

139. *Minister for Finance v McArdle* [2007] IEHC 98, [2007] 2 ILRM 438.
140. s.15 of the 2001 Act.
141. *Hamid v HSE Dublin Mid Leinster*, FTC/09/9, determination no. FTD 0910, 6 August 2009.

[6–93] In *Clare County Council v Power*[142] the Labour Court held that there were 'compelling reasons' for construing s.13(1)(d) as applicable to both the non-renewal of fixed-term contracts as well as dismissals at common law. The Court took the view that where a decision is made not to renew a fixed-term contract when no objective grounds for its extension have been given, this falls 'squarely within the ambit of cases which might be heard under Section 13(1)(d)'. In so holding, the Court was fortified by the judgment of the European Court of Justice in *Adeneler & Others v Ellinikos Organismos Galaktos*[143] which dealt with the thwarting of an employee's rights when the needs of the job are not of limited duration but fixed and permanent. In those circumstances, the Court ruled 'the protection of workers against the misuse of fixed-term employment contracts or relationships, which constitutes the aim of clause 5 of the Framework Agreement, is called into question'. The Labour Court in *Power* relied on this passage to arrive at its conclusion that 'real and effective judicial protection against abuse of fixed-term contracts can only be guaranteed if the non-renewal of a fixed-term contract, when used as an instrument of abuse, is rendered unlawful'.

[6–94] More recently, in *Hamid v HSE Dublin Mid Leinster*[144] the Labour Court upheld a claim for penalisation in circumstances where the claimant's contract had not been renewed, the respondent having argued unsuccessfully that this was due to the contract being designated as a training contract. Significantly, in addition to upholding the Rights Commissioner's award of a contract of indefinite duration, the Labour Court made an award compensation of €15,000 in relation to the penalisation claim, an amount it regarded as 'fair and equitable and a proportionate means of marking the gravity of the contravention of the Act found to have occurred'.[145]

3. Enforcement

[6–95] In this final section of the chapter, it is convenient to consider together some points of practice and procedure that pertain to both pieces of legislation.

Both the 2001 and the 2003 Acts provide that complaints under the Act may be referred in the first instance to a Rights Commissioner, whose decision shall do one or more of the following: (i) declare that the complaint was or was not well founded; (ii) require the employer to comply with the relevant provision; (iii) require the employer to re-instate or re-engage the employee (including on a contract of indefinite duration[146]); (iv) require the employer to pay to the

142. FTC/07/14, determination no. FTD 0812, 3 June 2008.
143. C-212/04 [2006] EUECJ C-212/04, [2006] ECR I-6057.
144. FTC/09/9, determination no. FTD 0910, 6 August 2009.
145. *Hamid v HSE Dublin Mid Leinster*, FTC/09/9, determination no. FTD 0910, 6 August 2009.
146. It is important to note that even where an employee is found to have been entitled to a contract of indefinite duration, it may be that the Rights Commissioner (or the Labour

employee compensation of such amount (if any) as is just and equitable having regard to all the circumstances, but not exceeding two years' remuneration. A significant point to note here is that, in awarding compensation, the Rights Commissioner (and the Labour Court on appeal[147]) must specify whether or not the award is 'in respect of remuneration including arrears of remuneration', as the distinction has significant income tax implications.[148]

Complaints must be made within six months of the date of contravention of the relevant Act, although this period may be extended by a further 12 months if the failure to refer the case within six months was due to 'reasonable cause'.[149] This power to extend the time limit was considered by the Labour Court in *Cementation Skanska v Carroll*,[150] where the Court held that, in considering if 'reasonable cause' existed, it was for the claimant to establish that there were reasons that both explain the delay and afford an excuse for it. The Court continued: [6–96]

> The explanation must be reasonable, that is to say it must make sense, be agreeable to reason and not be irrational or absurd. In the context in which the expression 'reasonable cause' appears in statute it suggests an objective standard but it must be applied to the facts and circumstances known to the claimant at the material time.

Related considerations in this context will include the length of the delay as well as possible prejudice to the opposing party.[151]

3.1. Appeals from and Enforcement of Decisions of Rights Commissioner

Both Acts provide for an appeal mechanism to the Labour Court by either party. A notice of appeal must be furnished in writing to the Labour Court within six weeks of the date of the decision to which the appeal relates. A copy of this notice is then given by the Labour Court to the other party concerned 'as soon as may be after the receipt of the notice by the Labour Court'. As noted below, a party to proceedings before the Labour Court under s.15 may appeal to the High Court from a determination of the Labour Court on a point of law; the determination of the High Court shall be final and conclusive. [6–97]

Court on appeal) may regard compensation as the more appropriate remedy. See for example *Health Service Executive v Oshodi*, FTC/08/20, determination no. FTD 0913, 24 September 2009 (effluxion of time meant that compensation more appropriate than reinstatement or re-engagement on a contract of indefinite duration).

147. See below in this chapter.
148. s.192A of the Taxes Consolidation Act 1997 (inserted by s.7 of the Finance Act 2004). For general comment on this area, see Farrelly, 'Taxation of Employment Awards: A Basic Understanding', 3(4) *IELJ* (2006), 113.
149. s.16(4) of the 2001 Act; s.14(4) of the 2003 Act.
150. WTC/03/2, determination no. DWT 0338, 31 October 2003.
151. See further the judgment of Laffoy J in *Minister for Finance v Civil and Public Service Union* [2006] IEHC 145, [2007] ELR 36.

Where a decision of a Rights Commissioner has not been carried out by the employer and an appeal has not been brought, the employee may refer the complaint to the Labour Court and the court, without hearing any evidence, shall make a determination to the like effect as the decision of the Rights Commissioner.

3.2. What Constitutes a Decision for the Purposes of Appeal?

[6–98] It was noted above that a decision of a Rights Commissioner may be appealed to the Labour Court within six weeks of the date of the decision. But what constitutes a decision for this purpose? In *Bus Éireann v SIPTU*,[152] a case concerning the equivalent provision under the Protection of Employees (Part-Time Work) Act 2001, the Labour Court held that the reference in that section to a decision of a Rights Commissioner could only be a reference to 'a complete or final decision which determines whether or not there has been an infringement of the Act'. In that case, the Labour Court was satisfied that the decision the company sought to appeal was merely a preliminary ruling on a single issue in the case, and consequently did not have the character of a 'decision' under the section. Nevertheless, the Court did recognise that there would be 'limited circumstances in which a preliminary point should be determined separately from other issues arising in a case'. The Court indicated that this would only normally be permitted 'where it could lead to considerable savings in both time and expense' and where the point was 'a question of pure law where no evidence is needed and where no further information is required'.

3.3. Enforcement of Determinations of the Labour Court

[6–99] Both Acts provide that the Labour Court's determination can be enforced by the employee, the employee's trade union or the Minister, in the Circuit Court without the employer or any evidence – other than in relation to non-implementation of the determination – being heard.

The procedures governing applications for enforcement are set out in Ord. 57, reg. 9 of the Circuit Court Rules 2001, as amended.[153]

3.4. Right of Appeal to High Court on Point of Law

[6–100] Under both the 2001 and the 2003 Acts, it is possible to institute a further appeal on a point of law only to the High Court.[154] The rarity of the circumstances in

---

152. PTW/04/4, determination no. PTD 048, 13 October 2004.
153. For part-time workers, see SI no. 721 of 2004; in the case of fixed-term workers, see SI no. 532 of 2006.
154. As to the procedural requirements for this appeal, see reg.2 of Order 84C, inserted by the Rules of the Superior Courts (Statutory Applications and Appeals) 2007, SI no. 14 of 2007, and the commentary by Kerr in his annotation to the 2003 Act: *Consolidated Irish Employment Legislation* (Thomson Round Hall, Release 22, June 2009), Division H.

which the High Court will overturn a decision of a specialist tribunal such as the Labour Court has been emphasised by the superior courts in many cases, of which the best-known example is *Henry Denny & Sons (Ireland) Ltd. v Minister for Social Welfare.*[155] In that case Hamilton CJ warned that:

> the courts should be slow to interfere with the decisions of expert administrative tribunals. Where conclusions are based upon an identifiable error of law or an unsustainable finding of fact by a tribunal such conclusions must be corrected. Otherwise it should be recognised that [when] tribunals which have been given statutory tasks to perform and exercise their functions, as is now usually the case, with a high degree of expertise and provide coherent and balanced judgments on the evidence and arguments heard by them it should not be necessary for the courts to review their decisions by way of appeal or judicial review.[156]

3.5. Mixed Questions of Fact and Law

This passage invites consideration of another fundamental question: when will a determination of the Labour Court properly be characterised as amounting to a matter of law, and when one of fact? On this point, it is instructive to have regard to the more recent Supreme Court decision in *National University of Ireland Cork v Ahern*,[157] where the Supreme Court considered what was meant by a 'question of law' in the context of an appeal from the Labour Court (in that case, under s.8(3) of the Anti-Discrimination Pay Act 1974). McCracken J, with whom the other members of the Supreme Court agreed, stated:

[6–101]

> The respondents submit that the matters determined by the Labour Court were largely questions of fact and that matters of fact as found by the Labour Court must be accepted by the High Court in any appeal from its findings. As a statement of principle, this is certainly correct. However, this is not to say that the High Court or this court cannot examine the basis upon which the Labour Court found certain facts. The relevance, or indeed admissibility, of the matters relied on by the Labour Court in determining the facts is a question of law. In particular, the question of whether certain matters ought or ought not to have been considered by the Labour Court and ought or ought not to have been taken into account by it in determining the facts, is clearly a question of law, and can be considered on an appeal…[158]

In considering whether or not to allow an appeal against a decision of the Labour Court, the High Court must consider whether that court based its decision on an identifiable error of law or on a finding of fact that is not sustainable.

---

155. [1997] IESC 9, [1998] 1 IR 34, [1998] ELR 36.
156. [1998] 1 IR 34, 37.
157. [2005] IESC 40, [2005] 2 IR 577.
158. [2005] 2 IR 577, 580.

3.6. Whether Arguments not Pursued below can be Advanced on High Court Appeal

[6–102] An important point for consideration concerning High Court appeals on points of law under both pieces of legislation is whether legal arguments not pursued in the Labour Court can be advanced on appeal to the High Court. In the High Court case of *Minister for Finance v McArdle*,[159] this issue arose in circumstances where the employer sought to advance legal arguments as to the jurisdiction of the fora below. Laffoy J described as 'correct in point of principle' the proposition that such legal arguments not presented before the Labour Court could not properly be canvassed on appeal to the High Court. She further emphasised the necessity for 'precision as to the points of law for determination by this Court… and the grounds on which it [is] asserted the Labour Court erred' in the special summons.

3.7. The Position Relating to Parallel Claims under the 2001 and 2003 Acts

[6–103] The question of parallel claims raises a number of distinct issues in the context of a consideration of these Acts. In s.18 of the 2003 Act, for example, it is provided that in the event that penalisation constitutes a dismissal of the employee within the meaning of the unfair dismissals legislation, relief may not be granted to the employee in respect of that penalisation both under the 2003 Act and under the unfair dismissals legislation. The section goes on to provide that an individual who is a fixed-term employee under the 2003 Act and a part-time employee under the 2001 Act may obtain relief[160] arising from the same circumstances under either, but not both, of the Acts.

Another point to be noted here is that s.18 of the 2003 Act, unlike s.15 of the Unfair Dismissals Act 1977, does not limit an employee's right of access to the High Court to enforce his or her common law rights.[161]

[6–104] In relation to employment equality claims, s.101A of the Employment Equality Act 1998 provides that, where an employer's conduct constitutes both a contravention of Pts III or IV of that Act and a contravention of the 2001 Act or the 2003 Act, relief may not be granted to the employee concerned in respect of the conduct under both the 1998 Act and the other Act. This section thus provides that a party may not obtain 'double relief', but does not preclude the *processing* of more than one claim. As an example, where an application under the unfair dismissals or the employment equality legislation has been unsuccessful, a claimant is not precluded by this section from pursuing a claim under the 2003 Act.[162]

---

159. [2007] IEHC 98, [2007] 2 ILRM 438.
160. Though this does not prevent two separate claims from being processed, as was confirmed by the Labour Court in *Galway City Council v Mackey*, FTC/06/5, determination no. FTD 065, 22 June 2006.
161. *Ahmed v Health Service Executive* [2008] ELR 117.
162. *Galway City Council v Mackey*, FTC/06/5, determination no. FTD 065, 23 June 2006.

PART III

Employment Equality

CHAPTER 7

Introduction to Employment Equality Law

Introduction

The *Oxford English Dictionary* defines 'discrimination' as 'the recognition of the [7–01] difference between one thing and another'.[1] Discrimination occurs in the workplace every day and is often perfectly acceptable. Employers make key decisions concerning, *inter alia*, recruitment, termination, promotion and career advancement on the basis of differences between individuals. Traditionally, the law has been reluctant to interfere with such managerial decisions and with the contractual and business arrangements entered into between an employer and his employees (or prospective employees). This *laissez faire* approach was clearly reflected in the oft-quoted passage from Lord Davey in *Allen v Flood*[2]:

> an employer may refuse to employ [a person] for the most mistaken, capricious, malicious or morally reprehensible motives that can be conceived, but [that person] has no right of action against him.[3]

However, in recent years, the law has adopted a more interventionist approach and [7–02] has greatly limited the employer's freedom in this regard. Where such decisions are based not on objectively verifiable criteria related to the individual's ability but rather on the basis of the employer's perception of certain inherent characteristics of the individual unconnected with their ability to do the work and deriving from certain listed grounds (for example the gender, age, race or religion of the worker),[4] then such discrimination is unlawful. More often than not, these perceptions are derived from a form of stereotyping or based on uninformed generalisations. For example, some employers may be reluctant to employ a mother of young children on the basis that she may not be as flexible in terms of hours of work as other employees. Yet, that employer may not hesitate in engaging a father of young children in similar circumstances. In the United Kingdom the Equal Opportunities Commission has highlighted the discriminatory effect of such attitudes:

---

1. *Oxford English Dictionary* (2nd ed., 2003).
2. [1898] AC 1.
3. *ibid.,* at 172.
4. The concept of discriminatory grounds is considered in Chapter 9.

It is common to hear jobs referred to as 'men's work' or 'women's work'. Such distinctions are no more than acceptance of existing conventions which are based upon nothing more than the customs of a bygone age. Women now do work which would have been regarded as utterly unsuitable for them before the first world war. No-one then would have accepted that women could do many of the jobs they are now doing, such as bus-driving or welding. Nor would they have accepted that men could be nurses and midwives, as they now are.

The convention that only women should use typewriters has no foundation in genuine sex differences in the abilities required. The irrational nature of the convention is shown by the fact that it is acceptable for journalists and authors to type. And it has been accepted for many years that men can operate keyboards (and be highly paid for it) provided they are setting type rather than typing on paper.[5]

The response of European and consequently of Irish law has been to prohibit acts of discrimination against employees where the discrimination is based on certain listed grounds which are regarded as being unmeritorious and inappropriate bases on which to distinguish one employee from another.

1. Historical Development of Irish Employment Equality Law

[7–03] While there is a guarantee of equality before the law under Art. 40.1 of the Constitution,[6] it was not until Ireland's accession to the European Economic Community in 1972 that real inroads were made into the area of employment equality. In terms of employment law, the introduction of Art. 141 (ex 119) of the Treaty of Rome 1957 guaranteeing equal pay for men and women for equal work changed the Irish legal landscape forever. Art. 141 was held to have direct horizontal and vertical effect, which meant that it could be relied upon by citizens before domestic courts and tribunals.[7] The Treaty was supplemented in this regard by Directives 76/207/EEC (the Equal Treatment Directive) and 75/117/EEC (the Equal Pay Directive).

[7–04] Ireland's accession to the EEC kick-started much legislative reform in the field of employment law and equality in particular. The equal pay provisions of the Treaty and Directive 75/117/EEC were enacted into Irish law in the form of the Anti-Discrimination (Pay) Act 1974. The Equal Treatment Directive (76/207EEC) was transposed into Irish law in the form of the Employment Equality Act 1977, which prohibited discrimination on the basis of the individual's sex or marital status.[8]

---

5. Equal Opportunities Commission, *Fair and Efficient Selection* (HMS, London, 1993), at 2–6.
6. For detailed analysis, see Bolger and Kimber, *Sex Discrimination Law* (Round Hall Sweet and Maxwell, 2000), at 25–45; see also Doyle, *Constitutional Equality Law* (Thomson Round Hall, 2004).
7. C-43/75, *Defrenne v SABENA* [1976] EUECJ, [1976] ECR 455.
8. See *Murphy v An Bord Telecom* [1986] ILRM 483.

Irish employment law underwent a further radical overhaul with the enact- [7–05] ment of the Employment Equality Act 1998. This legislation replaced the Anti-Discrimination (Pay) Act 1974 and the Employment Equality Act 1977, and consolidated Irish equality law in the form of a single enactment. Furthermore, the 1998 Act introduced a number of new grounds of discrimination, adding family status, sexual orientation, religion, age, disability, race and membership of the Travelling Community to the pre-existing grounds. The 1998 Act was, in many ways, ahead of its time. The legislation was introduced prior to the Treaty of Amsterdam 1997, which provided for the addition of new grounds of unlawful discrimination, including racial or ethnic origin, religion or belief, disability, age or sexual orientation.[9] The 1998 Act represents one instance where Ireland was 'ahead of the curve' in implementing legislation from Europe.

The consolidation of Irish employment equality law was also to be welcomed as it ensured that all aspects of equality legislation were contained within a single enactment, which should ensure consistency of approach and also eliminate confusion in this area.[10] The Employment Equality Act 1998 was amended, but not replaced by, the Equality Act 2004, which made a number of procedural changes to the 1998 Act.

2. Defining Discrimination

If discrimination involves the recognition of differences between one thing and [7–06] another, then the comparative approach to establishing unlawful discrimination under Irish law requires the victim to prove disparate or unfavourable treatment as against another person whose position is in all other respects similar to that of the victim, and to show that such discrimination arose on the basis of one of the listed grounds in the legislation. Possibly the simplest, and the best, definition of unlawful discrimination was provided by the European Court of Justice in *Gillespie v Health and Social Services Board and Others*[11] where it was said that, 'It is well settled that discrimination involves the application of different rules to comparable situations, or the application of the same rules to different situations.'[12]

This comparative approach towards combating inequality or discrimination, which [7–07] has been adopted under the legislation, has its drawbacks and has been criticised on the basis that it does little to dismantle historical discrimination in certain sectors of employment. It makes it difficult, for example, for a woman to prove that she

---

9. Art. 13 and Dir. 2000/78/EC (Framework Directive Establishing a General Framework for Equal Treatment in Employment and Occupation).
10. The same cannot be said for England and Wales, where similar provisions are contained in four Acts and three sets of regulations. Generally, see Smith and Thomas, *Smith & Wood's Employment Law* (9th ed., Oxford University Press, 2008), at pp.243–367.
11. C-342/93 [1996] EUECJ, [1996] ECR 475.
12. *ibid.* at para.16.

has been discriminated against on the basis of her sex when all her colleagues doing the same work are women. Furthermore, it raises the question as to whether the comparative approach towards discrimination allows the perpetuation of historically discriminatory practices where certain work (secretarial, nursing and so forth) was deemed, for prejudicial reasons alone, to be 'women's work', meaning that a worker would struggle to sustain a claim for sex discrimination due to the lack of a comparator. This issue has been alleviated but not eliminated, as we shall see in this chapter, by the introduction of the hypothetical comparator.

[7–08]   The Employment Equality Acts 1998 to 2008 provide that discrimination on one of the listed grounds in all its forms will be prohibited. The Acts distinguish between discriminatory measures that are illegal on their face (direct discrimination[13]) and more subtle forms of discrimination that, while superficially non-discriminatory, adversely affect one class of which the complainant is a member disproportionately more than other classes (indirect discrimination[14]). Both of these forms of discrimination are dealt with below.

3. Proving Discrimination

[7–09]   Discrimination is an inherently difficult thing to prove. It will be rare for the respondent to admit any deliberate wrongdoing in this regard. Indeed, there will be times where the respondent may not realise that [s]he is acting in a discriminatory manner but is doing so subconsciously, rationalising to him or herself that the complainant simply 'didn't fit in'. As the Labour Court pointed out in *Ntoko v Citibank*[15]:

> This approach is based on the empiricism that a person who discriminates unlawfully will rarely do so overtly and will not leave evidence of the discrimination within the complainant's power of procurement. Hence, the normal rules of evidence must be adapted in such cases so as to avoid the protection of anti-discrimination laws being rendered nugatory by obliging complainants to prove something which is beyond their reach and which may only be in the respondents' capacity of proof.[16]

Under the Employment Equality Act 2004, a complainant must establish a prima facie case of discrimination. Once this burden is discharged a presumption of discrimination is deemed to exist and it is then up to the respondent to rebut that presumption with evidence to the contrary. Thus s.38 of the 2004 Act (which amends the 1998 Act by the insertion of a new s.85A) states that:

---

13.   s.6(1) Employment Equality Act 1998, as amended by s.4 Equality Act 2004. For further discussion of direct and indirect discrimination please see below.
14.   s.31 Employment Equality Act 1998, as amended by s.20 Equality Act 2004.
15.   [2004] ELR 116.
16.   *ibid.*, at 127.

(1) Where in any proceedings facts are established by or on behalf of a complainant from which it may be presumed that there has been discrimination in relation to him or her, it is for the respondent to prove the contrary…

On the other hand, s.85A does not reverse the burden of proof. The complainant must establish the existence of facts from which a presumption that discrimination has occurred can be raised.[17] In *DPP v Sheehan*,[18] the Labour Court stated:

> What the complainant must establish is a factual matrix from which the Court may properly draw an inference that discrimination has occurred. There is no exhaustive list of factors which can be regarded as indicative of discrimination in the filling of employment vacancies. However, an inference of discrimination can arise where, for example, a less qualified man is appointed in preference to a more qualified woman… It can also arise from an unexplained procedural unfairness in the selection process.[19]

To what extent does the complainant have to establish facts that will give rise to the presumption of discrimination? The English Court of Appeal, in reference to a similar English provision,[20] gave detailed guidance as to what the complainant is obliged to prove in such circumstances in *Igen Ltd. v Wong*.[21] Here, the court stated that the claimant in such circumstances is required to prove on the balance of probabilities facts from which the tribunal could conclude – in the absence of adequate explanation – that the claimant has been unlawfully discriminated against. Once these facts are proven, it is the tribunal's function to examine those primary facts in order to determine what inferences of secondary fact could be drawn from them. Where facts are proven from which conclusions could be drawn that the claimant has been unlawfully discriminated against, then the burden of proof shifts to the respondent. It is for the respondent then to provide an explanation that is not only adequate to explain the primary facts as proven by the claimant, but also to discharge the burden of proof on the balance of probabilities that the discrimination was not unlawful. [7–10]

The Irish Supreme Court considered the matter in the context of a claim for indirect discrimination in *Nathan v Bailey Gibson*.[22] In that case, the plaintiff was a female employee who for 10 years assisted a man who operated a carton folder/gluer machine for the defendant. The man was a member of a traditionally male-dominated trade union. The union had an agreement with the defendant that should any union position become open, the defendant was required to offer the [7–11]

---

17. *Southern Health Board v Mitchell* [2001] ELR 201 (Labour Court determination no. DEE011/2001, 15 February 2001).
18. Determination no. EDA0416 (14 December 2004).
19. *ibid.*
20. s.63A Sex Discrimination Act 1975.
21. [2005] EWCA Civ 142, [2005] 3 All ER 812, [2005] ICR 931, [2005] IRLR 258, CA.
22. [1998] 2 IR 162.

position to a member of the union first. When the operator of the machine retired, the plaintiff (was not a member of that same union) applied for his job. As part of the 'closed shop' arrangement with the union, the defendant offered the position to a union member and not the plaintiff. The plaintiff alleged *inter alia* that she had been indirectly discriminated on the grounds of her sex and marital status because of the union's requirement that access to the vacant position of carton folder/gluer machine operator be confined to persons who held membership of the trade union. The Supreme Court held that both the Labour Court and High Court had erred in law in finding that it was necessary for the appellant to prove a causal link between the requirement and her sex. Hamilton CJ concluded that:

> In such a case the worker is not required, in the first instance, to prove a causal connection between the practice complained of and the sex of the complainant. It is sufficient for him or her to show that the practice complained of bears significantly more heavily on members of the complainant's sex than on members of the other sex. At that stage the complainant has established a *prima facie* case of discrimination and the onus of proof shifts to the employer to show that the practice complained of is based on objectively verifiable factors which have no relation to the complainant's sex.[23]

[7–12] The reasoning adopted in *Bailey Gibson* was applied by the Equality Tribunal in *Minaguchi v Wineport Lakeshore Restaurant*.[24] In that case, the claimant was a trainee chef on a CERT programme who alleged that she had been treated differently on the grounds of her age in relation to her placement with the respondent restaurant. The tribunal held that in order to establish a prima facie case of discrimination, the complainant was required to prove:

> (i) that s/he is covered by the relevant discriminatory ground(s), (ii) that s/he has been subjected to specific treatment and (iii) that this treatment is less favourable than the treatment someone, who is not covered by the relevant discriminatory [*sic*], has been or would be treated. In the instant case, I am satisfied that the complainant is covered by each of the three discriminatory grounds cited. I am also satisfied that as a result of having to undertake a trial period, she was treated less favourably than other students in her class. Finally, I am satisfied that she was the oldest student in her class (which numbered forty two and on the balance of probabilities, that she possessed a different marital status and family status from some of those students. In light of my foregoing comments, I consider that the complainant has discharged the burden placed on her to establish a *prima facie* case.

---

23. *ibid.*, at 178.
24. DEC-E-2002-20, 20 April 2002.

4. Forms of Prohibited Discrimination

As we have seen, there are two potential forms of discrimination under the legislation, namely direct or indirect discrimination. These will be considered in turn.

4.1. Direct Discrimination

Direct discrimination is defined under s.6(1) of the 1998 Act as occurring where [7–13] one person is treated less favourably than another is, has been or would have been treated, and the difference in treatment is on the basis of one of the discriminatory grounds listed in s.6(2) of the 1998 Act. This definition was amended and broadened by s.4 of the 2004 Act, which provides that discrimination shall be taken to occur where:

(a) a person is treated less favourably than another person is, has been or would be treated in a comparable situation on any of the grounds specified in subsection (2) (in this Act referred to as the 'discriminatory grounds') which—
  (i) exists,
  (ii) existed but no longer exists,
  (iii) may exist in the future, or
  (iv) is imputed to the person concerned,
(b) a person who is associated with another person—
  (i) is treated, by virtue of that association, less favourably than a person who is not so associated is, has been or would be treated in a comparable situation, and
  (ii) similar treatment of that other person on any of the discriminatory grounds would, by virtue of paragraph (a), constitute discrimination.

4.1.1. The Need for a 'Comparator'

Assessment of whether there has been direct discrimination involves a comparative [7–14] analysis between the situation of the claimant employee and that of a comparator who must currently be, have been or would have been in a comparable situation to the complainant. The choice of comparator is therefore crucial to the outcome of any decision as to whether or not the complainant had been discriminated against. For example, in *Field v Irish Carton Printers*,[25] the defendant company provided a free taxi service home for female employees once their shift ended. No such service was provided to male employees. This service was found to be discriminatory on the grounds of sex. In this case, clearly the position of the male employee was assessed having regard to the situation of a comparator female employee who was offered the free taxi service.

Fredman has noted when commenting on similar legislation in England, that the [7–15] need for a comparator has been one of the most problematic and limiting aspects

---

25. [1994] ELR 129.

of direct discrimination.[26] The 'less favourable treatment' definition, after all, may allow an employer to treat all of his or her other employees equally badly and yet to avoid liability under the equality legislation.[27] The definition provides for *less* favourable treatment and not *un*favourable treatment. Thus no liability would arise for an employer who treated one particular employee badly if it was shown that that was how [s]he treated all his or her employees.

[7–16] The difficulties that may arise with the comparative approach were highlighted by the decision of the Court of Appeal in *Pearce v Mayfield School*.[28] In that case, the complainant was a lesbian teacher who was subjected to verbal abuse by students over a number of years. She brought an action against the school alleging discrimination on the grounds of her sex (at that time there was no legislation expressly prohibiting discrimination on the grounds of sexual orientation). The identification of an actual comparator was critical to the outcome of the case. The complainant argued that for true comparison purposes in accordance with the legislation, an appropriate comparator would be someone who was male but who, in all other material respects, was in the same situation as she was – that is, a male with a preference for female sexual partners. Effectively, the complainant was contending that for women in her situation, 'it is their own sex, rather than the sex of their partners, which is the problem'.[29] Ultimately, the court did not accept this comparison and instead favoured comparison with a male homosexual, that is, the relevant question was whether, if the comparator was a homosexual man, he would have suffered similar abuse regarding his sexuality. The court concluded that there was no evidence that this (male) comparator would have suffered any more favourable treatment because of his sexual preferences than did the claimant. Hence there was no discrimination.

[7–17] Under the comparator approach, proof of mere bias by the employer against the complainant will be insufficient evidence of discrimination. In *Martins v Marks & Spencer's Plc*,[30] the complainant, Mrs Martins, was interviewed for a position as a trainee manager. Her performance on a written test was very good, but she was graded poorly in the interview. She alleged that the grade she had received could only be explained on the basis that the interview panel were biased against her because of her race. In the Court of Appeal, Mummery LJ stated that in order to prove direct discrimination the complainant had to first establish that she had suffered 'less favourable treatment', stating that:

> The answer to this question requires a comparison to be made between the treatment of Ms Martins and the treatment of a 27 year old applicant of a different racial group with similar experience and qualifications applying for the same job. The tribunal

26. Fredman, *Discrimination Law* (Oxford University Press, 2002), at pp.96–99.
27. It should, of course, be noted that in such circumstances the employer may attract liability under other statutes and indeed under the terms of the employment contract.
28. [2001] EWCA Civ 1347, [2002] ICR 198.
29. *per* Hale LJ, at para.7.
30. [1998] ICR 1005.

did not attempt to make the compulsory comparison. Instead, it simply asked itself whether there was 'bias' on the part of Mrs Cherrie and Mr Walters against Ms Martins and concluded that there was. This approach is defective. In a complaint under the 1976 Act the focus is not on whether the conduct of the employer or putative employer towards the complainant is biased or unreasonable or unfair ... the fact that an employer has acted unreasonably (e.g. in the sense relevant to a claim for unfair dismissal) casts no light whatsoever on the question whether he has treated the employee 'less favourably' for the purposes of the 1976 Act... it cannot be inferred *only* from the fact that the interviewers acted in a biased way towards Ms Martins, that the same interviewers would have acted in an unbiased way in dealing with another applicant in the same circumstances. The tribunal wholly failed to address itself to the issue, which Ms Martins had to establish in order to make out a claim for racial discrimination, whether she had been treated less favourably than the interviewers would have treated another applicant in the same circumstances. The finding that Marks & Spencer interviewers were guilty of 'bias' against Ms Martins is not a relevant or meaningful finding for the purpose of the 1976 Act.[31]

It was held that the members of the tribunal had substituted their own favourable impression of the complainant for that of the interviewers (Mrs Cherrie and Mr Walters) rather than assessing whether she had been treated less favourably on the basis of her race. Consequently, the tribunal applied the incorrect test as to whether or not there had been discrimination, and its findings could not be upheld.

It is for the complainant and not the tribunal to choose the comparator. In *Wilton* [7–18] *v Steel Company of Ireland Ltd.*,[32] the plaintiff worked in the credit control department of the defendant company. She alleged that she had been discriminated against on the grounds of her sex. Her predecessor in the role was a man who had been earning £14,000 per annum when he left the position, while she was only earning £11,000 per annum for what was essentially the same work. When considering the matter, both the Equality Officer and the Labour Court made a comparison between the complainant and another individual, a Mr Butler, and on that basis found that there was an objective justification for the difference in pay. The plaintiff appealed to the High Court, arguing that the Equality Officer had erred in law in choosing a different comparator to the one she had identified. While ultimately affirming the conclusion of the Equality Officer that there were objectively justifiable reasons for the difference in pay, the High Court did accept 'that the plaintiff is entitled to choose her comparator and in this case has chosen Mr Clarke whom she replaced in the credit control department of the defendant'.

4.1.2. *The Hypothetical Comparator*
A failure to identify an actual comparator may not necessarily be fatal to a claim for [7–19] unlawful discrimination. Were it otherwise, employers in workplaces or industries

---

31. [1998] IRLR 326 at 331–332.
32. [1998] IEHC 87, [1999] ELR 1.

that were populated mainly by women, for example, could act in a discriminatory manner because of the absence of an actual male comparator. In such circumstances, reliance may thus be placed on the 'hypothetical comparator' and involves an assessment of how such a hypothetical employee, similar in all aspects to the complainant (apart from the relevant alleged discriminatory ground), would have been treated by the employer.[33]

[7–20] Thus the definition of discrimination under the legislation now provides that the chosen comparator may be actual or hypothetical. The wording of s.6(1) of the 1998 Act provides that discrimination occurs where an individual is treated less favourably than another person is, has been or *would have been* treated. In *Phelan v Michael Stein*,[34] the claimant was asked at a job interview about her children and her caring arrangements for them. She was able to establish that no such questions would have been asked of a man in a similar position and as such they were held to be discriminatory in nature. Interestingly, the fact that the successful candidate for the position was also married with children did not affect the finding that the employer had acted in a discriminatory manner towards the claimant.

[7–21] The hypothetical comparator test was also utilised in *McDonald v Clonmel (Healthcare) Ltd*.[35] The female claimant alleged that during the course of two interviews for a position with the defendant company, she was asked questions about her marital and family status that would not have been asked of a man. These questions led to a discussion as to who would care for her children should she be offered the job. The other candidates for the position were all female and no actual comparator existed. While the case was brought under the Employment Equality Act 1977, which did not specifically provide for a hypothetical comparator, the Equality Officer held that to give proper effect to the provisions of that legislation, the Act should be interpreted as allowing for such comparison. Notwithstanding the fact that the position was offered to another woman who was also married with children, the Equality Officer concluded:

> With regard to the filling of the vacancy concerned, I believe that the fact that the claimant had children to look after was a consideration (though probably not the main one) which the interview board took into account and that this consideration would have been regarded as less of a factor if a male candidate was being considered for the post. I am, however, satisfied that there was little to choose between the quality of the candidate involved and that the company's decision to offer the position to a Dublin-based candidate was made for valid reasons unconnected with the claimant's sex.

---

33. The hypothetical comparator cannot be used for the purposes of comparison for 'like work' in a claim for equal pay: *Power v Blackrock College*, DEC-E2008-072, 23 December 2008. See also Chapter 8.
34. [1999] ELR 58.
35. DEC-E2000-012, 20 December 2000.

A similar approach was adopted by the Equality Tribunal in *Minaguchi v* [7–22]
Wineport Lakeshore Restaurant.[36] In that case, the complainant was a trainee chef
and mature student who asked for a 'family friendly' arrangement as part of her
placement, as she was married and had children. She was asked to work for a trial
period on her placement when other students in her class who were placed elsewhere were not expected to do the same and she alleged that this was discriminatory on grounds of marital status, family status and age. The Equality Officer
found that the appropriate comparator was not those classmates of hers who were
offered placement by other employers. Rather the correct comparison was with
the manner in which the respondent would have treated another member of her
class or previous students from that class. The Equality Officer ultimately held
that there was no discrimination, concluding that such individuals would have
been treated no differently than the complainant had been when asked to work
for the trial period while on placement.

4.1.3. Imputed and Associated Characteristics

Section 4 of the 2004 Act broadens the definition of discrimination to include [7–23]
unfavourable treatment based on characteristics *imputed* to the person and deriving
from one of the listed grounds within the legislation. This amendment will ensure
that an employee will not suffer discrimination because [s]he is presumed to have
certain characteristics. As a consequence, for example, it will now be unlawful for
an employer to treat a heterosexual employee less favourably because of his or her
employer's *mistaken* belief that the employee is homosexual.

Oliver has noted that the concept of imputed discrimination facilitates victims [7–24]
of sexual orientation discrimination, in particular, in bringing an action.[37] This is
because, inasmuch as discrimination is based on stereotypical perceptions, there
should be no need for the victim to reveal whether [s]he is actually gay or lesbian
in order to succeed in an action for discrimination. Oliver has concluded that:

> Sexual orientation is unique in being a 'hidden' characteristic, which is not gener-
> ally obvious to an outside observer. Many gay and lesbian employees choose not
> to be 'out' in the workplace, and this may be for a number of reasons, of which
> fear of discrimination is one. An individual's sexual orientation is an extremely
> personal issue, and many employees may choose to keep such information confi-
> dential simply because of its private nature. However, if individuals experiencing
> sexual orientation discrimination had to reveal their actual orientation in order to
> claim protection, clearly this would deter many employees from enforcing their
> rights. Indeed, for those employees who feared increased problems in the work-
> place if colleagues were aware of their actual orientation, it would make the right
> virtually meaningless.[38]

---

36. DEC-E2002-20, 20 April 2002.
37. Oliver, 'Sexual Orientation Discrimination: Perception, Definitions and Genuine Occupa-
    tional Requirements', 33, 1, *Industrial Law Journal* (March 2004), 1.
38. *ibid.*, at 5.

Direct discrimination under s.4 of the 2004 Act also extends to those persons who are treated less favourably because they have been *associated* with a person who falls within one of the listed grounds.[39] For example, if an employee is friendly with a homosexual employee and because of that friendship is treated less favourably, such treatment is discriminatory provided the complainant can establish that a person not so connected with the homosexual would not have been treated in a similar manner.

4.2. Indirect Discrimination

[7–25] Unlawful discrimination will not always be obvious. It is even less likely that such discrimination will be admitted. Rather it will tend to take a more subtle or disguised form. Section 13 of the 2004 Act (amending s.22 of the 1998 Act) has labelled this less obvious form of discriminatory treatment as 'indirect discrimination' and has defined it (in cases of gender) as occurring:

> where an apparently neutral provision puts persons of a particular gender (being As or Bs) at a particular disadvantage in respect of any matter other than remuneration compared with other employees of their employer.

In such circumstances,

> the employer shall be treated for the purposes of this Act as discriminating against each of the persons referred to (including A or B), unless the provision is objectively justified by a legitimate aim and the means of achieving that aim are appropriate and necessary.

Section 20 of the 2004 Act (amending s.31 of the 1998 Act) provides that indirect discrimination applied to a person on any of the other discriminatory grounds listed under the Acts shall also be unlawful.[40]

[7–26] Thus indirect discrimination occurs where a rule is imposed or a practice adopted that, although facially neutral in the sense that it applies to all workers, actually disadvantages a class within the workplace.[41] Crowley has noted that this provision 'has an important capacity, within limits, to focus on institutional systems and practices that can be discriminatory'.[42] For example, in *Price v CSC*[43] it was held that a rule that imposed a requirement that only those who fulfilled an age requirement (17.5–28 years) could be promoted to executive officer was discrimi-

---

39. C-303/06, *Coleman v Attridge Law* [2008] EUECJ C-303/06, [2008] ICR 1128.
40. Furthermore, ss.13 and 20 apply to matters other than remuneration.
41. Burger CJ of the United States Supreme Court described indirect discrimination as including 'practices that are fair in form but discriminatory in operation', in *Griggs v Power Duke Co* (1971) 401 US at 424.
42. Crowley, *An Ambition for Equality* (Irish Academic Press, 2006), at 68.
43. [1978] IRLR 3.

natory. While the rule applied to all workers, it was to the particular disadvantage of women as it was more likely that they would be out of the labour market during these years for reasons connected with pregnancy and motherhood.

4.2.1. 'Particular Disadvantage'

Under the Equality Act 2004, it is now easier to establish a prima facie case of [7–27] indirect gender discrimination because of amendments to the original definition provided for in s.22 of the 1998 Act. Section 22 provided that a rule or requirement that applied to both A and B was formerly deemed discriminatory if the proportion of persons who were disadvantaged by the rule or requirement was *substantially higher* in the case of those of the same sex as A than in the case of those of the same sex as B, and could not be justified on objective grounds unrelated to A's sex. Now under ss.13 and 20 of the 2004 Act, the claimant need only prove that the group to which [s]he belongs was *disadvantaged* by such rule, requirement or action.

The former approach taken under the 1998 Act was unsatisfactory, not least because [7–28] it was vague as to what constituted a 'substantially higher proportion'.[44] As a consequence, in proceedings alleging indirect discrimination, the parties relied heavily on statistical evidence in support of, or against the assertion that the complainant was actually disproportionately disadvantaged by the impugned measure.

In *Nathan v Bailey Gibson Ltd.*,[45] the female complainant worked as an assistant [7–29] machine operator. She applied for the senior position when the machine operator retired. The respondent had a closed-shop agreement with a trade union, which essentially provided that any new vacancies had to be offered to a member of their union first. The complainant, who was not a member of the union, did not obtain the job, which went to a male member of the union. The proportion of men versus women in this union was disproportionately high, with 80 per cent of the membership being male. The complainant alleged that the respondent had indirectly discriminated against her on the grounds of her sex. While the complainant ultimately failed in her action, the Supreme Court referred the matter back to the Labour Court for decision, finding that:

> It is sufficient for the complainant to show that the practice complained of bears significantly more heavily on members of the complainant's sex than on members of the other sex. At that stage the complainant has established a *prima facie* case of discrimination and the onus of proof shifts to the employer...[46]

In *North Western Health Board v Martyn*,[47] Barron J laid great emphasis on statis- [7–30] tics when assessing whether or not indirect discrimination had occurred:

---

44. s.22(1)(b) of the 1998 Act.
45. [1998] 2 IR 162.
46. [1998] 2 IR 162, 178.
47. [1985] ILRM 226.

For example, if a condition is imposed which makes it difficult for women to comply, then two sets of statistics must be considered:

1. The statistics of the particular application for employment;
2. The actual statistics of an application for similar employment on the same conditions but without the impugned condition.

If it is found that the proportion of men to women applicants in the first set of statistics is 80/20 and the second set of statistics 60/40, then as a matter of fact the particular requirement is one which discriminates against women.[48]

However, the old adage that there are 'lies, damned lies, and statistics' holds true. The use of statistics in these cases can be unreliable and much can depend on how they are presented and on the pool chosen for comparison purposes. In *Jones v Chief Adjudication Officer*,[49] Mustill LJ set out the following criteria to be followed when choosing the comparator group:

> (1) Identify the criterion for selection. (2) Identify the relevant population, comprising all those who satisfy all other criteria for selection... (3) Divide the relevant population into groups representing those who satisfy the criterion and those who do not. (4) Predict statistically what proportion of each group should consist of women. (5) Ascertain what are the actual male/female balances in the two groups. (6) Compare the actual with the predicted balances. (7) If women are found to be under-represented in the first group and over-represented in the second, it is proved that the criterion is discriminatory.[50]

[7–31] The Court of Appeal in *London Underground Ltd. v Edwards (No. 2)*[51] has warned that, depending on how it is presented, statistical evidence can produce misleading results. In that case, the respondent was a single mother who worked as a train operator. As a result of a change to her roster she was unable to work because of her parental responsibilities. In the Court of Appeal, a statistical comparison was made between all male train operators who could comply with the new roster and the female train operators who could so comply. The court found that 100 per cent of the male drivers (2,023) could comply with the roster changes whereas 95.2 per cent of the female drivers (20 out of 21) could comply with the roster changes. While statistically the difference was not particularly large in percentage terms, the actual numbers on which it was based (2,023 compared with 21) were disproportionate. The appellant challenged the finding that in such circumstances the tribunal was entitled to rely on statistics and their 'common knowledge that females are more likely to be single parents and caring for a child than males'.[52] The Court of Appeal, however, approved the decision of the tribunal stating that:

---

48. *ibid.*, at 231
49. [1990] IRLR 533.
50. [1990] IRLR 533 at 537.
51. [1999] ICR 494, [1998] IRLR 364.
52. *London Underground Ltd. v Edwards* [1995] ICR 574.

An Industrial Tribunal does not sit in blinkers. Its members are selected in order to have a degree of knowledge and expertise in the industrial field generally. The high preponderance of single mothers having care of a child is a matter of common knowledge. Even if the 'statistic' i.e. the precise ratio referred to is less well known, it was in any event apparently discussed at the hearing before the Industrial Tribunal without doubt or reservation on either side. It thus seems clear to me that, when considering as a basis for their decision the reliability of the figures with which they were presented, the Industrial Tribunal were entitled to take the view that the percentage difference represented a minimum rather than a maximum so far as discriminatory effect was concerned.[53]

The Irish Labour Court expressed similar concerns regarding the reliability of statistical information in cases such as *Inoue v NBK Designs Ltd.*[54] In that case, the complainant was a lone parent with a school-going child. She shared a position as a personal assistant with another employee in a small architectural practice. The business grew and the respondent wished to amalgamate the two part-time positions into one full-time position and asked the complainant to take the role. She refused and was subsequently dismissed. She claimed that her dismissal amounted to indirect discrimination on the grounds of sex and family status. The respondent argued that the complainant had to introduce comprehensive statistical evidence in order to support her claim. The complainant countered that statistical evidence together with the tribunal's own working knowledge of such situations would be sufficient for it to make a determination. In this regard, the Labour Court stated: [7–32]

> The procedures of the court are intended to facilitate parties whether they appear represented by solicitor or counsel, industrial relations practitioners or unrepresented alike. It would be alien to the ethos of the court to oblige parties to undertake the inconvenience and expense involved in producing elaborate statistical evidence to prove matters which are obvious to the members of the court by drawing on their own knowledge and experience.[55]

The modern requirement in the 2004 Act that a complainant need only prove that [s]he was at a 'disadvantage'[56] therefore greatly lessens the burden of proof on the complainant and will, in turn, also lessen the reliance on statistics in such cases. Thus s.13(1A) of the 2004 Act now provides that in any proceedings statistics are admissible, but not a necessity, for the purposes of determining whether or not indirect discrimination exists. [7–33]

Finally, it is worth noting that according to the wording of ss.13 and 20 of the 2004 Act it is necessary that the claimant alleging indirect discrimination prove that

---

53. *ibid.*, at para.24.
54. [2003] ELR 98.
55. *ibid.*, at p.104.
56. s.13(1)(a) of the 2004 Act.

[s]he was actually discriminated against as a result of the measure as it states that the measure must 'put persons… at a particular disadvantage'.⁵⁷

4.2.2. 'Objective Justification'

[7–34] In the case of indirect discrimination – though not in the case of direct discrimination, which can never be justified – notwithstanding the fact that the relevant measure may be capable of having a discriminatory effect it will not be considered unlawful where it can be 'objectively justified by a legitimate aim and the means of achieving that aim are appropriate and necessary'.⁵⁸ This test is very much based on the formula adopted by the European Court of Justice in *Bilka-Kaufhaus v Weber von Hartz*.⁵⁹ In that case the court, in interpreting Art. 141 of the EC Treaty, stated that if an employer is to justify such a measure [s]he must prove that it:

    (a) corresponds to a real need on the part of the employer;
    (b) is appropriate to that end; and
    (c) is necessary to that end.

Thus the employer is required to establish that the measure was a proportional and appropriate response to a real need. The test of proportionality was expressed by Balcombe LJ in the English Court of Appeal decision of *Hampson v Department of Education and Science*⁶⁰ as requiring 'an objective balance between the discriminatory effect of the condition and the reasonable needs of the party who applies the condition'.⁶¹

[7–35] The Irish Labour Court applied the test in favour of the respondent in *Bus Éireann v McLoughlin*.⁶² In that case, the complainant was 52 years of age and worked for the respondent from 1978 until 2001, when he left his employment on a voluntary severance scheme. The complainant challenged the company's policy not to rehire those employees who left on voluntary severance. It was the complainant's contention that this policy discriminated against him on grounds of age in that the vast majority of the workers who had availed of the voluntary severance scheme were aged 50 or over. While the court held that the policy was discriminatory, the provision was objectively justified on the basis of the need for the respondent to maintain stable and harmonious industrial relations between their employees. The means it had adopted were deemed appropriate and necessary.

---

57. *De Souza v Automobile Association* [1986] ICR 514.
58. s.13 Equality Act 2004. See also *Department of Justice, Equality & Law Reform v The Civil Public and Services Union*, determination no. EDA0713 (27 July 2007); *Barton v Investec PC Henderson Crosthwaite Securities Ltd.* [2003] ICR 1205, [2003] IRLR 332.
59. C-170/84 [1986] EUECJ, [1986] ECR 1607, [1987] ICR 110, [1986] IRLR 317.
60. [1990] 2 All ER 25, [1989] ICR 179, [1989] IRLR 69.
61. [1989] 1 ICR 179, 190. Balcombe LJ's decision was approved by the House of Lords on appeal in *Hampson v Department of Education and Science* [1991] 1 AC 171, [1990] 3 WLR 42, [1990] 2 All ER 513, [1990] ICR 511, [1990] IRLR 302.
62. Determination no. EDA0516 (21 November 2005).

5. Scope of Prohibited Discrimination

Section 8 of the Equality Act 2004 specifies that unlawful discrimination should   [7–36]
not exist in employment in the following areas:

(a) access to employment;
(b) conditions of employment;
(c) training or experience for or in relation to employment;
(d) promotion or re-grading; or
(e) classification of posts.

5.1. Access to Employment

Section 8(1) of the 1998 Act prohibits unlawful discrimination in relation to access   [7–37]
to employment. Section 8(5) provides that an employer shall be taken to have
discriminated against an employee or prospective employee:

(a) in any arrangements the employer makes for the purpose of deciding to whom
employment should be offered, or

(b) by specifying, in respect of one person or class of persons, entry requirements
for employment which are not specified in respect of other persons or classes of
persons, where the circumstances in which both such persons or classes would
be employed are not materially different.

Thus an employer is under an obligation to ensure that access to employment
is not denied to an employee or prospective employee on the basis of unlawful
discrimination. In particular, an employer must ensure that the integrity of the
selection/recruitment process is upheld. Proper training of staff in conducting
interviews is essential as questioning of candidates could, even inadvertently, indicate an intention to discriminate. In *Casey v Board of Management, Coachford
National School, Co. Cork*,[63] the complainant alleged that she had been discriminated against on gender grounds and on family status grounds when she had
been allegedly asked a question at an interview relating to the 'age/stage her children were at'. The Equality Officer held that such questioning was discriminatory,
observing that:

> I understand that the interviewer was endeavouring to be friendly and make the
> complainant feel at ease but the question, in whatever manner it was put, was
> discriminatory on the grounds of gender as there is no evidence that a similar ques-
> tion was put to the other applicant who was male even though it is clear from the
> notes of interview that he made reference to his wife and children.

---

63. DEC-E2007-008, 8 February 2007.

[7–38] In *Phelan v Michael Stein Travel*,[64] the Equality Officer found that the act of asking a candidate during the interview process about her child-minding arrangements was discriminatory. Similarly, in *MacGabhainn v Salesforce.com*,[65] the complainant was asked his age by an interviewer after she had noted he had not included it on his CV. The Equality Officer held that such questioning was also discriminatory.[66]

[7–39] In alleging unlawful discrimination during the interview process, the complainant must establish that [s]he has been 'treated less favourably' than another candidate on the basis of one of the listed grounds. In *Savage v Lantern Securities Ltd.*,[67] the complainant had applied for a security position with the respondent. During the course of his second interview, the complainant – who had long hair, which he wore in a ponytail – was asked whether he would consider having his hair cut. He submitted that such a question would not have been put to a female candidate in a similar position. However, the respondent denied that he asked the complainant to have his hair cut. The respondent contended that the issue was one of health and safety and stated that men or women with long hair would be required to wear it neatly by tying it up at the back of the neck or have it cut, a policy that applied to both sexes equally. The tribunal concluded that the complainant had failed to establish a prima facie case of discrimination.

[7–40] It is not for the tribunal or Equality Officer to determine which candidate was the most deserving of the position, or whether the complainant should, objectively, have got the job (although this may be evidence that there had been discrimination). Rather it must confine itself to the question of whether the interview panel were influenced by unlawful discriminatory matters. Thus in *Rodmell v University of Dublin, Trinity College*,[68] a reference by a member of the interview panel to the only female candidate as the 'lady electrician' was deemed to be discriminatory. Furthermore, a respondent facing an allegation of discrimination in such circumstances will fail to rebut prima facie evidence of discrimination at interview by arguing that the successful candidate was chosen because 'they performed best at interview' if they cannot produce evidence of this through the production of proper records.[69]

[7–41] In *Dunne v An Post*,[70] an employee was held to have suffered discrimination in relation to access to employment on the grounds of age where he was unfairly

---

64. [1999] ELR 58.
65. DEC-E2007-048, 3 September 2007.
66. While an award of €1,000 compensation was made, the Equality Officer found that the complainant had failed to prove that he would have been successful in obtaining the position had he not been asked the question about his age.
67. DEC-E2007–024.
68. DEC-E2001-016, 7 June 2001.
69. *Carroll v Monaghan Vocational Education Committee*, DEC-E2004-003, 5 February 2004.
70. DEC-E2007–034.

excluded from a severance package introduced as part of a cost-cutting plan by his employer. The severance package allowed certain employees 'under the age of sixty and with two years reckonable service' to apply for the 'Ownership Driver Scheme'. The Equality Officer held that the fact that the complainant was unable to qualify for the scheme because of his age amounted to unlawful discrimination in relation to access to employment on the grounds of age.

5.2. Advertisements

Section 10 of the 1998 Act provides that a person will be guilty of an offence if [7–42] [s]he publishes or causes to be published an advertisement relating to employment that (a) indicates an intention to discriminate, or (b) might reasonably be understood as indicating such an intention.

> (2) For the purposes of subsection (1), where in an advertisement a word or phrase is used defining or describing a post and the word or phrase is one which—
> (a) connotes or refers to an individual of one sex or an individual having a characteristic mentioned in any of the discriminatory grounds (other than the gender ground), or
> (b) is descriptive of, or refers to, a post or occupation of a kind previously held or carried on only by the members of one sex or individuals having such a characteristic, then, unless the advertisement indicates a contrary intention, the advertisement shall be taken as indicating an intention to discriminate on whichever discriminatory ground is relevant in the circumstances.

Because the gateway to most employment vacancies is initially via an advertise- [7–43] ment, a failure to regulate such forms of communication could allow discriminatory practices to develop that would result in potential candidates being unfairly refused entry into the employment market. Section 10 of the 1998 Act seeks to eliminate the possibility of such discrimination by ensuring a level playing field for all. Inasmuch as the wording of s.10(1) provides that 'a person shall not... *cause* to be published or displayed an advertisement...' (emphasis added), it would appear that breach of this provision can lead to liability being imposed not only on the employer but also on any media outlet that publishes the offending advertisement.

In *Equality Authority v Ryanair*,[71] a complaint was made by the Equality Authority [7–44] regarding a job advertisement placed in *The Irish Times* by Ryanair. The advertisement stated that Ryanair was seeking applications from 'a young and dynamic professional' and further provided that the 'ideal candidate will be young and dynamic'. The Authority argued that this advertisement unlawfully discriminated against candidates on the grounds of their age. Ryanair unsuccessfully argued that

---

71. DEC-E2000-14

the word 'young' simply indicated that they were seeking applications from candidates who were enthusiastic. The equality investigation officer held that Ryanair had caused to be published an advertisement that might reasonably be understood as indicating an intention to discriminate on the grounds of age. The use of the word 'young' could reasonably be understood as referring to candidates who were young in terms of chronological age rather than referring to a state of mind.

[7–45] Similarly, in *Equal Opportunities Commission v Robertson*,[72] it was held, not surprisingly, that a job advertisement that stated that the respondent was seeking 'a good bloke (or blokess to satisfy fool legislators)' was discriminatory on the grounds of sex. In *Noonan v Accountancy Connections*,[73] the complainant applied for two positions, which were advertised with a statement that the successful candidate was required to have 'two to three years' experience'. The complainant, who had twenty years' post-qualification experience, was unsuccessful in his application on the basis that he was considered too experienced for the positions advertised. The Equality Officer held that the complainant had been indirectly discriminated against on the grounds of his age.

[7–46] Section 85(1)(d) of the 1998 Act provided that actions under s.10 may not be brought by private individuals, and instead should be referred to the Equality Authority. This requirement would appear to be justified on the basis that were it otherwise, there would be a multiplicity of actions from members of the public regardless of whether they themselves had actually been discriminated against. In *Burke v FÁS*,[74] the complainant was 45 years old. He unsuccessfully applied for a job on foot of an advertisement that stated that the position was 'an ideal opportunity for a young candidate'. He alleged that the advertisement had discriminated against him on the ground of his age. The Equality Officer found that she had no jurisdiction to hear the matter as the complainant had no *locus standi* as there was no provision in the Act for an individual complainant to bring a claim.

[7–47] However, an action may be brought by an individual complainant in circumstances where it can be established that the advertisement proved an intention on the part of the employer to unlawfully discriminate during the selection process, thereby discouraging applications from certain classes of employee. In *O'Connor v GTS Reprographics*,[75] an advertisement that referred to 'young, confident, enthusiastic' applicants was found to be discriminatory of the complainant on the grounds of age. The Equality Officer stated that:

> I am satisfied that the publication of the initial advertisement specifying 'young' as a requirement constitutes *prima facie* evidence of an intention on the part of the

---

72. [1980] IRLR 44.
73. DEC-E2004-042, 30 June 2003.
74. DEC-E2004-016, 29 March 2004.
75. DEC-E2003-04.

respondent to discriminate in the selection process against older applicants and I regard the reasoning outlined by the Equality Officer's decision in the *Equality Authority v Ryanair* as applicable here also.

5.3. Conditions of Employment

Section 8(1) of the 1998 Act extends the prohibition of unlawful discrimination to conditions of employment. According to s.(8)6, if an employer does not offer to an employee or prospective employee: [7–48]

    (a) the same terms of employment (other than remuneration and pension rights),
    (b) the same working conditions, and
    (c) the same treatment in relation to overtime, shift work, short time, transfers, lay-offs, redundancies, dismissals and disciplinary measures,

as another worker, where the only material difference between the relevant employee or prospective employee is based on any one of the discriminatory grounds, then the employer will be found to have unlawfully discriminated against that employee or prospective employee in relation to the conditions of employment.

In *Maphoso v Chubb Ireland*,[76] the complainant was prohibited from using the canteen and toilet facilities at the site where he worked as a security officer. He alleged that he was discriminated against on the grounds of race in relation to the conditions of his employment. In the absence of an adequate explanation from the employer, the Equality Officer found in favour of the complainant. Similarly, in *Ntoko v Citibank*[77] a Nigerian employee of the respondent was dismissed because, contrary to company policy, he had made a personal telephone call from work. Evidence was produced that indicated that other employees who had committed similar breaches of policy were not dismissed. Such unequal treatment was discriminatory in the absence of an adequate explanation from the respondent.   [7–49]

5.4. Training or Experience for or in Relation to Employment

Section 8(1) prohibits unlawful discrimination in relation to training or experience for or in relation to employment. Section 8(7) further provides that an employer cannot unlawfully discriminate (on one of the listed grounds) against an employee in relation to facilities for employment counselling, training (whether on or off the job) and work experience. Thus in *Kelly v Department of Social Community & Family Affairs*,[78] the complainant was due to attend a week-long training course provided by her employer. The respondent agreed to provide some childcare facilities for those employees undertaking the training. However, most of the training   [7–50]

---

76. DEC-E2007-067, 15 November 2007.
77. [2004] ELR 116.
78. DEC-E2002-021, 1 May 2002.

took place on an evening basis and the childcare facilities were for the day only. The complainant requested extra payment for the additional childcare costs that would result from her attendance at the training. While the respondent did offer some payment, it was not considered sufficient by the complainant. She alleged that the respondent had discriminated against her on the grounds of her gender, family and marital status. The respondent contended that it was under no obligation to provide childcare in such circumstances and that the complainant's husband was also responsible for the care of their children, which should have defrayed some of the costs. The Equality Officer held the employer had acted reasonably in seeking information on the childcare costs the complainant had expected to incur and agreed that the amount she had quoted to her employer was excessive and proposed that a more reasonable costing – closer to the respondent's evaluation – should apply.

5.5. Promotion or Re-Grading

[7–51] Section 8(1) prohibits unlawful discrimination against an employee in relation to promotion. Section 8(8) provides that such discrimination will occur where:

> (a) the employer refuses or deliberately omits to offer or afford the employee access to opportunities for promotion in circumstances in which another eligible and qualified person is offered or afforded such access, or
>
> (b) the employer does not in those circumstances offer or afford the employee access in the same way to those opportunities.

Thus an employer is under an obligation to ensure that his or her treatment of employees in terms of promotion is non-discriminatory. It would be wise, therefore, for an employer to ensure that his or her policies and procedures in relation to promotion are clear and transparent. In *Mey v St. James Hospital*,[79] the complainant – a South African – was one of only two applicants for a specialist nurse position. The other applicant, who was Irish, was successful in her application. The complainant alleged that she had been unlawfully discriminated against on the grounds of her race. The Equality Officer observed that the respondent had 'failed to implement fair, open and transparent procedures in the interview process'. The Equality Officer held that the complainant was better qualified and had more experience than the successful candidate and, as the respondent failed to adequately explain why the complainant was not appointed, the respondent was deemed to be guilty of unlawful discriminatory treatment. The Equality Officer awarded the complainant €20,000 in compensation for the discriminatory treatment and €5,000 in respect of loss of earnings. The Equality Officer also ordered the respondent to introduce fair and transparent selection procedures.

---

79. DEC-E2007-016.

In *Revenue Commissioners v O'Mahony and Others*,[80] the Labour Court held that a question to one of the complainants asking why he was seeking promotion 'at this stage of his career' was evidence that age was of some relevance, probably subconsciously, during the selection process, and hence that the complainant had been the victim of unlawful discrimination.

[7–52]

This analysis indicates that it is of critical importance that an employer maintains comprehensive notes in relation to what happened during a job interview. In *Murtagh v Longford County Council*,[81] the complainant alleged that he had been discriminated against on the grounds of age when he was deemed not qualified for an engineering position by the respondent. The respondent failed to keep comprehensive notes of the original interviews, but did produce a summary of those interviews together with their application forms. Based on the information provided, the Equality Officer found that the marks awarded to the unsuccessful candidates had the appearance of being awarded in a cursory fashion. The Equality Officer held that the complainant had established a prima facie case of discrimination, which the respondent had failed to rebut due, in part, to the failure to retain comprehensive notes of the interview process.

[7–53]

5.6. Classification of Posts

Section 8(1) prohibits discrimination by an employer in relation to the classification of posts. In *Kane v Sligo Leitrim Home Youth Liaison Services Ltd.*,[82] the complainant alleged that she had been discriminated against on the grounds of her gender in relation to remuneration, access to promotion, conditions of work and classification of posts. The complainant was employed by the respondent in August 2000 as a home youth liaison officer. She claimed that there was only one other officer appointed to a similar role, a Mr H. The complainant alleged that her role and contract was the same as that of Mr H. In 2003 the complainant noticed that Mr H's role had changed and that he now had a supervisory function. She claimed that she had not been informed of the promotional opportunity and had been denied the opportunity of interviewing for the role. It transpired that Mr H was being paid an extra allowance from 2000 until 2002 when the payment of this allowance was altered and paid as a contribution to Mr H's allowance. The complainant alleged that this extra payment was in breach of the equal-pay provisions of the employment equality legislation as it was based on the grounds of her gender.[83] The Equality Officer held that the changes to the male comparator's post involved a simple formalisation of his role, as he had been carrying out the additional duties since prior to the commencement of the complainant's employment. The Equality Officer held that gender had no bearing on how the male comparator's role had changed and any formal restruc-

[7–54]

---

80. Determination no. EDA033 (27 January 2003).
81. DEC-E2007-026.
82. DEC-E2007-038.
83. s.19(1) Employment Equality Act 1998.

turing of roles that occurred in 2003 was simply giving formal effect to changes that had already occurred. The Equality Officer also held that the payment of the extra allowance to the Mr H had been made prior to the complainant's arrival as an employee and could not therefore be based on gender.

6. Exemptions

[7–55] In addition to a number of defences, the equality legislation also contains a number of exemptions or exceptions to the prohibition on discrimination. These provisions exclude the applicability of the legislation in certain circumstances.

6.1. Occupational Qualifications on Gender Grounds

[7–56] Under s.25(1) of the 1998 Act an employer will not be liable for gender discrimination if the sex of the candidate amounts to an occupational qualification for the post. Under s.25(2), therefore, it is acceptable for an employer to discriminate on the grounds of sex in relation to work on grounds of physiology (excluding physical strength and stamina) or on grounds of authenticity for the purpose of entertainment, if the nature of the post requires; (a) that it be filled by a person of that sex, and (b) it would be materially different if filled by a person of a different sex. So, for example, it has been held to be an acceptable choice for an employer to prefer a female nurse to act as midwife.[84]

Such exceptions will be construed narrowly, lest they be used as a cloak to disguise a more insidious form of discrimination. So, in *Wylie v Dee & Co (Menswear) Ltd.*,[85] the employer claimed that being male was a genuine occupational qualification to work in the menswear department of a shop as the job would involve the employee taking inside leg measurements. The defence was not accepted on the basis that the task was not a common occurrence in the job and when it would have been necessary to perform such tasks there were other male assistants available to do so.

Section 25(3) further provides that the sex of a person will be considered to be an occupational qualification where the job requires the performance of duties outside the State in a country where the laws or customs are such that those duties could not reasonably be performed by that person's sex.

6.2. Preserving a Religious Ethos

[7–57] Section 37 of the 1998 Act provides that certain religious, educational or medical institutions under the direction or control of a body established for religious purposes, or whose objectives include the provision of services in an environment

---

84. *Commission v United Kingdom* [1982] ECR 2001.
85. [1978] IRLR 103.

that promotes certain religious values, will not be taken to have discriminated against a person if:

(a) they give more favourable treatment, on the religion ground, to an employee or a prospective employee over that person where it is reasonable to do so in order to maintain the religious ethos of the institution, or

(b) they take action which is reasonably necessary to prevent an employee or a prospective employee from undermining the religious ethos of the institution.

Thus, a school with a certain religious ethos could discriminate in favour of teachers who support or would maintain that ethos. In *Flynn v Power*,[86] a case that occurred prior to the enactment of s.37, a single female teacher at a girls' secondary school run by a Catholic religious order was in a relationship with a married man and became pregnant. She was dismissed from her employment and her dismissal was successfully justified by the defendant on the basis that the school was established to promote a certain religious ethos and the plaintiff's lifestyle was in contravention of that ethos.

6.3. Positive Action

Positive action measures may be adopted in order to encourage greater participa- [7–58] tion from members of a protected group to break the dominance of a stronger group. In this regard, positive action should not be confused with positive discrimination. Positive action measures require that efforts be made to improve an imbalance in the workforce, whether it be a gender imbalance or otherwise. However, it is not a quota system, whereby in order to fulfill a requirement that there be a minimum number of members of a protected group or groups in the workplace, a member of one protected group is preferred over another employee who is not a member of that group, notwithstanding the fact that that other employee is better suited to the position. The non-mandatory nature of the posi- tive action provisions has been criticised on the basis that 'the voluntary nature of current provisions and the uncertainty around their scope has meant they are not deployed adequately or to sufficient effect'.[87]

Irish equality legislation does not require that positive action measures be imple- [7–59] mented. However, it does allow in certain limited circumstances the application of such measures. Section 24 of the Employment Equality Act 1998 (as amended by s.15 of the Equality Act 2004) provides that the provisions of the Act are without prejudice to measures:

---

86. [1985] IEHC 1, [1985] IR 648, [1985] ILRM 336.
87. Crowley, *An Ambition for Equality* (Irish Academic Press, 2006), at p.113.

(a) maintained or adopted with a view to ensuring full equality in practice between men and women in their employments, and

(b) providing for specific advantages so as—

    (i) to make it easier for an under-represented sex to pursue a vocational activity, or

    (ii) to prevent or compensate for disadvantages in professional careers.

Thus positive action measures may be adopted in relation to training and other vocational activities that make it easier for the under-represented sex (whether it be male or female) to pursue a professional career in that particular area.

[7–60] Similarly, s.33 of the Employment Equality Act 1998 (as amended by s.22 of the Equality Act 2004) provides that measures maintained or adopted with a view to ensuring full equality between employees will not be unlawful where they are measures designed:

(a) to prevent or compensate for disadvantages linked to any of the discriminatory grounds (other than the gender ground).

(b) To protect the health and safety at work of persons with a disability, or

(c) To create or maintain facilities for safeguarding or promoting the integration of such persons into the working environment.

6.4. Other Exemptions and Exclusions

[7–61] In addition, the legislation contains a number of other sections that permit discrimination in specific circumstances.

- Section 16(1) of the 1998 Act provides that an employer is not under an obligation to recruit, promote or retain an individual in a position or to provide training or experience to that individual in relation to a position where that individual will not accept the conditions under which the job is to be performed or is not fully competent, available and capable to undertake the duties attached to the position. Section 16(5) of the 1998 Act (as amended) further provides that an employer is not under an obligation to recruit, promote or retain an individual in a position if the employer is aware, on the basis of a criminal conviction or other reliable information, that the individual engages in, or has a propensity to engage in any sexual behaviour that is unlawful.
- Section 34(1) of the 1998 Act provides that certain benefits connected with family or marriage shall not be considered discriminatory; for example, the conferring of a benefit (such as a wedding present) on an employee or by reference to an event occasioning a change in the marital status of the employee. Furthermore, in accordance with s.34(3) of the Employment Equality Act 1998 (as amended), it shall not constitute discrimination on the age ground in relation to an occupational benefits

scheme for an employer to fix ages for admission to that scheme, to use age criteria in actuarial calculations for such a scheme and so forth. Section 34(5) expressly allows an employer to set maximum ages for recruitment, which may be justified on the grounds of cost.

- Section 35(1) of the 1998 Act (as amended) provides that an employer may pay a particular rate of remuneration to an employee with a disability if, because of that disability, the amount of work done by the employee during that period is less than the amount of similar work done, or which could reasonably be expected to be done, during that period by an employee without the disability.
- Section 36 of the 1998 Act allows for exemptions for certain State employees in relation to residence, citizenship and the Irish language.

7. Enforcement

As with most recent employment legislation, it is the purpose of the Employment Equality Acts to ensure that the system of enforcement applied is speedy, inexpensive and effective. Prior to the enactment of the 1998 Act, claims for discrimination under the Anti-Discrimination (Pay) Act 1974 and the Employment Equality Act 1977 were referred to the Labour Court. The court would appoint an Equality Officer to hear the case and that Officer would make a recommendation to the Labour Court. The parties could appeal the recommendation of the Equality Officer to the Labour Court, and from the Labour Court an appeal on a point of law only could be made to the High Court.[88] Additionally, where appropriate, employees had the option of pursuing a claim in the civil courts for breach of contract on the equality clause in the contract. [7–62]

With the enactment of the Employment Equality Act 1998 came a number of changes to the procedures by which Irish employment equality law is to be enforced.

7.1. Who Can Make a Complaint?

Section 77(1) of the 1998 Act simply provides that a complaint may be made by 'a person who claims'; there does not appear to be provision for another person to bring a claim on behalf of the complainant. Section 85 of the 1998 Act also provides that the Equality Authority may, under certain circumstances, refer a claim to the Director of Equality Investigations. In *A Complainant v FÁS*,[89] a complaint was referred by a father on behalf of his adult disabled son. The son had the intellectual ability to refer a claim himself but the father argued that because the son engaged in a training course delivered by Health Board staff and lived in Health Board accommodation, he was not comfortable in referring the claim himself and so that [7–63]

---

88. s.19 Employment Equality Act 1977; s.7 Anti-Discrimination (Pay) Act 1974.
89. DEC-E2003-029, 14 July 2003.

was why the father referred the claim on his behalf. The Equality Officer, concurring with the opinion of senior counsel on the matter, concluded that:

> the father did not have any legal or constitutional *locus standi* to refer a complaint, or to request relevant information, concerning alleged discrimination against his son. The father could represent his son, in a claim brought by his son, but it must be clear that the father is not the complainant and that the son is able and willing to bring the claim.

Under the Equality Act 2004, a complaint can now be referred on behalf of another person by his or her parent, guardian or other person acting in place of a parent 'where such a person is unable, by reason of an intellectual or a psychological disability, to pursue it effectively'.[90]

7.2. Mechanisms for Enforcement

[7–64] The manner by which the Equality Acts 1998-2008 are enforced involves respective roles for the Director of the Equality Tribunal, the Labour Court and the Circuit Court.

7.2.1. *The Director of the Equality Tribunal*

[7–65] This office was created under s.75(1) of the 1998 Act and was re-titled by an amendment contained in s.30 of the Employment Equality Act 2004. The Director is appointed by the Minister and may appoint Equality Officers and Equality Mediation Officers in order to delegate the enforcement of the office's functions.[91]

[7–66] The Director (and Equality Officers appointed by him or her) has a quasi-judicial function and hears cases involving alleged unlawful discrimination. Specifically, the office deals with cases where a person claims (a) to have been discriminated against by another in contravention of the Act; (b) not to be receiving the appropriate remuneration in accordance with equal remuneration terms; (c) not to be receiving the full benefit under the equality clause; (d) to have been penalised in circumstances amounting to victimisation.[92] According to s.77(2) of the Employment Equality Act 1998, the Director of the Equality Tribunal had no jurisdiction to deal with claims involving the dismissal of the complainant in circumstances amounting to discrimination or victimisation. However, s.46 of the Equality Act 2004 now provides that all claims will commence before the Director of the Equality Tribunal. A complainant may bypass the Director of the Equality Tribunal and the Labour Court and bring a claim to the Circuit Court at first instance in cases of gender discrimination only.[93] The decision of the Equality Tribunal may be appealed not later than 42 days from the date of the decision.[94]

---

90. s.77(4) Employment Equality Act 1998, as amended by s.32 Equality Act 2004.
91. s.75(4) *ibid.*, as amended by s.30 Equality Act 2004.
92. s.77(1) Employment Equality Act 1998.
93. s.77(3) *ibid.* For example, see *Atkinson v Carty* [2005] ELR 1.
94. s.83(1) Employment Equality Act 1998.

7.2.2. *The Labour Court*

Prior to the introduction of the 2004 Act, the Labour Court only heard cases of   [7–67]
discriminatory dismissal as a court of first instance.[95] However, now all claims
must first be heard by the Director of the Equality Tribunal[96] and the Labour
Court's jurisdiction is limited to appeals, which must be brought within 42 days
of a decision by the tribunal. The Labour Court may, if it deems it necessary to
assist it in its investigation, refer all or any of the matters at issue in the case to the
Director for investigation.[97] This power is also available to the Labour Court when
investigating appeals from the Director,[98] which would, as Bolger and Kimber
have noted, 'appear to be at the very least rather unorthodox as the Court is asking
the forum [the Director] from which the appeal is being brought to reconsider
the matters in issue'.[99] Section 24 of the 2004 Act (amending s.90 of the 1998
Act) provides that the decision of the Labour Court may be appealed to the High
Court, but on a point of law only. The Labour Court may also adjourn its decision
until the outcome of such a reference is known.[100]

7.2.3. *The Circuit Court*

Section 77(3) of the 1998 Act provides that in cases of discrimination on the   [7–68]
grounds of gender only, a claim under the legislation can be referred to the Circuit
Court at first instance.[101] While the 1998 Act puts a ceiling on the quantum of
compensation that can be awarded in a claim for discrimination,[102] s.82(3) of the
1998 Act provides that when a claim is directly referred to the Circuit Court, the
court may make an award that exceeds the normal civil jurisdiction of the Civil
Court. Bolger and Kimber surmise that this is because of the decision by the
European Court of Justice in *Marshall v Southampton Area Health Authority (No.
2)*,[103] which held that to put a cap on the quantum of damages awarded in cases of
unlawful discrimination would be contrary to the right to effective judicial process
under Art. 6 of the Equal Treatment Directive.[104]

---

95. Under s.79(2) *ibid.*, an investigation by the Labour Court shall be held in private unless, at
    the request of one of the parties to an investigation, the court decides to hold the investiga-
    tion (or part of it) in public.
96. s.46 Equality Act 2004.
97. s.84(1) *ibid.*
98. s.84(2) *ibid.*
99. Bolger and Kimber, *Sex Discrimination Law* (Round Hall Sweet and Maxwell, 2000), at 423.
100. s.24(2)(b) Equality Act 2004.
101. The jurisdiction of the Circuit Court as regards matters referred to it under s.77(3) of the
     1998 Act shall be exercised by the judge assigned to the circuit in which the respondent
     ordinarily resides or ordinarily carries on any profession, business or occupation: s.80(2)
     Employment Equality Act 1998.
102. s.82 *ibid.*
103. [1993] ECR I-4367.
104. It must now be questioned whether, in light of the advancements now made concerning
     discriminatory grounds other than gender, it is appropriate that the possibility of instituting
     proceedings at first instance in the Circuit Court ought to be limited to gender cases only.
     For discussion see Bolger and Kimber, *Employment Equality*, ch.13 in Regan, ed, *Employment
     Law* (Tottel Publishing, 2009), at p.446.

[7–69] The Circuit Court may nominate an Equality Officer to prepare a report on any aspect of the reference before it.[105] Where such a report has been prepared it must be furnished to any of the interested parties upon their request, will be introduced as evidence into the proceedings, and the Equality Officer nominated to prepare it may be called as a witness in the proceedings.[106] Finally, where the time for an appeal has elapsed or no appeal is made, the Circuit Court is authorised to enforce the determinations of the Director or the Labour Court,[107] or of any settlements reached by way of mediation.[108]

7.3. Time Limits

[7–70] The 1998 Act set strict time limits on the referring of claims for discrimination or victimisation under the legislation. Section 77(5) (as amended by s.32 of the 2004 Act) provides that such claims may not be referred under the legislation 'after the end of the period of 6 months from the date of occurrence of the discrimination or victimisation to which the case relates or, as the case may be, the date of its most recent occurrence'.

7.3.1. *Identifying when the Act of Discrimination or Victimisation Last Occurred*

[7–71] The wording of s.77(5) of the 1998 Act was unclear as to whether the time in which a claim must be referred started from the date of a specific act of discrimination or whether, in the case of discrimination, which was ongoing, the time in which a claim in respect of the totality of the discrimination could be brought could be deemed to start from the date of the most recent occurrence. In *Hawkins v Irish Life & Permanent Plc t/a TSB Bank*,[109] it was held that the wording of the provision implied that the time limit could be applied to a series of occurrences or instances of continuing discrimination. However, in such circumstances it was necessary for the complainant to show that the incidents referred to were similar and related incidents otherwise known as a 'chain of discriminatory incidents'. Thus in *Waldron v North Western Health Board*,[110] the complainant alleged that the respondent had committed discriminatory acts dating back to October 1999. Her complaint was only referred to the Director in June 2002. The Equality Officer held that the claim had been referred in time as the most recent occurrence of similar behaviour had occurred within the previous six months. The Equality Officer concluded that:

> the three alleged incidents appear to be closely related, given that they arise from issues between the same two employees over a continuous period, and involve discrimination on the same grounds namely family and marital status. Having

---

105. s.80(4) Employment Equality Act 1998.
106. s.80(5) *ibid.*
107. s.91(1) *ibid.*
108. s.91(2) *ibid.*
109. DEC-E2004-009, 19 February 2004.
110. DEC-E2003-021, 20 May 2003.

regard to section 77(5) of the 1998 Act, I am satisfied that the final incident is the most recent occurrence of the alleged acts of discrimination for which the complainant is seeking redress, and I have jurisdiction to investigate all three issues referred by the complainant.

The tribunal may take into consideration evidence of earlier incidents in order to establish whether a chain of discriminatory events exist, regardless of whether or not such events are within the time period.[111]

The matter was clarified by s.32(b) of the 2004 Act, which now provides that for the purposes of the section, discrimination or victimisation occurs: [7–72]

   (i) (if the act constituting it extends over a period), at the end of the period,

   (ii) (if it arises by virtue of a term in a contract), throughout the duration of the contract, and

   (iii) (if it arises by virtue of a provision which operates over a period), throughout the period.[112]

7.3.2. Application of Time Limits

The time limits provided for under the legislation will be applied strictly. In *A Complainant v A Company*,[113] the complainant alleged that the date of the most recent act of discrimination had occurred on 28 October 1999. The complainant's referral was received on 28 April 2000. The respondent argued that the six-month time period ended on 27 April 2000 and that the claim was therefore out of time. It was the complainant's assertion that the time period did not end until one day later, on 28 April 2000. The Equality Officer, referring to s.11(h) of the Interpretation Act 1937, held that the period expired on 27 April as the six-month time period in such cases should be interpreted as including the day of the most recent occurrence of discrimination and that where the period is expressed to end on a particular day, that day should also be included in the reference period. [7–73]

Moreover, the date of referral is the date on which the complaint is received by the relevant adjudicating body. In *A Named Female Employee v A Named Respondent*,[114] the complainant argued that the use of the transitive verb 'refer' suggested an act done by the referrer and not the adjudicating body to whom the complaint had been referred. On this basis it was argued that the date of referral should be taken as the date the complainant made first contact with the Office of the Director of Equality Investigations via telephone. The Equality Officer did not accept this argument and held that the date of receipt of the referral form in the [7–74]

---

111. *O'Mahony v Revenue*, DEC-E2002-018, 18 March 2002.
112. s.36(9) provides that where there is a delay in referring a case under this legislation because the respondent has misrepresented to the complainant the facts of the case, references to the date of referral under s.82 shall be construed as references to the date of the misrepresentation.
113. DEC-E2001-023, 3 August 2001.
114. DEC-E2003-001, 14 January 2003.

office of the Director of Equality Investigations should be the date of referral of a claim to the Director.

[7–75] It is perhaps worth noting in this regard that in *Figuerdo v McKiernan*[115] the High Court (in the context of a claim that a personal injury summons submitted to PIAB was statute barred) appeared to take a rather more lenient view of the question of whether the limitations clock will only stop running on the date of receipt of the said summons by PIAB. Dunne J was plainly uncomfortable with the notion that, in a situation where, for example, the summons was sent in what would normally constitute reasonable time, but for administrative reasons was not dated as having been received until a later date, the plaintiff could essentially lose his or her case through no fault of his or her own. Thus she commented:

> If the contention on behalf of the defendant is correct, it would appear that the effect of Rule 3(3) of S.I. No. 219 of 2004 is that a plaintiff could be statute barred in circumstances entirely outside their control. Clearly, such a consideration could result in significant hardship for a plaintiff. Whilst one might be critical of a plaintiff for leaving the issue of proceedings or, in the case of personal injuries applications the making of an application under s. 11 until the last moment, none-theless the Statute of Limitations 1957 has fixed a specific period within which to commence one's proceedings and it seems somewhat harsh, to say the least, that having taken every step that one can take in order to commence proceedings, that one could become statute barred by the actions of a third party over whom one has no control, in this case, the Personal Injuries Assessment Board.

Moreover, she noted the conclusions (in a different context) of the High Court in *Poole v O'Sullivan*[116] where the central office was closed on the date on which proceedings needed to be issued under the statute of limitations (being a Saturday), that the limitation period envisaged by the statute of limitations should be construed as ending on the next day on which the office was open and it was therefore possible to do the act required.[117]

7.3.3. Applications to Extend Time Limits

[7–76] Under s.77(6) of the 1998 Act a complainant could make an application for an extension of the limitation period by substituting the reference to six months with reference to a period not exceeding 12 months. The standard to be satisfied under the 1998 Act was very high. A complainant could only succeed in an application for the extension of the six month time limit where exceptional circum-stances prevented the timely referral. Thus the complainant was required to show not only that the circumstances were *exceptional* but that they also *prevented* the complainant from referring the complaint. Hence in *Reynolds v Limerick City*

---

115. [2008] IEHC 368, [2009] 2 ILRM 526.
116. [1993] IR 484, [1993] ILRM 55.
117. See on this Cox, 'Dismissal of An Action on the Grounds of Delay or Want of Prosecution', 3(4) *QRTL* (2008/9), 1.

Council,[118] where the reason why the application was delayed was because the applicant was attempting to elicit further information in respect of the alleged discrimination, it was found that there was nothing to prevent a complainant from referring a complaint while pursuing such nor was such delay excusable.

The standard set by s.77(5) of the 1998 Act has been modified by s.32(b) of the 2004 [7–77] Act, which now imposes a standard based on the reasonableness of the complaint's request rather than whether there were exceptional circumstances that prevented the application. Under the new section, where the complainant makes an application for an extension, the Director of the Equality Tribunal or the Circuit Court may, for *reasonable cause,* grant an extension to the time limits for a period of not more than 12 months. This approach allows the tribunal to adopt a more sympathetic view of the complainant's reasoning for the delay.

Finally, s.32(d) of the 2004 Act amends s.77 of the 1998 Act through the introduc- [7–78] tion of an appeals procedure from decisions of the Director to the Labour Court. Such appeals must be made not later than 42 days from the date of a decision of the Director on an application by a complainant for an extension of time. Section 90(1) of the 1998 Act provides for an appeal from the Labour Court to the Circuit Court not later than 42 days from the date of the determination of the Labour Court. The Circuit Court may order any form of redress that could be awarded by the Labour Court and, subject to any appeal on a point of law to the High Court, the decision of the Circuit Court will be final and conclusive.

7.4. The Right to Information

In accordance with s.76 of the 1998 Act a complainant, in order to formulate and [7–79] present his or her case in the most effective manner, may be able to question the respondent in order to obtain any material information in relation to the claim. According to s.76(2), where 'Y' is the potential respondent and 'X' the potential complainant, the information is deemed to be material if it is:

(a) information as to Y's reasons for doing or omitting to do any relevant act and as to any practices or procedures material to any such act,
(b) information, other than confidential information, about the remuneration or treatment of other persons who stand in relation to Y in the same or similar position as X, or
(c) other information which is not confidential information and which, in the circumstances of the case in question, it is reasonable for X to require.

Confidential information was defined as 'any information which relates to a [7–80] particular individual, which can be identified as so relating and to the disclosure of which that individual does not agree'.[119] Thus an objection can be made by any

118. DEC-E2003-032.
119. s.76(3) Employment Equality Act 1998.

party seeking to prohibit the disclosure of information about him or herself that is considered confidential. The right to information has been curtailed by s.31 of the 2004 Act, which provides for the replacement in s.76(2) of paragraph (c) with the following new paragraph:

> (c) other information which is not confidential information or information about the scale or financial resources of the employer's business and which, in the circumstances of the case in question, it is reasonable for X to require.

Additionally, therefore, it is no longer open to a party to an action to seek information that could be considered to relate to the scale or financial resources of the employer's business. This restriction may prove problematic in certain cases of discrimination, e.g. information on the scale or financial resources of the employer's business may be critical in determining whether that employer has taken steps to reasonably accommodate the complainant's disability.[120]

7.5. Mediation

[7–81] Section 78(1) of the 1998 Act provides that if at any stage the Director considers the case is one that can be resolved by mediation, the Director shall refer the case to an Equality Mediation Officer. Similarly, if the case is one the Labour Court considers can be resolved by mediation, the Labour Court shall either attempt to resolve the case in that way by itself or refer it to the Director for mediation by an Equality Mediation Officer.[121] The mediation process is entirely voluntary and if either the complainant or the respondent objects to mediation, the case shall not be dealt with in that manner.[122] The mediation process is, moreover, confidential, with meetings being held in private.[123]

[7–82] Where the dispute is resolved through the mediation process, the Equality Mediation Officer or the Labour Court, as the case may be, prepares a written record of the terms of the settlement, which is signed by the complainant and the respondent. The Equality Mediation Officer or the Labour Court, as the case may be, sends a copy of the record to the complainant and the respondent. A copy of the record is retained by the Director and the Labour Court.[124] Where the case cannot be resolved by mediation, the Equality Mediation Officer or the Labour Court shall issue a notice to the complainant and the respondent to that effect.[125] Where such a notice has been issued and the complainant makes an application to the Director

---

120. Similar criticisms have been levelled at s.76(3) of the Employment Equality Act 1998 by Bolger and Kimber, *Sex Discrimination Law* (Round Hall Sweet and Maxwell, 2000), at 431.
121. s.78(2) Employment Equality Act 1998.
122. s.78(3) *ibid.*
123. s.78(4) *ibid.*
124. s.78(5) *ibid.*
125. s.78(6) *ibid.*

or the Labour Court for the resumption of the hearing of the case, the Director or the Labour Court will proceed with its investigation of the case. Such an application must be accompanied by a copy of the notice with respect to the mediation.[126]

Mediation under the Employment Equality Act is designed to be an informal, voluntary and non-confrontational method of resolving disputes between parties. When one considers that in many cases involving employment disputes, the parties to the action must continue to work together, it is lamentable that so few cases, comparatively speaking, are resolved by mediation. In 2006, 185 complaints were dealt with by way of mediation and 129 (70 per cent) of those cases were disposed of through the mediation process and did not necessitate further investigation. However, closer examination of those figures shows that of those 185 cases only 84 resulted in mediation agreements, while 66 were non-resolved – a success rate of 56 per cent.[127] The statistics for 2007 did not show much sign of improvement. Of 99 closed cases in 2007, only one was settled at mediation while only four out of 261 open cases were awaiting mediation.[128] [7–83]

The benefits of mediation are often overlooked. For example, in 2006, some of the more imaginative solutions agreed upon following mediation included: [7–84]

- An acknowledgement from both parties that they were willing to accept in good faith the other party's interpretation of the incident that had led to the complaint of discrimination.
- The provision of a positive job reference.
- An offer to an unsuccessful job applicant of tuition in word processing skills in advance of an upcoming word processing examination for a position within that organisation.[129]

8. Redress

Section 82 of the 1998 Act outlines the form of redress available to a successful complainant under the legislation. The Director may, in cases involving a failure to pay equal remuneration, order compensation in the form of arrears of remuneration in respect of the period of employment as begins no more than three years before the date of the referral.[130] The Director may also make an order for equal remuneration from that date.[131] In cases involving discrimination or victimisation, the Director may make an order for compensation for the effects of acts that occurred no earlier [7–85]

---

126. s.78(7) *ibid.*
127. *Mediation Review* (Equality Tribunal, 2006), at 6. Available at www.equalitytribunal.ie.
128. *Equality Authority Annual Report* (Equality Tribunal, 2007), at 69–70. Available at www. equalitytribunal.ie.
129. *ibid.*, at 17.
130. s.82(1)(a) Employment Equality Act 1998.
131. s.82(1)(b) *ibid.*

than six years before the date of the referral of the case.[132] The Director may also make an order for equal treatment in relation to the case,[133] or may order that a person or persons specified take a course of action so specified in the order.[134]

[7–86] In accordance with s.82(2) of the 1998 Act, the Labour Court may similarly make orders for compensation for the effects of acts of discrimination or victimisation, or for equal treatment, or order that a person or persons take a course of action so specified.[135] Additionally, the Labour Court may, where appropriate, make an order for re-instatement or re-engagement, with or without an order for compensation.[136]

[7–87] Under s.82(3) of the 1998 Act, the Circuit Court may, in cases involving a failure to pay equal remuneration, order compensation in the form of arrears of remuneration in respect of the period of employment as begins no more than six years before the date of the referral.[137] The Circuit Court may also make an order for equal remuneration from the date of the referral.[138] The Circuit Court may also make an order for compensation for the effects of acts of discrimination or victimisation that occurred not earlier than six years before the date of referral of the case; an order for equal treatment; or order that the person or persons specified take a course of action that is so specified.[139] The Circuit Court may also make an order for re-instatement or re-engagement, with or without an order for compensation.[140]

[7–88] Section 82(4) of the 1998 Act sets a maximum amount on the quantum of damages that may be ordered by the Director or the Labour Court by way of compensation. The maximum amount provided for under that provision is limited to 104 times either his or her weekly remuneration or, where it is greater, the amount determined on a weekly basis that the complainant would have earned but for the act of discrimination or victimisation. This compensation is subject to an overall cap of what was then the equivalent of £10,000.[141] There is no ceiling on the quantum of compensation awarded by the Circuit Court under the legislation.[142]

---

132. s.82(1)(c) *ibid.*
133. s.82(1)(d) *ibid.*
134. s.82(1)(e) *ibid.*
135. s.82(2)(a) *ibid.*
136. s.82(2)(b) *ibid.*
137. s.82(3)(a) *ibid.*
138. s.82(3)(b) *ibid.*
139. s.82(3)(c) *ibid.*
140. s.82(3)(d) *ibid.*
141. Furthermore, the Director or the Labour Court may, when ordering the payment of compensation relating to a claim involving sex discrimination or any claim relating to the equal pay or equal treatment directives, make an award of interest: s.82(5) *ibid.*
142. s.82(3) of the 1998 Act provides that 'no enactment relating to the jurisdiction of the Circuit Court shall be taken to limit the amount of compensation or remuneration which may be awarded by the Circuit Court...' Thus not only is the Circuit Court not bound by the limita-

The removal of the upper limit on the awards of compensation by the Circuit Court [7–89] would appear to be giving full effect to the decision of the European Court of Justice in *Marshall v Southampton & South-West Hampshire Area Health Authority (No. 2)*.[143] In that case, the plaintiff was a senior employee with the Health Authority who challenged a State requirement that required female employees to retire aged 60 years, while similar male employees could retire at aged 65 years. These retirement ages could be postponed upon the mutual agreement of the parties. Miss Marshall was dismissed upon reaching the age of 62 years on the basis that she had reached the normal retiring age for such employees. She challenged the different retirement ages for men and women as being discriminatory under the Sex Discrimination Act and the Equal Treatment Directive 76/207. Ultimately, the European Court of Justice held that the plaintiff could rely on the Directive against a State Authority acting in its capacity as an employer. The Industrial Tribunal held that s.65(2) of the Sex Discrimination Act, which limited the compensation that could be awarded to victims of discrimination, did not provide an adequate remedy in accordance with Art. 6 of the Equal Treatment Directive. This aspect of the decision was appealed by Miss Marshall's employers. On this issue, the European Court of Justice held that any such ceiling on the award of compensation was unlawful:

> the fixing of an upper limit of the kind at issue in the main proceedings cannot, by definition, constitute proper implementation of Article 6 of the Directive, since its limits the amount of compensation *a priori* to a level which is not necessarily consistent with the requirement of ensuring real equality of opportunity through adequate reparation for the loss and damage sustained as a result of a discriminatory dismissal.[144]

Section 36 of the 2004 Act amends s.82 of the 1998 Act by adding a number of [7–90] subsections.

- Section 36 provides that the maximum amount of compensation identified under s.82(4) of the 1998 Act applies irrespective of whether (a) the discrimination occurs on more than one of the discriminatory grounds, or (b) whether the discrimination occurs on one or more of the discriminatory grounds and involves harassment or sexual harassment. Thus a complainant is prevented from receiving double-compensation for different offences under the legislation.
- Section 36(7) provides that an order for compensation may not be made in favour of the authority in a case referred by it to the Director.
- Section 36(8) provides that where an act constitutes victimisation under the employment equality legislation and the Equal Status Act 2000, redress may be provided under only one of them.

---

tions placed on the jurisdiction of the Director or the Labour Court as outlined in s.82(4), it is not bound by the Circuit Court's normal jurisdictional limit in civil cases of €38,000.
143. C-271/91 [1993] EUECJ C-271/91, [1993] ECR I-4367.
144. [1993] EUECJ C-271/91 at para.30.

CHAPTER 8

Equal Pay

1. The Concept of Equal Pay

Since Ireland's accession to the European Economic Community, much has been [8–01]
done to redress gender imbalance in terms of rates of pay. Art. 141(1) (ex-119) of
the EEC Treaty, which provides that men and women should be treated equally in
terms of pay, states that 'each Member State shall ensure that the principle of equal
pay for male and female workers for equal work or work of equal value is applied'.
This provision is directly effective and can be invoked by individuals in national
courts against public and private sector employers following the European Court of
Justice's decision in *Defrenne v SABENA*.[1] In that case, Ms Defrenne worked as an
air steward and argued that she was entitled to the same rate of pay as male air stew-
ards working for the same Belgian airline. As Belgian law did not provide for equal
pay between men and women she relied directly on Art. 119. The European Court
of Justice agreed and stated that the twin aims of the provision were as follows:

> First, in the light of the different stages of the development of social legislation in
> the various Member States, the aim of Article 119 is to avoid a situation in which
> undertakings established in States which have actually implemented the principle
> of equal pay suffer a competitive disadvantage in intra-Community competition as
> compared with undertakings established in States which have not yet eliminated
> discrimination against women workers as regards pay.

> Secondly, this provision forms part of the social objectives of the Community,
> which is not merely an economic union, but is at the same time intended, by
> common action, to ensure social progress and seek the constant improvement
> of the living and working conditions of their peoples, as is emphasised by the
> Preamble to the Treaty.[2]

The principles of equal pay were incorporated into Irish law by the Anti-Discrimination (Pay) Act 1974 and the Employment Equality Act 1977. Both of these
pieces of legislation were replaced by the Employment Equality Act 1998, which
was amended by the Equality Act 2004.

---

1. C-43/75 [1976] ECR 455.
2. *ibid.*, at 472.

1.1. Definition of Pay

[8–02] Section 2(1) of the 1998 Act defines 'pay' in a very broad manner, stating that it 'includes any consideration, whether in cash or in kind, which the employee receives, directly or indirectly, from the employer in respect of the employment'. The definition of 'pay' effectively provides that an employee's entire package will be taken into consideration when assessing an equal pay claim.³ Section 2(1) of the 1998 Act reflects the definition provided in Art. 141 of the Treaty of Rome in this regard, which itself has been broadly interpreted. Thus the payment of wages during sickness has been held to constitute pay,⁴ as has paid time off work for union training⁵ and payments made on foot of a statutory redundancy scheme.⁶ For the purposes of the legislation, the pay must be conferred on the employee by reason of his or her employment. Thus in *Garland v British Rail Engineering*,⁷ concessionary travel benefits for retired employees were held to amount to remuneration and in *R v Secretary of State for Employment, ex parte Seymour-Smith*,⁸ the European Court of Justice held that judicial award of compensation for unfair dismissal constituted pay within the meaning of Art. 141 (ex-119) of the EC Treaty.

1.2. Transparency of Pay Systems and the Burden of Proof

[8–03] In practical terms, it may be difficult for an employee making a claim for equal pay to prove that there is a difference in pay in circumstances where the pay system operated by his or her employer lacks transparency. In modern economies, pay systems have become more flexible and performance orientated. Thus the pay of employees may vary depending on bonuses, commission and so forth, which makes comparison with another worker very difficult. In *Handel-og Kontorfunk-tionaererernes Forbund I Danmark v Dansk Arbejdsgiverforening Ex p. Danfoss A/S*,⁹ the European Court of Justice stated that in such situations it would be virtually impossible for the employee to establish the exact pay of the comparator. It was held that where an employer operates a pay system lacking in transparency and a female employee 'establishes, in relation to a relatively large number of employees, that the average pay for women is less than that for men', then the burden of proof shifts to the employer to prove that the pay system in not discriminatory.¹⁰ This approach was reaffirmed by the European Court of Justice in *Enderby v Frenchay Health Authority and Secretary of State for Health*,¹¹ where it was held that:

---

3. Significantly, the definition of pay excludes pension rights that are now dealt with by the Pensions Act 1990.
4. *Rinner-Kuhn v FWW Spezial Gebaudereinigung GmbH*, C-171/88 [1989] EUECJ, [1989] ECR 2743, [1989] IRLR 493.
5. *Arbeiterwohlfahrt der Stadt Berlin v Botel*, C-360/90 [1992] EUECJ, [1992] ECR I-3589.
6. *Barber v Guardian Royal Exchange Assurance Group*, C–262/88 [1990] EUECJ, [1990] ECR I–1889.
7. C-12/81 [1982] EUECJ, [1982] ECR 359, [1982] IRLR 257.
8. C-167/97 [1999] EUECJ.
9. C-109/88 [1989] ECR 3199.
10. *ibid.*, at para.16.
11. C-127/92 [1993] EUECJ, [1993] ECR I-5535, [1993] IRLR 591.

where an undertaking applies a system of pay which is wholly lacking in transparency, it is for the employer to prove that his practice in the matter of wages is not discriminatory, if a female worker establishes, in relation to a relatively large number of employees, that the average pay for women is less than that for men.[12]

Moreover, the European Court of Justice further held in this case that a complainant will have established a *prima facie* case of discrimination where it could be shown that the difference in pay disproportionately affects one sex over another:

> where significant statistics disclose an appreciable difference in pay between two jobs of equal value, one of which is carried out almost exclusively by women and the other predominantly by men, Article 119 of the Treaty requires the employer to show that the difference is based on objectively justified factors unrelated to any discrimination on grounds of sex.[13]

Where the complainant can establish facts from which it can be presumed **[8–04]** that there has been unlawful discrimination, it shall be for the respondent to prove that there has been no breach of the legislation.[14] In *Irish Ale Breweries t/a Diageo European Global Supply v O'Sullivan*,[15] the complainant was employed as a cleaner/canteen assistant with the respondent in Ballyfermot. She sought to compare herself to two male comparators who were employed by the respondent as yardmen. The complainant worked as a cleaner, cleaning the kitchen, canteen, ladies toilets and so forth. The yardmen drove forklifts, cleaned the yard, cleaned the men's toilets and organised kegs into batches for delivery. The respondent had a grading system for pay which included all positions apart from cleaning. The complainant was paid at a lower rate than the lowest rate on the grading system. It was the complainant's contention that as cleaning is invariably work that is carried out by women the fact that cleaning was not included on the respondent's pay scale was an indication of an attitude which undervalued women. The complainant claimed that she was engaged in work of equal value as two yardmen – one named and located in Ballyfermot and the other unnamed and located in Waterford – and that she was being paid less than these comparators. Despite the complainant's efforts, the respondent was unforthcoming in providing information to her regarding the unnamed comparator's duties and remuneration. The Labour Court held that the fact that the complainant's post was excluded from the respondent's grading system without explanation was a fact from which discrimination could be inferred. Furthermore, the respondent's failure to provide information in relation to the unnamed comparator in Waterford led the court to infer that if that information had been given by the respondent it would have provided the complainant with evidence of 'like work'. Finally, the court held that

---

12. [1993] EUECJ C-127/92 at para.14.
13. [1993] EUECJ C-127/92 at para.19.
14. Art 19 of the Recast Equal Treatment Directive, Council Directive 2006/54/EC.
15. Determination no. EDA0611.

the failure to provide the complainant with explanation as to why she did not receive equal bonus and additional payments as the yardmen also gave rise to an inference of discrimination. The complainant succeeded in her action.

1.3. Elements of an Equal Pay Claim

[8–05]   Section 19(1),[16] reflecting the objectives of Art. 141,[17] provides that men and women should receive equal pay for like work. Section 19(1) provides that:

> It shall be a term of the contract under which A is employed that, subject to this Act, A shall at any time be entitled to the same rate of remuneration for the work which A is employed to do as B who, at that or any other relevant time, is employed to do like work by the same or an associated employer.

The provision for equal pay between men and women under s.19(1) only applies where a contractual relationship exists between the employer and the employee. Where no term providing for equal pay between men and women exists in the contract, one shall be implied into it by virtue of s.20 of the 1998 Act. Furthermore, where such an implied term conflicts with an express term, the implied term shall be taken to override the express term.

Thus an individual may bring a claim for equal pay under s.19(1) of the 1998 Act where [s]he can establish that the worker is: 'doing like work as a comparator who is working for the same or an associated employer at that or any other relevant time, and there is no objective justification for the difference in pay'.

1.3.1. Like Work

[8–06]   If an employee is to succeed in an equal pay claim [s]he must show that [s]he is being treated less favourably than another employee doing 'like work'. If it were a requirement that the comparator in question was doing exactly the same job as the complainant employee, this would severely curtail the effectiveness of the provision. Section 7 of the 1998 Act therefore defines 'like work' in the broadest possible terms, offering three alternative definitions. All three definitions refer to work 'performed', implying that the labels attached to the nature of the work by the parties (as expressed in the contract of employment, for example) may not necessarily be determinative. Rather it is what the worker actually does that is essential.[18] Section 7 provides the following definitions of 'like work':

---

16. s.19 is contained in Part III of the Employment Equality Act Act 1998, which deals specifically with discrimination between men and women.
17. s.29(1) of the 1998 Act also provides that the principle of equal pay for like work shall apply to the other areas of discrimination listed in s.6 of the Act.
18. *Shields v Coomes (Holdings) Ltd.* [1978] 1 WLR 1408, [1979] 1 All ER 456, [1978] ICR 1159, [1978] IRLR 263.

(a) Both perform the same work under the same or similar conditions, or each is interchangeable with the other in relation to the work;

(b) The work performed by one is of a similar nature to that performed by the other and any differences between the work performed or the conditions under which it is performed by each either are of small importance in relation to the work as a whole or occur with such irregularity as not to be significant to the work as a whole; or

(c) The work performed by one is equal in value to that performed by the other, having regard to such matters as skill, physical or mental requirements, responsibility and working conditions.

(a) Same Work

According to the definition provided under s.7(a), the work performed by the [8–07] complainant must be the same as that performed by the comparator and must be performed under the same or similar conditions. The definition also provides that if the work is 'interchangeable' then it is considered the same. Again, it is the *actual* work performed that will be compared and not simply the responsibilities that the workers have been assigned. In *Shields v Coomes Holdings Ltd.,*[19] a male counterhand was paid a greater hourly rate than a female counterhand. The difference was justified by the employer on the basis that the man was needed, in part, to deal with potential troublemakers who could have frequented the shop. In finding that the difference in pay was discriminatory, the Court of Appeal focused on the reality of the situation rather than the responsibilities outlined in the contract of employment. There was no evidence that the male counterhand was specifically trained for this additional function nor was there any evidence that disturbances that would require such an intervention had ever occurred in the shop. Most pertinently, there was nothing to suggest that a male counterhand would have been any more effective than a female counterhand in providing security. In the words of Lord Denning, 'he may have been a small nervous man who would not say "boo to a goose". She may have been as fierce and formidable as a battle axe.'[20]

Similarly, in *Department of Posts and Telegraphs v Kennefick,*[21] it was found that simply because the male employee was contractually liable for additional attendance duties which, in practice, rarely arose, was not a sufficient reason to distinguish the work as far as the pay was concerned.[22]

(b) Similar Work

The definition in the Act provides that the work of the comparator, while not [8–08] necessarily the same as that of the complainant, must be similar in nature and

---

19. [1978] 1 WLR 1408, [1979] 1 All ER 456, [1978] ICR 1159, [1978] IRLR 263.
20. [1978] ICR 1159, 1171.
21. EP 9/1979, DEP 2/1980.
22. See also *Electrolux v Hutchinson* [1977] ICR 252, [1976] IRLR 410, where a contractual requirement that men had to work overtime, at weekends or at night if required was rarely enforced and did not justify the difference in pay with female workers.

any differences in the work must be small in comparison to the work as a whole or occur with such irregularity that they are considered insignificant compared to the whole.[23] The concept of 'similar work' has been broadly interpreted in order to give full effect to the equal pay provisions. In *Capper Pass v Lawton*,[24] a female cook worked on her own in the director's dining room of a company, preparing 10 to 20 meals a day. She successfully sought to compare herself to male assistant chefs who worked supervised, in the staff canteen, and prepared approximately 350 meals a day. The work was generally of a similar type with similar skill and knowledge required to do it. The basic processes involved with both jobs was essentially the same.

[8–09]   If considered of practical importance, different responsibilities will justify a difference in pay even where the jobs are broadly similar. In *Eaton v Nuttall*,[25] a man and woman were doing the same work, but the woman handled goods whose value were no more than £2.50, whereas the man had responsibility for goods valued at £5–£1,000. The greater value of the goods carried with it greater responsibility and this responsibility was considered sufficient to distinguish the work of the man from that of the woman.

[8–10]   In *O'Leary v Minister for Energy, Transport and Communications*,[26] the Supreme Court held that, while the work of complainant and comparator may be similar in nature, the existence of significant differences that arise frequently could prove fatal to a claim that the work is 'like work' for the purposes of the legislation. In that case, the claimant worked as a communications assistant at Dublin Airport. She alleged that she had been discriminated against on the grounds of sex in relation to her pay as compared to male radio officers. The Equality Officer had rejected her claim on the basis that the comparators did not carry out like work since the work the men performed required additional qualifications, skills and had greater responsibility. Ultimately, Murphy J upheld the Equality Officer's decision in finding that the work was not 'like work'. While the work may have been similar, the court agreed with the conclusion of the Equality Officer that the work performed by the comparators frequently differed from that performed by the claimant, and the differences were of more than small importance as they required additional qualifications and skills of the comparators.

(c) Work of Equal Value
[8–11]   This is possibly the broadest definition of 'like work' as it allows the comparison of work that may be different in terms of content and process, but ultimately represents equal value to the employer. In order to make an assessment as to whether or

---

23. *An Comhairle Oiliuna Talmahiochta v Doyle and Others*, unreported, High Court, 13 April 1989.
24. [1977] QB 852, [1977] 2 WLR 261, [1977] 2 All ER 11, [1977] ICR 83.
25. [1977] 1 WLR 5491, [1977] 3 All ER 1131, [1977] ICR 272, [1977] IRLR 711.
26. [1998] 1 IR 588, [1998] ELR 113.

not the work is of 'equal value', s.7(c) of the 1998 Act has identified the following factors as being relevant: 'skill, physical or mental requirements, responsibility and working conditions'. In England and Wales,[27] a similar statutory definition of like work has been criticised because of its vagueness where it has been observed that:

> The immediate problem is that this takes the tribunals away from matters of relatively observable fact… and into the realm of assessment of value and the almost religious mysteries of job evaluation, for which arguably a tribunal as a judicial body is not particularly well suited.[28]

These difficulties were also recognised by the Supreme Court in *O'Leary v Minister* [8–12] *for Energy, Transport and Communications*,[29] where it was acknowledged that the more dissimilar in nature the work, the more difficult it may be to establish that the work is of 'equal value'. The court noted that:

> To liken patently different categories of work one with another by reference to the demands which they make on the skill, effort and responsibility of the workers involved may be a difficult task. Where, however, as in the present case, there is at the very least a significant degree of similarity between the work performed by the claimants and comparators it should be an easier task to compare the demands which each makes on those engaged in its performance. The possibility of establishing equality of demands or identifying the basis for any inequality must be enhanced in proportion to the degree of similarity between the allegedly different works.[30]

As a consequence, any claim that the work is of 'equal value' requires detailed [8–13] investigation by an Equality Officer as demonstrated in *24 Female Employees v Spring Grove Services*.[31] In that case, the claimants worked in a linen supply factory in the finishing and ironing section. Their comparators were men who worked in the wash-house area of the same service. It was the claimants' contention that they were doing work of equal value to that of the comparators and were therefore entitled to equal pay. In reaching her conclusions on the nature of the work, the Equality Officer interviewed an agreed representative number of claimants and comparators about their work. She then visited the workplace to observe the work at first hand. She assessed this work under each of the headings listed under s.7(1)(c) of the 1998 Act and reached the following conclusions on each point:

> *Skill* – Neither the claimant nor the comparator required any special qualifications for the work. The Equality Officer found that the work of the comparator required greater skill in the correct handling of detergents and other chemicals whereas the

27. s.1 Equal Pay Act 1970.
28. Smith and Thomas, *Smith & Wood's Employment Law* (9th ed., Oxford University Press, 2008), at p.299.
29. [1998] 1 IR 558, [1998] ELR 113.
30. [1988] 1 IR 558, 561.
31. [1996] ELR 147.

claimant was required to examine the clothing for damage or soiling and make a record of these items. The Equality Officer concluded that the skills demanded of the comparator were higher than those required of the claimant.

Physical Effort – The comparators were required to expend a great deal of physical effort. They had to carry big loads of linen, fill the washing machines and so forth. This required a lot of bending and lifting which had to be done at some pace. The work of the comparator had to be done by an individual who was relatively strong and fit. The claimant was required to stand in one position for long periods of time. From time to time she was required to stoop down to get cloths for insertion into the machines. At other times the claimant was required to pull trolleys a short distance to have them close to the machines. The Equality Officer concluded that the physical effort required of the comparator were greater than that required of the claimant.

Mental Effort – The Equality Officer decided that the attention to detail required of the comparator was much greater than that required of the claimant. The comparator was required to ensure that the washing machines were loaded correctly in order to achieve a correct balance. A failure to do this properly would result in damage to the machine's motor. Additionally, the comparator was required to know the proper level of detergents, bleach and other chemicals to put into each wash. A failure to do this properly could result in damage to the linen or lead to an ineffective wash. The claimant was required to be attentive enough so as to identify stains, repairs that were required and also to ensure that cloths are being fed in correctly. She was required to keep a record of those cloths that were damaged or stained. She was also required to stack cloths in defined bundles. The Equality Officer concluded that on balance the mental effort required of the comparator was higher than that required of the claimant.

Responsibility – The comparator was responsible for the set up, operation and cleaning of the washing machines; the balancing of the load in the machine; the correct use of detergents and other chemicals; the correct temperature and wash duration; recording details of each wash; reporting defects in machines and meeting expected output decided by management. The claimant had similar responsibility as the comparator in reporting defects in the machines and meeting expected output levels demanded by management. In addition, the claimant was responsible for identifying defects in the cloths and for ensuring that the clothing was stacked in appropriate quantities. The Equality Officer found that the demands made of the comparator, in terms of responsibility, were greater than those expected of the claimant.

Working Conditions – The Equality Officer did not find any significant difference in the working conditions of the claimant or the comparator. Both were required to work in a very warm and noisy environment. However, the comparator was required to handle soiled linen and this was not required of the claimant. The Equality Officer concluded that the demands made on the comparator, in terms of working conditions, were higher than those made on the claimant.

After this exhaustive review of the nature of the work carried out on a daily [8–14] basis by the comparator and the claimant, the Equality Officer concluded that the demands in terms of skill, responsibility, physical effort, mental effort and working conditions were much greater on the comparator than on the claimant. After taking all of these considerations into account the Equality Officer decided that the work was not equal in value.[32]

In assessing work of equal value the Labour Court has observed that it is not [8–15] simply necessary to consider the actual physical effort involved but also the relative physical effort involved. In *Irish Ale Breweries t/a Diageo European Global Supply v O'Sullivan*,[33] the facts of which are discussed at para 8–04 above, the Labour Court held that given the different physical demands which can be expected of men and women, the relative physical effort expected of the complainant (a female cleaner/ canteen assistant) was similar to that expected of the male comparators (male yardmen), even though the actual physical effort was very different.

(d) Work of Greater Value Is Work of Equal Value

Section 7(3) of the 1998 Act provides that where the work of the claimant is of [8–16] higher value than that of the comparator then for the purposes of the definition of 'like work', the work performed by the claimant shall be considered to be of 'equal value' to that of the comparator. This provision reflects the ruling of the European Court of Justice in *Murphy and Others v An Bord Telecom Éireann*,[34] where the employer unsuccessfully sought to avoid the application of the equal pay provisions by arguing that as the work of the claimant was greater in value than that of the male comparator, it could not be deemed to be work of 'equal value'.

1.3.2. Comparator

In order to succeed in an equal pay claim the complainant must establish the exist- [8–17] ence of an *actual* comparator doing like work for the same or associated employer at that or any other relevant time. In *Macarthys Ltd. v Smith*,[35] the European Court of Justice held that reliance on a hypothetical comparator was not possible. In that case, the claimant argued *inter alia* that a woman could not only claim the same salary as that received by a man who previously did the same work for her employer but that she could also claim the salary to which she would be entitled were she a man, 'even in the absence of any man who was concurrently performing, or had previously performed, similar work'.[36] However, the court refused to apply a hypothetical comparator to the claimant's equal pay claim, stating that such cases were:

---

32. See also *Sales and Clerical Assistants v Penneys Ltd.* [1996] ELR 78, EP 06/1994; *Sheridan & 12 Others v Health Services Executive*, DEC-E2008-010, 3 March 2008.
33. Determination no. EDA0611.
34. [1986] ILRM 483.
35. [1980] ECR 1275.
36. *supra* at para.14.

to be classed as indirect and disguised discrimination, the identification of which…
implies comparative studies of entire branches of industry and therefore requires,
as a prerequisite, the elaboration by the community and national legislative bodies
of criteria of assessment. From that it follows that, in cases of actual discrimination
falling within the scope of the direct application of Article 119, comparisons are
confined to parallels which may be drawn on the basis of concrete appraisals of
work actually performed by employees of different sex within the same establishment or service.[37]

[8–18] In *Brides v Minister for Agriculture, Food and Forestry*,[38] Budd J of the Irish High
Court, in applying the reasoning adopted in *Macarthys*, observed that:

> the European Court of Justice has clearly distinguished between direct and overt
> discrimination which can be dealt with solely on the criteria referred to in Article
> 119 and secondly, by way of contrast, indirect and disguised discrimination which
> can only be identified by reference to Community provisions, such as a directive, or
> by national legislation which spells out the tests to be applied in implementing the
> principle in Article 119. The European Court of Justice in those cases has confined
> the scope for location of a comparator and did not extend the range by allowing a
> comparison with a hypothetical comparator of the other gender. These cases seem
> to be clear authority on this issue and, in coming to these decisions, the Court must
> have been well aware of the difficulty which could arise in situations of the type
> of single gender establishments such as in the electrical board assembly business
> where there would be a dearth of male comparators. In short, the Applicants' argu-
> ment is that if equal pay legislation is to have a real effect in undermining gender
> discrimination then it should provide a mechanism for assuring that all women
> are able to secure what would be the male rate for the job. However, the European
> Court of Justice rejected this approach in both *Defrenne (No.2)* and *Macarthys v
> Smith* by holding that comparisons are confined to parallels which may drawn on
> the basis of concrete appraisals for the work actually performed by employees of
> the opposite sex within the same establishment or service.[39]

The refusal by the court to recognise the hypothetical comparator in such situations represents one of the biggest obstacles facing a claimant seeking parity in
respect of pay. If the claimant – usually a woman – is in a career or industry
dominated by her own sex (typically one of the five 'Cs' – catering, cashiering,
caring, cleaning and clerical[40]) then it may be difficult for her to find a suitable
candidate to whom she will be able to compare herself. Consequently, in the fields
where discrimination is most likely to occur, it will prove most difficult to sustain
a claim.

---

37. *supra* at para.15.
38. [1998] 4 IR 250.
39. [1998] 4 IR 250, 285-286.
40. The Women and Work Commission, *Shaping a Fairer Future*, February 2006, at 4.

While it has been held that it is for the claimant to choose her comparator,[41] the **[8–19]**
English Court of Appeal in *Cheshire and Wirral Partnership NHS Trust v Abbott*[42]
has held that the claimant cannot artificially limit the pool of comparators in order
to improve his or her chances of success. In that case, domestic staff (predominantly female) sought to compare themselves to hospital porters (exclusively male)
working in the same hospitals. In particular, the claimants argued that the failure
by the employer to apply a bonus payment scheme to them when it was available
to the porters was discriminatory. However, the employers succeeded in arguing
that the comparator group should have been extended to include catering workers
(also predominantly female), who performed like work. As the bonus scheme
applied equally to them, the claimants were unable to show that the scheme
adversely affected women.

The chosen comparator must work for a connected employer at that or any other **[8–20]**
relevant time. Section 19(2)(b) defines relevant time as any time during the three
years that precede or the three years that follow the particular time. The legislation
gives effect to the concept that equal pay 'may not be restricted by requirements
of contemporaneity'.[43] For these purposes, a comparison may also be made with
a complainant's successor.[44]

1.3.3. Same or Associated Employer
Section 19(1) of the 1998 Act further restricts the choice of comparator by requiring **[8–21]**
that the comparator must do like work for the same or an associated employer.
Section 19(3) provides that where the comparator is working for an associated
employer, he will not be considered to be doing 'like work' unless both have the
same or reasonably comparable terms and conditions of employment. Section 2(2)
of the 1998 Act provides that employers will be taken as being associated 'if one is a
body corporate of which the other (whether directly or indirectly) has control or if
both are bodies corporate of which a third person (whether directly or indirectly)
has control'. The element of 'control' is therefore essential.[45]

In *Malone v Royal Victoria Eye and Ear Hospital*,[46] the complainant worked as **[8–22]**
a domestic staff worker for the hospital that was part of the voluntary hospitals group. Part of her work involved store duties. She found that similar male
workers doing such duties received approximately 8 per cent more an hour than

41. *Lally v Citigroup*, DEC-E2006-016, *Wilton v Steel Co of Ireland Ltd.* [1998] IEHC 87, [1999] ELR 1, *Ainsworth v Glass Tubes and Components* [1977] ICR 347, [1977] IRLR 74.
42. [2006] EWCA Civ 523, [2006] IRLR 546.
43. *Macarthys Ltd. v Smith* [1980] IRLR 210, [1978] 1 WLR 849, [1978] ICR 500.
44. *Diocese of Hallam Trustee v Connaughton* [1996] ICR 860, [1996] IRLR 505.
45. *Brides v Minister for Agriculture, Food and Forestry* [1998] 4 IR 250. In that case, the necessary element of control was held not to exist where employees of Teagasc (an inde- pendent government unit) sought to compare themselves to employees of the Department of Agriculture. See also *Dublin Coporation v 16 Female Bath Attendants*, EP 5/1980.
46. [1999] ELR 328.

she received for carrying out these duties. She brought an action for equal pay, claiming that her male counterparts were receiving higher pay for doing similar work for an associated employer, i.e. the Department of Health and Children. Her action was unsuccessful. The comparators were not working for an associated employer. The hospitals were run by an independent hospital board and the Department of Health and Children had very little input in their running. The necessary 'control' as required under Act did not exist.

1.3.4. Absence of Objective Justification

[8–23] It is not the purpose or function of the equality legislation to eliminate all forms of discrimination. Employers retain the ability to discriminate against employees for reasons other than their gender (for example, differences in pay could be justified on the basis that the comparator has relevant qualifications the complainant does not have).[47] However, an employer must always tread carefully in this regard and must ensure that the process by which the difference in pay is calculated is completely free from the taint of discrimination. Otherwise such an employer will be in a position whereby [s]he must be able objectively to justify the difference.

[8–24] Direct discrimination in such circumstances cannot be justified. However, s.19(4) of the 1998 Act provides that where the difference in pay is as a result of indirect discrimination, the victim of such treatment shall be entitled to the higher remuneration where it cannot be justified by objective factors unrelated to the victim's sex.[48] Furthermore, s.19(5) provides that, subject to s.19(4), nothing in the legislation shall 'prevent an employer from paying, on grounds other than the gender ground, different rates of remuneration to different employees'.

1.3.4.1. Criteria for Objective Justification

[8–25] Member State governments have long pleaded that indirect gender discrimination related to pay could be objectively justified on the basis that it was necessary to achieve the a legitimate aim of that Member State's social or economic policy. One of the earliest decisions on objective justification arose in *Bilka-Kaufhaus GmbH v Weber von Hartz*.[49] In that case, a Mrs Weber was employed by Bilka as a sales assistant in a department store. She worked full-time in this position for a period of 11 years and worked for the remainder of her career on a part-time basis. As she had not worked for the minimum 15 years on a full-time basis, Bilka refused to pay her an occupational pension under its scheme. Mrs Weber challenged this scheme as being discriminatory on the grounds of gender, as the requirement that workers must be working full-time for a period of 15 years placed female workers at a disadvantage. Bilka argued that the discrimination was justified on the basis that

---

47. *An Chomhairle Oiliúna Talmhaíochta v Doyle*, unreported, High Court, Carroll J, 13 April 1989.
48. *Bilka-Kaufhaus GmbH v Weber von Hartz*, 170/84 [1986] EUECJ R-170/84, [1987] ICR 110, [1986] IRLR 317.
49. 170/84 [1987] ICR 110.

the decision to exclude part-time workers from the occupational pension scheme was simply to encourage more full-time workers, as part-time workers generally did not want to work late afternoons and on Saturdays and it was necessary to ensure the presence of an adequate workforce during these hours by making full-time work more attractive. The European Court of Justice held that it was for the national court to decide whether the restrictions placed on the occupational scheme were objectively justifiable. Such a scheme would be objectively justifiable, the European Court of Justice held, where it was 'found that the means chosen for achieving that objective correspond to a real need on the part of the undertaking, are appropriate with a view to achieving the objective in question and are necessary to that end'.[50]

In recent years, employers and governments have increasingly begun to argue that [8–26] the test for objective justification is more lenient than that initially laid down in *Bilka-Kaufhaus* and that that case should be limited to its own facts.[51] Instead it is argued that a difference in pay can be objectively justified on grounds unrelated to gender on the basis, for example, that it is necessary in order to fulfil a social or economic policy of an individual Member State. Following *Bilka-Kaufhaus,* the matter came before the European Court of Justice by way of a preliminary reference once again in *Rinner–Kuhn v FWW Spezial-Gebauderinigung GmbH.*[52] In that case, the question was whether German national legislation, which permitted employers to exclude from the continued payment of wages in the event of illness those employees whose normal hours of work did not exceed 10 hours a week (or 45 hours a month), amounted to indirect discrimination in relation to pay where that category of worker consisted predominantly of women. The European Court of Justice held that if a Member State could establish that the means chosen to achieve the necessary aim of its social policy were suitable and were required to attain that aim, then simply because it affected more female employees than male employees did not mean the measure was discriminatory.

That Member States enjoy a 'broad margin of discretion' in choosing the appro- [8–27] priate measures necessary to achieve the aim of their social and employment policy was confirmed by the European Court of Justice in *Nolte v Landesversicherung- santstalt Hannover.*[53] In that case, the court accepted that a national provision relating to old-age insurance – which excluded employment regularly consisting of a fewer than 15 hours a week and where the monthly remuneration did not exceed one-seventh of the average monthly salary of persons insured under the

---

50. *ibid.,* at 126.
51. That case concerned an occupational pension scheme operated by the employer that required employees to have a minimum period of full-time employment with the employer for a period of time. It could therefore be argued that the case was limited to employees of Bilka. Indeed this view was endorsed by the Equality Officer in *28 Named Employees v Courts Service* [2007] ELR 212.
52. 171/88 [1989] EUECJ R-171/88, [1989] ECR 2743.
53. C-317/93 [1995] ECR I-04625 at para.33.

statutory old-age insurance scheme (otherwise known as 'minor employment') – did not contravene Art. 141 (ex-119) on equal pay. While the national provision affected more women than men (as it was more likely that more women than men would be undertaking such minor employment), the national legislature was entitled to consider that such measures were necessary to meet the aims of their social and employment policy. In support of this argument, the German Government contended that the contributory scheme like the one at issue required that equivalence be maintained between the contributions paid by employees and employers and the benefits paid out under the scheme. It was the German Government's contention that the structure of the social security scheme could not be maintained if the provisions that excluded minor employment had to be abolished. It further successfully argued that its social policy demanded the fostering of minor employment and that the only way to do this within the German social security scheme was to exclude such employment from the compulsory insurance scheme.

[8–28] Whilst accepting that Member States retained a broad margin of discretion in meeting their aims of social and employment policy, the European Court of Justice, in *R v Secretary of State for Employment, ex parte Seymour-Smith*,[54] emphasised that in so doing discretion could not be used to frustrate the implementation of the principle of equal pay for men and women. In that case, two women sought to bring claims for unfair dismissal in the United Kingdom, but failed to do so because they lacked the two years' continuous service required under the relevant legislation. The women argued that the two-year qualifying period amounted to indirect discrimination as the proportion of women who could comply with it were considerably smaller than the proportion of men who could do so. In response, the United Kingdom government argued that the qualifying period of two years was necessary because otherwise there was a risk that employers would be exposed too easily to the threat of unfair dismissals claims, which could deter recruitment. The two-year qualifying period therefore was necessary to stimulate recruitment. Having accepted that compensation could be considered 'pay' for the purposes of Art. 119 (now Art. 141) of the EC Treaty, the European Court of Justice held that it is for the national court of each Member State to establish whether such objective factors exist. It warned that:

> Mere generalisations concerning the capacity of a specific measure to encourage recruitment are not enough to show that the aim of the disputed rule is unrelated to any discrimination based on sex nor to provide evidence on the basis of which it could reasonably be considered that the means chosen were suitable for achieving that aim.[55]

---

54. C-167/97 [1999] EUECJ C-167/97, [1999] ECR I-623.
55. [1999] EUECJ C-167/97at para.76.

The case was returned to the House of Lords[56] for consideration and on the ques- [8–29]
tion of objective justification, Lord Nicholls, in finding that the qualifying periods
in question could be objectively justified, held:

> The burden placed on the government in this type of case is not as heavy as previ-
> ously thought. Governments must be able to govern. They adopt general policies,
> and implement measures to carry out their policies. Governments must be able to
> take into account a wide range of social, economic and political factors. The Court
> of Justice has recognised these practical considerations. If their aim is legitimate,
> governments have a discretion when choosing the method to achieve their aim.
> National courts, acting with hindsight, are not to impose an impracticable burden
> on governments which are proceeding in good faith. Generalised assumptions,
> lacking any factual foundation, are not good enough. But governments are to be
> afforded a broad measure of discretion. The onus is on the Member State to show
> (1) that the allegedly discriminatory rule reflects a legitimate aim of its social policy,
> (2) that this aim is unrelated to any discrimination based on sex, and (3) that the
> Member State could reasonably consider that the means chosen were suitable for
> attaining that aim.[57]

The Irish Equality Tribunal was asked to consider what the appropriate test was [8–30]
for determining objective justification in *28 Named Employees v Courts Service*.[58] In
that case, the complainants were employed as court messengers by the respondent
at various court buildings throughout the country. The named comparators were
employed as staff officers at similar locations and in other government departments
and offices throughout the country. The complainants' union referred an equal
pay claim to the Equality Tribunal. The respondents argued that the complainants
were not performing 'like work' with the comparators and contended that even if
they were, the differences in pay could be objectively justified. In examining the
appropriate test to be applied, the Equality Officer favoured the more lenient test
outlined in *Rinner Kuhn/Nolte/Seymour-Smith* rather than that in *Bilka-Kaufhas*.
The Equality Officer was of the view that because these decisions concerned
national legislation or collective agreements they were of broader application than
Bilka-Kaufhas, which was quite specific, involving as it did the employer's occupational pension scheme. In applying the broader test, the Equality Officer observed
that the pay rates had developed as part of a series of national agreements negotiated between the government and trade unions under a partnership process. The
Equality Officer noted that:

> These agreements have not been restricted to pay determination in the public
> and private sectors, rather they have covered issues of housing, health, taxation,
> job creation, employment rights, social inclusion, etc. One of the objectives of

56. [2000] UKHL 12, [2000] 1 All ER 857.
57. [2000] 1 All ER 857, 873.
58. [2007] ELR 212.

the process was to create a stable environment for investment, job creation and growth. This entailed sound and orderly management of public finances, which included public sector pay rates. In pursuit of this objective the benchmarking process emerged from the PPF as a mechanism of evaluating public sector pay rates with comparable jobs in the private sector and required continued civil service productivity gains in response to any pay increase.[59]

[8–31] The Equality Officer held that this objective reflected the legitimate economic and social policy aims of the government and 'that if the respondent could show that the measures chosen reflect a necessary aim of its social policy and are suitable and necessary for achieving that aim, it has objectively justified the approach adopted'.[60] In reaching this conclusion, the Equality Officer examined the 'totality of factors' in making a determination of objective justification, including the historical reasons for the differences in pay, the grading structure within the civil service and the process of collective bargaining.

1.3.4.2. Specific Examples of Factors that May Amount to Objective Justification
[8–32] While neither Art. 119 of the Treaty nor s.19 of the 1998 Act clarify what constitutes an objectively justifiable reason for discrimination in this regard, case law has recognised a number of circumstances where the difference can be justified, some of which are dealt with in greater detail below:

[8–33] *1. Objective Grounds:* Where the difference in pay is based on objective grounds (unconnected with one of the discriminatory grounds) then it can be justified. In *National University of Ireland, Cork v 42 Named Claimants*,[61] the claimants were male workers that were employed as security operatives by the respondent. They sought to compare themselves to five female comparators who were employed as laboratory aides and switchboard operators. It was the respondent's contention that the difference in pay was not on the grounds of sex but rather to facilitate its employees – both male and female – to job-share in order to facilitate their family responsibilities in a manner which would not cause undue financial hardship. It transpired that the comparators had been initially employed on a full-time basis, but then had switched to part-time work for family reasons. To facilitate their family responsibilities, the comparators retained their original rate of remuneration. The Labour Court ultimately held that the sole reason for the retention of the comparators' pay when they had changed to part-time work was in order to facilitate them with their family responsibilities. Thus the difference in pay could be explained on grounds other than the gender and the difference in pay was therefore justified.[62]

59. [2007] ELR 212, 219.
60. [2007] ELR 212, 219.
61. Determination DEP061.
62. See also *Department of Justice, Equality and Law Reform v CPSU* [2008] ELR 140.

2. *Market Forces:* One of the main objectives of the Treaty of Rome 1957 was to   [8–34]
create a closer economic union among the nations of Europe. This Community
was based on a free-market model of perfect competition. However, legislation
on equal pay can act to disturb such market forces and thereby distort competition. Given the sometimes contradictory economic and social objectives of the
Community, it remains controversial as to whether a difference in pay can ever be
justified on free-market ideals allegedly unconnected with the employee's gender
or some other personal characteristic unconnected with job performance. In
particular, it is unclear whether or not this can be the case where the factors militating in favour of such pay differentials will inevitably affect a greater proportion
of one gender than of the other. [63]

One of the first successful cases to deal with market forces as a defence was that   [8–35]
of *Jenkins v Kingsgate*.[64] In that case, the employer had paid part-time staff a lower
hourly rate than full-time staff. The employer contended that the different rates
of pay were necessary in order to encourage full-time work with less reliance on
part-time work, which would, in turn, bring with it greater economic efficiencies
for the business. In particular, the employer argued that if the alternative was the
case, machinery would lay idle for part of the week when manned by part-time
staff. Furthermore, it was claimed by the employer that there was a higher rate of
absenteeism among part-time staff than full-time staff. The tribunal, after reference to the European Court of Justice, found that the payment of lower hourly
rates of remuneration to part-time workers was capable of amounting to indirect
discrimination because it was more likely that more women than men would work
on a part-time basis. However, it held that the tactic adopted by the employer in
this case was a genuine part of its business strategy and could be objectively justified on economic grounds.

The parameters of the defence were further explored in *Bilka-Kaufhaus v Weber*   [8–36]
von Hartz,[65] the facts of which are outlined earlier in this chapter at para 8.25. In
that case, the European Court of Justice held that an employer could justify this
disparity in pay on the basis that it was seeking to encourage its employees to work
full-time. The court held that:

> It falls to the national Court, which alone is competent to assess the facts, to decide
> whether, and if so to what extent, the grounds put forward by an employer to explain
> the adoption of a pay practice which applies irrespective of the employee's sex, but
> which in fact affects more women than men, can be considered to be objectively justi-
> fied for economic reasons. If the national Court finds the reasons chosen by Bilka:

---

63. The Court of Appeal of England and Wales initially rejected a claim by an employer that
    differences in pay between male and female workers could be justified on the basis that it
    was the only way to attract the male employee to the job: *Clay Cross (Quarry Services) v
    Fletcher* [1979] 1 All ER 474, [1979] ICR 1, [1977] IRLR 258.
64. [1981] 1 WLR, [1981] ECR 911, [1981] 2 CMLR 24, [1981] ICR 592, [1980] IRLR 6.
65. 170/84 [1986] EUECJ R-170/84, [1987] ICR 110, [1986] IRLR 317.

(a) meet a genuine need of the enterprise
(b) are suitable for attaining the objective pursued by the enterprise
(c) are necessary for that purpose;

the fact that the measure in question affects a much greater number of women than men is not sufficient to conclude that they involve a breach of Article 119.[66]

[8–37] The market forces defence was further clarified by the European Court of Justice in *Enderby v Frenchay Health Authority and Secretary of State for Health*,[67] where the court re-emphasised that the difference in pay must be proportionate to the requirement imposed. In that case, a comparison was made between speech therapists (who were predominantly women) and pharmacists (who were predominantly men). The employer had argued that the difference in pay was *inter alia* because of the need to attract suitably qualified candidates to the position where a labour shortage existed. Furthermore, the employer argued that if the employment market had played *some* part in the difference in pay, then that fact was sufficient to justify the *whole* of the difference between the two groups. The European Court of Justice held that the motives of the employer in the circumstances could constitute an objectively justified economic reason for differences in pay and reiterated that it was for the national court to determine how such a defence would be applied in each case. On the secondary issue as to whether the whole of the difference must be attributable to that reason, the court stated that:

> If... the national court has been able to determine precisely what proportion of the increase in pay is attributable to market forces, it must necessarily accept that the pay differential is objectively justified to the extent of that proportion. When national authorities have to apply Community Law, they must apply the principle of proportionality.

> If that is not the case, it is for the national court to assess whether the role of market forces in determining the rate of pay was sufficiently significant to provide objective justification for part or all of the difference... it is for the national court to determine, if necessary by applying the principle of proportionality, whether and to what extent the shortage of candidates for a job and the need to attract them by higher pay constitutes an objectively justified economic ground for the difference in pay between the jobs in question.[68]

[8–38] In *Sales and Clerical Assistants v Penneys Ltd.*,[69] the Labour Court was presented with the 'market forces' defence. In that case, over 550 female clerical assistants brought an equal pay claim against male storemen working at the same premises.

---

66. Bolger and Kimber, *Sex Discrimination Law* (Round Hall Sweet and Maxwell, 2000), at p.118.
67. C-127/92 1993] EUECJ C-127/92, [1993] ECR I-5535, [1993] IRLR 591.
68. [1993] EUECJ C-127/92 at para.27-29.
69. [1996] ELR 78.

The men's pay was greater than that of the women. The Labour Court decision was appealed to the High Court on a point of law.[70] Barron J of the High Court held that it was the function of the Labour Court to consider not merely whether there was a reason unconnected with sex for the difference in pay, but also whether the difference was justified on economic grounds. The High Court accepted that the work in question was of equal value, but it found that the differences in pay had been achieved through different negotiating routes. Thus the clerical assistants' pay was agreed with the employer directly, while the male storemen had agreed their pay through a collective bargaining process concluded during the 1970s. As a result of the industrial relations process that had taken place, the employer had obtained significant economic benefits in return. For the increased pay, the employer secured agreement to remove inflexible and unproductive work practices and as a result the employer achieved and continued to achieve economic benefits. The matter was referred to the Labour Court, which held that the difference in pay was justified on the basis that:

> the measures taken by the employer in the 1970's corresponded to a real need on the part of the company, were appropriate with a view to achieving the economic viability of the company and were necessary and that they continue today to be necessary to that end.[71]

The Labour Court decision was appealed to the High Court on the basis, *inter alia*, that the difference in pay could not currently be justified on economic grounds and that the difference in negotiation procedures alone could not constitute objective justification.[72] In the High Court, Laffoy J dismissed the appeal and held that not only could the difference in pay be objectively justified on historic grounds, in her view it would be to the economic disadvantage of the employer to revert back to the old work practices and that regardless, the extra pay agreed in return for the relinquishment of those bad work practices could not be given up without serious industrial unrest resulting. Thus the Labour Court's decision that the difference in pay could be objectively justified on the basis that the employer had obtained a historical economic advantage that continued to the present day was affirmed. The court noted that on foot of this agreement, one group of employees (the comparators) had, in return for extra pay, relinquished bad work practices for flexible ones. Furthermore, the court noted that the removal of the higher rate of pay from the comparators would result in industrial unrest for the employer and thus the status quo should remain. [8–39]

Bolger and Kimber have strongly criticised this outcome. It is their contention that the decision in *Penneys* does not dig deep enough into the reasons as to how the difference in pay arose in the first place: [8–40]

---

70. *Flynn and Others v Primark t/a Penneys Ltd.* [1997] ELR 218.

71. *Penneys Ltd. v MANDATE* [1998] ELR 94, 97.

72. *Flynn and Others v Primark t/a Penneys Ltd. & Others (No 2)* [1999] IEHC 119, [1999] ELR 89.

The reasoning here is not convincing. It may be that the unequal pay was due to the lesser negotiating leverage of the female sales assistants, but the possibility of that being on grounds of the sex of the employees is not addressed. To blame inequality on history without unpacking the inequality in that history is, at the very least, contrary to the spirit behind the principle of equal pay. The suggestion that the employer enjoyed continuing benefits accruing from the historical advantages given to the storemen is unconvincing as it is disingenuous to suggest that a finding of unequal pay would have resulted in the employer reverting back to the old work practices or that the additional pay could have been removed from the storemen. In fact it is arguable that a storeman who had his wages unilaterally reduced because his female sales assistant colleague had succeeded in her equal pay claim would be entitled to challenge the reduction of wages as unlawful pursuant to the Payment of Wages Act.[73]

There is merit in the view that the courts in *Penneys* too readily accepted the reasoning offered by the employer for the disparity in pay as justifiable. There was arguably a failure by the court to examine in greater detail the historical and social reasons that led one group (made up of men) to be in a stronger negotiating position than another group (made up of women) in the first place.

[8–41] The House of Lords also upheld the 'market forces' defence in *Rainey v Greater Glasgow Health Board*.[74] In that case, it had formerly been the practice of the health authority in Scotland not to employ prosthetists directly, but instead to engage private contractors, however it was later decided to bring such services within the remit of the health authority and to discontinue the practice of contracting the service. In order to attract qualified people it was necessary to offer candidates their current private sector salaries, with future changes and salaries to be negotiated by their trade union separately from other NHS employees. Following this once-off agreement, recruitment of further prosthetists would follow NHS salary guidelines and would be negotiated in a similar manner to all other NHS employees.

[8–42] The appellant was a female prosthetist who was paid at a lower rate to her male colleagues who had joined under the special arrangement. The House of Lords (which was heavily influenced by the fact that, had the special offer not been made to the male prosthetists, the new prosthetic service could never have been established within a reasonable time) upheld the respondent's claim that the difference in pay was objectively justifiable on the basis of market forces. The House of Lords observed that the disparity in pay had increased over the years by virtue of the different negotiating processes the appellant underwent to that of the male prosthetists, and found that this process was objectively justifiable. The House of Lords found in favour of the health authority on the basis that the respondent

---

73. Bolger and Kimber, *Sex Discrimination Law* (Round Hall Sweet and Maxwell, 2000), at p.121.
74. [1987] AC 224, [1987] 1 All ER 65, [1987] ICR 129, [1987] IRLR 26.

could not have been expected to single out all prosthetists and subject them to a negotiation process separate from all other NHS employees. The negotiation process by which the comparators' pay was reviewed was granted to this group as a once-off because of the particular market circumstances involved. Thereafter, however, all prosthetists employed by the respondent were subject to the standard rates and process.

One can sympathise with the rationale of the judgment in *Rainey*. Had the [8–43] respondent not made the offer it did, it is doubtful it would have attracted the necessary qualified staff to fill the positions within a reasonable period. It is note-worthy that each of the male prosthetists (totalling 20 in all) were offered the posi-tion on the basis either of normal NHS salary rates and subject to its negotiating processes, or to move to the NHS on their current salary level with future increases negotiated by their trade union,[75] and there was no evidence that the agreement was tainted by gender discrimination in any way. It was a once-off agreement, which applied to a select profession at a particular time when all members of the profession were male. Furthermore, all future prosthetists employed by the health board, both men and women, were subjected to the standard terms and condi-tions of employment. In other words, the relevant employer needed to deal with a specific situation and the male prosthetists in this case simply happened to be in the right place at the right time. That said, it could be argued that the employer's defence that its failure to raise the salaries of the other prosthetists to that of the comparators on the basis that it would not be 'administratively efficient' to do so is a dangerous precedent, which should not be used to allow sex discrimination in by the back door.

Recent decisions have re-emphasised the point that 'market forces' will not always [8–44] be accepted as an objectively justifiable reason for a difference in pay. Thus, in *Ratcliffe v North Yorkshire County Council*,[76] the respondent council had estab-lished a direct service organisation for the provision of school meals when compul-sory competitive tendering was introduced. After losing out on one such tender to a private company who had paid their all-female catering staff at a lower rate, the council made its staff redundant and re-employed them at a rate lower than their male comparators. The 'market forces' defence failed with Lord Slynn, who concluded that he was 'satisfied that to reduce the women's wages below that of their male comparators was the very kind of discrimination in relation to pay which the Act sought to remove'.[77]

In *Hill and Stapleton v The Revenue Commissioners*,[78] the European Court of [8–45] Justice similarly refused to accept the 'market forces' defence as a justification for

---

75. Each of the prosthetists chose the latter option.
76. [1995] 3 All ER 597, [1995] ICR 883.
77. [1995] 3 All ER 597 at 604.
78. C-243/95 [1998] ECR 3739.

differences in pay. In that case, Hill and Stapleton were female civil servants working for the Irish Revenue Commissioners as part of a job-share scheme. After securing full-time employment both women found that their pay had been re-classified and they were not treated comparably with other full-time civil servants. This apparently occurred on the basis that under the rules of the scheme two years' job-sharing was counted as one year's full-time service. The European Court of Justice held that this was a form of indirect discrimination (as the vast majority of job-sharing employees were women) and rejected the Revenue Commission-er's defence that the difference in pay could be objectively justified. The court concluded 'that an employer cannot justify discrimination arising from a job-sharing scheme solely on the ground that avoidance of such discrimination would involve increased costs'.[79]

[8–46]   *3. Collective Bargaining:* Differences in pay between employees may be explained by virtue of the fact that one group of employees, through a trade union, have leveraged their collective power in order to negotiate rates of pay for their members that are higher than those of another group who may not have the same collec-tive strength. This raises the question as to whether such reasoning will ever be considered an objectively justified explanation for the differences in pay, particu-larly where membership of that union was, for historic reasons, dominated by one sex.

[8–47]   In *Enderby v Frenchay Health Authority and Secretary of State for Health,*[80] the rates of pay of speech therapists (predominantly women) were different to those of phar-macists and clinical psychologists (predominantly men) doing like work. The pay was negotiated under the National Health Service Whitley Council negotiating procedures, but the pay of the therapists was negotiated by a separate bargaining unit from that of their comparators. The employer sought to objectively justify the difference in pay on the basis that the pay of the therapists and their compara-tors was determined by different collective bargaining processes, neither of which discriminated on the grounds of sex. The European Court of Justice held that while the role the collective bargaining process had played in the rates of pay was something that might have explained the differences in pay and was thus relevant, it was not sufficient, by itself, to justify the differences:

> The fact that the rates of pay at issue are decided by collective bargaining processes conducted separately for each of the two professional groups concerned, without any discriminatory effect within each group, does not preclude a finding of *prima facie* discrimination where the results of those processes show that two groups with the same employer and the same trade union are treated differently. If the employer could rely on the absence of discrimination within each of the collective bargaining processes taken separately as sufficient justification for the difference in pay, he

79. *ibid.*, at para.40.
80. C-127/92 [1993] EUECJ C-127/92, [1993] ECR I-5535, [1993] IRLR 591.

could... easily circumvent the principle of equal pay by using separate bargaining processes.

... the fact that the respective rates of pay of two jobs of equal value, one carried out almost exclusively by women and the other predominantly by men, were arrived at by collective bargaining processes which, although carried out by the same parties, are distinct, and, taken separately, have in themselves no discriminatory effect, is not sufficient objective justification for the difference in pay between those two jobs.[81]

The European Court of Justice, therefore, while willing to acknowledge the role collective bargaining played in determining the rates of pay, was unwilling to accept this fact alone as justification for the difference. The court observed that to do so too readily would allow the employer to avoid equal pay legislation through the adoption of different negotiation vehicles for each group.

The questions surrounding collective bargaining as an objective justification for **[8–48]** differences in pay also arose in *Flynn and Others v Primark t/a Penneys Ltd.*[82] In that case, the difference in pay between the two groups was attributable to five productivity agreements concluded in the 1970s, when the comparator group had enjoyed considerable industrial relations strength. The Labour Court had held that the difference in pay could be objectively justified on economic grounds and, furthermore, that the different rates of pay had been achieved by different industrial routes and were unisex rates even if one group was predominantly female and the other predominantly male.[83] As regards the validity of collective bargaining as a defence to differences in pay, the Labour Court distinguished the case from that of *Enderby*. In particular, the Labour Court emphasised that:

The claimants and the comparators are represented by different unions. The parties' representatives carry out different types of negotiations, and both of these types of negotiations end up with unisex rates of pay. But the comparators negotiate through their union directly with the company employer. The claimants negotiate on a very different basis, and not directly with the company at all. The claimants' rates of pay are fixed on an industry-wide basis through an industrial relations process which results in a registered employment agreement for the whole of the drapery trade ... The union, MANDATE, negotiates with the Irish Business and Employers Confederation (IBEC), as a result of which pay rates are fixed for all workers to whom the agreement applies, and those rates are then to be paid by all the employers in establishments selling certain classes of goods in the Dublin area.[84]

---

81. [1993] EUECJ C-127/92 at paras.22–23.
82. [1996] ELR 78, [1997] ELR 218, [1998] ELR 94, [1999] IEHC 119, [1999] ELR 89.
83. *Penneys Ltd. v MANDATE* [1998] ELR 94.
84. *ibid.*, at 97.

[8–49] The Labour Court concluded that to make an analogy with *Enderby* on these grounds was unjustified. On appeal to the High Court, the applicants contended that the Labour Court had erred in law in finding that the difference in pay was objectively justified on economic grounds. It was further argued that as collective bargaining (following *Enderby*) could not alone amount to an objective justification, absent any other justification, the difference in pay was discriminatory. On the market forces defence, the High Court found that the difference in pay could be justified. As to the question of whether the collective bargaining process could amount to an objective justification for the difference in pay, Laffoy J concluded:

> I have no doubt that the Labour Court correctly identified the significant factual distinction between the *Enderby* case and the instant case. However, it is not necessary for this Court to express any view on the Labour Court's conclusion that the bargaining processes which the two groups in the instant case follow are so different from each other '*as to make any analogy with the rationale of the Enderby judgment quite unjustified*', because it was acknowledged on behalf of the respondent that a difference in negotiating procedures cannot of itself constitute objective justification on economic grounds.[85]

[8–50] In reaffirming the decision of the Labour Court in *Flynn*, the High Court, by restricting *Enderby* to its own facts, has increased the scope of the collective bargaining defence as an objective justification for differences in pay. As a consequence, where rates of pay are negotiated from a position of industrial relations strength 'without any sex-based ingredient in the negotiating process', differences in pay may be justified.[86]

[8–51] *4. Length of Service:* At first glance it would seem that rewarding employees with incremental increases in their salary because of their loyalty and length of service would not be a policy that would fall foul of the provisions on equal pay, and that view appeared to be confirmed by the European Court of Justice in *Handel-og Konturfunktionaerernes Forbund I Danmark v Dansk Arbjdsgiverforening, ex parte Danfoss A/S.*[87] In that case, the European Court of Justice recognised that rewarding employees on the criterion of length of service could indirectly discriminate against female employees as it is more likely that such employees have entered the employment market more recently and are more likely to suffer an interruption of their career to have a family and so forth. However, the court noted that:

> since length of service goes hand in hand with experience and since experience generally enables the employee to perform his duties better, the employer is free to

---

85. [1999] ELR 89, 104-105.
86. In *28 Named Comparators v Courts Service* [2007] ELR 212, the Equality Tribunal approved of Laffoy J's decision in *Flynn* that a collective bargaining process could be included as a factor in deciding the issue of objective justification.
87. 109/88 [1989] ECR 3199.

reward it without having to establish the importance it has in the performance of specific tasks entrusted to the employee.[88]

The court concluded that as such the employer did not have to provide any special justification for using length of service as a criterion for calculating rates of pay.[89]

Handel-og was accepted as authority for the proposition that where a difference in **[8–52]** pay was based on criteria associated with length of service then it did not require to be objectively justified by the employer. However, the decision of the ECJ in *Cadman v Health and Safety Executive*[90] may now cast doubt on that view. In that case, Ms Cadman had five years' service with the Health and Safety Executive. She sought to compare herself to four male colleagues who were in the same managerial grade, but whose pay was greater than hers. The comparators had longer service with the Health and Safety Executive than Ms Cadman did. Her employer contended that because the male colleagues had greater length of service, the difference in pay was justifiable. The Court of Appeal referred the case to the European Court of Justice.

The ECJ acknowledged that its decision in *Handel-og* did provide that an employer **[8–53]** need not provide special justification for using experience as a criterion for determining rates of pay. However, it also noted that simply because an employee has greater experience does not automatically make them a better employee.[91] Thus, while on the facts Ms Cadman's claim was rejected, the court refused to rule out the possibility that in certain circumstances the employer would have to justify the imposition of a length-of-service criterion:

> That is so, in particular, where the worker provides evidence capable of giving rise to serious doubts as to whether recourse to the criterion of length of service is, in the circumstances, appropriate to attain the above mentioned objective. It is in such circumstances for the employer to prove that that which is true as a general rule, namely that length of service goes hand in hand with experience and that experience enables the worker to perform his duties better, is also true as regards the job in question.[92]

Thus, following *Cadman*, an employer may continue to rely on length of service as a criterion for determining rates of pay. However, it is open to an employee to challenge the criterion of length of service if the claimant can raise 'serious doubts' as to whether the purpose of the criterion – the greater the experience, the better the employee becomes – is appropriate to meet that objective.[93]

---

88. [1989] EUECJ R-109/88 at para.24.
89. *ibid.*, at para.25.
90. C-17/05 [2006] EUECJ, [2007] ELR 139.
91. CC-1/95, *Gerster v Freistaat Bayern*, [1997] EUECJ C-1/95.
92. [2007] ELR 139, 147.
93. The court in *Cadman* ([2006] EUECJ C-17/05 at para.39) also held that when seeking to

[8–54]   *5. Red Circling:* There may be situations where an employee, because of some past event or agreement, is being paid at a rate higher than that paid to his colleagues doing the same work. Because of his or her special situation, the employer may argue that such an employee should be insulated or 'red-circled' from an equal pay claim. Such arrangements may arise, for example, where the employee was originally employed to do higher level work at a higher rate of pay. However, due to personal circumstances (such as the occurrence of partial incapacity) the employee is no longer capable of performing the work. In those circumstances, the employer may agree to retain that employee on his or her original salary although [s]he is now doing lighter work. In such a case, the employer may be protected from an equal pay claim in which a claimant employee seeks to use that other employee as a comparator on the basis that the latter is 'red-circled'. In *Minister for Transport, Energy and Communications v Campbell and others*,[94] Keane J when describing when 'red circling' applies, affirmed the judgment of Lord Denning MR in *Clay Cross (Quarry Services) Ltd. v Fletcher*,[95] where he stated that:

> the issue depends on whether there is a material difference (other than sex) between her case and his. Take heed of the words between *her* case and *his*. They show that the Tribunal is to have regard to *her* and to *him* – to the personal equation of the woman as compared to the man, irrespective of any extrinsic forces which led to the variation in pay. As I said in *Shields v E. Coomes Holdings Ltd.* [1978] IRLR 263, *section 1(3)* applies '*when the personal equation of the man is such that he deserves to be paid at a higher rate than the woman*'. Thus the personal equation of the man may warrant a wage differential if he has much longer length of service or has superior skill or qualifications or gives bigger output or productivity or *has been placed, owing to downgrading, in a protected pay category, vividly described as red circled*, or to other circumstances personal to him. [Emphasis added]

[8–55]   The defence is subject to the important qualifier that the red-circling arrangement must not have come about as a result of past discrimination. In *Snoxell and Davies v Vauxhall Motors Ltd.*,[96] male and female employees working for the defendant employer were paid according to different pay scales. The scales were then merged, with the women's lower rate being fixed as the going rate for the work. Thus all new employees engaged after that point, whether male or female, were paid at the same rate. The men working for the employer prior to the merging of the two scales retained their higher rate of pay as they were 'red-circled'. The tribunal held that the defence could not succeed as its creation was tainted with sex discrimination and there were no plans by the employer to phase it out. In so holding, Philips J identified the following factors as being relevant

---

justify a job classification system 'there is no need to show in the context of such a system that an individual worker has acquired experience during the relevant period which has enabled him to perform his duties better'.

94. [1996] ELR 106.
95. [1978] IRLR 361.
96. [1978] QB 11, [1977] 3 WLR 189, [1977] 3 All ER 770, [1977] ICR 700, [1977] IRLR 123.

when determining whether the difference in pay could be justified on the basis of red circling:

> whether the 'red circling' is permanent or temporary, being phased out; whether the origin of the anomaly enshrined in the 'red circling' is to be found in sex discrimination, whether the group of 'red circled' employees is a closed group; whether the 'red circling' has been the subject of negotiations with the representatives of the work people, and the views of the women taken into account; or whether the women are able equally with the men to transfer between the grades?[97]

The existence of the defence of red circling allows the employer the flexibility **[8–56]** to adopt a compassionate approach towards loyal or hard-working employees who, for whatever reason, are no longer able to work to their normal level for their higher wage. However, where the defence is raised, it will be closely examined in order to ensure that it is not used as a disguise for what in reality is unlawful discrimination.[98] In *Minister for Transport, Energy and Communications v Campbell and Others*,[99] the claimants worked in the accounts unit processing charges levied to users of the Minister's communications services. The claimants, who were all female, were graded as communications assistants and sought to compare themselves to male radio assistants, who were paid a higher rate of pay under s.2(3) of the Anti-Discrimination (Pay) Act 1974. The employer defended the differentiation in pay on the basis that the male employees were red circled. The Labour Court held that in order for the defence to succeed under s.2(3) it was necessary to establish that the red circling had to be recognized, factual and acknowledged.[100]

On appeal, the High Court found that the Labour Court had erred in law in **[8–57]** attaching the above pre-conditions to the defence of red circling. It held that there was no obligation on the employer to satisfy the court that not only did the case involve a genuine case of red circling but also that a recognised, factual and acknowledged position of red circling existed. Thus the matter was returned to the Labour Court, which found that the real reason for the difference in pay was not based on red circling but on the fact that the radio officers were male and the communications assistants were female.[101]

The concept of red circling can work in reverse also. In *Benveniste v University of* **[8–58]** *Southampton*,[102] the Court of Appeal of England and Wales considered the case of a female employee who was hired on a lower rate of pay because of financial

---

97. [1977] 3 All ER 770, 775.
98. *Methven and Mussolik v Cow Industrial Polymers Ltd.* [1980] ICR 463, [1980] IRLR 289.
99. [1996] ELR 106.
100. Determination AEP 93/1.
101. *Department of Tourism, Transport and Communications (appellant/respondent) v Four Workers* [1998] ELR 1.
102. [1989] ICR 617, [1989] IRLR 122.

pressures on the university that existed at the time she was hired. It was held that the employee could no be longer red circled on such a lower rate of pay at a later time when those financial pressures had eased.

CHAPTER 9

The Discriminatory Grounds

In Chapter 7 we focused on the various contexts in which discrimination in the   [9–01]
workplace is prohibited. As was stressed, discrimination *per se* is not unlawful.
Thus, provided [s]he adheres to the terms of the employee's contract and operates in line with the general requirements of employment law, and provided that
[s]he is content to deal with industrial relations issues arising from such action,
an employer can generally discriminate against an employee or employees with
impunity. The exception to this principle, which is the foundation of modern
employment equality law, is that an employer is not permitted to discriminate
against an employee on the basis of specific and listed characteristics or grounds.
In other words, [s]he may not discriminate against an employee because that
employee is, for example, of a particular gender, martial or family status, religion,
race, ethnicity, age, sexual orientation, or is a member of the Travelling Community, or has a disability.[1] In this chapter we consider these listed grounds upon
which an employer may not discriminate.

1. Gender

Discrimination on the grounds of gender is the 'oldest' of all the discriminatory   [9–02]
grounds. Art. 141 (ex 119) EC originally provided for equality between the sexes as
regards pay. The principle of 'equal pay' was further strengthened in *Defrenne (No.
2) v Sabena*,[2] where the European Court of Justice (ECJ) held that Art. 119 applied
not only to the action of public authorities but also extended to contracts of
employment between private individuals. Subsequent directives 75/117 (the Equal
Pay Directive) and 76/207 (the Equal Treatment Directive) required Member
States to implement the principles of equal pay and also prohibited other forms
of discrimination on the grounds of sex. These directives were implemented
into Irish law via the Anti-Discrimination (Pay) Act 1974 and the Employment
Equality Act 1977 (which also introduced marital status as a listed ground) and
subsequent equality legislation.

---

1. s.6(2) Employment Equality Act 1998.
2. C-43/75 [1976] EUECJ, [1976] ECR 455.

[9–03] Gender discrimination arises in any circumstance where either there is directly preferential treatment given to an employee or employees of one gender over another, or where preferential treatment is given to an employee or employees on the basis of what might be seen as stereotypical views of the characteristics of persons of one gender. Gender discrimination was found to exist in *Field v Irish Carton Printers*,[3] where a free taxi service was provided to the female employees of the respondent company upon completion of their shift. The complainant alleged *inter alia* that he had been discriminated on the grounds of his sex in relation to pay. The taxi service was free and therefore was considered to be of benefit in kind and as such could be considered part of the female employees' pay for the purposes of the Anti-Discrimination (Pay) Act 1974. The Equality Officer held that the complainant had been unlawfully discriminated on the grounds of gender as he was treated less favourably than a female employee in similar circumstances. Similarly, in *Boland v Éircom*,[4] the complainant was assigned as a staff officer in 1980. She was employed to oversee the typing pool and the credit control section. She claimed that in 1995 she was passed over in terms of promotion. No explanation was given to her. In 1999, junior male colleagues were promoted ahead of her. She was told by her employer that it was because she lacked assertiveness with customers. The complainant stated that this shortcoming was never brought to her attention prior to this. The Equality Officer held that the complainant had established a prima facie case of discrimination. She held that the complainant had served the company for 18 years and the only changes to her position occurred because of restructuring agreements. She never received complaints regarding the non-performance of her duties. The Equality Officer held that between 1995 and 1999 five acting appointments were filled by junior male colleagues. In the absence of any lawful justification – which could not be found – it was held that the respondents were guilty of discrimination based on gender.

[9–04] In *Dublin City University v Horgan*,[5] gender discrimination was found to exist where the complainant was unsuccessful in her application for a promotion. In particular, the complainant stated that the respondent had rejected a number of referees she had put forward including one who had been accepted in the same circumstances on behalf of one of the successful male candidates for the position. Two female candidates and seven male candidates had applied for the promotion. Of 47 top academic posts at the university only five were filled by women. The Labour Court accepted the complainant's contention that the rejection of the referee in such circumstances raised an inference of gender discrimination which the respondent failed to rebut. Whereas some forms of gender discrimination will operate in an obvious fashion, others will be more subtle and are considered under various headings below.

---

3. [1994] ELR 129.
4. DEC-E2002-019, 19 April 2002. This decision was upheld on appeal by the Labour Court in *Eircom Ltd. v Boland*, determination no. DEE031.
5. Determination no. EDA0715.

1.1. Dress Codes

The enforcement of a dress code will not be discriminatory 'if it applies a common   [9–05]
standard of neatness, conventionality and hygiene to both men and women and
does not unreasonably bear more heavily on one gender than it does on the
other'.[6] A dress code that applies only to one gender (or more onerously to one
gender) will be deemed to be discriminatory. In *O'Byrne v Dunnes Stores Ltd.*,[7] the
complainant commenced employment with the respondent as a shop worker. He
had worn a goatee beard for 38 years. From the outset the complainant had been
informed that it was acceptable for him to wear a beard so long as it was kept neat
and tidy. Shortly after commencing work he was informed that he would have to
shave the beard. The complainant refused to do so. Following further meetings he
was informed that he would be required to wear a face mask at all times while at
work as an alternative to shaving off his beard. The complainant wore the mask
for one week but then refused to continue to do so because of the derogatory
comments he received from members of the public. Following further meetings
with the respondent and after the respondent's disciplinary proceedings had been
invoked, the complainant was dismissed. In finding that the complainant was
unlawfully discriminated against the Labour Court observed:

> In considering whether a dress code operates unfavourably with regard to one or
> other of the sexes, the conventional standard of appearance is the appropriate crite-
> rion to be applied. Other factors to be considered are the relative degree of comfort
> or discomfort which one or other of the sexes may experience in complying with
> the code and the relative degree to which it impinges on the right of men and
> women to determine their own appearance, particularly where it extends outside
> the workplace (where it relates to such matters as hair length or in this case a beard).
> A clear distinction must also be drawn between rules which relate to appearance
> and those imposed by the requirements of hygiene and safety.

In *Conlon v Arcourt Ltd. t/a Sheldon Park Hotel & Leisure Club*,[8] the complainant   [9–06]
was instructed by her manager to wear a skirt for work. She reluctantly agreed
on the basis that she considered that she would be dismissed if she did not. In its
defence, the respondent referred to the staff handbook – which did not make the
wearing of a skirt compulsory – as evidence that no such instruction was given. The
Equality Officer held the complainant's evidence as to this issue was more credible
and decided that the complainant had been treated differently from the respondent's
dress policy by being made to wear a skirt, and this occurred because of her gender.

In *Lantern Securities Ltd. v Savage*,[9] the complainant was interviewed by the   [9–07]
respondent for a position as a security officer. At the interview the complainant

---

6. *O'Byrne v Dunnes Stores Ltd.* [2004] 15 ELR 96.
7. *ibid.*
8. DEC-E2008-057, 21 October 2008.
9. Determination no. EDA081.

wore his hair in a ponytail neatly tied up at the base of his neck and was asked whether he would have a problem with getting his hair cut. The complainant informed the interviewer that he would. The complainant was unsuccessful in his application. He was later offered an alternative job but refused to take it. He unsuccessfully made a claim of gender discrimination before an Equality Officer on the basis that he was not successful in his application because he had long hair and that a woman in a similar position would not have been treated in a similar manner. The Labour Court affirmed the decision of the Equality Officer and held that the complainant had not established a *prima facie* case of discrimination. The court was satisfied that the requirement for neat dress applied equally to both men and women. It was noted that the respondent had already employed other men who had long hair and who were required to wear it in a tidy manner. The court therefore found that the requirement was not a factor which adversely influenced the decision of the respondent. This decision can be contrasted with that of the Labour Court in *Group 4 Securicor v Savage.*[10] In that case, the complainant, who wore his hair in a ponytail, applied for a job vacancy with the respondent. Upon arriving at the respondent's premises he was informed by an office assistant that 'it's short back and sides here' in reference to the company's dress code policy. The complainant felt demeaned by this comment and left the premises because he considered that there was no point in proceeding with his application. The Equality Officer upheld his claim and he was awarded €600 in compensation. He appealed the quantum to the Labour Court. The court affirmed the award pointing out that the complainant contributed to any loss or damage suffered by not remaining at the premises and clarifying with a more senior member of management the detail of the respondent's dress code.

1.2. Part-Time Work

[9–08] Despite the social changes of recent years it remains a fact that it is women who continue to bear the larger part of family responsibilities and, consequently, it is women who are more likely to avail of part-time/flexible work hours in order to carry out those responsibilities.[11] The Labour Court has acknowledged this fact by holding that a failure by an employer to reasonably consider a request by a female employee to work part-time/flexible hours due to her family commitments can amount to a form of indirect discrimination.[12] In *Byrne v*

---

10. Determination no. EDA079.
11. See, in particular, the following judgments of the European Court of Justice: C-170/84, *Bilka-Kaufhaus v Weber von Hartz* [1986] EUECJ R-170/84, [1986] ECR 1607; C-243/95, *Hill and Stapleton v The Revenue Commissioners and Department of Finance* [1998] EUECJ C-243/95, [1998] ECR I-3739; C-127/92, *Enderby v Frenchay Health Authority and Secretary of State for Health* [1993] EUECJ C-127/93, [1993] ECR I-5535; C-1/95, *Gerster v Freistaat Bayern* [1997] EUECJ C-1/95, [1997] ECR I-5253.
12. *Hand v the Minister for Justice, Equality and Law Reform and the Secretary, Department of Justice, Equality and Law Reform*, DEE 598. It is perhaps ironic that maternity protection, and especially adoptive leave legislation, are themselves starkly discriminatory in applying

Reynolds,[13] the complainant worked for the respondent as a receptionist/adminis-
trator in the respondent's dental practice from 1989 until 2005. In 1998, following
the birth of her second child, she entered into an agreement with the respondent
whereby she would work on a part-time basis for three days a week. In 2003,
following the birth of her third child, she agreed with the respondent that she
would continue working three days a week but in light of her family commitments she would work one morning and one afternoon from home. In April 2004,
the respondent unilaterally attempted to alter the arrangement. Thereafter, the
complainant's relationship with the respondent deteriorated and in June of that
year she went on sick leave and eventually resigned her position. The complainant
alleged that she was the victim of a discriminatory dismissal. The Equality Officer
held that while the arrangement regarding her working hours was not in writing,
he was satisfied that such an agreement was in place and that neither party had
put a time limit on its operation. In the opinion of the Equality Officer there was
no evidence in support of the respondent's assertion that he was unhappy with her
work. Thus the Equality Officer stated that:

> The complainant was unable to return to her previous working pattern not because
> she was a woman, *per se*, but because she was a mother of young children. I am satis-
> fied that the unilateral removal of this arrangement by the respondent amounts to a
> *prima facie* case of indirect discrimination contrary to the Acts. I note that section
> 31(5) of the Acts provides in effect that where a requirement on an employee is to
> be regarded as discriminating against that employee on grounds of marital status
> or family status and also as discriminating against that employee on grounds of
> gender, a finding of discrimination can only be made on grounds of gender and I
> therefore find that the behaviour of the respondent amounts to indirect discrimi-
> nation of the complainant on grounds of gender.

The Equality Officer did not find any objective justification for the respondent's
behaviour and held that the complainant's subsequent action in resigning was
reasonable in the circumstances.

Having said this, the employer is not under an obligation to provide part-time   [9–09]
work or enter into flexible working relationships simply because the employee
requests it. For example, the Labour Court held in *Hand v the Minister for Justice,
Equality and Law Reform and the Secretary, Department of Justice, Equality and
Law Reform*,[14] that the introduction of a job-share scheme did not guarantee the
employee access to such a scheme. Access to such employment schemes are within
the gift of the employer and not a right of the employee. According to the Labour
Court, such decisions are the:

> (in the main) only to women, thereby perpetuating the cultural presumption that it is
> women who would normally (and possibly should normally) take responsibility for looking
> after young children. See Chapter 13.

13. DEC-E2007-22, 26 April 2007.
14. DEE 598.

prerogative of the management charged with the efficient running of the Department... the fact that others, including the claimant, considered otherwise, does not change this situation, unless management were found to have made such decisions without genuine belief in their basis, or for perverse reasons.

[9–10] This position was affirmed in *Bank of Ireland Group v Morgan*.[15] In the case, the complainant had commenced employment with the respondent in 1990. In 2000 she applied to the respondent requesting that she be allowed work part time or to participate in a job-sharing arrangement. The complainant was not offered this facility until 2005. In the meantime, the claimant had adopted a child and had taken adoptive leave and had also availed of a career break. The complainant had referred a claim to the Equality Tribunal where she was awarded €30,000 by way of compensation. The respondent appealed to the Labour Court. It was the complainant's contention that a requirement to work fulltime by an employer is a form of indirect discrimination as such a requirement disadvantages a substantially higher proportion of women than men. However, the Labour Court rejected the assertion that the complainant had been indirectly discriminated against. The respondent did have arrangements in place to facilitate employees who required more flexible work arrangements. Evidence was to the effect that 98 per cent of those who participated in the job share scheme were women. Thus the court concluded that the manner in which the respondent allocated places on the job-sharing scheme did not place women at a particular disadvantage compared to men.

> It would be manifestly unreasonable to hold that an employer must provide a woman with a facility to job-share in every case in which such a facility is requested and such a result could not have been intended. It is self evident that such facilities can only be made available within the exigencies of the business. However, in allocating part-time or job-sharing opportunities, an employer must not discriminate on any of the grounds prescribed by the Act.

[9–11] However, the employer is expected at the very least to reasonably consider such requests. In *Black v Tesco Ireland*,[16] some weeks prior to taking maternity leave, the claimant made a request for part-time/flexible work upon her return. There was no response from the employer to this request and the claimant made a further request the week prior to her departure on maternity leave. The respondent ignored the request for a five-month period and subsequently contended that it was not in a position to make such arrangements on behalf of the claimant. The Equality Officer took a very dim view of the respondent's assertion that it was not enough that an employee seeking part-time/flexible work *want* such an arrangement, it was necessary that they show that they *needed* it. In the circumstances, the Equality Officer found that the respondent failed to reasonably consider the claimant's request and was guilty of indirect discrimination on gender grounds.[17]

15. Determination no. EDA096.
16. DEC-E2002-03, 30 January 2002.
17. See also *Weir v St Patrick's Hospital*, DEC-E2001-011, 26 February 2001; *NBK Designs Ltd. v Marie Inoue* [2004] ELR 98.

In *ICE Group Business Services Ltd. v Czerski*,[18] the complainant argued that a [9–12] requirement by the respondent that job applicants were required to produce two references was indirectly discriminatory towards women as it operated to the disadvantage of women who take a break from the workplace in order to care for their children. The complainant only produced one such reference and was not successful in her application. The court accepted the respondent's evidence that it had informed the complainant that one of the two required references could be a character reference. On that basis, the court held that there was no evidence that the requirement that the job applicant produce two references – one employment reference and one character reference – disadvantaged a substantially higher proportion of women than men. Interestingly, the court did note that a rigid requirement that the job applicants be required to produce two employment references could fall foul of the equality legislation.

1.3. Pregnancy

The history of pregnancy-related discrimination as a form of gender discrimina- [9–13] tion is a rather complex one, primarily because the definition of discrimination under successive legislation[19] required that the complainant in such cases show that she had been treated *less* favourably as opposed to *un*favourably on the basis of her pregnancy, thereby necessitating the plainly very difficult task of identifying a comparator in order for her to be successful.

The point is that, as it is only women who can become pregnant, it is difficult to [9–14] identify an appropriate comparator of a pregnant female employee. In the United Kingdom, (where, when interpreting equality legislation, the tribunal has developed a near-obsession with the need for establishing a relevant comparator as a precondition to establishing a claim[20]) in *Turley v Allders Department Stores Ltd.*[21] the tribunal found that the complainant had been dismissed because of the fact of her pregnancy and not because of the consequences thereof, i.e. unavailability for work. Therefore, the majority of the tribunal held that as there was no comparator for a pregnant woman unlawful discrimination could not be proven. To quote the rather quaint words of the majority, 'when she is pregnant a woman is no longer just a woman. She is a woman, as the Authorised Version of the Bible accurately puts it, with child, and there is no masculine equivalent'. In an arguably somewhat misguided attempt at assisting the complainant, the dissenting member of the tribunal sought to compare the complainant's position with that of a sick man, rationalising that:

> Pregnancy is a medical condition. It is a condition which applies only to women.
> It is a condition which will lead to a request for time off from work... A man is

---

18. Determination no. EDA0812.
19. s.2 Employment Equality Act 1977; s.6(1) Employment Equality Act 1998.
20. s.1(1)(a) Sex Discrimination Act 1975.
21. [1980] ICR 66, [1980] IRLR 4.

in similar circumstances… who in the course of the year will require time off for a hernia operation, to have his tonsils removed, or for other medical reasons. The employer must not discriminate by applying different and less favourable criteria to the pregnant woman than to the man requiring time off.[22]

[9–15] The question arose before the tribunal again in *Hayes v Malleable Working Men's Club and Institute*.[23] In that case, it was held that if a woman missed work because of pregnancy-related *medical* reasons and was subsequently dismissed because of her absence she *could* be compared to a man who missed work for a similar period because of illness. *Turley* was distinguished on the basis that in *Hayes* the complaint arose as a consequence of the complainant being pregnant, i.e. she was absent due to her medical condition.

[9–16] The approach that compared pregnant women with sick men was eventually ruled upon by the ECJ in *Dekker v Stichting Vormingscentrum voor Jonge Volwassen (VJV-Centrum)*.[24] In that case, the plaintiff had announced at interview that she was pregnant. She was not offered the position because her potential employer was concerned about certain insurance payments required by law for employees absent on maternity leave. The plaintiff alleged that in so doing, the defendant contravened the Equal Treatment Directive.[25] The ECJ upheld the complaint and found that discrimination on the grounds of pregnancy constituted direct discrimination on the grounds of sex:

> it should be observed that only women can be refused employment on grounds of pregnancy and such a refusal therefore constitutes direct discrimination on grounds of sex. A refusal of employment on account of the financial consequences of absence due to pregnancy must be regarded as based, essentially, on the fact of pregnancy. Such discrimination cannot be justified on grounds relating to the financial loss which an employer who appointed a pregnant woman would suffer for the duration of her maternity leave.[26]

[9–17] Consequently, discrimination on grounds related to pregnancy is now a form of direct gender discrimination. The *Dekker* decision is reflected in s.4(b) of the Equality Act 2004 (amending s.6 of the 1998 Act), which provides as follows:

> Without prejudice to the generality of subsections (1) and (2), discrimination on the gender ground shall be taken to occur where, on a ground related to her pregnancy or maternity leave, a woman employee is treated, contrary to any statutory requirement, less favourably than another employee is, has been or would be treated.

22. [1980] ICR 66, 71.
23. [1985] ICR 703, [1985] IRLR 367.
24. C-177/88 [1990] EUECJ R-177/88, [1990] ECR 3941.
25. 76/207/EEC.
26. [1990] EUECJ R-177/88 at para.12.

The expansion of sex discrimination to include discrimination on grounds of pregnancy was confirmed by the ECJ in *Handel-Og Kontorfunktionaerernes Forbund I Danmark v Dansk Arbejdsgiverforening*,[27] where the court limited the application of the protection to situations connected with the pregnancy or the period of confinement (statutory leave), concluding that:

> [T]he dismissal of a female worker on account of repeated periods of sick leave which are not attributable to pregnancy or confinement does not constitute direct discrimination on grounds of sex, in as much as such periods of sick leave would lead to the dismissal of a male worker in the same circumstances.[28]

The question of pregnancy-related illness as a form of sex discrimination arose once again before the English courts in *Webb v EMO Air Cargo (UK) (No. 2)*.[29] In that case, the complainant was hired to replace another employee who was going on maternity leave. Initially, her employer intended to retain the complainant after the pregnant employee returned to work. Soon after, the complainant also discovered that she was pregnant and would require maternity leave at virtually the same time as the woman for whom she was hired to provide cover. The complainant was dismissed on the basis that she was unavailable for work. The tribunal agreed with the complainant's employer, who argued that the complainant was not treated any differently to a man who was unavailable when hired to cover the same period. [9–18]

The decision was ultimately appealed to the House of Lords where their Lordships refused to accept that the case was one that amounted to sex discrimination. In their view, the precise reason the complainant was dismissed was not because of her pregnancy but because she was unavailable to perform the very thing she was hired to do, namely to replace another employee on maternity leave.[30] The matter was referred to the ECJ for a preliminary ruling. The court held that the dismissal of a pregnant employee appointed for an indefinite period simply because of her temporary inability to fulfil a fundamental term of the contract could not be justified.[31] The matter was returned to the House of Lords, who found in favour of the complainant. However, the House of Lords emphasised that, in its view, the ECJ's judgment was restricted to pregnant employees employed under a permanent contract. Consequently, it would not be discriminatory to dismiss a pregnant woman hired on foot of a fixed term contract who, because of her pregnancy, would be absent for all of that period if a man unavailable for a similar period would have been treated in the same manner. [9–19]

The ECJ clarified the extent of the protection offered to pregnant employees in *Brown v Rentokill*.[32] In that case, the court confirmed that a pregnant employee [9–20]

---

27. C-177/88 [1990] EUECJ R-177/88, [1990] ECR 3979.
28. At [14].
29. [1994] ICR 770, [1995] IRLR 645.
30. For more detailed analysis see Chapter 13.
31. *ibid.*
32. C-394/96 [1998] ECR 1-4185, [1998] All ER 791, [1998] ICR 790.

absent from work due to illness resulting from her pregnancy cannot be dismissed for that reason where the absence arose during the period from the start of her pregnancy to the end of her maternity leave. However, this special protection would not apply for an indefinite period and, where any such absence extended beyond the employee's maternity leave, dismissal would not be discriminatory if a man absent for a similar duration would have been treated in a similar manner. The court concluded that:

> Where pathological conditions caused by pregnancy or childbirth arise after the end of maternity leave, they are covered by the general rules applicable in the event of illness. In such circumstances, the sole question is whether a female worker's absences, following maternity leave, caused by incapacity for work brought on by such disorder, are treated in the same way as a male worker's absences, of the same duration, caused by incapacity for work; if they are, there is no discrimination on grounds of sex.[33]

[9–21] Thus the special protection provided to pregnant women under equality law relates only to their pregnancy or to illness connected with that pregnancy during the period of confinement. In *Rattigan v Boots the Chemists*[34] the complainant was frequently absent from work between May 1998 and February 1999. In March 1999 the respondent called a meeting with the complainant regarding these absences. The complainant became upset and left the meeting. The complainant argued that the initiation by the respondent of internal procedures governing its sick pay scheme and associated disciplinary code against her amounted to gender discrimination as her illness was due to a gynaecological condition, unique to women. It was the employer's contention that the initiation of the proceedings would have applied equally to a man absent for a similar duration because of illness and was therefore not discriminatory. The respondent further argued that the decisions in *Dekker* and *Brown* were not applicable as those cases involved dismissal of pregnant employees, while this case concerned the initiation of procedures against a female employee absent due to illness unconnected with pregnancy. The Equality Officer disagreed that the case was different to those in *Dekker* and *Brown*, holding that 'dismissal is the ultimate form of sanction against an employee and arises after all other avenues of discipline have been exhausted'. However, the Equality Officer did find that such protection was not unlimited and, where the relevant period of absence fell outside the 'pregnancy period', then as long as the pregnant employee was not treated any differently to a man in similar circumstances there was no discrimination. The Equality Officer concluded:

> The ECJ jurisprudence restricts the special protection against dismissal and disciplinary measures to circumstances connected with pregnancy, maternity and childbirth. To extend it beyond these parameters would, in my view, exceed what is envisaged by EU and national law and would undermine the special protection

33. *ibid.*, para.27.
34. DEC-E2001/10, 20 February 2001.

rightly afforded to pregnant employees. It would also place a significant and undue restraint on an employer to manage a business effectively.

In light of this, the Equality Officer found there was no evidence that the complainant had been treated less favourably than a man and held that there was no discrimination.

While great strides have been made in the prohibition of discrimination against [9–22] female employees based on the fact of pregnancy (particularly relating to their unfair dismissal), such workers, largely for economic reasons, will find that in other aspects of the employment relationship they are not as well protected. For example, while the gender ground in the Employment Equality Act 1998 ensures that any less favourable treatment of a pregnant employee during the period of her pregnancy and maternity leave will be unlawful, it does not guarantee such workers full pay while on maternity leave.[35] As long as the employee receives some pay (whether that be from the employer or in the form of social welfare payments), which is not so low as to undermine the purpose of maternity leave, then no discrimination will exist.[36]

[9–23]

The extent of this special protection for pregnant women under employment equality law was examined in *McKenna v North Western Health Board*.[37] In that case, the claimant was employed by the respondent but, due to a pregnancy-related illness, she was unable to work for virtually the entire period of her pregnancy. Under her contract of employment Ms McKenna was entitled to 183 days of absence on sick leave in any one 12-month period during which she would be fully paid. Thereafter, she would be entitled to half pay up to a maximum of 365 days during a four-year period. Having exhausted her contractual 183 day entitlement to sick pay because of her pregnancy-related illness, Ms McKenna's pay was reduced to half until the commencement of her maternity leave, when her full pay was reinstated. However, her pay was reduced once again at the end of her maternity leave period. Ms McKenna challenged the application of the sick-pay scheme to her situation, arguing that because her illness was pregnancy-related it should not be treated in the same manner as a 'normal' illness under her employer's sick pay scheme. To do otherwise, she contended, would amount to unequal treatment on the grounds of sex and was contrary to Directive 76/207. She further argued that the reduction of her pay following the expiration of the 183 days constituted unfavourable treatment in respect of pay contrary to Art. 141 and Directive 75/117. The Equality Officer upheld Ms McKenna's complaint, but the board appealed

---

35. For more detailed analysis, see Chapter 13.
36. C-342/93, *Gillespie v Northern Health and Social Services Board* [1996] EUECJ C-342/93, [1996] ECR I-475.
37. C-191/03, [2005] EUECJ C-191/03, [2006] ECR I-7631. For further discussion, see Ennis, '*McKenna v North Western Health Board* – The Recent Decision by the European Court of Justice Regarding Pregnancy-Related Illness and Conditions of Employment – A Missed Opportunity or a Sound Policy-Based Decision?', 3 *Employment Law Review* (2006), 63.

the decision to the Labour Court, which in turn referred the matter to the ECJ. As a preliminary point, the ECJ held that the application of the sick-pay scheme did not come within the ambit of Directive 76/207 (the Equal Treatment Directive) as its application was directly and indirectly related to pay. Ennis has criticised this aspect of the judgment, observing that:

> The significance of this particular conclusion should not be overlooked. This is based on the fact that the historic approach taken by the Court in relation to the issue of *pay* in respect of maternity... has not been as broad as that taken in regard to the issue of the *treatment* of pregnant employees. By finding that the application of the sick leave scheme in this case was to be viewed as an element of an employee's pay as opposed to treatment, opened the way for the Court to go on and hold that there was in fact, no discrimination on the grounds of sex.[38]

[9–24] Having designated the claim as one falling within the scope of Art. 141 EC Directive 75/117 on equal pay, the ECJ had then to consider whether the sick-pay scheme constituted discrimination on the grounds of sex. In particular, the court was required to assess whether the following aspects of the scheme were discriminatory:

(a) A rule which provided that employees absent from work due to illness (whether male or female, whether pregnancy-related or not) would have their pay reduced where the absence exceeds a certain duration.

(b) A rule which provides that any absences due to illness will be offset against a maximum of total number of days of paid sick leave to which the employee is entitled under the scheme, regardless of whether that illness is pregnancy-related or not.

As regards part (a) of the scheme, the Court held that different protections applied to pregnant workers where what was at stake was dismissal as compared to other facets of their work and concluded that the aspect of the scheme that dealt with pay was not discriminatory:

> so far as dismissals are concerned, the special nature of a pregnancy-related illness may only be accommodated by denying an employer the right to dismiss a female worker for that reason. By contrast, so far as pay is concerned, the full maintenance thereof is not the only way in which the special nature of a pregnancy-related illness may be accommodated. That special nature may, indeed, be accommodated within the context of a scheme which, in the event of the absence of a female worker by reason of a pregnancy-related illness, provides for a reduction in pay.[39]

---

38. *ibid.*, at 64.
39. [2005] EUECJ C-191/03 at para.58.

Therefore, the court concluded that treating the female worker who is absent on the grounds of illness related to her pregnancy in the same manner as a male worker who is absent on the grounds of illness in relation to pay is not discriminatory, provided that the amount of payment is not so low as to undermine the objective of protecting pregnant workers.

With respect to part (b) of the scheme, the court found that the special position [9–25] of pregnant workers did not absolutely preclude the possibility that their absence (on grounds related to their pregnancy) could be offset, within limits, against the total number of days of paid sick-leave. This would, in the court's opinion, be compatible with the possibility of reducing pay during pregnancy,[40] and was in line with the principle that after the 'protected period' a female employee whose illness is related to the fact that she was pregnant is to be treated the same as any other employee under a general scheme that applies to all.[41] However, the court qualified this by stating that any offsetting of absences during pregnancy 'cannot have the effect that, during the absence affected by that offsetting after the maternity leave, the female worker receives pay that is below the minimum amount to which she was entitled over the course of the illness which arose during her pregnancy'.[42]

The decision in *McKenna* is evidence of the strong reluctance by the ECJ to extend the protections provided to pregnant workers as regards discriminatory dismissal to other conditions of their employment, such as pay. As Ennis has noted, 'it would seem that the policy argument concerning the damaging financial repercussions of such a move, is proving to be more persuasive and for the moment at least, is winning the day at the Court'.[43]

1.4. Transsexuality

It is arguably one of the flaws of the equality legislation in Ireland that it does not [9–26] provide explicit protection to transsexuals against discrimination based on the fact that they have undergone gender reassignment surgery. Much like pregnant women, these individuals must have recourse to the gender ground of discrimination for protection of their rights.

The European Court of Human Rights has defined the term transsexual as applying:

---

40. C-342/93, *Gillespie v Northern Health and Social Services Board* [1996] EUECJ C-342/93, [1996] ECR 1–475.
41. C-177/88, *Handels-Og Kontorfunktionaerernes Forbund I Danmark v Dansk Arbejdsgiver-forening* [1990] EUECJ R-179/88, [1990] ECR 3979, C-394/96, *Brown v Rentokill* C-394/96 [1998] ECR 1-4185, [1998] All ER 791, [1998] ICR 790.
42. [2005] EUECJ C-191/03 at para.67.
43. Ennis, '*McKenna v North Western Health Board* – The Recent Decision by the European Court of Justice Regarding Pregnancy-Related Illness and Conditions of Employment – A Missed Opportunity or a Sound Policy-Based Decision?', 3 *Employment Law Review* (2006), 63 at 68.

to those who, whilst belonging physically to one sex, feel convinced that they belong to the other, they often seek to achieve a more integrated, unambiguous identity by undergoing medical treatment and surgical operations to adapt their physical characteristics to their psychological nature. Transsexuals who have been operated upon thus form a fairly well-defined and identifiable group.[44]

[9–27] If such an individual undergoes or proposes to undergo surgery in order to change the external physical characteristics of his or her gender and as a consequence is discriminated against by his or her employer, it is uncertain whether [s]he can bring a claim under the legislation, and if so, how the appropriate comparator in such a situation can be identified. An employer, after all, might argue that while it may have treated an individual who had 'male to female' surgery in an unfavourable manner, it would have treated an individual who had 'female to male' surgery in an identical manner, and hence there is no gender discrimination.

[9–28] The ECJ has held in *P v S and Cornwall County Council*[45] that the dismissal of a male to female transsexual (on the grounds that she *was* a transsexual) was contrary to EC Directive 75/117 on Equal Treatment. The court held that:

> the scope of the directive cannot be confined simply to discrimination based on the fact that a person is of one or other sex. In view of its purpose and the nature of the rights which it seeks to safeguard, the scope of the directive is also such as to apply to discrimination arising, as in this case, from the gender reassignment of the person concerned.

> Such discrimination is based, essentially if not exclusively, on the sex of the person concerned. Where a person is dismissed on the ground that he or she intends to undergo, or has undergone, gender reassignment, he or she is treated unfavourably by comparison with persons of the sex to which he or she was deemed to belong before undergoing gender reassignment.[46]

[9–29] Thus the ECJ interpreted the Equal Treatment Directive as prohibiting discrimination against transsexuals, but saw the discrimination as relating to the individual's gender. For comparison purposes the complainant may compare him or herself to persons of the sex to which [s]he was deemed to belong prior to the gender reassignment. A transsexual may bring an action for gender discrimination on the basis that [s]he has only been treated differently because [s]he is now a member of the opposite sex. Furthermore, in *KB v Health Service Pensions Agency and another*,[47] the ECJ held that it was discriminatory to treat transsexuals differently in relation to employment and pensions.

---

44. *Rees v United Kingdom*, [1986] ECHR 11 at para.38.
45. [1996] IRLR 347.
46. [2006] IRLR 347, 354.
47. [2004] All ER (EC) 1089, [2004] ICR 781.

Special protection for the transgendered was introduced in England and Wales by virtue of the Sex Discrimination (Gender Reassignment) Regulations 1999 (SI no. 1102 of 1999) and it is clear that similar legislative changes are necessary in this jurisdiction in order to provide full equality to this heretofore forgotten group in Irish society.

2. Marital Status

Art. 2(1) of EC Directive 75/117 (the Equal Treatment Directive) prohibits discrim- [9–30] ination on grounds of 'marital or family status'. In a similar vein s.6(2)(b) of the Employment Equality Act 1998 prohibits discrimination between two persons on the basis that they are of different marital status. 'Marital status' is defined under s.2(1) of the 1998 Act as including an individual's single, married, separated, divorced or widowed status. The definition provided in the 1998 Act was very comprehensive and included single persons for the first time.

This issue proved central to the decision in *Eagle Star Insurance Co. (Ireland) Ltd.* [9–31] *v A Worker.*[48] In that case, an employer provided an insurance discount scheme to its staff and their married partners. The claimant was unmarried and as such was not entitled to benefit under the scheme as his married colleagues were. He claimed that he was discriminated against on the grounds of his marital status under the Employment Equality Act 1977. The Labour Court upheld the claim. That said, similar schemes may now be exempt under s.34(1)(b) of the Employment Equality Act 1998, which provides that it will no longer be unlawful for an employer to provide 'a benefit to or in respect of a person as a member of an employee's family'. Section 34(1)(c) also provides that it will not be unlawful for an employer to provide 'a benefit to an employee on or by reference to an event occasioning a change in the marital status of the employee', for example, where an employer wishes to provide a wedding present to an employee.

In *44 Named Male and Female Complainants v Superquinn,*[49] the claimants chal- [9–32] lenged as discriminatory a sick-pay scheme adopted by the employer. Under this scheme, when calculating pay for employees absent through illness, employees were paid by the employer but a deduction was made based on the amount that could be claimed by them from the Department of Social, Community and Family Affairs. In so doing, the employer assumed that any married employees would be entitled to supplementary benefit on the basis of their 'dependant spouse'. The claimants argued that this scheme was discriminatory in that it assumed that all spouses of employees would be dependent and, where that was not the case, it would lead to an incorrect deduction from the employee's salary, which would not have happened in the case of an unmarried employee of the company in

---

48. [1998] ELR 306.
49. DEC-E2003-003.

a similar situation. In finding for the complainants on this issue, the Equality Officer concluded that:

> the practice complained of does place married employees in a more disadvantageous position than single employees in that (a) they have to ensure that they have not been over deducted and (b) if they have been over deducted to ensure that they receive a refund of the over deduction. The Company approach appears arbitrary and heavy handed in this respect.

Complaints of discrimination relating to marital status are often combined with claims involving discrimination on gender and family status grounds.[50]

3. Family Status

[9–33] The family has always enjoyed a privileged position in Irish law.[51] Section 6(2)(c) of the 1998 Act prohibits discrimination on the grounds of a person's family status. Family status is defined in s.2 of the 1998 Act as applying to anyone who has responsibility:

> (a) as a parent or as a person in *loco parentis* in relation to a person who has not attained the age of 18 years, or
>
> (b) as a parent or the resident primary carer[52] in relation to a person of or over that age with a disability which is of such a nature as to give rise to the need for care or support on a continuing, regular or frequent basis.

[9–34] Therefore, under the Act it is unlawful to discriminate against an employee simply because [s]he has a family and may not be as flexible as a single person.[53] In *Freeman v Superquinn*,[54] the complainant worked for over 16 years with the respondent. At the time of her complaint she was working on a part-time basis as a no. 3 cashier. She had previously been a no. 2 cashier on a full-time basis for a period of four years. She applied for a position as a no. 1 cashier, along with one other candidate who had three years' experience working with the respondent and who was at that time employed as a no. 2 cashier. The other candidate was successful in her application. The complainant challenged the selection process for the position of head cashier as being discriminatory against her on the basis *inter alia* of her family status. The Equality Officer held that the interview process was tainted with subjective bias against the complainant. In particular, the Equality Officer found that, given the senior nature of the position, the interview panel should have judged the interviewees according to a pre-prepared list of competencies rather than relying

---

50. *Marie Inoue v NBK Designs Ltd.* [2004] ELR 98.
51. Art. 41 of Bunreacht na hÉireann.
52. s.2 of the 1998 Act defines 'primary carer' as 'a resident carer in relation to a person with a disability if the primary carer resides with the person with the disability'.
53. *An Employee v An Employer* [1995] ELR 139.
54. DEC-E2002-13, 5 March 2002.

on a list they had drawn up themselves in preparation for the interview. In light of this, the Equality Officer concluded that the complainant had been treated less favourably than the successful candidate. When combined with the fact that the complainant was married with a child and the successful candidate was single and did not have any children, the Equality Officer held that the complainant had been discriminated against on the grounds of her family status.

In *O'Donnell and Others v Health Service Executive (North West Area)*,[55] the [9–35] complainants were employed as nurses on a roster that required them to work seven consecutive days and, on occasion, 13 out of 16 days, which meant that the complainants could be away from home for approximately 13 hours per day for continuous periods. The complainants alleged that the rosters impacted more heavily on them as mothers than on those nurses who were not mothers and thereby amounted to indirect discrimination on the grounds of family status. The Equality Officer held that the roster had indirectly discriminated against the complainants and the respondent failed to provide an objective justification for the imposition of the roster in this manner.

The protection under the family-status ground extends to employees caring for their [9–36] children. In *Kelly v Higgins*,[56] the complainant, a single mother, alleged that she was dismissed from her employment following an absence from work when she needed to take care of her daughter. After missing one week's work, the complainant reported for work on the Monday morning whereupon she was told by the respondent that the work roster had already been completed and that she was not scheduled to work until the Thursday of that week. Following a dispute over the roster, which the complainant refused to work, she was dismissed. The complainant challenged her dismissal on the basis that she had been unlawfully discriminated against on the grounds of her family status. The Equality Officer concluded that the complainant had been indirectly discriminated against as the change in the work roster impacted more heavily on her as a primary carer. While the Equality Officer held that the respondent's aim – running an efficient business – was legitimate, she concluded that it could have been achieved by methods other than dismissing the complainant. Thus there was no objective justification of the respondent's discriminatory actions.

4. Sexual Orientation

Section 6(2)(d) of the 1998 Act prohibits discrimination between two persons [9–37] based on sexual orientation, that is, on the basis of their being heterosexual, homosexual or bisexual.[57] Significantly, therefore, the section does not apply to persons who are transsexual or who have a gender-identity disorder.[58]

---

55. DEC-E2006-023.
56. DEC-E2007-002.
57. s.2 Employment Equality Act 1998.
58. Generally, see Ryan, 'Sexual Orientation Discrimination', *Discrimination Law* (Cavendish Publishing, 2005), at 97.

[9–38]   Prior to the enactment of the 1998 Act, Irish law did not provide protection to employees from discrimination on the grounds of sexual orientation. In such circumstances, claimants were therefore required to rely on the gender ground to base their claim. Such an approach, however, had its limitations. Thus it was felt that there could be no *gender* discrimination where it was proven that the employee treated a female who was attracted to other females as [s]he would have treated a male who was attracted to other males. In other words, a woman in such a situation could not use a man who was attracted to females (as she was) as an appropriate comparator. Thus in *Brookfield Leisure Centre Limited v A Worker*,[59] the complainant was dismissed from her job because of an allegation that she had been seen kissing another female employee in the centre. The claimant alleged that she had been discriminated against under the Employment Equality Act 1977 on the grounds of her gender, as lesbianism was a characteristic unique to women. The Labour Court rejected her argument, holding that the treatment of her did not occur because of any specific attribute connected with her sex, but rather because of her sexual orientation. It also found that it was likely that if a male employee had been found kissing another male employee he would have been treated in a similar manner and consequently there was no evidence of 'less favourable treatment' on the gender ground.

[9–39]   Until relatively recently, the English position was much the same. In *Grant v South-West Trains Limited*,[60] the respondent employer provided a benefits package to its employees, their spouses, partners and dependents, which included reduced travel rates. In order to claim under the benefits package, the employee was required to be in a stable relationship with a member of the opposite sex. The complainant's request for travel concessions in favour of her same-sex partner was rejected and she challenged her employer's policy as being discriminatory. The case was referred to the ECJ, who dismissed it. It held that there was no discrimination on the gender ground because a male homosexual would have been treated in a similar manner by the employer. The English position on the issue was challenged before the European Court of Human Rights, where it was found to be violation of an individual's right to a private life under Art. 8 of the European Convention on Human Rights.[61] Discrimination on the grounds of sexual orientation was subsequently prohibited in that jurisdiction by the adoption of the Employment Equality (Sexual Orientation) Regulations 2003.

5. Religious Beliefs

[9–40]   Section 6(2)(e) provides that to treat one person less favourably than another on the grounds that one has a different religious belief than the other, or that one has a religious belief and the other has not, will amount to unlawful discrimination.

59. [1994] ELR 79.
60. [1998] All ER (EC) 193, [1998] ICR 449, [1998] IRLR 206.
61. *Smith & Grady v UK* [2000] 29 EHRR 49, [1999] IRLR 734.

In prohibiting such discrimination, the 1998 Act was ahead of its time. This form of discrimination was not prohibited under European Union law until Directive 2000/78 EC was adopted, which required Member States to implement such a prohibition by 2 December 2003.

Significantly, s.6(2)(e) focuses on the person's religious *beliefs*[62] rather than his or her religion. As such, the prohibition does not concern itself with the definition of religion, nor does it assess whether the religion in question is one that comes within the protection of the Act. Indeed it is worth noting that s.6(2)(e) prohibits discrimination on the basis of *absence* of religious beliefs. In *Azmi v Kirklees MBC*,[63] a female Muslim teaching assistant was suspended following her refusal to follow her employer's instructions not to wear a full facial veil while in class assisting a male teacher. The tribunal found that this requirement amounted to direct discrimination against the claimant on the basis of her religious beliefs as a Muslim. However, it held that her employer's request was justified on the basis that she was unable to properly communicate with the schoolchildren, and it would have been impracticable for her employer to arrange her work situation such that she would not be working with a male teacher and therefore would not have to wear the full veil. [9–41]

In *Harris v NKL Automative Ltd. & Another*,[64] the Employment Appeals Tribunal in the United Kingdom accepted that Rastafarianism is a religious belief. In that case, the claimant argued that he had been discriminated against on the grounds of his race because he wore dreadlocks. However, the claim was rejected. The employer's dress code simply required that employees ensure that their hair was tidy. This could be done with dreadlocks as it could with other hairstyles and there was no discrimination. [9–42]

6. Age

In its 2007 annual report, the Equality Authority highlighted age as the most common grounds of complaint under the employment equality legislation, representing 24 per cent of all claims.[65] Section 6(2)(f) of the 1998 Act provides that it shall be unlawful to discriminate between two persons on the grounds that they are of different ages. This provision was qualified by s.6(3), which provides that any such discrimination will not be unlawful where: [9–43]

    (a) a person has attained the age of 65 years, or
    (b) a person has not attained the age of 18 years.

---

62. 'Religious beliefs' are defined in s.2 Employment Equality Act 1998 as including religious background or outlook.
63. [2007] UKEAT 0009 A 07 3003, [2007] ICR 1154.
64. [2007] UKEAT 0134 07 0310.
65. *Equality Authority Annual Report* (Equality Tribunal, 2007). Available at www.equality tribunal.ie.

Given that the purpose of s.6(2)(f) was to eliminate unlawful discrimination on the grounds of age, it was somewhat incongruous that the definition of 'age' under the 1998 Act only included those employees between the ages of 18 years and 65 years. In light of this, s.4 of the 2004 Act, which replaced subsection 3 of the 1998 Act, provides that: 'The age ground applies only in relation to persons above the maximum age at which a person is statutorily obliged to attend school.' Thus, by omission, the upper age limit no longer applies.[66] However, an employer may still reserve the right to set a minimum age for employees, not exceeding 18 years, for recruitment to a post.[67] The nature of the post might reasonably require that the successful candidate be of the age of majority (for example, where the job entails serving alcohol in a pub). Like all of the discriminatory grounds listed in s.6 of the 1998 Act, it shall be unlawful to discriminate against a person because it is *assumed* that they are younger or older than they actually are.[68]

[9–44] To establish a prima facie case of age discrimination it is necessary that the complainant not only show a difference in age between the two persons, but also that the complainant was treated differently because of the difference in age. In *McCormick v Dublin Port Company*,[69] the complainant could only satisfy the tribunal that the successful candidate for a senior position was older than her. Because there was no evidence that the complainant had greater skills than the successful candidate, her claim failed. Similarly, in *Concern v Martin*,[70] the complainant's assertion that he was discriminated against on the grounds of his age (56 years) simply because he was not short-listed for an interview when all the short-listed candidates were under the age of 40 years was not accepted by either the Equality Officer or the Labour Court as evidence of prima facie discrimination on the grounds of age.[71]

Age discrimination, like many other forms of discrimination, is more likely to arise at the point of entry into the workforce (through discriminatory recruitment and selection policies) or at the end of a person's career (through mandatory retirement requirements).

---

66. In this regard, it differs very much from the approach adopted in the United States, where under The Age Discrimination in Employment Act 1967 (as amended), discrimination because of a person's age is prohibited only where the person is over the age of 40 years. A person younger than 40 years cannot initiate a claim.
67. s.4(c) Employment Equality Act 2004. It should be noted that, for example, it is possible under minimum-wage legislation to pay a reduced wage to persons under the age of 18 in defined circumstances. See Chapter 12.
68. s.4(a) *ibid.*
69. DEC-E2002-046, 4 October 2002.
70. Determination EDA0518, Labour Court, 2005.
71. See also *Hawkins v Irish Life & Permanent*, DEC-E2004-009, 19 February 2004.

6.1. Recruitment and Selection

It is at the recruitment and selection stage that an employer faces greatest risk of [9–45] age-discrimination claims. To defend such an allegation it is crucial that all notes and records of the interview/selection process are retained by the employer for later examination, and that transparent and proper procedures are in place for the selection process. In *O'Conghaile v Mercy Mean Scoil Mhuire*,[72] the complainant applied for the position of principal. She was unsuccessful at interview. The successful candidate was younger than her. The complainant was an assistant principal post-holder and had worked at the school for 36 years. She submitted that she had been discriminated against during the selection process when she was asked a question as to why she was applying for the job 'at this time of her life'. The respondent stated that it had simply asked the complainant, '[W]hy [do] you feel, at this stage in your career, that you are the most suitable candidate for the position of Principal?' The complainant submitted that the question implied that she had to justify her application on the grounds of her age and as such it was discriminatory for her to be asked. While the Equality Officer was of the view that the evidence of the complainant as regards the conduct of the interview was to be approached with caution, it concluded that the limited notes retained by the respondent made it difficult for the respondent to rebut the presumption of discrimination. In finding for the complainant, the Equality Officer considered the following facts to be particularly relevant:

1. A much younger candidate had been appointed.
2. The nature of the 'offending' question asked at interview.
3. Changes made to the interview marking sheet, which appeared to favour the successful candidate.
4. The failure by the respondent to retain all notes of the interview process.
5. A general lack of transparency that surrounded the whole process.[73]

Unlawful discrimination may exist even where the best candidate was successful [9–46] at interview. In *MacGabhainn v Salesforce.com*,[74] it was found that asking the complainant about his age during an interview for a position was sufficient evidence to raise a presumption that the respondent had unlawfully discriminated against the complainant where the complainant was unsuccessful in his application. This was so notwithstanding the fact that the Equality Officer found that the complainant would not have been successful in the interview even if he had not been asked the question about his age. The Equality Officer accepted that the best candidate had succeeded in obtaining the position. Nonetheless, the complainant was awarded €1,000 compensation for the effects of the discrimination. Similarly, in *Hughes v Aer Lingus*,[75] the complainant submitted that she had been discriminated

---

72. [2008] ELR 107.
73. See also *Murtagh v Longford County Council*, DEC-E2007-026; *Carroll v Monaghan VEC*, DEC-E2004-003, 5 February 2004.
74. DEC-E2007-048, 3 September 2007.
75. DEC-E2002-049, 26 November 2002.

against on the grounds of her age when, during an interview for a cabin-crew position with the respondent, she was asked questions relating to how she would cope with younger people being in charge and how, being older, she would cope with starting her career with the respondent at the 'bottom of the ladder'. The respondent produced notes of the interview, which indicated that the complainant had not been successful in her application because she tended to 'lecture rather than communicate' and would have 'difficulty in taking direction'. The Equality Officer accepted that the complainant had failed to obtain the position for reasons other than her age. Nevertheless, it was held that she had been asked discriminatory questions at interview about her age. She was awarded €5,000 compensation for the distress caused by this discrimination and the Equality Officer ordered that the complainant be offered another opportunity to be re-interviewed for the position by a different interview board or, alternatively, be offered a similar position with the same airline.

[9–47] Recruitment advertisements that make reference to 'experience' may be considered to be discriminatory on grounds of age. In *O'Connor v Lidl Ireland GmbH*,[76] the complainant had applied for a position with the respondent following a recruitment advertisement that stated the ideal candidate should not have more than two/three years' experience in a commercial environment. The complainant, who was 51 years of age, was not called for interview. He alleged that the wording of the advertisement was designed or might reasonably be understood as indicating an intention to exclude older candidates. During the course of her investigation, the Equality Officer discovered that, after the complaint had been lodged, the respondent had destroyed all records of the dates of birth of all job applicants during the six-month period prior to the complainant's application. The Equality Officer held that the destruction of this information, in the knowledge that a complaint of discrimination had been made, raised an inference of indirect discrimination on grounds of age. Furthermore, the respondent 'could show no evidence suggesting objective or transparent merit criteria clearly unrelated to age'. The Equality Officer held that the complainant had been indirectly discriminated against on grounds of age.

[9–48] It is not a prerequisite for a complainant to establish that [s]he made an unsuccessful application to the respondent in order to establish a claim for discrimination. It will be sufficient if the complainant can establish that because of the discriminatory practice [s]he was discouraged from making an application because of a perception that [s]he would have been unsuccessful. In *Ruddy v SDS*,[77] the complainant submitted that he had been refused access to an owner-driver scheme as part of the respondent's overall restructuring programme. The complainant worked for the respondent from 1980 until his retirement in 2004. In mid-2003, the respondent developed the owner-driver scheme as part of its rationalisation plan.

---

76. DEC-E2005-012.
77. DEC-E2007-020, 26 April 2007.

The complainant never formally applied to take part in the scheme. At the time of its introduction, the scheme was limited to workers under 60 years of age. The complainant was over the age of 60 years at the time. The respondent submitted that as the complainant had never formally applied to take part in the scheme he could not bring a claim for age discrimination. The Equality Officer found that it was reasonable in the circumstances for the complainant to assume that an upper age limit applied to the scheme. The complainant had spoken with his trade union representative regarding the scheme, who confirmed the age limit. This fact was also confirmed by the Human Resource Department to the respondent in a later conversation. Furthermore, all the information received by the complainant from the respondent (in the form of booklets and so forth) confirmed the age limit. In these circumstances, it would not be reasonable to expect the complainant to make a formal application where he knew, based on the information available to him, what the actual outcome of any such application would be.

6.2. Retirement

The effectiveness of the protection offered by s.6(2)(f) to older workers is diluted [9–49] by the defences or exceptions provided in s.34 of the 1998 Act. For example, s.34(5) provides that:

> It shall not constitute discrimination on the age ground to set, in relation to any job, a maximum age for recruitment which takes account of—
> (a) Any cost or period of time involved in training a recruit to a standard at which the recruit will be effective in that job, and
> (b) The need for there to be a reasonable period of time prior to retirement age during which the recruit will be effective in that job.

Thus an employer could refuse to recruit an employee on the basis that [s]he was older if it could be established that it would not be economically viable for the employer to offer the position to that employee because his or her age would indicate that the employer would not receive a return on his or her investment in that the employee would not be available for work on a longer term basis. This provision threatens to undermine the entire basis of age discrimination under the Act. It treats all employees of a certain age in the same manner, irrespective of their ability or health. Section 34(5) effectively allows an employer to justify the exclusion of an individual from the workforce for no reason other than that [s]he has reached a chronological milestone.

6.3. Mandatory Retirement

The effects of s.6(2)(f) of the 1998 Act may also be avoided by the employer [9–50] through the imposition of a compulsory retirement age, or so it would appear. Section 34(4) of the 1998 Act provides that 'it shall not constitute discrimination on the age ground to fix different ages for the retirement (whether voluntarily or compulsorily) of employees or any class or description of employees'. Effectively, this subsection would appear to remove the imposition of compulsory retirement measures from the remit of the legislation completely. However, following a number of ECJ rulings, the validity of s.34(4) is now doubtful.[78]

[9–51] Mandatory retirement ages, as they have become known, were challenged as being discriminatory in *Leahy v Limerick City Council*.[79] In that case, the complainant challenged the compulsory retirement age of 55 years for firefighters as being discriminatory. The complainant also argued that the compulsory retirement age for fire officers was fixed at 65 years, and the difference in ages was also discriminatory. The Equality Officer held that the complainant had failed to establish a prima facie case of discrimination and that the fixing of different retirement ages for different classes of workers was justified under s.34(4) of the 1998 Act.

[9–52] Proponents of a mandatory retirement age claim that it encourages the regeneration of the workforce by facilitating the entry of younger people into that workforce, and also that having a mandatory retirement age takes account of disease and illnesses more common among older people and removes the personal element from retirement, therefore providing dignity to the older worker.[80]

[9–53] Notwithstanding the arguments in favour of it, it is submitted that mandatory retirement results in the treatment of employees differently solely on the grounds of their age. Mandatory retirement does not take into consideration the individual's actual skills or aptitudes and is stereotyping. Furthermore, it removes the decision to retire from the individual and assumes that age and incapability go hand in hand, thereby reinforcing a negative stereotype of the elderly. Cotter has observed:

> The growth of mandatory retirement has insured an increasing number of older workers being excluded from the labour force and denied access to earnings, as well as other economic, social and psychological aspects of the workplace. There is a valuable loss of important manpower, expertise and professional skills, because of mandatory retirement. However, more than ever as the population ages, the older generation is becoming a growing political, social and economic force.[81]

[9–54] A national mandatory retirement age was unsuccessfully challenged as being discriminatory before the ECJ in *Palacios de la Villa v Cortefiel Servicios SA*.[82] In that case Mr Palacios de la Villa had his contract of employment automatically terminated on the basis that he had reached the compulsory retirement age

---

78. Connolly, 'Compulsory Retirement Ages – A Thing of the Past?', 6(1) *IELJ* (2009), 4.
79. DEC-E2003-038, 11 September 2003.
80. Generally, see Eekelaar, *An Ageing World* (Clarendon, 1989).
81. Cotter, 'Age Discrimination', *Discrimination Law* (Cavendish Publishing, 2005), at p.146.
82. C-411/05, [2007] EUECJ C-411/05, [2007] ECR I-8531.

of 65 years provided for under a collective agreement. The court held that the mandatory retirement provision came within Council Directive 2000/78/EC on Equal Treatment and also concluded that it amounted to less favourable treatment on grounds of age. However, the ECJ ultimately decided that the provision in question was objectively and reasonably justifiable by a legitimate aim.[83] It held that the mandatory retirement provision was included in the contract of employment as part of a national policy seeking to promote better access to employment between the generations. The legitimacy of this public interest aim could not be questioned as it was among the objectives of the Directive and the Treaty, namely, the promotion of high employment. The ECJ concluded:

> the measure cannot be regarded as unduly prejudicing the legitimate claims of workers subject to compulsory retirement because they have reached the age limit provided for; the relevant legislation is not based only on a specific age, but also takes account of the fact that the persons concerned are entitled to financial compensation by way of a retirement pension at the end of their working life, such as that provided for by the national legislation at issue in the main proceedings, the level of which cannot be regarded as unreasonable.
>
> Moreover, the relevant national legislation allows the social partners to opt, by way of collective agreements – and therefore with considerable flexibility – for application of the compulsory retirement mechanism so that due account may be taken not only of the overall situation in the labour market concerned, but also of the specific features of the jobs in question.[84]

The decision in *Palacios* is significant as the ECJ definitively ruled that mandatory [9–55] retirement age requirements are capable of amounting to less favourable treatment on grounds of age. However, individual Member States retain a broad discretion to justify such mandatory retirement requirements, e.g. on the basis that such requirements are necessary to improve access to employment.

Palacios does raise questions, however, about the compatibility of s.34(4) of the [9–56] 1998 Act with Directive 2000/78 EC on Equal Treatment. While ruling that mandatory retirement ages were not discriminatory *per se*, *Palacios* did require that such requirements be objectively justified if they were not to fall foul of the Directive. This very point was recognised by the Labour Court in *Michael McCarthy v Calor Teoranta*.[85] In that case, a compulsory retirement age of 60 (which was linked to a pension scheme) was challenged. The Labour Court, while ultimately reserving its position on the compatibility of s.34(4) of the 1998 Act, did note the importance of the decision in *Palacios*, stating that:

---

83. Art. 6(1) Directive 2000/78/EC (Framework Directive Establishing a General Framework for Equal Treatment in Employment and Occupation).
84. [2007] EUECJ C-411/05 at paras.73–74.
85. [2008] ELR 269.

the Court of Justice appears to have held that a Member State cannot introduce a mandatory retirement age unless there is objective and reasonable justification for so doing. It would appear axiomatic that an individual employer would be similarly circumscribed in applying a contractual retirement age. If that is the law of the Community it is difficult to see how it can be reconciled with the apparent intendment of *s.34(4)*, at least in so far as it is to be interpreted as placing retirement ages outside the purview of the Act altogether.

[9–57] In *The Incorporated Trustees of the National Council on Ageing (Age Concern) England v Secretary of State for Business, Enterprise and Regulatory Reform*,[86] the National Council on Ageing (a charity that aims to promote the welfare of older people) challenged the legality of certain legislative provisions within the UK that allowed the dismissal of employees for retirement who were at or over the age of 65.[87] The matter was forwarded to the ECJ for a preliminary ruling. Art. 6(1) of Directive 2000/78 provided that such discrimination could be justified if it could be 'objectively and reasonably justified by a legitimate aim, including legitimate employment policy, labour market and vocational training objectives, and if the means of achieving that aim are appropriate and necessary'.[88] The second paragraph of Art. 6(1) listed some examples of differences in treatment that could be justified as being non-discriminatory. Age Concern England argued that by listing these objective and reasonable justifications, it was the intention of the Community legislature to impose an obligation on Member States to set out in their domestic legislation specific lists of the differences in treatment that may be justified, thereby precluding Member States from providing that a difference in treatment is not unlawful if it can be shown that it constitutes a proportionate means of achieving a legitimate aim.

[9–58] Having reviewed the principles of European Community law on the transposition of directives into national law,[89] the ECJ noted that the derogations from Directive 2000/78 provided in Art. 6(1) are by their public interest nature:

> distinguishable from purely individual reasons particular to the employer's situation, such as cost reduction or improving competitiveness, although it cannot be

---

86. C-388/07 [2009] EUECJ.
87. reg.30 Employment Equality (Age) Regulations 2006.
88. [2009] EUECJ C-288/07 at para.7. The following examples are listed in the Directive: '(a) the setting of special conditions on access to employment and vocational training, employment and occupation, including dismissal and remuneration conditions, for young people, older workers and persons with caring responsibilities in order to promote their vocational integration or ensure their protection; (b) the fixing of minimum conditions of age, professional experience or seniority in service for access to employment or to certain advantages linked to employment; (c) the fixing of a maximum age for recruitment which is based on the training requirements of the post in question or the need for a reasonable period of employment before retirement'.
89. C-388/07 [2009] EUECJ C-288/07, *The Incorporated Trustees of the National Council on Ageing (Age Concern) England v Secretary of State for Business, Enterprise and Regulatory Reform*, at para.41.

ruled that a national rule may recognise, in the pursuit of those legitimate aims, a certain degree of flexibility for employers.[90]

While concluding that Member States enjoyed 'a broad discretion' in achieving their social objectives, that discretion could not have the effect 'of frustrating the implementation of the principles of non-discrimination on the grounds of age'.[91]

While Age Concern England's challenge did not succeed in that the ECJ re-affirmed that mandatory age requirements could be justified by Member States on grounds of social and employment policy and the labour market, the court did warn that Member States could not hide behind such generalisations and did face a high burden of proof in justifying such discrimination: [9–59]

> Article 6(1) of Directive 2000/78 gives Member States the option to provide, within the context of national law, for certain kinds of differences in treatment on grounds of age if they are 'objectively and reasonably' justified by a legitimate aim, such as an employment policy, or labour market or vocational training objectives, and if the means of achieving that aim are appropriate and necessary. It imposes on Member States the burden of establishing to a high standard of proof the legitimacy of the aim relied on as a justification. No particular significance should be attached to the fact that the word 'reasonably' used in Article 6(1) of the directive does not appear in Article 2(2)(b) thereof.[92]

The decisions of the ECJ in *Palacios* and *Age Concern* do not bring an end to mandatory retirement ages, but should give employers and Member States pause for thought.[93] Now employers and Member States must be in a position to objectively justify the imposition of such mandatory retirement ages if such measures are not to be found to be discriminatory on grounds of age.

6.4. Other Defences

In addition to the imposition of mandatory retirement ages under s.34(4) and the proviso that an employer need not employ an older person where it would not be economically viable to do so under s.34(5), there are other defences the employer may plead in order to avoid the restrictions of s.6(2)(f) of the 1998 Act. [9–60]

Section 34(3) of the 1998 Act provides that it is not age discrimination 'where it is shown that there is clear actuarial or other evidence that significantly increased costs would result if the discrimination were not permitted in those circumstances'. Thus an employer can discriminate against an employee if it would be too costly [9–61]

---

90. *ibid.*, at para.46.
91. *ibid.*, at para.51.
92. *ibid.*, at para.67.
93. See further on this point *Age UK, R (on the application of) v Secretary of State for Business, Innovation & Skills & Ors* [2009] EWHC 2336 (Admin) 25 September 2009.

for him or her not to do so. In *Ruddy v SDS*[94] (discussed earlier at para.9-48), the respondent attempted to justify his refusal to allow the complainant access to the owner-driver scheme on the basis that it would have incurred significant increased costs had it not imposed the upper age requirement on the basis that employees over the age of 60 had, on average, a shorter working life than younger workers. The Equality Officer found that the actuarial evidence produced by the respondent was only prepared in the course of the investigation some three years after the introduction of the scheme. The respondent submitted that it would have incurred an increased cost in the region of €577,832 had it not imposed the age requirement. However, the Equality Officer observed that the savings incurred by the respondent through the retirement scheme was in the region of €11.8 million. It was also noted that the respondent had set aside €52.5 million to cover the costs of the restructuring programme. The Equality Officer therefore concluded that the respondent had not produced clear actuarial or other evidence that significantly increased costs would result if the discrimination was not permitted. The Equality Officer dismissed as 'speculative' the respondent's other submission that, should the complainant succeed, the respondent would incur significant extra costs in that up to 27 other claims might be brought against him.

[9–62] In accordance with s.34(3) of the 1998 Act (as modified by s.23 of the 2004 Act), it shall no longer be discrimination to use age as a basis for determining payments under an occupational benefits scheme. Section 34(3) provides that in such circumstances it shall not be unlawful for an employer:

> (a) to fix ages for admission to such a scheme or for entitlement to benefits under it,
>
> (b) to fix different such ages for all employees or a category of employees,
>
> (c) to use, in the context of such a scheme, age criteria in actuarial calculations, or
>
> (d) to provide different rates of severance payments for different employees or groups or categories of employees, being rates based on or taking into account the period between the age of an employee on leaving the employment and his or her compulsory retirement age, provided that that does not constitute discrimination on the gender ground.

7. Disability

[9–63] In May 2008 Oscar Pistorius, a South African sprinter, was deemed to be eligible to compete for a place on South Africa's Olympic team by the Swiss-based Court of Arbitration for Sport. The event was newsworthy because Pistorius is a double-amputee who uses carbon-fibre prosthetic limbs to compete in races. The ruling overturned an earlier decision by the International Association of Athletics Feder-

---

94. DEC-E2007-020, 26 April 2007.

ations (IAAF), which had determined that because Pistorius used artificial limbs he was ineligible for able-bodied competition. The Court of Arbitration, however, was not convinced that the sprinter had gained a 'metabolic advantage' over other able-bodied athletes through his used of the prosthetic limbs and cleared the athlete to compete.

While a sporting matter, the Oscar Pistorius case raised important issues regarding [9–64] modern society's perception of disability, including the meaning of disability and whether and when it is appropriate to regard a disability (for example, loss of limbs) as inevitably meaning that an employee can no longer do his or her job. Finally, a question arises as to whether an employee with a disability who can be reasonably accommodated by the provision of necessary special assistance should continue to be considered to be disabled.[95]

7.1. Definition

Section 6(2)(g) of the 1998 Act defines discrimination on the grounds of disability [9–65] as occurring where one person with a disability is treated less favourably than another is, has been or would be treated, where that other is either a person without a disability or a person with a different disability to that of the employee. The protection provided to those with a disability is much wider than that afforded to individuals under any of the other grounds. In particular, persons suffering under a disability are not limited to comparators who do not suffer from a disability, but may also compare themselves to those with a different disability.[96] Furthermore, as will be discussed below, the provision places positive obligations on employers to act to eliminate discrimination.

Section 2 of the 1998 Act defined disability as meaning: [9–66]

(a) the total or partial absence of a person's bodily or mental functions, including the absence of a part of a person's body,
(b) the presence in the body of organisms causing, or likely to cause, chronic disease or illness,
(c) the malfunction, malformation or disfigurement of a part of a person's body,
(d) a condition or malfunction which results in a person learning differently from a person without the condition or malfunction, or
(e) a condition, illness or disease which affects a person's thought processes, perception of reality, emotions or judgement or which results in disturbed behaviour, and shall be taken to include a disability which exists at present, or which

---

95. For general discussion, see Collins, 'Discrimination, Equality and Social Inclusion', 16 *MLR* (2003), 42; Smith, 'Disability, Discrimination and Employment: A Never-Ending Legal Story?', 8(1) *DULJ* (2001), 148.
96. *The Civil Service Commissions v A Complainant*, ADE/02/8, determination no. EDA024, 7 October 2002. For further discussion see Morgan, *Disability Discrimination – How Far Does it Extend?*, 6(3) *IELJ* (2009), 70.

previously existed but no longer exists, or which may exist in the future or which is imputed to a person…

[9–67] As a medical term, the definition of disability as outlined in s.2 is broad and encompasses a wide range of disabilities, both physical and mental. The definition has been held to include work-related stress and depression,[97] schizophrenia,[98] anorexia,[99] vertigo[100] and alcoholism.[101] It also encompasses disability of a temporary nature (that is to say, a disability that previously existed but exists no more). Thus in *Customer Perception Limited v Gemma Leydon*,[102] a whiplash-type injury qualified as a disability for the purposes of the legislation. The definition provided under the Equality Acts is not as restrictive as that provided under similar legislation in England and Wales, where disability is described as a physical or mental impairment that has a substantial and long-term adverse effect on that person's ability to carry out normal day-to-day activities.[103] Section 2 of the 1998 Act does not require that the disability have a substantial and long-term adverse effect on the person, nor does it identify any specific illness as qualifying as a disability.

[9–68] Notwithstanding its breadth, the approach towards disability adopted under the 1998 Act has been criticised as perpetuating the difficulties of those persons suffering with a disability in that it focused on the disability itself rather than on the disabled person's ability to do the job.[104] As Pitt has noted:

> the biggest problem facing people with disabilities is the blinkered attitude of the rest of the community, who frequently perceive them as having greater limitations than is in fact the case or who exhibit irrational prejudices. They therefore argue that a 'social model' of disability would be more appropriate, which would treat people as disabled if they are liable to be perceived as disabled or to suffer from prejudice against people with disabilities.[105]

The social model of disability recognises that in many cases the biggest barrier towards equality in the workforce is not an actual disability, but others' perceptions of it. While heavily reliant on the medical definition of disability, aspects of

---

97. *A Prison Officer v The Minister for Justice, Equality and Law Reform*, DEC-E2007-025; *Rattigan v Connacht Gold Co-operative Society*, DEC-E2008-026, 28 May 2008.
98. *Civil Service Commissions v A Complainant*, ADE/02/8, determination no. EDA024, 7 October 2002.
99. *A Health and Fitness Club v A Worker* determination no. EED037.
100. *Mr Z v A Building Contractor*, DEC-E2009-087, 7 October 2009.
101. *An Employee v A Government Department* [2006] ELR 224.
102. ED/02/1, determination no. EED0317, 12 December 2003.
103. s.1 Disability Discrimination Act 1995.
104. This is also known as the 'medical model of disability'. Generally, see McCrann and Kelleher, 'Disability Discrimination under the Employment Equality Act 1998 and the Equality Bill 2004', 1(2) *IELJ* (2004), 42.
105. Pitt, *Employment Law* (6th ed., Thomson, Sweet and Maxwell, 2007), at p.64.

the social model of disability are also evident in the Irish legislation. In particular, the inclusion in s.6 of factors such as the person's 'disfigurement, past, future and imputed disability' are issues that should have no bearing on the person's ability to do the job and yet are included within the definition.

Section 16(b) provides that an employer is under no obligation to recruit, promote [9–69] or train an individual where [s]he is not (or no longer is) fully competent to undertake the duties attached to that position, having regard to the conditions in which those duties are, or may be required to be, performed. Thus an employer can justifiably discriminate against an individual with a disability if, because of that disability, [s]he is not able to do the work. However, s.16(3)(b) of the 1998 Act creates a presumption that provides that all persons shall be considered 'fully competent' to do the work where they can do so with the assistance of special treatment or facilities. Furthermore, s.16(3)(b) places an obligation on an employer to 'do all that is reasonable to accommodate the needs of a person who has a disability by providing special treatment or facilities' that may be necessary for the employee to do the work.

The constitutional validity of s.16(3)(b) was questioned in *In the Matter of Article* [9–70] *26 of the Constitution of Ireland and In the Matter of the Employment Equality Bill, 1996*.[106] In particular, it was argued that the requirement that employers make 'reasonable accommodation' for employees with a disability failed to adequately protect the rights of employers to earn their livelihood and constituted an unjust attack on their property rights within the meaning of Art. 40.3.2 of the Constitution. The Supreme Court concluded in that case that:

> the difficulty with the section now under discussion is that it attempts to transfer the cost of solving one of society's problems on to a particular group. The difficulty the Court finds with the section is, not that it requires an employer to employ disabled people, but that it requires him to bear the cost of all special treatment or facilities which the disabled person may require to carry out the work unless the cost of the provision of such treatment or facilities would give rise to 'undue hardship' to the employer.

> There is no provision to exempt small firms or firms with a limited number of employees, from the provisions of the Bill. The wide definition of the term 'disability' in the Bill means that it is impossible to estimate in advance what the likely cost to an employer would be. The Bill does provide that one of the matters to be taken into consideration in estimating whether employing the disabled person would cause undue hardship to the employer is 'the financial circumstances of the employer' but this in turn implies that the employer would have to disclose his financial circumstances and the problems of his business to an outside party.

---

106. [1997] 2 IR 321.

It therefore appears to the Court that the provisions of the Bill dealing with disability, despite their laudable intention, are repugnant to the Constitution for the reasons stated.[107]

To redress the balance between the employer's property rights and the rights of those under a disability, s.16(3)(c) was introduced into the legislation by the 2004 Act, which provided that:

> A refusal or failure to provide for special treatment or facilities... shall not be deemed reasonable unless such provision would give rise to a cost, other than a nominal cost, to the employer.

[9–71] Prior to the inclusion of subsection (3)(c) there was a fear on the part of employers that the requirement of 'reasonable accommodation' would be judged in a wholly objective sense without having regard to the size of the employer's organisation or regard to the financial implications of the obligation. Section 16(3)(c) limited the employer's obligation in this regard to doing no more than that which amounts to a 'nominal cost'. However, the introduction of the nominal-cost provision greatly diluted the effectiveness of the requirement of reasonable accommodation, particularly where the word 'nominal' is given its literal meaning.[108] After all, taken to extremes of literalism, it is difficult to see how any effective action by an employer to reasonably accommodate an employee with a disability could avoid incurring more than nominal costs.

7.2. Reasonable Accommodation

[9–72] As we have seen, s.16(3)(b) of the 1998 Act placed an obligation on the employer to ensure that the disabled person was fully competent to do the job by requiring the employer to reasonably accommodate that person's disability. A failure to establish that [s]he had done so would mean that the employer could not defeat a claim of disability discrimination on the basis that the individual was not fully competent.[109] In *Humphries v Westwood Fitness Centre*,[110] the Labour Court, when assessing reasonable accommodation, outlined the nature and extent of the enquiries an employer should make in such circumstances:

> In practical terms this will normally require a two-stage enquiry, which looks firstly at the factual position concerning the employee's capability including the degree of

---

107. [1997] 2 IR 321, 367.
108. Research conducted in the United States would indicate that employers' fears that the requirement of 'reasonable accommodation' would place a crippling financial burden upon them are exaggerated. For further discussion, see Bruton, 'Reasonable Accommodation in Disability Law', 2, 1 *IELJ* (2005), 9 at 11.
109. *A Government Department v An Employee (Ms B)*, ADE/05/16, determination no. EDA061, 30 January 2006.
110. [2004] ELR 296.

impairment arising from the disability and its likely duration. This would involve looking at the medical evidence available to the employer either from the employee's doctors or obtained independently.

Secondly, if it is apparent that the employee is not fully capable Section 16(3) of the Act requires the employer to consider what if any special treatment or facilities may be available by which the employee can become fully capable. The Section requires that the cost of such special treatment or facilities must also be considered. Here, what constitutes nominal cost will depend on the size of the organisation and its financial resources.

Finally, such an enquiry could only be regarded as adequate if the employee concerned is allowed a full opportunity to participate at each level and is allowed to present relevant medical evidence and submissions.[111]

In *A Government Department v A Worker*,[112] the complainant was a civil service [9–73] worker who applied for promotion. He had suffered from an inflammatory bowel disease which flared up and as a consequence required surgery. While he was in hospital he was informed that the interviews were to take place at the same time. He contacted the personnel department in order to make it clear that he wished to remain in competition to be interviewed for the position. Following his discharge from hospital he informed the personnel department that he was available for interview but was told the position was closed. He claimed that he was discriminated against on the disability ground. The respondent claimed that it was not aware that the complainant had sought a deferral of his interview. The Labour Court accepted the complainant's evidence that it had requested a deferral of the interview from the respondent. The court concluded that the failure by the respondent to accommodate the complainant by moving the date of the interview constituted discrimination on the disability ground.

Section 16(3)(3) requires the employer to carry out an investigation into each of the following aspects of the employee's work:

7.2.1. Nature and Extent of the Disability
The employer must ensure that he has conducted a proper assessment of the individ- [9–74] ual's disability before he can make a decision as to whether [s]he can make reasonable accommodation for that individual. This assessment would include making adequate enquiries of the individual about his or her disability. This standard was not met in *A Computer Co. v A Worker*,[113] where an employer immediately dismissed an employee upon learning that the employee suffered from epilepsy on the basis that she would pose a danger to herself and others while operating heavy machinery

111. [2004] ELR 296, 301.
112. Determination no. EDA0612.
113. Determination no. EED013.

as part of her duties. The court held that the employer had failed in its duty to assess the nature and extent of her disability. In particular, it found that the employee's condition was well controlled by medicine and that the employer should have waited for a written medical report from a doctor that indicated that the employee could safely continue working. The court concluded that the employer:

> did not give the slightest consideration to providing the complainant with reasonable special facilities which would… overcome any difficulty which she or the respondent might otherwise experience.

[9–75] Similarly, in *Uwimana v TLC Centre*,[114] the claimant worked as a care assistant for the respondent. Her duties included lifting patients. The complainant was diagnosed with a degenerative back condition leading to arthritis. Her doctor issued her with a letter advising that she should find work that did not involve heavy lifting. This letter was forwarded to her employer. The Equality Officer found that upon receipt of this letter the respondent had effectively dismissed her on the basis that she was no longer fit to continue working. In relation to the respondent's obligation to assess the nature and extent of the complainant's disability, the Equality Officer concluded:

> The doctor's letter provides a statement as to the complainant's condition and suggestions in relation to her work as a care assistant. It does not provide a detailed assessment as to the complainant's capabilities. Also, the likely duration is unclear from this letter and is only clarified in the doctor's letter of 4 July 2005, which was after the complainant was dismissed and therefore could not have been taken into account by them. The complainant was not asked for any further medical evidence and the respondent did not seek any more information. I conclude that the respondent was correct in assessing that the complainant was not capable of carrying out the full range of duties of a care assistant at the time of her dismissal but they were incorrect in not seeking further medical evidence to determine the degree of impairment and its likely duration.

[9–76] Where possible, an employer should always seek a medical report on the individual's disability in order to fully assess how that individual may be reasonably accommodated. In *Kehoe v Convertec Ltd.*,[115] the complainant had been dismissed on the basis of poor work performance. The complainant contended that his poor performance was due to a disability that meant he could not work as quickly or as efficiently as other employees. The Equality Officer found that the employer's failure to send the complainant for a medical examination, in line with company policy, amounted to a failure to reasonably accommodate him. Such an examination would have assisted the employer in ascertaining what tasks the claimant was capable of performing in light of his disability.

---

114. DEC-E2008-009, March 2008.
115. DEC-E2001-034, 9 November 2001.

On the other hand, the employer is entitled to require that any request that reasonable accommodation be made for an employee is supported by appropriate medical documentation 'or other appropriate evidence outlining the reason for the request… and the nature of the accommodation required to enable the complainant to be fully competent and capable of undertaking the duties of the position'.[116]

In *A Government Department v A Worker*,[117] an employer was found to have [9–77] discriminated against an employee where it extended the employee's probationary period because the employee was persistently absent from work due to ill health. The employee in that case was appointed as a prison officer and was subject to a two-year probationary period. At the end of the probationary period the employee had been absent on sick leave for more than 70 days. The probationary period was extended for a further six months during which the employee missed a further 88 days. Thereafter, the employee's probationary period was extended for a further six months before the employee was made permanent. The employee had been suffering from a depressive condition which had caused her absences from work. The Labour Court held that the employee's illness was a disability for the purposes of the Act. The employer had discriminated against the employee by extending her probationary periods. The employer had failed to consider whether the employee's illness was a disability and had failed to consider whether any reasonable accommodation could be made for her prior to deciding whether any action should be taken to extend her probationary period.

7.2.2. Special Treatment or Facilities
Having assessed the nature and extent of the individual's disability, the employer [9–78] should be able to make an informed decision as to whether the individual, with the aid of special treatment or facilities, can be considered fully competent to do the work. In this respect, special treatment or facilities can range from the provision of a wheelchair-accessible room for interviewing the claimant[118] to the requirement to provide an appropriate headset to a hearing-impaired claimant working as a receptionist.[119] Essentially, all that the law requires is that the employer make reasonable efforts at accommodating the employee – and even that is subject to the principle that [s]he must do so only where [s]he would incur no more than nominal costs. In *A Company v A Worker*,[120] an employee suffering from cerebral palsy brought a claim for constructive dismissal on the basis that her employer failed to provide reasonable accommodation for her. The Labour Court held that the duties assigned to her, such as the sorting of post and so forth, were not suitable given her disability and the employer could have resolved the difficulties the employee had experienced by rotating certain tasks amongst the workforce.

---

116. *Mr D v A Government Department*, DEC-E2008-011, 5 March 2008.
117. Determination no. EDA094.
118. *Harrington v East Coast Area Health Board*, DEC-E2002-001, 23 January 2002.
119. *A Motor Company v A Worker*, determination no. EED026.
120. Determination no. EED021.

[9–79]   The duty to provide special treatment or facilities places positive obligations on the employer. In the words of the Labour Court in *A Government Department v A Worker*[121]:

> The duty to provide special treatment or facilities is proactive in nature. It includes an obligation to carry out a full assessment of the needs of the person with a disability and of the measures necessary to accommodate that person's disability…
>
> The scope of an employer's duty is determined by what is necessary and reasonable in the circumstances. It may… involve relieving the person with a disability from the requirement to undertake certain work which is beyond his or her capacity.

[9–80]   In *Mr A v A Government Department*,[122] the Equality Officer held that the respondent failed to take a proactive approach towards the provision of special treatment or facilities for the complainant and had consequently unlawfully discriminated against him. In that case, the complainant was employed in a technical specialist role with a government department since April 2005. He commuted daily to Dublin from a provincial town. In May 2006, the complainant sustained a spinal injury, as a result of which he experienced lower back pain when sitting for prolonged periods, including while driving a car. On 7 February 2007, the complainant was declared fit to return to work as long as he was not commuting for long periods of time. Since November 2006, the complainant had become aware that an advanced party of department staff would be decentralising to the provincial town where he lived. He sought, via letter, in November 2006 and again in February 2007, to be included in the advance party. On 28 February 2007, the complainant was advised that it was not possible to accommodate him as part of the advance party relocating to the town where he lived. On 5 April 2007, the complainant lodged his complaint with the tribunal. On 28 May 2007, the complainant's supervisor and an official from the respondent's HR department met with the complainant in order to discuss his return to work. The Equality Officer noted that this meeting took place three-and-a-half months after the complainant was declared fit for return to work and six weeks after the complainant had lodged a complaint. Consequently, the respondent had failed to pursue the assessment of the complainant's situation in a proactive fashion.

[9–81]   In *An Employee v A Local Authority*,[123] the complainant was engaged in a clerical post with the respondent. Following some negative assessments on his work performance, the complainant's contract was terminated and he was offered an alternative, non-administrative position. Soon afterwards, the complainant resigned his position, claiming that the respondent had failed to make reasonable accommodation for his disability (the complainant had undergone brain surgery and was suffering from

121. ADE/05/16, determination no; EDA061, 30 January 2006.
122. DEC-E2008-023, 6 May 2008.
123. DEC-E2002-04, 4 February 2002.

the residual after-effects). According to the complainant, the respondent had three options open to it by which it could have reasonably accommodated his disability. First, it could have ensured that the complainant undergo an independent vocational assessment in order to identify his work strengths and weaknesses. Secondly, the complainant could have benefited from the appointment of a specialised job coach, who could provide guidance, instruction and training on those areas of the job with which the complainant was struggling. Thirdly, the respondent could have received financial assistance from the Employment Support Scheme. This scheme offered financial support under certain circumstances to employers who employed persons with a disability. The Equality Officer noted that a subsequent expert occupational assessment of the complainant found that he had good potential for clerical work, including good work traits in areas including application, concentration and persistence – the very areas that the respondent highlighted as reasons for his poor work performance and subsequent dismissal. The Equality Officer observed that:

> I am satisfied, on balance, that the vocational assessment presents a more realistic outline of the complainant's capabilities than the views of the untrained staff involved with the complainant's performance evaluation within the respondent Authority. I note that whilst the respondent did not have any objection to a vocational assessment of the complainant, it only began to give active consideration to the idea in mid-November, 2000, some six weeks after it had decided that the complainant was not capable of performing his job as a Clerical Officer. I find therefore, that the respondent's conclusion that the complainant was not fully competent and capable to undertake his duties was a decision reached without proper consideration of all of the relevant factors and could not, therefore, have been reached in a reasonable and objective manner.

In relation to the appointment of a professional job coach, the Equality Officer [9–82] held that had such an appointment been made the complainant would have been able to carry out his job in a capable and competent manner. The Equality Officer concluded that the appointment of a job coach for a two- or three-month period would have been sufficient to render the complainant fully competent. Ultimately, the Equality Officer found that the respondent did not adequately examine the options open to it as regards special treatment and facilities and had therefore unlawfully discriminated against the complainant. The Equality Officer also held that the employer had not adequately examined whether it could receive adequate financial support from the Employment Support Scheme.

7.2.3. Nominal Cost

As we have seen, the constitutional compromise reached in the Supreme Court [9–83] decision in *In the Matter of Article 26 of the Constitution of Ireland and In the Matter of the Employment Equality Bill, 1996*[124] has meant that, in reasonably accommodating an employee with a disability, the employer need not incur more

---

124. [1997] 2 IR 321.

than nominal cost. In *An Employee v A Local Authority*,[125] the Equality Officer held that a 'nominal cost' was widely defined and considered that what amounted to a 'nominal cost' would vary depending on the size of the employer's organisation and would also be affected by whether the employer was in the public or private sector. In the view of the Equality Officer it was clear

> that the legislatures's understanding on the issue of 'nominal cost' was that all employers would not be treated in an identical fashion and that the particular circumstances would have to be evaluated in each case.

[9–84] In that case, the options made available to the employer, namely the professional independent assessment, the provision of a job coach, and access to the Employment Support Scheme were options available to the respondent from FÁS at no more than a nominal cost. In *Bowes v Southern Regional Fisheries Board*,[126] the complainant was employed as a fisheries officer with the respondent. He was diagnosed with multiple sclerosis. As a consequence of this disability, restrictions were placed on his driving licence, which permitted him to drive only vehicles fitted with hand controls. The complainant requested that the company car be fitted with such controls. This request was denied. The respondent argued that to do so would discriminate in favour of the complainant, particularly in light of the fact that it was the respondent's contention that the complainant was already undertaking lighter duties because of this illness. The Equality Officer held that the employer failed to adapt the car, which would have allowed the complainant to function normally and, furthermore, had failed to enter into any meaningful dialogue with the complainant regarding the issue. The Equality Officer noted that the controls could have been fitted at a cost of €400 and a person without a disability could still use the vehicle in the normal way, and as such the reasonable accommodation that would have rendered the complainant fully competent did not amount to more than a 'nominal cost'

[9–85] Similarly, in *A Motor Company v A Worker*,[127] the Labour Court found that the provision of an appropriate headset to the hearing-impaired complainant would have cost no more than €450 and therefore could not be considered more than a 'nominal cost'. However, in *Mr C v Iarnród Éireann*,[128] the complainant applied for a position as a gate-keeper with the respondent company. The complainant suffered from depression and, following medical advice, the respondent refused to offer the complainant the position. The complainant alleged that he had been discriminated against because of his disability and that the respondent had failed to make reasonable accommodation for it. The position was considered a safety-critical post as it involved allowing train users and cars to safely pass through. The

---

125. DEC-E2002-04, 4 February 2002.
126. DEC-E2004-008, 17 February 2004.
127. Determination no. EED026.
128. DEC-E2003-054, 26 November 2003.

respondent contended that it could only reasonably accommodate the complainant's disability by ensuring that he was accompanied at all times. The Equality Officer agreed that such accommodation would not be 'practical or affordable' and therefore amounted to something more than a 'nominal cost'. There was no unlawful discrimination.

7.2.4. Appropriate Measures

Art. 5 of the Directive on Equal Treatment (Directive 2000/78/EC) initiated [9–86] change to the concept of reasonable accommodation. This change was incorporated in s.9 of the Employment Equality Act 2004, which substituted s.16(3) of the 1998 Act. Under s.9 the term 'reasonable accommodation' was replaced with the term 'appropriate measures'. Crucially, under s.9 an employer is now obliged to undertake 'appropriate measures' in order to enable an employee to have access to employment, to participate or advance in employment, or to undergo training, unless the measures would impose a 'disproportionate burden' on the employer. In determining whether or not such measures would impose a disproportionate burden, s.9 provides that the financial and other costs to the employer, the scale and financial resources of the employer's business, and the possibility of obtaining public funding or other assistance would be taken into consideration. For the purposes of s.9, 'appropriate measures':

(a) means effective and practical measures, where needed in a particular case, to adapt the employer's place of business to the disability concerned,

(b) without prejudice to the generality of paragraph (a), includes the adaptation of premises and equipment, patterns of working time, distribution of tasks or the provision of training or integration resources, but

(c) does not include any treatment, facility or thing that the person might ordinarily or reasonably provide for himself or herself.

Section 9 represents a significant shift in favour of the disabled worker. Under the [9–87] 'nominal cost' provision the financial obligations for the particular employer would always remain comparatively low. Under the 2004 Act an employer will now be obliged to undertake 'appropriate measures', notwithstanding that the cost to the employer may amount to more than a nominal figure, provided it does not amount to a disproportionate cost on the employer in relation to his or her business as a whole. Thus on the financial sliding scale the balance has been tipped in favour of the disabled worker and should lessen the likelihood of an employer being able to hide behind financial cost in order to defeat claims of discrimination.

In *A Complainant v An Employer*,[129] the complainant, in response to an adver- [9–88] tisement, lodged a job application with the respondent. The complainant saw a call coming in on his mobile phone. Being deaf, he contacted the caller via text message asking to be text messaged with the content of their message. The

---

129. DEC-E2008-068, 30 December 2008.

respondent did so and requested that the complainant attend for interview the next day. The complainant contacted the Cork Deaf Society in order to arrange an interpreter for the interview. This could not be done on time. The complainant attempted to rearrange an alternative date for the interview, but the respondent indicated that this was not possible. The complainant then suggested that he could do the interview with the aid of a computer. The respondent indicated that this would not be possible either as the interviewer was not computer literate. As a result the complainant missed the interview. The Equality Officer decided that the respondent's outright rejection of the possibility that the interview be conducted with the aid of a computer because the interviewer was not computer literate was a failure to provide reasonable accommodation. Furthermore, it was held that the provision of such support would not have created a disproportionate burden for the respondent. The computer communication could have been as basic or elaborate as they chose. In addition, the provision of a person with typing skills for the duration of the interview could not be considered a disproportionate burden on the respondent.

8. Race

[9–89] With the great influx of inward migration to Ireland during the economic boom of the 'Celtic Tiger' era, the introduction of this ground of unlawful discrimination was an important and necessary development in the protection of employees of a racial, national or ethnic minority.

8.1. Definition

[9–90] Section 6(1)(h) of the 1998 Act provides that it shall be unlawful discrimination to treat a person less favourably than another person is, has been or would be treated because [s]he is of a different race, colour, nationality, or ethnic or national origins. No further definition is provided of these terms within the legislation. However, in England and Wales similar terminology is used in the Race Relations Act 1976. The definition of 'ethnic origins' was considered by the House of Lords in *Mandla v Dowell Lee*.[130] In that case, a Sikh boy was refused entry to a private school unless he agreed not to wear his turban and had his hair cut. The complainant argued that such requirements were contrary to his religion. In finding that the Sikh community was an 'ethnic group' for the purposes of the legislation, Lord Fraser identified the characteristics of an ethnic group as follows: 'it must, in my opinion, regard itself, and be regarded by others, as a distinct community by virtue of certain characteristics'.[131] The judge went on to state that those essential characteristics are:

---

130. [1983] 2 AC 548, [1983] 2 WLR 620, [1983] 1 All ER 1062, [1983] ICR 385, [1983] IRLR 209.
131. [1983] 2 AC 548, 562.

(1) a long shared history, of which the group is conscious as distinguishing it from other groups, and the memory of which it keeps alive; (2) a cultural tradition of its own, including family and social customs and manners, often but not necessarily associated with religious observance. In addition to those essential characteristics the following characteristics are, in my opinion, relevant; (3) either a common geographical origin, or descent from a small number of common ancestors; (4) a common language, not necessarily peculiar to the group; (5) a common literature peculiar to the group; (6) a common religion different from that of neighbouring groups or from the general community surrounding it; (7) being a minority or being an oppressed or a dominant group within a larger community, for example a conquered people...[132]

In *Dawkins v Department of the Environment*,[133] the Court of Appeal held that Rastafarians were not a separate ethnic group on the basis that, while they may have certain identifiable characteristics, they do not have a separate identity by virtue of their ethnic origins. There was nothing to distinguish them as a group from others of Afro-Caribbean descent.

The definition of race in the 1998 Act includes 'nationality or national origin'. There- [9–91] fore, a person holding Irish citizenship (nationality) but who originated from another country (national origin) could ground a claim for discrimination on the grounds of race. In *BBC Scotland v Souster*,[134] a sports broadcaster claimed that he was replaced by a Scotswoman simply because he was English. The court accepted that this was capable of amounting to discrimination on the basis of 'national origin'. Similarly, in *Northern Joint Police Board v Power*,[135] the tribunal held that to discriminate against a candidate simply because he was English and not Scottish was unlawful discrimination on grounds of national origin. In *Glennon v Bormac Ltd., t/a Carboni's Cafe*[136] it was held that the complainant had been discriminated against on the basis of her nationality where she was the only Irish employee of the respondent and had been dismissed while two non-national workers took up employment with the respondent at the same time. It was held that there was prima facie evidence of discrimination based on nationality because she was Irish in possession of language skills and consequently was able to stand over her rights successfully.

When dealing with employees of a different culture or language, an employer [9–92] must recognise that it may have to go to greater lengths to explain rules, procedures and rights to them than would be necessary in the case of a national or even an English-speaking worker. Miscommunication because of language or cultural barriers could lead to unfair treatment between national and non-national workers. Indeed, the ECJ has acknowledged that this area is one where discrimination can

---

132. [1983] 2 AC 548, 562.
133. [1993] IRLR 284.
134. [2001] IRLR 150.
135. [1997] IRLR 610.
136. DEC-E 2009-099.

arise not only through the application of different rules to similar situations but also to the application of the same rule to different situations.[137]

[9–93] In *Campbell Catering Ltd. v Rasdaq*,[138] the complainant was an African employee of the respondent catering company. The employee was summarily dismissed on the grounds that she had unlawfully taken company food off the premises without permission. The employee had been aware that while it was not an offence to eat such food on site, it was a serious offence to take such food off the premises. There was some conflict of evidence as to whether the complainant had the food in her possession in order to eat it on the premises at a later time or whether she had it in her possession with the intention of removing it from the premises. The Labour Court found that there was insufficient evidence available to the respondent to reasonably accuse the complainant of theft and as a consequence the respondent had failed to observe fair procedures in relation to her dismissal. This fact, together with the fact that the complainant was of a different racial origin, was sufficient to establish a prima facie case of discrimination, which the respondent was unable to rebut. The court warned employers that many non-nationals

> encounter special difficulties in employment arising from lack of knowledge concerning statutory and contractual employment rights together with differences of language and culture. In the case of disciplinary proceedings, employers have a positive duty to ensure that all workers fully understand what is alleged against them, the gravity of the alleged misconduct and their right to mount a full defence, including the right of representation. Special measures may be necessary in the case of non-national workers to ensure that this obligation is fulfilled and that the accused worker fully appreciates the gravity of the situation and is given appropriate facilities and guidance in making a defence. In such cases, applying the same procedural standards to a non-national worker as would be applied to an Irish national could amount to the application of the same rules to different situations, and could in itself amount to discrimination.[139]

[9–94] The principles enunciated in *Rasdaq* were approved by the tribunal in *Zhang v Towner Trading*.[140] In that case, the complainant, a Chinese national, had been working for the respondent in his shop for some eight months when she received a mobile phone text message from her employer. The message stated, 'I have u on camera robbing bus tickets. If that money or the tickets are not returned, I have your work and home address. I will call to your work and the police and show them the tape. You have until 5 o'clock tomorrow.' Following receipt of the message the complainant arranged to meet the respondent. At the meeting the complainant was accused of stealing bus tickets from the respondent's shop and presented with

---

137. C-279/93, *Finanzamt Koln-Altstadt v Schumacker* [1995] EUECJ C-279/93, [1995] ECR I-225.
138. [2004] ELR 310.
139. [2004] ELR 310, 318.
140. DEC-E2008-001, 16 January 2008.

CCTV footage in support of this allegation, which showed her handling a box of some description. The meeting had been called at the complainant's request and not as part of any investigation or disciplinary hearing. Following the meeting, the complainant sent the respondent a text enquiring as to whether she was on the roster for work the next day. She received a reply via text message from the respondent, which stated, 'You are not working here anymore.' The complainant arranged a further meeting with the respondent to which she brought a colleague to act as an interpreter. She was told at this meeting that an investigation would be conducted into the matter and a further meeting was arranged. This meeting was later cancelled by the respondent and the complainant was informed that the respondent was now only hiring full-time staff and she was no longer needed. The Equality Officer found that the complainant had been treated less favourably than another employee would be by virtue of the fact that the respondent had not followed fair procedures, did not conduct an investigation into the allegation and denied the complainant the opportunity to seek representation, prepare a defence and attend a disciplinary hearing. Based on these facts the complainant had proved a prima facie case of discrimination on the grounds of race, which the respondent had failed to rebut.

Similarly, in *Iurie Panuta v Watters Garden World and Watters Garden Sheds*,[141] [9–95] the respondent failed to issue the complainant with an employment contract or health and safety information in a language that he could understand. The Equality Officer decided that the complainant had established a prima facie case of less favourable treatment on the ground of race in that despite the complainant's limited English he was not provided with documentation in a language that he could understand, and did not receive explanation about the documentation from an interpreter or other competent third party contracted by the respondent for this purpose.[142]

In *Golovan v Porturlin Shellfish Ltd.*,[143] the complainant had given her passport to the respondent in support of a work-permit application. The fact that the respondent retained the passport (without justification) raised a prima facie case of less favourable treatment on grounds of race.

8.2. Indirect Discrimination in the Context of Application Procedures

A notable example of a claim for race discrimination being brought in the context [9–96] of application procedures is the case of *Ice Group Business Services Ltd. v Czerski*.[144]

---

141. DEC-E2008-059.

142. Similarly, in *Avizinis v J Ryan Haulage Ltd.* DEC-E2009-099, 9 October 2009, the employee was found to have contravened s.8(1) of the Act where he failed to ensure that the complainant was provided with health and safety information and training in a language which he could understand. See Chapter 15.

143. DEC-E2008-032, 13 June 2008.

144. ADE/06/14, determination no. EDA0812, 16 May 2008, appeal from the Equality Tribunal determination reported at [2007] ELR 221. While the Labour Court allowed the respondent's appeal,

This significant determination is instructive in that it involved the advancement of an interesting argument as to how an ostensibly routine requirement can become disproportionately burdensome on certain individuals so as to raise issues of indirect discrimination. In *Czerski*, an employment agency advertised for applications for positions as production operatives. The complainant stated that the application required applicants to furnish details of two referees; she was only in a position to furnish one employment-related reference. She maintained that the respondent never indicated to her that a character reference or some other form of reference would be acceptable and, if they had done so, she would have been in a position to comply with same. She further stated that she had offered to acquire a reference from an employer in Poland but this was rejected by the respondent. The complainant's case was that the absolute insistence by the respondent that she furnish two employment-related references constituted less favourable treatment of her on grounds of race.

[9–97] The Equality Officer stated that an employer is entitled to place a requirement for the furnishing of two references on applicants, but it must not do so in a manner that is contrary to the employment equality legislation. The Equality Officer was satisfied that the application of such a requirement operated to the disadvantage of a non-Irish national and that the requirement could be complied with by a substantially smaller number of non-Irish national prospective employees than Irish national prospective employees. Therefore, it was held that the complainant had established a prima facie case of indirect discrimination on the ground of race in relation to access to employment. Since the respondent failed to adduce evidence that the requirement was justified as reasonable in the circumstances of the case, the complainant was accordingly awarded €7,000 in compensation for distress suffered as a result of the discrimination.

[9–98] On appeal, the Labour Court explicitly accepted the respondent's evidence that it did inform the complainant that a character reference would be acceptable as one of the references. In light of its finding on this point, the court concluded:

> In those circumstances the Court cannot see how a non-national would be placed at any greater disadvantage than a National. While the Court accepts that there are inherent difficulties in applying any policy without regard for individual circumstances, the Court is of the view that a requirement to provide two references one of which might be a character reference, does not constitute indirect discrimination on the race ground. Furthermore, the Court accepts that in the circumstances of the Respondent's business as an employment agency, where it is dependent on its reputation for clients, the requirement to seek two named referees in order to recommend a person for employment with its clients, is a reasonable requirement in the circumstances.

---

it did so on the basis of arriving at a different finding of fact to that arrived at by the Equality Tribunal, as opposed to any divergence in approach concerning the applicable legal principles.

A number of observations may be made about the approach of the Labour Court   [9–99]
in *Czerski*. First, clearly critical to the appeal was the factual finding made by the
Labour Court as to the respondent's having communicated to the applicant that
a character reference would be sufficient. The significance of this point lies in
the fact that the indirect discrimination argument advanced before the Equality
Tribunal concerning the disproportionate impact of requiring two *employment*
references of a non-Irish person apparently remains valid. A second point that
emerges from the Labour Court determination is the importance when considering a claim for indirect discrimination of conducting an intense scrutiny of the
circumstances of the respondent: here, the importance for the agency of maintaining the confidence of its clients through the imposition of rigorous safeguards
was crucial in enabling the reference requirements to pass muster.

In *NUI Galway v McBrierty*,[145] the complainant was Welsh and a national of   [9–100]
the United Kingdom who had been educated in Wales. The complainant had
applied for a position with the respondent but her application was refused on
the basis that she did not hold a Leaving Certificate qualification or equivalent in
Irish. The Labour Court held that the respondent was justified in requiring that
its employees have proficiency in Irish. This was particularly the case given the
University's statutory obligations to promote the language and given its links with
Gaeltacht areas. The court therefore concluded that the requirement of having
proficiency in Irish was reasonable in all the circumstances of the case and was
therefore justified under s.31(d) of the Employment Equality Act 1998.

8.3. ECJ Approach to EC Race Directive

In July 2008, the ECJ delivered a very significant ruling under the Race Direc-   [9–101]
tive, *Centrum voor gelijkheid van kansen en voor racismebestrijding v Firma Feryn
NV*.[146] A Belgian body charged with the task (pursuant to Art. 13 of Directive
2000/43 implementing the principle of equal treatment between persons irrespective of racial or ethnic origin, hereafter the 'Race Directive') of promoting equal
treatment, applied to the Belgian labour courts for a finding that an undertaking
specialising in the sale and installation of up-and-over and sectional doors applied
a discriminatory recruitment policy. It sought this finding on the basis of the
public statements of a director to the effect that his undertaking was seeking to
recruit fitters, but that it could not employ 'immigrants' because its customers
were reluctant to give them access to their private residences for the period of the
work. On a preliminary reference under Art. 234 EC, the Court of Justice held
that the fact that an employer declares publicly that it will not recruit employees
of a certain ethnic or racial origin constitutes direct discrimination in respect of
recruitment within the meaning of Art. 2(2)(a) of the Race Directive, since clearly
such comments are likely to strongly dissuade certain candidates from submitting

---

145. Determination no. EDA091.
146. [2008] 1 ICR 1390.

their candidature and, accordingly, to hinder their access to the labour market. Crucially, the court held[147] that the establishment of the existence of such direct discrimination was not dependent on the identification of a complainant who claimed to have been the victim of that discrimination.

[9–102] In terms of the burden of proof, the court held[148] that such public statements made by an employer to the effect that, under its recruitment policy, it will not recruit any employees of a certain ethnic or racial origin are sufficient for a presumption of the existence of a recruitment policy that is directly discriminatory within the meaning of Art. 8(1) of the Race Directive. It is then for that employer to prove that there was no breach of the principle of equal treatment, which it can do by showing that the undertaking's actual recruitment practice does not correspond to those statements. In *Feryn*, the court held that it was for the national courts to verify that the facts alleged were established, and to assess the sufficiency of the evidence submitted in support of the employer's contentions that it had not breached the principle of equal treatment.

[9–103] From an Irish perspective, another interesting feature of the approach adopted by the ECJ in *Feryn* is the court's emphasis on the requirement in Art. 15 of the Race Directive that the rules concerning sanctions applicable to breaches of national provisions adopted in order to transpose that Directive must be effective, proportionate and dissuasive, even where there is no identifiable victim. As Bolger and Kimber have recently observed, this emphasis in *Feryn* on the need for effective, proportionate and dissuasive remedies may cast an uncertain shadow over s.82(4) of the Employment Equality Act 1998 (as amended), which imposes an upper monetary limitation of the relatively low sum of €12,697.38 on the amount of compensation that may be awarded to an unsuccessful job applicant at the access or recruitment stage.[149] Accordingly, the potential impact of *Feryn* and its underlying rationale may well be still to be felt if and when this point is tested.

9. Membership of the Travelling Community

[9–104] Section 6(1)(i) of the 1998 Act provides that it shall be unlawful discrimination to treat a person less favourably than another person is, has been or would be treated where they are so treated because one is a member of the Travelling Community and the other is not.

---

147. At para.25.
148. At para.34.
149. Bolger and Kimber, 'Employment Equality', ch.13 in Regan, ed., *Employment Law* (Tottel Publishing, 2009), at p.486.

9.1. Definition

The 1998 Act did not define the term 'Travelling Community', but it is now   [9–105]
defined under s.2 of the Equal Status Act 2000 as meaning 'the community of
people commonly called Travellers and who are identified (both by themselves
and others) as people with a shared history, culture and traditions including,
historically, a nomadic way of life on the island of Ireland'.

In *Nevin v The Plaza Hotel*,[150] the complainant was a member of the Travelling   [9–106]
Community who, through contact with OBAIR, the local employment service
network, obtained a position with the respondent as an accommodation assistant.
After completing her first day's work the complainant was informed that the day
had been a 'trial day'. She was later told that there was no more work for her as room
numbers in the hotel were down and other staff were having their hours reduced.
There was no evidence in the advertisement for the position that it was subject to a
trial-day period and the complainant's placement officer was not aware of this fact
either. The respondent maintained that the complainant had not been retained as
her work performance was not satisfactory. The Equality Officer found that the
'trial day', which the respondent claimed applied to all new staff members without
hotel experience, was actually applied in a selective manner by the hotel and did
not apply to all staff without such experience. Furthermore, the Equality Officer
did not accept the respondent's contention that the complainant's work was unsatisfactory, particularly in light of the fact that the she had subsequently obtained
employment with another hotel and the housekeeping manager of that hotel was
satisfied with her work. However, these facts, unfair though they were, were not
enough by themselves to make a finding that the complainant was the subject of
unlawful discrimination. Crucially, however, the Equality Officer did find that a
comment made by a supervisor working for the respondent to the complainant's
placement officer to the effect that she 'did not have the same concept of cleaning
as other employees would have, but how could she be expected, given the way
they live?' taken together with the events that preceded them was prima facie
evidence of discrimination, which the respondent failed to rebut.

Similarly, in *Sweeney v McHale Ltd.*,[151] evidence of discriminatory statements   [9–107]
proved determinative. In that case, the complainant had responded to an advertisement looking for saw-mill workers in the Sligo area. The complainant sent his
CV to the recruitment agency appointed by the respondent. Some time later, the
complainant enquired about his application with the employment agency and
was told that the respondent had remarked that the complainant was 'one of the
Sweeney's from Sligo' and was not acceptable for work with the saw mill. The
Equality Officer held that the complainant had been turned down for the position
simply on the basis that he was a member of the Travelling Community.

---

150. DEC-E2001-033, 07 November 2001.
151. DEC-E2003-050, 11 November 2003.

[9–108]   In *Stokes v The Irish Soccer Referees' Society*,[152] the complainant applied to transfer from the Longford branch of the Irish Soccer Referees' Society to the Roscommon branch. His request was refused. The complainant had made his application for a transfer in line with the Constitution of the Society and contended that his refusal by the respondent was based on his membership of the Travelling Community. The respondent claimed that the rejection of his transfer was based on the fact that the complainant's reason for leaving the Longford branch was contradicted by information provided by members of that branch when they sought to verify the matter. The Equality Officer held that if the reason for wanting to leave one branch is relevant when seeking transfer to another, then that should be clearly set out in advance and communicated to applicants. The Equality Officer also found that a local newspaper had reported that at a recent AGM, officials of the Roscommon branch had referred to the shortage of referees and said that five or six more referees were needed for the new season. Based on these facts the Equality Officer concluded that the complainant had established a prima facie case of discrimination on the grounds of membership of the Travelling Community.

---

152. DEC-E2007-033.

CHAPTER 10

Harassment and Victimisation

Introduction

As we have seen, various employment law statutes considered in other chapters in this book prohibit victimisation and harassment of employees who seek to assert their rights under legislation. In this chapter, however, we consider the concept of victimisation and harassment *per se*. The approach of the law has been to take the view that *as a matter of employment equality*, every employee is entitled to carry out his or her duties in an environment free from unwanted behaviour from others that can be considered to be an affront to one's dignity. Thus the Employment Equality Act 1998 provided explicitly for the first time that where an employee is harassed or victimised either in a sexual manner or on the basis of any of the other discriminatory grounds listed under s.6 this shall amount to unlawful discrimination. [10–01]

In this chapter we consider first the concept of *sexual* harassment; secondly, the concept of harassment of a non-sexual kind; and thirdly, the concept of victimisation focusing on the nature of the offence and the various defences that may be raised by an employer accused of such offences.

1. Sexual Harassment

Sexual harassment was first placed on a statutory footing under Irish law by s.23 of the Employment Equality Act 1998. Section 23 was repealed by s.14 of the Equality Act 2004, which replaces s.23 with a new section, 14A, which enhances the previous statutory position and deals comprehensively with this area.[1] [10–02]

Section 14A(1) of the Equality Act 2004 provides that sexual harassment will constitute discrimination by the victim's employer in relation to the victim's conditions of employment. Therefore, acts of sexual harassment are of themselves inherently discriminatory. Thus in order to succeed in a claim it is not necessary [10–03]

---

1. Art.2(1)(c) of Council Directive 2006/54/EC (the Recast Equal Treatment Directive) provided the following definition of sexual harassment: 'where unwanted conduct related to the sex of a person occurs with the purpose or effect of violating the dignity of a person, and of creating an intimidating, hostile, degrading, humiliating or offensive environment'.

for the victim, in addition to proving that the act of sexual harassment occurred, to establish that [s]he was treated less favourably than a comparator in accordance with the gender ground,[2] nor is it a defence to a sexual harassment claim for the employer to show that both men and women in his or her workplace were equally subjected to such behaviour.[3] This is significant in that, as we shall see, in order for a claim for harassment other than sexual harassment to be made out, it *is* necessary to show that one is being singled out on the basis of one of the listed grounds.[4]

[10–04] Section 14A(1)(a) provides that harassment or sexual harassment can occur where:

> an employee (in this section referred to as 'the victim') is harassed or sexually harassed either at a place where the employee is employed (in this section referred to as 'the workplace') or otherwise in the course of his or her employment by a person who is–
> (i) employed at that place or by the same employer,
> (ii) the victim's employer, or
> (iii) a client, customer or other business contact of the victim's employer and the circumstances of the harassment are such that the employer ought reasonably have taken steps to prevent it,

[10–05] An employer therefore may be made liable for acts of sexual harassment that are perpetrated by one of his or her employees, by the employer himself or herself or, in certain circumstances, by a client, customer or other business contact of the victim's employer. The extent of the employer's liability in this regard was evident in *Atkinson v Carty*.[5] In that case, the plaintiff was employed as a legal accountant by the defendant. The plaintiff worked closely with the managing partner and an independent contractor who provided accountancy services to the defendant. The plaintiff claimed that the independent contractor made unwanted sexual advances to her throughout the 1990s, culminating with the plaintiff making a written complaint in 2000 in response to the harassment. The plaintiff claimed that she had not made a complaint before then to the managing partner (who she claimed had bullied her) because of his close personal relationship with the independent contractor. An investigation into the plaintiff's complaint against the independent contractor was initiated by the managing partner. The plaintiff claimed that this investigation was tainted as the managing partner was investigating a complaint

---

2. s.14A(1)(a) of the Employment Equality Act 1998.
3. See, for example, *Stewart v Cleveland Guest (Engineering) Ltd.* [1996] ICR 535. In that case, it was held that a female employee had not been sexually harassed when she claimed that her employer had failed to act when she complained about nude pin-ups in the workplace. The tribunal held that no discrimination had taken place on the basis that a man could have equally found the posters to be offensive.
4. s.14(a)(7)(i) of the 1998 Act provides that such harassment refers to any form of unwanted conduct related to those discriminatory grounds, which has the purpose or effect of violating a person's dignity and creating an intimidating or hostile environment for the person.
5. [2005] ELR 1.

against his friend. The Circuit Court held that the plaintiff had been sexually harassed by the independent contractor and that the managing partner was liable for failing in his legal obligations towards her in this regard. However, because she did not make a complaint until 2000, Delahunt J was of the view that the plaintiff was guilty of contributory negligence and reduced her award by 25 per cent.

According to s.14A(4) of the Employment Equality Act 2004, the reference in [10–06] s.14A(1)(a) to the employer's client, customer or other business contact includes any other person with whom the employer might reasonably expect the victim to come into contact in the workplace or otherwise in the course of his or her employment. In *Ms BH v A Named Company t/a A Cab Company, Dublin*,[6] the complainant worked in the base office of a cab company. She alleged that she had been sexually harassed following a number of incidents including *inter alia* the placing of laxative tablets and steroids in the office kettle used by, amongst others, the complainant, which she claimed had been the result of a prank by the cab drivers who worked from the office. In finding that acts of sexual harassment had occurred and had been committed by a relevant person, the Director of the Equality Tribunal stated that:

> The respondent's representative did not put forward any evidence as to whether the cab drivers were employed by the respondent company or whether they were self-employed. However, they clearly come within the scope of the Act, either as employees or as business contacts with whom the employer might reasonably expect the complainant to come into contact in the workplace or otherwise in the course of her employment …

In *Ms A v A Contract Cleaning Company*,[7] the complainant was employed as a [10–07] cleaner for the respondent company and was assigned to cleaning duties at a shopping centre. The alleged harasser (Mr B) was a security guard at the shopping centre and was employed by a separate security company. The complainant alleged that during the course of his work, Mr B had made a number of crude and sexually offensive remarks and had also slapped her bottom. The complainant proceeded to bring a claim of discrimination against her employer because of Mr B's actions. The Equality Officer held that Mr B was someone with whom the complainant's employer might reasonably expect the complainant to come into contact in the workplace. Both the complainant and Mr B had worked in the shopping centre for a number of months and came into contact with each other on a frequent basis during their work, and the complainant's supervisor was aware of the close proximity in which she worked with Mr B. Consequently, the conduct of Mr B was found to amount to sexual harassment and thus her employer was found to have discriminated against her.

---

6. DEC-E2006-026, 9 June 2006.
7. DEC-E2004-068, 29 November 2004.

1.1. Unacceptable Types of Conduct

[10–08] A comprehensive description of the types of conduct that will be deemed unacceptable is provided under s.14A(7), which states that:

> (i) references to harassment are to any form of unwanted conduct related to any of the discriminatory grounds, and
> (ii) references to sexual harassment are to any form of unwanted verbal, non-verbal or physical conduct of a sexual nature,
> being conduct which in either case has the purpose or effect of violating a person's dignity and creating an intimidating, hostile, degrading, humiliating or offensive environment for the person.
> (b) … such unwanted conduct may consist of acts, requests, spoken words, gestures or the production, display or circulation of written words, pictures or other material.

[10–09] Unlike the definition provided under s.23(3) of the Employment Equality Act 1998, the definition from the 2004 Act is not inextricably linked to the gender ground of discrimination. The definition under s.23(3) of the 1998 Act had been criticised on the basis that the victim and harasser had to be of different sexes, thereby prohibiting a claim of same-sex harassment.[8] The definition in s.14A(7)(a)(i), however, now simply provides that sexual harassment will have occurred where the victim is subjected to any form of unwanted verbal, non-verbal or physical conduct of a sexual nature. As a consequence, an employee could now be found liable for sexual harassment by making unwanted overtures to another employee of the same sex. Bolger and Kimber had previously noted that an amendment to the 1998 Act of this kind would be welcomed observing that:

> A person who has been sexually harassed by a person of the same sex has not necessarily been harassed on grounds of their sexual orientation. In addition, sexual harassment is wider than simply *quid pro quo* harassment where a person is repeatedly requested to provide sexual favours, it also includes sexual harassment that creates detriment in the workplace for an employee who has rejected certain conduct. There is no reason why a person could not be subjected to sexual harassment of that nature without any suggestion of desired homosexual conduct.[9]

1.2. The Subjective Evaluation of whether Behaviour Constitutes Sexual Harassment

[10–10] Sexual harassment is defined under s.14A(7)(ii) as any form of *unwanted* conduct of a sexual nature. Consequently, if the conduct is flirtatious and reciprocated it cannot constitute sexual harassment under the Act. Whether the conduct is unwanted can only be answered by the person subjected to that conduct. Thus the

---

8. *A Male Employee v A Government Department*, DEC-E2002-024, 16 May 2002. See also Bolger and Kimber, *Sex Discrimination Law* (Round Hall Sweet and Maxwell, 2000), at pp.269–270.
9. *ibid.*, at p.270.

new provision represents a change from the former approach under s.23(3) of the 1998 Act, whereby actions by another could not ground a claim unless 'the request or conduct is unwelcome... and could *reasonably* [emphasis added] be regarded as sexually, or otherwise on the gender ground, offensive or intimidating...'. Now all that must be shown as far as objective indicia are concerned is that the unwanted behaviour 'has the purpose or effect of violating a person's dignity and creating an intimidating, hostile, degrading, humiliating or offensive environment for the person'.[10] In essence, then, the removal of this element of objectivity means that a person could be guilty of sexual harassment of another, whether or not the conduct was intended as such.

The earlier and more objective approach under the 1998 Act was applied in *A*   [10–11] *Company v A Worker*,[11] where the employee was, amongst other things, subjected to unwelcome touching of her shoulders by another employee and had also objected to the display of an offensive calendar. The respondent countered that the employee had overreacted and that such behaviour towards her was simply part of the 'easy' atmosphere of the workplace. In assessing whether or not the behaviour constituted sexual harassment it was held that:

> the worker must establish either directly or on the balance of probabilities that the alleged conduct took place, that it was offensive to and unwanted by her, and that the alleged perpetrators knew or could reasonably have been expected to know that it was offensive and unwanted.

The fact that the complainant did not complain at the time of the incident does not   [10–12] necessarily mean that a finding of sexual harassment cannot be made.[12] In *Moonsar v Fiveways Express Transport Ltd.*,[13] the claimant worked for the respondent on an evening basis with three male colleagues who downloaded pornographic images in the room where they were working. While the claimant was in close proximity to those who downloaded the pornography, she did not view the images, nor were they circulated to her. She did not complain about the behaviour at the time because she needed the job and decided to 'keep her head down'. The claimant successfully argued before the United Kingdom Employment Appeals Tribunal that she had established a *prima facie* case of discrimination. The tribunal held that, while she may not have been shown the images, her colleagues' behaviour was capable of affronting her dignity and also held that the claimant did find the behaviour to be unacceptable and the fact that she did not complain at the time of the behaviour was not necessarily fatal to her claim.

Sexual harassment can manifest itself through acts; requests; spoken words; gestures;   [10–13] or the production, display or circulation of written words, pictures or other

---

10. s.14(7)(a)(ii) 2004 Act.
11. [1992] ELR 73.
12. *Driskel v Pennisula Business Services Ltd.* [2000] IRLR 151.
13. [2005] IRLR 9.

material.[14] Thus the display of an offensive calendar,[15] a slap on the bottom,[16] the sending of text messages of a sexual nature,[17] and masturbatory gestures[18] have all been deemed to constitute acts of sexual harassment.

Furthermore, s.14(7) of the 2004 Act refers to unwanted conduct that has the purpose or effect of violating a person's dignity. Thus the conduct need not be deliberate but could also be the unintended consequence of the perpetrator's actions.

1.3. Burden of Proof

[10–14] The burden of proof in sexual harassment and/or harassment cases rests with the complainant.[19] The complainant must prove facts from which it can be inferred that [s]he suffered discriminatory treatment.[20] Where the complainant successfully raises the presumption the burden of proof shifts to the respondent to rebut that presumption. In *G v An Employer*,[21] the complainant worked as a quality assurance manager in a poultry factory for the respondent. She claimed that she had been sexually harassed, alleging that a male colleague (Mr A) touched her inappropriately as he passed her while she was inspecting carcasses on the killing line. Two witnesses attended the hearing. The first did not notice that anything untoward had occurred on the day in question. The second witness stated that Mr A had passed in front of the complainant and also noted that the complainant was crying and visibly upset that day. Mr A's statement was to the effect that he had passed behind the complainant and he placed his hand on her shoulder, in an effort to facilitate his getting past her. A Mr D, who was also present on the day, stated that he noticed that Mr A touched the complainant on the shoulder and waist. The Equality Officer noted from the evidence that the workplace was such that there was a continuous stream of poultry carcasses suspended on hooks moving along a production line at eye level directly in front of the area where the complainant had stood. In the Equality Officer's view it was extremely unlikely that Mr A would have passed in front of the complainant in these circumstances. He therefore found that:

> Having regard to the totality of the evidence presented on this issue I am satisfied, on balance, that the incident occurred as described by the complainant, i.e. that Mr A

---

14. s.14A(b) of the Employment Equality Act 1998.
15. *A Company v A Worker* [1992] ELR 73.
16. *Ms A v A Gym*, DEC-E2004-011, 1 March 2004.
17. *Ms CL v CRM*, DEC-E2004-027, 17 May 2004.
18. *A Complainant v A Financial Institution*, DEC-E2003-053, 20 November 2003.
19. s.38 Equality Act 2004.
20. Where the alleged harasser is the dominant party in the employment relationship (for example where [s]he is a manager or employer of the victim), the very nature of the relationship can be used as corroborating evidence that the behaviour was unwanted and amounted to harassment: *A Company v A Worker* [1992] ELR 73.
21. DEC-E2005-048, 11 October 2005.

touched her in an intimate and inappropriate manner as he passed her and that this behaviour constitutes a *prima facie* case of sexual harassment of the complainant

The Equality Officer weighed the factual evidence and concluded that there was *prima facie* evidence that the complainant was sexually harassed and held that the respondent had failed to rebut this finding.

The fact that there has been a history of flirtatious behaviour between the complainant and the respondent does not prevent the complainant from putting an end to the behaviour if [s]he so wishes. A claim of sexual harassment may thus be brought where the comparator has expressed a wish that formerly acceptable behaviour be discontinued and that request is ignored. In *A Company v A Worker,*[22] it was held that: [10–15]

> A sexual relationship between consenting adults does not imply that that consent is unlimited as regards either time-scale or acts which may take place between the parties. Each party has a continuing right to place limitations on what acts may take place and when they may take place, and also a right to withdraw consent totally.

1.4. Vicarious Liability

As we have seen, under equality legislation an employer may be found to be *directly* liable, for failing to prevent a situation in which sexual harassment occurs. In addition, however, s.15(1) of the Employment Equality Act 1998 provides that anything done by a person in the course of his or her employment shall, in relation to breaches of the Act, be treated under the Act as done also by that person's employer, irrespective of whether or not it was done with his or her knowledge or approval. Furthermore, s.15(2) provides that anything done by a person as an agent for another or with the authority of that other person, whether express or implied, shall be considered as done by that other person. [10–16]

Under the common law, the question as to whether or not an employer was liable for the tortious wrongdoing of his employees was determined by one of two tests: the *course* of employment test or the *scope* of employment test.[23] The scope test focuses on the expressed or implied authority of the employee to do the acts complained of.[24] With its emphasis on whether the employee had the relevant authority to do the acts complained of, the scope test was rather limited in its application, particularly in cases where the employee had committed an intentional wrong. The course of employment test, on the other hand, provides that if the act done is something that can be considered to be part of the job or is reasonably incidental to it, then it will be considered to be within the course of [10–17]

---

22. [1990] E.L.R. 187.
23. For more detailed discussion, see Chapter 3.
24. *Farry v GN Rly Co.* [1898] 2 IR 352; and which is reflected in s.15(2) of the 1998 Act.

employment, regardless of whether the employee was authorised to do it.[25] Thus the course of employment test leaves greater room for the imposition of liability on an employer for the intentional wrongs of an employee – such as sexual harassment – provided there exists a sufficiency of connection between the employee's actions and his or her work and in determining the existence of such a connection, much emphasis may be placed on the foreseeability of the employee's actions.[26]

[10–18] By their very nature it might seem that cases of sexual harassment or assault could never be considered to be committed by an employee in the scope/course of his or her employment. In *Health Board v BC*,[27] a decision reached prior to the enactment of s.15(1), the complainant was subjected to lewd and coarse remarks from two male colleagues who worked with her. They touched her without her consent and at one stage indecently assaulted her. Costello J of the High Court held that, in the absence of clear legislation to the contrary, employers could only be held liable for such conduct where it was committed by the employee acting in the course of his or her employment. In the circumstances, such was the seriousness of the assault the court found that it could in no way be considered to be connected with the work. Consequently, the employer was not liable for the actions of the employees who perpetrated the assault.

[10–19] However, in more recent years courts in other jurisdictions have been more willing to find that intentional wrongs committed by an employee (such as sexual assault) can render the employer liable at common law. In *Bazley v Curry*,[28] the Supreme Court of Canada addressed the issue from a 'policy' viewpoint. The court stated the following factors as being relevant:

(1) Ask the straightforward question – should liability lie against the employer?
(2) Is the wrongful act sufficiently related to conduct authorised by the employer? It is fair that an employer be made pay the generally foreseeable costs of running a business.
(3) In seeking to determine how foreseeable the wrongful act of the employee was the courts should take into consideration the following:
  (a) the opportunity that the enterprise afforded the employee to abuse his or her power
  (b) the extent to which the wrongful act may have furthered the employer's aims
  (c) the extent to which the wrongful act was related to the friction, confrontation or intimacy inherent in the employer's enterprise
  (d) the extent of power conferred on the employee in relation to the victim
  (e) the vulnerability of potential victims to wrongful exercise of the employee's power.[29]

25. As reflected in s.15(1) of the 1998 Act. For further detailed discussion see Chapter 3.
26. *Bazley v Curry* (1999) 174 DLR (4th) 45.
27. [1994] ELR 27.
28. (1999) 174 DLR (4th) 45. See also the House of Lords decision in *Lister v Hesley Hall Ltd.* [2002] 1 AC 215, [2001] 2 WLR 1311, [2001] 2 All ER 769, [2001] ICR 655, [2001] IRLR 472.
29. (1999) 174 D.L.R. (4th) 45 at 65.

The approach adopted by the Canadian Supreme Court in *Bazley* towards vicarious   [10–20]
liability and intentional wrongs committed by employees was heavily criticised by
Hardiman J in the Supreme Court decision of *O'Keeffe v Hickey & Others*.[30] In
that case, the appellant had been sexually abused by her school teacher while
he had been providing her with music lessons during her play-break or in the
afternoons after school.[31] The appellant argued that the Department of Education
should be held vicariously liable for the teacher's actions. The majority rejected
the appellant's claim. In refusing to find the respondent vicariously liable for the
teacher's actions, Hardiman J heavily criticised the 'close connection' test as it had
been developed from the Salmond test.[32] He stated:

> Properly understood, there is no rational connection between this formulation and
> the Canadian one of 'close connection', or a ground of vicarious liability, except
> that the word 'connection' is used in both. But Professor Salmond's 'explanation'
> as Lord Steyn regards it requires that the close connection be with acts which the
> employer has authorised and be such that what is actually done can be regarded as a
> mode, though an improper and unauthorised one, of doing what the employer has
> authorised. At the very least, the Canadian Supreme Court wholly dispensed with
> the second part of this test, requiring that what was in fact done must be a mode
> of doing what was authorised. The importance of the subject matter compels me
> to repeat, at the risk of tedium, that I cannot see anywhere in Professor Salmond's
> treatment of this subject the smallest 'germ' of what the Canadian Supreme Court
> did almost a century after Professor Salmond had first propounded his test.[33]

Notwithstanding the decision in *O'Keeffe*, it is submitted that the courts and   [10–21]
tribunal will continue to take a pragmatic approach towards the issue of vicarious liability and sexual harassment under the equality legislation and if there is
a sufficiency of connection between the employee's work and the harassment, the
employer will be made vicariously liable for the harasser's actions. Such a sufficiency of connection was held not to exist in *Ms O'N v An Insurance Company*[34]
where the complainant alleged that she had her breast violently groped by a work
colleague (Mr C) while in a nightclub with the social club from her work. In
considering whether the complainant's attendance at the nightclub as part of the
social club meant that she was acting within the course of her employment at the
time of the harassment, the Equality Officer concluded that:

> The respondent did not dispute that the Social Club was mentioned to the
> complainant at her induction training. However, there is no compulsion on
> anyone to join the Club and I note that approximately less than one third of the

---

30. [2008] IESC 72, [2009] 1 ILRM 490.
31. For more detailed discussion of this case, see Chapter 3.
32. *ibid.*
33. [2009] 1 ILRM 490, 521.
34. DEC-E2004-052, 1 September 2004.

employees are members. The Social Club was not set up by the respondent and has no connection with it other than its membership comprises employees of the respondent and it provides funding to it. Whilst it is not in question that the respondent provides considerable sponsorship to the Social Club, I do not consider that financial sponsorship by an employer at a social event where sexual harassment occurs is sufficient in itself and in the absence of other factors to bring an act of sexual harassment within the course of employment of a potential complainant. The complainant was employed as a Call Centre Agent in the Customer Desk Department of the respondent. The complainant did not attend the night club for the purposes of or in furtherance of her work and I therefore find that she was not sexually harassed in the course of her employment.

[10–22] When seeking to establish that the perpetrator had been acting in the course of his or her employment the foreseeability of the perpetrator's actions are likely to be crucial.[35] For example, if the perpetrator is placed in a position of manage-rial/supervisory control over the victim, then it will be readily foreseeable that such power or control could be abused if not checked. In *A Female Employee v Three Named Respondents*,[36] the claimant was taking a shower in the ladies' locker room after visiting the gym during her lunch break. A bag filled with cold water was thrown on top of her while she was in the shower. The shock caused her to turn round and as a result she found herself standing nude facing a male work colleague, who was laughing at her. In holding that the respondent was not liable, the Equality Officer concluded that:

> I cannot find that the act perpetrated against the claimant was in any way connected with the male employee's employment nor can I find, as he had no supervisory or responsibility over her, that it was improper exercise of managerial control over her.

[10–23] Similarly, in *Two Named Female Teachers and the Equality Authority v Board of Management and Principal of a Boys' Secondary School*,[37] the complainants were two female teachers in a boys' secondary school. They had alleged that they had been subjected to verbal and physical harassment of a sexual nature by the pupils. In finding that the Board of Management of the school were vicariously liable for the actions of the pupils, the Equality Officer laid great emphasis on the element of control exercised by the Board over the behaviour of the pupils:

> The perpetrators of the offending acts are not employees but pupils at the School, persons over whom the School has authority while they are engaged in School

---

35. For example, where an employer fails to adopt a sexual harassment policy or otherwise fails to adopt other preventative measures, the subsequent occurrence of harassment will be deemed to have been foreseeable and it will be more likely that the employer will be made vicariously liable for such acts – *A Male Employee v A Government Department*, DEC-E2002-024, 16 May 2002. See also *Persaud v The Shelbourne Hotel*, DEC-E2004-075, 20 December 2004.
36. EE-1997-04, 13 March 1997.
37. DEC-E2001-005, 25 January 2001.

activities, whether on the School premises or elsewhere. The acts complained of are acts of gross misbehaviour by adolescent pupils directed at female teachers which, if uncorrected, would in all likelihood continue, causing continued distress to female teachers. The board of management is clearly responsible for the disciplinary and working environment at the school and it is therefore in a position to exercise control over such behaviour.

However, under s.23(2) of the 1998 Act, where an act of harassment has occurred [10–24] *and* the complainant is treated differently in the workplace, or it could be reasonably anticipated [s]he would be so treated, then regardless of whether the act occurred during the course of the complainant's employment the employer will be guilty of discrimination. In *Ms O'N v An Insurance Company*,[38] Mr C had admitted that he had acted inappropriately towards the complainant. Following the incident, another work colleague asked the perpetrator to leave the complainant alone and then asked him to leave the night club. The complainant made an informal complaint to management upon her return to work and the matter was dealt with in accordance with the respondent's procedures on bullying and harassment. The Equality Officer held, on balance, that there was no evidence that the complainant had been treated differently in the workplace as a result of her rejection of Mr C's conduct. The Equality Officer concluded:

> Taking into account the actions of the colleague in question and the actions of management, on the balance of probability, I do not consider that it could reasonably be anticipated that the complainant would be treated differently in the workplace or otherwise in the course of her employment by reason of her rejection of Mr. C's behaviour. I therefore find that the sexual harassment does not constitute discrimination by the complainant's employer on the gender ground in relation to her conditions of employment…

2. Harassment Other Than Sexual Harassment

In addition to acts of sexual harassment, the Employment Equality Acts prohibit [10–25] all other forms of harassment connected to any of the discriminatory grounds listed under s.6 of the 1998 Act. Section 14(1)(a) of the 2004 Act provides that such harassment can occur at the employee's workplace or otherwise in the course of his or her employment. Like claims of sexual harassment, harassment may be committed by a person who is employed at that place or by the same employer, by the victim's employer, or a client, customer or other business contact of the victim's employer.

An employer will be liable for acts of harassment that have been committed [10–26] during the course of the perpetrator's employment. In *Maguire v North Eastern*

---

38. DEC-E2004-052, 1 September 2004.

Health Board,[39] the male complainant had attended the office Christmas party where a female co-worker invited other members of staff back to her house but added, referring to the complainant, 'the knacker's not coming'. The complainant reported the incident to his supervisor on his return to work. Nothing was done to resolve the situation. The respondent contended that the incident had occurred outside the course of employment and therefore it was not vicariously liable. The Equality Officer held that attendance at the Christmas party was sufficiently connected to the complainant's work and that the harassment by the employee consequently occurred during the course of employment. Moreover, the principles of vicarious liability discussed above in the context of sexual harassment apply equally to situations of non-sexual harassment.

2.1. Types of Conduct that amount to Harassment

[10–27] We have previously considered the types of conduct which, according to the legislation, can amount to sexual harassment. In a similar vein, the 1998 Act (as amended) provides a comprehensive definition of the types of conduct that will amount to non-sexual harassment. Section 14A(7)(i) of the 1998 Act provides that references to harassment in the Act relates to any form of unwanted conduct related to any of the discriminatory grounds that 'has the purpose or effect of violating a person's dignity and creating an intimidating, hostile, degrading, humiliating or offensive environment for the person'. Unlike sexual harassment (which, as we have seen, is a stand-alone form of discrimination) claims for other forms of harassment must be related to one of the nine discriminatory grounds listed in the Act. In other words, an act of harassment is only impugned under the legislation where the harassed employee is targeted because of one of the discriminatory grounds, and on this basis is being treated less favourably than another employee to whom that ground or grounds do not apply.

[10–28] Section 14A(7)(b) provides that such unwanted conduct 'may consist of acts, requests, spoken words, gestures or the production, display or circulation of written words, pictures or other material'. For example, in *A Complainant v A Company,*[40] persistent public ridicule of the complainant as being 'only a young fooling girl' amounted to harassment on the age and gender grounds and in *Ganusauskas, Zembrzowski and Guaizdauskas v All Purpose Stone Limited,*[41] it was held that references to two of the complainants as 'You f**king Pole!' and 'You stupid Russian!' amounted to harassment on the grounds of their nationality where both were Lithuanian nationals.

---

39. DEC-E2002-014.
40. DEC-E2002-014.
41. DEC-E2009-063.

Similarly, a successful claim of harassment related to the age ground is seen [10–29] in the determination of the Equality Tribunal in *Fortune v CARI*.[42] There the complainant began working as a psychotherapist with the respondent organisation in May 2004. She was instructed to work with an older colleague, Ms A, who from an early stage would regularly comment on the complainant's lack of client experience, lack of years of clinical practice and clinical hours prior to accreditation and general life experience. Ms A also stated that, in her opinion, entrants onto psychotherapy training courses should be at least over 30 years of age to ensure graduates had the necessary life experience, and that she had previously known a young therapist who was unable to cope with her case-load due to a lack of life experience and subsequently killed herself. The complainant, who was in her twenties at the time, understood this to be a criticism of her own age and experience: in evidence, she stated that when Ms A made that particular statement, she had looked directly at the complainant. Ms A occasionally embarrassed the complainant in front of clients, by referring to her as a 'little girl', or emphasising her own parental status in meetings with parents, in the presence of the complainant, by making statements like: 'As a parent, I understand.' The complainant stated that she felt undermined by these statements, and it was her contention that it was Ms A's intent to make her feel undermined. Based on this evidence, the Equality Officer was satisfied that the complainant had established a prima facie case of harassment on the ground of age. He explained:

> Ms A.'s constant references to 'life experience' and the connection she made in her statements to the complainant that trainee therapists should be over 30 years of age to ensure sufficient life experience make it clear that Ms A. took issue with the complainant's relative youth. I also find that being called 'little girl' in front of clients was indeed humiliating and undermined the complainant's dignity. I am satisfied that these statements had the effect of violating the complainant's dignity in the workplace and created a hostile environment in her working relationship with Ms A.

In *Valaithan v Martin Quigley (Nenagh) Ltd. t/a Quigley's Cafe & Bakery*,[43] the [10–30] complainant alleged that she had been the subject of harassment connected to her race. In that case, the complainant, who was from Malaysia, alleged that her supervisor constantly referred to her as 'blackie' and had made a number of other derogatory comments about the race of the complainant and her partner. After the complainant made a complaint about the supervisor's behaviour, she found that her hours were cut. A trade union representative contacted the respondent regarding the supervisor's treatment of the complainant. Soon after the complainant was issued with a disciplinary warning regarding her work performance. The complainant left the employment to study. The trade union representative met with the respondent, who refused to provide a statement in relation to the complaint as the complainant

---

42. Equality Tribunal, DEC-E2009-052, June 2009.
43. DEC-E2009-50, 19 June 2009.

had left the employment and had lodged a claim of discrimination. The respondent admitted that there had been banter between staff referring to the complainant's colour but said that such banter was meant as fun and the complainant had called her 'whitie' in response. The Equality Officer found that the comments made reference to her race and amounted to harassment, and it was not acceptable to say that such comments were made in fun. Furthermore, the respondent failed to take reasonable and practicable steps in dealing with harassment by the inadequate investigation by the respondent of the matter.[44]

3. Employer's Defence to Harassment Claims

[10–31] Where an employee has been the victim of sexual harassment and/or harassment occurring in the workplace or during the course of his or her employment, the employer may defend any such claim by pleading that [s]he had taken all reasonably practicable steps in dealing with the situation. Section 14A(2)(1)(a) of the 1998 Act as amended by the 2004 Act provides that where the sexual harassment occurs in the workplace or otherwise in the course of employment[45] the employer is obliged to take reasonably practicable steps to *prevent* the perpetrator from harassing or sexually harassing the victim. In circumstances where the employee has been harassed and is subsequently treated differently,[46] or it could reasonably anticipated that [s]he would be treated differently in the workplace, the employer must take reasonably practicable steps to prevent the victim from being treated so differently and, if and so far as any such treatment has occurred, *to reverse its effects*.[47]

[10–32] The term 'reasonably practicable steps' has not been defined in the legislation. However, the Labour Court and Equality Officers have put particular emphasis (in assessing whether 'reasonably practicable steps' have been taken) on whether adequate harassment policies were in place.[48] A failure to adopt or implement such policies has invariably been viewed as a failure to take 'reasonably practicable steps' and will more often than not render an employer vicariously liable for the actions of the perpetrator. In this regard, the temporal sequence of events is always highly significant: it has been emphasised that bringing in a policy in response to the situation that gave rise to the objectionable treatment cannot be interpreted as taking reasonably practicable steps to prevent situations of harassment from

---

44. Similarly, reference to another employee as a 'knacker' amounted to harassment on the membership of the Travelling Community ground in *Maguire v North Eastern Health Board* DEC-E2002-039, 22 August 2002.
45. In accordance with the definition of harassment provided in s.14A(1)(b) Employment Equality Act 1998, as amended by the 2004 Act.
46. *ibid.*
47. s.15(3) provides a more general defence to any breaches of the Act and requires the employer to take all reasonably practicable steps to prevent the employee from doing the relevant act or from doing in the course of his or her employment acts of that description.
48. *A Female Employee v A Candle Production Company*, DEC-E2006-035.

arising.[49] Thus the policy must be in place and communicated to all employees prior to the date that the act(s) of harassment complained of had occurred.[50]

In *Two Named Female Teachers and the Equality Authority v Board of Management* [10–33] *and Principal of a Boys' Secondary School*,[51] the claimants, female schoolteachers in an all boys' school, had alleged that on various occasions they had been subjected to sexual harassment of a physical, verbal and written nature by pupils of the school. On one such occasion a lewd and sexually suggestive note was placed on the back of one of the claimants while she was teaching in class. On another occasion one of the other claimants had suffered sexual harassment when she had been subjected to whistling and name calling of a sexually offensive nature by pupils. The claimants had alleged that the respondent had not taken reasonably practicable steps to deal with the actions of the students and consequently it was alleged that this inaction had helped to create an atmosphere in which such behavior was tolerated. The respondent rejected the claimants' allegations and pointed out that complaints of sexual harassment by the claimants had on two occasions resulted in pupils transferring to other schools, one incident involved a pupil being suspended for five weeks while another pupil was suspended for two weeks. Consequently, the Equality Officer was satisfied that the disciplinary action taken by the respondent against the perpetrators was what might reasonably be expected in the circumstances.

The Equality Authority alleged that the respondent's failure to adopt a Code [10–34] of Practice, policy statement or guidelines on sexual harassment amounted to a failure to adopt reasonably practicable steps to prevent the harassment. The Equality Officer found, however, that prior to the events that led to the claim the principal of the school had set in motion a number of initiatives to develop such policies. The principal had set up a sub-committee to review all aspects of discipline (including sexual harassment) and had also arranged a one-day seminar on sexual harassment, which was delivered by a recognised expert. Following this seminar, work had commenced on the drafting of a policy document on sexual harassment. The Equality Officer concluded that:

> Complaints of sexual harassment were dealt with as disciplinary matters coming within the scope of the School's disciplinary procedures and while the School had not implemented any new preventative policy or additional guidelines targeting sexual harassment up to the time of the first referral to the Labour Court by the First Named Claimant in April, 1998, I do not consider the absence of such a policy in itself to be adequate grounds for a finding of discrimination against the School. The Union and the Authority have challenged the adequacy of the School's

49. See the comments of the Equality Officer in this regard in *Fortune v CARI*, DEC-E2009-052, June 2009.
50. *An Employer v An Employee*, determination no. EDA0916.
51. DEC-E2001-005, 25 January 2001.

disciplinary code to deal with complaints of sexual harassment however I am satisfied that on balance, the School has taken all reasonably practicable steps in relation to complaints of sexual harassment and the implementation of a policy of education and prevention.

[10–35] The importance of internal grievance procedures was also highlighted in *Ms A v A Gym*.[52] In that case, the complainant worked as a receptionist for the respondent. Mr B, a fellow employee, allegedly made a number of sexually suggestive comments to the complainant about her appearance. One evening while in the office, the complainant alleged that as she walked past Mr B he gave her a 'robust slap' on her bottom. The complainant alleged that this occurred in the presence of another employee, Mr C. The complainant reported the incident to her manager, who appeared unsure as to what to do. Following the complaint, the manager contacted the complainant and said that Mr B denied any sexual harassment but that he had offered to apologise for any offence he may have caused. The complainant told her manager that she did not feel that it would be appropriate for Mr B to contact her directly and that she would prefer if company disciplinary procedures were followed in relation to the matter. The manager then informed the complainant that as Mr B had denied the incident, there was nothing more she could do. However, she did offer to place the complainant on alternate shifts to Mr B. The Equality Officer concluded that, on balance, the incident of sexual harassment had occurred as the complainant described it. In assessing whether the respondent had taken reasonably practicable steps in response to the claim, the Equality Officer observed:

> that the Manager did not know how to deal with an allegation of sexual harassment. There was no internal grievance procedure or code of practice on the matter, and the respondent had not introduced any procedures to comply with its responsibilities under the Employment Equality Act, 1998. In the circumstances, I cannot find that the respondent took any such steps as were *reasonably practicable*, in the terms of section 23(5), to provide it with a defence to the finding of discrimination on the ground of gender, and is therefore vicariously liable for the sexual harassment in accordance with section 23(1).

[10–36] A failure to adopt procedures and policies on sexual harassment also proved crucial in *Ms CL v CRM*.[53] In that case, the complainant had, during the course of her employment, accepted a lift from her colleague, Mr A. The complainant alleged that while in his car she had been touched inappropriately by Mr A and that he later sent her sexually explicit text messages. When she reported these incidents to the respondent she was given a commitment that she would no longer have to travel with Mr A. The respondent claimed that these allegations were never put to Mr A because the complainant did not wish Mr A to be called into a meeting. The

---

52. DEC-E2004-011.
53. DEC-E2004-027.

complainant stated that she had no objection to Mr A being called to a meeting but not in her presence. The Equality Officer accepted that the complainant's position was not made clear to the respondent at the meeting. The complainant alleged that she had been informed by the respondent at this meeting that a set of rules on sexual harassment would be posted in the workplace. The respondent denied making this commitment. Soon after this meeting, the complainant received another sexually explicit text message from Mr A. The Equality Officer noted that, had the respondent put in place a sexual harassment policy, the respondent would have called Mr A to a disciplinary hearing, undertaken an investigation, informed Mr A of the allegations against him and allowed him the opportunity to respond. However, this was not done and as a consequence the respondent failed to set out steps that were reasonably practicable to prevent the incidents from occurring and the respondent did not take any steps to resolve the situation after the complainant had registered her complaint. In these circumstances the respondent was found liable for the sexual harassment of the complainant.

It is not sufficient for an employer just to have a harassment policy in place it must [10–37] also take reasonable steps to bring such a policy to the attention of the employees. In *Dublin Airport Authority, Shannon Airport (formerly Aer Rianta) v Khatimy*,[54] the complainant was employed by the respondent on a fixed term contract. The complainant claimed that he had been racially abused by a fellow worker. The complaint was investigated by the respondent pursuant to its 'Respect and Dignity at Work Policy'. Following the investigation, both employees were found to have breached the policy and both received verbal warnings. The respondent failed to renew the complainant's contract when it expired. The Labour Court found that neither employee involved in the investigation were aware of the respondent's policy on Respect and Dignity at Work. While commending the existence of such a policy, the court concluded that the respondent had not taken reasonably practicable steps to bring the contents of the policy to the attention of its employees. The court held that the complainant had been harassed on racial grounds and the respondent was found liable.

In conclusion, a coherent sexual harassment policy in the workplace will be strong [10–38] *prima facie* evidence that the employer has taken reasonably practicable steps to deal with sexual harassment. In this respect, guidance on the appropriate nature of such a policy is provided in the Code of Practice on Sexual Harassment and Harassment at Work.[55] This code provides that a strong sexual harassment policy should *inter alia*:

- clearly prohibit harassment on any of the nine discriminatory grounds;
- be actively communicated to all staff;
- contain confidential, neutral grievance procedures;

---

54. Determination no. EDA067.
55. SI no. 78 of 2002.

- provide a quick, fair and sensitive internal investigation;
- provide for the imposition of effective and proportionate sanctions;
- ensure that victimisation following complaints is not tolerated; and
- ensure that the effectiveness of the procedures are monitored.

[10–39] However, the 'reasonably practicable steps' that the employer could have adopted to prevent the sexual harassment are not necessarily limited to the production, notification and implementation of a sexual harassment policy. In *A Worker v A Hotel*,[56] the complainant worked in a hotel as a waitress. She was working in the kitchen early one morning when she was approached from behind by a male customer (Mr X) of the hotel. The complainant alleged that the Mr X put his hands around her and she struggled to eventually break free. This occurred in the presence of the kitchen porter, who had security duties, and who knew Mr X. After the incident had occurred, the porter had asked Mr X to leave. The complainant made a complaint to the general manager of the hotel, Mr A, later that day. She was then summoned to Mr A's office where she found Mr A and Mr X waiting for her. At this meeting Mr X denied the incident and put his hand on her shoulder by way of – what the complainant considered to be – a token apology. The complainant alleged that the nature of the meeting and the behaviour of Mr X at the meeting was sexually offensive, humiliating and intimidating to her in light of what had occurred before. A number of days later the complainant made a formal written complaint regarding Mr X's behaviour and requested that the general manager inform her of the procedures in place at the hotel to deal with such an incident. After another meeting with the general manager, the complainant alleged that the general manager did not propose any further action in relation to the incident. Some time later the complainant discovered that Mr X was a personal friend of the general manager and when Mr X reappeared at the hotel she felt threatened. The complainant left work later that day and her partner called to the hotel and left a letter for Mr A regarding her reappearance at work. The complainant alleged that Mr A then rang her and expressed hostility towards her. From 22 December 2005 to 26 January 2006 the complainant was on certified sick leave for 'acute work-related stress'. On 26 January 2006 the complainant resigned in view of what she considered the unacceptable conditions of work imposed on her. The Equality Officer investigating the matter concluded that the touching of the complainant by Mr X, whether it was by wrapping his arms around her – as the complainant suggested – or whether he placed his hands on her hips by way of a greeting – as Mr X suggested – was 'a gesture of an equivocally sexual nature' that was offensive and intimidating to the complainant. As to whether the respondent should be held vicariously liable for Mr X's actions and what steps the respondent could have taken to prevent the sexual harassment, the Equality Officer concluded that:

> I am further satisfied that the respondent is vicariously liable for Mr. X's conduct pursuant to S.15 of the Acts, since it is undisputed that at the material time Mr X

---

56. DEC-E2009-062.

was a customer of the hotel within the meaning of S. 14A(1)(a)(iii) of the Acts, and, further to S.14A(1)(a)(iii), I am satisfied that the respondent had not taken any steps to prevent it. Not only did the respondent not have a policy in place to deal with such incidents, but did not even adhere to the widespread practice of mounting signs on the kitchen entrances to indicate that non-staff were not permitted access, which could otherwise be considered as a basic step taken to prevent the harassment of staff in the kitchen area where the incident occurred. Furthermore, the night porter, despite having express responsibility for security matters during the time in question, stood in the immediate vicinity of the complainant yet did nothing to stop Mr X from approaching her, and only requested that the harasser leave the kitchen after the incident.

The Equality Officer therefore held that the respondent had discriminated against [10–40] the complainant in relation to her conditions of employment by not taking reasonable and practicable steps to prevent her sexual harassment. The Equality Officer further held that the complainant had been discriminatorily dismissed contrary to s.8(6) of the Employment Equality Acts. The Equality Officer ordered that the respondent pay the complainant €30,000 in compensation for the discrimination and the discriminatory dismissal.

4. Victimisation

The comprehensive protection offered by the equality legislation would be of little [10–41] practical use if employees suffering discrimination were too intimidated to bring a claim for fear of reprisals from their employer. As a consequence s.74(2) of the Employment Equality Act 1998 (as amended by s.29 of the Equality Act 2004) prohibits the victimisation of an employee by his employer in reaction to:

    (a) a complaint of discrimination made by the employee to the employer,

    (b) any proceedings by a complainant,

    (c) an employee having represented or otherwise supported a complainant,

    (d) the work of an employee having been compared with that of another employee for any of the purposes of this Act or any enactment repealed by this Act,

    (e) an employee having been a witness in any proceedings under this Act or the Equal Status Act 2000 or any such repealed enactment,

    (f) an employee having opposed by lawful means an act which is unlawful under this Act or the said Act 2000 or which was unlawful under any such repealed enactment, or

    (g) an employee having given notice of an intention to take any of the actions mentioned in the preceding paragraphs.

Acts of victimisation can take many forms; all that is required by s.74(2) is that [10–42] the conduct has occurred in reaction to the employee's reliance on their rights under the employment equality legislation. Thus the failure by the respondent to provide references to a former employee who had brought a discrimination case against the respondent was held to amount to victimisation.[57] Similarly, leaving an employee isolated in an office by himself with little or no meaningful work to do after he made an allegation of bullying and harassment against his supervisor was considered to be victimisation.[58] Dismissing an employee who made good faith complaints of sexual harassment, which were found to be vexatious by her employer, has also been considered an act of victimisation.[59]

[10–43] The Labour Court has interpreted s.74(2) as applying in all circumstances where the employer acts in a manner which inflicts detriment on the worker in reaction to the worker exercising his or her rights under the legislation. Furthermore, the employer's impugned act(s) of victimisation may be conscious or unconscious, i.e. the employer's behaviour will be judged objectively and not subjectively. In *Watters Garden World Limited v Panuta*,[60] the complainant was a native of Moldova who worked for the respondent. He instigated proceedings before the Equality Tribunal on the basis that he had been treated less favourably by the respondent than a person of a different nationality would have been treated. In particular, the complainant alleged that the respondent had failed to apply to the Department of Enterprise, Trade and Employment for a work permit for him, had not provided him with a P60 tax certificate and failed to provide him with a statement of particulars of his contract of employment in a language that he understood. Furthermore, the complainant alleged that he had been victimised by his employer for bringing his complaint to the tribunal when the respondent informed An Garda Síochána of his immigration status. It was the respondent's contention that he only visited the Garda Síochána as he was unsure of the complainant's legal status. Following the respondent's visit to the gardaí, the complainant was threatened with prosecution and deportation because he had remained in the country following the expiration of his residency stamp. The court held that the complainant had been victimised contrary to the provisions of the equality legislation. The visit by the respondent to the Garda station was held to be a direct result of the complainant's equality claim which resulted in the adverse treatment of the complainant and irrespective of the respondent's subjective intentions it was foreseeable that the respondent's action could result in adverse consequences for the complainant.

[10–44] In *Waterford Institute of Technology v Moore-Walsh*,[61] the complainant was a US citizen employed by the respondent as an assistant lecturer. She held the US quali-fication of Juris Doctorate (JD). The complainant assisted a post graduate student to finalise her application for a masters' degree. When the student's application was received, the complainant's Head of Department questioned the status of her

---

57. *Coote v Granada Hospitality Ltd.* [1998] IRLR 656.
58. *Barrett v Department of Defence*, DEC-E2009-053, 29 June 2009.
59. *A Company v A Worker*, determination no. EED035.
60. Determination no. EDA098.
61. Determination no. EDA056.

JD qualification on the basis that he did not believe it a post graduate degree. Without a post graduate qualification the Head of Department decided that the complainant could not supervise a masters' degree. Following clarification from the Higher Education and Training Awards Council, the Head of Department informed the complainant and the student that the complainant's qualification was equivalent to the qualifications needed to supervise a masters' degree. The complainant alleged that the respondent was aware at all times that her qualifications were adequate. She claimed that since she had brought another case against her employer previously that the attitude of the respondent towards her had changed. The Labour Court held that the respondent had victimised the complainant when it questioned the validity of her degree.

[10–45] The Labour Court and Equality Officers have taken a dim view of employers who have been found to have victimised employees in the above manner and have awarded significant compensation to complainants who have suffered as a consequence. In *Two Named Female Teachers and the Equality Authority v Board of Management and Principal of a Boys' Secondary School*,[62] the claimants made an ultimately unsuccessful complaint of sexual harassment against their employer. However, after the claimants had referred their complaints of sexual harassment they were subjected to behaviour that they alleged amounted to victimisation. In particular, a notice was posted in the staff room of the school the day before the claimants' first hearing, which invited the staff to attend the hearing notwithstanding that an Equality Officer's hearing should be strictly private to the parties.[63] The Equality Officer concluded:

> I am further satisfied that the posting of the notice prior to the hearing had one purpose only i.e. to expose and embarrass the Claimants in the eyes of their colleagues as being the female teachers who were bringing complaints of sexual harassment against the School and to add to their trauma that day. I am satisfied that this action was a gross intrusion in the right of the Claimants to bring a complaint before an Equality Officer without fear of unfavourable consequences or victimisation.

The Equality Officer ordered that the school pay the first named claimant £7,000 and pay the second named claimant £12,000 in compensation for the distress they suffered as a result.

[10–46] Given its potential to undermine the effectiveness of the legislation, awards of compensation for victimisation mark the law's disapproval of such behaviour. In *McCarthy v Dublin Corporation*,[64] an employee had succeeded in an action against her employer and was subsequently marginalised by her manager and an in-house

---

62. DEC-E2001-005, 25 January 2001.
63. s.79(2) of the Employment Equality Act 1998.
64. DEC-2001-015.

magazine did not correct a misleading report, which stated that the employer had actually succeeded in the case. The Equality Officer ordered that the employee be awarded £40,000 in compensation. This award was reduced on appeal by the Labour Court to £25,000.[65] It should be noted that it is not necessary to succeed in a discrimination claim under the Employment Equality Acts in order to bring a successful claim for victimisation.[66]

4.1 Burden of Proof

[10–47] The burden of proof rests with the complainant in claims of victimisation. In *A Female Employee v A Candle Production Company*,[67] the complainant alleged that she had been discriminated against when she was subjected to sexual harassment in the course of her employment. The complainant alleged that warnings about her timekeeping and criticism of her work which followed immediately after her complaint of harassment constituted victimisation. In finding that the complainant had indeed been victimised, the Equality Officer explained how the burden of proof operates in such cases:

> The first issue for consideration … is whether the complainant in the present case has established a prima facie case of victimisation. I must therefore consider whether the claimant has adduced evidence to show that she was penalised and secondly, whether the evidence indicates that the penalisation was solely or mainly occasioned by the complainant having in good faith opposed by lawful means an act which is unlawful under the Employment Equality Act, 1998.

[10–48] In that case, the Equality Officer found that the complainant had been sexually harassed and that she had been victimised as a result of making a subsequent complaint. The Equality Officer ordered that the respondent pay the complainant the sum of £7,000 for the effects of the discrimination but ordered the respondent to pay the complainant £10,000 for the effects of the victimisation.

[10–49] In *An Engineering Company v A Worker*,[68] the complainant met with her employer (the respondent) on July 8, 2002 and made a verbal complaint against her manager who she alleged had sexually harassed her. The complainant was asked to put her complaint in writing. At this same meeting she was given a verbal warning regarding her poor timekeeping. On July 18, 2002 the complainant received a written warning about her poor timekeeping. On July 22, 2002 the respondent received the complainant's written complaint of sexual harassment. Following an investigation, the respondent concluded that there was no case to answer. On August 1, 2002 the complainant's employment was terminated. The complainant

---

65. Determination EDA022.
66. *Barrett v Department of Defence*, DEC-E2009-053, 29 June 2009.
67. DEC-E2006-035.
68. Determination no. EED071.

alleged that she had been dismissed because of making a complaint of sexually harassment. The respondent contended that she had been dismissed because of her continual poor timekeeping. The Labour Court found it significant that following her warning on July 18, 2002 the complainant had not been late for work on any occasion since that date and before her work was terminated on August 1, 2002. The court held:

> … that the dismissal was mainly occasioned by the complainant having, in good faith, opposed by lawful means an act which is unlawful under the Act and was therefore penalised in circumstances amounting to discrimination.

PART IV

The Operation of the Employment Relationship

CHAPTER 11

Organisation of Working Time

Introduction

Within this fourth section of the book we consider the impact of employment [11–01]
law as it applies during the course of the employment relationship. In this respect,
one of the most significant aspects of this relationship, and one which is governed
largely by statute, concerns the obligations and entitlements of employer and
employee in respect of working time as they apply to the following[1]:

---

1. It seems clear that the concept of 'working time' (defined in s.2 of the Act as meaning any
    time that the employee is at his or her place of work or at his or her employer's disposal
    and is carrying on or performing the activities or duties of his or her work) includes any
    time spent by a worker at a workplace while 'on call', including time spent asleep in this
    context. It does not include, however, time spent 'on call' but away from the workplace, nor
    does it include the time taken by an employee in travelling to and from work. See *Breffni
    Carpentry Services Ltd. v Solodounikovs*, WTC/08/2, DWT 0816, 6 May 2008. Thus in C-
    473/05 *Okrensi Soud v Ceskèm Krumlov District Court*, OJ C 36, 11 January 2007, the ECJ
    held that Directive 93/04/EC (Council Directive concerning certain aspects of the organisa-
    tion of working time) prohibited national legislation under which 'on call' duty performed
    by a doctor would not be treated as wholly amounting to 'working time', even if [s]he was
    physically present at the place of work, if [s]he did no actual work at the time. On the other
    hand, the ECJ accepted that it was legitimate for national laws to differentiate (in the case
    of workers who were on call) between those workers who were working while on call and
    those who were not for the purposes of setting levels of remuneration. Generally, for inter-
    pretation of the Framework Directive, see *Sinidicato de Medicos de Asistencia Publica (Simap)
    v Conselleria de Sanidad y Consumo de la Generalidad Valenciana*, C-303/98 [2000] ECR-I
    7963; *Landeshauptstadt Kiel v Norbert Jaeger* case C-151/02 [2003] ECR-1 08389; *Delllas and
    Others v Premier Ministre and Another* [2006] IRLR 225. Kerr, *Irish Employment Legislation*
    (Round Hall Sweet and Maxwell, 2000), at B60, makes the point that the definition in s.2
    appears to contain two separate elements joined by the conjunctive 'and', such that logically
    both elements of the definition would need to be proved (namely that the worker was at
    the workplace or at his employer's disposal *and* was carrying out duties), and hence that the
    approach of the ECJ in *Sinidicato de Medicos* in requiring that only *one* of these elements
    needed to be proved (and hence interpreting the two requirements in the definition as being
    separable) may be difficult to reconcile with the clear terms of the Irish Act. It is submitted
    that the approach of the ECJ in this case is, in fact, difficult even to reconcile with the defini-
    tion of working time within Art. 2 of the Framework Directive.

- the maximum number of hours in a week in which an employee can work;
- the entitlement of the employee to daily and weekly rest periods;
- the position of an employee who works predominantly at night;
- the regulation of Sunday work;
- the entitlement of an employee to holidays, including public holidays;
- the obligation of employers to inform employees for whom working hours are not certain of the days and times (including overtime) that they will be expected to work in a particular week; and
- the position of an employee who is expected to be available for work for an employer on given days but for whom there may not actually be any work on any particular day.

[11–02] As an introductory point, it should be noted that the Irish statutory provisions governing the maximum length of time employees can work and the minimum rest periods and holidays to which they are entitled are rooted in health and safety concerns, such that the primary purpose of the law in this area is arguably not to vindicate the rights of employees (many of whom in practice would be keen to work more than the statutorily permitted number of hours in that they will thereby receive more money), but rather to prevent a situation where, as a result of overwork, an employee poses a threat to the health, safety and welfare at work of him or herself, or of fellow employees or of the workplace generally.[2] Having said this, of course, as a consequence of fostering a situation where the employee's working hours do not pose health and safety concerns, the employee does naturally obtain entitlements under this legislation.

[11–03] The principal Irish legislation in this area, the Organisation of Working Time Act of 1997,[3] is itself based on, and transposes into force, the European Council Directive Concerning Certain Aspects of the Organisation of Working Time.[4] Its fundamental

2. This is the clear conclusion of the decision of the ECJ in *United Kingdom of Great Britain and Northern Ireland v Council of the European Union* [1997] IRLR 30. It is arguable, therefore, that many of the specific provisions of Irish working-time legislation simply give effect to what is implicitly required anyway under the health and safety code, considered in Chapter 15.
3. Generally, see Forde, *Employment Law* (2nd ed., Round Hall Sweet and Maxwell, 2001), at pp.85–93; Boyle, 'The Organisation of Working Time Act 1997 – An Overview', 15 *Irish Law Times* (1997), 130.
4. Directive 93/104/EC as amended by Directive 2000/34/EC and Directive 2003/88/EC. For analysis, see Barnard, *EC Employment Law* (3rd ed., Oxford University Press, 2006), at pp.573 *et seq.* Under s.2(2) of the 1997 Act, any word or expression used in the Act that is also used in this Directive is deemed to have the meaning that it has in the Directive unless the contrary intention appears. Significantly, in cases C-397/01 to C-403/01 *Pfeiffer & Others, Deutsches Rotes Kreuz, Kreisverband Waldshut e.v.,* [2004] EUECJ C-397/01-403/01, the ECJ held that the terms of this Directive were sufficiently precise and unconditional to be directly effective in the national courts of Member States. The reach or ambit of the Directive to particular categories of workers was expanded by the amending Directive on the Organisation of Working Time (Directive 2000/34/EC). For analysis, see O'Mara, European Developments, 1(1) *IELJ* (2004), 28.

purpose (as considered below) is to lay down certain maximum weekly working hours, minimum daily rest periods, and minimum holiday periods (including public holiday entitlements) and to lay down specific standards where the employee does the bulk of his or her work at night. In addition, the Act is concerned with its own enforcement, including the manner by which workplaces are inspected to ensure that their practices conform to the legislative requirements.

Much of the complexity in the Act (and indeed in the regulations made pursuant [11–04] thereto) derives from the fact that not all workers and not all activities are covered by its terms. Exemptions can be and are made for certain categories of activity, and indeed many of the specific terms of the Act can, to some extent, be ousted by the operation of a collective agreement, a Registered Employment Agreement (REA) or an Employment Regulation Order (ERO) dealing with such matters.[5] Thus before we consider the substance of the legislation we will focus on these two vital introductory questions:

- To what categories of worker does the Act not apply? and
- What are the procedural requirements that must be fulfilled in order for the terms of the legislation to be ousted by a valid collective agreement?

1. Categories of Workers to Whom the Act does not Apply

In essence it may be said that the terms of the Act do not apply to certain classes [11–05] of workers under four broad headings:

- where the statute itself specifically excludes that category of worker;
- where such category of worker is excluded by ministerial regulation;
- where the terms of the Act are not followed in a particular instance and for emergency reasons; or
- where such category of worker is excluded by some form of collective agreement.

1.1. Categories of Workers Specifically Excluded by the Legislation

Under s.3 of the 1997 Act, its terms (or in various cases, *some* of its terms) are [11–06] expressly deemed not to apply to certain categories of worker.[6] Thus the Act does not apply *in its entirety* to members of the Garda Síochána or defence forces.[7] In addition, Part II of the Act (which deals *inter alia* with minimum rest periods, work on Sundays, nightly working hours, provision of information in relation to

---

5. For consideration of the nature and operation of REAs and EROs, see Chapter 2.
6. See Barnard, *EC Employment Law* (3rd ed., Oxford University Press, 2006), at pp.592-597 for analysis of possible derogations under the terms of the Framework Directive.
7. s.3(1) Organisation of Working Time Act 1997.

working time, and provision in relation to zero hours working practices but not, pivotally, maximum working hours) does not apply to persons engaged in sea fishing or other work at sea; doctors in training[8]; persons who are employed by a relative[9] and are a member of the relative's household and whose place of employment is a private dwelling, house or a farm, on which he or she and the relative in question reside[10]; or persons whose working time is determined by themselves.[11] Finally, s.4 of the Act exempts from the application of ss.11 and/or 13 (which deal respectively with daily and weekly rest periods) persons who are employed in shift work who cannot avail of the statutory rest period each time they change shift,[12] and also persons who are employed in an activity consisting of periods of work spread over the day.[13]

It is, however, possible under s.3(4) of the Act, for the Minister by way of regulation to provide that a specified provision of the legislation *shall* for the time being apply to a particular class of workers who are generally exempt from the application of the legislation pursuant to ss.3(1) and (2).

1.2. Categories of Workers Excluded by Ministerial Regulation

[11–07] In addition, and pursuant to s.3(3) of the Act, the Minister (after consultation with any other Minister of the government who [s]he feels may be concerned with the matter), may, by regulation, exempt from the application of a specified provision or provisions of the Act persons employed in any specified class or classes of activity involving either transport (by whatever means) of goods or persons, or any activity in the civil protection services where, in the opinion of the Minister and of any other relevant Minister of the Government, the inherent nature of the activity is such that if the particular provision *was* to apply to the said person, the effective operation of the service concerned would be adversely affected.[14]

[11–08] Thus previously under the Organisation of Working Time (Exemption of Transport Activities) Regulations 1998[15] activities that are wholly or mainly connected with the operation of any vehicle, train, vessel, aircraft or other means of transport

---

8. s.3(2)(a) *ibid.* But see the European Communities (Organisation of Working Time) (Activities of Doctors in Training) Regulations of 2004, SI no. 494 of 2004.
9. The meaning of 'relative' in this sense is defined in s.3(6) Organisation of Working Time Act 1997.
10. s.3(2)(b) *ibid.* But see the Industrial Relations Act 1990 (Code of Practice for Protecting Persons Employed in Other People's Homes) (Declaration) Order 2007, SI no. 239 of 2007.
11. s.3(2)(c) Organisation of Working Time Act 1997.
12. s.4(1) *ibid.*
13. s.4(2) *ibid.*
14. Many categories of workers formerly excluded from the Act by reason of ministerial regulation are now included as a result of the amending Directive on the Organisation of Working Time (Directive 2000/34/EC).
15. SI no. 20 of 1998.

were exempt from the application of ss.11, 12, 13, 15 and 16[16]; however, these regulations were themselves abolished by the Organisation of Working Time (Inclusion of Transport Activities) Regulations of 2004.[17] Moreover, under the terms of the European Communities (Organisation of Working Time of Persons Performing Mobile Road Transport Activities) Regulations 2005[18] specific regulations are created for persons employed by companies based in an EU Member State who provide mobile road transport activities.[19] Finally, an ongoing exception existed for mobile staff in civil aviation as defined in the Annex to Council Directive 2000/79/EC of 27 November 2004 but this exemption was abolished in the terms of the European Communities (Organisation of Working Time) (Mobile Staff in Civil Aviation) Regulations of 2006.[20] In addition, under the Organisation of Working Time (Exemption of Civil Protection Services) Regulations of 1998[21] the activities of further specific classes of workers (essentially persons employed in prisons, persons employed by a fire authority as a retained fire fighter, persons other than a member of An Garda Síochána employed as an authorised officer within the meaning of the Air Navigation and Transport Acts 1950–1988, persons employed by the Dublin Port Company as a member of its harbour police and persons employed in the Irish Marine Emergency Service (whose activities are not of a clerical nature) are exempted from the application of ss.11,12,13,15 and 16.

In addition, under ss.4 and 7 of the Act, the Minister may by regulations exempt [11–09] certain activities (namely any activity referred to in para.2.2.1 of the Framework Directive or any) specified class or classes of such activity[22]) from the application of any or all of ss.11, 12, 13, 16 and 17.[23] Thus, under the Organisation of Working Time (General Exemption) Regulations 1998[24] an exemption is provided for certain categories of workers from the provisions of ss 11, 12, 13 and 16. The categories of activities to which this section applies are set out in the schedule to the

---

16. See *Coastal Line Container Terminal Ltd. v Services Industrial Professional Technical Union* [1999] IEHC 621, [2000] 1 IR 549, [2000] ELR 1 for the view that transport in this context involves some sense of movement, and hence would not cover activities that were stationary, such as crane driving.
17. SI no. 817 of 2004.
18. SI no. 002 of 2005.
19. The regulations transpose the terms of Directive 2002/15/EC of the European Parliament and of the Council of 11 March 2002. Essentially the regulations apply the 48-hour-maximum-average working week to the activities covered in the regulations, and require that no worker engaged in such activities work more than 60 hours in *any* week. The regulations also impose certain requirements in respect of night work and minimum breaks. For analysis see Kerr, 'Legislative Developments', 3(1) *IELJ* (2006), 29.
20. SI no. 507 of 2006. Generally, see *Goode Concrete Limited v 58 Workers*, WTC/09/83, DWT 0934, 30 April 2009.
21. SI no. 52 of 1998.
22. s.4(3) Organisation of Working Time Act 1997.
23. Such exemption may be provided on a conditional basis: s.4(3) *ibid.*
24. SI no. 21 of 1998.

regulations and include activities involving significant travel,[25] security work, seasonal-type work where the level of work will vary significantly from time to time, and work whose nature is such that employees are directly involved in ensuring the continuity of production or provision of services.[26] In all cases, the exemption only applies where the work in question genuinely relates to these activities and is not merely clerical in nature and only where the employee is 'wholly or mainly' engaged in such work.[27] Furthermore, in respect of these categories of workers it is provided that where, as a result of this exemption, such workers do not receive the statutory rest period, the employer is obliged to ensure that they have a rest period and break that, in all the circumstances, can be regarded as equivalent to the statutory entitlement.[28] Moreover, where employees to whom the exemption applies are required to work a shift or other period of work greater than six hours in length, the employer is required to give them a break of a duration that should be assessed having due regard to the age, health, safety and comfort of the employee.[29]

1.3. Justifiable Failure to Comply with Specific Provisions of the Act in Exceptional Circumstances

[11–10] In addition, under s.5 of the Act, an employer can justify a failure to comply with ss.11, 12, 13, 16 or 17 where, due to exceptional or emergency circumstances (including an accident or imminent risk of an accident) or any other unusual and foreseeable circumstances beyond the employer's control, it would not be practicable for him or her to comply with the section in question. Again this provision is without prejudice to the entitlement of an employee (under s.6) who has, for the stated emergency reasons, not been afforded the statutory rest period, to be afforded an equivalent rest period by way of compensation.

1.4. The Role of Collective Agreements under the Organisation of Working Time Act

[11–11] It is further provided under the legislation that ss.11–13 do not apply to any activity that is, in the case of specific employees, covered by express agreements in the form of

- a collective agreement approved by the Labour Court pursuant to s.24 of the Act[30];

---

25. Under the terms of the organisation of Working Time (Inclusion of Offshore Work) Regulations 2004, SI no. 819 of 2004, this is deemed to include offshore travel.
26. The schedule (as amended) lists specific examples of such work.
27. The regulations do not apply where the worker is a special category night worker or a worker who falls within a class of employee to which a Joint Labour Committee may perform functions under the Industrial Relations Acts 1946–2004.
28. para.4.
29. para.5(2).
30. s.4(5)(a) Organisation of Working Time Act 1997.

- an REA[31]; or
- an ERO.[32]

The nature and operation of REAs and EROs are considered in Chapter 2, but it is appropriate now to consider the role of collective agreements created specifically pursuant to the 1997 Act.

Various sections of the 1997 Act refer to the possibility of the stringent terms of the [11–12] Act not having application in circumstances where the employer and employee have instead agreed that the nature of the employment relationship will be determined by means of a collective agreement. Specifically this arises in s.4 (which provides for the non-application of ss.11, 12 and 13), s.15 (permitting a collective agreement to determine the reference period for calculating weekly working hours), and s.16 (permitting a collective agreement to set the reference period for assessing average nightly working hours).

In order for such collective agreement (defined in s.2 of the Act as 'an agree- [11–13] ment by or on behalf of an employer on the one hand, and by or on behalf of a body or bodies representative of the employees to whom the agreement relates on the other hand'[33]) to have any validity it must stand approved by the Labour Court, as also must any variation to an existing collective agreement.[34] Application to the Labour Court for such approval is made under s.24(2) of the Act. On receipt of such application the Labour Court is required to consult representatives of employees and employers whom it considers to have an interest in the matter to which the collective agreement relates.[35] In addition, the Labour Court shall not approve of a collective agreement unless certain specified conditions are fulfilled,[36] namely:

(a) in the case of a collective agreement referred to in ss. 4, 15 or 16, the Labour Court is satisfied that it is appropriate to approve of the agreement having regard to the provisions of the Council Directive permitting the entry into collective agreements for the purposes concerned;

---

31. s.4(5)(b) *ibid.*
32. s.4(6) Organisation of Working Time Act 1997.
33. It is worth noting that this is not the same definition of a 'collective agreement' as that contained in other pieces of Irish legislation such as the Anti-Discrimination (Pay) Act of 1974 and the Protection of Young Persons (Employment) Act of 1976. See Kerr, *Irish Employment Legislation* (Round Hall Sweet and Maxwell, 2000), at B59.
34. The Labour Court is required to determine the procedures to be followed (a) by persons applying to the Labour Court; (b) by the court in determining the application; and (c) by persons generally in matters related to this section (s.24(8) Organisation of Working Time Act 1997), and is required to publish such procedures (s.24(9) *ibid.*).
35. s.24(3) *ibid.*
36. s.24(4) *ibid.*

  (b) the agreement has been concluded in a manner usually employed in deter-
    mining the pay or other conditions of employment of employees in the
    employment concerned;

  (c) the body that negotiated the agreement on behalf of the employees concerned
    is the holder of a negotiation licence under the Trade Union Act 1941, or is an
    excepted body within the meaning of that Act that is sufficiently representative
    of the employees concerned; and

  (d) the agreement is in such form[37] as appears to the Labour Court to be suitable
    for the purposes of the agreement being approved of under this section.[38]

[11–14] The inference to be drawn from the terms of the section is that save where these
conditions are not met, the Labour Court should approve the collective agreement, although it can later withdraw such approval.[39]

Finally, the Labour Court is required to maintain a register of collective agreements standing approved by it, which register should be available for public
inspection.[40]

2. Substantive Obligations under the Organisation of Working Time Act

[11–15] We now turn to consider the substantive obligations and entitlements that exist
under the terms of the 1997 Act. These arise under the following headings[41]:

- maximum working hours;
- minimum rest periods;
- regulation of night work;
- regulation of work on Sundays;
- notice of working hours;
- zero-hours contracts; or
- holiday entitlements, including public holidays.

[11–16] There are various ways of classifying these categories of obligation. Thus under the
Framework Directive, the rules pertaining to maximum working hours and night
work constitute limitations on an employer's freedom, whereas the rest of the rules

---

37. In November 1997 the Labour Court published a guide in which sample outline agreements
  are included.

38. Where conditions (a) or (d) are not fulfilled but the others are, the Labour Court may request
  the parties to vary the terms of the agreement in order to fulfil these conditions: s.24(5) *ibid.*

39. s.24(7) *ibid.*

40. s.24(10) *ibid.* Where an agreement has been approved by the Labour Court but the parties
  thereto have varied it, then any of the said parties can apply to the Labour Court to have the
  varied agreement approved of by the Labour Court: s.24(6) *ibid.*

41. See Barnard, *EC Employment Law* (3rd ed., Oxford University Press, 2006), at Chapter 12.

constitute entitlements of an employee. An alternative method of classification is to say that the rules relating to maximum working hours, rest periods, night work and holidays are grounded in health and safety concerns, whereas the rules relating to zero-hour contracts, notice of working hours and Sunday work are grounded in a broader conception of social justice and the rights of workers. Equally, neither of these methods of classification is particularly satisfactory, and there will be cross-over between such justifications. Hence, whereas it is no doubt conducive to good health and safety within the workplace to ensure that a worker has proper holidays, equally a failure to provide such holidays quite clearly also represents a violation of the fundamental social rights of that worker. The reason, however, why such classifications are important is because they may go to the heart of explaining the extent of the employer's obligations under the law, and especially they may help to answer the important question of whether or not, in the context of the various issues dealt with by the legislation, an employer must simply provide conditions in which an employee *may* avail of the protections under the Act, or whether instead [s]he must *ensure* that the employee *does* so avail.

2.1. Maximum Working Hours

Naturally this is a key aspect of the legislation, and one that is clearly justifiable [11–17] by reference to health and safety concerns, in that there are obvious risks to the safety of a workplace where an employee is working an excessive number of hours and consequently is overly tired at a particular point during his or her working day. Thus the obligations imposed on employers in this section of the legislation are extremely onerous. In particular in interpreting this section, the Labour Court has held that the obligations it creates are obligations of strict liability in nature, such that the fact that the employer neither knows nor is negligent as to whether or not the employee is exceeding the maximum number of working hours (or indeed the fact that the employee may have been entirely responsible for exceeding the maximum number of working hours) is irrelevant. Employers must have some effective mechanism in place for monitoring the number of hours an employee works and some method of taking corrective action where the Act is being breached.[42] On the other hand, in *Conlon v Kruglijs*,[43] the Labour Court appeared to limit the amount of damages to which an employee (who had worked in excess of the permitted weekly working hours under the Act) would be entitled on the basis that he had colluded with the employer in breaching the Act (in the sense that he had requested that he be allowed to work overtime).

---

42. *IBM Ireland v Svoboda*, WTC/07/77, DWT 0818, 7 May 2008. Equally, and despite adopting this logic in this case, the Labour Court still found against a complainant who had plainly worked in excess of the statutory maximum number of hours, and found that any breach of the Act was 'technical and non-culpable in nature' ostensibly on the basis that the respondent had made a bona fide effort to ensure that the claimant would cease working in excess of the permitted number of hours. It is perhaps difficult to reconcile the logic of the court in this case with the factual result arrived at.

43. WTC/09/40, DWT 0939, 13 May 2009.

[11–18] Under the 1997 Act, an employer may not permit an employee covered by the legislation to work more than an average of 48 hours in each period of seven days as calculated over a reference period of consecutive days[44] that does not exceed four months. It is possible for the reference period to exceed four months, though the statutory rules in this regard are rather confused in their drafting. Thus in specific cases the reference period may be a six-month one[45] (namely in the case of an employee employed in an activity referred to in Art. 17 para.2.2.1 of the Framework Directive, and in the case of situations listed in s.15(5) – that is, where the weekly working hours vary on a seasonal basis or where the four-month reference period would not be practicable because of technical considerations or considerations relating to the conditions under which the work is organised). In addition, under s.15(5) it is provided that where either of these situations apply then it is possible for the reference period to be specified in a collective agreement approved by the Labour Court under s.24[46] and to be greater even than six months, though not more than 12 months.

[11–19] This reference period may not include the employee's minimum statutory period of annual leave granted under the terms of the Act (save so much of the leave period that exceeds the minimum period of annual leave required by the Act[47]), any absences of work constituting parental leave, *force majeure* leave, or carer's leave within the meaning of the Carer's Leave Act 2001,[48] any absences from work taken under the Maternity Protection Act 1994 or the Adoptive Leave Act 1995 as amended,[49] or any sick leave taken by the employee.[50]

2.2. Rest Periods

[11–20] As with the rules relating to the maximum number of hours an employee can work in a defined period, the rules covering the obligations imposed on employers in respect of the provision of rest periods for employees can be justified by reference to the potential threat to the safety of a workplace posed by an employee who has not had sufficient rest.[51]

[11–21] The question of the extent of the obligations arising in respect of rest periods is somewhat controversial. In *Tribune Publishing and Printing Group v GPMU*,[52] the Labour Court held that

---

44. s.15(3) Organisation of Working Time Act 1997.
45. s.15(1)(b) *ibid.*
46. s.15(5) *ibid.*
47. s.15(4)(a) *ibid.*
48. s.15(4)(a) as inserted by s.28 of the Carer's Leave Act 2001.
49. s.15(4)(b) *ibid.*
50. s.15(4)(c) *ibid.*
51. See, for example, *Goode Concrete v Munro*, WTC/04/59, DWT 051, 5 January 2005.
52. [2004] ELR 222.

The Company is under a duty to ensure that the employee receives his equivalent rest period and breaks. Merely stating that the employee could take rest breaks if they wished and not putting in place proper procedures to ensure that the employee receives these breaks, thus protecting his health and safety, does not discharge that duty.[53]

It may be argued, however, that this logic does not flow from the words of ss.11 and 12 of the Act. In the case of s.11, after all, it is provided that the employee is *entitled* to a weekly rest period, and in the case of s.12 it is similarly provided that an employer *shall not require* an employee to work for a designated period without taking a rest. This language is, therefore, plainly different to the language of ss.15 and 16 (dealing with maximum working hours and nightly working hours respectively), which provides in both cases that the employer *shall not permit* an employee to exceed the statutory limitations. In the latter case (as we have seen in our analysis of s.15), the statutory language *does* appear to require that the employer take positive steps to require the employee not to exceed the 48-hour working week (for example). In the case of ss.11 and 12, however, all that the language of the statute requires is that the employer respects the entitlement of the employee to have a weekly rest period and does not either explicitly or implicitly require the employee not to take daily breaks. On the other hand it may well be that what is required by the Framework Directive is greater than what is required by the Irish legislation. Thus in *Commission v United Kingdom*,[54] the ECJ, in interpreting the Directive, found that the UK was in breach of its obligations under the Directive for its failure to require employers to *ensure* that employees took their prescribed rest periods, although it did suggest that an employer should not be required to force an employee to do so.[55] [11–22]

Under the legislation, an employee is entitled to a rest period of at least 11 hours (a daily rest period) in every period of 24 hours during which [s]he works for his or her employer.[56] Moreover, an employee is entitled to a break of at least 15 minutes every four-and-a-half hours.[57] In addition, an employer must not require an employee to work for a period of more than six hours without allowing him or her a break of at least 30 minutes,[58] though this may include the 15 minutes [11–23]

---

53. [2004] ELR 222, 224.
54. C-484/04 [2006] ECR I-7471.
55. Kerr, 'Legislative Developments', 3(2) *IELJ* (2006), 63 questions whether, in light of the inadequate assessment of whether the statutorily required break periods are being taken in many workplaces, Ireland is compliant with its European norms in this regard. The same author ('Legislative Developments', 3(4) *IELJ* (2006), 133) notes that there may be a thin line between attempting to ensure that a workplace is compliant with the 1997 Act and forcing a worker to take breaks.
56. s.11 Organisation of Working Time Act 1997.
57. s.12(1) *ibid.*
58. s.12(2) *ibid.* It is provided that the Minister may provide as regards certain categories of employment that this minimum rest period be more than 30 minutes, though not more than one

referred to above.[59] Finally, this 15 or 30-minute break cannot be in the form of a break at the end of the working day.[60]

[11–24] Beyond this, an employee is entitled to a *weekly* rest period of at least 24 consecutive hours in each period of seven days,[61] which weekly rest period must be immediately preceded by an 11-hour *daily* rest period.[62] Alternatively, in lieu of such rest period within a given seven-day period, the employer may grant the employee two rest periods of 24 consecutive hours in the following seven-day period.[63] Where this happens, such rest periods may be consecutive or non-consecutive but the beginning of the first period if they are consecutive, and of both periods if they are not, must be preceded by an 11-hour daily rest period.[64] Finally, any rest period (or in the case above, any one of the two compensatory rest periods afforded under s.13(3)) must include a Sunday or, if the rest period is only 24 hours, must be a Sunday, unless alternative provision is made in the employee's contract.[65]

[11–25] As we have seen, it is possible for the legislative requirements in respect of rest periods to be effectively 'ousted' by the terms of a collective agreement, REA or ERO and by ministerial regulations, or where the failure to provide the statutory rest periods is justified by exceptional circumstances. Where this happens, such agreement, order or regulations must contain provision requiring that the employee has an equivalent rest period to that to which [s]he would be entitled under these

---

hour. Thus, under the Organisation of Working Time (Breaks at Work for Shop Employees) Regulations of 1998, SI no. 57 of 1998, a one-hour minimum break period is provided for shop employees (as defined in the regulations) whose hours of work include the hours from 11.30am to 2.30pm and who fulfil the statutory criteria of having worked for six hours.

59. s.12 (2) Organisation of Working Time Act 1997. This 15- or 30-minute rest period requirement as appropriate is not satisfied by a break at the end of the working day. Generally, see *Olhausens Ltd. v Murauskas* WTC/08/50, DWT 0852, 27 August 2008. On the other hand, provided that the complete rest period is afforded to the worker within the prescribed time period, it is not unlawful for an employer to ask the employee to interrupt his or her break and recommence it later. *Carlton Airport Hotel v Martin Patterson* WTC/08/26, DWT 0844, 30 July 2008.

60. s.12(4) Organisation of Working Time Act 1997.

61. s.13(2) *ibid.*

62. If this is justified by considerations of a technical nature or related to the conditions under which the work concerned is organised or other objective considerations, the employer may decide that the weekly rest period should not be preceded by a daily rest period (s.13(4) *ibid.*). Similarly this requirement does not apply where, by reason of a provision of the Act or an agreement, or instrument referred to in the Act, the employee is not entitled to a daily rest period in the circumstances concerned: s.13(6) *ibid.*

63. s.13(3) *ibid.*

64. This requirement that the weekly rest period be immediately preceded by a daily rest period may be dispensed with if this is justified by considerations of a technical nature or considerations related to the conditions under which the work concerned is organised or other objective considerations: s.13 *ibid.*

65. s.13(4) *ibid.*

sections.[66] The employer should either ensure that the employee has a period of rest available to him or herself that can, in the circumstances, be regarded as equivalent to the rest period(s) missed,[67] or where, for objectively justifiable reasons, this is not possible, then the employer must make such other arrangements *vis-à-vis* the employee's conditions of employment as will compensate the employee.[68] Equally such 'other arrangements' cannot include the granting of monetary compensation to the employee or providing him or her with any other material benefit other than one that will improve the physical conditions under which [s]he works or the amenities or services available to him or her while [s]he is at work.[69]

The Labour Relations Commission[70] has prepared a useful Code of Practice on [11–26] Compensatory Rest and Related Matters, which gives advice to employers on the question of how to provide for compensatory rest periods[71] where, by reason of regulations, collective agreement, REA or ERO, the basic statutory provisions in relation to rest periods cannot be followed.[72] The code (which operates very much from a 'common sense' standpoint) highlights the importance of minimum rest periods (both daily and weekly) for a safe and efficient workplace (pointing out, for example, the threat to safety where an employee who has not had adequate sleep reports for work) and makes a number of specific points in respect of how a non-statutory framework for providing rest periods should be managed. Thus for example, the code provides that any compensatory rest periods should be provided as soon as possible after the statutory period has been missed[73]:

> Exempted employees who miss out on their statutory rest entitlements should receive equivalent compensatory rest as soon as possible after the statutory rest has been missed out on. It is most important for employers to make rest time available to employees to allow them to recuperate from long periods of work without adequate rest. The Organisation of Working Time Act, 1997 and the EU Directive on Working Time do not specify any timeframes within which compensatory rest must be made available. However, when determining when compensatory rest is to be given, an employer should always have regard to the circumstances pertaining in the individual place of employment and to the health and safety requirements for adequate rest. In this context, it is important that the compensatory rest for

---

66. s.6(1) *ibid.* Complaints under s.6 should be made to the Rights Commissioner and, on appeal, to the Labour Court in the normal way pursuant to s.27 *ibid.*
67. s.6(2)(a) *ibid.*
68. s.6(2)(b) *ibid.*
69. s.6(3) *ibid.*
70. Pursuant to s.35 *ibid.*
71. This was brought into force in the terms of the Organisation of Working Time (Code of Practice on Compensatory Rest and Related Matters) (Declaration) Order 1998, SI no. 44 of 1998.
72. See also, for analysis of the provisions of the Framework Directive on compensatory rest, and especially the interpretation thereof provided by the ECJ in *Landeshaupstadt Kiel v Norbert Jaeger*, Bull and Bowery, 'ECJ Rests its Case', 48 *Employment Law Journal* (March 2004), 17.
73. para.3(1) of the Schedule to the code.

rest breaks at work and for daily rest breaks, in particular, be provided as soon as possible and, generally, in an adjacent time frame

[11–27]   In addition, the code deals with circumstances where equivalent rest periods cannot be provided and the employee is to be compensated in some other way pursuant to s.6(3) of the 1997 Act. Under the terms of this section, such compensation cannot take the form of monetary compensation or any other benefit except one that will improve the physical conditions under which the employee works or the amenities or services available to the employee while at work.[74] In assessing what this may mean in practice, the code provides as follows:

> A common sense approach should be adopted by employers and employees in such situations which takes account of the circumstances existing in the employment and has regard to the safety, health and well being of employees. It would be desirable that employers and employees and/or their representatives agree appropriate protection measures as respects an employee's conditions of employment.

> While it is not feasible to define such appropriate protection/conditions of employment measures, the concept might include measures which provide for, in addition to normal health and safety requirements:

> • enhanced environmental conditions to accommodate regular long periods of attendance at work;
> • refreshment facilities, recreational and reading material;
> • appropriate facilities/amenities such as television, radio and music;
> • alleviating monotonous work or isolation;
> • transport to and from work where appropriate.

2.3. Night Work

[11–28]   Again the very specific rules in the legislation relating to night work owe their existence to a concern with the safety of a workplace in which work is carried on at night. Thus in the case of a night worker (that is, a person who normally[75] works at least three hours of his or her daily working time and 50 per cent of his or her total annual working hours between midnight and 7.00am on the following day[76]) an employer shall not permit such worker to work more than an average of

---

74. para.3(4) *ibid.*
75. In *R v AG for Northern Ireland ex parte Burns* [1999] IRLR 315 it was held that the use of the word 'normally' in the section meant merely that the requirement of working at night be 'a regular feature' of the employee's employment and not necessarily that the worker work predominantly, let alone exclusively, at night. This rationale is plainly of limited application as far as the Irish legislation is concerned, with its requirement that a night worker work 50 per cent of his or her hours at night.
76. s.16(1) Organisation of Working Time Act 1997.

eight hours in each 24-hour period (calculated over a reference period of consecutive days[77] that does not exceed two months or such greater length of time as may be specified in a collective agreement that stands approved by the Labour Court under s.24).[78] Under the legislation, the reference period for assessing such averages may not include weekly rest periods (save where such rest period exceeds 24 hours),[79] annual leave periods (save any period of annual leave that exceeds the statutory minimum),[80] any absences from work that constitute carer's leave, parental leave or *force majeure* leave for the purposes of the Carer's Leave Act 2001,[81] absences that are authorised under the Maternity Protection Act 1994 or the Adoptive Leave Act 1995[82] (as amended) or any sick leave period.[83]

In addition, in the case of a 'special category night worker' – (defined as a night [11–29] worker in respect of whom an assessment carried out by his or her employer pursuant to health and safety legislation indicates that the work in question involves special hazards or a heavy physical or mental strain[84]) the employer is simply prohibited from allowing the employee to work more than 8 hours in any 24-hour period.[85]

Furthermore, under the terms of the Safety, Health and Welfare at Work (Night [11–30] Work and Shift Work) Regulations 2000,[86] an employer has a duty, both before a worker commences employment as a night worker and at regular intervals thereafter, to assess the health and safety implications for that employee of working at night,[87] and where there is a threat to his or her health *as a result of working at night* (as manifested in him or her becoming ill or showing symptoms of ill health) the employer should (where possible) assign day work to that employee.[88]

2.4. Holiday Entitlements

It has been held that the obligation to provide a worker with appro- [11–31] priate paid annual leave[89] is one that has its roots in health and safety

---

77. s.16(4) *ibid.*

78. s.16(2)(b) *ibid.*

79. ss.16(5)(a) and (b) *ibid.*

80. s.16(5)(c) *ibid.*

81. s.16(5)(c) as inserted by s.28 of the Carer's Leave Act 2001.

82. s.16(5)(d) *ibid.*

83. s.16(5)(e) *ibid.*

84. s.16(5) *ibid.*

85. s.16(5)(a) *ibid.*

86. SI no. 11 of 2000.

87. para.7.1 *ibid.*

88. para.7.5 *ibid.*

89. In *Royal Liver Assurance Ltd. v SIPTU*, WTC/01/27, DWT 0141, 8 October 2001, the Labour Court held that 'The term "paid annual leave" is not defined in the Act or in the Directive. It is, however, a term of common usage in industrial relations and is well understood as meaning a period of rest and relaxation during which a worker is paid his or her normal

concerns.[90] Unlike, for example, s.15, however, which deals with maximum working hours, s.20 presents the rules in respect of annual leave as an entitlement of the employee rather than as something the employer is obliged to ensure occurs. Thus there does not appear to be anything in the legislation prohibiting a situation where an employee voluntarily waives his or her right to annual leave. On the other hand, under Art. 7 of the Framework Directive, it is not legitimate for a worker to be given payment in lieu of holidays save where the employment relationship has ended, in which case such payment *may* be made.[91]

[11–32] The 1997 Act provides for a statutory minimum length of holidays to which an employee is entitled, although naturally this does not prevent an employer and employee from entering into private contractual arrangements that are more beneficial for the employee.[92] Thus under s.19 an employee is entitled to paid[93] annual holiday leave,[94] calculated as follows[95]:

---

wages without any obligation to work or provide any service to the employer. In the Court's view what is required by Article 7 of the Directive and by the Act, is not only that workers receive the requisite leave, but that they be unconditionally and automatically paid their normal weekly rate, specifically in respect of that leave.'

90. *Cementation Skanska (Formerly Kvaerner Cementation v Tom Carroll*, WTC/03/2, DWT 0338, 28 October 2003, citing comments from Advocate General Tizzano in *R v Secretary of State for Trade and Industry ex p Broadcasting, Entertainment Cinematography and Theatre Union* [2001] IRLR 559, in which the right to paid annual leave was referred to as a 'fundamental social right'. See also the decision of the High Court in *Royal Liver Assurance Ltd. v Macken* [2002] 4 IR 427.

91. See *Federatie Nederlandse Vakbeweging v Netherlands*, C-124/05, EUECJ, [2006] ECR I-3423, *Cementation Skanska (Formerly Kvaerner Cementation v Tom Carroll*, WTC/03/2, DWT 0338, 28 October 2003. Where the employment relationship *has* terminated, an employee who has been dismissed is entitled to be paid an amount equivalent to any untaken annual leave in that leave year or any untaken leave in the previous year when they are dismissed within the first six months of the current leave year.

92. s.20(3) Organisation of Working Time Act 1997.

93. For provisions in this regard, see s.20(2) *ibid.* In *Robinson-Steele v RD Retail Services, Clarke v Frank Staddon Ltd., Caulfield & Ors v Hanson Clay Products Ltd.*, C-131/04 and C-257/04 [2006] IRLR 386, the ECJ held that it was not lawful for an employer to provide 'rolled up' holiday pay (that is, to not pay an employee while on leave but rather to factor such holiday pay into his or her general hourly rate of pay) as was permitted in the UK, but rather that such payment would have to be made either before or while the employee was on annual leave. For analysis, see Last, 'Holiday Pay: Rolling Up Regardless', 70 *Employment Law Journal* (May 2006), 9.

94. If an employee produces relevant medical certification to an employer that would justify the taking of sick leave in respect of a particular day, that day shall not be regarded as a day of annual leave: s.19(2) Organisation of Working Time Act 1997.

95. In assessing the number of holidays to which an employee is entitled, an employer must include all days worked, all time spent on annual leave, maternity leave, paternal leave, *force majeure* leave or adoptive leave, and the first 13 weeks of carer's leave, but not periods of time spent on sick leave, leave in respect of occupational injury, temporary lay off or career break.

- four working weeks[96] for any leave year[97] in which [s]he works at least 1,365 hours[98];
- one-third of a working week for each month in the leave year in which [s]he works at least 117 hours; or
- Eight per cent of the hours that [s]he works in a year subject to a maximum of four working weeks.[99]

If more than one of these options applies, the employee is entitled to whichever of these periods of leave is greatest.[100] Moreover, if an employee has worked eight or more months in a year then, subject to the provisions of any ERO, REA, collective agreement or any agreement between employee and employer that may be in place, [s]he is entitled for such period of paid leave to include an unbroken period of two weeks' leave.[101]   [11–33]

In this respect, holiday pay (which should be paid in advance of the employee taking the leave[102]) should be at the normal weekly rate[103] or a proportionate   [11–34]

---

96. A working week refers to the number of days that the employee normally works in a week: s.19(6) Organisation of Working Time Act 1997. Thus in *Irish Ferries v SUI*, WTC/oo/62, DWT 0135, 23 August 2001, the Labour Court held that 'An amount of annual leave equal to four working weeks, to which an employee is entitled under Section 19(1) of the Act, must correspond to the amount of time which the employee would normally be required to work over a four-week period.'

97. For the purposes of the section a 'leave year' is any year beginning on 1 April (s.2 *ibid.*). Importantly this means that where there is an alleged breach of the holiday requirements under the 1997 Act in a given leave year, the time limit for bringing a complaint to a Rights Commissioner starts to run on the last day of that year (i.e. 31 March): *Cementation Skanska (Formerly Kvaerner Cementation v Tom Carroll*, WTC/03/2, DWT 0338, 28 October 2003; *Wastewise Limited v Hickey*, WTC/08/53, DWT 0850, 13 August 2008. In *Royal Liver Assurance Ltd. v SIPTU*, WTC/01/27, DWT 0141, 8 October 2001, the Labour Court suggested that under s.20(1) of the Act it is possible (by consent) for an employer to fix the period of annual leave for a worker at a date within six months after the end of the leave year. Hence the final date on which the terms of the legislation could have been breached was in fact 30 September (or 29 days previously in order that the worker be allowed to take the maximum possible period of annual leave) *after* the end of the previous leave year and thus the limitation period would start at this point. This logic was rejected by Lavan J in the High Court in *Royal Liver Assurance v Macken* [2002] 4 IR 427 on the basis that there was no evidence before the Labour Court that the employer had actually sought the consent of its employees to such an extension.

98. Time off granted to an employee under s.21 and s.19 is to be regarded as time worked by that employee: s.22(2) Organisation of Working Time Act 1997.

99. Specific provisions apply in the case of a part-time worker; these are considered in Chapter 6.

100. s.19(1) Organisation of Working Time Act 1997.

101. s.19(3) Organisation of Working Time Act 1997. This two-week continuous period can include a public holiday or a day on which the employee is ill: s.19(4) *ibid.*

102. s.20(2)(a) *ibid.*

103. s.20(2)(b) *ibid.* Under s.19(5) for the purposes of assessing payment, an employee is to be regarded as having worked on a day that [s]he is on annual leave, the normal hours that [s]he

rate and, where the employee receives board and lodging as part of his or her remuneration, it will include compensation for the board and lodging not being availed of while the employee is on leave.[104] The rate of pay for annual leave is to be calculated by reference to the mechanisms provided under the Organisation of Working Time (Determination of Pay for Holidays) Regulations 1997.[105]

[11–35] The times at which annual leave may be taken are determined by the employer,[106] but [s]he must bear in mind certain specific listed concerns in making such determination, namely the need for the employee to reconcile work and any family responsibilities and the opportunities for rest and recreation available to the employee.[107] In determining when annual leave is to be taken, the employer must consult with the employee or a relevant trade union.[108] Moreover, it is possible (with the consent of the employee) for the leave to which the employee is entitled in a leave year to be taken within six months after the expiry of that leave year.[109]

[11–36] In *Waterford County Council v O'Donoghue*[110] the Labour Court was faced with a somewhat unusual claim in respect of annual leave entitlements under the Organisation of Working Time Act 1997. It will be remembered that under s.2 of the 1997 Act, a 'leave year' is defined as a year beginning on the 1st of April in a given year and running until 31 March in the following year. In the present case the respondent body had altered its administrative leave year in November 2007 such that from then on, the leave year would run from 1 January until 31 December (the calendar year) rather than from 1 April until 31 March (the statutory leave year). As a result of such change, however, there would obviously be an anomalous nine month 'year' in the period between April 1 2007 until December 31 of the same year, and in order to deal with this anomaly, staff were informed that for this period (being 75 per cent of a year) they would be entitled to 75 per cent of the holidays that they would have accumulated in a full calendar year. The Union and the claimant in this case contended, however, that what the Respondent had done was in fact to define the period between April 1 and December 31 as a *year* (in other words that it had introduced a nine month leave year) and that workers

---

would have worked that day had [s]he *not* been on annual leave. Thus the Labour Court has recommended that where an employee is regularly rostered for overtime, such payments for overtime should be reflected in the amount of payment received while on annual leave. *Banagher Concrete v SIPTU*, CD/04/625, LCR 18118, 28 February 2005. For consideration, see Kerr, *Irish Employment Legislation* (Round Hall Sweet and Maxwell, 2000), at B-77.

104. s.20(2)(c) Organisation of Working Time Act 1997.

105. SI no. 475 of 1997. This is grounded in s.20(4) Organisation of Working Time Act 1997.

106. Thus an employee may be disciplined for taking annual leave other than at a time permitted by an employer *Costello v Gerard May Roofing* [1994] ELR 19.

107. s.20(1)(a) Organisation of Working Time Act 1997.

108. s.20(1)(b) *ibid.*

109. s.20(1)(c) *ibid.*

110. WTC/08/190 determination no. DWT0963 (14 July 2009)

(such as the claimant) who had worked the requisite number of hours in that period should be entitled to a full annual allowance of leave as provided under the terms of the 1997 Act (in this case, 23 days).

The Labour Court rejected this proposition. It noted that whereas the 1997 Act [11–37] referred to a leave year as commencing on April 1, nonetheless it still spoke very definitely in terms of a '*year*', and as the Labour Court pointed out

> 'As a matter of plain language that means a period of 12 months' and 'The period 1st April to 31st December is a period of nine months and is not capable of being regarded as a year for the purposes of the Act or otherwise'.

In other words, the period in which an employee can earn the maximum possible [11–38] number of days of annual leave is incontrovertibly a twelve month period. On this basis the court concluded that:

> The only leave year which is cognisable for the purpose of determining if an employee received his or her statutory entitlement is that prescribed by the Act itself, that is to say a year starting on 1st April and ending on 31st March the following year. While different arrangements may be put in place for administrative purposes, in determining if a contravention of the Act occurred that Court can only have regard to the leave allocated to an employees in the statutory period. Consequently the Claimant can only succeed in the present claim if it is shown that in the period 1st April 2007 to 31st march 2008 he was allocated less that 20 days annual leave.

> In the instant case the change in the 'leave year' is an administrative arrangement. Under the arrangement an employees affected will still accrue an entitlement to 20 days annual leave in the 12 month period 1st April and 31st March, or indeed any other 12 Month period. In accordance with s. 20(1) of the Act the statutory leave must be granted within the leave year, as defined, or within six months thereafter where the employee so consents.

Finally the Labour Court noted that the challenge in respect of the leave granted [11–39] had been originally brought to the Rights Commissioner in *January 2008*. Yet this was more than two months before the end of the relevant leave year April 2007-March 2008 – which was, of course the period of time which the Labour Court had concluded constituted the full year in respect of which the claimant had entitlements. Noting the conclusion of Lavan J in the High Court in case of *Royal Liver Assurance v Macken*[111] that where there had been an alleged contravention of s.19 of the 1997 Act then this contravention could only take place at the *end* of a leave year (in that the employee may, under the Act, exercise his or her discretion to allow his or her employees to take leave at any time during a leave year), the Labour Court concluded that in this case the action, apart from being ill

---

111. [2002] 4 IR 427

founded, was also premature in that it was 'in respect of an alleged contravention of the Act which could only have crystallised two months later'.

[11–40] It is worth noting that in a number of different cases under the Organisation of Working Time Act,[112] but most commonly where an employer has failed to provide an employee with appropriate annual leave, the Labour Court has tended to apply the logic of the European Court of Justice in *Von Colson and Kamann v Land Nordrhein-Westfalen*[113] – namely that judicial redress in cases where economic rights are under threat should not merely compensate but should also provide a real deterrent against future infractions – and to award not merely compensation but also additional damages aimed both at having an exemplary effect[114] and also at compensating the worker for the inconvenience and expense of pursuing the matter.[115] Thus in *Svetlana Kuzinsky t/a Assorti v Anastazjew*[116] and *Griffin Retail v Amimer*[117] the level of damages awarded by the Rights Commissioner was increased by the Labour Court to reflect the fact that there had been a deliberate and conscious breach of the Act. In *TJ & MA Construction Limited v Woldarczyk*[118] the Labour Court, accepting this logic, concluded:

> This means that the compensation awarded must fully compensate the complainant for the economic loss which he or she sustained as a result of the breach of their Community rights. It must also contain an element which reflects the gravity of the infringement and acts as a disincentive against future infractions.

[11–41] On the other hand, in *Patrick Callaghan v Leita*[119] the Labour Court held that limited damages would be awarded where what had occurred could only be classified as minor or technical breaches of the legislation. Moreover, very significantly in *Conlon v Kruglijs*,[120] the Labour Court appeared to limit the amount of damages to which an employee (who had worked in excess of the permitted weekly working hours under the Act) would be entitled on the basis that he had colluded

---

112. See, for example, *Feeney v Baquiram* [2004] ELR 304; *Goode Concrete v Munro*, WTC/04/59, DWT 051, 5 January 2005.
113. C-14/83 [1984] ECR 1891.
114. This is the logic of the approach of the Labour Court in *Solid Building Company v Sergejs Baranovs*, WTC/08/7, DWT 0821, 21 May 2008, where the Labour Court awarded significant damages to the claimant outside his simple annual-leave entitlements because of the flagrant nature of the breach of the legislation on the part of the respondent company.
115. *Cementation Skanska (Formerly Kvaerner Cementation v Tom Carroll)*, WTC/03/2, DWT 0338, 28 October 2003; *Wastewise Limited v Hickey*, WTC/08/53, DWT 0850, 13 August 2008; *Kennedy's Café Bar Ltd. v A Worker*, WTC/00/12, DWT 0026, 8 August 2000.
116. WTC/08/159, DWT 0918, 19 March 2009.
117. WTC/09/31, DWT 0940, 15 May 2009.
118. WTC/09/18, DWT 0929, 9 April 2009.
119. WTC/08/147, DWT 0910, 2 February 2009.
120. WTC/09/40, DWT 0939, 13 May 2009.

with the employer in breaching the Act (in the sense that he had requested that he be allowed to work overtime).

Finally, in the joined cases *Schultz-Hoff v Deutsche Rentenversicherung Bund* and *Stringer v Her Majesty's Revenue and Customs*[121] the ECJ made what could be enormously significant statements as far as Irish law is concerned, in respect of the connection between annual leave and sick leave, and in particular the question of the entitlement of an employee who is on an extended period of sick leave to his or her annual leave. The essence of the Court's conclusion is that, because of the huge significance of annual leave entitlements as far as EC law is concerned[122] the position of employees who are denied annual leave essentially because they are on sick leave requires special consideration.   [11–42]

The Court held that it is legitimate for a state to decide that annual leave may not be taken during the period when an employee is absent from work on sick leave.[123] Moreover Community law does not preclude, as a rule, national legislation which states that the right to annual leave will be lost at the end of a leave year or of a carry-over period. However, what is pivotal is that the employee in question must actually have had the opportunity to exercise the right conferred on him or her by the Directive.[124] Hence in the case of an employee   [11–43]

(a) who had been on sick leave for the whole leave year[125] or part of the leave year[126] and beyond the 'carry over' period following the end of the leave year and in which annual leave can be taken,

(b) who (under national law) was not permitted to take annual leave during this period and

(c) whose illness persisted until the termination of his employment,[127]

the ECJ determined that it would be necessary for the national law to provide that the entitlements to annual leave of that employee would not be extinguished

---

121. [2009] EUECJ C-350/06, C-520/06 [2009] All ER (EC) 906, [2009] IRLR 214, [2009] 2 CMLR 27, [2009] ICR 932

122. [2009] EUECJ C-350/06 at para.22

123. *ibid.*, at paras.28 and 29. This is because of the general entitlement under EC law of Member States to make provision for the specific manner in which annual leave may be taken. On the other hand, EC law does not preclude national legislation or practices which allow a worker on sick leave to take paid annual leave during that sick leave. *ibid.*, at para.31.

124. *ibid.*, at para.43.

125. *ibid.*, at para.44.

126. *ibid.,* at para.52.

127. *ibid.*, at paras.49 and 52. It is perhaps, not entirely clear why the ECJ felt that the fact that the illness persisted until the determination of the employment relationship was actually relevant as a matter of principle. Presumably the logic of the court would apply in any case where the employee was ill for the whole of a leave year and beyond and even if at some later stage [s]he became well enough to return to work.

by reason of the ending of that carry over period[128]. What is key in such a case is that the employee is *incapable* of taking his or her annual leave entitlements within the prescribed period. The essential conclusion of the Court in this case, therefore, is that the annual leave entitlements of an employee are so significant that the fact that [s]he is unable to avail of them within a defined period owing to illness should not mean that such entitlements are thereby lost. Moreover, where an employee has not taken his or her annual leave as a result of his or her being on sick leave, [s]he is entitled to be paid *in lieu* of such leave when their employment terminates and at his or her normal remuneration rate.[129]

[11–44] The significance of this decision as far as Irish employers are concerned is potentially enormous, in that it opens up the vista of employees who have been on very long and extended periods of sick leave making claims for perhaps years of back-dated holiday pay. It may be suggested that the best way for employers to manage the situation is not to focus on the issue of *annual* leave, but rather to focus on the issue of *sick* leave and to ensure in so far as is practicable that employees are not kept on sick leave for any extended period of time in which they may acquire holiday entitlements.[130]

2.4.1. Public Holidays

[11–45] Where an employee has worked at least 40 hours for his or her employer during the previous five weeks prior to any given public holiday,[131] [s]he is entitled to either

- a paid day off on that day[132];
- a paid day off within a month of that day[133];

---

128. *ibid.*, at paras.44–49.
129. *ibid.*, at para.61
130. For analysis see O'Mara, 'European Developments', 6(1) *IELJ* (2009), 30. O'Mara concludes (*ibid.*, at 32) that 'Employers will face major costs unless they manage sickness absence effectively and efficiently. Allowing absence to continue longer than is necessary will see workers "racking up" substantial holiday entitlement. This could create significant financial liability and, where employees seek to take significant periods of holiday following extended sick leave, it could cause severe disruption to the business.' The same author (*ibid.*) suggests that the requirement that a long term disabled employee be given four weeks annual leave might be seen as constituting no more than reasonable accommodation under Employment Equality law.
131. s.21(4) Organisation of Working Time Act 1997. Section 21(1) does not apply, as respects a particular public holiday, to a worker who is absent from work before the public holiday in any of the cases specified in the Third Schedule to the Act: s.21 (5) *ibid.*
132. s.21(1)(a) *ibid.* This paragraph does not have application if the day on which a public holiday falls is a day on which [s]he would, apart from the subsection, be entitled to a paid day off (and this is expressly deemed to include any day on which [s]he is not required to work): s.21(6) *ibid.*
133. s.21(1)(b) *ibid.*

- an additional day of annual leave, or[134];
- an additional day's pay,

whichever one of these four options is determined[135] by his or her employer.[136]

At present there are nine public holidays as set out in the second schedule to the 1997 Act.[137] The rate of pay for a public holiday is calculated by the mechanisms provided under the Organisation of Working Time (Determination of Pay for Holidays) Regulations 1997.[138]

Some uncertainty surrounds the position of an employee who is on sick leave at a time when a public holiday occurs. Undoubtedly that employee is entitled to some concession in respect of that public holiday – most usually a day's paid leave.[139] But the question is whether the fact that [s]he is sick is of any relevance. In other words,   [11–46]

---

134. s.21(1)(c). In *Royal Liver Assurance Ltd. v SIPTU*, WTC/01/27, DWT 0141, 8 October 2001, the Labour Court noted that, as far as the potential provision to a worker of an additional day's leave in lieu of a paid day off for a public holiday under s.20(1) of the Act is concerned, it is possible (by consent) for an employer to extend the date on which a worker can be given annual leave (and therefore, presumably, a day's extra annual leave in lieu of a public holiday) until up to six months after the end of the leave year (that is, 30 September). Hence it determined that the six-month time period for bringing a complaint in respect of public holidays within a particular leave year to a Rights Commissioner only starts to run from 30 September following the end of the relevant leave year. This logic was rejected by Lavan J in the High Court in *Royal Liver Assurance v Macken* [2002] 4 IR 427 on the basis that there was no evidence before the Labour Court that the employer had actually sought the consent of its employees to such an extension, and that such an approach would mean that no relief in respect of either annual leave or failure to provide public holidays could be sought until this later date.

135. An employee may, not later than 21 days before a public holiday, request his employer to make a determination as to which of the options under s.21(1) Organisation of Working Time Act 1997 the employer will take in respect of that employee. The employer must notify the employee within 14 days of the date of the public holiday of the result of this determination (s.21(2) *ibid.*) and should [s]he fail to do so, then [s]he shall be taken to have determined that the employee is entitled to a paid day off, or, if the employee would have been entitled irrespective of the section to have had a paid day off on that day, to an additional day's pay: s.21(3) *ibid.*

136. s.21(1)(d) *ibid.*

137. The public holidays listed in the second schedule to the Act are Christmas Day, St Stephen's Day, St Patrick's Day, 1 January, Easter Monday, the first Monday in May, June and August, and the last Monday in October. For an interesting analysis of the background to such public holidays, see Kerr, *Irish Employment Legislation* (Round Hall Sweet and Maxwell, 2000), at B-78–B-79.

138. SI no. 475 of 1997. Generally, see s.22 of the Act and see Kerr, *ibid.*, at B-80.

139. On the other hand, a similar entitlement does not apply where the employee is on so-called paid 'administrative leave' (that is, where the worker is relieved of the obligation to attend at his or her place of work or to perform work for his or her employer, but where all other aspects of the contract of employment are unaffected): *County Limerick VEC v Cotter*, WTC/08/83, DWT 0868, 29 October 2008.

can the employer (who may well be paying that employee some form of sick leave at the time) simply allow that employee the (paid) day off work by rolling up his or her public holiday entitlement into his or her sick pay entitlement, or must the employer treat that day off as a sick day such that the employee would retain the entitlement to some other form of compensation in respect of the public holiday – either in the form of another day's paid leave, or a day's extra pay?[140]

[11–47] This issue was revisited by the Labour Court in *Leitrim County Council v Martin*.[141] Here the employee in question was on certified sick leave over the Christmas holidays in 2006. There were three public holidays during the period of the workers' absence and these were paid for as public holiday benefit rather than sick leave. The employee claimed that the leave should have been classified as sick leave and that he should therefore have been able to claim the entitlements with respect to the public holiday at a later date. A Rights Commissioner had found that the complaint was well founded, and awarded the employee his public holiday entitlements and also €500 in compensation. This decision was appealed to the Labour Court.

[11–48] On the facts, the Labour Court found against the worker. It concluded that he had received paid days off for the three days in question, which were not offset against sick leave entitlements, that the (consistently applied) practice of the employer was to apply public holiday entitlements to workers who may be absent on sick leave on public holidays and not to offset the leave against entitlements under the sick pay scheme (in other words that one would not receive sick pay in respect of public holidays) and, most importantly, that in any event the employee's entitlements under the sick pay scheme had expired at the time (he was in fact given an extra three days of sick leave to reflect the fact that three of the days on which he was sick during the Christmas period were public holidays), and consequently, the only basis on which he could have received a paid day off work was by reference to his public holiday entitlements. The court noted its previous determinations in *Thermo King and Pat Kenny*[142] and *HSE West and Alison Meehan*[143] (which had led to the conclusion that an employee could not be paid public holiday pay

---

140. The Labour Court has concluded that if an employee is on paid sick leave (pursuant either to contract or to the terms of a collective agreement) over a period of time on which a public holiday falls, the employer does not discharge his or her statutory obligations by paying the employee under the terms of the sick-pay scheme. In other words, the entitlement to a paid day off on the public holiday is independent of any entitlements under a sick-pay scheme. See *Thermo King v Pat Kenny*, WTC/05/10, DWT 0611, 19 May 2006; *HSE West v Meehan*; WTC/08/73, DWT 0844, 1 December 2008; *Group 4 Securicor (Ireland) Ltd. v SIPTU*, CD08/166, LCR 19340, 22 September 2008 (this latter case arose by way of an application under s.26 Industrial Relations Act 1990 and hence does not constitute a definitive interpretation of the 1997 Act).
141. WTC/08/69, DWT 0914, 2 March 2009.
142. WTC/05/10 DWT 0611, 19 May 2006.
143. WTC/08/73 DWT 0884, 1 December 2008. See also *Group 4 Securicor (Ireland) Ltd. v SIPTU*, CD/08/166, LCR 19340, 22 September 2008.

on a public holiday on which [s]he was sick if a term in his or her contract of employment provided that [s]he was entitled to sick pay in such circumstances) but held that under s.21(1) of the 1997 Act an employer was free to provide any employee with a day's paid leave on a public holiday irrespective of whether that employee was or was not sick on that day. Finally, the court distinguished in principle between s.20 of the Act, which requires that annual leave must be granted at a time that affords an employee opportunity for rest and relaxation, and s.21 of the Act, which in dealing with public holidays makes no equivalent provision.[144]

2.4.2. Holiday Entitlements where the Employment Relationship Has Ended

Where an employee has holiday entitlements accruing against an employer but has [11–49] ceased to be employed by the employer,[145] [s]he is entitled to be paid the amount of the appropriate weekly rate[146] that [s]he would have received had [s]he been granted that annual leave.[147] Similar entitlements arise where an employee ceases to be employed during the week ending on the day before a public holiday and the employee has worked for his or her employer during the four weeks proceeding that week,[148] in which case the employee concerned is entitled to be paid an additional day's pay at the appropriate daily rate.[149]

2.4.3 Linking Claims

Finally, under s.40 of the 1997 Act it is provided that where there has been some [11–50] failure to comply with the provisions of Part III of the Act (dealing with holidays) then, if the claim in respect of holidays is linked with a claim pertaining to entitlements under another listed statute, the employee or his representative may, as an alternative to claiming relief under s.27, bring the Part III claim as an element of his or her claim under that other statute.

---

144. The court also made the point that in assessing the requirements in respect of public holidays, there was no EC law element to the case, which would, instead, be governed exclusively by domestic law.

145. If the employee has ceased to be employed by reason of his or her death then such compensation should be payable to the personal representative of the employee: s.23(3) Organisation of Working Time Act 1997.

146. The reference to the appropriate weekly and daily rate in this section means the appropriate rate determined in accordance with regulations made by the Minister (s.23(5) *ibid.*), namely the Organisation of Working Time (Determination of Pay for Holidays) Regulations 1997, SI no. 475 of 1997.

147. s.23(1) Organisation of Working Time Act 1997.

148. *Gazboro Ltd. v BATU* WTC/99/9, DWT 9916, 13 July 1999. A date for which a person receives an additional day's pay pursuant to s.23(2) Organisation of Working Time Act 1997 does not itself constitute a working day for the purposes of assessing the end of the relevant working week. Moreover, where compensation is payable under s.23(2) *ibid.*, the employee shall for social welfare purposes not be regarded as having been in the employment of the employer concerned on the relevant public holiday: s.23(4) *ibid.*

149. s.23(2) *ibid.*

2.5. Sunday Work

[11–51] Whereas the previous four categories of rule under the legislation are concerned with promoting health and safety within the relevant workplace, the next three categories of rule are far more concerned with securing entitlements for employees.

[11–52] As we have seen, the general rule in the Act is that, save as may be otherwise provided in the employee's contract of employment, the weekly rest period shall either be a Sunday or, if that weekly rest period is of more than 24 hours' duration, it shall *include* a Sunday.[150] Furthermore, where an employee *is* required, under the terms of his or her contract of employment, to work on a Sunday, and where this has not been otherwise factored into the determination of his or her rate of pay,[151] his or her employer must compensate him or her in some other fashion,[152] namely:

- by granting him or her an allowance of such amount as is reasonable having regard to all the circumstances[153];
- by otherwise increasing his or her rate of pay, by such amount as is reasonable having regard to all the circumstances[154];
- by granting him or her such paid time off work as is reasonable in the circumstances[155]; or
- by a combination of two or more of these options.[156]

[11–53] Finally, in assessing the premium to be paid for Sunday work (and in the case of a worker for whom such premium is not provided for in a collective agreement[157]) the Act takes the unusual step of permitting a Rights Commissioner or the Labour Court, in the context of proceedings under Part IV of the Act, to assess such premium by reference to the value or minimum value for Sunday work[158] that

---

150. s.13(5) *ibid.* In C-169/91 *Stoke on Trent City Council v B&Q* [1992] ECR I-6457, the UK government successfully challenged the validity of a similar provision within the Framework Directive, with the ECJ saying that there was no good reason why having Sunday as a day of weekly rest was more conducive to health and safety of workers than any other day of the week.

151. s.14(1) Organisation of Working Time Act 1997. See *Group 4 Securitas v SIPTU*, WTC/99/5, DWT 996, 16 April 1999, where the Labour Court rejected a claim for a general increase in the Sunday premium paid to workers in circumstances where there was an existing allowance paid to workers for working on Sundays.

152. See *Meaghers Tasty Bread v Eccles*, WTC/07/79, DWT 0817, 14 April 2009.

153. s.14(1)(a) Organisation of Working Time Act 1997.

154. s.14(1)(b) *ibid.*

155. s.14(1)(c) *ibid.*

156. s.14(1)(d) *ibid.*

157. s.14(2) *ibid.*

158. The concept of a 'minimum value' covers situations where the relevant collective agreement sets out a formula or procedures for calculating the minimum value in question, provided that such formula/procedures can be readily applied or followed by the Rights Commissioner or Labour Court in the relevant case: s.14(6) *ibid.*

should be paid to a comparable employee[159] under the terms of a collective agreement pertaining to that comparable employee.[160] In such circumstances, and save where the fact of such collective agreement specifying such premium has come to the attention of the Labour Court or Rights Commissioner, it is the duty of the person in the proceedings alleging that such premium is provided for in such collective agreement, to show that this is, in fact, the case.[161]

In assessing the form and level of such compensation for employees who work [11–54] in the retail sector and are contractually obliged to work on Sundays, employers should have regard to the Labour Relations Commission Code of Practice on the topic, which was brought into force via the Organisation of Working Time (Code of Practice on Sunday Working in the Retail Trade and Related Matters) (Declaration) Order 1998.[162] The essence of the recommendations in the code is that the level of such compensation should be set either in the form of a collective agreement or, where no such agreement exists, by reference to the arrangements in a collective agreement applying to comparable employees in the retail sector.[163] It is further recommended that the nature and value of the premium to be applied to Sunday work should be negotiated between employers and employees and should be based on a consensus approach. Moreover, the LRC will provide assistance to employers and trade unions and employers and employees who are not unionised in terms of negotiating such agreements.

Beyond this the code recommends that existing employees should have the option [11–55] to volunteer to opt into working patterns that include Sundays on a rota basis and that, whereas newly recruited employees may be contracted to work Sundays as part of a regular working pattern, employees who have at least two years' service on a Sunday-working contract should have the opportunity to seek to opt out of Sunday working for urgent personal or family reasons, giving adequate notice to employers. On the other hand, all employees should have the opportunity, irrespective of length of service, to volunteer to work on the peak Sunday trading days prior to Christmas in addition to their normal working week.

---

159. A 'comparable employee' means an employee who is employed to do, under similar circumstances, identical or similar work in the industry or sector of employment concerned to that which the relevant employee so far as the proceedings under Part IV are concerned is employed to do: s.14(5) *ibid.*

160. s.14(3) *ibid.* If there is more than one relevant collective agreement specifying different minimum values attaching to Sunday work, the value of compensation to be afforded to the claimant employee shall be the lesser or least of such different minimum values.

161. s.14(4) *ibid.*

162. SI no. 444 of 1998.

163. paras.3.1 and 3.2. The code also deals with matters such as entitlements to opt into a working pattern that includes Sundays, and entitlements to opt out of a Sunday working pattern for urgent family or personal reasons: para.3.3.

2.6. Provision of Information in Relation to Working Time

[11–56] Where the normal or regular starting and finishing times of work of an employee are not specified in his or her contract of employment, or in an ERO, REA or collective agreement, his or her employer is required to notify[164] such employee (in a working day at least 24 hours before the first day in each week that [s]he requires the employee to work) of the times at which the employee will normally be required to start and finish work on any or each day of that week.[165]

[11–57] In addition if, under the terms of his or her contract, the employee is also required to work additional hours as determined from time to time[166] by the employer (essentially overtime) the employee is again entitled to 24 hours' notice[167] before the first day (or, as the case may be, the day) of any week in which such additional hours are to be worked of the start and finishing times of such additional hours on each day of that week.[168]

[11–58] Finally, the provision of such notification does not prejudice the ability of the employer (subject to the provisions of the legislation) to require the employee to start or finish work or to start or finish any such additional hours at times other than those specified in the notification in circumstances that could not have been foreseen, and which justify the employer in changing the working times of the employee as notified to him or her.[169] In *Matrix Foods Limited v Klimenkovs*[170] the Labour Court dealt with the proper interpretation of this section and found, interpreting s.17(4), that it was acceptable that an employee was occasionally given very short notice that [s]he would be needed for work in the following week, in circumstances of emergency – for example, where a fellow employee was sick or had for some other reason not reported for work.

---

164. It is sufficient in this regard to post a notice in a conspicuous place in the employee's place of employment: s.17(5) Organisation of Working Time Act 1997.

165. s.17(1) *ibid.*

166. The use of the phrase 'from time to time' in the legislation has been interpreted by the courts as not covering a situation where such *ad hoc* determination of additional hours has occurred once (*Smart Scaffolding v Bunyahevych*, WTC/08/34, DWT 0877, 25 November 2008), nor where the additional hours are worked consistently and as a matter of the worker's contract: *Olhausens Ltd. v Murauskas* WTC/08/50, DWT 0852, 27 August 2008.

167. If the employee was not working for the employer in the 24-hour period before the first day of the week on which [s]he is required to work additional hours, then [s]he must be informed of his or her working hours, including additional hours of work during the last 24-hour period in which [s]he has been required to work for the employer: s.17(3) Organisation of Working Time Act 1997.

168. s.17(2) *ibid.*

169. s.17(4) *ibid.*

170. WTC/09/14, DWT 0931, 20 April 2009.

2.7. Zero-Hour Working Practices

Specific provision is made in the Act for what are termed 'zero-hour contracts' and   [11–59]
'zero-hour working practices'. These arise where, by virtue of his or her contract of
employment, an employee is either expected to be available for work for a certain
number of hours ('contract hours') or to be available as and when the employer
requires him or her to be so[171] (and this does not include a situation where an
employee is 'on call' – that is, required to be available to deal with emergencies,
which may not happen[172]) or both,[173] yet where, despite such mandatory availability, there is no guarantee that there will actually be paid work available for
the employee.[174] The objective of the legislation in this respect is to ensure that a
worker cannot be required to be available for work and receive no compensation
if [s]he ended up having no work to do. Hence, in such circumstances, where
the employee has not been required to work for at least 25 per cent of his or her
contract hours,[175] or (where [s]he was simply required to be available when an
employer required this) if [s]he was not required to work for at least 25 per cent of
the hours in which work of the kind that [s]he was to be available for was actually
done for that employer in that week,[176] then [s]he is nonetheless entitled to be

---

171. It is clear from s.18(1) Organisation of Working Time Act 1997 that this does not include
    situations where an employee claims to have a reasonable expectation of work by virtue only
    of the fact that the employer had engaged the employee to do casual work for him or her on
    occasions prior to the week in question.

172. s.18(5) *ibid.*

173. In *Ocean Manpower v MPGWU*, WTC/98/1, DWT 981, 11 August 1998, the Labour Court
    held that the fact that the relevant employer did not rigidly enforce such an arrangement did
    not preclude the application of s.18.

174. This does not include circumstances where the nature of the employee's contract is such
    that [s]he is entitled to be paid wages by the employer simply by reason of the fact that
    [s]he has made him or herself available for work (s.18(6) Organisation of Working Time Act
    1997). It also does not include situations where the fact that the employee concerned was
    not required to work of a lay off or a case of the employee being kept on for a short time for
    that week, or was due to exceptional circumstances or an emergency (including an accident
    or the imminent risk of an accident) or due to the occurrence of unusual and unforesee-
    able circumstances beyond the employer's control, all of whose consequences could not
    have been avoided despite the exercise of all due care (s.18(3)(a) *ibid.*). Finally, the section
    does not apply where the employee concerned would not actually have been available to
    work the relevant percentage of hours for the employer due to illness or any other reasons
    (s.18(3)(b) *ibid.*).

175. s.18(2)(a) *ibid.*

176. s.18(2)(b) *ibid.* This refers to a situation where another employee[s] does the relevant work
    for the employer. In calculating the relevant hours for which the employee was available for
    work, what is relevant is the number of hours that the other employee did such work for the
    employer and, where more than one employee is doing such work and the workload of such
    other employees is not identical, what is relevant is the greatest number of hours worked by
    any one such other employee: s.18(4) *ibid.*

paid for up to either 25 per cent of his or her contract hours, or of the hours that [s]he was required to be available,[177] or for 15 hours, whichever is less.[178]

3. Enforcement

[11–60]   The provisions of the 1997 Act can be enforced either through a claim for compensation taken by an employee or through criminal prosecution. This bifurcated method of enforcement reflects the dual concerns of the legislation, namely to foster safety in the workplace and to vindicate the interests of employees.[179] To some extent, however, it may be argued that the enforcement mechanisms within the legislation are somewhat unsophisticated, in that logically an employee should only be able to take a civil action in respect of a breach of those sections of the legislation that were designed to protect his or her interests (for example, where [s]he has not been given appropriate holiday pay or where [s]he has not received compensation for working on Sundays), whereas a criminal prosecution should be the appropriate remedy where there has been a breach of those aspects of the legislation that are designed to promote health and safety, save where the employee has actually suffered loss as a result of such breach. In other words, it is difficult to see why a worker who voluntarily works for a period in excess of the statutory maximum should then be entitled to take a civil action against the employer[180], whereas, because of the risk to workplace safety posed by an over-worked employer, this is the type of situation in which a criminal prosecution might well be appropriate.

---

177. In *Ocean Manpower v MPGWU*, WTC /98/1, DWT 981, 11 August 1998, the Labour Court held that the amount of money to which such a worker should be entitled should be calculated by reference to the number of hours the employee may be required to work in a week and not to the number of hours for which they are required to be available to undertake that work. It is respectfully submitted that such a conclusion does not follow from the terms of ss.18(1) and 18(2) of the Act.

178. s.18(2) Organisation of Working Time Act 1997. Naturally if [s]he has been paid for *any* hours that [s]he in fact worked in that week, then this will be deducted from the amount that [s]he must be paid under s.18. Thus if [s]he has worked and been paid for 15 hours, then s.18 has no application even though [s]he may not have worked 25 per cent of the hours for which [s]he was required to be available. Generally, see *Ocean Manpower v MPGWU*, WTC/98/1, DWT 981, 11 August 1998.

179. It has also been suggested that the terms of the legislation may be read into the contracts of employment of workers and hence that where an employer is in breach of such legislation (and hence in breach of contract) it is appropriate for a court to grant declaratory and injunctive relief. See *Barber v RJB Mining (UK) Ltd.* [1999] IRLR 308 and, generally, see Moffat, ed., *Employment Law* (2nd ed., Law Society of Ireland, 2006), at p.85.

180. As we have seen, in *Conlon v Kruglijs* (WTC/09/40, DWT 0939, 13 May 2009) the Labour Court appeared to limit the amount of damages to which an employee (who had worked in excess of the permitted weekly working hours under the Act) would be entitled on the basis that he had colluded with the employer in breaching the Act (in the sense that he had requested that he be allowed to work overtime).

3.1. Employee Compensation Claims

An employee or, with his or her consent, a trade union of which [s]he is a member, can bring a complaint[181] (in a written notice to the Rights Commissioner containing such particulars and in such form as may be specified by the Minister[182] and on notice to the other party concerned by the decisions[183]) to the Rights Commissioner in respect of any breach of s.6(2) or of ss.11 to 23, or in respect of a breach of any other relevant rule contained in regulations, or a collective agreement, REA or ERO.[184] **[11–61]**

In addition, a claim can be brought for compensation in circumstances where an employer (in breach of s.26 of the 1997 Act) penalises an employee for having in good faith and by lawful means opposed any action by the employer that is unlawful under the 1997 Act.[185] In *University College Cork v Keohane*[186] the Labour Court held that **[11–62]**

> In order to make out her complaint of penalisation it is necessary for the complainant to establish a causal link between her activities in seeking to have section 19 of the Act applied by the respondent and some detriment which she suffered in her employment. Such a link can be established by reference to particular facts or by inference from all of the surrounding circumstances. The activities alleged to have given rise to the detriment suffered must, however, relate to the claimant having opposed an act which is unlawful under the Act of 1997.

Finally, where a claim is for breach of Part III of the Act (pertaining to annual leave and holiday entitlements) then it can be instituted as part of a claim under any enactment listed in the table to s.39(2) of the 1997 Act and on the basis of the listed procedure contained in such enactment.

Complaints must be presented to the Rights Commissioner within six months beginning on the date of the contravention to which the complaint relates,[187] **[11–63]**

---

181. Naturally where the complainant, having been properly informed of the date of the hearing, fails to attend the hearing, his or her complaint can be struck out for want of prosecution. *Headway Security v Ryan*, WTC/08/75, DWT 0856, 16 September 2008.

182. s.27(6) Organisation of Working Time Act 1997.

183. 27(7) *ibid.*

184. ss.27(1) and (2) *ibid.*

185. s.26 *ibid.* This section has no application in cases where the penalisation by the employer is in response to a lawful and good-faith opposition by the employee to an act by the employer that is in fact not unlawful under the terms of the Act. *Carlton Airport Hotel v Martin Patterson*, WTC/08/26, DWT 0844, 30 July 2008. In addition, where the act of penalisation itself constitutes an unfair dismissal, relief may not be granted to the employee, both under the Organisation of Working Time Act and the Unfair Dismissals Act.

186. WTC/01/26, DWT 0147, 28 November 2001.

187. s.27(4) Organisation of Working Time Act 1997. See, for example, *Clare Community Radio v Kelly* WTC/08/24, DWT 0842, 21 July 2008. The Labour Court has held that where a

although the Rights Commissioner can extend this to a longer period not exceeding 12 months where [s]he feels that the failure to present the complaint within the six-month period was owing to reasonable cause.[188] In *Cementation Skanska v Carroll*[189] the Labour Court analysed what was meant by 'reasonable cause' in this regard and, having pointed out that the standard was patently less than that applying in other employment law statutes where an applicant has to show that there were exceptional circumstances explaining why the claim had not been brought in time, it proceeded as follows:

> It is the Court's view that in considering if reasonable cause exists, it is for the claimant to show that there are reasons, which both explain the delay and afford an excuse for the delay. The explanation must be reasonable, that is to say it must make sense, be agreeable to reason and not be irrational or absurd. In the context in which the expression reasonable cause appears in the statute it suggests an objective standard, but it must be applied to the facts and circumstances known to the claimant at the material time. The claimant's failure to present his or her claim within the six-month time limit must have been due to the reasonable cause relied upon. Hence, there must be a causal link between the circumstances cited and the delay and the claimant should satisfy the Court, as a matter of probability, that had those circumstances not been present he would have initiated the claim in time.[190]

> The length of the delay should be taken into account. A short delay may require only a slight explanation whereas a long delay may require more cogent reasons. Where reasonable cause is shown the Court must still consider if it is appropriate in the circumstances to exercise its discretion in favour of granting an extension of time. Here the Court should consider if the respondent has suffered prejudice by the delay and should also consider if the claimant has a good arguable case.

---

complaint was handed in to the receptionist's desk in the Rights Commissioner service on the last day of the six-month period the claim was not statute barred, even though the service itself did not actually receive it until the following morning. See *Department of Health and Children v Nestor*, WTC/08/134, DWT 0893, 11 December 2008. It may be suggested that a difficulty with this case on its facts was that the date from which the time period was deemed to start was the date on which the employee had left his job, which might not necessarily be a date on which there was a contravention of the Act.

188. s.27(5) Organisation of Working Time Act 1997. This would be the case, for example, where the claim was not brought in time owing to ill health on the part of the claimant. *Patrick T Durcan & Co. v Courtney*, WTC/07/91, DWT 0847, 1 August 2008.

189. WTC/03/2, DWT 0338, 31 October 2003.

190. So, for example, in *Manufacturing and Maintenance Engineering v Currams*, WTC/02/1, DWT 0215, 15 March 2002, the court allowed an employee what was in effect a 12-month extension to the normal six months in which to bring a claim on the basis that he believed he could only make a claim in respect of annual leave when his employment was over. With respect this is a strange decision, in that it appears to say that ignorance of the law is an objectively justifiable reason as to why such extension can be given, yet if this is the case then it may reasonably be asked why ignorance of the existence of the six-month time limit should not also constitute an objectively justifiable reason to extend such time limit.

Thus in the case of an ongoing breach of the Act it would seem that whereas a   **[11–64]** complaint may be brought at any point, the Rights Commissioner, in assessing both liability and the quantum of compensation, is confined to considering the events of the previous six (or, where appropriate and where the Labour Court allows an extension for submitting a claim, up to 18) months.[191]

Where such a case is brought in time, it must be heard[192] otherwise than in public   **[11–65]** by the Rights Commissioner,[193] and the Rights Commissioner must give both parties an opportunity to be heard and to present any evidence relating to the complaint. [194] The decision of the Rights Commissioner (which must be in writing and be communicated both to the parties[195] and to the Labour Court[196]) shall do one of the following[197]

    (a) declare that the complaint was or was not well founded;

    (b) require the employer[198] to comply with the relevant provision; or

    (c) require the employer to pay such compensation as is just and equitable having regard to all the circumstances but not exceeding two years' remuneration.

3.1.1. Employee Compensation Claims and the Obligation to Keep Records   **[11–66]**

Under s.25(4) of the 1997 Act it is provided that where an employer does not keep proper records to indicate fulfilment of the various obligations under the legislation, then the burden of proving that the terms of the Act have otherwise been complied with rests with that employer. In reality, in the context of civil proceedings taken by an employee against an employer under working-time legislation, where records have not been kept in a prescribed form by an employer[199]

---

191. See *Manufacturing and Maintenance Engineering v Currams*, WTC/02/1, DWT 0215, 15 March 2002; *Cementation Skanska (Formerly Kvaerner Cementation v Tom Carroll*, WTC/03/2, DWT 0338, 28 October 2003; *IBM Ireland v Svoboda*, WTC/07/77, DWT 0818, 7 May 2008; *Royal Liver Assurance Ltd. v SIPTU*, WTC/01/27, DWT 0141, 8 October 2001.

192. The Minister is empowered by regulations to provide for any matters relating to the proceedings before a Rights Commissioner that [s]he deems appropriate: s.27(10) Organisation of Working Time Act 1997.

193. s.27(8) *ibid.*

194. s.27(2) *ibid.*

195. s.27(2) *ibid.*

196. s.27(9) *ibid.*

197. s.27(3) *ibid.*

198. References in this section to 'the employer' include anyone who has taken ownership of what was formerly the employer's business after the contravention to which the complaint relates had occurred: s.27(3) *ibid.*

199. An employer is essentially required to keep records in respect of all of the various obligations under the legislation. So, for example, in *Schmidt Industries International Ltd. v Anisimovs*, WTC/08/54, DWT 0859, 3 October 2008, the Labour Court found (on a disputed question of fact as to whether or not an employee had been given adequate notice of overtime he would be required to work) against an employer who had not produced 'evidence' to support his argument of fact, but in reality this was a case where such 'evidence' could only have been in the form of appropriate records under the regulations.

then the onus of proving that the provisions of the Act have been complied with (which rests with the employer), may be extremely difficult to fulfil.[200] On the other hand, where accurate records *are* produced indicating compliance with the legislation, then this will be essentially determinative of the matter.[201] What is less certain, however, is whether the terms of s.25(4) can, by inference, be taken to mean that in all other circumstances (that is, other than those where the employer fails to produce appropriate records) the onus of proving that a breach has occurred rests with the employee. In other words, to take a hypothetical case in which an employee is of the view that, whereas the employer has kept records, nonetheless they have been falsified, normal principles of statutory interpretation would suggest that the burden of proving this (and moreover, of proving that there has been a breach of one of the obligations under the act) rests with the employee.

[11–67] While dealing with the obligation to keep records, it should be noted, furthermore, that complaints can only be made in respect of various sections of the Act (specifically ss.6(2), 11–23 and 26). Consequently, a Rights Commissioner and, on appeal, the Labour Court should neither investigate nor award damages for a failure to keep records *per se*.[202] Despite this there are various decisions of the Labour Court in which compensation appears to have been awarded expressly for breach of the statutory obligation to keep records.[203] Thus most recently in *Rianna Construction Limited v Nowak*,[204] *Patrick Callaghan v Leita*,[205] *Principal Construction Services Ltd. v Nikitins*[206] and *Traffic Management Services TMS v Bedo*,[207] compensation was apparently awarded to employees *inter alia* because of the employer's failure to provide records.

[11–68] With due respect, it is submitted that there is no statutory authority for such a course of action. Instead, it is arguable that the more appropriate response to such failure to keep records is evidenced in the decision of the Labour Court in *Weldon v Poleon*[208] and *Matrix Foods Limited v Klimenkovs*,[209] where it was held that the

---

200. s.25(4) Organisation of Working Time Act 1997. In such circumstances it would appear that the *standard* of proof for the employer is the civil standard of balance of probabilities. *Fergal Brodigan t/a FB Groundworks v Dubina*, WTC/08/105, DWT 0891, 10 December 2008; *Fergal Brodigan t/a FB Groundworks v Slupskis*, WTC/08/115, DWT 0890, 10 December 2008; *McHale Plant Hire v Cesna*, WTC/08/82, DWT 0874, 25 November 2008; *Feeney v Baquiran* [2004] ELR 304, 15 July 2004.

201. *Patrick T Durcan & Co. v Courtney*, WTC/07/91, DWT 0847, 1 August 2008.

202. *IBM Ireland v Svoboda*, WTC/07/77, DWT 0818, 7 May 2008.

203. See, for example, *Meaghers Tasty Bread v Eccles*, WTC/07/79, DWT 0817, 7 May 2008; *Erneside Construction Ltd. v Millers*, WTC/08/15, DWT 0832, 27 June 2008; *Tony Meegan Plant Hire v Cullivan*, WTC/08/19, DWT 0831, 27 June 2008; *Pauline Maguire t/a Toffee and Thyme v Parman*, WTC/08/18, DWT 0875, 24 November 2008.

204. WTC/08/123, DWT 095, 27 January 2009.

205. WTC/08/147, DWT 0910, 2 February 2009.

206. WTC/08/188, DWT 0920, 23 March 2009.

207. WTC/09/4, DWT 0922, 23 March 2009.

208. WTC/09/16, DWT 0928, 3 April 2009.

209. WTC/09/14, DWT 0931, 20 April 2009.

significance of an employer's failure in this regard lay in the fact that in such circumstances, and where a claim is taken by an employee, the onus of proving compliance with the legislation moves to the employer.[210] Hence if (as in these cases) there was directly conflicting uncorroborated testimony from both sides, it would be necessary (where the employer had not kept appropriate records) that the court decide questions of fact in the employee's favour. The net effect of this approach, however, is effectively to mean that the manner by which factual questions are answered in these cases is inevitably absolutely dependent on whether the employer has maintained records in an appropriate form. After all if [s]he does so, then they will display whether or not (and to what extent) there has been more general compliance with the legislation, and if [s]he does not do so, then factual questions will inevitably be determined in favour of the employee.

Finally, it should be noted that the impact of the Supreme Court decision in [11–69] *Ryanair v Labour Court*[211] (considered in detail in Chapter 2) applies in this context at well, such that in the absence of sworn testimony by one of the parties to the dispute, the Labour Court cannot determine a questions of fact in favour of such party where the other party *has* given evidence of a factual proposition.[212]

Where an employer has not carried out the terms of a decision of a Rights Commis- [11–70] sioner, and the time for bringing an appeal has expired and no such appeal has been taken, the employee may bring the complaint before the Labour Court which, without hearing the employer, may make a determination to the like effect as the decision.[213] Where the employer fails to carry out any determination of the Labour Court within six weeks, then the Circuit Court, on the application of the employee, his or her trade union or the Minister (where [s]he considers this appropriate), shall make an order directing the employer to carry out the terms of the determination.[214] Finally, where the Minister feels that an employer is not complying with a relevant provision of the Act, yet no complaint has been made to a Rights Commissioner in respect of such non-compliance, and in circumstances where (in the opinion of the Minister) it is unreasonable to expect the employee or his or her trade union to present such a complaint, the Minister him or herself may present a complaint in relation to the matter to a Rights Commissioner, and that complaint shall be dealt with as if it were a complaint presented by the employee.[215]

---

210. s.25(4) Organisation of Working Time Act 1997.

211. [2007] IESC 6, [2007] 4 IR 199.

212. *Solid Building Company v Sergejs Baranovs*, WTC/08/7, DWT 0821, 21 May 2008.

213. s.28(8) Organisation of Working Time Act 1997. See, for example, of the very many Labour Court determinations in this area: *Alert One Security Ltd. v Qureshi*, WTC/08/167, DWT 0889, 10 December 2008; *Arlington Lodge Ltd. v Mulhall*, WTC/08/166, DWT 0888, 9 December 2008; *RHD Transport Ltd. v Kasjaniuk*, WTC/08/168, DWT 0887, 8 December 2008.

214. s.29(1) Organisation of Working Time Act 1997. Applications in this regard are brought pursuant to Order 57 Rule 4 and using From 36D of the Circuit Court Rules 2001, SI no. 510 of 2001. See Circuit Court Rules (General) Regulations 2007, SI no. 312 of 2007.

215. s.31(1) Organisation of Working Time Act 1997.

3.1.2. Appeals to the Labour Court

[11–71] A decision of the Rights Commissioner can be appealed to the Labour Court within six weeks of the date on which the decision to which it relates was communicated to the party.[216] A notice of appeal must contain such particulars as are required by the Labour Court.[217] The Labour Court hearing is essentially a *de novo* one, such that even a decision of a Rights Commissioner to decline jurisdiction on the grounds that time limits have not been complied with may be revisited. In addition, a decision of the Labour Court may be appealed on a point of law to the High Court[218] (whose decision shall be final and conclusive) and moreover, the Minister may, at the request of the Labour Court, refer a question of law arising in proceedings before it to the High Court.[219]

3.2. Prosecution of Offences under the 1997 Act

[11–72] Various offences are created under the terms of the 1997 Act, namely:

- In specified ways, obstructing or failing to assist the work of an inspector.[220]
- Failing, without reasonable cause,[221] to keep such records in respect of employees that indicate whether the terms of the Act (or where appropriate, the Activities of Doctors in Training Regulations) are being complied with in relation to the employee, or failing to retain such records for at least three years from the date of their making.[222] In this respect directions as to the type of information that has to be recorded, as well as the precise form in which it is to be recorded, are contained in the Organisation of Working Time (Records) (Prescribed Form and Exemptions) Regulations of 2001.[223] Under the terms of these regulations, an employer is bound, either by way of clocking in facilities or by some other easily comprehensible form (of a kind similar to a form provided in the schedule to these regulations) to maintain a record of the days and hours worked by each employee (excluding breaks), any days and hours of leave granted by way of annual or public holiday leave, and the payment made to the employee in respect of that leave, and

---

216. s.28(2) *ibid.*
217. ss.28(2) and (4) *ibid.*
218. s.28(6) *ibid.* Under the Rules of the Superior Courts (Statutory Applications and Appeals) 2007, SI no. 14 of 2007, any such applications to the High Court should be brought in accordance with Order 84(c) r2 – that is, by way of originating notice of motion, which must state concisely the point of law on which the application is made.
219. s.28(5) Organisation of Working Time Act 1997.
220. s.8(8) *ibid.* Proceedings in respect of offences under this section may be brought by the Minister.
221. s.25(3) *ibid.*
222. s.25 *ibid.*
223. SI no. 473 of 2001.

details of any additional day's leave granted to an employee in lieu of a public holiday.[224] Breach of the terms of s. 25 and of the regulations is punishable on summary conviction by a fine not exceeding €1,900.[225] In addition, as we have seen, a failure to keep records will inevitably count against an employer where an employee is making a claim against him or her before a Rights Commissioner or the Labour Court.

- Failing to keep a register of particulars in respect of each outworker (as defined in s. 2[226]) for the time being employed by him or her, or failing to comply with Ministerial regulations in respect of the employment of such outworkers.[227]
- Employing an employee in circumstances where [s]he is also employed by someone else and where the total hours worked for both employers exceeds the maximum permitted working hours under the Act, save where the employer neither knew nor could reasonably have known that the employee had done work for another employer in the relevant period.[228]

A person found guilty of an offence under these sections is liable on summary conviction to a fine not exceeding €1,904.61.[229] Moreover, where the offence is continued after the date of conviction, [s]he can be liable on summary conviction to a further fine (not exceeding €634.87) for each day on which the offence continues.[230]   [11–73]

In order to facilitate the enforcement of its provisions, the Act provides for the Minister to appoint so many persons as [s]he thinks fit to be inspectors[231] for the purposes of the Act.[232] The general powers of such inspectors are considered in Chapter 1. It is an offence to obstruct or impede an inspector in the exercise of his powers[233], to refuse to produce any record which the inspector lawfully requires to be produced[234], to produce or cause to be produced any record which is false   [11–74]

---

224. regs.3 and 4.
225. reg.7.
226. Essentially these are persons who are working for the employer but at a place not under his or her control or management, and where such work involves the making of a product or the provision of a service specified by the employer.
227. s.32 Organisation of Working Time Act 1997.
228. s.33 *ibid.* Where an employer employs an employee in violation of this section, both the employer *and* the employee are guilty of an offence.
229. s.34(1) *ibid.*
230. s.34(3) *ibid.*
231. The role of such inspectors, as well as the limitations on the powers following from the decisions of the High Court and Supreme Court in *Gama Endustri Tesisleri Imalat Montag A.S. v Minister for Enterprise, Trade and Employment & Anor* [2009] IESC 37, [2005] IEHC 210 are considered in Chapter 1.
232. s.8(2) Organisation of Working Time Act 1997. The Minister may also appoint inspectors for the purposes of the Activities of Doctors in Training Regulations.
233. s.8(8)(a) Organisation of Working Time Act 1997.
234. s.8(8)(b) *ibid.*

or misleading in any material respect knowing it to be false or misleading[235], to give an inspector any information is false or misleading in any material respect knowing it to be false or misleading[236] or to fail to or refuse to comply with any lawful requirement of an inspector under s.8(3) of the Act

4. Miscellaneous Sections of the Act

[11–75]   Finally, it should be noted that ss.39 and 40 make important procedural changes with a view to ensuring increased administrative convenience in the enforcement of employment law. Thus under s.39 provision is made (under a number of different employment law statutes and regulations as listed in a table) for a relevant authority to amend one of its decisions to reflect correctly the name of the employer or some other relevant particular where this has not been correctly stated in the original decision.[237] In addition, where an employee wishes to bring a claim against a person for relief under any of those statutes, and has in fact instituted such a claim but, owing to inadvertence, the respondent named on the claim was not the person against whom [s]he wishes to bring such claim, then the employee may appeal to whichever authority is charged with enforcement of the relevant Act to institute proceedings against the correct respondent, and the relevant authority may grant such permission, provided that to do so would not, in its opinion, result in an injustice being done to the proposed respondent.[238]

[11–76]   Finally, under s.40 it is provided that as far as Part III of the 1997 Act (dealing with holidays) is concerned, an employee (or, with his or her consent, his or her trade union) may, instead of presenting a claim under s.27 of the 1997 Act, include in proceedings issued by him or her under any of the Acts referred to in s.39 of the 1997 Act, a complaint that his or her employer has failed to comply with the provisions of Part III of the 1997 Act.[239] In such circumstances, the procedure to be followed is that contained in the other relevant enactment,[240] but the reliefs that can be granted for the claim under Part III, including the amount of compensation that can be awarded, is confined to that which is provided for under s.27.[241]

---

235. s.8(8)(c) *ibid.*
236. s.8(8)(d) *ibid.*
237. s.39(2) *ibid.* This is subject to the requirement that this power not be exercised if it would result in a situation where a person who was not given the opportunity to be heard becomes the subject of any requirement or direction contained in the decision.
238. s.39(4) *ibid.*
239. s.40(1) *ibid.*
240. s.40(1)(a) *ibid.* On the other hand, any specific time limits under the relevant enactment shall not apply to the claim in respect of holidays, but rather the rules in respect of time limits laid down in ss.27(4) and (5) apply.
241. s.40(1)(b) *ibid.*

CHAPTER 12

Wages

Introduction

Of fundamental importance to the employer/employee relationship is the ques-   [12–01]
tion of the wages to which the employee is entitled. There are two conceptually different Irish statutes governing the issue of wages. The first, the National
Minimum Wage Act 2000, provides for a minimum hourly wage that must be
paid to employees. The second, the Payment of Wages Act 1991, deals with three
equally important issues as far as the employee is concerned, namely (a) the acceptable modes of payment of wages; (b) the entitlement of an employee to receive
a statement of his or her wages; and (c) the circumstances in which an employer
can make a deduction from the wages of an employee. In this chapter we consider
these various issues in turn.

1. National Minimum Wage[1]

Under the National Minimum Wage Act 2000,[2] provision is made for the Minister   [12–02]
to make regulations dealing with such matters as may be prescribed under the Act
and any such other concerns as are necessary or expedient for the purpose of giving
effect to the Act.[3] Of these, the most important such regulations are those referred
to under s.11 of the Act, namely regulations declaring a national minimum hourly
rate of pay.[4] In essence, therefore, what the 2000 Act does is to take the radical
step of creating a minimum hourly rate of pay to which all workers in the state

---

1. Generally, see Kerr, *Irish Employment Legislation* (Round Hall Sweet and Maxwell, 2000), at
   p.G-22; and Smith, 'Legislating against Low Pay', 18 *Irish Law Times* (2000), 222.
2. The Act does not apply to a person who is the spouse, parent, grandparent, step-parent,
   step-child, grandchild, sibling, half brother or sister of the employer, or who is an apprentice
   within the meaning of the Industrial Training Act 1967 or the Labour Services Act 1987.
3. s.3 Minimum Wage Act 2000.
4. Such national minimum hourly rate of pay can include an allowance for board and/or lodgings, but only at such rates as may be specified by the Minister in the National Minimum
   Wage Act 2000 (National Minimum Hourly Rate of Pay) Order 2000: SI no. 95 of 2000:
   s.11(2) Minimum Wage Act 2000. In addition, such allowance for board can only be deducted
   from the worker's wages if [s]he is actually in receipt of board: *An Oige YHA v SIPTU*,
   MWA/01/1, determination no. MWD012, 4 September 2001.

are entitled by law. What is laid down in the statute is a *minimum* requirement; naturally it is entirely possible for higher rates of pay for particular employees to be determined and set as a matter of contract.

1.1. Procedure for Setting a National Minimum Wage

[12–03] In the first instance, therefore, the Act permits the Minister to make an order setting the National Minimum Wage. Before making such an order, the Minister must take into account the impact that the proposed rate may have on employment, the overall economic conditions in the State, and national competitiveness.[5] Moreover, where, in the opinion of the Minister, a relevant national economic agreement is in existence[6] which includes a recommendation in relation to the national minimum hourly rate of pay, then, within three months of being advised of such recommendation the Minister must either accept, vary or reject the recommendation.[7] Should [s]he accept or vary it then [s]he must amend the relevant existing order to make the change to the national minimum hourly rate of pay and should [s]he vary or reject it[8] [s]he must as soon as possible make a statement to the Oireachtas explaining his or her decision.[9]

[12–04] Alternatively it is possible for an organisation (which the Labour Court is satisfied is substantially representative of employers or employees in the State) to request the Labour Court to examine the minimum wage and make a recommendation to the Minister.[10] The Labour Court must then consult with such persons as it thinks appropriate (including representatives of employers and employees in both the private and public sector).[11] Having done so, if it is satisfied that there is general agreement between the parties as to the appropriate minimum rate of pay, then it should make a recommendation to the Minister accordingly. Where such an agreement cannot be reached, however, it may still make a recommendation to the Minister, but in doing so it must have regard to the movement in earnings of employees since the Minister last set a minimum rate of pay, relevant exchange-rate movement, and the effect of any such change on employment, inflation and national competitiveness.[12] Once again, the Minister may accept,

---

5. s.11(1) Minimum Wage Act 2000.
6. Any organisation claiming to be substantially representative of employees or employers in he State can apply to the Minister for his opinion as to whether or not such a national economic agreement is in place: s.13(1) Minimum Wage Act 2000.
7. s.12(2) *ibid.* Generally on the impact of national economic agreements on the minimum rate of pay see Kerr, *Irish Employment Legislation* (Round Hall Sweet and Maxwell, 2000), at p.G-28.
8. s.12(2)(a) Minimum Wage Act 2000. The general power to review the national minimum wage is laid down in s.12(1).
9. s.12(3) *ibid.*
10. s.13(3) *ibid.* The Labour Court determines its own procedures in respect of any such application: s.13(6) *ibid.*
11. s.13(4) *ibid.*
12. s.13(5) *ibid.*

vary or reject the recommendation and must again make a statement to the Oireachtas explaining why [s]he proposes to vary or reject such recommendation.[13] In light of the economic downturn in Ireland since 2008 (and which obtains at the time of writing) it is far from inconceivable that either the Minister or the Labour Court will be petitioned by various interest groups to recommend a reduction in the National Minimum Wage in the near future.

1.2. The Effect of an Order Prescribing a National Minimum Wage

When such regulations have been made, all employees aged 18 years or older are   **[12–05]** entitled to be paid no less than that hourly rate, nor can an employer decide to pay a worker at less than that rate on the basis of a subjective valuation of the worth of his or her work.[14] Workers who have not reached the age of 18 must be remunerated at a level not less than 70 per cent of the minimum wage.[15] The Act further makes provision for sub-minimum wages to be paid to persons who are entering employment for the first time after reaching the age of 18 or those who reach the age of 18 while continuing to be employed.[16] Such reduced rates (80 per cent of the minimum wage in the first year and 90 per cent in the second) may be paid for two years from the point at which the person commences employment or turns 18, whichever applies. In addition, sub-minimum rates can be paid to 'trainees' under the terms of s.16 of the Act but this is strictly subject to the provisions of the National Minimum Wage Act 2000 (Prescribed Courses of Study and Training) Regulations 2000,[17]

It is possible under the 2000 Act for an employer (or his or her representative)   **[12–06]** to apply to the Labour Court[18] for a temporary exemption from the obligations under the legislation on the basis of financial difficulty and for the Labour Court to grant such exemption[19] for a period of between three months and one year.[20] In order for such exemption to be granted, the Labour Court must be satisfied that:

- In the case of an employer employing more than one employee, the employer has entered into an agreement with a majority of the employees or their representative, or else that there is a collective agreement in place covering the majority of employees to whom the exemption relates whereby the employees or their representative consent to the employer making the application and agree to abide by any

---

13. s.13(8) *ibid.*
14. *Carrabine Joinery Ltd. v Balodis*, MWA/08/4, determination no. MWD087, 5 August 2008.
15. s.14(b) Minimum Wage Act 2000.
16. s.15 *ibid.*
17. SI no. 99 of 2000. See *Enor Teoranta v SIPTU*, MWA/01/6, determination no. MWD015, 21 November 2001.
18. s.41(3) Minimum Wage Act 2000.
19. s.41(1) *ibid.*
20. s.41(2) *ibid.*

decision on the application that the Labour Court may make.[21]
- Where the employer makes an application in respect of only one employee, that the employer has entered into an agreement with that employee or his or her representative whereby [s]he consents to the application being made and to be bound by the decision of the Labour Court.[22]
- In either case, that the employer simply cannot meet the costs of paying an employee the minimum wage, such that if [s]he was forced to do so, the employee would be likely to be laid off or to have his or her employment terminated.[23]

When satisfied of these factors (as preliminary requirements), the Labour Court is required to convene a hearing of the parties to the application[24] and to give its decision in writing to the parties, stating the names and employment positions occupied by employees to whom the exemption applies,[25] the duration of the exemption and the average hourly rate of pay to be paid to employers during the period of exemption.[26]

[12–07] Beyond this, any contract or agreement that was in force before that point and which provides for a less favourable hourly[27] rate of pay for employees than such statutory minimum is modified to provide that the rate of pay is raised to the level of the statutory minimum.[28] Moreover, any provision in a contract of employment whether made before or after the coming into being of the relevant order, is void insofar as it purports to exclude or limit the operation of any provision of the Act.[29] In other words, the Act sets out the basic statutory entitlement of a worker as against his or her employer[30] as far as rates of pay are

---

21. s.41(6)(a) *ibid.*
22. s.41(6)(b) *ibid.*
23. *ibid.*
24. s.41(5) *ibid.* The Labour Court shall establish its own proceedings for such hearing: s.41(9) *ibid.*
25. If an employee to whom the exemption relates is replaced by another during the period of exemption, then the latter can be paid at the modified hourly rate of pay during the period of exemption: s.41(8) Minimum Wage Act 2000. On the other hand, the modified minimum hourly rate of pay does not apply in calculating an employee's redundancy entitlements (s.41(12) *ibid.*), entitlements under the Minimum Notice and Terms of Employment Acts (s.41(13) *ibid.*), or entitlements to payments from the Social Insurance Fund or the Protection of Employees (Employers' Insolvency) Acts: s.41(14) *ibid.*
26. s.41(7) *ibid.*
27. s.14(a) *ibid.* Rates of pay are calculated on a pro-rata basis for any time less than an hour in which the employee works: s.17 *ibid.*
28. s.7(2) *ibid.*
29. s.7(1) *ibid.* Naturally, the legislation does not invalidate a contract of employment that provides for a more favourable rate of play for employees than the statutory minimum: s.7(3) *ibid.*
30. Normal transfer of undertakings rules apply in respect of minimum wages (s.46 *ibid.*). These are considered in Chapter 23. In addition, in the event of the bankruptcy of a company,

concerned.[31] At the time of writing, the National Minimum Wage is €8.65 per hour.[32]

Finally, the Act also prohibits an employer from reducing an employee's hours of [12–08] work without reducing the *amount* of work that [s]he was required to do, in an effort to get around the increased financial liability arising from the fact of the National Minimum Wage being in place. Where this happens, and where the employer does not, within two weeks of being so requested, restore the employee's working hours to those that previously existed, then the employer and employee shall be deemed to have a dispute in respect of the appropriate pay to which the employee is entitled under the Act resulting in an alleged under-payment to the employee, and the employee shall be entitled to refer the matter to the Rights Commissioner for determination,[33] with the onus resting on the employer to show that the reduction in hours was not for the purpose of avoiding increased financial liability as a result of the National Minimum Wage being in place.[34]

1.3. Pay Reference Periods

The employee is entitled to be paid[35] at least the minimum rate of pay in respect of [12–09] his or her working hours within any pay reference period,[36] which period cannot be more than one month long.[37] The number of hours worked within a worker's pay reference period is calculated either by reference to the terms of any registered collective agreement, Registered Employment Agreement or Employment Regulation Order, by reference to any notification under s.17 of the Organisa-

---

any arrears of pay payable under the Act represent a debt which, pursuant to s.285 of the Companies Act 1963 is to be paid in priority to all other debts: s.49 *ibid.*

31. Nothing in the 2000 Act prevents deductions being made from pay to which an employee is entitled, or payments being made by that employee to an employer in accordance with the Payment of Wages Act 1991 (s.18(1)). Moreover, such deductions or payments cannot be allowed for in calculating the hourly rate of pay of an employee within a particular reference period: s.18(2) *ibid.*

32. This has been the case since 1 July 2007 under the National Minimum Wage Act 2000 (National Minimum Hourly Rate of Pay Order 2006). SI no. 667 of 2006. At the time of writing there is increased debate about the wisdom of reducing the minimum wage in light of the difficult economic times facing Ireland in late 2009. See 'Minimum Wage Levels May Need Adjustment Says Lenihan', *Irish Times* 22 July 2009.

33. s.25(1) Minimum Wage Act 2000. Such a claim must be brought within six months, though this can be extended to a longer period not exceeding 12 months, by the Rights Commissioner.

34. s.25(3) *ibid.*

35. Where the employment of an employee is terminated, [s]he is entitled to be paid at not less than the minimum hourly rate of pay in respect of the period commencing on the beginning of the pay reference period and ending on the day that his or her employment was terminated: s.21 *ibid.*

36. s.14(a) *ibid.*

37. s.10 *ibid.*

tion of Working Time Act 1997 or under the terms of s.18 of the same Act, or by reference to any other agreement made between employee and employer. Alternatively, it may simply be calculated by reference to the total hours during which the employee actually carries out the activities of his or her work at the employer's place of business or is required to be available for work (and is paid in respect of such availability), whichever of these is the greater number of hours.[38] If this latter method of calculating a reference period is taken and the employee's work is not normally controlled by the employer, the employee has a duty to provide his employer with a written record of his or her working hours in any given pay reference period (unless his or her hourly rate of pay is likely to be not less than 150 per cent of the minimum hourly rate of pay). It is an offence to provide information that the employee knows to be false and misleading in a material respect.

[12–10] The concept of 'working hours' in this context specifically includes overtime, time spent travelling on official business, time spent on training or a training course or course of study authorised by the employer within normal working hours (whether or not in the workplace), but does not include time spent on standby or call, time spent absent from work on annual leave, sick leave, protective leave, adoptive leave, parental leave, carer's leave, while laid off on strike or lock out, time during which the employee is paid *in lieu* of notice or time spent on travelling between an employee's residence and his or her place of work.[39] Finally, the Labour Court has determined that time spent on a daily rest break constitutes paid working time.[40]

1.4. Calculation of an Employee's Hourly Rate of Pay

[12–11] Calculation of the hourly rate of pay of an employee involves division of the gross remuneration of the employee in respect of a particular pay reference period[41] by the number of hours worked within that period. In assessing what the employee's rate of pay within a particular time period actually is, the employer should include all reckonable pay[42] (as referred to in the first schedule to the Act[43]), but should

---

38. s.8(1) *ibid.*
39. s.8(2) *ibid.*
40. *O'Sullivan & Maguire Ltd. t/a The Georgian Hotel v Oulidi*, MWA/05/4 determination no. MWD063, 8 May 2006.
41. s.19 Minimum Wage Act 2000. The first schedule to the Act sets out the reckonable components of an employee's income and the second schedule sets out the non-reckonable components for the purposes of assessing the overall gross pay of an employee during the pay reference period.
42. s.19(1) *ibid.* The amount that can be allowed for board and/or lodgings must be the amount declared as such by the Minister under s.11 of the Act.
43. Reckonable components of pay comprise: basic salary; shift premium; piece and incentive rates; commission and bonuses that are productivity related; the monetary value of board with lodgings or board only or lodgings only, not exceeding the amount, if any, prescribed for the purposes of this item; the amount of any service charge distributed to the employee through the payroll; any payments under s.18 of the Organisation of Working Time Act

exclude all benefits in kind[44] (of the types referred to in the second schedule to the Act[45]).

1.5. The Obligation to Keep Records

An employer is obliged to keep records to indicate that his or her business is in compli- [12–12] ance with its obligations under the terms of the Act,[46] and to keep such records for at least three years from the date of their making. Failure to do so (without reasonable cause) is an offence.[47] The role of records that are kept pursuant to the Organisation of Working Time Act 1997 for the purposes of the Minimum Wage Act is obvious, in that they will indicate the number of hours worked by the employee and will factor into the question of whether, having regard to his or her gross remuneration during that period, [s]he was paid at a level not below the minimum wage. As with the Organisation of Working Time Act, where an employer fails to keep such records, then the onus of proving that the Act was complied with (in the context of a complaint before a Rights Commissioner or the Labour Court) rests with the

---

1997 (zero hour protection); any amount in respect of any of the above items advanced in a previous pay reference period that relates to the specific pay reference period; and any amount in respect of any of the above items earned in the specific pay reference period and paid in the next pay reference period or, where s.9(1)(b) applies, paid in the pay reference period in which the record of working hours is received or due to be received by the employer or the pay reference period immediately after that.

44. s.19(2) Minimum Wage Act 2000. An employer is not permitted to recharacterise what is, in reality, a benefit in kind, as being a reckonable component of pay: s.19(3) *ibid.*

45. Non-reckonable components of pay comprise: overtime premium; call-out premium; service pay; unsocial hours premium; any amount distributed to the employee of tips or gratuities paid into a central fund managed by the employer and paid through the payroll; public holiday premium; Saturday premium and Sunday premium, where any such holidays or days are worked; allowances for special or additional duties including those of a post of responsibility; any payment of expenses incurred by the employee in carrying out his or her employment, including travel allowance, subsistence allowance, tool allowance and clothing allowance; on-call or standby allowance; any payments for or in relation to a period of absence of the employee from the workplace, such as sick pay, holiday pay, payment for health and safety leave under the Maternity Protection Act 1994, or pay in lieu of notice, but not including a payment under s.18 of the Organisation of Working Time Act 1997 (zero hour protection); any payment by way of an allowance or gratuity in connection with the retirement or resignation of the employee or as compensation for loss of office; pension contributions paid by the employer on behalf of the employee; any payment referable to the employee's redundancy; any advance of a payment referred to in Part 1 of this Schedule in the specific pay reference period relating to a subsequent pay reference period; any payment-in-kind or benefit-in-kind, except board with lodgings, lodgings only or board only; any payment to the employee otherwise than in his or her capacity as an employee; any payment representing compensation for the employee, such as for injury or loss of tools and equipment; an amount of any award under a staff suggestion scheme and any loan by the employer to the employee, other than an advance payment of the kind referred to above.

46. s.22(1) Minimum Wage Act 2000.

47. s.22(2) *ibid.*

claimant.[48] On the other hand, where an employer *does* keep appropriate records, then the onus switches back to the claimant to demonstrate that, as a matter of probability, the records are not a true reflection of the hours [s]he worked.[49] Moreover, where such records are kept properly, it will be relatively easy to demonstrate compliance or non-compliance with the terms of the legislation.[50]

[12–13]   In addition, an employee whose average pay is less than 150 per cent of the minimum wage or such other percentage as may be prescribed[51] may request a written statement from his or her employer of his or her average hourly rate of pay for any pay reference period (other than the current one) within the previous twelve months.[52] Where this happens the employer must, within four weeks, reply stating details of the employee's reckonable pay and also the hours worked, the average hourly pay as well as the minimum pay to which the employee is entitled under the Act.[53] Failure to do so, or knowingly providing false or misleading information in such a statement without reasonable excuse, is an offence.[54] Moreover, as we shall see, it is a prerequisite to making a complaint to the Rights Commissioner under the 2000 Act that such a statement has been sought by the employee making the complaint.[55]

1.6. Enforcement

[12–14]   The 2000 Act provides for three different ways in which its terms can be enforced, namely:

- through a complaint to a Rights Commissioner and thence to the Labour Court;
- through a civil action taken by or on behalf of an employee; or
- through criminal prosecution.

1.6.1. Reference of a Dispute to a Rights Commissioner/Labour Court

[12–15]   Where an employee and employer cannot agree on the appropriate entitlement of the employee in regards to pay in accordance with the Act resulting in an *alleged*

---

48. s.22(3) *ibid. Mansion House v Izquierado*, MWA/04/5, determination no. MWD043, 30 August 2004; *Zevas Communications Ltd. v A Worker*, MWA/04/13, determination no. MWD052, 23 June 2005. Generally, see Chapter 11.
49. *Pepper N Spice v Shahid Ali* MWA/07/14 determination no. MWD083 21 August 2008, *Pairc Nua Teoranta v Ligita Bartusevica*, MWA/08/2, determination no. MWD082, 2 May 2008.
50. *Porturlin Shellfish Ltd. v Golovan*, MWA/07/10, determination no. MWD0711, 29 November 2007.
51. s.23(2) Minimum Wage Act 2000.
52. s.23(1) *ibid.* Such request must be in writing and must state the pay reference period to which the application refers: s.23(3) *ibid.*
53. s.23(4) *ibid.* This must be signed and dated by the employer and kept for a period of 15 months by him or her.
54. s.23(6) *ibid.*
55. s.24(2)(a)(i) *ibid.*

underpayment to the employee, the employer or employee (or the representative of either of them) may refer the dispute to a Rights Commissioner for his or her decision.[56] As has been mentioned above, such dispute cannot be referred to or dealt with by a Rights Commissioner unless the employee has obtained a statement of the kind referred to in s.23 or has requested it but has not received it within the four-week time period set out in s.23(4) at some point within the six-month period before the reference was made.[57] Significantly, however, provided that the statement in question has been sought in the previous six months, it would appear that the Rights Commissioner may award compensation for under-payment of wages at any period in the reference period for which a statement has been sought.

In *Mansion House Ltd. t/a Fado Restaurant v Izquierdo*[58] the Labour Court held [12–16] that where a claimant had failed to seek such a statement then the proper course of action was for the Rights Commissioner to decline jurisdiction without prejudice to the possibility that the complaint might be made at a later period and when the relevant statement had been sought, rather than simply dismissing the claim on its merits. This course of action was also taken more recently by the Labour Court in *Harbour House Ltd. v Jurska*[59] in which, having determined that the Rights Commissioner was correct not to assume jurisdiction over the matter (on the basis that the claimant had not fulfilled the requirements under s.23) the Labour Court somewhat unusually decided nonetheless to examine the claim on its merits 'since the information which should have been requested by the complainant was before the Court at the hearing of the matter'.

In addition, the reference cannot be dealt with by the Rights Commissioner [12–17] where, in respect of the same alleged under-payment, the employer is or has been the subject of investigation by an inspector or the subject of a criminal prosecution.[60] Significantly, it does not appear to be the case that a Rights Commissioner is prohibited from investigating a dispute where there have been civil proceedings issued in respect of the same – although as we shall see, the Minister may not issue civil proceedings on behalf of an employee in respect of a matter that has been referred to the Rights Commissioner.

A Rights Commissioner's decision[61] (which must be made as soon as practicable [12–18] after the hearing of the dispute) may include an award of arrears for any shortfall

---

56. s.24(1) *ibid.* Such reference must be by way of written notice and must contain such particulars as may be prescribed.
57. s.24(2) *ibid.* This time period within which such written statement must have been sought may be extended by the Rights Commissioner, but to a maximum period of 12 months.
58. MWA/04/5, determination no. MWD043, 30 August 2004.
59. MWA/07/12, determination no. MWD081, 10 March 2008.
60. s.24(2)(b) Minimum Wage Act 2000. An inspector shall advise a Rights Commissioner as to whether this is the case: s.24(4) *ibid.*
61. The Rights Commissioner must keep a register of any decision made under this section, which must be available for public inspection during office hours: s.26(3) *ibid.*

in the payment of the employee compared to his or her entitlements under the
2000 Act and also the reasonable expenses of the employee in connection with
the dispute.[62] This latter provision (which is not replicated in, for example, the
Organisation of Working Time Act 1997) would seem to allow for an employee
to be paid his or her legal costs at the discretion of the Rights Commissioner,
although significantly there is no similar provision whereby the employer may be
paid his or her costs or reasonable expenses in defending any such claim. In addition, the Rights Commissioner may require an employee to remedy any breaches
of the Act within a specified period of time, though not longer than six weeks after
the date on which the decision was communicated to the employer.[63]

[12–19]   Where a decision of a Rights Commissioner has not been fully complied with and
the time for bringing an appeal has expired, and either no appeal has been brought or
any such appeal has been abandoned, the employee can refer the matter to the Labour
Court[64] and the Labour Court, without hearing the employer, shall make a determination to the like effect as the determination of the Rights Commissioner.[65]

[12–20]   The decision of the Rights Commissioner may be appealed to the Labour Court[66]
within six weeks of the date on which it was communicated to the relevant party[67]
and an appeal in this regard is deemed to be in the nature of a full rehearing.[68]
The prescribed powers of the Labour Court in hearing such an appeal are
more detailed in the Minimum Wage Act than is the case under, for example,
the Organisation of Working Time Act 1997, though realistically many of the
powers referred to in the 2000 Act are available in that context as well. Thus
it is provided within the 2000 Act that the Labour Court may take evidence
on oath or affirmation[69] (and it is an offence wilfully and corruptly to give false
evidence or to swear anything that is false),[70] and can require a person to attend at
hearing[71] and give evidence or to produce documents in his possession, custody or
control[72] (and again it is an offence to refuse or wilfully fail or neglect to do so).[73]

---

62. s.26(2) *ibid.*
63. s.26(2)(b) *ibid.*
64. This should be by way of written notice containing such particulars as may be determined
by the Labour Court: s.31(2) *ibid.*
65. s.31(2) *ibid.*
66. s.27(1) *ibid.*
67. In *Patricial Toscano t/a Ristorante Rossini v Mika*, MWA/08/3, determination no. MWD086, 29
July 2008, the Labour Court held that 'communicated' in this sense meant that the decision
must have actually reached the worker. Hence, in this case, where the communication was sent
to an address at which the employee (to the knowledge of the Rights Commission service) was
no longer resident, it could not have been said to have been communicated to the worker.
68. s.27(3) Minimum Wage Act 2000.
69. s.28(1) *ibid.*
70. s.28(2) *ibid.* Such offences carry a fine on summary conviction not exceeding €1,904.61.
71. Witnesses before the Labour Court have the same privileges and immunities as witnesses
before the High Court. 28(6) *ibid.*
72. s.28(3) *ibid.*
73. s.28(4) *ibid.* A document purporting to be signed by the chairperson of the Labour Court

In making its decision, the Labour Court is confined either to confirming the decision of the Rights Commissioner or, alternatively, to substituting any decision of its own that the Rights Commissioner could have made on the hearing of the dispute.[74] The Labour Court can specify a time frame in which any steps required within its determination (including payment of money) must be taken,[75] and in the absence of such specification, such steps must be taken within six weeks of the date on which the determination is communicated to the parties.[76] Where an employer fails to carry out the determination of the Labour Court within either the specified time or the six-week time limit then, on application by the employee, or (with the employee's consent) a trade union of which [s]he is a member, or the Minister, the Circuit Court shall make an order in the terms of the Labour Court determination.[77] Decisions of the Labour Court may be appealed to the High Court on a question of law.[78]

[12–21]

1.6.2. Criminal Prosecution

Various offences (prosecutable either summarily or on indictment) are created under the Act of which the most significant is the offence of refusing or failing to remunerate an employee at the minimum wage.[79] Significantly, the Act provides that it is a defence in proceedings for an offence under the legislation for the employer to prove that [s]he exercised due diligence and took reasonable precautions to ensure compliance with the law.[80] Significantly also, where an employer is found guilty of an offence under the section, then evidence may be given of any like contravention on his or her part during the previous three years before the offence.[81]

[12–22]

---

and saying that the person in question was given notice by which he was required to attend at the Labour Court on a given day or to produce evidence, that a hearing of the Labour Court occurred on that day and that the individual failed to comply with such requirements shall, in a prosecution, be evidence of the matters stated without further proof: s.28(5) *ibid.*

74. s.29(1) *ibid.*
75. s.32(1) *ibid.*
76. s.32(2) *ibid.*
77. s.32(3) *ibid.* An application to the Circuit Court shall be made to the judge of the Circuit Court for the circuit in which the employer concerned ordinarily resides or carries out any profession (s.32(6)) and should be brought pursuant to Order 57 Rule 10 of the Circuit Court Rules as inserted by the Circuit Court Rules (National Minimum Wage Act 2006, SI no. 531).
78. s.30(2) Minimum Wage Act 2000. In addition the Minister may, at the request of the Labour Court, refer a question of law arising in an appeal to the High Court for determination: s.30(1) *ibid.*
79. s.35 *ibid.* Where the offence is committed by a body corporate but can be shown to have been committed with the consent, connivance or approval of, or owing to the neglect of any person who at the time was a director, manager, secretary or other similar officer of the body corporate (or someone purporting to act in any such capacity), then that person shall be guilty of an offence and liable to prosecution as if guilty of the offence committed by the body corporate.
80. s.38 *ibid.*
81. s.35(2) *ibid.*

[12–23] In addition, as is the case under various other employment law statutes considered throughout this book, it is an offence for an employer to 'cause or suffer any action prejudicial to the employee' for having exercised or having proposed to exercise a right under the Act, for having in good faith opposed or proposed to oppose by lawful means an unlawful act, or for having become (or becoming in the future) entitled in accordance with the Act to remuneration at an hourly rate of pay that is not less than the minimum hourly rate of pay.[82] Moreover, where such victimisation takes the form of a dismissal of the employee then this will be deemed to be an unfair dismissal within the meaning of the unfair dismissals legislation, save that the employee in such a case does not need to have one year's continuous service for this to arise.[83]

[12–24] Details of sanctions and penalties in respect of such offences (including ongoing offences) are listed in s.37 of the Act and also in various sections of the Act in which such offences are created. Significantly, however, where, following a conviction of an employer in the context of a prosecution under the Act, it appears to a court that money is due to an employee from an employer, the court, in addition to any penalty it may impose under the Act, may order that the employer pay to the employee the amount owed.[84]

[12–25] Finally, the 2000 Act provides for the investigatory role of inspectors operating with the general powers discussed in Chapter 1 of this book.[85] In addition, however, an inspector may, either on his or her own initiative or on the request of an employee or his or her representative, investigate an allegation that an employer has failed to pay the minimum wage.[86] This kind of investigation may not, however, take place in cases where the alleged violation of the legislation has already been referred to a Rights Commissioner (and the inspector must cease any investigation that has already commenced on his or her becoming aware of such referral),[87] or where the alleged violations occurred more than three years before the date of the proposed investigation.[88] Following an investigation, if the inspector is satisfied that an offence has occurred (or if otherwise requested by the Minister) the inspector

---

82. s.36(1) *ibid.* In addition, where the employee alleges that [s]he has been victimized in this fashion and the employer, within two weeks of being so requested by the employee or his or her representative, does not restore him or her to conditions of employment that [s]he enjoyed immediately before allegedly being victimised, then, for the purposes of s.24(1), the employer and employee shall be deemed not to be able to agree on the appropriate entitlement of the employee as far as pay is concerned, resulting in an alleged underpayment to the employee and the Labour Court's complaint procedure under ss.24–32 shall apply: s.36(3) *ibid.*
83. s.36(2) *ibid.*
84. s.50(2) *ibid.*
85. s.33 *ibid.*
86. s.34(1) *ibid.*
87. s.34(5)(a) *ibid.* A Rights Commissioner shall, at the request of the inspector, inform him or her whether or not a dispute has been referred to him or her.
88. s.34(5)(b) *ibid.*

shall furnish a report on his or her investigation to the Minister.[89] Equally the conclusions of Supreme Court (and High Court) in *Gama Endustri Tesisleri Imalat Montag A.S. v Minister for Enterprise Trade and Employment & Anor*[90] considered earlier in Chapter 1 have application in this context as well.

1.6.3. Civil Proceedings

In addition, under s.39 of the Act, it is possible that compensation in respect of breaches of the Act may be sought by way of civil proceedings. This can occur in two ways. First, the Act speaks of the possibility that an employee may institute civil proceedings on his or her own behalf in respect of breaches of the legislation to recover such sums as a simple contract debt.[91] Such a claim (which may also be instituted and maintained on behalf of the employee by his trade union) does not appear to be dependent on the employee not having brought a complaint to the Labour Court or Rights Commissioner. In other words, it would appear possible that civil proceedings may be issued and a complaint to the Rights Commissioner brought in respect of the same alleged under-payment to the employee, though it would seem logical that the employee could not claim double compensation for the same offence. Significantly, a claim for compensation taken by way of civil proceedings would not be subject to the same limitation period as would a complaint to the Rights Commissioner, but offset against that is the fact that obviously an employee who unsuccessfully takes a civil action may be liable for his or her costs, which will not be the case where [s]he simply refers a dispute to the Rights Commissioner. [12–26]

Alternatively, where an employee has been paid less than the minimum wage and where there has been no reference of the dispute to a Rights Commissioner nor has the matter been referred to an inspector under s.34, and where in the opinion of the Minister it is not reasonable in the circumstances to expect the employee or his representative to make such references, or to institute civil proceedings on his or her own behalf, then the Minister may request an inspector to advise him or her on whether civil proceedings should be instituted by the Minister on behalf of and in the name of the employee.[92] Where such advice has been sought, received and considered, the Minister then has an absolute discretion on whether or not to institute such proceedings.[93] Significantly, though, where this happens, the employee is not liable for any of the costs of those proceedings which may, however, be awarded against the Minister. [12–27]

---

89. s.34(4) *ibid.*
90. [2009] IESC 37, [2005] IEHC 210.
91. s.50(1) Minimum Wage Act 2000.
92. s.39(1) *ibid.*
93. s.39(2) *ibid.*

2. Payment of Wages

[12–28] Beyond the concept of a minimum wage, Irish legislation in the form of the Payment of Wages Act 1991 also deals with the crucial issues of

- the method by which wages can be paid;
- the entitlement of a worker to a statement of his or her wages; and
- the circumstances in which deductions can be made from his or her wages.[94]

In this respect it should be noted that the concept of 'wages' is given a very broad definition in s.1 of the 1991 Act and refers to any sum payable to the employee by reason of his employment, and including:

(a) any fee, bonus[95] or commission, or any holiday, sick or maternity pay, or any other emolument, referable to his employment, whether payable under his or her contract of employment or otherwise; and

(b) any sum payable to the employee upon the termination by the employer of his or her contract of employment without his or her having given to the employee the appropriate prior notice of the termination, being a sum paid in lieu of the giving of such notice. So for example, where an employer does not pay the employee monies to which [s]he is entitled by reason of his or her statutory right to notice, theoretically the employee can seek compensation under the Minimum Notice and Terms of Employment Act 1973, but can also claim that this represents a deduction from his or her wages in breach of s. 4 of the Payment of Wages Act 1991.

[12–29] On the other hand, it is further provided in s.1 that the following shall not constitute wages for the purposes of the Act:

(a) any payment in respect of expenses incurred by the employee in carrying out his or her employment;

(b) any payment by way of a pension, allowance or gratuity in connection with the death, or the retirement or resignation from his or her employment, of the employee, or as compensation for loss of office;

(c) any payment referable to the employee's redundancy;

(d) any payment to the employee otherwise than in his capacity as an employee;

(e) any payment in kind or benefit in kind.

Finally, it is worth noting that unlike many of the other employment law statutes, there is nothing in the 1991 Act specifying thresholds of service necessary

---

94. For an analysis of the history of legislation of this nature, see Kerr, *Irish Employment Law* (Round Hall Sweet and Maxwell, 2000), at pp.G-3 *et seq.*

95. See, for example, *McGuirk v Irish Garden Publishers Ltd.*, PW75/2005.

for the Act to apply, or indeed specifying categories of employment to which the act expressly does *not* apply.[96] In other words, this is an Act that covers all employees[97] within the work force. Moreover, any provision in an agreement (including a contract of employment) whether or not it was made before the coming into being of the Act, which purports to preclude or limit the application of, or is inconsistent with any provision of the Act, shall be void.[98]

2.1. Modes of Payment of Wages

This issue is dealt within s.2 of the Payment of Wages Act 1991. This section sets out [12–30] eight different ways in which wages may be paid and provides that an employer who pays the wages other than in one of those eight ways shall be guilty of an offence and liable to summary conviction to a fine not exceeding €1, 269.74. The eight ways in which wages may be paid are as follows[99]:

(a) a cheque, draft or other bill of exchange within the meaning of the Bills of Exchange Act 1882;

(b) a document issued by a person who maintains an account with the Central Bank of Ireland or a holder of a licence under s. 9 of the Central Bank Act 1971, which, though not such a bill of exchange as aforesaid, is intended to enable a person to obtain payment from that bank or that holder of the amount specified in the document;

(c) a draft payable on demand drawn by a holder of such a licence as aforesaid upon him or herself, whether payable at the head office or some other office of the bank to which the licence relates;

(d) a postal, money or paying order, or a warrant, or any other like document, issued by or drawn on An Post, or a document issued by an officer of a Minister of the Government that is intended to enable a person to obtain payment from that Minister of the Government of the sum specified in the document;

(e) a document issued by a person who maintains an account with a trustee savings bank within the meaning of the Trustee Savings Banks Act 1989, that is intended to enable a person to obtain payment from the bank of the sum specified in the document;

(f) a credit transfer or another mode of payment whereby an amount is credited to an account specified by the employee concerned;

(g) cash;

96. In *Gaynor v Minister for Defence*, PW 12/2008. it was held that the 1991 Act would apply to members of the defence forces nor could its provisions be overridden by the terms of s.101 of the Defence Act 1954. Hence it was unlawful to deduct from the claimant's wages pending a court-martial-based inquiry into certain alleged absences from work on his part.
97. The concept of an employee is also given definition in s.1 of the Payment of Wages Act 1991.
98. s.11 *ibid.*
99. So in *Dunnes Stores v Buckley*, PW 18/2007 it was held that there was a breach of the Payment of Wages Act in circumstances where the appellant employer sought to pay a Christmas bonus to employees in the form of vouchers.

(h) any other mode of payment standing specified for the time being by regulations made by the Minister after consultation with the Minister for Finance.[100]

2.2. Statement of Wages

[12–31] The second major innovation introduced by the 1991 Act is the requirement that employers give employees a statement in writing specifying clearly the gross amount of the wages payable to the employee and the nature and amount of any deduction taken from such wages.[101] The employer is also bound to ensure so far as is reasonable that these issues remain confidential as between the parties.

[12–32] In terms of the time frame within which such a statement must be given to the employee, the norm is that it would be given at the time of payment.[102] On the other hand, if the payment is made by way of credit transfer or by some method whereby an amount is credited to an employee's bank or building society account (pursuant to s.2(1)(f)) then the statement should be made as soon as may be thereafter.[103] Similarly, if payment is made by a method specified in ministerial regulations pursuant to s.2(1)(h), the statement should be made at such time as may be specified in the regulations.[104]

Finally, an employer is obliged to inform an employee of changes to his or her wages.[105]

It is an offence to breach the requirements of this section both in terms of making this statement and in terms of adhering to the time period, and an employee who so breaches these requirements shall be liable of summary conviction to a fine not exceeding €1, 269.74.[106]

---

100. s.3(1) Payment of Wages Act 1991. Specific provision is made for situations where an employer is unable to pay an employee in the mode agreed owing to a strike or other industrial action affecting a financial institution (s.2(2)). In addition transitional provision is made in respect of circumstances for employees whose wages were paid either in cash or pursuant to s.3 of the Payment of Wages Act 1979 immediately before the 1991 Act.

101. s.4(1) Payment of Wages Act 1991.

102. s.4(2)(c) *ibid.*

103. s.4(2)(a) *ibid.*

104. s.4(2)(b) *ibid.* On the other hand, if the statement is found to contain an error or omission that was the result of clerical error or some accident made in good faith, then the statement is regarded as complying with the provisions of the section: s.4(3) *ibid.*

105. See *Sercom Solutions Ltd. v Hale*, PW70/2005.

106. s.4(4) Payment of Wages Act 1991.

2.3. Deductions from an Employee's Wages

The 1991 Act makes clear provision as to the circumstances in which deductions   **[12–33]**
may legitimately be made from an employee's wages.[107] The basic rule as set out
in s.5(1) of the Act is that an employer is not allowed to make a deduction[108]
from the wages of an employee or receive any payment from an employee. Hence
whenever an employee is paid less than [s]he should properly have been paid
on a given occasion, or where none of the wages that are properly payable to
him or her on that occasion are paid to him or her, save where such shortfall is
attributable to an error of computation, this is to be treated as a deduction from
the wages of the employee.[109] Unsurprisingly, in the interpretation of this clause,
controversy can surround the question of whether (in the case, for example, of
bonuses or other forms of additional pay) particular sums of money are 'properly
payable' to the employee. [110]

This general rule against deduction does not, however, apply where:

- the deduction or payment is required or authorised under statute or
statutory instrument[111];
- the deduction is required or authorised by virtue of a term of the
employee's contract[112]; or
- the employee has given his or her prior consent in writing to such
deduction.[113]

It is specifically provided in the legislation that a deduction may not *generally*   **[12–34]**
be made because of some act or omission of the employee[114] or in respect of any
goods or services supplied to or provided for the employee by the employer and

---

107. For analysis especially of the English case law in this area, see Kerr, *Irish Employment Law*
(Round Hall Sweet and Maxwell, 2000), at p.G-12.
108. For analysis of the UK position in this area, see Kerr, *Irish Employment Law*, at G-13 and
G-14.
109. s.5(6) Payment of Wages Act 1991. In assessing whether the employee has been paid less than
[s]he should have been paid, it is necessary to factor into the amount [s]he *was* paid and any
deductions lawfully taken from his or her wages under the terms of the 1991 Act.
110. See *Dunnes Stores v Lacey* [2005] IEHC 417.
111. s.5(1)(a) Payment of Wages Act 1991.
112. s.5(1)(b) *ibid*. See *Buckle v Lee Overlay Partners Ltd*. PW14/2005. Thus in *McGowan c/o Therese
Clinton v Clarke c/o St Anne's National School* PW 70/2007 where the respondent teacher had
employed the appellant as a part-time substitute at an agreed rate of pay but which was less
than the accepted *per diem* rate for teachers, it was held that in as much as the appellant was
being paid what had been agreed between the parties, the respondent was acting in fulfilment
of her obligations under the Payment of Wages Act 1991.
113. s.5(1)(c) Payment of Wages Act 1991. In *Potter v Hunt Contracts Ltd*. [1992] ICR 337, [1992]
IRLR 108, the English EAT in interpreting the equivalent English section held that there
would need to be a signed document authorising the deduction from the employee's wages.
114. s.5(2)(a) Payment of Wages Act 1991.

which are necessary for the employment,[115] unless all of the following conditions are satisfied[116]:

- the deduction is required or authorised by a term of the employee's contract of employment (whether oral or written);
- the deduction is fair and reasonable in the circumstances[117];
- the employee either has a copy of his or her contract (if it is in writing) or (if it is not in writing), [s]he has notice in writing of the existence and effect of such term[118];
- where the deduction is for an act or omission of the employee, the employee must be given particulars in writing of such act or omission and the amount of the deduction at least one week before making the deduction[119];
- if the deduction is made by way of compensation for damage suffered by the employer as a result of the act or omission, the amount of the deduction cannot exceed the amount of the loss suffered;
- if the deduction is for the cost of goods or services supplied to the employee, that amount of the deduction may not exceed the cost of such goods or services[120]; and
- the deduction (or where appropriate the first of a series of deductions) must not occur later than six months after the day on which the act or omission became known to the employer, or the goods or services were supplied.

[12–35] Finally, under s.5(5) of the Act it is expressly provided that this section does not apply to certain listed types of deductions, namely[121]:

- a deduction made by an employer from the wages of an employee, or any payment received from an employee by an employer, where the

---

115. s.5(2)(b) *ibid.* Equivalent rules apply in respect of payments made to the employee where there has been an act or omission or where goods or services have been applied to the employee.

116. A deduction cannot be made in respect of a matter referred to in s.5(2) Payment of Wages Act 1991 unless the requirements listed in that sub-section have been complied with (s.5(3) *ibid.*) and where this occurs, the employer is required to give a receipt of payment to the employee (s.5(3)(b) *ibid.*), and a contract that provides for such deduction or for a payment on the part of the employee where goods and services have been supplied to the employee shall not be valid unless it complies with the requirements in s.5(2): s.5(4) *ibid.*

117. In *Ryanair Limited v Downey*, POW6/2005, it was held that a deduction was not fair and reasonable as it had the effect of meaning that an employee would not be paid for the final period of his service.

118. On this point, see *Ballinalard Transport Limited v Reder*, PW 23/2007.

119. See, for example, *Ryanair Limited v Downey*, POW6/2005.

120. In addition, the deduction (or, if there is more than one deduction to be made, the first such deduction) cannot be made later than six months after the act or omission becomes known to the employer or after the provision of the goods or services.

121. s.5(5) Payment of Wages Act 1991.

purpose of the deduction is to compensate the employer for any previous overpayment to the employee in terms of wages or expenses incurred by the employee in carrying out his or her employment, and where the amount of the deduction or payment does not exceed the amount of the overpayment;

- a deduction made by an employer from the wages of an employee, or any payment received from an employee by an employer, in consequence of any disciplinary proceedings if those proceedings were held by virtue of a statutory provision;

- a deduction made by an employer from the wages of an employee in pursuance of a requirement imposed on the employer by virtue of any statutory provision to deduct and pay to a public authority, being a Minister of the Government, the Revenue Commissioners or a local authority for the purposes of the Local Government Act 1941, amounts determined by that authority as being due to it from the employee, if the deduction is made in accordance with the relevant determination of that authority[122]; or

- a deduction made by an employer from the wages of an employee in pursuance of any arrangements

  (i) which are in accordance with a term of a contract made between the employer and the employee to whose inclusion in the contract the employee has given his or her prior consent in writing; or

  (ii) to which the employee has otherwise given his or her prior consent in writing; and under which the employer deducts and pays to a third person amounts, being amounts in relation to which [s]he has received a notice in writing from that person stating that they are amounts due to him or her from the employee, if the deduction is made in accordance with the notice and the amount thereof is paid to the third person not later than the date on which it is required by the notice to be so paid; or

- a deduction made by an employer from the wages of an employee, or any payment received from an employee by his employer, where the employee has taken part in a strike or other industrial action and the deduction is made or the payment has been required by the employer on account of the employee's having taken part in that strike or other industrial action[123];

- a deduction made by an employer from the wages of an employee with his or her prior consent in writing, or any payment received from an employee by an employer, where the purpose of the deduction or payment is the satisfaction (whether wholly or in part) of an order of a

---

122. See, for example, *An Employee v An Employer* TE79/2006, PW99/2006 in which the EAT refused to make an award under the Payment of Wages Act which would have had the effect of preventing the employer from fulfilling his obligations to the Revenue Commissioners.

123. *Beaumont Hospital v McNally*, PW 29/1996.

court or tribunal requiring the payment of any amount by the employee to the employer; or

- a deduction made by an employer from the wages of an employee where the purpose of the deduction is the satisfaction (whether wholly or in part) of an order of a court or tribunal requiring the payment of any amount by the employer to the court or tribunal or a third party out of the wages of the employee.

2.4. Enforcement

[12–36]   Enforcement of the 1991 Act occurs at both a criminal and a civil level.[124] In the civil context (and quite apart from an employee's entitlement to issue proceedings for breach of contract in respect of any deduction of this kind) an employee may present a complaint of a breach of s.5 to a Rights Commissioner.[125] Such complaint (which must be presented in writing containing a statement of any particulars that are required by regulations and which must be on notice to both the Rights Commissioner and any party concerned by the case) must be brought within six months beginning on the date of the contravention to which the complaint relates, although the Rights Commissioner may extend this limitation period by up to a further six months where [s]he is satisfied that exceptional circumstances prevented the complaint being made within the initial six-month period.

[12–37]   Having given the parties an opportunity to be heard,[126] if the Rights Commissioner decides that a complaint in relation to a deduction or a payment is made out in whole or in part, [s]he shall order the employer to pay compensation to the employee in an amount that is reasonable in the circumstances[127] but not exceeding the net amount of the wages (that is, after the making of any lawful deductions from the employee's gross wages) that would have been paid to the

---

124. Significantly, in *An Employer v An Employee*, PW92/2007, the Employment Appeals Tribunal confirmed that neither it nor a Rights Commissioner had any jurisdiction under the Payment of Wages Act 1991 to enforce the pay-related terms of a Registered Employment Agreement on an employer. Rather (as is discussed in Chapter 2), this is a matter over which the Labour Court has jurisdiction under the terms of s.33 of the Industrial Relations Act 1946.

125. The complaint is made in writing to a Rights Commissioner, who must then give a copy of the notice to the other parties concerned. The notice must contain such particulars and be in such form as may be specified by the Minister.

126. Proceedings will generally be heard in public unless the Rights Commissioner on the application of one of the parties of the proceedings decides otherwise (s.6(6) Payment of Wages Act 1991). Moreover the Minister may by regulation provide for any matters relating to proceedings: s.6(8) *ibid.*

127. s.6(2) *ibid.* Such compensation shall not exceed the net amount of the wages that would have been paid to the employee if the deduction had not been paid; or where a payment has been made, the net amount of the wages paid the previous week to him or her or, if the amount of the deduction is greater than the net amount of the wages that would otherwise have been paid to the employee, twice that amount.

worker in the week immediately before the date of the deduction from his or her wages or the payment made by the employee to the employer if such deduction or payment had not occurred.[128] If the amount of deduction is greater than such net amount of wages, then the Rights Commissioner cannot order the employer to pay more than twice the amount of the deduction or payment.[129] Finally, a Rights Commissioner is not entitled to give a decision under this section at any point after the commencement of court proceedings taken by the claimant in respect of such deduction or payment and similarly, the employee is not entitled to recover money in court proceedings in respect of a deduction or payment for which the Rights Commissioner has already given a decision.[130] A decision of both the Rights Commissioner *and* of the EAT on appeal may provide that the relevant decision be carried out before a specified date,[131] but where this is not so provided, then it must be carried out within six weeks of the date on which it is communicated to the parties concerned.[132]

The decision of the Rights Commissioner[133] may be appealed to the EAT[134] within [12–38] six weeks of the relevant decision being communicated to him.[135] Significantly (and unlike other similar legislation), the Act does not provide for the EAT to extend this six-week limitation period, although it *is* stated that the Minister may, by regulation, provide for various matters connected with EAT proceedings, *including the possible extension by the EAT of such limitation periods.*[136] Decisions of

---

128. s.6(2)(a) *ibid.*
129. s.6(2)(b) *ibid.*
130. s.6(3) *ibid.*
131. s.8(2)(a) *ibid.*
132. The procedures governing applications for enforcement are set out in Order 57 Rule 2 of the Circuit Court Rules 2001 (SI no. 510 of 2001).
133. The Rights Commissioner is bound to furnish the tribunal with a copy of any decision given by him under the Act: s.6(7) Payment of Wages Act 1991.
134. Again the EAT must give the parties the opportunity to be heard and to present any evidence relevant to the appeal (s.7(1) *ibid.*) Moreover s.7(5) of the 1991 Act provides that s.39(17) of the Redundancy Payments Act 1967 shall apply to proceedings of the EAT under this Act, which essentially gives the EAT the power to require attendance at a hearing or production of documents by witnesses, and to take evidence on oath and administer oaths for this purpose.
135. s.7(2) *ibid.* Such an appeal is initiated by a party giving notice in writing to both the EAT and the other party concerned. In addition, when it is linked with, for example, a claim under the Terms of Employment (Information) Act 1994–2001, the EAT can hear an appeal from a decision of the Rights Commissioner in respect of the Payment of Wages Act 1991. On the other hand, however, a Payment of Wages Act claim can only be heard by the EAT as an appeal from a Rights Commissioner decision. Thus where an appeal is being taken against a Rights Commissioner decision pertaining to a different piece of legislation, it is not possible to include a novel claim under the Payment of Wages Act that had previously not been heard by the Rights Commissioner: *An Employer v 3 Employees,* C-PW55-57/2008.
136. See the Payment of Wages (Appeals) Regulations 1991 (SI no. 351 of 1991). In essence the appeal must contain the names, address and descriptions of the parties to whom the appeal relates, the date of the decision and the name of the Rights Commissioner and a brief outline

the EAT may be appealed by a party to the appeal to the High Court on a point of law[137] and the Minister may, at the request of the EAT, refer a question of law arising in an appeal to the High Court for a determination[138] (and in either event such determination shall be final and conclusive). Where no such appeal has been taken, decisions of a Rights Commissioner or determinations of the EAT may be enforced as if they were orders of the Circuit Court made in civil proceedings.[139]

[12–39]   In terms of criminal prosecution, as we have seen it is an offence to pay wages to an employee otherwise than by a method specified in s.2(1) of the Act,[140] to fail to comply with the transitional arrangements in s.3 of the Act,[141] and to fail to comply with the rules relating to the provision of statements of wages and deductions from wages.[142] Proceedings in relation to such offences may be brought and prosecuted by the Minister, with such proceedings having to be instituted within 12 months from the date of the offence.[143]

---

of the grounds of the appeal. The regulations also provide requirements as to the time-frame in which a respondent to such appeal must enter an appearance.

137. s.7(4)(b) Payment of Wages Act 1991.
138. s.7(4)(a) *ibid.*
139. s.8(1) *ibid.*
140. s.2(3) *ibid.*
141. s.3(3) *ibid.*
142. s.4(4) *ibid.*
143. s.10(1) *ibid.* Where the offence is committed by a body corporate, but can be proved to have been committed with the consent or connivance of, or to be attributable to the neglect of a director, manager, secretary or other officer of that body corporate (or a person purporting to act in that capacity), then both the body corporate and that person can be prosecuted.

CHAPTER 13

Protective Leave Entitlements

In separate chapters of this book we consider the entitlements of employees under [13–01] Irish law to both annual leave[1] and sick leave.[2] In this chapter we consider additional types of leave to which employees are entitled under Irish law. The link between these various types of leave is that they are afforded to employees so that they may take time off work for the purposes of looking after other people.[3] In most cases, the person to be looked after is someone who is already in a position of dependency on the employee in question – as is the case in respect of:

- maternity leave;
- adoptive leave;
- parental leave; and
- *force majeure* leave.

In addition, it is also possible to take *carer's leave* in respect of someone with whom [13–02] one has no previous connection but for whom it is agreed that one will provide full-time care. In respect of all of these kinds of leave, the grounding legislation emphasises that the leave in question is a stand-alone form of leave, not to be confused with any other leave, including annual leave and/or sick leave.[4]

The legislation grounding these kinds of leave (which are discussed in turn in [13–03] this chapter) is based in most cases on EC directives.[5] In all cases, the legislation provides that provisions in any agreement (whether or not a contract of employment and whether concluded before or after the coming into being of the statute) that purport to limit the application of the legislation or that are inconsistent therewith shall be void, and that any such provision which provides an employee

---

1. Chapter 11.
2. Chapter 4.
3. Obviously, in the case of maternity leave, the leave is afforded at least in part to enable a new mother to recuperate from the physical and other effects of pregnancy, labour and childbirth.
4. s.22(4) Maternity Protection Act 1994; s.13(4) Carer's Leave Act 2001; s.14(2) Parental Leave Acts 1998 and 2006; s.12(5) Adoptive Leave Acts 1995 and 2005. Generally, see Inverarity, 'Leave Matters', 2(2) *IELJ* (2005), 44, and Law Society of Ireland, *Employment Law* (2006), at pp.97–125.
5. The exceptions are adoptive leave and carer's leave.

with leave entitlements that are less favourable than those contained in the legislation shall be duly modified.[6]

[13–04] Two major areas of similarity in respect of all of these pieces of legislation relate to the protection afforded by law to employees while on leave, and the manner by which redress for breaches of the legislation is to be sought. Regrettably, however, the various pieces of legislation, while similar in these respects, are not actually identical. Accordingly in this chapter we will first consider the substantive entitlements of employees under the various pieces of legislation, and then consider in turn the protections afforded to employees while on leave and the manner by which redress is to be sought in general under all of the pieces of legislation: highlighting, where appropriate, differences in detail between the various statutes.

1. Maternity Leave

[13–05] Perhaps the most well known and significant form of leave under Irish law is maternity leave, provided for under the Maternity Protection Acts 1994[7] and 2004[8] and subsequent regulations.[9] This legislation, which is primarily aimed at implementing the provisions of Council Directive 92/85/EEC of 19 October 1992,[10] is, at root, an Act steeped in the ideology of equality, and in particular the view that it is an indispensable aspect of gender equality in the workplace that a woman should not be discriminated against, nor suffer any penalty or loss, direct or indirect, as a result of being pregnant.[11] Rather the underpinning ethic of the legislation is that a pregnant woman's needs should be accommodated insofar as is justly and reasonably possible by her employer. As such many aspects of the legislation are also discussed in Chapter 9.

---

6. s.4 of the Maternity Protection Act 1994, Adoptive Leave Act 1995, Parental Leave Act 1998 and Carer's Leave Act 2001. In all cases, the legislation provides that nothing contained therein prevents an employer from giving employees more favourable leave entitlements than those contained in the legislation.

7. For a general overview of the 1994 Act, see Barry, 'The Maternity Protection Act 1994', 13 *ILT* (1995), 15, and Masselot, 'Implementation of the Pregnant Workers Directive in the Republic of Ireland', 15 *ILT* (1997), 96. See also Meenan, 'Living to Work, Working to Live – New Statutory Domestic Arrangements', 1 *Employment Law Review* (2006), 19.

8. For analysis of the major changes generated by the 2004 Amendment Act, see Matthews, 'The Maternity Protection (Amendment) Bill 2003', 1(3) *IELJ* (2004), 68.

9. Most significantly the Maternity Protection Act 1994 (Extension of Periods of Leave) Order 2006. SI no. 51 of 2006, under which many of the periods of permitted leave under the 1994 Act have been significantly increased.

10. Prior to this, the entitlement to maternity leave was provided for in the Maternity Protection of Employees Acts of 1981 and 1991.

11. On the question of whether an employer discriminates if it withholds pension contributions from women on maternity leave, see Gater and Ramsey, 'Maternity Leave: Another Fine Mess?', 90 *Employment Law Journal* (May 2008), 5.

Thus, apart from providing for a woman's entitlement to a defined period of mater-   [13–06]
nity leave for which she is entitled to receive social welfare payments, the Act also
imposes obligations on an employer:

- to ensure that a pregnant woman's health and safety is not compromised
  by her work,
- to allow a mother the time and facility to breast-feed her child, and
- to render illegal any dismissal of an employee on the grounds of pregnancy.

1.1. Maternity Protection Legislation and Fathers

One final point should be made by way of introduction. Under s.7 of the Act it is   [13–07]
provided that the references to an 'employee' in the Maternity Protection Act 1994
are exclusively to a female employee – in other words, this is not leave that can be
taken by men.[12] One exception to this principle, as contained in s.16 of the 1994 Act
should, however, be noted: the father of a child (if he is employed under a contract
of employment) is entitled to leave[13] from his employment if the mother of that
child dies at any time before the expiry of the 40th week following the week of her
confinement.[14] In such circumstances, and where the mother dies before the 24th
week after the week of her confinement, he is entitled to leave up until the end of
the 24th week, and if the mother dies *after* the end of the 24th week he is entitled to
leave up until the end of the 40th week.[15] This leave[16] commences within seven days

---

12. This can, at least in part, be justified by the explanation that part of the reason for allowing
    maternity leave is in order to protect maternal health in the latter stages of pregnancy and
    after labour and childbirth. See, for example, *Boyle v Equal Opportunities Commission* [1998]
    ECR I-6401. As we will see, no similar justification would appear to cover the restriction of
    adoptive leave to a mother, such that an adopting father may only take adoptive leave where
    the adoptive mother of the child dies.
13. Significant increases in the time-frames in which leave can be sought under s.16 were
    provided for in the Maternity Protection Act 1994 (Extension of Periods of Leave) Order of
    2006, SI no. 5 of 2006. For an analysis of the equivalent English changes, see Parker, 'Work-
    Life Balance: New Maternity Provisions Arrive with a Bump', 76 *Employment Law Journal*
    (December 2006/January 2007), 10.
14. Under s.2 of the Act 'confinement' and 'the date of confinement' have the meanings assigned
    to them by s.41 of the Social Welfare (Consolidation) Act 1993. Thus confinement means
    'labour resulting in the issue of a living child, or a labour after 24 weeks of pregnancy
    resulting in the issue of a child whether alive or dead', and date of confinement means
    'where labour begun on one day results in the issue of a child on another day, to the date of
    the issue of a child, or if a woman is confined of twins or a greater number of children, to
    the date of the issue of the last of them'.
15. s.16(1) Maternity Protection Act 1994.
16. Such leave is conditional on the man notifying his employer in writing not later than the
    day on which his leave begins of the death of the mother, of his intention to take leave, and
    of the length of the leave to which he believes he is entitled (s.16(2) *ibid.*). If the employer
    requests it, the father is also obliged to cause his employer to be supplied with a copy of the
    death certificate of the mother and the birth certificate of the child.

of the mother's death.[17] Moreover, the father in question is entitled to sixteen further weeks of unpaid additional leave[18] following the expiry of the original period, which may either be taken as a consecutive period of leave or else may be wholly or partially postponed in the event of the hospitalisation of the child in question.[19]

[13–08] Having said that, it is still worth noting that Irish maternity protection legislation may be criticised for focusing exclusively on what may be termed a typical family structure. Thus under the legislation, where the mother dies it is only the father who can take leave to look after the child (subject to the capacity of someone else to take unpaid parental leave). Yet there are an increasing number of circumstances that fall outside of this paradigm. What of, for example, a lesbian couple, one of whom has conceived by way of sperm donation or in vitro fertilisation? What of a situation where a woman becomes pregnant in the context of a loose arrangement with a man (who, it is agreed, is to have no further interest in the child) and intends to raise the child either by herself or with a partner of either gender who is not the parent of the child? Should such woman die, there is no provision under the Act for her partner (or some other nominated person) to take *paid* leave to raise the child. On the other hand, s.16 of the Act appears to afford the father an entitlement to take such leave even if he has no more than a biological connection with the child, and even where he has no intention of using his leave period for any purpose connected with the child.[20] It is arguable that this state of affairs is inconsistent with the general thrust of EC equality law.

1.2. The Entitlement to Maternity Leave
[13–09] The basic essence of the Act in this regard is contained in s.8 of the Maternity Protection Act 1994 (as amended). Under this section (and since March 2007) a pregnant employee is now entitled to a minimum period of maternity leave of not less than 26 weeks.[21] Moreover, where the date on which the woman actually gives birth occurs in a week later than the week in which she was *due* to give birth, then the minimum period of maternity leave is extended in order to ensure that the

17. s.16(3) *ibid.*
18. This is again conditional on the employee giving notice to his employer of his intention to take such leave not later than four weeks before the date on which he was due to return to work ss.16(5) and 16(6) *ibid.* Any notification under s.16 may be revoked by a later notification given to the employer: s.16(7) *ibid.*
19. s.16(4) *ibid.* The context in which such leave may be postponed in the event of the hospitalisation of the child is discussed below in the context of maternity leave.
20. It is worth noting that, unlike the Parental Leave Act, there is no provision under the Maternity Protection Act 1994 for an employer to assess whether the maternity leave (or the leave taken by the father of a child whose mother has died) is being taken for the *bona fide* purpose of caring for that child, nor is there any reason why the leave must be taken for that purpose in the first instance.
21. The period of maternity leave was increased under the terms of the Maternity Protection Act 1994 (Extension of Periods of Leave) Order 2006, SI no. 51 of 2006, from 18 weeks to 22 weeks for the period between 1 March 2006 and to 26 weeks after 1 March 2007.

woman does not return to work earlier than two weeks[22] after the end of the week in which she gives birth.[23] The leave in question is unpaid[24] (although naturally the contract of employment may provide that the woman *is* to receive paid maternity leave), but in the absence of such agreement, and provided that the employee has the requisite qualifying contributions,[25] the employee in question is entitled to maternity benefit pursuant to ss.47-51 of the Social Welfare (Consolidation) Act of 2005[26] and at a rate of 75 per cent of her reckonable weekly earnings.[27]

1.2.1. Additional Maternity Leave

In addition, a woman who so desires is entitled to take an additional period of 12 [13–10] weeks' unpaid maternity leave.[28] Should she choose to do so, she is required[29] to notify her employer of this fact either at the same time as her original notification of maternity leave, or else at a time not later than four weeks before the date on which the employee was due to return to work following her period of maternity leave.[30]

Where an employee has notified her employer of her intention to take a period [13–11] of additional leave and becomes sick during the last four weeks of paid maternity

---

22. Under s.12 of the Maternity Protection Act 1994 it is provided that such leave cannot exceed four consecutive weeks after the date of confinement. On the other hand, this is to ensure compliance with the terms of s.10 of the Maternity Protection Act 1994, which, following amendment by the Maternity Protection (Amendment) Act of 2004, has reduced the number of weeks of maternity leave that must be taken after the week in which the woman gave birth from four weeks to two weeks. In other words, it would seem that, since 2004, a woman can only realistically be afforded an additional consecutive *two* weeks (rather than four) of maternity leave where the birth of her child is significantly overdue.

23. s.12(1) Maternity Protection Act 1994. Where such minimum period of maternity leave is proposed to be extended, the employee must, as soon as practicable after the proposal of such extension, notify her employer in writing of the proposed extension and, again as soon as practicable after the date of confinement, confirm the extension to her employer and specify the duration of the extension: s.12(2) *ibid.*

24. This is clear from the terms of s.22 *ibid.*

25. The rules in this regard are set out in s.48 of the Social Welfare (Consolidation) Act 2005.

26. Similarly, a father who is on leave following the death of the mother of his child, and pursuant to s.16 of the 1994 Act, is entitled to benefit of this kind: s.47(5) *ibid.*

27. The European Court of Justice (interpreting Article 11(3) of the Pregnant Workers Directive, which requires that pregnant women receive an 'adequate' allowance while on maternity leave) has held that whereas this does not require that a woman receive her full salary while on such leave, equally she must be awarded any pay rises that she would otherwise have been awarded either before or during maternity leave: C-342/93, *Gillespie v Northern Health and Social Services Board* [1996] ECR I-475.

28. s.14(1) of the Maternity Protection Act 1994, as amended both by s.5 of the Maternity Protection (Amendment) Act of 2004 and by the Maternity Protection Act 1994 (Extension of Periods of Leave) Order 2006, SI no. 51 of 2006.

29. s.14(3) Maternity Protection Act 1994.

30. s.14(4) *ibid.* A notification of this kind may be revoked by a further notification given by the employee not later than four weeks before the date on which she was due to return to work following her scheduled period of paid maternity leave: s.14(5) *ibid.*

leave, or during the additional maternity leave, she may request in writing that her employer terminate the additional maternity leave.[31] If the employer agrees to this (and it is a matter for that employer's discretion)[32] then the period of additional maternity leave will conclude on a date agreed by employer and employee, though not earlier than the date on which the employee's illness began, and not later than the date on which the additional maternity leave was due to end.[33] In such circumstances, and whereas the employee forgoes the entitlement to recommence her additional period of maternity leave at a later stage,[34] any further absence on her part from work on the grounds of sickness is to be treated in the same way as any normal sickness-based absence from work.[35]

1.2.2. *Postponement of Leave*

[13–12] Finally, an employee who is on either maternity leave or additional maternity leave may, if the child (in connection with whose birth she is on or is entitled to be on leave) is hospitalised, request in writing that her leave, or part of it, be postponed.[36] Such a request can only be made if, at the time of the request, the woman has taken not less than 14 weeks of her leave and where not less than four of those weeks occurred after the end of the week of confinement.[37] A mother who is on maternity leave and wishes to postpone her proposed *additional* maternity leave may make a request of this kind even though she has not yet notified the employer of her intention to take such additional leave and a request of this kind is deemed to constitute a notice of intention to take such additional leave.[38] Again the decision whether or not to agree to such postponement is at the discretion of the employer, but if [s]he agrees to such request,[39] then the employee concerned must return to work on a date agreed with her employer[40] and the

---

31. s.14A(1) Maternity Protection Act 1994 and 2004. Similar provision is made for a father who takes leave in the event of the death of the mother of his child: s.16A Maternity Protection Act 1994.

32. Kerr, *Irish Employment Legislation* (Round Hall Sweet and Maxwell, 2000), at p.C-61 makes the point that, whereas there is no right of appeal against a refusal of an employee to agree to terminate the additional maternity leave, nonetheless such refusal may amount to grounds for a trade dispute to be referred to the Labour Court.

33. s.14A(2) Maternity Protection Act 1994 and 2004.

34. s.14A(4)(b) *ibid.*

35. s.14A(4)(a) *ibid.*

36. s.14B(1) *ibid.* Similar provision is made in respect of a father who has taken leave under s.16 as a result of the death of the mother of the child in question: s.16B *ibid.*

37. s.14B(2) *ibid.*

38. s.14(3) *ibid.*

39. An employer is entitled to require an employee who wishes to postpone leave and subsequently to take resumed leave to furnish him or her with a letter or other appropriate document from the hospital in which the child concerned is hospitalised confirming such hospitalisation and a letter or other appropriate document from such hospital or from the child's medical practitioner, confirming that the child has been discharged from the hospital and giving the date of such discharge. Regulation 4 of the Maternity Protection (Postponement of Leave) Regulations 2004, SI no. 655 of 2004.

40. s.14B(4)(a) Maternity Protection Act 1994 and 2004. This date cannot be later than the date on which the leave concerned was due to end.

relevant leave is postponed (but by no more than six months[41]) from the date on which she returns to work.[42] The employee is then entitled to take what is termed 'resumed leave'[43] (that is, the part of her leave that was postponed) in one continuous period commencing not later than seven days after the discharge of the child from hospital.[44]

1.2.3. Notification Requirements

Subject to what is discussed above, in order to avail of statutory paid maternity leave,[45] a woman must cause her employer to be notified (in writing) of her intention to take such leave[46] 'as soon as reasonably practicable'[47] but not later than four weeks before the commencement of maternity leave.[48] In addition, she must at the time of such notification give her employer, or produce for his or her inspection, a medical or other appropriate certificate confirming that she is pregnant and specifying the expected week of confinement.[49] Provided that this is done, then the employee is entitled to take her minimum period of maternity leave commencing

[13–13]

---

41. reg.3 of the Maternity Protection (Postponement of Leave) Regulations 2004, SI no. 655 of 2004.

42. s.14B(4)(b) Maternity Protection Act 1994 and 2004. Where a mother is absent from work due to sickness during the period of postponement, she shall be deemed to have commenced resumed leave from the first day of such absence unless she notifies the employer as soon as is reasonably practicable that she does not wish to commence resumed leave, in which case the absence shall be treated as a routine absence from work of the employee due to sickness (s.14(b)(6) *ibid.*). It is further provided that where this happens 'the employee shall not be entitled to the resumed leave', but presumably in the interests of fairness this simply means that she shall not be entitled to resumed leave at that time, but must instead wait until she has informed her employer that she intends to take resumed leave.

43. Entitlement to such resumed leave is generally conditional on the employee having notified her employer, as soon as reasonably practicable and not later than the day on which the leave begins, of her intention to commence such leave (s.14(B)(8) Maternity Protection Act 1994 and 2004), although an employer may, at his or her discretion, waive the right to receive such notification (s.14(B)(10) *ibid.*). Moreover, a notification of intention to take resumed leave may be revoked by a subsequent notice (s.14(B)(9) *ibid.*).

44. s.14B(4)(c) *ibid.*

45. Under the previous relevant legislation (s.9 of the Maternity Protection of Employees Act of 1981) the EAT had held that compliance with an equivalent requirement was a mandatory prerequisite to the taking of maternity leave, and that a failure to do so could not be excused by reason of the employee's ignorance of the law.

46. This notice may be revoked by a subsequent notice from the employee: s.9(2) Maternity Protection Act 1994.

47. Where a woman gives birth in a week that is four weeks or more before the expected week of confinement, then the employee is deemed to have complied with the statutory notification requirements if she provides such notification within four days of the date on which she gives birth (s.13(1) *ibid.*) and her minimum period of maternity leave shall commence either on a date of her choosing in accordance with s.10(1) or on the date on which she gives birth (s.13(2) *ibid.*).

48. s.9(1)(a) *ibid.*

49. s.9(1)(b) *ibid.*

on the date that she selects,[50] provided that the date the leave begins is not later than two weeks before the expected week of confinement and the date it concludes is not earlier than two weeks after the expected week of confinement.[51]

1.3. Other Forms of Pregnancy-Related Leave

[13–14] Apart from maternity leave *per se*, there are various other contexts in which an employee may be entitled to what might loosely be termed 'pregnancy related leave':

- An employee is entitled to time off work without loss of pay in order to receive ante-natal or post-natal care.[52]
- An employee[53] is entitled to time off work without loss of pay for the purpose of attending one set of ante-natal classes (other than the last three classes in such a set[54]) during one or more pregnancies.[55] Moreover, an expectant father of a child is entitled once only to time off work[56] without loss of pay for the purpose of attending the last two ante-natal classes in a set that has been attended by the expectant mother.
- An employee who is breast-feeding[57] is entitled to time off from work

---

50. s.10(1) *ibid.* If a woman is employed on a fixed-term contract that is due to expire before the end of her maternity leave, then the last date of her maternity leave shall be the date on which the term expires, but nothing in the 1994 Act can be taken as affecting the termination of the employee's contract of employment on that date: s.10(2) *ibid.*

51. If an employee produces or causes to be produced to an employer a certificate by a registered medical practitioner (or otherwise to the satisfaction of the Minister for Justice, Equality and Law Reform and the Minister for Social and Family Affairs), stating that for a medical reason the employee's maternity leave should commence on a particular date, then the minimum leave for the employee shall commence on the date so specified (s.11(1) *ibid.*). Where a certificate of this kind is produced, then the notification requirements under s.9 are deemed to be complied with (s.11(2) *ibid.*).

52. s.15(1) *ibid.* The amount of time off to which an employee is entitled, the terms and conditions of such leave, the notice that must be given to an employer prior to such leave being taken, and the evidence to be furnished to the employer in order to justify such leave, may be provided for in regulations (s.15(2) *ibid.*). See the Maternity Protection (Time Off for Ante-Natal and Post-Natal Care) Regulations 1995, SI no. 18 of 1995.

53. The entitlement to leave to attend ante-natal classes does not apply to various categories of workers mentioned in s.15(A)(3) Maternity Protection Acts 1994 and 2004, which covers members of both the defence forces and the gardaí in specific circumstances.

54. These last classes would generally be attended when the mother is on maternity leave.

55. s.15A(1) Maternity Protection Act 1994 as inserted by s.8 of the Maternity Protection (Amendment) Act 2004.

56. s.15A(2) Maternity Protection Act 1994.

57. Under both s.2 of the Maternity Protection Act 1994 and the Maternity Protection (Protection of Mothers who are Breastfeeding) Regulations 2004, SI no. 654 of 2004, the definition of a employee who is breast-feeding is confined to a woman who gave birth six months previously (and who is breast-feeding and has informed her employer of this fact). For criticism, see Kerr, *Irish Employment Legislation* (Round Hall Sweet and Maxwell, 2000), at p.C-119.

for the purpose of breast-feeding[58] in the workplace[59] or to a reduction in her working hours for the purpose of breast-feeding outside of the workplace.[60] Both of these entitlements are without loss of pay.[61] If an employee who has exercised either of these entitlements ceases to breast-feed, she is required at the earliest practical time to notify her employer in writing that she has so ceased.[62] The specifics of how these entitlements operate are laid down in the Maternity Protection (Protection of Mothers who are Breastfeeding) Regulations 2004.[63] Thus the employee in question is entitled to an hour's paid break-time daily for breast-feeding, to be taken either as one break of 60 minutes, two breaks of 30 minutes, three breaks of 20 minutes, or in such other manner as is agreed by the employee and employer.[64] Alternatively, a woman whose employer has chosen that instead of such breaks from work, her working hours be reduced to accommodate breast-feeding, is entitled to have such hours reduced (without loss of pay) by 60 minutes, taken in one of the ways mentioned in this paragraph.[65]

- As is discussed in Chapter 15, under Irish health and safety legislation employers are required to conduct a risk-assessment for all workers to assess whether they are exposed to unacceptable risks. For present purposes, such assessment must occur in respect of pregnant employees, employees who have recently given birth and employees who are breast-feeding.[66] Where there is an unacceptable risk to the health either of a

---

58. Breast-feeding for the purposes of the Act means breast-feeding a child or expressing breast milk and feeding it to a child immediately or storing it for the purposes of feeding him or her later: s.15B(4) Maternity Protection Acts 1994 and 2004. Generally, see Daley and Baker, 'A right to Breastfeed', 46 *Employment Law Journal* (December 2003/January 2004), 5.

59. An employer is not required to provide facilities for breast-feeding in the workplace if the provision of such facilities would give rise to more than nominal cost: s.15B(2) Maternity Protection Act 1994.

60. s.15B(1) Maternity Protection Act 1994 and 2004.

61. s.15(B)(1) *ibid.*

62. s.15B(3) *ibid.* In addition, under Regulation 5 of the Maternity Protection (Protection of Mothers who are Breastfeeding) Regulations 2004, a breast-feeding employee is required to notify her employer as soon as reasonably practicable of her proposal to avail of her entitlements to time off for breast-feeding and, if requested by her employer, to furnish him or her with the child's birth certificate.

63. SI no. 654 of 2004. Section 15B(2) of the Maternity Protection Act 1994 and 2004 provides that the amount of time off and the number and frequency of breast-feeding breaks or the reduction of working hours to which an employee is entitled, the terms and conditions of such leave, the notice which must be given to an employer prior to such leave being taken, and the evidence to be furnished to the employer in order to justify such leave, may be provided for in regulations.

64. reg.3(1) Maternity Protection (Protection of Mothers who are Breastfeeding) Regulations 2004.

65. reg.3(2) *ibid.*

66. s.17(1) Maternity Protection Act 1994. See also Regulation 4 of the Safety, Health and Welfare

pregnant woman or her developing foetus,[67] she must be provided with alternative work to do that does not pose such unacceptable risks.[68] Where it is not technically or objectively feasible for this to happen, where such a move cannot reasonably be required on duly substantiated grounds or where the other work to which the employer proposes to move the employee is not suitable for her,[69] she is entitled to be granted leave from her employment.[70] In such circumstances, and for the first 21 days of such leave period, the employee is entitled to be paid an amount equal to three times her normal weekly pay[71] and thereafter can claim social welfare benefit under s.52 of the Social Welfare (Consolidation) Act 2005.[72]

1.4. Protection of Employees while on Leave and Enforcement Procedures

[13–15] One of the key aspects of Irish maternity protection legislation is that employees are protected from any unfavourable treatment (up to and including dismissal) by employers as a result of availing of leave entitlements. Most importantly, employees have a right to return to work at the end of their leave periods either in the same job or in some suitable alternative employment. As mentioned at the beginning of this chapter, however, this is an entitlement provided for in very similar ways in all the pieces of legislation considered in this chapter, and accordingly we deal with it (and with the question of how the legislation is enforced) later in this chapter.

---

at Work (pregnant employees, etc.) Regulations 1994, SI no. 218 of 2000. Under s.20(1) of the Maternity Protection Act 1994, where a woman who has taken leave under s.18 as a result of a risk posed in respect of breast-feeding ceases breast-feeding, she is obliged to inform the employer of this fact.

67. According to Regulation 4 of the 1994 Regulations, such risk must derive from 'any activity at the employer's place of work likely to involve a risk of exposure to any agent, process or working condition' that poses a risk to the pregnancy of or breast-feeding by employees.

68. An employee who has taken leave under s.18 is obliged to inform her employer as soon as practicable of any changes in her condition that mean she is no longer vulnerable to such risk: s.20(2) Maternity Protection Act 1994.

69. Work is deemed to be suitable for an employee where it is of a kind suitable for a pregnant employee, an employee who has recently given birth and/or an employee who is breast-feeding and where it is work that is appropriate for the employee to do in all the circumstances: s.18(3) *ibid.*

70. s.18(1) *ibid.*

71. reg.3(1) Maternity Protection (Health and Safety Leave Remuneration) Regulations 1995, SI no. 20 of 1995.

72. Entitlement to health and safety leave under s.18 of the Maternity Protection Act 1994 ends (a) on the date on which a pregnant employee commences maternity leave or ceases to be an employee to which Part III of the Act applies (that is, a pregnant employee, an employee who has recently given birth or a breast-feeding employee) (s.19(1) *ibid.*); (b) if the employee was employed under a fixed-term contract, on the date on which that contract expires; (c) where the employer informs the employee that the risk to which she was exposed no longer exists, or where the employee informs her employer that she is no longer vulnerable in respect of such risk (s.20 *ibid.*), then seven days after the notification either from employer or employee is received by the other party.

2. Adoptive Leave

Leave for parents who have adopted or are in the process of adopting children [13–16] is provided for in the Adoptive Leave Acts 1995–2005[73] and the various regulations made thereunder, most notably the Adoptive Leave Act 1995 (Extension of Periods of Leave) Order of 2006.[74] To some extent the 1995 Act, especially as it has been amended by the Adoptive Leave Act 2005, mirrors the various protections provided for in the Maternity Protection legislation considered in the previous section, and accordingly in dealing with such matters reference will occasionally be made to such protections. Unless there is provision in the employment contract for an employee to be paid while on adoptive leave, then that leave will be unpaid leave. On the other hand, an employee is entitled to adoptive benefit pursuant to ss.58–61 of the Social Welfare (Consolidation) Act of 2005. This benefit is paid at the rate of 75 per cent of the reckonable weekly earnings, reckonable weekly emoluments or reckonable income as the case may be of the adopting parent. Payment of such benefit is conditional on the relevant contribution requirements (as laid down in s.59 of the Social Welfare (Consolidation) Act) being fulfilled.

2.1. Entitlement to Adoptive Leave

The essential purpose of the legislation is to provide an entitlement to adopting [13–17] mothers or sole adopting fathers (that is, an adopting father where the adopting mother dies[75]) to take leave from employment for a minimum of 24 weeks[76] from the date of placement.[77] The fact that the legislation only permits an adopting father to take adoptive leave when the adopting mother has died is somewhat controversial.[78] After all, whereas in the context of maternity leave there may be

---

73. For analysis of the background to Irish adoptive leave legislation, see Kerr, *Irish Employment Legislation* (Round Hall Sweet and Maxwell, 2000), at p.D-4.
74. SI no. 51 of 2006.
75. In the case of an adoptive father, the period of adoptive leave must commence within seven days of the death of the adopting mother: s.9(3) Adoptive Leave Act 1995 and 2005.
76. s.6 Adoptive Leave Acts 1995 and 2005. The time limits in question were increased under the Adoptive Leave Act 1995 (Extensions of Periods of Leave) Order of 2006. Where it is an adoptive father who is the employee in question then the entitlement is to (a) in case the adopting mother dies on or after the day of placement, 24 weeks less the period between the date of placement and the date of her death; or (b) in any other case, 24 weeks (s.9 of the 1995 Act, as amended by s.5 of the 2005 Act and Regulation 10 of the 2006 Order).
77. The date of placement is defined in s.2 of the Adoptive Leave Acts 1995 and 2005 as either (a) the day on which the child is placed physically in the care of the adopting parent with a view to the making of an adoption order; (b) the day on which the child is placed physically in the care of the adopting parent with a view to the effecting of a foreign adoption; or (c) in the case of a foreign adoption, where the child has not previously been placed in the care of the adopting parent, the day on which the child has been so placed following the adoption.
78. In C-163-92 *Commission v Italy* [1983] EUECJ, [1983] ECR 3273 the ECJ concluded that the restriction of adoptive leave to women was justified in the interests of trying to ensure that the manner by which an adopted child became part of a family resembled as closely as possible the process by which a birth child did the same.

significant reasons (connected *inter alia* to maternal health) justifying this restriction, it is strongly arguable that such considerations do not apply in the context of adoptive leave. Indeed it is notable that in *Telecom Éireann v O'Grady*[79] the Supreme Court had previously concluded that a similar restriction in the appellant company's adoptive leave scheme (and operating prior to the coming into being of the Adoptive Leave Act 1995) contravened employment equality law as it then stood.[80] Moreover, as with maternity leave, it may be argued that the legislation is still very rooted in a traditional view of a family, and will have no application in, for example, a situation where two gay persons or indeed one single man adopts a child.

2.1.1. Notification Requirements

[13–18] This entitlement, like the other leave entitlements considered in this chapter, is subject to notification requirements.[81] Thus, in the cases of adoptions other than foreign adoptions, an employee who is seeking to avail of adoptive leave must, as soon as is reasonably practicable, but not later than four weeks before the expected date of placement, cause her employer to be notified in writing of her intention to take adoptive leave.[82] She must then cause her employer to be notified in writing as soon as is reasonably practicable of the expected date of placement,[83] and finally she must also supply her employer with the certificate of placement[84] as soon as is reasonably practicable but not later than four weeks after the date of placement.[85]

---

79. [1998] ELR 61.
80. See Inverarity, 'Leave Matters', 2(2) *IELJ* (2005), 44. It is worth noting, however, that in *Telecom Éireann v O Grady* [1998] ELR 61, Keane J noted that the new Employment Equality Act 1998 (which at that stage was pending) would expressly permit a law to confer benefits on women in connection inter alia with adoption.
81. The notifications to which reference is made can be revoked by further subsequent notifications given in writing to the relevant employer: s.7(3) Adoptive Leave Acts 1995 and 2005.
82. ss.7(1)(a) and 9(2) *ibid.* Where the employee in question is an adoptive father and the adopting mother dies after the date of placement, he must inform the employer of his intention to take such leave not later than the date on which he commences the leave: s.9(2)(a)(ii) *ibid.*
83. s.7(1)(b) Adoptive Leave Acts 1995 and 2005. Where the date of placement is postponed, commencement of the period of adoptive leave is also postponed, subject to the employee informing his or her employer of the expected new date of placement as soon as is reasonably practicable: s.7(4) *ibid.*
84. A certificate of placement under s.13 of the Adoptive Leave Acts 1995 and 2005 is issued to an adopting parent on request either by the relevant Health Board or the registering adopting society that arranges the placing of the child (or, where appropriate, by An Bord Uáchtala) and states the date on which it was issued, the date of placement, the sex and date of birth of the child, and the name and address of the adopting parents. Such certificate of placement or a copy thereof certified by the relevant body shall, unless the contrary be proved, be evidence of the matters referred to therein in any proceedings deriving from an effort by an adopting parent to exercise his or her rights under the Act: s.14 *ibid.*
85. s.7(1)(c) *ibid.* In the case of a sole adopting father the requirement is that the certificate be supplied either not later than four weeks after the date of placement or four weeks after the commencement of the leave, whichever is later: s.9(2)(c) *ibid.*

The first of these two notification requirements also apply in the case of foreign adoptions,[86] but instead of supplying his or her employer with the certificate of placement, an employee who is intending to take adoptive leave in respect of a foreign adoption must also have caused her employer to be supplied with a copy of the declaration made pursuant to s.5(1)(iii)(II) of the Adoption Act 1991[87] before the expected date of placement,[88] and must also cause her employer to be supplied with particulars in writing of the placement as soon as is reasonably practicable after the date of placement.[89] Finally, where an adopting parent commences work within the period of six weeks before the date of placement, then she must confirm in writing to her employer her intention to take adoptive leave as soon as practicable but not later than the date on which she commences adoptive leave.[90]

2.2. Additional Adoptive Leave

In addition, an employee is entitled to sixteen weeks' additional adoptive leave[91]   [13–19] commencing immediately after the end of her adoptive leave.[92] Again this is subject

---

86. ss.7(2)(a) and (b) *ibid.*

87. This is a declaration by An Bord Uáchtala that it is satisfied that the adopters are persons coming within the classes of persons in whose favour an adoption order may, by virtue of the said section 10, be made, and also that (having had regard to a report by the Health Board in whose functional area the adopters were ordinarily resident at the time of the assessment, or by a registered adoption society, of an assessment in relation to the adopters carried out by the board or the society, as the case may be) it is satisfied in relation to the adopters as respects the matters referred to in section 13 of the 1991 Adoption Act.

88. In the case of an adopting father this declaration must be supplied to the employer as soon as is reasonably practicable but not later than four weeks after the commencement of such leave: s.9(2)(c)(ii)(I) Adoptive Leave Acts 1995 and 2005.

89. s.7(2)(c) *ibid.* In the case of an adopting father such particulars must simply be supplied as soon as is reasonably practicable: s.9(2)(c)(ii)(II) *ibid.* In addition, the adopting father must, where this is requested by his or her employer, cause that employer to be supplied with a copy of the adopting mother's death certificate as soon as is reasonably practicable: s.9(2)(d) *ibid.*

90. s.41(1) *ibid.* An employer who receives a notification of this kind within two weeks of the notified date of commencement of the leave may require the adopting parent to delay commencement of the leave for up to two weeks from the day on which the notification was received: s.41(5) *ibid.*

91. In the case of an adopting father the period of additional leave is (a) in case the adopting mother dies on or after the expiration of 24 weeks from the day of placement, 16 weeks less the period between the date of that expiration and the date of her death; or (b) in any other case 16 weeks: s.10(1) *ibid.* This period was extended under the terms of Regulation 11 of the 2006 Order.

92. s.8 *ibid.* Again this period was extended under the 2006 Order. In the case of an adoptive father, the period of additional leave commences either within seven days of the death of the adoptive father or where the adopting father was on adoptive leave, on the date immediately following the end of such leave: s.10(5) *ibid.* Thus an adopting father can avail of additional adoptive leave even where he has not availed of adoptive leave *per se*, in circumstances where the adopting mother had availed of such adoptive leave.

to the employee informing her employer[93] (either at the time of informing her employer of her original intention to take adoptive leave, or at a point not later than four weeks before the date on which she was supposed to return to work following the original period of adoptive leave) of her intention to take such additional adoptive leave.[94] Where an adopting parent commences employment within a period of six weeks before the date of placement and wishes to take additional adoptive leave before the date of placement (pursuant to s.8(5) or s.11), then she must inform her employee in writing of her intention to take such additional adoptive leave as soon as practicable and not later than the date on which such leave is to commence.[95]

2.3. Miscellaneous Forms of Adoptive Leave

[13–20] In keeping with the approach taken by the Maternity Protection Act, an employee is entitled to time off from work, without loss of pay, to attend any pre-adoption classes and meetings[96] that she is obliged to attend.[97] This entitlement is subject to the employee informing her employer in writing of the dates and times of the classes concerned, as soon as practicable but not later than two weeks before the date of the relevant classes, and producing to the employer, on request, an appropriate document indicating the dates and times of the classes concerned.[98] Equally where the employee has failed to do so, but not as a result of any fault or negligence on her part, then such notification requirements will be deemed to

---

93. s.8(3) *ibid.* In the case of an adopting father, the notification requirements for additional adoptive leave are the same as for adoptive leave, and where such notification requirements have been complied with in the context of adoptive leave, it is not necessary to comply with the same requirements again in order to avail of additional adoptive leave. ss.10(2)–(4) *ibid.*

94. In the case of a foreign adoption, where it may be necessary for additional adoptive leave to be taken for the purposes of familiarisation with the child who is to be adopted, some or all of the adoptive leave may be taken before the date of placement (ss.8(5) and 11(1) *ibid.*). In such circumstances, an employee is required to notify the employer of the intention to take additional adoptive leave not later than four weeks before the intended date of commencement of such leave, and also to provide the employer with a copy of the declaration of the adoption board pursuant to s.5(1)(iii)(II) of the Adoption Act 1991 (s.8(6) Adoptive Leave Acts 1995 and 2005). Where the applicant is an adopting father he may also be required to furnish the employer with a copy of the adopting mother's death certificate (s.11(2)(c) *ibid.*). In general, additional adoptive leave of this kind expires immediately before the date of placement (s.8(8) *ibid.*) but there is no such provision in the event of such leave being taken by an adopting father. Rather it is provided that such period of adoptive leave shall commence as soon as is reasonably practicable after the death of the adopting mother: s.11(3) *ibid.*

95. s.41(2) *ibid.* Again an employer who receives a notification of this kind within two weeks of the notified date of commencement of the leave may require the adopting parent to delay commencement of the leave for up to two weeks from the day on which the notification was received: s.41(5) *ibid.*

96. This is taken to mean classes or meetings within the State: s.11A(4) *ibid.*

97. s.11A(1) *ibid.* This entitlement does not apply to members of the defence forces and members of the gardaí in listed circumstances under s.11A(2) of the Act.

98. s.11A(3)(b) *ibid.*

be fulfilled if, within one week of the class in question, she produces evidence to her employer of attendance at the class in question, and also an indication of the circumstances that gave rise to such non-compliance.[99]

2.3.1. *Postponement or Suspension of Adoptive Leave*

As with the approach taken under maternity protection legislation, where an adop-   [13–21]
tive parent becomes sick while on adoptive leave or additional adoptive leave, she may request her employer to suspend the period of additional adoptive leave[100] – in which case any further time taken off work owing to the sickness would simply count as a period of sick leave to which the employee may be entitled.[101] Where this happens the period of additional adoptive leave shall be deemed to be terminated on a date agreed by employer and employee but which is not earlier than the date on which the sickness began, and not later than the date on which the leave would otherwise have ended.[102] In such circumstances, the employee is deemed to lose any further additional adoptive leave.[103]

Again in keeping with the terms of the Maternity Protection Act, an employee   [13–22]
whose adoptive child has been hospitalised at the relevant time is entitled to request her employer that she be permitted to postpone her adoptive or additional leave or the remaining part thereof, whichever is appropriate.[104] Where the employer agrees to this proposal,[105] then the employee shall continue to work or, as the case may be, shall return to work on a date agreed by the employee and employer (albeit a date not later than that notified to the employer as the date on which the employee would otherwise have returned to work from adoptive or additional adoptive leave[106]) and the adoptive or additional adoptive leave shall be deemed to be postponed from that date. In such circumstances the employee is entitled for the leave not taken to be postponed and taken as a continuous period beginning not later than seven days after the child is discharged from hospital or such other date as may be agreed between the employer and the employee.[107]

---

99. s.11A(3)(c) *ibid.*

100. s.11B(1) *ibid.* The decision whether or not to accede to this request is a matter for the discretion of the employer.

101. s.11B(4)(a) *ibid.*

102. s.11B(2) *ibid.*

103. s.11B(4)(b) *ibid.*

104. s.11C(1) *ibid.*

105. An employer is entitled to require the employee to supply evidence of the child's hospitalisation and discharge from hospital.

106. The application to postpone adoptive or additional adoptive leave can be made even though the employee has not notified his or her employee of his or her intention to take adoptive leave or additional adoptive leave in the first instance: s.11(C)(5) Adoptive Leave Acts 1995 and 2005.

107. s.11C(2) *ibid.* The entitlement to take postponed leave is conditional on the employee notifying the employer (who may, however, waive his or her right to be so notified s.11(C)(5) *ibid.*) as soon as practicable after the employee becomes aware of the date of the child's discharge from hospital of his or her intention to take the postponed leave (s.11C(4) *ibid.*). Notification of this kind may be revoked by a subsequent notification (s.11C(4)(c) *ibid.*).

[13–23] Finally, where the employee who has applied for and been granted a postponement of her leave by reason of the hospitalisation of her adoptive child, has returned to work and then takes leave owing to sickness, this period of absence from work will be deemed to be the recommencement of her postponed leave unless she informs her employer to the contrary,[108] in which case it is regarded in the same way as any other period of sick leave and the employee shall cease to be entitled to the postponed leave.[109]

2.4. Termination of the Placement of a Child while Adoptive Leave is Ongoing

[13–24] Where the placement of a child with an adopting parent terminates before the expiration of the period of that parent's adoptive or additional adoptive leave (other than in circumstances where the child dies), the adopting parent is required to cause the employer to be notified in writing of the date of termination as soon as reasonably practicable but not later than seven days after that date.[110] In such circumstances, the employee is required to return to work on such date as is convenient to the employer[111] but not later than the date on which his or her adoptive or additional adoptive leave would otherwise have expired.[112] In the case of a proposed foreign adoption, where the adopting parent has taken additional adoptive leave *before* the date of placement and, in the event, no placement takes place, she must return to work no later than the date on which the notified period of leave expires, and must cause her employer to be notified of the intended date of her return as soon as is reasonably practicable.[113]

2.5. Protection of Employees while on Leave and Enforcement Procedures

[13–25] Finally, one of the key aspects of Irish adoptive leave legislation is that employees are protected from any unfavourable treatment (up to and including dismissal) by employers as a result of availing of leave entitlements. Most importantly, employees

---

108. s.11D(1) *ibid.*

109. s.11D(2) *ibid.* It will be remembered that, in the context of maternity leave, it was suggested that perhaps the fairest interpretation of this term is that the employee is not entitled to the resumed leave *at that time.*

110. s.12(1) *ibid.* Where, in the opinion of a Rights Commissioner or the Tribunal there are reasonable grounds for the failure of the employee to give the appropriate notice to his or her employer, or to give it within the designated time period, the Rights Commissioner or the Tribunal may extend the time for service of such notice (s.12(5) *ibid.*). Where there are not deemed to be such reasonable grounds, then the failure to give the appropriate notice or to give it within the prescribed period may be taken into account by the Rights Commissioner, the Tribunal or the Circuit Court in determining the entitlements of the employee under the Adoptive Leave Act, the Unfair Dismissals Acts or any other relevant enactment so far as the remedies of re-instatement, re-engagement or compensation are concerned (s.12(6) *ibid.*).

111. In such circumstances, the employer is required to give the employee one week's notice of the date on which she is expected to return to work.

112. s.12(2) Adoptive Leave Acts 1995 and 2005.

113. s.12(5) *ibid.*

have a right to return to work at the end of their leave periods, either in the same job or in some suitable alternative employment. As mentioned at the beginning of this chapter, however, this is an entitlement provided for in very similar ways in all the pieces of legislation considered in this chapter, and accordingly we deal with it (and with the question of how the legislation is enforced) later in this chapter.

3. Parental Leave

The entitlement to Parental Leave and to what is termed *force majeure* leave is   [13–26]
provided for under the Parental Leave Acts 1998 and 2006.[114] Apart from introducing the concept of emergency or *force majeure* leave (discussed below), these Acts
provide for the possibility of parents (and, significantly, not just mothers) taking a
certain period of unpaid leave in order to be with and take care of their young children.[115] The point has, however, been made that by reason of the fact that this kind
of leave *is* unpaid, it will inevitably be something that is only likely to be of significance to people from affluent or relatively affluent socio-economic backgrounds.

Furthermore, it is clear that parental leave is not to be regarded as a form of holiday   [13–27]
for employees, but exists on the condition that an employee is using it to take care of
the child concerned.[116] Thus, where an employee is on parental leave and his or her
employer has reasonable grounds for believing that [s]he is not using the leave to take
care of the child (that is, that [s]he is abusing the leave), then that employer may give
a written notice to the employee terminating the parental leave and summarising the
reasons for such termination,[117] in which case the employee is required to return to
work on the date specified in that notice and any absences from work after that date
shall be deemed not to be parental leave.[118] Furthermore, where an employee gives
an employer notice of his or her intention to take parental leave, and the employer
believes that [s]he is not entitled to such leave, then that employer may, by notice
to the employee summarising the reasons for the decision, refuse to grant the leave

---

114. This legislation is aimed at transposing into Irish law the terms of EC Council Directive on
the Framework Agreement on Parental Leave (Directive 96/34/EC). For analysis, see Kerr,
Irish Employment Legislation (Round Hall Sweet and Maxwell, 2000), at p.E-52. The 2006
Amendment Act was based on concerns raised in the Report of the Working Group on
the review of the Parental Leave Act 1998 (PN 11344, April 2002) and available at http://
www.justice.ie/en/JELR/reviewparentalleave.pdf/Files/reviewparentalleave.pdf. Moreover it
was the product of s.28 of the 1998 Act that required the Minister to consult with relevant
bodies and prepare a report on the Act starting at a point between two and three years after
commencement of the Act.
115. For consideration of how the equivalent English law has been interpreted, see *Forster v Cart-
wright Black* [2004] ICR 1728, [2004] IRLR 781; *Qua v John Ford Morrison Solicitors* [2003] ICR
482, [2003] IRLR 184; *South Central Trains v Rodway* [2005] ICR 75, [2004] IRLR 777.
116. s.12(1) Parental Leave Acts 1998 and 2006.
117. s.12(2) *ibid.*
118. s.12(3) *ibid.* The date for return to work cannot be later than the date on which the proposed
period of parental leave would otherwise have expired.

sought.[119] The superficial harshness of this provision is softened, however, by the fact that, before giving an employee either of these two kinds of notice, an employer is obliged to give him or her a proposal of such notice, stating in summary form the grounds for terminating or refusing the leave, and informing the employee that [s]he may make representations (which must be considered by the employer) to the employer within seven days of receiving such notice.[120]

3.1. The Entitlement to Parental Leave

[13–28] The basic entitlement to parental leave is contained in s.6 of the 1998 Act.[121] Under this section, a relevant parent[122] of a child[123] is entitled to 14 working weeks of parental leave from his or her employment,[124] to enable him or her to take care of the child. Such parental leave can be taken up until the date on which the child concerned attains the age of 8 years.[125] Alternatively, in the case of a child who is the subject of an adoption order, and who at the date of the making of that order had attained the age of six but not eight years, leave can be taken for up to two years from the date of the making of the order.[126] Moreover, in the case of a child who has a disability,[127] the period of parental leave can be taken up until the child attains the age of 16 years, or ceases to have that disability or any other disability, whichever first occurs.

---

119. s.12(4) *ibid.*

120. s.12(6) *ibid.* In the case of all notices under this section the employer and employee are required to retain notices given or sent by them.

121. As substituted by the terms of s.3 of the 2006 Act.

122. Under s.6(5), s.6(6) and s.6(9) of the Parental Leave Acts 1998 and 2006 a relevant parent in relation to a child means a person who is the natural parent, adopting parent, adoptive parent (that is, someone in whose favour an adoption order in respect of the child has been made and is in force), or someone acting in loco parentis to a child.

123. An employee is entitled to parental leave in respect of each child of which [s]he is a relevant parent (s.6(4) *ibid.*), but where an employee is a relevant parent in more than one capacity in respect of a child, [s]he is still only entitled to one period of parental leave in respect of that child: s.6(5) *ibid.*

124. The entitlement to the full statutory period of parental leave only accrues when the employee has completed one year's continuous employment with the employer from whose employment the leave is taken (s.6(3) ibid.). On the other hand, where an employee who has not completed one year's service has completed at least three months of such employment on the latest day for commencing a period of parental leave, then [s]he is entitled to one week's parental leave for each month of continuous employment that [s]he has completed with his or her employer at the time of commencement of that leave: s.6(8) ibid.

125. s.6(2)(a) *ibid.*

126. s.6(2)(b) *ibid.*

127. Under s.6(9) ibid. it is provided that a disability in relation to a child means an enduring physical, sensory, mental health or intellectual impairment of the child, such that the level of care required for him or her is substantially more than the level of care generally required for children of the same age who do not have any such impairment.

Prior to its amendment by the 2006 Act, s.6 of the 1998 Act had provided for a   **[13–29]**
14-week period of parental leave, which could be taken until the child in respect
of whom the leave was taken reached the age of five years (or, if the child was
adopted, and was older than three but younger than eight when the adoption
order was made, for two years from the date of the adoption order). Under s.6(8)
as amended, where a parent has taken 14 weeks' parental leave in respect of a
child before the date on which the 2006 Act came into force (18 May 2006), then
nothing in the new Act entitles him or her to any further leave.[128] On the other
hand, where the parent in question has *not* taken 14 weeks' parental leave, then the
provisions of the 1998 Act as amended by the 2006 Act will apply to so much of
the 14 weeks of parental leave as has not been taken before the date on which the
Act came into force.[129] This provision is of significance (albeit diminishing significance) in light of the new time frame in which leave can be taken since 2006.[130]

Where an employee is entitled to parental leave in respect of more than one child   **[13–30]**
(not being children of a multiple birth) then [s]he is still only entitled to 14 weeks
of parental leave within a 12-month period unless the employer consents to a
greater period of leave.[131] An exception to this rule is a situation where leave is
proposed to be taken in respect of a child who has either attained the age of seven
years before or on the date of commencement of the 2006 Act and before the first
anniversary of that date, or in respect of a child (presumably with a disability) who
has attained the age of 15 years before or on the date of commencement of the Act
and before the first anniversary of that date if, in either case, the new age limitation periods under the 2006 Act would have the effect of preventing the employee
from taking all or any part of parental leave to which [s]he was entitled.[132]

If any public holiday falls during the period when the employee is on parental leave,   **[13–31]**
a day must be added to the period of parental leave that the employee is entitled to
take.[133] In addition, if any *other* form of holiday to which an employee is entitled
falls during the period when [s]he is on parental leave and on a day where, but for
the leave and the holiday [s]he would have been working in the relevant employment, then [s]he is entitled to take the holiday in accordance with the terms of s.20
of the Organisation of Working Time Act 1997, which as we note in Chapter 11
essentially allows the employer to determine when such holidays may be taken.[134]

---

128. ss.6(8)(a) and (c) *ibid.*
129. ss.6(8)(b) and (d) *ibid.*
130. The weakening significance of this (in part) is that under the old rules such leave could only
    be taken up until the point when the child reached 5 years of age. Hence if a parent only
    managed to take (for example) 10 weeks of parental leave before his or her child turned 5, and
    if the child was under 8 on 18 May 2006, then the parents in question would have a further
    three weeks of leave available to them. Moreover, under the old legislation there was no exten-
    sion of the period in which leave could be taken where the child had a disability.
131. s.7(3) Parental Leave Acts 1998 and 2006.
132. s.7(3A) *ibid.*
133. s.7(4)(b) *ibid.*
134. s.7(4)(b) *ibid.*

3.1.1. Transfer of Leave Entitlements from One Parent to Another

[13–32] One of the most curious and confusing aspects of the legislation concerns the question of whether, in the event that both parents of a child are entitled to parental leave, it is possible for the leave entitlements of one to transfer to the other (thereby meaning that that parent was entitled to up to 28 weeks' parental leave). Under s.6(7) of the 1998 Act (prior to its amendment) the position had been that neither of the parents was entitled to the parental leave of the other. Under s.2 of the 2006 Act (substituting a new s.6 for that which had previously been in force) it was provided (s. 6(6)) that none of the relevant parents could transfer any part of their parental leave to another, or use the parental leave of another. In other words, the position appeared clear – namely that parental leave did not transfer from one parent to another. Remarkably, however, under s.3 of the 2006 Act an amendment was made to s.6(7) of the 1998 Act, essentially providing that where both parents were employed by the same employer, then '*either parent*' (as distinct from 'neither parent') could transfer their entitlements – in other words, a position diametrically opposed to what had gone before. Accordingly, it would seem that whereas the legislative intention may have been not to make such entitlements transferable, this has been thrown into confusion by a rather bizarre drafting error.[135]

3.1.2. The Manner in which Parental Leave can be Taken

[13–33] The manner in which such leave may be taken is provided for in s.7 of the Parental Leave Acts 1998 and 2006. An employee may take the leave either as a 14-week continuous period,[136] in two separate periods[137] each consisting of not less than six weeks and not exceeding 14 weeks in total,[138] or on the basis of an agreement[139] between the employer or representatives of the employer and other employers on the one hand and the employee or representatives of the employee and other employees on the other hand, the employee can take his or her parental leave in a number of periods being days or even hours [s]he would otherwise be working.[140]

---

135. For analysis, see Kerr, 'Legislative Developments' 3(2) *IELJ* (2006), 60; and Eardley & Cox *2006 Annual Review of Employment Law* (Firstlaw, 2007), at pp.111 and 112.

136. s.7(1)(a) Parental Leave Acts 1998 and 2006.

137. Unless (s.7(1B) *ibid.*) it is otherwise agreed between the parties, then where parental leave is taken in two periods, they must be not less than 10 weeks apart: s.7(1A) *ibid.*

138. s.7(1)(aa) *ibid.*

139. In the absence of such agreement, the employee will need to take parental leave in the form provided either in s.7(1)(a) or s.7(1)(aa) *ibid.* Generally, see *O'Neill v Dunnes Stores* [2000] ELR 306.

140. s.7(1)(b) *ibid.* Where this happens, the leave taken by the employee shall be such that the number of hours during which, but for the leave, the employee would be working equals the number of hours that [s]he would work in such continuous period of 14 weeks *before* the taking of the leave as shall be agreed between the employer and employee, or, where no such agreement is possible, the hours shall be equal to 14 times the average number of hours per week during which the employee worked in each of the periods of 14 weeks ending immediately before the commencement of each week in which [s]he takes any leave.

3.1.3. Notification Requirements

As with the other forms of leave considered in this chapter, an employee must give [13–34] his or her employer notice of his or her proposal to take such leave[141] as soon as is reasonably practicable but not later than six weeks before the commencement of the leave.[142] Where the employee proposes to take leave under s.7(1)(aa) (that is, in two periods of not less than six weeks) then [s]he will fulfil his or her notice obligations by providing either one notice specifying the two periods of parental leave that [s]he proposes to take, or two notices each specifying one of the periods of parental leave that [s]he proposes to take.[143] In either case, where the relevant notice requirements have been complied with, the employer is required not less than four weeks before the commencement of the leave, to prepare and sign (and, like the employee, to retain[144]) a confirmation document specifying the date of commencement of the leave, its duration and the manner in which it is to be taken.[145] Where a confirmation document has been prepared and signed, the employee is not entitled to work in the place of employment during the period of parental leave.[146]

3.1.4. Postponing, Suspending or Curtailing Parental Leave

Again, in common with the other forms of leave considered in this chapter, it is [13–35] possible for the parental leave to be curtailed or postponed or for the form in which it is taken to be varied. In the first instance, this may arise where the employer or his or her successor in title and the employee agree to this, in which case the leave is postponed, curtailed or varied to such extent as may be agreed.[147]

Alternatively, however, where the employee becomes sick and is consequently unable [13–36] to care for the child who is the subject of the parental leave, then the employee may by notice[148] (accompanied either by a medical certificate stating that the employee

---

141. Having said that, where the employee who is entitled to take parental leave purports to do so *without* having given the appropriate notice then the employer may, at his or her discretion, treat the leave as being parental leave, in which case the Act shall apply as normal: s.8(4) *ibid.*
142. s.8(1) *ibid.* The notice in question (which must be retained by the employee, s.8(5) *ibid.*) has to specify the date of commencement of the relevant leave, its duration and the manner in which it is proposed to be taken, must be signed by the employee (s.8(2) *ibid.*), and may subsequently be revoked by the employee (s.8(3) *ibid.*). Furthermore, where this is requested by the employer, the employee must give evidence reasonably required as to the date of birth of the relevant child, his or her status as a relevant parent of that child and, where appropriate, the disability of that child: s.8(6) *ibid.*
143. s.8(7) *ibid.*
144. s.9(3) *ibid.*
145. s.9(1) *ibid.* Where an employee has purported to take parental leave without giving the relevant notice, and where the employer has accepted this under s.8(4), the confirmation document must be prepared as soon as is practicable thereafter: s.9(2) *ibid.*
146. s.10(1) *ibid.*
147. s.10(2)(a) *ibid.* In such circumstances, the confirmation document is amended accordingly. Any parental leave not taken in this context may be taken at a later time agreed between the employer and employee.
148. Such notice must be given as soon as is reasonably practicable after the employee becomes sick.

is not capable of caring for the child[149] or by such other evidence as the employer may reasonably require[150]) either postpone the period of parental leave, if it has not commenced, or suspend the balance of the leave if it has.[151] Moreover, it is notable that the consent of the employer is not required in such circumstances.

[13–37] It is also possible for the employer (following consultation with an employee[152]) to give notice to an employee who intends to take parental leave (not later than four weeks before the proposed starting date) postponing that leave[153] to a period not later than six months after the date specified in the employee's original notice of parental leave.[154] This can only be done, however, where there are reasons justifying such postponement, and specifically where the employer is satisfied that the taking by that employee of parental leave at that time would have a substantial adverse effect on the operation of his or her business, profession or operation as a result of:

- seasonal factors;
- the unavailability of someone to do the duties of the employee;
- the nature of those duties;
- the number of employees in the employment or the number of employees whose periods of parental leave are due to fall within the period specified in that employee's notice; or
- any other relevant matters.[155]

---

149. s.10(5)(a) Parental Leave Acts 1998 and 2006. This medical certificate must be signed by a registered medical practitioner.
150. s.10(5)(b) *ibid.*
151. s.10(2)(b) *ibid.* Again, in such a situation, the confirmation document is amended accordingly. Moreover, if because of the postponement or suspension of leave, or the taking of the balance of parental leave, the statutory period in which such leave can be taken pursuant to s.6(2) expires, then the event that causes the period so to end (typically the child's eighth birthday) will be deemed to have occurred after the end of that period (s.10(4) *ibid.*). In other words, a parent will not be prevented from taking the statutory period of leave where such leave has been suspended or postponed, because of the normal operation of time limits.
152. s.11(2) *ibid.*
153. Where an employee has given notice under s.8(7)(a) *ibid.* – that is, one statement of notice in respect of both of two periods of parental leave that are to be taken pursuant to s.7(1)(aa) *ibid.* – then a notice from an employer postponing the leave must apply to both periods of parental leave that are the subject of the employee's notice, subject to any agreement between employer and employee.
154. s.11(1) *ibid.* Again, it is provided in s.11(6) that where such postponement of leave means that the statutory period in which such leave may be taken would in the normal course of events have expired (because, for example a child reached his or her eighth birthday), the employee will still be entitled to take such leave.
155. A notice given to an employee and postponing the leave must give a summary of the grounds for the postponement of the leave: s.11(3) *ibid.*

3.2. *Force Majeure* Leave

The concept of *force majeure* leave was introduced by s.13 of the Parental Leave [13–38]
Act of 1998 and the rules in respect of such leave were significantly amended by
the Parental Leave (Amendment) Act 2006.[156] The essence of the section is that
in certain tightly defined circumstances, it is possible for an employee to take a
brief and limited period of *paid* leave in order to deal with an emergency situation at home, which is sufficiently pressing that his or her immediate presence is
indispensable.

Thus, under s.13 of the Act, such paid *force majeure* leave is available to an employee
where:

> for urgent family reasons owing to an injury to or the illness of someone [coming within
> a defined category of persons]…the immediate presence of the employee at the place
> where the person is, whether at his or her home or elsewhere is indispensable

Section 13(2) as amended sets out the list of persons whose illness or injury may [13–39]
warrant the employee taking *force majeure* leave, namely:

* a child of the employee including an adoptive child;
* the spouse of the employee or a person with whom the employee is living
  as husband or wife;
* a person to whom the employee acts *in loco parentis*;
* a parent or grandparent of the employee;
* a brother or sister of the employee; or
* a person other than one specified in any of the preceding categories who
  resides with the employee in a relationship of domestic dependency.

In this respect, a person who resides with an employee is taken to be in a relationship [13–40]
of domestic dependency with the employee if, in the event of injury or illness, [s]he
reasonably relies on that employee to make arrangements for the provision of care
to him or her.[157] Moreover, it would seem possible that an employee's presence may
be indispensable owing to the illness of a dependent, but not because it is necessary
for him or her to take care of that dependent – most obviously where one parent
becomes sick and is consequently unable to take care of his or her child, such that it
is necessary for the other parent (the employee) to stay at home for that purpose.

This was the scenario at issue in *McGaley v Liebherr Container Cranes Ltd.*[158] In [13–41]
that case the EAT found that the employee's presence at home was not indispensable (on the facts); nonetheless there is nothing in either the EAT decision, the

---

156. The concept was introduced into Irish law pursuant to Council Directive 96/34/EC. See
   Barnard, *EC Employment Law* (3rd ed., Oxford University Press, 2006), at pp.464 *et seq.*
157. It is specifically provided that the sexual orientation of the persons concerned is immaterial
   (s.8(2A)(b) Parental Leave (Amendment) Act 2006).
158. *McGaley v Liebherr Container Cranes Ltd.* [2001] ELR 350.

High Court appeal in the case or, indeed, the terms of the statute that would rule out this possibility. If this *is* the case (namely that one can take *force majeure* leave where a family member's illness does not render him or her dependent on the employee but instead renders him or her unable to look after a dependent third party, for whom the employee is thus needed to care), then it is arguable that the decision of the High Court in this case is open to criticism. After all McCracken J appeared to attach some relevance (in assessing whether the appellant's immediate presence at home was indispensable) to the fact that the illness suffered by his wife was recognised by the parties at the time not to be a serious one. This conclusion would only have been relevant, however, if the employee had stayed at home to look after his wife, but was not relevant to the question of whether his wife's illness necessitated his presence to look after their child (who was under twelve months old and who was on a special diet). Of more relevance to this question in fact was surely the extent to which the wife's illness was debilitating (and McCracken J concluded that it was 'probably debilitating') in the sense of preventing her from being able to look after her infant child adequately.

[13–42] Where these criteria are established, an employee is entitled to one or more days of *force majeure* leave, but the leave taken cannot exceed three days in any consecutive 12-month period, nor can it exceed five days in any consecutive 36-month period.[159] Having taken the leave in question, the employee is required (as soon as possible thereafter) to notify his or her employer (in the form contained in the Schedule to the Parental Leave (Notice of *Force Majeure* Leave) Regulations[160] of the fact that leave was taken, of the name and address of the injured or ill person for whom *force majeure* leave was taken, of the relationship of that person to the employee, and of the dates of the leave, and should contain a statement of the facts entitling the employee to *force majeure* leave.[161]

[13–43] Naturally, because the entitlement to *force majeure* leave is couched in very strict terms, difficult factual questions can arise in individual cases as to whether the reason why *force majeure* leave was taken did genuinely constitute 'urgent family

---

159. s.13(4) Parental Leave Acts 1998 and 2006. In this respect where an employee is absent for *force majeure* reasons for part only of a working day, this is still deemed to be a day's *force majeure* leave. In *Murphy v Celtic Linen Ltd.*, PL1/2003, there is a suggestion that the Tribunal was prepared to allow the employee to exceed three days of *force majeure* leave in a 12-month period on the basis that she had not exceed the five-day limit in the 36-month period. It would seem, however, that the better construction of the statute is that an employee is not permitted to exceed either of the express maximum numbers of days (that is, [s]he cannot take more than three days in any 12-month period, nor can [s]he take more than five days in any 36-month period).

160. SI no. 454 of 1998. It is worth noting that there is no requirement in the regulations that the employee furnish the employer with relevant medical certification for the person whose illness has necessitated him or her in taking *force majeure* leave. See *Carey v Penn Racquet Sports Ltd.* [2001] IEHC 8, [2001] 3 IR 32, [2001] ELR 27.

161. s.13(3) Parental Leave Acts 1998 and 2006.

reasons' and whether the employee's *immediate* presence was genuinely 'indispensable'. This question can be of huge importance, both because it will determine whether or not an employee will receive remuneration for the time taken off work and, probably more importantly, because it is possible in a given case that if the employee takes a day or days off work and it is found that [s]he was *not* entitled to *force majeure* leave in the circumstances then [s]he will be subject to disciplinary measures for taking a day's unauthorised leave.

The question of whether the employee's immediate presence was indispensable as a   [13–44] result of urgent family reasons is a subjective question to be decided (presumably, having regard to the totality of the relevant circumstances) by the Rights Commissioner and, on appeal, by the Employment Appeals Tribunal – and it should be noted that the High Court, which can hear appeals on questions of law from the EAT, will not overturn decisions on questions of fact made by the EAT.[162] Despite the subjective nature of such evaluations, the following broad guiding principles may be seen to emerge from the decisions in this area:

3.2.1. *Matters are to be Assessed from the Standpoint of the Employee at the Relevant Time*

Where a dependent of an employee shows symptoms of serious illness and the   [13–45] employee in consequence takes *force majeure* leave, then it is irrelevant that the matter turns out, eventually, not to be as serious as was originally thought. Rather it is necessary that the Tribunal of fact evaluates the position from the standpoint of the employee at the time at which [s]he made the decision not to come into work.[163] Thus in *Carey v Penn Racquet Sports Ltd.*[164] a single mother was deemed to be entitled to two days' *force majeure* leave where her eight-year-old child, having been sick, developed a rash on her legs, despite the fact that, in hindsight, it was clear that the child was not seriously ill. Moreover, it must be accepted that in the vast majority of cases an employee will not have sufficient medical knowledge to make a judgment on how serious the symptoms displayed by the dependent person actually are.[165]

---

162. *McGaley v Liebherr Container Cranes Ltd.* [2001] ELR 350. An exception is where the factual conclusion reached by the EAT is deemed to be one which a reasonable Tribunal could have made on the facts.

163. *Carey v Penn Racquet Sports Ltd.* [2001] IEHC 8, [2001] 3 IR 32, [2000] ELR 27; *McGaley v Liebherr Container Cranes Ltd.* [2001] ELR 350. As far as this level of subjective analysis is concerned, it is not clear, for example, whether the fact that an employee is a naturally anxious or alarmist person (and hence more disposed to the view that his or her presence is indispensable in a given context) will be relevant. So, for example, if an employee had previously lost a child to meningitis it is strongly arguable that [s]he would be justified in regarding her presence with his or her other child as indispensable should that child start to display any symptoms, however remote, which might be connected with that illness.

164. [2001] ELR 27.

165. *Carey v Penn Racquet Sports Ltd.* [2001] IEHC 8, [2001] 3 IR 32, (2001) ELR 27.

[13–46] It might also be suggested that it would be appropriate to afford the employee some leeway on the question of whether his or her immediate presence was indispensable. Thus for example, a parent who fears in a moment of panic that his or her child has a life-threatening disease should arguably not have his or her entitlement to *force majeure* leave denied on the basis that, in the cold light of day, a reasonable person would not have made that evaluation of the situation.[166] At the other extreme, in *Murphy v Celtic Linen Ltd.*[167] the EAT somewhat remarkably held, 'In the final analysis we think it is for the parent to decide whether his/her immediate presence…at his/her home or elsewhere is indispensable'. It is submitted, however, that this cannot be the correct statement of the law in that it would permit employees to take their statutorily allotted maximum number of *force majeure* leave days essentially as and when they chose to do so. Perhaps the best interpretation of this phrase is simply that the perceptions of the employee as to whether or not his or her presence was indispensable is a factor to which the Tribunal should attach significant weight.

3.2.2. Could Anyone Else Have Taken Care of the Dependent Party?

[13–47] Of paramount importance in assessing whether the presence of the employee was indispensable will be the question of whether there was anyone else available to take care of the dependent person. So for example, it will obviously be more likely that the presence of a single mother with her sick child will be deemed to be indispensable than will be the case where the assistance of the other parent of the child could reasonably be relied upon. Similarly, where the employee is able to call on other persons for assistance with the dependent (or, it may be suggested, where [s]he calls on other persons as a matter of course), then it will be difficult to conclude that his or her presence was indispensable.

3.2.3. Was There Any Notice of the Emergency Situation?

[13–48] For this reason, it seems clear that *force majeure* leave will be far less likely to be deemed appropriate where the employee had notice that the situation of urgency was going to arise, both because [s]he would have more time to arrange alternative assistance with the dependent and also because [s]he could have informed his or her employer in advance and sought time off out of his or her annual leave allowance.

3.2.4. Force Majeure *Leave as Emergency Leave*

[13–49] *Force majeure* leave should always be regarded as emergency leave. In other words, it is not a form of compassionate leave for employees who would like to be with dependents who are sick (and whose presence is desired by those dependents).

---

166. A concession of this kind was made by the High Court to the appellant employee in *Carey v Penn Racquet Sports Ltd.* [2001] ELR 27, at p.28, where the court held that 'The matter should have been looked at from the Plaintiff's point of view at the time the decision was made not to go to work'.

167. PL1/2003.

Nor is it available simply because the presence of the employee would be of assistance at home.[168] Rather it is only available where the presence of the employee is genuinely indispensable – that is, where there is no other realistic option available for the dependent person.

3.2.5. *The Age of the Dependent may be Relevant*

It would appear that the age of the relevant dependent is a relevant factor in [13–50] assessing whether an employee's immediate presence is indispensable. The logic would appear to be that the presence of a parent will be more likely to be deemed to be indispensable where the child is a very young one than will be the case where the child is older.[169] In addition, as has been mentioned, if the employee is the sole person with responsibility for caring for the dependent (for example if [s]he is a single parent), then this will also be relevant.[170]

3.3. Codes of Practice

The Parental Leave Acts 1998 and 2006 make provisions for the Equality Authority [13–51] (either on its own behalf or if requested to do so by the Minister) to prepare for submission to the Minister a draft Code of Practice,[171] for providing practical guidance as to the steps that may be taken for complying with the Act.[172] The Minister may then declare that the draft (or possibly an amended version thereof) is a Code of Practice for the purposes of the Act, in which case it becomes admissible as evidence before a court, the Tribunal or a Rights Commissioner, and must be taken into account in determining any question to which a provision of the code appears to be relevant.[173]

3.4. Maintaining Records under the Parental Leave Acts

An employer is required to make a record of the parental leave and *force majeure* [13–52] leave taken by his or her employees during their period of employment, and the date and times on which each employee took such leave,[174] and to retain such records for eight years in a form specified by the Minister (where appropriate).[175] Moreover, an inspector, within the meaning of the Organisation of Working Time Act 1997 may exercise any of his or her functions under that Act for the

---

168. *McGaley v Liebherr Container Cranes Ltd.* [2001] ELR 350.

169. *Murphy v Celtic Linen Ltd.*, PL1/2003, 18 September 2003.

170. *Carey v Penn Racquet Sports Ltd.* (2000) ELR 27; *Murphy v Celtic Linen Ltd.*, PL1/2003.

171. Before submitting a draft Code of Practice, the Equality Authority must consult such other Minister of the government, or other person or persons as the Equality Authority considers appropriate or as the Minister may direct.

172. s.22A(1) Parental Leave Acts 1998 and 2006.

173. s.22A(4) *ibid.*

174. s.27(1) *ibid.* Failure to keep a record for the appropriate length of time is an offence that may be prosecuted by the Minister: s.27(6) *ibid.*

175. s.27(2) *ibid.* In addition, where the Act provides that a person retain a notice or copy of a notice under this Act, it should be retained for one year.

purposes of assessing whether such records or notices are being made and retained as required.[176]

3.5. Protection of Employees while on Leave and Enforcement Procedures

[13–53] One of the key aspects of Irish parental leave legislation is that employees are protected from any unfavourable treatment (up to and including dismissal) by employers as a result of availing of leave entitlements. Most importantly, employees have a right to return to work at the end of their leave periods, either in the same job or in some suitable alternative employment. As mentioned at the beginning of this chapter, however, this is an entitlement provided for in very similar ways in all the pieces of legislation considered in this chapter, and accordingly we deal with it (and with the question of how the legislation is enforced) later in this chapter.

4. Carer's Leave

[13–54] The concept of carer's leave – that is to say a period of temporary leave an employee can take in order to provide full-time care and attention to a person in need of the same – was introduced under the terms of the Carer's Leave Act of 2001.[177] It is a distinct form of leave that may not be treated as part of any other form of leave from the employment, including sick leave, annual leave, maternity leave, parental leave and *force majeure* leave to which the employee is entitled.[178]

4.1. Conditions for Taking Carer's Leave

[13–55] Under the terms of s.6 of the Act, an employee who has been employed for a continuous period of 12 months by the employer from whom [s]he proposes to take the carer's leave is entitled to take up to 65 weeks' carer's leave for the purpose of providing full-time care and attention to a relevant person.[179] The concept of a 'relevant person' is given definition (pursuant to s.2 of the 2001 Act) in the terms of s.99 of the Social Welfare (Consolidation) Act of 2005 and means a person who has such a disability that he or she requires full-time care and attention.

---

176. s.27(5) *ibid.* Generally see Chapter 1 for an analysis of the powers of such inspectors.
177. For analysis of the background to the legislation, see Kerr, *Irish Employment Legislation* (Round Hall Sweet and Maxwell, 2000), at p.D-30.
178. s.13(4) Carer's Leave Act 2001.
179. Under s.6(1) *ibid.* an employee is entitled to 65 weeks' leave 'for each relevant person', and therefore [s]he can take more than one 65-week period of carer's leave from his or her employer in order to care for more than one relevant person. An employer is required to make and retain records (for eight years) in respect of the carer's leave taken by all employees, and failure to do so is an offence. An employer or employee who is required under the Act to retain notices or copies of notices must retain such for three years: s.31 *ibid.*

In addition, it is necessary for the person seeking leave to provide 'full time care [13–56] and attention' to the relevant person[180] and in this respect the concept of full-time care and attention is construed in accordance with s.99(2) of the Social Welfare (Consolidation) Act 2005, whereby a relevant person is regarded as requiring full-time care and attention if and when [s]he requires from another person

(a) continual supervision and frequent assistance throughout the day in connection with normal bodily functions, or
(b) continual supervision in order to avoid danger to himself or herself,

and where the nature and extent of his or her disability has been certified in the prescribed manner by a medical practitioner.

It is specifically provided in the 2001 Act that the entitlement to take carer's leave [13–57] is conditional on the employee in question not engaging in employment or self-employment during the period of carer's leave.[181]

Under s.6(5) of the Act, in order to obtain carer's leave[182] the employee must apply [13–58] to the Minister for Social and Family Affairs for a decision by a Deciding Officer under s.300 of the Social Welfare (Consolidation) Act 2005[183] that the person in respect of whom the employee proposes to take carer's leave is actually a 'relevant person'.[184] The employee must then furnish his or her employer with a copy of this decision as soon as [s]he receives it. Unless and until the employee does so, [s]he will not be entitled to take carer's leave.

4.2. Notification Requirements

Where an employee intends or wishes to take carer's leave [s]he is required as [13–59] a preliminary step to provide his or her employer with notice in writing not later than six weeks before the proposed starting date of the leave[185] of his or her proposal to take carer's leave,[186] informing that employer that [s]he has applied

---

180. s.6(1)(c) *ibid.*
181. The exception is employment or self-employment prescribed under s.100(3) of the Social Welfare (Consolidation) Act of 2005.
182. s.6(1)(b) Carer's Leave Act 2001.
183. Originally the 2001 Act referred to the Social Welfare (Consolidation) Act of 1993 for its definitions, but this Act was repealed and replaced by the Social Welfare (Consolidation) Act of 2005.
184. The decision of the Deciding Officer may be appealed under s.311 of the 2005 Act.
185. Where exceptional or emergency circumstances mean that it is not reasonably practicable to comply with the normal six-week rule, the employee is simply required to give notice 'as soon as is reasonably practicable': s.9(2) Carer's Leave Act 2001.
186. s.9(1)(a) *ibid.* This notice may be revoked by an employee at a later stage by notice in writing, in which case [s]he is not entitled to take carer's leave at the date originally specified in the notice.

to the Minister for Social and Family Affairs for a decision under s.6(5) or has appealed the decision of the Deciding Officer under s.6(6),[187] and stating the proposed starting date of the carer's leave and the form in which it is intended to be taken.[188] Where these formalities have not been complied with, and where an employee nonetheless purports to take carer's leave, then his or her employer has discretion either to ignore the procedural failures and to treat the leave in question as being carer's leave[189] or, on reasonable grounds, to refuse to treat the leave as carer's leave. Where this latter option is taken an employer is required to specify in writing the grounds for such refusal.[190]

[13–60] On the other hand, where these formalities have been complied with (or where the employer exercises his or her discretion to overlook such procedural failings on the part of the employee), the employer and employee must, not less than two weeks before the proposed commencement of the carer's leave, prepare and sign a 'confirmation document' specifying the date of the commencement of the carer's leave, its duration and its form.[191] Following the date of the confirmation document (whether or not the agreed period of carer's leave has commenced), the leave may be postponed to a time agreed between the parties,[192] curtailed to an extent agreed between the parties,[193] or varied in a manner agreed between the parties,[194] and this fact should be recorded in an amended confirmation document. Moreover, more generally, an employee is required, as soon as practicable, to notify his or her employer of any change in circumstances that affect his or her entitlement to carer's leave.[195]

4.3. Extent of Carer's Leave
[13–61] Where an employee *is* entitled to carer's leave, then this cannot exceed 65 weeks for each relevant person, which may be taken either as one continuous period of 65 weeks[196] or in a number of periods, the aggregate duration of which does not exceed 65 weeks,[197] although in this latter context, an employer may refuse on

---

187. s.9(1)(b) *ibid.*
188. s.9(1)(c) *ibid.* An employer is required to retain all the documents given to him or her in accordance with s.9(1). Failure to do so is an offence under s.32 of the 2001 Act.
189. s.9(4) *ibid.*
190. s.9(8) *ibid.*
191. s.10(1) *ibid.* The employer is required to retain a confirmation document signed by him or her and to give a copy to the employee, who is also required to retain it: s.10(3) *ibid.*
192. s.12(1)(a) *ibid.*
193. s.12(1)(b) *ibid.*
194. s.12(1)(c) *ibid.*
195. s.7(1) *ibid.*
196. s.8(1)(a) *ibid.* Naturally, there is nothing in the Act that can be construed as prohibiting a local arrangement between employee and employer whereby the employee may take carer's leave on terms more favourable to him or her than those specified in the statute.
197. s.8(1)(b) *ibid.* The Minister may make regulations in respect of the form in which carer's leave may be taken by any specified class or classes of employees in circumstances where leave is to be taken other than as one consecutive block of 65 weeks: s.8(6) *ibid.*

reasonable grounds to permit an employee to take a period of carer's leave that is of less than 13 weeks' duration.[198] In normal circumstances, an employee is only entitled to a period of carer's leave for one relevant person at any one time[199] (and indeed must wait six months from the date of the expiry of his or her carer's leave before being entitled to commence another period of carer's leave in respect of a different relevant person,[200] or six weeks in respect of the same relevant person[201]), however, an exception is made in circumstances where an employee has taken carer's leave in respect of a relevant person and applies for carer's leave in respect of another person if that other person resides with the relevant person.[202] Similarly, an employee is not permitted to seek carer's leave to care for a relevant person in respect of whom another employee (not necessarily of the same employer) is absent from employment and on carer's leave.[203]

4.4. Social Welfare Payments and Carer's Leave

As we shall see, while on carer's leave, the majority of an employee's basic employ- [13–62] ment rights remain unaffected. An exception to this is the employee's right to remuneration[204] (and to superannuation benefits).[205] Thus, as far as the employer is concerned, carer's leave is effectively unpaid leave. From an employee's perspective, however, [s]he can seek carer's benefit pursuant to Chapter 14 of Part II of the Social Welfare (Consolidation) Act of 2005[206] in respect of full-time care and attention being provided for a relevant person.[207] Under this section, carer's benefit is payable to an employee if [s]he was engaged in remunerative full-time employ- ment[208] as an employed contributor for at least eight weeks (whether consecutive

---

198. s.8(2) *ibid.* Where the employer so refuses [s]he is required to specify in writing to the employee the grounds for such a refusal.

199. s.6(4) *ibid.*

200. s.8(4) *ibid.*

201. s.8(3) *ibid.*

202. s.7(2) *ibid.* In such circumstances, the employee is entitled to no more than 130 weeks leave in respect of the two relevant persons (s.7(4) *ibid.*). Moreover, where the employee has made an application under s.7(2) [s]he is then not entitled to make another application in respect of a third relevant person in the same circumstances (s.7(5) *ibid.*).

203. s.6(3) *ibid.*

204. s.13(1)(a)(i) *ibid.*

205. s.13(1)(a)(iv) *ibid.*

206. In addition, in specific circumstances it is possible to claim 'carer's allowance' where one resides with the person for whom one is caring, pursuant to the Social Welfare Consolidation Act 2005. One cannot, however, simultaneously claim for carer's benefit and carer's allowance.

207. Such relevant person may be required pursuant to regulations to attend for medical examina- tion and the carer's benefit may be denied to the carer should the relevant person fail to attend at such medical examination: s.104 of the Social Welfare (Consolidation) Act of 2005.

208. Under s.100(5) *ibid.* 'remunerative full-time employment' means remunerative employment for not less than 16 hours a week within the 8 weeks referred to in subsection (1)(a) or any period that may be prescribed under subsection (6), provided that where any two of those weeks are consecutive, the requirement in relation to those two weeks may be satisfied by an aggregate of not less than 32 hours in that fortnight.

or not) in the 26-week period immediately prior to the first day in respect of which a claim to carer's benefit is made.[209] Payment of such benefit is also conditional on the employee not engaging in employment or self-employment. [210] Furthermore, it is conditional on him or her having qualifying contributions of not less than 156 weeks in the period between his or her entry into insurance and the first date for which the benefit is claimed as well as qualifying contributions of not less than 39 contribution weeks in the second-last complete year before the beginning of the benefit year that includes the first date for which the benefit is claimed; or 39 weeks in the 12 months immediately prior to the first day for which the benefit is claimed, or 26 weeks in each of the second-last and third-last complete contribution years before the beginning of the benefit year that includes the first day for which the benefit is claimed.[211] The rate of such payment is calculated in accordance with Part 1 of the Second Schedule to the 2005 Act.[212] Previously it lasted for 65 weeks per relevant person for whom carer's leave is taken,[213] but since 7 December 2005 and under s.7 of the Social Welfare Law Reform and Pensions Act of 2006 it can now be claimed for 104 weeks per relevant person.

4.5. Termination of Carer's Leave

[13–63] In the normal course of events, the period of carer's leave terminates on the date specified in the confirmation document,[214] or on a date agreed between the employer and employee.[215] In addition, a change of circumstances *vis-à-vis* either the carer or the relevant person for whom the carer's leave has been taken may lead to termination of the leave. This will happen, for example, where the relevant person ceases to satisfy the conditions of a relevant person for the purposes of the Act,[216] or where the relevant person dies,[217] or where the employee ceases to satisfy the conditions for the provision of full-time care and attention for the purposes of the Act.[218]

---

209. s.100(1)(a) *ibid.* Under s.100(2) this requirement does not apply to a claimant who was in receipt of carer's benefit within the relevant period.

210. s.100(1)(b) *ibid.* The Minister may, however, make regulations providing that a carer may be employed or self-employed subject to prescribed limitations and conditions: s.100(3) *ibid.*

211. s.101 *ibid.* This requirement does not apply in the case of a claimant who was previously in receipt of carer's benefit: s.100(4) *ibid.*

212. s.102 *ibid.*

213. s.103 *ibid.* Only one carer's benefit can be payable to a carer and in respect of any one relevant person: s.105(a). In addition, carer's benefit is not payable where the relevant person is in receipt of a disablement pension or a carer's allowance has been claimed in respect of him or her under the 2005 Act. Finally, prescribed relative allowance ceases to be payable in respect of a relevant person for whom carer's benefit is being claimed.

214. s.11(1)(a) Carer's Leave Act 2001.

215. s.11(1)(b) *ibid.*

216. s.11(1)(c) *ibid.*

217. s.11(1)(f) *ibid.* In such circumstances the leave will terminate either six weeks after the date of death or else on the date of termination specified in the confirmation document, whichever is sooner.

218. s.11(1)(d) *ibid.*

In addition, an employer who is of the view either: [13–64]

- that the person in respect of whom the leave has been taken (or in respect of whom the employee proposes to take carer's leave) is not or is no longer fulfilling the criteria of a 'relevant person'[219];
- that the employee who proposes to take or is on carer's leave does not satisfy the conditions for providing full-time care and attention to the relevant person[220]; or
- that the employee in question is engaging in or has engaged in employment or self-employment (in violation of the conditions for taking carer's leave),[221]

must notify the Minister for Social and Family Affairs of his or her opinion and the grounds for that opinion. Where this happens, the matter is referred to a Deciding Officer for a decision (under the Social Welfare (Consolidation) Act of 2005) as to whether any of these opinions are substantiated.[222] In the event of the Deciding Officer or Appeals Officer concluding that this is the case, then the carer's leave shall terminate and the Deciding Officer or Appeals Officer is required as soon as practicable to notify the employer and employee of the decision.[223] Where this happens the employer is required, again as soon as practicable, to give the employee written notice[224] specifying the date on which the employee is to return to his or her employment (which date must be reasonable and practicable in the circumstances).[225]

4.6. Prosecutions Under the Legislation

Under s.33 of the Act provision is made for the prosecution of persons who commit   [13–65]
offences under the Act. In essence, however, the only offences to which this section can relate are (a) failure to maintain records or notices under s.31 of the Act; and (b) obstructing or failing to assist the work of inspectors under s.32 of the Act. In this respect the powers of inspectors under s.32 of the Act are of the kind discussed

---

219. s.18(1) *ibid.*
220. s.18(2) *ibid.*
221. s.18(3) *ibid.*
222. This decision may be appealed under s.311 of the 2005 Act. See s.18(5) *ibid.*
223. s.11(2) *ibid.*
224. The employee and employer are obliged to retain a copy of this notice (s.11(5) *ibid.*). Moreover, the giving of the notice may be effected by delivering it to the employee or by sending a copy of it by prepaid registered letter in an envelope addressed to the employee at the last known residence of the employee or, where appropriate, to the residence of the relevant person: s.11(7) *ibid.*
225. s.11(3) *ibid.* Where this happens, the employee is required to return to his or her employment on the date specified in the notice (which is the date on which the carer's leave is deemed to terminate, s.11(1)(e) *ibid.*) and any period between the date specified in the employer's notice and the date on which the employee is to return to his or her employment is deemed not to be carer's leave: s.11(4) *ibid.*

in Chapter 1. It is, however, difficult – given that there is no offence under the Act of failing to allow an employee to take carer's leave – to see how significant the work of the inspectors can be in this context, particularly given that there is nothing in s.33 that would permit the inspectors to divulge information that has been found to an individual employee who may wish to bring an action against his or her employer pursuant to the Act. It is worth remembering the conclusion of both the High Court and Supreme Court in *Gama Endustri Tesisleri Imalat Montag A.S. v Minister for Enterprise Trade and Employment & Anor*[226] (considered earlier in Chapter 1) that the powers of inspectors under legislation of this kind were confined to those expressed in its terms, and hence any actions outside of these terms that did not flow inevitably from such terms would be *ultra vires* the powers of such inspectors.

4.7. Protection of Employees while on Leave and Enforcement Procedures

[13–66] As with the other legislation considered in this chapter, one of the key aspects of Irish carer's legislation is that employees are protected from any unfavourable treatment (up to and including dismissal) by employers as a result of availing of leave entitlements. Most importantly, employees have a right to return to work at the end of their leave periods, either in the same job or in some suitable alternative employment. As mentioned at the beginning of this chapter, however, this is an entitlement provided for in very similar ways in all the pieces of legislation considered in this chapter. We now turn to consider how these protections operate, and thereafter consider how these pieces of legislation are enforced.

5. Protection of Employees

[13–67] Of vital importance as far as all the legislation considered in this chapter is concerned is the level of protection afforded to employees who take such leave. As has been mentioned throughout this chapter, the protection afforded in these pieces of legislation is very similar, although some slightly nuanced differences are discernible. We now consider the general strands of protection provided and refer, where appropriate, to such differences. For convenience, moreover, we group the protections in question into two categories, namely protections available while the employee is on leave and protections in terms of the employee's right to return to work.

5.1. Protections while the Employee Is on Leave

[13–68] The essence of the protection in all of the different pieces of legislation can be summed up in the rule that while employees are on leave they must, subject to certain exceptions, be treated as if they were not, in fact, absent from work. This is the case whenever an employee is:

---

226. [2009] IESC 37, [2005] IEHC 210.

- on 'natal care absence' (that is, absence permitted under regulations made pursuant to s.15 of the Maternity Protection Act for the purposes of receiving pre and/or post-natal care, attending ante-natal classes and breast-feeding)[227];
- on 'protective leave'[228] (that is, maternity leave, additional leave, leave to which a father is entitled under s.16 of the Maternity Protection Act, and leave under s.18 of the Maternity Protection Act in order to avoid exposure to risks to which the mother or her developing child is vulnerable[229]), whether or not such leave is or has been postponed[230] or is preceded or succeeded by protective leave of another description[231];
- on adoptive leave or additional adoptive leave[232];
- attending pre-adoption classes[233];
- on parental or *force majeure* leave[234];
- on carer's leave.[235]

In all these circumstances [s]he must be treated as if [s]he was not absent from work[236] such that the absence in question cannot affect his or her statutory and contractual rights save (in all cases other than *force majeure* leave or leave for the purposes of breast-feeding or attending ante-natal or pre-adoption classes) his or her right to remuneration and to superannuation benefits.[237] Similarly, for the purposes of the Social Welfare (Consolidation) Act 2005, an employee on maternity leave or adoptive leave (but not parental or carer's leave) is not deemed to be an employed contributor for any contribution weeks in a period of absence from work on such leave if the employee does not receive any reckonable earnings in respect of that week.[238] On the other hand, the employee who takes any form of leave is naturally relieved for that period of his or her obligations to pay contributions in respect of the employment.[239] **[13–69]**

---

227. ss.22(1) and (2) Maternity Protection Act 1994.
228. ss.22(1) and (2) *ibid.*
229. s.21(1) *ibid.*
230. s.21(3) *ibid.*
231. s.21(2) *ibid.*
232. ss.15(1) and (2) Adoptive Leave Acts 1995 and 2005.
233. s.15(3) *ibid.*
234. ss.14(1) and (4) Parental Leave Acts 1998 and 2006.
235. s.13(1) Carer's Leave Act 2001.
236. On the other hand, it would appear that if actual physical attendance at work is a necessary prerequisite to, for example, receipt of a bonus for attendance, then absence from work on the various forms of leave does not constitute attendance. *Byrne v Memorex Media Products Limited*, P9/1986.
237. The extent to which employees on adoptive, maternity and carer's leave are entitled to social welfare benefits is considered earlier.
238. s.22(5) Maternity Protection Act 1994; s.15(7) Adoptive Leave Acts 1995 and 2005.
239. s.13(1)(b) Carer's Leave Act 2001, s.15(2) Adoptive Leave Acts 1995 and 2005; s.22(4) Maternity Protection Act 1994; s.14(1) Parental Leave Acts 1998 and 2006.

5.1.1. Holiday Entitlements while on Leave

[13–70] As we have seen, certain exceptions exist in respect of the principle that an employee on protective leave must be treated as if [s]he is not absent from work. Some of these relate to holiday entitlements. Thus where an employee is on leave granted under s.18 of the Maternity Protection Act 1994 (that is the 'health and safety' form of maternity leave referred to above) [s]he is not entitled to benefits under s.21 of the Organisation of Working Time Act 1997 in respect of any public holiday falling during the period of absence.[240] On the other hand [s]he *is* entitled to be paid for public holidays that fall during her regular maternity leave.[241] Under the Parental Leave Acts, where a holiday other than a public holiday falls within the period of parental leave (and if the employee would otherwise have been working at the employment in question), [s]he is entitled to take that other holiday at a time as may be determined by the employer in accordance with working time legislation.[242] And if a public holiday falls during the period of parental leave a day must be added to the period of parental leave to which the employee is entitled.[243] Similarly, in the context of carer's leave, the prospective carer also loses entitlements as far as both annual leave and public holiday leave is entitled,[244] save that the first 13 weeks of the carer's leave *are* factored in as working time for the purposes of calculating such entitlements.[245] Curiously no equivalent provision exists in respect of adoptive leave and hence it is unclear as to whether or not an employee absent for this reason is entitled to public and other holiday leave falling during that period of absence.

5.1.2. Termination of Employment while on Leave

[13–71] In particular, any purported termination of the employment of an employee while [s]he is absent on protective leave,[246] during a period of natal care absence,[247] in order that [s]he can attend ante-natal classes,[248] while she is absent for breast-feeding purposes in accordance with s.15B of the Maternity Protection Act,[249] while

---

240. s.22(6) Maternity Protection Act 1994. Generally under s.15(4) of the Organisation of Working Time Act 1997, a reference period for calculating annual leave will not include any period during which the employee was absent from work *inter alia* on carer's leave, parental leave, *force majeure* leave, adoptive leave or maternity leave.

241. *Forde v Des Gibney Ltd.*, P8/1985. See Kerr, *Irish Employment Legislation* (Round Hall Sweet and Maxwell, 2000), at p.C-68/8.

242. s.7(4)(a) Parental Leave Acts 1998 and 2006.

243. s.7(4)(b) *ibid.* This is a curious provision in that the entitlement in respect of public holidays in s.21 of the Organisation of Working Time Act is to a *paid* day's leave, yet parental leave is unpaid leave. Consequently from the employee's standpoint, his or her right to a paid day's leave is converted in the Parental Leave Acts to a day of unpaid leave.

244. ss.13(1)(a)(ii) and (iii) Carer's Leave Act 2001.

245. s.13(2) *ibid.* It is specifically provided that s.21(1) of the Organisation of Working Time Act 1997 does not apply in the case of public holidays that occur after the first 13 weeks' absence from work on carer's leave: s.13(3) *ibid.*

246. s.23(a) Maternity Protection Act 1994.

247. s.23(b *ibid.*

248. s.23(bb) *ibid.*

249. s.23(bbb) *ibid.*

[s]he is absent on adoptive leave or additional adoptive leave[250] or while attending pre-adoption classes,[251] is invalid. Moreover, in all these cases, any notice of termination given while the employee is absent from work but expiring subsequent to such absence,[252] or any purported suspension of an employee imposed while [s]he is absent from work for such purposes,[253] is invalid. Curiously no equivalent provision exists in the Parental Leave Acts or Carer's Leave Act and hence (and whereas an employer may not penalise an employee for taking parental or carer's leave) it would appear that it *is* legal for an employer to terminate an employee's employment or to suspend him or her while [s]he is on parental or carer's leave.

Both the Parental Leave Acts[254] and the Carer's Leave Act[255] expressly provide that any penalisation of an employee for having taken parental or *force majeure* leave is prohibited. There is no such express provision in the Maternity Protection Act and the Adoptive Leave Acts but it may surely be suggested that this is implied in these statutes as well.   [13–72]

5.2. Right to Return to Work

The other key element of all of the relevant pieces of legislation is that an employee who has taken a period of protective leave shall be entitled to return to work (at its conclusion[256])   [13–73]

- with the employer with whom [s]he was working prior to taking leave, or in a transfer of undertakings situation, with the new owner of the business[257];

---

250. s.16(a)(i) Adoptive Leave Acts 1995 and 2005.

251. s.16 (a)(ii) *ibid.*

252. ss.23(c), (d), (dd) and (ddd) Maternity Protection Act 1994; ss.16(b) and 17(a) Adoptive Leave Acts 1995 and 2005.

253. s.23(e) Maternity Protection Act 1994; s.17(1)(b) Adoptive Leave Acts 1995 and 2005. Moreover, any notice of termination given before the employee begins a period of leave that is due to expire while the employee is absent from work for any of these reasons must be extended by the period of such absence: s.24 Maternity Protection Act 1994; s.17(2) Adoptive Leave Acts 1995 and 2005.

254. s.16A Parental Leave Acts 1998 and 2006.

255. s.16(1) Carer's Leave Act 2001. Such penalisation includes dismissal of the employee, unfair treatment of the employee or any unfavourable change in the conditions of employment of the employee (s.16(2) *ibid.*). Where the unfavourable treatment in question constitutes a redundancy or dismissal, then the appropriate form of redress is under unfair dismissals legislation, and not under the normal redress procedures contained in the Parental and Carer's Leave Acts.

256. In the case of all the legislation, where because of an interruption or cessation in the workplace that exists at the time of the expiration of the relevant leave it is unreasonable to expect an employee to return to work at the time, [s]he is entitled to return to work when work resumes at that place of employment, or as soon as reasonably practicable thereafter: s.29 Maternity Protection Act 1994; s.14(3) Carer's Leave Act 2001; s.15(3) Parental Leave Acts 1998 and 2006; s.21 Adoptive Leave Acts 1995 and 2005.

257. s.26(1)(a) Maternity Protection Act 1994; s.18(1)(a) Adoptive Leave Acts 1995 and 2005; s.14(1)(a) Carer's Leave Act 2001; s.15(1)(a) Parental Leave Acts 1998 and 2006.

- in the job[258] that [s]he held immediately before taking protective leave.[259] An exception to this general principle is where the job at which the employee was working immediately prior to taking protective leave was not his or her normal or usual job in which case [s]he is entitled to return to work either in that job, or his or her normal or usual job[260];
- under the contract of employment under which [s]he was formerly employed, or where there has been a transfer of undertakings situation, under a contract that is identical to his or her old one, under terms or conditions that are not less favourable than those that previously applied.[261] Moreover, the Maternity, Parental and Adoptive Leave Acts (but not the Carer's Leave Act) further require that, in either case, the employee's 'post-leave' contract incorporates any improvement to the terms and conditions of his or her contract to which [s]he would have been entitled had [s]he not been absent from work[262];
- where it is not reasonably practicable for the employer to permit the employee to return to his or her old job, the employer is entitled to offer him or her 'suitable alternative employment' – that is, work suitable in relation to the employee concerned,[263] which is appropriate for him or her to do in the circumstances, where the terms of his or her conditions of employment[264] are not less favourable to the employee than those of his or her former employment[265] (and under the Carer's leave Act the requirement is that the terms not be *substantially* less favourable than those of the former contract[266]). The Parental and Adoptive Leave Acts and the Maternity Protection Act further require that in such

---

258. For the purposes of the section 'job' means the nature of the work the employee is employed to do in accordance with his or her contract of employment and the capacity and place in which the employee is so employed (s.18(3) Adoptive Leave Acts 1995 and 2005; s.2 Parental Leave Acts 1998 and 2006; s.26(3) Maternity Protection Act 1994). No definition of the term appears in the Carer's Leave Act but it cannot be doubted that the definition provided in the three other pieces of legislation would apply equally here.

259. s.26(1)(b) Maternity Protection Act 1994; s.18(1)(b) Adoptive Leave Acts 1995 and 2005; s.14(1)(b) Carer's Leave Act 2001; s.15(1)(b) Parental Leave Acts 1998 and 2006.

260. s.26(2) Maternity Protection Act 1994; s.18(2) Adoptive Leave Acts 1995 and 2005; s.14(2) Carer's Leave Act 2001; s.15(2) Parental Leave Acts 1998 and 2006.

261. s.14(1)(c) Carer's Leave Act 2001; s.15(1)(c) Parental Leave Acts 1998 and 2006; s.18(1)(c) Adoptive Leave Acts 1995 and 2005; s.26(1)(c) Maternity Protection Act 1994.

262. s.15(1)(c) Parental Leave Acts 1998 and 2006; s.18(1)(c) Adoptive Leave Acts 1995 and 2005; s.26(1)(c) Maternity Protection Act 1994.

263. See Kerr, *Irish Employment Legislation* (Round Hall Sweet and Maxwell, 2000), at p.D-19 for suggestion that the question of whether the work is 'suitable' will be assessed subjectively from the employee's standpoint.

264. Such terms and conditions include the capacity in which [s]he is to be employed, the place in which [s]he is expected to work, and any other terms and conditions of employment.

265. s.19(2)(b) Adoptive Leave Acts 1995 and 2005; s.16(2)(b) Parental Leave Acts 1998 and 2006; s.27(2)(b) Maternity Protection Act 1994.

266. s.15(2)(b) Carer's Leave Act 2001. This had been the position under Maternity Protection Legislation prior to amendment under the Maternity Protection (Amendment) Act of 2004.

circumstances, the employee's terms and conditions of employment incorporate any improvements to which [s]he would have been entitled had [s]he not taken the leave[267];

- in all cases it is provided that where leave has been taken the employee's continuity of service is preserved[268]; and
- finally, where the employee, at the time of taking the relevant leave is on a probationary period, or undergoing training or is employed under a contract of apprenticeship, and if the employer is of the view that the employee's absence from work would not be consistent with the continuation of the probation, training or apprenticeship, the employer may require that the probation, training or apprenticeship be suspended during the period of leave and recommenced when that leave is completed.[269]

5.2.1. Notice of Intention to Return to Work

The one condition imposed on the employee's entitlement to return to work following maternity,[270] adoptive,[271] or carer's leave[272] is that [s]he must furnish his [13–74]

---

267. s.27(2)(b) Maternity Protection Act 1994; s.19(2)(b) Adoptive Leave Acts 1995 and 2005; s.16(2)(b) Parental Leave Acts 1998 and 2006.

268. s.27 Maternity Protection Act 1994; s.15 Carer's Leave Act 2001; s.20 Adoptive Leave Acts 1995 and 2005; s.15(2)(c) Parental Leave Acts 1998 and 2006.

269. s.13(5) Carer's Leave Act 2001; s.14(3) Parental Leave Acts 1998 and 2006. Under s.25 of the Maternity Protection Act 1994 and s.15(6) of the Adoptive Leave Acts 1995 and 2005, there is a mandatory requirement that where an employee on starting an employment is on a period of probation, apprenticeship or training when leave is taken, that period of probation, apprenticeship or training *shall* stand suspended and be recommenced following his or her return to work after the leave period.

270. s.28(1) Maternity Protection Act 1994. This is subject to the possibility of the leave being postponed in the event of the hospitalisation of the child under ss.14(b) and 16(b). In such circumstances, entitlement to return to work for an employee who has been absent on resumed leave (or who has been deemed to be such) is dependent on him or her notifying the employer of his or her intention to return to work either within four weeks before the intended date of return or, where the period of resumed leave is less than four weeks, at the same time as the notification of intention to take resumed leave (ss.14(b)(8) and 16(b)(7) *ibid.*) or, where the employer waives his or her right to such notification, not later than the day on which the employee expects to return to work: s.28(1)(a) *ibid.*

271. s.20(1) Adoptive Leave Acts 1995 and 2005. Hence if the leave is for a period of four weeks or less the employee is required to give notice of intention to return to work at the same time as [s]he informs his or her employer of his or her intention to take leave. Where an employee takes postponed leave under s.11(c), an employee is required to give notice of his or her return to work either at the time that [s]he notifies his or her employer of his or her intention to take postponed leave, or four weeks before the date of the expected return to work, whichever is later (s.20(1)(b) *ibid.*). Moreover, where an employee is *deemed* to be on postponed leave pursuant to s.11(d) then [s]he must give notice of his or her intention to return as soon as is reasonably practicable but not later than the date on which the employee expects to return to work: s.20(1)(b)(ii) *ibid.*

272. s.9(6) Carer's Leave Act 2001. This does not apply if the period of carer's leave is terminated in

or her employer (or where appropriate, the employer's successor) with a written notice of his or her intention to return to work and the proposed date of such return, not less than four weeks before the date on which [s]he is due to return to his or her employment. Formerly, failure to give such notice meant that the statutory entitlement to return to work was lost.[273] There is now statutory provision in the Adoptive Leave Acts and the Maternity Protection Act,[274] however, giving the Rights Commissioner or Tribunal a discretion in this regard, such that where it deems there to be reasonable grounds either for an employee's failure to give notification of intention to return to work, or his or her failure to do so within the specified time limits, then the Rights Commissioner (or Tribunal as the case may be) shall extend the time for giving the notification (nor is there any maximum length of time by which such time period can be extended).[275]

5.2.2. Dismissal or Redundancy at the Conclusion of a Leave Period

[13–75] Where an employee who is entitled to return to work having taken any of the various forms of leave is prohibited from doing so by his or her employer, then the date on which [s]he is deemed to be dismissed (for the purposes of the Redundancy Payments Acts 1967–2003, the Minimum Notice and Terms of Employment Act 1973 and the Unfair Dismissals Acts 1977–2001) shall be deemed to be the date on which [s]he was entitled to return to work.[276] Moreover, such a dismissal shall be deemed to be an unfair dismissal, unless there were substantial grounds justifying it.[277] In addition, any dismissal that results wholly or mainly from the fact that the employee exercises or proposes[278] to exercise his or her rights

circumstances where a Deciding Officer or Appeals Officer makes a determination under s.11(2) that the employee is, for whatever reason, no longer entitled to take carer's leave: s.9(7) *ibid.*

273. *Ivory v SkiLine Ltd.* [1988] IR 399.

274. s.28(2) Maternity Protection Act 1994; s.20(2) Adoptive Leave Acts 1995 and 2005.

275. In the absence of such reasonable grounds, the failure to give the relevant notification either at all or within the specified time limits are matters that may be taken into account by a Rights Commissioner, or the Tribunal or the Circuit Court in determining the employee's rights (if any) under unfair dismissals legislation, or any other legislation, to re-instatement, re-engagement or compensation. Thus Kerr, *Irish Employment Legislation* (Round Hall Sweet and Maxwell, 2000), at p.C-70, makes the point that irrespective of the statutory scheme, an employee in such circumstances may have a contractual right to return to work (*Scott v Yeates & Sons Opticians Limited* [1992] ELR 83), or the employer may be stopped by its conduct from deeming her not to be allowed to return to such work.

276. s.40 Maternity Protection Act 1994; ss.26(2), 29(2) and 30(2) Adoptive Leave Acts 1995 and 2005; s.25(3) Parental Leave Acts 1998 and 2006; s.16(4) Carer's Leave Act 2001.

277. s.40(4)(b) Maternity Protection Act 1994; s.24 Adoptive Leave Acts 1995 and 2005; s.16(4) Carer's Leave Act 2001; s.25(3)(a) Parental Leave Acts 1998 and 2006.

278. In respect of adoptive leave, s.6(2)(h) of the Unfair Dismissals Act says that an unfair dismissal will arise where an employee is dismissed because of the exercise or *contemplated* exercise of his or her rights under the legislation. It is not clear why the word *contemplated* is used here whereas the word *proposed* is used in respect of maternity, parental and carer's leave.

under the Maternity Protection Act,[279] the Adoptive Leave Acts,[280] or the Parental or Carer's Leave Acts[281] is deemed to be an unfair dismissal.[282] This issue is dealt with in more detail and in the contexts of our analysis of equality law and unfair dismissals law in Chapters 7–9 and 21.

6. Enforcement

As we shall see, in general the manner by which these various pieces of legislation are to be enforced is the same in all the different statutes. There are, however, certain minor and nuanced differences in approach, and these will be highlighted. Moreover, it should be noted that certain forms of dispute under the legislation cannot be referred in the general way provided for in the Acts – specifically disputes in relation to the dismissal or redundancy of the employee or disputes relating to minimum notice, which must be dealt with under the process specified in the specific statutes dealing with notice obligations and unfair dismissals.[283] [13–76]

Furthermore, under the Carer's Leave Act, an exception to the normal rules in respect of enforcement applies in the case of any matters relating to the decision of Deciding Officers and Appeals Officers under s.18, and ss.6(5) and 6(6) and paras.(a), (c) and (d) of s.6(1) of the Act.[284] All of these sections relate to the [13–77]

---

279. ss.6(2)(f) and (g) Unfair Dismissals Act 1977. Under s.6(2a) the normal requirement under unfair dismissals legislation that the employee have one year's continuous service does not apply in this context.

280. s.6(2)(h) Unfair Dismissals Act 1977. It is not clear whether under s.6(2a) of the 1977 Act, the normal requirement of one year's continuous service applies in this context. Section 6(2a) provides that for the purposes of paras.(f) and (g) of the section, an 'employee' or 'adopting parent' referred to in these sections will include a person who would otherwise be excluded from the operation of the Act because of the requirements in s.2 (which include the requirement that there be one year's continuous service). The confusion stems from the fact that paras.(f) and (g) do not include the term 'adopting parent' but para.(h) does.

281. s.6(2)(dd) Unfair Dismissals Act 1977.

282. On the other hand, under ss.2(2)(c) and (d) of the Unfair Dismissals Act, unfair dismissals legislation does not apply to a case where a temporary employee has been appointed to fill the position of a person on maternity, carer's or adoptive leave, where [s]he is informed that his or her employment will terminate when the person in question returns from adoptive leave, and where the dismissal of that employee duly occurs.

283. ss.30(1) and (2) Maternity Protection Act 1994; ss.32(1) and (2) Adoptive Leave Acts 1995 and 2005; ss.18(1) and (2) Parental Leave Acts 1998 and 2006. There is no express provision in this regard in the Carer's Leave Act 2001, but it would seem likely that the same principles would apply to that Act. The general enforcement procedures in all of these statutes also do not apply to disputes where the employee is a member of the Defence Forces. In addition, the general powers of enforcement contained in the Maternity Protection Act does not apply to disputes over which the Health and Safety Authority has jurisdiction under the Safety, Health and Welfare at Work Act 2005.

284. In addition, the terms of the Act do not apply to a member of the Defence Forces: s.17(4) Carer's Leave Act 2001.

question of whether the criteria are fulfilled for the employee to take carer's leave, namely whether the person for whom leave is sought is a relevant person, whether the employee will be providing full-time care and attention and whether or not the employee is employed or self-employed during the period of carer's leave and in violation of the conditions under the Act.[285] The reason why such questions are outside the jurisdiction of the Rights Commissioner is presumably that they are matters for the exclusive decision of the Deciding Officer or Appeals Officer under the Social Welfare (Consolidation) Act of 2005. Thus, if in any dispute before a Rights Commissioner there is a decision of a Deciding Officer or Appeals Officer in respect of such issues, the Rights Commissioner must accept that decision as a final determination of the matter.[286]

6.1. The Rights Commissioner

[13–78] Disputes between employers and employees under all of these statutes can be referred, in the first instance, by either the employee or the employer to a Rights Commissioner.[287] Such reference must be made in writing (containing such particulars as may be prescribed[288]) and must be made within six months of the date

- in the context of maternity protection legislation, on which the employer was initially informed of the initial circumstances relevant to the dispute, and which underpin the employee's entitlement to obtain leave under the Act (namely that the employee is pregnant, has given birth or is breastfeeding, or that, in the case of an expectant father, the mother of his child is pregnant, or that in the case of a father whose child has been born, the mother of his child has died)[289];
- in the context of adoptive leave legislation from the date of placement or, where no placement takes place, within six months of the date on which the employer receives notification of the employee's intention to take leave (either adoptive or additional adoptive leave) under the Act[290];
- in the context of parental leave legislation from the date of the occurrence of the dispute[291]; or

285. s.17(1) *ibid.*
286. s.17(2) *ibid.*
287. s.30(4) Maternity Protection Act 1994; s.19(1) Carer's Leave Act 2001; s.34(1) Adoptive Leave Acts 1995 and 2005; s.18(2) Parental Leave Acts 1998 and 2006.
288. These particulars are laid down in the Maternity Protection (Disputes and Appeals) Regulations 1995, SI no. 17 of 1995; the Parental Leave (Disputes and Appeals) Regulations 1999, SI no. 6 of 1999); the Adoptive Leave (Referral of Disputes and Appeals) (Part V) Regulations 1995, SI no. 195 of 1995. No such rules are laid down in any regulations made pursuant to the Carer's Leave Act 2001.
289. s.31(1)(a) Maternity Protection Act 1994. This notice should be given by the Rights Commissioner to the other party to the dispute as soon as possible: s.31(2) *ibid.*
290. s.24(1)(a) Adoptive Leave Acts 1995 and 2005.
291. s.18 Parental Leave Acts 1998 and 2006.

- in the context of the Carer's Leave Act, within six months of the date of the contravention of the legislation.[292]

Other than in the context of a hearing under parental leave legislation (where no [13–79] such extension appears possible), this limitation period may, however, be extended by the Rights Commissioner if in his or her view, exceptional circumstances prevented the giving of notice within the relevant time period, but where this happens the notice period may only be extended to a maximum of 12 months.[293] The Rights Commissioner, having conducted a hearing of the dispute,[294] is required to make a decision on the matter, and may (in the context of the Parental Leave Acts, the Maternity Protection Act and the Adoptive Leave Acts but not, strangely, the Carer's Leave Act) give such directions to the parties as [s]he considers necessary for the resolution of the dispute.[295]

6.2. Redress that May Be Awarded
Should [s]he find in favour of the employee, the Rights Commissioner (or, on [13–80] appeal, the Tribunal) can award him or her such redress as is deemed to be appropriate, including either or both of a grant of the relevant leave for a specified period[296] and/or an award of compensation[297] at a level that is deemed to be just

---

292. s.19(3) Carer's Leave Act 2001.
293. s.31(1)(b) Maternity Protection Act 1994; s.24(1)(b) Adoptive Leave Acts 1995 and 2005; s.19(8) Carer's Leave Act 2001. No such provision exists in respect of the Parental Leave Acts.
294. ss.31(3) and (4) Maternity Protection Act 1994; s.19(2) Carer's Leave Act 2001; s.32(3) Adoptive Leave Acts 1995 and 2005; s.18(2) and (6) Parental Leave Acts 1998 and 2006. Curiously under the Adoptive Leave Acts there is no provision (as there is in the other statutes) that the hearing take place otherwise than in public.
295. s.21(1) Parental Leave Acts 1998 and 2006; s.32(2) Maternity Protection Act 1994; s.33(1)(b) Adoptive Leave Acts 1995 and 2005.
296. Where such leave is awarded under the Parental Leave Act or Carer's Leave Act, the confirmation document concerned must be amended by the parties so as to accord with a decision, determination or direction under the section (s.21(8) Parental Leave Acts 1998 and 2006; s.21(1)(a) Carer's Leave Act 2001). It is further provided that in determining *when* such an award of *parental* leave is to be taken, the Rights Commissioner or Tribunal is entitled to postpone, curtail or vary such leave either because of the various factors listed in s.11(1) of the Parental Leave Acts 1998 and 2006 and considered earlier (s.21(6) *ibid.*), or because of a serious and substantial change in the circumstances affecting the employer or employee (s.21(7) *ibid.*). Moreover, where appropriate because of the illness or some other incapacity of the employee, the Rights Commissioner or Tribunal may order that the parental leave be taken at a time outside of the statutory time limits in which such leave can otherwise normally be taken: s.21(5) *ibid.*
297. ss.32(2) and (3) Maternity Protection Act 1994; s.33(3) Adoptive Leave Acts 1995 and 2005; s.21(2) Parental Leave Acts 1998 and 2006; s.21(1)(b) Carer's Leave Act 2001. The process for calculating maximum compensation under the various pieces of legislation is laid down respectively in the Maternity Protection (Maximum Compensation) Regulations of 1999, SI no. 134 of 1999; the Adoptive Leave (Calculation of Weekly Remuneration) Regulations 1995,

and equitable but not exceeding 20 weeks' remuneration in respect of the employee's employment where the Maternity Protection, Adoptive Leave and Parental Leave Acts are concerned, and 26 weeks' remuneration where the Carer's Leave Act is concerned.[298]

6.3. Appeals to the Tribunal

[13–81] A decision of the Rights Commissioner may be appealed to the Tribunal by written notice within four weeks of the date on which the relevant decision of the Commissioner was communicated to the parties.[299] The Tribunal has power to make a determination in respect of such appeal following a hearing of the matter[300] (varying, confirming or setting aside the decision of the Rights Commissioner), and to make the same awards as those that could be made by the Rights Commissioner.[301] A determination of the Tribunal can be appealed by either party to the High Court on a point of law[302] and, in addition, the Tribunal may itself refer a question of law arising before it to the High Court.[303]

SI no. 196 of 1995; the Parental Leave (Maximum Compensation) Regulations of 1999, SI no. 34 of 1999. No equivalent regulations are made in the context of carer's leave. Such an award of compensation shall be included among the debts which, under s.285 of the Companies Act 1963, are priority debts in the event of the company being wound up, and which under s.81 of the Bankruptcy Act 1988, are priority debts in the event of the bankruptcy of the employer: s.36 Maternity Protection Act 1994; s.38 Adoptive Leave Acts 1995 and 2005; s.24 Parental Leave Acts 1998 and 2006; s.25 Carer's Leave Act 2001.

298. s.21(1)(b) Carer's Leave Act 2001.

299. s.33(2) Maternity Protection Act 1994; s.35(2) Adoptive Leave Acts 1995 and 2005; s.19 Parental Leave Acts 1998 and 2006; s.20(1) Carer's Leave Act 2001. Under s.20(9) Carer's Leave Act 2001 (but none of the other statutes), this time period may be extended by the Tribunal for a further period of six weeks if it considers it reasonable to do so.

300. In all the statutes (s.33 Maternity Protection Act 1994; s.35 Adoptive Leave Acts 1995 and 2005; s.20 Carer's Leave Act 2001; s.19 Parental Leave Acts 1998 and 2006) it is provided that a witness appearing at such hearing has the same privileges and immunities as if the matter were being heard by the High Court and, similarly, that if someone lies under oath at the Tribunal, this is perjury for which [s]he can be prosecuted. Moreover, the Tribunal can take evidence on oath, and require persons to attend and to give evidence and produce relevant documentation. Failure to do so is an offence that may be prosecuted by the Minister and a document sworn by the chairman or vice-chairman of the Tribunal stating that the defendant failed to attend, or give evidence, or produce such documentation is sufficient evidence that the offence has occurred unless the contrary can be shown.

301. s.33(1) Maternity Protection Act 1994; s.21(1) Parental Leave Acts 1998 and 2006; s.21(1) Carer's Leave Act 2001; s.33(1) Adoptive Leave Acts 1995 and 2005.

302. s.34(2) Maternity Protection Act 1994; s.36(2) Adoptive Leave Acts 1995 and 2005; s.20(2) Parental Leave Acts 1998 and 2006; s.23(2) Carer's Leave Act 2001. Kerr in *Irish Employment Legislation* (Round Hall Sweet and Maxwell, 2000), at p.C-73 suggests that as far as time limits are concerned, in the absence of any specific time-frame in which to bring such an appeal, it would appear that it would need only to be brought within a reasonable time-frame and by way of a special summons.

303. s.34(1) Maternity Protection Act 1994; s.36(1) Adoptive Leave Acts 1995 and 2005; s.20(1) Parental Leave Acts 1998 and 2006; s.23(1) Carer's Leave Act 2001.

6.4. Enforcement by way of Circuit Court Order

Under the Maternity Protection Act and Adoptive Leave Acts (but not the Parental   [13–82]
Leave and Carer's Leave Acts), a decision of a Rights Commissioner and a determination of the Tribunal may specify a time limit in which that which it requires is
carried out.[304] Where this does not occur, then the default position is that it should
be done within four weeks from the date on which it has been communicated to
the parties.[305] Where this has not happened, and where the time period in which an
appeal can be brought has expired,[306] then, on application from either the Minister
or the party in whose favour the determination or decision was made,[307] the Circuit
Court shall make an order directing the relevant party to carry out the decision or
determination in accordance with its terms.[308] It is worth noting that, in the context
of parental leave[309] and carer's leave,[310] where the Circuit Court feels that owing to
lapse of time it would not be possible to comply with an order made by the Rights
Commissioner or Tribunal, it shall make an order providing for whatever other
form of redress it considers appropriate.

---

304. s.37(1) Maternity Protection Act 1994; s.39(1) Adoptive Leave Acts 1995 and 2005.

305. s.37(2) Maternity Protection Act 1994; s.39(1)(b) Adoptive Leave Acts 1995 and 2005. It is
arguable that there is no default position in respect of the time-frame in which an order of the
Rights Commissioner or Tribunal under the Parental Leave Acts and Carer's Leave Act must
be carried out.

306. As we have seen, there is no specific time-limit in which to appeal a Tribunal determination to
the High Court on a point of law.

307. s.22(1) Carer's Leave Act 2001; s.39(2) Adoptive Leave Acts 1995 and 2005; s.37(3) Maternity
Protection Act 1994; s.22(1)(a) Parental Leave Acts 1998 and 2006. Applications in this regard
should be made pursuant to Order 57 Rule 3 (Adoptive Leave), Rule 5 (Parental Leave) of the
Circuit Court Rules 2001, SI no. 510 of 2001. (See Kerr, *Irish Employment Legislation* (Round
Hall Sweet and Maxwell, 2000), at p.C-74 for suggestion that applications in respect of the
Maternity Protection Act should be brought in analogous fashion. Applications in respect of
a dispute under the Carer's Leave Act 2001 should be brought under the procedures as are set
out in the Circuit Court Rules (Carer's Leave Act 2001) 2005, SI no. 387 of 2005.

308. s.37(3) Maternity Protection Act 1994; s.39(2) Adoptive Leave Acts 1995 and 2005; s.22(1)
Parental Leave Acts 1998 and 2006; s.22(2) Carer's Leave Act 2001. Where the relevant determination or decision has included an order for compensation, the Circuit Court may make an
order requiring that interest be paid on top of the compensation, and in respect of the whole
or part of the period beginning four weeks after the decision or determination was communicated to the parties: s.37(5) Maternity Protection Act 1994; s.22(3) Carer's Leave Act 2001;
s.39(3) Adoptive Leave Acts 1995 and 2005; s.22(3) Parental Leave Acts 1998 and 2006.

309. s.22(2) Parental Leave Acts 1998 and 2006.

310. s.22(2) Carer's Leave Act 2001. The Circuit Court may also order that interest be paid on any
order of compensation that had been made: s.22(3) *ibid.*

CHAPTER 14

Information and Consultation Entitlements

Introduction

A relatively recent development in Irish employment law – albeit one that has [14–01] the potential to be of real significance as far as the role of employees within the decision-making processes of Irish businesses are concerned – is the movement to require employers to provide employees (or employees' representatives) with increased levels of information and consultation[1] about major developments affecting the business in which they work. These obligations are derived, as we shall see, in large part from European Community law,[2] but have the capacity, depending on how they are interpreted, to have a particular impact in a country like Ireland where there is no mandatory recognition of trade unions[3] and where, outside of the obligations under the Industrial Relations (Amendment) Act 2001 and the Industrial Relations (Miscellaneous Provisions) Act 2004, there is no obligation to negotiate collectively with employees.[4] Indeed the point has been made that the increased blurring of the lines between the conceptually distinct notions of consultation and negotiation at a European level may have the capacity to lead (albeit by a gradual process of accretion) to a situation where there is some level of mandatory obligation on employers throughout Europe to negotiate collectively with employees.[5]

---

1. s.3(1) Transnational Information and Consulation of Employees Act 1996 and s.1(1) Employees (Provision of Information and Consultation) Act 2006.
2. See Hayes, 'Informing and Consulting Employees – Irish and EU Developments', 2(3) *IELJ* (2005), 89. See also Barnard, *EC Employment Law* (3rd ed., Oxford University Press, 2006), at pp.701 *et seq.*
3. See Chapter 2.
4. It was further noted in Chapter 2 that the attempts in the Industrial Relations (Amendment) Act 2001, as amended to reduce the impact of 'voluntarism' as far as mandatory recognition of trade unions is concerned, were dealt a serious blow by the decision of the Supreme Court in *Ryanair v Labour Court* [2007] IESC 6, [2007] 4 IR 199.
5. See Connolly, 'Industrial Relations (Miscellaneous Provisions) Act 2004 – Implications for Industrial Relations Law and Practice of the Supreme Court decision in *Ryanair v Labour Court and IMPACT*', 4(2) *IELJ* (2007), 37 for the view that 'At European level, the distinction between consultation obligations and negotiation is increasingly becoming blurred. The ECJ judgment in *Junk v Kuhnel* ([2005] I.R.L.R. 301) in a collective redundancy context can be interpreted as indicating that the phrase 'consultation with a view to agreement' should be

[14–02] The law requiring employers to provide information to and to consult with employees is dominated by two key statutes,[6] namely the Transnational Information and Consultation of Employees Act 1996, which deals with the requirements in this regard of an employer whose workforce is based in at least two EU Member States, and the Employees (Provision of Information and Consultation) Act 2006, which is considered first and which applies more generally.

1. The Employees (Provision of Information and Consultation) Act 2006

[14–03] The purpose of the 2006 Act is to incorporate the European Information and Consultation Directive[7] into Irish law.[8] For its part, the Directive was aimed at ensuring that where matters pertaining to the operation of a large- or semi-large-scale business and that touch on the interests of employees are at issue, then there should be a process whereby (a) employees are informed about such developments, and (b) employees are consulted about the same.[9]

---

interpreted to mean negotiation. This phrase appears in directives and domestic legislation concerning collective redundancy, transfer of undertaking, and information and consultation, and will increasingly mean that employers will find themselves engaged in a negotiation process for specific purposes. Given the breadth of issues covered by the Information and Consultation Directive employers will increasingly be faced with the prospect of negotiation with employer representatives on key organisational issues.'

6. It should be noted that information and consultation obligations arise from other statutory sources, including the European Communities (Cross Border Mergers) Regulations 2008 (SI no. 157 of 2008) and the European Communities (European Public Limited-Liability Company) Regulations 2007 (SI no. 21 of 2007).

7. Directive 2002/14/EC. The Directive moreover gives effect to the call for greater dialogue between management and employees in Article 136 of the EC treaty and Point 17 of the Community Charter of Fundamental Social Rights of Workers. Finally, the 2006 Act also seeks to implement Article 3(2) of Council Directive 2001/23/EC in respect of the rights of employees in a Transfer of Undertakings situation. Generally, see Keane, 'The Consultation Directive and the Development of Workplace Relations: From Sweat Shops to Talking Shops?', 2 *Employment Law Review* (2006), 37; and Doherty, 'It's Good to Talk… Isn't it? Legislating for Information and Consultation in the Irish Workplace', 15(1) *DULJ* (2008), 120.

8. A clear and concise explanation of the nature and operation of the Act is provided in the Labour Relations Commission *Code of Practice on Information and Consultation* (2008), which was brought into force and declared to be a Code of Practice for the purposes of the Industrial Relations Act 1990 by the Industrial Relations Act 1990 (Code of Practice on Information and Consultation) (Declaration) Order 2008 (SI no. 132 of 2008).

9. See Keane, 'The Consultation Directive and the Development of Workplace Relations: From Sweat Shops to Talking Shops?', 2 *Employment Law Review* (2006), 37 for the view that the 2006 Act is in fact the culmination of a number of legislative developments aimed at fostering a culture of openness as far as management's relationship with employees is concerned.

This development was seen as being increasingly important in a globalised world   [14–04] where, in the case of multinational corporations, a decision made, for example, in New York or Tokyo could affect directly and significantly an Irish worker. Equally it should be noted from the outset that whereas this process involves *bona fide* provision of information[10] to and consultation with employees,[11] there is no obligation on an employer to act on the basis of such information and consultation. In other words, for all its promise, the provisions of the Act may exert relatively little ultimate impact on the rights and interests of employees beyond the fact that they are now being informed and consulted about what the employer will inevitably do whether they approve of such a step or not.

1.1. The Objective of the Act

The essence of the Act is summed up in s.3, which provides that 'Subject to the   [14–05] provisions of this Act, an employee employed in an undertaking employing 50 or more employees has a right to information and consultation'.[12]

This entitlement is expressly without prejudice to other entitlements in respect   [14–06] of information and consultation, which are provided under the Protection of Employment Act 1977 as amended by the Protection of Employment Order 1996,[13] the EC (Protection of Employment) Regulations 2000,[14] the EC (Protection of Employees on Transfer of Undertakings) Regulations 2003,[15] the Transnational Information and Consultation of Employees Act 1996, and the EC (Transnational Information and Consultation of Employees) Act 1996 (Amendment) Regulations 1999,[16] and such rights as are protected under any other Act or instrument thereunder.[17] Equally, however, the fact that an employer has provided employees with their entitlements under the Transnational Information and Consultation of Employees Act 1996 (considered below) does not mean that [s]he has complied with the terms of the 2006 Act.[18]

---

10. Provision of information for the purposes of s.1(1) Employees (Provision of Information and Consultation) Act 2006 means transmission by the employer to one or more employees, or their representatives, or both, of data in order to enable them to acquaint themselves with the subject matter and to examine it.
11. For the purposes of s.1(1) of the 2006 Act, consultation means the exchange of views and establishment of dialogue between either or both of one or more employees or the employees' representative(s) on the one hand, and the employer on the other.
12. The Act is expressly without prejudice to various other listed enactments under which the employee is entitled to information and consultation. See s.3(2) Employees (Provision of Information and Consultation) Act 2006. Moreover, under s.21 specific obligations arise where what is at issue is a Transfer of Undertakings.
13. SI no. 370 of 1996. See s.3(2)(a) Employees (Provision of Information and Consultation) Act 2006.
14. SI no. 488 of 2000. See s.3(2)(a) *ibid.*
15. SI no. 131 of 2003. See s.3(2)(b) *ibid.*
16. SI no. 386 of 1999. See s.3(2)(c) *ibid.*
17. s.3(2)(d) *ibid.*
18. See s.3(3) *ibid.*

1.2. The Meaning of 'Information and Consultation'

[14–07] The general rule in s.3 *vis-à-vis* the right to information and consultation is extremely broad, both in the fact that it applies generally and also in that the concepts of 'information and consultation' defined in s.1 are relatively pliable. To this end, some clarification as to what type of information and consultation is at issue is provided in s.3 of the First Schedule to the Act. As we shall see, the Act envisages the possibility either of a 'standard form' agreement or a negotiated agreement forming the basis of the manner by which the information and consultation obligations are to be fulfilled. Section 3 of the First Schedule provides that, where a 'standard form' information and consultation agreement for the purposes of s.10 and of the First Schedule to the Act is at issue, information and consultation includes:

(a) provision of information on the recent and probable development of the undertaking's activities and economic situation;

(b) provision of information and consultation on the situation, structure and probable development of employment within the undertaking and on any anticipatory measures envisaged, in particular where there is a threat to employment; and

(c) provision of information and consultation on decisions likely to lead to substantial changes in work organisation or in contractual relations (including those covered by the Protection of Employment Act 1977 (as amended by the Protection of Employment Order 1996 and the European Communities (Protection of Employment) Regulations 2000, and the European Communities (Protection of Employees on Transfer of Undertakings) Regulations 2003.

Equally it would appear that, where a negotiated agreement under s.8 of the Act is at issue, there is scope for other types of information and consultation to be provided.

1.3. What Undertakings Are Covered?

[14–08] The obligations under the Act only apply to certain undertakings depending on the 'relevant workplace threshold'[19] – that is the number of workers in the undertaking. In other words, the Act will only apply to those undertakings with a comparatively large number of employees. Moreover, the obligations under the legislation were phased in gradually to different undertakings depending on their size. Thus the Act applied from 4 September 2006 to undertakings with at least 150 employees,[20] from 23 March 2007 to undertakings with at least 100 employees[21] and from 23 March 2008 to undertakings with at least 50 employees.[22]

---

19. s.4(2) *ibid.*
20. s.4(1)(a) *ibid.* See the Employees (Provision of Information and Consultation) Act 2006 (Prescribed Dates) Regulations 2006, SI no. 383 of 2006.
21. s.4(1)(b) *ibid.*
22. s.4(1)(c) *ibid.*

Significantly, therefore, the Act has no application to undertakings with less than 50 employees.

In this respect, the number of employees in an undertaking is reckoned by calcu- [14–09] lating the average number of employees employed therein during the two years before a request for information as to the number of employees is made[23] or, where the undertaking has been in existence for less than two years, then by reference to the average number of employees during the period of the undertaking's exist-ence.[24] Furthermore, if the number of employees in an undertaking falls below the relevant threshold and remains so for 12 months, and if an information and consultation forum has already been set up in respect of that undertaking, then at the request either of the employer or of a majority of the employees, the forum shall stand dissolved unless both parties agree to its continuation.[25]

In terms of assessing the 'relevant workforce threshold' in an undertaking, one [14–10] or more employees or employees' representatives[26] may request the employer to provide details of the number of employees in his or her undertaking.[27] Alterna-tively one or more employees may request the Labour Court or a nominee of the Labour Court to make the request referred to.[28] Where such a request is received by the court (or a nominee thereof), it is required to notify the employer as soon as reasonably practicable that such a request has been made,[29] request from him or her details as to the numbers of employees in the undertaking[30] and issue a written notification to the employee or employees who made the request, confirming the number of employees in the undertaking.[31]

1.4. The 'Opt In' Procedure and the Role of Employee Representatives

Under the terms of the Framework Directive, it was envisaged that the consulta- [14–11] tion procedure to which it referred could operate either on an 'opt in' or an 'opt out' basis.[32] Under the former, in order for the procedure to be activated it would be necessary that a certain number of employees would make a formal request to open negotiations – in other words, the employer or management of the under-taking would have no proactive responsibility in this regard – whereas under the latter an employer would have a proactive obligation to open negotiations unless a

---

23. s.5(1) *ibid.*
24. s.5(3) *ibid.*
25. s.5(7) *ibid.*
26. The general role of employees' representatives is discussed throughout this chapter.
27. s.5(2) *ibid.*
28. s.5(4) *ibid.*
29. s.5(5)(a) *ibid.*
30. s.5(5)(b) *ibid.*
31. s.5(5)(c) *ibid.*
32. See Keane, 'The Consultation Directive and the Development of Workplace Relations: From Sweat Shops to Talking Shops?', 2 *Employment Law Review* (2006), 37.

specified number of employees declined to avail of the opportunity. The 2006 Act chooses the former option – in other words, the obligation is on the employees to seek to bring about the information and consultation procedure: there is no obligation on management to take proactive steps to do so.[33]

[14–12] Having said that, the employer *is* bound to take the initial step of ensuring that employees' representatives are elected or appointed for the purposes of the Act.[34] Thus in s.6(2) it is provided that an employer (obviously within an undertaking with a sufficient relevant workplace threshold) *shall* arrange for the election or appointment of one or more employee representatives who will engage with the employer in terms of the provision of information and the requirement of consultation.[35] Significantly, in this context 'appointed' means appointed by the employees with the basis for such appointment being (if the employees so determine) such as is agreed by them with the employer.[36] Equally where it is the practice of the employer to engage in collective bargaining negotiations with a trade union or excepted body, employees who are members of such trade union or excepted body that represents 10 per cent or more of the employees in the undertaking shall be entitled to elect or appoint at least one employee's representative from amongst their members,[37] with the eventual number of such representatives being determined on a pro-rata basis by reference to the percentage of workers represented by the relevant union or excepted body and the overall number of employees' representatives elected or appointed.[38]

---

33. See Doherty, 'It's Good to Talk… Isn't it? Legislating for Information and Consultation in the Irish Workplace', 15(1) *DULJ* (2008), 120.
34. Under s.13 of the Employees (Provision of Information and Consultation) Act 2006 an employer is prohibited from penalising an employees' representative (through dismissal, any unfavourable change to his or her conditions of employment, any unfair treatment including selection for redundancy, or any other action prejudicial to his or her employment (s. 13(2) *ibid.*)) for performing his or her functions under the Act (s.13(1) *ibid.*). Significantly where an employees' representative is dismissed in such circumstances then [s]he may not recover both for such penalisation and for an unfair dismissal under the Unfair Dismissals Acts (s.13(7) *ibid.*). Moreover, the employees' representative must be afforded reasonable facilities, including paid time off to enable him or her to fulfil his or her functions promptly and efficiently (ss.13(3) and (4) *ibid.*), with provision of such facilities being granted having regard to the needs, size and capabilities of the undertaking concerned (s.13(5)). Generally, see the Labour Relations Commission Code of Practice on *Duties and Responsibilities of Employee Representatives and the Protection and Facilities Afforded Them by Their Employers* (1993), which was brought into force by the Industrial Relations Act 1990 Code of Practice on Employee Representatives (Declaration) Order 1993 (SI no. 69 of 1993), which declared that the code was a Code of Practice for the purposes of the Industrial Relations Act 1990.
35. s.6(1) Employees (Provision of Information and Consultation) Act 2006.
36. s.1 *ibid.* It is notable that this is different to the definition of 'appointed' under s.3 of the Transnational Information and Consultation of Employees Act 1996 discussed below.
37. s.6(3) *ibid.*
38. s.6(4) *ibid.* Disputes under this section may be referred by the employer, trade union, excepted body or one or more employees to the Labour Court.

As has been mentioned at the outset, it remains unclear how the role of employees'   [14–13]
representatives and the general rules on information and consultation contained
in the 2006 Act will fit in with existing rules of union representation under general
industrial relations law. As is discussed in Chapter 2 after all, the decision of the
Supreme Court in *Ryanair v Labour Court*[39] would seem to indicate that it would
be possible, through informal consultation with such employee representatives,
for an employer to fulfil his or her obligations under the Industrial Relations
(Amendment) Act of 2001.

1.5. Information and Consultation Agreements

Where the relevant workforce threshold is established such that it is clear that the   [14–14]
terms of the 2005 Act apply to the relevant undertaking, and where employees'
representatives have been elected or appointed, the employer is required to enter
into negotiations with employees or their representatives or both, to establish
information and consultation arrangements either[40]

- at his or her own behest[41]; or
- at the written request of at least 10 per cent of employees[42] received by
  the employer[43] or by the Labour Court or its nominees.[44] Where the
  request is received by the Labour Court or its nominees, it or they are
  required to notify the employer as soon as is reasonably practicable that
  the request has been made, to request from the employer the information
  required to verify the number and names of the employees who made
  the request,[45] and to issue a written notification to the employer and
  employees who have made the request confirming how many employees
  have made the request, and whether the employee threshold has been
  met on the basis of the information provided by the employees and
  employer.[46]

---

39. [2007] IESC 6, [2007] 4 IR 199.
40. s.7(1) Employees (Provision of Information and Consultation) Act 2006.
41. s.7(1)(a) *ibid.*
42. This minimum requirement of 10 per cent of employees (known as the 'employee threshold')
    means the lesser of 10 per cent of the employees in the undertaking (but not less in any case
    than 15 employees) or 100 employees: s.7(2) *ibid.*
43. In s.7(8) *ibid.* it is provided that if, at the time of the making of a request by employees to
    the employer to enter into negotiations under s.7(1)(b) the employee threshold is *not* so
    established, the employees in the undertaking are not permitted to make a further request for
    negotiations for two years after the date on which the previous or initial request was received
    by the employer.
44. Specific procedures are laid down to apply in a situation where the request is made to the
    court. See ss.7(3)–(5) *ibid.*
45. s.7(3)(b) *ibid.* Where such information is requested, the employer is required to provide such
    information as soon as is reasonably practicable: s.7(4) *ibid.*
46. s.7(3)(c) *ibid.*

[14–15] In this respect, it is further provided that when defining or implementing practical arrangements for information and consultation under the Act, the employer and the employee(s) or representatives shall operate in a spirit of cooperation having regard to their reciprocal rights and duties and taking into account the interest both of the undertaking and the employees.[47]

[14–16] Within six months of commencing such negotiations (or such longer period as may be agreed by the parties[48]) the parties are required to agree to establish an information and consultation arrangement.[49] As has been mentioned, such an agreement may exist in one of two forms, namely a *Negotiated Agreement* (including, where appropriate, an agreement that predated the coming into being of the Act) or a *Standard Agreement* using the standard rules as set out in the First Schedule to the Act.[50] In both types of arrangement there are specific rules as to non-disclosure of confidential information (by members of an Information and Consultation Forum [ICF], employee participants, employee representatives, experts providing assistance and the Labour Court or any member, registrar or officer or servant thereof[51] – though not by employers) relating to the undertaking, and this duty of confidentiality continues to operate even after the individual in question is no longer employed within the undertaking or his or her term of office has expired.[52] Furthermore, an employer may refuse to communicate information or to engage in consultation where, by reference to objective criteria, to do so would seriously harm the functioning of the undertaking or, more broadly, would be prejudicial to the undertaking[53] or where disclosure of such information is prohibited by any enactment.[54]

---

47. s.12 *ibid.* See, however, Doherty, 'It's Good to Talk… Isn't it? Legislating for Information and Consultation in the Irish Workplace', 15(1) *DULJ* (2008), 120 for the view that 'one of the defining features of this legislation… has been the distinct lack of cooperation on view between employers and labour throughout its gestation' (at 134).
48. s.7(7) Employees (Provision of Information and Consultation) Act 2006.
49. s.7(6) *ibid.*
50. Doherty makes the point that the requirements as far as the standard rules are concerned are considerably more onerous than those emerging out of negotiated agreements and to this extent that it is in the interests of an employer to ensure that a negotiated agreement is reached. Doherty, 'It's Good to Talk… Isn't it? Legislating for Information and Consultation in the Irish Workplace', 15(1) *DULJ* (2008), 120.
51. s.14(6) Employees (Provision of Information and Consultation) Act 2006.
52. ss.14(1) and (2) *ibid.* Disclosure of such information to employees or third parties who themselves owe a duty of confidentiality under the Act is possible: s.14(3) *ibid.*
53. s.14(4) *ibid.*
54. s.14(5) *ibid.*

1.5.1. Negotiated Agreements[55]

An agreement establishing one or more information and consultation arrange-   [14–17]
ments may be negotiated between employers and employees either directly (which
may be the preferred choice for employers who are resistant to any possible inference that they are prepared to negotiate collectively or with unions) or through
employee representatives.[56] Alternatively, the said agreement may be pre-existing,[57]
in the sense of pre-dating the date of commencement of the Act or the date of
its application to the undertaking in question.[58] In either case, the agreement is
deemed to have been approved by the employees either

- where a majority of employees in the undertaking who cast a preference
  do so in favour of the agreement[59];
- where a majority of employee representatives elected or appointed under
  the Act approve of the agreement in writing[60]; or
- where any other agreed procedure for determining employee support
  indicates the presence of such support.[61]

Where the terms of a negotiated agreement are *not* approved in accordance with   [14–18]
s.8(3), then the Standard Rules under the Act will apply, but not until two years
have passed,[62] and if during that period the parties re-enter negotiations and do
approve a negotiated agreement, then the Standard Rules do not apply at all.[63]

---

55. s.8 *ibid.*
56. Where a system of direct involvement is in operation for the whole or part of the relevant
     undertaking, it is necessary (in order to change to a system of representation by employees'
     representatives) for at least 10 per cent of the employees to whom the direct involvement
     system applies to make a written request to the employer for such change, and for a majority
     of employees to approve of such change through the casting of preferences (ss.11(2), (3), (4) and
     (5) *ibid.*). Where there is approval of such change, the employer must arrange for the election
     or appointment of representatives by the employees: s.11(6) *ibid.*
57. s.9 *ibid.* Where the agreement has not been in force for six months then the requirements
     in s.7 pertaining to the manner by which information and consultation arrangements are
     to be established will apply to it (s.9(6) *ibid.*). Otherwise, and provided that the pre-existing
     agreement satisfies the requirements of s.9, then the employer is not obliged to comply with a
     request under s.7: s.9(1) *ibid.*
58. s.9(1) *ibid.* In the case of a pre-existing agreement, it is presumed to be valid unless proved to
     the contrary and remains in force (a) for the period, if any, specified in the agreement; (b) in
     the case of an open-ended agreement, until it is brought to an end in accordance with its terms;
     or (c) until it is brought to an end by agreement of the parties: s.9(5) *ibid.*
59. ss.8(3)(a) and 9(3)(a) *ibid.* In such circumstances, it is necessary for the employer to ensure
     that the mechanism for determining such support is confidential and capable of independent
     verification and of being used by all employees: ss.8(4) and 9(4) *ibid.*
60. s.8(3)(b) *ibid.* Naturally no such possibility applies in the context of an agreement that existed
     before the coming into being of the Act.
61. ss.8(3)(c) and 9(3)(c) *ibid.*
62. s.10(4) *ibid.*
63. s.10(5) *ibid.*

[14–19]   The negotiated agreement[64] is required to specify[65]:

- its duration and the procedure for its renegotiation or review[66];
- the subjects for information and consultation[67];
- the method and time-frame by which information is to be provided, including whether it is to be provided directly to employees or through one or more employees' representatives[68];
- the method and time-frame by which consultation is to be conducted, including whether it is to be provided directly to employees or through one or more employees' representatives[69]; and
- procedures for dealing with confidential information.[70]

1.5.2. Standard Agreements

[14–20]   Section 10 of the 2006 Act provides for the operation of standard agreements governing the provision of information and consultation with employees. These apply either

- where the parties agree to adopt the Standard Rules in the First Schedule in the Act, to which reference has been made earlier, as well as the procedures for the election of employees' representatives contained in the Second Schedule to the Act[71];
- where the employer refuses to enter into negotiations with employees within three months of receiving a written request from employees under s.7(1) of the 2006 Act or a written notification from the Labour Court under s.7(3)(c)[72]; or
- where the parties cannot agree to the establishment of an information and consultation arrangement within the time limits specified in s.7 of the 2006 Act.[73]

---

64. The agreement must be in writing and dated, signed by the employer and approved by the employees, applicable to all employees to whom it relates, and available for inspection by those persons and at the place agreed between the parties. ss.8(2) and 9(2) *ibid.*
65. s.8(5) *ibid.*
66. ss.8(5)(a) and 9(7)(a) *ibid.* At any time before its expiry or within six months of its expiry the parties may agree to renew an agreement under s.8 (s.8(6) *ibid.*). No such provision applies in the context of a pre-existing arrangement, and hence it would appear that where such an agreement is due to expire then it may be reviewed in accordance with its own terms, and if no provision is made in this regard and the pre-existing agreement expires, then an employer would logically at that point have to start from the outset as far as the procedures for creating an information and consultation arrangement under the Act are concerned.
67. s.8(5)(b) *ibid.*
68. ss.8(5)(c) and 9(7)(c) *ibid.*
69. ss.8(5)(d) and 9(7)(d) *ibid.*
70. s.8(5)(e) *ibid.* Curiously no equivalent provision is required in the case of a pre-existing agreement under s.9.
71. s.10(1)(a) *ibid.*
72. s.10(1)(b) *ibid.*
73. s.10(1)(c) *ibid.*

Where these Standard Rules apply, the employer is required as soon as practicable but within six months to comply with such Standard Rules.[74]

1.5.3. Standard Form Election of Employees' Representatives

Where a standard form agreement is at issue employees' representatives are elected   [14–21] rather than appointed to an ICF and in the manner prescribed in the Second Schedule to the 2006 Act. Any employee employed in the State by the relevant undertaking on the date of the election is permitted to vote in such election.[75] Moreover, any employee employed in the State by the relevant undertaking for a continuous period of not less than one year on the nomination day is eligible to stand for election to the forum, provided that [s]he is nominated by at least two employees or a trade union or excepted body with whom it is the practice of the employer to negotiate collectively.[76] Where an election is necessary (that is, where there are more candidates than places on the forum) a poll must be taken in secret ballot and under the auspices of a returning officer[77] appointed by the employer.[78] The cost of such election is to be borne by the employer.[79]

1.6. The Information and Consultation Forum

Under the Standard Rules, an employee representative is elected to an ICF and it is   [14–22] this forum that forms the basis of the standard form process for provision of information to and consultation with employees. The ICF is composed of employees' representatives elected in accordance with the Second Schedule to the 2006 Act,[80] and must have at least three but no more than 30 members[81] and, subject to certain listed constraints (including the rule that the forum has the right to meet with the employer twice a year or in exceptional circumstances[82]), it is permitted

---

74. s.10(2) *ibid.* Such rules may be altered by agreement after two years from the establishment of the Information and Consultation Forum and thereafter on a basis agreed by the parties: s.10(3) *ibid.*

75. para.1 of the Second Schedule *ibid.*

76. para.2 of the Second Schedule *ibid.*

77. para.3 of the Second Schedule *ibid.*

78. para.4 of the Second Schedule *ibid.* The returning officer must perform his or her duties in a fair and reasonable manner and in the interests of an orderly and proper conduct of nomination and election procedures: para.5 *ibid.*

79. para.6 of the Second Schedule *ibid.*

80. paras.1(1) and (2) of the Second Schedule *ibid.*

81. para.1(4) of the First Schedule *ibid.*

82. The other mandatory rules of procedure in para.2(1) are that (a) the arrangements for meetings of the forum are to be agreed by the employer in consultation with the employees, but the employer is not permitted unreasonably to withhold consent to proposals made by employees or their representatives; (b) minutes of the meetings of the forum must be approved by both the employer and employee representatives; and (c) before any meeting with the employer the forum may meet without the employer being present. Without prejudice to ss.14(1)(2) and (3) of the Act, the members of the forum shall inform employees of the content and outcome of the meetings of the forum.

to adopt its own internal procedures[83] as well as its own internal structures.[84]

[14–23]   The employer is obliged to give information to the forum to enable it to conduct an adequate study and, where necessary, to prepare for consultation.[85] In this regard, as was noted earlier, 'information and consultation' includes

- information on the recent and probable development of the undertaking's activities and economic situation[86];
- information and consultation on the situation, structure and probable development of employment within the undertaking and on any anticipatory measures envisaged, in particular where there is a threat to employment[87]; and
- information and consultation on decisions likely to lead to substantial changes in work organisations or in contractual relations, including those arising out of a transfer of undertakings situation.[88]

[14–24]   Consultation shall take place then on the basis of that information (and on the basis of the opinion the employees' representatives are entitled to formulate having regard to such information) and at the relevant level of management and representation depending on the subject under discussion.[89] Moreover, such consultation shall occur

> in such a way as to enable the Forum to meet the employer and contain a response and the reasons for that response to any opinion they might form and with a view to reaching an agreement on decisions that have been taken that might lead to substantial changes in work organisation or in contractual relations.[90]

[14–25]   The employer is bound to bear the expenses incurred in the operation of the forum and to provide the members of the forum with any necessary and reasonable financial resources to enable them to perform their duties in an appropriate manner.[91]

[14–26]   Finally, after a minimum initial period of two years and thereafter as regularly as is agreed by the parties, the application of the Standard Rules to the relevant undertaking may be reviewed by the ICF and the employer, and may be altered on the basis of negotiations between these parties.[92]

---

83. para.2(1) of the First Schedule *ibid.*
84. para.1(4) of the First Schedule *ibid.*
85. para.4 of the First Schedule *ibid.*
86. para.3(a) of the First Schedule *ibid.*
87. para.3(b) of the First Schedule *ibid.*
88. para.3(c) of the First Schedule *ibid.*
89. para.4(2) of the First Schedule *ibid.*
90. paras.4(2)(d) and (e) of the First Schedule *ibid.*
91. para.5(1) of the First Schedule *ibid.*
92. s.10(3) *ibid.*

1.7. Dispute Resolution and Enforcement

Any disputes between employers and one or more employees or their representa-   [14–27]
tives concerning

- the election or appointment of employees' representatives under s.6[93];
- the negotiation process under ss.8 or 10;
- the interpretation of a negotiated agreement or pre-existing agreement under ss.8 or 9[94];
- the interpretation of the Standard Rules under s.10 and the First Schedule;
- the procedures for electing representatives to an ICF under the Second Schedule; or
- the interpretation or operation of a system of direct involvement under s.11

may be referred to the Labour Court[95] by the employer, the employee (where there is direct involvement) or the employees' representatives.[96]

Having investigated a dispute, the Labour Court may make a recommendation   [14–28]
on the matter[97] and subsequently, where the dispute has still not been resolved,
it may at the request of the employer or one or more employees or their representatives (and following a review of all relevant matters) make a determination
in writing.[98]

In addition, any complaints that the employer has penalised an employees' repre-   [14–29]
sentative contrary to the terms of s.13 may be referred to a Rights Commissioner

---

93. s.6(5) *ibid.*

94. In this respect see *Health Service Executive v Health Service Staff Panel* ICC/07/1, RIC 081,
15 February 2008, at the time of writing the only determination of the Labour Court made
pursuant to the 2006 Act.

95. The normal rules in terms of procedures before the Labour Court, which are considered in
Chapter 1, including rules in respect of administering oaths and compelling witnesses, apply
in this context. See ss.15(6), (7) and (8) as well as s.16 of the Employees (Provision of Information and Consultation) Act 2006.

96. s.15(1) *ibid.* Such a dispute may only be referred to the court where recourse has been had
to the internal dispute resolution procedures in place in the employment concerned and to
the Labour Relations Commission, and in both cases it has not been possible to resolve the
dispute: s.15(2) *ibid.*

97. s.15(3) *ibid.*

98. s.15(4) *ibid.* In addition disputes concerning situations where the employer refuses to communicate allegedly confidential information to employees under ss.14(4) or (5), situations where
the employer discloses information to an individual subject to the condition that the information is not to be disclosed owing to its confidential nature (s.14(1) *ibid.*), and situations
where there has allegedly been a breach of the obligation not to disclose confidential information under s.14(1) may be referred directly to the Labour Court for a determination by an
employer or one or more employees or their representatives: s.15(5) *ibid.*

pursuant to the Third Schedule to the Act.[99] Such complaint must be brought (by written notice[100]) within six months of the alleged date of the contravention to which the complaint relates,[101] although the Rights Commissioner may decide to hear a complaint brought up to six months after the expiration of the original six-month limitation period where [s]he is satisfied that the failure to bring the complaint within the original six month period was due to reasonable cause.[102]

[14–30]   Following a hearing into the matter,[103] the Rights Commissioner must make a decision (which must be communicated to the parties), declaring that the complaint is or is not well founded, and if the latter, it may require the employer to take a particular course of action and may require him or her to pay compensation to the employee at a level that is just and equitable, but not exceeding two years' remuneration in respect of the relevant employee's employment.[104] The decision of the Rights Commissioner may be appealed by either party to the Labour Court[105] within six weeks from the date on which it was communicated to the party or such greater period as is determined by the court in the particular circumstances.[106] Following a hearing into the matter, the Labour Court is required to make a determination in writing which may affirm, vary or set aside the decision of the Rights Commissioner.[107]

[14–31]   If the party against whom a decision of a Rights Commissioner or a Labour Court determination is made (either generally or in the context of a dispute in respect of employees' representatives under s.6 of the 2006 Act) fails to carry out such determination within the time period specified in the determination (or, if no time period is specified, within six weeks from the date the determination or decision has been communicated to the parties[108]) and where any time period for bringing an appeal has expired or, if any such appeal has been brought, it has been abandoned,[109] the matter can be referred to the Circuit Court which, without hearing any evidence other than that in respect of the failure of the party concerned to carry out the terms of the determination, shall make an order directing the party

---

99. para.1(1) of the Third Schedule *ibid.*
100. paras.1(6) and (7) of the Third Schedule *ibid.* The complaint is made by giving a written notice to the Rights Commissioner and written notice must also be given to the other party to the complaint.
101. para.1(4) of the Third Schedule *ibid.*
102. para.1(5) of the Third Schedule *ibid.*
103. para.1(2) of the Third Schedule *ibid.* The hearing must be held other than in public: para.1(8) *ibid.*
104. para.1(3) of the Third Schedule *ibid.*
105. para.2(1) of the Third Schedule *ibid.*
106. para.2(2) of the Third Schedule *ibid.*
107. para.2(1) of the Third Schedule *ibid.*
108. s.17(1) *ibid.*
109. s.17(2) *ibid.*

to carry out the determination in accordance with its terms.[110] Finally, any party to a dispute may appeal from a determination of the Labour Court to the High Court on a point of law[111] and the Labour Court may itself refer a question of law to the High Court for determination.[112]

1.7.1. *The Role of Inspectors*

More generally in terms of proactive efforts to ensure that the new approach to [14–32] information and consultation is followed, the Act provides for the appointment by the Minister of inspectors, who will have the power *inter alia* to enter onto premises and make examinations and enquiries as may be necessary to ascertain whether or not the Act is being complied with.[113] The role and function of such inspectors is considered in Chapter 1. As we have seen in Chapter 1, the role and functions of inspectors under the Act are now circumscribed by the terms of the decision of the Supreme Court (and the High Court) in *Gama Endustri Tesisleri Imalat Montag A.S. v Minister for Enterprise, Trade and Employment & Anor.*[114]

1.7.2. *Offences*

Beyond this, various offences are created under the 2006 Act. Thus it is an offence [14–33]

- to refuse to provide details of the number of employees in the undertaking under s.5[115];
- to fail to arrange for the election or appointment of employees' representatives under s.6(2)[116];
- for an employer to fail to put in place a system of representation through employees' representatives where one has been requested and approved by employees under s.11[117];
- for any party to disclose confidential information contrary to s.14[118];
- to obstruct or impede the work of an inspector, or to fail to produce a record requested by an inspector, or to produce or cause to be produced or knowingly allow to be produced a false or misleading record, or to give the inspector information in the knowledge that it is false or misleading contrary to s.18; or
- generally to fail to comply with the requirements under ss.7, 8, 9, 10, or 13 of the Act (considered above).[119]

---

110. s.17(1) *ibid.* Where the relevant determination or decision includes an order requiring the relevant party to pay compensation, the Circuit Court in making such order may direct that interest is to be paid on such compensation: s.17(3) *ibid.*
111. s.15(9) *ibid.* and para.2(6) of the Third Schedule.
112. s.15(10) *ibid.* and para.2(5) of the Third Schedule.
113. s.18 *ibid.*
114. [2009] IESC 37 (SC), [2005] IEHC 210 (HC).
115. s.19(2) Employees (Provision of Information and Consultation) Act 2006.
116. s.19(3) *ibid.*
117. s.19(4) *ibid.*
118. s.19(5) *ibid.*
119. s.19(1) *ibid.*

[14–34]   A person guilty of such offence shall be liable on summary conviction to a fine not exceeding €3,000 and six months in prison or both and, on conviction on indictment, to a fine not exceeding €30,000[120] or three years in prison or both.[121] If the offence is an ongoing one, for which the person has received initial conviction, [s]he can be fined up to €500 (summarily) or €5,000 (on indictment) per day for each day on which the offence continues.[122]

1.8. Information on Transfer of Undertakings

[14–35]   Finally, the Act deals specifically with obligations of a transferor of a business to a prospective transferee as far as provision of information in the context of a transfer of undertakings situation is concerned.[123] Thus the transferor (that is, the former employer) is required to notify the transferee (that is, the new employer) of any rights or obligations [s]he knows or ought to know arise from a contract of employment on the date of transfer and will be transferred to the transferee.[124] Whereas a failure to provide such information does not affect the transfer of that right or obligation and the rights of employees as a result,[125] equally if the failure in question involves a failure to provide information and documents which are necessary for the transferee to fulfil an obligation owed to an employee, and if as a result the transferee has been required to pay an amount of compensation to the employee by a decision of a Rights Commissioner or a determination of the Employment Appeals Tribunal and has done so, then the transferee can recover from the transferor in any court of competent jurisdiction the amount of any such compensation or the proportion of such compensation that court decides is attributable to the failure of the transferor to provide the information in question.[126] Equally, such action can only be taken where the transferee has previously served a written notice on the transferor indicating (in everyday language) the relevant obligation owed to the employee[s]; the class of information the transferor has in his or her possession or control and which the transferee does not have but regards as necessary to fulfil the obligation in question; and requesting that the information in question be transferred to him or her within a specified period of not more than 21 days.[127]

---

120. For a suggestion that this fine may be insufficient to act as a deterrent for undertakings under the legislation, see Doherty, 'It's Good to Talk… Isn't it? Legislating for Information and Consultation in the Irish Workplace', 15(1) *DULJ* (2008), 120.

121. s.20(1) *ibid.*

122. s.20(2) *ibid.*

123. s.21 *ibid.* The issue of the of the information to be provided to employees in the context of a transfer of undertakings situation is considered in more detail in Chapter 23.

124. s.21(3) *ibid.*

125. s.21(4) *ibid.*

126. s.21(5) *ibid.* This action is to be regarded as one founded on quasi contract: s.21(7) *ibid.*

127. s.21(6)(a) *ibid.* The transferee is also required to comply with any reasonable request from the transferor for further details as to the items of information being requested. Where this happens, any time period that elapses before such request is fulfilled will not form part of the minimum specified period contained in the transferee's notice to the transferor: s.21(6)(b) *ibid.*

2. The Transnational Information and Consultation of Employees Act 1996

Whereas the 2006 Act applies generally in the context of all undertakings with [14–36] the relevant worker threshold, and seeks to generate a general culture of requiring employees to be informed about significant developments within the undertaking in which they are employed, the Transnational Information and Consultation of Employees Act 1996 is aimed rather at ensuring that employees in undertakings that have establishments in more than one EU Member State will be informed about decisions taken about the overall undertaking and which may therefore be of significance both to the particular localised establishment in which the employee works, and thus also to the employee him or herself. This Act was aimed at implementing Directive 94/45 EC of 22 September 1996,[128] and it may be suggested that in light of the developments wrought by the 2006 Act the importance of the 1996 Act has, at the very least, been considerably reduced. Put simply, many if not all employers of undertakings that would formerly have attracted obligations under the 1996 Act will now owe potentially more onerous obligations under the 2006 Act.

2.1. Community-Scale Undertakings and Groups of Undertakings

The Act applies only to a limited category of undertakings, namely 'commu- [14–37] nity[129]-scale undertakings' – defined as undertakings with at least 1,000 employees within the Member States of the EC and at least 150 employees in each of at least two Member States – and 'community-scale groups of undertakings' – defined as groups of undertakings with at least 1,000 employees within the Member States, and at least one group undertaking with at least 150 employees in one Member State and at least one other group undertaking with at least 150 employees in another Member State.[130]

In determining whether an undertaking is a community-scale undertaking/group [14–38] of undertakings, the number of employees employed therein is taken to be the average number of employees (including part-time employees[131]) employed in the

---

128. At the time of writing, there is a proposal to amend this Directive to introduce, *inter alia*, greater clarity in terms of definitions and scoping issues; see 'Proposal for a European Parliament and Council Directive on the Establishment of a European Works Council or a Procedure in Community-Scale Undertakings and Community-Scale Groups of Undertakings for the Purposes of Informing and Consulting Employees' (Recast), COM(2008) 419 of 2 July 2008.

129. Community is defined in s.3 of the Act as meaning the EC including Norway, Iceland and Liechtenstein. The United Kingdom had formerly been excluded but this was altered under the terms of the European Communities (Transnational Information and Consultation of Employees Act 1996) (Amendment) Regulations of 1999 (SI no. 386 of 1999).

130. s.3 Transnational Information and Consultation of Employees Act 1996.

131. A part-time employee in this context means an employee who is in the continuous service of the employer for not less than 13 weeks and who is normally expected to work not less than eight hours per week for the employer: s.4(3) *ibid.*

undertaking/group of undertakings in the two years immediately preceding the request for the establishment of a Special Negotiating Body under s.10(1).[132] Moreover, on request by an employee's representative, the central management of the relevant undertaking must give such information about the numbers and status of employees employed in the undertaking[s] to that representative as is reasonably necessary to enable the numbers of employees working in the undertaking to be assessed.[133] It is an offence for the employer to fail to give such information when requested.[134]

[14–39]   **2.2. The Provision of Information and Consultation**
The essence of the protection under the Act is contained in s.8 of the Act, which provides that in the case of all community-scale undertakings/groups of undertakings,[135] it is required that either a European Works Council or arrangements for the information and consultation of employees be established[136] in order to improve the rights of employees in such undertakings[137] to be informed and consulted.[138] Responsibility for creating such arrangements rests with the central management[139] of the community-scale undertaking/group of undertakings[140] or,

---

132. s.4(1) *ibid.*
133. s.4(2) *ibid.*
134. s.18(1) *ibid.*
135. Where a European Works Council or a European Employees' Forum is to be established in respect of a community-scale group of undertakings that consists of undertakings that are themselves community-scale undertakings/groups of undertakings, then the European Works Council or European Employees' Forum should be established at the level of the group unless an agreement created pursuant to s.11(1) specifically provides otherwise: s.8(2) *ibid.*
136. An exception to this rule exists in the case of a community-scale undertaking/group of undertakings in which on 22 September 1996 (the date on which the Act was brought into force pursuant to the Transnational Information and Consultation of Employees Act 1996 (Commencement) Order(SI no. 276 of 1996) there was a pre-existing agreement or multiplicity of agreements (s. 6(2) *ibid.*) (including an open-ended agreement subject to review and/ or alteration by the parties (s. 7(8) *ibid.*) covering the entire workforce, accepted by a majority of the workforce to whom it applies (s. 6(7) *ibid.*) and providing for the transnational information and consultation of employees (s. 6(1) *ibid.*). Where this is the case, such an agreement may be renewed within the period of six months before it expires (s. 6(4) *ibid.*) and where this does not happen, the 1996 Act applies to the relevant undertaking[s] thereafter (s. 6(5) *ibid.*).
137. Unless a wider application is provided for in an agreement created pursuant to s.11(1), the powers and competencies of any such European Works Council or other information and consultation procedure is deemed to cover all the establishments in the relevant community-scale undertaking and all the group undertakings in the case of a community-scale group of undertakings: s.8(3) *ibid.*
138. s.8(1) *ibid.* Consultation in this regard means the exchange of views and establishment of dialogue between employees' representatives and the central management: s.3 *ibid.*
139. For the purposes of s.3 *ibid.*, 'central management' means, in the case of a community-scale undertaking, the central management of the undertaking and, in the case of a community-scale group of undertakings, the central management of the controlling undertaking.
140. s.9(1) *ibid.*

where the central management is not located in an EU Member State, with the central management's representative agent in the Member State, provided that it has management responsibilities for the undertaking/group of undertakings and has been nominated in this regard by the central management.[141]

2.2.1. *The Special Negotiating Body*

The first step in facilitating the creation of an information and consultation [14–40] procedure is to establish a Special Negotiating Body (SNB), whose function is to negotiate[142] with central management[143] with the purpose of creating a written agreement or agreements for the information and consultation of employees and to agree on matters relating to such agreements.[144] Establishment of an SNB *may* be done on the initiative of the central management of the relevant undertakings or group of undertakings and *must* be done at the written request to central management[145] of at least a total of 100 employees or their representatives[146] spread over at least two undertakings or establishments that are themselves spread over at least two Member States.[147] The function of this body is to negotiate with central management for the establishment either of a European Employees' Forum or an information and consultation procedure.

In terms of its membership,[148] the SNB must contain no less than three members [14–41] and no more members than the number of EU Member States at the relevant

---

141. s.9(2) *ibid.* In the absence of any such representative, responsibility passes to the management of the establishment or group undertaking in which the greatest number of employees are employed in any one Member State.

142. The reasonable expenses of such negotiations must be borne by central management: ss.11(7) and (8) *ibid.*

143. In order to conclude such an agreement, the central management is required to convene a meeting with the SNB (s.11(2) *ibid.*). Equally, the SNB may decide by at least two-thirds of the votes of members present not to open negotiations with central management (s.11(4) *ibid.*), in which case the entire procedure to conclude an agreement with management shall cease (s.11(5) *ibid.*) and no request to convene a new SNB can be made for two years (s.11(6) *ibid.*).

144. s.11(1) *ibid.*

145. The request may be lodged with local rather than central management where the identity or location of central management is not readily discernible to the employees or representatives and, where this happens, local management must ensure that it is passed on to central management within 15 working days from its receipt: s.13(3) *ibid.*

146. Representatives in this context include representatives already recognised by the undertaking or group of undertakings for collective bargaining or information and consultation purposes: s.10(2) *ibid.*

147. s.10(1) *ibid.*

148. The central and local managements of the relevant undertakings must be informed in writing as soon as practicable after the election or appointment of members to the SNB of its composition: s.10(5) *ibid.* Representatives to an SNB, European Works Council or in connection with an arrangement for the information and consultation of employees must be either appointed (that is, appointed by employees or by central management on a basis agreed with employees) or elected in accordance with the terms of the First Schedule to the Act.

time.[149] Each Member State in which the relevant undertaking has an establishment or in which the relevant group of undertakings has the controlling undertaking of one or more controlled undertakings[150] must be represented by at least one member.[151] In addition, there must be one additional member from each Member State in which between 25 per cent and 50 per cent of the employees of the undertaking or group of undertakings are employed, two additional members from each Member State in which 50 per cent and 75 per cent of such employees are employed, and three additional members from a Member State in which more than 75 per cent of such employees are employed.[152] In the case of representatives to an SNB (as well as representatives to a European Employees' Forum or a European Works Council), such representatives must be elected or appointed by the employees whom they represent, or appointed by the central management on a basis agreed with those employees.[153] Moreover, as with the 2006 Act there is specific provision that such representatives may not be penalised in any way (up to and including dismissal) for exercising their functions under the Act,[154] and must instead be reasonably facilitated in their work including being given paid time off work to fulfil their functions.[155]

2.2.2. Information and Consultation Agreements

[14–42]   The objective of the negotiations to be carried out between central management and the SNB must be to reach an agreement or agreements[156] and in this

---

149. s.10(4)(a) *ibid.* as amended by the European Communities (Transnational Information and Consultation of Employees Act 1996) (Amendment) Regulations 2007 (SI no. 599 of 2007). Beyond Member States, it is provided that employees' representatives from countries that are *not* within the Community may be permitted to participate in the meetings and activities of the SNB but not entitled to vote: s.10(4)(d) *ibid.*

150. Guidance for determining whether or not an undertaking is a controlled or a controlling undertaking for the purposes of the legislation is provided in s.5 *ibid.*

151. s.10(4)(b) *ibid.*

152. s.10(4)(c) *ibid.*

153. s.14 *ibid.* In addition, the First Schedule to the Transnational Information and Consultation of Employees Act 1996 provides for a default mechanism for election of employees' representatives. Written notification to central management of their election or appointment shall, unless the contrary is proved, be regarded as proof that they have been duly elected or appointed.

154. s.17(1) *ibid.*

155. ss.17(2) and (4) *ibid.* Generally, see the Labour Relations Commission Code of Practice on *Duties and Responsibilities of Employee Representatives and the Protection and Facilities Afforded Them by Their Employers* (1993), which was brought into force by the Industrial Relations Act 1990 Code of Practice on Employee Representatives (Declaration) Order 1993 (SI no. 69 of 1993), which declared that the code was a Code of Practice for the purposes of the Industrial Relations Act 1990.

156. An agreement of this kind must determine *inter alia* the undertakings or establishments to which it refers, its duration and the procedure for its renegotiation, and the methods by which the information conveyed to representatives is to be renegotiated: s.12(3) Transnational Information and Consultation of Employees Act 1996.

regard, the various relevant bodies are required to work in a spirit of cooperation with due regard to their reciprocal rights and duties.[157] Essentially the purpose of such agreement is to create some arrangement where provision of information and consultation can occur, either through the establishment of a European Employees' Forum[158] or otherwise[159] through some other information and consultation procedure.[160] Where an agreement provides for a European Employees' Forum or an information and consultation procedure, then the forum itself (or the representatives to the consultation procedure) may renegotiate the agreement with central management rather than having this function performed by the SNB.[161] Moreover, where there is some dispute concerning the interpretation or operation of an agreement, then this may be referred by central management or employees' representatives to an independent arbitrator appointed by the parties,[162] or where they cannot agree on this, by the Labour Court.[163] Appeals against the decision of such arbitrator can only be made on a point of law.[164]

2.2.3. European Works Council

In the alternative (that is, where a European Employees' Forum or an information [14–43] and consultation procedure has not been created) a European Works Council shall be established either

- where the central management and the SNB agree to this[165];
- where central management refuses to commence negotiations within six months of a request from the employees or representatives under s.10(1) to establish a SNB[166]; or

---

157. s.16 *ibid.* See also s.12(1).

158. Where a European Employees' Forum is to be created, the agreement must also determine the composition of the forum, its functions and the procedure for information and consultation, the venue, frequency and duration of meetings, and the financial and other resources to be allocated to it: s.12(4) *ibid.*

159. s.12(2) *ibid.*

160. Where an alternative form of information and consultation procedure is envisaged, the agreement must specify what the procedure is, the issues for information and consultation, the methods by which representatives in the different Member States can meet to exchange views in respect of such information, and the financial and other resources to be allocated to the procedure: s.12(5) *ibid.*

161. s.12(8) *ibid.* In fact the SNB only remains in force for as long as it has the function of negotiating for an agreement and automatically dissolves when it ceases to have this function: s.12(9) *ibid.*

162. s.21(1) *ibid.* Such arbitrations are not governed by the Arbitration Acts 1954 and 1980: s.23 *ibid.*

163. s.21(2) *ibid.* Both parties pay their own costs of such arbitration: s.21(5) *ibid.*

164. s.21(6) *ibid.*

165. s.13(1)(a) *ibid.*

166. s.13(1)(b) *ibid.* It is specifically provided that where the request in question has been made to local management and there has been an avoidable or unreasonable delay in transferring this request to *central* management, this will not, of itself, justify extending the six-month time limit in s.13(1)(b). See s.10(3)(c) *ibid.*

- where after three years from the date of this request, the parties are unable to conclude an agreement and the SNB has not formally taken a decision not to negotiate with central management.[167]

[14–44] The procedural and other requirements in respect of a European Works Council are laid down in the Second Schedule to the Act.[168] Thus the council is to be composed of employees' representatives who are employees of the community-scale undertaking/group of undertakings and who are either appointed (by employees or by management on a basis agreed with employees[169]) or elected in accordance with the terms of the First Schedule to the Act. The council should have no less than three and no more than 30 members, although provision is made for election amongst its members of a select committee of no more than three members, if the size of the council warrants this.[170] Moreover, central management is required to ensure, so far as it is able to, that each Member State in which the community-scale undertaking has establishments or a controlling or controlled undertaking is represented by one member, and (like the procedures governing the composition of an SNB, discussed above) that there are supplementary members of the council from particular Member States as reflects the strength of the undertaking[s] in those Member States.[171]

[14–45] The competence of the council[172] is confined to information and consultation on matters that concern the undertaking[s] as a whole, or that concern at least two establishments or group undertakings situated in different Member States.[173] Within these parameters the council is entitled to meet with central management at least annually to be informed and consulted (on the basis of a report drawn up by central management) about the progress of the relevant undertaking/group of undertakings and its prospects.[174] The council (or a select committee

---

167. s.13(1)(c) *ibid.*
168. Significantly the expenses of the council are to be borne by central management: para.6 of the Second Schedule *ibid.*
169. s.3 *ibid.*
170. para.2 *ibid.*
171. See para.4 *ibid.*
172. After four years, the council is required to examine whether or not to open negotiations with central management with a view to concluding an agreement to create an information and consultation arrangement pursuant to s.11, in which case, ss.11 and 12 will apply, save that the references in those sections to a 'special negotiating body' should be read as referring to a 'European Works Council': para.7 of the Second Schedule *ibid.*
173. para.1(1) of the Second Schedule *ibid.* In the case of undertakings/groups of undertakings referred to in s.9(2) – that is, where the central management is not located in a Member State – the council's competence is confined to those matters concerning either all the establishments/group undertakings located within the Member States, or at least two establishments/group undertakings located in different Member States: para.1(2) *ibid.*
174. para.5(1) *ibid.* The meeting must relate in particular to the structure, economic and financial situation and probable trends in employment, investments and substantial changes concerning the organisation, introduction of new working methods or production processes, transfer of

thereof[175]) is also required to be informed and to meet central management (and such other level of management as central management regards as more appropriate) where there are exceptional circumstances affecting the employees' interests to a considerable extent in the event of relocation, the closure of establishments/ undertakings or collective redundancies.[176]

The council can determine its own rules of procedures, save that [14–46]

- arrangements for meetings are to be agreed by central management in consultation with employees or their representatives (and central management may not unreasonably withhold consent to proposals made by employees or their representatives)[177];
- the minutes of such meetings are to be approved jointly by management and the employees' representatives to the council[178];
- before any such meeting with central management the council or a select committee thereof is entitled to meet privately[179];
- save where confidential information is at issue, the council is required to inform the relevant employees' representatives or the workforce directly of the content and outcome of the relevant information and consultation procedures[180]; and
- the council or select committee may be assisted by such experts of its choice as are necessary for it to carry out its tasks.[181]

2.2.4. *Confidential Information*

As with the 2006 Act, the 1996 Act provides for the possibility that an SNB, [14–47] European Employees' Forum or European Works Council might be presented with confidential information. The general rule is that members of these bodies may not reveal such information provided to them in confidence.[182] Moreover, the central management may refuse to disclose information that it claims is commercially sensitive to such bodies, where it can show that the disclosure would be

---

production, mergers, cutbacks or closures of undertakings, establishments or important parts thereof and collective redundancies: para.5(2) *ibid.*

175. Where the meetings in question are between central management and a select committee of the council, those members who are representatives of undertakings that are directly concerned with the measures in question are also entitled to participate in the relevant meeting: para.5(5) *ibid.*

176. para.5(3) *ibid.*

177. para.3(a) *ibid.*

178. para.3(b) *ibid.*

179. para.3(c) *ibid.*

180. para.3(d) *ibid.*

181. para.3 (e) of the Second Schedule *ibid.*

182. s.15(1) *ibid.* An employees' representative or expert may, in accordance with his or her duties as a member, reveal such information to the body itself, to another employees' representative to the procedure, or to the member, body or person [s]he is or was then employed to advise.

significantly and adversely likely to prejudice the economic or financial position of the undertaking or group, and where the information should objectively be withheld on the basis of criteria agreed between the SNB, European Works Council, European Employment Forum, or representatives to the information and consultation procedure and the central management.[183]

2.3. Enforcement

[14–48] Somewhat curiously, there is no provision in the 1996 Act (as there is, for example, in the 2006 Act) whereby complaints can be made to a Rights Commissioner or the Labour Court in respect of breaches of the Act and whereby compensation can be awarded in respect of such breaches. Rather the only mechanism by which compliance with the Act can be compelled is through the prosecution of various offences created within the terms of the Act.

Thus it is an offence[184]:

- for the central management of an undertaking/group of undertakings to refuse to provide information about the number and status of its employees following a request by an employee under s.4(2), or for it unreasonably and wilfully to obstruct or delay the provision of such information[185];
- for the central management of an undertaking or group of undertakings to fail to comply with the requirements in respect of a European Works Council, pursuant to s.13(2) and the Second Schedule to the Act[186]; or

---

183. Disputes concerning the withholding of allegedly commercially sensitive information and concerning the question of whether information revealed to employees' representatives is confidential may be referred either by central management or the employees' representative to an independent arbitrator appointed by the Minister (s.20(1) *ibid.*). Such proceedings shall themselves endeavour to protect the confidentiality of the information (s.20(4) *ibid.*), nor is there any appeal from such arbitration save on a point of law (s.20(5) *ibid.*). Significantly, the terms of the Arbitration Acts 1954 and 1980 do not apply to such arbitrations.

184. Under s.18(4) of the Transnational Information and Consultation of Employees Act 1996, provision is made for a director, secretary or other officer of a body corporate to be personally liable for offences committed under the Act by the body corporate, where such offences were committed with the connivance or consent of, or were attributable to, the neglect of such person.

185. s.18(1) *ibid.* A person guilty of such offence is liable on summary conviction to a fine not exceeding €1,904.61 and/or six months in prison, and on indictment to a fine not exceeding €12,697.38 and/or three years in prison. Moreover, if the offence continues after conviction, the perpetrator shall be liable on summary conviction to a maximum fine of €253.95, and on indictment to a maximum fine of €1,269.74 per day for each day on which the offence continues. See ss.19(1) and (2) *ibid.*

186. s.18(2) *ibid.* A person guilty of such offence is liable on summary conviction to a fine not exceeding €1,904.61 and/or six months in prison, and on indictment to a fine not exceeding €12,697.38 and/or three years in prison. Moreover, if the offence continues after conviction,

- for a person to whom s.15(1) refers to reveal information that was provided to him or her in confidence, save in the circumstances permitted in s.15.[187]

---

the perpetrator shall be liable on summary conviction to a maximum fine of €253.95 and on indictment to a maximum fine of €1,269.74 per day for each day on which the offence continues. See ss.19(1) and (2) *ibid.*

187. s.15(3) *ibid.* A person guilty of such offence is liable on summary conviction to a fine not exceeding €1,904.61 and/or six months in prison, and on indictment to a fine not exceeding €12,697.38 and/or three years in prison: s.19(3) *ibid.*

CHAPTER 15

Health and Safety in Employment Law

Introduction

This chapter offers an analysis of the legal framework covering an employer's obli-   [15–01]
gations to employees in the context of health and safety. In this regard, it is necessary to focus not only on the well-established negligence principles applying to
health and safety issues, but also on the comprehensive – and, in many respects,
revolutionary – legislative scheme that now exists following the enactment of the
Safety, Health and Welfare at Work Act 2005.[1] This Act repeals and replaces in its
entirety its predecessor, the Safety, Health and Welfare at Work Act 1989. At the
time of writing, the 2005 Act has been in force for less than five years and as such
many aspects of the legislation still require clarification through judicial interpretation. Noteworthy examples of such aspects of the legislation are referred to
throughout this chapter.

1. Health and Safety in Employment: The Common Law Framework

At common law, an employer may be liable in negligence either for being person-   [15–02]
ally guilty of breaching a duty of care, or when vicariously liable for the wrongs
of an employee.[2] A separate section of this chapter is devoted to vicarious liability
in the context of health and safety, but reference will be made to the concept as
necessary in the course of analysis throughout.

1.1. The Common Law Position: Historical Overview

An outline of the history of the liability of employers is necessary for an under-   [15–03]
standing of the current common law position in the law of negligence in this area.
One of the most significant points to be made at the outset is that the development of the employer's personal and non-delegable duty to employees occurred

---

1. For detailed treatment generally, see Byrne, *Safety, Health and Welfare at Work Act 2005*
    (Thomson Round Hall, 2006); Shannon, *Health and Safety: Law and Practice* (Thomson
    Round Hall, 2007).
2. The concept of vicarious liability is analysed in detail in Chapter 3.

as a direct response to the now abolished defence of common employment, 'a doctrine which lawyers who are gentlemen have long disliked'.[3] This defence can be traced back to *Priestley v Fowler*,[4] but was more clearly articulated in *Hutchinson v York, Newcastle and Berwick Rwy Co.*[5] in 1850, where Baron Alderson held that an employer could not be held vicariously liable for tortious injury caused by one employee to another. This common employment rule was subsequently endorsed by the House of Lords[6] and by the Irish courts.[7] The doctrine was identified by Murnaghan J in the following terms in *Feeney v Pollexfen & Co.*: 'if the employer has selected a suitable and competent foreman or manager, by the doctrine of common employment the employer is not liable for injury which has been caused by the negligence of the foreman or manager'.[8]

[15–04] With contributory negligence – which was then a complete defence to any action – and *volenti non fit injuria*, this doctrine of common employment embodied one of the so-called 'unholy trinity'[9] of defences that enabled employers to defend actions brought against them by their employees. That the doctrine was widely regarded as harsh is evident from a number of prominent judicial and academic statements to that effect, with it being variously described as 'an embarrassment to the common law',[10] a rule that 'gave rise to much apparent hardship and to much debate',[11] and an illogical dogma that had 'little regard to reality or to modern ideas of economics or industrial conditions'.[12] This perception of the unfairness of the common employment doctrine led the courts to attempt to find ways to mitigate its harshness. In this regard, it became extremely important that the doctrine precluded only the employer's *vicarious* liability – it did not rule out its *personal* liability. This caused judicial attention to be shifted onto the capacity for holding an employer personally liable – and thus led to the development of the doctrine of the non-delegable duty of the employer. Under this doctrine, employers did not only have to ensure that they themselves took reasonable care for their employees' safety: they also had to ensure that all reasonable care was taken by any person(s)

---

3. *Speed v Thomas Swift & Co.* [1943] KB 557, 569 *per* MacKinnon LJ.
4. (1837) 3 M&W 1, 150 ER 1030.
5. (1850) 5 ex. ch.343.
6. *Bartonshill Coal Co. v Reid* (1858) 3 Macq 266 (Sco) at 284 *per* Lord Cranworth. The Law Lords in *Bartonshill* adopted the reasoning of Shaw CJ in the Supreme Court of the United States in *Farwell v Boston and Worcester Railroad Corporation*, 4 Metcalf 49, which 'was printed in Macqueen's Reports as a footnote to [*Bartonshill*], and has ever since been treated by judges and text writers as an authoritative exposition of the common law upon the subject' (*per* Fitzgibbon J in *Ewart v Polytechnic Touring Association* [1933] 1 IR 230, 240).
7. *Potts v Plunkett*, 9 ICLR 290; *Conway v Belfast and Northern Counties Railway Co.*, IR 11 CL 345.
8. [1931] 1 IR 589, *per* Murnaghan J at 615.
9. Fleming, *The Law of Torts* (9th ed., Sydney LBC Services, 1998), at 568.
10. Redgrave, *Health and Safety* (2nd ed., Butterworths, 1993), *liv.*
11. *Thomas v Quartermaine* (1887) 18 QBD 685 at 692, *per* Bowen LJ.
12. *Wilsons and Clyde Coal Co. Ltd. v English* [1938] AC 57 at 80, *per* Lord Wright.

they engaged to discharge this duty. The concept of the non-delegable duty – and, in particular, its relationship to the concept of vicarious liability – is discussed in detail below.[13]

1.2. Relationship between Common Law and Contractual Health and Safety Obligations

It is well established that the basis for the application of negligence principles in the employment context is an implied term in the contract of employment that the employer will provide a safe working environment for the employee.[14] The potential for inconsistencies between the contract of employment and common law negligence principles can, however, give rise to difficulties. In *Johnstone v Bloomsbury Health Authority*[15] the plaintiff, a junior hospital doctor, argued that he had been required by his employers to work such excessively long hours as to foreseeably damage his health. His employers argued that this contention, even if it were correct, gave rise to no cause of action in negligence since the plaintiff's contract expressly obliged him to work long hours. This express contractual provision, they argued, took priority over any duty in tort, or any implied term of the contract, to safeguard the health of the plaintiff as an employee. The Court of Appeal accepted that the express terms of the contract superseded any tortious or implied contractual duty, but a majority[16] refused to strike out the claim, holding that on the proper construction of the contract of employment, the express and implied duties were not inherently in conflict. Accordingly, the defendants had not established beyond argument that they had in fact secured by means of the contract the right to insist that the plaintiff work so hard as to endanger his health and well-being. It should be noted in this regard that in *Johnstone*, no cause of action premised on tort was apparently pleaded; rather, the focus of the case rested on the contractual sphere.

[15–05]

Notwithstanding the fact that the majority in *Johnstone* declined to strike out the plaintiff's case, the implications of the approach taken in that case will be regarded by some as troubling. As Buckley has remarked, 'the implication… that if the contract unambiguously so provides an employer can at common law acquire the right foreseeably to injure the health of his employees seems, to say the least, unattractive'.[17]

[15–06]

Subsequent developments, however, bear out this sense of unease with the prospect of the protection of the tort of negligence being emasculated by express

[15–07]

---

13. See below, paras.[2.1] – [2.2].

14. See for example, *Martin v Lancashire County Council/Bernadone v Pall Mall Services Group* [2000] 3 All ER 544, [2001] 1 ICR 197, [2000] IRLR 487.

15. [1992] QB 333. For comment, see Phang [1993] *JBL* 242.

16. Sir Nicolas Browne-Wilkinson VC and Stuart-Smith LJ; Leggatt LJ dissenting.

17. Buckley, *The Law of Negligence* (4th ed., LexisNexis Butterworths, 2005), 17.02, at p.360. See also White, 'The Employer's Duty and His Servant's Work-Load', 9 *ILT* (1991), 240.

contractual clauses. Thus in the leading House of Lords judgment in *Barber v Somerset County Council,*[18] *Johnstone* was referred to with approval, with Lord Rodger observing that a tortious duty of reasonable care to protect employees from stress may 'not sit easily with…contractual arrangements'.[19]

1.3. Relationship between Common Law and Statutory Health and Safety Obligations

[15–08] There is a close overlap between the common law duty of care in negligence and statutory obligations placed on employers under workplace health and safety legislation.[20] It is of course the case that a court must assess an employer's liability in negligence separately from any statutory obligations owed to the employee, but the reality is that the negligence inquiry is increasingly being informed and influenced by a consideration of statutory obligations. McMahon and Binchy suggest that the statutory code sends three messages to guide the courts in cases in which employers are sued in negligence: first, the statutory regime underlines the overall social support that exists for employees and what the authors refer to as 'paternalistic protective values'; secondly, the specificity of its provisions provides guidance as to what an employer might be expected to do in specific situations; and finally, 'the procedures prescribed by statutes may easily translate into useful models for what constitutes a "safe system of work" for the purposes of employers' liability litigation at common law'.[21] If the latter two functions are considered together, a number of high-profile examples from the recent Irish jurisprudence are apparent.

[15–09] A topical example of the interplay between statutory duties and the principles applicable in a negligence action is the approach taken by the courts in cases of workplace bullying, harassment and stress, dealt with in Chapter 16. Two significant instances in which the courts have clearly had regard to this interplay are the High Court judgments in *McGrath v Trintech Technologies*[22] and *Quigley v Complex Tooling and Moulding Ltd.*[23]

[15–10] In *McGrath v Trintech* the relevance of the health and safety legislation to a claim for occupational stress was considered by the High Court. The plaintiff claimed, *inter alia,* damages for personal injuries, which he alleged he suffered as a result of occupational stress. He argued that the defendant employer was in breach of its obligations pursuant to the Safety, Health and Welfare at Work Act 1989 and

---

18. [2004] UKHL 13, [2004] 1 WLR 1089, discussed in detail in Chapter 16.
19. [2004] 1 WLR 1089, 1101.
20. For detailed treatment of the action in breach of statutory duty in health and safety law, see Foster, 'Breach of Statutory Duty and Risk Management in Occupational Health and Safety Law: New Wine in Old Wineskins?', 14 *TLR* (2006), 79.
21. McMahon and Binchy, *Law of Torts* (3rd ed., Butterworths, 2000), 18.24, at p.488.
22. [2005] IEHC 342, [2005] 4 IR 382, [2005] ELR 49.
23. [2005] IEHC 71, [2009] 1 IR 349, [2005] ELR 305. Although the High Court judgment was reversed by the Supreme Court, this did not affect the approach taken by Lavan J on the law.

the 1993 Regulations made thereunder. Although the High Court (Laffoy J) ultimately found against the plaintiff on this point, in principle the court had no difficulty with the argument that the 1989 Act and the 1993 Regulations covered psychiatric health and psychiatric injuries. Laffoy J stated:

> It is undoubtedly the case that the general duties imposed by the Act of 1989 extend to the protection of the psychiatric health of employees and comprehend the obligation to provide assistance and measures which safeguard the employee against psychiatric injury induced by the stress and pressures of the employee's working conditions and work load. As is pointed out in McMahon & Binchy at p.605 (footnote 93), almost with exception, the 1993 Regulations provide 'for strict and even absolute duties'. However, in a civil action the plaintiff must establish that the injury was caused by the breach. The question which arises in this case is whether the plaintiff has established a breach of a statutory duty in consequence of which he has suffered the injury and loss of which he complains.[24]

Health and safety law was also expressly referred to in the case of *Quigley v Complex Tooling and Moulding*,[25] where Lavan J stated:　　[15–11]

> It has been a fairly recent movement towards thinking that an employer must take care not only of the physical health of their employees, for example by providing safe equipment, but also must take reasonable care to protect them against mental injury, such as is complained of by the plaintiff in this case. It follows on from this that employers now have an obligation to prevent their employees from such that would cause mental injury, i.e. stress, harassment and bullying in the workplace.[26]

The most important recent legislative initiative in this area is now the Safety,　[15–12] Health and Welfare at Work Act 2005.[27] In cases of accidents at work, breach of statutory duty is almost invariably pleaded in addition to negligence. There are important differences between the two claims, however, not least of which is that breaching a statutory duty does not in and of itself mean that liability in negligence will result, unless the existence of the statutory duty gives rise to the existence of a common law duty of care. As Healy has noted, 'The fact that a defendant is found to have breached a statutory duty enacted for the benefit of persons such as the plaintiff itself encourages the court to locate a corresponding duty under the common law'.[28]

Developments under the 2005 legislation are awaited with interest when its　[15–13] potential to inform the contours of the negligence action can be witnessed. To

---

24. [2005] 4 IR 382, 418–419.
25. [2009] 1 IR 349.
26. *ibid.*, at p.363.
27. For detailed analysis, see Byrne, *Safety, Health and Welfare at Work Act 2005* (Thomson Round Hall, 2006); Shannon, *Health and Safety: Law and Practice* (Thomson Round Hall, 2007).
28. Healy, *Principles of Irish Torts* (Clarus Press, 2006), 233.

date, however, the principal source of judicial comment on the relevance of health
and safety legislation remains the case law emanating from the previous health
and safety regime, the Safety, Health and Welfare at Work Act 1989. This legislation was primarily designed at ensuring regulation rather than as enhancing
civil liability – so much so that s.60(1) of the Act expressly provided that the
core duties owed by an employer under the statute (those laid down in ss.6–11)
were not to be taken independently to ground a civil cause of action, but were
instead enforceable by criminal prosecution. Section 28 of the 1989 Act enabled
the Minister to pass regulations applicable to all work activities, however, and
s.60(2) provided that the breach of a duty imposed by the regulations 'shall, so
far as it causes damage, be actionable except in so far as the regulations provide
otherwise'. The Safety, Health and Welfare at Work (General Application) Regulations 1993 adopted pursuant to this section did not preclude civil enforcement,
and in fact created broad and open-textured duties capable of tempering the
harshness of the s.60(1) denial of actionability. These regulations were preserved
in force under the 2005 Act,[29] unless and until repealed by further regulations
adopted under s.58 of the new Act,[30] but have now largely been repealed and
replaced by the Safety, Health and Welfare at Work (General Application) Regulations 2007.[31] A number of decided cases of the courts considering the 1989 Act
remain instructive as regards the relationship between general regulations and
the common law. Perhaps the most significant of these is the High Court decision in *Everitt v Thorsman Ireland Ltd.*,[32] a case that illustrates the capacity of the
regulations to fill the lacuna in the tort of negligence with which a plaintiff will
frequently be confronted. The plaintiff was injured when a lever with which he
was supplied by his employers snapped and broke causing him to fall backwards
onto the ground. The evidence established that a latent defect within the metal
lever caused it to snap and break. This was not known to the employer, who had
bought the lever in good faith and who blamed the supplier of the bin (and who
in turn blamed the manufacturer). The High Court (Kearns J) dismissed the
employee's common law claim in negligence on the basis that the employer had
not been unreasonable. Kearns J asked:

> What further steps could the employer have taken… Short of having the lever
> assessed by an expert in metallurgy or breaking the lever with a view to determining
> its maximum stress resistance, it is difficult to see what could have been done. It was

29. s.4(4).
30. See the Safety, Health and Welfare at Work (General Application) Regulations 2007, SI no.
    299 of 2007. For detailed treatment, see Byrne, 'Safety and Health' in Byrne and Binchy, eds,
    Annual Review of Irish Law 2007 (Thomson Round Hall, 2008), at pp.497–510. For other
    examples of new regulations enacted pursuant to the 2005 Act, see, for example, Safety,
    Health and Welfare at Work (Exposure to Asbestos) Regulations 2006, SI no. 386 of 2006;
    Safety, Health and Welfare at Work (Construction) Regulations 2006, SI no. 504 of 2006;
    Safety, Health and Welfare at Work (Work at Height) Regulations 2006, SI no. 318 of 2006.
31. SI no. 299 of 2007.
32. [2000] 1 IR 256.

a newly purchased tool which appeared strong enough for the job and had been purchased from a reputable supplier and there is no suggestion to the contrary.[33]

However, Kearns J regarded as of key relevance to the litigation s.19 of the General Application Regulations, which provided:

> It shall be the duty of every employer, to ensure that... the necessary measures are taken so that the work equipment is suitable for the work to be carried out or is properly adapted for that purpose and may be used by employees without risk to their safety and health.

Kearns J expressed in very clear terms his view that this section imposed a positive [15–14] obligation on the employer, describing it as placing 'virtually an absolute duty on employers in respect of the safety of equipment provided for the use of their employees'.[34] The aim of this statutory provision was inferred as being 'to ensure that an employee who suffers an injury at work through no fault of his own by using defective equipment should not be left without remedy'.[35]

Everitt was considered by the High Court in 2008 in *Doyle v ESB*,[36] where Quirke J similarly held that the employer had not breached its common law duty of care, but that recourse to the 1993 Regulations did enable the plaintiff to recover.

Cases such as *Everitt* and *Doyle* illustrate the capacity for statutory obligations to [15–15] provide routes to the imposition of liability upon employers where exclusive reliance on the tort negligence would not permit such a result. It is further submitted, however, that the inverse is also true: an employer might be found to have fulfilled its statutory obligations, but nevertheless to have breached its common law duty of care in negligence. Statutory obligations may exceed the common law duty, may equal it, or may fall some way short of it.[37] There is, however, authority for the proposition that where an employer has discharged its statutory obligation it will be difficult to establish negligence,[38] and this may prove accurate in a great many cases.

---

33. *ibid.*, at 262.
34. *ibid.*, at 263.
35. *ibid.* Kearns J noted, however, the lack of blameworthiness on the employer's part but, referring to *Connolly v Dundalk Urban District Council*, unreported, Supreme Court, 18 November 1992, discussed below in Chapter 2, laid emphasis on the employer's ability to seek indemnity against the supplier.
36. [2008] IEHC 88.
37. *Bux v Slough Metals Ltd.* [1973] 1 WLR 1358.
38. *Roberts v Dorman Long & Co.* [1953] 2 All ER 428, 436.

2. Employers' Duties Concerning Health and Safety at Common Law

[15–16] The Irish courts have repeatedly held that the duty of care of an employer is 'to take reasonable care for the servant's safety in all the circumstances of the case'.[39] This duty houses a number of distinct obligations to employees. These fundamental duties were first most clearly recognised by the former Supreme Court in *Dowling v Brown*[40] and fall into four distinct categories: the duty to provide and maintain a safe system of work; the duty to provide and maintain a safe place of work; the duty to provide competent staff; and the duty to provide and maintain safe equipment.

[15–17] The test the courts apply in this context is to ask whether an employer has taken reasonable care for the safety of his employees to prevent injury or damage to them from a foreseeable risk, having regard to all the circumstances of the particular case.[41] The foreseeability point in these cases can often be of special significance, a point that was highlighted in the well-known case of *Barclay v An Post*.[42]

[15–18] In June 1993, the plaintiff postman was delivering post to an area of townhouses and apartments in Terenure, Dublin, which were fitted with low letter-boxes; the letter-boxes were placed at the bottom of each door, not more than a few inches off the ground. The plaintiff alleged that when he bent down to reach a low letter-box he suffered a sudden and agonising attack of pain in his lower back. The plaintiff was diagnosed with acute lower back strain, with possible lumbar disc damage. He was treated with analgesics, anti-inflammatory drugs and rest; he was fit to return to work in or about the end of August or the beginning of September 1993. The next month the plaintiff was employed on overtime to deliver post to a new development of 350 houses, all of which had low letter-boxes. The plaintiff suffered a recurrence of his back problems; a CT scan subsequently showed disc protrusion at two levels. The plaintiff instituted proceedings for damages for personal injuries against his employer, alleging, *inter alia*, that the latter had not exercised reasonable care for the safety of the plaintiff, in that it had not done enough to deal with the problem of low letter-boxes.

[15–19] McGuinness J found in favour of the plaintiff in the context of the recurrence of his back problems in October 1993. She held that the employer's duty of care towards the plaintiff included a duty to ensure that, in the short term after his illness, he did not take up duties that would put undue and extraordinary strain on his back and the delivery the plaintiff undertook in October 1993 was such a

---

39. *Per* O'Higgins CJ in *Dalton v Frendo*, unreported, Supreme Court, 15 December 1977.
40. (1960) 94 ILTR 67.
41. *Kenny v Irish Shipping*, unreported, Supreme Court, 4 November 1968; approved in *Mulligan v Holland Dredging Company (Ireland) Ltd.*, unreported, Supreme Court, 21 November 1996.
42. [1998] IEHC 110, [1998] 2 ILRM 385.

duty. In the circumstances the defendant had not properly discharged the employer's reasonable duty of care in the case of the plaintiff's second injury and as such was liable for that injury.

Thus, as in all areas of the law of negligence generally, the principle of foreseeability is key in establishing breach of duty by an employer. This is well illustrated in the context of employment in *McLoughlin v Carr t/a Harloes Bar*,[43] a claim that arose out of somewhat unusual facts. The plaintiff worked in the bar owned by the defendant and suffered injury at the hands of armed robbers who gained entry to the premises. Earlier in the day, one of the robbers had telephoned the bar, pretending to be a friend of the owner, and saying that the gardaí were going to visit the premises that night. The plaintiff opened the door and saw a man wearing a garda pullover and a garda cap. The man pulled a balaclava down over his face and placed a shotgun against the plaintiff's neck. Two other raiders accompanied him into the premises. The raiders robbed money and caused damage to property inside. [15–20]

The plaintiff sued his employer, alleging breach of statutory duty and negligence. The allegations of breach of statutory duty focused on the failure of the defendant to train the plaintiff in relation to security measures and its failure to carry out a risk assessment or to have a safety notice in place. [15–21]

Peart J dismissed the plaintiff's claim. Peart J held that the manner in which the raiders had gained entry was so unforeseeable that compliance with the statutory obligations would not have prevented the plaintiff's injury. Peart J explained thus: [15–22]

> The employer's duty is, *inter alia*, to provide a reasonably safe place of work for his employee. He cannot reasonably be expected to provide a place of work, guaranteed to exclude any potential hazard no matter how remote a possibility, or unforeseeable it is. In my view the plaintiff has failed to establish that any act or omission on the part of the defendant was the cause of the undoubted injury which the plaintiff has suffered. Harsh as it will seem, the law has provided that certain things must be established by a plaintiff if he is to be successful in a claim of negligence against his employer, and unfortunately the plaintiff has fallen short of satisfying me of these matters in the present case.[44]

The reasoning of Peart J is likely to be followed in other cases where the allegation of negligence concerns the employer's failure properly to train staff to minimise the risk of a criminal attack, and/or as to how to respond should such an attack take place. This is not to say that such claims are unsustainable; simply that it is likely that a plaintiff may face difficulties regarding foreseeability and or establishing that the harm suffered would not have been caused had there been no negligence. [15–23]

---

43. [2005] IEHC 358, [2007] 3 IR 496.
44. *ibid.*, at 509.

[15–24] In *Eyres v Atkinsons Kitchens and Bedrooms Ltd.*,[45] the claimant had been driving the defendant employer's van on a motorway when he lost control and sustained serious injuries. He had been awake continuously for about 19 hours before the accident and had complained of being tired during the journey. The central issue in the case was what had caused the complainant's loss of control. The claimant's case was that the defendant had permitted him to drive when he had been too tired, and that he must have fallen asleep at the wheel.

[15–25] It was accepted that if the accident was caused by tiredness, the company was liable to him in negligence and/or breach of statutory duty in permitting him to drive when he was too tired, after having worked excessively long hours without a proper break. There was evidence from a sleep medicine expert, including the risks and consequences of a brief period of drowsiness or a 'micro-sleep'. At first instance, the judge held that the accident had been caused by the claimant's inattention through using his mobile phone and not by his falling asleep.

[15–26] Allowing the appeal, however, the Court of Appeal held that on the balance of probabilities, the claimant had shown that he had fallen asleep and that that had caused the accident. The employer was liable for the accident, but the claimant had to bear some responsibility for it also. There must have been some time, albeit a short time before the accident, when he must have realised that he was at risk of falling asleep. His overall contributory negligence was assessed at 33 per cent, which appears to be somewhat generous to the plaintiff, given that it encompassed a finding of 25 per cent for his failure to wear a safety belt.

2.1. A Non-Delegable Duty

[15–27] The duty of care owed by the employer is a personal duty that is non-delegable. This means that the employer must not simply take care, but must actually see that care is taken by all persons engaged by him or her. So, while employers can and do delegate the performance of their duties to others, the employer will remain liable for the negligent performance of those duties.

[15–28] Although the language of non-delegable duty suggests primary liability that is personal to the employer, the late Professor Fleming has described the concept as 'a disguised form of vicarious liability'.[46] Fleming lamented the lack of any coherent theory to determine when a duty would be classified as 'non-delegable', but noted that a common thread in several of the authorities was the existence of a 'special protective relationship' and a corresponding special reliance or dependence by the person who suffered the loss. So too do McMahon and Binchy agree

---

45. [2007] EWCA Civ 365.
46. Fleming, *The Law of Torts* (9th ed., Sydney LBC Services, 1998), at p.433. See also Swanton, 'Non-Delegable Duties: Liability for the Negligence of Independent Contractors', 4 *JCL* (1991), 183 and 5 *JCL* (1992), 26.

that the non-delegable duty of care is 'in truth... a form of vicarious liability'. This is on the basis that the recognition of a non-delegable duty is not predicated upon any requirement of establishing proof of control or even an ability to control on the part of an employer.[47]

This characterisation of the non-delegable duty as a form of vicarious liability has [15–29] prompted considerable academic debate, and a strong case can be put forward for maintaining that the concept of the non-delegable duty must be distinct from that of vicarious liability. One strong argument of this type is the point that, if non-delegable duties are indeed a form of vicarious liability, then they offend against the general rule that it is not possible to be vicariously liable for independent contractors.[48]

In *Connolly v Dundalk UDC and Mahon & McPhillips*,[49] the plaintiff was a care- [15–30] taker at the council's waterworks and suffered serious injury after inhaling a dense cloud of chlorine gas, which had escaped from a pipe. The point of connection of the pipe had been inadequately secured. The council sought to escape liability by arguing that this was the fault of the second defendant – a firm of independent contractors who had installed the piping and were responsible for the service and maintenance of it. O'Hanlon J rejected this argument, stating that 'an employer owes a duty to his employee to provide a safe place of work and cannot escape liability for breach of such duty by employing an independent contractor – no matter how expert – to perform the duty for him'.[50]

O'Hanlon J's judgment was upheld by the Supreme Court.[51] O'Flaherty J, speaking [15–31] of the employer's duty of care, said that it 'cannot be delegated to independent contractors so as to avoid the primary liability that devolves on employers'. O'Flaherty J went on to say that if an employer engages an independent contractor to perform work, and the contractor's negligence causes injury to an employee, 'the employer retains a primary liability for the damage suffered though if he is not himself negligent he may obtain from the contractor a contribution to the damages and costs which he has to pay which will amount to full indemnity'.

In the later case of *McCarthy v Garda Commissioner*,[52] the plaintiff sued his [15–32] employers in negligence for failing to take reasonable care in relation to the uniform with which he had been provided. His claim was dismissed in the High Court, and the Supreme Court dismissed the appeal. Murphy J in the course of an *ex tempore* Supreme Court judgment noted that the defendant had given the correct specifications for pocket size to the tailors with whom they contracted.

---

47. McMahon and Binchy, *Law of Torts* (3rd ed., Butterworths, 2000), 18.34, at p.490.
48. Generally, see Stevens, 'Non-Delegable Duties and Vicarious Liability', ch.13 in Neyers, Chamberlain and Pitel, eds, *Emerging Issues in Tort Law* (Hart, 2007), at p.331.
49. [1990] 2 IR 1.
50. [1990] 2 IR 1, 7.
51. Unreported, Supreme Court, 18 November 1992.
52. Unreported, Supreme Court, 27 February 1998.

[15–33] Interestingly, and as noted by McMahon and Binchy,[53] there is no mention of the defendant having been under a non-delegable duty of care in relation to the supply of uniforms to its employees. On one reading of the judgment of O'Flaherty J in *Connolly*, in *McCarthy* the defendants might have been held liable, with it being presumably open to them to sue the tailors.

2.2. Duty to Hired Worker

[15–34] Where the plaintiff is or was a hired worker, as opposed to an employee, of the defendant, the courts tend, nevertheless, to determine liability by reference to principles relevant in the context of employers' liability. The Supreme Court decision in *Phillips v Durgan*[54] provides a clear manifestation of this. The defendant had casually hired the first plaintiff, who was his sister, to paint and decorate his home. The second plaintiff, her husband, drove her to the house. The evidence was to the effect that the premises was extremely neglected, unsafe, and so unclean that before the first plaintiff could set about her task she was obliged to clean the kitchen thoroughly as its floors, walls and cooker had become literally caked with grease. The linoleum covering the kitchen floor was broken. While engaged in this clean-up operation, the first plaintiff slipped on the grease, which caused a cloth she was carrying to come into contact with flames from the cooker. This started a fire in the kitchen which, due to the grease, spread rapidly and ultimately caused both plaintiffs to sustain severe burns. In the Supreme Court, Finlay CJ expressed his preference for assessing the case by reference to principles applicable to employers', rather than to occupiers', liability. In the instant case, Finlay CJ held that amongst the duties of the defendant there existed 'a duty to the people whom he was asking to carry out the work for him to give some consideration to how it might be done with safety'.[55]

2.3. Agency Workers

[15–35] A situation yet more difficult is that involving agency workers.[56] Such workers will generally have a contract with the agency through which they secure work. It is unlikely that this contract will be a contract of employment. The entity for which the agency worker goes to work – the end user – will probably have a contract with the agency. But this will not be a contract of employment, and in any case the agency worker will not be a party to it. The issue, then, is whether the end user owes a duty of care to the agency worker and may be liable to that worker in negligence.

[15–36] It is submitted that, where an issue of health and safety in the workplace is involved, it would be undesirable as a matter of policy to conclude that no duty

---

53. McMahon and Binchy, *Law of Torts* (3rd ed., Butterworths, 2000), p.494.
54. [1991] ILRM 321.
55. [1991] ILRM 321, 327.
56. The status of agency workers in employment law is considered in Chapter 4.

of care could be owed. This would be to promote different standards as between different classes of worker, and would yield different and probably highly anomalous results as to liability in what might be identical factual circumstances, as far as the defendant's want of care was concerned. Most objectionably, such an approach would permit lesser standards of protection of the safety of some individuals than the levels of protection enjoyed by others in the same workplace. Whilst this may be fully understandable so far as benefits and privileges are concerned, it seems undesirable in the area of health and safety.[57]

In this context, it is significant to note the terms of s.2(4) of the Safety, Health and Welfare at Work Act 2005, which provides as follows: **[15–37]**

> For the purposes of the relevant statutory provisions, where an individual agrees with a person who is carrying on the business of an employment agency within the meaning of the Employment Agency Act 1971, and is acting in the course of that business to do or perform personally any work or service for another person (whether or not the latter person is a party to the contract and whether or not the latter person pays the wages or salary of the individual in respect of the work or service), then the latter person shall be deemed to be the individual's employer for the purposes of the relevant statutory provisions.

Given the potential impact of this statutory regime in the context of the negligence action considered above, it is submitted that this is a notable example of the potential for the common law position in negligence to be infused with statutorily inspired imperatives of workplace health and safety law.

2.4. Employer not an Insurer of an Employee's Safety

The courts have 'repeatedly confirmed',[58] though, that an employer is not an insurer of the safety of an employee. A clear example of this principle is to be seen in the case of *Bradley v CIÉ*,[59] which has been described judicially as 'the classic case in this jurisdiction on the standard of care owed by an employer to an employee in regard to safety'.[60] In that case the plaintiff, a railwayman, was injured when he fell from a ladder attached to a signal post. Engineering evidence suggested that a protective cage would have prevented such a fall but there was no evidence that such cages were provided by other railway companies. There had been no similar accidents within the previous ten years. The Supreme Court held that the suggested precaution had not been shown either to have been commonly taken by other railway operators or to have been such that a reasonably prudent **[15–38]**

---

57. See Cotter and Bennett, eds, *Munkman on Employers' Liability* (14th ed., LexisNexis Butterworths, 2006), at p.126.
58. *Donnelly v Commissioner of An Garda Síochána* [2008] IEHC 7, *per* Quirke J.
59. [1976] IR 217.
60. *Per* McGuinness J in *Barclay v An Post* [1998] 2 ILRM 385, 395.

employer would think was obviously necessary in the prevailing circumstances for the protection of its employees. Henchy J stated that:

> The law does not require an employer to ensure in all circumstances the safety of his workmen. He will have discharged his duty of care if he does what a reasonable and prudent employer would have done in the circumstances.[61]

Henchy J went onto say:

> Even where a certain precaution is obviously wanted in the interest of the safety of the workman, there may be countervailing factors which would justify the employer in not taking that precaution.[62]

[15–39] However, subsequent judgments of the Supreme Court would appear to have cast a degree of doubt over the validity of the above-mentioned 'countervailing factors' in circumstances of obvious danger. Thus, in *Daly v Avonmore Creameries Ltd.*[63] McCarthy J arguably distanced himself from the above proposition when he observed that it was 'not to be taken as supporting the view that where lives are at stake considerations of expense are any more than vaguely material'.[64]

McCarthy J continued this theme in his later judgment in *Kennedy v Hughes Dairy Ltd.*,[65] when he stated:

> The essential question in all actions of negligence is whether or not the party charged has failed to take reasonable care whether by act or omission. That prime question may be broken down to subsidiary questions appropriate to the circumstances of different cases. In actions resulting from injuries sustained in what may be termed static conditions – those prevailing in a particular employment or a particular premises or the like, expert evidence may properly point, as a primary matter, to the foreseeable risk of injury and the consequent requirement of special care. The practice of the trade or of occupiers of similar premises may be powerful rebutting evidence but, in my view, in a changing world, it should seldom, if ever, be conclusive.[66]

[15–40] As against this, it should be noted that Finlay CJ, dissenting in *Kennedy*, stated his preference for the *Bradley v CIE*[67] formulation: he held that the mere fact that a precaution that could be considered necessary to prevent a different type of accident would, by sheer coincidence, have also ameliorated or prevented injury from

---

61. [1976] IR 217, 223.
62. *ibid.*, at 223.
63. [1984] IR 131.
64. [1984] IR 131, 147.
65. [1989] ILRM 117.
66. *ibid.*, at 122.
67. [1976] IR 217.

the accident that had occurred was not, in his view, a good reason for concluding that it was a precaution a reasonable and prudent man would consider obviously necessary to provide against the happening of the accident or injury.[68]

2.4.1. The Relevance of Individual Circumstances

Employees' individual circumstances are naturally of relevance in determining the scope of the duty of care in negligence owed by an employer. In *Dalton v Frendo*,[69] Griffin J stated that: 'Actions of negligence are concerned with the duty of care as between a particular employer and a particular workman… That duty may vary with the workman's age, knowledge and experience.'   [15–41]

An emerging, and controversial, area in employers' liability, therefore, is the extent to which an employer has to tailor its practices to accommodate the circumstances peculiar to an individual employee.[70] What of an 'emotionally fragile' employee? Or an employee known to suffer from some form of disability?[71]   [15–42]

It is undoubtedly the position that an employer must take care having regard to a known susceptibility or weakness of an employee that makes injury likely, or serious if it happens.[72] Similarly, where an employee from a foreign country is not fluent in English, it will be necessary to ensure that certain instructions regarding safety are understood or translated.[73] It is submitted, however, that there is no legal duty on an employer to refuse to employ an adult employee for work he is willing to do because the employer thinks it is not in the employee's best interests to do such work. Such a rule would be imposing a restriction on the freedom of the individual, and would be oppressive to the employee by limiting his ability to find work.[74] It has, however, been questioned whether this approach has survived developments in European legislation.[75]   [15–43]

---

68. *ibid.*, at 119.

69. Unreported, Supreme Court, 15 December 1977.

70. The duty of care is concerned with the relationship between an employer and an individual employee, although it is of course the case that many duties are general and are owed by the employer to his entire workforce.

71. In *Coxall v Goodyear Great Britain Ltd.* [2002] EWCA Civ 1010, [2003] 1 WLR 536, [2003] ICR 152, [2002] IRLR 742, liability was imposed where an employee's asthma condition worsened because, given the magnitude of the risk, it would have been proper to move him to other work or to dismiss him.

72. As in *Paris v Stepney Borough Council* [1957] AC 367.

73. This seems sensible; though authorities in the common law context appear thin on the ground. For an example, see *Hawkins v Ian Ross (Castings) Ltd.* [1970] 1 All ER 180. This issue is affected by the coming into force of s.9 Safety, Health and Welfare at Work Act 2005, discussed below.

74. *Withers v Perry Chain Co. Ltd.* [1961] 1 WLR 1314.

75. Cotter and Bennett, eds, *Munkman on Employers' Liability* (14th ed., LexisNexis Butterworths, 2006), at p.134.

2.4.2. *Where the Risk is Manifest and May Be Easily Overcome*

[15–44] When a risk or danger becomes manifest in the course of employment, and a simple means of overcoming it is available, an employer will be negligent if he permits the danger to continue. In *Fortune v P.E. Jacob and Co. Ltd.*[76] the Supreme Court held that the case should not have been withdrawn from the jury in the following circumstances. The plaintiff employee was injured when he fell from the platform of a lorry, which he was loading at the defendant's premises. There was evidence to the effect that a strip of timber was habitually nailed along the platform edge of the defendant's lorries, to indicate to the workers that they were standing near the edge of the platform, since the loading operation required them to look upwards at a chute through which sacks were propelled to the lorries from the defendant's premises. Evidence was also given that four of the six lorries belonging to the defendant had such a wooden strip. On the day of the accident, the lorry in use had no wooden strip, but the plaintiff, who was accustomed to the presence of a strip, assumed that it was there. At the trial, the judge withdrew the case from the jury on the ground that there was no evidence to go before it. On appeal, the Supreme Court held that there was evidence of negligence that should have gone to the jury.

2.4.3. *Where the Employment is Inherently Dangerous*

[15–45] Even where the employment is inherently dangerous, the employer is still under a duty to take reasonable care. Thus, while it has recently been judicially observed that it is 'the very nature of military life that a soldier must expect to find himself, on occasion, in harm's way and a witness to horrific and barbaric events',[77] there is still an obligation on the employer to safeguard the employee's welfare. This is well illustrated by the landmark ruling of the Supreme Court in *Ryan v Ireland*,[78] where the Supreme Court held that the plaintiff soldier was owed a duty of care in negligence by the army.[79]

While serving as a soldier with the United Nations Interim Force in Lebanon, and in the course of lengthy hostile engagement, the plaintiff was ordered by his commanding officer to take rest from sentry duty in an exposed and unprotected billet near his guardpost. He was injured in the legs by shrapnel from a mortar-attack that hit the billet. In the course of his negligence action in the High Court, the defendants sought a direction of no case to answer, which was refused.[80] On appeal to the Supreme Court, they argued that at common law the plaintiff was

---

76. [1976–7] ILRM 277.
77. *Per* de Valera J in *Corbett v Ireland* [2008] 1 IR 495, 497.
78. [1989] IR 177.
79. For a more recent example of a similar case, see *Clarke v Minister for Defence* [2008] IEHC 105.
80. However, the High Court judge Keane J dismissed the plaintiff's case in ruling that the plaintiff had failed to join the proper defendants. The plaintiff appealed to the Supreme Court on this point; the defendants cross-appealed in relation to, *inter alia*, the refusal to grant a direction of no case to answer.

precluded from suing the State for injury or damage occasioned by any negligence of his superior officers.

The Supreme Court accepted that, although in volunteering for active army service [15–46] the plaintiff had accepted the risks inherent in being involved in armed conflict, this did not include a risk of being unnecessarily exposed to injury by negligence. Finlay CJ explained the principles governing the inquiry to be embarked upon by the courts in such cases:

> In broadest terms the duty can be stated to be to take such care for the safety of the plaintiff as is reasonable in all the circumstances of their relationship and the activity in which they were engaged. Quite clearly those circumstances in this case are unusual for they are the circumstances of military service in which the carrying out of the task allotted to the forces concerned could involve an unavoidable risk of death or serious injury. In such situations considerations of standards of care drawn from the experience of the workplace may be of little assistance. There could, I think, be no objective in a master and servant relationship which would justify exposing the servant to risk of serious injury or death other than the saving of life itself. In the execution of military service exposing a soldier to such risk may often be justified by the nature of the task committed to the forces concerned. Furthermore, there can, in relation to armed conflict, be many situations where those in authority must make swift decisions in effect in the agony of the moment. Mere proof of error in such decisions would not of itself establish negligence. Importance may be attached, I am satisfied, in regard to alleged negligence in a military situation, to the question as to whether the role of the soldier at the time of the alleged negligence is one of attack or defence, or, to put the matter in another way, whether he is engaged actively in armed operations or is only passively engaged in them. Where, as occurred in this case, the plaintiff was, whilst on guard duty, acting in a defensive role and was in effect standing by, I am satisfied that his commanding officer owed to him a duty to take such precautions as were reasonable and practical, having regard to the functions which as a member of the guard the plaintiff was obliged to perform, to try and reduce the risk of his being wounded or killed.[81]

The point is also seen in cases taken by employees whose jobs are inherently [15–47] dangerous, such as firemen. In *Heeney v Dublin Corporation*[82] the plaintiff was the widow of a deceased fire man who had been employed as a station master with the Dublin Fire Brigade. He died due to inhaling gas while fighting a fire without having breathing apparatus. The man died in 1985, and the evidence was that the defendant had started to provide its crews with breathing apparatus and to organise training for fire fighters. By 1984, all permanent fire brigades in Ireland had been issued with breathing apparatus, but certain brigades, including the one

---

81. *Per* Finlay CJ at pp.183–184.
82. Unreported, High Court, Barron J, 16 May 1991.

with which the deceased was employed, had not yet been issued with the apparatus. Barron J imposed liability, concluding that the fire authority should have provided the breathing apparatus, and should not have sent the deceased to tackle the fire in question without the protection of such apparatus.

Equally, the mere existence of a risk to the employee's safety does not necessarily establish any breach of duty. The common law has long insisted that employees are free to pursue risky endeavours that involve an unavoidable risk of injury or even death.[83]

2.4.4. No Such Thing in Law as Employment that is Inherently Dangerous to Mental Health

[15–48]   In recent years, the courts have repeatedly emphasised that as a matter of assessing an employer's liability in negligence for the infliction of psychiatric injury, there is no such thing as an occupation that is intrinsically dangerous to mental health. In the landmark case of *Barber v Somerset County Council*,[84] discussed at length in Chapter 16, Hale LJ (as she then was) in the course of her judgment in the Court of Appeal[85] formulated some 16 practical propositions applicable to cases where a complaint is made of psychiatric illness brought about by stress at work. On the question of whether psychiatric harm to the particular employee was reasonably foreseeable, the list included the proposition that 'there are no occupations which should be regarded as intrinsically dangerous to mental health'.[86] This proposition has recently been affirmed by the High Court of Australia in the case of *New South Wales v Fahy*.[87]

[15–49]   Another way of expressing a similar idea may be to say the factors that may cause stress, and the circumstances in which an individual might suffer stress-related injury, are so various that to single out any occupation and treat it as intrinsically dangerous in this respect is unwarranted. There are circumstances, for example, in which caring for children might be at least as stressful as law enforcement.

2.5. Exposing Employees to Particular Danger

[15–50]   The question of whether an employer is under a duty of care in negligence to warn a prospective employee of risks inherent in a post offered to him or her does not

---

83.   Grubb, ed., *Tort* (London: Butterworths LexisNexis, 2007), 20.12; *Smith v Charles Baker & Sons* [1891] AC 325, 356; *Reid v Rush & Tompkins Group Plc* [1990] 1 WLR 212, 221 (work at sea considered to be an example of a job carrying an unavoidable risk).

84.   [2004] UKHL 13, [2004] 1 WLR 1089.

85.   The judgment was subsequently reversed on appeal by a majority in the House of Lords, but the practical propositions were expressly endorsed and indeed have since been frequently applied and followed in numerous cases, including judgments of the Irish courts. For full treatment of this area, see Chapter 16.

86.   [2004] 1 WLR 1089 at 1092 [7], [2004] 2 All ER 385 at 389.

87.   [2007] HCA 20, (2007), 81 ALJR 1021.

appear to have arisen in Ireland. It is submitted that there would be held to be a duty to inform a prospective employee of risks to health and safety associated with the job. In a Court of Appeal decision such a duty was recognised, albeit in a situation where the action was taken by a present employee who had applied for a new job in the same organisation.[88] In that case, however, where the failure to warn was of the risk of vibration-induced white finger, the employer was acquitted of breach of duty because the condition was then believed only to cause minor discomfort, not limiting capacity to work, and the plaintiff took on the job knowing that others doing the same work had experienced numbness in their fingers.

Even if an employer is shown to have negligently failed to warn of risks inherent in the work, the plaintiff will still have to prove that this caused the injury [s]he subsequently suffered at work.

Instructive in this regard are cases taken by employees of security firms who have   [15–51] been injured in the course of an armed robbery. Because it is eminently foreseeable that criminals may target employees carrying large amounts of cash and or valuable goods, the courts require that security firms have put in place sophisticated and well-thought out safety systems.

In *Walsh v Securicor (Ireland) Ltd.*,[89] the Supreme Court addressed the issue in detail.   [15–52] The plaintiff was an employee of the defendant security company. He collected a large amount of cash from a bank in Cork city and drove a van in the direction of Cobh, where he was to deliver the money to smaller banks and a post office. He was accompanied in the van by an employee, and the van had a garda escort. The van was ambushed; a tractor blocked its path and bullets were fired at the van, shattering the windscreen. The plaintiff was forced to open the door of the van and was hit on the head with a rifle. In his negligence action against his employers, the plaintiff succeeded both before Barrington J at first instance, and in the Supreme Court.

In evidence, the plaintiff established that the time of delivery had been the same   [15–53] every week for a period of seven years. Negligence was alleged by the failure of the defendant to vary the delivery time on what was a high-risk route. Expert evidence established what might be thought to be a matter of common sense – that it was unwise to retain a clockwork precision in relation to the time the deliveries were to be carried out.

The defendant maintained that it was contractually tied to the delivery time. Egan J (Finlay CJ and Hederman J concurring) noted that there had been 'no evidence at all of any discussions at the appropriate levels about the desirability of reviewing or changing the times of delivery from time to time'. [90]

---

88. *White v Holbrook Precision Castings* [1985] IRLR 215.
89. [1993] 2 IR 507.
90. [1993] 2 IR 507, 509–510.

[15–54]   In affirming the High Court's imposition of liability, the Supreme Court concluded that 'this was a high risk operation and the defendant was bound to avail of every safety precaution, not just the provision of a Garda escort'.[91] Significantly, the court relied on the earlier dictum of Finlay CJ in *Ryan v Ireland*[92] that 'there could… be no objective in a master and servant relationship which would justify exposing the servant to a risk of serious injury or death other than the saving of life itself'.[93]

[15–55]   The allegation of negligence took a more nuanced form in *McCann v Brinks Allied and Ulster Bank Ltd*.[94] The plaintiffs worked as security men, employed by Brinks Allied Ltd. They were seriously injured by armed robbers who held them up whilst they were delivering £1 million in cash to a branch of Ulster Bank. This particular branch was a modern purpose-built bank with a paved forecourt. Bollards had been erected because the bank was unhappy with vans driving over the paved slabs, which were incapable of supporting the weight of a van. As a result, the closest the van could get to the door of the bank was 47 feet. It was while the plaintiffs were walking from the van to the door that they were set upon by the armed robbers. The first named plaintiff was shot in the leg.

[15–56]   The particulars of negligence concentrated on the fact that the plaintiffs were required to walk the 47 feet to the door, and more generally, to work at a location that was peculiarly attractive to bank robbers. The branch in question had been raided on three earlier occasions, and two of those raids involved robbery or attempted robbery from security men making a delivery. The plaintiffs maintained that their employer should have ensured that arrangements were put in place to allow the van to be driven very close to the bank door; in the alternative, the employer should have provided a chute or bank-link facility into which the cash could be deposited without putting the security men in danger.

[15–57]   These arguments were accepted by Morris J, who imposed liability. Although Morris J accepted that it was not the practice in banking circles to use bank link units or chutes, on the facts of this particular case the employer should have

---

91. [1993] 2 IR 507, 510.
92. [1989] IR 177.
93. [1989] IR 177, 182. In *Clarke v Minister for Defence* [2008] IEHC 105 the plaintiff unsuccessfully argued that the effect of the Supreme Court judgment in *Walsh* was to oblige the defendants to take every precaution or use every device available to seek to eliminate a risk to its troops. Irvine J rejected this contention, observing that: 'The particular duty of care arising in the *Walsh* case was one which was directly related to the high risk of the likelihood of an attack being made on an armoured vehicle known to be transporting monies and for this reason must be distinguished from those very different facts which arise for the consideration of the Court in this case, which demonstrated the unlikelihood of an unannounced mortar attack.' Irvine J went on to state her view that the attack in *Walsh* was 'much more foreseeable' than that which occurred in *Clarke*.
94. [1997] 1 ILRM 461, Supreme Court, affirming High Court judgment of Morris J, 12 May 1995.

ensured that such arrangements were put in place. Morris J noted in particular that there had been previous raids on the branch, and that the cost of installing such bank link units and making them compatible with a corresponding unit on the side of the van was small. Morris J was persuaded that if the steps contended for by the plaintiffs had been taken by their employer, the injuries suffered by the plaintiffs would not, on the balance of probabilities, have occurred.[95]

The Supreme Court decision in 2003 in *Corkery v Bus Éireann*[96] is also of relevance [15–58] here. The plaintiff worked as a bus driver in Cork city. He was assaulted by a person from behind for the cash he had taken on the journey, at a time when he thought that the bus was empty. He was cut with a knife, and although the physical injuries suffered were minor, he suffered serious psychological consequences, which led to sexual impotence. The trial judge held that the attack was reasonably foreseeable in that the defendant's sister company had experienced the same problem in Dublin, and there had been isolated assaults in Cork. The trial judge held that the provision of screens that precluded physical conduct with the driver was a reasonable precaution the defendant should have taken. Evidence was led to the effect that this was standard in Dublin Bus and in various urban centres in the UK, to which personnel of the defendant had travelled for the purpose of learning how the problem of assaults was managed there. The Supreme Court unanimously dismissed the defendant's appeal, holding that the provision of such protective screens was a standard precaution in the industry and one that a reasonable employer should have adopted.

In *O'Neill v Dunnes Stores*[97] the plaintiff was employed as a storeman by a company [15–59] named Premier Foods in Thurles, Co. Tipperary. The defendant was the principal tenant of the shopping centre in Thurles. On the relevant evening, the plaintiff went to the defendant's store. He was approached by a woman he did not know who said to him, 'Help, there's been a robbery.' Responding to the woman's cry, the plaintiff went to the rear of the building where he saw a security officer employed by the defendant involved in a struggle with a man named Colville. The plaintiff went to the assistance of the security officer. After the guards had arrived, the plaintiff was struck in the face by a motorcycle chain brandished by Colville.

Kelly J had no hesitation in concluding that the security arrangements the defendant had in place on the evening in question were substandard. In Kelly J's view, to ask one person to take responsibility for the security of the entire of the defendant's shop consisting of drapery, grocery and off-licence was not reasonable.

---

95. In a 2006 case in the Circuit Court, Judge Linnane dismissed a negligence action taken by employees of Dunnes Stores who had been traumatised after being confronted by armed raiders. Negligence was not established. See 'Dunnes Workers Lose Claim for Raid Damages', *The Irish Times*, 21 February 2006.
96. Supreme Court, *ex temp*, 6 May 2003.
97. [2007] IEHC 33, unreported, High Court, 21 February 2007.

[15–60] It was common case that the plaintiff went to the rescue of the security officer, and that accordingly the case fell to be determined by reference to the law on rescuers. At the conclusion of the plaintiff's case, Kelly J declined to accede to an application for a non-suit, taking the view that there was a prima facie case made out against the defendant. Kelly J upheld the plaintiff's claim. The security officer failed to adhere to the protocol in place, which does not require a security officer to attempt an arrest in circumstances where he is outnumbered, and this amounted to negligence on the part of the security officer for which the defendant was vicariously liable.

Kelly J held that the 'situation requiring assistance of a rescuer was reasonably foreseeable and was brought about by [the security officer's] non-adherence to the protocol and the defendant's failure to provide appropriate backup for [him]'.

Kelly J went on to refer to the

> shabby way the plaintiff was treated by the defendant. Despite his bravery in going to the assistance of one of his security men he received not a word of thanks or acknowledgement from Dunnes Stores until the commencement of his cross-examination in this case, four and a half years after the event. No real effort was made to make any contact with the plaintiff to enquire as to his welfare or to thank him for what he had done.

2.6. Duty to Provide 'Light Work'

[15–61] The potential for employers to be held liable in negligence for failing to respect an employee's request that [s]he only be given light work raises a number of difficult questions. The classic case would be where medical opinion, verified by a certificate or letter, is presented by the employee to the effect that [s]he is unfit for anything other than light work. If the employer ignores this, and the employee ends up doing heavy work and suffers injury, there is at least the potential for liability to be imposed. The leading Irish case is *Rafferty v Parsons (CA) of Ireland Ltd*.[98] The plaintiff had been employed as a storeman by the defendants. He began to experience recurring back pain. His doctors advised him only to do light work. A doctor gave him a note to give to his foreman requesting that he only be given light work. The foreman told the plaintiff that the employers had no light work for him to carry out, and that there would be no work for the plaintiff unless he was able to do the full work. In evidence in the High Court, the plaintiff maintained that he only resumed the full work because of the need to support his family, and that doing this work caused him further back pain in the years ahead.

[15–62] The trial judge withdrew the case from jury and the Supreme Court, by a 2-1 majority, dismissed the appeal. Finlay CJ thought it would be 'a wholly artificial and unreal standard of care' to impose liability when the employer had simply told

98. [1987] ILRM 98.

the employee that there was no light work, and when the employee 'voluntarily' resumed ordinary work and continued at it for some years afterwards.

More than twenty years on from *Rafferty*, the question of whether an employer [15–63] may be liable for allowing an employee to do his normal work when he was known only to be fit for light work remains open. In *Rafferty*, Henchy J pointedly did not address that issue, although he did remark *obiter* that 'It may well be that it would be evidence of negligence on the part of an employer that he allowed his employee to do his normal work when he was known to be fit only for light work'[99]; and the dissent of McCarthy J quite obviously was consistent with there being potential liability on these facts.

Conversely, there is also a duty of care in negligence on the employer not to over- [15–64] burden an employee with an excessive workload.[100] This duty has been the subject of considerable development in a series of cases in the last decade involving claims for workplace stress and psychological injury, considered separately in Chapter 16.

2.7. Duties in Respect of Protective Clothing

Where the type of work is such that a reasonable employer would provide his [15–65] employees with protective clothing or equipment while doing the work, there is a duty to provide it and to take reasonable care to see that it is used.

In *Crouch v British Rail Engineering*,[101] an employee regularly had to perform tasks that carried a reasonably foreseeable risk of eye injury. It was held to be insufficient for the employer to make goggles available in a store and inform him of the need to wear them; the employer should have actually provided the goggles into the hand of the employee. The fact that the employees had to go some distance to get the safety goggles gave those employees an incentive to 'take a chance'.

2.8. Duty to Insist on Adherence to Safety Measures

It is submitted that it may well amount to negligence for an employer not to insist [15–66] that safety measures are followed where the employee is working in a dangerous environment or with dangerous materials. That is, it may not be sufficient merely to provide the equipment or issue instructions.

As Lord Denning said in the course of one judgment:

> When [an employer] asks his men to work with dangerous substances, he must set in force a proper system by which they use the appliances and take the necessary precautions; and he must do his best to see that they adhere to it.[102]

---

99. *ibid.*, at 102.
100. See further White, 'The Employer's Duty and His Servant's Work-Load', 9 *ILT* (1991), 240.
101. [1988] IRLR 404.
102. *Clifford v Charles Challen & Sons* [1951] 1 KB 495, 497.

[15–67] In *Pape v Cumbria County Council*,[103] the defendant employer was under a duty of care to warn cleaners of the dangers of handling chemical substances and to instruct them as to the necessity for wearing gloves at all times. The employer was held to have been negligent in simply providing gloves without giving clear instructions. Accordingly, a warning might not be sufficient to discharge the duty where a danger exists in the workplace. As Walsh J said in the course of a Supreme Court judgment, 'Instruction and warning, however explicit, cannot be equated to the presence of a physical guard.'[104]

2.9. Duty of Employer to Implement Promised Health and Safety Change

[15–68] In some circumstances, a failure by an employer to implement a promised change in working conditions might amount to negligence. The crucial question is whether the promised change sets the standard of reasonableness. The issue surfaced in the English case of *Pratley v Surrey County Council*.[105] The plaintiff was a care manager at a residential home for the elderly. She began to suffer stress-related symptoms as a result of her heavy workload. She spoke to her superior, who acknowledged that Ms Pratley was under considerable pressure. At a supervision meeting in 1996 it was suggested that a system of stacking be introduced to slow down the number of incoming cases. This system of stacking would operate so as to ensure that new cases would not be allocated to individual case managers unless and until there was space in an existing workload. After this meeting, Ms Pratley took a summer holiday. Her superior decided to wait and see how Ms Pratley was feeling when she returned from her holidays before taking any action. Ms Pratley was expecting the stacking system to be introduced in her absence. When she returned to work in the same conditions and without the stacking system having been introduced, she suffered psychiatric injury, which caused her to leave work.

[15–69] Although both the trial judge and the Court of Appeal felt that the psychiatric illness was caused by the return to work and the absence of the stacking system, the claim failed because the psychiatric illness suffered was not foreseeable. The risk of injury to the plaintiff in the long term was foreseeable, but not the risk of immediate injury upon her return to work after her holiday if the promised change was not implemented.

[15–70] On the issue of potential liability for failure to implement a promised change in working conditions, then, it is submitted that such a failure does not automatically demonstrate negligence. If it is not foreseeable that injury will be suffered as a result of the failure to implement a promised change, there can be no liability, as the decision in *Pratley* shows.

---

103. [1992] 3 All ER 211, [1992] ICR 132, [1991] IRLR 463.
104. *Swords v St Patrick's Copper Mines Ltd.*, Supreme Court, 30 July 1963.
105. [2003] EWCA Civ 1067, [2003] IRLR 794.

2.10. Duty of Employer in Respect of Psychiatric Damage

In this section, consideration is given to the potential for imposing liability in [15–71] negligence upon employers for injuries other than physical injuries sustained by employees – an issue also considered in detail in Chapter 16. As McMahon and Binchy ask, 'Why should an employer, who owes a duty of care to an employee not to cause him or her physical injury, not also owe a duty of care to avoid causing the employee psychiatric injury resulting from nervous shock?'[106]

A leading Irish case on the employer's duty in the context of psychiatric injury is [15–72] the much-discussed judgment of the Supreme Court in 2002 in the case of *Fletcher v Commissioner of Public Works*,[107] where the Supreme Court, reversing the decision of O'Neill J in the High Court, denied recovery in a 'fear for the future' claim brought by an employee who had been negligently exposed to asbestos dust in the course of his employment.

Fletcher was heard at the same time as four other appeals. As Keane CJ pointed [15–73] out, all five cases arose out of what was admitted to be the failure of the defendants, as employers, to take proper precautions for the safety, health and welfare of the plaintiffs, their employees. As a result of that failure (as was conceded by the defendants) the plaintiffs were exposed to significant quantities of asbestos dust in the course of their employment and, as a further consequence, were exposed to the risk of contracting in later life the disease of mesothelioma which, when contracted, is potentially fatal. There was evidence in each case from psychiatrists that the plaintiffs, as a result of their having been informed of that risk, suffered from a recognisable psychiatric disorder. In each case the High Court found that the defendants were liable to pay damages in respect of the psychiatric illness. The defendants appealed successfully to the Supreme Court.[108]

The Supreme Court in *Fletcher* declined to impose liability for the plaintiffs' 'fear [15–74] for the future argument', a refusal essentially based on two grounds identified in the judgment of Keane CJ. The first was 'the undesirability of awarding damages to plaintiffs who have suffered no physical injury and whose psychiatric condition is solely due to an unfounded fear of contracting a particular disease'.[109] The second concern that weighed with Keane CJ was the adverse effect on funds available for health care that would inevitably follow from the flood of claims to be expected following such a ruling. Keane CJ concluded that he was satisfied

> in cases where there is no more than a very remote risk that [the plaintiff] will contract the disease, recovery should not be allowed for such a psychiatric illness.

---

106. McMahon and Binchy, *Law of Torts* (3rd ed., Butterworths, 2000), 18.64, at p.1498.
107. [2003] IESC 13, [2003] 1 IR 465, [2003] 2 ILRM 94.
108. The refusal to allow recovery was apparently based on the fact that the plaintiff could demonstrate no sign of having developed a physical injury as a result of the employer's breach of duty.
109. [2003] 1 IR 465, 484.

That is because... policy considerations... point clearly to the necessity for imposing some limitation on the number of potential claims which might otherwise come into being.[110]

[15–75] Geoghegan J expressed similar concerns in very clear terms in a judgment that is perhaps best captured in his observation: 'mechanisms are necessary to control the potential number of claims that may be made arising out of negligent exposure to asbestos'.[111] Having conducted an extensive comparative inquiry, Geoghegan J, in allowing the appeal, emphasised that the claim in *Fletcher* was 'quite different from the case of a plaintiff who suffers from traumatic neurasthenia linked with physical illness directly resulting from an accident'.[112]

[15–76] It is submitted that much remains unclear post *Fletcher* about what will satisfy the minimum actionable damage requirement. This is hardly surprising given the narrow question at issue in that case regarding what ultimately came to be viewed as the plaintiff's irrational fear. It will be recalled that in *Fletcher*, the sole basis for the plaintiff's claim was a fear of the future argument and damages were sought only for the psychiatric injury allegedly caused by the defendants' negligence. Significantly, Keane CJ did apparently consider[113] it possible that, at common law, inferred simple permanent penetration by asbestos fibres occasioning the risk of the possible future occurrence of mesothelioma could amount to 'injury' so as to found an action for damages. The reason this point was not canvassed further was that the point was not argued on behalf of the plaintiff. Speaking of whether a physiological change to the plaintiff resulted from the defendant's negligence, Geoghegan J stated

> I have deliberately refrained from expressing any view as to whether the implantation of fibres into the lung (which did occur in this case) or the development of pleural plaques (which did not occur), in neither case involving any immediate symptoms, could be described as a physical injury especially having regard to the definition of injury in the Civil Liability Acts.[114]

[15–77] In *Melville v The Home Office*,[115] a Court of Appeal judgment, the plaintiff worked as a prison officer and from time to time had to participate in recovering the bodies of prisoners who had committed suicide. Evidence indicated that the defendant knew that employees who had to deal with such incidents might suffer psychiatric injury and thus should receive support from the prison care team after such an incident. Liability was made out.

110. [2003] 1 IR 465, 485.
111. [2003] 1 IR 465, 510.
112. [2003] 1 IR 465, 518.
113. [2003] 1 IR 465, 472.
114. [2003] 1 IR 465, 519.
115. [2005] PIQR P255.

2.10.1. Embarrassment and Humiliation Caused to Employee in the Context of Error Concerning Promotion

In *Larkin v Dublin City Council*,[116] the plaintiff advanced what Clark J described as 'an unusual case'. He sought damages for the humiliation and disappointment he suffered when, owing to an administrative error concerning examination results, he was wrongly advised that he had been successful in applying for promotion, only to have this good news withdrawn days later when the error was discovered. Although he had not sustained any psychiatric illness and as such did not seek damages for nervous shock, the plaintiff contended that the negligence of the employer had occasioned him considerable upset and disappointment. [15–78]

It is interesting that Clark J accepted that a duty of care was owed by the employer in these circumstances, and had been breached. She observed that [15–79]

> it seems to me, in all the circumstances of the case that there was a duty to ensure that the results were not presented to candidates until their accuracy had been checked. This was not a case of a moment of momentary inadvertence where someone accidentally hit the wrong button. The mistake which occurred was multifaceted and required the omission of an entire set of written exam results from inclusion in the spread sheet in the final calculation of marks.[117]

However, because the plaintiff in *Larkin* could show no recognised psychiatric injury, his claim was dismissed as disclosing no actionable damage. The significant point to note here is that the expansive approach taken to the questions of duty and breach may very well avail a future plaintiff who can show such psychiatric injuries.

2.11. Duty in Respect of Pure Economic Loss Suffered by an Employee

It is likely that – broadly speaking – an employee's economic interests would be held to be beyond the scope of the employer's duty of care in negligence. (An exception here is in relation to references, where there may be liability in negligence for loss suffered due to an employer's negligence in preparing a reference[118]). [15–80]

There is scant authority on the point, but it appears that for a duty to arise in respect of pure economic loss there would have to be special factors or circumstances in the employment relationship that made it just to impose such a duty. In *Scally v Southern Health and Social Services Board*,[119] it was said that this was essentially a matter of contract law into which the law of negligence should not

---

116. [2007] IEHC 416, [2008] 1 IR 391. This case is also analysed in Chapter 16.
117. [2008] 1 IR 391, 396-397.
118. *Spring v Guardian Assurance Plc* [1995] 2 AC 296.
119. [1992] 1 AC 294.

interfere. In the words of Lord Bridge: 'If a duty of the kind in question was not inherent in the contractual relationship, I do not see how it could possibly be derived from the tort of negligence.'[120]

[15–81] *Scally* was approved by the Supreme Court in *Sweeney v Duggan*[121]; it would thus appear that the general rule is that the employer's duty of care extends only to protecting employees against physical injury, and unless there is an express term in the contract of employment, there will be no liability for an employee incurring economic loss.[122]

2.12. Duty to Provide Safe System of Work

[15–82] If an employee suffers injury at work, due to a risk in the system of work that the employer should have taken steps to eliminate or minimise, the employer will be liable in negligence. It is submitted that an employer must address, in advance, the foreseeable risks inherent in the work [s]he is going to require an employee to carry out, so as to ensure that the method or procedures to be followed in carrying out the work are sufficient so as to reasonably protect the employee from those risks.[123]

> The extent of the duty owed by an employer in respect of the system of work may vary from case to case. As was said in the course of a recent Supreme Court judgment:

> The extent of the duty will vary considerably according to the circumstances of the case. In cases where the work is complex and/or highly dangerous the duty may involve the establishment of an elaborate system which is strictly supervised and enforced. In other circumstances a mere warning or specific instruction may suffice.[124]

[15–83] In this respect, it is submitted that it is not necessary as such for the plaintiff who claims that an employer has an unsafe system of work to prove that an alternative system would have been far safer. Nor does the plaintiff have to establish in pleadings, or in evidence adduced at trial, what precise alternative system of work ought to have been in place. Authority for this proposition can be found in the decision of the former Supreme Court in *Connor v Malachy Bourke Contractors Ltd.*[125] In practical terms, plaintiffs in some cases may face major difficulties if they

---

120. *ibid.*, at 303.
121. [1997] 2 IR 531, [1997] 2 ILRM 211.
122. See also *Reid v Rush & Tompkins Group Plc* [1990] 1 WLR 212, [1990] ICR 61.
123. In this respect, it is well established that an employer will owe a duty of care not to expose an employee to a level of noise that the employers know (or ought to know) to be dangerous. It is now common practice to limit the volume of sound with ear protection and any difficulties in providing such protection are not insurmountable.
124. *McSweeney v J S McCarthy Ltd.* [2000] IESC 162, *per* Murray J.
125. Supreme Court, 31 March 1955.

are unable to point to an alternative system free of the dangers that arose with the impugned system. However, it is not a rule that the plaintiff, in order to succeed, must highlight another system that should have been used. In *Dixon v Cementation Co. Ltd.*,[126] Devlin LJ stated 'there are…cases…in which a plaintiff can fairly say: "If this is dangerous, then there must be some way of doing it that can be found by a prudent employer and it is not for me to devise that way or say what it is." '

That said, however, if the plaintiff can provide evidence that other employers have put precautions in place that minimise risk of the type of accident in question, this may strengthen the plaintiff's hand in two ways. First, it *may* be evidence that standard industry practice is safer than that adhered to by the defendant, and secondly, it will be evidence that precautions are widely available and can be implemented relatively easily. [15–84]

2.12.1. Meaning of Safe System of Work not a Term of Art

In *Caulfield v George Bell & Co. Ltd.*[127] Murnaghan J noted that the expression 'a safe system of work' had not previously, to his knowledge, been defined. He continued: [15–85]

> The obligation has to be considered in every case, to which it is appropriate, in relation to the particular circumstances of the job in hand. In the expression the word 'safe' means no more than 'as safe as is reasonably possible in the circumstances'. The degree of safety would depend on the particular job and would vary between wide limits.[128]

In *Kennedy v Hughes Dairy Ltd.*,[129] the plaintiff was working as a fork-lift driver at the defendant's dairy. His work involved preparing crates of bottled milk for delivery and tidying up broken bottles at the end of loading sessions. While carrying a crate, the plaintiff tripped on a bottle and fell, and his arm was cut by broken glass that fell on him from the crate. The plaintiff sued his employer, alleging negligence on the basis that he had not been supplied with proper protective clothing such as appropriate gloves or gauntlets. The plaintiff claimed that there was a foreseeable and major risk of a person in his position becoming injured by broken bottles in the manner described. Blayney J withdrew the case from the jury in the High Court holding that, in the absence of evidence that the management had been imprudent or unreasonable in not providing the particular gloves, the plaintiff had failed to establish that employers in the same business followed a practice of providing the appropriate safety equipment. On the plaintiff's appeal, however, the Supreme Court in a majority judgment allowed the appeal and ordered a new trial. The court was of the view that the plaintiff's evidence and the expert evidence, if accepted, had been sufficient to warrant the conclusion that [15–86]

---

126. [1960] 1 WLR 746, 748.
127. [1958] IR 326.
128. [1958] IR 326, 333.
129. [1989] ILRM 117.

there had been a foreseeable risk of injury to the plaintiff in the area in which he was injured, because of the nature of his work. There had been sufficient evidence to support a conclusion that the failure of the employer to provide the plaintiff with adequate protective gloves could have exposed the plaintiff to unnecessary risks of injury.

[15–87]   In *Coyle v An Post*,[130] the plaintiff worked as the sub-postmaster in Raphoe, County Donegal. He had to drive, on an icy winter's morning, to Lifford in order to collect cash. He crashed en route, suffering personal injury, and alleged negligence on behalf of his employer in its failing to have funds available elsewhere, which would have meant that he did not have to make the journey to Lifford. The argument was somewhat ambitious, and was rejected by the Supreme Court, albeit in a majority decision.

[15–88]   It is submitted in this regard that there is no liability where an employee suffers injury whilst performing a task requiring basic common sense for which no instructions can be appropriately given. In *Devizes Reclamation Company Ltd. v Chalk*,[131] the Court of Appeal in England relieved an employer of liability in the following circumstances. The action arose from an accident in the scrap metal yard owned by the defendants where the plaintiff was employed as a labourer. A large lump of lead fell off a pallet while being unloaded from a lorry. It was necessary to move the lead so, on his own initiative, the plaintiff bent down to slew it round and felt a sudden sharp pain in his back. The Court of Appeal, reversing the decision of the trial judge, held that it was impossible to find negligence without ascertaining what the instructions should have been and it was difficult to see what possible instruction would have been relevant in a one-off situation where the plaintiff was doing something on his own initiative and when he should have been using his common sense.

2.12.2. Where the Plaintiff is Injured Whilst Working Alone

[15–89]   Permitting the plaintiff to work on his own when it is foreseeable that he may need the help of a co-worker may amount to negligence, as is illustrated by the Supreme Court judgment in *McSweeney v McCarthy Ltd*.[132] The plaintiff was an experienced painter and decorator who worked for the defendant contractors. The plaintiff suffered injuries after ascending to the top of a ladder for the purpose of painting certain pipes, when the ladder slipped away from underneath him, causing him to fall some 10 feet to the tiled factory floor. There was nobody holding the ladder at the base nor was it tied, or otherwise secured at either the top or the bottom. The allegation of negligence was that, *inter alia*, the employer should have ensured that somebody was at the foot of the ladder securing it while the plaintiff mounted the ladder. The Supreme Court, reversing the trial judge, held that it was negligent to

---

130. [1993] ILRM 508.
131. *The Times*, 2 April 1999.
132. [2000] IESC 162.

leave the plaintiff to his own devices. The court emphasised that it was at all times foreseeable that the plaintiff working without assistance was likely to need assistance to secure the ladder. The foreman did not inspect the site to identify when or where this was likely to arise or how the plaintiff should deal with this situation, or how he might or should be contacted by the plaintiff when assistance was needed. Assigning a man on his own to use a ladder to work at a height poses immediately the question as to how he is to mount an unsecured ladder, whether it is for the purpose of tying it at the top or getting to his place of work. That was an inherent danger, which was primarily, though not exclusively, under the control of the defendants as the employer.

The court observed that a straightforward but specific instruction to postpone the work until the plaintiff sought out and located the foreman, whatever delay was involved, would have been one means of addressing the risk. A deduction of 40 per cent was made for contributory negligence.

2.12.3. Where the Employer Acquiesces in or Condones Dangerous Practices
In a case where employees have fallen into the habit of adopting a dangerous [15–90] practice, negligence may be found through an employer turning a blind eye so as to be said to have acquiesced in or condoned the dangerous practice. The point is illustrated by *O'Reilly v CIÉ*.[133] The case arose out of an accident that occurred while the plaintiff was in the employment of Iarnród Éireann as a guard. On the day in question he was travelling as a guard on a freight train. It was the practice pursued by both the plaintiff and his other colleagues acting as guards to get off the train while it was actually in motion, in the course of performing a particular task. He suffered very serious injury. In the course of upholding the trial judge's finding of liability, the Supreme Court noted that the dangerous practice had 'been acquiesced in and condoned by the employers over a number of years'.

In this respect, putting in place a safe system may not be enough if the employer [15–91] does not take steps to ensure that that system is followed. If safety measures are being routinely ignored by staff, an employer might be liable for failing to insist that such safety practices be adhered to. In one English case, liability was imposed when an employee suffered a serious eye injury as a result of not wearing protective goggles. Goggles were made available, but workers generally did not wear them because they thought the goggles impeded their work. The Court of Appeal held that the employer was negligent in not making it a rule to wear goggles and enforcing such a rule through supervision.[134]

---

133. Supreme Court, *ex temp*, 8 May 2002.
134. *Bux v Slough Metals Ltd.* [1973] 1 WLR 1358.

2.13. Duty to Provide Adequate Plant and Equipment

[15–92] An employer is bound at common law to take reasonable care to provide employees with the necessary plant and equipment. Accordingly, the employer will be liable for injury caused by defective equipment, or where injury arises from the absence of equipment that was obviously necessary.[135] Thus, if the work an employee is required to do involves a known risk, the employer is under an obligation to devise, insofar as is possible, a method of working that minimises that risk, and also to provide adequate safety equipment or facilities. So, in *General Cleaning Contractors v Christmas*,[136] the House of Lords imposed liability upon the defendant employers for failing to take suitable precautions, which could have prevented their employee from falling and suffering serious injuries while cleaning the windows of a building from the outside. Lord Reid articulated the correct position in negligence in the following terms:

> Where the problem varies from job to job it may be reasonable to leave a great deal to the man in charge, but the danger in this case is one which is constantly found, and it calls for a system to meet it. Where a practice of ignoring an obvious danger has grown up I do not think that it is reasonable to expect an individual workman to take the initiative in devising and using precautions. It is the duty of the employer to consider the situation, to devise a suitable system, to instruct his men what they must do and to supply any implements that may be required… No doubt he cannot be certain that his men will do as they are told when they are working alone. But if he does all that is reasonable to ensure that his safety system is operated he will have done what he is bound to do.[137]

[15–93] So too can liability be imposed where an employee is injured by defective equipment at work even where that equipment is not provided by the employer. In *Keenan v Bergin*,[138] the plaintiff was a foreman who was employed by the second defendants. The first defendant drove his articulated vehicle, consisting of a motor cab and trailer, onto the property of the second defendants, where he left the trailer to be unloaded. The trailer was supported at the rear by ordinary lorry wheels and in front by struts attached to jockey wheels, which were designed to be retracted under the trailer when it was being drawn by the motor cab. The locking mechanism of the struts and jockey wheels was defective but the second defendants did not know this. After the trailer had been unloaded, it was manhandled in the usual manner so as to remove it from the unloading area and, as it passed over some uneven ground, its forward supports collapsed and that end of the trailer fell to the ground and caused severe injuries to the plaintiff who was helping to manhandle the trailer. The plaintiff claimed damages in the High Court for the

---

135. In the old case of *Deegan v Langan* [1966] IR 373 an employer was held liable for supplying the plaintiff employee, a carpenter, with nails that the employer knew to be of a type that could disintegrate when struck by a hammer.
136. [1952] AC 180.
137. *ibid.*, at p.194.
138. [1971] IR 192.

negligence of the defendants. At the trial of the action each defendant was found to have been negligent, with an apportionment of fault of 20 per cent to the employer. This apportionment was upheld by the Supreme Court, which held that the employers had been negligent as the trailer and its forward supports were equipment with which they were familiar, and they had failed in their duty to their employee by omitting to inspect the trailer's support mechanism, and thus discover a patent defect, before allowing the plaintiff to manhandle the trailer.

Burke v John Paul & Co.[139] is one of the leading Irish authorities on point. The [15–94] plaintiff worked as a labourer for the defendant, who claimed that the defendant had been negligent in furnishing the plaintiff with defective equipment for his work and that he had been injured as a result of the extra physical strain imposed on him when using the defective equipment. It was established that the plaintiff's abdominal muscles had been ruptured and that he had developed a hernia; there was evidence that a hernia usually develops where there is an area of congenital weakness of the abdomen. The Supreme Court held that there had been evidence to support a finding by the jury that the defendant had been negligent either by failing to supply the plaintiff with proper equipment or by failing to maintain in proper condition the equipment that had been supplied, thus exposing the plaintiff to an avoidable risk of injury; and that there had been ample evidence to support a finding by the jury that the plaintiff's hernia resulted from the extra strain imposed on him when using the defective equipment.

In some cases, negligence may be shown by virtue of the employer's failure to keep [15–95] up to speed with improved practices, and to update and modernise his equipment in line with such practices. In *Connolly v Dundalk UDC*,[140] the defendant employer was negligent in failing to install an alarm and ventilation system that would have prevented the emission of chlorine gas, which caused harm to the plaintiff employee. Such a ventilation system was commonplace in other places of employment in the same industry. Similarly, in *English v Anglo-Irish Meat Co.*,[141] the employer was negligent in failing to provide an employee working as a meat boner with modern protective clothing that would have prevented injuries he sustained when using a razor-sharp knife for boning meat.

As regards equipment, the 2006 decision of the House of Lords in *Robb v Salamis* [15–96] *(M & I) Ltd.*[142] is important. The case reaffirmed the position that an employer is under a duty to anticipate accidents. Mr Robb had been working as a scaffolder on an oil-and-gas production platform. The accommodation provided for men working on the platform had been equipped with two-tier bunks with suspended ladders providing access to the top bunks.

139. [1967] IR 277.
140. [1990] 2 IR 1, aff'd Supreme Court, O'Hanlon J, 18 November 1992.
141. [1988] IEHC 18.
142. [2006] UKHL 56, [2007] 2 All ER 97.

On the day of the accident, Mr Robb had attempted to descend from the top bunk, but the ladder had not been properly engaged within the retaining brackets, it had fallen to the floor and he had been injured. After the accident the owners of the platform had fixed them permanently with screws. That was a simple operation it would have been reasonably practicable to carry out before Mr Robb had had his accident.

[15–97] Interestingly, Lord Hope, delivering the leading judgment, stated that when an employer was assessing the risks to which his employees might be exposed when using equipment that [s]he provided for them to work with, the employer had to consider not only the skilled and careful man but also the contingency of carelessness and the frequency with which that contingency was likely to arise. The employer's obligation, however, was to anticipate situations that might give rise to accidents; he was not permitted to wait for them to happen.

[15–98] What of the situation where an employer does provide the appropriate facilities, and makes the employees aware of this, but the plaintiff argues that no or no sufficient pressure was put on him or her to make use of those facilities? In such cases, it appears correct to say that a plaintiff 'will understandably find it much harder to succeed than… in cases where the defendants failed to provide safety equipment at all'.[143]

2.13.1. Employer's Duty to Provide Safe Plant and Equipment in the Context of a 'Dangerous Job'

[15–99] The Court of Appeal case of *Buck and Others v Nottinghamshire Healthcare NHS Trust*[144] concerned an interesting question: whether a hospital was in breach of its duty of care to its employees when a patient in high-security conditions injured several nurses. In the circumstances, it was held that there was a breach of a duty and the defendant's appeal against a first-instance finding of liability was dismissed. Six nurses at a high-security hospital were assaulted by a 26-year-old patient who was classified as having a psychopathic personality disorder. It is submitted that the important point to take from the Court of Appeal decision in this case is that the duty of care owed by an employer is no different in a situation where the nature of the job is dangerous. Whilst employees accept the risks inherent in their work, they do not accept risks that could be avoided by the exercise of reasonable care by their employers in providing safe equipment and a safe system of work. It had been open to the trial judge in this case to conclude that Miss A was a patient who posed an exceptional risk, and that if there had been a policy in place that involved confining patients to their rooms at night if a rigorous risk assessment indicated that it was necessary, it would have been applied to her, thereby preventing the events that led to the injuries to nursing staff.

143. Buckley, *The Law of Negligence* (4th ed., LexisNexis Butterworths, 2005), at p.365, discussing *Qualcast (Wolverhampton) Ltd. v Haynes* [1959] AC 743 and *James v Hepworth & Grandage Ltd.* [1968] 1 QB 94, [1967] 3 WLR 178, [1967] 2 All ER 829.
144. [2006] EWCA Civ. 1576, [2006] 1 MHLR 351.

2.13.2. *Lifting Excessive Weight*

Injuries suffered at work as a result of lifting heavy weights have given rise to much   [15–100]
litigation. As to heavy weights, this is governed by the Factories Acts and statutory
instruments relating to safety, health and welfare at work.[145] The preponderance
of common law negligence actions in this area appear to focus on the question of
whether adequate training has been provided to the plaintiff in respect of lifting
technique. *Kirby v South Eastern Health Board*[146] was a claim by a nurse who had
suffered injury to her back when lifting a patient. The method of turning used
was outdated and had been criticised in medical publications as being dangerous.
Prior to the plaintiff's suffering injury, the defendant employer had published
instructions for the training of nurses that expressly repudiated the practice the
plaintiff was using.

In imposing liability, Morris J had regard to expert evidence that it had been well   [15–101]
known for many years that, in order to protect employees' safety, lifting must not
be performed in the manner carried out by the plaintiff. Morris J refused to make
a deduction for contributory negligence; after all, the plaintiff 'could not reasonably have been aware of the danger present in using this method of lifting without
instruction from the defendants'.

2.14. Duty to Provide Competent Staff

An employer owes a duty of care to provide competent staff. Clearly, in some   [15–102]
instances engaging an incompetent employee may threaten the physical safety of
another employee; if personal injury results, the employer may well be liable in
negligence.

Liability may arise if injury is caused by a person performing a task for which they
are untrained. Conceivably, an employer may be negligent in hiring an individual
whose bad character was apparent. Alternatively, the employer may be vicariously
liable, assuming the other employee has committed a tort, and that tort is within
the scope of the employment.

2.14.1. *Practical Jokers*

If an employee is injured as result of joking or horseplay of another employee,   [15–103]
an employer may also be liable in negligence. If the employer was aware of the
employee's mischievous propensities, the employer may be liable for failing to take
steps to prevent the employee from causing injury to colleagues.

---

145. See McMahon and Binchy, *Law of Torts* (3rd ed., Butterworths, 2000), at p.515, and the Safety,
    Health and Welfare at Work (General Application) Regulations 2007, SI no. 299 of 2007.
146. DPIJ: Trinity and Michaelmas Terms 1993, at p.234, discussed amongst a number of similar
    cases in McMahon and Binchy, *Law of Torts* (3rd ed., Butterworths, 2000), 18.115, at p.516.

[15–104]   The issue of an employer's liability for the actions of a practical joker was addressed by the Supreme Court more than 40 years ago in *Hough v Irish Base Metals*.[147] The plaintiff was injured when jumping away from a gas fire, which had been placed near him for 'a bit of devilment' by another employee. The evidence was that this was a 'lark' often practised in the repair shop where the employees worked. The Supreme Court held that negligence had not been established. The messing about in question had not been reported to anyone in authority, and was not something that would have been easily detectable. It was artificial to say that the employer's failure to be aware that this larking was taking place amounted to a failure to take reasonable care. After all, 'the larking in question was of such recent origin and was not of such frequency as must necessarily have been detected in any system of reasonable supervision'.[148]

[15–105]   By contrast, in *Hudson v Ridge Manufacturing Co. Ltd.*,[149] liability was imposed where the plaintiff was tripped up by a co-worker who had persistently been engaging in 'horse-play and skylarking' and who had 'an almost incurable habit of tripping people up'. The employer had repeatedly upbraided him but this had had no effect, and they did not dismiss him. Streatfeild J found that this amounted to a danger in the system of work for which the employer should be held liable. He emphasised, however, that if the incident had been an isolated one, or if it had occurred once before and followed by a reprimand so as to provide a basis for assuming there would be no recurrence, then liability would not be imposed.[150] Similarly, in *Nagle v Tippler's Tavern Ltd.*,[151] a 15-year-old worker was injured when tricked by two 17-year-old colleagues into drinking a tumbler of dishwasher detergent that looked like water. Barr J imposed liability in negligence on the employer, holding that there had been a breach of the duty to warn employees, especially young employees, as to the nature and properties of the detergent.

2.15. Duty to Provide and Maintain a Safe Place of Work
2.15.1. Where Injury Occurs Off Premises

[15–106]   An employer may owe a duty of care to his employee in relation to the safety of premises to which the employee is sent in the course of his duties. The position is conveniently summarised by White,[152] who states thus:

---

147. Unreported, Supreme Court, 8 December 1967.
148. *Hough* may be compared with an earlier English case, *Smith v Crossley Brothers* (1951) 95 Sol Jo 655. There, injury was caused to the plaintiff when compressed air from a pipe was directed at his rectum. The employers were relieved of liability because there was no reason to anticipate that the employees responsible would behave in such a manner since they had never done anything like it before.
149. [1957] 2 QB 348.
150. *ibid.*, at 350.
151. Unreported, High Court, Barr J, 11 October 1991.
152. White, *Civil Liability for Industrial Accidents* (vol. 1, Oak Tress Press, 1993), at p.434.

The employer owes the like duty of care with regard to the safety of the premises of third parties on which he requires his servants to work as he does in respect of his own premises, but what reasonable care requires in relation to the latter is not necessarily the same as what reasonable care requires in relation to the former.[153]

What of the situation where the employer is aware of the off-site hazard? In the [15–107] English case of *Smith v Austin Lifts Ltd.*,[154] the plaintiff was employed as a fitter by a firm of lift repairers and was injured when he went to overhaul a lift on certain premises. The machine house in which the winding mechanism was situated was on the roof and was reached by a ladder through double doors secured by bolts. The fitter knew that the left-hand door was defective in that a hinge was broken, and had reported this to his employers, who had informed the occupiers. On the day of the accident he found the left-hand door jammed inside the machine house and the right-hand door open; he put his hand on the left-hand door to help himself up, but the door gave and he fell from the ladder. When the employee was injured as a result of the hazard, the House of Lords held[155] that the employer had indeed been negligent. Lord Denning said:

> Notwithstanding what was said in *Taylor v Sims & Sims* [1942] 2 All ER 375, it has since been held, I think rightly, that employers who send their workmen to work on the premises of others cannot renounce all responsibility for their safety. The employers still have an over-riding duty to take reasonable care not to expose their men to unnecessary risk. They must, for instance, take reasonable care to devise a safe system of work (see *General Cleaning Contractors v Christmas* [1952] 2 All ER 1110) and, if they know or ought to know of a danger on the premises to which they send their men, they ought to take reasonable care to safeguard them from it. What is reasonable care depends of course on the circumstances: see *Wilson v Tyneside Window Cleaning Co.* [1958] 2 All ER 265.

> Applying this principle, I think that the judge was entitled in this case to find the employers liable. If the workmen had not reported any difficulty or defect on the premises, the employers would not have been responsible. They would have been entitled to assume that the means of access provided by the occupiers was reasonably safe. But when the workmen reported – as they did – that the machine house door was broken and needed re-fixing in position, the employers were, I think, put on enquiry whether the means of access provided by these doors was reasonably safe. They ought to have done something but they did nothing beyond report the defect to the occupiers. Report after report, four in all, produced no results. Thereupon the employers ought, I should have thought – and, indeed, as the judge thought – to have gone themselves to see if the means of access was reasonably safe. If they had done so they would have found it unsafe and would have done

---

153. *ibid.*
154. [1959] 1 WLR 100, [1959] 1 All ER 81.
155. Lord Reid dissenting on this point.

something. They might have insisted on the door being mended, or they might have sent a long ladder to enable the men to get safely to the machinery. Having done nothing, they cannot escape liability.[156]

[15–108]   The courts may be wary of imposing too high a standard on employers here, however, as evidenced by the decision in *Mulcare v Southern Health Board*.[157] The plaintiff in *Mulcare* was working as a home help in a dilapidated old house. She instituted proceedings in negligence against the Health Board after suffering injury when she fell on an uneven floor in the house. Her claim was dismissed by Murphy J in the High Court. The Court noted that the plaintiff had worked as a home help in the house for seven years without any previous incident occurring. It was also noted that even if the defendant had inspected the house to ensure it was safe, it would have been powerless to order the occupier to improve. Regard was also had in the judgment to the social utility of the defendant's service of home help.

[15–109]   It is submitted that *Mulcare* is correctly decided, but the point about the defendant being unable to order the occupier to make the property safe is perhaps the least compelling aspect of the reasoning. There will be cases in which an employer simply cannot permit an employee to work in an environment that is dangerous, although *Mulcare* was not such a case.

[15–110]   The issue of injury being suffered off-site also arose in *McMahon v Irish Biscuits*.[158] The plaintiff worked for Irish Biscuits as a sales representative. He was often sent to various client supermarkets to inspect stock levels. On the occasion in question, he was under time pressure to visit a number of such client supermarkets. In one such supermarket, the stockroom was overcrowded with boxes, and in order to get the job done speedily, the plaintiff, ignoring cautionary warnings, climbed shelving. He fell and suffered personal injuries. O'Donovan J apportioned liability between the employer (30 per cent) and the client supermarket (60 per cent), with a deduction of 10 per cent for contributory negligence. Speaking of the duty of the employer to ensure the safety of the client's premises, O'Donovan J stated:

> It is my view that [the employers] had a duty to acquaint themselves of [sic] the facilities which were provided by their customers to enable… their sales staff to carry out duties, which were for their mutual benefit, and to satisfy themselves that those facilities and the system operated by their customers… did not pose a threat to their well being.[159]

[15–111]   In *Dunne v Honeywell Control Systems Ltd.*,[160] Barron J dealt with the situation where an employee is working on a third party's premises. The first defendant

---

156. [1959] 1 WLR 100, 117–118.
157. [1988] ILRM 689.
158. [2002] IEHC 15.
159. At para.5 of the judgment.
160. [1991] ILRM 595.

carried on business as a supplier of control systems and had a service contract with the second defendant whereby they maintained equipment they had sold to the second defendant. The plaintiff, an electrical technician employed by the first defendant, sustained serious injuries when he fell from a ladder on the second defendant's premises, where, in the course of his employment with the first defendant, he was engaged on a repair job. Expert evidence indicated that the ladder in question did not comply with accepted standards of safety; other evidence showed that the plaintiff had carried a case of tools when ascending and descending the ladder. Barron J found as a fact the both the defendants contributed to his accident. The tool case carried by the plaintiff was one that had been provided for him by the first defendant. The plaintiff sought damages for negligence against the first defendants, and for negligence and breach of statutory duty against the second. Barron J, in finding both defendants liable, but in apportioning liability between the defendants, stated:

> An employer has a duty to take reasonable care for the safety of his employee. Where an employee is working on premises other than that of his employer the duty of the employer to use reasonable care for his safety does not in any way diminish. Nevertheless what might be reasonable for an employer to do for the safety of his employee on his own premises may no longer be reasonable where the employee is working elsewhere.[161]

2.16. No Right of Action in Negligence for Manner of Employee's Dismissal

It is submitted that there is no action in negligence for personal injuries arising [15–112] out of the manner in which an employee is dismissed.[162] This is because the legislature, by virtue of the Unfair Dismissals Acts 1977 (as amended), has provided a statutory mechanism by which an action for unfair dismissal may be pursued. As such, it is not appropriate for the common law of negligence to intervene and to offer an alternative remedy. The leading English decision on the point is *Johnson v Unisys Ltd.*,[163] where the House of Lords was clear that a right of action in negligence in respect of the manner of one's dismissal cannot co-exist with one's statutory entitlement not to be unfairly dismissed. *Johnson* has been approved in the High Court case of *Orr v Zomax*[164] and is referred to with apparent approval in other Irish cases.[165]

However, the mere fact that an employee has been dismissed cannot be used by [15–113] the employer to extinguish any pre-existing negligence action the employee might

---

161. [1991] ILRM 595, 600.
162. See also chapters 16 and 21.
163. [2003] 1 AC 518, [2001] UKHL 131, [2001] 2 WLR 1076, [2001] 2 All ER 801, [2001] ICR 480, [2001] IRLR 279.
164. [2004] IEHC 47, [2004] 1 IR 486.
165. It was, for example, referred to by Laffoy J in her judgment in *McGrath v Trintech Technologies* [2004] IEHC 342, [2005] 4 IR 382.

have against the employer. Clarke J made this quite clear in *Maher v Jabil Global Services*.¹⁶⁶ This is consistent with the approach taken by the House of Lords in *Eastwood v Magnox Electric*¹⁶⁷ and *McCabe v Cornwall County Council*,¹⁶⁸ holding that outside the *Johnson v Unisys* exclusion area, a cause of action can accrue for breach of the employment contract prior to dismissal, which cause of action exists independently of the dismissal.

In an important passage in *Eastwood*, Lord Nicholls explained:

> The existence of this boundary line means that in some cases a continuing course of conduct, typically a disciplinary process followed by dismissal, may have to be chopped artificially into separate pieces. In cases of constructive dismissal a distinction will have to be drawn between loss flowing from antecedent breaches of the trust and confidence term and loss flowing from the employee's acceptance of these breaches as a repudiation of the contract. The loss flowing from the impugned conduct taking place before actual or constructive dismissal lies outside the Johnson exclusion area; the loss flowing from the dismissal itself is within that area. In some cases this legalistic distinction may give rise to difficult questions of causation in cases such as those now before the House, where financial loss is claimed as the consequence of psychiatric illness said to have been brought on by the employer's conduct before the employee was dismissed. Judges and tribunals, faced perhaps with conflicting medical evidence, may have to decide whether the fact of dismissal was really the last straw which proved too much for the employee, or whether the onset of the illness occurred even before he was dismissed.¹⁶⁹

3. The Safety, Health and Welfare at Work Act 2005

[15–114] The legal framework of health and safety law has been transformed due to the introduction of the Safety, Health and Welfare at Work Act 2005. This piece of legislation is framework in nature, pursuing the general objective of preventing workplace accidents and illnesses. The strength of the enforcement provisions in the legislation also places a renewed emphasis on deterrence. Although a complete study of this piece of legislation is outside the scope of the present work,¹⁷⁰ emphasis is placed here on the sections of the legislation of most significance for the employment relationship. As already discussed above, one of the most significant implications for employment law of the coming into force of the 2005 Act is the extent to which the statutory provisions will inform the development of the common law position already analysed in this chapter.

---

166. [2005] IEHC 130, [2008] 1 IR 25, [2005] ELR 233.
167. [2004] UKHL 35, [2005] 1 AC 503, [2004] 3 WLR 322, [2004] 3 All ER 991, [2004] IRLR 733. See also chapters 21 and 22.
168. [2003] ICR 501, [2003] IRLR 87.
169. [2005] 1 AC 503, 528-529.
170. See further Shannon, *Health and Safety: Law and Practice* (Thomson Round Hall, 2007), ch.3.

Part II of the 2005 Act sets out in general terms a range of distinct duties upon employers. Thus s.8(1) of the 2005 Act provides that it shall be the duty of every employer to do everything [s]he can, as far as is reasonably practicable, to ensure the safety, health and welfare of his or her employees.[171] It should be noted that any breach of s.8 of the 2005 Act attracts criminal liability.[172]

Before analysing the employer's duties in greater detail, a preliminary point should [15–115] be noted concerning the concept of an employee. Section 2(1) of the 2005 Act defines an employer in relation to an employee as:

    (a) the employer under the terms of a contract of employment;
    (b) a person (other than an employee of that person) under whose control and direction an employee works; and
    (c) the successor of the employer or an associated employer of the employer, where appropriate.

It is clear from this section that where an employer engages employees from [15–116] another business or company for temporary purposes, the engaging employer bears the responsibility for ensuring the place of work is safe, since [s]he is in control of the working environment. This is the case regardless of whether [s]he is the true employer of the employee. In summary, an employer/employee relationship, for the purposes of the 2005 Act, arises where an employee is working in the capacity of an employee (regardless of whose employee [s]he is) and is under an employer's direction and control.

Amongst the new duties identified in s.8(2) of the 2005 Act are:

    (a) managing and conducting work activities in such a way as to ensure, so far as is reasonably practicable, the safety, health and welfare at work of his or her employees[173];
    (b) managing and conducting work activities in such a way as to prevent, so far as is reasonably practicable, any improper conduct or behaviour likely to put the safety, health or welfare at work of his or her employees at risk.[174]

Section 8(2)(b) is significant in that it imposes an obligation on employers to iden- [15–117] tify in their human resources policies behaviour that will not be acceptable. Such policies should, of course, also identify the action to be taken where employee behaviour poses a threat to the health and safety of other employees. Clearly, this provision is of significance in the context of bullying, harassment and stress in

---

171. s.8(1) Safety, Health and Welfare at Work Act 2005 provides: '(1) Every employer shall ensure, so far as is reasonably practicable, the safety, health and welfare at work of his or her employees.'
172. See s.77(2)(a) *ibid.*
173. s.8(2)(a) *ibid.*
174. s.8(2)(b) *ibid.*

the workplace, dealt with separately in this work. Thus, as Shannon observes,[175] were the Health and Safety Authority to consider that an employer was exposing employees to unacceptable levels of stress at work, for example, the potential is here for the invocation of the enforcement mechanisms available under the 2005 Act.

Section 8(2)(b) refers to 'improper conduct', a term that is not defined in the 2005 Act. It has been noted, however, that this is likely to cover 'horse play', which did not, as such, come within the scope of the 1989 Act.[176]

Section 8(2) of the 2005 Act either amends or restates many of the particular duties set out in the 1989 Act and the 1993 Regulations. Examples include s.8(2)(e) of the 2005 Act, which extends the duty to provide safe systems of work by obliging the employer to revise and update as appropriate.

[15–118] Another interesting example of the broadening out of the employer's duties is contained in s.8(2)(h) of the 2005 Act, which may impose new obligations on employers to address stress in the workplace. This provision requires employers to determine and implement the safety measures necessary for the protection of the safety, health and welfare of employees when identifying hazards and carrying out a risk assessment under s.19 of the 2005 Act, or when preparing a safety statement under s.20 of the 2005 Act.

[15–119] Section 8(2)(c) of the 2005 Act provides that an employer's duty extends, as regards the place of work concerned, to ensuring, so far as is reasonably practicable:

(i) the design, provision and maintenance of it in a condition that is safe and without risk to health;
(ii) the design, provision and maintenance of safe means of access to and egress from it; and
(iii) the design, provision and maintenance of plant and machinery or any other articles that are safe and without risk to health; …

While the foregoing duties correspond to the duties previously contained in ss.6(2)(a) to (c) of the 1989 Act, the old provisions only applied to 'any place of work' that was 'under the employer's control'.[177] It is significant that these words have been deleted from the 2005 Act, with the result that an employer is now required to ensure, so far as is reasonably practicable, compliance with the duties set out in s.8(2)(c) of the 2005 Act, even if the place of work is not under his or her control.

175. See Shannon, *Health and Safety: Law and Practice* (Thomson Round Hall, 2007), at p.18, para.3.25.
176. *ibid.*, at para.3.26.
177. s.6(2)(a) Safety, Health and Welfare at Work Act 1989.

3.1. Breach of Statutory Duty under the 2005 Act

The 2005 Act appears to admit the possibility that an employer might be sued [15–120] civilly for breach of the various obligations imposed on him or her under the Act. It is, however, a matter of conjecture as to how this will operate in practice. It is clear, generally, that not every breach of a statutory obligation will give rise to a cause of action for breach of statutory duty. Rather, if a plaintiff is to sue for a breach of statutory duty [s]he must be able to show both that [s]he is a member of a class of people that the statute was designed to protect, and must have suffered harm over and above that suffered by other members of that class.[178] In a case where a prospective plaintiff wishes to sue under the 2005 Act, the second element of the test is not problematic, presuming that such plaintiff has actually suffered harm. The first element, however, is – especially given that it may be suggested that in the relevant case law, there is a certain amount of evidence that courts are reluctant to be overly expansive in deciding the limits of the class of persons that the legislation was designed to protect.

The key question, then, is, 'What category of persons is the 2005 Act designed to [15–121] protect?', for the answer to this question will also answer the question of who may sue for a breach of statutory duty. It is beyond doubt, having regard to the terms of the 2005 Act, that employees are protected and also, that the category of persons protected is not restricted to employees.[179] It is submitted, however, that in fact inasmuch as s.12 of the Act does not make any attempt to impose any restriction on the category of persons whom the employer should be seeking to protect (it refers merely to 'individuals at the place of work') it is, therefore, entirely arguable that anyone injured in that workplace, whether or not they are connected with the work that is ongoing, will have an action against the employer or person in control of the workplace for breach of statutory duty, should they suffer harm by reason of the employer or person in control not having done all that was reasonably practicable to make the workplace safe by identifying those hazards that might cause injury to health and/or by putting in place measures to deal with them. The only limitation to the application of s.12 would seem to be that the risk to the non-employee must arise 'in the course of work being carried on'. Significantly even this limitation does not apply in the case of a defendant non-employer in control of a workplace (s. 15) or in the case of a plaintiff employee under s.8.

3.2. Duty to Provide Information to Employees

Section 9 of the 2005 Act imposes a duty on an employer regarding information [15–122] to his or her employees.[180] Section 9(1) includes an additional requirement that the

---

178. *Lonrho Ltd. v Shell Petroleum* [1982] AC 173, [1981] 3 WLR 331, [1981] 2 All ER 456; *McDaid v Milford Rural District Council* [1919] 2 IR 1; *Doherty v Bowaters Irish Wallboard Mills* [1968] IR 277; *Gallagher v Mogul of Ireland* [1975] IR 204; *Daly v Greybridge Co-Operative Creamery Ltd.* [1964] IR 497; *Roche v Kelly* [1969] IR 100; *Moyne v Londonderry Port & Harbour Commissioners* [1986] IR 299.

179. s.12 Safety, Health and Welfare at Work Act 2005.

180. Pursuant to s.77(2)(a) *ibid.*, any breach of s.9 attracts criminal liability.

employer, when providing information to employees regarding health and safety matters, do so in a manner, form and, as appropriate, language that is reasonably likely to be understood by his or her employees. Section 9(1) requires employers to provide information 'on matters relating to' employees' safety, health and welfare 'that is reasonably likely to be understood by the employees concerned'. Section 9(1)(b) sets out the information that every employer should give to his or her employees. It requires that the information provided should include information on:

(i) the hazards to safety, health and welfare at work and the risks identified by the risk assessment,

(ii) the protective and preventive measures to be taken concerning safety, health and welfare at work under the relevant statutory provisions in respect of the place of work and each specific task to be performed at the place of work, and

(iii) the names of persons designated under *section 11* [i.e. persons to contact in an emergency situation] and or safety representatives selected under *section 25* if any.

This section is thus of significance in addressing the needs of non-English speaking employees although it does not, as Shannon points out, require an employer to ensure an employee has understood the relevant information.[181]

3.3. Duties of Employees under the 2005 Act

[15–123] Another very significant element of the 2005 Act is that it imposes a number of new obligations on employees. Amongst the obligations imposed upon employees under s.13 of the 2005 Act are:

• to comply with the relevant statutory provisions, as appropriate[182];

• not to engage in improper conduct or behaviour that is likely to endanger his or her own safety or that of any other person[183]; and

• to attend such training and, as appropriate, undergo such assessment as may reasonably be required by his or her employer or as may be prescribed relating to safety, health and welfare at work or relating to the work carried out by the employee.[184]

The section also imposes significant obligations on employees to report to their employer or any other appropriate person any dangerous practice or contravention of statutory provisions where this may endanger the safety, health and welfare at work of an employee or any other person.[185]

---

181. Shannon, *Health and Safety: Law and Practice* (Thomson Round Hall, 2007), at p.21, para.3.32.

182. s.13(1)(a) Safety, Health and Welfare at Work Act 2005.

183. s.13(1)(e) *ibid.* This section is discussed below in this chapter in the context of vicarious liability for bullying, harassment and stress at work.

184. s.13(1)(f) *ibid.*

185. s.13(1)(h)(i) *ibid.*

3.3.1. *Duty of Employees to Submit to Testing for Intoxicants*[186]

One of the most important and controversial additions to the duties of employees [15–124] is the inclusion of a duty to submit to any appropriate testing for intoxicants.[187] At the time of writing, regulations under this section have not been introduced. It should be emphasised, however, that this does not preclude employers from operating random intoxicant testing policies: such policies may validly be introduced and operated by way of contractual agreement.

The manner in which an employer operates such a testing regime was considered [15–125] by the Labour Court in the case of *Alstom Ireland Ltd. v A Worker*.[188] This was an industrial relations trade dispute referral that arose when a LUAS worker failed a random drugs test even though the quantity of intoxicant found was very low. The individual's union argued that it was of such a low percentage that the test should properly be classified as negative. The company, however, operated a zero-tolerance policy. The Labour Court stated that it had:

> consistently supported the use of drug and alcohol testing in safety critical employments. However, given the inevitable consequences for employees who test positive it is crucial that the modalities of all aspects of the testing conform to predetermined standards, which as far as possible, are agreed between the employer and the trade unions representing staff.

The Labour Court ruled that the worker should be given the benefit of the doubt given the fact that the particulars of the testing had not been agreed.

This controversial requirement on employees, with all its implications for constitutional rights, claims of victimisation, and unfair dismissal, seems likely to generate litigation once the relevant regulations are introduced.

3.4. Protection Against Penalisation under Section 27 of the 2005 Act

Section 27 of the 2005 Act introduces a very significant new provision in rela- [15–126] tion to health and safety in Irish employment law: that an employee should not be penalised for acting in good faith in the interests of health and safety.[189]

---

186. An 'intoxicant' is defined in s.2(1) *ibid.* as 'alcohol and drugs and any combination of drugs or of drugs and alcohol'. As Shannon observes, this definition 'does not discriminate between prescription and non-prescription drugs and provides no guidance on what is an acceptable quantity of drugs or alcohol'. Shannon, *Health and Safety: Law and Practice* (Thomson Round Hall, 2007), at p.28, para.3.50.
187. s.13(1)(c) Safety, Health and Welfare at Work Act 2005. On the privacy implications of this area of the law, see Chapter 17.
188. CD/07/413, appeal decision no. AD0765, 18 December 2007.
189. On this and other examples of penalisation in Irish employment law, see Curran, 'Victimisation: A New Remedy for Employees', 5(1) *IELJ* (2008), 4.

'Penalisation' for this purpose includes any act or omission by an employer or a person acting on behalf of an employer that affects, to his or her detriment, an employee with respect to any term or condition of his or her employment.[190]

[15–127] Section 27(3) prohibits an employer from penalising or threatening the penalisation of an employee for:

- acting as a safety representative;
- acting in compliance with the relevant statutory provisions;
- making a complaint or a representation about health and safety to the safety representative, or to the employer, or to an inspector[191];
- giving evidence in enforcement proceedings; and
- leaving, or while the danger persisted, refusing to return to his or her work in the face of serious or imminent danger.[192]

The dismissal of an employee following such penalisation will be deemed to be unfair under the Unfair Dismissal Acts,[193] though it should be noted that in such a case relief may not be granted to the employee under both Acts.[194] Section 27(7) provides that if an employee is dismissed, the employee shall not be regarded as unfairly dismissed if the employer shows that it was (or would have been) so negligent for the employee to take the steps [s]he took (or proposed to take) that a reasonable employer might have dismissed him or her for taking (or proposing to take) them.

[15–128] Under s.27(1) of the 2005 Act, penalisation includes any act or omission by an employer, or person acting on behalf of an employer that affects an employee to his or her detriment with respect to any term or condition of his or her employment, including:

- suspension, lay-off or dismissal (including a dismissal within the meaning of the Unfair Dismissals Acts 1977 to 2001), or the threat of suspension, lay-off or dismissal;
- demotion or loss of opportunity for promotion;
- transfer of duties, change of location of place of work, reduction in wages or change in working hours;
- imposition of any discipline, reprimand or other penalty (including a financial penalty);
- coercion or intimidation.

---

190. s.27(1) Safety, Health and Welfare at Work Act 2005.
191. See, for example, *HSE Dublin North East v Tiernan*, HSC/07/13, determination no. HSD 088, 9 October 2008.
192. See, for example, *Aranbel Construction Ltd. v Braney and Lacey*, HSC/08/7, determination no. HSD 086, 5 September 2008.
193. s.27(4) Safety, Health and Welfare at Work Act 2005.
194. s.27(5) *ibid.*

The causation inquiry that will attend consideration of this section was well [15–129] captured by the Labour Court in its 2009 determination in *Toni & Guy Blackrock v Paul O'Neill*[195] when it observed:

> It is clear from the language of this section that in order to make out a complaint of penalisation it is necessary for a claimant to establish that the determent of which he or she complains was imposed *for'* having committed one of the acts protected by subsection 3. Thus the detriment giving rise to the complaint must have been incurred because of, or in retaliation for, the Claimant having committed a protected act. This suggested that where there is more than one causal factor in the chain of events leading to the detriment complained of the commission of a protected act must be an operative cause in the sense that *'but for'* the Claimant having committed the protected act he or she would not have suffered the detriment. This involves a consideration of the motive or reasons which influenced the decision maker in imposing the impugned determent.

Two points can be made about the significance of this penalisation provision. First, [15–130] the open-ended nature of the concept of penalisation is illustrated by an analysis of determinations of the Labour Court in this area, which demonstrate, for example, how the manner in which an employer responds to a complaint may in and of itself be relevant when considering whether that response amounts to penalisation. Thus, in *LW Associates Ltd. v Lacey*,[196] the Labour Court considered that

> the precipitous manner in which the decision to place the Complainant on Health and Safety Leave was taken and the absence of any real and considered deliberation of the matter without affording the Complainant the benefit of representation, constitutes penalisation for having invoked the Act and comes within the meaning of S. 27 of the Act.

Secondly, it is clear from even a cursory perusal of the above list that the concept of 'penalisation' under the 2005 Act may thus have significant implications for other areas of employment law (including areas that are ostensibly distinct and separate segments of employment law). A good example is the legal framework concerning bullying, harassment and stress at work.[197]

3.4.1. *Examples of Labour Court Determinations Concerning Penalization under Section 27*

The Labour Court has repeatedly illustrated in its determinations the serious- [15–131] ness with which this penalisation provision will be treated. Thus, in *Allied Foods Ltd. v Sterio*,[198] for example, the complainant was employed as a General

---

195. HSC/09/5, determination no. HSD095, 18 June 2009.
196. HSC/08/2, determination no. HSD 085, 18 July 2008.
197. See Chapter 16.
198. HSC/09/4, determination no. HSD 097, 29 July 2009.

Operative. In May 2008 he discovered that his forklift licence was out of date and he alerted the company to this. Following clarification from the Health and Safety Authority, the complainant was moved to alternative duties. The company set up a refresher training course for workers with expired licences; the complainant claimed that he was initially overlooked for this training and that he was impeded in returning to the contract on which he was working. He referred his case to the Rights Commissioner under s.27 of the 2005 Act. The Rights Commissioner held that the complaint was well founded, and directed that the employer relocate the claimant back to the duties he had been performing immediately before he had reported the licence issue. In addition, the Rights Commissioner directed that compensation in the amount of €5,000 be paid to the complainant. The employer appealed the Rights Commissioner's decision to the Labour Court.

Disallowing the appeal, the Labour Court was satisfied that what occurred subsequent to the complaint being made – not placing the claimant on the refresher course, and his subsequent loss of earnings – constituted penalisation within the meaning of s.27.

[15–132] Significantly, the Labour Court relied on the decision of the European Court of Justice in *Von Colson and Kamann v Land Nordrhein-Westfalen*[199], and the principles emphasised therein to the effect that where an individual right is infringed, the judicial redress provided should not only compensate for the claimant's economic loss but must also provide a real deterrent against future infractions. Accordingly, the Labour Court varied the Rights Commissioner's determination to provide for total compensation of €6,000.

Another instructive recent authority on the nature of a claim for penalisation under s.27 of the 2005 Act is *Flynn Concrete Products Ltd. v Timma Gundars*.[200] The claimant contended that his dismissal was a direct result of his making a complaint under the 2005 Act which, he alleged, constituted penalisation within the terms of s.27(3)(c).

[15–133] The employer rejected this contention and claimed that the dismissal flowed from the claimant's failure to co-operate fully with, and in other respects to act properly concerning, an internal investigation of a complaint made by the claimant against his supervisor; and the claimant's attitude towards the company and his work prior to the termination of his employment. The company insisted that there was no connection between the complaint and the dismissal. There was no evidence that the letter had arrived in the company before the complainant was dismissed. The Labour Court emphasised that, given the fact that there was a complaint, followed by a dismissal, the onus was on the company to demonstrate that there was no causal connection. In the view of the Court, the company had not succeeded in so demon-

---

199. (C14/83) [1984] ECR 1891.
200.HSC/08/9, determination no. HSD 096, 20 July 2009.

strating, and the Court, on the balance of probabilities, preferred the evidence put on behalf of the claimant, concluding that penalisation under s.27 of the 2005 Act had been made out. The Court took the view that an award of compensation was appropriate and measured the level of this compensation at €10,000.

In *Toni & Guy Blackrock v Paul O'Neill*,[201] the Labour Court noted that the 2005   [15–134] Act was 'silent on the question of how the burden of proof should be allocated as between the parties'. Referring to its earlier determinations in *Department of Justice, Equality and Law Reform v Philip Kirwan*[202] and *Fergal Brodigan T/A FB Groundworks v Juris Dubina*[203] which had acknowledged that the normal rule of he who asserts must prove is subject to the exception of the 'peculiar knowledge principle', the Court in *O'Neill* continued:

> In the instant case what is at issue is the motive or reason for the Claimant's dismissal. That is to be found in the thought process of the decision makers at the time the decision to dismiss the Complainant was taken. That is something which is peculiarly within the knowledge of the Respondent. It would be palpably unfair to expect the Claimant to adduce direct evidence to show that the Respondent was influenced by his earlier complaints in deciding to dismiss him. Conversely, it is perfectly reasonable to require the Respondent to establish that the reasons for the dismissal were unrelated to his complaints under the Act.

> Having regard to these considerations, it seems to the Court that a form of shifting burden of proof, similar to that in employment equality law should be applied in the instant case. Thus the Claimant must establish, on the balance of probabilities, that he made complaints concerning health and safety. It is then necessary for him to show that, having regard to the circumstances of the case, it is apt to infer from subsequent events that his complaints were an operative consideration leading to his dismissal. If those two limbs of the test are satisfied it is for the Respondent to satisfy the Court, on credible evidence and to the normal civil standard, that the complaints relied upon did not influence the Claimant's dismissal.

Applying this test to the facts of *O'Neill*, the Labour Court concluded that the claimant had been penalised in that his dismissal had flowed from his having made the relevant complaints, and awarded the substantial sum of €20,000 in compensation.

3.4.2 Points of Practice and Procedure Concerning Section 27 Claims

Under the 2005 Act, an employee alleging a breach of s.27 is permitted to bring   [15–135] his or her claim before a Rights Commissioner, with proceedings being heard *in camera*. Section 28(2) of the 2005 Act provides that a Rights Commissioner shall:

---

201. HSC/09/5, determination no. HSD 085, HSD095, 18 June 2009.
202. HSC/07/12, determination no. HSD082, 16 January 2008.
203. HSC/08/12, determination no. HSD0810, 10 December 2008.

(a) give the parties an opportunity to be heard... and... present any evidence relevant to the complaint;

(b) give a decision in writing in relation to [the complaint]; and

(c) communicate the decision to the parties.

A Rights Commissioner has the power to declare that the complaint is or is not well founded. The Rights Commissioner may also direct the employer to take a specific course of action or to pay compensation. It is significant that the Rights Commissioner is accorded considerable discretion as regards the awarding of compensation, being entitled to direct the payment of such compensation 'as is just and equitable having regard to all the circumstances'.

[15–136] A Rights Commissioner must receive a complaint (made by giving notice in writing) within the period of six months, beginning on the date of the contravention to which the complaint relates, or within such further period not exceeding six months as the Rights Commissioner considers reasonable. The complaint, which must be given to the defendant by the Rights Commissioner, must contain such particulars and be in such form as may be specified by the Minister for Enterprise, Trade and Employment.[204]

[15–137] Section 29 of the 2005 Act provides that a decision of a Rights Commissioner can be appealed to the Labour Court. This appeal, which must be made within six weeks of the date on which the decision of the Rights Commissioner has been communicated to the parties, comprises a new hearing, with the Labour Court being empowered to affirm, vary or set aside the decision of a Rights Commissioner. A determination of the Labour Court can be enforced in the Circuit Court.[205] An appeal from the Labour Court to the High Court is only possible on a point of law.[206]

4. Vicarious Liability and the Safety, Health and Welfare at Work Act 2005

[15–138] In Chapter 3 it has been emphasised that one of the consequences of the categorisation of the relationship between the parties as one of employment is the potential for vicarious liability to be imposed. An issue of some importance at the present time in Irish employment law is the imposition of vicarious liability of employers for wrongs committed by their employees, particularly in the context of intentional wrongdoing performed by one employee against another. In the context of health and safety law, the classic example of such a situation is a bullying at work

---

204.s.28(5) Safety, Health and Welfare at Work Act 2005.
205.s.30 *ibid.*
206.s.29(6) *ibid.*

scenario. Although the Supreme Court judgment in *O'Keeffe v Hickey*[207] displays a degree of judicial unease with the prospect of the parameters of vicarious liability being expanded in tort law generally, it is important to note that a number of important developments in the UK and elsewhere may prove to be of significant persuasive authority in the development of vicarious liability principles in Irish law, at least in the context of bullying, harassment and stress at work.

5. The Significance of Codes of Practice

Finally, it should be noted that under s.60 of the Act, the Health and Safety [15–139] Authority is empowered to create codes of practice. Under s.61, it is provided that, in the context of criminal proceedings,

> (2) (*a*) Where a code of practice referred to in *subsection (1)* appears to the court to give practical guidance as to the observance of the requirement or prohibition alleged to have been contravened, the code of practice shall be admissible in evidence.
>
> (*b*) Where it is proved that any act or omission of the defendant alleged to constitute the contravention—
>> (i)   is a failure to observe a code of practice referred to in *subsection (1)*, or
>> (ii) is a compliance with that code of practice, then such failure or compliance is admissible in evidence.

It is submitted that, despite the fact that s.61 specifically refers to criminal proceedings, it may be argued that such rules of admissibility will also apply to civil proceedings, in that a failure to follow such codes of practice may well be important in seeking to establish negligence on the part of the employer.[208]

A prominent example of such a Code of Practice is the Health and Safety Authority's [15–140] *Code of Practice for Employers and Employees on the Prevention and Resolution of Bullying at Work*,[209] which came into effect on 1 May 2007. This latest new Code of Practice is aimed at both employers and employees and refers, in particular, to the duties in the Safety, Health and Welfare at Work Act 2005. The new code provides practical guidance for employers on identifying and preventing bullying at work, arising from their duties under s.8(2)(b) of the 2005 Act as regards 'managing and conducting work activities in such a way as to prevent, so far as is reasonably practicable, any improper conduct or behaviour likely to put the safety, health

---

207. [2008] IESC 72, [2009] 1 ILRM 490. This case is also discussed in Chapter 3.
208. In this respect, employers should have regard to the various codes of practice listed on the www.hsa.ie website. In particular it is important to consider the HSA *Strategy for the Prevention of Workplace Accidents, Injuries and Illnesses* (2004–2009) and the 2007 Code of Practice in respect of bullying in the workplace.
209. Available at www.hsa.ie.

and welfare at work of his or her employees at risk'. It also applies to employees in relation to their duties under s.13(1)(e) of the 2005 Act to 'not engage in improper conduct or behaviour that is likely to endanger his or her own safety, health and welfare at work or that of any other person'. In practice, it is highly likely to be taken into account in civil cases alleging bullying and harassment at work, in light of the judicial instances of its being cited analysed above, the most prominent example of which to date is the judgment of the High Court in the case of *Quigley v Complex Tooling and Moulding*,[210] where Lavan J referred to the definition of bullying as contained in the Code of Practice detailing procedures for addressing bullying in the workplace made under the Industrial Relations Act 1990[211] and expressly applied it to the plaintiff's evidence. On appeal to the Supreme Court, the parties were agreed that this was appropriate and it was on this basis that the Supreme Court analysed the factual matrix of the plaintiff's claim.[212]

---

210. *Quigley v Complex Tooling and Moulding* [2005] IEHC 71, [2009] 1 IR 349, [2005] ELR 305. Both this judgment and the subsequent appeal to the Supreme Court are analysed in Chapter 16.
211. SI no. 17 of 2002.
212. Analysed in Chapter 16.

CHAPTER 16

Legal Obligations for the Employer in Respect of Workplace Stress and Bullying

Introduction

The last couple of decades have witnessed significant developments in Irish employ-   [16–01]
ment law as well as Irish tort law, such that it is now abundantly clear that employers
owe duties of care to employees to provide reasonable protection not merely against the
risk of *physical* harm[1], but also against the risk of psychological harm where such harm
is caused by factors connected with the workplace. Where an employer is in breach
of such duties then this may (depending on the circumstances) justify a constructive
dismissal claim on behalf of the employee, ground a personal injuries action or, theoretically, form the basis of a criminal prosecution under Health and Safety legislation.

The psychological harm that can ground such causes of action may be divided into   [16–02]
three categories:

- harm caused as a result of what is colloquially known as 'workplace
  stress';
- harm caused by bullying in the workplace; and
- harm caused by victimisation.

In reality, however, this method of dividing up the issues is a very inexact one,   [16–03]
and fails to acknowledge the high degree of cross-over between them, both in that
victimisation can be regarded as a form of bullying and also in that, aside from
any physical injuries that may arise as a result of bullying, the likely harmful effects
of bullying and victimisation will be psychological, and the root cause of such
psychological injuries will, in fact, be stress. Indeed it is worth bearing in mind
the conclusion of Lavan J in *Quigley v Complex Tooling & Moulding*[2] (considered
in detail later in this chapter) that where an employee who has been bullied suffers
stress-related psychological harm, this is still a stress claim, albeit one where the
cause of the stress is the bullying.

---

1. The concept of employers' liability for *physical* harm is considered in Chapter 15.
2. [2005] IEHC 71, [2009] 1 IR 349, [2005] ELR 305.

[16–04] Finally, and by way of introduction, it will be remembered that many of the employment law statutes considered in the course of this book prohibit specific forms of victimisation – for example, victimisation of an employee for failing to comply with an order that would be unlawful under the particular statute; victimisation in the form of sexual harassment under equality legislation; or victimisation on the basis of membership or otherwise of a trade union under industrial relations legislation.[3] These rules are considered throughout this book in the various chapters dealing with such statutes.

[16–05] Before we look at the substance of the issues under discussion and in particular at the relevant case law, it is important to focus on two key introductory points: the various contexts in which what is known as a 'stress' or a 'bullying' claim may arise and the appropriate definition of stress.

1. Contexts in which a Stress or Bullying Claim can be Brought

[16–06] The most high-profile context in which recovery can be sought for stress or bullying is through a personal injuries action brought either in tort or in contract, and the bulk of this chapter represents an analysis of such claims. For now it is worth considering briefly some other contexts where such a claim might arise.[4]

1.1. Stress, Bullying and Equality Legislation

[16–07] As far as bulling is concerned, s.8 of the Equality Act 2004 characterises harassment and sexual harassment as unlawful discrimination.[5] Significantly, s.23 represents a conceptual change from the old approach under the 1998 Employment Equality Act. Previously, the position had been that in order for a claim of harassment to be made out, the impugned conduct had to be unwelcome and had to reach an objective threshold where it could reasonably be regarded as offensive, humiliating or intimidating either sexually or on the ground of gender. Under the new dispensation, it would seem that the standard is a subjective one – in other words, that it remains up to the person alleging harassment to determine whether the conduct in question is acceptable or not.[6] Moreover, in order to escape liability for the actions

---

3. Generally, see Curran, 'Victimisation: A New Remedy for Employees', 5(1) *IELJ* (2008), 4.
4. Generally, on the various contexts in which a claim for stress, bullying and harassment may arise, see Neligan, 'Jurisdictions and Causes of Action: Commercial Considerations in Dealing with Bullying, Stress and Harassment Cases', parts I and II, 15(1) *CLP* (2008), 3 and 15(2) *CLP* (2008), 38.
5. Generally, see the Equality Authority's *Code of Practice on Harassment and Sexual Harassment at Work* (2002), which has been given legal effect under the Employment Equality Act 1998 (Code of Practice) (Harassment) Order 2002, SI no. 78 of 2002, which is admissible in evidence in all relevant hearings.
6. Bolger, 'Claiming for Occupational Stress, Bullying and Harassment', 3(4) *IELJ* (2006), 108 makes the point that where bullying (as distinct from harassment) is at issue the standard of

of an employee in this regard, it is necessary that the employer take such steps as are 'reasonably practicable' to protect employees. It has been suggested that such steps might include informing employees (and other relevant personnel)

> that certain behaviour is unacceptable, that if a person is being treated in that way they are entitled to bring a complaint and that any such behaviour shall be treated as a disciplinary matter.[7]

Indeed, it has been held that the absence of such a complaints procedure is strongly indicative that the employer is failing in his or her obligation to employees to provide a safe place and system of work – even in circumstances where it is far from certain that the injured employee would have availed of such a procedure.[8] [16–08]

It is notable that under s.2 of the Employment Equality Act a worker who is being harassed or bullied on the basis of one of the listed grounds may claim for constructive dismissal, which is included in the definition of dismissal under the terms of the Act.[9] [16–09]

Finally, it should be noted that inasmuch as the definition of 'disability' in the Employment Equality Acts 1998–2004 is clearly broad enough to cover someone suffering mental problems as a result of stress, there is almost certainly a *statutory* obligation to provide reasonable accommodation for someone suffering from stress. In this respect it should be further noted that whereas prior to 2004 an employer merely had to accommodate a person with a disability if this involved him or her incurring no more than nominal expense, under s.9 of the Equality Act 2004 the obligation is now to accommodate unless this would impose a 'disproportionate burden' on the employer. Once again, however, the precise definition of what is meant by reasonable accommodation in this sense remains a matter of uncertainty. [16–10]

---

whether one has been bullied is plainly an objective one. For a UK perspective, see Feinstein, 'Protection From Harassment Act: Extreme Solutions for Extreme Behaviour', 64 *Employment Law Journal* (October 2005), 4; and Middlemiss, 'Liability of Employers for Verbal Harassment in the Workplace', 6(1) *IELJ* (2009), 8.

7. Bolger, 'Stress, Bullying and Harassment in the Workplace: Recent Developments', paper presented at the Legal Island Annual Review of Employment Law in Ireland Conference, 10 November 2005.

8. *Atkinson v Carty and Others* [2005] ELR 1. See also *CL v CRM*, DEC-E2004-027, 17 May 2004 – a case involving alleged sexual harassment by one employee of another in which the Equality Officer found against the respondent employer *inter alia* because of the absence of a sexual harassment policy in his workplace at the time at which the events occurred.

9. See O'Sullivan, 'Preventing and Defending Stress and Bullying at Work Cases', 1 *Employment Law Review* (2006), 14. For analysis of the position in the UK, see Middlemiss, 'The Right to Dignity at Work? Recent Developments in Harassment Law in the United Kingdom', 25 *ILT* (2007), 95 and 25 *ILT* (2007), 111.

1.2. Stress, Bullying and Health and Safety Legislation

[16–11]   The provisions of the Safety, Health and Welfare at Work Act 2005 (which are discussed in more detail in Chapter 15) can also be applied to the issues of stress and bullying.[10] Thus in listing the obligations of an employer, s.8(2) of the 2005 Act includes the requirement that work activities be managed and conducted 'in such a way as to prevent, so far as is reasonably practicable, any improper conduct or behaviour likely to put the safety, health or welfare at work of his or her employees at risk', and in assessing what is necessary in order to do that which is reasonably practicable, s.2(6) of the Act says that the obligation is on the employer to be proactive – to put 'in place the necessary protective and preventative measures, having identified the hazards and assessed the risks to safety and health likely to result in accidents or injury to health at the place of work concerned'.

[16–12]   Furthermore, under s.13 of the Act it is clear that employees have a statutory duty not to bully fellow employees (and hence a situation of bullying may in fact generate criminal liability). Thus under s.13 employees have a duty to take reasonable care to protect the health, safety and welfare both of themselves and of others who might be affected by their acts and omissions. Most specifically of all, under s.13 an employee is bound to 'not engage in improper conduct or other behaviour that is likely to endanger his or her own safety, health and welfare at work or that of any other person.'

[16–13]   Finally, under s.61 of the Safety, Health and Welfare at Work Act 2005 it is provided that the Health and Safety Authority is entitled to create codes of practice in specific areas relating to health and safety in the workplace, and that failure by an employer to adhere to the standards in such codes (including codes created prior to the coming into being of the Act) can be used as evidence in criminal proceedings.[11] In addition, it may be suggested that a failure to live up to the standards in such codes of practice may be evidence of negligence on the part of the employer in civil proceedings.[12] In this respect it is vital for the employer to be aware of and to implement the following relevant codes of practice:

---

10. Generally, see Bolger, 'Claiming for Occupational Stress, Bullying and Harassment', 3(4) *IELJ* (2006), 108; O'Connell, 'Bullying in the Workplace', 2(4) *IELJ* (2005), 119. In this respect it is notable that the *Report of the Expert Advisory Group on Workplace Bullying* (2005) recommended *inter alia* that there be a legal requirement that a bullying policy be contained in all safety statements for workplaces.

11. For the suggestion that injunctive relief may be available to employees to secure the performance of obligations under health and safety legislation in the context of bullying, see Codd and McDonald, 'Bullying in the Workplace and the Interlocutory Injunction: Protections Available to "Niche Employees"', 4 *Employment Law Review* (2007), 7.

12. This is the logic of the Labour Court as quoted by the High Court in *Health Board v BC and the Labour Court* [1994] ELR 2,7 and in *Saehan Media Ireland Ltd. v A Worker* [1999] ELR 41. Generally, see Compton and Waters, 'Practice and Procedure', 1(1) *IELJ* (2004), 18.

- the Code of Practice on Procedures for Addressing Bullying in the Workplace made under the Industrial Relations Act 1990[13];
- the Code of Practice on guidance on prevention and procedures for dealing with sexual harassment and harassment at work under the Employment Equality Act 1998[14]; and
- The HSA Code of Practice on the prevention of workplace bullying of 2007. This last code provides a particularly useful practical guide to employers on how to construct and operate a scheme aimed at preventing workplace bullying.[15]

1.3. Stress, Bullying[16] and Constructive Dismissal Actions

Naturally, it is possible for employees who claim to have been bullied to resign and [16–14] claim constructive dismissal (although it is clear that there is a substantial onus on claimants wishing to succeed on this basis).[17] The issue of constructive dismissal generally is discussed in Chapter 21 but for present purposes it may be suggested that the determinations of the EAT in cases of alleged bullying indicate two firm points of principle. First, from the employee's standpoint, it is vital to ensure that he or she avails as far as possible of internal grievance procedures before seeking to sue for damages or to claim constructive dismissal.[18] Secondly, from the employer's standpoint it is vital to ensure both that working conditions are not conducive to bullying and that there is a workable and working grievance procedure in place[19] (and ideally a counselling procedure) to enable complaints to be made, listened to and acted upon.[20] In other words, a failure to deal with bullying is the single most prevalent contributory factor in cases where bullying has been found to generate a

---

13. SI no. 117 of 1996.

14. SI no. 17 of 2002.

15. For further analysis of practical measures an employer can take to deal with workplace bullying, see Jenner and Finn, 'Ensuring Dignity at Work', 74 *Employment Law Journal* (October 2006), 7.

16. Most constructive dismissal cases do arise (in this context) as a result of bullying, however, it is possible for a constructive dismissal situation to arise on the basis of stress *per se* depending on whether or not the employer is at fault. See *Linnane v Bettabuy*, UD 683/2002, as a case where, whereas there had been some bullying in the past, arguably at the time of his resignation, the employee was suffering from a more general form of workplace stress. Indeed it is arguable that this logic also explains the decisions in *Allen v Independent Newspapers (Ireland) Ltd.* [2002] ELR 84; and *Monaghan v Sherry Brothers* [2003] ELR 293.

17. *Tobin v Cadbury Ireland Ltd.*, UD 1295/2002; *Deane v Thermo Air Machines Ltd.*, UD 430/2001, *Baker v Ceramicx Ireland Ltd.*, UD 41/2003. Generally, see O'Sullivan, 'Preventing and Defending Stress and Bullying at Work Cases', 1 *Employment Law Review* (2006), 14; O'Connell, 'Bullying in the Workplace', 2(4) *IELJ* (2005), 119.

18. *Tobin v Cadbury Ireland Ltd.*, UD 1295/2002; *Harrold v St Michael's* House [2008] ELR 1; *Donnellan v Dunnes Stores*, UD 827/2007.

19. *Martin v Doonane Ltd.*, UD 715/2007.

20. See, for example, *Leonard v ISME*, UD 269/2002; *Daly v Gallagher*, UD 1095/2002.

constructive dismissal situation.[21] Moreover the EAT has recently held that where there is an inordinate delay by the employer in addressing the relevant issues this may lead to a finding that a constructive dismissal situation has arisen.[22]

1.4. Stress, Bullying and Industrial Relations Law

[16–15] It is conceivable that where a situation of stress or bullying has arisen in the workplace, and where it is not being dealt with appropriately, then this could be classified as a trade dispute (under the broad definition given in s.3 of the Industrial Relations Act 1946)[23] and referred either to the Labour Court under s.20 of the Industrial Relations Act 1990, or to the Labour Relations Commission pursuant to s.25 of the 1990 Act or s.13(2) of the Industrial Relations Act 1969.[24]

1.5. Claiming Damages for Stress in the Context of an Unfair Dismissals Action

[16–16] As is well known and, as is discussed in chapters 19 and 21, it is generally the case that the common law claim for damages for wrongful dismissal and the statutory claim for unfair dismissal are mutually exclusive, such that where an employee has sued for unfair dismissal under the statutory scheme [s]he is precluded from suing for damages at common law in respect of that dismissal.[25] In *Eastwood v Magnox Electric*[26] (which was heavily relied on by Esmond Smyth J in his High Court judgment in *Microsoft v Pickering*[27]), however, the House of Lords held that irre-

---

21. See *Baker v Ceramicx Ireland Ltd.*, UD 41/2003, where the relevant human resources officer in the defendant company did not deal with a bullying situation because she said she did not want to get involved and the EAT found that there had been a situation of constructive dismissal.

22. *Fitzimons v Mount Carmel Hospital*, UD 855/2007.

23. In *Bell Security v TEEU*, CD/07/654, LCR 19188, 10 April 2008, the Labour Court rejected the suggestion from an employer that a trade dispute could not occur where the internal dispute-resolution procedures within a company had not been exhausted, and hence, in order to prove that a trade dispute existed one would also have to prove that such internal procedures no longer worked.

24. See, for example, *Saehan Media Ltd. v A Worker* [1999] ELR 41. Generally, see O'Sullivan, 'Preventing and Defending Stress and Bullying at Work Cases', 1 *Employment Law Review* (2006), 14.

25. *Orr v Zomax* [2004] IEHC 47, [2004] 1 IR 486; *Parsons v Iarnród Éireann* [1997] ELR 203; *Johnson v Unisys Ltd* [2001] UKHL 13, [2003] 1 AC 518, [2001] 2 WLR 1076, [2001] ICR 480, [2001] IRLR 279; *Dunnachie v Kingston upon Hull City Council* [2004] UKHL 36, [2005] 1 AC 226, [2004] 3 WLR 310, [2004] ICR 227, [2004] 2 All ER 501; *Eastwood v Magnox Electric* [2004] UKHL 35, [2005] 1 AC 503, [2004] 3 WLR 322, [2004] ICR 1064, [2004] 3 All ER 991; *MG v North Devon NHS Primary Care Trust* [2006] EWHC 850; *McGrath v Trintech*, High Court, [2004] IEHC 342; [2005] 4 IR 382. See Temperton, 'Non-Economic Loss: Is Johnson v Unisys Dead?', *Employment Law Journal*, 42 (July/August 2003) 2.

26. [2005] AC 503. See Temperton, 'Manner of Dismissal: Lords Revisit *Johnson* Exclusion Zone', 53 *Employment Law Journal* (September 2004), 15.

27. [2006] ELR 65.

spective of which approach was taken when the challenge to the dismissal arose, equally if *before* that dismissal a separate cause of action had been acquired by the plaintiff, that cause of action would remain unimpaired by his or her subsequent dismissal. In other words, whereas a plaintiff who has proceeded by the statutory unfair dismissal route cannot take a common law action in respect of stress suffered as a result of such dismissal, [s]he can still claim common law damages for injuries, including stress-related psychological injuries suffered *prior to his or her dismissal.* The same approach was taken by Lavan J in *Quigley v Complex Tooling and Moulding*[28] – a case considered in some detail below.[29] Moreover, whereas it would appear likely that damages for personal injures *per se* cannot be awarded in the context of an unfair dismissals action,[30] it has been suggested that the approach of the EAT in *Allen v Independent Newspapers*[31] and *Browne v Ventelo Telecommunications (Ireland) Limited*[32] indicates that in calculating damages in the context of an unfair dismissal (including a constructive dismissal) case, the extent to which the employee may suffer a future loss of earnings as a result of stress endured prior to the dismissal is relevant and irrespective of whether the damage suffered is actual or potential.[33]

It is somewhat less certain as to whether the same logic applies to a construc- [16–17] tive dismissal situation – in other words, can an employee who claims [s]he was constructively dismissed (perhaps because of the level of stress to which [s]he was exposed[34]) also take a personal injuries action in respect of damage suffered before such 'dismissal'? The answer (by extension from the normal principles relating to unfair dismissal actions) would appear to be that in theory it would be open to the employee to do so, but only where [s]he could demonstrate that the factors that caused his or her stress-related illness were somehow distinct from the factors that made his or her working life so unbearable that a constructive dismissal action was warranted. Naturally in most cases this will not be possible to do, in that a constructive dismissal action is essentially rather similar to a personal injuries action for stress in the sense that both involve work situations that become unbearable from the employee's standpoint. Thus it may be suggested that in practice, if not in theory, a claimant who has suffered psychiatric harm as a result of a workplace situation in respect of which [s]he also has a potential constructive dismissal action will be required to make a choice between the two options of a personal injuries action or a claim for constructive dismissal.

---

28. [2005] IEHC 71, [2009] 1 IR 349, [2005] ELR 305.
29. [2005] IEHC 71. See also *Nolan v EMO Oil Services Ltd.* [2009] IEHC 15, [2009] ELR 122.
30. See Bowers and Lewis, 'Non-Economic Damage in Unfair Dismissal Cases: What's Left after *Dunnachie*', 34(1) *Industrial Law Journal* (March 2005), 83.
31. [2002] ELR 84.
32. UD 597/2001.
33. This is pursuant to s.7(3) Unfair Dismissals Act 1977. See Eardly, 'Psychiatric Injury and the Employment Appeals Tribunal: A Double Bite at the Compensation Cherry', 1 *Employment Law Review* (2007), 12.
34. *Riehn v DSPCA*, UD 947/2002.

1.6. Tort and Contract-Based Actions

[16–18] Finally, in assessing the contexts in which a 'stress' claim may arise, it should be noted that workplace stress claims may be brought on the basis either of a tort action or an action for breach of contract (obviously depending on the circumstances),[35] although, as we shall see, there is some uncertainty as to how a contractual claim of this kind actually works.

[16–19] Previously, in the case of *Carroll v Bus Átha Cliath*[36] Clarke J had seemed to suggest that it would be very difficult to recover general (that is unliquidated) damages through a claim for breach of contract. He held that it was 'not possible to award general damages for frustration, mental distress, injured feelings or annoyance occasioned by the breach [of contract]'.[37] Indeed, in his view, the only exception to this principle were cases where the contract in question was for a holiday, in which circumstances the contract itself is one to provide 'peace of mind or freedom from distress'.[38] Clarke J accepted that the traditional workplace stress cases could 'of course be mounted in contract (based on an implied term)' but he also felt that 'such claims more neatly fit into the law of tort'.[39]

[16–20] On the other hand, more recent case law has appeared to accept that stress claims can be brought for breach of an implied contractual term, nor has there been any reference to the above dicta of Clarke J in such cases. Hence in the High Court decision in *Berber v Dunnes Stores*[40] Laffoy J held that the claim for stress in contract was indistinguishable from that in tort, and she proceeded to hold that the scope of the duty of care owed to an employee to take reasonable care to provide a safe system of work was 'co-extensive with the scope of the implied term as to the employee's safety in the contract of employment'.[41] Whereas the decision of the High Court has been reversed on its facts by the Supreme Court, the latter did not appear to have any difficulty with the fact of the claim being brought both in contract and in tort.[42] Similarly, in *Pickering v Microsoft*,[43] Esmond Smyth J

---

35. See, for example, *Green v DB Group Services (UK) Ltd.* [2006] EWHC 1898, [2006] IRLR 764. In this case it was accepted that there was a contractual duty on the part of an employer to exercise reasonable care for the safety of employees, but it was also accepted that if the claimant failed to demonstrate the type of negligence on the part of an employer that would ground a tort-based personal injuries action, it would necessarily follow that she would be unable to succeed in a claim that a breach of this implicit contractual term had occurred.
36. [2005] IEHC 278, [2005] 4 IR 184, [2005] ELR 192.
37. [2005] 4 IR 184, 214. For analysis of this general proposition outside the standpoint of a workplace stress claim, see Carey, 'Breach, Distress and Damages', *Commercial Law Practitioner* 9(1) (January 2002), 3.
38. [2005] 4 IR 184, 214.
39. [2005] 4 IR 184, 215.
40. [2006] IEHC 327, [2007] ELR 1.
41. [2007] ELR 1, 19.
42. [2009] IESC 10, [2009] ELR 61.
43. [2006] ELR 65.

awarded a substantial sum of money to a plaintiff for workplace stress, and did so on the basis that the stress was caused by a serious and ongoing breach of an implied term in her contract.

What is curious about the High Court judgments in both *Berber* and *Pickering*, however, is that whereas the claims appear to be dealt with on the basis of contract law, nonetheless the language adopted by the courts seems far more rooted in tort law. It is arguable, in fact, that cases of this kind (and cases like *O'Byrne v Dunnes Stores*[44]) involve a merging of contract and tort principles, such that what the employer is being sued for is in fact negligence, but the negligent act for which [s]he is being sued also involves a breach of the employee's contract in circumstances where it was foreseeable that this breach would cause harm to him or her.[45] If this is the case then of course the dicta of Clarke J in *Carroll v Dublin Bus*[46] referred to above holds good. We consider these cases and this question in more detail later in this chapter.

[16–21]

2. The Nature of Stress

Workplace stress represents a major source of problems to individual employers and employees and indeed to the European economy as a whole.[47] According to the European Commission, work-related stress costs the EU at least €20 billion annually in lost work time and health bills, and indeed is the second biggest occupational health problem in the EU after back pain. The World Mental-Health Committee is predicting that by 2020 it will in fact be the primary cause of workplace ill health.[48] It is further estimated that 16 per cent of male and 22 per cent of female cardiovascular diseases derive from stress. It is also estimated that over 50 per cent of absenteeism has its roots in work-related stress.[49] Stress is estimated to affect over 40 million employees in the EU, with 28 per cent of employees reporting that they are affected by work-related stress generally (though not always) deriving from causes such as:

[16–22]

---

44. [2003] ELR 297. In this case Smyth J concluded that damages for stress would be awarded to the plaintiff *inter alia* because of foreseeable psychological harm arising from a breach of his contract. See Bolger, 'Claiming for Occupational Stress, Bullying and Harassment', 3(4) *IELJ* (2006), 108; O'Sullivan, 'Preventing and Defending Stress and Bullying at Work Cases', 1 *Employment Law Review* (2006), 14.

45. Generally, see Bolger, 'Claiming for Occupational Stress, Bullying and Harassment', 3(4) *IELJ* (2006), 108.

46. [2005] IEHC, [2005] 4 IR 184, [2005] ELR 192.

47. See, for example, Quinlan, 'Workers Get £200,000 for Illness Due to Stress', *Irish Examiner*, 7 September 2001.

48. See Humphries, 'Stress Will Be the Main Cause of Workplace Illness by 2020', *Irish Times*, 7 July 2005.

49. From an Irish perspective the National Absenteeism Report of the Small Firms Association (9 April 2007) found that stress was the single biggest cause of absenteeism. See http://www.sfa.ie/Sectors/SFA/SFAADoclib4.nsf/wvPRYCS/B90F9F9604BAC8DA802572B4004866

- lack of job security and control;
- work overload;
- monotony;
- demotion and consequent humiliation; and
- bullying.[50]

[16–23]   Indeed the problem has become so serious at a European level that in 2004 the European Social Partners produced a (voluntary) framework agreement on work-related stress, which committed signatory states to adopt measures to ensure that the stress concerns referred to in the document were addressed *inter alia* by means of national legislation. On the other hand, a 2007 report by the National Economic and Social Forum found that whereas 60 per cent of employers said that the issue of work-related stress had arisen in their workplace, nonetheless 74 per cent of employers did not have a written mental health policy.[51]

Despite all of this, there is a good deal of popular and judicial uncertainty as to what stress is, and to how it should be treated by the courts.

2.1. Attitudes to Stress

[16–24]   It may perhaps be suggested that the greatest area of controversy in respect of this aspect of the law is in the different views people take of whether 'stress' as a concept should be taken seriously. Thus whereas one person may say that mental illness, no more and no less than physical illness, is a condition for which one should receive sympathy, treatment and concession, another person may equally say that life is pressurised, the workplace is particularly pressurised and the claim that someone is 'stressed' is just an excuse for weakness, and it should consequently be treated with contempt. Alternatively, it is argued that if one's fellow employees can cope with the pressure of their work, then this is an indicator that one should be able to cope with the pressure of one's own work, and that if one does not or cannot so cope, then this is one's own fault, nor should liability be imposed on the employer in this context. It is arguable that variants of these two views find expressions in judicial decisions in this area.

2.2. The Definition of Stress

[16–25]   Much of the complexity of Irish case law in this area, as well as the basis for this diversity in attitudes to stress, stems, it is submitted, from inconsistencies in the judicial and popular understanding of what stress is and what stress does. Hence it is important at the outset to try to provide some clarity in this area.

---

50. See http://www.hsa.ie/publisher/index.jsp?aID=216&nID=203&pID=201. See also European Commission, *EU Guidance on Work Related Stress* (2000).
51. See National Economic and Social Forum, *Report on Mental Health and Social Inclusion* (report no. 36), November 2007. See also Harvey, 'Mental Health Hits One in Four', *Irish Times*, 14 November 2007.

The first point to be made in defining 'stress' (both as a medical condition and [16–26]
as a basis for a legal claim) is that it is clearly more than merely the routine
strain connected with the day-to-day business of work or of life in general. After
all, situations can frequently be pressurised or even stressful for many people,
most of whom will never have any health problems as a result (and it is virtually
axiomatic as a matter of legal principle that an employer will not be liable for
mental problems experienced by the employee if the only alleged breach of duty
lies in the fact that the employer has exposed that [willing] employee to life in the
workplace, with all its routine attendant stress).[52] Indeed within traditional negligence language, the extent to which an employee assumes the risks inherent in a
particular employment situation will necessarily limit the duty of the employer
not to expose him or her to such risks. Furthermore, such day-to-day burdens
to which we are all exposed are more properly termed 'pressure' – nor is pressure
inevitably a bad thing. Indeed psychologists tell us that some level of pressure in
the workplace is advantageous as a motivational force. Stress, on the other hand,
as it is properly understood relates to a person's *inability to cope with such pressure*
– and the consequent vulnerabilities of that person as a result of that fact. Moreover, such inability to cope, whereas it may relate to the extent of the pressure
being imposed on the worker, is, in essence, an inexplicable and totally subjective reaction. Finally (and again depending on the individual employee), the
vulnerability generated by the employee's inability to cope may mean that, unless
something is done to assist him or her, [s]he may suffer long-lasting psychological
harm as a result of being unable to cope with such pressure. Hence the confusion
in the definition of stress arises *inter alia* from the fact that, at least in colloquial
terms, the same term 'stress' is being used to describe both the *cause* of a problem
(pressure), the problem itself (stress) and the harmful consequences connected
with the problem (psychological injury).

The question of which of the above situations is regarded as the 'stress' for which [16–27]
an employee is bringing a personal injuries action is obviously very significant for
legal purposes. Thus if a court understands stress to refer to the level of workplace
pressure *simpliciter* (i.e. the cause of the problem), then it may assess whether the
employer is liable by reference to objective factors such as the level of pressure
imposed on the worker, and may determine whether such pressure was excessive
by examining whether or not other workers were able to cope with it. On the
other hand, if the court sees stress as relating to the individual employee's subjective inability to cope with such pressure then (a) the reaction of other employees to
the pressure is irrelevant, and (b) the duty of the employer will presumably extend
beyond ensuring that an objectively excessive level of pressure is not imposed
on workers and will cover some sort of obligation to the individual employee in
respect of his or her personal circumstances.

---

52. See, for example, the dissenting judgment of Lord Scott in *Barber v Somerset District Council*
[2004] UKHL 13, [2004] 1 WLR 1089, [2004] 2 All ER 385.

[16–28] The second point to be made about the definition and nature of stress is that it is a personal and subjective illness, which can often cause people to act irrationally. In other words, whereas if I suffer from a physical injury I will go to the doctor, or seek time off work or admit to my suffering; on the other hand, if I suffer a psychological sickness I am far more likely (because of the stigma attached to mental health issues in Ireland) to try to pretend that there is nothing wrong with me and to fail to communicate my problem to colleagues or my boss. Accordingly, stress is not just something that arises without any need for an objectively probable causal action, but in addition a stressed person may not give any objectively discernible indication that [s]he is suffering from it. This issue was summed up by Hale LJ in the English Court of Appeal in *Sutherland v Hatton*[53]:

> Their causes will often be complex and depend upon the interaction between the patient personality and a number of factors in the patient's life. It is not easy to predict who will fall victim, how, or when... For the same reason, treatment is often not straightforward or its outcome predictable: while some conditions may respond comparatively quickly and easily to appropriate medication others may only respond, if at all, to prolonged and complicated 'talking treatments' or behavioural therapy. There are strong divergences of views among psychiatrists on these issues.[54]

Lady Justice Hale also accepted that

> as with many words in a living language, the word 'stress' has acquired a vague, catch-all meaning, used by different people to mean different things. It is used to describe both physical and mental conditions and the pressures which cause these conditions. It is also used to describe stress which is beneficial and harmful in its sources and its effects.[55]

What this means, however, is that an entirely objective approach to stress, focusing on objective characteristics of workers, etc., will never deal properly with the problem.

[16–29] Finally, in defining the concept of stress it should be emphasised that there is plainly a difference between workplace stress (which is a reaction to an ongoing situation) and a nervous shock situation (which typically involves a reaction to a one-off stimulus).[56] On the other hand, there is arguably an analogy between the case of workplace stress and the situation where an employee exposed to asbestos has an irrational fear of illness – the type of situation that was at issue in the unsuccessful claim brought in *Fletcher v Commissioner of Public Works*.[57] Yet it is

---

53. [2002] EWCA Civ 76, [2002] ICR 613, [2002] All ER 1, [2002] IRLR 263.
54. [2002] ICR 613, 618.
55. [2002] ICR 613, 619.
56. For consideration of this point and especially the type of situation where, as a result of exposure to the risk of *physical* injury, the plaintiff suffers *psychological* damage, see *Page v Smith* [1996] 1 AC 155, [1996] 1 WLR 855, [1996] 3 All ER 272; *Donachie v Greater Manchester Police* [2004] EWCA Civ 405; *Schofield v Chief Constable of the West Yorkshire Police* [1999] ICR 193.
57. [2003] IESC 13, [2003] 1 IR 465.

most notable that in *Fletcher*, Keane CJ expressly said that his decision should not be taken to have application to occupational stress cases.

2.3. Stress and Public Policy

To some extent, the various cases dealing with workplace stress reflect an ongoing [16–30] tension that has its roots in policy and involves a balance between psychiatric reality on the one hand and intuitive views of justice on the other. After all, if the law were to side completely with psychiatric reality (that stress is an absolutely personal, subjective and inexplicable reaction to pressure) then the question of whether an employee had suffered a stress-related illness would be an entirely subjective one, nor could the employer seek to rely on an absence of objective indicia of that illness as a defence to his or her failure to protect his employee. Indeed this is compounded by the fact that because stressed people do not act in objectively rational ways, the extent to which it is possible to monitor for stress in the workplace and to remedy such stress when it is found may require a great deal of skill on the part of the employer. To require an employer to deal with stress effectively, therefore, may lead to an extremely onerous burden for him or her. Hence the intuitive views of justice mentioned may suggest that it would be unjust to impose such a burden on him or her. Rather, provided that [s]he fulfils certain objective criteria (of ensuring that, for example, the burdens of work are not unreasonable and there is some counselling service available for stressed employees), then an employer's job in respect of guarding against stress should be seen as being done. It is arguable – certainly on one view of justice – that this is an appropriate state of affairs. Equally it means that, to a large extent, the law on workplace stress is unrealistic and hence represents something of a meaningless sop to mental health.

2.4. The Nature of a Stress Claim

In reality, however, a typical stress claim tends to fuse the three popular definitions [16–31] of stress referred to above. It is, in other words, a claim that the plaintiff suffered serious injury as a result of his or her personal inability to cope with the pressure of the workplace, and that the employer was to blame for this because of a breach of duty (be it through action or omission), either by exposing the employee to excessive pressure or by not managing the situation properly when it was foreseeable that the individual employee was suffering from stress (that is to say, was unable to cope with the situation with which [s]he was faced). From the standpoint of an employer, this means that obligations arise (both in contract and in tort) in respect of

- managing the level of pressure imposed on employees;
- monitoring employees to ensure that they can cope with such excessive pressure; and
- ensuring that all that is reasonable is done to prevent an inability to cope from turning into serious illness.[58]

---

58. In its 2002 *Guide for Employers on Work-Related Stress*, the Health and Safety Authority classifies these three different levels of responsibility as primary (prevention), secondary (management) and tertiary (minimisation).

[16–32] On the other hand the employee is not an insurer of his or her employees' well-being. It may be that after the employer has done all that is reasonable an employee still suffers, for example, a nervous breakdown. In such circumstances this cannot be traced to a breach of an employer's duty and hence no question of liability arises.

3. Case Law in Respect of Workplace Stress

[16–33] We move now to consider the various principles created by the Irish courts in workplace stress cases. Whereas it is the Irish case law that we are analysing, much of this case law is grounded on the decision of the Court of Appeal in *Sutherland v Hatton*,[59] and hence this is our starting point.

3.1. *Sutherland v Hatton*

[16–34] *Sutherland v Hatton*[60] is, certainly from the standpoint of the Irish law in respect of workplace stress, by far the most important decision of the English courts in this area. Prior to this decision, it had been decided that the question of whether the employer was in breach of its duty to the employee hinged on the question of foreseeability – that is whether or not it was foreseeable that an employee would suffer the psychological harm that [s]he did, in fact, suffer. Thus in *Walker v Northumberland County Council*[61] a social services officer who was an area manager and had significant responsibility for field-workers dealing with child care had suffered a nervous breakdown in 1987 because of the stresses of work. Before he returned from a three-month period of sick leave related to this breakdown, he requested that his work load should be decreased, but not only did this not happen, in fact he had to cope with the backlog of the work that had built up in his absence as well as a number of new cases. Unsurprisingly, he suffered a second breakdown six months later, and was certified as permanently unfit to work and on this basis he was dismissed by his employer. The court held that whereas his *first* breakdown was not foreseeable nor was any duty of care owed by the employer in respect of it, on the other hand, his *second* breakdown was eminently foreseeable and thus a duty of care would arise.

[16–35] In *Sutherland v Hatton*[62] (a composite judgment in relation to four entirely disparate claims brought by four separate employees against four separate employers), the Court of Appeal (Lady Justice Hale) said that a stress claim taken under the tort of negligence was effectively like any other negligence-based personal injuries claim. Thus it would be necessary to establish the four traditional common law prerequisites of the tort of negligence, namely:

---

59. [2002] EWCA Civ 76, [2002] ICR 613, [2002] All ER 1, [2002] IRLR 263.
60. [2002] EWCA Civ 76, [2002] ICR 613, [2002] All ER 1, [2002] IRLR 263.
61. [1995] ICR 702, [1995] 1 All ER 737, [1995] IRLR 35.
62. [2002] EWCA Civ 76, [2002] ICR 613, [2002] All ER 1, [2002] IRLR 263.

- the existence of a duty of care;
- a breach of the standard of care;
- a causal link between the breach and the harm; and
- damage resulting from such breach.

Very significantly, Hale LJ laid down what she termed 16 'practical propositions' [16–36] for determining liability in stress cases. Inasmuch as these propositions still represent the starting point for most judges both in the UK and Ireland when dealing with cases of this nature, it is worth setting them out in their entirety.

(1) There are no special control mechanisms applying to claims for psychiatric (or physical) illness or injury arising from the stress of doing the work the employee is required to do. The ordinary principles of employer's liability apply.

(2) The threshold question is whether this kind of harm to this particular employee was reasonably foreseeable: this has two components (a) an injury to health (as distinct from occupational stress) which (b) is attributable to stress at work (as distinct from other factors).

(3) Foreseeability depends upon what the employer knows (or ought reasonably to know) about the individual employee. Because of the nature of mental disorder, it is harder to foresee than physical injury, but may be easier to foresee in a known individual than in the population at large. An employer is usually entitled to assume that the employee can withstand the normal pressures of the job unless he knows of some particular problem or vulnerability.

(4) The test is the same whatever the employment: there are no occupations which should be regarded as intrinsically dangerous to mental health.

(5) Factors likely to be relevant in answering the threshold question include: (a) The nature and extent of the work done by the employee. Is the workload much more than is normal for the particular job? Is the work particularly intellectually or emotionally demanding for this employee? Are the demands being made of this employee unreasonable when compared with the demands made of others in the same or comparable jobs? Or are there signs that others doing this job are suffering harmful levels of stress? Is there an abnormal level of sickness or absenteeism in the same job or the same department?

(b) Signs from the employee of impending harm to health. Has he a particular problem or vulnerability? Has he already suffered from illness attributable to stress at work? Have there recently been frequent or prolonged absences which are uncharacteristic of him? Is there reason to think that these are attributable to stress at work, for example because of complaints or warnings from him or others?

(6) The employer is generally entitled to take what he is told by his employee at face value, unless he has good reason to think to the contrary. He does not generally have to make searching enquiries of the employee or seek permission to make further enquiries of his medical advisers.

(7) To trigger a duty to take steps, the indications of impending harm to health

arising from stress at work must be plain enough for any reasonable employer to realise that he should do something about it.

(8) The employer is only in breach of duty if he has failed to take the steps which are reasonable in the circumstances, bearing in mind the magnitude of the risk of harm occurring, the gravity of the harm which may occur, the costs and practicability of preventing it, and the justifications for running the risk.

(9) The size and scope of the employer's operation, its resources and the demands it faces are relevant in deciding what is reasonable; these include the interests of other employees and the need to treat them fairly, for example, in any redistribution of duties.

(10) An employer can only reasonably be expected to take steps which are likely to do some good: the court is likely to need expert evidence on this.

(11) An employer who offers a confidential advice service, with referral to appropriate counselling or treatment services, is unlikely to be found in breach of duty.

(12) If the only reasonable and effective step would have been to dismiss or demote the employee, the employer will not be in breach of duty in allowing a willing employee to continue in the job.

(13) In all cases, therefore, it is necessary to identify the steps which the employer both could and should have taken before finding him in breach of his duty of care.

(14) The claimant must show that that breach of duty has caused or materially contributed to the harm suffered. It is not enough to show that occupational stress has caused the harm.

(15) Where the harm suffered has more than one cause, the employer should only pay for that proportion of the harm suffered which is attributable to his wrongdoing, unless the harm is truly indivisible. It is for the defendant to raise the question of apportionment.

(16) The assessment of damages will take account of any pre-existing disorder or vulnerability and of the chance that the claimant would have succumbed to a stress-related disorder in any event.[63]

It is, perhaps, helpful in order fully to understand what this case says about this area of the law to classify these principles according to the relevant aspect of the tort of negligence that is at issue.

3.1.1. *Duty of Care*

[16–37] Principles 1–7 above can be classified as relating to the question of whether a specific duty of care is owed by the employer to the individual employee as far as preventing or managing stress is concerned (as distinct from a general duty of care being owed to all employees by reason of respect of their general well-being). The key question in this respect is foreseeability of harm such that once the harm

---

63. [2002] ICR 613, 631-632.

is foreseeable then the duty will be deemed to arise.[64] It is arguable that both in Ireland and in England the primary reason stress claims fail is that the claimant is unable to prove the harm suffered was, in fact, reasonably foreseeable.[65]

It is notable that in assessing foreseeability, Hale LJ moved away from the position [16–38] in *Walker v Northumberland County Council*[66] that liability could only be imposed on an employer if [s]he failed to react to a known vulnerability in an employee, such that liability (so it would appear) could also be imposed where the actions of the employer, viewed objectively, created an inherent and foreseeable risk of stress as far as employees were concerned (as might occur, for example, if the employer bullied employees or imposed an objectively excessive level of work on them).[67] Foreseeability of harm in this sense thus will derive from the nature of the work[68] and any known vulnerabilities of the employee.[69] Moreover, it seems clear from the decision of the Court of Appeal in *Melville v Home Office*[70] that it is sufficient to show foreseeability of injury to *all* persons in a particular job by virtue of the objectively demanding or stressful nature of that job rather than necessarily having to show that injury to the individual employee was reasonably foreseeable having regard to his or her particular vulnerabilities. Equally, of course, foreseeability may arise in this latter context as well. In addition, the general approach of the courts appears to be that inasmuch as most workers are able to withstand the stress of a heavy workload, thus the starting point for any assessment should be that the employer is entitled to assume that his or her employees are capable of coping with such pressures.[71] Finally, it is unclear (at least in theory) whether

---

64. An alternative way of putting it is, 'The test is whether there were indications of impending harm arising from stress at work that were plain enough for the defendants to realise that they should do something about it': *McCotter v McNally and Anor* [2004] NIQB 59. See also *Garrett v Camden London Borough Council* [2001] EWCA Civ 395; *Green v DB Services* [2006] IRLR 764, [2006] EWHC 1898; *Hammond v International Network Services UK Ltd.* [2007] EWHC 2604, [2007] 1 WLR 26; *Clark v Chief Constable of Essex Police* [2006] EWHC 2290. See also *Beattie v Ulster Television Plc* [2005] NIQB 36 for the view that 'It is foreseeable injury flowing from the employer's breach of duty that gives rise to the liability. It does not follow that because a claimant suffers stress at work and that the employer is in some way in breach of duty in allowing that to occur that the claimant is able to establish a claim in negligence.' Similarly, see *Banks v Ablex Ltd.* [2005] ICR 819 at 829 for the view that 'So proof that the defendants foresaw or ought to have foreseen the particular type of injury suffered by the claimant as a possible consequence of the conduct complained of is a pre-requisite to a finding of liability.'
65. See, for example, the High Court decision in *Shortt v Royal Liver Ltd.* [2009] ELR 240, [2009] ELR 240.
66. [1995] ICR 702, [1995] 1 All ER 737, [1995] IRLR 35.
67. This appears to be the approach taken by the Northern Irish Court of Appeal in *Rongland v South Eastern Education and Library Board* [2004] NIQB 89.
68. *MG v North Devon NHS Primary Care Trust* [2006] EWHC 8500.
69. See, for example, *Bonsor v RJB Mining (UK) Ltd.* [2004] IRLR 164.
70. [2005] IRLR 293.
71. *Hartman v South Essex Mental Health and Community Care NHS Trust* [2005] EWCA Civ 6, [2005] ICR 782; *Bonsor v RJB Mining (UK) Ltd.* [2004] IRLR 164; *Croft v Broadstairs Town Council* [2003] EWCA Civ 676.

application of these rules will be modified in any sense where the stress is caused intentionally (for example through bullying) rather than negligently.[72]

[16–39] In one sense this approach to duty of care is remarkably broad from an English standpoint, and is more akin to the now somewhat discredited language of broad principles associated to an extent with *Donoghue v Stevenson*[73] and in particular with *Anns v Merton London Borough Council*[74] than to the more incremental approach taken in subsequent cases in which the courts set stringent limits on the question of whether a duty of care would arise, most significantly in requiring that it be 'just and reasonable' that such duty be found to exist.[75] In another sense, however, the courts' approach to the question of the meaning of foreseeability (and indeed the approach of Hale LJ in her 16 propositions) is a very measured one, which will often not favour an employee who is genuinely suffering from stress. Thus the employer is only required to act where it is obvious that there is a problem[76] – and is not required to engage in any proactive analysis in this regard; [s]he is entitled to take what the employee says at face value, and does not have to make searching enquiries of him or her, and [s]he is entitled to assume that the employee can withstand the 'normal' pressures of the workplace, with the further comfort that there is no workplace with an inherent risk of stress.

[16–40] This attitude to foreseeability ignores, however, the psychological reality that if an employee is genuinely suffering a mental illness as a result of stress then it is highly unlikely that [s]he will behave rationally, for example in informing the employer of his or her problems. Indeed it is considerably more likely that [s]he will tell that employer that all is well rather than create a situation of enquiry. This is a significant point. In applying the law to the facts, the court in *Sutherland v Hatton*[77] strongly implied that liability should not be imposed where the employee had not given an indication to the employer that problems he had previously had and of which he had made the employer aware, were in fact continuing. Indeed in something of a throw-back to the logic in *Walker v Northumberland County Council*[78] the court appeared to be arguing that 'an employer should not be expected to be a mind reader and an employee needs to make an employer aware of problems when

72. See *Clark v Chief Constable of Essex Police* [2006] EWHC 2290 for some discussion of this point.
73. [1932] AC 562, [1932] All ER 1.
74. [1978] AC 728.
75. *Yuen Kun-Yeu v AG of Hong Kong* [1987] 2 All ER 705; *Caparo v Dickman* [1990] 2 AC 605; *Murphy v Brentwood* [1991] 1 AC 398.
76. See, for example, *Hone v Six Continents Retail Ltd.* [2005] EWCA Civ 922, where the Court of Appeal upheld the conclusion of the trial judge that a situation of stress was reasonably foreseeable in a case where an employee was patently overworked and had complained that he was tired as a result.
77. [2002] EWCA Civ, [2002] ICR 613, [2002] All ER 1, [2002] IRLR 263.
78. [1995] ICR 702, [1995] 1 All ER 737, [1995] IRLR 35.

they exist'.[79] It may, however, be argued that such an approach does not correspond with what the court had previously said was the touchstone for imposing liability in such cases – that is, the general principles of employers' liability. It is surely arguable that under normal tortious principles, a failure on the part of an employee to draw the employer's attention to problems that [s]he was suffering would not absolutely absolve the employer from his or her duty of care (or alternatively would not absolutely indicate that the employer was acting in accordance with the relevant standard of care), but might at most be a factor that would go towards indicating contributory negligence.

3.1.2. *Standard of Care*

Once the duty of care has been established by showing the harm was foreseeable, the next question is whether there has been a breach of the standard of care – in other words, whether the employer has acted unreasonably in the circumstances. Again it is arguable that the position adopted by Lady Justice Hale in this regard (in principles 8–13) is entirely favourable for employers. The employer is only required to take measures that might actually do some good; what [s]he will be required to do is conditioned by the resources available to him or her; [s]he may, where appropriate, dismiss the employee if this is the only way to ease the pressure and finally, if [s]he offers a confidential counselling service then this would strongly indicate that his or her duty is fulfilled.[80] This final rule arguably lifts the 16 principles firmly out of the realm of reality. It is entirely possible, after all, that someone suffering from stress will emphatically *not* want to 'tell all' to an employer, nor will [s]he necessarily want to avail of a counselling service if this is provided. As has been mentioned, it is unrealistic to expect someone who is suffering from a mental illness to behave rationally. [16–41]

3.1.3. *Causation*

In theory principles 14 and 15, which deal with causation, are not particularly controversial. It is, after all, a basic element of the tort of negligence that the harm must be caused by the breach of duty. What is significant, however, is the fact that the concept of psychiatric harm (rather than physical harm) does not fit neatly into the 'single cause' logic adopted by the court. In fact the most usual scenario is that an employee who suffers a breakdown in such circumstances will generally have pre-existing vulnerabilities, which are exacerbated or brought to the surface as a result of his or her work (and possibly the failure of the employer properly to deal with the situation), such that the employee then suffers a recognisable psychiatric illness. In such circumstances perhaps the best way to regard the matter is to [16–42]

---

79. Kimber, 'Stress at Work: Searching For Guidance', 1(3) *IELJ* (2004), 80, 83.
80. It is arguable that in *Hartman v South Essex Mental Health and Community Care NHS Trust* [2005] EWCA Civ 6, [2005] ICR 782, the presence of a counselling service was given less significance than was the case in *Sutherland v Hatton*. In the latter, the suggestion was that the provision of such a service was strong evidence that the standard of care was met, whereas in the former, the Court of Appeal merely described the availability of counselling as 'a relevant matter to consider in stress at work cases' (para.58).

see the breach of duty that causes the harm (the psychiatric illness) as involving a failure by the employer to take reasonable steps to prevent a vulnerable employee from suffering from stress, or a failure on his or her part to manage the situation properly when it is clear that the employee *is* suffering from stress. It is arguable that whereas the pre-existing vulnerabilities of the employee represent a factual cause of the eventual harm, nonetheless the failures of the employer should be classified as its legal cause.

3.1.4. Harm Suffered

[16–43] This issue is dealt with in principle 16. Two points are notable here. First, it would appear that this principle only becomes relevant where there has been found to be a breach of duty. In other words, following the finding of a breach of duty it would seem that the damages owed can be reduced by reference to pre-existing vulnerabilities on the part of the victim.[81] But this is completely at odds with the traditional egg-shell-skull rule for assessing damages whereby one is required to take one's victim as one finds him or her.[82] Secondly, as has been mentioned, under equality law it is entirely possible to regard stress as a form of disability, and hence to regard a failure on the part of an employer to take any account of pre-existing stress as a form of discrimination. On such logic it is difficult to see why the fact that an employee was suffering from a disability should be relevant as a reason for reducing the quantum of damages to be paid where a breach of duty has been found to have occurred.

[16–44] As has been mentioned, *Sutherland v Hatton* is a particularly important decision, and one that has been referred to in many subsequent decisions from both Irish and English courts. The precise legal status of the 16 principles remains, perhaps, a matter of uncertainty; as a very broad proposition, it may be suggested that in England, the principles are, at best, seen as being useful guidelines – indeed this is the logic of the House of Lords decision in *Barber v Somerset County Council*[83] and that of the Court of Appeal in *Hartman v South Essex Mental Health and Community Care NHS Trust*[84] as well as a host of other

---

81. See, for instance, *Allan v British Rail Engineering* [2001] EWCA Civ 242, [2001] ICR 942; *MG v North Devon NHS Primary Care Trust* [2006] EWHC 850.

82. For a suggestion in this regard, certainly in cases where the individual with a pre-existing vulnerability to stress has suffered psychiatric injury in a 'nervous shock' type of situation, see *Donachie v Greater Manchester Police* [2004] EWCA Civ 405, [2004] 1 Pol L R 204.

83. [2004] UKHL 13, [2004] 1 WLR 1089, [2004] 2 All ER 385. This was an appeal against the decision of the Court of Appeal decision in *Sutherland v Hatton*, in which the holding in that case was actually reversed. It is a peculiarity that Hale LJ's decision has received so much prominence in subsequent cases (particularly Irish cases), whereas the decision in *Barber v Somerset CC* which, on one interpretation, greatly undermined the decision in *Sutherland v Hatton*, has been virtually ignored. For analysis of *Barber* see McKenna, 'Lords Uphold Landmark Stress Guidelines', *Employment Law Journal* (July/August 2004, no. 52) 11.

84. [2005] EWCA Civ 6, [2005] ICR 782. In this case the Court of Appeal appeared to take a different (and arguably even more objective) approach to psychological injury caused by

cases[85] – whereas in Ireland they have become the central basis on which questions of duty and standard of care in stress cases are resolved. It is to the Irish position thus that we now turn.

3.2. The Irish Position[86]

Whereas there had previously been cases in which the Irish courts had consid- [16–45]
ered the question both of damages for workplace stress[87] and indeed for nervous
shock consequent on witnessing an industrial accident[88] the first major case on the
specific area of workplace stress (and one which took a particularly robust approach
to the question of employee protection) is *McHugh v Minister for Defence*.[89]

---

exposure to trauma (as distinct to ongoing stress) than did their Lordships in *Barber v Somerset CC*. Thus it held that if an employer foresaw that exposure to the particular trauma might pose a risk of psychiatric injury to employees *generally* then the requisite foreseeability would be established irrespective of whether the employer could have foreseen the risk of injury to the injured individual employee specifically. On the other hand, the Court of Appeal also held that there must be 'a real risk of breakdown which the claimant's employers ought to have foreseen' and a situation where 'a claimant suffers stress at work and... the employer is in some way in breach of duty in allowing that to occur'. For consideration, see Scott, 'The Lessons of Hartman', 58(2) *Employment Law Journal* (March 2005), 21. See also *Garrett v Camden London Borough Council* [2001] EWCA Civ 395.

85. *Pratley v Surrey County Council* [2003] EWCA Civ 1067, [2004] ICR 159, [2003] IRLR 794 – employer not liable for stress arising out of the fact of disappointment that a procedure to ward off another type of stress had not been put in place; *Young v Post Office* [2002] EWCA Civ 661, [2002] IRLR 606 – obligation on employer not just to devise a scheme for accommodating an employee who had suffered a nervous breakdown but also to ensure that that scheme was being applied; *Bonser v RJB Mining (UK) Ltd.* [2004] IRLR 164 – an employer will be liable if [t]he subjects employee to severe pressure of work in circumstances where the employer knows or ought to foresee that this is likely to result in psychiatric injury; *Croft v Broadstairs Town Council* [2003] EWCA Civ 676 – the fact that two members of the employer town council knew that the employee was undergoing counselling was not enough to establish that the council knew of her psychiatric vulnerability; *Vahidi v Fairstead House School Trust* [2005] EWCA Civ 765 – employer school not liable for stress suffered by an employee as a result of reorganisation and change within the school; *Packenham-Walsh Ltd. v Connell Residential & Anor* [2006] EWCA Civ 90 – no breach of duty where the employee showed no visible signs of suffering from stress through, for example, absenteeism; *Deadman v Bristol City Council* [2007] EWCA Civ 822 – defendant council not liable when a person who showed no signs of propensity to suffer from stress did so as the result of the ordinary operation of its procedure for investigating complaints of harassment, which was not, itself, something likely to cause stress.

86. For analysis of whether workplace stress claims must in the first instance be brought to the Personal Injuries Assessment Board, see Canny, 'Stress at Work Claims and the Personal Injuries Assessment Board Act 2003', 2 *Employment Law Review* (2007), 5.

87. *Sullivan v Southern Health Board* [1997] 3 IR 123.

88. *Curran v Cadbury (Ireland) Ltd.* [2000] 2 ILRM 343.

89. [1999] IEHC 91, [2001] IR 424.

3.2.1. *McHugh v Minister for Defence*

[16–46] This case concerned a soldier in the defence forces who had served in Lebanon in the early 1990s and had been exposed to certain traumatic sights. As a result, he manifested signs of post-traumatic stress disorder (PTSD), as was not unusual for people in his position, and this was brought to the attention of his platoon commander. Despite the fact that the defence forces had been aware for a long time of the problem of PTSD, nothing was done to assist the plaintiff until about a year later, by which time the disorder had developed into a full-blown psychiatric condition, leaving the plaintiff seriously ill. Significantly the plaintiff did not claim for damages based on the fact that he had been exposed to a stressful situation and that such exposure had led to him suffering from stress. Rather his claim was that the extent of the damage he had suffered had been gravely increased by reason of the fact that his condition had not been detected by his employers when it should have been, and by the fact that he did not receive appropriate treatment, including a referral to a clinical psychologist.

[16–47] In the High Court, Budd J found for the employee. He emphasised that liability did not arise simply because the soldier had been exposed in the course of his work to the inherent pressures that went with it. The employer was liable, rather, because the extent of the injuries to the employee was the fault of his employer. In this case such fault existed because, despite the fact that the employee had manifested uncharacteristic behaviour and other symptoms of stress, this was not brought to the attention of the medical officers and hence he was not adequately treated. In other words, according to the court, an employer owes a duty to ensure that stress is detected in an employee and also where this happens that appropriate treatment is provided. In both respects the court held that the duty on the employer was significant in that [s]he was required to 'keep abreast with contemporary knowledge in the field of reduction in the effects of potential afflictions to which soldiers are inevitably exposed in the course of duty'.[90]

[16–48] It may be said that this decision (which admittedly has not been a significant point of reference in subsequent cases) is authority for three separate propositions:

- An employer is required to keep up to date to some extent with the science of stress and with developments in this area.
- An employer has a responsibility to be proactive in checking the health of employees – a responsibility that arises even where the employee does not inform the employers of his or her ongoing difficulties. Indeed Budd J made the point (which Lord Walker would later make in *Barber*) that individuals suffering from stress will often attempt, for their own reasons, to suppress this fact, and that this was also something of which employers should be aware.

---

90. [2001] IR 424, 429. A similar conclusion had been reached in the British courts in the case of *Cross v Highlands and Islands Enterprise* [2001] IRLR 336.

- The employer's responsibilities carry on after the point at which stress has been deducted. Thus [s]he will be required to continue to monitor the health of the stressed employee and to take appropriate remedial action.

Since this case the issue of workplace stress has arisen with some measure of regu-   [16–49]
larity before the Employment Appeals Tribunal in the context of claims in which
an employee suffering from factors such as stress, harassment and bullying has
resigned from work and sued for constructive dismissal.[91] It was not until 2004,
however, that the High Court dealt again in any concerted fashion with the issue
of workplace stress, in the important case of *McGrath v Trintech Technologies*.[92]

3.2.2. McGrath v Trintech Technologies

The plaintiff in *McGrath v Trintech*[93] was a senior project manager in a multina-   [16–50]
tional IT company who was accustomed to working abroad on foreign projects.
During his first two-and-a-half years with the company he suffered bouts of ill
health and while on sick leave he was requested to go on an assignment to Uruguay
to work for a company recently purchased by the defendants. He accepted the job
but while in Uruguay claimed that he was subjected to serious work-related stress
resulting in injury to his psychological health and well-being. On his return to
Ireland, the plaintiff went on paid sick leave until he was made redundant. The
plaintiff issued proceedings seeking various reliefs in respect of his dismissal. In
addition, however, he claimed damages for personal injury and loss of good health
deriving from the stress suffered, and he grounded his claim both on the common
law duty of care that he claimed he was owed by his employer and also on an
alleged breach of statutory duty under health and safety legislation.

Laffoy J took the opportunity to review much of the existing Irish and English   [16–51]
case law in the area. In so doing, she concluded that the practical propositions that
Lady Justice Hale had endorsed in *Sutherland v Hatton*[94] should be seen as being
helpful in the application of Irish legal principle in this area and that the English
approach of assimilating liability for both physical and psychological injury under
the general heading of employers' liability[95] should be adopted in Ireland. She
further quoted the judgment in *McHugh v Minister for Defence*[96] and also the decision of Swanwick J in *Stokes v Guest, Keen & Nettlefold*,[97] in which it was held that
the standard of care to be expected for employees was to act as a reasonable and
prudent employer, taking positive thought for the safety of his or her workers in

---

91. See, for example, *Beate Riehn v DSPCA*, UD 947/2002; *A Worker v An Employer* [2005] ELR 132.
92. [2004] IEHC 342.
93. [2004] IEHC 342, [2005] 4 IR 382.
94. [2002] EWCA Civ 76, [2002] ICR 613, [2002] All ER 1, [2002] IRLR 263.
95. *Hartman v South Essex Mental Health and Community Care NHS Trust* [2005] EWCA Civ 6, [2005] ICR 782.
96. [1999] IEHC 91, [2001] 1 IR 424.
97. [1968] 1 WLR 1776.

the light of what was known or ought to have been known, and bearing in mind both recognised and general practice and developing knowledge.[98]

[16–52]   As was the case in *Sutherland v Hatton*[99], the concept of foreseeability of risk as a prerequisite to any finding that a duty of care existed in the case was of paramount importance and Laffoy J concluded that on the facts of this case, the harm suffered by the plaintiff was not foreseeable. In reaching this conclusion, Laffoy J referred to the corporate culture in which he worked.

> It clearly emerged from the evidence that the corporate culture in the defendant's companies is competitive and demanding of their employees… the American modal where employees work hard and play hard against the background of economic ups and downs. It was not a place where one would admit weakness… On the evidence I conclude that there was no reason why the defendant should not assume that the plaintiff could withstand the stresses and pressures of this type of work environment and of the workload which he was prepared to undertake.[100]

[16–53]   Laffoy J further noted that whereas the pressure under which he was operating was substantial and exacerbated by certain crises, equally it did not amount to 'greater pressure than was assumed by any other member of the management team'.[101] Moreover, whereas she accepted that he had a 'subjective perception' that he was not being properly supported by his employers, nonetheless the appropriate standard for assessing such matters was an objective one, and objectively the employer had at all stages acted reasonably towards him.[102] What is significant about these conclusions read together is the inference that Laffoy J was looking to the question of the objective level of workplace pressure as the relevant factor in determining whether liability should be imposed. In other words, the questions of whether the individual employee had suffered psychological harm as a result of his personal reaction to such pressure and whether the defendant employer had behaved reasonably in terms of adequately monitoring and treating the situation was not addressed. This is despite the fact that it is at least arguable that because this *was* a workplace where 'one would not admit weakness' meant that it was highly unlikely an employee genuinely suffering from stress would have reported the situation to the employer – a conclusion that should arguably have meant that a greater obligation should lie on the employer to ensure that no such weakness lay beneath the surface.

---

98. This view of the law was approved by Lord Walker in *Barber v Somerset CC*. It was also approved by Coghlin J in *McClurg v Chief Constable of the RUC* [2007] NIQB 53.
99. [2002] EWCA Civ 76, [2002] ICR 613, [2002] All ER 1, [2002] IRLR 263.
100. [2005] 4 IR 382, 433. See Brennan, '*Maher v Jabil*: Stress Claims and the Failure to Complain', 2 *Employment Law Review* (2005), 44, for the view that the conclusion from the Irish courts that a certain level of stress is to be expected in an Irish workplace is a remarkable one and is at variance with the approach taken in *Barber v Somerset County Council*.
101. [2005] 4 IR 382, 434.
102. See Bolger, 'Claiming for Occupational Stress, Bullying and Harassment', 3(4) *IELJ* (2006), 108.

Laffoy J did not give any particular consideration of the extent to which an [16–54] employer is required to be proactive in routinely 'checking out' the ongoing well-being of those employees who do not report that they are suffering from stress. Put another way, whereas the judge outlined in some depth the nature of the *Suther-land* and *Barber* cases, there is little consideration of the key difference between the approach of Lord Walker in the House of Lords and Lady Justice Hale in the Court of Appeal – namely that the former was prepared to require much more of employers than the latter. Equally, though, this was an unusual case where in fact there had been some efforts on the part of the employer to assess the employee's situation nor, on the evidence, was there anything that could reasonably have alerted even the most proactive employer to the impending problems for the plaintiff. In addition, Laffoy J (quite appropriately given the facts) did not make any comment as to whether *at Irish law* there was an obligation on employers to keep up-to-date with modern scientific developments in the area. Hence these two key areas that go to the heart of the extent of the obligations owed by an employer remain uncertain at Irish law.

The plaintiff also sued for a breach of statutory duty under the Safety, Health [16–55] and Welfare at Work Act 1989 (and the 1993 Safety, Health and Welfare at Work (General Application) Regulations[103]). In this respect, the plaintiff claimed that the employer was under 'virtually an absolute duty… in relation to the health and safety obligations imposed by the Act of 1989 and the 1993 regulations' – a proposition which, if accepted, would of course have meant that there was no need to show blameworthiness on the part of the employer.[104] Laffoy J accepted that the 1989 Act and the 1993 regulations clearly applied to both physical and mental health, but found that in the present case, even if there had been a breach of the statutory duty by the employer, it was not the case that such breach had caused the harm suffered – in the sense that even if such duty as outlined by the plaintiff had been followed, the problems would still have been suffered by him. As a general observation, Laffoy J did remark that 'if the submissions made on behalf of the plaintiff were correct, in my view the law would impose a wholly unrealistic burden on employers'.[105]

3.2.3. *Maher v Jabil Global Services Ltd*

A particularly important (and succinct) statement of Irish law in this area was [16–56] given by the High Court in *Maher v Jabil Global Services Ltd*.[106] This case is interesting, not least because (as well as certain claims in respect of harassment and bullying) it dealt with a claim that the plaintiff – a shift supervisor who was an employee of the defendant – had suffered stress at two different periods in his

---

103. SI no. 44 of 1993.
104. Authority for this proposition is to be found in *Everitt v Thorsman Ireland Ltd.* [1999] IEHC 7, [2000] 1 IR 256.
105. [2005] 4 IR 382, 437.
106. [2005] IEHC 130, [2008] 1 IR 25. See Brennan, '*Maher v Jabil:* Stress Claims and the Failure to Complain', 2 *Employment Law Review* (2006), 44.

working life (separated by a period of sick leave and discussions with his employer about his state of health), and that the cause of the stress was radically different in the two periods.

[16–57] For the first period of his employment with the defendants, the plaintiff claimed that the stress he suffered was the result of his being *over*worked and of his working in what even the defendants admitted was a high pressure (albeit, according to the defendants, not an unrealistic) environment.[107] In this respect, Clarke J accepted that the evidence indicated that the productivity targets the management set for the employees were not objectively excessive, in light of the level of staffing and equipment available. Interestingly, however, Clarke J did accept the possibility that an actionable claim could arise on the basis of the simple level of work that was being demanded by an employer. Thus he held that:

> There may be occasions where it would be possible for a court to come to its own assessment as to whether the level of work being asked of an employee was such as might expose a reasonable or typical employee to an unreasonable level of stress. However… there are also areas where it would be most difficult for a court to reach such a conclusion without expert evidence that targets or other demands and the like were unreasonable.[108]

[16–58] In this instance, however, the level of pressure imposed was deemed not to be objectively excessive. Thus Clarke J placed considerable reliance on the testimony of one of the plaintiff's fellow employees, who said that in her view the level of pressure on employees was 'absolutely not' unacceptable.

[16–59] The plaintiff then took a period of sick leave, and underwent some medical examination by medical representatives of the employers, which led the employers to the view that the plaintiff should not return to the kind of employment that had led to him being stressed in the first place. Instead he should return to a lighter level of work where he could be in his comfort zone and was the type of work he had been engaged in before a recent promotion. Equally, it should be noted that the psychiatrist who recommended this move also warned the employers that as a result of it the plaintiff might suffer some ego problems because of his inevitable perception that he was being demoted. This led to the second allegedly stressful period of the employee's working life, where he claimed that the stress he suffered was the result of his being *under* worked. In short he claimed that he was shunted into a 'non-job'. Again, on the facts, Clarke J concluded that the claim was not made out – that in fact there was good reason for the plaintiff's employers to retain him in a low-pressure job – not least the fact that his attendance record had been poor since his return to the workplace.

---

107. For a similar claim in the English courts, see *Hone v Six Continents Retail Ltd.* [2005] EWCA Civ 922.
108. [2008] 1 IR 25, 30.

In his general observations on the law in this area, Clarke J then reviewed the   [16–60] recent developments in Irish law – and specifically the cases of *McGrath v Trin- tech*[109] and *Quigley v Complex Tooling and Moulding*,[110] which will be considered shortly. Clarke J accepted that there was no difference in principle between the responsibility of the employer in the provision against physical and mental injury in the workplace, although he also accepted that the practical way in which such provision would be made would vary as between the two types of case. The judge also held that the starting point for analysis of liability in such cases would be to ask three questions, and these have been subsequently been adopted by the Supreme Court as an appropriate statement of Irish law:

(a) Has the plaintiff suffered an injury to his or her health as opposed to what may be described as ordinary occupational stress?

(b) If so is that injury attributable to the workplace?

(c) If so was the harm suffered [by] the particular employee concerned reasonably foreseeable in all the circumstances?[111]

From a tort law perspective it is worth noting that these three principles relate to   [16–61] only three of the four elements of the tort of negligence – and indeed this may have resulted in some confusion in later cases. Thus question (a) goes to the issues of presence of harm and remoteness of damage, (b) goes to causation, and (c) with its reference to foreseeability goes to duty of care (and arguably this should be the first rather than the third of the questions asked). Yet what is missing is a fourth question asking whether or not, in fulfilment of a duty that came into being on the basis of foreseeability, the employer acted reasonably – which is of course the basis for assessing whether the standard of care required of him or her has been fulfilled. After all, whereas one may have caused real psychological harm in circumstances where the risk of such harm being suffered was foreseeable, one will not be liable if one did not act unreasonably. Indeed it may more generally be suggested that whereas the later Irish cases in this area appear clear in principle on what activates the *duty* of care (foreseeability of damage), they are considerably less clear on what an employer must do to *fulfil* that duty. We will return to this point later.

In any event, on the facts of the case, Clarke J concluded that it was the third of the   [16–62] questions above that was pivotal. Following the rationale of the Court of Appeal in *Sutherland v Hatton*[112] Clarke J held that foreseeability of injury would depend on two factors, the burden of work involved (and the reaction of 'any normal employee' thereto) and the particular vulnerabilities of an individual employee that were *known to the employer*. In this last respect, it is arguable that Clarke J

---

109. [2004] IEHC 342, [2005] 4 IR 382.
110. [2005] IEHC 71, [2009] 1 IR 349, [2005] ELR 305.
111. [2008] 1 IR 25, 39.
112. [2002] EWCA Civ 76, [2002] ICR 613, [2002] All ER 1, [2002] IRLR 263.

followed the approach of Lady Justice Hale in *Sutherland v Hatton*[113] in coming to the view that if such vulnerability was to lead to a finding of foreseeability, then it would have actually to be known to the employer. In other words the obligation of the employer to a vulnerable employee was *reactive* rather than *proactive*.[114] Thus whereas Clarke J held that the stress deriving from the first period of work was not foreseeable because of the low threshold of work demanded, he found that the stress deriving from the second period was not foreseeable because the plaintiff's complaints were not particularly frequent (and certainly not as frequent as he had claimed).[115] It is notable that this approach is arguably at variance with that adopted in *McHugh v Minister for Defence*[116] – a decision which, like *Barber v Somerset County Council*[117], is not mentioned in Clarke J's judgment.

[16–63] Finally, in dealing with the question of the standard of care, Clarke J emphatically adopted the 11th of Hale LJ's propositions in *Sutherland v Hatton*[118] (that if there was a counselling service offered an employer would not be in breach of its duty of care), subject only to the proviso that this counselling service could not be a mere smokescreen for a concerted effort to get rid of the employee. This heavy reliance on the presence or absence of a counselling service is perhaps a curious approach.[119] It is certainly one inference to be drawn from Clarke J's judgment in *Maher v Jabil*[120] that (save in circumstances where an employer is imposing an objectively excessive workload on employees,[121] in which case it is obvious what he must do to act reasonably, namely reduce the workload[122]) where stress is reasonably and objectively foreseeable, the provision of a confidential counselling service is all that needs to be done in order for the standard of care to be met. If this is

113. [2002] EWCA Civ 76, [2002] ICR 613, [2002] All ER 1, [2002] IRLR 263.
114. See Brennan, '*Maher v Jabil:* Stress Claims and the Failure to Complain', 2 *Employment Law Review* (2006), 44.
115. *ibid.*
116. [1999] IEHC 91, [2001] 1 IR 424.
117. [2004] UKHL 13, [2004] 1 WLR 1089, [2004] 2 All ER 385.
118. [2002] EWCA Civ 76, [2002] ICR 613, [2002] All ER 1, [2002] IRLR 263.
119. The point has been made that stress cases often arise in circumstances where there is also an allegation of bullying and self-evidently provision of a counselling service will not be enough to satisfy the standard of care in a bullying situation where matters would need to be formally investigated by the employer. See O'Sullivan, 'Preventing and Defending Stress and Bullying at Work Cases', 1 *Employment Law Review* (2006), 14.
120. [2005] IEHC 130, [2008] 1 IR 25, [2005] ELR 233.
121. There is thus an obvious link between the obligations of an employer not to impose excessively onerous burdens on an employee and his or her obligations under working-time legislation. See Cox, 'Health, Safety and Working Time', 9 *Employment Law Journal* (April 2000), 22.
122. The clear inference to be drawn from the decisions of the High Court in *McGrath v Trintech* [2004] IEHC 342, [2005] 4 IR 382 and *Maher v Jabil Global Services* [2005] IEHC 130, [2008] 1 IR 25, [2005] ELR 233 is that it is up to the employee to demonstrate that the level of burden imposed on him or her is excessive and that it will realistically be necessary to adduce expert evidence in support of this conclusion. See Brennan, '*Maher v Jabil:* Stress Claims and the Failure to Complain', 2 *Employment Law Review* (2006), 44.

the case, then the burden on employers is a light one indeed. Indeed it is notable that in its more recent decision in *Intel Incorporation Ltd. v Daw*[123] the Court of Appeal stressed that the mere presence of a counselling service would not necessarily satisfy the standard of care.

> The reference to counselling services in *Hatton* does not make such services a panacea by which employers can discharge their duty of care in all cases. The respondent... pointed out the serious management failures which were causing her stress and the failure to take action was that of management. The consequences of that failure were not avoided by the provision of counsellors who might have brought home to management that action was required.[124]

Moreover, it is also notable that the presence or absence of a counselling service has not been of relevance in any of the subsequent Irish stress cases in which the courts have given judgment.[125]

Since the decision in *Maher v Jabil*,[126] the three questions raised by Clarke J have come to represent the basis for the Irish law in this area, and this is clear from subsequent case law. In essence the following broad propositions emerge from these cases: **[16–64]**

3.2.3.1. Genuine Harm Must Be Suffered

First, it is clear that there must be genuine psychiatric harm suffered by the plaintiff as distinct from anything less. Thus in *Larkin v Dublin City Council*[127] – a case where an employee had been wrongly told he had been promoted and suffered humiliation and grave disappointment when he was subsequently told that there had been a mistake and he would not be promoted – Clark J, with great sensitivity to the unfortunate plaintiff, emphasised that it would be necessary in a case of this kind to prove genuine psychiatric harm, as distinct from merely an unpleasant emotional reaction.[128]   **[16–65]**

---

123. [2007] EWCA Civ 70.

124. para.45 *ibid.*

125. See O'Sullivan, 'Preventing and Defending Stress and Bullying at Work Cases', 1 *Employment Law Review* (2006), 14 at 19, for the view that 'Employers should not and cannot hide behind a counselling service when matters need to be investigated'.

126. [2005] IEHC 130, [2008] 1 IR 25, [2005] ELR 233.

127. [2007] IEHC 416, [2008] 1 IR 391.

128. Similarly, in a case in which judgment was given the day after the judgment in *Berber v Dunnes Stores*, namely *Cronin v Eircom Ltd.* [2006] IEHC 380, [2007] 3 IR 104, [2007] ELR 84, it was held that a plaintiff who had suffered only 'ordinary stress' from her working life would not be entitled to general damages. In a similar vein in *Devlin v The National Maternity Hospital* [2007] IESC 50, [2008] 2 IR 222, [2008] 1 ILRM 401, Denham J, speaking in the context of a nervous shock claim, concluded ([2008] 2 IR 222, 238) that 'Grief and sorrow are not a basis upon which to recover damages. There has to be a proven psychiatric illness.' For an analysis of the types of harm that can arise in this sense, see *McClurg v Chief Constable of the RUC* [2007] NIQB 53.

3.2.3.2. The Harm Must Be Foreseeable

[16–66] Secondly, the question of foreseeability of injury continues to be the central marker in assessing whether a duty of care may be found to exist. Thus in *Shortt v Royal Liver Ltd.*[129] Laffoy J rejected a personal injuries claim from a man who alleged that he had suffered stress as a result of a disciplinary investigation into his conduct. Laffoy J decided, having regard to Clarke J's three principles in *Maher v Jabil*,[130] that even if there had been an injury caused by the workplace (which she did not accept), there was no question that this was foreseeable. Thus she concluded that

> The harm which the plaintiff alleges he suffered, even if it constituted an injury in the sense of a recognised psychological injury, was not reasonably foreseeable. While it is reasonable to assume that being subjected to a disciplinary process in the workplace and being transferred to a different position in the workplace against one's will are events which are accompanied by a certain degree of stress, they are events which are encountered in the normal course of the management of a business or organisation. *In the absence of any reason for a contrary conclusion* [emphasis added], an employer is entitled to assume that an employee is able to withstand such stress. On the basis of the evidence in this case, the management of the defendant did not know, and there was no reason why the management personnel ought to have known, that the plaintiff was vulnerable or likely to succumb to psychiatric or psychological injury because of the implementation of the disciplinary process... Indeed, the plaintiff deliberately, if understandably, concealed from the defendant that he was suffering from, and being treated for, stress.[131]

[16–67] This statement accurately sums up the Irish position: that the duty of the employer is only activated where it is objectively likely that stress will be suffered by employees *in the presence of obvious indicia* suggesting that a particular employee is unusually vulnerable to stress. Thus the best advice to lawyers representing an employee is to put employers on notice as soon as there is any suggestion that the employee may be in difficulties, that that employee is suffering from stress, and to continue to re-emphasise the point as often as possible. Indeed this was the principal reason why both the High Court and the Supreme Court accepted the plaintiff's claim that a duty of care arose in *Berber v Dunnes Stores.*[132]

[16–68] As far as the issue of foreseeability is concerned, and beyond situations where an employer is actually notified that the employee is suffering from stress, it may be that there remain some obligations on the part of employers to act proactively to spot obvious signs of stress – as was suggested in *McHugh v Minister for Defence.*[133] In assessing more fully the nature of their obligations in this regard, it would be

---

129. [2008] IEHC 108, [2009] ELR 240.
130. [2005] IEHC 130, [2008] 1 IR 25, [2005] ELR 233.
131. [2009] ELR 240, 256.
132. [2006] IEHC 327, [2007] ELR 1, [2009] IESC 10, [2009] ELR 61.
133. [1999] IEHC 91, [2001] 1 IR 424.

useful for employers to have recourse to *Work Positive*, a document revised in 2005 that is the brainchild of the Irish Health and Safety Authority and Health Scotland, and is aimed at helping Irish employers comply with their obligations under health and safety legislation.[134] The document, available on the Health and Safety Authority website, gives clear and practical advice (as well as employee questionnaires and so on) for employers. In the future it may well be that failure to follow such advice will be seen as an inherent act of negligence on the part of employers in their management of occupational stress. In addition, employers should have regard to the practical advice given in the HSA's *Work-Related Stress – Guide for Employers* from October 2002 which, again, is available on the HSA website, and which highlights the signs of stress, its effects and appropriate ways of dealing with it.[135]

3.2.3.3. *The Harm Must Be Attributable to the Workplace*

Finally, as far as the causation element of Clarke J's three questions in *Maher v Jabil*[136] is concerned, it is clearly the case that in order to be liable for harm suffered by an employee, the employer must be causally responsible for such harm. On one level this should be perhaps the most complicated aspect of the rules relating to workplace stress, in that in many if not most cases it will be impossible to detect a single cause of a person's stress, and whereas the pressures of the workplace may, no doubt, play a part, it is surely difficult to expect a judge to give the answer to what is essentially a medical or psychological question, namely whether that part is sufficient for it to be deemed to be the cause of the recognisable mental illness from which the person is suffering. [16–69]

To this extent, it is notable that, when dealing with the issue of causation in a stress case, Finnegan J, giving judgment for the Supreme Court in *Berber v Dunnes Stores*,[137] concluded that 'Causation is not an issue [in this case] in that the personal injury arose out of the circumstances existing in the workplace'.[138] There are, perhaps, two difficulties with this conclusion. First, it is surely the case that the mere fact that the injury suffered by a plaintiff arose out of circumstances existing in the workplace does not, of itself, mean that the defendant employer necessarily caused that injury. Thus, for example, if an employee owing to personal vulnerability is simply unable to cope with a job in which he is voluntarily employed, [16–70]

---

134. Generally, see Dean, 'Handling Stressed Employees', 3 *Employment Law Journal* (September 1999), 15.
135. Also of significance is the European Commission Document *Guidance on Work-Related Stress – Spice of Life or Kiss of Death?* (2002).
136. [2005] IEHC 130, [2008] 1 IR 25, [2005] ELR 233.
137. [2009] IESC 10, [2009] ELR 61. For analysis, see Kimber, 'Editorial', 6(1) *IELJ* (2009), 2; Cox, 'Recent Developments in the Rules Relating to Workplace Stress: The Supreme Court Decision in *Berber v Dunnes Stores*', 3(3) *Tort Quarterly Review* (2009), 17; and Cox and Ryan, 'Bullying, Harassment and Stress at Work: The Implications of the Supreme Court Decisions in *Quigley* and *Berber*', 1(1) *Employment Law Review* (January–April 2009), 17.
138. [2009] ELR 61, 79.

it is difficult to see how the employer can be causally responsible (in the sense of being the legal cause) for this, even though at a literal level the personal injury 'arose out of the circumstances existing in the workplace'. Secondly, moreover, on the facts of this case, it is strongly arguable that the plaintiff's injuries were at least partially caused by his own inherent vulnerabilities.

3.3. Contract-Based Stress Claims in the Irish Courts

[16–71] We now turn to consider the 'contract based' claim for damages deriving from stress – a type of claim that first achieved huge success in the High Court decision in *Pickering v Microsoft*.[139] As has been mentioned, the cases in this area tend to fuse principles of contract law and tort law, such that recovery occurs (where it does occur) on the basis both of a breach of the employer's duty of care *and* on the basis of some breach of contract.

3.3.1. *Pickering v Microsoft*

[16–72] In *Pickering v Microsoft*,[140] the plaintiff had been employed by the defendant company for some years and, in June 1999, her line manager asked her to take up a senior post within a restructuring of the organisation, which would have been a significant promotion, but would also have entailed relocating to America. The plaintiff declined this offer not because she did not want the job but exclusively because she did not want to relocate, and she indicated that fact to her line manager. Instead of discussing the issue further with her, the line manager indicated that another Microsoft employee would be taking up the position originally offered to the plaintiff. At a meeting with her line manager in September 2000 the latter informed the plaintiff that he knew that the transition during the restructuring would be hard for her, but suggested that she should continue in her job for six months and that if the situation became impossible for her at that stage, then he would help her to find another job in the company. Moreover (and pivotally), the line manager promised the plaintiff that he would ensure she was party to the resolution of any difficulties that would arise, that she would be 'kept in the loop' so to speak and would be involved in such processes.

[16–73] In fact, according to the plaintiff, the reality of the situation was entirely different, and she was systematically left out of the loop, leaving her feeling undermined and isolated – a situation that was compounded by comments made to the plaintiff by her line manager in a phone call, when he suggested she take some time out to see if that would help the situation. From this point, the plaintiff alleged that she started to suffer from a stress-caused psychiatric illness. She claimed that her feelings of being undermined and isolated in the workplace had been exacerbated by the fact that she had been totally unsupported by management. As a result the plaintiff went on paid sick leave from February 2001 until her employment termi-

---

139. [2006] ELR 65.
140. [2006] ELR 65.

nated on 16 August 2001. From this point she was not contacted or visited by any senior member of management (although she was referred to and attended both the company doctor and the company psychologist) and, at a particular point, her company e-mail account was cut off. During this period, the plaintiff suffered from chest pains, sweating palms, breathing difficulties, headaches and low self-esteem. She became reluctant to leave her home, to interact with other people, and especially to visit the Microsoft plant. She was prescribed tranquilisers, sleeping tablets and anti-depressants, and was diagnosed by her doctor as suffering from an anxiety disorder and, later, depression. Her doctor's prognosis was that, whereas the plaintiff would recover well in time, she might reasonably expect to continue to suffer some anxiety symptoms for some time. Her doctor also concluded that such anxiety attacks were the direct result of her working environment. In particular, according to the doctor, the plaintiff operated from the standpoint of the 'just world view' – the view that life is basically fair, a view which when shattered can have very grave consequences for the individual. Following the termination of her employment, the plaintiff sued the defendant, claiming *inter alia* damages for constructive dismissal and for stress-related psychiatric injuries.

Esmond Smyth J found that the defendant had breached an express clause in its [16–74] (unwritten) contract with the plaintiff that she would be involved in discussions and negotiations consequent upon a restructuring of the company that would necessarily alter her job, and that this had caused her stress. In his analysis the judge arguably straddled the divide between contract and tort, eventually concluding:

> I should add that this is a case, where in the absence of an express term, it would have been inappropriate to deal with the case on the basis of negligence principles alone. The duty of care that I am satisfied arises in this case is an incident of the plaintiff's contract of employment and the breach thereof. Finally I am of the view that this is precisely the type of case where a term of mutual trust and confidence can be and ought to be imported into the plaintiff's contract of employment. It is surely entirely consistent with the particular contractual term in the instant case that the defendant would not, without reasonable and proper cause, conduct itself in a manner likely to destroy or seriously damage the relationship of trust and confidence between the plaintiff and the defendant to ensure that the plaintiff was in a position to fully discharge her duties as a Senior Executive and Director of the defendant. The imposition of the implied term in this case is clearly independent of, and unconnected with, the manner of the plaintiff's dismissal. In my view there was a clear breach of this implied term in the failure to involve the plaintiff in the process which had been agreed for her and that this was a causative factor according to the medical evidence of the plaintiff's illness.[141]

Ultimately Esmond Smyth J held that the defendant corporation was liable both [16–75] because of the breach of contract that arose before the plaintiff took sick leave

---

141. [2006] ELR 65, 130-131.

(when her stress was not reasonably foreseeable) and the ongoing breach when she went on sick leave (when it was). In this latter respect the judge was critical of the defendant's management of the situation when the plaintiff was on sick leave. Despite the fact that the defendant company provided the plaintiff with the services of a psychiatric nurse, a doctor and a counselling service/psychologist, the judge found that there was a breach of duty because management within the company had made no effort to contact the plaintiff while she was on sick leave to discuss her grievances with her.

[16–76] From a tort law perspective, this may seem like a significant ratcheting up of the standards traditionally required of employers, not least because, as we have seen, in *Maher v Jabil*[142] Clarke J had endorsed the proposition of Hale LJ in *Sutherland v Hatton*[143] to the effect that as far as *standard of care* was concerned, a defendant employer, in order to act reasonably would merely have to provide a confidential counselling service. On the other hand, it should be remembered that the judge was applying contractual rather than tort-based principles in his analysis of the case. In other words the best interpretation of the holding in the case may be that, whereas a good deal of tort law language was used, arguably this case has little application to traditional tort-based personal injuries actions. Equally, as we shall shortly see, an uncertainty remains as to the precise relationship between tort law and contract law in this judgment.

3.3.2. Berber v Dunnes Stores

[16–77] The significance of a contract law based action for stress was again highlighted by the decision of the High Court in *Berber v Dunnes Stores*.[144] Here, the plaintiff was an employee of the defendants and had been since he was 18 years of age in 1980, and had worked successfully in the company for some years. At a particular point in his employment relationship with the defendants he felt that his superiors' view of him changed. Thus he was given far less opportunity to travel abroad for work purposes. He also felt that there was an increased interest in the state of his health. This centred largely on the fact that he had Crohn's disease – and indeed had had this condition since he was a teenager. He felt that various events over the course of a year involved him being demoted and ignored by management within the company – and despite the fact that his solicitors had put the company on notice that he was suffering from stress. Eventually his employment relationship with the defendant company was terminated.

Following these events, the plaintiff issued proceedings, suing for:

- breach of contract (in particular of the implied term of mutual trust and confidence);

---

142. [2005] IEHC 130, [2008] 1 IR 25, [2005] ELR 233.
143. [2002] EWCA Civ, [2002] ICR 613, [2002] All ER 1, [2002] IRLR 263.
144. [2006] IEHC 327, [2007] ELR 1.

- personal injuries – a claim made both in contract and tort – in the form of stress; and
- defamation (in respect of the incorrect description of the plaintiff in one roster as a 'new trainee', which the defendants had admitted was an error).

The first and third of these claims are not relevant for the purposes of this chapter **[16–78]** – hence our exclusive focus is on the stress claim. In this respect, there were two strands to the plaintiff's personal injuries claim:

(a) that the stress to which he had been exposed had exacerbated his ongoing problems with Crohn's disease; and

(b) that this stress had also led to him suffering recognisable psychological harm.

As has been mentioned, the plaintiff's claim in this regard was brought both in **[16–79]** contract and in tort. Laffoy J had no difficulty with this approach (regarding the two as 'indistinguishable') and, quoted the view of the English High Court in *Walker v Northumberland County Council* to the effect that[145]

> the scope of the duty of care owed to an employee to take reasonable care to provide a safe system of work is co-extensive with the scope of the implied term as to the employee's safety in the contract of employment[146]

More generally, Laffoy J adopted the 'three questions' approach to the issue of **[16–80]** workplace stress taken by Clarke J in *Maher v Jabil Global Services Ltd.*[147] and she then answered these questions as follows:

(a) She accepted that the plaintiff *had* suffered a genuine injury to his health (a psychiatric condition known as adjustment disorder), as distinct from mere ordinary occupational stress. Moreover, she concluded that this disorder had exacerbated the plaintiff's Crohn's disease symptoms and hampered the treatment thereof.

(b) She also accepted that these conditions were caused by workplace stress – in other words, that it was not the symptoms and treatment of his Crohn's disease that were the stressors affecting his mental health. Equally, the court was not prepared to find that a particular flare up in his Crohn's disease in March 2000 or a deterioration in his symptoms in 2005 could be attributed to the manner with which he was dealt by the defendants.

(c) Finally, she felt that the possibility of the plaintiff suffering from psychological injury as a result of the manner in which he was treated

---

145. [1995] ICR 702, [1995] 1 All ER 737, [1995] IRLR 35.
146. [1995] 1 ICR 702, 721.
147. [2005] IEHC 130, [2008] 1 IR 25, [2005] ELR 233.

after 23 November 2000 was reasonably foreseeable, especially in light of the fact that the defendants had been informed on 7 December 2000 that the plaintiff was suffering from stress.

[16–81] Laffoy J proceeded to address the vexed question of what the nature and scope of an employer's duty of care should be, once it was found that one existed. She accepted that the obligation on the employer was not to act as an insurer of the employee's safety but merely to do what a reasonable and prudent employer would have done in the circumstances. Equally in this case, where, as she had already concluded, the defendants had actually breached the implied term of trust and confidence, there was no difficulty in concluding that their conduct fell short of what a reasonable and prudent employer would have done in the circumstances. Accordingly damages (both for the psychological symptoms suffered by the plaintiff *and* for the exacerbation of his physical symptoms) were assessed at €40,000.

[16–82] What is perhaps slightly surprising about Laffoy J's judgment in this case is the absence of reference to the previous case law on workplace stress, and in particular to Lady Justice Hale's 16 practical propositions in *Sutherland v Hatton*.[148] Indeed this is particularly notable given that these principles underpinned the decisions both of Clarke J in *Maher v Jabil*[149] and also of Laffoy J herself in *McGrath v Trintech*.[150] Furthermore, it will be remembered that in *Sutherland v Hatton*[151] and in *Maher v Jabil*[152] it was stated that if an employer offered a confidential advice service with referral to appropriate counselling or treatment services then it would be unlikely to be found in breach of duty. It is unclear whether or not the defendants operated such a service, but it is perhaps surprising that no reference to this possibility was made, nor is it clear whether or not this suggests that an employer who offers such a service will now not be able to claim that [s]he has thereby fulfilled all the obligations pursuant to the duty of care [s]he owes to his or her employees.

[16–83] In assessing whether or not the employer had acted reasonably in the circumstances and thereby in fulfilment of such duty, Laffoy J's judgment seems to link the breach of contract with the fact of negligence. Laffoy J had already held that the defendant employer was in breach of the implied term of mutual trust and confidence in the plaintiff's contract, and, having reached this conclusion, she had no difficulty in further concluding that the employer had acted unreasonably in the circumstances. In other words, it would appear that the acts of negligence of the employer whereby the duty of care was breached were the same acts as those that led to the breakdown of the relationship of mutual trust and confidence

---

148. [2002] All ER 1. Generally, see Cox, 'Employers' Liability for Workplace Stress: New Legal Developments', 1(2) *Quarterly Review of Tort Law* (Spring 2006), 10.
149. [2005] IEHC 130, [2008] 1 IR 25, [2005] ELR 233.
150. [2004] IEHC 342, [2005] 4 IR 382.
151. [2002] EWCA Civ, [2002] ICR 613, [2002] All ER 1, [2002] IRLR 263.
152. [2005] IEHC 130, [2008] 1 IR 25, [2005] ELR 233.

between the parties, and the logic of the court seems to suggest an inevitable corollary between the two, such that, wherever the employer is responsible for the breakdown in trust and confidence between the parties, this will inevitably constitute an unreasonable act of negligence in breach of a duty of care to the employee that is capable of causing psychological harm.

Perhaps the best explanation of the manner in which the tort and contract claims were framed and dealt with by the High Court in *Berber v Dunnes Stores*[153] and *Pickering v Microsoft*[154] (and especially of why in *Pickering* the language of foreseeability was so pivotal to a claim ostensibly taken under contract law) is that recovery of unliquidated damages should probably have been sought on the basis of the tort of negligence, but the negligent action of the employer that grounded the claim in those cases (whereas it would have been sufficient *per se* to justify the claim) also happened to represent a breach by the employer of some aspect of the employee's contract. If that *is* the case, however, it is arguable that the conclusions on the facts in these cases (especially in *Pickering v Microsoft*[155]) were extremely harsh as far as the employer was concerned. After all in *Pickering v Microsoft*[156] the employer had actually taken significant steps to assist its allegedly stressed employee by providing her *inter alia* with a range of counselling services and by allowing her a lengthy period of sick leave. **[16–84]**

The Supreme Court decision in *Berber v Dunnes Stores*[157] is somewhat unusual, in that whereas the Court appeared to endorse the approach taken by the High Court to the law on workplace stress, it nonetheless overturned many of the conclusions of fact reached by the High Court and, in doing so, it may have generated a situation where it is harder than ever for a plaintiff to win a stress claim. It is, however, a decision of great significance in that it is the first Supreme Court decision in respect of a 'pure' stress claim – that is a claim that does not have a bullying component to it. **[16–85]**

In terms of the theoretical position of the law on workplace stress, Finnegan J for the Supreme Court accepted that this was represented correctly in the decisions of the High Court in *Maher v Jabil*[158] and of the UK Court of Appeal in *Sutherland v Hatton*.[159] Indeed Finnegan J cited the 16 practical propositions laid down in this **[16–86]**

---

153. [2009] IESC 10, [2009] ELR 61.
154. [2006] ELR 65.
155. [2006] ELR 65.
156. [2006] ELR 65.
157. [2009] IESC 10, [2009] ELR 61. For analysis, see Kimber, 'Editorial', 6(1) *IELJ* (2009), 2; Cox, 'Recent Developments in the Rules Relating to Workplace Stress: The Supreme Court Decision in *Berber v Dunnes Stores*', 3(3) *Tort Quarterly Review* (2009), 17; Cox and Ryan, 'Bullying, Harassment and Stress at Work: The Implications of the Supreme Court Decisions in *Quigley* and *Berber*', 1(1) *Employment Law Review* (January–April 2009), 17.
158. [2005] IEHC 130, [2008] 1 IR 25, [2005] ELR 233.
159. [2002] EWCA Civ, [2002] ICR 613, [2002] All ER 1, [2002] IRLR 263.

case, and the inference would appear to be that these principles are of considerable authority in Irish law. Nonetheless, on the basis of these principles, he held that the defendant was not liable for any injuries caused to the plaintiff.

[16–87] As far as the plaintiff's constructive dismissal claim was concerned, Finnegan J concluded that the actions of the defendant did not constitute a repudiation of the plaintiff's contract of employment – indeed the court found that it was the plaintiff who had acted unreasonably – and on this basis his purported 'acceptance of repudiation of the contract of employment by the respondent was neither justified nor effective'.[160] The court found that the employer was simply not responsible for any breakdown in the relationship of mutual trust and confidence between the parties – a conclusion of obvious importance as far as the stress claim was concerned, in that Laffoy J in the High Court had essentially held that what negligence there was on the part of the employer was manifest in it being responsible for the breakdown in the contractual relationship between the parties.

[16–88] The court then proceeded to look at the stress aspect of the claim. As far as *duty of care* was concerned, Finnegan J felt that because the plaintiff had put the employer on notice of his vulnerability to mental injury, therefore it was reasonably foreseeable on the part of the employer that 'if it should fail to take reasonable care, it would cause stress'.[161] In addition, as we have seen earlier, Finnegan J felt that causation was not an issue in the case. Moreover, it was clear that the plaintiff had suffered psychological harm. Hence the key issue was whether the employer had breached the standard of care by acting unreasonably in the circumstances. On the facts, Finnegan J found that the defendant employer *had* acted reasonably in dealing with the plaintiff's known vulnerabilities and consequently that the claim must fail – a conclusion that was not surprising given that he had previously held the employer was not responsible for the breakdown in mutual trust and confidence between the parties.

[16–89] Two final points are, however, worth making in respect of Finnegan J's analysis of the case:

- It is, perhaps, unusual for a Supreme Court to reverse a decision of the High Court exclusively on a factual and not a legal basis.
- This was a case where the court found that there *was* a duty of care on the part of the employer on the basis of the foreseeability of the injury, but that the duty had not been breached on the basis of the reasonableness of the actions of the employer. Yet at the conclusion of his judgment, Finnegan J commented that 'The injury sustained by the respondent being unforeseeable, the respondent's claim based on breach of duty must

160. [2009] ELR 61, 75.
161. [2009] ELR 61, 79.

fail.'¹⁶² This phrase, with its reference to foreseeability is, perhaps, an unfortunate one, in that the concept of foreseeability goes to the question of *duty* rather than *standard* of care, and the court had already concluded that such a duty did exist because the risk of injury *was* foreseeable if the defendants did not act reasonably. It is arguable that what was meant by this phrase was simply that in light of the employer's reasonable responses to the plaintiff, no breach of duty such as might cause the injuries that were suffered could be found to have happened.

It may be argued that two seminal questions remain unanswered after the *Trintech*,   [16–90]
Maher, Pickering and *Berber* decisions.

- First, it remains a matter of some uncertainty as to the extent to which an employer must be proactive in seeking to detect whether individual employees are suffering from stress. Equally, it is notable that, amongst the various statutory obligations that exist for an employer in dealing with stress, s.22 of the Safety, Health and Welfare Act 2005 imposes an obligation on employers to ensure that 'health surveillance' is available to employees, with health surveillance being seen as a periodic review for the purpose of protecting health and preventing occupationally related disease so that any adverse variations in health can be defined as early as possible. In other words, it may be that, regardless of the approach of the common law in this area, there is a *statutory* obligation to undertake periodic and proactive investigations into the mental health of employees.
- Secondly, it is unclear from a view of Irish case law in this area as to what precisely an employer must do to satisfy the standard of care owed to an employee in cases where, by reason of the foreseeability of injury, a duty of care arises. This is not least because, as has been noted, Clarke J's pivotal three questions in *Maher v Jabil*⁶³, which have been widely accepted in subsequent cases, simply do not deal with issues of standard of care. Although it seems obvious that this is something that is dependent on the precise facts of any case that may arise, it is equally the case that Irish case law is remarkably unclear on this point. Thus Clarke J in *Maher v Jabil*⁶⁴ intimated that the duty would be fulfilled by reason of having a working and effective counselling service in place.¹⁶⁵ But, on the other hand, in *Pickering v Microsoft*¹⁶⁶ considerably more was

---

162. [2009] ELR 61, 80.
163. [2005] IEHC 130, [2008] 1 IR 25, [2005] ELR 233.
164. [2005] IEHC 130, [2008] 1 IR 25, [2005] ELR 233.
165. Indeed, in this respect, it has been suggested that s.8(2)(f) of the Safety, Health and Welfare at Work Act 2005, which obliges an employer to maintain facilities and arrangements for the welfare of employees, could include an obligation to provide a counselling facility.
166. [2006] ELR 65.

required of the employer and in *Berber v Dunnes Stores*[167] the implication, certainly in the High Court, was that the duty of care would only be fulfilled by the employer ensuring that the relationship of mutual trust and confidence between the parties was not undermined.

3.3.3. More Restrictive Contractual Approach Taken by High Court of Australia

[16–91] In relation to this breach of contract point, the High Court of Australia delivered an important judgment in this area in the case of *Koehler v Cerebos (Australia) Ltd*.[168] This approach is striking for the emphasis placed on the employee's contract of employment. It has been said that the decision in *Koehler* 'means that it is now going to be very difficult for Australian workers to claim for psychiatric injury caused by stress at work, at least in cases... where the stress was caused by being given too much work to do.'[169]

[16–92] The plaintiff in *Koehler* was a sales representative negotiating sales of the defendant's products to independent supermarkets. She was made redundant, but was offered a substitute job setting up displays in supermarkets, working three days a week. When she saw the list of stores she was required to visit she immediately complained to her superiors that there was too much territory to cover in the three days a week for which she was paid, and that she would have to have help, or more time to do the work. She made these complaints on a number of different occasions. After five months, she resigned. She went to see her doctor, complaining of aches and pains and difficulty in moving as a result of lifting heavy cartons, but the doctor said that she was suffering from a stress-related illness. Over the next few months, this developed into a relatively severe depressive illness.

[16–93] In the High Court of Australia, the defendant was relieved of liability on the basis that a reasonable employer would not have foreseen the risk of psychiatric injury to the employee. Since the complaints made had related to the physical problem of getting the work done in the available time, and did not reveal that any difficulties she was encountering were affecting her health, the defendant employers could not reasonably be expected to work out for themselves that her health might be at risk. The anomalous result of such an approach, as Mullany and Handford have noted, is that 'the employee who stoically battles on, or who makes some sort of reference to his or her workload but is hesitant to disclose personal medical details, will be in a poorer position than someone who pours out a litany of problems at the earliest opportunity'.[170]

---

167. [2006] IEHC 327, [2007] ELR 1, [2009] IESC 10, [2009] ELR 61.
168. *Koehler v Cerebos (Australia) Ltd.* [2005] HCA 15, (2005) 222 CLR 44, (2005) 214 ALR 355, (2005) 79 ALJR 845. For analysis, see Hor, 'Psychiatric Injury in the Workplace: The Implications of *Koehler*', 27 *Sydney Law Review* (2005), 557.
169. Mullany and Handford, *Tort Liability for Psychiatric Damage* (2nd ed., Sydney Law Book Company, Sydney, 2006), at p.560.
170. *ibid.*, p. 561.

Interestingly, the High Court of Australia in *Koehler* expressly endorsed the judg- [16–94] ment of Lord Rodger in *Barber v Somerset County Council.*[171] In that case, Lord Rodger referred to the contract between the plaintiff and the defendant and concluded that the demands placed on the plaintiff were not excessive in themselves, but only because of some factor in the plaintiff's personality that made him more vulnerable to developing a mental illness as a result of work stress.

The High Court of Australia in *Koehler* was convinced, as Lord Rodger appears [16–95] to have been in *Barber*, that the introduction of a tortious duty of care did not sit easily with contractual arrangements between the parties. The court in *Koehler* held that not only was the psychiatric injury not foreseeable, but Mrs Koehler had agreed to perform the duties that were the cause of her injury. Insistence by an employer that an employee perform his or her contractual obligations cannot amount to a breach of a duty of care in negligence. The court stated that developing the law of negligence in a way that undermined or inhibited freedom of contract would be a big, and perhaps unwelcome, step to take.

If the *Koehler*/Lord Rodger type of approach is to gain currency, it is clear that [16–96] many plaintiffs will be unable to successfully argue that a duty of care is consistent with the terms of their contract of employment.

4. The Connection Between Stress and Bullying

One factor in the workplace that can clearly lead to stress is bullying.[172] The [16–97] definition of bullying provided by the Industrial Relations Act 1990 (Code of Practice detailing Procedures for Addressing Bullying in the Workplace) (Declaration) Order 2002[173] and adopted by Lavan J in *Quigley v Complex Tooling and Moulding*[174] and by the Supreme Court in the same case[175] is as follows:

> Workplace bullying is repeated inappropriate behaviour, direct or indirect, whether verbal, physical or otherwise, conducted by one or more persons against another or others, at the place of work and/or in the course of employment which could

---

171. *Barber v Somerset County Council* [2004] UKHL 13, [2004] 1 WLR 1089, [2004] ICR 457.
172. See Stewart and Fahey, 'Bullying and the Workplace', 5(4) *IELJ* (2008), 114; O'Connell, 'Bullying in the Workplace', 2(4) *IELJ* (2005), 119. For a comparative analysis having regard to developments in the UK, see Middlemiss and Hay, 'Legal Redress against Employers for Victims of Workplace Bullying', 21 *Irish Law Times* (2003), 250. For suggested statutory reform in the area of workplace bullying, see *Dignity at Work: Report of the Task Force on the Prevention of Workplace Bullying* (2001); *Report of the Expert Advisory Group on Workplace Bullying* (2005); and also Smith, 'What Can Be Done? Suggestions for Amended and New Legislation Dealing with Workplace Bullying', 1(3) *Employment Law Review* (2006), 57.
173. SI no. 17 of 2002.
174. [2005] IEHC 71, [2005] ELR 305.
175. [2008] IESC 44, [2009] 1 IR 349.

reasonably be regarded as undermining the individual's right to dignity at work. An isolated incident of the behaviour described in this definition may be an affront to dignity at work but, as a once off incident, is not considered to be bullying.[176]

[16–98]   According to the Health and Safety Authority,[177] examples of bullying include:

- purposely undermining someone;
- targeting someone for special negative treatment;
- manipulation of an individual's reputation;
- social exclusion or isolation;
- intimidation;
- aggressive or obscene language;
- jokes that are obviously offensive to one individual by spoken word or email;
- intrusion by pestering, spying and stalking;
- unreasonable assignments that are obviously unfavourable to one individual; and
- repeated requests with impossible deadlines or impossible tasks.

[16–99]   As far as Irish law is concerned, an employee who has been injured as a result of bullying has a range of legal options:

- to take an action under equality legislation;
- to take an action under health and safety legislation;
- to issue constructive dismissal proceedings;
- to bring a personal injuries action against either the bully or his or her employer, either directly or as a matter of vicarious liability.[178]

The first three of these different avenues have already been considered. We now turn to the last of them.

4.1. Workplace Bullying and Personal Injuries Actions

[16–100]   It is quite clear that a cause of action exists for victims of workplace bullying to bring personal injury actions against employers in respect of harm suffered as a result of such bullying.[179] Indeed where the harm in question is stress-related psychological harm, the presence of bullying (or a failure on the part of an employer to deal with a situation of bullying or harassment) is arguably a factor that will greatly increase

---

176. Generally, for analysis see O'Connell, 'Bullying in the Workplace', 2(4) *IELJ* (2005), 119.

177. See www.hsa.ie/eng/Work_Safely/Workplace_Health/Bullying/

178. It is also possible that a bullying situation could lead to a claim for a trade dispute under the Industrial Relations Act 1969. See O'Sullivan, 'Preventing and Defending Stress and Bullying at Work Cases', 1 *Employment Law Review* (2006), 14.

179. See, for example, *Green v DB Group Service (UK) Ltd.* [2006] EWHC 1898, [2006] IRLR 764.

the chances of a claimant succeeding in a stress claim.[180] In this respect, important statements of principle emerge from the recent High Court decision in *Quigley v Complex Tooling and Moulding*[181] and, though the decision was reversed on appeal by the Supreme Court[182] on one particular ground (namely that the claimant had not proved that the mental health problems from which he was suffering were caused by such bullying[183]), nonetheless the legal principles developed by the High Court in this case stand.[184]

In this case the plaintiff was employed by the defendant as a factory operative.   [16–101]
Having enjoyed a happy and healthy working relationship with the defendant's predecessor in title, the plaintiff alleged that his working relationship with his current employer was quite the opposite – especially after he refused to take voluntary redundancy. He claimed that he was victimised, mocked, insulted and demeaned, and that despite frequent complaints to management nothing was done about this (indeed he felt that he was being ridiculed for making such complaints): as a result he had suffered significant stress leading to him being diagnosed as clinically depressed. Eventually he was dismissed and, having successfully secured relief from the EAT for unfair dismissal, he brought a civil action against his former employer for the personal injuries he had suffered in the lead up to that dismissal. Significantly – and it is noteworthy that by this stage the company had gone into liquidation – nine fellow workers testified that his version of events was correct and that he had been the victim of bullying.

Having concluded that the fact that the plaintiff had proceeded under the unfair   [16–102]
dismissals procedure did not preclude him from seeking damages in respect of harm suffered in the lead up to and prior to his dismissal, Lavan J then gave an important and incisive analysis of the question of the duty of employers generally where issues of bullying are concerned.

Lavan J noted that whereas the recognition of the responsibility of the employer   [16–103]
towards the employee in respect of his or her mental health was a recent one, nonetheless it was one that was now firmly established at Irish law:

---

180. *Clark v Chief Constable of Essex Police* [2006] EWHC 2290; *Banks v Ablex Ltd.* [2005] EWCA Civ 173, [2005] ICR 819.
181. [2005] IEHC 71, [2005] ELR 305.
182. [2008] IESC 44, [2009] 1 IR 349.
183. This conclusion was reached largely on the basis of the written medical report from the plaintiff's doctor, which had concluded that the stress from which he was suffering was the result of his having been dismissed and not the result of his having been bullied. It should be noted that the same doctor appeared to reach a different conclusion (that the stress from which he was suffering *was* caused by the bullying) in his oral testimony in the case. The authors are grateful to Padraig McCartan SC for his kind assistance in this matter.
184. For analysis generally, see Brennan, '*Maher v Jabil:* Stress Claims and the Failure to Complain', 2 *Employment Law Review* (2006), 44.

It has been a fairly recent movement towards the thinking that an employer must take care not only of the physical health of their employees, for example by providing safe equipment, but also take reasonable care to protect them against mental injury, such as is complained of by the plaintiff in the case.

It follows on from this that employers now have an obligation to prevent their employees from such that would cause them mental injury, i.e. stress, harassment and bullying in the workplace.[185]

[16–104] Thus employers could be liable for instances of workplace bullying, either vicariously, or personally for failure to notice bullying going on around them, or for failure to provide a safe system of work. Moreover, as far as the High Court was concerned, such bullying cases would in fact be a species of stress claims – in other words, the fact that the bullying was the cause of the stress did not make this other than a stress claim. The employer was liable for an unreasonable failure to manage a factor within the workplace that quite clearly increased the risk the employee would suffer stress. Thus Lavan J held that:

> the action of the defendant in not preventing any further injury to the plaintiff's mental health by taking no action whatsoever against the bullying falls short of the standard of a reasonable prudent employer.[186]

[16–105] On this basis he gave judgment in favour of the plaintiff. As has been mentioned, the Supreme Court subsequently reversed this finding,[187] not because the defendant had not been negligent (it had), but because such negligence could not be shown to have caused the harm that the claimant alleged he had suffered in terms of depression and anxiety. Nonetheless the statement of law from Lavan J in the High Court appears to have been untouched. In this respect the Irish law in this area would appear to mirror its English counterpart as laid down by the House of Lords in *Waters v Commissioner of Police for the Metropolis*,[188] where their lordships held that:

---

185. [2005] ELR 305, 317.
186. [2005] ELR 305, 320. See Brennan, '*Maher v Jabil:* Stress Claims and the Failure to Complain', 2 *Employment Law Review* (2006), 44 for the view that this conclusion was a questionable one in light of the fact that the plaintiff gave no evidence to the effect that he had actually informed his employer that the incidents of bullying in question were causing a threat to his health. Indeed it will be remembered that the Supreme Court later concluded that the bullying in question was *not* the cause of the plaintiff's mental illness and reversed the decision of the High Court on this basis.
187. For analysis of the Supreme Court decision, see Cox and Ryan, 'Bullying, Harassment and Stress at Work: The Implications of the Supreme Court Decisions in *Quigley* and *Berber*', 1(1) *Employment Law Review* (January–April 2009), 17.
188. [2000] 1 ICR 1064, (2000) IRLR 720.

If an employer knows that acts being done by his employees during their employment may cause mental or physical harm to a particular fellow employee and he does nothing to supervise or prevent such acts, when it is in his power to do so, it is clearly arguable he may be in breach of his duty to that employee.[189]

4.2. Bullying and Vicarious Liability

Finally, cases of this nature raise the question of the extent to which an employer [16–106] can properly be vicariously liable for the actions of employees.[190] As is well known, vicarious liability arises where the negligent act causing the harm has been done by the employee *in the course of employment*. This is conceptually different to a situation where an employer is directly liable for the kind of systemic negligence that arose in *Quigley v Complex Tooling and Moulding* (where the employer knew or should have known that the bullying was occurring but did not take appropriate remedial action).[191] Naturally, for the purposes of a bullying action the question of when exactly an act can be regarded as having occurred in the course of employment becomes of huge significance.[192]

There is, of course, an argument that most persons employed in whatever setting [16–107] are employed to act reasonably, and hence whenever such a person commits a tort or, more obviously still, a crime, the action is by definition outside the course of employment and hence vicarious liability should not arise. Obviously if such a proposition were to be accepted it would mean that the entire concept of vicarious liability would be illusory in nature. Hence certain unreasonable (and possibly

189. [2000] 1 ICR 1064, 1068. See also *Barlow v Borough of Broxbourne* [2005] EWHC 50; *Banks v Ablex Ltd.* [2005] EWCA Civ 173, [2005] ICR 819; *Clark v Chief Constable of Essex Police* [2006] EWHC 2290; *Green v DB Services* [2006] EWHC 1898, [2006] IRLR 764. In the latter case, the court accepted that bullying may be found to exist even where no single action by the 'bully' was particularly harmful where the cumulative effect of 'a course of conduct pursued over a considerable period' is such as to amount to bullying in the ordinary meaning of the term. For a less-successful attempt to ground a workplace stress claim *inter alia* on an allegation of bullying, see *Packenham-Walsh Ltd. v Connell Residential & Anor* [2006] EWCA Civ 90.
190. See *Clark v Chief Constable of Essex Police* [2006] EWHC 2290. For analysis of the general question of vicarious liability for employers, see Ryan and Ryan, 'Vicarious Liability of Employers – Emerging Themes and Trends and their Potential Implications for Irish Law', 4(1) *IELJ* (2007), 3; O'Connell, 'Bullying in the Workplace', 2(4) *IELJ* (2005), 119. For analysis of the UK position in this regard, see Jones, 'Bosses Face Blame for Workers' Bullying', 60 *Employment Law Journal* (May 2005), 9.
191. See, for example, a decision of the Equality Tribunal on this point: *Ms A v A Gym*, DEC-E2004-011, 1 March 2004; and *Ms CL v CRM*, DEC-E2004-027, 17 May 2004.
192. See, for instance, *Green v DB Services* [2006] EWHC 1898, [2006] IRLR 764 (where bullying by a line manager was deemed to be directly and intimately connected to the work that he was engaged to perform and hence where vicarious liability was found to exist); *Bernard v AG of Jamaica* [2005] IRLR 398; *Hammond v International Network Services UK Ltd.* [2007] EWHC 264.

illegal) actions are deemed to be done in the course of employment. Nonetheless the question of precisely *when* a person is acting in the course of his or her employment remains somewhat uncertain.

[16–108] In England the theoretical position is that a person is acting in the course of employment (and vicarious liability therefore arises) where the conduct of the employee was so closely connected with the nature and circumstances of the employment, and/or the risk of the breach was one so reasonably incidental to it, that it would be fair and just and reasonable to hold the employer vicariously liable for it.[193] This is, however, a question of fact to be answered on a case-by-case basis.[194] On this basis, for example, authorities in charge of children's homes have been held liable for sexual assaults perpetrated by employees thereof,[195] as has a nightclub where a bouncer (trained to act aggressively) who had been hit by someone he ejected from the defendants' club, returned to his flat, found a knife and stabbed the claimant.[196] Similarly the employers of a policeman were held vicariously liable where he assaulted someone while off duty, having told the victim that he was a police officer.[197] Perhaps even more controversially, on this basis the Privy Council found a security company vicariously liable for the action of one of its employees in shooting dead (from two paces) a man who was trying to gain entry to a football stadium.[198] On the other hand, vicarious liability has not been found, for example, where a policeman who offered to escort an inebriated female to a police station actually took her to his house and raped her as she slept,[199] or where a policeman while off duty simply and randomly shot someone with his service revolver.[200]

[16–109] The approach of the Irish courts on this issue is somewhat uncertain. In the Northern Irish case *McCready v Securicor*,[201] the plaintiff and a colleague were playing with large trolleys. The colleague pushed the plaintiff, who was on top of such a trolley, into a vault and then, as a prank, tried to slam the vault door shut on the plaintiff. Unhappily, in doing so, he seriously injured the plaintiff's hand. The plaintiff sued the company, claiming that the colleague was negligent in his action and that the company was vicariously liable for this negligence. The Court of Appeal rejected

193. *Majrowski v Guy's and St Thomas's NHS Trust* [2005] QB 848 [2006] UKHL 34, [2006] 3 WLR 125, [2007] 1 AC 224.
194. *Dubai Aluminium Co Ltd. v Salaam* [2003] 2 AC 366.
195. *Lister v Hesley Hall Ltd.* [2001] UKHL 22, [2002] 1 AC 215; *Bernard v Attorney General of Jamaica* [2004] UKPC 47, [2005] IRLR 398 para.23; *Bazley v Curry* [1999] 2 SCR 534, (1999) 174 DLR (4th) 45. A less-expansive approach to this question is perhaps manifest in the decision in *Godden v Kent and Medway Strategic Health Authority* [2004] EWHC 1629.
196. *Mattis v Pollock* [2003] 1 WLR 2158.
197. *Weir v Chief Constable of Merseyside Police* [2003] ICR 708.
198. *Brown v Robinson* [2004] UKPC 56, 14 December 2004.
199. *N v Chief Constable of Merseyside Police* [2006] EWHC 3041.
200. *AG of British Virgin Islands v Hartwell* [2004] 1 WLR 1273.
201. [1991] NI 229.

this argument, saying that the negligence did not arise in the course of the man's employment. Equally this is an obvious case with an obvious result.

Far less clear cut is the scenario that arose in *Delahunty v South Eastern Health* [16–110]
Board.[202] Here a young boy who had visited (but was not resident in) an industrial school managed by the defendants was sexually assaulted by a housemaster working within the school. The defendants were deemed *not* to be vicariously liable for the actions of the housemaster on the basis that there was not a sufficient connection between the functions of the housemaster in question and the assault on the plaintiff for it to be regarded as within the scope of his employment.[203] This approach is, however, arguably at variance with much of the English case law in the area, where an expansive approach has been taken (albeit on a case-by-case basis) to the question of whether and when it can be said that a person who commits a crime does so in the course of his or her employment. It is perhaps significant that in *L O'K v LH and Others*[204] Mr Justice de Valera adopted the approach taken in *Delahunty v South Eastern Health Board*,[205] but also seemed implicitly to endorse the expansive view taken by the House of Lords in *Lister v Hesley Hall Ltd*.[206] As has been discussed at length elsewhere in this book, however, the recent Supreme Court decision in this case signals a strong disagreement amongst members of the Supreme Court on the question of whether an approach such as that taken in *Lister* could represent the law in this jurisdiction.[207]

A significant recent development in English law on this point is the decision of the [16–111]
House of Lords in *Majrowski v Guy's and St Thomas's NHS Trust*.[208] In *Majrowski*, it was held that an employer could be held vicariously responsible for the breach of a statutory duty by an employee even where that statutory duty was only owed by the employee. The case arose from the harassment of one employee by another, contrary to the UK's Protection from Harassment Act 1997. The employee alleged that he was bullied, intimidated and harassed by his departmental manager over a period of time. He pointed to excessive criticism, ostracism, abusive conduct and the setting of unreasonable work targets, and alleged that this treatment was motivated by homophobia on the part of his departmental manager. When Mr Majrowski complained, the departmental manager was suspended and, after an internal investigation, which found that Mr Majrowski had been subjected to homophobic harassment, she resigned.

---

202. [2003] 4 IR 361.
203. For the Canadian position on this, see *Bazley v Curry* [1999] 2 SCR 534, (1999) 174 DLR (4th) 45; *Jacobi v Griffiths* [1999] 2 SCR 570, (1999) 174 DLR (4th) 71.
204. [2006] IEHC 13.
205. [2003] 4 IR 361.
206. [2001] UKHL 22, [2002] 1 AC 215.
207. For more detailed discussion, see Chapter 3.
208. *Majrowski v Guy's and St Thomas's NHS Trust* [2006] UKHL 34, [2006] 3 WLR 125, [2007] 1 AC 224.

[16–112]   In instituting legal proceedings, Mr Majrowski elected not to sue the departmental manager herself, but rather the employer, whom he alleged was vicariously liable. He claimed damages for distress and anxiety and consequential losses caused by the harassment he suffered while employed by the defendants. The departmental manager, Mr Majrowski claimed, was at all times acting in the course of her employment. Significantly, Mr Majrowski did not make any claim against the employer for negligence or breach of his contract of employment. His claim was based exclusively on the employer's vicarious liability for the departmental manager's alleged breach of the statutory prohibition of harassment.

[16–113]   At first instance, the proceedings were struck out summarily. The judge held that the statutory framework to combat harassment was not designed to create another level of liability in employment law, since employees were already adequately protected by the common law. On appeal, the Court of Appeal ruled by a majority (Auld and May LJJ, Scott Baker LJ dissenting in part) that the employer could be vicariously liable for the employee's breach of statutory duty. Accordingly, the Court of Appeal held that the case should be permitted to go to trial. On appeal to the House of Lords, it was acknowledged that there was little judicial authority for the proposition that vicarious liability could (in the absence of express statutory guidance) be imposed upon an employer for an employee's breach of statutory duty. Notwithstanding this, all of the judges in the House of Lords were in agreement about the correctness of the result reached in the Court of Appeal.

[16–114]   Another significant English case involving the imposition of vicarious liability for bullying at work is that of *Green v DB Group Services (UK) Ltd.*,[209] a case that attracted considerable media attention when judgment was delivered, not least because of the size of the award for bullying and harassment in the workplace, which was in excess of £800,000. The claimant sued her former employer, Deutsche Bank, after persistent bullying by colleagues at the bank caused her to suffer two nervous breakdowns. The judge concluded that Ms Green had been 'subjected to a relentless campaign of mean and spiteful behaviour designed to cause her distress'.[210]

[16–115]   Of particular interest for present purposes is the approach taken by Owen J in finding the employer vicariously liable for the bullying suffered by the claimant at the hands of some of her colleagues. The claimant asserted that her psychiatric injury, and consequential loss and damage, were the result of bullying and harassment on the part of a number of the defendant's employees, for whom the defendant was vicariously liable; and also that there was a negligent failure on the part of the management and of the defendant's human resources department to take any or any adequate steps to protect her from such conduct.

209. *Green v DB Group Services (UK) Ltd.* [2006] EWHC 1898, [2006] IRLR 764.
210. *ibid.* 99.

The claimant in *Green* succeeded on both grounds. Interestingly, Owen J cited   [16–116]
the House of Lords' decision in *Majrowksi,* then just days old. Owen J noted that
the defendant in no sense condoned the bullying carried out by its employees;
it genuinely was appalled that this should have taken place, and was sorry that
the claimant was subjected to it. Equally, however, the defendant argued that it
could not fairly be held vicariously liable. The bullying had nothing to do with
the work of either the bullies or the claimant. All that could be said was that the
fact that they were employed by the defendant gave the bullies the opportunity to
behave as they did. Owen J rejected this argument and imposed vicarious liability.
He identified a close connection between the wrongdoers' employment and the
behaviour in issue. The bullying directly affected the working environment in
which the claimant worked; and some aspects of the wrongful behaviour involved
work that one or other of the wrongdoing employees were required to undertake
in the course of their employment. By way of example on this latter point, Owen
J noted that one of the bullies was responsible for distributing post, and had
deliberately withheld the claimant's post and would then fill her in-tray with what
seemed like a week's internal post. A further example given was that a colleague
of the claimant's, when asked to compile a list of all staff to give to security, had
deliberately omitted the claimant's name and details. Owen J applied the test
set out by Lord Steyn in the Privy Council case of *Bernard v Attorney General
of Jamaica,*[211] where Lord Steyn explained the correct approach to the issue of
vicarious liability in the following terms:

> The correct approach is to concentrate on the relative closeness of the connection
> between the nature of the employment and the particular tort, and to ask whether
> in looking at the matter in the round, it is just and reasonable to hold the employer
> vicariously liable.[212]

It is to be noted that in *Green* the court also held the employer negligent in failing   [16–117]
to have put in place any or any adequate system of protecting Ms Green from
bullying or harassment. The court gave a more detailed analysis of the negligence
of the employer as opposed to its vicarious liability. However, it is still important
that vicarious liability was found on the facts of this case: if Ms Green had failed
to establish breach of duty by her employer she would still have won her case by
virtue of vicarious liability having been imputed to the employer for bullying by
its employees.

In the context of bullying, it should of course be remembered that as far as   [16–118]
personal injury claims for workplace bullying are concerned, it seems clear that
an employer can be held directly liable either where [s]he himself or herself is
the bully or where, owing to systemic negligence, bullying is allowed to go on
unchecked in the workplace. In addition, it is possible, depending on the facts,

---

211. *Bernard v Attorney General of Jamaica* [2004] UKPC 47, [2005] IRLR 398.
212. *ibid.* 18.

that that employer may also be held vicariously liable for the bullying actions of an employee. It may, however, be conjectured that the latter scenario will most typically arise where the bully has some position of responsibility over the victim, such that the bullying actions may be regarded as connected to the exercise of his or her authority.

4.3. Health and Safety Authority Code of Practice 2007

[16–119] The Health and Safety Authority's *Code of Practice for Employers and Employees on the Prevention and Resolution of Bullying at Work*[213] came into effect in 2007. This latest new Code of Practice is aimed at both employers and employees and refers, in particular, to the duties in the Safety, Health and Welfare at Work Act 2005 ('the 2005 Act'). The new code provides practical guidance for employers on identifying and preventing bullying at work arising from their duties under s.8(2)(b) of the 2005 Act as regards 'managing and conducting work activities in such a way as to prevent, so far as is reasonably practicable, any improper conduct or behaviour likely to put the safety, health and welfare at work of his or her employees at risk'. It also applies to employees in relation to their duties under s.13(1)(e) of the 2005 Act to 'not engage in improper conduct or behaviour that is likely to endanger his or her own safety, health and welfare at work or that of any other person'.

[16–120] The code recognises (in s.3.1) the established definition of bullying at work as 'repeated inappropriate behaviour, direct or indirect, whether verbal, physical or otherwise, conducted by one or more persons against another or others, at the place of work and/or in the course of employment, which could reasonably be regarded as undermining the individual's right to dignity at work'.[214] It confirms that an isolated incident of the behaviour in this definition may be an affront to dignity, but as a once-off incident is not considered to be bullying. The code thus articulates a vision of bullying that coheres with that accepted by the courts – most recently, by the Supreme Court in *Quigley v Complex Tooling and Moulding*.[215]

4.3.1. Key Procedural Changes in New Code

[16–121] Although the new code does not differ very markedly from its 2002 predecessor, the most significant changes relate to the procedures for resolution of complaints and the proposed involvement of the Labour Relations Commission.[216]

[16–122] In terms of the procedure for resolution of complaints, a 'contact person' remains the first port of call for an employee who feels that [s]he has been bullied, although

---

213. Available at www.hsa.ie

214. *Report of the Task Force on the Prevention of Workplace Bullying, 2001*; also used in the *2005 Report of the Expert Advisory Group on Workplace Bullying*, and in the surveys conducted by the ESRI to determine the incidence of workplace bullying.

215. *Quigley v Complex Tooling and Moulding* [2008] IESC 44, [2009] 1 IR 349.

216. See also the Industrial Relations Act 1990 Code of Practice detailing procedures for Addressing Bullying in the Workplace (Declaration) Order 2002, SI no. 17 of 2002.

the role of this 'contact person' has been altered slightly in that, under the new Code, the contact person has no involvement in the complaints procedure and does not act as an advocate for either party. [S]he is simply required to listen and give guidance to a complainant in relation to the procedures available under internal policies. The complainant may then use an informal procedure and, in the absence of a successful conclusion, proceed to the formal stage.

The Code recommends that the employer should first decide if the facts constitute 'bullying' and put in place a monitoring system to the satisfaction of the parties. The purpose of this informal procedure is to establish if agreement can be reached between the parties to bring to an end the behaviour complained of. Naturally, the importance of retaining records of the procedure as it progresses is emphasised in the Code. [16–123]

Where the complaint is made against a senior member of the organisation, it may be necessary to have recourse to external services, such as the mediation services of the Labour Relations Commission. The formal procedure requires the complaint to be made in writing and to be signed and dated by the complainant. The person against whom the complaint is made should also be notified, in writing, of the complaint and thereafter a formal investigation will take place pursuant to the employer's internal bullying policy, which should reflect the new Code. The Code stipulates that there must be an appeals procedure available to the parties following the outcome. [16–124]

Where internal procedures fail to resolve the complaint, the Code provides that the Rights Commissioner Service should be accessible to the persons involved in the complaint. The Rights Commissioner may look at the internal procedures applied and may opt to carry out a new investigation. [16–125]

4.3.2. Status of Code in Criminal and Civil Proceedings

Although failure to adhere to the Code is not an offence, the Code is admissible in evidence in criminal proceedings under s.61 of the 2005 Act. In practice, it is highly likely to be taken into account in civil cases alleging bullying and harassment at work, in light of the judicial instances of its being cited analysed above, the most prominent example of which to date is the judgment of the High Court is the case of *Quigley v Complex Tooling and Moulding*,[217] where Lavan J referred to the definition of bullying as contained in the Code of Practice, and expressly applied it to the plaintiff's evidence. On appeal to the Supreme Court, the parties were agreed that this was appropriate and it was on this basis that the Supreme Court analysed the factual matrix of the plaintiff's claim.[218] [16–126]

---

217. *Quigley v Complex Tooling and Moulding* [2005] IEHC 71, [2005] ELR 305.
218. Analysed above in this chapter.

CHAPTER 17

Privacy and Employment

Introduction

As employees spend more and more time at work, the line between the employee's [17–01] private life and his or her work life has become increasingly blurred. In such circumstances, an obvious tension will arise between the employee's right to privacy while at work on the one hand and the employer's right to monitor his or her employee's activities in order to protect his or her business on the other. To compound matters, in the modern workplace, employees have access to a plethora of technological communication tools, from the internet to e-mail and the telephone, and whereas access to such technology facilitates more effective communication it can also have a negative impact on productivity, as well as representing an opportunity for the employee to abuse the privileges of his or her workplace, and for the employer covertly to engage in surveillance of aspects of the employee's private life. In this chapter we focus on the nature of the employee's privacy rights within the workplace, as well as the circumstances in which an employer may legitimately limit such rights.

1. Sources of Employee Privacy in Employment

The employee's right to privacy may be sourced from the Constitution,[1] the Euro- [17–02] pean Convention on Human Rights,[2] data protection legislation[3] and the contract of employment.[4] These are considered in turn.

1.1. The Constitutional Right to Privacy

It has been established in a series of court decisions that the right to privacy is [17–03] guaranteed as an unenumerated personal right under Art. 40.3 of the Constitu-

---

1. Art. 40.3.
2. Art. 8 European Convention on Human Rights.
3. The Data Protection Acts 1988–2003.
4. For example, the right may be implied as a term of mutual trust and confidence *per* Browne-Wilkinson J in *Woods v WM Car Services (Peterborough) Ltd.* [1981] ICR 666.

tion.[5] In *McGee v AG*[6] (a case that recognised an unenumerated constitutional right to *marital* privacy), and *Norris v AG*[7] (a case in which the court appeared to recognise a constitutional right to *individual* privacy), the courts used the concept of privacy to represent an entitlement of citizens to some measure of autonomy of choice in matters that, on one analysis, were private to them – use of birth control and engaging in same-sex sexual activity respectively. More relevantly for present purposes, in *Kennedy v Ireland*[8] (where the plaintiffs were awarded damages for unlawful interference with their privacy after the State was found to have tapped their telephones and recorded their private conversations), the court used privacy as a right (albeit not an absolute right) that permitted a citizen to restrict another entity (here the State) from engaging in surveillance of his or her private life. Thus Hamilton P commented:

> The dignity and freedom of an individual in a democratic society cannot be ensured if his communications of a private nature, be they written or telephonic, are deliberately, consciously and unjustifiably intruded upon and interfered with.[9]

[17–04] The principles in *Kennedy v Ireland*[10] and *Kearney v Minister for Justice*[11] (in which a prisoner's constitutional rights were held to be violated as a result of overly excessive scrutiny of his mail in prison by officers of the State) were further developed in *Cogley v RTÉ, Aherne v RTÉ*[12] in which, in the context of a combined defamation and privacy action (and where the plaintiffs were seeking an interlocutory injunction restraining the transmission of a broadcast on the defendant television station), Clarke J accepted that privacy operated at both a vertical and a horizontal level (that is, against both the State and other individuals) and also that it could be violated either where information was obtained in a manner where the right to privacy was violated, or where the publication of that information itself represented a violation of the right to privacy. This logic was applied in *Herrity v Associated Newspapers (Ireland) Limited*[13] when the court awarded damages for breach of an individual's privacy against a newspaper that published salacious details of her private life in circumstances where the information on which such story was based was obtained both illegally (that is, in violation of the terms of the Postal and Telecommunications Services Act 1983) and in violation of her right to privacy.[14]

---

5. For detailed analysis, see Delany and Carolan, *The Right to Privacy* (Thomson Round Hall, 2008).
6. [1974] IR 284.
7. [1984] IR 36.
8. [1987] IR 587.
9. *ibid.*, at 593.
10. [1987] IR 587.
11. [1986] IR 116.
12. [2005] IEHC 180, [2005] 2 ILRM 529.
13. [2008] IEHC 249.
14. Cox, 'Recent Developments in Defamation and Breach of Privacy Law', 3(2) *QRTL* (2008), 18.

1.2. The European Convention on Human Rights

The individual's right to privacy is further strengthened under the European [17–05]
Convention on Human Rights. Article 8 of the Convention provides:

> 1. Everyone has the right to respect for his private and family life, his home and
> his correspondence.

> 2 There shall be no interference by a public authority with the exercise of this right
> except such as is in accordance with the law and is necessary in a democratic society
> in the interests of national security, public safety or the economic well-being of the
> country, for the prevention of disorder or crime, for the protection of health or
> morals, or for the protection of the rights and freedoms of others.

Following the enactment of the European Convention on Human Rights Act [17–06]
2003 into Irish law, Irish courts must also have regard to the European Convention and the jurisprudence of the European Court of Human Rights when interpreting domestic law. The right to private life guaranteed under Art. 8 may be
applied horizontally between private individuals and was famously held to apply
to individuals even when in public places in *Von Hannover v Germany*[15] – a case
where a member of the Royal Family of Monaco successfully challenged a German
law, which did not prevent the publication by the media of photographs of her
and her family engaged in private activities, such as, for example, holidaying with
her children. In a judgment that is significant for employees asserting a right to
privacy while at work, the court stated that 'there is… a zone of interaction of a
person with others, even in a public context, which may fall within the scope of
"private life"'.[16] Later in the judgment the importance of protecting private life
even when in a public place was emphasised when the court acknowledged:

> the fundamental importance of protecting private life from the point of view of the
> development of every human being's personality. That protection – as stated above
> – extends beyond the private family circle and also includes a social dimension.
> The Court considers that anyone, even if they are known to the general public,
> must be able to enjoy a 'legitimate expectation' of protection of and respect for
> their private life.[17]

This approach is significant in that it could be argued that once the individual [17–07]
enters the workplace [s]he leaves his or her personal life at the door and therefore, while on his or her employer's time, should have no reasonable expectation
of privacy. However, in the modern workplace it is not so easy to draw a clear
dividing line between work life and personal life. As Oliver has noted:

---

15. [2004] ECHR 294.
16. *ibid.*, at para.50; approving *P.G. & J.H. v United Kingdom*, application no. 44787/98,
25 September 2001.
17. *supra*, at no. 15 at para.69.

Workers invest much of their lives in their workplace and have an interest in the maintenance of working conditions which acknowledge their existence as autonomous beings. This is particularly the case in today's society, where the traditional 'nine-to-five' working hours are no longer the reality for many workers, and working hours often begin early and continue into the evenings and weekends. In these circumstances, it becomes even more 'implausible' to expect employees to put their private lives on hold and devote 100% of working time to work related matters. This is especially true of private communications – it seems inherently unreasonable to prevent all private communications by workers during the course of a long working day, especially as some workers may have no choice but to carry out some private business during working hours. Of course, the realities of the workplace require some comprise of values such as privacy and autonomy, in order that the employer can plan and control work effectively. However, the question is one of where this compromise and balance should be struck, rather than whether individuals can be denied privacy protection altogether when at work.[18]

[17–08] The European Court of Human Rights recognised the difficulties in separating one's private life from one's work life in *Niemitz v Germany*.[19] In that case, police searched a lawyer's office including confidential filing cabinets containing confidential client information. The European Court of Human Rights rejected the narrow interpretation of private life under Art. 8 of the Convention, which provided that a clear distinction existed between private life and home, on the one hand, and professional and business life, on the other. The court stated:

> Respect for private life must also comprise to a certain degree the right to establish and develop relationships with other human beings. There appears, furthermore, to be no reason of principle why this understanding of the notion of 'private life' should be taken to exclude activities of a professional or business nature since it is, after all, in the course of their working lives that the majority of people have significant, if not the greatest, opportunity of developing relationships with the outside world. This view is supported by the fact that, as was rightly pointed out by the Commission, it is not always possible to distinguish clearly which of an individual's activities form part of his professional or business life and which do not.[20]

[17–09] The decision in *Niemitz* was approved by the Irish High Court in *Hanahoe v Hussey*.[21] In that case, gardaí conducted a search of a solicitor's offices. The search was leaked to the media in advance, who were waiting for the gardaí when they arrived to effect the search. The court held that the solicitors concerned were entitled to a right to privacy in their place of work (even more so as they were legal professionals where client confidentiality was essential).

---

18. Oliver, 'Email and Internet Monitoring in the Workplace: Information Privacy and Contracting-Out', 31 *ILJ* (2002), 321.
19. (1993) 16 EHRR 97.
20. *ibid.*, at para.44.
21. [1998] 3 IR 69.

The employee's right to privacy may also extend to the use by the employee of [17–10] the employer's property. In *Halford v United Kingdom*,[22] Ms Halford was an assistant chief constable in the police force. She initiated a claim for discrimination against the police force when she failed to gain promotion. During the course of these proceedings she was provided with a phone in her office, which was for her personal use in the conduct of her case for discrimination. She alleged that the police force had intercepted her communications when using this phone in breach of her right to privacy. Her employers argued that they were entitled to monitor the communications of their employees during work time and when using the employer's property. The European Court of Human Rights upheld Ms Halford's claim on the basis that she had a 'reasonable expectation of privacy' in the circumstances. This was particularly so because she had her own office from which the communications occurred and the communications in question had been made from a telephone specifically provided to her for her private use. Furthermore, her employer had not provided her with any warnings that her communications when using this telephone would be liable to interception.

1.3. Data Protection Law

In addition to a personal right to privacy enshrined under the Constitution and [17–11] under the European Convention on Human Rights, every citizen's privacy with respect to the processing of personal data is protected under the Data Protection Acts 1988–2003.[23] Thus an employer processing such employee data must be cognizant of the provisions of data protection legislation.[24]

1.3.1. Definitions

Section 1(1) of the Data Protection Act 1988 defines a data subject as 'a person who [17–12] is the subject of personal data', and personal data is defined as 'data relating to a living individual who can be identified either from the data or from the data in conjunction with other information in the possession of the data controller'. The data controller is defined under s.1(1) as 'a person who, either alone or with others, controls the contents and use of personal data.' Data processing is defined under s.1(1) as the act of 'performing any operation or set of operations on the information or data, whether or not by automatic means'. The Act provides that such processing can occur through the obtaining, recording or keeping of information or data, the collecting, storing or organising such information or data, retrieving, consulting or using such information or data, and the disclosing of such information or data.[25]

---

22. (1997) 24 EHRR 253.
23. Which transposed Directive 95/46/EC into Irish law.
24. An exhaustive analysis of this area is beyond the scope of this text. For a more detailed treatment on the subject, see Kelleher, *Privacy and Data Protection Law in Ireland* (Tottel Publishing, 2006).
25. s.2 Data Protection (Amendment) Act 2003.

[17–13]   In addition to questions of invasion of privacy, it is clear that for the employer who wishes to monitor his or her employee's activities during working hours, the data protection legislation poses a number of challenges. The monitoring of an employee's e-mail or Internet activity, the use of CCTV footage, the requirement to submit to alcohol or drug testing by an employer all have the have the potential to expose the employer, as data controller, to liability under the legislation. Consequently, the employer must be familiar with the general principles of data protection and the rules on the lawful use of the processing of personal data. In particular, the employer must ensure that [s]he is in compliance with the principles relating to data quality and the criteria for making data processing legitimate.

1.3.2. Principles on Data Quality

[17–14]   Section 2(1) of the Data Protection Act 1988 provides that when collecting, processing, keeping, using and disclosing personal data the data controller (in this context, the employer) must comply with the following provisions:

(a) *The data must be processed 'fairly'* – personal data cannot be processed fairly unless certain information is disclosed to the data subject, such as who the data controller is, who the information might be disclosed to and for what purpose the data is being processed.

(b) *The data shall be accurate and, where necessary kept up to date* – the data controller is under an obligation to ensure that any personal data is kept up to date and is accurate. An employer, therefore, should be careful that employment files are kept up to date and are accurate. For example, a disciplinary warning placed on an employee's file should be removed following an appropriate passage of time and in line with the provisions of the employee handbook or his or her contract of employment.

(c) *The data shall be kept only for one or more specified and lawful purposes* – thus the data cannot be used in any manner that is incompatible with that purpose or purposes. The data collected by an employer in furtherance of a specific concern about security, for example, cannot then be used to monitor employees for suspected wrongdoing that has no security element to it. Furthermore, the collection of such data should only be adequate, relevant and not excessive in relation to that specified purpose or purposes. Such data shall not be kept for longer than is necessary for that purpose.

(d) *The data must be properly secured* – the employer must ensure that any personal data is protected from unauthorised access, alteration, disclosure or destruction. The principle obliges the employer to implement appropriate technical and organisational measures to ensure that any personal data held by him or her is secure and safe from outside intrusion. It also encompasses the right of the employer to protect his or her system against viruses and may involve the automated scanning of e-mails and network traffic data.

1.3.3. *Making Data Processing Legitimate*

Before the processing of personal data regarding an employee can be consid- [17–15]
ered legitimate, s.4 of the Data Protection (Amendment) Act 2003 provides that
the employer must ensure that the principles of data quality outlined above are
complied with *and* that at least one of the following requirements has been met:

(a) *Consent*

Processing of personal data by an employer may be unlawful unless the employee [17–16]
has given consent to such processing. While the Act does not define 'consent',
Art. 7 of Directive 95/46 provides that personal data cannot be processed unless
the consent of the data subject has been unambiguously given. Consent is defined
under Art. 2(h) of Directive 95/46 as meaning consent that is freely given, is
specific and is informed. Thus it would appear that consent in this context must
be explicitly given and it is submitted that for the purposes of the legislation it is
advisable for the employer to request in the most direct manner possible that the
employee gives written consent to the use of personal data in this way.

Kelleher has noted that, in the context of employment law, 'consent is arguably [17–17]
the least attractive criterion for making data processing legitimate',[26] simply
because the power imbalance in the relationship between employer and employee
makes it that much harder to establish that the consent was 'freely given'. Indeed
it has been suggested that 'reliance on consent should be confined to cases where
the worker has a genuinely free choice and is subsequently able to withdraw the
consent without detriment'.[27] This statement would also suggest that in certain
circumstances an employee may be able to withdraw consent already given. On
this basis, it would appear that an employer would have to be extremely careful
in obtaining such consent (for example, through a provision in the employee's
contract of employment), and must take the appropriate steps to ensure that it can
subsequently demonstrate that the employee's consent in such circumstances has
not been tainted by undue influence (for example, by including such a term in the
contract only after extensive consultation with employees and, where appropriate,
their union representatives).

(b) *Necessity*

This principle means that the employer must be satisfied that any form of moni- [17–18]
toring is absolutely necessary for a specified purpose before proceeding to engage in
any such activity.[28] Moreover, before seeking to rely on the necessity principle, it is
essential that consideration be given to whether other means of securing the objective aimed are available. Thus, traditional methods of supervision, less intrusive for
the privacy of individuals, should be carefully considered and, where appropriate,

---

26. Kelleher, *Privacy and Data Protection Law in Ireland* (Tottel Publishing, 2006), at p.213.
27. Art. 29 Working Party on Data Protection, Opinion 8/2001.
28. Such data processing may be deemed necessary by the contract of employment: s.2A(1)(b)(i)
    Data Protection Act 1988.

implemented before the employer engages in any monitoring of electronic communications. Kelleher has observed that the processing of information on sick leave by an employee, for example, would be necessary where that employee was the Human Resources Manager or the data subject's line manager. If such processing were carried out by an employee not in either such position, then such processing could not be considered necessary for the purposes of the legislation.[29]

[17–19] Alternatively, such data processing may be deemed necessary as a condition precedent to the formation of the contract of employment.[30] For example, the employer may wish to make it a prerequisite of entry to the contract of employment that the prospective employee submits to a drugs' test prior to the commencement of the employment relationship.

Data processing may be deemed necessary 'for compliance with a legal obligation to which the data controller is subject other than an obligation imposed by contract'.[31] Thus in certain kinds of employment an employer may deem it necessary to process the personal data of a prospective employee on the basis that a failure to do otherwise could expose the employer to liability. For example, an employer seeking to engage a crèche worker would be under a legal duty of care to carry out a background check on any potential employee in order properly to assess whether they are suitable to work with children.

[17–20] The Act further provides that the processing may be legitimate where it is necessary in order to protect the health or property of the data subject.[32] Furthermore, s.2A(1)(c) provides that the processing of personal data may be legitimate where it is necessary for the administration of justice[33]; the performance of a function conferred on another by way of enactment[34]; the performance of the Government[35]; or for the performance of any other function of a public nature.[36] Finally, such processing may be legitimate where it is necessary 'for the purposes of the legitimate interests pursued by the data controller or by a third party to whom the data are disclosed'.[37]

---

29. Kelleher, *Privacy and Data Protection Law in Ireland* (Tottel Publishing,2006), at 225.
30. s.2A(1)(b)(ii) Data Protection Act 1988, as amended by the Data Protection (Amendment) Act 2003.
31. s.2A(1)(b)(iii) Data Protection Act 1988, as amended by the Data Protection (Amendment) Act 2003.
32. s.2A(1)(b)(iv) *ibid.*
33. s.2A(1)(c)(i) *ibid.*
34. s.2A(1)(c)(ii) *ibid.*
35. s.2A(1)(c)(iii) *ibid.*
36. s.2A(1)(c)(iv) *ibid.*
37. s.2A(1)(d) *ibid.*

1.4. The Contract of Employment

The contract of employment may also be a source of privacy rights. It is well estab- [17–21]
lished that there exists an implied term in the contract of employment between
employer and employee that the employer will not act in a manner calculated
to destroy the relationship of 'trust and confidence' between the parties.[38] Thus
any unjustified invasion of the employee's right to privacy could give rise to an
action for breach of contract if it would have this effect. In *Bliss v South East
Thames Regional Health Authority*,[39] the employer's unjustifiable demand that
an employee submit for psychiatric examination before he would be allowed to
return to work was held to have destroyed the relationship of trust and confidence between the employer and employee and was a breach of the contract of
employment between them.

2. Limiting Employee Privacy

Whether privacy protection arises from constitutional principles, the Euro- [17–22]
pean Convention on Human Rights, data protection legislation, the contract of
employment, or from all of these sources, there is a definite legal basis for the
assertion that the employee enjoys a right to their private space even while at
work. However, that right is not unrestricted and an employer is entitled to take
steps that will limit the scope of that privacy if it can be justified in order to effectively manage and protect the business. We now consider various situations where
potentially justifiable instances in which an employee's privacy is compromised
may arise.

2.1. Monitoring of Employees in the Workplace

Workplace monitoring can take many forms. It can be obvious, where the [17–23]
employer is physically present and visibly supervising staff, or it can be covert, for
example, where the employer uses hidden cameras or where [s]he implements an
e-mail or Internet monitoring policy. It is during the monitoring process that it is
most likely an employer will infringe an employee's right to privacy.

As already outlined, it is well established that an employee is entitled to privacy [17–24]
while at work, but also that the right to privacy is not unlimited and may be
restricted in particular by the rights of others.[40] Thus an employer may be justified in breaching an employee's privacy where it is deemed necessary in order
to protect the employer's property or business. In *Pay v United Kingdom*,[41] Mr

---

38. *per* Browne-Wilkinson J in *Woods v WM Car Services (Peterborough) Ltd.* [1981] ICR 666. The
   appeal to the Court of Appeal ([1982] ICR 693) is not relevant for this point. Generally, see
   Chapter 4 on implied terms.
39. [1987] ICR 700.
40. *Kennedy v Ireland* [1987] IR 587.
41. Application no. 32792/05, [2008] ECHR 1007, [2009] IRLR 139.

Pay was a probation officer who worked with sex offenders for the Probation Service. The employer learned through a tip-off that Mr Pay was a director of a company that supplied products associated with bondage and sadomasochism. The company was advertised on the Internet and its website had links to other bondage and sadomasochistic websites, which hosted photographs of Mr Pay semi-naked and performing various sex acts. Following the discovery of this information, Mr Pay's employer requested that he cease such activities on the basis that if such information became public it would damage his employer's reputation and, moreover, such activities were incompatible with Mr Pay's work with sex offenders. Mr Pay was then dismissed by his employer and he initiated proceedings for unfair dismissal, arguing that the employer's decision had infringed his right to privacy guaranteed under Art. 8 and his right to freedom of expression guaranteed under Art. 10. Having exhausted domestic remedies, Mr Pay made an application to the European Court of Human Rights.

[17–25] The court proceeded on the basis that the applicant's right to privacy had been infringed. While the photographs were of acts performed in public, the occasion was attended by a limited group of like-minded people and the court was of the opinion that Mr Pay's right to privacy had been engaged. The court accepted that the employer's dismissal may have been excessive, but acknowledged that the employee did also owe certain duties to his employer. Given the nature of the applicant's work, the embarrassment that the publication of this information could cause and the fact that the applicant refused to accept that his connection with the company and his activities could be damaging to his employer, the court held that the employer's dismissal of the applicant was not a disproportionate response in the circumstances. While accepting that the applicant's dismissal was in contravention of his right to freely express his sexual identity, the court concluded that the employer's response was 'necessary in a democratic society' for the reasons already stated above.

2.1.1. Monitoring of Electronic Communications

[17–26] In today's workplace, ready access to e-mail communication and the Internet is an essential part of business. However, while the ease of electronic communication has certainly facilitated business, it has increased the employer's exposure to liability where misused or abused by employees. The proliferation of social networking sites and their popularity amongst the younger members of the workforce in particular create special difficulties, as one commentator has observed:

> Social networking sites have muddied the waters between an individual's private and personal life. The sheer number of people using these sites, as well as the easy access to unvetted discussion boards, means that the risks to employers and individual privacy remain high. One of the prime causes of these risks is that users tend to let their guard down when using the sites, exposing views and information about themselves that they would withhold in a professional environment. The relative infancy of these sites combined with their substantial growth and users' naivety of

what they are exposing themselves to raises new and potentially damaging legal and company practice issues.[42]

From the user's point of view, the use of these sites involves great personal exposure [17–27] in the form of identity theft, extortion and targeted 'phishing' (a form of Internet fraud where fraudsters pose as well-known brands in order to steal sensitive information from users, such as account details).[43] The threat to the user's privacy and personal data protection is obvious in that [s]he is exposing the most sensitive information about himself or herself for others to see, including employers who might, for example, access the employee's personal site in order to obtain evidence to be used in disciplinary proceedings against that employee.[44]

Monitoring an employee's use of electronic communications creates special prob- [17–28] lems. Unlike traditional methods of supervision, monitoring of an employee's electronic communications can enable the employer to access detailed information on the employee's private activities, and this can be done without the knowledge of the employee. Oliver has pointed out how such monitoring can amount to an infringement of the employee's right to privacy:

> Perhaps the most obvious example is that of deliberate monitoring of the content of personal emails – an employer who reads the content of such communications is clearly obtaining personal information about its employees relating to their private lives. Similarly, an employer who looks at non-business related internet sites visited by its employees will be obtaining personal information about them, including such matters as details of their interests and lifestyles outside work … an employer may monitor 'traffic data' rather than actual content of communications. Although less personal information may be obtained through this method than through content monitoring, an employer will obtain information about the people with whom the employee has communicated through their email addresses, and the titles of email messages may also reveal their subject matter and some or all of the content. Monitoring of the names of the internet sites visited would similarly reveal information about an employee's private activities. Even firewalls could potentially reveal personal information about employees, as where a communication is blocked the employer would know that an employee had been attempting to access prohibited information. These examples may involve a less serious infringement of privacy than content monitoring, on the basis that less detailed information is being obtained, but nevertheless dignity is still affected and conduct may still be inhibited.[45]

---

42. James, 'Social Networking Sites: Regulating the Online "Wild West" of Web 2.0', 19 *Ent LR* (2008), 47 at p.47.
43. The European Network and Information Security Agency (ENISA), 'Security Issues and Recommendations for Social Networks', position paper, 25 October 2007. See further James, *ibid.*
44. 'Bosses Using Internet to Monitor Activities of Staff', *The Irish Times*, 25 September 2008.
45. Oliver, 'Email and Internet Monitoring in the Workplace: Information Privacy and Contracting-Out', 31 *ILJ* (2002), 321.

[17–29]   Art. 29 of the European Commission on Data Privacy Directive (95/46/EC) established a Working Party of Data Privacy Commissioners in order to examine the issue of surveillance of electronic communications.[46] This group produced a working document, (which, while not legally binding, would certainly prove persuasive), that identified that in order for any monitoring measure to be considered legitimate it must satisfy the following tests:

1.   Is the measure necessary?
2.   Is the measure transparent to the employees?
3.   Is the measure adopted proportionate?
4.   Is the data obtained as a result of such monitoring accurate and retained no longer than necessary?
5.   Is the data obtained as a result of such monitoring secured safely?

2.1.1.1. Monitoring Must be Necessary

[17–30]   The Working Party document notes that before the employer engages in the monitoring of electronic communications of employees, traditional, less-intrusive methods of supervision should be considered. Monitoring of an employee's e-mail or Internet use should only occur in exceptional circumstances.[47]

However, an employee's wrongful actions committed during the course of his or her employment may expose the employer to liability on the basis of the doctrine of vicarious liability.[48] When such actions occur during the course of employment or by using an employer's property, the employer may be entitled to carry out such monitoring activities as is necessary in order to protect his or her interests.[49] An employer may also deem it necessary to monitor an employee's electronic communications on the basis that [s]he is protecting his or her property. First, the employer can argue that monitoring is necessary in order to ensure that employee

---

46.   Article 29 – Data Protection Working Party, *Working Document on the Surveillance of Electronic Communications in the Workplace* (5401/01/EN/Final WP 55). This working document was adopted on 29 May 2002. The document does not prejudice the application of national law in related to data protection. The working group offers guidance about what constitutes legitimate monitoring activities and acceptable limits of worker's surveillance by the employer although it is open to Member States to establish higher standards of protection for workers.

47.   *ibid.*, at 13.

48.   An employer's vicarious liability can occur in number of different ways. First, the misuse of an employer's communication technology can expose the employer to an action for defamation. Secondly, the improper use of e-mail by the employee may expose the employer to a claim for bullying and harassment (including sexual harassment) (see *Mehigan v Dyflin Publications Ltd.* UD/2001). Thirdly, an employee could expose an employer to liability for infringement of another's intellectual property rights, and finally, an employer could be exposed to unwanted contractual liability by an employee's careless use of e-mail because the Electronic Commerce Act 2000 makes it clear that legally binding contracts can be entered into via e-mail.

49.   See Chapter 3 for further discussion of the application of the doctrine of vicarious liability.

productivity is maintained at a high level during working hours. Secondly, the employer may deem it necessary to introduce monitoring technology to the workplace in order to ensure that his or her property is adequately protected from theft or vandalism.

2.1.1.2. Monitoring Must be Transparent

Where possible, an employer must not carry out any surveillance of his or her [17–31] employees in a covert manner.[50] The employer should inform and warn the employee that any such surveillance is being conducted. In order to comply with the requirement of transparency, the employer should ensure that the employee is provided with a clear statement of the employer's monitoring policy. This policy should be readily accessible to the employee. The Working Party suggests the following information, at the very least, should be made available to the employee:

1. E-mail/Internet policy within the company describing in detail the extent to which communication facilities owned by the company may be used for personal/ private communications by the employees (e.g. limitation on time and duration of use).

2. Reasons and purposes for which surveillance, if any, is being carried out. Where the employer has allowed the use of the company's communication facilities for express private purposes, such private communications may under very limited circumstances be subject to surveillance, e.g. to ensure the security of the information system (virus checking).

3. The details of surveillance measures taken, i.e. who? what? how? when?

4. Details of any enforcement procedures outlining how and when workers will be notified of breaches of internal policies and be given the opportunity to respond to any such claims against them.[51]

The Working Party advises that where a system of monitoring identifies a breach of [17–32] the employer's policy then the employer should immediately notify the employee of any misuse detected unless there are good reasons why such notification should not take place.[52] Finally, the Working Party recommends that the employer should enter into a consultative process with the employees before introducing any worker-related monitoring policies.[53]

---

50. Art. 13 of the European Commission on Data Privacy Directive (95/46/EC) provides that covert surveillance may be legitimate when it is considered necessary to safeguard important public interests such as national security or the prevention, detection, investigation and prosecution of criminal offences, or is necessary for the protection of the data subject or of the rights and freedoms of others.
51. *supra*, no. 46 at 15.
52. *ibid.*
53. *ibid.*

[17–33] Furthermore, an employee has a right of access to any data related to him or her processed by his or her employer. The employee may request the rectification or erasure of such data that does not comply with the provisions of the Directive. The employee's right of access to such information without excessive delay or expense is, in the words of the Working Party, 'a powerful tool that workers individually can exercise to make sure that the monitoring activities in the workplace remain lawful and fair to the workers'.[54] However, the Working Party does acknowledge that in exceptional circumstances granting full access to all such data may cause difficulties, particularly in the case of what is called 'evaluation data'.[55]

[17–34] In Recommendation 1/2001 of the Working Party on employee evaluation data,[56] it was recommended that such data could qualify as 'personal data' even where that information contained subjective judgment of the employee, i.e. performance reviews. The Working Party suggested that:

> Personal data can be… found in subjective judgments and evaluations which can actually include elements specific to the physical, physiological, psychical, economic, cultural or social identity of data subjects. This is equally true if a judgment or a evaluation is summarised by a score or rank or is expressed by means of other evaluation criteria.

> The fact that under national law a few of these subjective data cannot be always accessed and rectified directly, or that they can be rectified by the inclusion of statements or notes made by data subjects, does not prevent them from being personal data, with a view to transparency of processing and the exercise of right of access.

> Similar considerations apply in respect of the fact that direct access to the data included in subjective judgments or evaluations can be deferred or limited under national law.[57]

2.1.1.3. Monitoring Must be Proportionate

[17–35] The Working Party recommends 'that personal data including those involved in monitoring must be adequate, relevant and not excessive with regard to achieving the purpose specified'.[58] Thus the employer is under an obligation to ensure that the system of monitoring introduced must be specifically devised with the perceived threat identified by the employer in mind. That rules out the blanket monitoring of individual employee e-mails and employee use of the internet unless such monitoring can be justified on security or other grounds and places an

---

54. *supra*, no. 46 at 16.
55. *ibid.*
56. Art. 29 Working Party, *Recommendation 1/2001 on Employee Evaluation Data* (5008/01/EN Final WP 42), 22 March 2001.
57. *ibid.*, at 2–3.
58. *ibid.*, at 17.

obligation on the employer to consider whether there were less intrusive methods by which the employer's objectives could have been achieved.[59]

2.1.1.4. Accuracy and Retention

The data must be kept up-to-date by the employer and must be retained by the [17–36] employer no longer than is necessary. Under the principles of transparency, as part of its monitoring policy, for example, the employer should inform its employees of the retention period for e-mails sent by employees stored on their servers for business needs. The Working Party recommended that a period of retention of longer than three months would not normally be justified.[60]

2.1.1.5. Security

An employer is obliged to adopt technical and organisational measures in order [17–37] to protect the security of any personal data retained by him or her. Equally, the employer is entitled to secure his or her property from viruses and so forth by introducing technology that automatically scans e-mails and traffic data. In the view of the Working Party, this can be done through the use of modern technology that minimises the infringement of the employees' right to privacy. The employer is also under an obligation to implement organisational measures in order to secure such data. Thus great responsibility lies on the systems administrator to ensure that all personal data is adequately secured. The Working Party also noted that an employer should place employees with such security responsibilities 'under a strict duty of professional secrecy with regard to confidential information, to which they have access'.[61]

2.1.2. E-mail and Internet Usage Policy

As already explained, an employer is entitled and/or obliged to take steps in [17–38] order to protect his or her business interests and may be justified in taking action that would otherwise be considered an invasion of an employee's privacy. In the context of e-mail and Internet monitoring, the employer (in line with the principles on transparency as outlined by the Art. 29 Working Party) can warn employees that such monitoring is taking place and the nature and extent of such monitoring. The existence of an e-mail and Internet usage policy that is communicated to all employees can have the two-fold effect of meeting the requirements of transparency under data protection principles, while also providing certainty to an employee in terms of the level of privacy that it is reasonable for him or her to expect in the workplace. The Art. 29 Working Party recommended that the following minimum information should be provided by an employer to its employees regarding e-mail monitoring:

---

59. *ibid.*
60. *supra*, no. 46 at 18.
61. *ibid.*, at 19.

a) Whether a worker is entitled to have an e-mail account for purely personal use, whether use of web-mail accounts is permitted at work and whether the employer recommends the use, by workers, of a private web-mail account for the purpose of using e-mail for purely personal use…

b) The arrangements in place with workers to access the contents of an e-mail, i.e. when the worker is unexpectantly absent, and the specific purposes for such access.

c) When a backup copy of messages are made, the storage period of it.

d) Information as to when e-mails are definitively deleted from the server.

e) Security issues.

f) The involvement of representatives of workers in formulating the policy.[62]

[17–39]   The Working Party warned that there is a continual obligation on the employer to ensure that the policy on usage of e-mail in the workplace is kept up to date.[63] Furthermore, it strongly encouraged employers to consider a policy of allowing employees to use their own private e-mail accounts if they found it necessary to send private e-mails while at work. The use of such e-mail accounts 'would clarify the distinction between e-mails for professional and for private use, and would reduce the possibility of employers invading their workers' privacy'.[64] The Working Party concluded that encouraging an employer to adopt a policy on employee web-mail or private e-mail accounts would facilitate a form of monitoring that might be considered less intrusive. For example, in a situation where an employee is suspected of misusing e-mail, the employer could simply monitor the time that that employee spent on the computer for personal reasons by reference to the time spent on web-mail or personal e-mail accounts, thereby obviating the need to trawl through the content of all employees' e-mail communications.[65]

[17–40]   As regards Internet use, the Working Party has recognised the importance and benefits of free access to the Internet for employees in enabling them to carry out their duties in an efficient manner. Thus the Working Party recommends that the employer should concentrate his or her efforts on preventing misuse of the Internet by employees rather than detecting it.[66] Thus blocking access to certain non-essential websites might be less intrusive than monitoring the employee's actual use of the Internet. The Working Party also recommends that the issuing of a prompt warning to an employee in relation to any suspicious use of the Internet

---

62. *ibid.* at 22.
63. *ibid.*
64. *ibid.*, at 23.
65. *ibid.*, at 23.
66. *ibid.*, at 24.

will minimise problems, and further recommends that the employer should always treat suspicious behaviour regarding Internet misuse with caution given the ease by which websites can be inadvertently accessed by an employee.[67] The Working Party recommended that the following information – at a minimum – should be contained as part of the employer's Internet usage policy:

1. The information specified… under the transparency principle.

And more specifically in relation to Internet use in particular the following points should be addressed:

2. The employer must set out clearly to workers the conditions on which private use of the Internet is permitted as well as specifying material which cannot be viewed or copied. These conditions and limitations have to be explained to the workers.

3. Workers need to be informed about the systems implemented both to prevent access to certain sites and to detect misuse. The extent of such monitoring should be specified, for instance, whether such monitoring may relate to individuals or particular sections of the company or whether the content of the sites visited is viewed or recorded by the employer in particular circumstances. Furthermore, the policy should specify what use, if any, will be made of any data collected in relation to who visited what sites.

4. Inform workers about the involvement of their representatives, both in the implementation of this policy and in the investigation of alleged breaches.[68]

2.1.2.1. Enforcement of an E-mail and Internet Usage Policy

Employers must tread carefully when seeking to enforce an e-mail and Internet [17–41] usage policy. As is the case with any employment disciplinary process, the employer should be guided by the principles of natural justice and fair procedures when enforcing such a policy.[69] Thus an employer should ensure that the requirements of the policy are clearly communicated to the employees so that they are properly understood,[70] and furthermore, that the employees have prior knowledge of the sanctions that will be imposed should any aspect of the policy be breached.[71] In *Mehigan v Dyflin Publications Ltd.*,[72] the Employment Appeals Tribunal held that:

---

67. *ibid.*
68. *ibid.*, at 25.
69. For further discussion of the employer's obligations when applying a disciplinary process, see Chapter 18.
70. *Byrne v Security Watch (Dublin) Ltd.* [1991] ELR 35.
71. *Harris v PV Doyle Hotels* UD 150/1978.
72. UD 582/2001.

Any disciplining or dismissal of staff for unauthorised use or misuse of company e-mail systems and the internet must be carried out having regard to the employee's fundamental rights to fair procedures and natural justice. Therefore, where the 'offence' is not sufficiently serious to justify dismissal, employers are expected to apply the different stages in the company disciplinary procedure. Where there is no disciplinary procedure then the employer must act in a fair and reasonable manner. Where an employer feels that an employee's conduct is sufficiently serious to justify summary dismissal then the fairness of the dismissal will be judged against the standard of what the reasonable employer would have done in the circumstances; whether the punishment fits the crime and whether there were any mitigating circumstances in favour of the employee. Under the Unfair Dismissals Acts 1977–2001, the burden of proof falls on the employer to justify a dismissal as not being unfair.

[17–42] In *O'Leary v Eagle Star Life Assurance Company of Ireland Ltd.*,[73] the claimant worked as a trainee accountant and was called to a meeting with the HR department of the respondent company regarding the claimant's alleged misuse of the company e-mail. Apparently, a lot of material had been discovered on the company's internal e-mail system regarding a group called 'the Legends'. It was alleged that this group were harassing staff and forming hitlists of people within the company that they identified as 'company men'. It was alleged that the claimant was heavily involved in this group. At the meeting the claimant was told that the company was treating the matter most seriously and would be conducting an investigation. The claimant was then issued with a letter informing him that the matter was one that required further investigation and he was suspended. He was informed that he was required to attend a disciplinary hearing, at which he was entitled to representation. The claimant wrote to the respondent company seeking details of the allegations and was provided with copies of the offending e-mail exchanges. At the meeting the claimant apologised and explained that the e-mail exchanges were sent between a number of employees who were simply engaged in some 'laddish' banter. He maintained that the group had been in existence for a year before he joined it and its members were only involved in such banter communicated through e-mail. The claimant was dismissed by the respondent without any right of appeal. Prior to this incident, the respondent had circulated the employer's policy on the acceptable usage of e-mail and Internet to all employees and the claimant was well aware that his actions were in breach of that policy, however, the abuse of the e-mail system was not defined within the company's policies as an act of gross misconduct which could result in dismissal. The claimant brought an action for unfair dismissal. The tribunal held that the employer's failure to provide the claimant with a right of appeal gave rise to the likelihood of bias in the investigation. Furthermore, in all the documentation produced by the respondent as regards its e-mail and Internet usage policy, at no stage did such documentation state that the penalty for breach of that policy could

73. [2003] ELR 223.

be the dismissal of the employee. Based on the foregoing, the tribunal held that the dismissal of the employee was disproportionate and unfair.

2.1.3. CCTV Surveillance

Employers increasingly rely on CCTV in order to monitor the workplace for a [17–43] myriad of reasons. The processing of data from CCTV footage or surveillance involving employees will be considered data processing for the purposes of the legislation. Consequently, the use of CCTV in the workplace must follow general data protection principles.

The use of CCTV surveillance must be necessary. Thus, an employer might argue [17–44] that CCTV was implemented for security reasons or in order to enhance the productivity of the workforce. In *Fair Oak Foods v SIPTU*,[74] an employer justified the introduction of CCTV surveillance as being necessary in order to prevent accidents in the workplace. Following a number of accidents in a factory, the company introduced CCTV surveillance on the basis that its installation was at the insistence of the company's insurers given the number of claims that were being made. It defended the introduction of the cameras on the basis that if it had not introduced them it would no longer be able to obtain public liability insurance cover and would be forced to close its business. The workers' union argued that the installation of such cameras was in breach of their members' right to privacy and that the company's poor accident record was a result of the employer's poor training and failure to provide adequate safety equipment. The Labour Court recommended that the employer seek insurance that was not dependent on the introduction of such cameras. Failing that, it was recommended that the cameras only be directed at scenes where accidents had already occurred and that the employer guarantee that a shop steward or union official receive an invitation to be present prior to any viewing of such footage. The placing of such cameras in sensitive parts of the workplace – such as bathrooms or locker rooms – can be particularly problematic and must be specially justified.[75]

The use of CCTV surveillance must be transparent. Where an employer chooses to [17–45] adopt such a system [s]he would be advised to inform employees of such surveillance, state clearly through signage the whereabouts of such cameras, and explain the purpose for which the footage captured by such surveillance is going to be used. Employees should be warned of the presence of such cameras and the use to which the footage is to be put. In *Tytex v SIPTU*,[76] a number of video cameras were concealed in the workplace. One camera was hidden in the clock on the canteen wall, five were aimed at the factory floor and one in the car park. The cameras had been in place for two years when they were discovered. The employer argued that the cameras were necessary in order to prevent ongoing theft of company

---

74. CD/00/198, recommendation no. LCR 16531, 6 June 2000.
75. *Meadow Meats v SIPTU*, CD/98/72, recommendation no. LCR 15878, 15 May 1998.
76. CD/97/132, recommendation no. LCR 15502, 18 April 1997.

property. The Labour Court found that the installation of these cameras without consulting the workers was unacceptable and was detrimental to the development of good industrial relations between the parties. The employer agreed to transfer to an open system where the cameras were in full view, provided there was agreement from the workers that such cameras were not interfered with.

[17–46] An employer must inform the employee of the purposes for which such footage is to be used. Thus, if an employer informs an employee that the cameras are being installed in order to prevent theft of company property, the employer cannot attempt to use the information gathered from such surveillance as evidence in an unrelated disciplinary matter. In *Case Study 10/2008*,[77] the Data Protection Commissioner received a complaint from two employees regarding their employer's intention to use CCTV recordings for disciplinary purposes. In that case, the employer used CCTV footage to compile a log recording the employees' pattern of entry and exit from their place of work. The employees' trade union representative was informed that this information was going to be used as evidence in disciplinary proceedings against the employees and the trade union representative was provided with a copy of the log. The employees objected to the use of the recorded footage in this way. They complained that they had never been informed of the purpose of the CCTV cameras at their place of work. The employer was advised that its planned use of the footage was in contravention of the Act. The Data Protection Commissioner concluded:

> This case demonstrates how data controllers are tempted to use personal information captured on CCTV systems for a whole range of purposes. Many businesses have justifiable reasons, related to security, for the deployment of CCTV systems on their premises. However, any further use of personal data captured in this way is unlawful under the Data Protection Acts unless the data controller has made it known at the time of recording that images captured may be used for those additional purposes. Transparency and proportionality are the key points to be considered by any data controller before they install a CCTV system. Proportionality is an important factor in this respect since the proposed use must be justifiable and reasonable if it is not to breach the Data Protection Acts. Notification of all proposed uses will not be enough if such uses are not justifiable.

2.2. Alcohol and Drug Testing Policies

[17–47] The question of whether employees are obliged to submit to alcohol or drug testing at the request of their employer gives rise to a number issues relating to employee rights to privacy and bodily integrity.[78] An employee may argue that information as to the amount of alcohol or drugs that [s]he may have ingested is a

---

77. Available at www.dataprotection.ie.
78. Generally, see Doran, 'Drug and Alcohol Testing under the Safety, Health and Welfare at Work Act 2005', 3(2) *IELJ* (2006), 36.

matter personal to them and of no business of the employer. The employer, on the other hand, may argue that such information is of vital importance, depending on the nature of the employment. For example, an employer could maintain that whether an employee is intoxicated or not is a matter of workplace security, or that an intoxicated employee is unlikely to be as productive as an employee who is not so intoxicated, or that the question is one that could affect staff morale. However, the strongest justification for the implementation of an alcohol and drug testing policy in the workplace is that it is one of safety.

The Safety, Health and Welfare at Work Act 2005 is primarily concerned with **[17–48]** ensuring insofar as is practicable that the workplace is safe.[79] Section 13 of the Act sets out the general duties of the employer in this regard and identifies the dangers created by an employee under the influence of an intoxicant while at work. Section 13(b) provides that an employee is under a duty to ensure that [s]he is not under the influence of an intoxicant to the extent that they pose a danger to him or herself or any other person at work. Furthermore, s.22 of the Act provides that an employer is required, as part of a risk assessment of the workplace (under s.19 of that Act), to ensure that 'health surveillance' is made available to his or employees. In this context, 'health surveillance' essentially involves a 'periodic review for the purpose of protecting health and preventing occupationally related disease, so that any adverse variations in their health that may be related to working conditions are identified as early as possible'.[80] Thus, depending on the nature of the work, an employer could be justified in requiring the employee to submit to periodic drug or alcohol testing. Section 23 of the Act provides that:

> (1) an employer may require an employee of a class or classes, as may be prescribed, to undergo an assessment by a registered medical practitioner, nominated by the employer, of his or her fitness to perform work activities referred to in subsection 2 and the employee shall co-operate with such a medical assessment.

> (2) An employer shall ensure that employees undergo assessment by a registered medical practitioner of their fitness to perform work activities, as may be prescribed, which, when performed, give rise to serious risks to the safety, health and welfare of persons at work.

Under s.23 of the 2005 Act an employer can only require that an employee is **[17–49]** assessed by a registered medical practitioner regarding their fitness to perform where the employee is involved in work that gives rise to 'serious risks' to the safety, health and welfare of persons at work. Thus it would appear that an employer seeking to justify imposing an alcohol or drug testing policy at work under the Act would need to prove that there is a real possibility that failing to do otherwise could expose other persons to serious risk of injury at work. Furthermore, it will

---

79. See Chapter 15 for further discussion.
80. s.2 Safety, Health and Welfare at Work Act 2005.

be noted that the legislation only allows such tests to be carried out by a registered medical practitioner and cannot be carried out by the employer him or herself.

[17–50] As it may be difficult under health and safety law for an employer to justify the imposition of alcohol and drug testing policies on employees in work that is not considered 'safety critical', employers have increasingly sought to impose such policies by agreement through the contract of employment. Any term that provides that an employee will be obliged to submit to such screening will be governed by the principles of fair procedures and the requirements of data protection already outlined. It must be established that the employee was made aware of the employer's rules on alcohol and drug testing and that the employee was aware of the consequences of breach of those rules. Furthermore, any information obtained following such tests would be subject to the general principles on data protection provided for under the legislation. Thus, an employer would be obliged to prove that the implementation of the testing procedures was a necessary, transparent and proportionate response to a real need.

[17–51] Provisions on alcohol and drug testing were upheld as being legitimate by the tribunal in *Kennedy v Veolia Transport Ireland*[81] (discussed in Chapter 15). In that case, the employee's contract of employment stated that he was required to comply with the employer's policy on testing for drugs and alcohol. After providing a breath sample, the employee was found to be clearly over the limit for driving purposes. The employee was dismissed for gross misconduct. While the employee's contract of employment provided for such testing and while such testing had been agreed with his union, the employee had never received a copy of the procedures. Nevertheless, the employee's action for unfair dismissal was unsuccessful. Equally, if an employer is successfully to rely on a contractual provision regarding alcohol and drug testing it is imperative that any such provision is detailed and that all aspects of the procedure are agreed between the parties. In *Alstom Ireland Ltd. v A Worker*,[82] an employee who worked for a company for over two years was dismissed for an alleged breach of the company/union agreed alcohol and drug testing procedures. The employee tested positive for a banned substance. However, the employee argued that the traces of the banned substance were of such a low amount that his test should have been properly classified as negative. The Labour Court recognised the importance of alcohol and drug testing in the workplace and stated that:

> The Court is conscious that drug and alcohol testing is becoming an increasingly common feature of many employments, particularly in safety critical areas. Changed societal factors, including increased drug abuse, has heightened the need, and the justification, for such testing.

---

81. UD 240/2006.
82. CD/07/413, Appeal No: AD0765, 18 December 2007.

The Court has consistently supported the use of drug and alcohol testing in safety critical employments. However, given the inevitable consequences for employees who test positive it is crucial that the modalities of all aspects of the testing conform to predetermined standards, which as far as possible, are agreed between the employer and the trade unions representing staff.

The court concluded that because there was some confusion between the parties [17–52] as to whether the testing policy adopted by the employer should have reported the result as positive or negative, then the employee should be given the benefit of the doubt. The court recommended that the procedures should be reviewed in order to ensure no such confusion would occur in the future. It also recommended that the employee be re-engaged in his former position without loss of accrued service with the company.

2.3. Biometric Testing

Security-conscious employers are increasingly relying on advances in technology [17–53] and science to develop systems that provide greater security in terms of access to the workplace. For example, employers may rely on fingerprint- or iris-scanning of employees in order to determine who may gain access to a particular site. The development of such systems go beyond the key-code or key-card systems of entry and exit and also raise data protection concerns. In particular, it could be argued that a biometric system (such as one that scans employee fingerprints) would be in breach of s.2(1)(c)(iii) of the Data Protection Act 1988, which provides that the data shall be adequate and not excessive in relation to the purpose for which it is sought. Consequently, an employer would have a substantial hurdle to overcome in proving that security was so vital to the employer that it was necessary to adopt such an intrusive scheme. Before introducing any such system it would therefore be recommended that the employer examine all avenues in order to assess whether or not the purpose of providing greater security could be achieved in a less invasive way.

In *Case Study 12/2007*,[83] the Data Protection Commissioner received a number of [17–54] complaints from employees regarding their employer's intention to introduce a biometric fingerprint-scanning system for the purpose of time and attendance. The employer submitted a report to the Data Protection Commissioner where it had assessed the viability of using other, less intrusive systems. The employer came to the conclusion that other systems were open to abuse and the system that it had chosen was the most cost effective. The employer agreed that the complaining employees would not be obliged to use the biometric system as it was accepted that the use of fingerprint-scanning does give rise to data protection issues. The employer accepted that those employees could use a pin-code system, which would not give rise to any data protection concerns.

---

83. Available at www.dataprotection.ie.

3. Employees' Right to Privacy Outside the Workplace

[17–55] A particularly complex area of privacy law in the employment context concerns the issues of employees' private lives beyond and outside the workplace, and whether what an employee does in his or her private life can ever constitute grounds for dismissal or other adverse treatment. The subject has come under intense academic analysis in recent years as conceptions of both privacy and the employment relationship have altered. Indeed, one commentator has proposed that a new framework be adopted for considering cases in this context:

> A fresh approach to privacy, resting on the idea of domination, is proposed, which is sensitive to the particularities of the employment relationship. Considering the fairness enquiry in dismissal, it argues that off duty conduct may lead to lawful termination of employment only if there is a clear and present impact or a high likelihood of such impact on business interests; a speculative and marginal danger does not suffice. It further proposes that a particularly meticulous test is appropriate when certain suspect categories, such as the employees' sexual preferences, are at stake.[84]

[17–56] The starting point for analysis of this question must begin with the decision in *Flynn v Power*,[85] In this case, Ms Flynn, a 30-year-old teacher in a New Ross convent school, sought a determination from the Employment Appeals Tribunal and subsequently, on appeal, from the Circuit Court and from the High Court, that she had been unfairly dismissed. The grounds of dismissal concerned her liaison with a local married man with whom she cohabited and by whom she had become pregnant. Following several admonitory interviews with her employer she was dismissed. She contended that she had been dismissed by reason of her pregnancy contrary to s.6(2)(f) of the Unfair Dismissals Act 1977; that her contract of employment imposed no express constraints on the conduct of her private life; and that consideration of her private affairs was an improper ground for dismissal. The respondents justified the dismissal by emphasising the conflict between the appellant's conduct of her private life and the principles sought to be fostered in a religious school.

[17–57] Rejecting her claim that her dismissal was unfair, having regard to s.6(2)(f) of the Unfair Dismissals Act 1977, as it resulted wholly or mainly from her pregnancy, Costello J held that Ms Flynn was not dismissed as a result of her pregnancy but rather because she refused to terminate the relationship with her partner. He added:

---

84. Mantouvalou, 'Human Rights and Dismissal: Private Acts in Public Spaces', 71(6) *MLR* (2008), 917 at p.917. See also discussion of *Pay v United Kingdom*, application no. 32792/05 [2008] ECHR 1007, [2009] IRLR 139, at para.17-24 above.
85. [1985] IEHC 1, [1985] IR 648, [1985] ILRM 336.

No doubt the pregnancy confirmed (if a confirmation was needed) the nature of the relationship, but the warning of dismissal had been given before such confirmation had been obtained and had it continued dismissal would have occurred in any event.[86]

Emphasising that, in considering a claim under the 1977 Unfair Dismissals Act, the test is whether, in all of the circumstances of the case, there were substantial grounds to justify the dismissal, Costello J cited, *inter alia*, various UK authorities in support of his conclusion that one of the principles applicable to the 1977 Act is that an employee's conduct in sexual matters outside the contract of employment may justify dismissal if it can be shown that it is capable of damaging the employer's business. Costello J acknowledged that in certain circumstances it was unreasonable to dismiss an employee for conduct not prohibited by the terms of the contract. As he pointed out, however, the 1977 Act lays down a threshold question of whether there are substantial grounds to justify the dismissal and not whether the impugned conduct is prohibited in the contract. Notwithstanding its successful defence of the claim, it seems fair to state, as Redmond observes, that 'a constructive approach to discipline' would better have facilitated the employer's decision in *Flynn*.[87]

As *Flynn v Power*[88] was taken under the Unfair Dismissals 1977, no constitutional [17–58] argument was put to Costello J in the High Court. This is, however, a type of case in which competing constitutional rights are at issue.[89] In *Re Article 26 and the Employment Equality Bill 1996*[90] the Supreme Court considered the constitutionality of, *inter alia*, ss.12 and 37 of the Employment Equality Bill 1996, which purported to allow certain vocational training bodies and religious bodies operating religious, educational or medical institutions to discriminate on grounds of religion so as to maintain the religious ethos of the institution. Upholding the constitutional validity of both sections, the court (per Hamilton CJ) said:

> It is constitutionally permissible to make distinctions or discriminations on grounds of religious profession, belief or status insofar – but only insofar – as this may be necessary to give life and reality to the guarantee of the free profession and practice of religion in the Constitution.[91]

Hence s.37(1) of the Employment Equality Act 1998 now provides:

---

86. [1985] IR 648, 654.
87. Redmond, *Dismissal Law in Ireland* (2nd ed., Tottel Publishing, 2007), at p.367.
88. [1985] IEHC 1, [1985] IR 648, [1985] ILRM 336.
89. In an analogous context, the courts have taken the view that the promotion of a religious ethos may qualify the constitutional prohibitions on religious discrimination. For detailed analysis in the context of religion, see Whyte, 'Protecting Religious Ethos in Employment Law: A Clash of Cultures', 27 *DULJ* (2005), 169.
90. [1997] 2 IR 321.
91. *ibid.*, at 358.

A religious, educational or medical institution which is under the direction or control of a body established for religious purposes or whose objectives include the provision of services in an environment which promotes certain religious values shall not be taken to discriminate against a person for the purposes of this Part or Part II if—

... it takes action which is reasonably necessary to prevent an employee or a prospective employee from undermining the religious ethos of the institution.

3.1. The European Convention on Human Rights

[17–59]   The incorporation of the ECHR provides 'a glimmer of light' in terms of challenging the reasonableness of a dismissal relating to private conduct outside the workplace.[92] In the UK case of *X v Y*,[93] it was accepted that a relevant provision of UK employment legislation must be interpreted in light of the Human Rights Act 1998 and, as Mummery LJ observed:

> Some unfair dismissal cases naturally attract arguments based on Convention rights and the HRA: the employee dismissed for refusing, on religious grounds, to work on a particular day (article 9); the employee dismissed for engaging in party politics (article 10); or the employee whose activities, even in the privacy of his own home, may constitute a criminal offence and lead to dismissal (article 8). In general, whenever HRA points are raised in unfair dismissal cases, the employment tribunals should properly consider their relevance, dealing with them in a structured way (though not necessarily at great length), even if it is ultimately decided that they do not affect the outcome of the claim for unfair dismissal.[94]

In that case, the applicant was a homosexual who worked for a charity that assisted young offenders. He was dismissed after failing to inform his employer that he had been cautioned by the police after engaging in consensual sexual activity with another man in a public toilet. While it was acknowledged that the Employment Rights Act 1996 had to be considered in light of Art. 8 of the European Convention on Human Rights, it was held that because the sexual activity occurred in a public place and involved criminal activity, the applicant's right to privacy was not engaged.

[17–60]   However, in the recent case of *Pay v United Kingdom*,[95] the European Court of Human Rights appeared to adopt a broader view to such issues. In that case (the facts of which have been considered earlier), whereas Mr Pay's application before

---

92. Mantouvalou, 'Human Rights and Dismissal: Private Acts in Public Spaces', 71 *MLR* (2008), 917, citing Ewing, 'The Human Rights Act and Parliamentary Democracy', 62 *MLR* (1999), 79, 89; and Ford, 'Two Conceptions of Worker Privacy', 31 *ILJ* (2002), 135–136.
93. [2004] ICR 1634.
94. *Per* Mummery LJ in *X v Y* [2004] ICR 1634 at [49].
95. Application no. 32792/05 [2009] IRLR 139.

the European Court of Human Rights was ultimately unsuccessful, the court did state that the facts of the case were such that Art. 8 of the Convention had been engaged. The court did not accept the view that simply because Mr Pay's image appeared on the Internet or that he had been photographed in a club necessarily made those pictures 'public'. The photographs did not name Mr Pay and the club, while public, was one that would only be attended by certain, like-minded people. The decision in *Pay* certainly casts doubts over the decision reached in *X v Y*, and would appear to provide a strong indication that in future cases, the court will be more likely to adopt a broader approach to the interpretation of private life when considering whether or not the dismissal was justified. As Mantouvalou has commented:

> Just because an employer does not approve of what an employee does at weekends on moralistic grounds and worries that it might attract some adverse publicity, that concern does not necessarily mean that it is possible do dismiss the employee fairly. On the contrary, such a dismissal is likely to be unfair even in cases concerning activities related to the nature of the employee's job, provided that she cooperates to minimise any risk of adverse publicity for the employer. The fact that the employee's conduct takes place in public or in a place to which the public have access does not necessarily take it outside the zone of the right to privacy.[96]

---

96. Mantouvalou, 'Private Life and Dismissal', 38 *ILJ* (2009), 133 at 138.

PART V

The Breakdown of the Employment Relationship

CHAPTER 18

Procedural Fairness and Disciplinary Action

Introduction

In this final section of the book we consider the law in relation to issues that may [18–01]
arise at the *end* of an employee's relationship with his or her employer. One context
in which the ending of this relationship may generate legal controversy is where
the employee is being dismissed for misconduct. Hence it is appropriate that we
begin the section with an analysis of the legal obligations on employers in respect
of their workplace disciplinary procedures generally, and in particular of whether
such procedures adequately vindicate an employee's rights – both contractual and
constitutional – to be treated fairly by his or her employer. As we shall see, the
level of fair procedures to which an employee will be entitled will depend on the
facts of his or her case and, in particular, the seriousness of what is at stake for him
or her, which can be assessed by reference *inter alia* to the level of sanction [s]he
is facing; however, an employee will be entitled to *some* measure of fair procedures
irrespective of the sanction that might be imposed.

In this respect, it should of course be noted that there is a considerable overlap [18–02]
between the disciplinary rules within a workplace and the industrial relations
procedures considered in Chapter 2, both in that the precise content of the disciplinary rules operative within a workplace will often be the fruit of negotiations
between management and employee representatives, and also in that a failure
by an employer to follow appropriate procedures when exercising such rules is a
common reason for a trade dispute.[1]

Furthermore, it should also be noted that many of the concepts touched on in this [18–03]
chapter – issues of disciplinary investigations, summary dismissal and proportionality of sanction, for example – are also dealt with in more detail in later chapters,

---

1. For the particular position of non-unionised employees in the context of disciplinary
    procedures, see Redmond, *Dismissal Law In Ireland* (2nd ed., Tottel Publishing, 2007), at
    paras.13.99 *et seq*. See also Industrial Relations Act 1990 (Code of Practice on Grievance
    and Disciplinary Procedures) (Declaration) Order 2000, SI no. 146 of 2000, at para.3(1)
    for the view that by following appropriate procedures prior to taking disciplinary action,
    an employer can increase the likelihood of a good industrial relations atmosphere in the
    workplace being maintained.

and particularly in Chapter 21 on unfair dismissals. Finally, as we shall see, the Irish courts are typically reluctant to interfere with the operation of 'in house' disciplinary procedures in a workplace (and, in particular, an incomplete disciplinary process[2]) unless there is a particularly egregious breach of fair procedures, and this concept is dealt with in more detail in Chapter 24 on employment injunctions.[3]

[18–04]   As has been mentioned, the most usual context in which a disciplinary process in a workplace attracts legal scrutiny is where it fails to accord with standards of fair procedures. Thus the central legal obligation as far as an employer is concerned in this regard is to ensure both that the nature and also the operation of his or her disciplinary rules accord with appropriate standards of fair procedures. Accordingly in this chapter we consider:

- the nature of the disciplinary rules of a typical workplace;
- the nature of an employee's right to fair procedures; and
- the manner in which this right applies to the various aspects of a workplace disciplinary process.

[18–05]   In this regard, significant reference will be made (and generally should be made by employers) to the Labour Relations Commission Industrial Relations Act 1990 (Code of Practice on Grievance and Disciplinary Procedures) (Declaration) Order 2000.[4] This code (which, like all such codes, may be regarded as setting basic standards such that a failure to comply with such standards will indicate that an employer's disciplinary rules are defective) outlines the basic levels of fair procedures that can and should be expected from workplace disciplinary rules, while also accepting that the precise nature of what is required insofar as fair procedures are concerned will inevitably vary from workplace to workplace.[5]

[18–06]   Finally, by way of introduction, the point is worth making that there are various contexts in which an employee may be penalised by his or her employer but not as a result of disciplinary infractions – most obviously where [s]he is not doing his or her job properly owing to illness or incompetence. Aspects of these situations are considered in Chapter 21, and moreover the procedural entitlements of employees in such situations will be broadly analogous to those that apply where [s]he is being disciplined by an employer. Equally in this chapter our focus is exclusively on the nature and operation of the disciplinary rules in a workplace, and not on these other types of situations.

---

2. *Carroll v Bus Átha Cliath* [2005] 4 IR 184, [2005] ELR 192. Generally, see McCrann, 'Investigations in the Workplace', 3(3) *IELJ* (2006), 68.
3. Generally, see *Khan v Health Service Executive* [2008] IEHC 234, [2009] ELR 178.
4. Industrial Relations Act 1990 (Code of Practice on Grievance and Disciplinary Procedures) (Declaration) Order 2000, SI no. 146 of 2000.
5. *ibid.* at para.2 refers to 'a wide variety of factors including the terms of contracts of employment, locally agreed procedures, industry agreements and whether trade unions are recognised for bargaining purposes' as being relevant in determining the precise arrangements for handling discipline and grievance issues in any workplace.

1. Elements of a Workplace Disciplinary Procedure

In most workplaces,[6] the disciplinary procedures operate by reference to what may   [18–07]
be termed a 'staged' approach to disciplinary offences, with increasingly severe
consequences applying based on:

- the seriousness of the alleged disciplinary offence under discussion; and
- whether the offence was a 'once off' incident, or whether it represents one
  of a series of events for which the employee in question is responsible,[7]
  with the penalties that are imposed increasing with each successive
  disciplinary offence that [s]he commits.

As we shall see, the level of fair procedures to which an employee is entitled in the   [18–08]
context of such disciplinary procedures is dependent, *inter alia*, on the seriousness
of what is at stake for him or her which, in turn, can be assessed in large measure
by reference to the sanction [s]he faces. Thus whereas presumably *any* finding that
an employee has committed a disciplinary offence will have negative consequences
for him or her, it is clearly far more serious if [s]he faces dismissal in respect of the
same, as compared to a situation where [s]he faces, for example, no more than a
verbal warning. Naturally, therefore, the further along in the 'staged procedures'
at which a particular disciplinary offence committed by an employee is located,
the higher the level of fair procedures that must be adopted by the employer in
dealing with that offence.

1.1. Informing Employees about Disciplinary Procedures

One of the most important lessons for employers in respect of their disciplinary   [18–09]
rules is the necessity (in order to ensure that such rules are legally acceptable insofar
as fair procedures and the contractual entitlements of employees are concerned) of
putting employees on notice both of the existence and content of the disciplinary
rules *per se* and, should they be the subject of a disciplinary investigation, of all
aspects of that investigation and of the charges that they are facing, not least so
that they can properly defend themselves. In other words, such disciplinary procedures should be clear and transparent.[8]

---

6. For analysis of the specific disciplinary rules that apply under the Civil Service Disciplinary Code to members of the civil service, see Redmond, 'The New Civil Service Disciplinary Code', 4(2) *IELJ* (2007), 42. For analysis of the related issue of the appropriate
   disciplinary jurisdiction in respect of persons appointed to a job pursuant to statute, see
   Turner, 'Case Focus: Disciplinary Procedures and Appointments Governed by Statute',
   3(1) *IELJ* (2006), 16.
7. On the question of when an offence is so serious that it is appropriate for the employer
   to transfer responsibility for dealing with it to the police, see Redmond, *Dismissal Law In
   Ireland* (2nd ed., Tottel Publishing, 2007), at para.13.94.
8. *Higgins v Irish Rail* [2008] ELR 225.

[18–10]   In this respect it is advisable that employees are made aware (typically in an employees' handbook, which may possibly be attached to each employee's contract) of the employer's disciplinary procedures, coupled with an indication of the types of conduct that may generate particular sanctions.⁹ This information should be in writing, and should be readily accessible in a language that employees *and management* can understand.¹⁰ Simply having delineated procedures of this kind is of huge importance because they can enable management to maintain satisfactory standards in conducting disciplinary investigations and will also provide employees with a mechanism for defending their rights and entitlements.¹¹

[18–11]   The employer is statutorily obliged to provide an employee, within 28 days of his or her entering into a contract of employment with that employer, with a statement of the procedure that will be observed by the employer before and for the purpose of dismissing the employee.¹² Beyond this, however, there is no statutory obligation to provide the employee with a statement in respect of the employer's disciplinary procedures (where dismissal is not on the line) unless the procedures are annexed to the employee's contract of employment, in which case a statement thereof must be provided to the employee under the Terms of Employment (Information) Act 1994. Equally, it is clearly best practice to provide such information¹³ and to provide it *at the commencement of employment.*¹⁴ This is also in the interests of the employer, in that it reduces the likelihood of an employee being able to successfully challenge such rules on fair procedures grounds (by alleging

9.   See Redmond, *Dismissal Law In Ireland* (2nd ed., Tottel Publishing, 2007), at para.13.33 for the view: 'It is crucial for an employer to list all possible forms of disciplinary action in addition to warnings, suspension and dismissal in the contract of employment… Otherwise the employer would be in breach of contract if it were to impose such sanctions. It is advisable to provide examples of wrongs that will attract the different types of disciplinary action, such lists being explicitly non-exhaustive and illustrative only.' Generally, see *Harris v PV Doyle Hotels*, UD 150/1978; *Byrne v Security Watch (Dublin) Ltd.* [1991] ELR 35; *Gavin v Kerry Foods* [1990] ELR 162; *Higgins v Irish Rail* [2008] ELR 225; *Brooks & Son v Skinner* [1984] IRLR 379. See also Industrial Relations Act 1990 (Code of Practice on Grievance and Disciplinary Procedures) (Declaration) Order 2000, SI no. 146 of 2000, at para.4(9). Equally there may be some instances of misconduct that are so patently unacceptable that there is no need to communicate the fact that they constitute disciplinary offences to employees. See *Parsons (CA) & Co v McLoughlin* [1978] IRLR 65 (fighting in the workplace near dangerous machinery).
10. Industrial Relations Act 1990 (Code of Practice on Grievance and Disciplinary Procedures) (Declaration) Order 2000, SI no. 146 of 2000, at para.3(3).
11. *ibid.* at para.3(2).
12. s.14(1) Unfair Dismissals Act 1977. In addition, an employee must be told of the type of conduct that could ultimately lead to him or her being dismissed: *Cavanagh v Dunnes Stores*, UD 820/1994; *Allen v Dunnes Stores* [1996] ELR 203; *Houlihan v Central Shopping* [1990] ELR 34.
13. See Redmond, *Dismissal Law In Ireland* (2nd ed., Tottel Publishing, 2007), at paras.13.29 and 13.30.
14. Industrial Relations Act 1990 (Code of Practice on Grievance and Disciplinary Procedures) (Declaration) Order 2000, SI no. 146 of 2000, at para.3(3).

that [s]he was subject to disciplinary rules but was not aware of some aspect of
the matter[15]).

Moreover, as we shall see later, there may be considerable merit in making such   [18–12]
disciplinary rules a part of the employee's contract, because this will ensure that
the employee (and obviously the employer) is bound by such rules even though
they may well have been created by the employer with him or herself in mind.[16]
Furthermore in *Mooney v An Post*[17] Barrington J in the Supreme Court, in dealing
with the question of what would be required of an employer insofar as the
employee's right to fair procedures was concerned, appeared to make a significant
concession to employers who adhere to the terms of agreed disciplinary procedures contained within the employment contract. Thus he commented that

> If the contract or the statute governing a person's employment contains proce-
> dure whereby the employment may be terminated it usually will be sufficient for
> the employer to show that he has complied with this procedure. If the contract
> or the statute contains a provision whereby an employee is entitled to a hearing
> before an independent board or arbitrator before he can be dismissed then clearly
> that independent board or arbitrator must conduct the relevant proceedings with
> due respect to the principles of natural and constitutional justice. If however the
> contract (or the statute) provides that the employee may be dismissed for miscon-
> duct without specifying any procedure to be followed the position may be more
> difficult. Certainly the employee is entitled to the benefit of fair procedures but
> what these demand will depend upon the terms of his employment and the circum-
> stances surrounding his proposed dismissal. Certainly the minimum he is entitled
> to is to be informed of the charge against him and to be given an opportunity to
> answer it and to make submissions.[18]

1.2. The Nature of a Staged Disciplinary Procedure

The precise content of the disciplinary rules and procedures that apply in a partic-   [18–13]
ular workplace is a matter for the relevant employer who will, no doubt, be influenced both by his or her own concerns and also by the interests of employees'
groups and, where appropriate, unions. As a matter of principle, however, the
Labour Relations Commission recommends that for all such rules:

> The essential elements of any procedure for dealing with grievance and disciplinary
> issues are that they be rational and fair, that the basis for disciplinary action is clear, that
> the range of penalties that can be imposed is well defined and that an internal appeal
> mechanism is available.

---

15. See Redmond, *Dismissal Law In Ireland* (2nd ed., Tottel Publishing, 2007), at para.13.43
    for the view that where, given the nature of the work, particular standards are required of
    employees in specific areas, this must also be communicated to employees.
16. *Stoskus v Goode Concrete* [2007] IEHC 432.
17. *Mooney v An Post* [1998] 4 IR 288, [1998] ELR 238.
18. [1998] 4 IR 288, 298.

Procedures should be reviewed and up-dated periodically so that they are consistent with changed circumstances in the workplace, developments in employment legislation and case law and good practice generally.[19]

[18–14]   As has been mentioned, the normal approach in workplace disciplinary rules is to take a staged approach to disciplinary offences.[20] The 'staging' in this regard refers to the increasing level of penalties that can be imposed (as well as more senior levels of management who will deal with the matter[21]) both as the offences become more serious or as the employee in question re-offends in the relatively short term after having committed an earlier infraction.[22] Thus, where a serious offence has been committed, it is not necessary for the employer to proceed through all the stages referred to below, but rather [s]he can dispense with some of these stages and impose a more serious penalty even though it may be a first offence as far as the employee concerned, with the most obvious example being a situation where an employee faces dismissal or even summary dismissal for gross misconduct – a concept we consider in Chapter 21.[23] Alternatively it is possible for an employee who is persistently in violation of disciplinary rules (albeit without ever having committed any act of gross misconduct) to be dealt with sequentially through these stages until [s]he eventually faces the ultimate sanction of dismissal.[24]

[18–15]   Having said this, irrespective of the stage of a disciplinary procedure at which an employee is being investigated, the approach of the employer (both in terms of deciding whether or not to discipline an employee and also in terms of the manner in which [s]he deals with that employee) should be reasonable and, as we shall see, should provide the employee with an appropriate level of fair procedures.[25] Where an employer does not act reasonably, after all, or does not provide the

---

19. Industrial Relations Act 1990 (Code of Practice on Grievance and Disciplinary Procedures) (Declaration) Order 2000, SI no. 146 of 2000, at paras.4(1) and 4(2).
20. For the alternative 'constructive approach' to disciplinary procedures, whereby an employer will put considerable effort into rehabilitating an offending employee, see Redmond, *Dismissal Law In Ireland* (2nd ed., Tottel Publishing, 2007), at paras.13.34 *et seq.*
21. The Industrial Relations Act 1990 (Code of Practice on Grievance and Disciplinary Procedures) (Declaration) Order 2000, SI no. 146 of 2000, para.4(13) recommends that the disciplinary procedures make it clear as to the different levels in the enterprise or organisation at which the various stages of the procedures will be applied.
22. The Labour Relations Commission regards such a staged process as stemming from good practice. See *ibid.* at para.4(3).
23. *ibid.* at para.4(11) for the view that, whereas it is possible for more serious sanctions, including dismissal, to be warranted before the preliminary stages of the disciplinary process are completed, equally the steps in the procedure will generally be progressive.
24. See, for example, Redmond, *Dismissal Law In Ireland* (2nd ed., Tottel Publishing, 2007), at para.13.31.
25. The Industrial Relations Act 1990 (Code of Practice on Grievance and Disciplinary Procedures) (Declaration) Order 2000, SI no. 146 of 2000, at para.4(8) recommends that as a general rule, attempts should be made to resolve disciplinary issues between the employee concerned and his or her immediate manager or supervisor on an informal or private basis.

employee with an appropriate standard of fair procedures, then in extreme cases the employee can allege that [s]he is being persecuted and can thus resign and claim constructive dismissal.[26]

It is further worth noting that it is entirely possible for an employer to take disci-   [18–16] plinary action against an employee for behaviour which occurred *outside of* the workplace or outside of the employee's working hours. In such circumstances, however, it would be necessary that the misconduct for which the employee was being investigated would actually relate, in some way to his or her work[27]. Thus for example the Tribunal held that it was legitimate for disciplinary action to be taken against an employee who had posted derogatory comments about her employer on her Bebo page[28]. As ever, moreover, it would be necessary that appropriate standards of fair procedures are followed.

Finally, as with so much in the relationship between employer and employee, the   [18–17] employer is advised to keep appropriate records of all disciplinary investigations and hearings that have occurred.[29]

The various sanctions that represent the stages of a typical workplace disciplinary procedure are as follows:

1.2.1. Verbal Warning

This penalty (which would be for relatively minor offences such as, for example,   [18–18] persistent lateness) is in fact something of a misnomer, in that whereas the warning may originally be given in verbal fashion it should also be followed up by a written confirmation that a verbal warning has been given, and by a written statement that the warning remains on the employee's personnel file for a defined period (generally approximately one month) after which it will be removed.[30] As with all

---

26. *Troy v Ennis Handling Systems Ltd.*, UD 601/1991. See Redmond, *Dismissal Law In Ireland* (2nd ed., Tottel Publishing, 2007), at para. 13.71 for the suggestion that it may be counterproductive to issue an excessive number of warnings to an employee, as this may indicate that [s]he is being poorly managed and 'suggests an indifference to improving the shortcomings of the individual'.

27. *Browne v Delaney* UD 1127/2003, *Moloney and Feeney v The Old Quarter* UD 187 and 189/99.

28. *Kiernan v A Wear Limited* UD 643/2007. In this case, however, it was held that the sanction which was imposed on the employee in question (namely dismissal) was disproportionate. Importantly, though, the Tribunal felt that the actions of the employee deserved 'strong censure and possibly disciplinary action'.

29. Industrial Relations Act 1990 (Code of Practice on Grievance and Disciplinary Procedures) (Declaration) Order 2000, SI no. 146 of 2000, at para.4(15).

30. In the case of all of the warnings that go on to an employee's personnel file, when they are removed the slate is wiped clean for the purposes of the disciplinary rules, such that if that employee commits a further infraction *after* the defined period (and assuming it is a minor one), the procedure will recommence *ab initio* and [s]he will receive only a *verbal* warning. On the other hand, the fact that such warnings have been given may have a practical impact (even after such warnings have been removed from the file) both in terms of the contents of

of the sanctions referred to below (other than dismissal) the employee should be informed in writing both of the fact that the warning *will* be removed after the defined period and should be further informed in writing that it has been removed when this point in time is reached.[31] Again as with *all* of the various stages in a disciplinary procedure other than dismissal, this written confirmation of such a warning should also make it clear that, should the employee commit another infraction within the defined period in which the warning remains on his or her personnel file, then more serious disciplinary action will follow, and that it is not necessary (in order for this to happen) that the second infraction be of the same kind as the one that generated the earlier warning.[32]

1.2.2. Written Warning

[18–19] A written warning is simply a more serious form of warning, which remains on the employee's file for a longer period (typically six months). Again the employee should be informed of the fact of such warning and should be told that, should another infraction occur during the period in which the written warning remains on file, then it will be followed by a further disciplinary measure. Depending on the terms of the employer's disciplinary rules, a written warning may be followed by a second written warning or a final written warning. Alternatively (and in any event depending on how serious any subsequent offence is), the employer's disciplinary rules may provide that any subsequent offence while a written warning remains on an employee's personnel file will lead not merely to a warning but rather to more serious and tangible penalties.[33]

---

any reference the employee may receive and also in a redundancy situation, where a matrix system of calculating entitlements is used, in which case the fact of such disciplinary action being taken against employees may count against them.

31. Industrial Relations Act 1990 (Code of Practice on Grievance and Disciplinary Procedures) (Declaration) Order 2000, SI no. 146 of 2000, at para.4(14).

32. See Redmond, *Dismissal Law In Ireland* (2nd ed., Tottel Publishing, 2007), at para.13.68 for the sound advice that in all cases where any type of warning is communicated to an employee it is advisable to ask that employee to confirm receipt of the same, in order to prevent a situation where [s]he subsequently denies ever having received such a warning. See for example *Zinenko v Chapel Hill Stores Limited* UD 275/2007.

33. It is almost inevitable, save in cases of summary dismissal for gross misconduct, that if an employer is to dismiss an employee for misconduct, it will be necessary that that employee will previously have received a warning indicating that it is a final warning and that, should a further infringement occur within a specified period, the consequence will be dismissal: *O'Reilly v Dodder Management*, UD 311/1978. See Redmond, *Dismissal Law In Ireland* (2nd ed., Tottel Publishing, 2007), at para.13.65 for the view that where this happens, a reasonable employee should seek to determine whether or not there is some way of correcting the employee's behaviour.

1.2.3. Tangible Penalties Short of Dismissal

Such penalties, albeit rather unusual, can include: [18–20]

- demotion;
- an increased probationary period (where the relevant employee is on probation at the time of the offence);
- short-term deduction of pay without demotion;
- short-term suspension without pay[34]; and
- transfer to another task or section of the enterprise.

In all instances, the employee must be notified of the relevant penalty and of the   [18–21]
length of time for which the fact of the penalty will remain on his or her file, and
of the consequences should [s]he commit another offence during this period. In
this respect, a punitive suspension of this kind should be distinguished from a
'holding' suspension *with* pay, which may arise where an employee is being investigated in respect of a disciplinary matter. This type of holding suspension will
be discussed shortly, but the point is worth making that even in such a case it is
important that such a suspension – because it may generate an inference of guilt
– be handled carefully in order to prevent a trade dispute from occurring.[35]

1.2.4. Dismissal

Naturally this is the ultimate disciplinary sanction as far as an employee is concerned,   [18–22]
and hence the highest level of procedural fairness must be afforded to the employee
when dismissal is a possibility. Whereas the procedural entitlements of an employee
before [s]he is dismissed are discussed throughout this chapter, a more complete
analysis of the rules relating to dismissals is provided in Chapter 21.

---

34. In many instances, such short-term suspensions without pay are not necessarily a good idea, as this entails crossing a definite rubicon as far as employer/employee relationships are concerned, and may well lead to a trade dispute. In any event, it is clear that an employee must be afforded a high level of fair procedures before being suspended as a disciplinary sanction. *Deegan v Minister for Finance* [2000] ELR 190; *McNamara v South Western Area Health Board* [2001] ELR 317; *McKenzie Ltd. v Smith* [1976] IRLR 345. See also McCrann, 'Investigations in the Workplace', 3(3) *IELJ* (2006), 68 for the view that 'the party affected is entitled to know why he is being suspended and to know this with some particularity'.

35. In *Dowling v Cumann na Daoine Aontaithe Teo* UD 545/2007 the EAT suggested that as the provisional suspension which had been imposed in that case was not a punishment, the principles of natural justice could not apply. It is respectfully submitted that this logic does not inevitably follow. The impact of such a provisional suspension on the rights (*inter alia* to a good name) of the employee could be substantial and hence [s]he would be entitled to have been treated with appropriate standards of fair procedures.

2. The Right to Fair Procedures

[18–23] As has been mentioned, irrespective of which stage in this process is at issue, an employee has an entitlement – both constitutional *and* contractual – to an appropriate level of fair procedures. We will shortly consider the manner in which this right to fair procedures applies to the various stages of a disciplinary investigation. Before doing so, however, we consider the nature of the right to fair procedures and natural and constitutional justice.

[18–24] As far as an Irish employee is concerned, there are two key and related legal bases upon which [s]he can claim to be entitled to be treated in accordance with standards of fair procedures in the context of any disciplinary action being taken against him or her, namely the Irish Constitution and his or her contract of employment. Each of these bases is now considered in turn.

2.1. Constitutional Rights to Fair Procedures

[18–25] The Constitution provides the basic starting point as far as the entitlement of an employee to fair procedures in respect of any disciplinary process that might be operating against him or her is concerned.[36] Thus it is clear from the decision of the Supreme Court in the case of *In re Haughey*[37] that Art. 40.3 of the Constitution includes a guarantee of fair procedures for all citizens, such that in any proceedings before any body in the course of which a person's rights are at stake,[38] the State is required to ensure that [s]he is treated fairly, in the sense of being given appropriate entitlements that will enable him or her to attempt to defend and vindicate these rights.

[18–26] The right to fair procedures is strongly connected to the individual's constitutional rights to natural and constitutional justice,[39] which are again exercisable against both the State and, more importantly, against private individuals.[40] The net result,

---

36. It is possible that the claim that an employee has a right to fair procedures might also be made by reference to the terms of Art. 6 of the European Convention on Human Rights.
37. [1971] IR 217.
38. Quite clearly, where an employee is facing disciplinary proceedings his or her rights to livelihood and a good name under Art. 40.3 of the Constitution are also at stake. For the view that the right to fair procedures in cases of allegedly unfair dismissals may be an element of the right to a livelihood, see *Pacelli v Irish Distillers Limited* [2004] ELR 25.
39. For the holding that the right to natural and constitutional justice is available to all employees and not merely office-holders, see *Gunn v Bord an Choláiste Ealaíne is Deartha* [1990] 2 IR 168.
40. The constitutional question of the tripartite relationship between the right to fair procedures, the right to natural justice and the overarching concept of constitutional justice is a difficult one, and one that is beyond the scope of a comprehensive employment law textbook of this kind. Generally, see *State (Gleeson) v Minister for Defence* [1976] IR 280; *McCormack v Garda Complaints Board* [1997] IEHC 200, [1997] 2 IR 489. For discussion, see Hogan and

therefore, is that if an employer acts other than fairly towards an employee in the context of disciplinary proceedings, then [s]he will be violating that employee's constitutional rights to fair procedures and natural and constitutional justice and, as Redmond points out, this is significant in that 'pragmatism could not take precedence over breach of a constitutional right and the court's obligation to defend and vindicate the constitutional rights of the citizen'.[41] Equally, as we shall see, the mere fact that an employee possesses a constitutional right to fair procedures generates significant uncertainty as far as the operation of workplace disciplinary rules is concerned, in that it leaves open the potentially enormous question of what, on the facts of any given case, an employer must do in order to afford the employee his or her constitutional rights. [42]

2.2. Contractual Rights to Fair Procedures

In light of the constitutional imperatives discussed above, the Supreme Court has [18–27] held that there is an implied term of fair procedures to be read into all employment contracts,[43] and irrespective of the position of the relevant employee (that is to say, whether or not [s]he is an office holder).[44] The obvious significance of this is that it means that an employee has a contractual right to be treated fairly by his or her employer where the operation of his or her employment contract is concerned, and hence, where this does not happen, that [s]he will have not merely a potential constitutional action against his or her employer but, of more practical importance, a potential action for breach of contract. Moreover, depending on the circumstances, if [s]he is *not* treated fairly by his or her employer, this may provide a basis for claiming that there was a frustration (by the employer) of a term of the contract that was sufficiently fundamental to justify him or her resigning and claiming for constructive dismissal.

Morgan, *Administrative Law in Ireland* (3rd ed., Round Hall Sweet and Maxwell, Dublin, 1998), at chapters 10 and 11; Hogan and Whyte, *Kelly: The Irish Constitution* (4th ed., Lexis-Nexis Butterworths, London, 2003), at paras.6.1.79 *et seq.* and Redmond, *Dismissal Law In Ireland* (2nd ed., Tottel Publishing, 2007), at paras.7.01 *et seq.*

41. Redmond, *Dismissal Law In Ireland* (2nd ed., Tottel Publishing, 2007), at para.17.05.
42. The European Convention on Human Rights as well as the European Convention on Human Rights Act 2003 may also be relevant in this context, in particular where what is at stake is a State-run employer. Generally, see Redmond, *Dismissal Law In Ireland* (2nd ed., Tottel Publishing, 2007), at paras.13.108 *et seq.*
43. This is discussed in Chapter 4.
44. *Glover v BLN Ltd.* [1973] IR 388. The authority of *Glover* was doubted in its immediate aftermath (see, for example, *Lupton v AIB Ltd.* (1984) 3 JISSL 107; *Goldrick and Mooney v Lord Mayor, Aldermen and Burgesses of Dublin*, unreported, 10 November 1986), but was firmly endorsed by the Supreme Court in *Gunn v Bord an Choláiste Ealaíne is Deartha* [1990] 2 IR 168; *Hickey v Eastern Health Board* [1991] 1 IR 208, [1990] ELR 177; and *Mooney v An Post* [1998] 4 IR 288, [1998] ELR 238. Generally, see Redmond, *Dismissal Law In Ireland* (2nd ed., Tottel Publishing, 2007), at paras.5.05 *et seq.*

[18–28]   On the other hand, and from an employer's perspective, it is uncertain as to whether and to what extent an employer can put an express provision in a contract requiring an employee to waive his or her entitlements as far as natural and constitutional justice is concerned.⁴⁵ Thus in *Stoskus v Goode Concrete*⁴⁶ the High Court suggested that even if the employee in that case had a right to be legally represented at a disciplinary hearing, he had waived this right in signing up to a contract that precluded this possibility.

2.3. The Maxims of Fair Procedures

[18–29]   Whatever the source of the employee's entitlements in this regard, and however the relationship between fair procedures and natural and constitutional justice play out, it is clear both constitutionally and as a matter of contract that an employee must be treated with fair procedures when an employer is taking any form of disciplinary action against him or her. The traditional administrative rules of fair procedures are, of course, summed up in the maxims *audi alteram partem* (requiring a decision-maker to hear both sides of a case before deciding on it) and *nemo iudex in causa sua* (requiring the decision-maker not to be a judge in his or her own case, and therefore not to be biased in the matter), although there is a measure of uncertainty as to what additional protections are afforded to employees by reason of the constitutionalisation of the entitlement to such fair procedures.⁴⁷ We will shortly consider how these basic rules of fair procedures apply in the specific context of workplace disciplinary investigation.

[18–30]   Before doing so, however, one vitally important point is addressed (which should be borne in mind in respect of all aspects of the relationship between fair procedures and disciplinary rules), namely that whereas an employee must always be treated fairly, this does not mean that [s]he will have the same practical entitlements in every case. The concept of fair procedures, after all, is not a static one, and what is required in any given case will depend on the facts of that case.⁴⁸ Most

---

45.   *Glover v BLN* [1973] IR 388. See also *Stoskus v Goode Concrete* [2007] IEHC 432. On the question of whether it is possible to waive constitutional rights, see *inter alia Murphy v Stewart* [1973] IR 97; *Meskill v CIÉ* [1973] IR 121; *G v An Bord Uchtála* [1980] IR 32.

46.   [2007] IEHC 432.

47.   The Supreme Court has recognised that these maxims and especially the *audi alteram partem* maxim may have limited application in a case where an employee is challenging his or her dismissal. See *Mooney v An Post* [1998] 4 IR 288, [1998] ELR 238.

48.   Thus, for example, it may be possible in a particular case that hearsay evidence can be admitted in circumstances where the witness who provided the evidence is for some reason incapable of appearing before the relevant disciplinary hearing (*A Worker v A Hospital* [1997] ELR 214). Similarly, it may be necessary to allow an employee who, for example, has a speech impediment to be legally represented (in circumstances where such representation would not normally be permitted) in order that [s]he can present his or her case properly. See *Duke v Sherlock Bros Ltd.*, UD 75/1993 and, by analogy, *Jones & Ebbw Vale RFC v Welsh Rugby Union*, unreported, Queen's Bench, 27 February 1997; *The Times*, 6 January 1998 (Court of Appeal), noted at Jan./Feb. 1998, 'Sports Law Administration and Practice', at p. 10.

importantly, the extent of fair procedures that must be afforded to an employee will depend on the seriousness of what is at stake[49] as well as other relevant factual aspects of the case,[50] including, arguably, the seniority of the employee.[51]

Accordingly, and as a general principle, it may be stated that, whereas any investigation and disciplinary process will need to be attended by appropriate standards of fair procedures, equally the further along the various stages of disciplinary action at which a particular investigation and disciplinary process may be located, the higher the level of fair procedures that may be required, to the point that where dismissal is a possible sanction for the employee, [s]he will be entitled to all the various protections outlined below, which flow from a very high standard of fair procedures.[52]   [18–31]

Finally in any given case where an employee is not afforded a perfect level of procedures it will still be necessary for him or her to demonstrate that any such departure from accepted procedures actually had the effect of imperilling the overall fairness and reliability of the result of the disciplinary investigation.[53]   [18–32]

In this light, the point is worth making that, whereas from an employee's perspective any disciplinary investigation and particularly one at the conclusion of which [s]he may be dismissed will be extremely serious, nonetheless it is not as serious as, for example, a situation in which a person faces criminal proceedings. Thus the courts have repeatedly stated that the level of fair procedures (for example, in terms of evidential standards) that must apply in the context of a workplace disciplinary hearing are less onerous than those that apply in the context of a criminal trial in court.[54] Equally, the courts have always stressed that any departure from such formalised rules of evidence and so on cannot be used to 'imperil a fair hearing or a fair result'.[55]   [18–33]

---

49. *Mooney v An Post* [1998] 4 IR 288, [1998] ELR 238; *Shortt v Royal liver Assurance Ltd.* [2008] IEHC 332, [2009] ELR 240; *Flanagan v UCD* [1989] ILRM 469.

50. See Redmond, *Dismissal Law In Ireland* (2nd ed., Tottel Publishing, 2007), at para.7.27 for the view that it is not legitimate for an employer to deny an employee the right to fair procedures simply because that employee has him or herself behaved in unmeritorious fashion. See *Gallagher v Revenue Commissioners* [1995] 1 IR 55, [1995] ILRM 108; *Casey v Daughters of Charity*, UD 62/2007.

51. Thus it is possible that the seniority of the employee may be relevant in assessing what level of fair procedures are at stake, both because of the potentially greater losses to such a person should [s]he be dismissed, and also because of the potential impact on the company as a whole of, for example, a disciplinary investigation into a senior manager. See, by analogy, *Murphy v Eyrefield House Stud Ltd.*, UD 441/1992.

52. Generally, see *Flanagan v University College Dublin* [1989] ILRM 469.

53. *Loftus and Healy v An Bord Telecom* [1987] IEHC 40; *Shortt v Royal Liver Assurance Ltd.* [2008] IEHC 332, [2009] ELR 240.

54. So, for example, it is entirely possible for disciplinary tribunals to admit hearsay evidence. See *Maher v Irish Permanent Plc (No. 2)* [1998] 4 IR 302, [1998] ELR 89.

55. *Kiely v Minister for Social Welfare* [1977] IEHC 2, [1977] IR 267, 281.

[18–34] Beyond this, and as a matter of policy, the courts have indicated that they are reluctant to interfere with the disciplinary procedures operating in a particular workplace in that it is desirable that such in-house processes can operate in a full and free manner.[56] In other words, it is only where an investigation is manifestly unfair or where there is a serious risk that a miscarriage of justice has occurred that the courts are likely not to stand over the legitimacy of such investigations. This point is, however, discussed in more detail in Chapter 24 dealing with employment injunctions.

3. Application of Fair Procedures to Workplace Disciplinary Procedures

[18–35] For the remainder of this chapter, we will consider broadly how the rules of fair procedures and natural and constitutional justice apply to the various stages of the operation of disciplinary procedures within a workplace, namely:

- the investigation of an alleged wrongdoing;
- the hearing of the matter following such investigation;
- the sanction(s) imposed should the employee be found to be guilty of such wrongdoing.

[18–36] As a preliminary point, and whilst recognising that these rules of natural justice will frequently place an onerous burden on employers, it is salutary to recall the following note of caution sounded by the Court of Appeal as to the fundamental importance of their being followed:

> It may be that there are some who would decry the importance which the courts attach to the observance of the rules of natural justice. 'When something is obvious,' they may say, 'why force everybody to go through the tiresome waste of time involved in framing charges and giving an opportunity to be heard? The result is obvious from the start'. Those who take this view do not, I think, do themselves justice. As everybody who has anything to do with the law well knows, the path of the law is strewn with examples of open and shut cases which, somehow, were not; of unanswerable charges which, in the event, were completely answered; of inexplicable conduct which was fully explained; of fixed and unalterable determinations that, by discussion, suffered a change. Nor are those with any knowledge of human nature who pause to think for a moment likely to underestimate the feelings of resentment of those who find that a decision against them has been made without their being afforded any opportunity to influence the course of events.[57]

---

56. *Carroll v Bus Átha Cliath* [2005] 4 IR 184, [2005] ELR 192. Generally, see McCrann, 'Investigations in the Workplace', 3(3) *IELJ* (2006), 68.
57. *John v Rees* [1969] 2 WLR 1294, *per* Megarry J at 1335.

3.1. The Investigation[58]

The courts have accepted that where an investigation involves the making of find-   **[18–37]**
ings of fact then the rules of fair procedures apply to that investigation.[59] Thus, in
all cases the imposition of a sanction (as well as the finding of a disciplinary infraction) must be preceded by a properly focused[60] investigation that is conducted
promptly,[61] fairly, completely[62] and with no bias on the part of the investigator.[63]
This is, for obvious reasons, in that without such an investigation there is a risk
that the employee may be found to have committed an offence without the requisite standard of proof being reached, and indeed there is a further risk that the
ultimate decision-maker will not be apprised of – and hence will not fully take
into account – the employee's arguments. As has been mentioned before, where
an employee is subject to a disciplinary investigation that is not conducted fairly,
this may lead to a situation in which [s]he can resign and claim constructive
dismissal.[64]

The precise scope of what is necessary in order for an investigation to be 'fair'   **[18–38]**
will, however, obviously vary from case to case, depending on what is at stake.[65]
In other words, much less will be required of an investigation where an employee
has demonstrably been guilty of persistent lateness, which may lead to a verbal
warning, than will be required of an investigation into a complex factual situation

---

58. Generally, see McCrann, 'Investigations in the Workplace', 3(3) *IELJ* (2006), 68.

59. In both *Minnock v Irish Casing Company Ltd. and Stewart* [2007] ELR 229 and *O'Brien v AON Insurance Managers (Dublin) Ltd.* [2005] IEHC 3, Clarke J suggested that where a disciplinary enquiry had no fact-finding purpose or was not responsible for the imposition of a sanction, no right to fair procedures would arise.

60. *Redmond v Ryanair Ltd.*, UD 123/05.

61. See *Zambra v Duffy*, UD 154/1978; *Sheehan v H&M Keating & Sons Ltd.*, UD 534/1991; *Marley Home Care v Dutton* [1981] IRLR 380; *Allman v Minister for Justice* [2002] IEHC 45, [2002] 3 IR 546, [2003] ELR 7.

62. See *Preston v Standard Piping Ltd.* [1999] ELR 233; *Dermody v Dunnes Stores*, UD 1350/2003; *Walsh v Cuisine de France*, UD 479/05; for instances where a disciplinary sanction imposed on an employee was deemed to be unfair because it had not been preceded by a sufficiently comprehensive investigation. It may be that there are cases where the guilt of an employee is so immediately manifest that [s]he can be disciplined immediately with no need for any further investigation (*Meath County Council v Creighton*, UD 11/1977). Equally an employer would be advised that such instances would arise only in rare circumstances.

63. *Atkinson v Carty* [2005] ELR 1. For analysis of the particular concerns faced by an employer in the context of a situation where the investigation relates to a complaint made against one employee by another, see Redmond, *Dismissal Law In Ireland* (2nd ed., Tottel Publishing, 2007), at paras.13.78 *et seq.*, and Wilkinson, 'Workplace Investigations: Factors that Contribute to a Fair Procedure Being Conducted', 5(1) *IELJ* (2008), 14.

64. *McKenna v Pizza Express Restaurants Ltd.* [2008] ELR 234.

65. In *Maher v Irish Permanent* [1998] 4 IR 302, [1998] ELR 77, Laffoy J suggested that in assessing what level of fair procedures would be necessary in a given factual situation, regard would have to be made to the practicalities of the situation. Generally, see McCrann, 'Investigations in the Workplace', 3(3) *IELJ* (2006), 68.

at the end of which an employee may be suspended or even dismissed. Inevitably, however, and irrespective of the relevant offence or the degree of sanction that it may attract, there will be a need, however informally, to interview the employee concerned in order to assess his or her side of the matter.[66] In this respect, failure on the part of the employee to cooperate with such investigation can be used against him or her in the overall determination of the matter.[67] In addition, depending on the circumstances, it may be necessary to interview other members of staff who were present at the time of the alleged disciplinary infraction[s] or who could otherwise shed light on the matter.[68] Furthermore, in certain cases where an employee learns that [s]he is the subject of a disciplinary investigation, [s]he will raise a grievance against the employer or possibly against a co-worker who has testified against him or her. In such circumstances it may be necessary to temporarily suspend the disciplinary investigation in order to allow the employee to avail of the workplace grievance procedures.[69] Beyond this, however, the employer will have a significant discretion in how [s]he conducts any disciplinary investigation, subject only to concerns both with fair procedures and also with the employee's right to privacy and to protection of personal data, which we consider in Chapter 17.[70]

[18–39] Most especially, however, the investigation must genuinely be an investigation – that is, a process aimed ultimately at fact-finding. It cannot be a formality undertaken by an employer prior to the imposition of a sanction, nor can it be used merely as a means of securing sufficient evidence to justify the imposition of such sanction, without seeking to assess whether there is evidence available that would support the employee's position. In other words (and having regard generally to an employee's right to a good name, and the consequent relevance of the notion of his or her presumption of innocence), the investigator should start from a neutral perspective, assuming that the employee is *not* guilty of the alleged offence, and

66. See, for example, *O'Sullivan v Mercy Hospital Cork Limited* [2005] IEHC 170.
67. *Farrell v Minister for Defence*, unreported, High Court, 10 July 1984. See also *Cahill v Trinity College Dublin*, UD 476/1985 for the view that inconsistencies in the evidence presented by an employee may also count against him or her. Generally, see Redmond, *Dismissal Law In Ireland* (2nd ed., Tottel Publishing, 2007), at paras 13.47 *et seq.*
68. *Vita Context Ltd. v Dourellan*, UD 131/1992.
69. *Casey v Daughters of Charity*, UD 62/2007. Generally, see *McNamara v Dublin City University*, UD 381/2005; *Porter v Atlantic Homecare Ltd.* [2008] ELR 95.
70. For consideration of the role of informants, private investigators, surveillance cameras, handwriting experts and test purchasers/mystery shoppers, see Redmond, *Dismissal Law In Ireland* (2nd ed., Tottel Publishing, 2007), at paras.13.81 *et seq.* It may (rather simplistically) be suggested that whereas such information may be used (subject to concerns with privacy and data protection), fair procedures require that it be treated like all other evidence against the employee, namely in a critical manner and without any suggestion that it is, of itself, absolutely probative. See *Linfood Cash and Carry v Thomson* [1989] ICR 518, [1989] IRLR 235; *Frizelle v New Ross Credit Union* [1997] IEHC 137; *McArdle v Superquinn* [1991] ELR 171; *McGarry v Jury's Hotel Plc*, UD 775/1992; *Harte v Iarnród Éireann*, UD 149/1990; *Clery v TSB Bank*, UD 754/199.

should use the investigation as a way of establishing all relevant factors by which [s]he can evaluate whether or not the employee was guilty of any wrongdoing.[71] This is nothing more than the simple application of the rule against bias.

In cases where there is allegedly gross misconduct justifying summary dismissal, [18–40] the requirements as to the requisite level of investigation may involve a reconciliation of two competing factors. In such circumstances, after all, the infraction may be a blatantly obvious one, such that there is little need to undertake much further investigation into the facts (and again inasmuch as the level of fair procedures to which an employee is entitled will be fact dependent, it is clear that where the facts do not require an excessively large investigation, it is not necessary to contrive one simply to accord with all conceivable standards of fair procedures[72]). On the other hand, however, the sanction is the most serious one possible, and hence the investigation must be a complete one. The net result is that whereas normal principles apply (that is to say, the investigation must be sufficient to represent a thorough and complete factual analysis of the situation in order to ward off the possibility of an unfair hearing), and whereas this requirement is particularly strict in light of the fact that so much is at stake for the employee, equally the nature of the facts of the case may mean that a relatively truncated investigation will serve to provide such a complete factual analysis.

3.1.1. Precautionary Suspensions During an Investigation

While the investigation is ongoing, the employer may decide that it is appro- [18–41] priate to suspend the employee until it is complete.[73] Such a suspension is, however, a 'holding' or 'precautionary' one and this fact must be made clear to the employee.[74]

The distinction between a holding and a punitive suspension was explained by [18–42] Barr J in *Quirke v Bord Lúthchleas na hÉireann*[75] (a case involving the imposition

---

71. *Kelly v An Post*, UD 974/1986.
72. Redmond, *Dismissal Law In Ireland* (2nd ed., Tottel Publishing, 2007), at para.13.76.
73. Such a process is in conformity with para.4(12) of the Industrial Relations Act 1990 (Code of Practice on Grievance and Disciplinary Procedures) (Declaration) Order 2000, SI no. 146 of 2000. See *Morgan v Trinity College* [2003] IEHC 167, [2003] 3 IR 157.
74. Redmond, *Dismissal Law In Ireland* (2nd ed., Tottel Publishing, 2007), at paras.13.32 and 13.72 *et seq*. It may be suggested that the practice is that an invariable inference will be drawn (*inter alia* by other employees) that even a precautionary suspension *is* punitive in nature and thus that the right to a good name of the employee is to that extent compromised. Hence there may be circumstances where, if the precautionary suspension is not actually necessary in order for the investigation to be conducted, the fact that it was imposed may be a factor that indicates that the employer has breached the implied contractual term of mutual trust and confidence. Accordingly, Redmond, *Dismissal Law In Ireland* (2nd ed., Tottel Publishing, 2007), at para.13.72 counsels against a 'knee jerk reaction of suspension in all cases'.
75. [1988] IR 83.

of a suspension on an athlete for an alleged infraction of an anti-doping rule), when he stated that:

> suspension… may take two different forms. On the one hand, it may be imposed as a holding operation pending the investigation of a complaint. Such a suspension does not imply that there has been a finding of any misbehaviour or breach of rules by the suspended person, but merely that an allegation of some such impropriety or misconduct has been made against the member in question. On the other hand, a suspension may be imposed not as a holding operation pending the outcome of an inquiry, but as a penalty by way of punishment of a member who has been found guilty of misconduct or breach of rules. The importance of the distinction is that where a suspension is imposed by way of punishment, it follows that the body in question has found its member guilty of significant misconduct or breach of rules.[76]

[18–43] The importance of this brightline distinction between a holding suspension and a punitive suspension was illustrated in the High Court judgment in *Morgan v Trinity College Dublin*.[77] The plaintiff was employed as a senior lecturer in the English Department of Trinity College Dublin. He was suspended with pay with immediate effect on foot of a complaint made by a female colleague who alleged physical intimidation and harassment. The plaintiff applied, *inter alia*, for an interlocutory injunction restraining the defendants from removing him from office and restraining them from embarking on a disciplinary inquiry. He contended that there was a failure to comply with natural justice in that he did not have an opportunity to challenge his accusers during the investigation, and that his suspension was invalid as it constituted a second suspension and should in any event be lifted by reason of its duration.

[18–44] Kearns J refused the relief sought and held that whether a suspension amounted to a sanction such as would invoke concepts of natural justice or give rise to an inference that the person concerned had been found guilty of significant misconduct was, in every case, a question of fact and degree. Significantly, Kearns J emphasised the importance of the distinction between a holding suspension and a punitive suspension, citing the above passage from the judgment of Barr J in *Quirke*. Kearns J stressed that in the context of a punitive suspension, the person affected was entitled to be afforded natural justice and fair procedures before the decision to suspend was taken; by contrast, in the latter case, the rules of natural justice might not apply. It should, however, be noted that Kearns J did point out that the period of the suspension had to be sufficiently reasonable to allow the investigation to take place.

[18–45] In relation to holding or precautionary suspensions, then, the point is worth making that inasmuch as even a precautionary suspension is something that can

---

76. *ibid.*, at 87.
77. [2003] IEHC 167, [2003] 3 IR 157.

have significant impact on the reputation and well-being of an employee, it is not something that should be imposed unless it is actually necessary in order for the investigation to proceed properly.[78] Furthermore, fair procedures should of course be followed both in determining whether or not to impose such a suspension and in the manner of any such suspension.[79] Thus the employee should be told why [s]he is being suspended[80] and, most importantly (given that it is not intended to be punitive in nature), the suspension in question must be *with pay*[81] and (as we have seen) should not be for an indefinite or excessively long period of time.[82] Indeed if a suspension was on a 'without pay' basis or for a prolonged period of time, then, irrespective of whether it was described as a holding suspension, it would almost certainly be capable of being characterised as being punitive in nature.[83] In this context, regard might be had to the earlier decision of *Martin v Nationwide Building Society*,[84] where a suspension had been allowed to continue for a period of time that was both 'inordinate and unjust'.[85] There, the High Court granted an injunction allowing the plaintiff to return to work, even though he had been suspended, to allow an investigation into allegations of misconduct. Thus if an employee *is* suspended pending the investigation, the employer should make all efforts to ensure a speedy, albeit thorough, investigation, at the end of which, if his or her actions were found not to merit any serious sanction, the employee could be restored to his or her former employment.[86] In this regard, a useful statement of the general principles that apply where an employee is the subject of a 'holding suspension' was provided by Clarke J in *Mulcahy v Avoca Capital Holdings*,[87] who stated that

---

78. This is distinct from a situation in which an employee has been found to have committed an offence (for example, fighting or bullying) and the employer determines that in order for a cooling-off period to occur that employee should be suspended by way of sanction, with or without pay.

79. *Khan v Health Service Executive* [2008] IEHC 234, [2009] ELR 178. See also *O'Donoghue v South Eastern Health Board* [2005] 4 IR 127. For discussion of the EAT determination in *Dowling v Cumann na Daoine Aontaithe Teo* UD 545/2007 see *supra* n.35.

80. *Flynn v An Post* [1987] 1 IR 68. Generally, see McCrann, 'Investigations in the Workplace', 3(3) *IELJ* (2006), 68.

81. In circumstances where the salary of the employee is not fixed (being *inter alia* bonus or commission related) the appropriate response is to calculate the amount that the employee should be paid by reference to the amount that [s]he would be paid while on annual leave – which will entail factoring in an appropriate percentage the amount of any such bonuses or commission. See *Ferris v Royal Liver Friendly Society*, UD 877/1983 and generally Chapter 11.

82. It is possible that an excessively long holding suspension may come to be regarded as a punitive sanction. *Mulcahy v Avoca Capital Holdings Ltd.* [2005] IEHC 70; *Martin v Nationwide Building Society* [1999] IEHC 163, [1999] ELR 241. Generally, see McCrann, 'Investigations in the Workplace', 3(3) *IELJ* (2006), 68.

83. See *McNamara v South Western Health Board* [2001] IEHC 24, [2001] ELR 317.

84. [2001] 1 IR 228.

85. At p. 235, *per* Macken J.

86. *Deegan v Dunnes Stores* [1992] ELR 184.

87. [2005] IEHC 70.

Finally, before leaving this topic I think it is important to make two points. They are factors that are relevant in considering what period of time might be considered to be inordinate and unjust. They would tend in the one case to favour a shorter period and in the other case to favour a longer period on the facts of this case; therefore their cumulative effect may not be very significant, but it is nonetheless important to note them. On the one hand the question of whether someone has been suspended with or without pay seems to me to be a significant factor. Obviously, someone who has been suspended without pay is entitled to an even greater degree of expedition in the completion of a disciplinary process than someone who has been suspended with pay. Obviously the plaintiff in this case has been suspended on pay and therefore that factor does not lead to perhaps an even greater level of expedition being required. On the other hand, there can be no doubt that the absence from work for a prolonged period, particularly someone who is in a significant position, is the kind of thing which can be noticed to an extent that it can affect that person's reputation in the relevant economic community in which the employment is situated. While some element of that may be an inevitable consequence of the necessity to suspend in the first place, the nature of the job involved, and the likelihood of an absence from that job being in practice something which will mitigate against an employee, is also a factor that needs to be taken into account, and is a factor which, I think, would favour additional expedition in this case, having regard to the position which the plaintiff holds, and the fact that any significantly longer period not actively engaged in the carrying out of his duties could have a significant effect on him.[88]

3.2. Providing the Employee with Appropriate Notice of the Investigation

[18–46] Appropriate and timely notice must be given to the party against whom the disciplinary process is being invoked both of the fact of the investigation[89] and of the fact that a disciplinary hearing is to take place,[90] and also of the precise nature of the charge against him or her.[91] The extent of the information and the amount of notice that must be provided to the relevant employee will vary from

---

88. At p.4 of the judgment.
89. It has been held that where professionals are concerned, they are entitled to be put on notice even of a preliminary enquiry into their behaviour. *O'Ceallaigh v An Bord Altranais* [2000] 4 IR 54; *O'Callaghan v Disciplinary Tribunal* [2002] 1 IR 1, [2002] 1 ILRM 89. On the other hand, in *Mulcahy v Avoca Capital Holdings Ltd.* [2005] IEHC 70, Clarke J held that it was not the case that an employee had to be kept constantly in the loop insofar as developments in the investigation were concerned. Clarke J noted that, after all, there may be any number of circumstances where it would be counterproductive to the investigation if this was to happen.
90. Thus an employee must be told that a meeting to which [s]he has been invited or summoned is a disciplinary one that could lead to him or her being sanctioned: *Paul Collins v Tesco Ireland Ltd.*, UD 85/2005.
91. The Industrial Relations Act 1990 (Code of Practice on Grievance and Disciplinary Procedures) (Declaration) Order 2000, SI no. 146 of 2000, para.4(7) suggests that the right to fair procedures may mean that the allegations against an employee should be set out in writing.

case to case, but in all cases it must be sufficient to enable him or her to mount a proper defence.⁹²

Thus if any report is made at the conclusion of an investigation, the employee is [18–47] generally entitled to such report.⁹³ [S]he is also entitled to know of the existence of and to have access to any statements made in respect of him or her either generally or specifically pertaining to the relevant investigation by any other person.⁹⁴ In addition, [s]he is generally entitled to have access to any other information or evidence against him or her.⁹⁵ On the other hand, the guiding principle is that the employee's entitlement to such material stems from the need to ensure that [s]he is being treated fairly, and hence, logically, an employer can deny certain material to an employee if this does not imperil the fairness of the disciplinary process.⁹⁶ Equally (and quite apart from the fact that an employee facing disciplinary proceedings may, depending on the circumstances, have an entitlement to cross-examine and challenge the evidence of witnesses who give evidence against him or her), it may be inadvisable for disciplinary proceedings to go ahead exclusively on the basis of evidence that has been obtained in confidence and is not to be released to the employee who is being investigated.⁹⁷

3.3. The Nature of a Fair Hearing

As with the other matters considered in this chapter, the question of what consti- [18–48] tutes a fair hearing will depend on the facts of an individual case, and in particular the significance or seriousness of what is at stake.⁹⁸ Thus it is clear that there must

---

92. *Maher v Irish Permanent Plc (No. 2)* [1997] IEHC 150, [1998] 4 IR 302, [1998] ELR 89; *State (Gleeson) v Minister for Defence* [1976] IR 280; *Bunyan v United Dominions Trust (Ireland) Ltd.* [1982] ILRM 406; *Mooney v An Post* [1998] 4 IR 288, [1998] ELR 238; *State (Irish Pharmaceutical Union) v Employment Appeals Tribunal* [1987] ILRM 36.
93. Surprisingly, in *Mooney v An Post* [1998] 4 IR 288, [1998] ELR 238, the employee was held *not* to be entitled to see the investigating officer's report.
94. *Magham v Janssen Pharmaceuticals BV*, UD 1127/1984. Generally, see Redmond *Dismissal Law In Ireland* (2nd ed., Tottel Publishing, 2007), at para.13.52.
95. *C v Mid-Western Health Board* [2000] ELR 38; *Magham v Janssen Pharmaceuticals*, UD 1127/1984; *Sheerin v Deantusiocht Dane-Elec Teoranta*, UD 402/2006; *Cassidy v Shannon Castle Banquets and Heritage Ltd.* [2000] ELR 248. In *Maher v Aim Group*, UD 398/2004 it was held that an employee could not claim that he was prejudiced by not being given access during a disciplinary hearing to certain evidence that was being used against him (CCTV footage) in circumstances where he had previously declined to look at the evidence during the investigation.
96. *Hussain v Elonex Plc* [1999] IRLR 420.
97. See Redmond, *Dismissal Law In Ireland* (2nd ed., Tottel Publishing, 2007), at para.13.55. See *McNamara v Lannit (Ireland) Ltd.*, UD 910/1984. But see also *Kiernan v Our Lady's Hospital for Sick Children*, UD 1129/1992.
98. The Industrial Relations Act 1990 (Code of Practice on Grievance and Disciplinary Procedures) (Declaration) Order 2000, SI no. 146 of 2000, at para.4(6) envisages a fair hearing as one where the employee's grievances are fairly examined and processed; details of any

be appropriate evidence produced against an employee as a result of the investigation[99] to justify a finding that the offence has occurred. Subject to the doctrine of necessity,[100] moreover, any disciplinary hearing of the matter must be conducted by persons who may be regarded as being independent,[101] and, in particular, *must* be conducted by persons other than the person or persons responsible for investigating the matter.[102] In particular the employee must be given some opportunity of being heard[103] and the person judging the matter (like the person conducting the investigation) must, insofar as is possible, start from the perspective that the employee is innocent, and must only find him or her guilty where this is warranted by the evidence. In other words, there must be no prejudgment of the issue.[104]

[18–49] Almost inevitably, and irrespective of what type of disciplinary sanction is at issue, an employee must have the evidence against him or her put to him or her and

---

allegations or complaints are put to the employee concerned; [s]he is given the opportunity to respond fully to any such allegations or complaints; [s]he is given the opportunity to avail of the right to be represented during the procedure; and [s]he has the right to a fair and impartial determination of the issues concerned, taking into account any representations made by or on behalf of the employee and any other relevant or appropriate evidence factors or circumstances. Generally, see *Flanagan v UCD* [1989] ILRM 469; *O'Brien v Asahi Synthetic Fibre*, UD 25/1992.

99. On the correct relationship between a disciplinary investigation and a police investigation into the same act or acts of the employee, and in particular the question of whether evidence garnered as a result of a *police* investigation can be used to justify *the employer* taking disciplinary action against an employee, see Redmond, *Dismissal Law In Ireland* (2nd ed., Tottel Publishing, 2007), at para.13.94 *et seq.* and McCrann, 'Investigations in the Workplace', 3(3) *IELJ* (2006), 68. See also *Mooney v An Post* [1998] 4 IR 288, [1998] ELR 238; *Mahon v Cummins Graphic Supplies Ltd.* [1991] ELR 53.

100. *Flynn v Great Northern Railway* (1955) 89 ILTR 46. See Redmond, *Dismissal Law In Ireland* (2nd ed., Tottel Publishing, 2007), at para.17.37.

101. *Cassidy v Shannon Castle Banquets and Heritage Ltd.* [2000] ELR 248; *Heneghen v Western Regional Fisheries Board* [1986] ILRM 225.

102. *Dowling v Cumann na Daoine Aontaithe Teo* UD 545/2007. On the question of whether it is legitimate for a person who was involved in the investigation that led to the disciplinary hearing also to be present on the occasion of that hearing, other than as a witness, see *Connelly v McConnell* [1983] IR 172; *O'Donoghue v Veterinary Council* [1974] IEHC 1, [1975] IR 398; *Mooney v An Post* [1998] 4 IR 288, [1998] ELR 238.

103. *State (Gleeson) v Minister for Defence* [1976] IR 280.

104. *Glover v BLN* [1973] IR 88; *Ridge v Baldwin* [1961] 2 WLR 1054. In other words, as Redmond puts it (*Dismissal Law In Ireland* (2nd ed., Tottel Publishing, 2007), at para.7.30) there is 'no such thing as an open and shut case'. On the other hand, see *McGrath and Ó Ruairc v The Trustees of the College of Maynooth* [1979] ILRM 166 at 170 for the suggestion that it was acceptable for the disciplinary panel to take a preconceived view of the matter, provided that it was 'willing to hear what may be said by the party charged and [to] afford... him a full and real opportunity of making his defence'. See Redmond, *Dismissal Law In Ireland* (2nd ed., Tottel Publishing, 2007), at para.7.41 for the view that what was permitted here was administrative expertise rather than prejudgement and that 'the latter... should always be a fatal flaw in any decision'.

will be entitled to present evidence on his or her own behalf and to have that evidence taken into account by the body hearing the matter.[105] Indeed in *Mooney v An Post*[106] the Supreme Court regarded this as a basic minimum entitlement as far as the right to fair procedures was concerned. As we have seen, this entitlement exists both at any disciplinary hearing that may occur but also more generally in the context of any pre-hearing investigation. Thus an employee is entitled to be informed of the nature of the complaint being made against him or her, and given an opportunity to respond to this, either orally or preferably in writing. Moreover, such response should be taken into account by the person conducting the investigation as well as by the overall decision-maker in the case. In this context it has been described as 'axiomatic' that the person who will make the ultimate determination in respect of the disciplinary matter meets with the employee concerned and hears his or her side of the story.[107]

It is a basic aspect of the right to fair procedures that the entire disciplinary [18–50] process and especially any disciplinary hearing must be conducted without any bias or appearance of bias. In this respect, it is necessary to ensure that procedures are applied consistently between all employees in the workplace.[108] Thus it is important where a disciplinary rule has *not* traditionally been enforced within a workplace, that if it is henceforth to be enforced, employees are made aware of this change of policy.[109] The alternative, after all, would be a situation where an employee who was penalised for such an infraction could claim to have been discriminated against when compared to other employees who formerly had committed such offences with impunity. Again, moreover, this comes back to a point made consistently throughout this chapter, namely that the best way for an employer to ensure that his or her disciplinary procedures can survive scrutiny is to communicate all aspects thereof to his or her employees and, ideally, to make the disciplinary rules a part of the employees' contracts of employment.[110]

3.3.1. Right to an Oral Hearing

Depending on the circumstances of the case, the employee's right to fair proce- [18–51] dures may require that [s]he be afforded an oral hearing into his or her case.[111] This is not, however, inevitable[112] and will depend on how serious the matter

---

105. See, for example, *McGarrigle v Donegal Sports and Golf Centre Ltd.*, UD 680/2002; *Daly v Somers*, UD 94/2005; *Ryan v Molloy's Confectionary & Bakery (Roscommon) Ltd.* [2006] ELR 61.
106. *Mooney v An Post* [1998] 4 IR 288, [1998] ELR 238.
107. Redmond, *Dismissal Law In Ireland* (2nd ed., Tottel Publishing, 2007), at para.13.57.
108. *O'Neill v RSL* [1990] ELR 31; *Kelly v Power Supermarkets* [1990] ELR 141.
109. See, for example, *Hayes & Others v Waterford Carpets Ltd.*, UD 257, 258 & 259/2007; *O'Connell v Garde's Coffee Shop* [1991] ELR 105; *O'Neill v RSL (Ire) Ltd.* [1990] ELR 31; *Kelly v Power Supermarkets Ltd.* [1990] ELR 41.
110. Generally, see Redmond, *Dismissal Law In Ireland* (2nd ed., Tottel Publishing, 2007), at para.13.41.
111. *Kiely v Minister for Social Welfare (No. 2)* [1977] IR 267.
112. See *Curtin v An Post*, UD 1409/2005. Thus in *Mooney v An Post* [1998] 4 IR 288, [1998] ELR

is.[113] There may, after all, be cases where it is entirely possible for a disciplinary issue to be dealt with perfectly fairly on the basis of an investigation (during the course of which a statement is taken from the employee whose conduct is being investigated) and written reports, with no oral hearing into the matter. Indeed this would arguably be the norm where a low-level sanction is envisaged. It is only when the absence of an oral hearing would compromise the fairness of a disciplinary hearing that one should be held.

3.3.2. Right to Legal Representation

[18–52] In a number of recent cases,[114] the Irish courts have revisited the thorny question of whether and when an employee who is facing disciplinary action is entitled to legal representation.[115] The logic would appear to be that, whereas the employee is generally entitled to *some form of representation* in the context of a disciplinary investigation,[116] and whereas it is possible if a serious sanction is being considered, that [s]he may be entitled to what may be termed legal representation (that is, representation by a solicitor or by counsel),[117] there is, however, no inherent right to legal representation in a workplace disciplinary setting, not least because in many cases,

---

238 the Supreme Court upheld the conclusion of the trial judge that the employee had no right to an oral hearing before his employer. See, however, Redmond, *Dismissal Law In Ireland* (2nd ed., Tottel Publishing, 2007), at paras.7.20–7.21 for a convincing explanation as to why the possibility of an oral hearing was simply inappropriate on the facts of the case. In *Sheriff v Corrigan* [1999] ELR 146 it was stated that there were no hard-and-fast rules for determining when an oral hearing would be required.

113. See *Martin v Blooms Hotel* [1999] ELR 116.

114. *Burns v Governor of Castlerea Prison* [2009] IESC 33, [2009] ELR 109; *Stoskus v Goode Concrete* [2007] IEHC 432. Generally, see Compton and Dillon, 'Practice and Procedure', 6(2) *IELJ* (2009), 58; Duffy, 'Lawyers in the Workplace – When Are the Services of a Lawyer Appropriate?', 3(1) *IELJ* (2006), 4; Farrell, 'Opening the Door to Injunctions? – Refusing Legal Representation at Disciplinary Hearings', 3(1) *IELJ* (2006), 7; Hayes, 'Lawyers in the Workplace', 3(1) *IELJ* (2006), 14; McCrann, 'Investigations in the Workplace', 3(3) *IELJ* (2006), 68.

115. The Industrial Relations Act 1990 (Code of Practice on Grievance and Disciplinary Procedures) (Declaration) Order 2000, SI no. 146 of 2000, at para.4(4) envisages an employee having an employee representative with him or her when disciplinary proceedings are ongoing against him or her but defines the term 'employee representative' as 'includ[ing] a colleague of the employee's choice and a registered trade union *but not any other person or body unconnected with the enterprise*' [emphasis added], which appears to exclude lawyers from having any role in the matter.

116. *Devlin v Player & Wills Ltd.*, UD 90/1978,; *O'Brien v Asahi Synthetic Fibre*, UD 25/1992. Generally, see Redmond, *Dismissal Law In Ireland* (2nd ed., Tottel Publishing, 2007), at paras 13.60 *et seq.* Redmond submits (at para.13.62) that 'Fairness suggests that representation should be extended to employees at every stage of the disciplinary procedures except, possibly, where an oral warning is concerned.'

117. *Stoskus v Goode Concrete* [2007] IEHC 432; *Gallagher v Minister for Justice, Equality and Law Reform* [2006] 1 ILRM 486; *Aziz v Midland Health Board* [1995] ELR 49; *Flanagan v University College Dublin* [1989] ILRM 469; *Gallagher v Revenue Commissioners* [1991] ILRM 632; *Maher v Irish Permanent* [1998] 4 IR 302; *Galvin v Kerry Foods* [1990] ELR 162.

this is simply not demanded by the facts.[118] After all, in many if not most cases, the issues under discussion at any disciplinary tribunal will be factual rather than legal in nature and the employer him or herself will not be legally represented.[119]

Equally it is possible for an employer to make it a term of an employee's contract **[18–53]** that in the event of a disciplinary hearing [s]he is entitled to legal representation,[120] or in alternative that she may be accompanied and represented by a colleague or a trade union official, but not by any other party (including a lawyer).[121] Should the employer be legally represented, it would appear to stand to reason that the employee in such circumstances would have a reciprocal right to legal representation.[122]

These issues were recently revisited in *Burns v Governor of Castlerea Prison*[123] when **[18–54]** the Supreme Court overturned a decision of the High Court (Butler J) in which it was held that, where a serious disciplinary matter was under investigation, the relevant employee would be entitled to legal representation. The net issue in the case was whether the relevant employer had a discretion to allow legal representation to be used by an employee and, if so, whether or not that discretion should have been exercised in favour of the employee on the facts of the present case. Geoghegan J held that the employer in this case properly exercised its discretion not to allow the employee to have legal representation. Indeed he was of the view that in cases of this nature 'legal representation should be the exception rather than the rule. In most cases the provisions of the rules will simply apply'.[124] Moreover, in this case it was simply unnecessary for the employee to be legally represented. Thus Geoghegan J held that

> While there is obviously room for legitimate difference of opinion as to the proper exercise of a discretion in any given set of circumstances, I would take the view

---

118. See, for example, *Burns v Governor of Castlerea Prison* [2009] IESC 33, [2009] ELR 109; *Stoskus v Goode Concrete* [2007] IEHC 432; *Murphy v College Freight Ltd.*, UD 867/2007; *O'Neill v Iarnród Éireann* [1991] ELR 1; *Garvey v Minister for Justice, Equality and Law Reform and Others* [2006] IESC 3, [2006] 1 IR 548, [2006] ILRM 486.
119. *Aziz v Midland Health Board* [1995] ELR 48; *Mooney v An Post* [1998] 4 IR 288, [1998] ELR 238.
120. See Farrell, 'Opening the Door to Injunctions? – Refusing Legal Representation at Disciplinary Hearings', 3(1) *IELJ* (2006), 7.
121. *Stoskus v Goode Concrete* [2007] IEHC 432. See, however, Hayes, 'Lawyers in the Workplace', 3(1) *IELJ* (2006), 14, for the view, 'It is clear that declining union density creates a representation vacuum at the enterprise level.'
122. It has been held (*Georgopoulos v Beaumont Hospital Board* [1993] ELR 246) that where an employer has received legal advice in respect of disciplinary proceedings being taken against an employee, it is not required to disclose that advice to that employee. Equally it must surely be the case that where that advice amounts to part of the case against the employee, this would necessarily have to be disclosed, and may, indeed, justify the employee being legally represented as a matter of fair procedures.
123. [2009] IESC 33, [2009] ELR 109.
124. [2009] ELR 109, 115.

that legal representation was clearly unnecessary in this case. On one view, none of the charges were serious enough in the objective sense. However, I am reluctant to use that terminology given that at least one of them involves the alleged making of a deliberately false statement with intent to deceive. From a human point of view, that is a serious allegation in the mind of an accused but in the context of the factual matrix to this case, the charges could very easily be defended without a lawyer. The issues were factual issues connected with the day to day running of the prison. It is difficult to see why a lawyer would be required. The rules specify who is to be an advocate and, therefore, subject to the overall obligation of fairness they should be followed. The cases for which the Governor would be obliged to exercise a discretion in favour of permitting legal representation would be exceptional. They would not necessarily be related even to the objective seriousness of the charges if the issues of proof were purely ones of simple fact and could safely be disposed of without a lawyer. In any organisation where there are disciplinary procedures, it is wholly undesirable to involve legal representation unless in all the circumstances it would be required by the principles of constitutional justice.[125]

[18–55] In assessing *when* it would be appropriate to permit an employee to have legal representation, Geoghegan J referred to various matters that Webster J had deemed relevant to this question in *R v Secretary of State for the Home Department ex parte Tarrant*,[126] namely:

1. The seriousness of the charge and of the potential penalty.
2. Whether any points of law are likely to arise.
3. The capacity of a particular prisoner to present his own case.
4. Procedural difficulty.
5. The need for reasonable speed in making the adjudication, that being an important consideration.
6. The need for fairness as between prisoners and as between prisoners and prison officers.

Geoghegan J concluded:

I would approve of that list but it is a list merely of the kind of factors which might be relevant in the consideration of whether legal representation is desirable in the interests of a fair hearing. Ultimately, the essential point which the relevant Governor has to consider is whether from the accused's point of view legal representation is needed in the particular circumstances of the case.[127]

---

125. [2009] ELR 109, 114.
126. [1985] 1 QB 251.
127. [2009] ELR 109, 115.

3.3.3. *Right to Present One's Case, Cross-Examine Witnesses and Challenge Evidence*

As we have seen, it is vital in order for fair procedures to be followed that an   [18–56]
employee facing disciplinary proceedings is presented with all the evidence against
him or her[128] and is permitted to challenge that evidence and to present rebutting
evidence in his or her defence.[129] In addition, however, if an oral hearing *is* to be
permitted, [s]he should be entitled to challenge such evidence by cross-examining
witnesses[130] provided that this is necessary in order to ensure a fair result.[131] As
has been mentioned earlier, it is for this reason that an employer should be reluctant to proceed with a disciplinary process against an employee where the only
evidence that can be used has been obtained in confidence.[132]

3.3.4. *Standard of Proof*

In *Georgopoulos v Beaumont Hospital Board*,[133] Murphy J rejected the proposition   [18–57]
that the criminal standard of proof beyond reasonable doubt would have to be
reached by a disciplinary tribunal before an employee could be found guilty of the
disciplinary infraction for which [s]he was being investigated. Hence the standard
of proof that must be reached would appear to be the civil standard (balance
of probabilities), but subject to the general rule that this standard is sufficiently
flexible that it can take into account the varying circumstances of the case.[134]
Thus it might be suggested that, where a particularly serious offence is at issue
with a particularly onerous penalty, the standard of proof required by the relevant
tribunal should reflect this fact.[135]

3.3.5. *Right to an Appeal*

There may, depending on the seriousness of the matter, be an entitlement where a   [18–58]
decision has been made against an employee, for that employee to appeal against
this decision.[136] As a result (and in order to ensure that an employee is able to
determine appropriate grounds on which to bring such an appeal), it may also be

---

128. *C v Mid-Western Health Board* [2000] ELR 38.
129. *Gallagher v Revenue Commissioners* [1995] ILRM 108; *Sheehan v Commissioner for An Garda Síochána and Others* [1998] IEHC 202.
130. *Mooney v An Post* [1998] 4 IR 288, [1998] ELR 238. See also Industrial Relations Act 1990 (Code of Practice on Grievance and Disciplinary Procedures) (Declaration) Order 2000, SI no. 146 of 2000, at para.4(7).
131. In *Shortt v Royal Liver Assurance Ltd.* [2008] IEHC 332, [2009] ELR 240, Laffoy J held that the fact that an employee who was the subject of a disciplinary hearing was not permitted to cross-examine a witness did not imperil the fairness of the proceedings and hence was not a reason to deem the disciplinary process to be unfair.
132. See Redmond, *Dismissal Law In Ireland* (2nd ed., Tottel Publishing, 2007), at para.13.57.
133. [1993] ELR 246.
134. *Georgopoulus v Beaumont Hospital Board* [1993] ELR 246.
135. Generally, on standard of proof, see Redmond, *Dismissal Law In Ireland* (2nd ed., Tottel Publishing, 2007), at paras.17.34 *et seq.*
136. See *O'Leary v Eagle Star Life Assurance Co of Ireland Ltd.* [2003] ELR 223.

necessary in such circumstances that the original decision be a reasoned one.[137] In any event, and subject to the doctrine of necessity (that is to say, that it may simply be impossible in a small workplace to find someone who can hear an appeal and who has not been affected even tangentially by the original hearing), the appeal should be to someone other[138] than the person[s] who was/were involved in[139] or who made the decision at the original hearing.[140]

[18–59] The point has been made, however,[141] that the concept of an appeal raises various difficult questions that should, ideally, be dealt with in the company's disciplinary procedures and can be reduced to two issues:

- Is such an appeal to be heard on a *de novo* basis, with a brand-new panel that is unaware of the basis for the original decision and will (presumably on the basis of the existing investigation) hear witnesses and consider evidence in the same way as the original panel,[142] or is it to be a challenge to the decision of the original panel, whereby the appeal focuses merely on deficiencies (or perceived deficiencies) within that decision? Moreover, can the appeal body actually impose a different decision to the original disciplinary body or is it confined to quashing such decision and referring the matter back for a fresh investigation and/or hearing?
- What is the position of the worker (who may, for example, have been suspended or dismissed on foot of the decision of the original disciplinary body) pending the appeal, and does the fact that an appeal has been taken represent a stay on the operation of the penalty originally imposed and in respect of which the appeal now lies?

---

137. Generally, see *Garvey v Ireland* [1981] IR 75.

138. For the suggestion that the party hearing the appeal should not be more junior in the workplace than the party hearing the original matter, see *Jameson v Harris Calorific Ltd.*, UD 372/1991.

139. Thus the appeal should not be heard by someone who advised the original decision-maker as inevitably [s]he can be taken to have supported the original decision: *Quinn v Tenants (Ireland) Ltd.*, UD 249/1922.

140. *Hobson v Liebherr Great Britain Ltd.*, UD 451/2004. See, however, *Kurfey v Dublin Gas Company*, UD 483/1986 for the view that any defect in a situation where the same party was involved in both the original hearing and the appeal could be cured if there was a further appeal step to someone completely independent. See also *State (Sheehan) v McMahon* [1976–77] ILRM 305 for the view that a defective appeal system does not render the entire process (including the original finding of the disciplinary panel) invalid.

141. See Redmond, *Dismissal Law In Ireland* (2nd ed., Tottel Publishing, 2007), at paras.13.95 *et seq.*

142. A question also arises as to the impact of evidence discovered *subsequent* to the original hearing and whether any exculpatory evidence of this kind can justify an appeal on a *de novo* basis. Again this is something in respect of which provision should be made in the relevant disciplinary procedures.

3.4. Fair Sanctions

A final point to consider is the question of whether it is appropriate that a [18–60] reviewing body (such as the EAT) should be able to have regard not merely to the decision-making process but also to the decision that was reached. In other words (and aside from the operation of unfair dismissals and redundancy law considered in chapters 21 and 22), can the reviewing body ever strike down the sanction that was imposed on an employee as being unfair, while not impugning the manner by which the decision was reached?

In general, after all – and in keeping with the approach generally taken to review [18–61] decisions of public authorities[143] – a decision in a disciplinary matter will only be reviewed by the EAT (for example) on the question of whether fair procedures were followed in the decision-making process and, possibly, on the question of whether there was evidence before the decision-maker that justified the decision that was made.[144] In other words the merits of the actual decision will only be challengeable for irrationality – that is, on the basis that there was no evidence before the decision-maker that supported the decision, and not because the reviewing body (typically the EAT) would have made a different decision on that evidence.[145]

Having said this, however, there is perhaps something unsatisfactory in a situation [18–62] where, for example, an employee can follow fair procedures (as outlined above) and thereby escape any liability, other than in the form of a trade dispute, while imposing a manifestly excessive penalty on an employee – for example, by suspending him or her for a first time incident of bad time-keeping. To some extent it may be that the full impact of the right to constitutional justice has not been explored in this regard. The constitutional doctrine of proportionality is, after all, a well-established one,[146] and it remains to be seen whether it might be used in this context to ensure that there is an objective link between the offence of which an employee is found guilty and the penalty that [s]he receives as a result.[147]

---

143. *O'Keeffe v An Bord Pleanála* [1993] 1 IR 39.
144. *Murphy v College Freight Ltd.*, UD 867/2007; *Hestor v Dunnes Stores* [1990] ELR 12; *Pacelli v Irish Distillers Ltd.* [2004] ELR 25; *Looney & Co Ltd. v Looney.*, UD 843/84; *Bunyan v United Dominions Trust (Ireland) Ltd.* [1982] ILRM 404; *Hennessy v Read and Write Shop*, UD 192/78.
145. *Moloney v Bolger* [2000] IEHC 63; *Zockoll Group Limited v Telecom Éireann* [1998] 4 IR 287 at 318.
146. *Cox v Ireland* [1992] 2 IR 503; *Heaney v Ireland* [1994] 3 IR 593; *Rock v Ireland* [1997] 3 IR 484; *Iarnród Éireann v Ireland* [1995] 2 ILRM 161; *In re Article 26 and the Employment Equality Bill* [1997] 2 IR 321. Generally, see Hogan and Whyte, *Kelly: The Irish Constitution* (4th ed., LexisNexis Butterworths, London, 2003), at paras.7.1.56 *et seq.*
147. For the suggestion that it is necessary that there be some proportionality of response, see *McCurdy v Adelphi* [1992] ELR 14; *McGee v Peamount Hospital*, UD 136/1984; *Tierney v An Post* [2000] 1 IR 536, [2009] ELR 293.

CHAPTER 19

Termination of Employment

Introduction

In chapters 21 and 22 we consider two particular situations in which there have [19–01] been significant statutory developments regulating the ability of an employer to terminate an employment contract: redundancy and instances of what is termed unfair dismissal. In this chapter we consider the rules relating to five further miscellaneous categories of termination:

- wrongful dismissal at common law;
- frustration of contract;
- death or dissolution of one of the parties;
- mutual consent; and
- employer's insolvency.

1. Wrongful Dismissal

Wrongful dismissal is a common law action for breach of contract that may be [19–02] brought by an employee in response to a repudiatory breach by the employer (which usually takes the form of an unjustified termination of the contract of employment by the employer). The wrongful dismissal action is entirely dependent on the terms of the contract of employment. Thus in the absence of a justifiable reason an action for wrongful dismissal will arise where the employee has been dismissed:

(a) without adequate notice, or no notice at all (and hence there is a significant connection between the concept of wrongful dismissal and that of entitlement to notice, considered in Chapter 20);

(b) contrary to any express (or possibly implied) term on termination contained within the contract;

(c) in the case of a fixed term contract, before the expiry of that fixed term; or

(d) in the case of a contract to perform a specific task, before the completion of that task.

[19–03] The wrongful dismissal action centres on the *form* of the dismissal rather than on the substantive reasons surrounding it. Therefore, as long as the employer's dismissal was in strict accordance with the terms of the contract and principles of natural justice, no right to a claim for wrongful dismissal would exist even if the employer's motives were improper. However, while it may be true that, under strict contractual principles, an employer has great freedom as regards the dismissal of employees, this power is still subject to restriction. An employer's power to dismiss may be limited by the terms (express and implied) of the contract itself or by the constitutional principles of natural justice and fair procedures (as discussed in Chapter 18).

1.1. Limitations on the Power to Dismiss – The Contract

[19–04] An employee may bring a claim for wrongful dismissal where the employer fails to adhere to procedural safeguards on termination expressly provided for in the contract of employment. In *Gunton v Richmond-upon-Thames London Borough Council*,[1] a college attempted to dismiss its registrar on disciplinary grounds without following the disciplinary procedure that was found to be part of his contract of employment. In strict accordance with the terms of his contract of employment on termination, the employee was to be given one month's notice of his dismissal by his employer. It was held that the employee's dismissal was wrongful because of the employer's failure to follow its own disciplinary procedures and the employee's damages were assessed by reference to a reasonable period of time by which the employer could have enacted the appropriate disciplinary procedures. Thus the employee was entitled to his salary for this 'reasonable period' in addition to his one month's notice period.

[19–05] Where the dismissal of an employee entails or involves a breach of an implied term in his or her employment contract, this may also give rise to a claim for wrongful dismissal.[2] Employees have increasingly relied on the development of the implied term of trust and confidence[3] in order to strengthen the express safeguards contained within the contract of employment. In this context, the term has been used to provide additional protection to the employee on the basis that the 'trust and confidence' between the parties has broken down. In *Johnson v Unisys*,[4] the House of Lords refused to hold that the implied term of trust and confidence justified imposing a term in the contract of employment that, notwithstanding an express term that provided the employee could be dismissed at four weeks' notice without any reason, the employer could not terminate the contract without just cause and after giving the employee a reasonable opportunity to demonstrate that no such cause existed. Lord Hoffmann held that no such term could be implied

---

1. [1981] Ch 448, [1980] 3 WLR 714, [1980] IRLR 321.
2. For detailed discussion of implied terms, see Chapter 4.
3. *Malik and Mahmood v Bank of Credit and Commerce International SA* [1997] UKHL 23, [1998] AC 20, [1997] 3 WLR 95, [1997] 3 All ER 1, [1997] ICR 606, [1997] IRLR 462.
4. [2001] UKHL 13, [2003] 1 AC 518, [2001] 2 WLR 1076, [2001] ICR 480, [2001] IRLR 279.

where it ran contrary to an express term of the contract of employment. In a dissenting judgment, Lord Steyn, however, rejected the notion than an implied term of mutual trust and confidence would always be inferior to an express contractual term, stating that such an argument:

> loses sight of the particular nature of the implied obligation of mutual trust and confidence. It is not a term implied in fact. It is an over-arching obligation implied by law as an incident of the contract of employment. It can also be described as a legal duty imposed by law – Treitel, *The Law of Contract* (10th ed., 1999) at p.190. It requires at least express words or a necessary implication to displace it or to cut down its scope. Prima facie it must be read consistently with the express terms of the contract... The interaction of the implied obligation of trust and confidence and express terms of the contract can be compared with the relationship between duties of good faith or fair dealing with the express terms of notice in a contract. They can live together.[5]

Essentially, Lord Steyn was asserting that the duty of trust and confidence was imposed by law rather than by fact. That being so, the term could be implied regardless of the presumed intention of the parties and in Lord Steyn's view could co-exist with a contradictory express term within the contract of employment.　[19–06]

The issue was reviewed by the Irish High Court in *McGrath v Trintech Technologies Ltd. and Trintech Group Plc.*[6] In that case, the plaintiff worked as a project manager with the first named defendant. During his employment he suffered bouts of physical illness. It was while on sick leave that he was asked to go on an assignment to work in a Uruguayan company recently acquired by the defendant. The plaintiff worked in Uruguay for over five months. In June 2003 the plaintiff returned from Uruguay and went on certified sick leave and did not return to work. In August 2003 he was informed that he was to be made redundant with effect from September 2003. The plaintiff's contract of employment contained the following express termination clause: 'One month's notice will be required for the termination of employment. Employees are requested to confirm a resignation in writing, confirming the date when he/she shall cease.'[7]　[19–07]

The plaintiff claimed *inter alia* that a term should be implied into the contract of employment to the effect that he would not be dismissed without due or reasonable cause, or consultation, and that the defendant would adopt fair procedures in any selection process for dismissal or redundancy. Furthermore, any breach of such a term would give rise to an action in common law for wrongful dismissal. In essence, the plaintiff was seeking to copper-fasten the protection expressly provided within the contract of employment by implying a term that required the　[19–08]

5.　[2003] 1 AC 518, 536.
6.　[2004] IEHC 342, [2005] 4 IR 382, [2005] ELR 49. See Chapter 16.
7.　[2005] 4 IR 382, 392.

defendant to act reasonably and fairly when exercising the option to dismiss. The High Court followed the decision of the House of Lords in *Johnson* and refused to imply such a term. Laffoy J observed that the added protection that would be provided by such a clause was superfluous because it was already provided for under the unfair dismissals legislation:

> The essence of the plaintiff's case… is that there should be implied into his contract with the defendant a term that mere compliance with the express notice provision in the contract would not validly and effectively terminate the contractual relationship at common law. There is no authority for this proposition. I am persuaded by the authorities cited by the defendant's counsel that the proposition is not sound in principle. Accordingly, I have come to the conclusion that terms in relation to dismissal and redundancy on the lines pleaded by the plaintiff cannot be implied into the plaintiff's contract of employment with the defendant so as to give rise to a cause of action at common law. Such protection and remedies as are afforded by statute law to the plaintiff in the circumstances which prevailed in August 2003 cannot be pursued at first instance in a plenary action in the High Court.[8]

[19–09] A breach of an implied term of trust and confidence formed the basis of a claim for wrongful dismissal before the Supreme Court in *Berber v Dunnes Stores Ltd.*[9] In that case the respondent had been employed for 21 years by the appellant. He suffered from Crohn's Disease since his teens and his employer was aware of the condition. The respondent had worked his way up in the appellant's company to the position of 'buyer'. In 2000 he noticed a perceptible change in management's attitude towards him. In that year he did not travel abroad on as many business trips and he noticed an increased interest in his health from his employers. At this stage he was asked by the managing director to report his condition to the appellant's HR department. In October 2000, the respondent was informed that he was being transferred from his role as buyer to that of department manager. The respondent saw this as a demotion and demanded a meeting with the managing director. At this meeting it was agreed that he would return to store management. It was proposed that he be 'fast tracked' through training in order to become a store manager in the company's flagship store in the Blanchardstown shopping centre. A disagreement subsequently arose in relation to the transfer, the terms of which the plaintiff considered to be inconsistent with the assurances he had been given; this resulted in his refusing to move, which in turn gave rise to his being suspended from work by the defendant. At this juncture the plaintiff's solicitors wrote to the defendant setting out the plaintiff's understanding of the assurances he was given by the defendant, and further alleging that the defendant's conduct towards the plaintiff and the stress it had caused had resulted in his becoming ill. Although the plaintiff did subsequently report for work in the Blanchardstown

---

8. [2005] 4 IR 382, 395.
9. [2009] IESC 10, [2009] ELR 61. This case is considered in different contexts in Chapter 16 and Chapter 4.

store at the end of December 2000, he ultimately spent very little time there due to various periods of sick leave and annual leave. The plaintiff wrote to the defendant claiming that the defendant had repudiated his contract of employment and that his contract was at an end. He specifically referred to a disagreement with the store manager and to his medical advice that, in the interests of his health, he should cease working in the environment immediately. The plaintiff sought, *inter alia*, a declaration that the defendant had unlawfully repudiated his contract of employment and further sought damages for (1) breach of contract, the essence of this aspect of his claim being that the plaintiff was constructively and wrongfully dismissed by the defendant; (2) personal injuries, this aspect of his claim being formulated both in contract and in tort; and (3) defamation, as regards the incorrect description of the plaintiff as a *'new trainee'* in a managers' weekly roster.

The High Court upheld the employee's claim for wrongful dismissal. Laffoy J was [19–10] of the view that the employer's treatment of the plaintiff up until the meeting referred to above was objectively fair. However, the learned judge held that after that meeting the employer acted unreasonably and failed to have proper regard to the plaintiff's medical condition. This was particularly so after the solicitor's letter informing the employer of the stress caused by the suspension.

The decision of the High Court was reversed on appeal to the Supreme Court. In [19–11] determining whether or not the appellant's behaviour towards the respondent was such as to justify the appellant's resignation, the court restricted itself to a consideration of the matters that had occurred between the parties after the meeting referred to above. On the question of whether or not the behavior of either party was so unreasonable as to amount to a repudiatory breach of contract, Finnegan J noted the following:

1. The test is objective.
2. The test requires that the conduct of both employer and employee be considered.
3. The conduct of the parties as a whole and the accumulative effect must be looked at.
4. The conduct of the employer complained of must be unreasonable and without proper cause and its effect on the employee must be judged objectively, reasonably and sensibly in order to determine if it is such that the employee cannot be expected to put up with it.

In applying the test outlined above, Finnegan J concluded that because of:

the history of interaction between the appellant and the respondent and looking at each event individually and at the events cumulatively, [Finnegan J was] satisfied that the conduct of the appellant judged objectively was not such as to amount to a repudiation of the contract of employment. The conduct judged objectively did not evince an intention not to be bound by the contract of employment. On the other hand the conduct of the respondent was in the instances mentioned above unreasonable or in error and the employer's conduct must be considered in the light of the same. In these circumstances the purported acceptance of repudiation of the contract of employment by the respondent was neither justified nor effective.[10]

1.2. Limitations on the Power to Dismiss – Fair Procedures

[19–12] An action for wrongful dismissal may be sustained by an employee where the employer breaches that employee's right to natural and constitutional justice in dismissing him or her.[11] In *Glover v BLN Ltd.*,[12] the plaintiff was an office-holder who was dismissed from his position for misconduct in accordance with the terms of his contract of employment. The contract provided that the plaintiff could only be dismissed for misconduct of a serious kind and only after the board of directors so held and voted. The Supreme Court implied a term into the contract of employment that the inquiry into the allegation of misconduct and the deter-mination of the board of directors must be held in accordance with the principles of natural and constitutional justice. Because this was not done, the dismissal was wrongful. However, it was unclear from the decision whether the constitu-tional principles of fair procedures and natural justice applied equally to 'ordinary' employees as well as 'office-holders'.[13]

[19–13] Following the *Glover* decision, there was some confusion as to whether it should be limited to its own particular facts[14] or whether it created a general principle that the concept of natural and constitutional justice should be implied into all contracts of employment, regardless of the status of the employee.[15] It would now seem that, following the Supreme Court decision in *Mooney v An Post*,[16] there is no distinction between 'normal' employees and office-holders when implying prin-ciples of natural and constitutional justice into a contract of employment. While not clearly advocating that principles of natural and constitutional justice should be implied into all contracts of employment, Barrington J held that if:

> the contract (or the statute) provides that the employee may be dismissed for misconduct without specifying any procedure to be followed the position may be

---

10. [2009] ELR 61, 75.
11. For an assessment of the nature of the right to fair procedures enjoyed by the employee in such circumstances, see Chapter 18.
12. [1973] IR 388. For further discussion of fair procedures in the context of unfair dismissal, see Chapter 21.
13. An 'office holder' was described by Kenny J of the High Court, in *Glover v BLN Ltd.* [1973] IR 388, at p.414–415, as an office that 'is created by Act of the National Parliament, charter, statutory regulation, articles of association of company or of a body corporate formed under the authority of a statute, deed of trust, grant or by prescription'.
14. *Lupton v Allied Irish Banks Ltd.* (1984) 3 JISSL 107.
15. *Gunn v Bord an Choláiste Ealaíne is Deartha* [1990] 2 IR 168.
16. [1998] 4 IR 288, [1998] ELR 238.

more difficult. Certainly the employee is entitled to the benefit of fair procedures but what these demand will depend upon the terms of his employment and the circumstances surrounding his proposed dismissal. Certainly the minimum he is entitled to is to be informed of the charge against him and to be given an opportunity to answer it and to make submissions.[17]

Thus an employee can bring an action for wrongful dismissal where his or her employer fails to adhere to the principles of natural and constitutional justice when following a termination procedure expressly provided for in the contract of employment. Where no such procedure exists within the contract of employment, the employee is entitled, at a minimum, to be informed of the charge, be given an opportunity to answer, and be provided with the opportunity to make submissions on his or her own behalf. [19–14]

1.3. Failure to Give Notice

Undoubtedly the most common instance where there has been a wrongful dismissal is where the employer has failed to give the employee any or adequate notice of the termination of his or her employment. Damages in such circumstances are limited to the amount of the employee's salary for the period of notice to which [s]he was entitled. This issue is considered in depth in Chapter 20. [19–15]

1.4. Consequences of the Breach of Contract

Wrongful dismissal involves a repudiatory breach of the contract of employment by the employer. A repudiatory breach occurs where one of the parties to the contract clearly signals their intention that they are no longer willing to be bound by the terms of the agreement.[18] Under general principles of contract law, a repudiatory breach does not, without acceptance by the innocent party, bring a contract to an end[19] as 'an unaccepted repudiation is a thing writ in water and of no value to anybody'.[20] Thus in strict contract law terms, the innocent party may elect to affirm the contract, in which case the original contract may be deemed to have been varied, or to enter into a new contract.[21] On the other hand, the innocent party can elect to treat the breach as bringing the contract to an end and claim that [s]he has been wrongfully dismissed. [19–16]

The concept of repudiatory breach does not rest well within the context of employment contracts. In theory, if an employer were wrongfully to dismiss an employee, that employee should be entitled to choose whether or not to accept the dismissal by the employer. In practice, the situation can be very different and the employee [19–17]

---

17. [1998] 4 IR 288, 298.
18. McDermott, *Contract Law* (LexisNexis Butterworths, 2001), at pp.1074–1103.
19. *Marshall (Thomas) (Exports) Ltd. v Guinle* [1978] 3 All ER 193.
20. *per* Asquith LJ, *Howard v Pickford Tool Co Ltd.* [1951] 1 KB 417 at 421.
21. For more detailed discussion, see Chapter 4.

may have no choice but to accept his or her dismissal. Therefore, while in theory the employer's unjustified termination of the contract should not automatically end the employment relationship, in practice, it usually does and the courts will readily infer that this is automatically the case (automatic theory).[22]

[19–18] While the automatic theory will be applied by the courts in cases of outright dismissal, it would seem that repudiatory actions by the employer that fall short of outright dismissal will only bring the contract to an end at the election of the employee (elective theory). In *Bliss v South East Thames Regional Health Authority*,[23] an employer required a returning employee (a surgeon) to submit to a psychiatric examination without reasonable cause, and suspended him when he refused to do so. It was held that the employer's actions were in breach of the implied term of trust and confidence and amounted to a repudiatory action. After lifting the suspension and removing the requirement to submit to the examination, the employer offered to give the employee time to consider his position and agreed to pay him while he did so. It was held that the employer's repudiatory actions did not automatically bring the contract to an end. Furthermore, the employee had accepted his salary, thereby generating an inference that he was of the view that the contract had not been repudiated. It was held that notwithstanding his acceptance of his salary he was still entitled to accept the repudiation. This was because the employer had been prepared to give the plaintiff time to decide whether or not to return to his post and to pay his salary in the meantime: accordingly, the plaintiff could not be criticised for continuing to receive his salary and his action in so doing did not amount to an affirmation of the contract or preclude him from electing to treat the contract as at an end.

[19–19] In *Rigby v Ferodo Ltd*.[24] the employee was a lathe operator. He was a member of a union and in 1982 the employer was experiencing financial difficulties. The employer informed the union that it would seek to impose a 5 per cent wage reduction. The employer warned the union that if the proposal was not accepted, it would be imposed in any event. Ultimately, the union did not agree to the wage reduction but indicated that no industrial action would be taken if the reductions were imposed. In 1984, the employee instituted proceedings for damages. Lord Oliver summarised the employer's argument, which was based on the 'automatic theory', as follows:

> It was not contended and could not, in the light of the trial judge's findings of fact, be contended that the appellant's repudiation of its contractual obligation to pay the agreed wages in full was ever expressly accepted by Mr Rigby. Equally it is accepted that, as a general rule, an unaccepted repudiation leaves the contractual obligations of the parties unaffected. It is, however, argued that contracts of

22. *Decro-Wall SA v Practitioners in Marketing Ltd.* [1971] 1 WLR 361, [1971] 2 All ER 216.
23. [1987] ICR 700.
24. [1988] ICR 29, [1987] IRLR 61.

employment form a special category of their own, constituting an exception to the general rule. The wrongful repudiation of the fundamental obligations of either party under such a contract, it is said, not only brings to an end the relationship of employer and employee (which, as a practical matter, cannot continue in the face of a refusal to perform or accept the services which the employee has agreed to perform) but also, of itself and by itself, terminates the contract of service forthwith without the necessity of any acceptance, express or implied, by the party not in default. Thus, it is argued, when the appellant's management implemented the reduction of Mr Rigby's wages without his agreement and against his will, his contract of employment with the appellant was terminated – wrongfully terminated, no doubt, but terminated – and could no longer be claimed by him to be subsisting. His sole remedy, therefore, was to sue for damages and the only damage suffered was the amount of the shortfall from the original contractual wage over the period of 12 weeks on the expiration of which the contract could have been lawfully terminated.[25]

However, Lord Oliver held that the 'automatic theory' should not apply to the facts of the case before him. He stated that: [19–20]

> Whatever may be the position under a contract of service where the repudiation takes the form either of a walk-out by the employee or of a refusal by the employer any longer to regard the employee as his servant, I know of no principle of law that any breach which the innocent party is entitled to treat as repudiatory of the other party's obligations brings the contract to an end automatically.[26]

The House of Lords concluded that because the employee had continued to work and receive reduced payment under protest he had not accepted a variation of the terms of the contract and was entitled to seek recovery for the losses incurred.

The issue arose most recently in *Robinson v Tescom Corporation*.[27] In that case, the employee refused to agree to proposed changes (which involved increased time spent away from home while travelling) in his contract of employment. After similar changes were agreed with other employees, the employer announced that the changes were to be imposed on the employee. The employee responded in writing as follows, 'I will work under the terms of the varied job description... but under protest... I do not accept the terms and I am treating the change as a breach of contract and dismissal from the original contract.' [19–21]

The employee refused to work the new terms and conditions and, following a disciplinary meeting, was summarily dismissed for gross misconduct. The employee sued for breach of contract and claimed that the employer had unilater- [19–22]

---

25. [1988] ICR 29 at 33.
26. [1988] ICR 29 at 35.
27. Appeal no. UKEAT 0567 07 JOJ (decision of Nelson J), [2008] IRLR 408.

ally imposed the new terms, which the employee had not affirmed. The tribunal held in favour of the employer and concluded:

> There was not an affirmation of the amended contract as such, as the Claimant made it clear that he rejected the new terms and was only working to them under protest. He was however, albeit under protest, agreeing to work to the contract of employment as amended until such time as he felt a satisfactory agreement had been reached or was incapable of being reached. Whilst that process was going on however he had agreed to work under the terms of the varied job description which he then failed to do.[28]

[19–23] One could not but have sympathy with the employee in that particular case, which would appear to turn on the construction of his written response.[29] The tribunal's interpretation was that the employee's written response indicated that he was willing to work the new terms – albeit under protest – and yet then refused to do so. In other words, he had agreed to work under the new terms until the matter was resolved. His failure to follow reasonable instructions under the terms of the contract was unjustifiable.

[19–24] Much of the foregoing debate surrounding the 'automatic' and 'elective' theories may seem academic because the reality is that the employee may rarely have a choice as to whether [s]he remains in his or her job. As has been noted:

> The question of which theory (elective or automatic) is to be preferred remains at best undecided; in the context of common law claims it has the same intellectual fascination as the question as to how many angels may dance on the head of a pin and (except perhaps in a case where some collateral or incidental matter relies upon the technical continued existence of the contract) about as much practical relevance.[30]

However, the question as to whether or not the purported dismissal by an employer automatically brings the relationship to an end can have significant implications on the nature of the remedies that the employee may be entitled to. For example, whether the employee still has a contractual relationship with the employer could be significant should that employee seek injunctive relief preventing his dismissal.[31]

---

28. para.31.
29. White, *Case Comment: Working Under Protest and Variation of Employment Terms* [2008] ILJ 365.
30. Smith and Thomas, *Smith & Wood's Employment Law* (9th ed., Oxford University Press, 2008), at p.437.
31. For detailed discussion of the remedies available to an employee in such circumstances, see Chapter 24.

1.5. Summary Dismissal

An employer may dismiss an employee without notice provided [s]he has suffi- [19–25]
cient cause.[32] This form of dismissal is otherwise known as summary dismissal.
Summary dismissal can only be justified in exceptional circumstances and is
acceptable where it can be proven that the *employee's* actions were so serious that
they amounted to a repudiation of the essential terms of the contract.[33] The test
to be applied was outlined by Lord Jauncey in *Neary v Dean of Westminister*[34]
as follows: 'conduct amounting to gross misconduct justifying dismissal must so
undermine the trust and confidence which is inherent in the particular contract
of employment that the master should no longer be required to retain the servant
in his employment'.[35]

Whether the behavior of the employee amounts to a repudiatory breach is a ques- [19–26]
tion of fact and will depend on the circumstances of each case. Much will depend
on the nature of the misconduct, the nature of the employer's business, and the
position of the employee. The test as to what kind of misconduct would justify
instant dismissal was summarised as follows by Kenny J in *Glover v BLN Ltd.*[36]: 'all
that one can say about serious misconduct is that it is misconduct which the court
regards as being grave and deliberate. And the standards to be applied in deciding
the matter are those of men and not of angels.'[37]

Thus in *Pepper v Webb*,[38] a refusal by an employee to obey lawful and reason- [19–27]
able orders and the use of foul and abusive language, together with previous incidents of misconduct, amounted to a repudiation of the contract of employment
by the employee. Similarly, in *Sinclair v Neighbour*,[39] the dismissal of a manager
who removed some money from the till and left an IOU was upheld. While the
manager may have intended to return the money, given the position of trust he
held, his employer regarded his behavior as dishonest and his subsequent dismissal
was justified. Single acts of negligence do not generally amount to conduct justifying dismissal unless the consequences or potential consequences of such negligence are particularly severe.[40]

---

32. See Chapter 18 and Chapter 20.
33. *Jupiter General Insurance Co v Shroff* [1937] 3 All ER 67.
34. [1999] IRLR 288.
35. [1999] IRLR 288, 288.
36. [1973] IR 388.
37. [1973] IR 388 at 405.
38. [1969] 2 All ER 216, [1969] 1 WLR 514. However, that decision can be contrasted with that in
Wilson v Raucher [1974] ICR 428, where a gardener also swore at his employer. In that case,
his behavior was not considered to amount to gross misconduct as the employer's conduct
had provoked the gardener's reaction. Furthermore, the gardener's outburst towards the
employer was not a 'last straw' situation like that in *Pepper*.
39. [1967] 2 QB 279, [1967] 2 WLR 1, [1966] 3 All ER 988.
40. *Taylor v Alidair Ltd.* [1978] ICR 445, [1978] IRLR 82.

1.6. Continued Importance of Wrongful Dismissal

[19–28] Since the introduction of the unfair dismissals legislation, the importance of the common law action for wrongful dismissal has diminished somewhat. As we have seen elsewhere,[41] the statutory regime is inexpensive in that disputes may first be referred to a Rights Commissioner or the tribunal and not a civil court; the burden of proof favours the employee and the remedies of re-instatement and re-engagement, which would theoretically allow the employee to get his or her job back, are available. This is compounded by the fact that in accordance with s.15 of the Unfair Dismissals Act 1977, once an employee initiates proceedings for unfair dismissal they are precluded from taking proceedings for wrongful dismissal in respect of that dismissal. Furthermore, damages are generally the only remedy available in an action for wrongful dismissal.

[19–29] Notwithstanding these facts, for many employees an action for wrongful dismissal can have considerable advantages over an action for unfair dismissal.

- First, the statutory protection provided only applies to employees who satisfy minimum service criteria[42]; no such requirement is necessary for the wrongful dismissal action.
- Secondly, compensation for unfair dismissal is limited to a maximum of two years' of the employee's salary.[43] The award of compensation in wrongful dismissal claims is limited to the amount of wages, however, that the employee would have been paid during the notice period. For a high-earning employee with a long notice period, a claim for wrongful dismissal could provide him or her with substantially more damages than a claim for unfair dismissal ever could.
- Thirdly, a claim for unfair dismissal under the legislation is statute-barred if not initiated within six months of the date of the employee's dismissal.[44] An action for wrongful dismissal is subject to a much greater limitation period of six years.[45]
- Finally, as is considered in Chapter 16, where an employee suffers personal injuries (including psychiatric injuries) as a result of his dismissal (as distinct from in the period *before* such dismissal) then [s]he is precluded from suing at common law in respect of such injuries and also taking the dismissal itself before the EAT under the unfair dismissals legislation.

---

41. See Chapter 21.
42. s.2(1)(a) Unfair Dismissals Act 1977.
43. s.7(1)(c) Unfair Dismissals Act 1977.
44. s.8(2) *ibid.* Section 7 of the Unfair Dismissals (Amendment) Act 1993 provides that this period may be extended to a maximum of 12 months in exceptional circumstances.
45. s.11 Statute of Limitations 1957.

2. Frustration of Contract

A contract of employment will be terminated by frustration where performance   [19–30]
of the contract becomes impossible to perform due to an unforeseen event outside
the control of either party.[46] In such situations the contract is terminated by operation of law.[47] Lord Radcliffe, in *Davis Contractors v Fareham UDC*,[48] held that
frustration occurs:

> whenever the law recognizes that without default of either party a contractual obli-
> gation has become incapable of being performed because the circumstances in
> which performance is called for would render it a thing radically different from
> that which was undertaken by the contract. *No haec in foedera veni.* It was not this
> I promised to do.[49]

Because the doctrine arises by operation of law, an employee whose contract of   [19–31]
employment has been terminated by frustration cannot avail of the statutory
protection of unfair dismissals legislation as there is no dismissal by the employer.[50]
The temptation of evading the statutory protection available to employees where
the contract has been terminated may prove too much to an employer who might
attempt to disguise what was in fact a dismissal as a frustrating event. Consequently,
the courts will closely scrutinise the application of the doctrine in employment law
cases. In *Zuphen v Kelly Technical Services*,[51] the plaintiffs were South African techni-
cians who were recruited under contracts by the defendant recruitment agencies to
work in Ireland. The defendants had anticipated that the plaintiffs would work for
Éircom Plc. However, when the defendants' contractual relationship with Éircom
Plc fell through, the defendants contended that the contracts of employment with
the plaintiffs had been frustrated as a result of loss of the Éircom Plc contract. In
the High Court it was held that the contract between the plaintiffs and the defendants had not been frustrated by the events. In particular, the court noted that the
defendants continued to seek alternative employment for the plaintiffs after the
arrangements with Éircom Plc had fallen through and consequently was of the
view that the contract had not been rendered impossible to perform by the events
in question. In delivering his judgment, Murphy J did warn of the dangers of
applying the doctrine without caution in cases involving employment contracts:

> the relationship entered into with the plaintiffs was one of master and servant to
> use the old fashioned term. It seems to me to be inappropriate in that circumstance

---

46. *Taylor v Caldwell* (1863) B. & S. 826.
47. Generally, see Clark, *Contract Law in Ireland* (6th ed., Thomson Round Hall, 2008), at
    pp.569–588; McDermott, *Contract Law* (LexisNexis Butterworths, 2001), ch.20; and Kelly,
    'Frustration and Employment Contracts', 11 (1) *CLP* (2004), 286.
48. [1956] AC 696.
49. [1956] AC 696 at 728.
50. For further discussion, see Chapter 21.
51. [2000] IEHC 117, [2000] ELR 277.

to apply a strict contract law approach to employment disputes. Attempts to apply tend to obscure the social implications of certain kinds of conduct or events by reducing them to legalistic principles.[52]

2.1. Illness

[19–32] The long-term illness of the employee is one of the most common reasons pleaded as a frustrating event by the employer.[53] Such a plea will succeed when, due to the employee's unavoidable absence, it has become impossible to continue with the contract of employment. In *Flynn v Great Northern Railway Co*,[54] Budd J stated that whether or not illness constituted a frustrating event depended on whether the incapacity was such as to frustrate the business object of the engagement.[55]

[19–33] Whether or not the illness will have such an effect on the contract is not a straight-forward factual issue and will depend on the length of the employee's absence, his or her prospects for recovery, and the importance of the employee's role to the business. The test to be applied in determining whether or not the illness of the employee will frustrate the contract of employment was elaborated upon by the tribunal in *Donegal County Council v Langan*.[56] In that case, the employee worked as a general labourer since 1974. Between 1985 and 1988 the employee was unable to work due to back pain. While on sick leave he submitted sick certificates to his employer. In April 1988 he was informed by his employer that it was not the employer's intention to re-employ him. In July 1988 the employee was declared medically fit. In finding that the contract of employment had not been frustrated, the tribunal took into consideration the following factors:

(i)   the length of the previous employment.
(ii)   how long it had been expected that the employment would last.
(iii) the nature of the job.
(iv)   the nature, length and effect of the illness or disabling event.
(v)   the need of the employer for the work to be done.
(vi)   whether wages have continued to be paid.
(vii) the actions of the employer in relation to the employment.
(viii) whether consideration was given to retaining the employee on the books if not in employment.
(ix)   whether the employer discussed with the employee and his trade union the employee's problems and prospects.

---

52. [2000] ELR 277, 291.
53. For greater discussion in the context of unfair dismissal, see Chapter 21.
54. (1953) 89 ILTR 46.
55. *ibid.*, at 59.
56. UD 143/89. See also *Marshall v Harland and Wolff Ltd.* [1972] 1WLR 899, [1972] 2 All ER 715, [1972] ICR 97, [1972] IRLR 90; and *Egg Stores (Stamford Hill) Ltd. v Leibovici* [1977] ICR 260, [1976] IRLR 376.

(x) whether adequate medical investigation was carried out…

(xi) Whether, in all the circumstances, a reasonable employer could be expected to wait any longer.

A contract of employment may still be held to have been frustrated despite the **[19–34]** fact that the employee has produced medical certificates. In *Hart v Marshall & Sons (Bulwell) Ltd.*,[57] the employee contracted dermatitis, which caused him to be absent from work for 20 months. He kept his employer constantly informed of his condition by forwarding medical certificates. The medical certificates were received by the employer, who did not respond. When the employee was fit to return to work he was informed that he had been replaced. It was held that the employee's contract of employment had been frustrated. Holland and Burnett have explained this decision on the basis that the provision of medical certificates by the employee did not necessarily exclude frustration as being the cause of the termination. The doctrine arises by the operation of law and it is something that the parties to the agreement cannot control. Thus whether or not medical certificates are supplied and whether or not they are accepted is not determinative of the issue; the frustrating event 'has either happened or not happened'.[58]

2.2. Imprisonment

The contract of employment may be frustrated by the imprisonment of the **[19–35]** employee. Again, whether a prison sentence will amount to a frustrating event will depend on the nature of the employee's work and the length of the sentence. In *Hare v Murphy Brothers*,[59] the Court of Appeal of England and Wales held that the employee's contract of employment was frustrated when he was sentenced to 12 months' imprisonment for an assault not connected with the work. Lord Denning set out the factors to be taken into consideration when deciding whether a prison sentence amounted to a frustrating event:

> you must look at the length of time he has been employed, the position which he held, and, of course, most importantly of all, the length of time which he is likely to be away from his work and unable to perform it – and the importance of getting someone else to do his job in the meantime … if it then appears that his job has been effectively brought to an end, the contract is frustrated.[60]

It would appear that an employee cannot plead that because his or her imprison- **[19–36]** ment was his or her fault it was self-induced and therefore not a frustrating event. In *Shepherd FC & Co Ltd. v Jerrom*,[61] an apprentice was sentenced to at least six months in a borstal while working under a four-year apprenticeship contract. The court held that the contract had been frustrated given the length of the sentence

---

57. [1977] 1 WLR 1067, [1978] 2 All ER 413, [1977] ICR 539.
58. Holland and Burnett, *Employment Law* (Oxford University Press, 2006), at 237.
59. [1974] 3 All ER 940, [1974] ICR 603.
60. [1974] ICR 603 at 607.
61. [1987] QB 301.

in comparison to the length of the apprenticeship. The court also held that the employee could not claim that his imprisonment was 'self-induced' and therefore could not be considered a frustrating event. To allow such a claim, the court stated, would be 'an affront to common sense, an infringement of... the fundamental legal and moral rule that a man should not be allowed to take advantage of his own wrong'.[62]

2.3. Death or Dissolution

[19–37] In brief, the death of one of the parties to the contract of employment will generally bring an end to the contract where it is one that requires personal performance.[63] Similarly, if the contract is of a personal character, then a contract of employment with a partnership which has dissolved due to the death of one of the partners will be terminated upon the dissolution of the partnership.[64]

3. Mutual Consent

[19–38] The contract of employment may be terminated by the mutual consent of the parties. Consent must be genuinely and voluntarily given by both parties. Thus the courts will be wary of what Selwyn termed the 'did he jump or was he pushed' question.[65] If the employee's consent was vitiated in some way by the wrongful actions of the employer, then the employee's 'agreement' to end the contract will amount to a dismissal and may be subject to the protection of the unfair dismissals legislation or a claim for wrongful dismissal. In *O'Reilly v Minister of Industry and Commerce Ireland and the Attorney General*,[66] the plaintff had worked for the civil service for over 45 years. He was called to the office of his superior, Mr Dorgan, and his retirement from the civil service was discussed. The plaintiff understood from the meeting that he was no longer wanted and that he had no choice in the matter of retirement. It was not made clear to the plaintiff at this meeting that he could decide against voluntary retirement if he so wished. A couple of days later the plaintiff submitted his resignation. The High Court held that the resignation was not a voluntary one. Carroll J concluded:

> I am satisfied that Mr O'Reilly was deeply shocked when the question of his retirement was raised. He could not think clearly. There were long silences and it is not an exaggeration to say the he was devastated. Mr Dorgan was aware of his condition. It was not made clear to Mr O'Reilly by Mr Dorgan that he was not talking about compulsory retirement for Mr O'Reilly, that he was only raising the

---

62. [1987] QB 301 at 325.
63. *Stubbs v Holywell Rly Co* (1867) LR 2 Exch. 311.
64. *Harvey v Tivoli (Manchester) Ltd.* (1907) 23 TLR 592.
65. Selwyn, *Selwyn's Law of Employment* (15th ed., Oxford University Press, 2008), at p.416.
66. [1997] ELR 48.

question of retirement on a voluntary basis, that he did have a choice, and that he could decide against voluntary retirement. Why was compulsory retirement under the *Civil Service Regulations Act* mentioned at all when it had nothing to do with the purpose of the meeting? In my opinion, the whole tenor of the conversation as far as Mr O'Reilly was concerned, was that he was to retire because the Minister and Mr Dorgan wanted him to. Mr O'Reilly had reasonable grounds for taking that view because of the way the interview progressed. He was not told to the contrary even though he clearly indicated his understanding of what was being said to him.[67]

In *Sandhu v Jan de Rijk Transport*,[68] the Court of Appeal of England and Wales [19–39] was asked to consider a similar issue. In that case, the employee was called to a meeting, where he was informed that his contract was going to be terminated. The employee then reached an agreement with his employer regarding his departure. It was held that the employee's resignation was not one that was genuine or voluntary. The employee had very little time to consider his options and in particular did not have the opportunity of seeking independent advice on the matter. In these circumstances his resignation was actually considered to be a dismissal.

4. Employer's Insolvency

The insolvency of the employer will terminate the contract of employment but [19–40] will not be considered a frustrating event as the employer is deemed to be responsible for the solvency of the business. The legal effect that the employer's financial difficulties will have on the employee's contract of employment will depend on whether the business has entered into liquidation or receivership.[69]

4.1. Liquidation
An employer's business may enter into liquidation either by way of: (a) a compul- [19–41] sory winding up order of the court, or (b) on a voluntary basis through a creditors' voluntary winding up or a members' voluntary winding up.[70] A winding-up order constitutes the end of the company and will lead to the dismissal of the employee.[71]

In the case of a compulsory court winding up, two scenarios may arise for the [19–42] employee whose employment is being terminated. In the first, the employment

---

67. [1997] ELR 48, 51.
68. [2007] EWCA Civ 430, [2007] ICR 1137, [2007] IRLR 519.
69. Generally, see Barrett, 'The Effect of Insolvency on the Contract of Employment', 3(1) *DULJ* (1996), 15. See further discussion of the relevant European Community and Irish Laws in respect of Transfer of Undertakings in Chapter 23.
70. Generally, see Courtney, *The Law of Private Companies* (2nd ed., LexisNexis Butterworths, 2002), ch.25.
71. Generally, see Regan (ed.), *Employment Law* (Tottel Publishing, 2009), ch.12.

ceases from the time the order is made. Where it is the employer who seeks to bring the employment to an end, then the winding-up order will constitute notice of dismissal and the employee may, depending on the circumstances, have an action for wrongful dismissal.[72] Where the employment is terminated at the behest of the employee following a court winding-up order, then the order is considered a repudiation of the contract of employment by the employer, which is accepted by the employee. In the second scenario, the employee continues to be employed after the making of the winding-up order. In such circumstances, the traditional view has been that the winding-up order operated as notice to the employee that the employer could no longer fulfill his or her contractual obligations to the employee and accordingly that the contract of employment was being terminated.[73] An alternative approach was adopted by the court in *Re English Joint Stock Bank, ex parte Harding*,[74] where Wood J stated:

> if the company be a continuing company (and it is to be observed that the appointment of an official liquidator does not destroy a company – the official liquidator is, in effect, the company), and there be actual business to occupy the services of clerks – they must then, I think, go on under the old contract.[75]

[19–43] However, the traditional approach was restated in *Re Oriental Bank Corporation*.[76] In that case, the court held that the winding-up order constituted valid notice operating from the date of the order. The employee had continued to work for more than three months after the date of the winding-up order. As the employee's notice period was three months, it was held that his claim for damages because of the employer's failure to provide adequate notice was unsuccessful. In *Re Forster & Co Ltd., ex parte Schumann*,[77] the court held that the winding-up order constituted implied notice of discharge of the contract of employment. This was so notwithstanding the fact that the employee in question was not aware that the order would change his status and consequently had not sought alternative employment. His claim for damages was rejected. The principle that the winding-up order constitutes notice of dismissal was upheld by the Irish High Court on two separate occasions since.[78] However, in *Re Evanhenry Ltd.*, Murphy J did state that the winding-up order was only an 'ordinary presumption as to termination'.[79]

---

72. *In re General Rolling Stock Company* (1866) LR 1 Eq. 346.
73. Graham, 'The Effect of Liquidation on Contracts of Service', 15 *MLR* (1952) 48.
74. (1867) LR 3 eq. 341.
75. *ibid.* See also Barrett, 'The Effect of Insolvency on the Contract of Employment', 18 *DULJ* (1996), 15 at 18, where the author agreed with Wood J, arguing that 'a more convincing basis for a finding that a contractual repudiation had occurred might be that when a compulsory winding-up order is made against a company, this is tantamount to a renunciation of contractual obligations from the date on which the company is *finally dissolved*'.
76. (1886) 32 ch. D 366.
77. (1887–88) 19 LR IR 240.
78. *Donnelly v Gleeson*, High Court, unreported, 11 July 1978; and *Evanhenry Ltd., in re* High Court, unreported, 15 May 1986.
79. *Evanhenry Ltd., in re* High Court, unreported, 15 May 1986.

Barrett has criticised the approach adopted in *Re Oriental* and *Re Forster* on two **[19–44]** grounds.[80] First, he has pointed out that it is a general requirement for valid notice that the date of termination be either stated or ascertainable and that requirement is generally not satisfied in circumstances where the employee continues to work after the winding-up order. Secondly, the idea that 'the winding-up order, which is advertised in the newspapers, constitutes notice to all the world of the winding-up'[81] is capable of producing unjust results on the basis that it is dependent first, on the employee reading the particular newspaper containing the notice, and second, on whether or not [s]he understands the impact such a notice has on his or her contract of employment.

There may be circumstances in which the winding-up order is not deemed to be **[19–45]** notice of dismissal, for example, where the liquidator is held to have implicitly waived the notice of dismissal. In *Dodd v Local Stores (Trading) Ltd.*,[82] the claimants were employed in a number of retail shops trading under the name 'Seven-Eleven'. Following the appointment of a receiver, a liquidator was appointed to the ailing company on 22 April 1991. The shops continued to trade following the appointment of the liquidator. The liquidator did not deal with or communicate to the staff and all matters relating to staff were dealt with by the receiver. The claimants' trade union had dealings with the receiver but only heard of the appointment of the liquidator unofficially 'through the grapevine'. At various dates between May and July 1991, the claimants were dismissed without notice. The tribunal held that the liquidator, who had utterly failed to communicate with the employees, had waived the notice of discharge on the winding-up order. Thus, the claimants were dismissed without due notice and were therefore entitled to an award of damages. *Dodd* can be contrasted with *Irish Shipping Ltd. v Byrne and the Minister for Labour*[83] where the liquidator expressly terminated the appointment of the respondents by writing letters to the employees immediately after his appointment. Thus in that case there could be no doubt that the liquidator had not, either explicitly or implicitly, waived notice of discharge on the winding up order.

In other circumstances it can be argued that the liquidator's appointment does not **[19–46]** serve as notice of the discharge of the contract because the employee's continued employment is based on the creation of a new contract. In *Re Evanhenry Ltd.*,[84] the court held that the continuing employment of the two employees for more than three months after the appointment of the liquidator was an indication that, either expressly or implicitly, the liquidator had agreed with the employees to continue working but under new contracts of employment (although the terms were very similar to those of the former contracts). However, the courts will not readily infer

---

80. Barrett, 'The Effect of Insolvency on the Contract of Employment', 18 *DULJ* (1996), 15 at 19 *et seq.*
81. *per* Romilly MR, *Re General Rolling Stock Co Ltd.* (1866) LR 1 Eq. 346 at 347.
82. [1992] ELR 61.
83. [1987] IR 468.
84. High Court, unreported, 15 May 1986.

the creation of such a new contract and in *Irish Shipping Ltd. v Byrne*,[85] the court refused to imply a new contract notwithstanding the fact that the employees had continued to work for four months after their 'dismissal' by the liquidator.

In the case of a voluntary liquidation,[86] whether it occurs by way of a creditors' winding-up or a members' winding-up, it would seem that the resolution for the voluntary winding-up will act as notice of termination in cases where the employee continues in employment after the passing of the resolution.[87]

4.2. Receivership

[19–47] A receiver is appointed to a company 'whose function it is to "receive" a debtor's assets and property for and on behalf of a creditor who is entitled to take them in satisfaction of the debtor's obligations'.[88] A receiver may be appointed by a debenture holder or by the court.[89] Where the receiver is appointed on foot of a debenture [s]he is deemed to be the agent of the company and it has been held that his or her appointment does not act as notice of termination of the contract of employment.[90] However, this statement can be qualified in three situations.

- First, where the appointment of the receiver is accompanied by the sale of the business; that will operate to discharge the contracts of employment.
- Secondly, where a receiver and manager enters into a new agreement with the employee that is inconsistent with his or her original contract of employment, that new agreement may discharge the old contract of employment.
- Thirdly, where the role of 'receiver-manager' is inconsistent with the role and function of a particular employee, i.e. the managing director, then the appointment of the 'receiver-manager' may have the effect of discharging the contract of employment of that employee.[91]

---

85. [1987] IR 468.
86. Generally, see Courtney, *The Law of Private Companies* (2nd ed., LexisNexis Butterworths, 2002), ch.25.
87. *per* Chatterton VC, *Re Forster & Co, ex parte Schumann* (1887) 19 LR IR 240 at 244.
88. Courtney, *The Law of Private Companies* (2nd ed., LexisNexis Butterworths, 2002), ch.25 at pp.1275–1276.
89. For detailed analysis, see Courtney, *ibid.*, ch.25.
90. *Griffiths v Secretary of State for Social Services* [1974] QB 468, [1973] 3 WLR 831, [1973] All ER 1184.
91. *ibid.*, at 485–486.

CHAPTER 20

Notice

Introduction

The concept of the notice to which an employee who is to be dismissed is entitled is extremely important within Irish employment law. This is for a number of reasons, not least because, owing to the rule at common law that an employer is entitled to dismiss an employee for no reason or no sufficient reason, the only redress for an employee who has been dismissed and to whom the terms of the unfair dismissals acts do not apply may be compensation for unpaid notice. Conversely, from the standpoint of the employer, and outside of the context of the statutory unfair dismissals situation, it will generally be the case that provided that [s]he gives the employee appropriate notice of his or her impending dismissal (or pays the employee *in lieu* of such notice), the employee has no further cause of action against him or her. [20–01]

Accordingly, it is vital that an employer is aware of the extent of notice to which the employee is entitled. Such entitlements derive both from contract and from statute and these are now assessed in turn.

1. Contractual Notice Entitlements

The contract of employment may be terminated whenever either party provides the other with the appropriate notice of such termination. Furthermore, once notice has been given, it can only be withdrawn by the agreement of the parties.[1] Where the contract is silent as to the length of the notice period, the courts will imply a reasonable notice period, which will be calculated based *inter alia* on the nature of the employee's work,[2] the length of service of the employee, and the custom and practice in the industry.[3] The test of what constitutes reasonable notice was explained by Gilligan J in *Carey v Independent Newspapers (Ireland) Ltd.*[4] as follows: [20–02]

---

1. *Riordan v War Office* [1959] 1 WLR 1046, [1959] 3 All ER 552.
2. *Lyons v MF Kent (International) Ltd.* [1996] ELR 103.
3. *Produce Brokers Co Ltd. v Olympia and Cake Co Ltd.*[1916] 1 AC 314, [1916] 2 KB 296.
4. [2004] 3 IR 52, 77, [2004] ELR 45.

what is a reasonable notice, depends upon the capacity in which the employee is engaged, the general standing in the community of the class of persons, having regard to their profession, to which the employee belongs, the probable facility or difficulty the employee would have in procuring other employment in case of dismissal, having regard to the demand for persons of that profession, and the general character of the services which the engagement contemplates.[5]

[20–03] Communication of the notice period to the other party must be clear and certain.[6] In *Morris v CH Bailey Ltd.*,[7] a notice of termination was communicated to the plaintiff's union but not to him personally. The Court of Appeal held that the communication of the notice was ineffective and not valid.

The contract of employment only comes to an end after the expiration of the notice period irrespective of whether the parties have agreed that the employee shall receive payment in lieu of notice.[8]

1.1. Garden Leave Clauses

[20–04] An employer may seek to include a very long notice period in the contract of employment, which might act as a form of restraint on the employee should [s]he serve notice with the intention to set up in competition or join a competitor. During this notice period the employer will continue to pay the employee his or her salary and, as we have already seen, [s]he will be entitled to all benefits associated with being an employee, but will not be required to work – leaving time for him or her to 'tend the garden'. As a corollary, the employee will be subject to a continuing duty of fidelity to his or her employer, thereby preventing him or her from working for a competitor during the notice period or from disclosing trade secrets and other information to the employer's competitors.[9] Thus the employee has the benefit of being paid while the employer can ensure that the employee does not divulge important trade secrets or other information.

[20–05] A garden leave clause may be construed or implied from the terms of notice contained in the contract of employment. In such circumstances, an employer may agree to continue to pay the employee during the notice period, but not expect him or her to work. Because of his or her duty of fidelity, that employee will be restrained from acting contrary to his or her employer's best interests, thereby protecting the employer's interests during the notice period. However, employers must be careful about relying on long notice periods as a disguised means of enforcing a garden leave clause in that, as we have discussed

---

5. Expressly approving the words of Beck J in *Speakman v Calgary (City)* (1908) 9 WWR 264 at 265.
6. *Bolands Ltd. v Ward and Others* [1987] IESC 1, [1988] ILRM 382.
7. [1969] 2 Lloyd's Rep 215, CA.
8. *Adams v GKN Sankey Ltd.* [1980] IRLR 416.
9. *Evening Standard Co Ltd. v Henderson* [1987] ICR 588.

elsewhere,[10] an employee may have an implied right to be provided with work by his or her employer.[11] In such circumstances, the courts may be reluctant to enforce an implied garden leave term on the basis that the employer's refusal to provide work to the employee could be damaging to his or her future career and might therefore be unduly restrictive.[12] Thus an employer paying an employee his or her salary *in lieu* of notice may find that [s]he is in breach of contract for failing to provide that employee with work. As a result of such a breach, the employee could treat the employer's actions as having terminated the contract of employment, thereby freeing the employee immediately to commence employment with a competitor.

Given the dangers of relying on an implied term in these circumstances, an [20–06] employer would be on a more secure legal footing if an express garden leave term were incorporated into the contract of employment. However, even then difficulties may arise regarding the enforceability of such clauses. Because a garden leave clause is a form of restraint, the courts will treat such clauses in a similar manner to restrictive covenants and will examine carefully whether the restraint is necessary to protect the employer's legitimate interests.[13] That said, once an employer can establish that the period of leave was reasonably necessary to protect those interests, the courts may be willing to enforce the clause. For example, in *Eurobrokers Ltd. v Rabey*,[14] the court upheld a six-month express garden leave clause. The employer satisfied the court that the period was necessary in the circumstances. The employee had built up relationships with the employer's customers at his employer's expense and the six-month period was considered a reasonable period in which to allow the employer to re-establish a relationship with those customers, thereby nullifying the potential impact of the employee's departure.

The validity and enforceability of a garden leave clause may, furthermore, depend [20–07] on whether it is followed by a post-employment restraint of trade clause. If the combined effect of both terms proves to be unreasonably restrictive, the courts may not fully enforce both terms.[15]

An express garden leave clause can provide much security and effective protection [20–08] to an employer seeking to limit the damage caused by the departure of a valuable employee to a competing rival. While garden leave clauses may be more expensive (for the employer) than restraint of trade clauses, they can be more effective as it is more likely that they will be enforced by the courts, particularly if reasonable in their duration.

---

10. See the detailed discussion in Chapter 4 of the employee's implied right to work.
11. *Cronin v Eircom Ltd.* [2006] IEHC 380, [2007] 3 IR 104, [2007] ELR 84; *William Hill Organisation v Tucker* [1999] ICR 291, [1998] IRLR 313, CA.
12. *William Hill Organisation v Tucker* [1999] ICR 291, [1998] IRLR 313, CA.
13. See the discussion in Chapter 4 on restrictive covenants.
14. [1995] IRLR 206.
15. *Credit Suisse Asset Management Ltd. v Armstrong* [1996] ICR 882, [1996] IRLR 450.

2. Statutory Minimum Notice Entitlements

[20–09] Having examined the contractual position, we now turn to consider the basic statutory entitlements of an employee to notice.[16] Such entitlements are laid out in the Minimum Notice and Terms of Employment Act of 1973.[17] The most important practical effect of the legislation is that workers who have worked for the employer for a continuous period of 13 weeks or more[18] are provided with a minimum statutory entitlement of at least one week's notice of the impending termination of their employment relationship, with such minimum statutory notice period increasing depending on the length of service of the employee. In addition (albeit less significantly), the Act also provides that an employee who has been in continuous employment with an employer for at least 13 weeks must give one week's notice of his or her intention to terminate his or her contract of employment.[19]

2.1. Circumstances in Which Statutory Notice Requirements Do Not Apply

[20–10] The general notice provisions contained in the 1973 Act do not apply in certain listed circumstances. Thus under s.3 it is provided that the Act does not apply to:

- an employee who is normally expected to work for his employer for less than 21 hours a week[20];
- employment by an employer who is the parent, grandparent, step-parent, child, step-child, grandchild, sibling or half-sibling of the employee, where the employee is a member of the employer's household and where the place of employment is a private dwelling house or farm in or on which both the employee and employer reside[21];
- employment in the civil service[22] other than in an unestablished position[23];

---

16. The notice requirements in question only apply to employees rather than sub-contractors or self-employed persons with whom an employer has a contract for services: *Employee v Employer* MN 106/2007.
17. This Act operates with the Protection of Employees (Part-Time Work) Act of 2001 such that its terms apply to part-time workers as defined under the 2001 Act. Generally see Kerr, *Irish Employment Legislation* (Round Hall Sweet and Maxwell, 2000), at pp.A-53 *et seq.*
18. For assessment of whether there had been 13 weeks' continuous service in a controversial situation see *Employee v Employer* MN 299/2007.
19. s.6 Minimum Notice and Terms of Employment Act 1973. This is subject to the right of the employee to give counter-notice under s.10 of the Redundancy Payments Act 1967 or to give notice of intention to claim redundancy payment in respect of lay off or short time under s.12 of the 1967 Act.
20. s.3(1)(a) Minimum Notice and Terms of Employment Act 1973, as substituted by s.3 of the Protection of Employees (Employers' Insolvency) Act 1984.
21. s.3(1)(b) *ibid.*
22. Within the meaning of the Civil Service Commissioners Act 1956.
23. s.3(1)(c) Minimum Notice and Terms of Employment Act 1973.

- employment as a member of the Permanent Defence Forces other than a temporary member of the army nursing service[24];
- employment as a member of the gardaí[25]; and
- employment under an employment agreement pursuant to Part II or Part IV of the Merchant Shipping Act.[26]

In addition, the Minister may, by regulations, provide for further categories of [20–11] employment to which the Act shall not apply,[27] or may, alternatively, provide that particular sections of the Act *shall* apply to a designated class of employment.[28]

2.2. Summary Dismissal and Statutory Notice

Section 8 of the 1973 Act provides that the terms of the Act do not prevent an [20–12] employer from summarily dismissing an employee *without notice* for misconduct[29]. Equally, and for obvious reasons (considered in Chapters 4 and 18), it would be necessary that such summary dismissal take place in accordance both with the terms of the employee's contract and also that any disciplinary process resulting in such dismissal should be conducted in accordance with the rules of natural and constitutional justice. For now it is worth noting that because the concept of misconduct is not defined within the 1973 Act,[30] and because of the rules relating to interlocutory injunctions which are considered in Chapter 24, the act of summary dismissal without notice is a step that should only be taken in the most obvious cases of gross misconduct.[31]

In this respect, the EAT has tended to take a very strict view of what is necessary [20–13] in order for a summary dismissal to be justified.[32] Thus in one case, the EAT, in holding that the onus for showing that the dismissal was for misconduct rested with the employer, rejected the employer's claim that a summary dismissal was warranted, on the basis that the employer had only heard hearsay evidence before coming to its decision.[33] Similarly the EAT awarded an employee damages for

---

24. s.3(1)(d) *ibid.*
25. s.3(1)(e) *ibid.*
26. s.3(1)(f) *ibid.*
27. s.3(2) *ibid.*
28. s.3(3) *ibid.* Any such orders under s.3 may be amended or revoked by further ministerial order: s.3(5) *ibid.*
29. s.8 *ibid.*
30. Indeed, it is impossible to define the misconduct that will justify summary dismissal: *Glover v BLN Ltd.* [1973] IR 388.
31. In *Employee v Employer* MN 699/2007, the respondent summarily dismissed the claimant (who had herself given notice of her resignation) in circumstances where it was learned that she was about to start work with a neighbouring competitor of the respondent – a course of action that the respondent alleged represented a breach of her contract.
32. See, for example, *Creed v KMP Co-Op Society Ltd.* [1991] ELR 140.
33. *Employee v 2 Employers* MN 178/2006.

failure to give notice, while apparently refusing to decide whether there had been a legitimate and fair summary dismissal. In this case, and despite having accepted that 'there may have been misconduct on the part of the employee', the EAT concluded nonetheless that, in light of the fact that another employee had claimed responsibility for such misconduct, it would award the appellant compensation for failure to give notice.[34] If this is the approach the EAT will continue to take, then it is submitted that the thrust of s.8 of the 1973 Act is rendered useless, because in essence the determination seems to suggest that whereas an employer is entitled under the Act to justify summary dismissal by reference to misconduct on the part of the employee and whereas the EAT must be satisfied that the dismissal for misconduct was justifiable, yet it will also be, at best, reluctant to decide whether or not such misconduct is present other than in the context of an unfair dismissals hearing.

[20–14] In reality, moreover, it is arguable that in these cases the EAT engaged in a process that is simply not warranted under the terms of the 1973 Act. After all, on one analysis, s.8 of the 1973 Act simply permits an employer to dismiss an employee summarily and without notice. Should this dismissal be unfair or in breach of natural and constitutional justice or the employee's contract, then that employee has a range of remedies available to him or her, ranging from an unfair dismissals action to a claim for injunctive relief in the High Court, and these are the proper fora for vindicating the rights of the employee. Under s.8 of the 1973 Act, on the other hand, all that is necessary (in order to avoid obligations *vis-à-vis* notice) is for the employer to show that, rightly or wrongly, the dismissal *was* for misconduct, and where this can be done, then the terms of s.8 should apply and no stand-alone claim for notice should be granted. As against this, however, it may also be argued that under s.8 what is protected is the *right* of the employer to summarily dismiss the employee without notice for misconduct and that this right will only exist where the dismissal is a fair one in the circumstances. In either event, it is perhaps true that the operation of s.8 involves greater complexities than have been considered thus far in decisions of the EAT on this point.[35]

[20–15] In addition, the High Court has held that where the employee breaches an implied obligation to act with good faith and fidelity and hence effectively repudiates his or her contract of employment, then there is no obligation on the part of his or her employer to give him or her any notice, whether under statute or contract.[36]

---

34. *Employee v Employer* MN 729/2007.
35. A further complicated issue that has not been considered with any great sophistication concerns the question of whether, if the employee subsequent to his or her summary dismissal demonstrates that such dismissal was unfair, [s]he should receive *inter alia* compensation for failure to provide notice periods by reason of the employer relying on his power under s.8 of the 1973 Act to dismiss an employee summarily and without notice for misconduct.
36. *B-Lex v Fields* [2007] IEHC 437. See also *Sinclair v Neighbour* [1967] 2 QB 279.

Finally, it is possible for an employee (or an employer) either to waive his or her   [20–16]
right to notice,[37] or alternatively to arrange that instead of working out the notice
period, [s]he will accept payment in lieu of notice.[38]

2.3. The Requirement that the Employee Has Been Dismissed

Significantly, in order for the minimum notice rules to apply, there must actually   [20–17]
be a dismissal of the employee,[39] and depending on the facts it may be difficult to
establish whether or not the actions of the employer constitute an act of dismissal
or whether such actions have been misconstrued as such by the employee.[40] So,
for example, in one case[41] the EAT refused to find that there had been a dismissal
(and hence that a notice period should have been given) in circumstances where
the employer and employee had fought but the employer had subsequently sought
to use a third party to persuade the employee to return to work.

Clear lines of principle are somewhat difficult to distil from the various EAT   [20–18]
determinations in this area. It has been suggested, for instance, in one case that the
fact of a dismissal could be established on the basis that the tribunal was satisfied
on the balance of probability that the claimant *understood* certain comments made
by the respondent to him to mean that he was being summarily dismissed.[42] Yet
it can scarcely be the case that a dismissal can be found to have occurred in any
and all cases where the employee is subjectively of the opinion that he has been
dismissed, but where there are no objective indicia to support such a subjective
viewpoint. Indeed, it is particularly notable that in *Halal Meat Packers (Bally-
haunis) Ltd. v EAT*[43] Murphy J in the High Court held – admittedly in a relatively
controversial conclusion – that notice did not have to be given or paid in circumstances where an employee had been constructively dismissed.

On the other hand, from the employer's standpoint it may, on occasion, be   [20–19]
difficult in the circumstances to determine whether and when an employee has
resigned and thus can be replaced. This is significant because naturally if the
employee has resigned [s]he can be replaced nor can [s]he insist on being taken
back into employment in the job that [s]he previously worked at, but if [s]he has

---

37. s.7(1) Minimum Notice and Terms of Employment Act 1973.
38. s.7(2) *ibid.* In such circumstances, the date of termination of the employment is deemed to
    be the date on which the notice period, had it been given, would have elapsed. Generally see
    Employee v Employer MN 141/2008. Kerr, *Irish Employment Legislation* (Round Hall Sweet
    and Maxwell, 2000), at p.A-57 makes the point that it is not clear under the legislation
    whether an employee could refuse to accept wages in lieu of notice.
39. This issue has also been considered in the context of unfair dismissals in Chapter 21.
40. See *Employee v Employer* MN 474/2008 and MN 475/2008; *Employee v Employer* MN
    260/2008; *Employee v Employer* MN 836/2007.
41. *Employee v Employer* MN 649/2006.
42. *Employee v 2 Employers* MN 178/2006.
43. [1990] ILRM 293, [1990] ELR 49.

not resigned, then such refusal to employ him or her may amount to a termination of his or her employment, for which [s]he will need to be given notice.[44] Equally, it is possible that the 1973 Act may apply even where the employee *has* resigned, depending on the facts of the case. Thus in one case an employee agreed to leave the company for which she had worked for over 15 years on the understanding that she would get paid 'what she was entitled to'. The EAT, while accepting that neither party fully understood the import of this phrase, nonetheless concluded that amongst the claimant's entitlements was minimum notice and hence the employer was ordered to pay her six weeks' salary in lieu of notice.[45]

2.4. Substantive Notice Requirements

[20–20] Beyond cases of justified summary dismissals, an employee whose employment is to be terminated is entitled to a notice period (or payment in lieu of notice)[46] calculated as follows[47]:

- if [s]he has been in the continuous service[48] of his or her employer for less than two years, one week[49];
- if [s]he has been in the continuous service of his or her employer for between two and five years, two weeks;
- if [s]he has been in the continuous service of his or her employer for between five and ten years, four weeks;
- if [s]he has been in the continuous service of his or her employer for between ten and fifteen years, six weeks;
- if [s]he has been in the continuous service of his or her employer for in excess of fifteen years, eight weeks.

[20–21] The second Schedule to the Act lays down rules for computing continuous service. Thus it is provided that:

- any week in which a person is not normally expected to work for at least 18 hours[50] or where [s]he was absent from his or her employment because [s]he was taking part in a strike in relation to the trade or

---

44. *Employee v Employer* MN 704/2007.
45. *Employee v Employer* MN 372/2007.
46. The EAT has stressed that an inability to pay notice is not a defence for an employer who has failed either to give an employee appropriate notice of termination, or to pay him or her money in lieu of notice: *Employee v Employer* MN 478/2008.
47. s.4(2) Minimum Notice and Terms of Employment Act 1973. The Minister may, by regulations, amend the minimum notice periods that must be provided: s.4(4) *ibid.*
48. The concept of continuity of service is discussed in more detail in the context of unfair dismissals legislation at Chapter 21.
49. The EAT has held that the reference to a 'week's notice' denotes a full working week: *Supple v Period Properties Ltd.* MN 609/2001.
50. This is subject to the requirements of the Protection of Employees (Part Time Work) Act 2001.

business in which [s]he was employed *shall not* count as a period of service, but any week or part of a week in which [s]he was absent from work because of a lock out by his or her employer or by reason of a strike or lock out in some other business *shall* count as a period of service;

- any occasions where an employee is absent from his or her work because of service in the Reserve Defence Forces *shall* count as a period of service;
- where an employee is absent from employment (in a period between consecutive periods of employment) for not more than 26 weeks[51] by reason of a lay off, sickness or injury, or an agreement with his or her employer, this *shall* constitute a period of service.

Moreover, such service will be deemed to be continuous (and it should be noted [20–22] that service can be deemed to be continuous even where aspects of the service are not computable) unless an employee is either dismissed or voluntarily leaves his or her employment, or claims and receives redundancy payments in respect of lay off or short time. Hence service will be deemed continuous where the employee goes on strike, where there is a lock out or, more controversially, where the employer dismisses the employee and then immediately reinstates him or her. Finally, normal transfer of undertakings rules apply,[52] such that where there is a transfer of undertakings, the service of the employee with the transferor shall be reckoned as part of his or her service with the transferee, nor shall the fact of the transfer break the continuity of such service save where the employer received and retained redundancy payment from the transferor at the time of and by reason of the transfer.[53]

According to the EAT, in order to ensure that there is no doubt but that such notice [20–23] is being given to the employee, it is necessary that a notice period be preceded by an 'unqualified statement, either verbal or written...to the employee, to confirm to him that his employment would end'.[54] Equally in *Bolands Ltd. v Ward*[55] the Supreme Court, overturning decisions of both the High Court and the EAT, held that sufficient notice had been given in circumstances where an employer, having given a clear statement of notice to employees on a given day, then proceeded on a weekly basis to extend the employees' employment for successive further weeks with the final such extension, coming only one week before the employment was eventually terminated. The employees claimed that the final date on which their

---

51. See Kerr, *Irish Employment Legislation* (Round Hall Sweet and Maxwell, 2000), at p. A-63 for analysis of whether, in circumstances where the break in service is in excess of 26 weeks, the whole period should be discounted in computing continuous service, or only the period in excess of 26 weeks.
52. These are considered in Chapter 23.
53. For the question of whether this approach is consistent with the Transfer of Undertakings Directive (Directive 2001/23/EC) see *Brett v Niall Collins Ltd.* [1995] ELR 69.
54. *Employee v Employer* MN 478/2008. In addition, it would seem that where notice has once been given it cannot be unilaterally withdrawn. See *Brennan v Lindley & Co Ltd.* [1974] IRLR 153.
55. [1987] IESC 1, [1988] ILRM 382.

contracts had been extended for an additional week (and not the first date on which they had been given notice of their impending dismissal) should be deemed to be the date on which they were given their statutory notice, and accordingly that the notice period that they were given was less than the statutory minimum. The Supreme Court rejected this logic, holding that as the employees had worked well in excess of their statutorily designated notice period since the original date on which they were given notice, they could not complain that the employer had provided ongoing work for them for a period greater than the length of that notice period. Thus, the date on which they were deemed to be given notice was regarded as the original date on which notice was first given, and they had worked out this notice period, albeit in circumstances where they were subsequently retained on a weekly basis.[56]

2.5. Entitlements while on Notice

[20–24] While on notice (where such notice is given either by the employee or the employer but not where the employee gives notice to terminate his or her employment in response to a notice of lay off[57] or short time by the employer[58]), an employee is entitled to be paid by his employer in accordance with the terms of his or her contract of employment, and to have the same rights to sick pay and holiday pay as if such notice had not been given. Payment, where appropriate, should be made in respect of normal working hours that the employee would be expected to work, including overtime and also any working hours where [s]he was ready and willing to work but no work was provided for him by his or her employer. Alternatively, where the employee's pay is not calculated by reference to working hours, or where there are no 'normal working hours', the employee should be paid at a rate not less than the average weekly earnings of the employee in the 13 weeks immediately prior to the point at which [s]he was given notice, provided that the

---

56. See also *Waterford Multiport Ltd. v Fagan* [1999] IEHC 158, [1999] ELR 185.

57. In *Irish Leathers Ltd. v Minister for Labour* [1986] IR 77, Barrington J in the High Court held that where an employee who had been temporarily laid off was then given notice of redundancy [s]he should be paid during the notice period and under the terms of the 1973 Act. Barrington J held that at the point at which the notice of redundancy was issued, the employee ceased to be 'laid off' for the purposes of the Redundancy Payments Act 1973 and was instead an employee 'under notice of dismissal'. The situation appears different where an employee takes a voluntary redundancy. For cases where the EAT found that, albeit in a situation of considerable uncertainty, the employee had taken a voluntary redundancy having been temporarily laid off (in a *bona fide* lay off situation in which the employer had not engineered matters to misrepresent a normal redundancy situation in order to avoid paying significant amounts of money in lieu of notice) and hence that he was not entitled to any notice under the 1973 Act, see *Employee v Employer* MN 95/2007 and MN 126/2007. On the other hand, in *Employee v Employer* MN 694/2007 the EAT *did* award compensation for a failure to give notice to an employee in circumstances where that employee had sought and obtained a voluntary redundancy package (rather than having resigned as was contended by the respondent employer).

58. s.5(2) Minimum Notice and Terms of Employment Act 1973.

employee is ready and willing to do work of a reasonable nature and amount to earn remuneration at that level.[59]

2.6. Relationship between Statutory Notice and Contractual Notice Entitlements

Where an employee's contract of employment provides for a notice period that is [20–25] less than the statutory minimum, then that contract must be read as if it provided for a notice period at the level of the statutory minimum.[60] Naturally, however, such statutory minimum entitlements can be replaced in an employee's contract of employment by a more substantial entitlement for an employee.[61] There is some conflicting authority from the EAT as to whether it is entitled to award compensation to an employee for failure of his or her employer to provide him or her with the contractual notice period, or whether it is confined to awarding compensation for breach of statutory entitlements.[62] It is surely the case, however, that inasmuch as the EAT derives its authority from statute, its jurisdiction is confined to that prescribed by statute. In other words, where an employee is not given his or her *contractual* notice period, then the appropriate remedy is a civil action for breach of contract (or possibly an action for unauthorised deduction of wages under payment of wages legislation[63]), nor would it be *intra vires* the powers of the EAT under minimum notice legislation to award compensation for such a breach. Thus the most recent authority from the EAT indicates that it will only award damages in respect of an employee's statutory notice entitlements.[64]

3. Enforcement

Naturally where an employer is in breach of his or her contractual obligations to [20–26] an employee *vis-à-vis* notice, the appropriate method of enforcing such contractual entitlements is through a breach of contract action in the civil courts. Similarly, as we have seen in Chapter 19 the wrongful dismissal action is one rooted in common law, and hence to be enforced through the civil courts. The EAT, however, has a dual role as far as enforcement of the terms of the Minimum Notice and Terms of Employment Act of 1973 is concerned.

---

59. Second Schedule to the Minimum Notice and Terms of Employment Act 1973. Any term of a contract purporting to exclude or limit such obligations on the part of an employer shall be void: s.5(3) *ibid.*
60. s.4(5) Minimum Notice and Terms of Employment Act 1973.
61. In *Jameson v MCW Ltd.* MN 878/1983 the EAT accepted this premise but also held that in such circumstances the statutory period of notice should occupy the last appropriate number of weeks of any contractual period.
62. See the conflicting authorities in *Foley v Labtech Ltd.* M 259/1978 on the one hand and *Benson v Switzers Ltd.* M 850/1984 on the other.
63. This is considered in Chapter 12.
64. *An Employee v An Employer* MN 496/2008.

[20–27]   First, where any disputes arise in relation to the legislation, then they should be referred to the tribunal,[65] which will make a final determination in respect of such dispute,[66] save that a party may appeal such determination to the High Court on a point of law,[67] and that the Minister, on the request of the EAT, may refer any question of law arising in the course of a dispute to the High Court.[68]

[20–28]   Secondly, if the employer fails to give the employee the level of notice to which [s]he is entitled under statute, or fails to afford the employee his or her statutory rights during the period of notice, then the employee may refer the matter to the EAT for arbitration and the EAT may award the employee compensation[69] for any loss suffered,[70] with the amount of any such award being recoverable as a simple contract debt[71] in proceedings issued either by the employee, or his or her trade union or the Minister.[72] Significantly, under this procedure there must be *loss* on the part of the employee if compensation is to be awarded.[73] Hence, for example, whether or not notice is given, if the employee would, for whatever reason, have been unable to have worked for the relevant notice period (for example if [s]he was away on holiday[74] or physically incapable of working[75] or had started work in

---

65. Disputes should be referred in the manner prescribed by the Minimum Notice and Terms of Employment (Reference of Disputes) Regulations 1973 (SI no. 243 of 1973).

66. s.11(1) Minimum Notice and Terms of Employment Act 1973.

67. s.11(2) *ibid.* Such an appeal should be brought pursuant to Order 105 of the Rules of the Superior Courts. See also for the form of such appeal the decision of the Supreme Court in *Bates v Model Bakery Limited* [1993] 1 IR 359.

68. s.11(3) Minimum Notice and Terms of Employment Act of 1973. Such questions should be referred pursuant again to Order 105 of the Rules of the Superior Courts.

69. Any outstanding compensation owed under this Act shall, in the event of the winding up and bankruptcy of a company, constitute a debt under s.285 of the Companies Act 1963 (as amended) and s.81 of the Bankruptcy Act 1988 to be paid in priority to all other debts. Payment of such compensation can also be sought under the Employers (Employees' Insolvency) Acts 1984 to 2001.

70. s.12(1) Minimum Notice and Terms of Employment Act 1973.

71. s.12(2) *ibid.*

72. s.12(3) *ibid.*

73. *Irish Shipping Ltd. v Byrne* [1987] IR 468. The inference to be drawn is that awards under s.12 are genuinely compensatory in nature, and hence, although the principle that a litigant must seek to mitigate his or her loss does not appear to apply, there is no blanket entitlement to compensation on the part of an employee who has not been given his or her statutory notice period. Kerr *Irish Employment Legislation* (Round Hall Sweet and Maxwell, 2000), at p.A-60 makes the point that this conclusion sits uneasily with both the conclusion of Barrington J in *Irish Leathers Ltd. v Minister for Labour* [1986] IR 177 that social welfare payments received by an employee during what should have been his or her notice period cannot be deducted from an award for compensation under s.12 and, perhaps more importantly, with the general approach of the EAT to make awards under s.12 based on the claimant's *gross* rather than his or her *net* salary.

74. *Employee v Employer* MN 278/2008.

75. *Employee v Employer* MN 884/2007.

a new job[76]) then there will be no loss, and no compensation can be awarded. A special exception to this principle (and an arguably illogical one) appears to exist for workers who are on maternity leave or are absent for reasons connected with pregnancy when they are dismissed, with the EAT concluding that even though they would not be capable of working, nonetheless they should be compensated for a failure to provide notice periods on the basis of the high level of protection generally given by Irish employment law to such workers.[77]

It is notable that, whereas disputes under the legislation can be referred to the [20–29] EAT either by the employee or the employer,[78] the EAT can only award compensation to the employee. Hence the best that the employer can achieve is essentially a declaration from the tribunal to the effect that the employee was in breach of his or her obligations to the employer.[79]

Unlike the position under various other employment law statutes there are no [20–30] mandatory time limits within which a matter must be referred to the EAT under the 1973 Act[80] and hence, whereas a matter can be referred under the 1973 Act to arbitration in the EAT at any time, equally insofar as recovery of any compensation awarded by the EAT is concerned, the normal time limits under the Statute of Limitations would seem to apply. On the other hand, as with the other legislation, a failure by either side to attend or give evidence at the hearing will be fatal to their case.[81]

Finally, as we have seen, the terms of ss.39 and 40 of the Organisation of Working [20–31] Time Act 1997 allow claims under that Act to be joined with any related claims under *inter alia* the Minimum Notice and Terms of Employment Acts – an approach that makes great sense given that at the end of a person's employment there may well be extant claims in respect of outstanding leave entitlements, as well as possible claims about adequacy of notice.

---

76. *Employee v Employer* MN 564/2007. In this case the claimant who was entitled to two weeks' notice but only received three days', was awarded compensation only for that part of the remaining portion of the notice period to which he was entitled by statute in which he was not working in a new job.
77. *Kelly v Wexford Electronics Ltd.* MN 1252/2002.
78. See *Leopard Security Ltd. v Campbell* [1997] ELR 227.
79. *Employee v Employer* MN 613/2006.
80. In *Employee v 2 Employers* 527/2006, the EAT struck out a claim on the basis that it was 'made outside the time limit for making a claim' and the tribunal found that the claimant had not shown exceptional circumstances prevented him from making a claim on time. It is difficult to see the basis for such a determination if the claim was (as appears from the EAT determination) one made exclusively under the Minimum Notice and Terms of Employment Act 1973.
81. See, for example, *Employee v Employer* MN 322/2008, WT 165/2008; *Employee v Employer* MN 422/2007, WT 183/2007. For a refusal by the EAT to allow a hearing to be adjourned in the unreasonable absence of one of the parties, see *Employee v Employer* MN 663/2007.

CHAPTER 21

Unfair Dismissals

Introduction

As far as the protection available to an employee in the context of the termina- [21–01]
tion of his or her employment was concerned, it was clear by the middle of the
1970s that the traditional action for *wrongful* dismissal (considered in Chapter 19)
was inadequate, and that the absence of some more substantive protection for
employees was compromising industrial peace in Ireland. Wrongful dismissal
actions, after all, were expensive and time-consuming to maintain (as they necessitated the employee taking a court action); the burden of proof in such actions
rested with the employee; and, most significantly, such actions involved little, if
any, scrutiny of the procedural fairness of the manner by which the employee
was dismissed. Rather, provided that the relevant notice periods and the basic
principles of natural justice were complied with, the motives and intentions of the
employer in deciding to dismiss were irrelevant to the question of the fairness of
the dismissal.

The acute pressure on the Irish government to legislate in this area in the 1970s [21–02]
was three-pronged in nature.

- First, the lack of appropriate protection for employees as regards the
  termination of their employment increased the risk of such employees
  resorting to industrial action in an attempt to resolve their disputes.
  Thus when introducing the Bill at the second stage in the Dáil, the
  Minister for Labour observed that during the period 1972–1975 there
  were approximately 187 disputes relating to employees' termination of
  employment, in which 26,299 people were involved. These disputes had
  accounted for a quarter of a million days lost in industry.[1]
- Secondly, the International Labour Organisation had issued
  Recommendation 119 on the Termination of Employment (Geneva) 1963,
  which provided that the dismissal of an employee should not take place
  unless the employer had valid reasons for doing so. The ILO also required
  each Member State to update the organisation on its law in this area.
- Finally, the Council of the European Economic Community requested

---

1. *Dáil Debates*, 4 November 1976.

that the Commission conduct a report on the status of the law in this area from each of the Member States.[2] Both of these reports reinforced the need for legislative reform in the area.

[21–03] These influences culminated in the passing of the Unfair Dismissals Act 1977 ('the 1977 Act'). During the Second Reading of the Bill in the Seanad, the Minister for Labour set out the main objective of the Bill as follows:

> The basic proposal of this Bill is that the dismissal of an employee will be regarded as unfair unless the employer can show grounds which justify the dismissal. Its objective is to limit the area of arbitrary decision by employers in relation to dismissals of employees.

> The employer at present has the absolute legal right to hire and fire at his discretion. The Bill seeks to foster better relations between management and employees in relation to discipline and dismissals. It is accepted by successful employers that industrial efficiency must be based on management practices which respect employees' rights. Arguments in the past about the rights and wrongs of decisions in relation to dismissals have led to costly strikes…

> For the employee's part, the Bill seeks to correct a serious omission in our statute law in respect of the individual's right to fair treatment in circumstances where the employer decides on dismissal. As the law stands, apart from the employee's rights to the requisite notice under the Minimum Notice and Terms of Employment Act, 1973, the employer could implement dismissal in circumstances where the culpability of the individual worker need not be soundly based. The employee's only legal recourse up to now against the unjust dismissal lay in a common law action for wrongful dismissal in the civil courts which could entail considerable costs and delays. This omission in our worker protection legislation has resulted in arguments about the rights and wrongs of dismissal decisions which have frequently led to costly strikes. Frequently an employee who has felt aggrieved at his dismissal has resorted to the support of his fellow employees.[3]

[21–04] The 1977 Act therefore recognised that each employee had a stake in his or her own job and that to allow an employer to terminate the relationship without good reason was to cause a grave injustice to the employee that only succeeded in cementing the power imbalance that already existed between employer and employee.

The 1977 Act was amended by the Unfair Dismissals (Amendment) Act 1993 ('the 1993 Act'), which introduced a number of improvements to the existing legislation, including *inter alia* an extension of the coverage of the Act to include

---

2. V/812/75-E.
3. *Seanad Debates*, vol. 86, 29 March 1977.

employees employed through employment agencies[4] and an expansion of the list of grounds for dismissal deemed automatically unfair.[5]

1. To Whom Does the Legislation Apply?

Section 2(1) provides a long list of categories of employees excluded from its protection. The primary restriction that applies to all employees is that in order for the Act to apply the employee must, at the date of dismissal, have at least 52 weeks' continuous service with the employer. This restriction does not apply to employees who are dismissed because of: [21–05]

- trade union membership or activity[6];
- pregnancy or the exercise of their rights under the Maternity Protection Acts 1994–2003[7];
- the exercise of their rights under the National Minimum Wage Act 2000,[8] and in certain circumstances under the Safety, Health and Welfare at Work Act 2005.[9]

1.1. Continuous Service

The method of computation of 52 weeks' continuous service has been set down in the First Schedule of the Minimum Notice and Terms of Employment Act 1973. Under this Act any employee who worked less than eight hours per week before the legislation was amended would be excluded from the protection of the 1977 Act. Following the enactment of s.9 of the Protection of Employees (Part-Time Work) Act 2001, 'a part-time employee shall not, in respect of his or her conditions of employment, be treated in a less favourable manner than a comparable full-time employee'. As a result, an employee is no longer required to work eight hours per week in order to avail of the protections under the Act. [21–06]

The First Schedule to the 1973 Act provides *inter alia* that a lock-out,[10] lay-off[11] or a strike[12] by the employee shall not amount to a break in the continuity of employment. Further, where the employee has been dismissed by the employer [21–07]

---

4. s.13 of the 1993 Act.
5. For example, s.5(a) of the 1993 Act provides that dismissal of an employee on grounds of the employee's race, colour, sexual orientation, age or membership of the Travelling Community is automatically deemed to be unfair.
6. s.14 of the 1993 Act.
7. s.6(2)(a) of the 1977 Act, as amended by s.38(5) Maternity Protection Act 1994.
8. s.36(2) National Minimum Wage Act 2000.
9. s.27(4) Safety, Health and Welfare at Work Act 2005.
10. para.2 of the First Schedule of the Minimum Notice and Terms of Employment Act 1973.
11. para.3 *ibid.*
12. para.4 *ibid.*

and immediately re-employed, there is no break in the continuity of service.[13] The Act does not define what is meant by 'immediate re-employment' and the tribunal has offered different interpretations of the words. In *Ennis v Toyota*,[14] it was held that re-employment within one month did not break the continuity of service, whereas a break of four months was deemed to lack immediacy in *Myles v O'Kane*,[15] and was held to amount to a break in the continuity of employment. The 1973 Act also provides that if an employee is absent from his or her employment for not more than 26 weeks between consecutive periods of employment because of (a) a lay-off; (b) sickness or injury; or (c) by agreement with his or her employer; such a period will count as a period of service.[16]

1.2. Other Categories of Employee Excluded from the Act

[21–08] There are other categories of employee excluded from the 1977 Act (as amended by the 1993 Act), such as persons employed by a family member in a private dwelling, house or farm where both reside,[17] members of the Defence Forces or An Garda Síochána,[18] FÁS trainees and apprentices,[19] managers of a local authority for purposes of the Local Government Act 2001,[20] officer of a vocational education committee established by the Vocational Education Act 1930,[21] the chief executive officer of the Health Services Executive[22] or persons dismissed during a period of probation where the probation period does not exceed one year.[23] Civil servants were originally excluded from the application of the Act, but following the implementation of the Civil Service Regulations (Amendment) Act 2005 this exclusion has been abolished.

[21–09] In addition, the 1977 Act does not apply to employees who on or before the date of dismissal have reached the normal retiring age for employees of the same employer in similar employment.[24] This indicates that it is in the interests of employers (in order to avoid application of the 1977 Act) to make express provision for a retirement age in all contracts of employment. Thus in *Donegal County Council v Porter and Others*,[25] four employees were employed as part-time firemen. Each of the claimants was dismissed upon attaining the age of 55 years,

---

13. para.6 *ibid.*
14. UD 597/1983.
15. [1991] ELR 181.
16. para.10.
17. s.2(1)(c) of the 1977 Act.
18. See s.2(1)(d) and s.2 (1)(e) of the 1977 Act.
19. s.2(1)(g) *ibid.*
20. s.144 Local Government Act 2001.
21. s.2(1)(j) of the 1977 Act.
22. s.17 Health Act 2004.
23. s.3(1) of the 1977 Act.
24. s.2(1)(b) of the 1977 Act.
25. [1993] ELR 101.

which at the time of their dismissal was considered to be the normal retirement age for firemen. The claimants were employed in the 1960s and at that time there was no clause in their contract that specified their retirement age. However, since the 1980s any firemen engaged by the council had a written term in their contract of employment that provided for a retirement age of 55 years. The High Court found that, in the absence of a written agreement to the contrary, the claimants were entitled to believe that the 'normal' retirement age was 60 years. Nothing in the intervening period occurred to change their minds. There was never any negotiation with the claimants to change that age. The court held that the attempt unilaterally to force them to accept the younger retirement age was in breach of contract and unjustifiable.

1.3. Types of Contract Excluded from the Application of the Act

Under s.2(2) of the 1977 Act, an employee engaged under a fixed-term or speci- [21–10] fied purpose contract will not fall within the remit of the legislation where his or her employment ends as a result of the expiry of that contract. Equally, if such contracts are to be excluded from the application of the legislation, the following conditions must be satisfied:

(1) the contract must be in writing;
(2) it must be signed by both parties; and
(3) it must contain a statement that the Act shall not apply to a dismissal consisting only of the expiry or cesser aforesaid.

Thus in *Sheehan v Dublin Tribune*,[26] the failure by the employer to include a specific clause stating that the 1977 Act did not apply meant that the contract could not be excluded from the application of the legislation.

The tribunal will not, however, allow unscrupulous employers to use these types of [21–11] contracts as a means of evading their obligations under the 1977 Act. The tribunal will examine whether the contract was in reality a fixed-term contract or whether it was an open-ended arrangement designed to avoid the application of the 1977 legislation. In *FitzGerald v St Patrick's College, Maynooth*,[27] the claimant was appointed as a lecturer on a temporary basis on foot of a fixed-term contract for one academic year. At the end of the academic year the claimant was re-appointed under another fixed-term contract for another academic year. The second contract was not renewed and the claimant brought an action for unfair dismissal. The tribunal found that there had been a dismissal with the non-renewal of the claimant's contract. It was not sufficient for an employer to dismiss the employee simply with the expiration of time. The employer must show that the circumstances have changed. Otherwise, as the tribunal noted:

---

26. [1992] ELR 239.
27. UD 244/1978.

If the mere expiry of a fixed-term contract of employment were to be regarded as a substantial ground for the non-renewal of the employment, the Unfair Dismissals Act could be rendered abortive in many cases. An employer could side-step its provisions by employing his employees on fixed-term contracts only. Then to get rid of an employee on whatever grounds, be they trivial or substantial, fanciful or solid, fair or unfair, he need only wait until that employee's fixed-term contract expired and then refuse to renew it. The threat of non-renewal of his contract might well be enough to make many an employee submit to oppressive conditions or treatment at the hands of an employer.

1.3.1. Successive Fixed-Term Contracts

[21–12]   Notwithstanding the fact that fixed-term contracts fell outside the ambit of the 1977 Act, s.3(b) of the 1993 Act does now provide that if the employee is dismissed only because of the expiry of the term of the contract or the purpose of the contract ended and:

(i)   the employee is re-employed by the employer within three months of the expiry of the previous contract;

(ii) the nature of the employment is the same or similar to the employment under the previous contract; and

(iii) in the opinion of the Rights Commissioner, EAT or Circuit Court, as the case may be, the entry by the employer into the subsequent contract is wholly or partly connected with the purpose of avoidance of liability under the 1977 Act,

then the 1977 Act shall apply to the dismissal and the term of the previous contract and any antecedent contracts (which expired not more than three months before the commencement of the prior contract) shall be added together for the purposes of determining whether or not the requisite period of service has been complied with. Such periods taken together will be treated as continuous service for the purposes of the legislation.

1.3.2. Fixed-Term Contracts Related to Protected Leave

[21–13]   Fixed contracts can be entered into by an employer with an employee and to which the unfair dismissals legislation does not apply, where that employee is engaged simply to provide cover for another employee who is absent on protective leave under the Maternity Protection Act 1994,[28] the Adoptive Leave Act 1995[29] or the Carer's Leave Act 2001.[30] In each of these situations the employer must inform the replacement employee in writing at the commencement of the employment that it will terminate upon the return to work of the employee absent on such protective leave. Furthermore, such dismissal must occur only to facilitate the return to work of the employee who was absent on protective leave.

---

28. s.38(2) Maternity Protection Act 1994 (amending s.2(2) of the 1977 Act).

29. s.23 Adoptive Leave Act 1995 (amending s.2(2) of the 1977 Act).

30. s.27(1) Carer's Leave Act 2001 (amending s.2(2) of the 1977 Act).

2. The Fact of Dismissal as a Prerequisite to Application of the Legislation

A crucial point at the outset of any proceedings under the 1977 Act is to estab-   [21–14]
lish whether or not the employee was dismissed by the employer. Effectively, this
question will determine where the burden of proof will lie. If the employee can
establish the fact of his or her dismissal, then the burden shifts and it is left to the
employer to prove that the dismissal was justified. Otherwise, it is the employee
who must go first in evidence in the proceedings.

Dismissal is defined under s.1 of the 1977 Act as follows:

> (*a*) the termination by his employer of the employee's contract of employment
> with the employer, whether prior notice of the termination was or was not given
> to the employee;

> (*b*) the termination by the employee of his contract of employment with his
> employer, whether prior notice of the termination was or was not given to the
> employer, in circumstances in which, because of the conduct of the employer, the
> employee was or would have been entitled, or it was or would have been reasonable
> for the employee, to terminate the contract of employment without giving prior
> notice of the termination to the employer; or

> (*c*) the expiration of a contract of employment for a fixed term without its being
> renewed under the same contract or, in the case of a contract for a specified purpose
> (being a purpose of such a kind that the duration of the contract was limited but
> was, at the time of its making, incapable of precise ascertainment), the cesser of
> the purpose.

Whether or not a dismissal occurred is determined in accordance with an objec-   [21–15]
tive standard. In many cases, the fact of dismissal will be obvious and undis-
puted: for example, where an employer writes a formal letter of termination to the
employee. However, complications may arise where the employer has not acted
with clarity as to his or her intentions.[31] The test in such circumstances is whether
a reasonable employee in the circumstances would consider that the employer's
words and/or actions amounted to a dismissal.[32] In *Tanner v DT Kean Ltd.*,[33] the
claimant, contrary to company policy, used his employer's van outside of working
hours. Upon learning of this his employer became abusive and shouted, 'That's it,
you're finished with me.'[34] Did these words constitute a dismissal of the claimant

---

31. See *Employee v Employer*, MN 474/2008 and MN 475/2008; *Employee v Employer*, MN
    260/2008; *Employee v Employer*, MN 836/2007; *Employee v Employer*, MN 649/2006.
32. *Devaney v DNT Distribution Company Ltd.*, UD 412/1993; *Cooke v Ashmore Hotels Ltd.* [1992]
    ELR 1.
33. [1978] IRLR 110.
34. *ibid.* at 110.

by his employer? The tribunal held that when dealing with ambiguous words in such circumstances the incident must be viewed in its entirety. In particular, it noted that 'a relevant and perhaps the most important question is how would a reasonable employee in all the circumstances have understood what the employer intended by what he said and did?'[35] The employer had uttered the words in the heat of the moment and it could not be reasonably said that he intended to dismiss the employee with the use of such language.

[21–16]   A similar approach was adopted by the tribunal in *Devaney v DNT Distribution Company Ltd.,*[36] where it held that what was necessary was to determine the employer's intention towards the employee in all the circumstances. To answer this question it was necessary to consider 'how a reasonable employee in all the circumstances would have understood the employer's intention'. Thus an employer's intention can be determined from the nature of the industry and 'just because an employer speaks sharply to an employee is not sufficient reason for the employee to walk away'.[37] In *Futty v D & D Brekkes Ltd.,*[38] the complainant, a fish filleter who worked on the docks, entered into an argument with his foreman. The foreman eventually said to the complainant, 'If you do not like the job, f**k off.'[39] The complainant left the job and did not return. In response to a claim for unfair dismissal, the employer maintained that there had been no dismissal. It was the employer's contention that in the context of work on the docks, language such as that used by the foreman was commonplace and merely amounted to banter. Properly interpreted, in light of the circumstances, the foreman was telling the complainant to clock-off and return the next day. The Employment Appeals Tribunal in England and Wales agreed and held that the words must not be viewed in isolation but against the background of the workplace, in this case the 'rough and tumble' of the docks. It found, ironically, that in this atmosphere formality was used when dismissing employees and its absence in this case was strong evidence that the employee had not been dismissed.

[21–17]   The tribunal will be sympathetic towards employers who may have spoken in the heat of the moment. In *Martin v Yeoman Aggregates Ltd.,*[40] the employee was asked to collect a part for a car that needed repair. When he returned with the incorrect part he had a row with his employer (one of the directors of the company). He refused to return and collect the correct part and his employer dismissed him for disobeying the order. Within a couple of minutes the director realised that by summarily dismissing the employee he had breached his own company's disciplinary procedures. He immediately informed the employee that he was instead suspended without full pay for two days. The tribunal held that, as a matter of policy, it made

---

35. [1978] IRLR 110 at 111.
36. UD 412/1993.
37. *Maher v Walsh*, UD 605/1983.
38. [1974] IRLR 130.
39. *ibid.* at 130.
40. [1983] ICR 314, [1983] IRLR 49.

good industrial relations sense to allow employers and employees an opportunity of recanting words said in the heat of the moment. There was no dismissal.

Even in the absence of a formal statement from the employer that the employee is [21–18] dismissed, the actions of an employer may also be deemed to amount to a dismissal of an employee. Thus the indefinite suspension of an employee in *McKenzie Ltd. v Smith*[41] was considered to amount to a dismissal. Similarly, in *Deegan v Dunnes Stores Ltd.*,[42] the claimants were suspended indefinitely as they refused to give undertakings in relation to certain management decisions. The suspension was found to be tantamount to a dismissal as their return to work was conditional on their agreement to certain issues to which they had already indicated they were opposed.

2.1. The Date of Dismissal

The date of dismissal can be of critical importance in determining whether or not [21–19] the employee is in a position to make a claim for unfair dismissal under the legislation. The definition of the date of dismissal under s.1 of the 1977 Act provides that the date may be a different date to the date of the actual dismissal. Section 1 provides that the date of dismissal may be determined in one of the following three ways:

(1) where notice has been given in accordance with the statutory provisions of the Minimum Notice and Terms Act 1973 and also complies with the provisions of the contract, the date that such notice expires;

(2) where no notice is given in breach of the statutory provisions of the 1973 Act or the provisions of the contract, the later of the following dates will be considered the date of dismissal:
  a. the earliest date that would be in compliance with the provisions of the contract; or
  b. the earliest date that would be in compliance with the provisions of the Minimum Notice and Terms of Employment Act, 1973 (as amended);

(3) where the contract is a fixed term/specific purpose contract the date of dismissal will be the date of the expiry of the term or the ending of the purpose.

The later date provided for in s.1(1) and s.1(2) applies regardless of whether the [21–20] employee has worked the notice period or not. The provision of artificial dates of dismissal in the legislation is beneficial to the employee in two important respects. First, the date of dismissal will be used to determine whether the requirement of having completed one year's continuous service with the employer is met. Secondly, s.8(2) of the 1977 Act provides that a claim for unfair dismissal under

---

41. [1976] IRLR 345.
42. [1992] ELR 184.

the legislation must be brought within six months of the date of dismissal. In both situations, the definition provided under s.1 gives the employee more time to build up the requisite continuous service or to bring a claim.

3. Categories of Dismissal under the 1977 Act

[21–21]   The Unfair Dismissals Act 1977 provides for three categories of dismissal:

(1) constructive dismissal;
(2) fair dismissal; and
(3) unfair dismissal.

3.1. Constructive Dismissal

[21–22]   In order to avoid a situation where an employer who, wishing both to dismiss a troublesome employee and also to evade liability for unfair dismissal proceedings, does not actually dismiss the employee but instead makes his or her position so unbearable that it becomes essentially untenable for him or her, such that [s]he is forced to resign, s.1 of the 1977 Act provides that such an employee may bring an action against his or her employer in such circumstances for what is termed constructive dismissal, that is, a situation where, because of the employer's behaviour, the employee feels that he or she is left with no other option but to resign his or her position. In defining dismissal, the section includes the following:

> The termination by the employee of his contract of employment with his employer whether prior notice of the termination was or was not given to the employer in circumstances in which, because of the conduct of the employer, the employee was or would have been entitled or it was or would have been reasonable for the employee to terminate the contract of employment without giving prior notice of the termination to the employer.

Thus constructive dismissal is an unfair dismissal, and the essence of such a claim is that in the circumstances, what the employer has done is tantamount to dismissing the employee, and hence, if such actions were unreasonable, it should be deemed to constitute a form of unfair dismissal.

3.1.1. The Fact of a Dismissal

[21–23]   In cases of constructive dismissal, the *fact* of the employee's dismissal will be in dispute as the employer will argue that the employee's resignation was entirely voluntary and had nothing to do with his or her behaviour and therefore did not constitute a dismissal at all. It will be for the employee to prove that [s]he would never have resigned from the position but for the employer's behaviour and that [s]he had, in fact, been dismissed.

In *Farrell v Sheils Plant Hire Ltd.*,[43] the claimant worked as a fitter for the [21–24]
respondent. The claimant was of the view that he had been left short in terms
of his wages. He had inquired about the discrepancy but was told to contact the
managing director of the company in relation to the matter, which he tried but
failed to do. Before leaving for his Christmas holidays the quarry manager told him
to leave his mobile phone so that it could be updated for the following year. He
explained to the manager that he did not have the phone with him and was told
that he could drop it in after Christmas. The manager then asked him to leave the
company van as the managing director's brother wanted to use it over Christmas.
The claimant had taken the van home over previous holidays and drove it home
every evening. He told the manager that he needed to take it home in order to
unload his tools. The claimant approached the managing director's brother in
relation to the van but was told that it was the managing director who wanted to
use the van over the holidays. The claimant took the van home and did not return
it. The next day the claimant's wife told him that an employee of the company
had called to the house to collect the van. The claimant contacted his employer
and told them of his belief that the managing director did not want the claimant
to come back to work after the Christmas holidays; the claimant also sought the
back pay and holiday pay that he was owed. A half-hour later a member of the
gardaí called seeking the return of the van. Because of the respondent's behaviour
the claimant felt that he had no option but to resign. The tribunal held that the
claimant had been unfairly dismissed. The behaviour of the employer would give
any reasonable employee the impression that [s]he was dismissed. The request for
the return of the van and phone indicated to the claimant that the respondent
intended to terminate the contract of employment.

In practical terms, the requirement that there be a dismissal indicates that an [21–25]
employer should be wary of too readily accepting the resignation of an employee
lest it be interpreted as further evidence that the employer had deliberately engineered a situation in which the employee would have no choice but to resign.
This is particularly pertinent given that the tribunal has decided that there is a
positive obligation on the employer to enquire as to the reasons behind the resignation. In *May v Moog Ltd.*,[44] the respondent had employed the claimant for a
number of years. Due to an illness, the claimant missed some time at work. As
a result of these health problems, the claimant requested a part-time position.
The respondent did not provide this work. Some time later, the claimant became
seriously ill again. While she was on sick leave, the respondent visited her and
warned her that if she did not return to work, her position would be advertised.
The claimant returned to work before the expiry of her sick leave and still did not
receive an official response to her query for part-time work. She resigned her position as she felt that she could not continue to work under those circumstances.
The respondent alleged that the claimant only resigned because part-time work

---

43. UD 585/2008.
44. [2002] ELR 261.

was not made available to her, and while the company facilitated such requests, they were not under an obligation to do so. The majority of the tribunal determined that the employer had acted unreasonably in the circumstances. The visit to the claimant in hospital, in particular, was wholly inappropriate. As a result of this visit, and against medical advice, the claimant returned to work earlier than she should have. One day later she resigned.

[21–26] The majority of the tribunal held that the employer's failure to look into the reasons of the claimant's resignation (which occurred within one day of her return from sick leave) and the employer's request that she finish 'there and then', despite the fact that she offered two weeks' notice, was unreasonable and showed little regard for the employee:

> The claimant's resignation must be looked at in the context of her return to work. The claimant who was in a vulnerable state of mind, returned to work because, as a result of the manager's visit and what he said, she was afraid she would lose her job. She was not in a fit state either physically or psychologically for work and the medical evidence was that she would remain so for some months. The respondent ought to have been aware of the state of her health as it had the certificate of May 29 in its possession on June 9, the date she tendered her resignation. In the circumstances the majority finds that the real reason for the claimant's resignation was that she was unfit for work. For the reasons outlined earlier and for its failure to demonstrate any concern or consideration for the state of the claimant's health, the majority finds that the respondent acted unreasonably.

> Applying the reasonableness [*sic*] in this constructive dismissal case the majority finds that in the exceptional circumstances of this case, the claimant's resignation due to the state of her health was reasonable. Her failure to use the grievance procedure because she felt *'isolated and depressed and could cope with no more either physically or mentally'* is not fatal to her claim in the exceptional circumstances outlined. The majority determines that the claim for constructive dismissal succeeds.[45]

3.1.2. Onus of Proof

[21–27] More generally, the onus of proof in a constructive dismissal case rests with the employee, who must prove that the behaviour of the employer justified his or her action in resigning.[46] The burden of proof on the employee is quite onerous in such cases as [s]he must prove not only that his or her employer's behaviour was unreasonable, but also that his or her response in resigning was reasonable.[47] Key to this question will be whether the aggrieved employee had the option of having recourse to any internal grievance procedures within the company, and whether [s]he had, in fact, availed of such procedures.

---

45. [2002] ELR 261, 274.
46. *Riehn v Dublin Society for the Prevention of Cruelty to Animals* [2004] ELR 205.
47. *Healy v Credit Card Systems Ireland Ltd.*, UD 148/2003.

In *Carthy v Clydale Investment*,[48] the claimant had some rows with fellow employees, [21–28] after which her general manager had ensured that each employee involved apologised to her. Nevertheless, the claimant felt that she had been bullied and resigned her position. Her general manager visited her at home to discuss the resignation with her. The tribunal held that the employee had not discharged the burden of proof that she had been constructively dismissed in the circumstances. In particular, it found that her failure to utilise the company's grievance procedures before resigning was unreasonable.

In *Martin v Xtra Vision Ltd.*,[49] the claimant was suspended with pay pending inves- [21–29] tigation into missing stock from the store in which she worked. It was alleged that she had failed in her management of the store and had not informed management of the missing stock. Following a disciplinary hearing she was informed that she was to be demoted two grades. She appealed and the sanction was lessened. Nevertheless, she felt that she was not trusted afterwards and consequently submitted a letter of resignation. The tribunal held that the claimant failed to discharge the onus of proof required to establish that she was constructively dismissed. In the circumstances, the respondent was entitled to conduct an investigation of the matter. In the course of an internal appeal, the claimant had requested and received a lesser sanction. She could not claim then that the sanction she received was unfair. There was not constructive dismissal.[50]

3.1.3. Assessing the Employer's Behaviour

Therefore, the constructive dismissal action centres on the employer's conduct. [21–30] That in turn raises the question as to how bad an employer's behaviour must be before an employee is justified in resigning and bringing an action for constructive dismissal. It would appear that two tests can be gleaned from the statutory definition of constructive dismissal, which may be utilised to measure whether the employer's behaviour in any given situation has become so intolerable as to justify the employee resigning and bringing an action for unfair dismissal. In the first instance, an employee may bring an action for constructive dismissal where [s]he is *entitled* to do so by virtue of his or her contract of employment.[51] The circumstances when an employee might be entitled to end the contract because of the behaviour of the employer have been discussed elsewhere in this work,[52] however, based on general contract law principles it could be said that an employee would be entitled to end the contract of employment where the employer has repudiated that contract, i.e. the employer acts in a manner that amounts to a fundamental breach of the employee's contract, thereby allowing the employee to terminate the

---

48. UD 1091/2004.
49. UD 265/2006.
50. See also on the issue Chapter 16.
51. s.1(b) of the 1977 Act.
52. See Chapter 19.

contract with or without notice.[53] This is also known as the 'contract test'.[54] In the second, an employee may be entitled to terminate his or her employment where the employer acts so *unreasonably* that the employee is left with no option but to terminate the contract.[55] Under this test, it need not be proven that the employer's behaviour strictly amounted to a breach of the contract of employment. This is known as the 'reasonableness test'.[56]

3.1.3.1. The Contract Test

[21–31] As a means of measuring whether the employer's behaviour was so unreasonable as to justify the employee resigning his or her position, the contract test is much stricter than the reasonableness test. To satisfy this test, the employee must show that the employer was guilty of conduct so serious as breaching a term that goes to the root of the contract, or is guilty of conduct that is tantamount to a repudiation of the essential terms of the contract.[57] In *Western Excavating v Sharp*,[58] the employee was suspended without pay as a disciplinary sanction. The employee, who was suffering from cash-flow difficulties, asked his employer for his holiday pay. This was refused. He then asked his employer for a loan, which was also refused. He resigned his position and brought an action for constructive dismissal, citing his employer's behaviour as the reason. In refusing the employee relief on the basis that his employer's behaviour, while not generous, did not amount to a breach of contract, Lord Denning MR held that:

> If the employer is guilty of conduct which is a significant breach going to the root of the contract of employment, or does something to show that he no longer intends to be bound by one or more of the essential terms of the contract, then the employee is entitled to treat himself as discharged from any further performance... [T]he conduct must... be sufficiently serious to entitle him to leave at once...[59]

Thus in order to determine whether the employer's behaviour is sufficient to justify the employee's resignation, much will depend on whether that behaviour can be considered as breaching an essential term (express or implied) of the contract, and thereby amounting to an act that repudiates the contract and justifies the decision of the employee to resign.[60]

---

53. See, for example, *Athlone RDC v Campbell and Son (No. 2)* [1912] 47 ILTR 142.
54. Redmond, *Dismissal Law in Ireland* (2nd ed., Tottel Publishing, 2007), at paras.19.11–19.16.
55. s.1(b) of the 1977 Act.
56. Redmond, *Dismissal Law in Ireland* (2nd ed., Tottel Publishing, 2007), at paras.19.17–19.18.
57. *Lewis v Motorworld Garages Limited* [1986] ICR 157, [1985] IRLR 465; *Higgins v Donnelly Mirrors Ltd.* UD 104/1979; *Western Excavating v Sharp* [1978] QB 761, [1978] 2 WLR 344, [1978] 1 All ER 713, [1978] ICR 221, [1978] IRLR 27.
58. [1978] ICR 221.
59. *ibid.*, at 226.
60. *Jones v F Sirl & Son Ltd. (Furnishers) Ltd.* [1997] IRLR 493.

Employment tribunals have found that an employee has been constructively [21–32]
dismissed where the employer has unilaterally and unjustifiably reduced the
employee's pay,[61] or where the employer imposes a change of location for work
not contractually provided for.[62] In *Furlong v Amarosa Ltd. t/a Joels Restaurant*,[63]
the unjustified unilateral alteration of the employee's hours of work amounted to
a repudiation of the contract of employment, entitling the employee to resign. In
that case, the claimant was employed as a lounge person in late 1999. In 2000 he
was promoted to the position of barman, and by 2001 he had been appointed as
a bar supervisor. However, following a number of minor indiscretions, the claimant's position was given to another employee in the summer of 2001. The claimant's relationship with the new supervisor was not good. The claimant had an
unwritten agreement with his employer that he would not have to work Saturdays
or Sundays. However, the supervisor informed him that he would be required to
work shifts on Saturday and Sunday from 6pm to 12am. The claimant was humili-
ated at his demotion and the changes to his contract of employment and did not
return to work. The tribunal found that the changes to the claimant's terms of
employment were unreasonable in the circumstances and found that he had been
constructively dismissed.

Similarly, in *Vaughan v McGaughey*,[64] the claimant worked as a painter for the [21–33]
respondent. He worked as part of a five-man team. The claimant had not been
provided with a written contract of employment. The other members of the
team were smokers and the claimant was not. The claimant made a number of
complaints to his colleagues and to the respondent regarding smoking in the workplace but nothing was done to alleviate the problem. A dispute arose as to the
agreed finishing time of the claimant. The claimant and another colleague were
adamant that the agreed finishing time each day was 5pm. The respondent claimed
that the correct finishing time was 5.30pm. The claimant resigned because of the
respondent's failure to deal with his complaints regarding the smoking and what
he perceived to be the respondent's unilateral alteration of a term of his contract
of employment. The tribunal, having regard to all the circumstances, was satisfied that the claimant's colleagues were smoking in the workplace and that the
claimant brought this to the attention of the respondent. Furthermore, the tribunal
preferred the evidence of the claimant and his colleague as to the agreed finishing
time and pointed out that had the claimant been provided with a written contract
of employment the dispute never would have arisen. The tribunal held that the
employee was entitled to consider that he had been constructively dismissed.

The 'contract test' has been extended to apply to situations where there has been [21–34]
a breach of an implied term or terms of the contract, such as the amorphous

---

61. *Hill Ltd. v Mooney* [1981] IRLR 258.
62. *Bass Leisure Ltd. v Thomas* [1994] IRLR 104.
63. UD 140/2002.
64. UD 357/2008.

obligation of 'trust and confidence',[65] discussed in detail in Chapter 4 of this work. In *Byrne v RHM Foods (Ireland) Ltd.*,[66] the tribunal found that the employee's trust and confidence in her employer had been destroyed where the claimant was treated differently subsequent to the termination of her manager's employment with the respondent. Following her manager's departure the claimant was given little work or responsibility. She was isolated within the workplace and felt that she was identified as being 'guilty by association' with her former manager. The tribunal found that the relationship of trust and confidence had broken down to such an extent that she was entitled to resign her position and claim constructive dismissal. The employer should have spoken directly with her in order to reassure her of her position during that turbulent time.

[21–35] The failure by an employer to treat the employee fairly regarding disciplinary matters can amount to conduct that will be interpreted as repudiation of the contract of employment. In *British Broadcasting Corporation v Beckett*,[67] the complainant worked as a carpenter, preparing background scenes for the respondent, and was summarily dismissed when an accident was caused as a result of his negligence. Following an appeal under the respondent's grievance procedures, he was reinstated as a maintenance carpenter, which was effectively a demotion. The complainant refused to work in his new role, resigned and brought an action for constructive dismissal. The tribunal found that the punishment imposed on the complainant was wholly disproportionate to his wrong. The treatment of the complainant by his employer during the disciplinary process amounted to a fundamental breach of his contract and the claim of constructive dismissal was upheld.

[21–36] Similarly, in *MacLehose v R&G Taverns Ltd.*,[68] the claimant was employed as a manager of the respondent's bar. His employers became aware of discrepancies in relation to the till and stock. As a result, the employer introduced video cameras into the bar area. The tapes showed till irregularities on the part of the claimant, but did not show him actually taking any money. The claimant was only informed of his employer's concerns when he was arrested by the gardaí at home and taken in for questioning. He explained that his practice of not charging for all drinks could be for any number of reasons, including the fact that the drinks may have been paid for earlier by the customer or he may have been getting rid of an over-ring (i.e. not registering a drink in order to balance an earlier over-ring), or the customers could have been running a tab. Following his questioning, the claimant did not return to work and claimed constructive dismissal. The tribunal found that it was reasonable in the circumstances for the claimant to believe that the mutual bond of trust and confidence between the employer and employee had

---

65. *Courtaulds Northern Textiles Ltd. v Andrew* [1979] IRLR 84; *Higgins v Donnelly Mirrors Ltd.*, UD 104/1979.
66. UD 69/1979.
67. [1983] IRLR 43.
68. [1999] ELR 180.

broken down, entitling him to leave his employment. The employer failed to carry out a fair and proper investigation of the discrepancies in relation to the till and as a consequence had caused the relationship of mutual trust and confidence irretrievably to break down, and thus had led to a situation where the applicant could validly claim to have been constructively dismissed.

3.1.3.2. The 'Reasonableness' Test

Under the 'reasonableness' test, the claimant will assert that the employer's behav- [21–37] iour was so unreasonable that [s]he could not be fairly expected to put up with it any longer and was therefore justified in resigning his or her position. While the distinction between the two tests can become blurred, the 'reasonableness' test is much wider in scope than the 'contract' test.

(A) Reasonableness of the Employer's Behaviour

Under the 'contract' test the employee's claim is limited to conduct that amounts [21–38] to a repudiatory breach of the terms (express and implied) of the contract itself. The application of the 'reasonableness' test, on the other hand, is not limited to 'contractual misbehaviour' and can encapsulate the poor behaviour of the employer, which is deemed to be so unreasonable as to justify the employee resigning his position.

For example, an employer who acts unreasonably during the course of a discipli- [21–39] nary process may expose him or herself to an action for constructive dismissal. In *McKenna v Pizza Express Restaurants Ltd.*,[69] the claimant had been employed with the respondent for over 10 years and had worked her way up to a managerial position. The claimant had deducted the price of a pizza from a customer's bill because a hair had been found in the pizza. Her manager found the discrepancy in the bill and felt that it was deliberate. The claimant was contacted while on holiday and asked to attend a meeting about the matter. On her first day back from holidays the claimant attended a meeting with her manager, where it was alleged that she had tried to mislead the auditor in relation to the bill. She was told that she was to be suspended with full pay and was then escorted out of the restaurant in full view of other staff members and customers. The claimant was later informed of the date of the disciplinary hearing, but she had to adjourn the meeting for health reasons. The employer informed the employee that because she was certified as being unfit for work she was entitled to sick pay. The claimant's solicitors then informed the employer that she was pregnant and suffering from stress. The employer informed her of a new date for the disciplinary hearing. The claimant's solicitors informed the employer that she would not be able to attend the disciplinary hearing due to her ongoing health issues. Her employer set a new date for the disciplinary hearing and informed her that her sick pay would cease before the date of that hearing. The claimant's solicitors sought assurances that her sick pay would continue until she was medically fit to attend the hearing and set a date by which a response

---

69. [2008] 19 ELR 234.

would be expected by the claimant. No response was received and the claimant resigned and brought a claim for constructive dismissal. The tribunal concluded that the claimant had been constructively dismissed:

> The Tribunal came to the conclusion by reason of the fact of the manner in which the employer conducted the investigation into the incident that occurred in relation to the docket in question. The manner and the level in which the investigation was conducted was totally disproportionate to the incident itself. The necessity for a member of management to escort her to her place of work in front of employees whom she had managed, and off the premises, was distasteful and unnecessarily embarrassing to the claimant.

> The Tribunal also find that the company acted in a very hasty manner in precipitating the disciplinary hearing when there was uncontroverted medical evidence that the claimant was unfit to attend such a hearing.[70]

[21–40] In *Kennedy v Foxfield Inns Ltd. t/a The Imperial Hotel*,[71] the claimant worked as a waitress for the respondent company. She had a difficult relationship with her manager, whom she reported to her supervisor for being rude to her and calling her names in front of customers. The behaviour did not improve and the final straw for the claimant came when the manager slapped her on the back and stood on her foot at the cash desk. She resigned her position and the manager called her for a meeting, where he apologised to the claimant and explained that he had 'only been messing'. The claimant subsequently brought an action for constructive dismissal. In finding in favour of the claimant the tribunal stated that:

> The question for the Tribunal is to decide whether the claimant's decision to terminate her employment was reasonable. We are satisfied on the evidence that, by virtue of the type of conduct of which she had complained, coupled with the status of the perpetrator of that conduct, the claimant's situation in her employment became intolerable to the extent that she was left with no option but to terminate her employment.[72]

Furthermore, in *Byrne v Furniture Link International Ltd.*,[73] the tribunal held that the employer's failure to follow its own internal grievance procedures when dealing with an employee was unreasonable behaviour, which justified the employee's subsequent claim for constructive dismissal.

[21–41] It is axiomatic in constructive dismissal cases that, whereas there is a significant obligation on employees to avail of internal grievance procedures within the work-

---

70. *ibid.*, at 244.
71. [1995] ELR 216.
72. [1995] ELR 216, 219.
73. [2008] ELR 229.

place, there is a similarly onerous obligation on *employers* to ensure both that such internal grievance procedures exist and also that they are genuinely effective. In *O'Doherty v John Paul Hennessy Junior and Harrow Holdings Ltd.*,[74] the tribunal held that it was reasonable for the employee to resign her position and claim constructive dismissal where she had been the victim of sexual harassment by a colleague. The claimant reported the complaint to the bar manager and did not bring it to her employer directly as the individual involved was a member of her employer's family. The employer's failure to deal adequately with the complaint was deemed to constitute unreasonable behaviour, which justified her resignation. Similarly, in *Kelly v Stuart*,[75] the claimant worked as a carer in a respite home. She made an informal verbal complaint to her employer that she was being harassed by one of the patients. As nothing was done to resolve her complaint she resigned her position and claimed constructive dismissal. While the tribunal noted that the claimant could have done more to inform her employer of the situation, such as making a formal complaint, it did find on balance that the harassment 'subjectively made the claimant's place of employment a very uncomfortable place to be'. The claimant was therefore justified in her resignation and her claim for constructive dismissal was upheld.[76]

A leading case in this area is *Allen v Independent Newspapers Ltd.*[77] In a high-profile [21–42] appointment, the claimant was engaged as a crime reporter for the respondent. Since then she claimed that she experienced a negative atmosphere in the workplace from some colleagues. Some time after her appointment she was asked to take over the writing of the weekly 'Keane Edge' social column. While she perceived this move to be a demotion, she nevertheless agreed to the move on a temporary basis. However, one week later she told the editor she was no longer willing to work in the role. The claimant also heard rumours that the respondent was actively seeking to employ another crime correspondent. She approached the editor with these fears but was told that she had nothing to worry about. Her flexible work hours were later changed by her line manager, Mr Kealy, and she made a further complaint regarding this. The claimant also complained to Mr Kealy regarding the conduct of one of her colleagues, Mr Jody Corcoran. Mr Kealy told her that he would speak with Mr Corcoran regarding the matter, but the claimant alleged that Mr Kealy never got back to her in relation to the complaint. Soon after, in an administrative change within the office, Mr Corcoran was appointed as the claimant's manager. Some time after that, the claimant requested 16 days' annual leave, which she had accumulated in order that she could work on a book. She was warned by Mr Kealy that such a situation (the gathering of holidays) should not occur again. The claimant was of the view that the position taken by her employer ran contrary to what she had previously agreed in her contract of employment.

---

74. [1993] ELR 161.
75. UD 670/2006.
76. For application of this principle in the context of an employee suing for constructive dismissal as a result of stress or bullying within the workplace, see Chapter 16.
77. [2002] ELR 84.

In finding that the reaction of the claimant to these changes in her employment was understandable, the tribunal found that it was 'not an unreasonable belief on her part that once again strictures were being put on how she did her work'.

[21–43] The claimant put her complaints regarding the hostile working environment in writing to Mr Kealy and asked him to respond in kind. However, she did not receive a response. The claimant made a further complaint to the respondent's group managing editor, Mr Roche. In response, Mr Roche attempted to arrange a meeting with the editor in order to resolve the situation. It was his contention that this meeting was just the first step in the process of implementing the company's grievance procedures. However, the claimant did not view it this way and was upset that a meeting was arranged with those she was having difficulties with and whom she felt had done nothing to resolve the problems. As a consequence she developed a stress-related condition and soon after resigned her position, claiming constructive dismissal. In finding in favour of the claimant, the tribunal noted the poor behaviour of the respondent in failing to deal with the claimant's concerns in any meaningful manner and concluded that it was 'reasonable in all the circumstances' for the claimant to have had no confidence in the respondent to properly or effectively address her grievances.

[21–44] As is discussed in Chapter 16, an employee who suffers from a stress-related illness caused by his or her employment may be justified in resigning his or her position and claiming for constructive dismissal where the employer fails to notice the employee's illness or to take appropriate steps to alleviate it. In *Riehn v Dublin Society for the Prevention of Cruelty to Animals*,[78] the claimant worked as the general manager of the DSPCA until 2002. She claimed that she had been constantly undermined by her employer since taking up her employment. She had made complaints regarding lines of communication within the organisation and her workload in particular. She received a verbal promise that assistance would be provided. This did not happen. As a consequence of her difficulties at work, her health began to deteriorate and she was advised by her doctor to take time off work. Her employer claimed that the first it became aware of her illness was upon the production of a medical certificate by her doctor to explain her absence from work. After an eight-week absence, the claimant met with her employer in order to negotiate certain safeguards into her contract designed to protect her health. After the lapse of a period of time with no response from her employer, she considered herself to have been dismissed. In upholding her claim for constructive dismissal, the tribunal observed that:

> the nature and general remoteness of the employer in terms of everyday contact with the employee may have been a significant contributory factor in relation to what happened. However, we did not regard this factor as a sufficient ground to absolve the employer from responsibility in the matter. We fully accept that the

78. [2004] ELR 205.

severe stress suffered by the employee was job-related and feel that it should have
been noticed by the employer and not allowed to continue for as long as it did
without any positive intervention.[79]

An employer must always tread carefully with employees who are suffering from   [21–45]
a stress-related illness. In *Curran v Graham Anthony & Co Ltd.*,[80] the claimant
worked in the respondent company's wholesale company. During that time she
began a personal relationship with the owner of the respondent company. The
relationship broke down and then the complainant noticed that the atmosphere
in work was deteriorating. The claimant became ill and while on sick leave her
mobile phone was disconnected and the respondent refused to pay her sick pay.
She returned to work, but the atmosphere did not improve. She felt isolated and
eventually had a nervous breakdown. While on sick leave the respondent company
contacted her by letter informing her that certain operational irregularities were
being investigated and would be discussed with her upon her return. The claimant's
psychiatrist advised her that it would be detrimental to her health if she returned
to work, and she resigned her position and claimed constructive dismissal. The
tribunal found that the claimant had been constructively dismissed. The conduct
of the respondent in contacting the claimant and inferring misconduct of a serious
nature while she was still on sick leave was particularly inappropriate:

> The employer did not provide any details of any irregularities. The claimant did
> not know to what irregularities the employer was referring. This paragraph [in the
> letter] conveyed the clear implication that the claimant was somehow involved in
> serious irregularities of an unspecified nature regarding the operational dealings of
> the respondent company. No evidence was adduced at the hearing in this regard.
> Whilst the Tribunal must decide the claim for constructive dismissal on what was
> operating on the claimant's mind at the time of her resignation it can have regard
> to the latter fact as corroborative evidence. In the circumstances the Tribunal finds
> that the employer's conduct, in referring to serious irregularities of an unspecified
> nature and doing so while the claimant was out sick due to stress, was so unreason-
> able as to justify the claimant's resignation and claim for constructive dismissal.

A breach of the implied duty of trust and confidence between an employer and   [21–46]
employee may occur following a series of actions by the employer which, by themselves, may not amount to a breach but which cumulatively amount to a breach of
the term.[81] The last in the series of such incidents, which results in the employee
resigning, is also known as the 'last straw' situation, i.e. the latest act when taken
in conjunction with the earlier acts amounts to a breach of the implied term
of trust and confidence.[82] Such a situation arose before the Supreme Court in

---

79. [2004] ELR 205, 212.
80. UD 495/2006.
81. *Woods v W.M. Car Services (Peterborough) Limited* [1981] ICR 666.
82. *Omilaju v Waltham Forest London Borough Council* [2004] 3 All ER 129, [2005] ICR 481.

Berber v Dunnes Stores Ltd.,[83] where an employee unsuccessfully claimed that his employer had, through a series of negative interactions, breached the implied duty of trust and confidence between the parties. In the first of these incidents, the court found that the appellant's (employer's) initial decision to move the respondent (employee) from his former role as buyer to store manager at the Blanchardstown store was a bona fide decision and within the appellant's rights. At that stage it was held that the appellant was not aware nor should have been aware of the respondent's mental condition or the fact that it was affecting his Crohn's Disease. Instead the court held that the respondent's refusal to move until he had spoken to senior management. was unreasonable. Notwithstanding the respondent's unreasonable refusal to comply with the direction of the appellant, the court found that the appellant continued to act reasonably when it did not seek to dismiss him for his insubordination and instead adopted the much less severe measure of suspending him with pay. Following receipt of the respondent's solicitor's letter in December 2000 informing the appellant of the respondent's deteriorating medical condition the appellant informed the respondent that it would be willing to overlook the previous incidents provided that he returned to work as soon as possible after he was certified medically fit to do so.

[21–47] Following the respondent's return to work another incident arose regarding the roster, which described the respondent as a new trainee. The respondent objected to this description of him – given his many years of experience – and to a personalised training plan set for him by the appellant. The appellant admitted that a genuine mistake had been made regarding the naming of the respondent on the roster. As regards the personalised training plan, the appellant pointed out that, while the respondent had many years' experience, he had been absent from store management for a number of years and a lot had changed during that intervening period. Nevertheless, the appellant made reasonable attempts to accommodate the respondent's concerns and had drafted a new training plan. The court did not find that the appellant's behaviour in this regard was unreasonable or oppressive and, while the correction of the roster was not in the form agreed, attempts had been made to rectify the situation.

[21–48] The final incident that involved a dispute regarding the hours the respondent was scheduled to work. The disagreement ended with the respondent refusing to work the longer hours (which his manager believed he was obliged to), telling the manager that he could deal with his solicitor in future, and refusing to communicate directly with the appellant. Having reviewed both the employer's and the employee's pattern of behaviour throughout each of these incidents, Finnegan J concluded:

> That being the history of interaction between the appellant and the respondent and looking at each event individually and at the events cumulatively, I am satisfied

---

83. [2009] IESC 10, [2009] ELR 61. The facts of this case are discussed extensively in Chapter 16 and in Chapter 4.

that the conduct of the appellant judged objectively was not such as to amount to a repudiation of the contract of employment. The conduct judged objectively did not evince an intention not to be bound by the contract of employment. On the other hand the conduct of the respondent was in the instances mentioned above unreasonable or in error and the employer's conduct must be considered in the light of the same. In these circumstances the purported acceptance of repudiation of the contract of employment by the respondent was neither justified nor effective. The respondent must fail on his claim under this heading.[84]

(B) Reasonableness of the Employee's Behaviour
The question of reasonableness in the context of constructive dismissal works both [21–49] ways. The employee must, in all the circumstances, act reasonably in response to the employer's behaviour. Thus an employee's failure to genuinely engage in a meaningful manner or to exhaust available procedures will make it very difficult for that employee to claim that [s]he has been constructively dismissed.[85]

In *Conway v Ulster Bank Ltd.*,[86] the employee resigned his position without fully [21–50] engaging with the respondent company's grievance procedures in order to resolve his difficulties. The tribunal found his resignation was unreasonable in the circumstances and his claim for constructive dismissal failed. However, the tribunal did accept that an employee is not required to 'jump through the hoops' of following grievance procedures simply to satisfy the tribunal that he has acted reasonably.[87]

In *Harrold v St Michael's House*,[88] the tribunal held that a refusal to engage with [21–51] the employer's grievance procedures may be deemed to be unreasonable behaviour on the part of the employee. In that case the claimant had started working for the respondent in 1991 as a psychologist. In 2001, he started having difficulties with the respondent. In a letter to the chairperson of the board, the claimant expressed concern regarding bullying within the organisation. The chairperson referred the claimant to the respondent's internal grievance procedure to have these concerns addressed. Three individuals were nominated as part of a board to investigate the matter. The claimant maintained two of these individuals were involved in the bullying and stated that he would engage in the process, but not with the two individuals, and would only engage with the process if the board members were independent. The claimant was threatened with disciplinary action if he did not cooperate with the respondent's internal grievance procedures. The respondent then wrote to the claimant outlining a formula for an investigative sub-committee of the board that could investigate the complaints. The claimant objected to this solution because of the presence of a member of the committee on the grounds of

84. [2009] ELR 61, 75.
85. *Walker, Walker and Keating v Sodexho Ireland Ltd.* [2008] ELR 156; *Donnellan v Dunnes Stores* UD 827/2007. Generally see Chapter 16.
86. UD 474/1981.
87. *Lakey v Dunnes Stores Ltd.*, UD 1085/2002.
88. [2008] ELR 1.

his being a friend of the chief executive. In 2002, the board wrote to the claimant, informing him that because he had not cooperated with either of the respondent's procedures the case was now closed. In 2003, he wrote to the Minister for Health highlighting his concerns. The Minister organised for the Eastern Regional Health Authority to set up an investigation. The investigation resulted in the claimant being informed that he had not cooperated with the investigation. Approximately one month later he received a letter from the respondent outlining complaints about his work performance, and in response he wrote a letter enquiring about the status of the investigation. He did not receive a response to this letter and resigned in 2004, and brought an action for constructive dismissal on the basis that he had been the subject of persistent bullying by the respondent. The tribunal held that there was no evidence that the claimant was bullied in such a manner and the claimant's failure to engage with the two processes offered to him by the respondent in response to his complaints was unreasonable behaviour.

[21–52]   However, a failure to engage with the employer's grievance procedures may not always be deemed unreasonable. In *Porter v Atlantic Homecare Ltd.*,[89] the claimant worked as a sales assistant for the respondent. Following the appointment of a new manageress, the claimant began to experience difficulties. She had been subjected to name-calling, had been shouted at and had been required to take holidays in place of *force majeure* leave. She was also wrongly accused of taking money from the till (it was subsequently discovered that the discrepancy had arisen due to a banking error). The claimant received no warnings from her manageress. The claimant went on sick leave and soon after resigned her position and claimed that she had been constructively dismissed. Notwithstanding the fact that the claimant had not utilised the respondent's grievance procedures, the tribunal held that her resignation had been involuntary and she had been constructively dismissed. Her failure to follow the employer's grievance procedures was excused on the basis that the existing problems at work had made her afraid of availing of such procedures.

3.1.3.3. Delay
[21–53]   Whether it be under the 'contract' or 'reasonableness' test, the behaviour of the employer must have caused the claimant's resignation. As such, any unjustified delay between the alleged incident(s) that caused the resignation and the actual date of resignation itself could prove fatal to a claim for constructive dismissal as any such delay could be interpreted as amounting to an affirmation of the contract by the employee. This, however, is not a strict rule, and the significance of delay is a question of fact to be determined in each case. Browne-Wilkinson J in *WE Cox Toner (International) Ltd. v Crook*[90] stated:

> Mere delay by itself (unaccompanied by any express or implied affirmation of the contract) does not constitute affirmation of the contract; but if it is prolonged it

89. [2008] ELR 95.
90. [1981] IRLR 443.

may be evidence of an implied affirmation... Affirmation of the contract can be implied...[91]

Browne-Wilkinson J qualified this statement by reiterating that where the victim elects to continue with the contract, but reserves the right to resign at a later date, [s]he may do so:

> if the innocent party further performs the contract to a limited extent but at the same time makes it clear that he is reserving his right to accept the repudiation... such further performance does not prejudice his rights subsequently to accept the repudiation.[92]

However, where delay exists, a causative relationship between the employer's [21–54] behaviour and the employee's decision to resign must exist. In *O'Leary v Cranehire Ltd.*,[93] the claimant was the victim of an assault by his employer in January 1978. However, it was not until January 1979 that the claimant resigned and claimed constructive dismissal because of the incident. Because of the delay of one year between the assault and the resignation, the tribunal was not convinced that it was the assault that led to the claimant's resignation, hence the claim for constructive dismissal failed.

Thus, delay will not be fatal to a constructive dismissal claim where the claimant can [21–55] show there was good reason for the delay and that the incident was the main reason for their resignation. In *Jones v F Sirl & Son (Furnishers) Ltd.*,[94] the fact that the employee did not resign immediately and instead waited until she found a new job did not necessarily mean she could not make a claim for constructive dismissal.[95] In *Curran v Graham Anthony & Co Ltd.*,[96] a delay of a couple of weeks between the offending behaviour and the resignation of the claimant was not deemed to affect her claim of constructive dismissal as she was under medical care at that time as a result of a stress-related illness caused by her employment situation.

3.2. 'Fair' Dismissals

The second type of dismissal to which the 1977 Act refers are those that are, at [21–56] least potentially, 'fair'. While the 1977 Act may have been introduced in order to offer greater job security to employees, a constant theme running throughout the legislation is that, subject to natural justice and fairness, the employer must retain the discretion and the ultimate authority to dismiss an employee for stated reasons if it is in the best interests of the business.

---

91. [1981] IRLR 443, 444.
92. *ibid.*
93. UD 167/1979.
94. [1997] IRLR 493.
95. *Walton & Morse v Dorrington* [1997] IRLR 488.
96. D 495/2006.

[21–57]   Accordingly, s.6(1) of the 1977 Act lists the grounds on which it may, depending on the circumstances, be deemed 'fair' to dismiss an employee. Conscious that these grounds could be used as convenient labels by employers to hide the real reasons for the employee's dismissal, the legislation and subsequent decisions of the tribunal have adopted a twin-track approach by which the legitimacy of every dismissal can be examined. First, the tribunal must assess whether the *grounds* on which the decision to dismiss was based were fair (substantive fairness). Secondly, the tribunal must assess whether the *manner* in which the decision was reached was fair (procedural fairness). This issue of procedural fairness and specifically the obligations of the employer in this regard are discussed in more detail in Chapter 18.

3.2.1. Substantive Fairness
[21–58]   Section 6(1) of the 1977 Act provides that a dismissal shall be deemed to be an unfair dismissal unless, having regard to all the circumstances, there were substantial grounds justifying it. The onus of proof is therefore placed on the employer to justify the dismissal on 'substantial grounds'.[97]

[21–59]   Section 6(4) of the 1977 Act provides that if the employer can establish that the dismissal resulted, wholly or mainly, from one of the following grounds, it will be deemed a fair dismissal:

> (i)   the capability, competence or qualifications of the employee[98];
> (ii) the employee's conduct[99];
> (iii) redundancy of the employee[100];
> (iv) the employee's continued employment would be in contravention of statute.[101]

3.2.1.1. Capability
[21–60]   Section 6(4)(a) of the 1977 Act provides that a dismissal will be not be unfair if it arises due to the fact that the employee has been deemed incapable of performing work of a kind for which [s]he had been employed to do. Section 6(4)(a) does not define the word, however, the jurisprudence of the EAT has taken 'capability' in this context to mean that the employee is *inherently* incapable of carrying out the work [s]he was employed to do.[102]

---

97. However, not only must the reasons for the employee's dismissal be deemed to be substantively fair but also the decision to dismiss itself must, according to s.5 of the 1993 Act, be reasonable and in line with constitutional principles of natural justice and fair procedures (procedural fairness): *Garvey v Ireland* [1981] IR 75; *Glover v BLN Limited* [1973] IR 388. This is considered in detail in Chapter 18.
98. s.6(4)(a) of the 1977 Act.
99. s.6(4)(b) *ibid.*
100. s.6(4)(c) *ibid.*
101. s.6(4)(d) *ibid.*
102. However, the employer must establish that the decision to dismiss on the grounds of incapability was necessary to protect the business.

Such incapability can often arise through no fault of the employee, for example, [21–61] where it derives from medical illness.[103] In *Reardon v St Vincent's Hospital*,[104] the claimant was employed as kitchen porter. He had a history of prolonged absences from work. Each absence was explained by way of medical certificates produced by the claimant. The employer warned the claimant that his continued absences from work were a source of concern. He was also warned that if his attendance record did not improve, his continued employment would be reviewed. The claimant's attendance did not improve and he was dismissed. The claimant challenged the dismissal on the basis *inter alia* that each of his absences had been explained by way of medical certificates. The claim failed, however, with the tribunal finding that, whereas the claimant was not at fault for the situation, ultimately he was not capable of performing his work and the employer had acted reasonably in reaching the decision to dismiss.[105]

In this respect, dismissal simply because the employee has a poor attendance [21–62] record will not be sufficient.[106] On the other hand, where an employee is absent from work for a prolonged period, an employer may be justified in dismissing the employee (provided he has acted reasonably) notwithstanding the fact that the reason for the absence relates to the employee's medical condition. In such circumstances, the employer should evaluate all the information available to him or her, including the nature of the illness, the probability of recovery, the expected date of return, the needs of the business and so forth.[107] Thus the EAT noted in *McElhinney v Templemore Co-opearative Society Ltd.* that:

> the basic question that has to be determined in every case is whether in all the circumstances the employer can be expected to wait any longer and, if so, how much longer. The nature of the illness, the likely length of the continuing absence, the need of the employers to have done the work which the employee was engaged to do – and these presumably will vary with the size of the employing organisation. In some cases four to six weeks may justify dismissal, in others six months may not.[108]

In such circumstances, the question will also arise as to whether or not the [21–63] contract between the parties has become frustrated.[109] Frustration in the context

---

103. Shubotham, 'Illness and Incapacity in the Workplace', 1(1) *IELJ* (2004), 6.
104. UD 74/1979.
105. s.6(4)(a) states that this ground must render the employee incapable of doing the work [s]he was employed to do, nor is there any obligation on the employer to find alternative work for an incapacitated employee where it would be unreasonable to expect him to do so. *Gurr v Office of Public Works*, UD 919/1987; *Corless v Steiner (Galway) Ltd.*, UD 535/1982.
106. *McGrane v Mater Private Nursing Home*, UD 369/1985.
107. *Mooney v Rowntree Mackintosh Ltd.*, UD 473/1990.
108. UD 434/1982.
109. For greater discussion see Chapter 19.

of employment law has been described as incapacity[110] that makes it appear 'that further performance of [the employee's] obligations in the future would either be impossible or would be a thing radically different from that undertaken by him and agreed to be accepted by the employer'.[111] Naturally, given that a frustrating event would terminate a contract by operation of law, it could be argued by an employer that a long-term incapacitated employee was not dismissed, but rather that the contract had simply terminated as a result of the failure of the employee to honour its fundamental terms. In other words, the doctrine of frustration could be used as a cloak to hide the dismissal. As a consequence, the EAT, both in Ireland and the UK, have been loathe to allow employers plead that a contract had been frustrated in such circumstances. The EAT for England and Wales in *Williams v Watsons' Luxury Coaches*[112] have considered the following factors to be relevant when seeking to confirm whether or not the contract of employment has been frustrated in such circumstances:

(1) the length of employment prior to the event and the length of future foreseeable employment;
(2) the nature of the work;
(3) the nature of the illness and its length;
(4) the prospects for recovery;
(5) the employer's need for a replacement;
(6) whether wages or sick pay have continued to be paid;
(7) whether in all the circumstances a reasonable employer would have waited longer.

[21–64] The fact that the employee has been rendered incapable of working because of an illness or injury *caused by his or her work* should not affect the validity of the decision to dismiss on the grounds of incapability.[113] Thus in *London Fire and Civil Defence Authority v Betty*,[114] the EAT for England and Wales confirmed that:

> An employer does not disable himself from fairly dismissing an employee whom he has injured. The employer's duty to act fairly in dismissing an employee on the grounds of ill health is unaffected by consideration as to who was responsible for the employee's unfitness for work. The question is whether the dismissal was fair having regard to the employee's medical condition and the enquiries and procedures which the employer made and used before deciding to dismiss.[115]

110. A contract of employment may also be frustrated due to the employee's incapacity where that employee has been imprisoned: *Kingston v British Railways Board* [1984] IRLR 146.
111. *Marshall v Harland & Wolff Ltd. and the Secretary of State for Employment* [1972] ICR 101, 106.
112. [1990] ICR 536, [1990] IRLR 164. This decision followed and expanded earlier decisions of the EAT for England and Wales in *Marshall v Harland & Wolff Ltd.* [1972] 1 WLR 899 and *Egg Stores Ltd. v Leibovici* [1977] ICR 260. These decisions were followed, for the most part, by the Irish EAT in *Donegal County Council v Langan*, UD 143/1989.
113. *Caulfield v Waterford Foundry Ltd.* [1991] ELR 137.
114. [1994] IRLR 384.
115. *ibid.*, at 384.

Before dismissing an employee on the grounds of incapability, the employer must ensure that the employee was given fair warning of the possibility of dismissal and a fair hearing before such a decision is made.[116]

3.2.1.2. Competence
Competence in this regard relates to the employee's ability to do the work satisfacto- [21–65] rily. Continual poor work performance, with no sign of improvement, may be a justi-fiable reason for dismissal under this heading. Of crucial importance, then, is how an employee's performance is to be measured. In some jobs work performance may be easily measurable, however, in many others, particularly in management roles, performance may be somewhat more difficult to assess. In such instances, therefore, the EAT for England and Wales has tended to rely on the views of management as to whether the employee was incompetent. In *Cooke v Thomas Linnell & Sons Ltd.*,[117] the claimant was a non-food manager in the respondent's company. He was promoted to a position where he was managing the food section – a position for which he had no previous experience. He was dismissed on the basis of poor work performance. The claimant argued that, while there was evidence that the management had lost confidence in the claimant's ability to do his job, there was no objective on factual evidence that this opinion was justified. The claimant contended that irrespective of how strong the criticism by an employer was, it was not sufficient by itself to prove that [s]he was incompetent. It was the respondent's contention that evidence of management's opinion of the employee's performance should be taken as conclusive proof of that employee's incompetence. However, Philip's J did not agree:

> It seems to us that this goes too far, although we accept that there is something in the point. When responsible employers have genuinely come to the conclusion over a reasonable period of time that a manager is incompetent we think that it is some evidence that he is incompetent.[118]

This test was further developed by the English Court of Appeal in *Alidair Ltd. v Taylor*,[119] where Lord Denning MR stated that, when dismissing an employee for incompetence, 'it is sufficient that the employer honestly believed on reasonable grounds that the man is incapable and incompetent. It is not necessary for the employer to prove that he is in fact incapable or incompetent.'[120]

The Irish tribunal, in *McDonnell v Rooney t/a Spar Supermarket*[121] developed a twin [21–66] test to determine whether an employee's dismissal was justified on the grounds of his or her incompetence. In that case, the claimant was dismissed following a number of irregularities with the operation of cash registers. Despite warnings,

---

116. *Bolger v Showerings (Ireland) Ltd.* [1990] ELR 184.
117. [1977] IRLR 132.
118. [1977] IRLR 132, 134.
119. [1978] ICR 445, [1978] IRLR 82.
120. [1978] ICR 445, 451.
121. UD 504/1991.

these irregularities continued and the claimant was eventually dismissed due to a lack of competence. The tribunal held that the test for dismissal in cases involving alleged incompetence should be divided into two parts:

    (i) Does the employer honestly believe that the employee is incompetent or unsuitable for the job?

    (ii) Are the grounds for his belief reasonable?

[21–67]   The test contains both a subjective and objective element. While the subjective opinion of the employer as to whether the employee is competent will be relevant in determining the issue, it will only be valid as proof of incompetence where such a belief is justified on objectively reasonable grounds. Ultimately, the tribunal in *McDonnell* found that the grounds justifying the employer's decision to dismiss were not reasonable. In particular, it found that the claimant was not solely responsible for all cash register requirements, the system of monitoring operators was flawed, and there was no proper investigation of the problem carried out by the employer.

[21–68]   It should also be noted that an employee could, depending on the nature and seriousness of the work, be dismissed for a single act of incompetence. In *Alidair Ltd. v Taylor*,[122] the employee was a commercial pilot who was dismissed because he made a faulty landing with 77 passengers during reasonable weather conditions. While none of the passengers were hurt, the aircraft was badly damaged. The pilot's claim was not only rejected by the tribunal, but also by the Court of Appeal.

Where an employer considers that an employee is not performing to the appropriate standard, he or she must warn the employee of that fact and provide them with a reasonable opportunity to effect the necessary improvement.[123]

3.2.1.3. Qualifications

[21–69]   The dismissal of an employee may be justified on the basis that [s]he does not possess the necessary qualifications to perform the work that [s]he was employed to do. In this respect, the concept of qualifications has not been defined under the 1977 Act. Taken in its ordinary meaning, qualifications are obtained where an individual passes an examination or course. The term 'qualifications' for the purposes of the equivalent English legislation was defined by the EAT for England and Wales in *Blue Star Ship Management Ltd. v Williams*[124] as qualifications that have a bearing on ability or aptitude. Therefore, a mere permit or authorisation is not considered a qualification unless so connected with the employee's ability or aptitude to do the work.

[21–70]   If an employee is to be fairly dismissed on the grounds of lack of qualifications, the qualifications that [s]he is lacking must be necessary for him or her to perform

---

122. [1978] ICR 445, [1978] IRLR 82.
123. *Richardson v H Williams & Co Ltd.*, UD 17/1979.
124. [1978] ICR 770, [1979] IRLR 16.

the work that [s]he was employed to do. In *Lister v Thom & Sons Ltd.*,[125] an employee was employed as a fitter and driver. In order to drive heavy vehicles he was required to hold a HGV licence. The employee did not hold such a licence and, when he sat the driving test, he failed it. He was told by his employer that the licence was necessary (although this requirement had never formed part of his contract of employment) for his continued employment. He tried the test again and failed. He was then dismissed. The EAT for England and Wales found that the dismissal was unfair. The requirement to hold a licence never formed part of his contract of employment and did not prevent him from continuing to work as a fitter. By contrast, in *Tayside Regional Council v McIntosh*,[126] it was found by the same tribunal that the dismissal of a car mechanic who had lost his driver's licence was justified, as the qualification was necessary to do his job.

Where the nature of the work changes such that it is necessary that the employee [21–71] undergo further training, then the employer may be justified in dismissing an employee where he or she fails to obtain those qualifications within a reasonable time.[127] However, the employee must be afforded a reasonable opportunity to obtain the necessary qualifications.[128]

3.2.1.4. Conduct

The manner in which one behaves as an employee could be grounds for a fair [21–72] dismissal under the 1977 Act and an employee can thus be fairly dismissed because of his or her conduct. Redmond has observed that the Act does not refer to 'misconduct', but simply 'conduct'.[129] Therefore, the legislation gives the employer greater scope for dismissal of an employee on grounds that may not, in the ordinary sense, be considered bad behaviour.

In order to justify a dismissal on the grounds of the employee's conduct, it must be [21–73] established by the employer that he acted reasonably in dealing with the employee at all times. This would include carrying out a reasonable and proper investigation into the alleged behaviour and drawing a reasonable conclusion from the information unearthed by any such investigation.[130] The tribunal is less concerned with establishing guilt or innocence in such cases, and more concerned with establishing whether the employer's actions in all the circumstances were reasonable.[131] The tribunal will seek to satisfy itself that the employer believed that the employee had not conducted himself properly and the employer had reasonable grounds for such belief.[132]

---

125. [1975] IRLR 47.
126. [1982] IRLR 272.
127. *Ryder and Byrne v Commissioners of Irish Lights*, unreported, High Court, 16 April 1980.
128. *Coyle v Dun Laoghaire Vocational Education Committee*, UD 993/1996.
129. Redmond, *Dismissal Law in Ireland* (2nd ed., Tottel Publishing, 2007), at para.16.01.
130. *Hennessy v Read and Write Shop Ltd.*, UD 192/1978; *BHS v Burchell* [1978] IRLR 379.
131. *Dunne v Harrington*, UD 166/1979; *Looney and Co Ltd. v Looney*, UD 843/1984.
132. *Noritake (Irl) Ltd. v Kenna*, UD 88/1983.

[21–74]   Conduct for these purposes covers a wide range of activities and behaviour. The one common thread throughout, however, is that the conduct must have destroyed the relationship of trust and confidence between the employer and the employee. The type of behaviour that could justify dismissal is not exhaustive, but includes the following:

(1) dishonesty;
(2) breach of loyalty and fidelity;
(3) persistent absenteeism;
(4) refusal to obey reasonable orders;
(5) breach of employer's rules;
(6) physical injury or damage to property; and
(7) crimes committed outside of employment.

(1) Dishonesty

[21–75]   Dishonest behaviour towards an employer or his or her suppliers or customers is always likely to damage the relationship of trust with the employer.[133] Indeed, in certain types of work, where honesty and truth is of paramount importance, dishonesty may be seen as the worst kind of misconduct.[134] Dishonesty can mean different things to different people. In *John Lewis Plc v Coyne*,[135] Bell J proposed the following test for determining whether or not the behaviour of the employee in the circumstances could be considered dishonest:

> In summary, there are two aspects to dishonesty, the objective and the subjective, and judging whether there has been dishonesty involves going through a two-stage process. Firstly, one must first of all decide whether according to the ordinary standards of reasonable and honest people what was done was dishonest? Secondly, if so, then one must consider whether the person concerned must have realised that what he or she was doing was by those standards dishonest. In many, but not all, cases where actions are obviously dishonest by ordinary standards, there will be no doubt about it.[136]

[21–76]   Dishonesty is measured in accordance with objective standards of proper behaviour, but should also take into account the employee's particular situation and his or her subjective awareness as to whether or not his or her behaviour was dishonest. Like the category of conduct itself, there are a wide range of activities that have constituted dishonest behaviour on the part of the employee, thereby justifying dismissal. In *Hardy v Cadbury Ireland Ltd.*,[137] it was held that abuse of

---

133. *Hardyside v Tesco Stores (Irl) Ltd.*, UD 932/1982.
134. *Patel v General Medical Council* [2003] IRLR 316.
135. [2001] IRLR 139.
136. *ibid.*, at para.27, quoting Lord Lane in *Regina v Ghosh* [1982] QB 1053 with approval.
137. UD 727/1983.

a sick-pay scheme by an employee (the employee had been working elsewhere when claiming to be unable to work for the respondent due to illness) constituted dishonesty and was a justifiable reason to dismiss. In *Malone v Burlington Industries (Ireland) Ltd.*,[138] the claimant's dismissal for abusing his sick leave when he was discovered working on his farm at a time when he was certified as being unable to work due to illness was deemed to be unfair. The tribunal found that there was a big difference between being fit enough to 'do a bit around the farm' and being fit enough to work a strenuous eight-hour shift and thus concluded that the dismissal was unfair.

It has been held that falsely completing overtime work sheets where no such over- [21–77] time was worked amounted to dishonest behaviour,[139] as also did the act of an employee in obtaining 'secret profits' through his work, and in both cases the employee's dismissal could be justified on the basis of this dishonesty.[140] Proof that the employee has been found guilty of theft from his employer, clients or customers may amount to dishonest behaviour, justifying the employee's dismissal. However, where the allegations of theft are the subject of continuing police investigation, the employer may be justified in dismissing the employee before the outcome of such an investigation but only if it is reasonable for him or her to do so[141]; the fact that the employee is later cleared by the police investigation will not necessarily render the dismissal unfair. The employer is entitled to make a reasonable decision based on the information before him at the time of dismissal.[142]

(2) Breach of Loyalty and Fidelity

It has long been held that there exists a mutual duty of loyalty or fidelity between [21–78] an employer and an employee that is founded on the contract of employment.[143] It is also clear that, where an employee breaches this duty, this may justify his or her dismissal.

Thus, in *Mulchrone v Feeney*,[144] the tribunal held that an employee could be dismissed where she worked part-time for a competitor as there was a danger she could pass on, however inadvertently, confidential information. Similarly, because of the damage that can be caused to the employer's business, acting in direct competition with one's employer can amount to a breach of the duty of loyalty

---

138. UD 947/1982.
139. *Grimes v Otis Elevator Group Ireland*, UD 292/1988.
140. *Murray v Michael Grant Ltd. t/a Michael Grant Opel Centre*, UD 559/1987.
141. *Sheehan v H.M. Keating & Son Ltd.* [1993] ELR 12.
142. *Hestor v Dunnes Stores Ltd.* [1990] ELR 12; *Harris and Shepherd v Courage* [1981] IRLR 153; *Monie v Coral Racing Ltd.* [1981] ICR 109, [1980] IRLR 96.
143. *Boston Deep Sea Fishing & Ice Co v Ansell* (1888) 39 Ch D 339. For further detailed discussion see Chapter 4.
144. UD 1023/1982.

and fidelity.[145] In *Shortt v Smurfit Corrugated Ireland Ltd.*,[146] the claimant was a specialist designer who was found to have been fairly dismissed when it was discovered that he was using his skills to carry out similar work for a competitor. Indeed, in one extreme example, the requirement not to directly compete has even been held to extend to the activities of the employee's spouse.[147]

[21–79] It should, however, be noted that working a 'second job' is not of itself grounds for dismissal unless it can be shown that by working in the 'second job' the employee is capable of damaging the employer's business. In circumstances where the 'second employer' is not a direct rival or where the employee is not in a position to disclose confidential information then, unless the 'second job' is affecting the employee's performance, any dismissal under this heading will be deemed unfair.[148]

[21–80] It is not a breach of the duty of loyalty and fidelity for an employee to hold out an intention to set up in competition with his employer. However, once the employee actively engages in activity to establish a competitor and abuses his position as an employee through the use of confidential information or approaching other employees, then he will be in breach. To seek alternative employment without an intention to abuse one's confidential position would not constitute a breach.[149] In *Laughton and Hawley v Bapp Industries Supplies Ltd.*,[150] it was held that an employee was not in breach of his duty of loyalty or fidelity where he had simply contacted suppliers asking for price lists. While his activities indicated an intention to set up in competition with his employer, there was no evidence that he was not completely focused on his work for his employer or that he intended to abuse confidential information. This case can be contrasted with the case of *Marshall v Industrial Systems and Control Ltd.*[151] In that case the claimant was the managing director of a software company. With another manager in the company, he approached one of his employer's biggest customers with a view to setting up in competition with his employer. He had also approached another employee to join him in the new venture. On learning of these events, the claimant was dismissed. The EAT for England and Wales found that the employee had been justifiably dismissed by his employer. By directly approaching his employer's clients and other employees the claimant had breached the duty of loyalty and fidelity. *Laughton* was distinguished on the basis that, while the employee may have indicated his intentions, there was no evidence that he was not continuing to perform satisfactorily for his employer and, crucially, he had not acted upon his intentions.

---

145. *Higgins v Aer Lingus*, UD 410/1986.
146. UD 40/1986.
147. *Fairbrother v Steifel Laboratories (Ireland)*, UD 665/1985.
148. *Nova Plastics Ltd. v Froggatt* [1982] IRLR 146.
149. *Harris and Russell Ltd. v Slingsby* [1973] 3 All ER 3, [1973] ICR 454, [1973] IRLR 221.
150. [1986] ICR 634, [1986] IRLR 245.
151. [1992] IRLR 294.

This issue arose in an Irish context in the case of *McDermott v Kemek Ltd/Irish* [21–81]
Industrial Explosives Ltd.[152] In that case the claimant arranged a dinner meeting
with one of his employer's customers. At the meeting he discussed setting up in
business with this individual. At the meeting the proposed business venture was
discussed in general terms. When the employer learned of this, he summoned
the claimant to a meeting, where he asked the claimant whether or not he had
discussed sensitive company information with persons outside the company. The
claimant responded in the negative and was then dismissed. The tribunal found
that, while the claimant was certainly guilty of an indiscretion, the tribunal was
not of the opinion that it was of such a serious nature that it should lead to the
claimant's dismissal. The tribunal found that the information released was of a
general nature, much of which was either in the public domain or could have been
obtained by the customer elsewhere. In finding that the dismissal was unjustified,
the tribunal laid down the following general principles on the matter:

> (1) It is perfectly legitimate for an employee to aspire to set up in business on his
> own account.

> (2) Such a person would consider it normal to work in the industry with which he
> was familiar. It would be contrary to public policy to prevent someone from setting
> up in competition with his existing employer.

> (3) However, an employee's duty of fidelity continues so long as he remains in
> employment. There may be a point at which preparations to set up a new business
> might be incompatible with continuing to serve the existing employer.

> (4) If an employer believes that an employee's actions in pursuit of his ambition
> have become so incompatible, he owes the same duty not to dismiss unfairly as he
> would in any other type of case.[153]

Ultimately, the tribunal found that the employee's actions, while inappropriate,
were general in nature and had not reached a stage where they could be deemed
to be incompatible with continuing to serve his existing employer. The dismissal
was deemed to be unfair.

(3) Persistent Absenteeism
As we have seen, employee absenteeism from work for health reasons generally [21–82]
comes under the heading of incapacity.[154] However, the existence of different
reasons for persistent absenteeism is in reality an issue of conduct, even where
such absences are justified by the production of medical certification. In *Inter-*

---

152. [1996] ELR 233.
153. [1996] ELR 233, 235.
154. See para.21-60 above.

national Sports Co Ltd. v Thomson,[155] the claimant was persistently absent from work with a number of different minor complaints. Each absence was justified with the production of a medical certificate. The employee was warned about her attendance record and was told that if it did not improve she could be dismissed. No such improvement occurred. Before dismissing the claimant, the employer consulted with a general practitioner in order to discuss the claimant's medical certificates. The doctor advised the employer that there was no point in examining the claimant at the time of his request as the effects of her illnesses were transitory and therefore could not be verified after the event. The claimant was dismissed. In upholding the dismissal, the EAT for England and Wales held that:

> Where an employee has an unacceptable level of intermittent absences due to minor illness what is required is firstly that there should be a fair review by the employer of the attendance record and the reasons for it and secondly appropriate warnings after the employee has been given an opportunity to make representations. If there is then no adequate improvement in the attendance record in most cases the employer will be justified in treating the persistent absences as a sufficient reason for dismissing the employee. It would be placing too heavy a burden on an employer to require him to carry out a formal medical investigation in such a case… This is a case where the employer is entitled to say 'enough is enough'.[156]

However, notwithstanding the fact that an employer may have the authority to do this, [s]he should tread carefully in this regard.

[21–83] In very limited circumstances an employer may be justified in dismissing an employee for absenteeism or lateness as a first offence, e.g. where the employee's conduct directly caused the loss of a big order.[157] However, such circumstances will be very rare and the employer should always provide the employee with adequate warnings and conduct a proper investigation prior to dismissal on such grounds.[158]

(4) Refusal to Obey Reasonable and Lawful Orders

[21–84] An employee may be in breach of his contract of employment where he fails to follow a reasonable order of his employer.[159] As Lord Evershed MR observed in *Laws v London Chronicle*[160]:

> It is, in no doubt… generally true that wilful disobedience of a lawful and reasonable order shows a disregard – a complete disregard – of a condition essential to the contract of service, namely, the condition that the servant must obey the proper

---

155. [1980] IRLR 340.
156. *ibid.,* at 340.
157. *Galloway v K Miller (Contractors)* (1980) COIT 243/1980.
158. For more detailed discussion see Chapter 18.
159. *Brewster v Burke and the Minister for Labour* (1985) 4 JISLL 98.
160. [1959] 1 WLR 698.

orders of the master and that, unless he does so, the relationship is, so to speak, struck at fundamentally.[161]

There is no obligation on an employee to follow an order of his or her employer **[21–85]** where it is unlawful or illegal. Thus in *Morrish v Henlys (Folkestone) Ltd.*,[162] an employee was entitled to refuse his employer's request to falsify the accounts where he worked. In assessing whether or not the employee's failure to obey a reasonable order will amount to justifiable grounds for dismissal, the employer must also consider whether or not the employee had valid reasons for refusing to comply with the order. In *Cavanagh v Dunnes Stores*,[163] the claimant was group head of security for the respondent. The claimant had worked for the respondent since 1984. In 1994 the claimant was asked to move from head office to the location of one of the respondent's stores at the ILAC centre. The move caused the claimant some concern. The new office space he was allocated was insufficient for his needs, no other employee of a similar standing in the company had been asked to move from head office, and it appeared that his responsibilities were no longer as head of security for the respondent at a national level, but rather for the ILAC centre store alone. When the claimant sought assurances as to his position within the organisation he received an evasive response from management. The claimant refused to move and was subsequently dismissed. The tribunal held *inter alia* that given the nature of the circumstances surrounding the claimant's refusal to obey the instructions of the respondent in relation to the move, in particular the lack of assurances as to his role within the company, the actions of the employer were not reasonable and the dismissal was unfair.

The simple fact that the order by the employer relates to an action that does not **[21–86]** form part of the employee's contract of employment does not justify the employee in failing to obey that order where [s]he has no good reason for refusing. In this regard, reasonable orders will be interpreted in a manner that will entitle the employer to expect a certain amount of flexibility from the employee.[164] Thus in *Horrigan v Lewisham London Borough Council*,[165] an employee was dismissed where he suddenly refused to work overtime, having done so for the previous ten years. Notwithstanding the fact that he was not contractually obliged to work the overtime, in the absence of a justifiable reason for his refusal, the employer was entitled to dismiss him.

(5) Breach of Employer's Rules

Failure to abide by company rules may be considered conduct that justifies the **[21–87]** dismissal of an employee. The employee must have prior notice of the rules and

---

161. *ibid.*, 700.
162. [1973] 2 All ER 137, [1973] ICR 482, [1973] IRLR 61. See also *Brown v McNamara Freight*, UD 745/1987.
163. [1995] ELR 164.
164. Generally, see Lockton, *Employment Law* (5th ed., Palgrave MacMillan, 2006), at pp.103–105.
165. [1978] ICR 15.

be made aware of the possible consequences of their breach. In *Costello v Gerard F May Roofing Ltd.*,[166] the respondent had issued its employees with a circular that advised them as to the times during which holidays could be taken. The claimants booked their holidays at a time that contravened the circular. As a consequence the respondent suffered a financial loss because a contract could not be completed on time. The tribunal was satisfied that the claimants were fully aware of the respondent's position on the taking of holidays and as such were responsible for their own dismissals. That said, the rules on the taking of holidays must be applied in a reasonable manner, taking all the circumstances into consideration.[167] In *Conroy v Iggy Madden Transport Ltd.*,[168] the claimant had taken her holidays outside the standard period preferred by her employer. Upon her return from holidays she was served with notice of her dismissal. The tribunal held that the employer's response in the circumstances to her taking holidays against management's wishes was disproportionate and her dismissal was unfair.

[21–88] The employee's length of service should also be taken into consideration if the rules are to be applied in a reasonable manner. In *Johnson Matthey Metals Ltd. v Harding*,[169] the employee was found to have been wearing the wristwatch of a co-worker, which had gone missing some months before. The employer dismissed him. The tribunal held that in such circumstances the 15 years of loyal service given by the employee should have been taken into consideration and the dismissal was deemed unfair. Loyal service, however, will not immunise the employee from dismissal. In *AEI Cables Ltd. v McLay*,[170] an employee had been dismissed when it was discovered that he had been defrauding his employer by making false claims for diesel fuels. The dismissal was found to be fair notwithstanding the employee's past work record.

(6) Physical Injury or Damage to Property

[21–89] The conduct of an employee that causes physical injury or damage to the property of another may be grounds justifying the dismissal of the employee. Such conduct would include 'horseplay' or 'goofing around' in circumstances where such actions represented a danger to others. In *Creed v KMP Co-Op Society Ltd.*,[171] the claimant worked in a meat factory. The environment was dangerous as the employees worked with knives. The respondent was very safety conscious and inserted a clause into the employees' terms of employment that stated that 'fighting, provoking or instigating a fight when on company's premises' would lead to the culprit's immediate dismissal. The claimant was involved in a non-aggressive incident with another employee, which involved the throwing of fat. Following an investigation the respondent dismissed the claimant. The tribunal approved the dismissal. In an

---

166. [1994] ELR 19.
167. *Laws Stores Ltd. v Oliphant* [1978] IRLR 251; *Ladbroke Racing Ltd. v Arnott and Others* [1983] IRLR 154.
168. [1991] ELR 29.
169. [1978] IRLR 248.
170. [1980] IRLR 84.
171. [1991] ELR 140.

environment where safety was of such importance given the nature of the work, the claimant's behaviour was unacceptable as his actions had caused risk to others. However, where the employer has failed to control the workplace to such an extent that horseplay is the norm, then an employer may not be justified in dismissing an employee involved in such activity.[172]

Whether or not an employee can be dismissed because of his or her conduct [21–90] outside normal work hours would appear to depend on whether it was deemed to be sufficiently related to his or her work. In *Keane v Westinghouse Electric Ireland Ltd.*,[173] the employee was involved in an altercation with his supervisor in a disagreement over the fact that the supervisor had reported the employee on another occasion, causing his suspension. Despite the fact that the assault had taken place sometime after 11pm at a company function it was found that it was sufficiently connected with the employee's work to justify his dismissal.

(7) Crimes Committed Outside Employment

It is uncertain as to whether and when an employee's conviction for a crime [21–91] committed *outside* of his or her employment would entitle his or her employer to dismiss him or her. In such circumstances, an employer would presumably argue that any such conviction would justify dismissal as it destroys the relationship of trust and confidence between the employer and employee.[174] However, it would appear that such a dismissal can only be justified where there is a sufficient connection between the crime and the employee's work, such that it could be said that the employee's criminal conviction makes him or her unsuitable for the job, or is capable of damaging the employer's business reputation.[175] For example, in *Clarke v CIÉ*,[176] the claimant, who worked as a carriage cleaner for the respondent, was dismissed following his conviction for house breaking and larceny. The tribunal found that the dismissal was unfair. It determined that a policy whereby all criminal convictions justified dismissal would be contrary to public policy. The respondent's argument that the employee's conviction had destroyed the relationship it had with the employee was not accepted by the tribunal, which was of the view that the position did not require a high level of trust. Redmond has criticised this argument, pointing out that it is:

> difficult to think of any job that does not involve trust. Opportunities to betray trust exist in every employment. For example, market-sensitive papers left lying around a boardroom, or discarded in a wastepaper bin, may be accessed by anyone.[177]

---

172. *Dunphy v Largo Food Exports Ltd.* [1992] ELR 179.
173. UD 643/1986.
174. *Clarke v CIÉ*, UD 104/1978.
175. *Singh v London Country Bus Services* [1976] IRLR 176. See also *Robb v Mersey Insulation Co Ltd.* [1972] IRLR 18.
176. UD 104/1978.
177. Redmond, *Dismissal Law in Ireland* (2nd ed., Tottel Publishing, 2007), at para.16.22.

[21–92]   The connection between the criminal conviction and the employee's work was plain in *Barry and French v Irish Linen Service Ltd.*[178] In that case the claimants were involved in an attempted robbery and one of the company's vehicles had been used in the attempt. The dismissals were considered fair by the tribunal. Also, in *Martin v Dunnes Stores (Enniscorthy),*[179] the claimant had broken into and stole from another retailer in the town. The dismissal was deemed not to be unfair.[180] On the other hand, no such connection was found in *Noonan v Dunnes Stores (Mullingar),*[181] where an employee had been convicted of a minor assault of a garda late one night. The employer only learned of the incident some time after it had occurred. Similarly, in *Brady v An Post,*[182] the dismissal of an employee following his conviction for assault was deemed unfair. The claimant was not in a high level position of trust and the conviction did not bring disrepute to the employer's business reputation.

3.2.1.5. Redundancy of the Employee
[21–93]   Section 6(4)(c) of the 1977 Act provides that if the dismissal of the employee arises wholly or mainly because of the redundancy of the employee it will not be unfair.[183] There is a real temptation for employers to disguise what is actually a dismissal as a redundancy, thereby avoiding liability under the 1977 Act. There are essentially three aspects to redundancy in this regard. First, the dismissal of the employee must arise – wholly or mainly – because of redundancy. Secondly, notwithstanding the fact that a genuine redundancy situation may exist, the employer must not unfairly select an employee for redundancy. Such unfair selection will be deemed to be an unfair dismissal under s.6(3) of the 1977 Act. Thirdly, s.6(7) of the 1977 Act (as inserted by s.5(g) of the 1993 Act) now requires that the employer act reasonably when dismissing on the grounds of redundancy.

Definition of Dismissal by Reason of Redundancy
[21–94]   The definition of dismissal by way of redundancy under the 1977 Act is the same as that contained in the Redundancy Payments Acts 1967 to 2003.[184] Section 7(2) of the Redundancy Payments Act 1967 (as amended by s.4 of the Redundancy Payments Act 1971) states:

> [A]n employee who is dismissed shall be taken to be dismissed by reason of redundancy if the dismissal is attributable wholly or mainly to:
>
> (a) The fact that his employer has ceased, or intends to cease, to carry on the business for the purposes of which the employee was employed by him, or

---

178. UD 905 and 906/1986.
179. UD 571/1988.
180. See also *Moore v C & A Modes* [1981] IRLR 71.
181. Unreported, Circuit Court (Neery J) 14 July 1989.
182. UD 463/1991.
183. For more detailed discussion see Chapter 22.
184. s.1 of the 1977 Act.

has ceased or intends to cease, to carry on that business in the place where the employee was so employed; or

(b) The fact that the requirements of that business for employees to carry out work of a particular kind in the place where he was so employed have ceased or diminished or are expected to cease or diminish; or

(c) The fact that his employer has decided to carry on the business with fewer or no employees, whether by requiring the work for which the employee had been employed (or had been doing before his dismissal) to be done by other employees or otherwise; or

(d) The fact that his employer has decided that the work for which the employee has been employed (or had been doing before his dismissal) should henceforward be done in a different manner for which the employee is not sufficiently qualified or trained; or

(e) The fact that his employer has decided that the work for which the employee had been employed (or had been doing before his dismissal) should henceforward be done by a person who is also capable of doing other work for which the employee is not sufficiently qualified or trained.

Crucially, then, dismissal by way of redundancy is not related to the individual. Genuine redundancy arises in circumstances where the work disappears, diminishes or changes. Therefore, to be a valid redundancy the dismissal must not be connected to the individual employee's personality but rather to the state of the business. This is explored further in Chapter 22.

3.2.1.6. Statutory Restrictions

An employer may justifiably dismiss an employee in circumstances where his or her continued employment would be in breach of statute. Thus an employee whose work is based on his or her ability to drive could be dismissed under this heading should [s]he lose his or her licence.[185] Also in *Brennan v Blugas Ltd.*,[186] the fact that an employer could not obtain insurance for one of his employees in order that they could carry out his or her duties was deemed sufficient grounds for dismissal. However, it would appear that the employer would have to be satisfied that [s]he could not provide the employee with suitable alternative work.[187]

[21–95]

In recent years, cases involving work permits for migrant workers have arisen before the tribunal. The tribunal takes a dim view of employers who fail to renew a migrant employee's work permit and then use the fact that the employee no

[21–96]

---

185. *Haugh and Haugh v Atlanta Nursing Home Ltd.*, UD 490 and 491/1994.
186. UD 591/1993.
187. *Appleyard v Smith (Hull) Ltd.* [1972] IRLR 19 and *Mathieson v WJ Noble & Son Ltd.* [1972] IRLR 76.

longer has such a permit as a reason to dismiss him or her. The application for, or renewal of, the employee's work permit is at the very least an implied term of their contract.[188] In *Golovan v Porturlin Shell Fish Ltd.*,[189] the claimant worked for the respondent company. The respondent claimed that it had attempted to secure a work permit for the claimant without success. After 16 months in the employment of the respondent, the claimant was dismissed with one week's notice. The tribunal found that the dismissal was unfair. The claimant had been working in breach of the Employment Permits Act 2003 and it was the respondent's duty to obtain the necessary work permit, which it failed to do.

3.2.1.7. Other Substantial Reasons for Dismissal

[21–97] Finally, s.6(6) of the 1977 Act represents a 'catch-all' provision, whereby a decision to dismiss may be deemed to be fair if there were other substantial grounds not covered in the previous sections that justified the dismissal. Naturally this is a broad principle, and the case law generated by the section represents merely examples of situations where it may have application.

[21–98] For example, in *Flynn v Power*[190] a female school teacher who was in a relationship with a married man was employed at a convent school run by nuns. The board of management of the school asked her to end the relationship as it was setting a bad example for the children of the school. The teacher refused and was dismissed. The dismissal was upheld by the High Court, which held that there were substantial grounds justifying it. The school was established to promote a certain ethos; the management believed that the teacher was damaging that ethos and, having offered her an opportunity to desist from the behaviour, they were entitled to dismiss her.

[21–99] It has been further held that in some instances an unreasonable refusal by an employee to agree to changes in his or her contract of employment in circumstances where an employer is seeking to reorganise his or her business may constitute a 'substantial reason' justifying that employee's dismissal. Thus in *RS Components v Irwin*,[191] the employer sought to introduce restraint of trade clauses into all his employee's contracts. This move was made as a consequence of the fact that the employer had been losing employees to competitors. The employee refused to agree to the change and was dismissed. The dismissal was justified as it was based on sound business reasons. However, if the imposition of the restraint of trade clause is unreasonable, then the employer cannot use the refusal as a reason to justify the dismissal.[192]

In certain circumstances, a dismissal may be justified under s.6(6) where a major customer or client or even fellow workers pressurise the employer to dismiss the

---

188. *Dubyna v Hourican Hygiene Services Ltd. t/a Master Clean Services,* UD 781/2004. Generally, see Redmond, *Dismissal Law in Ireland* (2nd ed., Tottel Publishing, 2007), at paras.15.46 –15.53.
189. UD 428/2006.
190. [1985] IR 648.
191. [1974] 1 All ER 41, [1973] ICR 535, [1973] IRLR 239.
192. *Forshaw v Archcraft Ltd.* [2006] ICR 70, [2005] IRLR 600.

employee. The threat to the employer's business must be real and based on reasonable grounds if the dismissal is to be justified.[193]

3.2.2. Procedural Unfairness

Irish employees enjoy both a contractual and a constitutional right to fair procedures.[194] Moreover, inasmuch as this right will be most keenly enforced by the courts and the tribunal in circumstances where that employee faces the ultimate sanction of dismissal, a dismissal of an employee may be deemed to be unfair in circumstances where, even though there is no *substantive* difficulty with the dismissal (that is, where it is for one of the listed reasons contained in the Act for which a dismissal will be deemed to be fair), the manner in which the decision to dismiss was reached was somehow procedurally flawed. From an employer's standpoint, therefore, it is vital that his or her business have in place a fair set of disciplinary rules and that they be adhered to strictly. This issue is dealt with in Chapter 18, in which we focus on the procedural entitlements of employees both generally and in the specific context of a dismissal situation. [21–100]

3.3. Automatically Unfair Reasons for Dismissal

Section 6(2) of the 1977 Act provides that where the dismissal arises wholly or mainly from any one of the following grounds it will automatically be deemed to be unfair: [21–101]

(i)   trade union membership or activities;
(ii)   civil or criminal proceedings against the employer;
(iii)   religious or political beliefs of the employee;
(iv)   race, colour or sexual orientation of the employee;
(v)   employee's pregnancy and pregnancy-related issues;
(vi)   exercise of other statutory rights;
(vii)   age of the employee;
(viii) membership of the Travelling Community; or
(ix)   unfair selection for redundancy.

3.3.1. Trade Union Membership or Activities

Section 6(2)(a) of the 1977 Act states that the dismissal of an employee will be deemed automatically unfair where it arises due to the fact of: [21–102]

> the employee's membership, or proposal that he or another person become a member, of, or his engaging in activities on behalf of, a trade union or excepted body under the Trade Union Acts, 1941 and 1971, where the times at which he engages in such activities are outside his hours of work or are times during his hours of work in which he is permitted pursuant to the contract of employment between him and his employer so to engage.

---

193. *Merrigan v Home Counties Cleaning Ireland Ltd.*, UD 904/1984.
194. For detailed treatment see Chapter 18.

Under s.6(2)(a) the employee must prove that his or her dismissal arose wholly or mainly from his or her membership or proposed membership of a trade union or as a result of his or her activities on behalf of the trade union during hours of work where [s]he had the permission of the employer to do so. Section 14 of the 1993 Act amended the 1977 Act by providing that an employee alleging that [s]he has been dismissed for the reasons outlined in s.6(2)(a) is no longer required to establish one year's continuous service. Section 14 also places the burden of proving that the employee had been dismissed because of his or her association with a trade union on the shoulders of the claimant.

[21–103] Proving the employer's actual intentions in this regard can be very difficult. However, the tribunal has adopted a common-sense approach to the issue and will not readily accept claims of 'coincidence' by employers who have dismissed an employee in such circumstances.[195] In *White v Betson*,[196] for example, the claimant was out of work sick for a number of days. While out sick on 14 August, he joined a trade union. The union wrote to the respondent on that day regarding the claimant's pay and conditions. The claimant returned to work on 17 August and was told by the respondent that he was no longer needed. The respondent claimed that he had never received a letter from the claimant's trade union and that that decision to dismiss him had nothing to do with his trade union membership. The respondent's evidence in this regard was not accepted by the tribunal, who held that he had received the letter from the trade union prior to his decision to dismiss the claimant. It was its view that the decision to dismiss resulted from the claimant's membership of the union and was therefore unfair.

[21–104] Similarly in *Wixted v Sang Mann*,[197] the claimant worked as a trainee chef for the respondent. He joined a union because of poor working conditions. The union wrote to the respondent, seeking a meeting to discuss these working conditions. The claimant was then dismissed. The respondent contended that the dismissal was due to the claimant's poor work performance. The claimant had only received one warning (from the respondent's brother) and did not receive any other communication from the respondent as to his performance prior to his dismissal. The tribunal found that the dismissal was not because of the claimant's poor work performance, but due to the fact that he had joined a trade union. Accordingly, the dismissal was deemed to be unfair.

[21–105] A dismissal will also be automatically unfair where the employee is dismissed because [s]he had the intention of joining a trade union. In *O'Riordan v Killine Eyewear Ltd.*,[198] the claimant was employed on a temporary short-term contract

---

195. Equally, the employee who claims that [s]he was dismissed for trade union membership must show that the employer knew of his union membership/activity.
196. [1992] ELR 120.
197. [1992] ICR 221, [1991] ELR 208.
198. [1991] ELR 89.

with the respondent company. He had met with other employees in a public house to discuss some grievances they had with the respondent, their employer. In particular, all were unhappy with the amount of overtime they were required to work. At the meeting it was decided to seek legal advice about joining or forming a trade union. The next morning, management called the workers together, explained that they understood the workers were unhappy with the amount of overtime and promised that the hours would be reduced. Six days after the meeting in the public house, the claimant was dismissed due to poor work performance. The claimant had not been warned about the standard of his work prior to his dismissal. The tribunal held that the respondent had been aware of the meeting in the public house and found that the claimant was dismissed because of his involvement and the dismissal was deemed unfair. The EAT for England and Wales reached a similar conclusion in *Fitzpatrick v British Railways Board*.[199] In that case, the claimant deliberately failed to inform her employer of her previous employment and history as a trade union activist. When the employer discovered this he dismissed her on the basis that she had not been truthful. The Court of Appeal held that the true reason for her dismissal was because of her past as a trade union activist and the fear that she would continue such activity in her new employment. The dismissal was deemed to be unfair.

'Membership of a trade union' in this context (referring to similar legislation in England and Wales[200]) has been interpreted by the EAT for England and Wales as including situations where an employee avails of the services of the union. In *Discount Tobacco and Confectionary Ltd. v Armitage*,[201] the claimant was dismissed after she had asked her trade union to enter into a dialogue with her employer regarding the terms of her contract of employment. The employer claimed that she had been dismissed because of poor work performance, while the claimant argued that she had been dismissed because of her union membership. The tribunal held on appeal that: [21–106]

> For the purpose of s.58(1)(a) there is no genuine distinction between membership of a union on the one hand and making use of the essential services of a union officer on the other. The activity of a trade union officer in elucidating and negotiating terms of employment is an important incident of union membership and the outward and the visible manifestation of it. To construe the section so narrowly as to apply only to the fact that a person was a member of the union without regard to the consequences of that membership would be to emasculate the provision altogether.[202]

It is submitted that the Irish tribunal would draw similar conclusions when assessing s.6(2)(a). Limiting the protection to situations where the employee was

199. [1991] IRLR 376.
200. s.152 Trade Union and Labour Relations (Consolidation) Act 1992.
201. [1990] IRLR 15.
202. *ibid.*, at 15.

dismissed solely because of union membership would hardly constitute sufficient protection.

[21–107] Section 6(2)(a) of the 1977 Act also provides that the dismissal of an employee for engaging in trade union 'activities' will be unfair. It would appear that such activities would have to be connected to core aspects of trade union activity. In *Chant v Aquaboats*,[203] an employee organised a petition regarding unsafe machinery. He was a member of a trade union, but the petition was not organised on its behalf. It was held that his dismissal was because of his personal actions and had nothing to do with his union membership and therefore was not an unfair dismissal. In *Bass Taverns v Burgess*,[204] the claimant was a shop steward and was dismissed from the trainer manager aspect of his post. He had delivered a presentation as part of an induction programme for trainee managers. During the presentation he referred to his union and the services that it provided to staff members. His employer felt that the presentation was very biased in favour of the union. The claimant resigned his position as a result. The Court of Appeal held that the claimant was undertaking a trade union activity at an appropriate time. The court concluded:

> A consent to recruit must include a consent to underline the services which the union can provide and that may reasonably involve a submission to prospective members that in some respects the union will provide a service which the company does not.[205]

[21–108] The distinction between 'trade union activities' and industrial action is not always clear. In *Drew v St Edmundsbury Borough Council*,[206] an employee was dismissed after a couple of weeks in his job because he made a number of complaints to his employer regarding health and safety in the workplace. The employee claimed that he had been dismissed following a directive from his union to go slow. It was held that the true reason that the employee had been dismissed was because of his complaints regarding health and safety, which had nothing to do with the trade union directive, and the dismissal was unfair.

[21–109] In order for a dismissal based on trade union activity to be unfair, the activity in question must take place outside of the employee's hours of work. Otherwise, such activities can only take place during hours of work where the employer has consented to such activity. A literal interpretation of the phrase 'hours of work' would mean that the consent of the employer would not be required where the activities in question took place outside of the actual hours that the employee is contracted to work, for example, during statutory rest times.[207]

203. [1978] ICR 643.
204. [1995] IRLR 596.
205. [1995] IRLR 596, 597.
206. [1980] ICR 513, [1980] IRLR 459.
207. *Zucker v Astrid Jewels Ltd.* [1978] ICR 1088, [1978] IRLR 385; *Marley Tile Co Ltd. v Shaw* [1980] ICR 828, [1980] IRLR 25.

3.3.2. Employee Involvement in Civil or Criminal Proceedings against the Employer

Where an employee is dismissed wholly or mainly because of his involvement in [21–110]
civil or criminal proceedings against his employer then such a dismissal will be
automatically deemed unfair. Involvement in proceedings for these purposes will
include direct or indirect involvement. In *Hanon v Prendergast*,[208] the claimant,
against his employer's wishes, gave evidence regarding a case of assault that had
occurred on his employer's premises. The day after giving his testimony, the
claimant was dismissed due to redundancy. The tribunal held that no genuine
redundancy situation existed and the dismissal was therefore unfair.

3.3.3. Religious or Political Beliefs of the Employee

Dismissal due wholly or mainly to the employee's religious or political beliefs will [21–111]
be deemed automatically unfair unless there are substantial reasons justifying such
dismissal.[209] An employee dismissed by reason of religious or political beliefs may
also pursue an action under the Employment Equality Acts 1998–2008.[210]

3.3.4. Race, Colour or Sexual Orientation of the Employee

Dismissal because of the employee's race, colour or sexual orientation will be [21–112]
deemed automatically unfair.[211] An employee may also bring an action for discrimination under the Employment Equality Acts 1998–2008 regarding any dismissal
under this heading.[212]

3.3.5. Employee's Pregnancy and Related Issues

Any dismissal of an employee on the grounds of her pregnancy or for reasons [21–113]
related to her pregnancy, such as maternity leave, will be deemed automatically
unfair unless there are substantial grounds justifying any such dismissal.[213] In
Maxwell v English Language Institute,[214] the claimant was employed as a secretary.
The claimant submitted a form regarding her statutory maternity leave, which was
to be completed by her employer. He failed to do so. When she later advised her
employer that she was taking maternity leave she was told that she was dismissed.
The employer contended that the reason for her dismissal was unconnected to her
pregnancy and asserted that her work had been unsatisfactory. The tribunal found
no evidence that prior to her dismissal the claimant had ever been spoken to
regarding her poor work performance. It was held that her dismissal was actually
connected with her pregnancy and was therefore automatically unfair.

---

208. UD 274/1985.
209. s.6(2)(b) of the 1977 Act as amended by s.5(a) of the 1993 Act. See also *Merriman v St James's Hospital*, unreported, Circuit Court, Clarke J, 24 November 1986.
210. See Chapter 9.
211. s.6(2)(e) of the 1977 Act as amended by s.5(a) of the 1993 Act.
212. *ibid.*
213. For more detailed discussion see Chapter 13.
214. [1990] ELR 226.

[21–114] However, in certain limited circumstances, an employer may be justified in dismissing an employee on the grounds of her pregnancy. Section 6(2)(f) of the 1977 Act provides that an employee may be dismissed where she was unable by reason of the pregnancy or matters connected with it:

> (I) to do adequately the work for which she was employed, or
> (II) to continue to do such work without contravention by her or her employer of a provision of a statute or instrument made under statute, and

> (ii) (I) there was not, at the time of the dismissal, any other employment with her employer that was suitable for her and in relation to which there was a vacancy,
>
> or
>
> (II) she refused an offer by her employer of alternative employment on terms and conditions corresponding to those of the employment to which the dismissal related, being an offer made so as to enable her to be retained in the employment notwithstanding her pregnancy.

[21–115] However, as discussed earlier in Chapters 15 and 13, an employer is obliged to conduct a risk assessment of the workplace to assess whether workers are exposed to unacceptable risks. In the case of a pregnant employee, where the workplace poses an unacceptable risk the employer is required to provide the employee with alternative work that does not pose such risks. If it is technically or objectively feasible for this to happen or the alternative work is not suitable, the pregnant employee is entitled to be granted leave from her employment.[215]

3.3.6. Exercise of other Statutory Rights

[21–116] This category was introduced under s.5(a) of the 1993 Act and provides that dismissal of the employee simply because [s]he has exercised his or her statutory rights under other employment legislation is *prima facie* unfair. For example, s.25(1) of the Parental Leave Acts 1998–2006 provides that it shall be an unfair dismissal to dismiss an employee simply because [s]he exercises or proposes to exercise his or her right to parental or *force majeure* leave under the Acts; s.36(1) of the National Minimum Wage Act 2000 provides that an employee should not be penalised through dismissal for exercising his or her rights under the Act; and s.16(3) of the Carer's Leave Act 2001 also provides that an employee should not be penalised for proposing to exercise or having exercised his or her entitlement to carer's leave under that enactment.

3.3.7. Age of the Employee

[21–117] This category was introduced under s.5(a) of the 1993 Act and provides that an employee cannot be dismissed because of his or her age. Often the dismissal of employees because of age, particularly where such employees are older, is disguised

---

215. s.18(1) Maternity Protection Act 1994.

behind the cloak of redundancy. In *Kerrigan v Peter Owens Advertising and Marketing Ltd.*,[216] the claimant, an account director, was informed that due to a loss of clients he was to be made redundant. It transpired that the claimant's age was a factor in his dismissal as his employer was of the opinion that their clients wanted to deal with somebody younger in his position. The tribunal found that no redundancy situation actually existed, that the primary reason for the claimant's dismissal was because of his age and, consequently, that the dismissal was unfair.

3.3.8. Membership of the Travelling Community
This category was another introduced under s.5(a) of the 1993 Act. If an employee [21–118] is dismissed because of his membership of the Travelling Community then it will be deemed automatically unfair. Discrimination on this ground is considered in detail Chapter 9.

3.3.9. Unfair Selection for Redundancy
Section 6(4) of the 1977 Act provides that if the dismissal arises wholly or mainly [21–119] because of the redundancy of the employee it will not be unfair. However, s.6(3) of the 1977 Act provides that the unfair selection of the employee for redundancy will automatically amount to an unfair dismissal for the purposes of the legislation.[217]

4. Redress for Unfair Dismissal

Section 7 of the 1977 Act (as amended) makes provision for the remedies that may [21–120] be available to an unfairly dismissed employee. These remedies reflect the legislation's laudable aim of bringing about, insofar as is practicable, conciliation between the disputing parties. The nature of the remedies, particularly those of reinstatement and re-engagement, recognise the proprietary interest that employees have in their jobs by providing that, in appropriate circumstances, they may be entitled to return to those jobs.[218]

Section 14 of the 1977 Act (as amended by s.9 of the 1993 Act) provides that where requested, an employer must provide the employee with particulars in writing of the grounds for the employee's dismissal within 14 days. However, for the purposes of the Acts, when determining whether the dismissal was unfair, account may be taken of any other grounds that are substantial grounds and would justify the dismissal.

Unfair dismissal claims shall be brought in the first instance to a Rights Commis- [21–121] sioner, or, if there is an objection, to the Tribunal.[219] The Rights Commissioner's

---

216. UD 31/1997.
217. For detailed discussion see Chapter 22.
218. Generally, see Redmond, *Dismissal Law in Ireland* (2nd ed., Tottel Publishing, 2007), at ch.23.
219. s.8(1) of the 1977 Act.

decision may be appealed to the Tribunal,[220] and the Tribunal's determination may be appealed to the Circuit Court.[221] In either case, the time limit for bringing such an appeal is six weeks.[222] Where the employer fails to act in accordance with the determination of the Rights Commissioner or tribunal within six weeks from the date on which the determination was communicated to the parties, then proceedings can be instigated in the Circuit Court against the employer for redress under the Act.[223] The High Court has expressly confirmed that a right of appeal to the High Court exists from Circuit Court decisions under the Unfair Dismissals Acts[224]; amongst the many examples of such appeals is the famous decision in *Flynn v Power*,[225] discussed above in this chapter.

[21–122] Section 8(2) of the 1977 Act provides that a claim for unfair dismissal under the legislation must be brought either to the Rights Commissioner or the tribunal within six months of the date of dismissal. Section 7 of the 1993 Act provides, however, that the six-month period may be extended up to a maximum period of 12 months in circumstances where a Rights Commissioner or the tribunal determines that exceptional circumstances exist that prevented the employee from bringing their claim within the initial six-month period. The tribunal has been quite strict in its interpretation of the words 'exceptional circumstances'. In *Byrne v PJ Quigley Ltd.*,[226] the claimant was dismissed from his employment in November 1993. He had been engaged as an independent contractor; however, he later discovered that for the purposes of social welfare his status was that of an employee from March 1992 until September 1993. Upon learning this fact he instigated a claim for unfair dismissal against his former employer in August 1994. He made a submission to the tribunal seeking an extension of the time limit available under s.7 of the 1993 Act. The tribunal rejected the application for an extension and outlined three tests that must be satisfied before an extension is granted:

1. The exceptional circumstances must be something out of the ordinary or unusual, although it need not be highly unusual.
2. The exceptional circumstances must have prevented the lodging of the claim within the 6 month period. Thus there must be a causative link between the exceptional circumstances and the failure to lodge the claim.
3. The exceptional circumstances must therefore have arisen during the initial 6 month period.

[21–123] The tribunal concluded that the social welfare investigation into his status as a worker instigated the bringing of a claim but did not prevent him from bringing

220. s.9(1) *ibid.*
221. s.10(4) *ibid.*
222. s.9(1) *ibid.*; s.11 of the 1993 Act.
223. s.10(1) of the 1977 Act.
224. *The Commissioners of Irish Lights v Sugg* [1994] ELR 97.
225. [1985] IEHC 1, [1985] IR 648.
226. [1995] ELR 205.

one. Nothing had occurred during this period that was exceptional and that would have prevented him from lodging a claim. In *McDonagh v Dell Computer Corporation*,[227] the tribunal accepted the claimant's evidence that the treatment of him by his employer had caused him to suffer from a stress-related illness, which was an exceptional circumstance that had prevented him from lodging his claim within the necessary time period.

The tribunal has also held that where the claimant fails to comply with the six-month limitation period solely because of a mistake made by the claimant's solicitor, such a mistake will not constitute exceptional circumstances justifying an extension of the limitation period. In *Baxter v Kildare County Council*,[228] with two or three weeks to go to the end of the six-month limitation period, the claimant instructed her solicitor to proceed with an unfair dismissal action by lodging a claim with the Rights Commissioner. Unfortunately, this was not done within the time limits and the tribunal refused to extend the limitation period based solely on the solicitor's mistake. [21–124]

Once an employee elects to pursue his or her claim through the statutory unfair dismissals route and a recommendation has been made by a Rights Commissioner, or proceedings before the tribunal have commenced, that employee is not entitled to pursue a common law claim for wrongful dismissal arising from the same incident.[229] Conversely, an employee cannot bring a claim for unfair dismissal under the legislation where the hearing by the court of proceedings for wrongful dismissal has commenced.[230] [21–125]

Section 7 of the 1977 Act identifies three remedies that may be awarded as a Rights Commissioner, the tribunal or the Circuit Court may deem appropriate, having regard to all the circumstances surrounding the complaint.

4.1. Re-instatement

In recommending or ordering the re-instatement of an employee a Rights Commissioner, tribunal or court is effectively putting on record that the employee was entirely blameless as regards his or her dismissal. While not always practicable, it is possibly the highest form of vindication a dismissed employee can obtain under the legislation. [21–126]

227. [2004] ELR 197.
228. UD 1255/2005.
229. s.15(2) of the 1977 Act, as amended by s.10 of the 1993 Act.
230. s.15(3) *ibid.* Generally, see Chapter 16 for further analysis of the circumstances when an employee is precluded from bringing a claim under the legislation because [s]he has already initiated a claim under the common law. Generally, see *Pickering v Microsoft Ireland Operations Ltd.* [2006] ELR 65; *Eastwood v Magnox Electric Plc*; *McCabe v Cornwall County Council* [2004] UKHL 35, [2005] 1 AC 503, [2004] 3 WLR 322, [2004] 3 All ER 991, [2004] ICR 1064.

[21–127] Essentially re-instatement requires the employer to treat the employee as if [s]he had never been dismissed and is usually granted when the employee has not contributed in any way to the dismissal. Significantly, the employee will be entitled to any arrears of salary from the date of dismissal to the date of termination and his or her continuity of service will not be considered to have been broken.

[21–128] Under s.7(1)(a) of the 1977 Act, where an employee is re-instated, [s]he is entitled to the same terms and conditions on which [s]he was employed immediately before his or her dismissal, including salary,[231] as well as all rights and privileges [s]he might reasonably be expected to have but for the dismissal. Thus in *Rapple v Irish Press Newspapers*,[232] the claimant had been dismissed, with consequences for his pension entitlements. The company went into liquidation and the claimant's colleagues received redundancy. The trust governing the pension was wound up. If the claimant was deemed to have been dismissed at the time of the winding up of the trust he would not benefit to the same extent as if he had been in employment. The tribunal, whilst acknowledging that the claimant had no job to go back to, ordered re-instatement.

[21–129] Section 2 of the 1993 Act has now amended s.1(2) of the 1977 Act in this regard and provides that the re-instated employee is entitled to the terms and conditions of other employees of the employer in a similar position (or, if no such employees exist, the terms and conditions of his or her employees generally) if those terms and conditions are more favourable than they were at the date of the employee's dismissal. This provision has essentially encapsulated in statutory form what had formerly been the position of the tribunal.[233]

4.2. Re-engagement

[21–130] Like re-instatement, the remedy of re-engagement entitles the employee to return to work. However, re-engagement differs from re-instatement in that the employee is not entitled to his or her 'old job' on the same terms and conditions. Instead, an order of re-engagement may enable an employer to offer the employee a different, albeit comparable, job to the one from which [s]he had been dismissed. The tribunal has the power to set down the terms and operative dates of the re-engagement. This could entail continuity of employment from the date of dismissal to date of re-engagement.[234]

[21–131] Re-engagement is usually ordered where the relationship between the parties has deteriorated so badly that it is impossible to re-instate the employee into his or

---

231. For the purposes of the legislation, 'salary' includes all associated benefits, as noted by the tribunal in *Groves v Aer Lingus Teo* UD 562/1979.

232. UD 841/1995.

233. See, for example, *Clarke v Hogan*, UD 135/1978.

234. Indeed the continuity of employment is preserved for the purposes of the Minimum Notice and Terms of Employment Act 1973 and the Unfair Dismissals Acts when immediate re-engagement is ordered.

her old position. It may also be ordered where the circumstances in the workplace have altered – for example, where the work has changed or where the employer's former job no longer exists. An order of this kind may not guarantee continuity of service and may entail loss of associated benefits.[235]

Re-engagement may be ordered, for example, where the employee has not been [21–132] entirely blameless in the events leading to the dismissal. Thus in *Parsons v Liffey Marine Ltd.*,[236] the tribunal ordered:

> that the claimant be re-engaged and restored to his apprenticeship in the respondent company with effect from 1 April 1992, with the period from the date of dismissal to the date of re-engagement to be considered as a period of suspension without pay, with all the claimant's rights and entitlements deriving from his employment to be preserved.[237]

The remedy of re-engagement allows the tribunal great scope to impose redress that takes into account the culpability of both parties. In *O'Connell v CTF Ltd.*,[238] the claimant was dismissed partly because of a poor attendance record. The tribunal ordered re-engagement, but the claimant was to be monitored for a number of months before he was fully reinstalled as an employee. The remedy was also used in *Breslin v Calvinia Ltd.*[239] where the employee was only awarded re-engagement from a date some time after the date of his dismissal, with the interim period being deemed to be a period of unpaid suspension.

4.3. Limitations on Re-instatement and Re-engagement as Remedies

Reinstatement and re-engagement represent the primary remedies for unfair [21–133] dismissal.[240] The availability of these remedies under the legislation is significant in that it recognises what the employee has invested in the job and allows him or her in certain circumstances to have that job returned to him or her. However, the realities of the workplace mean that these remedies are somewhat aspirational and it seems that they will only be awarded where it is *practicable* to do so, rather than when it is *reasonable* to do so.[241] Cognisant of the fact that it is ultimately the parties who will have to work together, the tribunal will take the parties' wishes into account, although it will ultimately be its discretion that will determine the issue.[242]

235. *Mulligan v Bus Éireann*, UD 567/1987.
236. [1992] ELR 136.
237. [1992] ELR 136, 139.
238. UD 588/1991.
239. UD 60/1988.
240. These remedies may be varied by the Circuit Court: s.11 Unfair Dismissals (Amendment) Act 1993.
241. For example, before a particular remedy is awarded the tribunal may take into consideration the wishes of the parties – as in *Marsh v University College Dublin*, UD 27/1997 – or whether either or both of the parties is or are opposed to the particular remedy: *Fitzmaurice v Hele PVC Windows*, UD 385/1990.
242. *McArdle v Kingspan Ltd.*, UD 1342/2003.

[21–134]   Therefore, re-instatement or re-engagement will generally not be ordered where the relationship between the parties has irretrievably broken down,[243] where the job is no longer in existence because of a redundancy situation,[244] or where the return of the employee could cause industrial relation difficulties for the employer.[245] In *Enessy Co SA v Minoprio*,[246] Lord McDonald observed in an *obiter* statement that the size of the organisation could be determinative in this regard:

> It was not realistic to make an order of this nature in a case where the parties involved were in close personal relationships with each other such as they were in the present situation. It is one thing to make an order for reinstatement where the employee concerned works in a factory or other substantial organisation. It is another to do so in the case of a small employer with a few staff. [247]

[21–135]   It is submitted that if one of the aims of the legislation was to redress the imbalance of power between the employer and the employee by allowing the employee to be returned to the job that was rightfully his or hers, then in this sense, it has not been a success. In using 'practicability' as a yardstick rather than whether it was 'reasonable' to order the employee to be given his or her job back, the tribunal is in effect legitimising what the employer has already done – namely unfairly removing the employee from the workplace. Redmond has concluded on this issue that:

> The fact that either of the primary remedies will be awarded only where it is practicable represents a serious qualification to the view that unfair dismissals legislation protects a worker's *proprietas* in employment thus achieving a supposed new balance in the employment relationship. The vast majority of claimants before the EAT who are declared to have been unfairly dismissed do not receive their jobs back.[248]

4.4. Compensation

[21–136]   In many disputes over dismissal, the relationship between the parties is broken beyond repair. It is not surprising, therefore, that the most common remedy imposed by the tribunal in such cases is that of compensation. Section 7(1)(c) of the 1977 Act provides that an employee is entitled to compensation up to a maximum of 104 weeks' remuneration. Section 6(a) of the 1993 Act amends the 1977 Act and provides that, where there is no financial loss attributable to the dismissal, the employee is entitled to compensation of up to a maximum of four weeks' remuneration. Section 7(3) of the 1977 Act defines 'remuneration' as including 'allowances in the nature of pay and benefits in lieu of or in addition to pay'.

---

243. *Moore v Xnet Information Systems* [2002] IEHC 6, [2002] 4 IR 362, [2002] 2 ILRM 278.
244. *Trusler v Lummus Co Ltd.* [1972] IRLR 35.
245. *Coleman v Magnet Joinery Ltd.* [1975] ICR 46, [1974] IRLR 343.
246. [1978] IRLR 489.
247. *ibid.*, at 489.
248. Redmond, *Dismissal Law in Ireland* (2nd ed., Tottel Publishing, 2007), at para.23.22.

4.4.1. Calculation of Financial Loss

Section 7(1)(c) provides that compensation is available in respect of any financial [21–137] loss incurred by the employee that is *attributable* to the dismissal, and is just and equitable having regard to all the circumstances. Thus the legislation recognises only financial loss that has come about as a direct result of his or her unfair dismissal by the employer.

The legislation under s.7(2) of the 1977 Act (as amended) provides guidance as [21–138] to the factors that influence the calculation of the compensation. In particular, it refers to:

(a) the extent (if any) to which the financial loss referred to in that sub-section was attributable to an act, omission or conduct by or on behalf of the employer;

(b) the extent (if any) to which the said financial loss was attributable to an act, omission or conduct by or on behalf of the employee;

(c) the measures (if any) adopted by the employee or, as the case may be, his failure to adopt measures, to mitigate the loss aforesaid; and

(d) the extent (if any) of the compliance or failure to comply by the employer, in relation to the employee, with the procedure referred to in sub-section (1) of s 14 of this Act or with the provisions of any code of practice relating to procedures regarding dismissal approved of by the Minister;

Section 6(b) of the 1993 (Amendment) Act inserted the following provisions into the legislation:

(e) the extent (if any) of the compliance or failure to comply by the employer, in relation to the employee, with the said section 14, and

(f) the extent (if any) to which the conduct of the employee (whether by act or omission) contributed to the dismissal.

Section 7(2) requires that the financial loss be 'attributable to the conduct', and therefore it is quite clear that the employer must establish a causal relationship between the employee's conduct and the dismissal.[249]

The wording of s.7(2) of the 1977 Act raised questions as to whether or not the [21–139] tribunal (or other body), when calculating the financial loss suffered by the employee, could take into consideration the actions of the employer or employee that had occurred *prior* to the dismissal of that employee. This issue came, by way

---

249.*Hutchinson v Enfield Rolling Mills Ltd.* [1981] IRLR 318.

of case stated, before the Supreme Court in *Carney v Balkan Tours (Ireland) Ltd.*[250] In that case, the applicant was employed in the Dublin office of the respondent travel agency and had responsibilities regarding bank lodgements. She was summarily dismissed, and according to the respondent company, this was because she had failed to follow its procedures for dealing with the Revenue Commissioners. She was awarded £200 compensation by the tribunal for her dismissal, who took into account the extent to which she had contributed to that dismissal. She appealed this decision on a point of law regarding the proper interpretation of s.7(2), arguing that the tribunal was not entitled to take her own contribution to her dismissal into consideration as it was conduct that had occurred *prior* to her dismissal. It was her contention that her 'financial loss' only arose from the dismissal and as the wording of s.7(2) referred to 'conduct which was attributable to her financial loss' and not 'conduct which was attributable to her dismissal' therefore by definition her conduct prior to the dismissal could not be taken into consideration. It was further argued that whereas the introduction of s.7(f) under the 1993 Act now empowered the tribunal to act in the manner that it had done in this case (that is, to consider the employee's actions prior to dismissal), such power was not in place at the time the tribunal made its decision. In other words, the fact that the legislature deemed it necessary to reform the law along the lines of s.7(f) was evidence that the power provided in that subsection did not previously exist.

[21–140] The case came before the Supreme Court by way of case stated from the Circuit Court. Murphy J in delivering the judgment of the Supreme Court disagreed with the appellant's contentions. In so doing, the court noted that s.7(1)(c) of the 1977 Act provided for the award of compensation where it is 'just and equitable having regard to all the circumstances', thus automatically providing the tribunal (or other body) with a great deal of latitude when considering the quantum of such compensation. Thus, Murphy J concluded that:

> It does seem to me that the discretion conferred upon the Tribunal (or other adjudicating body) by *Section 7* of the 1977 Act in relation to the computation of a payment by way of compensation is very wide. Moreover whilst the specific directives given to the adjudicating body by paragraphs (a), (b) and more particularly (c) (dealing with mitigation) may be interpreted as referring to events subsequent to the dismissal the provisions of *paragraph (d) of subsection 2* unquestionably refer to the machinery which was or should have been resorted to in relation to the dismissal rather than events subsequent thereto. That provision coupled with the discretion conferred upon the adjudicating tribunal in the widest terms would seem to me compelling reason for inferring that the legislature intended that the body determining the nature or extent of the redress to which the employee was entitled should look at all of the circumstances of the case including the conduct of the parties prior to the dismissal. I am fortified in this view by the judgment of Ellis J in *McCabe v Lisney & Son* (delivered 16 March 1981) and the jurisprudence

---

250. [1997] 1 IR 153, [1997] ELR 102.

which has evolved based thereon. The fact that the legislature in 1993 made express provision in that regard must in the circumstances be interpreted as a provision made *ex abundante cautela* and to avoid the doubts which might well and, indeed, have arisen in the circumstances.[251]

Therefore, the Supreme Court concluded that the EAT in determining the payment to be made to the appellant by the respondent of compensation for unfair dismissal was entitled to have regard to her contribution to the dismissal as one of the relevant circumstances in determining the amount to be paid.

The Supreme Court decision in *Carney* was pleaded with good effect by the claimant [21–141] in *Allen v Independent Newspapers (Ireland) Ltd.*[252] In that case the claimant had resigned her position with the respondent following a series of incidents that left her feeling undermined. The tribunal accepted that she had been constructively dismissed and that her stress-related illness was caused by the factors that led to her dismissal. The claimant argued that the behaviour of her employer prior to her dismissal, which had caused her illness, should be taken into consideration in determining the level of the award. The tribunal upheld the claimant's argument and concluded that her illness caused her financial loss and that as that loss was caused by the respondent, the resulting financial loss was attributable to the conduct of the employer. The claimant was awarded compensation equivalent to 78 weeks' remuneration.

The reasoning of the tribunal in *Allen* was followed and extended in *Browne v* [21–142] *Ventelo Telecommunications (Ireland) Ltd.*[253] In that case, the claimant's manager sexually harassed her. In accordance with her company's grievance procedures she filed a complaint against her manager. Her claim was upheld and she received a written apology from the offender but was also asked to sign a document waiving her rights to pursue further legal action in relation to the matter. She refused to do this and was subjected to a campaign of bullying and harassment as a result. She resigned her position and brought an action for constructive dismissal. Her claim was upheld by the tribunal. She was awarded damages of £10,000 despite the fact that she had only been out of work for one month after her resignation. The large award was made on the basis that the tribunal found that it was likely that the claimant would suffer future financial losses as a result of the nature of her dismissal. In particular, the tribunal relied on the terms of the Code of Practice on Sexual Harassment and Harassment at Work, stating that in light of this code, it was possible that the claimant had not come to terms with the conduct of her employer and this could negatively affect the claimant regarding her potential earnings in the future.

---

251. [1997] 1 IR 153, 158.
252. [2002] ELR 84.
253. UD 597/2001.

[21–143] The extent of the compensation awarded to the claimants by the tribunal in both *Allen* and *Browne* has attracted criticism. By awarding compensation for future loss caused by a stress-related illness, it has been said that the tribunal has overstepped the bounds of its authority. Eardly has criticised such a development, warning that it may allow the claimant 'a double bite at the compensation cherry'.[254] In particular, he has argued that in granting compensation to a claimant who maintains that their future work opportunities may be diminished as a result of their stress-related illness, a tribunal may be awarding compensation in circumstances where a civil court would not:

> On this basis, once a tribunal were to satisfy itself that the conduct and associated working conditions justified the resignation of the employee in the first place, then the issue would simply come down to the simple connection being made between the illness caused and the conduct alleged. There is little scope for the vital requirement of the civil courts that the employer must also *reasonably foresee* the injury before liability attaches.[255]

Thus the claimant bringing a claim for financial loss under the dismissals legislation would simply have to establish causation, but would not have to prove the foreseeability of the harm as required under common law negligence.

[21–144] This may not always be the case, however. Eardly's criticism appears to be predicated on the assumption that the loss in the statutory action is the same as that that would be compensated in an action for personal injury. The express purpose of compensation under s.7 of the 1977 Act is to award compensation for the financial loss attributable to the dismissal. Damages for personal injury in tort law are awarded – where appropriate – for financial loss *and* pain and suffering. The purpose of compensation under ordinary negligence principles is to put the plaintiff back into the position that [s]he was in before the injury had occurred. In *Allen*, the claimant did not receive compensation for personal injury. She was compensated for financial loss her unfair dismissal had caused, or was likely to cause, her. Thus the claimant in *Allen* could legitimately pursue a common law action for negligence. However, any damages awarded as a result of such an action would reflect the claimant's actual loss, i.e. pain and suffering and financial loss (other than that related to the dismissal). In such circumstances there is little chance of the claimant having 'a double-bite of the compensation cherry'. A failure by the tribunal in *Allen* to consider the role that the employer's behaviour had to play in her illness and related subsequent dismissal would lead to situations where claimants would obtain inadequate compensation as the award would fail to take into consideration the impact of the employer's behaviour on the claimant's employability.

---

254. Eardly, 'Psychiatric Injury and the Employment Appeals Tribunal: A Double Bite of the Compensation Cherry', 1 *Employment Law Review* (2007), 12.

255. *ibid.*, at 13.

Under s.7(2), the tribunal may take into consideration the conduct of the employee **[21–145]** in contributing to his or her own dismissal. This has been described 'loosely' as a form of contributory negligence.[256] Section 7(2) requires that the financial loss be 'attributable to the conduct', therefore the employer must establish a causal relationship between the employee's conduct and the dismissal.[257]

A finding that the claimant was in some way to blame for his or her dismissal **[21–146]** may justify a reduction in the award of compensation by the tribunal. Consideration of the employee's conduct when calculating the award of compensation arises frequently in circumstances where the dismissal may have been found to have been unfair on the grounds that, whereas there is no substantive unfairness, nonetheless the decision involved a measure of procedural unfairness. In *Shiels v Williams Transport Group (Ireland) Ltd.*,[258] the claimant was dismissed following an allegation that he was in possession of illegal drugs while on his employer's premises. His employer failed to follow fair procedures in dismissing him and this failure resulted in a finding that his dismissal was unfair. It transpired that the employee was in possession of illegal drugs and had used them while at work. Notwithstanding the finding of unfair dismissal, and having regard to the employee's own contribution to it, his compensation was reduced to nil by the tribunal.

4.4.2. Duty to Mitigate Loss
Section 7(2)(c) of the 1977 Act introduces the traditional contractual principle **[21–147]** that the claimant will not be entitled to compensation for losses that could have been avoided had [s]he taken reasonable steps, e.g. seeking suitable alternative employment after his or her dismissal. Thus the claimant cannot use the fact of his or her unfair dismissal as reason not to seek alternative employment in anticipation of obtaining a 'windfall' in compensation. Instead, the claimant should, according to the tribunal in *Sheehan v Continental Administration Co Ltd.*[259]:

> employ a reasonable amount of time each weekday in seeking work. It is not enough to inform agencies that you are available for work nor merely to post an application to various companies seeking work… The time that a claimant finds on his hands is not his own, unless he chooses it to be, but rather to be profitably employed in seeking to mitigate his loss.

The nature of the mitigation inquiry is well captured in the following passage from the judgment of Roskill LJ in *Bessenden Properties v Corness*[260]:

256. *per* Viscount Dilhorne in *W Devis & Sons Ltd. v Atkins* [1977] AC 391, 956.
257. *Hutchinson v Enfield Rolling Mills* [1981] IRLR 318.
258. UD 191/1984; *Sheehan v H M Keating & Sons Ltd.* [1993] ELR 12; *O'Loughlin v Climatic Building Systems Ltd.*, UD 500/1984.
259. UD 858/1999.
260. [1977] ICR 821.

Questions of mitigation are questions of fact. When one party seeks to allege that another party has failed to mitigate a loss, the burden of proof is upon the party making that allegation.[261]

The duty does not require the claimant to take the very first opportunity that comes his or her way but rather it is a question of reasonableness and is based on the circumstances of the case.[262]

Setting up in business for oneself rather than seeking alternative work will not constitute a failure to mitigate one's loss simply because the salary is lower than that the claimant would have received had [s]he accepted other employment.[263]

4.4.3. Heads of Loss

[21–148] Section 7(3) of the 1977 Act defines 'financial loss' as including any 'actual loss and any estimated prospective loss of income attributable to the dismissal'. Thus a claimant may seek compensation under two distinct headings: (1) actual loss and (2) prospective loss.

4.4.3.1. Actual Loss

[21–149] The employee is entitled to compensation for the actual loss that [s]he has suffered from the date of his or her dismissal. Under this heading, the employee may be awarded compensation for the actual losses – such as salary, wages and pension[264] – [s]he has incurred as a result of the dismissal. Thus, notwithstanding the fact that the employee has been unfairly dismissed, no compensation for actual loss will be awarded in circumstances where [s]he was unavailable for work regardless, including where due to ill health [s]he had been declared unfit for work.[265] Under s.6(c) of the 1993 Act, payments made under the Social Welfare Acts 1981–1993 for the period following any dismissal, or payments made under the Income Tax Acts arising by reason of the dismissal, are now disregarded from the calculation of actual loss.

Section 6(a) of the 1993 Act has amended the 1977 Act and provides that where the employee has not suffered any actual financial loss as a result of the dismissal, compensation (up to a maximum four weeks' remuneration) may be awarded as is considered just and reasonable in the circumstances.

4.4.3.2. Prospective/Future Losses

[21–150] Under s.7(2)(a) of the 1977 Act, an employer may be rendered liable for future losses where those losses were attributable to the actions or conduct of the employer.

---

261. *ibid.*, at 823.
262. *McCabe v Lisney & Son*, UD 5/1977; *AG Bracey Ltd. v Iles* [1973] IRLR 210.
263. *Bunyan v United Dominions Trust (Ireland) Ltd.* [1982] ILRM 404; *Cavanagh v Dunnes Stores Ltd.* [1995] ELR 164; *Gardiner-Hill v Roland Berger Technics Ltd.* [1982] IRLR 498.
264. *Bunyan v United Dominions Trust (Ireland) Ltd.* [1981] ILRM 404.
265. *Coyle v Tipper House Trust Ltd.*, UD 904/1993.

Furthermore, s.7(3) provides that financial loss includes any prospective loss attributable to the dismissal (as distinct from the conduct of the employer).[266]

These losses are calculated in a manner similar to the award of damages in tort.   [21–151] Thus the tribunal is required to engage in speculation as to the claimant's future losses that may be considered attributable to his dismissal. Such calculations are, by their very nature, vague and difficult to ascertain but will take into consideration the fact that, as a result of the dismissal, the employee may not secure employment at a similar wage,[267] or may have benefited from a redundancy payment had [s]he not been dismissed.[268] The claimant may introduce expert evidence in order to establish the likely extent of his or her future loss. Thus in *Allen v Independent Newspapers (Ireland) Ltd.*,[269] the claimant had not found alternative work since her resignation from her employment with the respondent precisely because of the psychiatric illness she had suffered, which had been caused by her working situation. In assessing the extent of the financial loss she was likely to incur, the tribunal undertook the following analysis of her claim:

> It is clear that [the claimant] is unable to work since her dismissal and at the time of this hearing she remains unfit for work. We are satisfied that she has sustained financial loss to date. There is a dispute between the parties' medical experts not just in relation to the nature of the claimant's illness, but also the likely duration of same. We have considered the evidence of the medical witnesses and overall the Tribunal accepts on balance the evidence of Dr Brophy as to diagnosis and the prognosis for recovery. In his evidence given on February 6, 2001 he envisaged from that time a period of recovery of some 18 months. The Tribunal estimates therefore, that because of her illness, the claimant will suffer financial loss for a period of almost two years from the date of dismissal. The Tribunal also accepts as not unreasonable the submission made on behalf of the claimant that, following recovery (even allowing for some earlier element of recovery) a period of time will elapse before she will achieve a salary commensurate with that of her pre-dismissal earnings. The Tribunal assesses as reasonable, following recovery, that it will take a period of at least a year for the claimant to achieve similar earnings. We accept therefore that she will incur financial loss in this period.[270]

---

266. Both these subsections are subject to the generality of s.7(1), which provides that the compensation payable must be attributable to the dismissal.

267. *Bux v Toohey & Co Ltd.*, UD 137/1978.

268. *McDermott v Allied Irish Banks*, UD 166/1978.

269. [2002] ELR 84.

270. *ibid.*, at 106.

CHAPTER 22

Redundancy

Introduction

An employer is entitled to dismiss an employee where that employee's position [22–01] becomes redundant. Redundancy may affect one individual employee, part of a workforce, or an entire workforce where the situation is one of complete closure.[1] Employers may in the first instance offer voluntary redundancies before or instead of requiring redundancy compulsorily. In circumstances of redundancy, an employee with more than two years' continuous service is entitled to the payment of a lump sum; the amount of that lump sum varies according to the employee's seniority and salary. In this chapter, the circumstances amounting to a redundancy situation within the meaning of the relevant legislative regimes are analysed. Analysis is then provided of the requirement of fair procedures in the redundancy selection process, before turning to consider the recent developments in the law concerning collective redundancies. In the final part of the chapter, an overview is provided of the nature of the entitlements of an employee made redundant.

1. The Legislative Framework

As in almost all areas of employment law, the legislative framework underpin- [22–02] ning the law relating to redundancy is complex. The entitlement to redundancy payments was introduced into Irish law pursuant to the Redundancy Payments Act 1967, which has been amended on a number of occasions (most significantly in 1971, 1979, 2003 and 2007). As already stated in Chapter 21, however, the Unfair Dismissals Acts 1977–2007 are also relevant in this area of employment law. As noted in that chapter, s.6 of the Unfair Dismissals Act 1977 – while it recognises the entitlement of an employer to dismiss an employee in circumstances of redundancy – imposes a number of requirements to be met in this context. These are discussed in detail in this chapter.

---

1. See further Redmond, *Dismissal Law in Ireland* (2nd ed., Tottel Publishing, 2007), ch.17; Higgins and McCrann, ch.15 in Regan, ed., *Employment Law* (Tottel Publishing, 2009). For discussion of the background to the redundancy legislation in this jurisdiction generally, see Barrett, 'The Law on "Downsizing" – Some Reflections on the Experience of Redundancy Payments Legislation in Ireland', 5(1) *DULJ* (1998), 1.

[22–03] In addition, other distinct legislative initiatives may well have significant implications for circumstances of redundancy. Pertinent examples are the specific procedural requirements laid down by the Protection of Employment Acts 1997–2007 and the various regulations introduced thereunder, and, in the context of so-called 'exceptional collective redundancies', the provisions of the Protection of Employment (Exceptional Collective Redundancies and Related Matters) Act 2007.

1.1. Definition of Redundancy

[22–04] The statutory definition of redundancy is located in the Redundancy Payments Act 1967, s.7(2), as amended,[2] which provides that:

> An employee who is dismissed shall be taken to be dismissed by reason of redundancy if for one or more reasons not related to the employee concerned the dismissal is attributable wholly or mainly to—
>
> (a) the fact that his employer has ceased, or intends to cease, to carry on the business for the purposes of which the employee was employed by him, or has ceased or intends to cease, to carry on that business in the place where the employee was so employed, or
>
> (b) the fact that the requirements of that business for employees to carry out work of a particular kind in the place where he was so employed have ceased or diminished or are expected to cease or diminish, or
>
> (c) the fact that his employer has decided to carry on the business with fewer or no employees, whether by requiring the work for which the employee had been employed (or had been doing before his dismissal) to be done by other employees or otherwise, or
>
> (d) the fact that his employer has decided that the work for which the employee had been employed (or had been doing before his dismissal) should henceforward be done in a different manner for which the employee is not sufficiently qualified or trained, or
>
> (e) the fact that his employer has decided that the work for which the employee had been employed (or had been doing before his dismissal) should henceforward be done by a person who is also capable of doing other work for which the employee is not sufficiently qualified or trained.

This definition is now analysed in detail.

---

2. Amended by s.4 Redundancy Payments Act 1971, and s.5 Redundancy Payments Act 2003.

1.2. Termination 'Wholly or Mainly' because of Redundancy

In order to be considered a dismissal by reason of redundancy it must be established   [22–05]
by the employer that the termination of the contract of employment was 'wholly or
mainly' because of the redundancy. Effectively, the legislation requires not only that
a redundancy situation must exist, but also that causation be established – that is, it
must be shown that the redundancy situation caused the dismissal.[3] Thus in *Daly v
Hanson Industries Ltd.*,[4] the Employment Appeals Tribunal found that the claimant
had been dismissed soon after giving evidence in favour of a former employee
of the company in a hearing before the tribunal. While there was a redundancy
element in the circumstances of the claimant's dismissal, the tribunal ultimately
decided that it was not the main reason for her dismissal. Similarly, in *Edwards
v Aerials and Electronics (Ireland) Ltd.*,[5] it was determined that notwithstanding
the fact that the respondent company was experiencing losses, the dismissal of
the claimant was deemed not to arise mainly by reason of redundancy as there
was evidence that showed disagreements between the claimant and other members
of management. Finally, in *Elbay v Iona National Airways Ltd.*,[6] while a genuine
redundancy situation did exist within the company, it did not affect the claimant's
job. His purported dismissal by reason of redundancy was not valid.

2. The Requirements of Impersonality and Change

The legislative definition of redundancy set out in detail above was described by   [22–06]
Kenny J in *Minister for Labour v O'Connor*[7] as being 'remarkable for its obscurity'.
Notwithstanding this, a number of propositions can be stated with confidence
about the definition. Thus, according to the Employment Appeals Tribunal in
its leading determination in *St Ledger v Frontline Distributors Ireland Ltd.*,[8] the
statutory definition of 'redundancy' has two important characteristics, namely
'impersonality' and 'change':

> Impersonality runs throughout the five definitions in the Act. Redundancy impacts
> on the job and only as a consequence of the redundancy does the person involved
> lose his job…

> Change also runs through all five definitions. This means change in the workplace.
> The most dramatic change of all is a complete close down. Change may also mean

---

3. See also *Safeway Stores Plc v Burrell* [1997] ICR 523, [1997] IRLR 220; *Murray v Foyle Meats
    Ltd.* [2000] 1 AC 51, [1999] 3 WLR 356.
4. UD 719/1986. The employer's appeal to the Circuit Court was dismissed: for detailed discus-
    sion see Stewart and Dunleavy, *Compensation on Dismissal: Employment Law and Practice*
    (First Law, 2007), 398-399.
5. UD 236/1985.
6. [1993] ELR 166.
7. (1985) 4 JISLL 72, 74.
8. [1995] ELR 160, 161–162.

a reduction in needs for employees, or a reduction in number. Definition (d) and (e) involve change in the way the work is done or some other form of change in the nature of the job. Under these two definitions change in the job must mean qualitative change. Definition (e) must involve, partly at least, work of a different kind, and that is the only meaning we can put on the words 'other work'. More work or less work of the same kind does not mean 'other work' and is only quantitative change.

2.1. The Impersonality Requirement

[22–07] The two phrases used at the outset of s.7(2) – 'one or more reasons not related to the employee concerned', and 'wholly or mainly' – are significant in that they serve to emphasise a necessary characteristic of redundancy: impersonality. In order for a valid redundancy situation to exist, it must be unconnected to the particular employee who is to be made redundant.

Crucially, then, dismissal by way of redundancy is not related to the individual. Genuine redundancy arises in circumstances where the work disappears, diminishes or changes. Therefore, to be a valid redundancy the dismissal must not be connected to the individual employee's personality but rather to the state of the business. Authority for this proposition is to be found in a great many oft-quoted determinations of the EAT. In *Moloney v W Deacon & Sons Ltd.*,[9] for example, the tribunal emphasised that one of the key features of redundancy is impersonality and where a dismissal refers to a claimant's personality it cannot be a genuine redundancy. In that case, the respondent purported to dismiss the claimant by way of redundancy due to the automation of the company's processes. The claimant insisted that his dismissal was because he had lodged an arrears of payment claim against his employer. The respondent, on the other hand, maintained that the claimant was selected for redundancy as he was the third most junior employee in the company, but, very significantly, the reasons presented by the respondent to the tribunal for the redundancy also referred to the claimant's failure to satisfactorily complete a statutory probationary period and to his claim for arrears of payment. These reasons referred to the claimant's personality and therefore it was not a true redundancy.

[22–08] Because of the dangers of redundancy being used as a cloak to disguise the true reasons for a dismissal, the tribunal has consistently applied a very strict approach towards recognising dismissals by way of redundancy. In the much-cited case of *St Ledger v Frontline Distribution Ltd.*,[10] the claimant was a warehouse supervisor who was replaced by a more qualified individual – Mr Kennedy – who had passed an examination that could lead to further qualifications. The respondent argued that the claimant had lost his position due to redundancy under s.7(2)(e) of the

---

9.   [1996] ELR 239.
10. [1995] ELR 160.

1967 Act (as amended),[11] namely, that Mr Kennedy was doing other work for which the claimant was not sufficiently qualified. The tribunal could not find any difference in the nature of the work carried out by the claimant and that carried out by Mr Kennedy. The only discernible difference was that Mr Kennedy was able to complete the work without the assistance of a part-time helper. The tribunal found that 'other work' for the purposes of s.7(2)(e) must be work of a different kind, not more or less work of the same kind. Effectively, the claimant had been replaced because he was not as capable as Mr Kennedy. The tribunal, having availed of the opportunity to elaborate on the definition of redundancy set out earlier, concluded:

> For redundancy to arise in the present case, the respondent would have to satisfy us that the nature of the job changed, and that in connection with the change, and only in connection with the change, Mr Kennedy had certain training that the claimant had not.[12]

The fact that Mr Kennedy may have been a more efficient employee and was able to do more work with less assistance was not grounds for making the claimant redundant under s.7(2)(e). The termination of the claimant's contract of employment was anything but impersonal and the day-to-day work did not change.[13]

Similarly, in *Hurley v Royal Cork Yacht Club*,[14] the tribunal warned against the [22–09] dangers of accepting an employer's assertion that the dismissal was by way of redundancy, particularly in cases involving the position of only one employee. In that case, the claimant was dismissed, it was alleged, because of the poor financial state of the club. However, the minutes of meetings from the club committee made no reference to redundancy and actually commented on the sound financial position of the club. The minutes did refer to the committee's dissatisfaction with the claimant's work at the club. The tribunal held that there was no evidence that the claimant's dismissal was by reason of redundancy and warned that:

> Especially where there is a single redundancy the Tribunal must be on guard for the *'redundancy cloak'*. Because the Act recognises redundancy as a substantial ground justifying dismissal, and because only the employer knows the true reason for dismissal, it is easy to dress up as redundancy a dismissal for some other reason.[15]

---

11. Considered in more detail below in this chapter.
12. [1995] ELR 160, 162.
13. For other examples where no redundancy was found to justify dismissal, see *Melroy v Floraville Nurseries Ltd.*, UD 703/1993; *Coyle v Dublin Institute of Technology*, RP 67/1998.
14. [1999] ELR 7.
15. [1999] ELR 7, 9.

2.2. The Change Requirement

[22–10] Beyond the requirement of impersonality there is also a need for the redundancy to reflect a change in the relevant business.[16] Such change can occur in a number of different ways.

2.2.1. Purpose or Location of the Business

[22–11] Section 7(2)(a) includes in the definition of redundancy the following situation:

> (a) the fact that his employer has ceased, or intends to cease, to carry on the business for the purposes of which the employee was employed by him, or has ceased or intends to cease, to carry on that business in the place where the employee was so employed...

This section clearly applies to situations where the purpose of the business changes or where the business (or that particular part of same in which the employee is employed) closes. One of the most interesting and complex questions arising in this regard concerns the issue of mobility clauses, that is, where the employee's contract of employment includes a clause providing that the employee may be required to work at another location. The key question arising here is whether s.7(2) imposes a contractual test or a primarily factual test to determine 'the place where the employee was so employed'. It could be argued that since in s.7(2) the word 'employed', and not 'worked', is used, this connotes 'employed under the contract of employment'. Thus, in the context of the subsection and having regard to the definitions of 'employee' and 'employer' in s.2 of the 1967 Act, the question of what place the employee was so employed in must be determined by reference to the contract of employment: if the contract contains a mobility clause allowing the employer to require the employee to work elsewhere, 'the place where the employee was so employed' extends to every place the employee may be required to work.

[22–12] By contrast, it could be argued that on a plain language construction of s.7 of the 1967 Act, the words 'the place where he was so employed' clearly refer to the place where the employee actually worked and not where in theory the employer could require the employee to work.

There is a dearth of Irish case law on the specific definition of the 'place of employment' within s.7(2). It is in decisions of the English courts that analysis is to be found of the precise meaning of the wording of the above subsection, which is identical in the relevant UK legislation,[17] and such decisions indicate a gradual shift in the law.

---

16. See Chapter 23 for the application of a similar requirement that there be a change in the workforce if the so-called 'Economic, Technical and Organisational' defence to a dismissal in the context of a transfer of undertakings situation is to be allowed to apply.

17. s.1(2)(b) Redundancy Payments Act 1965.

Older case law in this area tended to involve the adoption of a strict approach [22–13] to this question of place of employment and tended to take the view that the employee was not entitled to consider himself or herself redundant in these circumstances, particularly in cases where a mobility or equivalent clause was built in to the employment contract. Thus, in the early English case of *Sutcliffe v Hawker Siddely Ltd.*,[18] where consideration was given to the meaning of such phrases in the equivalent British legislation, it was held that such phrases meant 'where under his contract of employment [the employee] could be required to work'.[19]

More recent case law illustrates a shift away from this approach and, significantly, [22–14] regards the question as a factual one rather than one that hinges on the construction of the particular contract of employment. Hence, the position now seems to be that even in cases where the contract of employment contains a mobility clause, the court or tribunal will still determine what, on the facts, amounts to the place of employment within the meaning of s.7 of the Redundancy Payments Act 1967.

In *Bass Leisure Ltd. v Thomas*,[20] for example, the English EAT ruled that the place [22–15] where an employee was employed for redundancy payment purposes does not extend to any place where [s]he could be contractually required to work. The place of employment was to be established 'by a factual inquiry, taking into account the employee's fixed or changing place or places of work and any contractual terms which go to evidence or define the place of employment and its extent, but not those (if any) which make provision for the employee to be transferred to another'.[21] Significantly, in *Bass Leisure*, the fact that the contract reserved the right to transfer any employee to a suitable place of work did not result in the claimant losing her right to a redundancy payment when she resigned after being relocated to a depot some 20 miles away.

Delivering the judgment of the EAT, Judge Hicks QC analysed the wording in the [22–16] UK statute, which is identical to s.7 of the 1967 Act, as follows:

> The use of the words 'so employed', relating back to the phrase 'employed by [the employer]', directs attention to the relationship between the parties, and the definite article in 'the place' suggests a certain fixity which tends against equating the place of employment with, for instance, each location of a peripatetic 'place of work' successively. Without needing to consider or decide whether the parties could arbitrarily define the 'place where the employee is employed' in terms outside the limits of the objective realities, we see no reason why there cannot be valid and effective contractual terms, express or implied, evidencing or defining the place

---

18. [1973] ICR 560.
19. [1973] ICR 560, 566.
20. [1994] IRLR 104.
21. [1994] IRLR 104, 112-113.

of employment and its extent within those limits, so that (for example) the place where a steel erector is employed could be the area within which he can be required to attend at construction sites to perform his duties. That is supported by the fact that the preposition before the expression to be construed is 'in' not 'at'.[22]

[22–17] The judgment in *Bass Leisure* was approved by the English Court of Appeal in *High Table Ltd. v Horst*.[23] In that case, the applicant employees worked as waitresses for an employer whose business was providing catering services to corporate clients. The employees' contracts of employment contained a mobility clause stating that they might sometimes have to be transferred to locations other than the normal place of work stated in their letters of appointment. For some years the employees worked at the offices of one particular client of the employer. When the client reduced its requirements for the employer's services, it became necessary for the employer to reduce the catering staff. The applicant employees were informed that they were being made redundant due to staff restructuring and cost savings within the client's organisation. They complained of unfair dismissal or unfair selection for redundancy in that employees with shorter periods of service had not been selected. The Industrial Tribunal ruled that the employees had been dismissed for redundancy and that their dismissals were not unfair. The EAT allowed the employees' appeal and remitted the case to the Industrial Tribunal for rehearing on the ground, *inter alia*, that, in considering whether there was a redundancy situation at the place where the employees were employed for the purposes of the employer's business, the Industrial Tribunal had not heard evidence so as to determine the place where the employees were employed and whether by virtue of the mobility clause their place of work included all the sites at which the employer operated.

[22–18] On the employer's appeal, the Court of Appeal held that the question of the place where the employee was employed for the purposes of the employer's business was to be answered primarily by a consideration of the factual circumstances that obtained until the dismissal. Crucially, the Court confirmed that if an employee had worked in only one location under the contract of employment for the purposes of the employer's business, the extent of the place 'where he was so employed' could not be widened merely because of the existence of a mobility clause. The contract of employment was thus not the sole determinant of where the employee was employed regardless of where the employee actually worked. Peter Gibson LJ observed:

> If an employee has worked in only one location under his contract of employment for the purposes of the employer's business, it defies common sense to widen the extent of the place where he was so employed, merely because of the existence of a mobility clause… It would be unfortunate if the law were to encourage the inclusion of mobility clauses in contracts of employment to defeat genuine redun-

22. [1994] IRLR 104, 110.
23. [1998] ICR 409, [1998] IRLR 513.

dancy claims. Parliament has recognised the importance of the employee's right to a redundancy payment. If the work of the employee for his employer has involved a change of location, as would be the case where the nature of the work required the employee to go from place to place, then the contract of employment may be helpful to determine the extent of the place where the employee was employed. But it cannot be right to let the contract be the sole determinant, regardless of where the employee actually worked for the employer.[24]

In a subsequent determination of the EAT for England and Wales, Elias J described   [22–19]
the above case as 'the leading authority on the question of place of work' in the redundancy context.[25] By way of conclusion, then, it is clear that 'contractual terms are not determinative'[26] of the application of the subsection.

As Higgins and McCrann have observed, one consequence of this approach is that it 'potentially allows the employer the best of both worlds in so far as mobility clauses are concerned',[27] in that the clause can be relied upon to defend a claim for unfair dismissal by an employee unwilling to move, but could also be invoked by the employer in the context of redundancy.

2.2.2. *Diminution in Requirements of Business or in Required Number of Employees*
Section 7(2)(b) includes in the definition of redundancy the following situation: [22–20]

> the fact that the requirements of that business for employees to carry out work of a particular kind in the place where he was so employed have ceased or diminished or are expected to cease or diminish…

Amongst the examples of the tribunal adopting a 'qualitative'[28] approach to the interpretation of the phrase 'work of a particular kind' in this section are its findings that day work is of a different kind to night work[29]; that part-time work is different to on-call work[30]; and that off-site work differs from work on the employer's premises.[31]

It is important to note that the employer is not obliged to wait until the diminu-   [22–21]
tion in work actually occurs: the section speaks of the work ceasing or diminishing, but also of it being 'expected to cease or diminish'. The tribunal has emphasised,

---

24. [1998] ICR 409, 419.
25. *Pitman v Foreign & Commonwealth Office*, EAT/0416/DA, 28 November 2002.
26. *Per* Lord Irvine of Lairg LC in *Murray v Foyle Meats Ltd.* [2000] 1 AC 51, 60.
27. Higgins and McCrann, ch.15 in Regan, ed., *Employment Law* (Tottel Publishing, 2009), [15.14].
28. See Redmond, *Dismissal Law in Ireland* (2nd ed., Tottel Publishing, 2007), at paras.17.21 *et seq.*
29. *Dinworth v Southern Hotel Board*, UD 284/1977.
30. *Kelleher v St James's Hospital Ltd.*, UD 59/1977.
31. *Shine v SKS Communications Ltd.*, UD 975/2007.

however, that the diminution must be imminent. Thus in *Keenan v Gresham Hotel*[32] the EAT explained that the diminution must be expected to occur 'at or within a short time after the alleged redundancy' since

> otherwise an employer who merely expects that his requirements for employees to do work of a particular kind may diminish at some distant time in the future could greatly reduce the redundancy entitlements of such employees by serving [the relevant statutory forms] on them prematurely.

Section 7(2)(c) includes in the definition of redundancy the following situation:

> the fact that his employer has decided to carry on the business with fewer or no employees, whether by requiring the work for which the employee had been employed (or had been doing before his dismissal) to be done by other employees or otherwise...

[22–22] Unlike the situation considered immediately above, this situation does not necessarily involve a reduction in the volume of work, but instead a reduction in the number of employees needed to carry out the work. Thus an employer may introduce a technological innovation that reduces the number of persons necessary to perform a particular task and this can lead to a redundancy situation. Even if such a diminution was foreseen at the time of engagement, there can still be a redundancy.[33]

2.2.3. Change in the Manner of Work Being Done Renders it Incompatible with Employee's Qualifications or Training

[22–23] Section 7(2)(d) includes in the definition of redundancy the following situation:

> the fact that his employer has decided that the work for which the employee had been employed (or had been doing before his dismissal) should henceforward be done in a different manner for which the employee is not sufficiently qualified or trained...

It is important to note that, for a redundancy situation to be captured by this subsection, the redundancy must relate to the employee's qualifications or training. Thus, in *Lefever v Trustees of the Irish Wheelchair Association*,[34] the tribunal observed that it was 'important that qualifications or training be the deciding factor rather than personal qualities'[35] in this context. There the claimant was employed as a supervisor of workers employed by the respondents to assist disabled people. Funding for the work was provided by FÁS. The claimant was employed on

---

32. UD 478/1988.
33. *Nottinghamshire County Council v Lee* [1980] ICR 635, [1980] IRLR 294.
34. [1996] ELR 220.
35. [1996] ELR 220, 222.

two supervision schemes; a position for a third scheme was then advertised, but the claimant was unsuccessful in her application for the job. In holding that no redundancy existed within the meaning of the legislative framework, the tribunal expressly referred to the inability of the employer to identify any difference in the qualifications or training that would be needed for the third as opposed to the earlier schemes.

A case that may helpfully be contrasted with *Lefever* is that of *Daniels v County*   [22–24]
Wexford Community Workshop (New Ross) Ltd.[36] The respondent company engaged a consultant to recommend improvements to its operations. Amongst the latter's recommendations was the appointment of a manager with a third-level qualification. The claimant did not have a third-level qualification and it was her case that she was more than qualified to run the company in view of her extensive experience and years of service in the business. The company acknowledged her contribution and resolved to make a position available to her under the same conditions, and at the same rates of financial remuneration, as she had previously enjoyed. The only exception was that she was not to be allowed access to the workshop floor. The claimant contended that this was demeaning to her and affected her good standing in the community. She refused to accept the offer of alternative employment. The tribunal held that such a situation constituted a valid redundancy on the qualification ground.

A similar situation is that provided for in s.7(2)(e):

> (e) the fact that his employer has decided that the work for which the employee had been employed (or had been doing before his dismissal) should henceforward be done by a person who is also capable of doing other work for which the employee is not sufficiently qualified or trained…

The most significant point to note about this subsection is the holding by the EAT   [22–25]
in the *St Ledger* case discussed above to the effect that the reference to 'other work' in this category means work of a different kind. The tribunal explained:

> Definitions (d) and (e) involve change in the way the work is done or some other form of change in the nature of the job. Under these two definitions change in the job must mean qualitative change. Definition (e) must involve, partly at least, work of a different kind, and that is the only meaning we can put on the words 'other work'. More work or less work of the same kind does not mean 'other work' and is only quantitative change.[37]

---

36. [1996] ELR 213.
37. [1995] ELR 160, 160. (Emphasis added).

3. Fair Selection for Redundancy

[22–26] There are at least three reasons why it is imperative for employers to be able to identify and demonstrate the use of a fair selection process in circumstances of redundancy. First, even where a genuine redundancy situation exists, an employee may be able to bring a successful unfair dismissals action under the Unfair Dismissals Acts where [s]he has been unfairly selected for redundancy.[38] Secondly, heavily infused with this analysis of unfair selection is the question of whether an employer has acted reasonably. This is due to the provision in the Unfair Dismissals Acts to the effect that, when determining if a dismissal is unfair, regard may be had to, *inter alia*, the reasonableness or otherwise of the employer's conduct.[39] In addition, however, it is important to emphasise that a lack of transparency or objectivity in selection processes can in and of itself raise questions about the genuineness of the putative redundancy in the first place. It is, therefore, essential that employers can demonstrate the existence of and adherence to a fair selection procedure.

3.1. Meaning of Unfair Selection

[22–27] Under s.6(3) of the 1977 Act there may be a finding of unfair selection for redundancy where an employee is dismissed but the circumstances constituting the redundancy 'applied equally to one or more other employees in similar employment with the same employer who have not been dismissed' and either:

> (a) the selection of that employee for dismissal resulted wholly or mainly from one or more of the matters specified in subsection (2) of this section or another matter that would not be a ground justifying dismissal, or

> (b) he was selected for dismissal in contravention of a procedure (being a procedure that has been agreed upon by or on behalf of the employer and by the employee or a trade union, or an excepted body... representing him or has been established by the custom and practice of the employment concerned) relating to redundancy and there were no special reasons justifying a departure from that procedure, then the dismissal shall be deemed, for the purposes of this Act, to be an unfair dismissal.

Case law has established that where paragraph (b) does not apply to the particular organisation, the fairness of the selection for redundancy will be assessed having regard to the general provisions of s.6(1) and s.6(7) of the Unfair Dismissals Act 1977.[40]

[22–28] This statutory wording of s.6(3) envisions a broad, non-prescriptive array of approaches to what might be characterised as fair procedures. Clearly, the section envisages procedures that are expressly or implicitly agreed upon by employers

---

38. s.6(3) Unfair Dismissals Act 1977.
39. *ibid.*, s. 6(7).
40. *Boucher v Irish Productivity Centre* [1994] ELR 205.

and employees, but it also envisages a procedure being established by custom and practice. Regardless of whether the procedure is one that is agreed or is customary, the employer should normally adhere closely to that procedure: any departure from same must be justified by 'special reasons'.

3.2. Guiding Principles in Relation to Fair Selection

The general wording of the statute leaves considerable latitude for employers in terms of the criteria that will be appropriate to apply in a given context. It has correctly been observed that 'much depends on the facts of the case and what is fair in one instance will not necessarily be fair in another'.[41] The fact-specific nature of this area of redundancy law does not mean, however, that guidance cannot be sought from the decided case law. Amongst the most comprehensive judicial exegesis of fair selection in redundancy is that of Browne-Wilkinson J (delivering judgment for the EAT of England and Wales) in *Williams v CompAir Maxam Ltd*.[42] Whilst recognising that it was impossible to lay down brightline rules all employers must follow concerning the question of fair selection, the tribunal identified the following as 'generally accepted'[43] principles governing how reasonable employers will typically act:

[22–29]

1. The employer will seek to give as much warning as possible of impending redundancies so as to enable the union and employees who may be affected to take early steps to inform themselves of the relevant facts, consider possible alternative solutions and, if necessary, find alternative employment in the undertaking or elsewhere.

2. The employer will consult the union as to the best means by which the desired management result can be achieved fairly and with as little hardship to the employees as possible. In particular, the employer will seek to agree with the union the criteria to be applied in selecting the employees to be made redundant. When a selection has been made, the employer will consider with the union whether the selection has been made in accordance with those criteria.

3. Whether or not an agreement as to the criteria to be adopted has been agreed with the union, the employer will seek to establish criteria for selection which so far as possible do not depend solely upon the opinion of the person making the selection but can be objectively checked against such things as attendance record, efficiency at the job, experience, or length of service.

---

41. Higgins and McCrann, ch.15 in Regan, ed., *Employment Law* (Tottel Publishing, 2009), at para.15.31.
42. [1982] 1 ICR 156.
43. *ibid.*, at 162. The tribunal noted that not all of these factors are present in every case, since circumstances may prevent one or more of them being applied. Departure from these principles, however, would be expected only 'where some good reason is shown to justify such departure' (at 162).

4. The employer will seek to ensure that the selection is made fairly in accordance with these criteria and will consider any representations the union may make as to such selection.

5. The employer will seek to see whether instead of dismissing an employee he could offer him alternative employment.[44]

[22–30] Analysing the above principles – and noting what has been referred to as 'the grave danger of erecting what was said in *Williams v CompAir Maxam Ltd.* into the terms of a statute'[45] – a number of imperatives stand out: objectivity, fairness, consultation, and the contemplation of alternative solutions to redundancy. Browne-Wilkinson J helpfully captured these characteristics of the fair selection process when he added:

> The basic approach is that, in the unfortunate circumstances that necessarily attend redundancies, as much as is reasonably possible should be done to mitigate the impact on the work force and to satisfy them that the selection has been made fairly and not on the basis of personal whim.[46]

[22–31] An illustration of an unfair selection procedure is given in *Boucher v Irish Productivity Centre.*[47] In this case, no agreement was reached as to the method of selection for redundancy: the chief executive of the relevant business simply selected the people most suitable to continue with the employer. His criteria revolved around maintaining a core of employees with a balance of skills and flexibility, having regard to their ability to sell, work, and generate new business, and to their financial contribution to the organisation. The selection process was carried out without any consultations or interviews, either at the time of making his selection or at the hearing before a Rights Commissioner, although those selected for redundancy were notified of the criteria on which the decisions were based.

[22–32] In describing this selection procedure as unfair and holding that the claimants had been unfairly dismissed, the EAT emphasised that, where selection involves consideration of particular employees' contributions and versatility to the respondent, those in the group likely to be dismissed should be made aware that such assessment is being made and they should be given an opportunity to give their views, which should be considered. Significantly, the EAT in *Boucher* emphasised that it was not for the tribunal to determine whether such input by the employees would or would not have made a difference: the key point in such cases is that the

---

44. [1982] 1 ICR 156, 162.
45. *Rolls Royce Motor Cars Ltd. v Price* [1993] IRLR 203, *per* Knox J at 208. See also *Rolls Royce Motor Cars Ltd. v Dewhurst* [1985] ICR 869, [1985] IRLR 184 where the EAT emphasised that failure to adhere to the *Williams* principles does not necessarily nullify a selection process.
46. [1982] 1 ICR 156, 162.
47. [1994] ELR 205.

employees are afforded the right to contribute. *Boucher* is authority for the further proposition that where assessments are used as a means of selection, the onus is on the employer to establish that reasonable criteria are applied to all employees and that the selection of an individual employee is fairly made in the context of those criteria.

3.3. Difficulties in Including Conduct as a Criterion in Selection Procedure

Another example of a case in which the EAT held selection criteria to be unfair is [22–33] *Fox v Des Kelly Carpets Ltd.*[48] The claimant's employment was terminated because of restructuring within the company. Three employees were made redundant: the claimant and the last two employees to join the company. The employer's position was that when choosing people for redundancy the employer used its own judgment in an attempt to keep the better employees. The claimant had been made redundant because of his behaviour and because of his ability. He had been verbally warned about his behaviour in the context of an incident that had occurred early in the period of employment. The claimant's position, however, was that verbal warnings were a common feature of the workplace; at no stage was he told that his conduct was a factor in choosing him for redundancy. The EAT, in finding that the claimant had been unfairly dismissed, held that the employer was 'estopped' from relying on the previous misconduct in circumstances where the employee continued to work as normal after the particular incident.[49]

More generally, this case demonstrates the inherent difficulty in an employer seeking [22–34] to include conduct as a selection criterion: such an approach will, as Redmond observes, give rise to the risk that 'the dismissed employee will argue that redundancy is a sham and merely a pretext for getting rid of him'.[50]

3.4. Duty of Employer to Consider Other Options

It is important that employers identify and explore the feasibility of pursuing less [22–35] drastic measures to redundancy. Failure to do so may result in a dismissal in an alleged redundancy situation being deemed unfair. This is illustrated, for example, in the approach of the EAT in *Keogh v Mentroy Limited.*[51] There the claimant was promoted from his position as sales assistant to that of manager in the employer's store. A downturn in business demand prompted the decision to make the position of manager redundant, as this position was the most financially costly for the employer. The employer had also received complaints from other staff members about the employee and his management style. The employee was not given the option of returning to his former role. In the days immediately following the employee's redundancy another staff member resigned and a notice advertising

---

48. [1992] ELR 182.
49. Generally, see Chapter 18.
50. Redmond, *Dismissal Law in Ireland* (2nd ed., Tottel Publishing, 2007), [20.55].
51. UD 209/2009.

full- or part-time positions was placed in the employer's shop window. The EAT held that in deciding to make the employee redundant the employer had taken into account factors other than the decline in business, namely the complaints from other staff members. The EAT also found, however, that the employer did not adequately consider other alternatives to redundancy and that the reasons given by him were not in fact the reasons for the dismissal. Accordingly the EAT found that the employee had been unfairly dismissed.

[22–36] In *Sheehan and O'Brien v Vintners Federation of Ireland Ltd.*[52] the EAT held that the claimants had been unfairly dismissed even though the redundancy was found to be genuine. The employees provided proposals to the company on how their jobs could be retained and the company did not take these into consideration. The tribunal was critical of, *inter alia*, the employer's failure to 'consider earnestly the claimants' proposals regarding the reorganisation of the work which would have realised significant savings'.[53]

[22–37] Finally, an important point to be noted regarding alternative employment is that, pursuant to s.15 of the Redundancy Payments Act 1967 as amended, an employee will lose his or her entitlement to redundancy payment – set out in detail below in this chapter – where [s]he unreasonably refuses an offer of alternative employment.

3.5. 'Last in, First Out' (LIFO) and Similar Criteria

[22–38] 'Last in, First Out' (LIFO) is 'a revered principle in redundancy selection, and continues to be respected'.[54] Even where a LIFO policy is in place in the particular organisation, however, there may be legitimate reasons justifying its non-application in any given case.[55]

[22–39] A related point to be emphasised is that care must be taken in relation to the inclusion of any criterion that could run contrary to employment equality protection, discussed in detail in Part III of this book. A topical example at the time of writing concerns the taking into account as a selection criterion an employee's length of service, with the implications this may have for age discrimination. In the 2009 case of *Rolls-Royce Plc v Unite the Union*[56] Wall LJ upheld the legitimacy of such a criterion and rejected the argument that it breached the prohibition on age discrimination in the EU Framework Directive.[57] He said:

---

52. [2009] ELR 155.
53. [2009] ELR 155, 168.
54. Redmond, *Dismissal Law in Ireland* (2nd ed., Tottel Publishing, 2007), [20.58].
55. *Board of Management Rushbrooke National School v Geary* [2009] ELR 30; *Rolls-Royce Motor Cars Ltd. v Price* [1993] IRLR 203.
56. [2009] EWCA Civ 387, [2009] IRLR 576.
57. Council Directive 2000/78/EC, establishing a General Framework for Equal Treatment in Employment and Occupation.

In my judgment, to reward long service by employees in any redundancy selection process is, viewed objectively, an entirely reasonable and legitimate employment policy, and one which a conscientious employer would readily and properly negotiate with a responsible Trade Union.[58]

Notwithstanding this judicial support for the inclusion of such a criterion, it is important to stress that such criteria should be applied with extreme care by employers, as should any capable of engaging other protective legislation such as the Protection of Employees (Part-Time) Work Act 2001 or the Protection of Employees (Fixed-Term) Work Act 2003. [22–40]

4. Collective Redundancies: Protection of Employment Act 1977

Determining the fairness of a selection procedure may also be affected by procedures relating to collective redundancies and, in particular, by a consideration of whether the requirements of the Protection of Employment Act 1977 have been respected by the employer.[59] The term 'collective redundancies' in this context means[60] dismissals effected by an employer for one or more reasons not related to the individual concerned, where in any period of 30 consecutive days the number of such dismissals is: [22–41]

    (a) at least five in an establishment normally employing more than 20 and less than 50 employees;

    (b) at least 10 in an establishment normally employing at least 50 but less than 100 employees;

    (c) at least 10 per cent of the number of employees in an establishment normally employing at least 100 but less than 300 employees; and

    (d) at least 30 in an establishment normally employing 300 or more employees.

The 1977 Act[61] sought to transpose into Irish law Council Directive 75/129 EC on Collective Redundancies (now replaced by Council Directive 98/59 EC on Collective Redundancies, which led to the passing in this jurisdiction of the European Communities (Protection of Employment) Regulations 2000[62]). The essential purpose of this Directive, which was introduced amidst concerns about 'social dumping', is to ensure that employers follow certain procedures when making [22–42]

---

58. *Rolls-Royce Plc v Unite the Union* [2009] EWCA Civ 387, *per* Wall LJ, [95].

59. Collective redundancies may arise in, *inter alia*, the context of a transfer of undertakings situation, considered in detail in Chapter 23.

60. s.6(1) Protection of Employment Act 1977, as amended.

61. For detailed analysis see Kerr, *Consolidated Irish Employment Legislation* (Thomson Round Hall, Release 23, September 2009), Division I.

62. SI no. 488 of 2000.

a number of employees redundant over a specified period. The obligations laid down in the Directive can be distilled into two key duties: that of consultation with employees' representatives and that of notification of the proposed redundancies to the relevant authorities in the State.

4.1. Employers' Obligations in the Context of Collective Redundancies

[22–43] Where it is proposed to create collective redundancies, an employer should, 'with a view to reaching agreement', initiate consultations with employees' representatives.[63] The representatives may be a trade union, a staff association or an excepted body[64] with which the employer has had a practice of conducting collective bargaining negotiations.[65] If there is no such body in existence, the employees may choose their representative from amongst their number to represent them in negotiations with the employer.[66]

These consultations should include the following matters:

(a) the possibility of avoiding the proposed redundancies, reducing the number of employees affected by them or mitigating their consequences; and

(b) the basis on which it will be decided which particular employees will be made redundant.[67]

4.1.1. Junk v Kuhnel *and the Meaning of Consultation*

[22–44] The legislation provides that these consultations are to be initiated at the earliest opportunity and in any event at least 30 days before the first dismissal takes effect. In its landmark ruling in *Junk v Kuhnel*,[68] the European Court of Justice held that the consultation process required pursuant to the Directive must occur prior to employees being given notice of dismissal, as opposed to after individual notices have been issued but before they take effect. Having interpreted Art. 2 of the Directive as essentially imposing an obligation to negotiate, the court continued:

> The effectiveness of such an obligation would be compromised if an employer was entitled to terminate contracts of employment during the course of the procedure or even at the beginning thereof. It would be significantly more difficult for workers' representatives to achieve the withdrawal of a decision that has been taken than to secure the abandonment of a decision that is being contemplated.[69]

---

63. s.9(1) Protection of Employment Act 1977, as amended.
64. s.6(3) Trade Union Act 1941, as amended.
65. s.2 Protection of Employment Act 1977, as amended.
66. s.2(d) Protection of Employment Act 1977, as amended; Regulation 3 of the European Communities (Protection of Employment) Regulations 2000, SI no. 488 of 2000.
67. s.9(2) Protection of Employment Act 1977, as amended.
68. [2005] EUECJ C18803, [2005] 1 CMLR 42.
69. At [44].

More recently, the European Court of Justice has held that the obligation in Art. [22–45] 2 of the Directive must be interpreted to mean that the adoption, within a group of undertakings, of strategic decisions or of changes in activities that compel the employer to contemplate or to plan for collective redundancies, gives rise to an obligation on that employer to consult with workers' representatives.[70] This is so regardless of whether the employer is directly responsible for making the decision: this decision thus has clear implications for multi-national employers.

4.1.2. *Provision of Information*

The employer is obliged[71] to supply in writing to the employees' representatives all [22–46] relevant information, including but not limited to:

(a) the reasons for the proposed redundancies,
(b) the number, and description of categories, of employees whom it is proposed to make redundant,
(c) the number of employees, and description of categories, normally employed,
(d) the period during which it is proposed to effect the proposed redundancies,
(e) the criteria proposed for the selection of the workers to be made redundant, and
(f) the method of calculating any redundancy payments other than those methods set out in the Redundancy Payments Acts 1967 to 2007 or any other relevant enactment for the time being in force or, subject thereto, in practice.

Significantly, it has been held that employers may provide this information as [22–47] and when it comes to light throughout the consultation process: the fact that such information is not available does not preclude the consultation process from commencing. This approach has recently been explained by the European Court of Justice in the following observation:

> Flexibility is essential, given, first, that that information may become available only at various stages in the consultation process, which implies that the employer both can and must add to the information supplied in the course of that process. Secondly, the purpose of the employer being under that obligation is to enable the workers' representatives to participate in the consultation process as fully and effectively as possible, and, to achieve that, any new relevant information must be supplied up to the end of the process.[72]

---

70. *Akavan Erityisalojen Keskusliitto AEK & Ors v Fujitsu Siemens Computers Oy* [2009] EUECJ C-44/08.
71. s.10(2) Protection of Employment Act 1977, as amended.
72. *Akavan Erityisalojen Keskusliitto AEK & Ors v Fujitsu Siemens Computers Oy* [2009] EUECJ C-44/08, 10 September 2009, [53].

4.2. Consequences of a Failure to Inform or Consult

[22–48] Regulation 6(2) of the European Communities (Protection of Employment) Regulations 2000[73] provides that an employee, trade union, staff association or excepted body on behalf of an employee may present a complaint to a Rights Commissioner arising out of a failure to inform or consult concerning collective redundancies. The Rights Commissioner may require the employer to comply with the provision of the Act of 1977 concerned and, for that purpose, to take a specified course of action, and/or require the employer to pay to the employee compensation of such amount (if any) as is just and equitable having regard to all of the circumstances, but not exceeding four weeks' remuneration in respect of the employee's employment.

[22–49] Such failures to inform or consult also constitute criminal offences; upon conviction, an employer may be fined up to €5,000 per offence. Should the employer seek to effect collective redundancies before the expiry of the 30-day period discussed above, the employer shall be guilty of an offence and shall be liable on conviction on indictment to a fine not exceeding €250,000.[74]

4.3. The Notification Obligation

[22–50] The other main obligation upon employers[75] in relation to collective redundancies is that of notification. An employer is obliged to notify the Minister of the proposed redundancies at the earliest opportunity, and in any event at least 30 days before the first dismissal takes effect.[76] The key objective behind this obligation is that it enables the Minister to explore solutions to the proposed collective redundancies.[77] Regulation 2 of the Protection of Employment Act 1977 (Notification of Proposed Collective Redundancies) Regulations 1977[78] stipulates that the following information must be provided to the Minister:

---

73. SI no. 488 of 2000.

74. s.14(2) Protection of Employment Act 1977, as amended.

75. In the case of collective redundancies arising from the employer's business being terminated following bankruptcy or winding up proceedings, or for any other reason as a result of a court decision, the Act provides that the person responsible for the affairs of the business need comply with this notification obligation 'only if the Minister so requests': s.12(4) Protection of Employment Act 1977, as inserted by Art. 11 of the Protection of Employment Order 1996, SI no. 370 of 1996.

76. s.12 Protection of Employment Act 1977, as amended.

77. See Art. 4.2 of the Directive in this regard. For the purpose of seeking solutions to the problems caused by the proposed redundancies, the Minister may request the employer to enter into consultations with him or her, or with an authorised officer. Where this takes place, the employer is obliged to supply the Minister or authorised officer 'with such information relating to the proposed redundancies as the Minister or the officer may reasonably require' (s.15 Protection of Employment Act 1977). It is important to note that employers are obliged to keep records showing that all the requirements applicable to collective redundancies have been complied with. These records must be retained for at least three years (s.18 Protection of Employment Act 1977, as amended).

78. SI no. 140 of 1977.

(a) the name and address of the employer, indicating whether he is a sole trader, a partnership or a company;

(b) the address of the establishment where the collective redundancies are proposed;

(c) the total number of persons normally employed at that establishment;

(d) the number and descriptions or categories of employees whom it is proposed to make redundant;

(e) the period during which the collective redundancies are proposed to be effected, stating the dates on which the first and the final dismissals are expected to take effect;

(f) the reasons for the proposed collective redundancies;

(g) the names and addresses of the trade unions or staff associations representing employees affected by the proposed redundancies and with which it has been the practice of the employer to conduct collective bargaining negotiations;

(h) the date on which consultations with each such trade union or staff association commenced and the progress achieved in those consultations to the date of the notification.

A copy of the notification must be supplied as soon as possible by the employer to the employees' representatives, who may forward to the Minister in writing any observations they have relating to the notification.[79]

5. Exceptional Collective Redundancies

The Protection of Employment (Exceptional Collective Redundancies and Related Matters) Act 2007 introduced new and specific provisions for what are termed 'exceptional collective redundancies'.[80] The key objective of the 2007 legislation is to increase the expense of exceptional collective redundancies so that their attractiveness as an option for employers is diminished. [22–51]

5.1. Overview of the Key Effects of the 2007 Act

Exceptional collective redundancies are, in essence, compulsory collective redundancies in circumstances where the redundant employees are to be replaced within [22–52]

---

79. s.12(3) Protection of Employment Act 1977.
80. For analysis of this legislation generally, see Meenan, 'Exceptional Collective Redundancies', 4(3) *IELJ* (2007), 74.

the State, whether at the same location or elsewhere, by new employees who will carry out similar functions but who will enjoy less favourable terms and conditions of employment.[81] The 2007 Act introduces yet another statutory body into Irish employment law: the Redundancy Panel, which is responsible for determining at first instance whether collective redundancies constitute exceptional collective redundancies for the purposes of the legislation. Either an employer or the employee representative may refer a proposal to create collective redundancies to this panel, so that the latter can determine whether such collective redundancies would constitute exceptional collective redundancies.[82] This reference must be made within the 30-day window for consultation considered above as set out under the Protection of Employment Act 1977 as amended. The panel must be satisfied that the referring party has:

- unsuccessfully sought to resolve the matter through local engagement, that is, all or any of the following:

  1. Established dispute resolution procedures;

  2. Procedures in place, or availed of by custom or usual practice, in the employment concerned;

  3. Ordinary consultative procedures;

- acted reasonably and has not acted in a manner that, in the opinion of the Panel, has frustrated the possibility of agreement to restructuring, or other changes, necessary to secure the viability of the business of the employer, and, as a consequence, the best possible levels of employment and conditions, and

- not had recourse to industrial action since the proposal was referred to the Panel.[83]

[22–53] Where it appears to the panel that the proposed collective redundancies are exceptional collective redundancies, it must, within seven working days of receipt of the reference, either request the Minister to seek an opinion from the Labour Court as to whether or not the proposal creates exceptional collective redundancies, or inform the Minister that the conditions for referring the proposal outlined above have not been satisfied.

[22–54] Should the panel request the Minister to refer the matter to the Labour Court, the Minister has seven days from the receipt of the request to do so.[84] The Minister

---

81. s.7(2)(A) Redundancy Payments Acts, as inserted by 2007 Act.
82. s.6(1) Protection of Employment (Exceptional Collective Redundancies and Related Matters) Act 2007.
83. *ibid.*, s.6(3) as amended.
84. *ibid.*, s. 7.

may, however, make such a request to the Labour Court of his or her own initiative – regardless of whether or not a reference has been made to the panel – where it appears to him or her that the proposed collective redundancies amount to exceptional collective redundancies and the relevant time limits have not elapsed.[85] The Labour Court must, within 16 days, hold a hearing and issue an opinion to the Minister as to whether or not the proposed redundancies are exceptional collective redundancies.[86] The Labour Court may, however, only issue such an opinion where it is satisfied that the same conditions outlined above of which the panel must be satisfied have been met. The Minister is obliged to notify the affected parties within seven days of receiving the opinion of the Labour Court.

Where the Labour Court determines that the redundancies do constitute exceptional collective redundancies and the employer nevertheless decides to proceed with these redundancies, the Minister may refuse the employer the redundancy rebate from the Social Insurance Fund to which the employer would, as seen in the section immediately below in this chapter, ordinarily be entitled upon payment of a lump sum on redundancy.[87] [22–55]

Another important feature of the 2007 legislation to be noted here is that the Act extends the time period during which dismissals may not occur where a reference is made to the panel or the Minister's request is lodged with the Labour Court. Where a reference is made to the panel, a dismissal cannot take place earlier than after the expiry of seven working days from the date on which the panel received the request. Should the panel request the Minister to refer the matter to the Labour Court, this period will be extended by a further seven working days. Where the Minister lodges a request with the Labour Court, the period will be further extended by 16 days, running from the date of that lodgment. [22–56]

6. Employee Entitlements under the Redundancy Payments Acts

In the final section of this chapter, a brief overview is provided of employees' entitlements under the Redundancy Payments Acts in this jurisdiction. The analysis is necessarily concise and is concerned with the legislative framework: for this reason, schemes to which employers frequently have recourse in the redundancy context but which do not come within the scope of the Redundancy Acts or the jurisdiction of the EAT – such as *ex gratia* payments, for example – are not considered. It is therefore important to emphasise that legal and other professional advice should be sought in this area as appropriate.[88] [22–57]

---

85. *ibid.*, s. 7(3).
86. *ibid.*, s. 8(1).
87. *ibid.*, s.9.
88. Generally, see also Higgins and McCrann, Chapter 15 in Regan, ed., *Employment Law* (Tottel Publishing, 2009), at paras.15.77 *et seq*. The Department of Enterprise, Trade and Employment has issued a *Guide to the Redundancy Payments Scheme*, available free of charge

[22–58] Under the Redundancy Payments Acts, employees who come within the scope of the legislation and are dismissed on the grounds of redundancy, or placed on short time or are laid off for an amount of time exceeding a temporary period, shall be entitled to a redundancy certificate and a lump-sum payment from their employer, as well as (in the case of employees dismissed on grounds of redundancy) to notice of their dismissal.

6.1. To Whom Do the Entitlements Apply?

[22–59] The Redundancy Payments Acts apply to all employees in both the public and private sector who have been at least 104 weeks in continuous employment that is insurable for all benefits under social welfare legislation, or who have ceased to be ordinarily employed in employment that was so insurable in the period of four years ending on the date of termination.[89] An individual's employment is presumed under the legislation to be continuous[90] unless it is terminated by dismissal or by the employee voluntarily leaving the employment.[91] Continuity of employment will not be affected by interruptions of not more than 26 consecutive weeks arising from holidays, lay-offs, or any other cause authorised by the employer.[92]

[22–60] Section 2 of the Redundancy Payments Act 1967 (as amended) defines an employee as any person of 16 years and upwards who has entered into or works under (or, where the employment has ceased, entered into or worked under) a contract of employment; the same section defines 'employer' as the person with whom the employee has entered into or for whom the employee works under (or, where the employment has ceased, entered into or worked under) a contract of employment. Where the employee is an agency worker, the employer is the entity responsible for paying the employee's salary.[93]

[22–61] The legislation confers a right to a redundancy payment not only upon those employees dismissed due to redundancy, but also upon those who are laid off or kept on short time for a period of four or more consecutive weeks, or for a period of six or more weeks within a period of 13 consecutive weeks.[94] In this respect, it is important to be aware of what is meant by an employee being 'laid off' or kept on 'short time'.

---

from the Department of Enterprise, Trade and Employment, Davitt House, Adelaide Road, Dublin 2, at Social Welfare Offices and FÁS Offices, and also available on the Department's Website at www.entemp.ie.

89. ss.4(1) and 7(1) Redundancy Payments Act 1967, as amended.
90. s.10(a) Redundancy Payments Act 1971.
91. Third Schedule to the Redundancy Payments Act 1967, as amended.
92. See *Irish Shipping Ltd. v Adams* (1987) 6 JISLL 186, and the commentary thereon by Kerr, *Consolidated Irish Employment Legislation* (Thomson Round Hall, Release 23, September 2009), Division I.
93. s.2 as amended.
94. ss.7(1) and 7(3) Redundancy Payments Act 1967.

Thus s.11(1) of the Redundancy Payments Act 1967, as amended, provides that an [22–62]
employee will be regarded as having been laid off where his or her employment
ceases by reason of the employer's being unable to provide the work for which the
employee was employed to do, and

(a) it is reasonable in the circumstances for that employer to believe that the
cessation of employment will not be permanent, and
(b) the employer gives notice to that effect to the employee prior to the
cessation.

Similarly, s.11(2) provides that an employee will be regarded as being on short time [22–63]
where his or her hours of work or remuneration are less than half of their normal
weekly amount owing to a diminution in the work provided by the employer. Here
again, it must be reasonable in the circumstances for the employer to believe that
the diminution in work will not be permanent and [s]he must give notice to that
effect to the employee prior to the reduction in remuneration or hours of work.

Where an employee is either laid off of placed on short time for the periods [22–64]
outlined above, then [s]he may give his or her employer written notice of his or
her intention to claim a redundancy payment, after the expiry of the time period
and in any event not later than four weeks after the cessation of the lay-off or short
time.[95] Alternately, the employee may choose to terminate his or her contract
of employment either by giving the employer the notice thereby required or, if
none is so required under the contract, by giving the employer not less than one
week's notice in writing of intention to terminate the contract.[96] An employee
will not, however, be entitled to a redundancy payment in these circumstances if
the employer establishes that on the date the notice was served, it was reasonably
expected that the employee would, not later than four weeks from that date, enter
into a period of full employment for not less than 13 weeks.[97] In order to establish this, the employer must serve within seven days a counter-notice informing
the employee that the employer will contest any liability to pay a redundancy
payment in pursuance of the notice of intention to claim.[98]

It should be noted that the legislation expressly excludes certain employees from [22–65]
the ambit of the payments entitlements. Thus, for example, an apprentice who is
dismissed within one month after the end of the apprenticeship will not be entitled
to a redundancy payment.[99] Section 14 of the 1967 Act provides that employees
who are dismissed for misconduct in circumstances where the employer is entitled
to terminate the employee's contract without notice are not entitled to a redundancy payment.

---

95. s.12 Redundancy Payments Act 1967, as inserted by s.11 Redundancy Payments Act 1971.
96. *ibid.*, s. 12(2).
97. *ibid.*, s. 13(1).
98. *ibid.*, s. 13(2).
99. *ibid.*, s. 7(4).

6.2. The Requirement to Provide Notice of Dismissal for Redundancy and Redundancy Certificate

[22–66] Where an employer proposes to dismiss an employee on the grounds of redundancy, it must furnish to the employee, at least two weeks before the date of dismissal, a written notice of the proposed dismissal.[100] The relevant documentation here is Part A of Form RP50: detailed stipulations as to what must be contained in the notice may be found in the Redundancy (Notice of Dismissal) Regulations 1991.[101]

[22–67] The employer is also obliged to provide to the employee a redundancy certificate, which must be supplied no later than the date of the dismissal.[102] In circumstances where the employee has already given the employer notice of his or her intention to claim a redundancy payment, then the employer must provide the certificate within seven days of receipt of that notice.[103] The relevant documentation here is Part B of Form RP50: detailed stipulations as to what must be contained in the certificate may be found in the Redundancy Certificate Regulations 1991.[104]

6.3. Employee's Entitlement to Time Off during Notice Period

[22–68] An employee is, during the course of the two weeks of the redundancy notice period, entitled to a reasonable amount of (paid) time off 'in order to look for new employment or make arrangements for training for future employment'.[105]

6.4. Lump-Sum Payments

[22–69] Section 19 of the Redundancy Payments Act 1967 confers upon employees an entitlement to a lump-sum payment on dismissal. This lump sum consists of a sum equivalent to two weeks' normal remuneration for every year of service, in addition to one bonus week's payment.[106] The remuneration is capped at €600 per week or €31,200 per annum.[107] Earnings that are in excess of this amount will be disregarded for the purposes of arriving at a calculation of the redundancy payment.

[22–70] The employer is responsible for making this payment to the employee; the employer can then claim a 60 per cent rebate of that sum from the Social Insurance Fund by submitting the RP50 Form to the department within six months of the payment.[108] Where the employer refuses or is not in a position to make

---

100. *ibid.*, s.17. On notice generally, see Chapter 20.
101. SI no. 348 of 1991.
102. s.18 Redundancy Payments Act 1967.
103. *ibid.*, s.18(2).
104. SI no. 347 of 1991, as amended by s.7 Redundancy Payments Act 2003.
105. s.7(2) Redundancy Payments Act 1979.
106. Third Schedule to the Redundancy Payments Act 1967, as amended.
107. Redundancy Payments (Lump Sum) Regulations 2004.
108. s.29(1) Redundancy Payments Act 1967, as amended.

the lump-sum payment – and where the employee has (except in the case of the employer's insolvency or death) taken all reasonable steps to obtain the lump-sum payment from the employer – the Minister will pay the sum or whatever part of same the employer has refused to pay.[109] The Minister will then seek to recoup this amount from the employer.[110]

The lump-sum payment must be paid within 52 weeks commencing from the date [22–71] of dismissal or termination. Where the 52 weeks have expired without payment being made, the employee may apply to the EAT during the subsequent 52 weeks claiming the lump sum. The EAT may award the sum if satisfied that the delay in question was owing to a reasonable cause.[111] Where the employee can establish to the satisfaction of the EAT that failure to make a claim for a lump sum before the end of the period of 104 weeks was caused either:

- by his or her ignorance of the identity of his or her employer or employers, or
- by his or her ignorance of a change of employer resulting in his or her dismissal and engagement under a contract with another employer, and
- that in either case such ignorance arose out of or was contributed to by a breach of a statutory duty (on the part of the employer) to give the employee either notice of the proposed dismissal or a redundancy certificate,

then the period of 104 weeks shall commence from such date as the EAT at its discretion considers reasonable having regard to all the circumstances.[112]

109. s.32(2) Redundancy Payments Act 1967.
110. This may include a deduction of the rebate from the Social Insurance Fund to which the employer would have had access had the employer paid the lump sum in the first place; however, the Minister may withhold the rebate where it appears to him or her that there was no reasonable excuse for the refusal or failure to pay (s.32(4) Redundancy Payments Act 1967, as amended).
111. *ibid.*
112. *ibid.*, s.24(3) as amended.

CHAPTER 23

Transfer of Undertakings

Introduction

Since the mid-1970s, European Community law has been concerned with the need to protect the employment interests of an employee whose employer sells the business in which [s]he is employed to another organisation. The objective of the Community measures in this regard has been to 'protect workers in a business which is transferred',[1] essentially by seeking to provide them with some measure of continuity of employment (that is to say, employment on the same conditions as they had previously enjoyed[2]) following such transfer.[3] In other words, it is intended that the transferee[4] of the undertaking should be obliged to provide employees with the same terms and conditions of employment as they had formerly enjoyed with the transferor.[5]

[23–01]

Various efforts were made at a European Union level to legislate for such protection,[6] culminating in Council Directive no. 2001/23/EC of 12 March 2001, which

[23–02]

---

1. Advocate General Slynn in C-24/85, *Spijkers v Gebroeders Bendik Abbatoir CV* [1986] ECR 1119. Generally, see Kimber and O'Doherty, 'Transfer of Undertakings – Perspectives from Litigation', 5(2) *IELJ* (2008), 56.
2. C-287/86, *Landsorganisationen I Danmark v Ny Molle Kro* [1987] EUECJ R-287/86, [1987] ECR 5465. The point is made (Law Society of Ireland, in Moffatt, ed., *Employment Law* (2nd ed., Oxford University Press, 2006), at para.1.2.3) that the Directive and the transposing regulations are given a purposive interpretation both by the ECJ and by domestic tribunals. See also *Bannon v Employment Appeals Tribunal and Drogheda Town Centre* [1992] ELR 203.
3. The previous position had been that in such circumstances, unless the transferee consented to this, [s]he would have no responsibility for the former employees of the transferor, and hence the sale of the business would terminate all existing employment contracts: *Nokes v Doncaster Amalgamated Collieries Ltd.* [1940] AC 1014, [1940] 3 All ER 549.
4. Under reg.2 European Communities (Protection of Employees on Transfer of Undertakings) Regulations 2003, a 'transferee' is defined as 'any natural or legal person who, by reason of a transfer within the meaning of these regulations, becomes the employer in respect of the undertaking, business or part of the undertaking or business'.
5. Under reg.2 European Communities (Protection of Employees on Transfer of Undertakings) Regulations 2003 a 'transferor' is defined as 'any natural or legal person who, by reason of a transfer within the meaning of these regulations, ceases to be the employer in respect of the undertaking, business or part of the undertaking or business'.
6. From a European perspective, the Acquired Rights Directive (Directive 77/187/EEC) –

was transposed into Irish law through the European Communities (Protection of Employees on Transfer of Undertakings) Regulations 2003.[7] It is this Directive and, more particularly, these regulations that are the principal focus of this chapter.

[23–03] On balance it may be said that all of the various directives and regulations dealing with this area have been less than satisfactory in the sense that many uncertainties remain as far as the law is concerned. This is not least because there is a wealth of case law in the area from which, on occasion, conflicting principles emerge. In this chapter, therefore, we seek to assess not merely the terms of the relevant regulations in this area, but also the manner in which the various terms and concepts dealt with in these regulations have been interpreted in the various courts and tribunals and most importantly (given the European Community Law dimensions to this issue) within the European Court of Justice (ECJ). Equally it should be noted that the body of law relating to transfer of undertakings is vast and very detailed, and there are specialist texts dealing with the issue in more detail than is possible within a comprehensive employment law text of this nature.[8]

[23–04] As a final introductory point, it is worth noting that whereas the provisions of the Directive (and hence the regulations) will apply to all transfer of undertakings

---

which was brought into force in Ireland through the European Communities (Safeguarding of Employees' Rights on Transfer of Undertakings) Regulations 1980, SI no. 306/1980 – was replaced by Directive 98/50/EC – which was brought into force through the European Communities (Safeguarding of Employees' Rights on Transfer of Undertakings) Regulations, SI no. 487 of 2000. All of these directives and regulations were repealed and replaced by the third Acquired Rights Directive (Council Directive No. 2001/23/EC) brought into force by the European Communities (Protection of Employees on Transfer of Undertakings) Regulations 2003, SI no. 131 of 2003, which sought to deal with some of the uncertainties of interpretation that bedevilled the previous rules. See Byrne, 'Transfer of Undertakings', in Regan, ed., *Employment Law* (Tottel Publishing, 2009), at paras.19.01–19.05; Codd, 'The Transfer of Undertakings and Commercial Agreements: Advising Clients and some Practical Pitfalls', 5 *Employment Law Review* (2007), 7; and Barrett, 'Report on the Implementation by Ireland of Directive 2001/23/EC on the Approximation of Laws of the Member States Relating to the Safeguarding of Employees' Rights in the Event of Transfers of Undertakings, Businesses or Parts of Businesses' (European Commission, Brussels, 2006).

7.   SI no. 131 of 2003. For a general analysis of the lead-up to and the nature of the regulations, see O'Mara, 'Third Time Lucky? The New European Communities (Protection of Employees on Transfer of Undertakings) Regulations 2003', 10(7) *Commercial Law Practitioner* (2003), 179. For analysis of the equivalent English regulations (The Transfer of Undertakings (Protection of Employment) Regulations 2006, see McMullen, 'An Analysis of the Transfer of Undertakings (Protection of Employment) Regulations 2006', 35(2) *Industrial Law Journal* (2006), 113.

8.   See, for example, McMullen, *Business Transfers and Employee Rights* (Butterworths, 2000), plus subsequent loose-leaf supplements; *Business Transfers and Contracting: A Practical Guide to TUPE* (EEF, 2006): Byrne, *Transfer of Undertakings: Employment Aspects of Business Transfers in Irish and European Law* (Blackhall, 1999); Wynn Evans, *Blackstone's Guide to the New Transfer of Undertakings Legislation* (Oxford University Press, 2006); Hyams, *Employment Aspects of Business Reorganisation* (Oxford University Press, 2006).

situations within the relevant jurisdiction in which they are in force, and, whereas any provision in any agreement that purports to exclude or limit the application of or is inconsistent with any provision of the regulations is void[9] and any term in any agreement that is less favourable than a similar or corresponding entitlement conferred by the regulations will be modified so as not to be less favourable,[10] equally the Irish regulations appear to permit their terms to be replaced by the terms of an agreement – provided that the effect of such an agreement is to put the employee in a more favourable position than would be the case as a result of the application of the regulations.[11]

I. The Scope of the Directive

Given the significance of the rights protected under the terms of the regulations, [23–05] the first point of analysis as far as this chapter is concerned is the question of what types of commercial situation are covered by the regulations. Reg. 3(1) states that the regulations cover

> any transfer of an undertaking, business, or part of an undertaking or business from one employer to another employer as a result of a legal transfer (including the assignment or forfeiture of a lease[12]) or merger.[13]

Yet this apparently simple rule has generated significant uncertainty. We consider the nature of this uncertainty under three headings:

- defining an undertaking;
- defining a transfer; and
- having regard to these two factors, defining a transfer of undertakings.

---

9. reg.9(1) European Communities (Protection of Employees on Transfer of Undertakings) Regulations 2003.

10. reg.9(2) *ibid.*

11. reg.9(3) *ibid.* This is arguably at variance with the conclusion of the ECJ in C-324/84, *Foreningen af Arbejdsledere I Danmark v Daddy's Dance Hall A/S* [1988] EUECJ R-324/86, [1988] ECR 739. It has been suggested that any such changes cannot be consequent on the fact of the transfer and hence must arise where the first pre-transfer contract has come to an end. See Law Society of Ireland, in Moffatt, ed., *Employment Law* (2nd ed., Oxford University Press, 2006), at 11.8.9.4. For analysis by the English Court of Appeal, see *MD Power v Regent Security Services Ltd.* [2007] EWCA Civ 1188.

12. On this point, see C-144 and C-145/87, *Berg and Busschers v Besselsen* [1998] EUECJ R-145/87, [1988] ECR 2559.

13. This was the approach taken by the European Court of Justice in C-324/84, *Foreningen af Arbejdsledere I Danmark v Daddy's Dance Hall A/S* [1988] ECR 739. Under reg.2, a 'merger' is defined as having the meaning assigned to it by the European Communities (Mergers and Divisions of Companies) Regulations 1987, SI no. 137 of 1987, which means 'merger by acquisition' or 'merger by formation of a new company'.

1.1. Defining an Undertaking

[23–06] What must be transferred is an 'undertaking', yet neither the regulations nor the EC Directive (nor any previous regulations or directives) define the concept of an undertaking *per se*.[14] Some clue is given in reg. 3(3), which states that the regulations apply 'to public and private undertakings engaged in economic activities whether or not they are operating for gain'. Thus it may be suggested (and by analogy with, for example, the approach of EC Competition Law) that an undertaking for these purposes is any entity if and when it is engaged, even indirectly or tangentially, in economic activity.[15] Thus, for example, a non-profit-making organisation, which will normally not be targeted by competition law, will constitute an undertaking whenever it is engaged in economic activity.[16]

[23–07] In this regard, a further and more useful clue to the meaning of an 'undertaking' is provided in the regulations as they define the concept of a 'transfer'. Thus the regulations refer to the transfer of 'an economic entity which retains its identity'.[17] In other words, it would seem that an 'undertaking' for the purposes of the Directive and regulations is an economic entity that retains its identity following the transfer process. This is a significant point, in that the approach at EC law to the interpretation of the Transfer of Undertakings Directive appears to be to regard the distinct terms 'undertaking' and 'economic entity'[18] as being essentially identical,[19] and indeed (insofar as the ECJ is concerned) to refer far more regularly to 'economic entities' and 'economic units' than to 'undertakings' when speaking of transfers that have been caught by the Directive.

[23–08] In defining what an 'economic entity' is, the regulations (essentially encapsulating the approach of the ECJ in this area) state that the term

> means an organised grouping of resources which has the objective of pursuing an

---

14. It is, however, provided that the regulations do not apply to sea-going vessels: reg.2(5) European Communities (Protection of Employees on Transfer of Undertakings) Regulations 2003.

15. C-209-215 and C-2184/78, *Heintz van Landewyck Sarl and others v Commission* [1990] ECR 3125.

16. C-41/90, *Hofner and Elser v Macrotron GmBH* [1993] 4 CMLR 306; C-160/91, *Pourcet and Pistre v AGF and Cancava* [1993] 1 ECR 637.

17. In C-48/94, *Ledernes Hovedorganisation (Rygaard) v Dansk Arbejdsgiverforening (Stro Molle Akustik A/S* [1995] EUECJ C-48/94, [1995] ECR I-2745, the ECJ held that the Directive would apply wherever there was a transfer of a stable economic entity.

18. It was suggested by Advocate General van Gerven in C-392/92, *Schmidt v Spar und Leihkasse der Fruheren Amter Bordesholm* [1994] ECR I-1311, [1994] EUECJ, [1994] IRLR 302, [1995] 2 CMLR 331, [1995] ICR 237 that the concept of an economic entity was synonymous with that of an economic unit. For the significance of this (particularly in terms of the question of whether or not the transfer of the activities of the undertaking may be regarded as a transfer of undertakings, see Law Society of Ireland, in Moffat, ed., *Employment Law* (2nd ed., Oxford University Press, 2006), at 11.8.2.

19. See C-13/95, *Süzen v Zehnacker Gebaudereinigung GmbH Krankenhausservice* [1997] EUECJ C-13/95, [1997] ECR I-1259.

economic activity whether or not that activity is for profit or whether it is central or ancillary to another economic or administrative entity.[20]

Again the breadth of this definition is of significance in that, as we shall see shortly, the ECJ has concluded on occasion that it is possible, if a business transfers some of its activities to another business, that this may, depending on the facts, constitute a transfer of an economic unit, which will consequently be caught by the terms of the Directive and regulations. [23–09]

1.1.1. A 'Part' of an Undertaking

The regulations make it clear that they will apply not merely to the transfer of the whole of a business but also (where what is at stake is a self-contained economic unit with a definable identity) to the transfer of *part* of an undertaking. Nonetheless, there is no particularly clinical test for determining *when* a part of an undertaking will be regarded as being sufficiently organised and possessed of an independent identity that its transfer will be caught by the Directive and regulations. This is a question that will be decided on the facts of individual cases, with the key question being whether what is being transferred constitutes a stable economic entity that retains its identity following the point of transfer.[21] In other words, what must be shown is that what has been transferred is the business itself (or a definable part thereof) rather than simply something that the business possessed – for example its assets.[22] [23–10]

We will return to these issues shortly as we explore the overall concept of a 'transfer of undertakings'. Before we do so, however, it is necessary to consider briefly what is meant by a 'transfer' under the terms of the regulations. [23–11]

1.2. Defining a Transfer

The concept of a 'transfer' is a notoriously uncertain one, which will inevitably be caught up with the question of what is meant by an undertaking.[23] [23–12]

---

20. reg.3(2) European Communities (Protection of Employees on Transfer of Undertakings) Regulations 2003.

21. C-392/92, *Schmidt v Spar und Leihkasse der Fruheren Amter Bordesholm* [1994] ECR I-1311, [1994] EUECJ, [1994] IRLR 302, [1995] 2 CMLR 331, [1995] ICR 237. It has been suggested that in this case (where a bank's cleaning work was transferred to an independent contract cleaning company) 'basic logic suggests that there is a transfer of part of the economic entity in such circumstances': Law Society of Ireland, in Moffatt, ed., *Employment Law* (2nd ed., Oxford University Press, 2006), at para.11.4.2.

22. Thus in C-24/85, *Spijkers v Gebroeders Bendik Abbatoir CV* [1986] ECR 1119 it was held that the simple fact that the assets of a company were being sold would not mean that there was a transfer of undertakings situation unless the economic identity of the undertaking was retained.

23. Generally, see Bracebridge and Sanford, 'TUPE: All Change or No Change?', 79 *Employment Law Journal* (April 2007), 11. On the question of whether and when it is appropriate for a tribunal to pierce the corporate veil in order to establish whether a transfer has, in fact, taken place see *Print Factory v Millam* [2006] UKEAT0253060108.

[23–13] Again the text of the regulations is not particularly helpful as an aid to defining the term 'transfer'. Thus it is simply provided that a 'transfer means the transfer of an economic entity which retains its identity'.²⁴ Significantly in this regard it has been held that the fact that at the date of transfer, the business being transferred has ceased trading or has been substantially downsized does not mean that there cannot be a transfer, provided that the business has the infrastructure and employees to enable it to carry on its operations, and provided that these are being transferred.²⁵ In other words, there can be a transfer of the entity without any concomitant transfer of goodwill if what is transferred retains its identity after the event. Equally, the fact (and the duration) of such cessation and the absence of such goodwill may be factors from which it can be inferred that no such transfer has occurred.

[23–14] The regulations further provide that 'an administrative reorganisation of public administrative authorities, or the transfer of administrative functions between public administrative authorities is not a transfer for the purposes of these regulations'.²⁶ On the other hand, it is clear that where a public body that previously used a particular undertaking to work on a project then transfers the work in question to another undertaking, this may involve a transfer of undertakings situation even though there is no direct relationship between the transferor and transferee.²⁷ This was the situation, for example, in *Redmond Stichting v Bartol*,²⁸ a case in which a Dutch local authority had formerly used one particular group to provide a drug-treatment programme to recovering addicts and had provided it with, for example, funds and facilities, and then transferred responsibility for the drug-treatment programme to a different undertaking and provided them with the relevant funds and facilities and had, perhaps most importantly, transferred the patients (and some of the employees) from one undertaking to the other. In the circumstances, and despite the lack of any nexus between the first and second

24. reg.3(2) European Communities (Protection of Employees on Transfer of Undertakings) Regulations 2003. Kerr (*Irish Employment Legislation* (Round Hall Sweet and Maxwell, 2000), at p.M-118) says that 'The new definition of "transfer" singularly fails to add clarity because it simply consolidates the jurisprudence of the Court of Justice which itself contains a series of confusing and sometimes unclear indications regarding what must be taken into consideration.'
25. C-24/85, *Spijkers v Gebroeders Bendik Abbatoir CV* [1986] ECR 1119.
26. reg.3(4) European Communities (Protection of Employees on Transfer of Undertakings) Regulations 2003. This encapsulates the position of the ECJ as held in C-298/94, *Henke v Gemeinde Schierke and Verwaltungsgemeinschaft Brocken* [1996] EUECJ, a case in which the functions of an administrative body in one municipality were transferred to another body set up for that purpose by various different municipalities.
27. In a similar vein, the transfer of functions from a public body to a private body and vice versa can, depending on the circumstances, constitute a transfer of undertakings for the purposes of the Directive. C-175/99, *Mayeur v Association Promotion de l'Information Messine (APIM)* [2000] EUECJ C-343/98, [2002] ECR I-7755; *Collino and Chiappero* [2000] EUECJ C-343/98.
28. C-29/91, *Redmond Stichting v Bartol* [1992] EUECJ C-29/91, [1992] ECR I-3189.

undertaking, the ECJ concluded that there had been a transfer of undertakings situation, and hence that the Directive applied to it.

This case, it is submitted, presents a number of problematic points as far as the [23–15] development of the law on transfer of undertakings is concerned. As shall be discussed later, after all, it is arguable that on the facts of the case what was transferred was merely an activity in which the first company was involved, but this activity should not have been seen as being synonymous with the business itself. For present purposes, it is worth making the point, however, that the court's conclusion that a transfer of undertakings situation can arise where the alleged transferor has no contractual link with the alleged transferee (and indeed where either party may be entirely opposed to the concept of the transfer that is being foisted on it by a third party) does present difficulties, in that if the regulations and the Directive apply to such a set of circumstances, then the transferee will attract obligations towards former employees of the transferor in circumstances where it may have no knowledge of such employees. The reason why this is problematic is that the interventionist nature of the transfer of undertakings rules may be justified *inter alia* by the argument that whereas a transferee will become responsible for the employees of the transferor following the transfer, this is not particularly harsh on him or her, in that [s]he would have been aware of the existence of such employees in advance of the transfer and could presumably factor the cost of dealing with them into the price that [s]he was prepared to pay for the business[29]. Yet the decision in *Redmond Stichting v Bartol*[30] allows him or her to incur such costs without ever having been aware that they were likely to arise.[31]

In *Dietmar Klarenberg v Ferrotron Technologies GmbH*[32] the ECJ addressed the [23–16] question of whether the requirement that the transferred undertaking retain its identity following the transfer meant that the organisational structure of the economic entity allegedly transferred must also be retained, such that it was necessary that the former structural link between the employees and the other factors of production be the same before and after the alleged transfer. The court, noting that any restrictions or potential restrictions on the impact of the Directive should be strictly construed, rejected this suggestion, holding that the requirement that the independent identity of the transferred entity:

> should be interpreted, not as requiring the retention of the specific organisation imposed by the undertaking on the various elements of production which are

---

29. The entitlement of a transferee to be aware of the obligations which [s]he owes to former employees of the transferor underpins the obligations of the transferor under s.21 of the Employees (Provision of Information and Consultation) Act 2006, considered in Chapter 14.
30. C-29/91, *Redmond Stichting v Bartol* [1992] EUECJ C-29/91, [1992] ECR I-3189.
31. The significance of this argument may be greatly diluted by the terms of the Employees (Provision of Information and Consultation) Act 2006, which imposes obligations on the transferor to inform the transferee of such obligations. This is considered in Chapter 14.
32. C-466/07 [2009] EUECJ, [2009] IRLR 301.

transferred, but as… requiring the retention of a functional link of interdependence, and complementarity, between those elements.[33]

and moreover that:

> The retention of such a functional link between the various elements transferred allows the transferee to use them, even if they are integrated, after the transfer, in a new and different organisational structure, to pursue an identical or analogous economic activity… [and i]t is for the referring court to ascertain, in the light of the foregoing elements, in the context of a global assessment of all the facts characterising the transaction in question in the main proceedings…whether the identity of the economic entity transferred was preserved.[34]

1.2.1. The Concept of a 'Legal Transfer'

[23–17] Whereas the concept of a transfer is an uncertain one, it is clear, however, that there must be a *legal* transfer, and the manner in which this term is used within the Irish regulations and the grounding Directive has come to denote a situation where a stable economic entity[35] (or part thereof) has retained its identity following the alleged transfer, but where there has been a change in the identity of the person responsible for the operation of the undertaking and, most importantly, responsible for the legal obligations owed to employees who are employed by the undertaking.[36] Moreover, the ECJ has concluded that a flexible interpretation should be given to the question of whether a *legal* transfer has occurred: it has not required, for example, that this arise by way of written agreement.[37]

---

33. C-466/07, [2009] EUECJ C-466/07 at para.47.
34. [2009] EUECJ C-466/07 at para.48-49.See also on this point C-171/94 and C-172/94, *Merckx and Neuhuys* [1996] EUECJ C-171/94, [1996] ECR I-1253, *Mayeur*; and C-458/05, *Jouini and Others v Princess Personal Service GmbH (PPS)* [2007] EUECJ C-458/05, [2007] ECR I-7301, [2007] IRLR 1005, [2008] ICR 128. In *Joiuini* the ECJ stressed that where the transferred entity constituted a 'temporary employment business' there was even less need to demonstrate that what was transferred retained an organised structure.
35. Defined as 'an organised grouping of persons and assets enabling an economic activity which pursues a specific objective to be exercised'. See C-127/96, C-229/96 and C-74/97, *Hernández Vidal and Others* [1998] EUECJ C-127/96, [1998] ECR I-817; C-48/94, *Ledernes Hovedorganisation (Rygaard) v Dansk Arbejdsgiverforening (Stro Molle Akustik A/S* [1995] EUECJ; C-13/95,[1995] ECR I-2745; *Süzen v Zehnacker Gebaudereinigung GmbH Krankenhausservice* [1997] EUECJ C-13/95, [1997] ECR I-1259; *Hernandez v Gomez Perez* [1999] IRLR 132; C-137/96 and C-247/96, *Hidalgo v Associacion de Servicios Aser* and *Ziemann v Ziemann Sicherheit GmbH* [1999] IRLR 136.
36. C-48/94, *Ledernes Hovedorganisation (Rygaard) v Dansk Arbejdsgiverforening (Stro Molle Akustik A/S)* [1995] EUECJ C-48/94, [1995] ECR I-2745. In this case it had been suggested (Advocate General Cosmas) that the transfer would need to arise as a result of some contractual relationship between transferor and transferee. Whereas it may be suggested that this is an appropriate conclusion, it is of very doubtful authority given the decision of the ECJ in C-29/91, *Redmond Stichting v Bartol* [1992] EUECJ C-29/91, [1992] ECR I-3189.
37. In C-458/05, *Jouini and Others v Princess Personal Service GmbH (PPS)* [2007] EUECJ

It has been further held that there may be a transfer of an undertaking in circum- [23–18] stances where the legal owner of the relevant undertaking does not change, but where the management changes.[38] The key factor is that there must be a change in the legal identity of the entity that owes obligations as employer towards the relevant employees.[39] This position is now given legislative force in reg. 3(1) of the 2003 regulations, which states that a transfer for the purposes of the regulations involves

> any transfer of an undertaking, business, or part of an undertaking or business from one employer to another employer as a result of a legal transfer (including the assignment or forfeiture of a lease) or merger.

1.3. Defining a Transfer of Undertakings

On the basis of all of the above, therefore, it is necessary to determine what is [23–19] meant in the regulations by a transfer of undertakings. In theory, the term can be defined easily: A transfer of undertakings will occur whenever there is a changed legal identity of the person responsible for the management of the employees of a stable economic entity that retains its identity[40] following such transfer. However, behind this relatively clear definition there are significant uncertainties of inter-pretation and, whereas in many cases it will be beyond dispute or doubt that there has been a transfer of undertakings, in other cases it will be considerably less certain.

The courts dealing with this issue (including the ECJ) are clear that the question of [23–20] whether there is a transfer of undertakings is a factual one that must be answered on a case-by-case basis. The ECJ has said that, in answering this question, tech-nical rules of interpretation should be avoided, and instead what is needed is an assessment of whether 'the transferee has obtained a business or an undertaking

---

C-458/05, [2007] ECR I-7301, [2007] IRLR 1005, [2008] ICR 128, the ECJ concluded, 'The concept of legal transfer is thus capable of covering, as the case may be, a written or oral agreement between the transferor and the transferee relating to a change in the person responsible for the operation of the economic entity concerned and a tacit agree-ment between them resulting from aspects of practical co-operation which imply a common intention to make such a change.'

38. C-324/84, *Foreningen af Arbejdsledere I Danmark v Daddy's Dance Hall A/S* [1988] EUECJ R-324/86, [1988] ECR 739. See also C-287/86, *Landsorganisationen I Danmark v Ny Molle Kro* [1987] EUECJ R-287/86, [1987] ECR 5465; C-144 and C-145/87, *Berg and Busschers v Besselsen* [1988] ECR 2559, *Guidon v Hugh Farrington and Ushers Island Petrol Station* [1993] ELR 98.

39. See C-171 and C-172/94, *Merckx and Neuhuys v Ford Motors Belgium SA* [1996] EUECJ C-171/94, [1996] ECR-I 1253. But see *Sheehy v Ryan* [2008] IESC 14, [2008] 4 IR 258, [2005] IEHC 419, for the view that no transfer of undertakings had taken place in circumstances where a diocesan secretary had been employed by successive bishops. In other words, the mere fact that the claimant's direct employer (the bishop) had changed did not mean that there had been a transfer of undertakings.

40. C-29/91, *Redmond Stichting v Bartol* [1992] EUECJ C-29/91, [1992] ECR I-3189.

or a part thereof, which he can continue to operate'[41] and whether that business retains its identity following the alleged transfer.[42] In this regard, various factors have consistently been identified and relied upon by the courts as being relevant (though not determinative) in answering this question, including[43]:

- the type of business or undertaking concerned;
- the extent to which the undertaking/part of the undertaking has sufficient structural organisation to enable it properly to be termed an economic entity;
- whether tangible and/or intangible assets are being transferred,[44] and the value of any such intangible assets at the time of transfer[45];
- whether machinery that was formerly used is still being used;
- whether goodwill has been transferred;
- the degree of similarity of activities between the original and allegedly transferred undertaking and the duration of any interruption in the activities; and
- whether or not customers and/or employees are transferred.[46]

[23–21] It may be suggested that these factors are largely 'common-sense' in nature. Thus, where the owners of a business have sold an aspect thereof to a competitor, providing it with all their client bases, machinery, and other assets, the intuitive response would almost certainly be to see this as a case where part of the business has been transferred. Importantly, however, these factors are merely evidence from which the broader question of whether there has been a transfer of the relevant entity may be answered, and they will not necessarily have any application in

---

41. See, for example, C-24/85, *Spijkers v Gebroeders Bendik Abbatoir CV* [1986] ECR 1119. Naturally this necessitates an evaluation whether there was a stable economic entity both before *and* after the alleged transfer. See Curran, 'Transfer of Undertakings and Changing Sub-contractors – Does the Directive Apply?', 4(1) *IELJ* (2007), 15.

42. For the view that there should be a flexible interpretation of whether the identity of the allegedly transferred undertaking has been retained, see C-458/05, *Jouini and Others v Princess Personal Service GmbH (PPS)* [2007] EUECJ C-458/05, [2007] ECR I-7301, [2007] IRLR 1005, [2008] ICR 128.

43. C-24/85, *Spijkers v Gebroeders Bendik Abbatoir CV* [1986] ECR 1119; C-29/91, *Redmond Stichting v Bartol* [1992] EUECJ C-29/91, [1992] ECR I-3189. Generally, see Law Society of Ireland, in Moffatt, ed., *Employment Law* (2nd ed., Oxford University Press, 2006), at 11.8.6.2; Curran, 'Transfer of Undertakings and Changing Sub-contractors – Does the Directive Apply?', 4(1) *IELJ* (2007), 15.

44. This is a particularly relevant factor as far as the ECJ is concerned. Equally it is clear that there does not necessarily have to be asset transfer in order for the Directive to apply. See C-392/92, *Schmidt v Spar und Leihkasse der Fruheren Amter Bordesholm* [1994] ECR I-1311, [1994] EUECJ, [1994] IRLR 302, [1995] 2 CMLR 331, [1995] ICR 237; C-171 and C-172/94, *Merckx and Neuhuys v Ford Motors Belgium SA* [1996] EUECJ C-171/94, [1996] ECR-I 1253.

45. *Betts v Brintel Helicopters* [1997] EWCA Civ 1340, [1997] IRLR 361.

46. C-13/95, *Süzen v Zehnacker Gebaudereinigung GmbH Krankenhausservice* [1997] EUECJ C-13/95, [1997] ECR I-1259.

a given case.[47] Furthermore, whereas all of these factors are relevant, it may be suggested that some are particularly important – notably the questions of whether there has been a transfer of assets and whether a significant proportion of the workforce of the alleged transferor has moved to the transferee. Thus the case law of the ECJ is not always consistent on the point, but it would appear that what the Court is primarily trying to assess in such cases is whether or not 'the wherewithal to carry on the business such as plant, building and employees are available and are transferred'.[48]

1.4. Transfer of Activities as a Transfer of Undertakings

As we have seen, it is clear from reg. 3(1) of the 2003 regulations that the transfer [23–22] of undertakings rules can apply where what is transferred is not the whole of the undertaking but merely a part thereof.[49] As we have also seen, in many cases it will not be difficult to determine that a sufficiently identifiable part of the business has been transferred and therefore that the process is caught by the terms of

---

47. Thus it has been said that 'The *Spijkers* tests for identifying the existence of a transfer have survived the passage of time and are still relevant. It must be kept in mind, however, that each of the tests is in itself merely guidance and when each test has been answered the totality has to be assessed to see whether or not it adds up to there being a transfer.' See Byrne, 'Transfer of Undertakings', in Regan, ed., *Employment Law* (Tottel Publishing, 2009), at para.119, and by the same author in Law Society of Ireland, in Moffatt, ed., *Employment Law* (2nd ed., Oxford University Press, 2006), at 11.5.1.1.

48. C-24/85, *Spijkers v Gebroeders Bendik Abbatoir CV* [1986] ECR 1119. Kerr, *Irish Employment Legislation* (Round Hall Sweet and Maxwell, 2000), at p.M-118 notes that whereas the ECJ jurisprudence in this area highlights, in particular, the significance of the fact that assets or a section of the workforce has been transferred as evidence that there has been a transfer of undertakings, the English Court of Appeal has found a prima facie transfer of the legal ownership of an entity where there has been no such transfer of assets, but where there has been a deliberate decision by the transferor *not* to transfer any employees or assets in order to negate the suggestion that there has been a transfer of undertakings. See *ECM (Vehicle Delivery Service) Ltd. v Cox* [1999] 4 All ER 669, [1999] IRLR 559; *ADI (UK) Ltd. v Firm Security Group Ltd.* [2001] EWCA Civ 971, [2001] IRLR 542; *RCO Support Services v UNISON* [2002] IRLR 401.

49. It is also clear that where this happens, it is only employees assigned to the part of the undertaking that is transferred that obtain entitlements under the terms of the Directive and for whom the transferee becomes responsible. C-392/92, *Schmidt v Spar und Leihkasse der Fruheren Amter Bordesholm* [1994] ECR I-1311, [1994] EUECJ, [1994] IRLR 302, [1995] 2 CMLR 331, [1995] ICR 237. In *Sunley Turriff Holdings Ltd. v Thompson* [1995] IRLR 184 it was held that this principle applied even where the employee in question worked within the part of the business that had been transferred actually continued *de facto* to work for the transferor company. In R-186/83, *Botzen v Rotterdamsche Droogdok Maatschappij* [1985] EUECJ R-1861/83, [1986] ECR 519, Advocate General Slynn suggested that it would be necessary (in order for the transferee to acquire obligations towards him or her) that the employee be wholly engaged in the part of the business that was transferred subject only to an exception where his or her work for a part of the business that was *not* transferred was at a *de minimis* level.

the Directive and regulations. If assets are sold, or if the employees or clientele of the transferor are transferred to the transferee, then in most cases this will indicate that there has been a transfer of part of the undertaking or of the business. Much more controversial, however, is the situation where there is no tangible transfer of (for example) assets, but rather where a company simply transfers one of its activities to another entity – for example, where a car manufacturing company that had previously also sold cars directly to the public transfers its retail activity to a designated car dealership or dealerships. In such a situation can there be said to have been a transfer of part of the undertaking?

[23–23] On one level, after all, this may simply be regarded as a situation where the company is reducing the number of its activities, yet where the undertaking itself remains intact. There are quite clearly instances where this will be the case – for example where there has been no transfer of assets, infrastructure or employees but where the business has (for example) discontinued an activity[50] and sold its client base in respect of that activity to another company. In such a situation, it can be persuasively argued that there is not a genuine transfer of undertakings situation.[51] On another level, however (and given that very many businesses may, on one view, be seen to be composed of or even synonymous with their activities), there will also be cases of undertakings where if one or more such activity is transferred to another entity this does represent a transfer of part of the undertaking.[52]

[23–24] The key question in assessing whether what has happened is a transfer of undertakings situation as distinct from the mere transfer of an activity is the same as applies generally in determining whether any activity of an undertaking constitutes a transfer of undertakings – namely whether what was transferred is capable of being regarded in itself as a stable economic activity,[53] and whether it retained its distinct identity following the alleged transfer. This is, of course, a question of fact and the relevant matters discussed earlier (and which derive from the logic of the ECJ in cases such as *Spijkers v Gebroeders Bendik Abbatoir CV*[54] and *Redmond*

---

50. Thus in C-13/95, *Süzen v Zehnacker Gebaudereinigung GmbH Krankenhausservice* [1997] EUECJ C-13/95, [1997] ECR I-1259, the ECJ had stressed that a company or undertaking could not be reduced to its activities. A range of other factors would also be relevant in assessing the make-up of an entity, including its workforce, assets, organisational structure and management.
51. From the earlier analysis it is submitted that this was the case in C-29/91, *Redmond Stichting v Bartol* [1992] EUECJ C-29/91, [1992] ECR I-3189 in that the transfer of activity was generated by no desire or intentional action on the part of the company that originally was responsible for the activity.
52. See, for example, *Michael Peters Ltd. v Farnfield & Michael Peters Group* [1995] IRLR 190; *Sunley Turriff Holdings Ltd. v Thompson* [1995] IRLR 184; *Botzen v Rotterdamsche Droogdok Maatschappij* [1985] EUECJ R-186/83, [1986] ECR 519.
53. C-48, *Ledernes Hovedorganisation (Rygaard) v Dansk Arbejdsgiverforening (Stro Molle Akustik A/S)* [1995] EUECJ C-48, [1995] ECR I-2745; *Wynnwith Engineering Co Ltd. v Bennett* [2002] IRLR 170; *Temco Service Industries SA v Imzilyen* [2002] IRLR 214.
54. C-24/85, *Spijkers v Gebroeders Bendik Abbatoir CV* [1986] ECR 1119.

Stichting v Bartol[55]) will have application in this regard. So, for example, the courts will *inter alia* look closely at the question of whether or not the purported transfer of an *activity* involves the transfer of assets or of a significant proportion of the workplace to the new undertaking responsible for the activity.

It has already been respectfully submitted that the decision in *Redmond Stichting v Bartol*[56] is perhaps open to criticism for endorsing the notion that a transfer of undertakings can be found even where there is no contractual link between transferor and transferee. The decision may, however, be further criticised for its factual conclusion that there had genuinely been a transfer of undertakings in the case. What happened here, after all, was that a local authority removed a tender from one undertaking and gave it to another undertaking. In other words, a significant aspect of the activity of the first undertaking was taken from it, but this was something over which it had no control, and indeed which occurred against its will.[57] More to the point, whereas it lost its client base and some of its employees in connection with the tender it had formerly enjoyed, equally, on the facts it is still arguable that the undertaking was potentially significantly more than the tender, and hence that the identity of the undertaking (or even a part thereof) was not the same as the activity in which it had formerly been engaged.[58] Rather, the activity might at best be regarded as an asset which the undertaking formerly possessed, but which, as a result of the decision of the local authority, it had lost. Yet it is clear from decisions of the ECJ in this area that transfer of assets is not the same as a transfer of undertakings.[59]

[23–25]

---

55. C-29/91, *Redmond Stichting v Bartol* [1992] EUECJ 29/91, [1992] ECR I-3189.
56. *ibid.*
57. It is true that, in C-171 and C-172/94, *Merckx and Neuhuys v Ford Motors Belgium SA* [1996] EUECJ C-171/94, [1996] ECR I-1253, the ECJ, noting that a transfer of undertakings could occur in circumstances where there was no contractual nexus between the transferor and the transferee, held that it was possible that a transfer of undertakings could be found in circumstances where a franchise had been removed from one undertaking and given to another. Equally this was a very specific situation in which there had been considerable transfer of employees from the first to the second firm, where the first firm had recommended the second to its former clients and, most importantly, where the entity that granted the franchise was the main shareholder in the first firm and had undertaken to bear the costs of any responsibilities the second firm might owe to employees or former employees of the first firm. It is, however, notable that in *Zhao v Valken Ltd.*, UD 356/2006, the Irish EAT determined that the transfer of undertakings regulations would apply where a franchise had been transferred.
58. The point made by Advocate General van Gerven in this case was that the activity for which the employees had originally been employed was continuing (albeit with some minor differences) and hence that this constituted a transfer of undertakings.
59. Thus, in C-24/85, *Spijkers v Gebroeders Bendik Abbatoir CV* [1986] ECR 1119, it was held that the simple fact that the assets of a company were being sold would not mean that there was a transfer of undertakings situation unless the economic identity of the undertaking was retained.

[23–26] On the other hand, it is clear as a matter of legal principle that as far as the various courts dealing with this question (including the ECJ) are concerned, it is certainly possible that the transfer of an activity from one undertaking to another *can* (provided that the normal criteria for a transfer of undertakings are fulfilled) represent a transfer of undertakings and irrespective of whether the activity that is being transferred represents either an integral or even an ancillary[60] part of the relevant business.[61] Thus in *Schmidt v Spar und Leihkasse der Fruheren Amter Bordesholm*[62] the ECJ famously found that a transfer of undertakings situation existed in circumstances where cleaning operations in a bank (which had previously been carried out by staff of the bank) were to be contracted out to an external service provider.[63] The court held that what was relevant was that there had been a transfer of a distinct economic entity within the bank, whereby the entity had retained its identity after the transfer,[64] and whereby the transferee assumed the responsibility of employer towards persons who had responsibility in respect of such activities.[65]

1.5. Outsourcing and Transfer of Undertakings

[23–27] This leads to a further issue of controversy, namely if a business contracts out or outsources certain of its functions, whether and when this may represent a transfer

---

60. *Rask and Christensen v ISS Kantineservice A/S* [1993] IRLR 133.
61. C-392/92, *Schmidt v Spar und Leihkasse der Fruheren Amter Bordesholm* [1994] ECR I-1311, [1994] EUECJ, [1994] IRLR 302, [1995] 2 CMLR 331, [1995] ICR 237; *Rask and Christensen v ISS Kantineservice A/S* [1993] IRLR 133.
62. C-392/92 [1994] ECR I-1311, [1994] EUECJ C-392/92, [1994] IRLR 302, [1995] 2 CMLR 331, [1995] ICR 237.
63. It has been suggested that 'Most of the confusion in the minds of commentators on *Schmidt* and the difficulties caused by the subsequent application of the *Schmidt* criteria have been caused by the failure to accept or understand that the cleaning work carried out in *Schmidt* was in itself an economic entity which became the subject of a transfer' (See Law Society of Ireland, in Moffatt, ed., *Employment Law* (2nd ed., Oxford University Press, 2006), at para.11.8.1.2) It is respectfully submitted that in fact, and whereas the reasoning of both Advocate General van Gerven and of the ECJ in this case on the question of what constitutes an economic entity is sound, the decision is confusing precisely because of the result reached. In other words, the reasoning in the case as to what constitutes an economic entity (and indeed the more general approach in C-24/85, *Spijkers v Gebroeders Bendik Abbatoir CV* [1986] ECR 1119; and C-29/91, *Redmond Stichting v Bartol* [1992] EUECJ C-29/91, [1992] ECR I-3189 as to what constitutes a transfer of undertakings) should, it is submitted, have led to the conclusion that what had occurred here was *not* the transfer of a stable economic entity.
64. As indicated by the fact that the activity in question was identical after and before the transfer. For the significance of this fact see C-24/85, *Spijkers v Gebroeders Bendik Abbatoir CV* [1986] ECR 1119; and C-29/91, *Redmond Stichting v Bartol* [1992] EUECJ C-29/91, [1992] ECR I-3189.
65. Generally, see *Berg and Busschers v Besselsen* [1989] IRLR 447; *Botzen v Rotterdamsche Droogdok Maatschappij* [1985] EUECJ R-186/83, [1986] ECR 519.

of undertakings.[66] Cases like *Schmidt v Spar und Leihkasse der Fruheren Amter Bordesholm*[67] and *Rask and Christensen v ISS Kantineservice A/S*[68] indicate clearly that this is theoretically possible. Nonetheless, not least because of some arguably conflicting case law from the ECJ, it is difficult to pinpoint exactly when this is likely to happen.

There are three types of situation in which such outsourcing can occur and which [23–28] may possibly be caught by the Directive and regulations. These are:

- cases where services that were previously performed on an 'in house' basis have been contracted out to external service providers – the type of situation that existed in *Schmidt v Spar und Leihkasse der Fruheren Amter Bordesholm*[69] (a first-generation transfer);
- cases where services previously performed by external contractors are now to be performed on an in-house basis (a third-generation transfer); and
- cases where services previously performed by one particular external contractor have been transferred to another (a second-generation transfer).[70]

The case law, especially of the ECJ, indicates, moreover, that it is in the first (and [23–29] possibly second) of these types of situation (first- and third-generation transfers) that a transfer of undertakings will be more likely to be found, and that it is only where there has been a transfer of assets or of a considerable proportion of the workforce that the third of these scenarios (a second-generation transfer) will be likely to be caught by the Directive.

The reason why the ECJ has been reluctant to deem second generation transfers to [23–30] constitute genuine transfers of undertakings is arguably because decisions such as *Schmidt v Spar und Leihkasse der Fruheren Amter Bordesholm*[71] (which, it has been suggested above, may be wrongly decided on its facts) naturally caused controversy and also concern for employers and business owners because of the remarkably expansive nature of their conclusion. After all, what was at issue on the facts of *Schmidt* was undeniably an ancillary activity of the business which had nothing

---

66. Generally, see Curran, 'Transfer of Undertakings and Changing Sub-contractors – Does the Directive Apply?', 4(1) *IELJ* (2007), 15.
67. C-392/92 [1994] ECR I-1311, [1994] EUECJ, [1994] IRLR 302, [1995] 2 CMLR 331, [1995] ICR 237.
68. [1993] IRLR 133.
69. C-392/92 [1994] ECR I-1311, [1994] EUECJ, [1994] IRLR 302, [1995] 2 CMLR 331, [1995] ICR 237.
70. See Kerr, *Irish Employment Legislation* (Round Hall Sweet and Maxwell, 2000), at p.M-117. See also Law Society of Ireland, in Moffatt, ed., *Employment Law* (2nd ed., Oxford University Press, 2006), at 11.8.1.
71. C-392/92 [1994] ECR I-1311, [1994] EUECJ, [1994] IRLR 302, [1995] 2 CMLR 331, [1995] ICR 237.

to do with its overall commercial objectives, and was, indeed, an activity in which only one employee was employed and which involved no assets to speak of. Yet when this activity was outsourced, the ECJ still concluded that what had occurred was a transfer of undertakings. Put another way, this conclusion is remarkable because virtually none of the factual criteria (considered above) that might indicate that there had been a transfer of undertakings were present on the facts.[72]

[23–31]   In this respect, the more recent decisions of the ECJ in both *Ledernes Hovedorganisation (Rygaard) v Dansk Arbejdsgiverforening (Stro Molle Akustik A/S*[73] (in which it was stressed that what must be transferred was a stable economic entity whose work was not limited to performing one specific works contract[74]) and in *Süzen v Zehnacker Gebaudereinigung GmbH Krankenhausservice*[75] provide more comfort to businesses that are changing the identity of sub-contractors performing services for them.[76] In *Süzen* the ECJ refused to find a transfer of undertakings situation on the facts where an undertaking (a school), having previously employed one firm of contractors for cleaning purposes, at the end of its contract entered into a contract with a different cleaning firm. The ECJ concluded that the first firm's contract with the school should properly be regarded not as part of the undertaking that was the firm but as one of its assets, and hence when the cleaning contract for the school was given to a different firm, this represented at best the transfer of one of its assets and not a transfer of undertakings.[77] Pivotally, what

---

72. In *Power v St Paul's Nursing Home and T&M Cleaning Ltd.* [1998] ELR 212, the EAT appeared to apply the logic in *Schmidt v Spar und Leihkasse der Fruheren Amter Bordesholm* [1994] EUECJ C-392/92, [1994] ECR I-1311, finding that there was a transfer of undertakings situation where an undertaking that had previously directly employed cleaners decided to outsource such work and had provided certain equipment (which they had formerly used in the internally run cleaning operation) to the firm to whom they had outsourced this work. The EAT found that there had been an organised group of workers and tangible assets as far as the former cleaning process was concerned, that this had been transferred to the new cleaning firm and hence that there had been a transfer of undertakings.

73. C-48/94, *Ledernes Hovedorganisation (Rygaard) v Dansk Arbejdsgiverforening (Stro Molle Akustik A/S)* [1995] EUECJ C-48/94, [1995] ECR I-2745.

74. See also C-458/05, *Jouini and Others v Princess Personal Service GmbH (PPS)* [2007] ECR I-7301, [2007] EUECJ, [2007] EUECJ, [2007] IRLR 1005, [2008] ICR 128.

75. C-13/95, *Süzen v Zehnacker Gebaudereinigung GmbH Krankenhausservice* [1997] EUECJ C-13/95, [1997] ECR I-1259.

76. In light of the decision in *Süzen v Zehnacker Gebaudereinigung GmbH Krankenhausservice* it is submitted that the decision of the UK EAT in *ECM (Vehicle Delivery Service) Ltd. v Cox* [1999] 4 All ER 669, [1999] IRLR 559 (a decision in which the Directive was deemed to apply to a situation where a business had changed the external sub-contractors that did certain work for it) is somewhat difficult to understand. Equally it is arguable that the principle rationale for this decision was the conclusion of the EAT that there had been a deliberate decision *not* to transfer any of the workforce who had provided the service for the first contractor in a bid to avoid application of the Directive.

77. In fact, inasmuch as the contract of the first firm had been terminated, it is difficult to see how this could even be seen as a transfer of a company's assets, in that there was nothing the company had that could be transferred.

had happened here was not the transfer of a stable economic entity nor could such a transfer necessarily be inferred from the fact that the activity conducted by the second firm was similar to that conducted formerly by the first firm.[78] The ECJ highlighted the fact that there had been no transfer of assets as between the transferor and transferee (other than the contract itself), and appeared to afford the question of whether such transfer of assets had taken place a particular importance in the list of factors that would be relevant in assessing whether or not there was a transfer of undertakings.

It may be suggested that, whereas the conclusion of the ECJ in this case was a correct one (and fits neatly with the general approach of the Court to the question of whether and when a transfer situation has occurred), equally it becomes difficult to reconcile this decision (as the Court attempted to do) with the decision in *Schmidt v Spar und Leihkasse der Fruheren Amter Bordesholm.*[79] The logical effect of the combination of the two decisions in *Schmidt v Spar und Leihkasse der Fruheren Amter Bordesholm*[80] and *Süzen v Zehnacker Gebaudereinigung GmbH Krankenhausservice*[81] in the context of the outsourcing of an operation may be that where a firm that has previously done something 'in house' outsources such operations or, presumably, vice versa[82] (that is, first and third generation transfers) then this is more likely to amount to a transfer of undertakings situation than where a firm that has always employed a group of external contractors switches contractors (a second generation transfer).[83] As has been mentioned earlier, in this latter type

[23–32]

---

78. The ECJ did accept that in certain labour-intensive industries (where workers were the main factor of production and where there were likely to be limited tangible or intangible assets) it was conceivable that the simple fact that there was a group of workers engaged permanently in a joint of activity within an undertaking could mean that where that activity was transferred this would constitute a transfer of undertakings situation, provided that the new employer takes over a significant number of the former workforce after such transfer. The ECJ has, in particular, applied this logic to the cleaning industry. See *Süzen v Zehnacker Gebaudereinigung GmbH Krankenhausservice* [1997] EUECJ C-13/95, [1997] ECR I-1259. See also *Hernandez v Gomez Perez* [1999] IRLR 132; *Hidalgo v Associacion de Servicios Aser,* and *Ziemann v Ziemann Sicherheit GmbH* [1999] IRLR 136. Generally, see C-458/05, *Jouini and Others v Princess Personal Service GmbH (PPS)* [2007] ECR I-7301, [2007] EUECJ, [2007] EUECJ, [2007] IRLR 1005, [2008] ICR 128 for the view that 'Indeed, in certain economic sectors, those assets are often reduced to their most basic and the activity is essentially based on the labour force. Thus, an organised grouping of wage earners who are specifically and permanently assigned to a common task may, in the absence of other factors of production, amount to an economic entity' (at para.32).
79. C-392/92 [1994] EUECJ, [1994] ECR I-1311.
80. *ibid.*
81. C-13/95, *Süzen v Zehnacker Gebaudereinigung GmbH Krankenhausservice* [1997] EUECJ C-13/95, [1997] ECR I-1259.
82. See *Hernandez v Gomez Perez* [1999] IRLR 132.
83. See *Gray v ISPCA* [1994] ELR 225; *Cannon v Noonan Cleaning* [1998] ELR 153; *Power v St Paul's Nursing Home* [1998] ELR 212; *Shiels v Noonan Cleaning Ltd.,* UD 461/1997; *Ryan v O'Flaherty* [2004] ELR 180; *Bruton v Knights Cleaning Services Ltd.,* UD 803/97; *Digan v*

of case, it would seem (from *Süzen v Zehnacker Gebaudereinigung GmbH Krank-enhausservice*[84]) that unless there is a significant transfer of tangible and intangible assets (where this is the essence of the transfer) and of workers (where the economic entity is an essentially labour-intensive one), either as between the two contracting firms or from the organisation itself of assets formerly used by the first sub-contractor to the second sub-contractor,[85] it will be unlikely that a transfer of undertakings situation will be found to have occurred.[86]

[23-33]   In this regard it may further be suggested that the principal intuitive difference of substance between cases where the undertaking outsources activities formerly conducted 'in house' and cases where the undertaking simply switches sub-contractors is that in the former there is a contractual link between the transferor and the transferee that justifies the finding that the transferee incurs obligations towards the employees of the transferor. Again it is arguable that it is the decisions of the ECJ in cases such as *Redmond Stichting v Bartol*[87] to the effect that no such contractual nexus was necessary in order for a transfer of undertakings situation to apply that are the source of confusion. Put another way, whereas it is, presumably, possible on the facts that a transfer of undertakings situation could validly be found to exist in the absence of such a contractual nexus, it may be suggested that the absence in question must surely be a very significant factor militating against such a finding.

1.6. Conclusion on the Concept of Transfer of Undertakings
[23-34]   The above analysis is complicated – not least because of the various (often arguably conflicting) judgments of the ECJ in this area. As such, it may be helpful to summarise such analysis in a brief statement of what is arguably the current legal view as to the meaning of a 'transfer of undertakings', having regard both to the terms of the Directive and regulations and also of the major conclusions of principle reached by the ECJ and other courts and tribunals.

Sheehan Security Corporation Ltd. [2005] ELR 222; *Bannon v Employment Appeals Tribunal* [1993] 1 IR 500. For a succinct analysis of the issues and a critique of the circular reasoning in *Süzen v Zehnacker Gebaudereinigung GmbH Krankenhausservice* [1997] EUECJ C-13/95, [1997] ECR I-1259 see McMullen, 'TUPE: Transfers Continue to Confuse', 47 *Employment Law Journal* (February 2004), 22. See also Wynn Evans, 'The Ghost of TUPE Past', 72 *Employment Law Journal* (July/August 2006), 5.

84. C-13/95, *Süzen v Zehnacker Gebaudereinigung GmbH Krankenhausservice* [1997] EUECJ C-13/95, [1997] ECR I-1259.

85. This was the case in C-340/01, *Abler v Sodexho & CO* [2004] IRLR 168. See also *Oy Liikenne Ab v Pekka Liskojarvi and Pentti Juntunen* [2001] IRLR 171.

86. In *Keenan v Professional Contract Services Ltd.*, UD 454-456/98 a transfer *was* found to have occurred where an undertaking switched sub-contractors, but in circumstances where the transferee appeared to have accepted at the time that this was a transfer of undertakings situation and that it had responsibility for the employees of the transferor.

87. C-29/91 [1992] EUECJ, [1992] ECR I-3189.

- The question of whether there has been a transfer of undertakings is an entirely factual one to be determined on a case-by-case basis.
- In order for there to have been a transfer of undertakings there must have been a transfer of a stable economic unit or entity (which retains its own identity following the alleged transfer), such that the legal identity of the body with responsibility for employees (although not necessarily the legal owner of the undertaking) changes as a result of the alleged transfers.
- The various factors identified by the court in *Spijkers v Gebroeders Bendik Abbatoir CV*[88] and *Redmond Stichting v Bartol*,[89] considered above, will be useful in answering this question but will not, *per se*, be determinative thereof.
- Whereas the Directive will come into operation when there is even a transfer of *part of* an undertaking, nonetheless, there is, in general, a difference between a transfer of undertakings and a transfer of the activities of the undertaking, in that an undertaking is usually more than its activities.
- On the other hand, it may be that a particular activity of an undertaking represents in itself a stable economic entity and where this happens (and this must also be determined on the facts) the Directive and regulations will apply.
- This logic has application in situations where what has happened is an outsourcing of services formerly performed on an 'in-house' basis to an external contractor, and arguably in a situation where formerly outsourced services are henceforth to be carried out in house. It may also have application (albeit less usually) in a situation where an undertaking replaces one external contractor with another, although in order for a transfer of undertakings situation to be deemed to arise in such circumstances, it will probably be necessary for there to have been a transfer of assets or of a significant proportion of the workforce of the transferor to the transferee.

1.7. Time and Date of Transfer

As we shall shortly see, the major substantive rules within the regulations apply from the date of transfer – that is to say, the entitlements and obligations of the transferor *on the date of transfer* are what transfer to the transferee. Accordingly, it is important to be aware of what is meant by *the date of transfer*.[90] Indeed, this can be very controversial because the phrase 'date of transfer' may, on a literal analysis, suggest a single point in time, whereas in actuality the transfer may be a process that has extended

[23–35]

---

88. C-24/85, *Spijkers v Gebroeders Bendik Abbatoir CV* [1986] ECR 1119.
89. C-29/91 [1992] EUECJ, [1992] ECR I-3189.
90. It would appear that, provided there has been a transfer of undertakings on a particular date (and if an employee was dismissed at this point), the Directive will apply even if the transfer later falls through. *Dabell v Vale Industrial Services (Nottingham) Ltd.* [1988] IRLR 439.

over a period of time.⁹¹ In any event, what is pivotal is that if no employment relationship subsists between the transferor and an employee *at the date of transfer* then nothing in this respect is passed to the transferee, and [s]he consequently incurs no obligations under the regulations in respect of that employee.⁹²

[23–36] The ECJ has held that the date of transfer is the date on which the obligations and responsibilities of the relevant employer move from the transferor to the transferee – a date that could not be postponed or altered at the behest of either party.⁹³ Equally, and in order to avoid the possibility that a transferor/transferee could evade the legislation by the simple expedient of dismissing employees in advance of the transfer, it has also been suggested that the Directive protects not merely employees who were employed in the undertaking at the date of transfer, but also employees who *should* have been so employed but who were, instead, unfairly dismissed.⁹⁴ Furthermore, it has been suggested that where the transfer takes place over a period of time, the Directive and regulations can apply to employees who were employed in the undertaking at any period during that time,⁹⁵ although the question of whether or not there has been a 'date of transfer' during this period is one of fact, and the fact that parties are in negotiations aimed at such a transfer will not constitute a transfer in itself.⁹⁶

1.8. Jurisdictional Issues

[23–37] The final issue of significance in assessing the scope of the Directive (more so than the regulations) is a jurisdictional one. Quite clearly the regulations apply within Ireland and the Directive applies throughout the territory of the EEA. But what of a situation where an undertaking *within* the territory of the EEA transfers an economic entity to an undertaking *outside* of the EEA? Does the Directive have any applica-

---

91. It is notable that in reg.4(4) European Communities (Protection of Employees on Transfer of Undertakings) Regulations 2003 (dealing with non-transfer of certain pension rights), the regulations (following the Directive) speak in terms of the *time of transfer* and it may be that the two terms are intended to be interchangeable.

92. *Wendleboe v LJ Music ApS (in liquidation)* [1985] ECR 457; *Secretary of State for Employment v Spence* [1986] 3 WLR 380, [1986] 3 All ER 616, [1986] ICR 651, [1986] IRLR 248.

93. C-478/03, *Celtec Limited v Astley* [2005] IRLR 647. See also Bracebridge and Sanford, 'TUPE: All Change or No Change?', 79 *Employment Law Journal* (April 2007), 11.

94. *Lister v Forth Dry Dock and Engineering Co Ltd.* [1989] IRLR 161, *Macer v Abafast Ltd.* [1990] ICR 234, [1990] IRLR 137. For consideration, see *Dynamex Friction and others v Amicus and others* [2008] EWCA Civ 381, [2008] IRLR 515. Generally, see Law Society of Ireland, in Moffatt, Ed., *Employment Law* (2nd ed., Oxford University Press, 2006), at 11.8.8.1. Equally, in such a situation where the employees have been dismissed in order to make the transfer more attractive for the potential transferees, it could easily be argued that the dismissal was as a result of the transfer, and hence was invalid under the regulations in any event.

95. See Law Society of Ireland, in Moffatt, ed., *Employment Law* (2nd ed., Oxford University Press, 2006), at 11.8.8.2.

96. *Longden and Paisley v Ferrari Ltd.* [1994] IRLR 157.

tion in this context?[97] In *Holis Metal Industries Ltd. v GMB*[98] the EAT for England and Wales suggested that this was a possibility.[99] It would seem more appropriate, however, to conclude that in such a situation the transferor (being based in the territory of the EEA) is bound by the terms of the Directive, but there is no basis in law for finding that the transferee (being based outside the EEA) could be subject to the jurisdiction of EC law and hence, following the transfer, the employees in question have no rights as against either the transferor or the transferee.[100]

2. Rights and Obligations in the Event of a Transfer

The basic impact of the Directive (in circumstances where a transfer of an economic entity has been found to have taken place[101]) is to ensure that the full extent of the rights[102] and obligations[103] of the transferor arising from a contract of

[23–38]

---

97. The European Commission has noted that this is a matter of uncertainty in its 2007 report on the Acquired Rights Directive: COM 2007 334, 4 July 2007.

98. [2008] ICR 464, [2008] IRLR 187.

99. See Byrne, 'Transfer of Undertakings', in Regan, ed., *Employment Law* (Tottel Publishing, 2009), at para.19.40 for the suggestion that this decision 'is logical and it would seem, though it is not beyond question, that the [Irish] regulations would apply to such a transfer'.

100. See Law Society of Ireland, in Moffatt, ed., *Employment Law* (2nd ed., Oxford University Press, 2006), at 11.2.2.1. Generally, see Jeffreys, 'The Acquired Rights Directive – Ripe for Reform', 82 *Employment Law Journal* (July/August 2007), 15.

101. An exception to this general rule exists (from reg.6(1) European Communities (Protection of Employees on Transfer of Undertakings) Regulations 2003) in circumstances where there is a transfer of an undertaking or business (or part of an undertaking of a business) but where the transferor is the subject of bankruptcy or insolvency proceedings (as defined in reg.6(2)). See Codd, 'The Transfer of Undertakings and Commercial Agreements: Advising Clients and some Practical Pitfalls', 5 *Employment Law Review* (2007), 7. Equally this exception will not apply where the sole or main reason for the institution of such bankruptcy or insolvency proceedings is to evade legal obligations under these regulations (reg.6(3)). Generally, see *Mythen v Employment Appeals Tribunal* [1990] 1 IR 98, [1989] ILRM 844; *Abels v Administrative Board of the Bedrijfsvereniging voor de Metaalindustrie* [1985] ECR 470; C-319-94, *Jules Dethier Equipment v Dassy* [1998] EUECJ C-319/94, [1998] ECR I-1061; C-399/96 *Europieces SA v Sanders* [1998] EUECJ C-399/96, [1998] ECR I-6965; *Blaney v Vanguard Plastics Ireland Ltd.*, UD 271/2000. See also *Kelly v Cavanagh Hiester Ltd. (in liquidation) and Dubshad Ltd.*, UD 222-224/96 for the view that the exception to the regulations will not apply where there is a *voluntary* liquidation. See C-561/07, *Commission v Italy* [2009] EUECJ for the view that it is not possible for a Member State to permit an undertaking to avail of the insolvency exception on the basis that that undertaking is undergoing 'critical difficulties'.

102. The point is made (Byrne, 'Transfer of Undertakings', in Regan, ed., *Employment Law* (Tottel Publishing, 2009), at para.19.28) that whereas the principle focus of the regulations relates to the transfer of the employer's obligations, equally his or her *rights* will also transfer. Thus, for example, the transferee will be able to reply on any restrictive covenants in the transferred employees' employment contracts with the transferor. See *Morris Angel & Sons Ltd. v Hollander* [1993] 3 All ER 569, [1993] ICR 71, [1993] IRLR 169; and Law Society of Ireland, in Moffatt, ed., *Employment Law* (2nd ed., Oxford University Press, 2006), at 11.11.5 and 11.11.6.

103. See Byrne, *ibid.*, at paras.19.25 and 19.26 for analysis of the types of employee entitlements

employment[104] that existed on the date of the transfer[105] shall, by reason of the transfer, be transferred to the transferee.[106] Hence from the standpoint of employees[107] of the undertaking, the transfer will not (subject to the exceptions considered below) affect their contracts of employment, or the terms and conditions[108] governing their employment.[109]

---

that will transfer, including, for example, the bonus structures, disciplinary procedures and other schemes that may have been specifically created and moulded as far as the transferor's undertaking was concerned and may simply not fit within the structure of the transferee's undertaking. Thus in *Computershire Investor Services Plc v Jackson* [2006] UKEAT0503061512, the UK EAT held that where following a transfer an employee had joined a transferee's benefit scheme, she was entitled to benefits based on the period of her continuous employment with both transferor and transferee. See Bracebridge and Sanford, 'TUPE: All Change or No Change?', 79 *Employment Law Journal* (April 2007), 11.

104. It is only the rights and obligations arising out of a contract of employment that transfer. Thus in C-313/07, *Kirtruna v Red Elite de Electrodomésticos SA* [2008] EUECJ, [2009] 1 CMLR 14 the ECJ held that following a transfer the transferee was not required to preserve the lease of commercial premises entered into by the transferor of the undertaking with a third party (because it did not arise out of a contract of employment) even though the termination of that lease was likely to entail the termination of contracts of employment transferred to the transferee.

105. In *Gutridge v Sodexo North Tees & Hartlepool NHS Trust* [2009] EWCA Civ 729, [2009] ICR 70, [2009] IRLR 721, a case in which a group of female employees who had acquired equal pay rights relative to various male comparators, had been transferred to a new undertaking but without any such male comparators, the English Court of Appeal held that their right to equal pay would, nonetheless, survive the transfer. The court concluded that their right to equal pay, albeit based on the pay afforded to men in the transferor undertaking, had crystallised prior to the transfer and hence could be enforced against the transferee.

106. reg.4(1) European Communities (Protection of Employees on Transfer of Undertakings) Regulations 2003. See Byrne, 'Transfer of Undertakings', in Regan, ed., *Employment Law* (Tottel Publishing, 2009), at para.19.26 for the point that 'One of the main problems for a transferee is where the contractual matters that transfer were particularly tailored to the transferor's identity. The transferee may simply not be in a position to replicate these contractual benefits even if the transferee wished to do so.'

107. An employee is defined (in reg.2 European Communities (Protection of Employees on Transfer of Undertakings) Regulations 2003) as a person of any age who has entered into or works under (or, where the employment has ceased, entered into or worked under) a contract of employment, and a contract of employment is defined to mean a contract of service or apprenticeship and any other contract whereby an individual agrees with another person who is carrying on the business of an employment agency and is acting in the course of that business to do or perform personally any work or service for a third person (whether or not the third person is a party to the contract) and in either case, whether the contract is express or implied and, if express, whether it is oral or in writing.

108. See, for example, *Zhao v Valken Ltd.*, UD 356/2006; *Lennon v BDS Security* RP 139/2007.

109. Specific provision as to the application of this principle in respect of various entitlements of an employee is made in various employment law statutes that are considered in different chapters in this book. Equally, in *Rask and Christensen v ISS Kantineservice A/S* [1993] IRLR 133, the point was made that minor alterations to the terms and conditions of an employee's contract 'such as would be permitted in any event under national law' would not be prohib-

2.1. Automatic Transfer and the Discharge of the Transferor's Obligations

Under the Directive, it is possible for Member States to make both the transferor [23–39] and the transferee jointly and severally liable in respect of the entitlements of employees from the date of the transfer,[110] but where this has *not* happened then the position under the Directive is that the transferee becomes exclusively liable in this regard.[111] The Irish regulations do not provide for this possibility of joint and several liability and hence, as far as Irish law is concerned, from the date of transfer the rights and obligations imposed by the regulations as far as the status of the employees of the relevant undertaking is concerned automatically pass to the transferee,[112] and the transferor will be discharged from any such rights and obligations.[113] Equally, the point has been made that it can be extremely difficult, particularly where the full panoply of an employee's rights under an existing employment relationship have not been written down, to work out in detail the totality of what may have transferred.[114]

2.2. Collective Agreements

Where there is a collective agreement in place on the date of transfer, the trans- [23–40] feree is required to continue to observe the terms and conditions agreed in such agreement and on the same terms as bound the transferor under the terms of that agreement, until the point at which the agreement expires or is terminated or

---

ited under the terms of the regulations, provided that such alterations were not the result of the transfer in question.

110. Art. 3(1) Directive 2001/23/EC. Generally, see Kimber and O'Doherty, 'Transfer of Undertakings – Perspectives from Litigation', 5(2) *IELJ* (2008), 56.

111. C-144 and C-145/87, *Berg and Busschers v Besselsen* [1988] EUECJ R-147/87, [1988] ECR 2559. Significantly, in *Rotsart de Hertaing v J Benoit SA (in liquidation)* [1996] ECR I-52927, the ECJ held that this was an automatic consequence of a transfer and could not be avoided by a contrary agreement or intention as between the transferor and transferee. See also *North Wales Training & Enterprise Council Ltd. v Astley and Others*, unreported, 23 December 1999. Generally, see McMullen, 'The "Right" to Object to Transfer of Employment under TUPE', 37(2) *Industrial Law Journal* (2008), 169.

112. In *Secretary of State for Trade & Industry v Cook* [1997] ICR 288, [1997] IRLR 150, the UK EAT held that an employer could not prevent the automatic transfer of an employee's contract of employment simply by refusing to inform employees of the transfer or the identity of the purchaser. See McMullen, 'The "Right" to Object to Transfer of Employment under TUPE', 37(2) *Industrial Law Journal* (2008), 169.

113. For recent authority on this point, see *Gutridge v Sodexo North Tees & Hartlepool NHS Trust* [2009] EWCA Civ 729, [2009] ICR 70, [2009] IRLR 721. The point has been made that in a number of cases (*Zhao v Valken Ltd.*, UD 356/2006) the Irish EAT appears to have concluded (almost certainly wrongly) that transferor *and* transferee could be jointly and severally liable in the event of a transfer. See Kimber and O'Doherty, 'Transfer of Undertakings – Perspectives from Litigation', 5(2) *IELJ* (2008), 56.

114. Law Society of Ireland, in Moffatt, ed., *Employment Law* (2nd ed., Oxford University Press, 2006), at 11.8.6.4.

replaced.[115] This is a significant provision, in that it may lead to a situation where the law enforces an exception to the general principle (considered in Chapter 2) that an employer cannot be required to recognise or negotiate with trade unions. The logic of the regulations suggests that where there was such a process of recognition and negotiation on the date of transfer, then this amounts to an obligation on the part of the transferor that is passed to the transferee.[116] On the other hand, it is possible that the transferee may not be caught by the terms of a Registered Employment Agreement (REA) or Employment Regulation Order (ERO) that bound the transferor in cases where the transferee is not an undertaking operating within the industry to which the relevant agreement or order applies[117]. It is a matter of uncertainty whether, as a result of the regulations, the transferee remains bound by the REA or ERO, but it is submitted that this can simply not be the case, given that the relevant agreement is not one between the employer and employees within the specific undertaking but rather between all employers and employees within the relevant sector of the economy.

[23–41] In a similar vein, where the economic entity being transferred retains its autonomy after the transfer, then the regulations provide that the status and functions of the representatives[118] of the employees affected by the transfer shall be preserved by the transferee and on the same terms and conditions as specified in any enactment or in any agreement between the employer and the employees' representatives.[119] Moreover, where the autonomy of the undertaking is *not* preserved, the

---

115. reg.4(2) European Communities (Protection of Employees on Transfer of Undertakings) Regulations 2003. See C-499/04, *Werhof v Freeway Traffic Systems* [2006] EUECJ C-499/04, [2006] IRLR 400 for the view that the transferee is not bound under the regulations by any collective agreements entered into *subsequent* to the date of transfer and that bind the transferor and indeed would have covered the relevant undertaking prior to the date of transfer, but that where such *new* collective agreements terminate existing agreements that *do* bind the transferee, then [s]he will no longer be bound by such agreements. Generally, see Codd, 'The Transfer of Undertakings and Commercial Agreements: Advising Clients and some Practical Pitfalls', 5 *Employment Law Review* (2007), 7.

116. For analysis of this question and of the related question of whether it is valid for employees of a transferor to stage a picket directed at the transferee, see Law Society of Ireland, in Moffatt, ed., *Employment Law* (2nd ed., Oxford University Press, 2006), at 11.9.3 and 11.9.4, where it is suggested that where there has been a transfer of undertakings situation, and where the general rules in respect of picketing contained in the Industrial Relations Act 1990 have been fulfilled, then such a picket should be deemed to be valid.

117. This would apply, for example, where an architectural firm (which is not bound by the REA for the construction industry) purchased some aspect of the business of a construction firm.

118. Under reg.2 European Communities (Protection of Employees on Transfer of Undertakings) Regulations 2003, employees' representatives are defined as (a) a trade union, staff association or excepted body with which it has been the practice of the employer to conduct collective bargaining negotiations or (b) in the absence of such a trade union, staff, association or excepted body, a person or persons chosen by such employees (under an arrangement put in place by the employer from among their number to represent them in negotiations).

119. reg.7(1) *ibid*.

transferee is obliged to arrange for the employees who were transferred (and who had formerly been represented before the date of transfer) to choose (if necessary by election) a person or persons from among them to represent them during the period necessary for the reappointment of the representatives of the employees or the reconstitution of their representation.[120]

Finally, where the term of office of the employees' representatives in question expires as a result of the transfer, they continue to be protected against a dismissal on the grounds of their involvement with trade-union-related activity.[121]   [23–42]

2.3. Prohibition against Dismissal Arising out of the Transfer

Specifically, the regulations provide that the transfer of an undertaking cannot in itself constitute grounds for a dismissal either by the transferor or by the transferee and that any dismissal that is, in fact, the result of such transfer is prohibited.[122] Consequently (and self-evidently), a transferee cannot dismiss employees who were formerly employed by the transferor when the undertaking is transferred to him or her but, perhaps less obviously, a transferor may also not dismiss employees in advance of the transfer in order to make the undertaking more attractive as a commercial proposition, and thus to encourage a transfer.[123] The precise effect of these rules is, however, uncertain, in that either the transferor *or* the transferee may, as we shall shortly see, dismiss employees if there are economic, technical or organisational reasons for doing so. It may, in other words, be very difficult to see whether a dismissal is for such reasons or is a response either of transferor or transferee to an impending or recent transfer.   [23–43]

---

120. reg.7(2) *ibid.*
121. reg.7(3) *ibid.* Under s.6(2)(a) Unfair Dismissals Act 1977 a dismissal on the grounds of the employee's membership, or proposal that [s]he or another person become a member of, or his or her engaging in activities on behalf of, a trade union or excepted body under the Trade Union Acts 1941 and 1971, where the times at which [s]he engages in such activities are outside his or her hours of work or are times during his or her hours of work in which [s]he is permitted pursuant to the contract of employment between the employee and employer so to engage is deemed to be an inherently unfair dismissal. See Kerr, *Irish Employment Legislation* (Round Hall Sweet and Maxwell, 2000), at p.M-117, and reg.2 European Communities (Protection of Employees on Transfer of Undertakings) Regulations 2003 for analysis of what constitutes an excepted body in this regard.
122. reg.5(1) European Communities (Protection of Employees on Transfer of Undertakings) Regulations 2003. If a dismissal of this kind constitutes an unfair dismissal for the purposes of the Unfair Dismissals Acts, relief may not be granted to the employee under both those Acts and the regulations: reg.5(4) *ibid.* The ECJ has interpreted the equivalent term in the Directive as requiring Member States to hold the transferee employer responsible for any such dismissals, but not as requiring that where a dismissal in this context occurs, the entitlements of the employees are identical to those of employees who are dismissed by employers in the normal course of an employment relationship: C-296/07, *Mirja Juuri v Fazer Amica Oy* [2008] EUECJ.
123. C-101/87, *P. Bork International A/S* [1988] EUECJ R-101/87, [1988] ECR 3057.

Employment Law in Ireland

[23–44] Where the dismissals in question *are* found to have been the result of the transfer, then the approach of the courts is to deem them to be invalid and hence to hold that the employee[s] in question must be regarded as still being employed either by the transferor or, if the transfer has taken place, by the transferee. Moreover, if the transfer involves a change in working conditions to the detriment of the employee concerned, such that the contract of employment is terminated as a result, then the employer must be regarded as having been responsible for the termination of the contract.[124]

2.4. Pension Entitlements

[23–45] The one exception to the general principle contained in reg. 4(1) relates to pension entitlements.[125] Thus the regulations do not apply in relation to employee's rights to old-age, invalidity or survivors' benefits under supplementary company or inter-company pension schemes that do not fall within the Social Welfare Acts.[126] Equally the ECJ has said that because the equivalent provision in the Directive represents an exception to the general approach towards transfer of undertakings situations, it must be interpreted strictly,[127] such that a very narrow interpretation is taken of the concept of 'old-age, invalidity or survivor's benefits'.[128]

[23–46] On the other hand, the interests of persons no longer employed in the undertaking at the time of the transfer in respect of immediate or prospective entitlements to old-age and survivors' benefits under a supplementary company pension scheme that is an occupational pension scheme for the purposes of the Pensions Acts 1990 to 2003 are protected[129] and, moreover, the transferee is required to ensure that the interests of such persons in respect of immediate or prospective entitlements to old-age and survivors' benefits under a supplementary company pension scheme, other than an occupational pension scheme for the purposes of the Pensions Acts 1990–2003, are protected.[130]

---

124. reg.5(3) European Communities (Protection of Employees on Transfer of Undertakings) Regulations 2003.
125. Generally, see Brettle, 'The Shrinking Pensions Exemption', 59 *Employment Law Journal* (April 2005), 11.
126. reg.4(3) European Communities (Protection of Employees on Transfer of Undertakings) Regulations 2003.
127. C-561/07, *Commission v Italy* [2009] EUECJ; *Beckmann v Dynamco Whicheloe Macfarlane Ltd.* [2002] EUECJ C-164/00, [2002] ECR I-4893.
128. So, for example, early retirement benefits and redundancy benefits do not come within this rubric: C-164/00, *Beckmann v Dynamco Whicheloe Macfarlane Ltd.* [2002] EUECJ C-164/00, [2002] ECR I-4893; C-4/01, *Martin v South Bank University* [2004] EUECJ C-4/01, [2004] ECR I-12859, [2004] IRLR 74.
129. reg.4(4)(a) European Communities (Protection of Employees on Transfer of Undertakings) Regulations 2003.
130. reg.4(4)(b) *ibid.* See C-561/07, *Commission v Italy* [2009] EUECJ.

826

2.5. Employee Objections to Transfer

It should be noted that an employee can, of course, object to the transfer and can [23–47]
refuse to work within the 'new' undertaking after it has been transferred to the
transferor.[131] The legal consequences of such a step for that employee is a matter
for individual Member States as far as the Directive is concerned,[132] although the
Irish regulations are silent on the issue. It is arguable, however, that inasmuch as
the regulations provide a specific form of protection to employees (the right to
continuity of service) and inasmuch as they also replace a legal position where
the ending of an employer's interest in an undertaking meant the termination
of all employment contracts as far as that employer and that undertaking was
concerned, an employee who refuses to avail of the new protections afforded by
the law should be taken as having resigned, or alternatively his or her employment
contract should simply be regarded as having expired.[133]

In Ireland, however, in *Symantec v Leddy, Symantec v Lyons*[134] the EAT had [23–48]
suggested that in circumstances where there had been a transfer of undertakings
to which certain employees objected, it was open to those employees to claim
redundancy payments from their former employer given that their employment
with him no longer existed.[135] This was, it is submitted, a puzzling conclusion,
in that it appeared to involve an assessment of the facts that did not appreciate
the reality of the transfer itself. It was not, after all, the case that the employees'
contracts of employment with the transferor had come to an end, but rather, that
those contracts remained extant but were now with a different employer. Unsurprisingly, the EAT decision was overturned on appeal,[136] with Edwards J in the
High Court concluding that the regulations did not

> make any particular provision as to what will occur if employees decide not to
> transfer. However, contrary to [the respondent's] belief… It does not follow that if
> an employee decides not to transfer a situation of redundancy automatically arises
> vis-à-vis the transferor. It cannot do so because the fact that an employee objects
> to the transfer does not of itself have the effect of negativing the transfer. It is just

---

131. See C-132, C-138, and C-139/91, *Katsikas v Konstantinidis* [1993] ECR-I6577. In *Nokes v Doncaster Amalgamated Collieries Ltd.* [1940] AC 1014, Lord Atkin had suggested that it would be 'astonishing' for power to be given to a court or anyone else to transfer an employee from one employer to another without his or her knowledge and against his or her will.
132. See C-171 and C-172/94, *Merckx and Neuhuys v Ford Motors Belgium SA* [1996] ECR-I 1253.
133. This is the approach taken in England and also by the ECJ in *Mikkelson v Danmols Inventar A/S* [1986] 1 CMLR 316. See Byrne, 'Transfer of Undertakings', in Regan, ed., *Employment Law* (Tottel Publishing, 2009), at para.19.23; and McMullen, 'The "Right" to Object to Transfer of Employment under TUPE', 37(2) *Industrial Law Journal* (June 2008), 169. See also *New ISG Ltd. v Vernon and Others* [2008] IRLR 115 for the question of whether or not an employee can validly object to a transfer *after* it has taken place.
134. [2009] IEHC 256, [2009] ELR 169.
135. *Leddy v Symantec*, UD 471/2007.
136. [2009] IEHC 256, [2009] ELR 169.

that an employee is not obliged to continue his employment relationship with the transferee. However, the transfer still goes ahead unless a member state expressly provides for the contrary in its implementing legislation. That this is so is clear from the judgment of the ECJ in *Cassias*. That Court explained that the purpose of the Directive is to allow the employee to remain in the employ of his new employer on the same conditions as were agreed with the transferor. However, he is not obliged to avail of this facility. As the Court said 'the directive does not preclude an employee from deciding to object to the transfer of his contract of employment or employment relationship and hence deciding not to take advantage of the protection afforded him by the directive.' However, 'the purpose of the directive is not to ensure that the contract of employment or employment relationship with the transferor is continued where the undertaking's employees do not wish to remain in the transferee's employ.'

In my view nothing could be clearer. If the Irish legislature had wished the employment relationship with the transferor to continue so as to facilitate the employee in making a claim for redundancy it could have enacted legislation to that effect. It has not done so. This court is completely satisfied that by virtue of regulation 4 (1) it is not possible for the Defendants/Respondents in this case to make a redundancy claim against the Plaintiff/Appellant.[137]

[23–49] Accordingly, it may now be regarded as settled that, at Irish law, where a transfer has occurred and where employees object to the fact of such transfer, they are entitled not to transfer their employment, but equally they cannot seek to claim that their employment relationship *with the transferor* survives the transfer, or that their objection thereto somehow negates the impact of the transfer[138]. In other words, whereas they may refuse to transfer, equally (and in line with the principle discussed earlier that following the transfer the transferor is discharged from all obligations in respect of the employees for which [s]he was formerly responsible) they have no subsequent cause of action against the transferor deriving from their former employment relationship with him or her.

2.6. Information and Consultation Obligations

[23–50] In Chapter 14 we consider the general obligations imposed by the law on employers insofar as providing information to and consulting with employees is concerned. It was noted in that chapter that the obligations in this regard include informing and consulting with employees in respect of an impending transfer of undertakings, and also that the Employees (Provision of Information and Consultation) Act 2006 provides for the mechanisms by which such consultation is to take place.[139]

---

137. [2009] ELR 169, 177-178.
138. Generally see Redmond, 'Employment Objections to TUPE Transfers – Key Questions', 6(3) *IELJ* (2009), 68.
139. Thus as we have seen the Employees (Provision of Information and Consultation) Act 2006 gives effect to the requirements of reg.8(5) European Communities (Protection of Employees

Reg. 8 of the 2003 Regulations, however, gives a detailed statement of the nature of the information that must be provided and in respect of which consultation must occur in the context of such transfer of undertakings.[140] Breach of such obligations can lead to an award of damages being made against the defaulting party.[141]

Thus the transferor *and* transferee are required (where reasonably practicable not later than 30 days before the transfer[142] and in any event, in good time before the transfer[143]) to provide employees' representatives or, where there are no representatives of the employees in the relevant undertaking through no fault of the employees,[144] each of the employees, in writing[145] with information[146] in respect of: [23–51]

- the date or proposed date of the transfer;
- the reasons for the transfer;
- the legal implications of the transfer for the employees and a summary of any relevant economic and social implications of the transfer for them; and
- any measures envisaged in relation to the employees.[147]

Moreover, where any such measures are envisaged in relation to the employees the transferor or transferee (as appropriate) is required where reasonably practicable, not later than 30 days before and in any event in good time before the transfer is carried out, to consult with the representatives of employees in relation to meas-   [23–52]

---

on Transfer of Undertakings) Regulations 2003 by putting in place a mechanism by which employees' representatives can be appointed in order for information and consultation to occur.

140. Such obligations arise irrespective of whether the decision resulting in the transfer is taken by the employer of the relevant employees or an undertaking controlling the employer, and irrespective of whether (in the latter scenario) the relevant information was not provided to the employer by the undertaking controlling it: reg.8(7) European Communities (Protection of Employees on Transfer of Undertakings) Regulations 2003.

141. *McCabe v Greenhills Peat Ltd.*, UD 810/2006. See Kimber and O'Doherty, 'Transfer of Undertakings – Perspectives from Litigation', 5(2) *IELJ* (2008), 56.

142. In the case of the transferee the information must be provided not later than 30 days before the transfer is carried out and in any event in good time before the employees are directly affected by the transfer as regards their conditions of work and employment: reg.8(3) European Communities (Protection of Employees on Transfer of Undertakings) Regulations 2003.

143. reg.8(2) *ibid.*

144. This may well be the case, for example, in an undertaking that employs insufficient persons for the terms of the Employees (Provision of Information and Consultation) Act 2006 to apply to it.

145. reg.8(6) European Communities (Protection of Employees on Transfer of Undertakings) Regulations 2003.

146. The transferor/transferee has a duty to ensure that such information is correct. See *King v Aer Lingus* [2002] 3 IR 481, [2003] ELR 173.

147. See McMullen, 'The "Right" to Object to Transfer of Employment under TUPE', 37(2) *Industrial Law Journal* (June 2008), 169.

ures with a view to reaching an agreement.[148] Equally it should be noted that all that is necessary is consultation with a view to reaching an agreement; there is no obligation on the employer to ensure that such agreement is actually reached.

2.7. The ETO Defence

[23–53] The general obligations in the regulations as far as the obligations of transferees not to dismiss employees of the transferred undertaking are concerned are tempered by the existence of the so-called ETO defence – that is to say, the rule that nothing in the regulations can be taken to prohibit dismissals for economic, technical or organisational reasons that entail changes in the workforce.[149] This is a difficult concept in that it may be possibly to classify any measure taken either by a transferor or transferee to reduce the size of the workforce (because of an impending or recent transfer) as having been done for economic, technical or organisational reasons. Equally, it is clear that for the so-called ETO defence to apply there must be a genuine need to dismiss employees[150] – essentially on the same basis as a traditional redundancy situation at Irish law[151] – and that it will be a question of fact as to whether this was the case or whether the reason for the termination is the transfer itself (in which case, obviously, it will be invalid).[152]

[23–54] A number of principles emerge from the relevant case law in this area. First, and inasmuch as this defence only applies in a situation where the dismissal is connected with the transfer (in that in the normal course of events either the transferor or transferee are free – subject to unfair dismissals legislation – to dismiss employees provided that it is not the transfer that is the reason for such dismissal), the reality is that it is only the transferee who can rely on the ETO defence. This is because the courts, including the ECJ, have refused to permit a prospective transferor to rely on the ETO defence to justify a dismissal or dismissals on the basis that it or they will make his or her business a more attractive commercial proposition for the transferee.[153] In other words, where a transferee is of the view that following

---

148. reg.8(4) European Communities (Protection of Employees on Transfer of Undertakings) Regulations 2003.

149. reg.5(2) *ibid.*

150. See *Dynamex Friction and others v Amicus and others* [2008] EWCA Civ 381, [2008] IRLR 515, for the holding that what is relevant here is the view of the person responsible for such dismissals. Hence where an administrator of a pre-transfer undertaking (acting in the course of his bona fide professional duties) genuinely felt it was necessary that employees be dismissed (as there was no money to pay them) then the ETO defence would apply despite the fact that, unbeknownst to the administrator, the managing director of the company had 'stage-managed' events by placing the business into administration knowing that dismissals would occur and that the business would thereby become a more attractive commercial proposition for potential transferees.

151. *Powell and McHugh v Bewleys Manufacturing* [1990] ELR 68; *Trafford v Sharpe & Fisher (Building Supplies) Ltd.* [1994] IRLR 325; *Morris v Smart Brothers Ltd.*, UD 688/93.

152. See C-101/87, *P. Bork International A/S* [1988] EUECJ R-101/87, [1988] ECR 3057.

153. But see *Anderson v Dalkeith Engineering Ltd.* [1984] IRLR 429 for the suggestion that where

the transfer it will be necessary to lose some of the staff of the undertaking that has been transferred for operational reasons, [s]he must still take such employees on and subsequently dismiss them or make them redundant (regardless of the cost to him or her in so doing) and rely on the ETO defence as a justification for doing so.[154] Alternatively, it may be open to him or her to seek indemnities from the employer in respect of the obligations that [s]he will owe to employees on foot of the transfer. As has been stated:

> A transferee should not seek to have liability for [severance payments which must be paid to employees] imposed on the transferor by having the transferor reduce or reorganise the workforce on the basis of someone else's (the transferee's) reasons or plans for doing so. The transferee is better placed to deal with all issues arising consequent on termination of employment of any of the workforce as a result of the transfer. If the transferee does not want to be exposed to the cost of having done so, provision may be made to recover the cost from the transferor or make some provision for the reservation of sufficient funds for this purpose; however, the level of severance payments the workforce might seek may not be easily predictable. If the workforce were to hold out for substantially higher payments than may have been paid in the past, and parties have done their calculations based on such historical payments, difficulties may arise and great care must be taken by both parties in planning for the costs of rationalisation or reduction in the workforce consequent on a transfer.[155]

Secondly, the ETO defence will only apply where the economic, technical or **[23–55]** organisational reasons in question entail bona fide changes in the workforce.[156] Hence the mere fact that an undertaking is undergoing 'critical difficulties' will not permit it to avail of the ETO defence if there are to be no such changes in the workforce.[157] Moreover, the defence only applies to justify dismissals. In other words, economic, technical and organisational reasons cannot be relied upon as a defence to altering the terms and conditions (or remuneration[158]) of workers

---

it is necessary to reduce staff in order to sell the undertaking (and where there was no pressure from the transferee in this regard) the ETO defence may apply.

154. *Rotstart de Hertaing v J Benoit S/A* [1997] IRLR 127; *Wendelboe v LJ Music ApS* [1985] ECR 457; *Wheeler v Patel* [1987] ICR 631, [1987] IRLR 211; *Gateway Hotels Ltd. v Stewart* [1988] IRLR 287; *Ibex Trading Co Ltd. v Walton* [1994] ICR 907, [1994] IRLR 594. This logic is, in part, based on the view that an ETO justification must relate to the conduct of the business and not to a desire to get the best possible price for the sale thereof.

155.Law Society of Ireland, in Moffatt, ed., *Employment Law* (2nd ed., Oxford University Press, 2006), at 11.9.7.

156. This means changes in the composition of the workforce as distinct from merely change in the conditions thereof. *Berriman v Delabole Slate Ltd.* [1985] ICR 546, [1985] IRLR 305. See Byrne, 'Transfer of Undertakings', in Regan, ed., *Employment Law* (Tottel Publishing, 2009), at para.19.37.

157. C-561/07, *Commission v Italy* [2009] EUECJ.

158. *Meikle v McPhail* [1983] IRLR 351.

retained following the transfer. Where the exception *is* likely to apply is where, following a transfer, the transferee deems it necessary to reduce the number of staff [s]he employs in a manner akin to a traditional redundancy situation.[159]

[23–56] Thirdly, there is authority for the proposition that a dismissal as a result of a transfer will still be invalid even if it takes place some time after the transfer, in circumstances where the reason for the dismissal relates to the fact of the transfer rather than to any broader economic, technical or organisational reasons. Thus in *LMU v Sackur & Others*[160] the United Kingdom EAT found a breach of the regulations in circumstances where employees were dismissed some two years after the transfer in order to achieve post-transfer harmonisation of wages.

3. Enforcement[161]

[23–57] Where any alleged contravention of the regulations[162] has occurred, the employee or a trade union, staff association or excepted body acting on behalf of and with the consent of the employee[163] is entitled to make a complaint (within six months of the date of the alleged contravention[164]) to the Rights Commissioner (on notice to the other party or parties concerned[165]). Having heard the matter,[166] the Rights

---

159. *Gorictree Ltd. v Jenkinson* [1985] ICR 51, [1984] IRLR 391; *Trafford v Sharpe & Fisher (Building Supplies) Ltd.* [1994] IRLR 325.

160. [2006] UKEAT0286061708.

161. For analysis of the use of injunctive relief by employees seeking either to restrain a transfer of undertakings or to restrain any alleged breaches of the regulations, see Law Society of Ireland, in Moffatt, ed., *Employment Law* (2nd ed., Oxford University Press, 2006), at 11.11.14.

162. Other than reg.4(4)(a) European Communities (Protection of Employees on Transfer of Undertakings) Regulations 2003 (relating to the entitlements of employees and persons no longer employed in the transferor's business at the time of the transfer to benefits under a supplementary company pension scheme) and reg.13 *ibid.* (relating to infringements of the rules of the EAT in terms of, for example, lying under oath).

163. reg.10(1) *ibid.*

164. reg.10(6) *ibid.* This six-month period may be extended by up to a further six months by the Rights Commissioner where [s]he concludes that the failure to bring the complaint within time was due to exceptional circumstances. See *Gutridge v Sodexo North Tees & Hartlepool NHS Trust* [2009] EWCA Civ 729, [2009] ICR 70, [2009] IRLR 721, for consideration of whether, in the event of an employee seeking to enforce statutory rights under a different employment statute (in this case one guaranteeing equal pay) that had been breached by the transferee on foot of the transfer, the limitation period would run from the date on which the transfer had occurred or the date on which the claimant's contract of employment with the transferee concluded. On this point, see also *Preston v Wolverhampton Health NHS Trust (No.3)* [2006] ICR 606; *Slack v Cumbria CC* [2009] EWCA Civ 293, [2009] IRLR 463.

165. reg.10(3) European Communities (Protection of Employees on Transfer of Undertakings) Regulations 2003.

166. As usual, complaints before the Rights Commissioner are heard other than in public: reg.10(7) *ibid.*

Commissioner may in his or her decision declare that the complaint was or was not well founded, may require the employer[167] to take a specified cause of action, and may require the employer to pay such compensation[168] as is just and equitable in the circumstances but, in the case of a contravention of reg. 8 (dealing with information and consultation), not exceeding four weeks' remuneration and, in the case of any other contravention, not exceeding two years' remuneration in respect of the employee's employment.[169]

As with other statutes considered in this book, the decision of the Rights Commis- [23–58] sioner can be appealed to the Employment Appeals Tribunal[170] within six weeks from the date on which it was communicated to the prospective appellant, or such greater period as the tribunal may determine in the circumstances,[171] and the tribunal, following a hearing of the matter, may affirm, vary or set aside the decision of the Rights Commissioner.[172] The decision of the tribunal may be appealed by either party to the High Court on a point of law,[173] and the Minister may, at the request of the tribunal, also refer a question of law arising in proceedings before it to the High Court for determination.[174]

Where a decision of a Rights Commissioner or a determination of the tribunal has [23–59] not been carried out within six weeks of being communicated to the parties (and no appeal has been brought against such decision or any such appeal has been abandoned[175]), then on the application either of the employee, any trade union of which [s]he is a member (with his or her consent), or the Minister, the Circuit Court, (if [s]he considers such an application appropriate), without hearing the matter, shall make an order directing the employer to carry out the determination in accordance with its terms.[176]

---

167. A reference to an employer in this context means, where ownership of the relevant economic unit of the employer changes after the contravention to which the complaint relates occurred, the person who, by virtue of the change, becomes entitled to such ownership.

168. Any such compensation represents a priority debt to be paid under s.285 of the Companies Act 1963 in the event of the winding-up of a company (para.5(1) of the Second Schedule to the Employment Permits Acts 2003 and 2006) and under s.81 of the Bankruptcy Act 1988 in the event of bankruptcy (para.5(2) of the Second Schedule).

169. reg.10(5)(c) European Communities (Protection of Employees on Transfer of Undertakings) Regulations 2003. The remuneration in question is calculated in accordance with regulations made under s.17 of the Unfair Dismissals Act 1977.

170. The tribunal is possessed of the normal powers in respect of determining its own procedures, and in respect of evidence and witnesses: regs.11(4) and 13 European Communities (Protection of Employees on Transfer of Undertakings) Regulations 2003.

171. reg.11(2) *ibid.*

172. reg.11(1) *ibid.*

173. reg.12(1) i*bid.*

174. reg.12(2) *ibid.*

175. reg.14(2) *ibid.*

176. reg.14(1) *ibid.* Such order may include an order to pay interest on any outstanding compensation owed by the employer to the employee: reg.14(3) *ibid.*

CHAPTER 24

The Employment Injunction

Introduction

In comparatively recent times, Irish law has witnessed a significant increase in the [24–01] use of what has come to be known as the 'employment injunction'[1]. This is a form of relief that may be sought by either an employee or an employer (though in the vast majority of cases it is sought by the employee) and, if granted, will have the effect of requiring the party against whom it is granted either to do or to refrain from doing something, or both. Naturally where what is at issue is a serious employment dispute, an order of this kind becomes a potent tool in the armoury of the successful applicant.

As we shall see, the types of relief sought in employment injunction applications [24–02] tend to come within one of four categories, namely:

- an order requiring that an employee who has been dismissed be reinstated;
- an order restraining the dismissal of an employee (but not requiring his reinstatement), which essentially means that the employer is bound to pay the employee for the duration of the order;
- an order preventing the employer from taking steps inconsistent with the employee's status in the place of employment, most obviously by appointing a replacement to his or her position; or
- an order preventing the employer from carrying out disciplinary proceedings in respect of the employee otherwise than in accordance with the applicable rules of fair procedures and natural and constitutional justice that are considered in Chapter 18.

In addition, an employer may seek an injunction in order to enforce a negative undertaking in an employee's contract of employment, preventing him or her, for

---

1. Generally, see Horan, 'Employment Injunctions: Current Status and Future Developments', 1 *Employment Law Review* (2006), 8; Mallon, 'Recent Developments in Employment Injunctions', 5(2) *IELJ* (2008), 48; McDermott, '*Carroll v Bus Átha Cliath*: Strengthening the Right to an Employment Injunction', 5 *Employment Law Review* (2006), 104; Delany, 'Case and Comment: Employment Injunctions: The Role of Mutual Trust and Confidence', 13(1) *DULJ* (2006), 363.

example, from working for a competitor for a defined period of time following the termination of that employee's employment contract.[2]

[24–03] It has been fairly said that the number of conflicting judgments in this area mean that it is difficult to predict with any degree of certainty whether an interlocutory injunction will actually be granted in a given case, and that 'broadly speaking a court will be likely to grant injunctive relief to an employee where it would be unjust not to do so and where the order sought is workable'.[3] Indeed, the position was summed up neatly by Clarke J in *Bergin v Galway Clinic Doughiska Ltd*.[4]:

> There have been a significant number of decisions over the last number of years both of this court, and to a lesser extent, of the Supreme Court, in relation to what might loosely be called employment injunctions. I think it is fair to state that this area of the jurisprudence of the courts is in a state of evolution and the precise current state of that jurisprudence is far from clear. This situation is not, in my view, helped by the fact that a great many of the cases do not proceed to trial so that by far the greater number of the authorities consist of decisions of the court at an interlocutory stage rather than after a full hearing. While such authorities may be of very considerable assistance in defining the jurisprudence in relation to the grant or refusal of interlocutory injunctions, same may do little to advance the cause of clarity in respect of employment law generally, for the court is required to approach issues of general employment law, at the interlocutory stage, on the basis of arguability or, perhaps, where the injunction sought is mandatory in substance, likelihood of success. In either case a definitive decision on the legal issues arising (with the exception of those which are relevant solely to the grant or refusal of interlocutory relief) has to await a full trial. In practice the full trial rarely arises. It is the frequent experience of the court dealing with such matters that a great many of the cases which are the subject of an interlocutory ruling are resolved by agreement between the parties before the matter comes to trial. It would be somewhat naïve not to surmise that a significant feature of the interlocutory hearing is concerned with both parties attempting to establish the most advantageous position from which to approach the frequently expected negotiations designed to lead to an agreed termination of the contract of employment concerned. The employee who has the benefit of an interlocutory injunction can approach such negotiations from a position of strength as can the employer who has successfully resisted an interlocutory application.[5]

2. *Capital Radio Productions Ltd. v Radio 2000*, unreported, Supreme Court, 26 May 1998. (O'Flaherty J observed that 'while a person cannot be forced to work against his will for someone he can, if in breach of contract, be prevented from working for anyone else'.)
3. McDermott, '*Carroll v Bus Átha Cliath:* Strengthening the Right to an Employment Injunction', 5 *Employment Law Review* (2006), 104, 108.
4. *Bergin v Galway Clinic Doughiska Ltd.* [2007] IEHC 386, [2008] 2 IR 205.
5. [2008] 2 IR 205, 212.

1. An Exceptional Remedy

Traditionally, the courts were very slow to grant injunctions in cases involving [24–04] employment contracts.[6] This reluctance was founded on a number of different grounds all of which are only really relevant where an employee is seeking an order of reinstatement (as distinct from some other kind of injunctive relief, such as an order directing that [s]he continue to be paid his or her salary).

First, the courts both in Ireland and the UK are simply opposed to the idea of [24–05] compelling specific performance of contracts for personal services[7] and as we shall see there is an ongoing judicial reluctance to require employees and employers whose employment relationship has broken down to continue to work together, even on an interim basis. Hence in a number of cases, the courts have used the question of whether the relationship of mutual trust and confidence between the parties has broken down as a determining factor in deciding whether or not to grant injunctive relief. As Clarke J pointed out in *Yap v Children's University Hospital Temple Street*[8]

> It is not the function of the courts to deal with the day-to-day operation of contracts of employment, and the courts would be required to almost act in an industrial relations role if the courts were to make orders as to precisely how contracts of employment were to work. Therefore there are very limited circumstances in which the court will intervene to force a continuation of a contract of the employment, particularly where there is a serious controversy.[9]

Secondly, the courts are equally reluctant to make an order whose performance either can not be supervised or might require constant supervision,[10] and which

---

6. *Whitwood Chemical Co v Hardman* [1891] 2 Ch. 416. See Redmond, *Dismissal Law in Ireland* (2nd ed., Tottel Publishing, 2007), at para.10.03.
7. Generally, see *Reynolds v Malocco* [1999] 2 IR 203, [1999] 1 ILRM 289; *Garrahy v Bord na gCon* [2002] IEHC 147, [2002] 3 IR 566; *Evans v IRFB Services Ireland Ltd.* [2005] IEHC 107, [2005] 2 ILRM 358; *Yeates v Minister for Posts and Telegraphs* [1978] ILRM 22; *De Francesco v Barnum* (1890) 45 Ch. 430; *Phelan v BIC (Ireland) Ltd.* [1997] ELR 208. See also McDermott, 'Carroll v Bus Átha Cliath: Strengthening the Right to an Employment Injunction', 5 *Employment Law Review* (2006), 104. On the other hand it was possible to get an injunction to enforce a negative undertaking in a contract – for example preventing an employee from working for someone else (*Capital Radio Productions Ltd. v Radio 2000* unreported, Supreme Court, 26 May 1998), although even this would not be granted if it would have the indirect effect of compelling performance of a contract for personal services (*Warren v Mendy* [1989] 1 WLR 853, [1989] ICR 525, [1989] All ER 103, [1989] IRLR 210).
8. [2006] IEHC 308, [2006] 4 IR 298.
9. [2006] 4 IR 298, 301.
10. *Ryan v Mutual Tontine Westminster Chambers Association* [1893] 1 Ch. 116; *Co-Operative Insurance Society Ltd. v Argyll Stores (Holdings) Ltd.* [1998] AC 1. See Redmond, *Dismissal Law in Ireland* (2nd ed., Tottel Publishing, 2007), at para.10.04; Delany, 'Case and Comment: Employment Injunctions: The Role of Mutual Trust and Confidence', 13(1) *DULJ* (2006), 363.

consequently would not be workable[11] in the sense that it would not be possible to see whether or not it was being obeyed.[12]

Finally, Redmond notes that a further reason why the courts were traditionally slow to grant injunctive relief in employment cases was because of the absence of mutuality in such issues – in other words, it appeared unfair to force an employer to continue employing a worker where it was patently impossible that the same worker could be required to continue working for the employer.[13]

[24–06] On the other hand, this traditional refusal to grant so-called employment injunctions was never an absolute one.[14] There are, after all, a number of different kinds of order that can be sought to which the objections mentioned above do not apply – for example, an injunction requiring an employee's salary to be paid pending the trial of the action without requiring him or her to be reinstated, an injunction requiring that a disciplinary process be carried out in accordance with fair procedures and natural and constitutional justice, or an injunction to enforce a negative undertaking in a contract, for example preventing an employee from working for somebody else, or breaching a non-compete or confidentiality clause.[15] Clearly in such circumstances, even if it were to grant the order sought, (a) the court would not be violating the normal rule against compelling specific performance of a contract for personal services, (b) such orders can be monitored and (c) the breakdown in the employment relationship between employer and employee will not mean that the order in question is inherently unworkable.[16]

2. Emerging Principles

[24–07] As has been mentioned, there is considerable uncertainty, even with the increasing Irish jurisprudence in this area, as to when exactly a court will grant injunctive relief in an employment case. Nonetheless certain broad guiding principles (which operate in tandem with the general rules at Irish law relating to interlocutory injunctions, which are considered below)[17] can be discerned in the case law on this question. Some of these principles are specific to the type of relief being sought and these are considered later in this chapter. Others, however, apply generally and are considered now.

---

11. See *Robb v London Borough of Brent* [1991] ICR 514, [1987] IRLR 72.
12. *Ó Murchú v Eircell Ltd.*, Supreme Court, 21 February 2001.
13. *Page One Records Ltd. v Britton* [1968] 1 WLR 157, [1967] 3 All ER 822. Redmond at 10.04 notes that to require mutuality in such circumstances is to ignore the reality of the employer/employee relationship where the employer will necessarily enjoy a measure of dominance.
14. *CH Giles & Co Ltd. v Morris* [1972] 1 All ER 960.
15. Generally, see Redmond, *Dismissal Law in Ireland* (2nd ed., Tottel Publishing, 2007), at para.10.06.
16. *CH Giles & Co Ltd. v Morris* [1972] 1 All ER 960.
17. Redmond, *Dismissal Law in Ireland* (2nd ed., Tottel Publishing, 2007), at para.10.25.

2.1. The Relevance of the Identity of the Parties

It seems clear that the nature of the relevant parties may play a part in the deter- [24–08]
mination of whether injunctive relief should be granted. Thus, for example, it is
clearly far easier to obtain such relief against a public body than a private body. It
is also easier to obtain injunctive relief where what is sought to be injuncted is the
dismissal of an office holder who has a contract of employment as distinct from
that of a normal employee.[18]

2.2. The Requirement that the Employee's Rights have been Undermined

Most importantly, it may be suggested that injunctive relief will not be granted [24–09]
unless either the impugned action was *ultra vires* the powers of the person taking
the action[19] or where what occurred was in breach of the employee's constitutional rights[20] or, most commonly, where what is sought to be injuncted allegedly constitutes a breach either of a substantive or a procedural clause (express
or implied) in the applicant's contract of employment.[21] This would arise, for
example, where an employee is being dismissed in breach of his or her contract,[22]
where agreed disciplinary procedures have not been followed, or where the implied
term of fair procedures in his or her contract (and thereby his or her constitutional
right to fair procedures and natural and constitutional justice) is being violated.
In other words, there must be some right – constitutional or contractual – of the
employee which is under threat.

---

18. See *Garvey v Ireland* [1981] IR 75; *Shortt v Data Packaging* [1994] ELR 251; *Sharkey v Dunnes Stores* [2004] IEHC 163, [2005] 1 ICLMD 24. This was also of considerable significance as far as the High Court was concerned in *Nolan v EMO Oil Services Ltd.* [2008] IEHC 15, [2009] ELR 122. It is not clear why the fact that someone is an office holder should be relevant to this extent, though it may be suggested that it is either because the complexity of the issues involved will mean that it is easier for the applicant to show that there is a fair issue to be tried, or the amount of money and prestige that may be at stake may be a weighty factor as far as the balance of convenience is concerned. See *Boland v Phoenix Shannon* [1997] IEHC 63, [1997] ELR 113.

19. *Shortt v Data Packaging* [1994] ELR 251; *O'Donnell v Chief State Solicitor* [2003] ELR 268.

20. *Maher v Irish Permanent* [1997] IEHC 150 [1998] 4 IR 302, [1998] ELR 77; *Meskell v CIÉ* [1973] IR 121.

21. And in this respect it is worth noting the comments of the Supreme Court in *Sheehy v Ryan* [2008] IESC 14, [2008] 4 IR 258, that 'every contract of employment is different and [there-fore] caselaw is of marginal assistance only in construing the terms of any given contract'. See *Fennelly v Assicurazioni Generali SpA* [1985] ILTR 73; *Courtenay v Radio 2000 Ltd.* [1997] ELR 198; *Maher v Irish Permanent Plc* [1997] IEHC 150, [1998] 4 IR 302, [1998] ELR 77; *Lonergan v Salter-Townshend* [1999] IEHC 205, [2000] ELR 15; *O'Donnell v Chief State Solicitor* [2003] ELR 268; *Cahill v Dublin City University* [2007] IEHC 20, [2007] ELR 113; *Irani v Southampton and South West Hampshire Health Authority* [1985] ICR 590, [1985] IRLR 203; *Anderson v Pringle of Scotland* [1998] IRLR 64.

22. See, for example, *O'Donnell v Chief State Solicitor* [2003] ELR 268; *Lonergan v Salter-Townshend* [1999] IEHC 205, [2000] ELR 15.

2.3 Normal Workplace Practices should not be Restrained

[24-10] As a further guiding principle it may be said that the courts are not in favour of relief of this kind being used to prevent the normal operation of the agreed employment contract and of employment law generally. So, for example, it has been held that the courts should be slow to grant injunctive relief in respect of an ongoing disciplinary process,[23] or indeed an investigation process (including possibly a process whereby the employee is suspended on full pay[24]) occurring prior to any disciplinary proceedings.[25]

2.4. Mere Dismissal of an Employee is not a Reason to Grant Injunctive Relief

[24-11] Finally, it is absolutely clear that the courts will never grant injunctive relief simply because someone has been dismissed and in the absence either of a procedural defect in the manner of his or her dismissal or some other breach of a term of his or her employment contract. The logic of the courts in this regard would appear to be threefold, namely:

- First, where someone is unfairly dismissed (for the purposes of unfair dismissals legislation, and thus including being unfairly selected for redundancy[26]) then [s]he has a statutory remedy, and should proceed to seek relief under such legislation. Nor can such persons raise the issue of *unfair* dismissal outside of the prescribed statutory fora.[27] In this respect the decision of the High Court in *Nolan v EMO Oil Services*[28] is significant. Here the High Court was faced with an applicant who claimed that he had been unfairly selected for redundancy and sought

---

23. *Carroll v Bus Átha Cliath* [2005] 4 IR 184, [2005] ELR 192; *Becker v Board of Management of St Dominic's Secondary School* [2005] IEHC 169.

24. *Morgan v The Provost, Fellows and Scholars of Trinity College Dublin* [2003] 3 IR 157; *O'Brien v AON Insurance Managers (Dublin) Ltd.* [2005] IEHC 3. In *Yap v Children's University Hospital Temple Street* [2006] IEHC 308, [2006] 4 IR 298, Clarke J accepted that it might be possible for the courts to intervene in a situation where an employer was purporting to suspend an employee *without* pay pending an investigation and in light of the seriousness of what was alleged against the employee.

25. *Foley v Aer Lingus* [2001] 3 IR 158, [2001] ELR 193; *O'Brien v Avon Insurance Managers (Dublin) Ltd.* [2005] IEHC 3.

26. See *Nolan v EMO Oil Services Ltd.* [2009] IEHC 15.

27. *Parsons v Iarnród Éireann* [1997] 2 IR 523. Redmond, *Dismissal Law in Ireland* (2nd ed., Tottel Publishing, 2007), at para.10.74 quotes the view of Tom Mallon BL that one of the real drawbacks of this rule is that there can be a considerable waiting period even for EAT hearings to occur and for the matter to be resolved, and that the absence of any interlocutory relief (and it should be remembered that the EAT is not permitted to grant such interlocutory relief) may prove disastrous for an employee who has been dismissed without pay. See also Horan, 'Employment Injunctions: Current Status and Future Developments', 1 *Employment Law Review* (2006), 8.

28. [2009] IEHC 15, [2009] 20 ELR 122.

interlocutory relief restraining implementation of this decision by the employer. Laffoy J, noting that the question of whether a redundancy was valid was one for the Employment Appeals Tribunal, appeared to conclude that the High Court on this basis had no jurisdiction to consider any aspects of that question. The message, therefore, from an applicant's perspective would appear to be that if his or her ultimate claim is one over which the High Court does not have jurisdiction, then it will be most unlikely that it will grant interlocutory relief in respect of the matter.

- Secondly, where someone is wrongly dismissed (at common law) then, as is discussed in Chapter 19 this merely means that [s]he was not given appropriate notice of dismissal, in that there is no restriction at common law on an employer's ability to dismiss an employee (even, it would seem, where the job is described as being permanent[29]) with or without cause provided that reasonable notice has been given.[30] Even if it *is* made out, moreover, a claim for *wrongful* dismissal will only ever lead to an award of damages (for failure to give notice). Hence where an employee is dismissed *with* notice then there is no wrongful dismissal no matter how malicious the motives behind such dismissal,[31] and where there *is* a question as to whether the requisite notice has been given then there is a strong argument that if any wrong has been done to the employee, then damages will by definition be an adequate remedy and hence injunctive relief should not be granted.[32]

- Finally, it is clear that a dismissal that is in accordance with both the employee's contract of employment and in line with statutory notice requirements cannot violate any implied term of mutual trust and confidence within the employee's contract of employment.[33]

---

29. *Sheehy v Ryan* [2008] IESC 14, [2008] 4 IR 258; *Walsh v Dublin Health Board* 98 ILTR 82; *Dooley v Great Southern Hotel* [2001] IEHC 115, [2001] ELR 340. But see also *Grehan v NE Health Board* [1989] IR 422.

30. *Sheehy v Ryan* [2008] IESC 14, [2008] 4 IR 258; *Maha Lingham v Health Service Executive* [2006] ELR 137; *Nolan v EMO Oil Services Ltd.* [2008] IEHC 15, [2009] ELR 122. In *Cahill v Dublin City University* [2007] ELR 113 it was held that whereas no such restriction existed in principle at common law, nonetheless the respondent university was constrained in its dealings with the plaintiff lecturer by reason of the terms of the Universities Act 1997.

31. *Sheehy v Ryan* [2004] 15 ELR 87 (HC), [2008] IESC 14 (SC), [2008] 4 IR 258 (SC); *Orr v Zomax Ltd.* [2004] IEHC 47, [2004] 1 IR 486, [2004] ELR 161; *McGrath v Trintech Technologies* [2005] 4 IR 382, [2005] 16 ELR 49.

32. *Philpott v Ogilvy & Mather Ltd.* [2000] 3 IR 206 [2000] ELR 225. For criticism of the logic used in this case, see Redmond at 10.63.

33. *Maha Lingham v Health Service Executive* [2006] ELR 137; *Nolan v EMO Oil Services Ltd.* [2008] IEHC 15, [2009] ELR 122.

[24–12]   Naturally, therefore, from the perspective of someone seeking an interlocutory injunction to restrain his or her dismissal, it is necessary to claim that what has occurred is not simply a dismissal *per se* or even a wrongful or unfair dismissal, but that the manner of his or her dismissal either involved a substantive breach of his or her contract of employment, or else that there were procedural flaws in the lead up to that dismissal. Naturally also, the employer in such a case will seek to claim that what was at issue was a dismissal *simpliciter* rather than one generating such procedural concerns. Alternatively, the applicant in such circumstances may say that [s]he was dismissed for disciplinary reasons but without any fair hearing having taken place, whereas the employer in response may say either that there *was* a fair disciplinary process or, even more clinically, may say that the employee's employment was terminated on a whim and that [s]he was not dismissed for disciplinary reasons – and will thus seek to claim that there was no contractual difficulty with what occurred. Hence the manner in which this area of the law has developed provides an incentive to employers who are faced with an employee whom they regard as having contravened disciplinary rules, to hold no investigation and no disciplinary proceedings, but rather simply to dismiss the employee for no stated reason having given him or her the notice to which [s]he was entitled.

3. The Interlocutory Injunction

[24–13]   In practical terms, the most significant type of injunction in employment cases has been the interlocutory injunction[34] – a short-term remedy directing that certain orders be obeyed pending the trial of the action.[35] In many cases, the practice is that the grant or refusal of such interlocutory orders can have the effect of ending the matter, in that, particularly where the relationship of mutual trust and confidence between the parties has broken down, there will generally be no long-term future to the employment relationship, hence what can be secured on a short-term basis will often dictate at least in part the terms on which the employment relationship will be determined in the long run. Indeed because of this the issuing of proceedings for interlocutory relief can often be seen as a tactical mechanism aimed at securing some form of settlement on behalf of an employee who has been disciplined or dismissed[36] – and it should be pointed out that the vast

---

34.   In addition, it is, of course, possible to obtain an interim injunction on an *ex parte* basis as a very short-term remedy and pending the application for interlocutory relief.
35.   See Delany, *Equity and the Law of Trusts in Ireland* (4th ed., Thomson Round Hall, 2007), at p.557. See also Redmond, *Dismissal Law in Ireland* (2nd ed., Tottel Publishing, 2007), at para.10.09 for consideration of the potential for use of a *quia timet* injunction in employment cases. See also *Garrahy v Bord na gCon* [2002] IEHC 147, [2002] 3 IR 566, [2003] ELR 274.
36.   Indeed because proceedings for interlocutory relief of this kind are brought by way of notice of motion and grounding affidavit, the applicant may well seek to make as many damaging and embarrassing allegations as possible against the employer in his or her grounding affidavit in the knowledge that when they are read in court they, and fair and accurate reporting

majority of such applications do not go to trial. In other circumstances, however, an interlocutory injunction may be sought in circumstances where an employee may be looking for a different and longer-lasting benefit as a result of his or her application – for example where [s]he has been dismissed for disciplinary reasons but where there has not been an appropriate disciplinary hearing and where [s]he believes that such an appropriate hearing would, in fact, lead to a situation where [s]he would be exonerated.

3.1. General Principles Governing the Grant of Interlocutory Injunctions

Unsurprisingly, the principles used to answer the question of whether what is [24–14] colloquially known as an *employment injunction* should be granted derive from the more general rules governing the grant of interlocutory injunctions in Ireland and it is to these rules that we now turn.

As is well known, these rules are derived from the case *Campus Oil v Minister for* [24–15] *Industry and Commerce (No. 2)*,[37] which was itself largely based on the opinion of the House of Lords in *American Cynamid Limited v Ethicon*.[38] The net effect of these principles is that in order for interlocutory injunctive relief to be granted the plaintiff must show that there is a fair *bona fide* question to be tried and, when this has been established, the court should consider whether the balance of convenience supports the granting of the relief or not.[39] Among the various factors to be considered in assessing where the balance of convenience lies in any case the question of whether damages would be an adequate alternative remedy for the plaintiff is a primary consideration,[40] with relief only being granted where this is not the case. Indeed it has been suggested that, in fact, it is only where damages would *not* be an adequate remedy, that the court should even begin to analyse the question of whether the balance of convenience favours the grant of the relief or not.[41] Beyond this, however, the drawing of the balance of convenience in a given

---

of them, will be privileged as far as defamation law is concerned, and hence an employer might prefer to settle the case than to risk the possibility of such embarrassing allegations against him or her being publicly reported.

37. [1983] IR 88, [1984] ILRM 47.
38. [1975] AC 396.
39. For analysis, see Kirwan, '*Campus Oil* Turns Twenty-Five: Is There Much to Celebrate?', 15(1) *DULJ* (2008), 325.
40. *Garrahy v Bord na gCon* [2002] IEHC 147, [2002] 3 IR 566, [2003] ELR 274; *Ryanair Ltd. v Aer Rianta*, High Court (Kelly J), 25 January 2001. There is perhaps some uncertainty as to whether the issue of adequacy of damages is an aspect of the balance of convenience or whether it precedes the application of balance of convenience analysis, in the sense that, on occasion, courts have seemed to assess first whether damages would be an adequate remedy and if so have automatically refused the relief sought, and if not have only then proceeded to consider where the balance of convenience lies.
41. In *Garrahy v Bord na gCon* [2002] IEHC 147, [2002] 3 IR 566, [2003] ELR 274 the court said that the relevant issue was not whether damages would be an adequate remedy but rather whether there was a *doubt* as to whether damages would be an adequate remedy.

case will involve analysis of concerns of policy as well as of intuitive views of the justice of the matter in hand.

[24–16] Hence, in the context of the 'employment injunction' it is necessary in the first instance for the applicant employee or employer to show that there is a fair question to be tried – which, as mentioned above, will generally only be the case if what occurred involved some possible breach – substantive or procedural – of the relevant contract of employment. Where this has been done, it will be necessary to show that the balance of convenience favours the granting of the relief and that damages at trial will not be an adequate remedy should the interlocutory relief not be granted. So, for example, where an employee is seeking payment of salary pending the hearing of the action, [s]he will tend to point to the disastrous consequences for him or her of the *non-payment* of that salary when set beside the relatively innocuous consequences for the employer should such payment be made, as indicating that the balance of convenience favours the grant of the relief sought. Finally, the applicant for such relief must make an undertaking as to damages – that is, an undertaking that if the relief is granted at an interlocutory or interim stage and if [s]he is unsuccessful at the full hearing of the action, [s]he will compensate the person against whom the interlocutory order was granted for any loss arising as a result.

[24–17] The application of these rules in the context of the various kinds of orders that can be sought will be considered shortly. Before this, however, two more specific aspects of these rules (as they apply in the context of an employment dispute) require more detailed consideration. The first is the now settled proposition that where the application is for mandatory as distinct from prohibitory relief the employee will need to show not merely that [s]he has a fair question to be tried but rather that [s]he has a *strong case*, and the second is the question of whether damages will inevitably be an adequate remedy in the case of an employee who is seeking payment of his or her wages pending the hearing of the action, but who has no realistic prospect of being reinstated thereafter (in other words for whom, realistically, the best possible result at trial is an award of damages).

3.1.1. *The Strong Case Needed to Ground an Application for Mandatory Relief*

[24–18] From an employment law perspective, a most important development in terms of the criteria for granting an interlocutory injunction occurred in the Supreme Court decision in *Maha Lingam v Health Service Executive*.[42] Here the court explicitly held that where *mandatory* as distinct from merely *prohibitory* relief was

---

42. [2006] ELR 137. This principle has been consistently applied in subsequent cases. See, for example, *Nolan v EMO Oil Services Ltd.* [2008] IEHC 15, [2009] ELR 122; *Turner v O'Reilly* [2008] IEHC 92; *Bergin v Galway Clinic Doughiska Ltd.* [2007] IEHC 386, [2008] 2 IR 205; *Naujoks v National Institute of Bioprocessing, Research and Training* [2006] IEHC 358, [2007] ELR 25; *Stoskus v Goode Concrete* [2007] IEHC 432.

being sought (that is, where an employer was being required to do something, as distinct from refraining from doing something), the risk of injustice being done to the defendant by way of the grant of the relief sought was increased.[43] Accordingly, in such circumstances the plaintiff would have to show not merely that there was a fair question to be tried but that in fact [s]he had a *strong case* that [s]he was likely to succeed at hearing.

Naturally this development ratchets up the standards of what is required of an [24–19] applicant in order for him or her to obtain the relief sought. As a result, it makes sense for applicants in cases of this kind to plead their claims as if they were seeking a prohibitory rather than a mandatory order even where, in essence, what is being sought is more properly to be construed as mandatory relief. So, for example, where an employee is in fact looking for a court order requiring his or her employer to continue paying, or indeed employing him or her (which order is inherently mandatory in nature), it would seem to make sense to phrase his or her claim as one requiring the employer to desist from operating as if the employee is not employed by him or her. Equally (and significantly) it would seem that the courts are becoming wise to such tactics, and are regarding such pleas as being 'essentially' mandatory if not mandatory on the precise words of the pleadings.[44] Thus in *Bergin v Galway Clinic Doughiska Ltd.*[45] Clarke J held that

> in any case in which an employee seeks to prevent a dismissal or a process leading to a dismissal…and in whatever terms the claim is couched, the employee concerned is seeking what is, in substance, a mandatory injunction which has the effect of necessarily continuing his contract of employment…In those circumstances it is necessary for the employee concerned to establish a strong case in order to obtain interlocutory relief.[46]

Moreover, it is surely arguable that this logic applies equally to cases where an [24–20] order is sought to require an employer to pay an employee his or her salary prior to the hearing, where an employee is seeking to restrain an employer from making a decision to dismiss him or her on foot of a disciplinary investigation,[47] and even where an order is sought requiring an employer to hold a disciplinary hearing in accordance with rules of fair procedures and natural and constitutional justice.

---

43. As Kirwan puts it, 'it is much harder to undo the consequences of a mandatory order than a prohibitory order after the trial of an action'. See Kirwan, '*Campus Oil* Turns Twenty-Five: Is There Much to Celebrate?', 15(1) *DULJ* (2008), 325 at 336 for analysis.
44. *Coffey v William Connolly and Sons Ltd.* [2007] IEHC 319; *Stoskus v Goode Concrete* [2007] IEHC 432.
45. [2007] IEHC 386, [2008] 2 IR 205, 216.
46. See also *Turner v O'Reilly* [2008] IEHC 92; *Coffey v William Connolly & Sons Ltd.* [2007] IEHC 319. See Kirwan, '*Campus Oil* Turns Twenty-Five: Is There Much to Celebrate?', 15(1) *DULJ* (2008), 325.
47. *Bergin v Galway Clinic Doughiska Ltd.* [2007] IEHC 386, [2008] 2 IR 205.

[24-21] This requirement – that where mandatory or essentially mandatory relief is being sought in employment injunction cases, the claimant must demonstrate a strong case that [s]he will succeed at trial – has been accepted in all relevant subsequent cases and may now be seen as a settled aspect of Irish law.[48] So, for example, in *Stoskus v Goode Concrete*[49] the plaintiff sought an interlocutory injunction to restrain his dismissal and to require that he be paid pending the trial of the action, on the basis that his employers had dismissed him following a disciplinary hearing at which he was permitted to have a union representative present, but was not permitted to be represented by a solicitor[50]. Irvine J accepted that the traditional test for interlocutory relief was to ask whether there was a serious question to be tried, but she also noted the recent developments such that where plaintiffs had sought mandatory relief in relation to an employment contract, the courts had increasingly required that the employee concerned must establish a strong case in order to obtain interlocutory relief.

[24-22] On behalf of the applicant it was submitted that the relief sought was not truly mandatory in nature given that it was seeking to restrain the defendants from ceasing to pay the plaintiff's salary pending the hearing of the action. Irvine J rejected this logic, however, noting that whereas the relief sought by the plaintiff was framed as prohibitory in nature, the plaintiff was in effect seeking mandatory relief as he was asking the court to require the defendant to perform an obligation (namely to pay his salary), which obligation only exists in the context of an ongoing contractual relationship between the parties. On this basis, the court concluded that the relief sought was mandatory in nature and therefore, that the onus of proof on the plaintiff at the interlocutory hearing was to establish that he had a strong case to make at the hearing of the action. The court further held that the applicant had failed to make out the strong case required because, whereas principles of natural and constitutional justice might indicate that a solicitor should be present at disciplinary hearings of this nature, on the other hand the fact that the plaintiff had signed a contract that appeared to involve him accepting that he would not be entitled to legal representation in disciplinary proceedings told against him strongly. In the opinion of the court, the plaintiff's claim was no more than merely stateable and had not reached the level of a strong case the recent cases demanded.

[24-23] The potential impact of this recent line of Supreme Court and High Court authority is enormous. To recap, the courts have concluded that where mandatory relief is being sought, the plaintiff must establish that [s]he has a strong case

---

48. *Kurt Naujoks v National Institute of Bioprocessing Research and Training Limited* [2006] IEHC 358, [2007] ELR 25; *Bergin v Galway Clinic Doughiska Limited* [2007] IEHC 386, [2008] 2 IR 205; *Coffey v William Connolly and Sons Ltd.* [2007] IEHC 319; *Stoskus v Goode Concrete* [2007] IEHC 432.
49. [2007] IEHC 432.
50. The question of whether and when an employee is entitled to be legally represented at a disciplinary hearing is considered in Chapter 18.

that [s]he will succeed at trial (and they have taken a relatively hard line on what constitutes a strong case in this sense), and they have also taken a strict view on what constitutes an application for mandatory relief, and have regarded various reliefs as mandatory even when they are pleaded as prohibitory.[51]

The net effect of these two factors would seem to be that of the four types of order [24–24] that can be sought in proceedings for an interlocutory injunction, at least two (the order requiring reinstatement, and the order restraining dismissal and requiring payment of salary) are mandatory in nature and hence will require that a strong case be shown by the applicant at the interlocutory stage. Moreover, it is arguable that where the employee is seeking to compel an employer to hold a disciplinary hearing, or to conduct such hearing in accordance with natural and constitutional justice, this is also an application for mandatory relief (although where a plaintiff has been disciplined without fair procedures it will presumably be relatively easy to establish a strong case at the interlocutory stage). In other words the only contexts in which an interlocutory injunction is genuinely prohibitory in nature, and hence where a strong case would *not* need to be established, is where an employee is seeking to prevent the employer from appointing a replacement for him or her or where an employer is seeking to enforce a negative covenant in the employee's contract.

These changes may mean that the employment injunction becomes a less signifi- [24–25] cant weapon for employees than had previously been the case.[52] Traditionally, after all, the law on interlocutory injunctions arguably favoured the applicant in employment disputes, and particularly where [s]he was seeking payment of salary pending the trial of the action given that all [s]he had to do was to prove that [s]he had a fair question to be tried, after which the balance of convenience element of the test for an interlocutory injunction would generally be found to favour him or her – particularly if [s]he claimed that [s]he would be left financially destitute as a result of non-payment of his or her salary. Now, however, the pendulum appears to have swung the other way, and the law appears to favour the defendant in such a case in that it may be increasingly difficult for an applicant to prove a strong case and thus to take the matter to the balance of convenience stage of the test.

3.1.2. Adequacy of Damages Where an Employee Has No Realistic Prospect of Reinstatement

There is conflicting authority on the question of whether interlocutory relief [24–26] should be refused in circumstances where there has been an irretrievable break-down in the relationship of mutual trust and confidence between the parties, in

---

51. The point is worth making that at the interlocutory stage the employee's task of proving a strong case (largely if not completely on the terms of his or her grounding affidavit) will be an onerous one in any context and one which may in fact be impossible if the case in question involves highly complex questions of law and fact that can only be resolved at trial

52. For the opposite view see Mallon, 'Recent Developments in Employment Injunctions', 5(2) *IELJ* (2008), 48.

that in such circumstances there is no reasonable prospect of the employee being re-employed, and hence, should [s]he succeed at trial the best that [s]he could hope for would be an award of damages, which in turn means that an award of damages is by definition an adequate remedy for such an applicant. This was the view taken by the High Court in *Orr v Zomax*,[53] where Carroll J, having concluded that there was no fair question to be tried that would justify an inter-locutory injunction being granted in the case, further concluded that, even if such a fair question *was* deemed to exist, in the circumstances an award of damages at the trial if the applicant was successful would still be an adequate remedy. Thus she held that

> In the event that I am wrong to hold that this issue is not a fair issue…I will go on to consider whether damages are an adequate remedy. In my opinion they are. The plaintiff cannot seriously hope that he will be re-instated in employment where the defendants are unwilling to take him back and have no place for him. Therefore his remedy if he is successful, is in damages.[54]

[24–27] On the other hand, in *Doyle v Grangeford Precase Concrete Ltd.*,[55] an interlocu-tory order restraining dismissal and directing that the employee's salary continue to be paid was granted despite the fact that there was no realistic prospect an order of reinstatement would be made at the trial of the action because of the breakdown in the relationship of mutual trust and confidence between the parties. Commenting on this case, Professor Delany says that:

> it is the fact that damages would not be an adequate remedy pending trial that is the crucial factor and provided that the plaintiff gives an undertaking in damages as he will invariably be required to do, orders of this nature [that is a *Fennelly* order] will be fairly readily granted.[56]

[24–28] An alternative way of putting matters is that, whereas the key question is whether the award of damages at the trial of the action would be an adequate remedy having regard to any wrong the applicant has suffered and for which [s]he is claiming, nonetheless in circumstances where non-payment of his or her salary pending the trial of the action would lead to serious deprivation, a subsequent award of damages at what may be a considerably later date would not adequately compensate him or her for the suffering undergone in the interim period.[57]

---

53. *Orr v Zomax Ltd.* [2004] IEHC 47, [2004] 1 IR 486, [2004] ELR 161.

54. [2004] 1 IR 486, 493-494.

55. [1998] ELR 260.

56. Delany, 'Cases and Comment: Employment Injunctions: The Role of Mutual Trust and Confidence', 13(1) *DULJ* (2006), 363.

57. This is the essence of the conclusion reached by Kelly J in *Mullarkey v Irish National Stud Co Ltd.* [2004] IEHC 116.

On the other side of the coin, however, it may perhaps be mentioned in passing [24–29] that the undertaking of damages in the context certainly of an application for an order directing that an employee be paid pending the hearing of the action will often be something of a fallacy. After all, if it is necessary to order that an employee be paid his or her salary pending trial as an alternative to serious financial hardship, it is scarcely realistic to expect that the undertaking as to damages will be met should [s]he lose the substantive action. Indeed this reality spawns a further reality, namely that in cases of this nature, the application for interlocutory relief (let alone the grant of such relief), will often, in fact, be little more than the basis for settlement negotiations between the parties.

4. Types of Injunctive Orders in Employment Cases

These, then, are the basic principles that have been developed by the courts in [24–30] respect of injunctions (and in particular interlocutory injunctions) in the context of the employment relationship. On the other hand, it should be noted that the precise manner in which these principles are applied in any case will depend in large measure on the type of order that is being sought. So, for example, very different concerns will arise where an employee is seeking to be reinstated to the job from which [s]he has been dismissed than will apply where [s]he is simply seeking to ensure that any disciplinary procedures that apply against him or her are conducted in accordance with basic standards of fair procedures and natural and constitutional justice. Finally in this chapter, therefore, we look at the four conceptually different types of order that may be sought where an employee applies for an injunction against his or her employer, and we assess how the various principles referred to above have played out in these different contexts. We do not, however, consider the type of situation where it is the employer who is seeking to enforce a negative covenant in a contract of employment against an employee, both because of the absence of any case law in this area and because it is arguably the case that the specific policy concerns that have informed the development of principles in the area of the employment injunction simply do not have application in this context.

4.1. An Order of Reinstatement

The first kind of order that may be sought, then, is an order reinstating an employee [24–31] who has been dismissed to his or her former position. This type of order is particularly difficult to obtain (on a permanent or an interlocutory basis) in that all of the traditional arguments against granting employment injunctions (opposition to enforcing specific performance of a contract of services, opposition to making unworkable orders, and opposition to requiring people to work together where the relationship of mutual trust and confidence between them has broken down) militate against the granting of such orders.[58] It is, after all, virtually inconceivable that an order of this kind could be sought other than in a context where an employer is being asked to reemploy somebody with whom [s]he clearly does not want to work. Indeed the level of opposition to the grant of such orders means that in reality an employee who has been dismissed and who wishes to obtain injunctive relief should be advised as a matter of course to apply not for an order of reinstatement but rather for an order requiring his or her employer not to proceed with his or her dismissal.

[24–32] It is in the context of an application for reinstatement, therefore, that the principles that have developed regarding the significance of the presence or absence of an ongoing relationship of mutual trust and confidence in the context of an application for injunctive relief have particular application.[59] To repeat points that were made earlier, the general rule remains that 'it is undesirable to force individuals to work together where a relationship of trust and confidence no longer exists between them'.[60] The courts (and especially the English courts[61]) remain extremely reluctant to grant injunctive relief where it would be unworkable and an order of reinstatement will clearly not be workable where there is a breakdown in the relationship between employer and employee.[62] As Professor Delany puts it

---

58. So, for example, in *Cahill v Dublin City University* [2007] IEHC 20, [2007] ELR 113, the High Court had originally felt prepared to make an order of reinstatement in favour of an academic who had had his contract of employment terminated in a manner that violated the terms of the Education Act 1997, on the basis that no compelling arguments had been proffered as to why he could not continue with his employment, but by the time the matter came to full hearing the court concluded that 'much water has passed under the bridge' and hence that it would no longer be possible for the applicant to be restored to his former position and as such, the only appropriate order would be one declaring that he remained in office and was entitled to his salary but not reinstating him in any practical way.

59. *Powell v London Borough of Brent* [1987] IRLR 466. See Redmond, *Dismissal Law in Ireland* (2nd ed., Tottel Publishing, 2007), at para.10.19.

60. Delany, *Equity and The Law of Trusts in Ireland* (4th ed., Thomson Round Hall, 2007), at p.557 and, by the same author, 'Case and Comment: Employment Injunctions: The Role of Mutual Trust and Confidence', 13(1) *DULJ* (2006), 363. See *Hill v CA Parsons Ltd.* [1972] ch.305; *Chappell v Times Newspapers* [1975] 1 WLR 482, [1975] ICR 145; *Sanders v Earnest A Neale* [1974] ICR 565; *Garrahy v Bord na gCon* [2002] IEHC 147, [2002] 3 IR 566, [2003] ELR 274; *Evans v IRFB Services (Ireland) Limited* [2005] IEHC 107, [2005] 2 ILRM 358; *Warren v Mendy* [1989] 1 WLR 853, [1989] ICR 525, [1989] 3 All ER 103, [1989] IRLR 210.

61. See Mallon, 'Recent Developments in Employment Injunctions', 5(2) *IELJ* (2008), 48 for the view that the Irish courts have shown themselves to be considerably more likely to grant interlocutory relief than their English counterparts in cases where there has been a breakdown in the relationship of mutual trust and confidence between the parties.

62. *Fennelly v Assicurazioni Generali SpA* [1985] ILT 73; *Carroll v Dublin Bus* [2005] 4 IR 184, [2005] ELR 192; *Powell v London Borough of Brent* [1987] IRLR 466; *Hughes v London Borough of Southwark* [1988] IRLR 72. Equally in *Robb v London Borough of Hammersmith and Fulham* [1991] ICR 514, [1991] IRLR 72 the court held that there was no blanket rule that an interlocutory injunction could not be granted where there was a breakdown in the

The reality that in the absence of a continuing relationship of mutual trust and confidence there is no basis on which to make an order requiring parties to continue to work together even on a temporary basis has been generally accepted.[63]

It is arguable, however, that the concept of mutual trust and confidence *simpliciter* has received an excessive amount of attention where employment injunctions are concerned. Thus it has been suggested that because of the limitations of these rules, and because the courts will only be prepared to grant an order of reinstatement where mutual trust and confidence is found to exist as between the parties,[64] the English courts have, on occasion, (and in the interests of a particular view of justice that favours reinstatement of the employee) strained logic in finding that mutual trust and confidence continued to exist in cases where it patently did not.[65] The risk is that a general principle has emerged that injunctive relief should not be granted in any case where there is no mutual trust and confidence *inter partes*. But, as we have seen, the concept is only relevant in the context of an application for an order of reinstatement, and not where what is sought is an order requiring that a disciplinary process be held in accordance with natural and constitutional justice,[66] or an order requiring that the employee be paid pending the trial of the action, without necessarily being reinstated.[67]

[24–33]

---

relationship of mutual trust and confidence. See also Redmond at 10.19–10.20 and especially at 10.22 for the view that the significance of the absence of mutual trust and confidence goes to the question of whether, in the circumstances, the order sought would be workable.

63. Delany, 'Case and Comment: Employment Injunctions: The Role of Mutual Trust and Confidence', 13(1) *DULJ* (2006), 363, 370.

64. *Hill v CA Parsons & Co Ltd.* [1972] Ch. 305; *Hughes v London Borough of Southwark* [1988] IRLR 55.

65. See Delany, 'Case and Comment: Employment Injunctions: The Role of Mutual Trust and Confidence', 13(1) *DULJ* (2006), 363, referring to *Irani v Southampton and South-West Hampshire Health Authority* [1985] ICR 590, [1985] IRLR 203 and *Powell v London Borough of Brent* [1987] IRLR 466.

66. *Robb v Hammersmith and Fulham London Borough Council* [1991] ICR 514, [1991] IRLR 72; *Jones v Lee* [1980] ICR 310.

67. Whereas in *Fennelly v Assicurazioni Generali SpA* [1985] ILT 73 the court found that there *was* a relationship of mutual trust and confidence between the parties, as we shall see, such a relationship has not been seen in subsequent cases as a prerequisite to a grant of a *Fennelly* order. On the other hand, in *Hennessy v St Gerard's School Trust* [2003] IEHC 49, and *O'Malley v Aravon School Ltd.*, High Court, 13 August 1997, the court held that the extent to which the mutual trust and confidence between the parties had been fractured by events meant that no interlocutory relief should be granted, as any harm suffered could be assessed in calculating damages when the matter came to trial. Moreover, as we shall see, in *Stoskus v Goode Concrete* [2007] IEHC 432, Irvine J took the view that because the relationship between employee and employer had been so damaged that there was no possibility of it being resuscitated, the balance of convenience militated *against* granting the relief sought (an order directing payment of salary pending the trial of the actions) given that from the employee's perspective this would simply mean postponing the inevitable moment at which he would have to seek employment elsewhere.

To this end, as has been mentioned, the preferable approach is to ask whether the relief sought is workable and to grant such relief only where this is the case. Naturally where there is no mutual trust and confidence between the parties then an order requiring that an employee who has been dismissed be temporarily reinstated will in most, if not all, circumstances be unworkable.[68]

[24–34] Finally, there is authority for the proposition that a breakdown in the relationship of mutual trust and confidence will be less of an obstacle to an order of reinstatement where the employee has been suspended for an excessively long time rather than dismissed.[69] On the other hand, it has been suggested more generally that the courts are far less likely to grant relief where what it is sought to injunct is conduct short of dismissal of an employee.[70]

[24–35] In conclusion however, it is now virtually axiomatic that injunctive relief will not be granted to require a dismissed employee to be restored to his or her former position.[71] Moreover, following the decision in *Parsons v Iarnród Éireann*[72] it would seem both that the courts are not supportive of an application for interlocutory relief which is, in effect, an attempt to obtain relief for unfair dismissal,[73] and also, as has been mentioned earlier, that where a claimant has pursued the injunction route [s]he may thereby be precluded from taking an unfair dismissals action.

---

68. *Robb v Hammersmith and Fulham London Borough Council* [1991] ICR 514, [1991] IRLR 72.
69. *Martin v Nationwide Building Society* [1999] IEHC 163, [2001] 1 IR 228. But see also *Joyce v Health Service Executive* [2005] IEHC 174. For analysis, see Delany, 'Cases and Comment: Employment Injunctions: The Role of Mutual Trust and Confidence', 13(1) *DULJ* (2006), 363.
70. See Mallon, 'Recent Developments in Employment Injunctions', 5(2) *IELJ* (2008), 48 referring to decisions such as *Foley v Aer Lingus* [2001] 3 IR 158, [2001] ELR 193; *Morgan v Trinity College Dublin* [2003] 3 IR 158; *Becker v Board of Management of St Dominic's School* [2006] IEHC 130.
71. *Cassidy v Shannon Heritage and Others* [1999] IEHC 245, [2000] ELR 248; *Maher v Irish Permanent Plc* [1997] IEHC 150, [1988] IR 302; *Carroll v Bus Átha Cliath* [2005] 4 IR 184, [2005] ELR 192; *Cahill v Dublin City University* [2007] IEHC 20, [2007] ELR 113. In this last case Clarke J concluded that whereas, in light of the demands of academic freedom and the desirability of ensuring that an academic office holder had his entitlements maintained in accordance with the Education Act of 1997, he would *lean* in favour of granting an order that restored the plaintiff to his former position, nonetheless he would not grant the order in question because of difficulties that had arisen between the parties that made such a step effectively impossible. Generally, see Mallon, 'Recent Developments in Employment Injunctions', 5(2) *IELJ* (2008), 48. In *Carroll v Bus Átha Cliath* [2005] 4 IR 184, [2005] ELR 192, Clarke J said that an order restoring an employee to a former position should only be granted 'where it was clear that no other difficulties could reasonably be expected to arise by virtue of the making of the order', and naturally this will never be the case where there is any kind of a breakdown in the relationship of mutual trust and confidence between the parties – which will almost inevitably exist if the need to seek interlocutory relief arises in the first instance.
72. [1997] 2 IR 523.
73. *Orr v Zomax Ltd.* [2004] IEHC 47, [2004] 1 IR 486, [2004] ELR 161.

4.2. The '*Fennelly* Order'

The more usual application from an employee's standpoint therefore (and one [24–36] which is far more likely to be successful) is for an order which does not require the reinstatement of an employee who has been dismissed, but instead requires that his or her employer not proceed with his or her dismissal. From the employer's perspective, such an order will have the effect of preventing him or her from appointing someone else to the employee's position, and equally importantly will mean that the employee must be paid pending the hearing of the action. From the employee's perspective, it will typically entail an obligation that [s]he give an undertaking that [s]he would be available for such work as is in accordance with his or her contract of employment and that the employer may require of him or her.[74] Naturally, this kind of undertaking is necessarily made in the knowledge that it is highly unlikely (and not in the interest of both parties as well as of the broader community within the relevant place of employment[75]) that the employee will be called in to work in such a manner.[76] On the other hand, without such an undertaking the court will not be able to make an order restraining dismissal. Thus in *Carroll v Bus Átha Cliath*[77] one of the reasons why an application for interlocutory relief of this kind was refused was that the applicant (owing to the health problems that were at the root of his difficulties with his employer) would not have been available to work as and when he was required by his employer.[78] Finally, and because of the serious unlikelihood that the employee *will* be called in to work with his or her employer, such an order may be made notwithstanding the breakdown in mutual trust and confidence between the parties, nor does such a breakdown affect the workability of the order in question.[79]

Alternatively, the employee's application may simply be for an order requiring the [24–37] employer to pay his or her salary pending the hearing of the action (or possibly

---

74. *Moore v Xnet Information Services Ltd.* [2002] IEHC 6, [2002] 4 IR 362, [2002] 2 ILRM 278, [2002] ELR 65; *Courtenay v Radio 2000 Ltd.* [1997] ELR 198. See McDermott, '*Carroll v Bus Átha Cliath:* Strengthening the Right to an Employment Injunction', 5 *Employment Law Review* (2006), 104, and Delany, 'Case and Comment: Employment Injunctions: The Role of Mutual Trust and Confidence', 13(1) *DULJ* (2006), 363. See, for example, *Carroll v Bus Átha Cliath* [2005] 4 IR 184, [2005] ELR 192 as an example of a case where this kind of order was not made on the basis that, owing to the applicant's ill health, there was no work that he could make himself available for, nor could it be argued that there was either an established custom and practice within the business or that it was a term of the employee's contract that he would be permitted to return to work and be provided with alternative employment that he could carry out in his current state of health.
75. *Harte v Kelly* [1997] IEHC 124, [1997] ELR 125.
76. *Fennelly v Assicurazioni Generali SpA* [1985] ILTR 73.
77. [2005] 4 IR 184, [2005] ELR 192.
78. See Delany, 'Case and Comment: Employment Injunctions: The Role of Mutual Trust and Confidence', 13(1) *DULJ* (2006), 363.
79. See, for example, *Shortt v Data Packaging* [1994] ELR 251; *Courtenay v Radio 2000 Ltd.* [1997] ELR 198.

to pay sick pay pending the trial of the action).[80] As far as this type of case is concerned, the approach taken in a number of judgments has been to say that where an employee would be left in a financially precarious position pending trial (and provided that [s]he can show either a stateable or a strong case of success at trial – whichever is applicable on the principles discussed above) then the balance of convenience will favour the employee and interlocutory relief should be granted.[81] After all, for an employee in such a position, any award of damages that might be made to him or her some six months to one year after the application for interlocutory relief (should [s]he be successful at trial) will not remedy the problems that [s]he would face in the intervening period,[82] nor, in the usual scheme of things, would the risk to the employer arising from having to pay the employee's wages be at the same level of intensity as would the threat to the impoverished employee who was being denied his or her income.[83] This type of order has colloquially come to be known as a '*Fennelly* order' and has become one which, since the original decision in *Fennelly v Assicurazioni Generali SpA*[84], has been made in an expanding number of circumstances.[85]

[24–38] It appears that, in drawing the balance of convenience in the context of applications of this kind, the judicial perception of the injustice of a situation where an employee who may have a stateable case is being left without any income pending the hearing of the action will be enormously significant. Thus in *Courtney v Radio 2000*[86] the court appeared to link what it intuitively saw as the justice of the matter (that is, that it would be unjust *not* to ensure that the employee was paid pending a hearing of the matter) with the way in which the court should assess the balance of convenience in the case. Similarly, in *Fennelly v Assicurazioni Generali SpA*,[87]

---

80. *Mullarkey v Irish National Stud Company Ltd.* [2004] IEHC 116, [2004] ELR 172.

81. For analysis, see Kirwan, '*Campus Oil* Turns Twenty-Five: Is There Much to Celebrate?', 15(1) *DULJ* (2008), 325.

82. For suggestion that the reason why the employment injunction has developed is to protect employees from the potentially disastrous financial consequences of being dismissed, see Horan, 'Employment Injunction: Current Status and Future Developments', 1 *Employment Law Review* (2006), 8.

83. It is possible that in light of the economically difficult situation for businesses in Ireland at the time of writing, this balance may need to be recalibrated and that there may be an increasing number of situations where the long term cost to the employer of paying the employee's salary pending the hearing of the action will be greater than the long-term cost to the employee (who can, of course, claim social welfare) should [s]he not be paid.

84. [1985] ILTR 73.

85. For comment, see *Orr v Zomax Ltd.* [2004] IEHC 47, [2004] 1 IR 486, [2004] ELR 161. See also *GEE v Irish Times* [2001] ELR 249. In *Yap v Children's University Hospital Temple Street* [2006] IEHC 308, [2006] 4 IR 298, however, Clarke J suggested that there were a 'very limited [number] of cases where it is appropriate or possible for the court to direct that there be payment pending trial'.

86. [1997] ELR 198.

87. [1985] 3 ILTR 73.

the court, in deciding to grant the relief sought, was clearly and significantly influenced by the plaintiffs' claim that it would be financially disastrous for them if the relief sought was not granted.[88] Moreover, it may be suggested that this logic is particularly apposite where the employee faces a lengthy delay before any hearing into the matter[89] and indeed it is worth noting that, in a number of cases where an order of this kind was refused, the court *did* conclude that the most appropriate course of action was to have an early trial of the matter.[90]

The flexibility of this approach, whereby the question of balance of convenience [24–39] is linked with intuitive views of the justice of the matter, has meant that whereas originally such orders were only made in cases where the plaintiff would be destitute if no such relief was granted,[91] in later cases they have been granted even where this would not be the case but where the situation was financially difficult for the employee.[92] On the other hand, it should be pointed out that in all the cases where relief *was* granted on the basis of the financial risk to the plaintiff, there plainly *were* serious questions to be tried, and the plaintiffs tended to be highly paid executives who would be likely to lose a lot of money between the date of the application for the interlocutory relief and the date of trial.[93]

From the employer's perspective, it may be argued that, in assessing the financial [24–40] aspects of the situation for balance of convenience purposes, the courts do not, as a generality, attach sufficient significance to the reality that, should the relevant interlocutory relief be granted, and should the applicant *lose* at trial, it will generally be very difficult for the defendant to rely on the applicant's undertaking as to damages in order to recover the money already paid in salary let alone any more general costs that had been incurred by him or her.[94] Moreover, in the currently straitened economic climate for businesses in Ireland, it is arguable that the automatic conclusion that it is the employee who will suffer more if his or her salary is *not* paid than will the employer if the salary *is* paid, no longer holds. On the other hand, as far as balance of convenience analysis goes, it is worth noting that beyond money, there are other factors (the employee's reputation or his sense of self-confidence or self worth, for example) that may be under threat as a result of the actions

---

88. See also *Harte v Kelly* [1997] IEHC 124, [1997] ELR 125; *Courtenay v Radio 2000* [1997] ELR 198.
89. *O'Donnell v Chief State Solicitor* [2003] ELR 268. See Horan, 'Employment Injunctions: Current Status and Future Developments', 1 *Employment Law Review* (2006), 8.
90. See, for example, *Orr v Zomax Ltd.* [2004] IEHC 47, [2004] 1 IR 486, [2004] ELR 161.
91. *Fennelly v Assicurazioni Generali SpA* (1985) 3 ILTR 73; *Shortt v Data Packaging* [1994] ELR 251.
92. *Phelan v BIC (Ireland) Ltd.* [1997] ELR 208; *Harte v Kelly* [1997] IEHC 124, [1997] ELR 125; *Boland v Phoenix Shannon Plc* [1997] IEHC 63, [1997] ELR 113.
93. Generally, see Redmond, *Dismissal Law in Ireland* (2nd ed., Tottel Publishing, 2007), at para.10.07.
94. An exception to this is the decision of the High Court in *Orr v Zomax Ltd.* [2004] IEHC 47, [2004] 1 IR 486, [2004] 15 ELR 161.

of the employer, which the employee is seeking to injunct and regarding which the employer has no similar concerns.[95]

[24–41] It is therefore arguable that the courts have been overly prone to conclude that, as far as balance of convenience is concerned, the respective balance of interests of employer and employee will all but inevitably mean that (where there is a stateable case) an employee should be paid his or her salary pending the hearing of the action, if [s]he would otherwise suffer financial difficulty in this period. In this respect, the decision of Irvine J in *Stoskus v Goode Concrete*[96] is again instructive. Here counsel for the plaintiff had admitted during the course of the proceedings that his client did not want to return to work, nor was there any possibility that he would do so. In other words, the relief sought was essentially aimed at securing payment of his salary until trial, after which, irrespective of the result at trial, he would not return to work. As we have seen, this fact pattern is arguably the norm where the relationship between employer and employee has reached the point where one is taking a High Court action seeking injunctive relief against the other. In previous cases, it is arguable that the balance of convenience analysis undertaken by the court (as between the allegedly impoverished employee and the allegedly affluent company) would generally favour the employee. In *Stoskus v Goode Concrete*, however, Irvine J took what is arguably a radical if holistically sensible approach to this issue.

[24–42] She noted that there was no prospect of the employee ever returning to work for the employer and that therefore, there would, in the future, be a need for him to obtain a different job. If she were to grant the relief sought, therefore, and require the employer to continue paying his salary, this would merely be putting off the evil hour when he would have to get different work, and as it was in no one's interests (including those of the applicant) that this would happen, this was a reason for finding that the balance of convenience did not favour granting the relief sought. It should be pointed out that in this case the judge had already concluded that the plaintiffs would fail because they had not demonstrated that they had a strong case, hence this comment on the balance of convenience question was not in any way determinative of the matter. Nonetheless, if this rationale were adopted – that in the context of an application for a *Fennelly* order where an employee has no intention of returning to work for the employer then it is in the interests of all parties (and thus of the balance of convenience) that the dying relationship between the two not be strung out artificially pending the hearing of the action – it would be a significant development creating a serious obstacle for an employee seeking interlocutory relief of this kind.

---

95. *Powell v Brent LBC* [1988] ICR 176, [1988] IRLR 466; *Robb v London Borough of Hammersmith and Fulham* [1991] ICR 514, [1991] IRLR 72. Generally, see Horan, 'Employment Injunctions: Current Status and Future Developments', 1 *Employment Law Review* (2006), 8.
96. [2007] IEHC 432.

It is clear that an application for a *Fennelly* order is an independent application in [24–43]
and of itself, such that it does not need to be accompanied by an application that
the employee be allowed to return to work pending the hearing of the action.⁹⁷
On the other hand, as has been noted, in *Carroll v Bus Átha Cliath*,⁹⁸ Clarke J
refused to grant a *Fennelly* order in circumstances where the employee (who had
particular health concerns that prevented him from carrying out the work he had
originally done) was seeking *inter alia* an order entitling him to return to work but
with lighter duties. He was not being paid at the time, but this was not for disciplinary reasons but simply because he was unable to work by virtue of ill health,
and his contractual entitlement to sick pay had expired. In the circumstances,
Clarke J, who had already ruled that the applicant was *not* entitled to an order
requiring the defendant to re-employ him but assign him lighter duties, held that
an order requiring the defendants to pay his salary pending the trial of the action
would not be appropriate as 'the only basis upon which he can argue that he is
entitled to be paid is the same basis upon which he argues that he is entitled to
return to work'.⁹⁹

4.3. Orders Restraining the Employer from Replacing the Employee

An alternative type of order that may be sought is an injunction restraining the [24–44]
employer from taking steps that compromise the position of the employee within
the business – for example by appointing a replacement to his or her position,¹⁰⁰
or by reorganising the business in a way that involves the employee effectively
being frozen out (for example by a recruitment process that involves the creation
of new positions within the workforce and has the effect of rendering his or her
position redundant).¹⁰¹ Such an order (which is plainly workable irrespective of the
absence of mutual trust and confidence between the parties) may be granted even
where the court is not prepared to grant an order requiring that the employee be

---

97. *Lonergan v Salter-Townshend and Others* [1999] IEHC 205, [2000] ELR 15; *Moore v Xnet Information Systems Ltd. and Others* [2002] IEHC 6, [2002] 4 IR 362, [2002] 2 ILRM 278, [2002] ELR 65. Generally, see McDermott, 'Carroll v Bus Átha Cliath: Strengthening the Right to an Employment Injunction', 5 *Employment Law Review* (2006), 104.
98. [2005] 4 IR 184, [2005] ELR 192.
99. For a similar conclusion see *Yap v Children's University Hospital Temple Street* [2006] IEHC 308, [2006] 4 IR 298, and *Mullarkey v Irish National Stud Co Ltd.* [2004] IEHC 116, [2004] ELR 172. In both of these cases it was held that there would not be a legal right to sick pay (outside of any contractual entitlements an employee might have) pending the trial of any action against an employer, even where the employer was responsible for the illness of the employee.
100. *Powell v London Borough of Brent* [1988] ICR 176, [1987] IRLR 466; *Lonergan v Salter Townshend* [1999] IEHC 205, [2000] ELR 115.
101. *Harkins v Shannon Foynes Port Company* [2001] IEHC 6, [2001] ELR 75; *Garrahy v Bord na gCon* [2002] IEHC 147, [2002] 3 IR 566, [2003] ELR 274; *Evans v IRFB Services Ltd.* [2005] IEHC 107, [2005] 2 ILRM 358. For cases where orders of this kind have not been granted, see *Hennessy v St Gerard's School Trust* [2003] IEHC 49; *Orr v Zomax Ltd.* [2004] IEHC 47, [2004] 1 IR 486, [2004] ELR 161.

reinstated.[102] After all, as has been noted, the difficulties connected with supervision of an order of reinstatement do not arise where the employer is being required not to create a new position or positions within the company.[103] Moreover, in light of the fact that this, of all the categories of injunctive reliefs that may be sought in employment cases, is an order that is genuinely prohibitory rather than mandatory in nature, it will only be necessary for the employee to demonstrate that [s]he has a stateable as distinct from a strong case that [s]he will succeed at trial. On the other hand, it has been suggested that such an order would obviously be extremely restrictive and troublesome for the employer and that this would have to be factored into the balance of convenience.[104]

4.4. Orders Requiring that Disciplinary Hearings Be Conducted in Accordance with Fair Procedures

[24–45]   Finally, an employee may seek injunctive relief against an employer in respect of the manner in which [s]he was subject to disciplinary action by him or her. It should be stressed that it is highly unlikely that an order of the kind will ever be granted against an employer that would have the effect of preventing him or her from instituting disciplinary procedures in respect of an employee, or of requiring him or her to reinstate an employee who has been so disciplined.[105] In particular, the employment injunction will not operate to restrain the operation or effect of a disciplinary process that is being or has been conducted in accordance with an appropriate level of fair procedures.[106] Rather it will be used by an employee who faces disciplinary action as a mechanism for ensuring that any such action is taken only pursuant to a disciplinary process that complies with

---

102. Delany, 'Case and Comment: Employment Injunctions: The Role of Mutual Trust and Confidence', 13(1) *DULJ* (2006), 363.

103. *Garrahy v Bord na gCon* [2002] IEHC 147, [2002] 3 IR 566, [2003] ELR 274. See Delany, 'Cases and Comment: Employment Injunctions: The Role of Mutual Trust and Confidence', 13(1) *DULJ* (2006), 363, for the view that, in addition, such an order does not generate the difficulties involved where parties with no effective working relationship are being required by law to work together. Professor Delany rightly points out, however, that in cases where the effect of requiring an employer *not* to employ somebody else would in practice entail requiring the employer and employee to work together, the normal principled opposition to an injunction requiring reinstatement in such circumstances should continue to apply. *Page One Records v Britton* [1968] 1 WLR 157, [1967] All ER 822; *Warren v Mendy* [1989] 1 WLR 853, [1989] ICR 525, [1989] All ER 103, [1989] IRLR 210.

104. *Mullarkey v Irish National Stud Co Ltd.* [2004] IEHC 116, [2004] ELR 172. Thus in *Bergin v Galway Clinic Doughiska Ltd.* [2007] IEHC 386, [2008] 2 IR 205, Clarke J permitted the defendant employer to appoint someone to replace the applicant, but in circumstances where the appointment of that new person contained terms sufficient to permit the applicant to return to his former duties should this be ordered by the court at the full hearing of the matter.

105. See Redmond, *Dismissal Law in Ireland* (2nd ed., Tottel Publishing, 2007), at para.10.39.

106. *O'Malley v Aravon School*, High Court (Costello J), 13 August 1997.

(a) the terms of his or her contract;
(b) any rules or procedures agreed between the parties; and
(c) basic rules and principles of fair procedures and natural and constitutional justice of the kind discussed in Chapter 18.[107]

Naturally the presence or absence of an ongoing relationship of mutual trust and confidence is simply irrelevant to the question of whether an order of this kind can and should be granted.

Thus, in a line of authority dating from the English case *Hill v Parsons*,[108] the courts **[24–46]** in both Ireland and England have shown themselves to be prepared to grant injunctions in cases where an employee has been dismissed in a manner that is either in breach of the terms of his or her contract or in breach of fair procedures. Typically this will arise where [s]he was dismissed for disciplinary reasons without a proper disciplinary hearing[109] or where, in any case, the procedures that were adopted were not sufficiently fair having regard to the seriousness of what was at issue in the case.[110] Equally, however, given that all employment contracts contain an implied term of fair procedures, it is perhaps appropriate to say that all cases in which an employee successfully obtains an employment injunction against an employer can be classified as cases where there is a perceived breach of contract.[111]

---

107. *Cassidy v Shannon Heritage and Others* [1999] IEHC 245, [2000] ELR 248; *Maher v Irish Permanent (No. 1)* [1998] 4 IR 302, [1998] ELR 77; *Carroll v Bus Átha Cliath* [2005] 4 IR 184, [2005] ELR 192.

108. [1972] Ch. 305, [1971] 3 WLR 995, [1971] All ER 1345.

109. See, for example, *Phelan v BIC (Ireland) Ltd.* [1997] ELR 208; *Moore v Xnet Information Systems Ltd.* [2002] IEHC 6, [2002] 4 IR 362, [2002] ELR 65; *Hickey v Eastern Health Board* [1991] 1 IR 208; *Martin v Nationwide Building Society* [1999] ELR 241.

110. *Moore v Xnet Information Systems Ltd.* [2002] IEHC 6, [2002] 4 IR 362, [2002] ELR 65; *O'Malley v Aravon School*, High Court, 13 August 1997; *Maher v Irish Permanent Plc (No. 1)* [1998] 4 IR 302, [1998] ELR 77; *Deegan v Minister for Finance* [1998] IEHC 68, [1998] ELR 280. The issue of the level of fair procedures that is required in any given situation is considered in Chapter 18. In *Gallagher v The Revenue Commissioners (No. 2)* [1995] 1 IR 55, [1995] 1 ILRM 241, Hamilton CJ adopted the following passage from the judgment of Henchy J in *Kiely v Minister for Social Welfare* [1977] IESC 2, [1977] IR 267, 281: 'Tribunals exercising quasi-judicial functions are frequently allowed to act informally – to receive unsworn evidence, to act on hearsay, to depart from the rules of evidence, to ignore courtroom procedures, and the like – but they may not act in such a way as to imperil a fair hearing or a fair result.' Thus it is clear that the courts do not require procedures to be at the level of a High Court hearing: *Maher v Irish Permanent Plc (No. 1)* [1998] 4 IR 302, [1998] ELR 77; *Traynor v Ryan* [2002] IEHC 76, [2003] 2 IR 508.

111. See, for example, *Jones v Lee and Guilding* [1980] ICR 310, [1980] IRLR 67; *Gunton v Richmond upon Thames* [1980] ICR 755, [1980] IRLR 321; *Irani v Southampton and SW Hampshire Health Authority* [1985] ICR 590, [1985] IRLR 203.

[24–47]   As far as applications for interlocutory injunctions in the case of perceived problems with disciplinary processes are concerned, a number of principles emerge
from the relevant Irish cases.

- The courts should be slow to interfere with disciplinary processes
  that are not yet completed, even in situations where an employee has
  been provisionally suspended pending the outcome of an ongoing
  investigation.[112]
- There are exceptions to this principle, however, notably where the
  disciplinary process is being conducted in a way that is manifestly in
  breach of contract, in breach of the procedures that the employer clearly
  indicated would be followed, or in breach of the employee's rights to
  fair procedures, and especially where the effect of an adverse finding as
  a result of such flawed disciplinary processes would be unlikely to be
  substantially reversed at any later stage, such that the employee would
  suffer significant prejudice as a result.[113]
- In Chapter 18 we consider in more detail the requirements of employers
  in so far as disciplinary processes are concerned but, so far as the case law
  on injunctions is concerned, it is clear that where a disciplinary process
  is to occur, an employee is entitled that the basic rules of fair procedures
  (*audi alterem partem* and *nemo iudex in causa sua*) are fulfilled. In giving
  effect to these rules, it is clear that employees are entitled to 'at least a
  reasonable account of the complaint which they are asked to answer',[114]
  and possibly a right to legal representation, and to call appropriate
  witnesses. Moreover, where the matter has been prejudged by the party
  or parties charged with the investigation, then this so egregious a breach
  of the constitutional rights of the employee that [s]he will be able to
  demonstrate that [s]he has a sufficiently strong case that mandatory relief
  should be awarded.[115]
- Where a disciplinary process has been found to have been conducted
  otherwise than in accordance with fair procedures, it is not entirely
  clear what the appropriate relief is for the employee. Thus in *Maher
  v Irish Permanent Plc*[116] Laffoy J held that a decision emerging from a
  disciplinary process was fatally flawed and hence invalid from the point

---

112. *Carroll v Bus Átha Cliath* [2005] 4 IR 184, [2005] ELR 192; *Turner v O'Reilly* [2008] IEHC
      92; *Foley v Aer Lingus* [2001] 3 IR 158, [2001] ELR 193; *Becker v Board of Management of
      St Dominic's Secondary School and Others*, Clarke J, unreported, 13 April 2006; *Bergin v
      Galway Clinic Doughiska Ltd.* [2007] IEHC 386, [2008] 2 IR 205; *O'Brien v AON Insurance
      Managers (Dublin) Ltd.* [2005] IEHC 3; *Morgan v The Provost, Fellows and Scholars of Trinity
      College Dublin* [2003] 3 IR 157.
113. *Carroll v Bus Átha Cliath* [2005] 4 IR 184, [2005] ELR 192.
114. *Carroll v Bus Átha Cliath* [2005] 4 IR 184, *Carroll v Bus Átha Cliath* [2005] ELR 192.
115. *Bergin v Galway Clinic Doughiska Ltd.* [2007] IEHC 386, [2008] 2 IR 205.
116. [1997] IEHC 150, [1998] 4 IR 302.

at which it was made.[117] On the other hand, in *Carroll v Bus Átha Cliath*,[118] Clarke J did not deem the decision emerging from such flawed disciplinary process to be invalid, but simply required that an appeal be held against such a decision. In either event, it would seem clear that the most that an employee can hope for is that an order be granted requiring that the impugned disciplinary hearing be re-held, but this time in accordance with the agreed procedures, with the terms of the employee's contract and with basic rules of fair procedures and natural and constitutional justice.

---

117. See McDermott, '*Carroll v Bus Átha Cliath:* Strengthening the Right to an Employment Injunction', 5 *Employment Law Review* (2006), 104.
118. *Carroll v Bus Átha Cliath* [2005] 4 IR 184, [2005] ELR 192.

Index

as emergency leave 13-49
generally 11-28, 13-38–13-44
notice of emergency situation 13-48
standpoint of employee at relevant time
13-45–13-46
see also parental leave; protective leave
foreign workers *see* employment permits
foul language
use of 4-104
frustration of contract
death or dissolution 19-37
generally 19-30–19-31
illness 19-32–19-34, 21-61–21-63
imprisonment 19-35–19-36
termination of employment 19-30–19-36

gardaí
age discrimination 7-61
disability discrimination 7-61
privacy and 17-09
working time 11-06
garden leave 20-04–20-08
gender discrimination
access to employment 7-37, 7-38, 7-39,
7-40
advertisements 7-45
Circuit Court 7-68–7-69
classification of posts 7-54
comparator 7-07, 7-18, 7-20–7-22
pregnancy 9-14
compensation 7-68
dress codes 9-05–9-07
generally 7-02, 7-07, 9-02–9-04
indirect discrimination 7-25, 7-26, 7-27,
7-29–7-32
occupational qualifications on gender
grounds 7-56
part-time work 9-08–9-12
particular disadvantage 7-27, 7-29–7-32
pregnancy 9-13–9-25
comparator 9-14–9-16
less favourable treatment 9-13, 9-22
maternity pay 9-22
pregnancy-related illness 9-18–9-21,
9-23–9-25
promotion 9-03, 9-04
sexual harassment *see* sexual harassment
training or experience for or in relation
to employment 7-50

transsexuality 9-26–9-29, 9-37
gender reassignment
discrimination and 9-26–9-29
graduate scheme 5-32–5-34
see also employment permits
green card scheme 5-26–5-28, 5-44
grievance procedures
contract of employment 4-42

harassment
code of practice 10-38, 16-13
conduct amounting to harassment
10-27–10-30
defence to claims 10-31–10-40
generally 10-01, 10-25–10-26
racial harassment 10-30
'reasonably practical steps' 10-31–10-40
sexual harassment 10-02–10-07
burden of proof 10-14–10-15
defence to claims 10-31–10-40
'reasonably practical steps'
10-31–10-40
same-sex harassment 10-09
subjective evaluation 10-10–10-13
unacceptable conduct 10-08–10-13
vicarious liability 10-16–10-14
victimisation and 10-45
vicarious liability 10-26, 15-138,
16-111–16-113
sexual harassment 10-16–10-14
see also bullying; victimisation
health and safety
agency workers 15-35–15-37
breach of statutory duty 15-120–15-121
bullying 16-11–16-13
codes of practice 15-139–15-140
common employment defence 15-03
common law 15-02
common employment defence
15-03–15-04
contributory negligence 15-04
employers' duties 15-16–15-113
historical overview 15-03–15-04
implied duty of care 4-98
relationship with contractual
obligations 15-05–15-07
relationship with statutory
obligations 15-08–15-15
volenti non fit injuria 15-04

verbal warning
disciplinary procedures 18-18
vicarious liability
bullying 15-138, 16-106–16-118
course of employment test 3-60, 3-63–3-
65, 10-17, 16-107
e-mail and Internet use 17-30
employment status 3-02, 3-25–3-26, 3-
55–3-95, 10-17
harassment 10-26, 15-138, 16-111–16-113
sexual harassment 10-16–10-14
health and safety 15-02, 15-138
non-delegable duty of care
15-28–15-29